SAS/STAT® User's Guide

Version 8

Volume 1

SAS Institute Inc.
SAS Campus Drive
Cary, NC 27513

The correct bibliographic citation for this manual is as follows: SAS Institute Inc., *SAS/STAT® User's Guide, Version 8*, Cary, NC: SAS Institute Inc., 1999. 3884 pp.

SAS/STAT® User's Guide, Version 8

ISBN 1–58025–494–2

SAS Institute Inc., SAS Campus Drive, Cary, North Carolina 27513.

1st printing, October 1999

Table of Contents

Credits

Documentation

Writing	Tim Arnold, Maura E. Stokes
Editing	Donna M. Sawyer, Maura E. Stokes
Documentation Support	Kevin D. Smith
Editorial Support	Dee Doles, Ozkan Zengin
Production Support and Cover Design	Creative Solutions Division
Technical Review	Rob Agnelli, Shu An, Jack J. Berry, Phil Gibbs, Kelley M. Graham, Duane Hayes, Gerardo I. Hurtado, Elizabeth S. Edwards, Kathleen Kiernan, Eddie Routten, Annette Sanders, Paul T. Savarese, David Schlotzhauer, Mike Stockstill, Fouad G. Younan

Software

The procedures in SAS/STAT software were implemented by members of the Applications Division. Program development includes design, programming, debugging, support, documentation, and technical review. In the following list, the names of the developers currently supporting the procedure are listed first. Other developers previously worked on the procedure.

ACECLUS	Ann Kuo, Warren S. Sarle, Donna Lucas Watts
ANOVA	Randall D. Tobias, Yang C. Yuan
BOXPLOT	Bucky Ransdell, Robert N. Rodriguez
CALIS	Yiu-Fai Yung, Wolfgang M. Hartmann
CANCORR	Ann Kuo, Warren S. Sarle, Donna Lucas Watts
CANDISC	George MacKenzie, Warren F. Kuhfeld, Warren S. Sarle, Yang C. Yuan
CATMOD	Robert E. Derr, John P. Sall, Donna Lucas Watts
CLUSTER	Bart Killam, Warren S. Sarle
CORRESP	Warren F. Kuhfeld
DISCRIM	George MacKenzie, Warren F. Kuhfeld, Warren S. Sarle, Yang C. Yuan
FACTOR	Yiu-Fai Yung, Wolfgang M. Hartmann, John P. Sall, Warren S. Sarle

FASTCLUS	Bart Killam, Warren S. Sarle, Donna Lucas Watts
FREQ	Donna Lucas Watts, John P. Sall
GENMOD	Gordon Johnston
GLM	Randall D. Tobias, James H. Goodnight, John P. Sall, Warren S. Sarle, Yang C. Yuan
GLMMOD	Randall D. Tobias
INBREED	Anthony Baiching An, Meltem Narter
KDE	Russell D. Wolfinger
KRIGE2D	Bart Killam
LATTICE	Russell D. Wolfinger
LIFEREG	Gordon Johnston
LIFETEST	Ying So
LOESS	Robert Cohen
LOGISTIC	Ying So, John Castello
MDS	George MacKenzie, Warren S. Sarle
MIXED	Russell D. Wolfinger
MODECLUS	Ann Kuo, Warren S. Sarle
MULTTEST	Russell D. Wolfinger
NESTED	Randall D. Tobias, Leigh A. Ihnen
NLIN	Don Erdman, James H. Goodnight, Leigh A. Ihnen
NLMIXED	Russell D. Wolfinger
NPAR1WAY	Donna Lucas Watts, Jane Pierce, John P. Sall
ORTHOREG	Randall D. Tobias, Wolfgang M. Hartmann, John P. Sall
PHREG	Ying So
PLAN	Randall D. Tobias, Leigh A. Ihnen
PLS	Randall D. Tobias
PRINCOMP	Ann Kuo, Warren S. Sarle
PRINQUAL	Warren F. Kuhfeld
PROBIT	Gordon Johnston
REG	Robert Cohen, Leigh A. Ihnen, John P. Sall
RSREG	Randall D. Tobias, John P. Sall
SCORE	Ann Kuo, Donna Lucas Watts
SIM2D	Bart Killam
STDIZE	Ann Kuo
STEPDISC	George MacKenzie, Warren F. Kuhfeld, Warren S. Sarle, Yang C. Yuan
SURVEYMEANS	Anthony Baiching An
SURVEYSELECT	Donna Lucas Watts
SURVEYREG	Anthony Baiching An
TPSPLINE	Dong Xiang
TRANSREG	Warren F. Kuhfeld
TREE	Bucky Ransdell, Warren S. Sarle
TTEST	Padraic Neville, James H. Goodnight
VARCLUS	George MacKenzie, Wolfgang M. Hartmann, Warren S. Sarle
VARCOMP	Russell D. Wolfinger, James H. Goodnight, Randall D. Tobias

VARIOGRAM	Bart Killam
Probability Routines	Georges Guirguis
Other Numerical Routines	Robert Cohen, Georges Guirguis, Warren F. Kuhfeld, Randall D. Tobias, Donna Lucas Watts, Wolfgang M. Hartmann, Leigh A. Ihnen, Richard D. Langston, Katherine Ng, Jane Pierce, John P. Sall, Warren S. Sarle, Brian T. Schellenberger, Yang C. Yuan

The following staff members made special contributions to this release in the form of leadership and support for other developers: Robert Cohen, Warren F. Kuhfeld, Christopher R. Olinger, Robert N. Rodriguez, Warren S. Sarle, and Randall D. Tobias.

Acknowledgments

Many people make significant and continuing contributions to the development of SAS Institute's software products. The following persons are some of the people who have contributed significant amounts of their time to help us make improvements to SAS/STAT software. This includes research and consulting, testing, or reviewing documentation. We are grateful for the involvement of these members of the statistical community and the many others who are not mentioned here for their feedback, suggestions, and consulting.

Alan Agresti, University of Florida; Douglas Bates, University of Wisconsin; Suzette Blanchard, Frontier Science Technology Research Foundation; Mary Butler Moore, formerly of University of Florida at Gainesville; Wilbert P. Byrd, Clemson University; Vincent Carey, Harvard University; Sally Carson, RAND; Love Casanova, CSC-FSG; Helene Cavior, Abacus Concepts; George Chao, DuPont Merek Pharmaceutical Company; Daniel M. Chilko, West Virginia University; Jan de Leeuw, University of California, Los Angeles; Dave DeLong, Duke University; Sandra Donaghy, North Carolina State University; David B. Duncan, Johns Hopkins University; Michael Farrell, Oak Ridge National Laboratory; Stewart Fossceco, SLF Consulting; Michael Friendly, York University: Rudolf J. Freund, Texas A & M University; Wayne Fuller, Iowa State University; Andrzej Galecki, University of Michigan; A. Ronald Gallant, University of North Carolina at Chapel Hill; Joseph Gardiner, Michigan State University; Charles Gates, Texas A & M University; Thomas M. Gerig, North Carolina State University; Francis Giesbrecht, North Carolina State University; Harvey J. Gold, North Carolina State University; Kenneth Goldberg, Wyeth-Ayerst Research; Donald Guthrie, University of California, Los Angeles; Gerald Hajian, Schering Plough Research Institute; Bob Hamer, UMDNJ-RWJ Medical School; Frank E. Harrell, Jr., University of Virginia; Walter Harvey, Ohio State University; Ronald W. Helms, University of North Carolina at Chapel Hill; Joseph Hilbe, Arizona State University; Gerry Hobbs, West Virginia University; Ronald R. Hocking, Texas A & M University; Julian Horwich; Camp Conference Company; Jason C. Hsu, Ohio State University; David Hurst, University of Alabama at Birmingham; Emilio A. Icaza, Louisiana State University; Joerg Kaufman, Schering AG; William Kennedy, Iowa State University; Gary Koch, University of North Carolina at Chapel Hill; Kenneth L. Koonce, Louisiana State University; Rich La Valley, Strategic Technology Solutions; Charles Lin, InterLeap, Inc.; Ardell C. Linnerud, North Carolina State University; Ramon C. Littel, University of Florida; J. Jack McArdle, University of Virginia; Roderick P. McDonald, Macquarie University; J. Philip Miller, Washington University Medical School; George Milliken, Kansas State University; Robert J. Monroe, North Carolina State University; Robert D. Morrison, Oklahoma State University; Keith Muller, University of North Carolina at Chapel Hill; Anupama Narayanen, Sabre Technologies; Ralph G. O'Brien, Cleveland Clinic Foundation; Kenneth Offord, Mayo Clinic; Robert Parks, Washington University; Richard M. Patterson, Auburn University; Virginia Patterson, University of Tennessee; Cliff Pereira, Oregon State University; Hans-Peter Piepho, Universitaet Kassel; Edward Pollak, Iowa State University; C. H. Proctor, North Carolina State University; Dana Quade, University of North Carolina at Chapel Hill; Bill Raynor, Kimberly Clark; James Roger, Live Data Process Limited; William L. Sanders, University of Tennessee; Robert Schechter, AstraZeneca Pharmaceuticals; Shayle Searle, Cornell University; Pat Hermes Smith, formerly of Ciba-Geigy; Roger Smith, formerly of USDA; Phil Spector, University of California, Berkeley; Michael Speed, Texas A & M University at College Station; William Stanish, Statistical Insight; Rodney Strand, Orion Enterprises, LLC; Walter Stroup, University of Nebraska; Robert Teichman, ICI Americas Inc.; Edward Vonesh, Baxter Healthcare Corporation; Grace Wahba, University of Wisconsin at Madison; Glenn Ware, University of Georgia; Peter H. Westfall, Texas Tech University; Edward W. Whitehorne, CI Partners, LLC; William Wigton, USDA; William Wilson, University of North Florida; Philip Wittall, Unilever; Forrest W. Young, University of North Carolina at Chapel Hill; and Scott Zeger, Johns Hopkins University.

The final responsibility for the SAS System lies with SAS Institute alone. We hope that you will always let us know your opinions about the SAS System and its documentation. It is through your participation that SAS Software is continuously improved.

Please send your comments to **suggest@sas.com**.

Chapter 1

Changes and Enhancements to SAS/STAT Software in Versions 7 and 8

Chapter Table of Contents

Chapter 1
Changes and Enhancements to SAS/STAT Software in Versions 7 and 8

Overview

This chapter summarizes the major changes and enhancements to SAS/STAT software in Versions 7 and 8. All of these changes and enhancements are incorporated into the individual procedure chapters and are described in greater detail.

With Version 7 of SAS/STAT software, the PLS, KRIGE2D, and VARIOGRAM procedures became production. These procedures were experimental in Release 6.12. With Version 8, the SURVEYSELECT, SURVEYMEANS, SURVEYREG, KDE, LOESS, TPSPLINE, and NLMIXED procedures become production. These procedures were experimental in Version 7. ***V8***

Output Delivery System

All procedures now incorporate the Output Delivery System (ODS). This is a system for managing the results of a procedure. By default, the results for a procedure are directed to the SAS listing file as in previous releases, but with ODS you can create HTML or RTF files, create SAS output data sets of any table in the output, select or exclude pieces of output from a procedure, or modify the organization and style of that output. Chapter 15, "Using the Output Delivery System," describes some typical uses of ODS with SAS/STAT software and provides a description of the basic features. Refer to *The Complete Guide to the SAS Output Delivery System* for complete documention of ODS.

As part of the ODS implementation, some of the output of the SAS/STAT procedures has been reorganized to be consistent across procedures.

In Version 8, some of the table names have been changed for various reasons. However, note that the table names that were in effect for the Version 7 release are still accepted, so programs written for Version 7 will still work. ***V8***

ANOVA Procedure

The NAMELEN= option enables you to specify the length of effect names to be between 20 and 200 characters.

BOXPLOT Procedure

The new BOXPLOT procedure creates side-by-side box-and-whisker plots of measurements organized in groups. A box-and-whisker plot displays the mean, quartiles, and minimum and maximum observations for a group. You can specify multiple PLOT statements and also control the layout and appearance of the plots.

CATMOD Procedure

V8

The NOPRINT option has been added to the PROC and MODEL statements. The ESTIMATE= and ALPHA= options have been added to the CONTRAST statement.

CORRESP Procedure

V8

The CORRESP procedure provides adjusted inertias with the BENZECRI and GREENACRE options.

FACTOR Procedure

The NOPRINT option is now supported in the PROC FACTOR statement. The FUZZ, ROUND, and FLAG options are no longer supported. You can duplicate this functionality by creating the appropriate data sets from PROC FACTOR using ODS and then modifying them with the DATA step.

FASTCLUS Procedure

In the FREQ statement, frequencies are no longer truncated to integers.

When the IMPUTE option is specified in the PROC FASTCLUS statement, imputed values are no longer used in computing cluster statistics. This change causes the cluster standard deviations and other statistics computed from the standard deviations to be different than in previous releases.

The new INSTAT= option reads a SAS data set previously created by the FASTCLUS procedure using the OUTSTAT= option. If you specify the INSTAT= option, no clustering iterations are performed and no output is displayed. Only cluster assignment and imputation are performed as an OUT= data set is created.

The OUTSTAT= data set also contains the cluster seeds, and observations that were previously designated _TYPE_='SCALE' are now _TYPE_='DISPERSION'.

FREQ Procedure

The FREQ procedure now includes a TEST statement that provides asymptotic tests for selected measures of association and measures of agreement. A new BINOMIAL option in the TABLES statement computes the binomial proportion for one-way tables. You can compute the confidence bounds of a one-way table and request the test that the proportion equals a specified value as well as produce exact confidence bounds for the binomial proportion and an exact p-value for the binomial proportion test. You can now request that Fleiss-Cohen scores be used to compute the weighted kappa coefficient with the AGREE(WT=FC) option. The SCOROUT option requests that the row and column scores used for computing statistics such as Cochran-Mantel-Haenzsel statistics and Peason correlation be displayed.

The PCHI option in the EXACT statement computes the exact chi-square goodness-of-fit test for one-way tables as well as the exact Pearson chi-square test for two-way tables. The MAXTIME= option in the EXACT statement specifies the maximum time that PROC FREQ uses to compute an exact p-value.

The EXACT statement also includes the MC option for computing Monte Carlo estimates of exact p-values. **V8**

The Robins, Breslow, and Greenland (1986) estimate of variance is now used to compute the confidence bounds for the odds ratio and relative risk.

GENMOD Procedure

The earlier version of PROC GENMOD used a prototype Output Delivery System. This system has been totally rewritten; as a consequence, some of the syntax associated with ODS has changed. In particular, the ODS statement now replaces the use of the MAKE statement and _PRINT_ and _DISK_ global variables. The MAKE statement continues to be supported (except for its NOPRINT option), but the ODS statement provides much greater functionality and you should convert to using it. In addition, several of the table names and associated variable names in the GENMOD procedure have changed; see the chapter on the GENMOD procedure for complete information. The OUTPUT and the TEMPLATE procedures have changed. See Chapter 15, "Using the Output Delivery System," in this book for more information about the Output Delivery System.

PROC GENMOD now includes an LSMEANS statement that provides an extension of least squares means to the generalized linear model. In addition, the ESTIMATE statement is now supported. The new DIST=NEGBIN option in the MODEL statement specifies the negative binomial distribution, and the DIST=MULT option specifies the multinomial distribution. The log function is the default link for the negative binomial distribution, and the cumulative logit is the default link function for the multinomial distribution. Note that only the ordinal model is supported for the multinomial distribution, including the links CLOGIT for cumulative logit, CPROBIT for cumulative probit, and CCLL for cumulative complementary log-log.

The GEE facilities have also been updated. Type 3 tests are now provided for model effects, and the CONTRAST statement can be used for the GEE parameter estimates. The LSMEANS and ESTIMATE statements also apply to GEE parameter estimation. The method of alternating logistic regressions (ALR) is available with the LOGOR option in the REPEATED statement, which specifies the regression structure of the log odds ratio used to model the association of the responses from subjects for binary data. You can also fit the GEE model to ordinal data now, using the independent working correlation structure.

The NAMELEN= option in the PROC GENMOD statement enables you to specify the length of effect names to be between 20 and 200 characters.

V8

The DESCENDING option in the PROC statement specifies that the levels of the response variable be sorted in reverse order. The RORDER= option defines the ordering of the levels of the response variable. The procedure now includes an ID option in the MODEL statement for the OBSTATS table, and new variables have been added to the OUTPUT= data set.

GLM Procedure

The new ALPHA= option in the PROC GLM statement specifies the level of significance for confidence intervals computed from the LSMEANS, MEANS, MODEL, and OUTPUT statements. The ALPHA= option in all of these statements overrides the ALPHA value in the PROC GLM statement. The NAMELEN= option enables you to specify the length of effect names to be between 20 and 200 characters

The ALIASING option in the MODEL statement specifies that the estimable functions should be displayed as an aliasing structure, such that each row specifies the linear combination of the parameters estimated by each estimable function. This option is very useful in fractional factorial experiments that can be analyzed without a CLASS statement. The CLPARM option in the MODEL statement produces confidence limits for the parameter estimates (when you specify the SOLUTION option) and for the results of all ESTIMATE statements.

GLMMOD Procedure

The NAMELEN= option enables you to specify the length of effect names to be between 20 and 200 characters. The PREFIX= option specifies a prefix to use in naming the columns of the design matrix in the OUTDESIGN= data set. The ZEROBASED option specifies that the numbering for the columns of the design matrix in the OUTDESIGN= data set should begin at 0.

KDE Procedure

The KDE procedure performs either univariate or bivariate kernel density estimation. Statistical density estimation involves approximating a hypothesized probability density function from observed data. Kernel density estimation is a nonparametric technique for density estimation in which a known density function (kernal) is averaged across the observed data points to create a smooth approximation. PROC KDE uses a Gaussian density as the kernel, and its assumed variance determines the smoothness of the resulting estimate. PROC KDE outputs the kernel density estimate into a SAS data set, which you can then use with other procedures for plotting or analysis.

KRIGE2D Procedure

The KRIGE2D procedure performs ordinary kriging in two dimensions. Both anisotropic and isotropic semivariogram models can be handled. Four semivariogram models are supported: the gaussian, exponential, spherical, and power models. A single nugget effect is also supported. The locations of kriging estimates can be specified in a GRID statement or read from a SAS data set. The grid specification is most suitable for a regular grid; the data set specification can handle any irregular pattern of points. PROC KRIGE2D writes the kriging estimates and associated standard errors to an output data set.

LIFETEST Procedure

The plotting facility in the LIFETEST procedure has been upgraded, and high resolution plots are now the default. The CENSOREDSYMBOL= option and the EVENTSYMBOL= option specify the symbol for the censored and event observations, respectively.

LOGISTIC Procedure

The LOGISTIC procedure includes several new MODEL statement options that provide additional control over the model-fitting process. The ABSFCONV= option specifies the absolute function convergence criterion, the FCONV= option specifies the relative function convergence criterion, the GCONV= option specifies the relative gradient convergence criterion, and the XCONV= option specifies the relative parameter convergence criterion. The RIDGING= option specifies the technique used to improve the log-likelihood function when its value is less than that of the previous step.

PROC LOGISTIC now supports the PREDPROBS= option in the OUTPUT statement. This option requests individual, cumulative, or cross validated predicted probabilities. The LACKFIT option now enables you to specify a number n to be subtracted from the number of partitions to give the correct degrees of freedom for the Hosmer and Lemeshow test.

V8

The LOGISTIC procedure supports the CLASS statement and the specification of model effects similar to the GLM procedure. You can specify the type of parameterization to use, such as effect coding and reference coding, the ordering of the classification variables, and the reference level. Such specifications can be done globally or for individual variables. See the information on the CLASS statement for more detail.

LOESS Procedure

The LOESS procedure implements a nonparametric method for estimating regression surfaces. The LOESS procedure allows great flexibility because no assumptions about the parametric form of the regression surface are needed. The LOESS procedure is suitable when there are outliers in the data and a robust fitting method is necessary. PROC LOESS fits nonparametric models, supports the use of multidimensional data, supports both direct and interpolated fitting using kd trees, and performs statistical inference.

MDS Procedure

The DIMENSION option in the PROC MDS statement now includes a BY parameter.

MIXED Procedure

Earlier versions of PROC MIXED used a prototype Output Delivery System. This system has been totally rewritten in Version 7; as a consequence, some of the syntax associated with ODS has changed. In particular, the ODS statement now replaces the use of the MAKE statement and _PRINT_ and _DISK_ global variables. The MAKE statement continues to be supported (except for its NOPRINT option), but the ODS statement provides much greater functionality and you should convert to using it. In addition, several of the table names and associated variable names in the MIXED procedure have changed; see the chapter on the MIXED procedure for complete information. The OUTPUT procedure and the TEMPLATE procedure have changed. See Chapter 15, "Using the Output Delivery System," in this book for more information about the Output Delivery System.

The METHOD= option in the PROC MIXED statement has three new specifications: TYPE1, TYPE2, and TYPE3. These request analysis-of-variance estimates of variance components corresponding to type 1, 2, or 3 expected mean squares, respectively. These methods apply only to variance component models with no SUBJECT= effects and no REPEATED statement. The NAMELEN= option enables you to specify the length of effect names to be between 20 and 200 characters. The NCLPRINT option suppresses the display of the "Class Level Information" table, and the NOINFO option suppresses the display of the "Model Information" and "Dimensions" tables (this option replaces the INFO option).

The ID statement specifies the variables from the input data set to be included in the new OUTP= and OUTM= data sets from the MODEL statement.

In the MODEL statement, the OUTP= and OUTPM= options specify data sets containing predicted values and predicted means, respectively. These options replace the earlier P and PM options.

The PRIOR statement includes the following new options. The ALG=INDCHAIN option specifies a new default independence chain algorithm for generating the posterior sample, and the ALG=RWCHAIN option specifies the earlier random walk chain algorithm. The BDATA= option enables you to input the base densities used by the sampling algorithm. The GRID= and GRIDT= options specify grids and transformed grids, respectively, over which to evaluate the posterior density. The OUTG= and OUTGT= options specify output data sets to be created from the grid and transformed grid evaluations. The TRANS= option specifies the particular algorithm used to determine the transformation of the covariance parameters. The NOFULLZ option in the RANDOM statement eliminates the columns in Z corresponding to the missing levels of random effects involving CLASS variables.

PROC MIXED provides the Kenward-Rogers method of computing degrees of freedom with the DDFM=KENWARDROGER option in the MODEL statement. **V8**

NLMIXED Procedure

The NLMIXED procedure fits nonlinear mixed models, that is, models in which both fixed and random effects enter nonlinearly. These models have a wide variety of applications, two of the most common being pharmacokinetics and overdispersed binomial data. PROC NLMIXED enables you to specify a conditional distribution for your data (given the random effects) having either a standard form (normal, binomial, Poisson) or a general distribution that you code using SAS programming statements. PROC NLMIXED fits nonlinear mixed models by maximizing an approximation to the likelihood integrated over the random effects.

NPAR1WAY Procedure

The NPAR1WAY procedure now provides tests for scale differences: the AB, KLOTZ, MOOD, and ST options in the PROC NPAR1WAY statement request tests based on Ansari-Bradley, Klotz, Mood, and Siegel-Tukey scores, respectively. The SCORES=DATA option requests analysis with raw input data values. This option provides the flexibility of constructing any set of scores and then analyzing these scores directly with PROC NPAR1WAY. The option is available for both two-sample and multi-sample data. You can request exact p-values in the EXACT statement for all of the preceding options. Also, the EXACT statement now includes the MC option for computing Monte Carlo estimates of exact p-values and the MAXTIME= option to specify the maximum time that PROC NPAR1WAY uses to compute an exact p-value. In addition, the NPAR1WAY procedure now has a FREQ statement.

ORTHOREG Procedure

The ORTHOREG procedure now supports the CLASS statement and allows the same specification of effects in the MODEL statement as the GLM procedure does. The NOINT option is also supported.

PHREG Procedure

The PHREG procedure includes several MODEL statement options that provide additional control over the optimization process. The ABSCONV= option specifies the absolute function convergence criterion, the FCONV= option specifies the relative function convergence criterion, the GONV= option specifies the relative gradient convergence criterion, and the XCONV= option specifies the relative parameter convergence criterion. The RIDGING= option specifies the technique used to improve the log-likelihood function when its value is less than that of the previous iteration.

PROC PHREG supports the NOTRUNCATE option in the FREQ statement to allow noninteger frequency values to be used in the computations. The default value for the ORDER= option in the OUTPUT statement has been changed from SORTED to DATA.

PLAN Procedure

The PLAN procedure can now be used to produce all possible permutations of n values and all possible combinations of n values taken k at a time.

PLS Procedure

The PLS procedure fits models using any one of a number of linear predictive methods, including partial least squares (PLS). Ordinary least squares regression has the single goal of minimizing sample response prediction error, seeking linear functions of the predictors that explain as much variation in each response as possible. The techniques implemented in the PLS procedure have the additional goal of accounting for variation in the predictors, under the assumption that directions in the predictor space that are well sampled should provide better prediction for new observations when the predictors are highly correlated. All of the techniques implemented in the PLS procedure work by extracting successive linear combinations of the predictors, called *factors*, that optimally address one or both of these two goals, explaining response variation and explaining predictor variation. In particular, the method of partial least squares balances the two objectives, seeking factors that explain both response and predictor variation.

REG Procedure

The ALPHA= option in the PROC REG statement sets the significance level for the construction of confidence intervals. Plots are now high resolution graphics by default, and you must specify the LINEPRINTER option if you want lineprinter plots. The TABLEOUT option now also outputs the upper and lower confidence limits to the OUTEST= data set.

In the MODEL statement, the CLB option requests confidence limits for the parameter estimates. The ALPHA= option in the MODEL statement can be used to set the significance level for the confidence limits produced by the current MODEL statement. Otherwise, the ALPHA= option in the PROC REG statement can be used to change the α level. The MAXSTEP option specifies the maximum number of steps to take when SELECTION=STEPWISE is used, and the SINGULAR= option for tuning singularity-checking overrides the same option in the PROC REG statement.

RSREG Procedure

The RSREG procedure no longer requires the data to be sorted in order to test lack-of-fit.

SIM2D Procedure

The SIM2D procedure produces a spatial simulation for a Gaussian random field with a specified mean and covariance structure in two dimensions using an LU decomposition technique. The simulation can be conditional or unconditional. If the simulation is conditional, a set of coordinates and associated field values are read from a SAS data set. The resulting simulation will honor these data values. The mean structure can be specified as a quadratic in the coordinates. The covariance is specified by naming the form and supplying the associated parameters. The locations of simulation points can be specified in a GRID statement or read from a SAS data set. The grid specification is most suitable for a regular grid; the data set specification can handle any irregular pattern of points. The SIM2D procedure writes the simulated values for each grid point to an output data set. The SIM2D procedure does not produce any displayed output.

STDIZE Procedure

The STDIZE procedure standardizes one or more numeric variables in a SAS data set by subtracting a location measure and dividing by a scale measure. A variety of location and scale measures are provided, including estimates that are resistant to outliers and clustering. You can also multiply each standardized value by a constant and add a constant. You can replace missing values by the location measure or by any specified constant; you can suppress standardization if you only want to replace missing values.

SURVEYMEANS Procedure

The SURVEYMEANS procedure produces estimates of survey population means and totals from sample survey data. The procedure also produces variance estimates, confidence limits, and other descriptive statistics. When computing these estimates, the procedure takes into account the sample design used to select the survey sample. The sample design can be a complex survey sample design with stratification, clustering, and unequal weighting.

SURVEYREG Procedure

The SURVEYREG procedure performs regression analysis for sample survey data. This procedure can handle complex survey sample designs, including designs with stratification, clustering, and unequal weighting. The procedure fits linear models for survey data and computes regression coefficients and their variance-covariance matrix.

SURVEYSELECT Procedure

The SURVEYSELECT procedure provides a variety of methods for selecting probability-based random samples. The procedure can select a simple random sample or a sample according to a complex multistage sample design that includes stratification, clustering, and unequal probabilities of selection.

TPSPLINE Procedure

The TPSPLINE procedure uses the penalized least squares method to fit a nonparametric regression model. It computes thin-plate smoothing splines to approximate smooth multivariate functions observed with noise. The TPSPLINE procedure allows great flexibility in the possible form of the regression surface. In particular, PROC TPSPLINE makes no assumptions of a parametric form for the model. The generalized cross validation (GCV) function can be used to select the amount of smoothing.

TRANSREG Procedure

The TRANSREG procedure now supports smoothing spline transformations in the MODEL statement. The SMOOTH option specifies a noniterative transform, and the SSPLINE option specifies an iterative smoothing spline transformation. You can specify the smoothing parameter with the PARAMETER= option or the new SM= option. The DESIGN option has been enhanced. Other new options in PROC TRANSREG provide control over output data set variable names and labels.

TTEST Procedure

The TTEST procedure now performs t tests for one sample, two samples, and paired observations. The ALPHA= option in the PROC TTEST statement specifies the alpha level for the confidence intervals produced. The CI= option specifies that a confidence interval be produced for the standard deviation and that the confidence interval be either an equal tailed confidence interval or an interval based on the uniformly most powerful unbiased test of $H_0{:}\, \sigma = \sigma_0$. The H0= option requests tests against m instead of 0.

The FREQ and WEIGHT statements are now supported. The new PAIRED statement identifies the variables to be compared in paired comparisons.

VARIOGRAM Procedure

The VARIOGRAM procedure computes sample or empirical measures of spatial continuity for two-dimensional spatial data. These continuity measures are the regular semivariogram, a robust version of the semivariogram, and the covariance. These measures are written to an output data set, allowing plotting or parameter estimation for theoretical semivariograms or covariance models. Both isotropic and anisotropic measures are available. You can then use the KRIGE2D procedure for spatial prediction.

References

Robins, J.M., Breslow, N., and Greenland, S. (1986), "Estimators of the Mantel-Haenszel Variance Consistent in Both Sparse Data and Large-Strata Limiting Models," *Biometrics*, 42, 311–323.

Chapter 2
Introduction

Chapter Table of Contents

Chapter 2
Introduction

Overview of SAS/STAT Software

SAS/STAT software, a component of the SAS System, provides comprehensive statistical tools for a wide range of statistical analyses, including analysis of variance, regression, categorical data analysis, multivariate analysis, survival analysis, psychometric analysis, cluster analysis, and nonparametric analysis. A few examples include mixed models, generalized linear models, correspondence analysis, and structural equations. The software is constantly being updated to reflect new methodology.

In addition to 54 procedures for statistical analysis, SAS/STAT software also includes the Market Research Application (MRA), a point-and-click interface to commonly used techniques in market research. Also, the Analyst Application in the SAS System provides convenient access to some of the more commonly used statistical analyses in SAS/STAT software including analysis of variance, regression, logistic regression, mixed models, survival analysis, and some multivariate techniques.

About This Book

Since SAS/STAT software is a part of the SAS System, this book assumes that you are familiar with base SAS software and with the books *SAS Language Reference: Dictionary*, *SAS Language Reference: Concepts,* and the *SAS Procedures Guide*. It also assumes that you are familiar with basic SAS System concepts such as creating SAS data sets with the DATA step and manipulating SAS data sets with the procedures in base SAS software (for example, the PRINT and SORT procedures).

Chapter Organization

This book is organized as follows.

Chapter 1, "Changes and Enhancements to SAS/STAT Software in V7 and V8," contains information about the updates that are included in this release (Version 8). Chapter 2, this chapter, provides an overview of SAS/STAT software and summarizes related information, products, and services. The next ten chapters provide some introduction to the broad areas covered by SAS/STAT software. Subsequent chapters describe the SAS procedures that make up SAS/STAT software. These chapters appear in alphabetical order by procedure name.

The chapters documenting the SAS/STAT procedures are organized as follows:

- The *Overview* section provides a brief description of the analysis provided by the procedure.
- The *Getting Started* section provides a quick introduction to the procedure through a simple example.
- The *Syntax* section describes the SAS statements and options that control the procedure.
- The *Details* section discusses methodology and miscellaneous details.
- The *Examples* section contains examples using the procedure.
- The *References* section contains references for the methodology and examples for the procedure.

Following the chapters on the SAS/STAT procedures, Appendix A, "Special SAS Data Sets," documents the special SAS data sets associated with SAS/STAT procedures.

Typographical Conventions

This book uses several type styles for presenting information. The following list explains the meaning of the typographical conventions used in this book:

roman	is the standard type style used for most text.
UPPERCASE ROMAN	is used for SAS statements, options, and other SAS language elements when they appear in the text. However, you can enter these elements in your own SAS programs in lowercase, uppercase, or a mixture of the two.
UPPERCASE BOLD	is used in the "Syntax" sections' initial lists of SAS statements and options.
oblique	is used for user-supplied values for options in the syntax definitions. In the text, these values are written in *italic*.
helvetica	is used for the names of variables and data sets when they appear in the text.
bold	is used to refer to matrices and vectors.
italic	is used for terms that are defined in the text, for emphasis, and for references to publications.
`monospace`	is used for example code. In most cases, this book uses lowercase type for SAS code.

Options Used in Examples

Output of Examples

Most of the output shown in this book is produced with the following SAS System options:

```
options linesize=80 pagesize=200 nonumber nodate;
```

The template STATDOC.TPL is used to create the HTML output that appears in the online (CD) version. A style template controls stylistic HTML elements such as colors, fonts, and presentation attributes. The style template is specified in the ODS HTML statement as follows:

```
ODS HTML style=statdoc;
```

If you run the examples, you may get slightly different output. This is a function of the SAS System options used and the precision used by your computer for floating-point calculations.

Graphics Options

The examples that contain graphical output are created with a specific set of options and symbol statements. The code you see in the examples creates the color graphics that appear in the online (CD) version of this book. A slightly different set of options and statements is used to create the black and white graphics that appear in the printed version of the book.

If you run the examples, you may get slightly different results. This may occur because not all graphic options for color devices translate directly to black and white output formats. For complete information on SAS/GRAPH software and graphics options, refer to *SAS/GRAPH Software: Reference*.

The following GOPTIONS statement is used to create the online (color) version of the graphic output.

```
filename GSASFILE  '<file-specification>';

goptions gsfname=GSASFILE   gsfmode =replace
         fileonly
         transparency       dev     = gif
         ftext    = swiss   lfactor = 1
         htext    = 4.0pct  htitle  = 4.5pct
         hsize    = 5.625in vsize   = 3.5in
         noborder           cback   = white
         horigin = 0in      vorigin = 0in ;
```

The following GOPTIONS statement is used to create the black and white version of the graphic output, which appears in the printed version of the manual.

```
filename GSASFILE  '<file-specification>';

goptions gsfname=GSASFILE   gsfmode =replace
         gaccess = sasgaedt fileonly
         dev     = pslepsf
         ftext   = swiss    lfactor = 1
         htext   = 3.0pct   htitle  = 3.5pct
         hsize   = 5.625in  vsize   = 3.5in
         border             cback   = white
         horigin = 0in      vorigin = 0in ;
```

In most of the online examples, the plot symbols are specified as follows:

```
symbol1 value=dot color=white height=3.5pct;
```

The SYMBOL*n* statements used in online examples order the symbol colors as follows: white, yellow, cyan, green, orange, blue, and black.

In the examples appearing in the printed manual, symbol statements specify COLOR=BLACK and order the plot symbols as follows: dot, square, triangle, circle, plus, x, diamond, and star.

The %PLOTIT Macro

Examples that use the %PLOTIT macro are generated by defining a special macro variable to specify graphics options. See Appendix B, "Using the %PLOTIT Macro," for details on the options specified in these examples.

Where to Turn for More Information

This section describes other sources of information about SAS/STAT software.

Accessing the SAS/STAT Sample Library

The SAS/STAT sample library includes many examples that illustrate the use of SAS/STAT software, including the examples used in this documentation. To access these sample programs, select **Help** from the pmenu and select **SAS System Help**. From the Main Contents list, choose **Sample SAS Programs and Applications**.

Online Help System

You can access online help information about SAS/STAT software in two ways. You can select **SAS System Help** from the **Help** pmenu and then select **SAS/STAT Software** from the list of available topics. Or, you can bring up a command line and issue the command **help STAT** to bring up an index to the statistical procedures, or issue the command **help CATMOD** (or another procedure name) to bring up the help for that particular procedure. Note that the online help includes syntax and some essential overview and detail material.

SAS Institute Technical Support Services

As with all SAS Institute products, the SAS Institute Technical Support staff is available to respond to problems and answer technical questions regarding the use of SAS/STAT software.

Related SAS Software

Many features not found in SAS/STAT software are available in other parts of the SAS System. If you don't find something you need in SAS/STAT software, try looking for the feature in the following SAS software products.

Base SAS Software

The features provided by SAS/STAT software are in addition to the features provided by base SAS software. Many data management and reporting capabilities you will need are part of base SAS software. Refer to *SAS Language Reference: Concepts*, *SAS Language Reference: Dictionary*, and the *SAS Procedures Guide* for documentation of base SAS software.

SAS DATA Step

The DATA step is your primary tool for reading and processing data in the SAS System. The DATA step provides a powerful general purpose programming language that enables you to perform all kinds of data processing tasks. The DATA step is documented in *SAS Language Reference: Concepts*.

Base SAS Procedures

Base SAS software includes many useful SAS procedures. Base SAS procedures are documented in the *SAS Procedures Guide*. The following is a list of base SAS procedures you may find useful:

CORR	compute correlations
RANK	compute rankings or order statistics
STANDARD	standardize variables to a fixed mean and variance
MEANS	compute descriptive statistics and summarizing or collapsing data over cross sections

TABULATE	print descriptive statistics in tabular format
UNIVARIATE	compute descriptive statistics

SAS/ETS Software

SAS/ETS software provides SAS procedures for econometrics and time series analysis. It includes capabilities for forecasting, systems modeling and simulation, seasonal adjustment, and financial analysis and reporting. In addition, SAS/ETS software includes an interactive time series forecasting system.

SAS/GRAPH Software

SAS/GRAPH software includes procedures that create two- and three-dimensional high resolution color graphics plots and charts. You can generate output that graphs the relationship of data values to one another, enhance existing graphs, or simply create graphics output that is not tied to data.

SAS/IML Software

SAS/IML software gives you access to a powerful and flexible programming language (Interactive Matrix Language) in a dynamic, interactive environment. The fundamental object of the language is a data matrix. You can use SAS/IML software interactively (at the statement level) to see results immediately, or you can store statements in a module and execute them later. The programming is dynamic because necessary activities such as memory allocation and dimensioning of matrices are done automatically. SAS/IML software is of interest to users of SAS/STAT software because it enables you to program your methods in the SAS System.

SAS/INSIGHT Software

SAS/INSIGHT software is a highly interactive tool for data analysis. You can explore data through a variety of interactive graphs including bar charts, scatter plots, box plots, and three-dimensional rotating plots. You can examine distributions and perform parametric and nonparametric regression, analyze general linear models and generalized linear models, examine correlation matrixes, and perform principal component analyses. Any changes you make to your data show immediately in all graphs and analyses. You can also configure SAS/INSIGHT software to produce graphs and analyses tailored to the way you work.

SAS/INSIGHT software may be of interest to users of SAS/STAT software for interactive graphical viewing of data, editing data, exploratory data analysis, and checking distributional assumptions.

SAS/OR Software

AS/OR software provides SAS procedures for operations research and project planning and includes a point-and-click interface to project management. Its capabilities include the following:

- solving transportation problems
- linear, integer, and mixed-integer programming
- nonlinear programming
- scheduling projects
- plotting Gantt charts
- drawing network diagrams
- solving optimal assignment problems
- network flow programming

SAS/OR software may be of interest to users of SAS/STAT software for its mathematical programming features. In particular, the NLP procedure in SAS/OR software solves nonlinear programming problems, and it can be used for constrained and unconstrained maximization of user-defined likelihood functions.

SAS/QC Software

SAS/QC software provides a variety of procedures for statistical quality control and quality improvement. SAS/QC software includes procedures for

- Shewhart control charts
- cumulative sum control charts
- moving average control charts
- process capability analysis
- Ishikawa diagrams
- Pareto charts
- experimental design

SAS/QC software also includes the ADX interface for experimental design.

Chapter 3
Introduction to Regression Procedures

Chapter Table of Contents

Chapter 3
Introduction to Regression Procedures

Overview

This chapter reviews SAS/STAT software procedures that are used for regression analysis: CATMOD, GLM, LIFEREG, LOGISTIC, NLIN, ORTHOREG, PLS, PROBIT, REG, RSREG, and TRANSREG. The REG procedure provides the most general analysis capabilities; the other procedures give more specialized analyses. This chapter also briefly mentions several procedures in SAS/ETS software.

Introduction

Many SAS/STAT procedures, each with special features, perform regression analysis. The following procedures perform at least one type of regression analysis:

CATMOD — analyzes data that can be represented by a contingency table. PROC CATMOD fits linear models to functions of response frequencies, and it can be used for linear and logistic regression. The CATMOD procedure is discussed in detail in Chapter 5, "Introduction to Categorical Data Analysis Procedures."

GENMOD — fits generalized linear models. PROC GENMOD is especially suited for responses with discrete outcomes, and it performs logistic regression and Poisson regression as well as fitting Generalized Estimating Equations for repeated measures data. See Chapter 5, "Introduction to Categorical Data Analysis Procedures," and Chapter 29, "The GENMOD Procedure," for more information.

GLM — uses the method of least squares to fit general linear models. In addition to many other analyses, PROC GLM can perform simple, multiple, polynomial, and weighted regression. PROC GLM has many of the same input/output capabilities as PROC REG, but it does not provide as many diagnostic tools or allow interactive changes in the model or data. See Chapter 4, "Introduction to Analysis-of-Variance Procedures," for a more detailed overview of the GLM procedure.

LIFEREG — fits parametric models to failure-time data that may be right censored. These types of models are commonly used in survival analysis. See Chapter 10, "Introduction to Survival Analysis Procedures," for a more detailed overview of the LIFEREG procedure.

LOGISTIC	fits logistic models for binomial and ordinal outcomes. PROC LOGISTIC provides a wide variety of model-building methods and computes numerous regression diagnostics. See Chapter 5, "Introduction to Categorical Data Analysis Procedures," for a brief comparison of PROC LOGISTIC with other procedures.
NLIN	builds nonlinear regression models. Several different iterative methods are available.
ORTHOREG	performs regression using the Gentleman-Givens computational method. For ill-conditioned data, PROC ORTHOREG can produce more accurate parameter estimates than other procedures such as PROC GLM and PROC REG.
PLS	performs partial least squares regression, principal components regression, and reduced rank regression, with cross validation for the number of components.
PROBIT	performs probit regression as well as logistic regression and ordinal logistic regression. The PROBIT procedure is useful when the dependent variable is either dichotomous or polychotomous and the independent variables are continuous.
REG	performs linear regression with many diagnostic capabilities, selects models using one of nine methods, produces scatter plots of raw data and statistics, highlights scatter plots to identify particular observations, and allows interactive changes in both the regression model and the data used to fit the model.
RSREG	builds quadratic response-surface regression models. PROC RSREG analyzes the fitted response surface to determine the factor levels of optimum response and performs a ridge analysis to search for the region of optimum response.
TRANSREG	fits univariate and multivariate linear models, optionally with spline and other nonlinear transformations. Models include ordinary regression and ANOVA, multiple and multivariate regression, metric and nonmetric conjoint analysis, metric and nonmetric vector and ideal point preference mapping, redundancy analysis, canonical correlation, and response surface regression.

Several SAS/ETS procedures also perform regression. The following procedures are documented in the *SAS/ETS User's Guide*.

AUTOREG	implements regression models using time-series data where the errors are autocorrelated.
PDLREG	performs regression analysis with polynomial distributed lags.
SYSLIN	handles linear simultaneous systems of equations, such as econometric models.
MODEL	handles nonlinear simultaneous systems of equations, such as econometric models.

Introductory Example

Regression analysis is the analysis of the relationship between one variable and another set of variables. The relationship is expressed as an equation that predicts a *response variable* (also called a *dependent variable* or *criterion*) from a function of *regressor variables* (also called *independent variables, predictors, explanatory variables, factors,* or *carriers*) and *parameters*. The parameters are adjusted so that a measure of fit is optimized. For example, the equation for the ith observation might be

$$y_i = \beta_0 + \beta_1 x_i + \epsilon_i$$

where y_i is the response variable, x_i is a regressor variable, β_0 and β_1 are unknown parameters to be estimated, and ϵ_i is an error term.

You might use regression analysis to find out how well you can predict a child's weight if you know that child's height. Suppose you collect your data by measuring heights and weights of 19 school children. You want to estimate the intercept β_0 and the slope β_1 of a line described by the equation

$$\text{Weight} = \beta_0 + \beta_1 \text{Height} + \epsilon$$

where

Weight	is the response variable.
β_0, β_1	are the unknown parameters.
Height	is the regressor variable.
ϵ	is the unknown error.

The data are included in the following program. The results are displayed in Figure 3.1 and Figure 3.2.

```
data class;
   input Name $ Height Weight Age;
   datalines;
Alfred  69.0 112.5 14
Alice   56.5  84.0 13
Barbara 65.3  98.0 13
Carol   62.8 102.5 14
Henry   63.5 102.5 14
James   57.3  83.0 12
Jane    59.8  84.5 12
Janet   62.5 112.5 15
Jeffrey 62.5  84.0 13
John    59.0  99.5 12
Joyce   51.3  50.5 11
Judy    64.3  90.0 14
```

```
Louise  56.3  77.0 12
Mary    66.5 112.0 15
Philip  72.0 150.0 16
Robert  64.8 128.0 12
Ronald  67.0 133.0 15
Thomas  57.5  85.0 11
William 66.5 112.0 15
;
symbol1 v=dot c=blue height=3.5pct;
proc reg;
   model Weight=Height;
   plot Weight*Height/cframe=ligr;
run;
```

```
                          The REG Procedure
                            Model: MODEL1
                     Dependent Variable: Weight

                        Analysis of Variance

                                    Sum of           Mean
Source                   DF        Squares         Square    F Value    Pr > F

Model                     1     7193.24912     7193.24912      57.08    <.0001
Error                    17     2142.48772      126.02869
Corrected Total          18     9335.73684


             Root MSE             11.22625    R-Square     0.7705
             Dependent Mean      100.02632    Adj R-Sq     0.7570
             Coeff Var            11.22330


                        Parameter Estimates

                      Parameter       Standard
     Variable    DF    Estimate          Error    t Value    Pr > |t|

     Intercept    1  -143.02692       32.27459      -4.43      0.0004
     Height       1     3.89903        0.51609       7.55      <.0001
```

Figure 3.1. Regression for Weight and Height Data

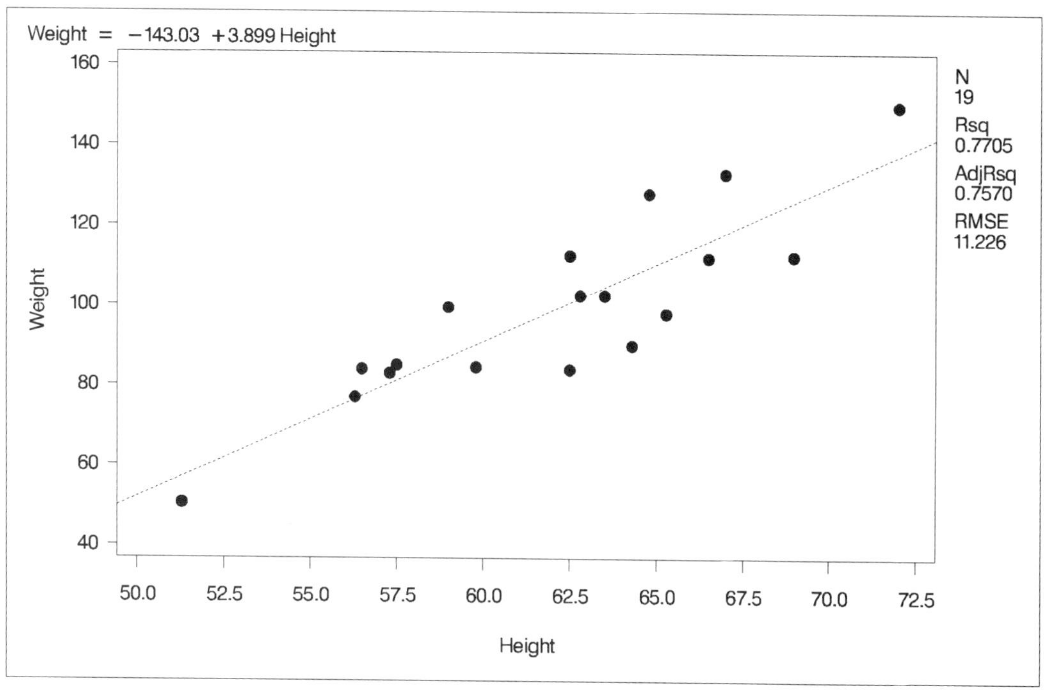

Figure 3.2. Regression for Weight and Height Data

Estimates of β_0 and β_1 for these data are $b_0 = -143.0$ and $b_1 = 3.9$, so the line is described by the equation

$$\text{Weight} = -143.0 + 3.9 * \text{Height}$$

Regression is often used in an exploratory fashion to look for empirical relationships, such as the relationship between Height and Weight. In this example, Height is not the cause of Weight. You would need a controlled experiment to confirm scientifically the relationship. See the "Comments on Interpreting Regression Statistics" section on page 40 for more information.

The method most commonly used to estimate the parameters is to minimize the sum of squares of the differences between the actual response value and the value predicted by the equation. The estimates are called *least-squares estimates*, and the criterion value is called the *error sum of squares*

$$\text{SSE} = \sum_{i=1}^{n} (y_i - b_0 - b_1 x_i)^2$$

where b_0 and b_1 are the estimates of β_0 and β_1 that minimize SSE.

For a general discussion of the theory of least-squares estimation of linear models and its application to regression and analysis of variance, refer to one of the applied regression texts, including Draper and Smith (1981), Daniel and Wood (1980), Johnston (1972), and Weisberg (1985).

SAS/STAT regression procedures produce the following information for a typical regression analysis.

- parameter estimates using the least-squares criterion
- estimates of the variance of the error term
- estimates of the variance or standard deviation of the sampling distribution of the parameter estimates
- tests of hypotheses about the parameters

SAS/STAT regression procedures can produce many other specialized diagnostic statistics, including

- collinearity diagnostics to measure how strongly regressors are related to other regressors and how this affects the stability and variance of the estimates (REG)
- influence diagnostics to measure how each individual observation contributes to determining the parameter estimates, the SSE, and the fitted values (LOGISTIC, REG, RSREG)
- lack-of-fit diagnostics that measure the lack of fit of the regression model by comparing the error variance estimate to another pure error variance that is not dependent on the form of the model (CATMOD, PROBIT, RSREG)
- diagnostic scatter plots that check the fit of the model and highlighted scatter plots that identify particular observations or groups of observations (REG)
- predicted and residual values, and confidence intervals for the mean and for an individual value (GLM, LOGISTIC, REG)
- time-series diagnostics for equally spaced time-series data that measure how much errors may be related across neighboring observations. These diagnostics can also measure functional goodness of fit for data sorted by regressor or response variables (REG, SAS/ETS procedures).

General Regression: The REG Procedure

The REG procedure is a general-purpose procedure for regression that

- handles multiple regression models
- provides nine model-selection methods
- allows interactive changes both in the model and in the data used to fit the model
- allows linear equality restrictions on parameters
- tests linear hypotheses and multivariate hypotheses
- produces collinearity diagnostics, influence diagnostics, and partial regression leverage plots
- saves estimates, predicted values, residuals, confidence limits, and other diagnostic statistics in output SAS data sets
- generates plots of data and of various statistics

- "paints" or highlights scatter plots to identify particular observations or groups of observations
- uses, optionally, correlations or crossproducts for input

Model-selection Methods in PROC REG

The nine methods of model selection implemented in PROC REG are

NONE — no selection. This method is the default and uses the full model given in the MODEL statement to fit the linear regression.

FORWARD — forward selection. This method starts with no variables in the model and adds variables one by one to the model. At each step, the variable added is the one that maximizes the fit of the model. You can also specify groups of variables to treat as a unit during the selection process. An option enables you to specify the criterion for inclusion.

BACKWARD — backward elimination. This method starts with a full model and eliminates variables one by one from the model. At each step, the variable with the smallest contribution to the model is deleted. You can also specify groups of variables to treat as a unit during the selection process. An option enables you to specify the criterion for exclusion.

STEPWISE — stepwise regression, forward and backward. This method is a modification of the forward-selection method in that variables already in the model do not necessarily stay there. You can also specify groups of variables to treat as a unit during the selection process. Again, options enable you to specify criteria for entry into the model and for remaining in the model.

MAXR — maximum R^2 improvement. This method tries to find the best one-variable model, the best two-variable model, and so on. The MAXR method differs from the STEPWISE method in that many more models are evaluated with MAXR, which considers all switches before making any switch. The STEPWISE method may remove the "worst" variable without considering what the "best" remaining variable might accomplish, whereas MAXR would consider what the "best" remaining variable might accomplish. Consequently, MAXR typically takes much longer to run than STEPWISE.

MINR — minimum R^2 improvement. This method closely resembles MAXR, but the switch chosen is the one that produces the smallest increase in R^2.

RSQUARE — finds a specified number of models having the highest R^2 in each of a range of model sizes.

CP — finds a specified number of models with the lowest C_p within a range of model sizes.

ADJRSQ — finds a specified number of models having the highest adjusted R^2 within a range of model sizes.

Nonlinear Regression: The NLIN Procedure

The NLIN procedure implements iterative methods that attempt to find least-squares estimates for nonlinear models. The default method is Gauss-Newton, although several other methods, such as Gauss or Marquardt, are available. You must specify parameter names, starting values, and expressions for the model. For some iterative methods, you also need to specify expressions for derivatives of the model with respect to the parameters. A grid search is also available to select starting values for the parameters. Since nonlinear models are often difficult to estimate, PROC NLIN may not always find the globally optimal least-squares estimates.

Response Surface Regression: The RSREG Procedure

The RSREG procedure fits a quadratic response-surface model, which is useful in searching for factor values that optimize a response. The following features in PROC RSREG make it preferable to other regression procedures for analyzing response surfaces:

- automatic generation of quadratic effects
- a lack-of-fit test
- solutions for critical values of the surface
- eigenvalues of the associated quadratic form
- a ridge analysis to search for the direction of optimum response

Partial Least Squares Regression: The PLS Procedure

The PLS procedure fits models using any one of a number of linear predictive methods, including *partial least squares* (PLS). Ordinary least-squares regression, as implemented in SAS/STAT procedures such as PROC GLM and PROC REG, has the single goal of minimizing sample response prediction error, seeking linear functions of the predictors that explain as much variation in each response as possible. The techniques implemented in the PLS procedure have the additional goal of accounting for variation in the predictors, under the assumption that directions in the predictor space that are well sampled should provide better prediction for *new* observations when the predictors are highly correlated. All of the techniques implemented in the PLS procedure work by extracting successive linear combinations of the predictors, called *factors* (also called *components* or *latent vectors*), which optimally address one or both of these two goals—explaining response variation and explaining predictor variation. In particular, the method of partial least squares balances the two objectives, seeking for factors that explain both response and predictor variation.

Regression for Ill-conditioned Data: The ORTHOREG Procedure

The ORTHOREG procedure performs linear least-squares regression using the Gentleman-Givens computational method, and it can produce more accurate parameter estimates for ill-conditioned data. PROC GLM and PROC REG produce very accurate estimates for most problems. However, if you have very ill-conditioned data, consider using the ORTHOREG procedure. The collinearity diagnostics in PROC REG can help you to determine whether PROC ORTHOREG would be useful.

Logistic Regression: The LOGISTIC Procedure

The LOGISTIC procedure fits logistic models, in which the response can be either dichotomous or polychotomous. Stepwise model selection is available. You can request regression diagnostics, and predicted and residual values.

Regression With Transformations: The TRANSREG Procedure

The TRANSREG procedure can fit many standard linear models. In addition, PROC TRANSREG can find nonlinear transformations of data and fit a linear model to the transformed variables. This is in contrast to PROC REG and PROC GLM, which fit linear models to data, or PROC NLIN, which fits nonlinear models to data. The TRANSREG procedure fits many types of linear models, including

- ordinary regression and ANOVA
- metric and nonmetric conjoint analysis
- metric and nonmetric vector and ideal point preference mapping
- simple, multiple, and multivariate regression with variable transformations
- redundancy analysis with variable transformations
- canonical correlation analysis with variable transformations
- response surface regression with variable transformations

Regression Using the GLM, CATMOD, LOGISTIC, PROBIT, and LIFEREG Procedures

The GLM procedure fits general linear models to data, and it can perform regression, analysis of variance, analysis of covariance, and many other analyses. The following features for regression distinguish PROC GLM from other regression procedures:

- direct specification of polynomial effects
- ease of specifying categorical effects (PROC GLM automatically generates dummy variables for class variables)

Most of the statistics based on predicted and residual values that are available in PROC REG are also available in PROC GLM. However, PROC GLM does not produce collinearity diagnostics, influence diagnostics, or scatter plots. In addition, PROC GLM allows only one model and fits the full model.

See Chapter 4, "Introduction to Analysis-of-Variance Procedures," and Chapter 30, "The GLM Procedure," for more details.

The CATMOD procedure can perform linear regression and logistic regression of response functions for data that can be represented in a contingency table. See Chapter 5, "Introduction to Categorical Data Analysis Procedures," and Chapter 22, "The CATMOD Procedure," for more details.

The LOGISTIC and PROBIT procedures can perform logistic and ordinal logistic regression. See Chapter 5, "Introduction to Categorical Data Analysis Procedures," Chapter 39, "The LOGISTIC Procedure," and Chapter 54, "The PROBIT Procedure," for additional details.

The LIFEREG procedure is useful in fitting equations to data that may be right-censored. See Chapter 10, "Introduction to Survival Analysis Procedures," and Chapter 36, "The LIFEREG Procedure," for more details.

Interactive Features in the CATMOD, GLM, and REG Procedures

The CATMOD, GLM, and REG procedures do not stop after processing a RUN statement. More statements can be submitted as a continuation of the previous statements. Many new features in these procedures are useful to request after you have reviewed the results from previous statements. The procedures stop if a DATA step or another procedure is requested or if a QUIT statement is submitted.

Statistical Background

The rest of this chapter outlines the way many SAS/STAT regression procedures calculate various regression quantities. Exceptions and further details are documented with individual procedures.

Linear Models

In matrix algebra notation, a linear model is written as

$$\mathbf{y} = \mathbf{X}\boldsymbol{\beta} + \boldsymbol{\epsilon}$$

where $\mathbf{X}$ is the $n \times k$ design matrix (rows are observations and columns are the regressors), $\boldsymbol{\beta}$ is the $k \times 1$ vector of unknown parameters, and $\boldsymbol{\epsilon}$ is the $n \times 1$ vector of unknown errors. The first column of $\mathbf{X}$ is usually a vector of 1s used in estimating the intercept term.

The statistical theory of linear models is based on strict classical assumptions. Ideally, the response is measured with all the factors controlled in an experimentally determined environment. If you cannot control the factors experimentally, some tests must be interpreted as being conditional on the observed values of the regressors.

Other assumptions are that

- the form of the model is correct (all important explanatory variables have been included)

- regressor variables are measured without error
- the expected value of the errors is zero
- the variance of the errors (and thus the dependent variable) is a constant across observations (called σ^2)
- the errors are uncorrelated across observations

When hypotheses are tested, the additional assumption is made that the errors are normally distributed.

Statistical Model

If the model satisfies all the necessary assumptions, the least-squares estimates are the best linear unbiased estimates (BLUE). In other words, the estimates have minimum variance among the class of estimators that are unbiased and are linear functions of the responses. If the additional assumption that the error term is normally distributed is also satisfied, then

- the statistics that are computed have the proper sampling distributions for hypothesis testing
- parameter estimates are normally distributed
- various sums of squares are distributed proportional to chi-square, at least under proper hypotheses
- ratios of estimates to standard errors are distributed as Student's t under certain hypotheses
- appropriate ratios of sums of squares are distributed as F under certain hypotheses

When regression analysis is used to model data that do not meet the assumptions, the results should be interpreted in a cautious, exploratory fashion. The significance probabilities under these circumstances are unreliable.

Box (1966) and Mosteller and Tukey (1977, chaps. 12 and 13) discuss the problems that are encountered with regression data, especially when the data are not under experimental control.

Parameter Estimates and Associated Statistics

Parameter estimates are formed using least-squares criteria by solving the normal equations

$$(\mathbf{X}'\mathbf{X})\mathbf{b} = \mathbf{X}'\mathbf{y}$$

for the parameter estimates $\mathbf{b}$, yielding

$$\mathbf{b} = (\mathbf{X}'\mathbf{X})^{-1}\mathbf{X}'\mathbf{y}$$

Assume for the present that $(\mathbf{X}'\mathbf{X})$ is full rank (this assumption is relaxed later). The variance of the error σ^2 is estimated by the mean square error

$$s^2 = \text{MSE} = \frac{\text{SSE}}{n-k} = \frac{1}{n-k}\sum_{i=1}^{n}(y_i - \mathbf{x}_i\mathbf{b})^2$$

where $\mathbf{x}_i$ is the ith row of regressors. The parameter estimates are unbiased:

$$\begin{aligned} E(\mathbf{b}) &= \boldsymbol{\beta} \\ E(s^2) &= \sigma^2 \end{aligned}$$

The covariance matrix of the estimates is

$$\text{VAR}(\mathbf{b}) = (\mathbf{X}'\mathbf{X})^{-1}\sigma^2$$

The estimate of the covariance matrix is obtained by replacing σ^2 with its estimate, s^2, in the formula preceding:

$$\text{COVB} = (\mathbf{X}'\mathbf{X})^{-1}s^2$$

The correlations of the estimates are derived by scaling to 1s on the diagonal.

Let

$$\begin{aligned} \mathbf{S} &= \text{diag}\left((\mathbf{X}'\mathbf{X})^{-1}\right)^{-\frac{1}{2}} \\ \text{CORRB} &= \mathbf{S}\left(\mathbf{X}'\mathbf{X}\right)^{-1}\mathbf{S} \end{aligned}$$

Standard errors of the estimates are computed using the equation

$$\text{STDERR}(b_i) = \sqrt{(\mathbf{X}'\mathbf{X})^{-1}_{ii}s^2}$$

where $(\mathbf{X}'\mathbf{X})^{-1}_{ii}$ is the ith diagonal element of $(\mathbf{X}'\mathbf{X})^{-1}$. The ratio

$$t = \frac{b_i}{\text{STDERR}(b_i)}$$

is distributed as Student's t under the hypothesis that β_i is zero. Regression procedures display the t ratio and the significance probability, which is the probability under the hypothesis $\beta_i = 0$ of a larger absolute t value than was actually obtained. When the probability is less than some small level, the event is considered so unlikely that the hypothesis is rejected.

Type I SS and Type II SS measure the contribution of a variable to the reduction in SSE. Type I SS measure the reduction in SSE as that variable is entered into the model in sequence. Type II SS are the increment in SSE that results from removing the variable from the full model. Type II SS are equivalent to the Type III and Type IV SS reported in the GLM procedure. If Type II SS are used in the numerator of an F test, the test is equivalent to the t test for the hypothesis that the parameter is zero. In polynomial models, Type I SS measure the contribution of each polynomial term after it is orthogonalized to the previous terms in the model. The four types of SS are described in Chapter 12, "The Four Types of Estimable Functions."

Standardized estimates are defined as the estimates that result when all variables are standardized to a mean of 0 and a variance of 1. Standardized estimates are computed by multiplying the original estimates by the sample standard deviation of the regressor variable and dividing by the sample standard deviation of the dependent variable.

R^2 is an indicator of how much of the variation in the data is explained by the model. It is defined as

$$R^2 = 1 - \frac{\mathrm{SSE}}{\mathrm{TSS}}$$

where SSE is the sum of squares for error and TSS is the corrected total sum of squares. The Adjusted R^2 statistic is an alternative to R^2 that is adjusted for the number of parameters in the model. This is calculated as

$$\mathrm{ADJRSQ} = 1 - \frac{n-i}{n-p}\left(1 - R^2\right)$$

where n is the number of observations used to fit the model, p is the number of parameters in the model (including the intercept), and i is 1 if the model includes an intercept term, and 0 otherwise.

Tolerances and variance inflation factors measure the strength of interrelationships among the regressor variables in the model. If all variables are orthogonal to each other, both tolerance and variance inflation are 1. If a variable is very closely related to other variables, the tolerance goes to 0 and the variance inflation gets very large. Tolerance (TOL) is 1 minus the R^2 that results from the regression of the other variables in the model on that regressor. Variance inflation (VIF) is the diagonal of $(\mathbf{X}'\mathbf{X})^{-1}$ if $(\mathbf{X}'\mathbf{X})$ is scaled to correlation form. The statistics are related as

$$\mathrm{VIF} = \frac{1}{\mathrm{TOL}}$$

Models Not of Full Rank

If the model is not full rank, then a generalized inverse can be used to solve the normal equations to minimize the SSE:

$$\mathrm{b} = (\mathbf{X}'\mathbf{X})^{-}\mathbf{X}'\mathbf{y}$$

However, these estimates are not unique since there are an infinite number of solutions using different generalized inverses. PROC REG and other regression procedures choose a nonzero solution for all variables that are linearly independent of previous variables and a zero solution for other variables. This corresponds to using a generalized inverse in the normal equations, and the expected values of the estimates are the Hermite normal form of $\mathbf{X}'\mathbf{X}$ multiplied by the true parameters:

$$E(\mathbf{b}) = (\mathbf{X}'\mathbf{X})^{-}(\mathbf{X}'\mathbf{X})\beta$$

Degrees of freedom for the zeroed estimates are reported as zero. The hypotheses that are not testable have t tests displayed as missing. The message that the model is not full rank includes a display of the relations that exist in the matrix.

Comments on Interpreting Regression Statistics

In most applications, regression models are merely useful approximations. Reality is often so complicated that you cannot know what the true model is. You may have to choose a model more on the basis of what variables can be measured and what kinds of models can be estimated than on a rigorous theory that explains how the universe really works. However, even in cases where theory is lacking, a regression model may be an excellent predictor of the response if the model is carefully formulated from a large sample. The interpretation of statistics such as parameter estimates may nevertheless be highly problematical.

Statisticians usually use the word "prediction" in a technical sense. *Prediction* in this sense does not refer to "predicting the future" (statisticians call that *forecasting*) but rather to guessing the response from the values of the regressors in an observation taken under the same circumstances as the sample from which the regression equation was estimated. If you developed a regression model for predicting consumer preferences in 1958, it may not give very good predictions in 1988 no matter how well it did in 1958. If it is the future you want to predict, your model must include whatever relevant factors may change over time. If the process you are studying does in fact change over time, you must take observations at several, perhaps many, different times. Analysis of such data is the province of SAS/ETS procedures such as AUTOREG and STATESPACE. Refer to the *SAS/ETS User's Guide* for more information on these procedures.

The comments in the rest of this section are directed toward linear least-squares regression. Nonlinear regression and non-least-squares regression often introduce further complications. For more detailed discussions of the interpretation of regression statistics, see Darlington (1968), Mosteller and Tukey (1977), Weisberg (1985), and Younger (1979).

Interpreting Parameter Estimates from a Controlled Experiment

Parameter estimates are easiest to interpret in a controlled experiment in which the regressors are manipulated independently of each other. In a well-designed experiment, such as a randomized factorial design with replications in each cell, you can use lack-of-fit tests and estimates of the standard error of prediction to determine whether the model describes the experimental process with adequate precision. If so, a regression coefficient estimates the amount by which the mean response changes when the regressor is changed by one unit while all the other regressors are unchanged. However, if the model involves interactions or polynomial terms, it may not be possible to interpret individual regression coefficients. For example, if the equation includes both linear and quadratic terms for a given variable, you cannot physically change the value of the linear term without also changing the value of the quadratic term. Sometimes it may be possible to recode the regressors, for example by using orthogonal polynomials, to make the interpretation easier.

If the nonstatistical aspects of the experiment are also treated with sufficient care (including such things as use of placebos and double blinds), then you can state conclusions in causal terms; that is, this change in a regressor causes that change in the response. Causality can never be inferred from statistical results alone or from an observational study.

If the model that you fit is not the true model, then the parameter estimates may depend strongly on the particular values of the regressors used in the experiment. For example, if the response is actually a quadratic function of a regressor but you fit a linear function, the estimated slope may be a large negative value if you use only small values of the regressor, a large positive value if you use only large values of the regressor, or near zero if you use both large and small regressor values. When you report the results of an experiment, it is important to include the values of the regressors. It is also important to avoid extrapolating the regression equation outside the range of regressors in the sample.

Interpreting Parameter Estimates from an Observational Study

In an observational study, parameter estimates can be interpreted as the expected difference in response of two observations that differ by one unit on the regressor in question and that have the same values for all other regressors. You cannot make inferences about "changes" in an observational study since you have not actually changed anything. It may not be possible even in principle to change one regressor independently of all the others. Neither can you draw conclusions about causality without experimental manipulation.

If you conduct an observational study and if you do not know the true form of the model, interpretation of parameter estimates becomes even more convoluted. A coefficient must then be interpreted as an average over the sampled population of expected differences in response of observations that differ by one unit on only one regressor. The considerations that are discussed under controlled experiments for which the true model is not known also apply.

Comparing Parameter Estimates

Two coefficients in the same model can be directly compared only if the regressors are measured in the same units. You can make any coefficient large or small just by changing the units. If you convert a regressor from feet to miles, the parameter estimate is multiplied by 5280.

Sometimes standardized regression coefficients are used to compare the effects of regressors measured in different units. Standardizing the variables effectively makes the standard deviation the unit of measurement. This makes sense only if the standard deviation is a meaningful quantity, which usually is the case only if the observations are sampled from a well-defined population. In a controlled experiment, the standard deviation of a regressor depends on the values of the regressor selected by the experimenter. Thus, you can make a standardized regression coefficient large by using a large range of values for the regressor.

In some applications you may be able to compare regression coefficients in terms of the practical range of variation of a regressor. Suppose that each independent variable in an industrial process can be set to values only within a certain range. You can rescale the variables so that the smallest possible value is zero and the largest possible value is one. Then the unit of measurement for each regressor is the maximum possible range of the regressor, and the parameter estimates are comparable in that sense. Another possibility is to scale the regressors in terms of the cost of setting a regressor to a particular value, so comparisons can be made in monetary terms.

Correlated Regressors

In an experiment, you can often select values for the regressors such that the regressors are orthogonal (not correlated with each other). Orthogonal designs have enormous advantages in interpretation. With orthogonal regressors, the parameter estimate for a given regressor does not depend on which other regressors are included in the model, although other statistics such as standard errors and p-values may change.

If the regressors are correlated, it becomes difficult to disentangle the effects of one regressor from another, and the parameter estimates may be highly dependent on which regressors are used in the model. Two correlated regressors may be nonsignificant when tested separately but highly significant when considered together. If two regressors have a correlation of 1.0, it is impossible to separate their effects.

It may be possible to recode correlated regressors to make interpretation easier. For example, if X and Y are highly correlated, they could be replaced in a linear regression by $X + Y$ and $X - Y$ without changing the fit of the model or statistics for other regressors.

Errors in the Regressors

If there is error in the measurements of the regressors, the parameter estimates must be interpreted with respect to the measured values of the regressors, not the true values. A regressor may be statistically nonsignificant when measured with error even though it would have been highly significant if measured accurately.

Probability Values (p-values)

Probability values (p-values) do not necessarily measure the importance of a regressor. An important regressor can have a large (nonsignificant) p-value if the sample is small, if the regressor is measured over a narrow range, if there are large measurement errors, or if another closely related regressor is included in the equation. An unimportant regressor can have a very small p-value in a large sample. Computing a confidence interval for a parameter estimate gives you more useful information than just looking at the p-value, but confidence intervals do not solve problems of measurement errors in the regressors or highly correlated regressors.

The p-values are always approximations. The assumptions required to compute exact p-values are never satisfied in practice.

Interpreting R^2

R^2 is usually defined as the proportion of variance of the response that is predictable from (that can be explained by) the regressor variables. It may be easier to interpret $\sqrt{1 - R^2}$, which is approximately the factor by which the standard error of prediction is reduced by the introduction of the regressor variables.

R^2 is easiest to interpret when the observations, including the values of both the regressors and response, are randomly sampled from a well-defined population. Nonrandom sampling can greatly distort R^2. For example, excessively large values of R^2 can be obtained by omitting from the sample observations with regressor values near the mean.

In a controlled experiment, R^2 depends on the values chosen for the regressors. A wide range of regressor values generally yields a larger R^2 than a narrow range. In comparing the results of two experiments on the same variables but with different ranges for the regressors, you should look at the standard error of prediction (root mean square error) rather than R^2.

Whether a given R^2 value is considered to be large or small depends on the context of the particular study. A social scientist might consider an R^2 of 0.30 to be large, while a physicist might consider 0.98 to be small.

You can always get an R^2 arbitrarily close to 1.0 by including a large number of completely unrelated regressors in the equation. If the number of regressors is close to the sample size, R^2 is very biased. In such cases, the adjusted R^2 and related statistics discussed by Darlington (1968) are less misleading.

If you fit many different models and choose the model with the largest R^2, all the statistics are biased and the p-values for the parameter estimates are not valid. Caution must be taken with the interpretation of R^2 for models with no intercept term. As a general rule, no-intercept models should be fit only when theoretical justification exists and the data appear to fit a no-intercept framework. The R^2 in those cases is measuring something different (refer to Kvalseth 1985).

Incorrect Data Values

All regression statistics can be seriously distorted by a single incorrect data value. A decimal point in the wrong place can completely change the parameter estimates, R^2, and other statistics. It is important to check your data for outliers and influential observations. The diagnostics in PROC REG are particularly useful in this regard.

Predicted and Residual Values

After the model has been fit, predicted and residual values are usually calculated and output. The predicted values are calculated from the estimated regression equation; the residuals are calculated as actual minus predicted. Some procedures can calculate standard errors of residuals, predicted mean values, and individual predicted values.

Consider the ith observation where $\mathbf{x}_i$ is the row of regressors, $\mathbf{b}$ is the vector of parameter estimates, and s^2 is the mean squared error.

Let

$$h_i = \mathbf{x}_i(\mathbf{X}'\mathbf{X})^{-1}\mathbf{x}_i' \ \ \text{(the leverage)}$$

Then

$$\begin{aligned} \hat{y}_i &= \mathbf{x}_i\mathbf{b} \ \ \text{(the predicted mean value)} \\ \text{STDERR}(\hat{y}_i) &= \sqrt{h_i s^2} \ \ \text{(the standard error of the predicted mean)} \end{aligned}$$

The standard error of the individual (future) predicted value y_i is

$$\text{STDERR}(y_i) = \sqrt{(1+h_i)s^2}$$

The residual is defined as

$$\begin{aligned} \text{RESID}_i &= y_i - \mathbf{x}_i\mathbf{b} \ \ \text{(the residual)} \\ \text{STDERR}(\text{RESID}_i) &= \sqrt{(1-h_i)s^2} \ \ \text{(the standard error of the residual)} \end{aligned}$$

The ratio of the residual to its standard error, called the *studentized residual*, is sometimes shown as

$$\text{STUDENT}_i = \frac{\text{RESID}_i}{\text{STDERR}(\text{RESID}_i)}$$

There are two kinds of confidence intervals for predicted values. One type of confidence interval is an interval for the mean value of the response. The other type, sometimes called a *prediction* or *forecasting interval*, is an interval for the actual value of a response, which is the mean value plus error.

For example, you can construct for the ith observation a confidence interval that contains the true mean value of the response with probability $1-\alpha$. The upper and lower limits of the confidence interval for the mean value are

$$\begin{aligned} \text{LowerM} &= \mathbf{x}_i\mathbf{b} - t_{\alpha/2}\sqrt{h_i s^2} \\ \text{UpperM} &= \mathbf{x}_i\mathbf{b} + t_{\alpha/2}\sqrt{h_i s^2} \end{aligned}$$

where $t_{\alpha/2}$ is the tabulated t statistic with degrees of freedom equal to the degrees of freedom for the mean squared error.

The limits for the confidence interval for an actual individual response are

$$\begin{aligned} \text{LowerI} &= \mathbf{x}_i\mathbf{b} - t_{\alpha/2}\sqrt{(1+h_i)s^2} \\ \text{UpperI} &= \mathbf{x}_i\mathbf{b} + t_{\alpha/2}\sqrt{(1+h_i)s^2} \end{aligned}$$

Influential observations are those that, according to various criteria, appear to have a large influence on the parameter estimates. One measure of influence, Cook's D, measures the change to the estimates that results from deleting each observation:

$$\text{COOKD} = \frac{1}{k}\text{STUDENT}^2 \left(\frac{\text{STDERR}(\hat{y})}{\text{STDERR}(\text{RESID})} \right)^2$$

where k is the number of parameters in the model (including the intercept). For more information, refer to Cook (1977, 1979).

The *predicted residual* for observation i is defined as the residual for the ith observation that results from dropping the ith observation from the parameter estimates. The sum of squares of predicted residual errors is called the *PRESS statistic*:

$$\begin{aligned} \text{PRESID}_i &= \frac{\text{RESID}_i}{1 - h_i} \\ \text{PRESS} &= \sum_{i=1}^{n} \text{PRESID}_i^2 \end{aligned}$$

Testing Linear Hypotheses

The general form of a linear hypothesis for the parameters is

$$\mathbf{H}_0 : \mathbf{L}\boldsymbol{\beta} = \mathbf{c}$$

where $\mathbf{L}$ is $q \times k$, $\boldsymbol{\beta}$ is $k \times 1$, and $\mathbf{c}$ is $q \times 1$. To test this hypothesis, the linear function is taken with respect to the parameter estimates:

$$\mathbf{Lb} - \mathbf{c}$$

This has variance

$$\text{Var}(\mathbf{Lb} - \mathbf{c}) = \mathbf{L}\text{Var}(\mathbf{b})\mathbf{L}' = \mathbf{L}(\mathbf{X}'\mathbf{X})^{-}\mathbf{L}'\sigma^2$$

where $\mathbf{b}$ is the estimate of $\boldsymbol{\beta}$.

A quadratic form called the *sum of squares due to the hypothesis* is calculated:

$$\text{SS}(\mathbf{Lb} - \mathbf{c}) = (\mathbf{Lb} - \mathbf{c})'(\mathbf{L}(\mathbf{X}'\mathbf{X})^{-}\mathbf{L}')^{-1}(\mathbf{Lb} - \mathbf{c})$$

If you assume that this is testable, the SS can be used as a numerator of the F test:

$$F = \frac{\text{SS}(\mathbf{Lb} - \mathbf{c})/q}{s^2}$$

This is compared with an F distribution with q and dfe degrees of freedom, where dfe is the degrees of freedom for residual error.

Multivariate Tests

Multivariate hypotheses involve several dependent variables in the form

$$\mathbf{H}_0 : \mathbf{L}\boldsymbol{\beta}\mathbf{M} = \mathbf{d}$$

where $\mathbf{L}$ is a linear function on the regressor side, $\boldsymbol{\beta}$ is a matrix of parameters, $\mathbf{M}$ is a linear function on the dependent side, and $\mathbf{d}$ is a matrix of constants. The special case (handled by PROC REG) in which the constants are the same for each dependent variable is written

$$(\mathbf{L}\boldsymbol{\beta} - \mathbf{cj})\mathbf{M} = \mathbf{0}$$

where $\mathbf{c}$ is a column vector of constants and $\mathbf{j}$ is a row vector of 1s. The special case in which the constants are 0 is

$$\mathbf{L}\boldsymbol{\beta}\mathbf{M} = \mathbf{0}$$

These multivariate tests are covered in detail in Morrison (1976); Timm (1975); Mardia, Kent, and Bibby (1979); Bock (1975); and other works cited in Chapter 6, "Introduction to Multivariate Procedures."

To test this hypothesis, construct two matrices, $\mathbf{H}$ and $\mathbf{E}$, that correspond to the numerator and denominator of a univariate F test:

$$\begin{aligned} \mathbf{H} &= \mathbf{M}'(\mathbf{LB} - \mathbf{cj})'(\mathbf{L}(\mathbf{X}'\mathbf{X})^{-}\mathbf{L}')^{-1}(\mathbf{LB} - \mathbf{cj})\mathbf{M} \\ \mathbf{E} &= \mathbf{M}'\left(\mathbf{Y}'\mathbf{Y} - \mathbf{B}'(\mathbf{X}'\mathbf{X})\mathbf{B}\right)\mathbf{M} \end{aligned}$$

Four test statistics, based on the eigenvalues of $\mathbf{E}^{-1}\mathbf{H}$ or $(\mathbf{E}+\mathbf{H})^{-1}\mathbf{H}$, are formed. Let λ_i be the ordered eigenvalues of $\mathbf{E}^{-1}\mathbf{H}$ (if the inverse exists), and let ξ_i be the ordered eigenvalues of $(\mathbf{E}+\mathbf{H})^{-1}\mathbf{H}$. It happens that $\xi_i = \lambda_i/(1+\lambda_i)$ and $\lambda_i = \xi_i/(1-\xi_i)$, and it turns out that $\rho_i = \sqrt{\xi_i}$ is the ith canonical correlation.

Let p be the rank of $(\mathbf{H}+\mathbf{E})$, which is less than or equal to the number of columns of $\mathbf{M}$. Let q be the rank of $\mathbf{L}(\mathbf{X}'\mathbf{X})^{-}\mathbf{L}'$. Let v be the error degrees of freedom and $s = \min(p, q)$. Let $m = (|p-q|-1)/2$, and let $n = (v-p-1)/2$. Then the following statistics have the approximate F statistics as shown.

Wilks' Lambda

If

$$\Lambda = \frac{\det(\mathbf{E})}{\det(\mathbf{H}+\mathbf{E})} = \prod_{i=1}^{n} \frac{1}{1+\lambda_i} = \prod_{i=1}^{n}(1-\xi_i)$$

then

$$F = \frac{1-\Lambda^{1/t}}{\Lambda^{1/t}} \cdot \frac{rt-2u}{pq}$$

is approximately F, where

$$\begin{aligned} r &= v - \frac{p-q+1}{2} \\ u &= \frac{pq-2}{4} \\ t &= \begin{cases} \sqrt{\frac{p^2q^2-4}{p^2+q^2-5}} & \text{if } p^2+q^2-5>0 \\ 1 & \text{otherwise} \end{cases} \end{aligned}$$

The degrees of freedom are pq and $rt-2u$. The distribution is exact if $\min(p,q) \leq 2$. (Refer to Rao 1973, p. 556.)

Pillai's Trace

If

$$\mathbf{V} = \text{trace}\left(\mathbf{H}(\mathbf{H}+\mathbf{E})^{-1}\right) = \sum_{i=1}^{n} \frac{\lambda_i}{1+\lambda_i} = \sum_{i=1}^{n} \xi_i$$

then

$$F = \frac{2n+s+1}{2m+s+1} \cdot \frac{\mathbf{V}}{s-\mathbf{V}}$$

is approximately F with $s(2m+s+1)$ and $s(2n+s+1)$ degrees of freedom.

Hotelling-Lawley Trace

If

$$\mathbf{U} = \text{trace}\left(\mathbf{E}^{-1}\mathbf{H}\right) = \sum_{i=1}^{n} \lambda_i = \sum_{i=1}^{n} \frac{\xi_i}{1-\xi_i}$$

then

$$F = \frac{2(sn+1)\mathbf{U}}{s^2(2m+s+1)}$$

is approximately F with $s(2m+s+1)$ and $2(sn+1)$ degrees of freedom.

Roy's Maximum Root

If

$$\Theta = \lambda_1$$

then

$$F = \Theta \frac{v-r+q}{r}$$

where $r = \max(p, q)$ is an upper bound on F that yields a lower bound on the significance level. Degrees of freedom are r for the numerator and $v - r + q$ for the denominator.

Tables of critical values for these statistics are found in Pillai (1960).

References

Allen, D.M. (1971), "Mean Square Error of Prediction as a Criterion for Selecting Variables," *Technometrics*, 13, 469–475.

Allen, D.M. and Cady, F.B. (1982), *Analyzing Experimental Data by Regression*, Belmont, CA: Lifetime Learning Publications.

Belsley, D.A., Kuh, E., and Welsch, R.E. (1980), *Regression Diagnostics*, New York: John Wiley & Sons, Inc.

Bock, R.D. (1975), *Multivariate Statistical Methods in Behavioral Research*, New York: McGraw-Hill Book Co.

Box, G.E.P. (1966), "The Use and Abuse of Regression," *Technometrics*, 8, 625–629.

Cook, R.D. (1977), "Detection of Influential Observations in Linear Regression," *Technometrics*, 19, 15–18.

Cook, R.D. (1979), "Influential Observations in Linear Regression," *Journal of the American Statistical Association*, 74, 169–174.

Daniel, C. and Wood, F. (1980), *Fitting Equations to Data*, Revised Edition, New York: John Wiley & Sons, Inc.

Darlington, R.B. (1968), "Multiple Regression in Psychological Research and Practice," *Psychological Bulletin*, 69, 161–182.

Draper, N. and Smith, H. (1981), *Applied Regression Analysis*, Second Edition, New York: John Wiley & Sons, Inc.

Durbin, J. and Watson, G.S. (1951), "Testing for Serial Correlation in Least Squares Regression," *Biometrika*, 37, 409–428.

Freund, R.J., Littell, R.C., and Spector P.C. (1991), *SAS System for Linear Models*, Cary, NC: SAS Institute Inc.

Freund, R.J. and Littell, R.C. (1986), *SAS System for Regression, 1986 Edition*, Cary, NC: SAS Institute Inc.

Goodnight, J.H. (1979), "A Tutorial on the SWEEP Operator," *The American Statistician*, 33, 149–158. (Also available as SAS Technical Report R-106, *The Sweep Operator: Its Importance in Statistical Computing*, Cary, NC: SAS Institute Inc.)

Hawkins, D.M. (1980), "A Note on Fitting a Regression With No Intercept Term," *The American Statistician*, 34, 233.

Hosmer, D.W, Jr and Lemeshow, S. (1989), *Applied Logistic Regression*, New York: John Wiley & Sons, Inc.

Johnston, J. (1972), *Econometric Methods*, New York: McGraw-Hill Book Co.

Kennedy, W.J. and Gentle, J.E. (1980), *Statistical Computing*, New York: Marcel Dekker, Inc.

Kvalseth, T.O. (1985), "Cautionary Note About R^2," *The American Statistician*, 39, 279.

Mallows, C.L. (1973), "Some Comments on C_p," *Technometrics*, 15, 661–75.

Mardia, K.V., Kent, J.T., and Bibby, J.M. (1979), *Multivariate Analysis*, London: Academic Press.

Morrison, D.F. (1976), *Multivariate Statistical Methods*, Second Edition, New York: McGraw-Hill Book Co.

Mosteller, F. and Tukey, J.W. (1977), *Data Analysis and Regression*, Reading, MA: Addison-Wesley Publishing Co., Inc.

Neter, J. and Wasserman, W. (1974), *Applied Linear Statistical Models*, Homewood, IL: Irwin.

Pillai, K.C.S. (1960), *Statistical Table for Tests of Multivariate Hypotheses*, Manila: The Statistical Center, University of Philippines.

Pindyck, R.S. and Rubinfeld, D.L. (1981), *Econometric Models and Econometric Forecasts*, Second Edition, New York: McGraw-Hill Book Co.

Rao, C.R. (1973), *Linear Statistical Inference and Its Applications*, Second Edition, New York: John Wiley & Sons, Inc.

Rawlings, J.O. (1988), *Applied Regression Analysis: A Research Tool*, Pacific Grove, California: Wadsworth & Brooks/Cole Advanced Books & Software.

Timm, N.H. (1975), *Multivariate Analysis with Applications in Education and Psychology*, Monterey, CA: Brooks-Cole Publishing Co.

Weisberg, S. (1985), *Applied Linear Regression*, Second Edition. New York: John Wiley & Sons, Inc.

Younger, M.S. (1979), *Handbook for Linear Regression*, North Scituate, MA: Duxbury Press.

Chapter 4
Introduction to Analysis-of-Variance Procedures

Chapter Table of Contents

Chapter 4
Introduction to Analysis-of-Variance Procedures

Overview

This chapter reviews the SAS/STAT software procedures that are used for analysis of variance: GLM, ANOVA, CATMOD, MIXED, NESTED, NPAR1WAY, TRANSREG, TTEST, and VARCOMP. Also discussed are SAS/STAT and SAS/QC software procedures for constructing analysis of variance designs: PLAN, FACTEX, and OPTEX.

The flagship analysis-of-variance procedure is the GLM procedure, which handles most standard problems. The following are descriptions of PROC GLM and other procedures that are used for more specialized situations:

ANOVA
: performs analysis of variance, multivariate analysis of variance, and repeated measures analysis of variance for *balanced* designs. PROC ANOVA also performs several multiple comparison tests.

CATMOD
: fits linear models and performs analysis of variance and repeated measures analysis of variance for categorical responses.

GENMOD
: fits generalized linear models and performs analysis of variance in the generalized linear models framework. The methods are particularly suited for discrete response outcomes.

GLM
: performs analysis of variance, regression, analysis of covariance, repeated measures analysis, and multivariate analysis of variance. PROC GLM produces several diagnostic measures, performs tests for random effects, provides contrasts and estimates for customized hypothesis tests, performs several multiple comparison tests, and provides tests for means adjusted for covariates.

MIXED
: performs mixed-model analysis of variance and repeated measures analysis of variance via covariance structure modeling. Using likelihood-based or method-of-moment estimates, PROC MIXED constructs statistical tests and intervals, allows customized contrasts and estimates, and computes empirical Bayes predictions.

NESTED
: performs analysis of variance and analysis of covariance for purely nested random models.

NPAR1WAY
: performs nonparametric one-way analysis of rank scores.

TTEST
: compares the means of two groups of observations.

TRANSREG
: fits univariate and multivariate linear models, optionally with spline and other nonlinear transformations.

VARCOMP
: estimates variance components for random or mixed models.

The following section presents an overview of some of the fundamental features of analysis of variance. Subsequent sections describe how this analysis is performed with procedures in SAS/STAT software. For more detail, see the chapters for the individual procedures. Additional sources are described in the "References" section on page 61.

Statistical Details for Analysis of Variance

Definitions

Analysis of variance (ANOVA) is a technique for analyzing experimental data in which one or more *response* (or *dependent* or simply Y) variables are measured under various conditions identified by one or more classification variables. The combinations of levels for the classification variables form the cells of the experimental design for the data. For example, an experiment may measure weight change (the dependent variable) for men and women who participated in three different weight-loss programs. The six cells of the design are formed by the six combinations of sex (men, women) and program (A, B, C).

In an analysis of variance, the variation in the response is separated into variation attributable to differences between the classification variables and variation attributable to random error. An analysis of variance constructs tests to determine the significance of the classification effects. A typical goal in an analysis of variance is to compare means of the response variable for various combinations of the classification variables.

An analysis of variance may be written as a linear model. Analysis of variance procedures in SAS/STAT software use the model to predict the response for each observation. The difference between the actual and predicted response is the *residual error*. Most of the procedures fit model parameters that minimize the sum of squares of residual errors. Thus, the method is called *least squares regression*. The variance due to the random error, σ^2, is estimated by the mean squared error (MSE or s^2).

Fixed and Random Effects

The explanatory classification variables in an ANOVA design may represent fixed or random effects. The levels of a classification variable for a fixed effect give all the levels of interest, while the levels of a classification variable for a random effect are typically a subset of levels selected from a population of levels. The following are examples.

- In a large drug trial, the levels that correspond to types of drugs are usually considered to comprise a fixed effect, but the levels corresponding to the various clinics where the drugs are administered comprise a random effect.
- In agricultural experiments, it is common to declare locations (or plots) as random because the levels are chosen randomly from a large population of locations and you assume fertility to vary normally across locations.

- In repeated-measures experiments with people or animals as subjects, subjects are declared random because they are selected from the larger population to which you want to generalize.

A typical assumption is that random effects have values drawn from a normally distributed random process with mean zero and common variance. Effects are declared random when the levels are randomly selected from a large population of possible levels. Inferences are made using only a few levels but can be generalized across the whole population of random effects levels.

The consequence of having random effects in your model is that some observations are no longer uncorrelated but instead have a covariance that depends on the variance of the random effect. In fact, a more general approach to random effect models is to model the covariance between observations.

Tests of Effects

Analysis of variance tests are constructed by comparing independent mean squares. To test a particular null hypothesis, you compute the ratio of two mean squares that have the same expected value under that hypothesis; if the ratio is much larger than 1, then that constitutes significant evidence against the null. In particular, in an analysis-of-variance model with fixed effects only, the expected value of each mean square has two components: quadratic functions of fixed parameters and random variation. For example, for a fixed effect called A, the expected value of its mean square is

$$E(\mathrm{MS(A)}) = \mathrm{Q}(\boldsymbol{\beta}) + \sigma_e^2$$

Under the null hypothesis of no A effect, the fixed portion $\mathrm{Q}(\boldsymbol{\beta})$ of the expected mean square is zero. This mean square is then compared to another mean square, say MS(E), that is independent of the first and has expected value σ_e^2. The ratio of the two mean squares

$$F = \frac{\mathrm{MS(A)}}{\mathrm{MS(E)}}$$

has the F distribution under the null hypothesis. When the null hypothesis is false, the numerator term has a larger expected value, but the expected value of the denominator remains the same. Thus, large F values lead to rejection of the null hypothesis. The probability of getting an F value at least as large as the one observed given that the null hypothesis is true is called the *significance probability value* (or the p-value). A p-value of less than 0.05, for example, indicates that data with *no* real A effect will yield F values as large as the one observed less than 5% of the time. This is usually considered moderate evidence that there *is* a real A effect. Smaller p-values constitute even stronger evidence. Larger p-values indicate that the effect of interest is less than random noise. In this case, you can conclude either that there is no effect at all or that you do not have enough data to detect the differences being tested.

General Linear Models

An analysis-of-variance model can be written as a linear model, which is an equation that predicts the response as a linear function of parameters and design variables. In general,

$$y_i = \beta_0 x_{0i} + \beta_1 x_{1i} + \cdots + \beta_k x_{ki} + \epsilon_i \quad i = 1, 2, \ldots, n$$

where y_i is the response for the ith observation, β_k are unknown parameters to be estimated, and x_{ij} are design variables. Design variables for analysis of variance are indicator variables; that is, they are always either 0 or 1.

The simplest model is to fit a single mean to all observations. In this case there is only one parameter, β_0, and one design variable, x_{0i}, which always has the value of 1:

$$\begin{aligned} y_i &= \beta_0 x_{0i} + \epsilon_i \\ &= \beta_0 + \epsilon_i \end{aligned}$$

The least-squares estimator of β_0 is the mean of the y_i. This simple model underlies all more complex models, and all larger models are compared to this simple mean model. In writing the parameterization of a linear model, β_0 is usually referred to as the *intercept*.

A one-way model is written by introducing an indicator variable for each level of the classification variable. Suppose that a variable A has four levels, with two observations per level. The indicator variables are created as follows:

Intercept	A1	A2	A3	A4
1	1	0	0	0
1	1	0	0	0
1	0	1	0	0
1	0	1	0	0
1	0	0	1	0
1	0	0	1	0
1	0	0	0	1
1	0	0	0	1

The linear model for this example is

$$y_i = \beta_0 + \beta_1 A1_i + \beta_2 A2_i + \beta_3 A3_i + \beta_4 A4_i$$

To construct crossed and nested effects, you can simply multiply out all combinations of the main-effect columns. This is described in detail in "Specification of Effects" in Chapter 30, "The GLM Procedure."

Linear Hypotheses

When models are expressed in the framework of linear models, hypothesis tests are expressed in terms of a linear function of the parameters. For example, you may want to test that $\beta_2 - \beta_3 = 0$. In general, the coefficients for linear hypotheses are some set of Ls:

$$H_0\colon L_0\beta_0 + L_1\beta_1 + \cdots + L_k\beta_k = 0$$

Several of these linear functions can be combined to make one joint test. These tests can be expressed in one matrix equation:

$$H_0\colon \mathbf{L}\boldsymbol{\beta} = 0$$

For each linear hypothesis, a sum of squares (SS) due to that hypothesis can be constructed. These sums of squares can be calculated either as a quadratic form of the estimates

$$\mathrm{SS}(\mathbf{L}\boldsymbol{\beta} = 0) = (\mathbf{Lb})'(\mathbf{L}(\mathbf{X}'\mathbf{X})^{-}\mathbf{L}')^{-1}(\mathbf{Lb})$$

or, equivalently, as the increase in sums of squares for error (SSE) for the model constrained by the null hypothesis

$$\mathrm{SS}(\mathbf{L}\beta = 0) = \mathrm{SSE(constrained)} - \mathrm{SSE(full)}$$

This SS is then divided by appropriate degrees of freedom and used as a numerator of an F statistic.

Analysis of Variance for Fixed Effect Models

PROC GLM for General Linear Models

The GLM procedure is the flagship tool for analysis of variance in SAS/STAT software. It performs analysis of variance by using least squares regression to fit general linear models, as described in the section "General Linear Models" on page 56. Among the statistical methods available in PROC GLM are regression, analysis of variance, analysis of covariance, multivariate analysis of variance, and partial correlation.

While PROC GLM can handle most common analysis of variance problems, other procedures are more efficient or have more features than PROC GLM for certain specialized analyses, or they can handle specialized models that PROC GLM cannot. Much of the rest of this chapter is concerned with comparing PROC GLM to other procedures.

PROC ANOVA for Balanced Designs

When you design an experiment, you choose how many experimental units to assign to each combination of levels (or cells) in the classification. In order to achieve good statistical properties and simplify the computations, you typically attempt to assign the same number of units to every cell in the design. Such designs are called *balanced designs*.

In SAS/STAT software, you can use the ANOVA procedure to perform analysis of variance for balanced data. The ANOVA procedure performs computations for analysis of variance that assume the balanced nature of the data. These computations are simpler and more efficient than the corresponding general computations performed by PROC GLM. Note that PROC ANOVA can be applied to certain designs that are not balanced in the strict sense of equal numbers of observations for all cells. These additional designs include all one-way models, regardless of how unbalanced the cell counts are, as well as Latin squares, which do not have data in all cells. In general, however, the ANOVA procedure is recommended only for balanced data. **If you use ANOVA to analyze a design that is not balanced, you must assume responsibility for the validity of the output.** You are responsible for recognizing incorrect results, which may include negative values reported for the sums of squares. If you are not certain that your data fit into a balanced design, then you probably need the framework of general linear models in the GLM procedure.

Comparing Group Means with PROC ANOVA and PROC GLM

When you have more than two means to compare, an F test in PROC ANOVA or PROC GLM tells you whether the means are significantly different from each other, but it does not tell you which means differ from which other means.

If you have specific comparisons in mind, you can use the CONTRAST statement in PROC GLM to make these comparisons. However, if you make many comparisons using some given significance level (0.05, for example), you are more likely to make a type 1 error (incorrectly rejecting a hypothesis that the means are equal) simply because you have more chances to make the error.

Multiple comparison methods give you more detailed information about the differences among the means and enables you to control error rates for a multitude of comparisons. A variety of multiple comparison methods are available with the MEANS statement in both the ANOVA and GLM procedures, as well as the LSMEANS statement in PROC GLM. These are described in detail in "Multiple Comparisons" in Chapter 30, "The GLM Procedure."

PROC TTEST for Comparing Two Groups

If you want to perform an analysis of variance and have only one classification variable with two levels, you can use PROC TTEST. In this special case, the results generated by PROC TTEST are equivalent to the results generated by PROC ANOVA or PROC GLM.

In addition to testing for differences between two groups, PROC TTEST performs a test for unequal variances. You can use PROC TTEST with balanced or unbalanced groups. The PROC NPAR1WAY procedure performs nonparametric analogues to t tests. See Chapter 13, "Introduction to Nonparametric Analysis," for an overview and Chapter 47 for details on PROC NPAR1WAY.

Analysis of Variance for Mixed and Random Effect Models

Just as PROC GLM is the flagship procedure for fixed-effect linear models, the MIXED procedure is the flagship procedure for random- and mixed-effect linear models. PROC MIXED fits a variety of mixed linear models to data and enables you to use these fitted models to make statistical inferences about the data. The default fitting method maximizes the restricted likelihood of the data under the assumption that the data are normally distributed and any missing data are missing at random. This general framework accommodates many common correlated-data methods, including variance component models and repeated measures analyses.

A few other procedures in SAS/STAT software offer limited mixed-linear-model capabilities. PROC GLM fits some random-effects and repeated-measures models, although its methods are based on method-of-moments estimation and a portion of the output applies only to the fixed-effects model. PROC NESTED fits special nested designs and may be useful for large data sets because of its customized algorithms. PROC VARCOMP estimates variance components models, but all of its methods are now available in PROC MIXED. PROC LATTICE fits special balanced lattice designs, but, again, the same models are available in PROC MIXED. In general, PROC MIXED is recommended for nearly all of your linear mixed-model applications.

PROC NLMIXED handles models in which the fixed or random effects enter nonlinearly. It requires that you specify a conditional distribution of the data given the random effects, with available distributions including the normal, binomial, and Poisson. You can alternatively code your own distribution with SAS programming statements. Under a normality assumption for the random effects, PROC NLMIXED performs maximum likelihood estimation via adaptive Gaussian quadrature and a dual quasi-Newton optimization algorithm. Besides standard maximum likelihood results, you can obtain empirical Bayes predictions of the random effects and estimates of arbitrary functions of the parameters with delta-method standard errors. PROC NLMIXED has a wide variety of applications, two of the most common being nonlinear growth curves and overdispersed binomial data.

Analysis of Variance for Categorical Data and Generalized Linear Models

A *categorical variable* is defined as one that can assume only a limited number of values. For example, a person's sex is a categorical variable that can assume one of two values. Variables with levels that simply name a group are said to be measured on a *nominal scale*. Categorical variables can also be measured using an *ordinal scale*, which means that the levels of the variable are ordered in some way. For example, responses to an opinion poll are usually measured on an ordinal scale, with levels ranging from "strongly disagree" to "no opinion" to "strongly agree."

For two categorical variables, one measured on an ordinal scale and one measured on a nominal scale, you may assign scores to the levels of the ordinal variable and test whether the mean scores for the different levels of the nominal variable are significantly different. This process is analogous to performing an analysis of variance on continuous data, which can be performed by PROC CATMOD. If there are n nominal variables, rather than 1, then PROC CATMOD can do an n-way analysis of variance of the mean scores.

For two categorical variables measured on a nominal scale, you can test whether the distribution of the first variable is significantly different for the levels of the second variable. This process is an analysis of variance of proportions, rather than means, and can be performed by PROC CATMOD. The corresponding n-way analysis of variance can also be performed by PROC CATMOD.

See Chapter 5, "Introduction to Categorical Data Analysis Procedures," and Chapter 22, "The CATMOD Procedure," for more information.

GENMOD uses maximum likelihood estimation to fit generalized linear models. This family includes models for categorical data such as logistic, probit, and complementary log-log regression for binomial data and Poisson regression for count data, as well as continuous models such as ordinary linear regression, gamma and inverse Gaussian regression models. GENMOD performs analysis of variance through likelihood ratio and Wald tests of fixed effects in generalized linear models, and provides contrasts and estimates for customized hypothesis tests. It performs analysis of repeated measures data with generalized estimating equation (GEE) methods.

See Chapter 5, "Introduction to Categorical Data Analysis Procedures," and Chapter 29, "The GENMOD Procedure," for more information.

Nonparametric Analysis of Variance

Analysis of variance is sensitive to the distribution of the error term. If the error term is not normally distributed, the statistics based on normality can be misleading. The traditional test statistics are called *parametric tests* because they depend on the specification of a certain probability distribution except for a set of free parameters. Parametric tests are said to depend on distributional assumptions. Nonparametric methods perform the tests without making any strict distributional assumptions. Even if the data are distributed normally, nonparametric methods are often almost as powerful as parametric methods.

Most nonparametric methods are based on taking the ranks of a variable and analyzing these ranks (or transformations of them) instead of the original values. The NPAR1WAY procedure performs a nonparametric one-way analysis of variance. Other nonparametric tests can be performed by taking ranks of the data (using the RANK procedure) and using a regular parametric procedure (such as GLM or ANOVA) to perform the analysis. Some of these techniques are outlined in the description of PROC RANK in the *SAS Procedures Guide* and in Conover and Iman (1981).

Constructing Analysis of Variance Designs

Analysis of variance is most often used for data from designed experiments. You can use the PLAN procedure to construct designs for many experiments. For example, PROC PLAN constructs designs for completely randomized experiments, randomized blocks, Latin squares, factorial experiments, and balanced incomplete block designs.

Randomization, or randomly assigning experimental units to cells in a design and to treatments within a cell, is another important aspect of experimental design. For either a new or an existing design, you can use PROC PLAN to randomize the experimental plan.

Additional features for design of experiments are available in SAS/QC software. The FACTEX and OPTEX procedures can construct a wide variety of designs, including factorials, fractional factorials, and D-optimal or A-optimal designs. These procedures, as well as the ADX Interface, provide features for randomizing and replicating designs; saving the design in an output data set; and interactively changing the design by changing its size, use of blocking, or the search strategies used. For more information, see *SAS/QC Software: Reference*.

References

Analysis of variance was pioneered by R.A. Fisher (1925). For a general introduction to analysis of variance, see an intermediate statistical methods textbook such as Steel and Torrie (1980), Snedecor and Cochran (1980), Milliken and Johnson (1984), Mendenhall (1968), John (1971), Ott (1977), or Kirk (1968). A classic source is Scheffe (1959). Freund, Littell, and Spector (1991) bring together a treatment of these statistical methods and SAS/STAT software procedures. Schlotzhauer and Littell (1997) cover how to perform *t* tests and one-way analysis of variance with SAS/STAT procedures. Texts on linear models include Searle (1971), Graybill (1976), and Hocking (1984). Kennedy and Gentle (1980) survey the computing aspects.

Conover, W.J. and Iman, R.L. (1981), "Rank Transformations as a Bridge Between Parametric and Nonparametric Statistics," *The American Statistician*, 35, 124–129.

Fisher, R.A. (1925), *Statistical Methods for Research Workers*, Edinburgh: Oliver & Boyd.

Freund, R.J., Littell, R.C., and Spector, P.C. (1991), *SAS System for Linear Models*, Cary, NC: SAS Institute Inc.

Graybill, F.A. (1976), *Theory and Applications of the Linear Model*, North Scituate, MA: Duxbury Press.

Hocking, R.R. (1984), *Analysis of Linear Models*, Monterey, CA: Brooks-Cole Publishing Co.

John, P. (1971), *Statistical Design and Analysis of Experiments*, New York: Macmillan Publishing Co.

Kennedy, W.J., Jr. and Gentle, J.E. (1980), *Statistical Computing*, New York: Marcel Dekker, Inc.

Kirk, R.E. (1968), *Experimental Design: Procedures for the Behavioral Sciences*, Monterey, CA: Brooks-Cole Publishing Co.

Mendenhall, W. (1968), *Introduction to Linear Models and the Design and Analysis of Experiments*, Belmont, CA: Duxbury Press.

Milliken, G.A. and Johnson, D.E. (1984), *Analysis of Messy Data Volume I: Designed Experiments*, Belmont, CA: Lifetime Learning Publications.

Ott, L. (1977), *Introduction to Statistical Methods and Data Analysis*, Second Edition, Belmont, CA: Duxbury Press.

Scheffe, H. (1959), *The Analysis of Variance*, New York: John Wiley & Sons, Inc.

Schlotzhauer, S.D. and Littell, R.C. (1997), *SAS System for Elementary Statistical Analysis*, Cary, NC: SAS Institute Inc.

Searle, S.R. (1971), *Linear Models*, New York: John Wiley & Sons, Inc.

Snedecor, G.W. and Cochran, W.G. (1980), *Statistical Methods*, Seventh Edition, Ames, IA: Iowa State University Press.

Steel R.G.D. and Torrie, J.H. (1980), *Principles and Procedures of Statistics*, Second Edition, New York: McGraw-Hill Book Co.

Chapter 5
Introduction to Categorical Data Analysis Procedures

Chapter Table of Contents

Chapter 5
Introduction to Categorical Data Analysis Procedures

Overview

Several procedures in SAS/STAT software can be used for the analysis of categorical data:

CATMOD	fits linear models to functions of categorical data, facilitating such analyses as regression, analysis of variance, linear modeling, log-linear modeling, logistic regression, and repeated measures analysis. Maximum likelihood estimation is used for the analysis of logits and generalized logits, and weighted least squares analysis is used for fitting models to other response functions.
CORRESP	performs simple and multiple correspondence analyses, using a contingency table, Burt table, binary table, or raw categorical data as input. For more on PROC CORRESP, see Chapter 6, "Introduction to Multivariate Procedures," and Chapter 24, "The CORRESP Procedure,".
FREQ	builds frequency tables or contingency tables and produces numerous tests and measures of association including chi-square statistics, odds ratios, correlation statistics, and Fisher's exact test for any size two-way table. In addition, it performs stratified analysis, computing Cochran-Mantel-Haenszel statistics and estimates of the common relative risk. It performs a test of binomial proportions, computes measures of agreement such as McNemar's test, kappa, and weighted kappa.
GENMOD	fits generalized linear models with maximum-likelihood methods. This family includes logistic, probit, and complementary log-log regression models for binomial data, Poisson regression models for count data, and multinomial models for ordinal response data. It performs likelihood ratio and Wald tests for type I, type III, and user-defined contrasts. It analyzes repeated measures data with generalized estimating equation (GEE) methods.
LOGISTIC	fits linear logistic regression models for binary or ordinal response data with maximum-likelihood methods. It performs stepwise regression and provides regression diagnostics. The logit link function in the logistic regression models can be replaced by the normit function or the complementary log-log function.

PROBIT computes maximum-likelihood estimates of regression parameters and optional threshold parameters for binary or ordinal response data.

Other procedures that perform analyses for categorical data are the TRANSREG and PRINQUAL procedures. PROC PRINQUAL is summarized in Chapter 6, "Introduction to Multivariate Procedures," and PROC TRANSREG is summarized in Chapter 3, "Introduction to Regression Procedures."

A *categorical variable* is defined as one that can assume only a limited number of discrete values. The measurement scale for such a variable is unrestricted. It can be *nominal*, which means that the observed levels are not ordered. It can be *ordinal*, which means that the observed levels are ordered in some way. Or it can be *interval*, which means that the observed levels are ordered and numeric and that any interval of one unit on the scale of measurement represents the same amount, regardless of its location on the scale. One example of a categorical variable is litter size; another is the number of times a subject has been married. A variable that lies on a nominal scale is sometimes called a *qualitative* or *classification variable*.

Categorical data result from observations on multiple subjects where one or more categorical variables are observed for each subject. If there is only one categorical variable, then the data are generally represented by a *frequency table*, which lists each observed value of the variable and its frequency of occurrence.

If there are two or more categorical variables, then a subject's *profile* is defined as the subject's observed values for each of the variables. Such categorical data can be represented by a frequency table that lists each observed profile and its frequency of occurrence.

If there are exactly two categorical variables, then the data are often represented by a two-dimensional *contingency table*, which has one row for each level of variable 1 and one column for each level of variable 2. The intersections of rows and columns, called *cells*, correspond to variable profiles, and each cell contains the frequency of occurrence of the corresponding profile.

If there are more than two categorical variables, then the data can be represented by a *multidimensional contingency table*. There are two commonly used methods for displaying such tables, and both require that the variables be divided into two sets.

In the first method, one set contains a row variable and a column variable for a two-dimensional contingency table, and the second set contains all of the other variables. The variables in the second set are used to form a set of profiles. Thus, the data are represented as a series of two-dimensional contingency tables, one for each profile. This is the data representation used by PROC FREQ. For example, if you request tables for RACE*SEX*AGE*INCOME, the FREQ procedure represents the data as a series of contingency tables: the row variable is AGE, the column variable is INCOME, and the combinations of levels of RACE and SEX form a set of profiles.

In the second method, one set contains the independent variables, and the other set contains the dependent variables. Profiles based on the independent variables are called *population profiles*, whereas those based on the dependent variables are called *response profiles*. A two-dimensional contingency table is then formed, with one row for each population profile and one column for each response profile. Since any subject can have only one population profile and one response profile, the contingency table is uniquely defined. This is the data representation used by PROC CATMOD.

Sampling Frameworks and Distribution Assumptions

This section discusses the sampling frameworks and distribution assumptions for the CATMOD and FREQ procedures.

Simple Random Sampling: One Population

Suppose you take a simple random sample of 100 people and ask each person the following question: Of the three colors red, blue, and green, which is your favorite? You then tabulate the results in a frequency table as shown in Table 5.1.

Table 5.1. One-Way Frequency Table

	Favorite Color			
	Red	Blue	Green	Total
Frequency	52	31	17	100
Proportion	0.52	0.31	0.17	1.00

In the population you are sampling, you assume there is an unknown probability that a population member, selected at random, would choose any given color. In order to estimate that probability, you use the sample proportion

$$p_j = \frac{n_j}{n}$$

where n_j is the frequency of the jth response and n is the total frequency.

Because of the random variation inherent in any random sample, the frequencies have a probability distribution representing their relative frequency of occurrence in a hypothetical series of samples. For a simple random sample, the distribution of frequencies for a frequency table with three levels is as follows. The probability that the first frequency is n_1, the second frequency is n_2, and the third is $n_3 = n - n_1 - n_2$ where π_j is the true probability of observing the jth response level in the population.

$$\Pr(n_1, n_2, n_3) = \frac{n!}{n_1!n_2!n_3!}\pi_1^{n_1}\pi_2^{n_2}\pi_3^{n_3}$$

This distribution, called the *multinomial distribution*, can be generalized to any number of response levels. The special case of two response levels is called the *binomial distribution*.

Simple random sampling is the type of sampling required by PROC CATMOD when there is one population. PROC CATMOD uses the multinomial distribution to estimate a probability vector and its covariance matrix. If the sample size is sufficiently large, then the probability vector is approximately normally distributed as a result of central limit theory. PROC CATMOD uses this result to compute appropriate test statistics for the specified statistical model.

Stratified Simple Random Sampling: Multiple Populations

Suppose you take two simple random samples, fifty men and fifty women, and ask the same question as before. You are now sampling two different populations that may have different response probabilities. The data can be tabulated as shown in Table 5.2.

Table 5.2. Two-Way Contingency Table: Sex by Color

	Favorite Color			
Sex	Red	Blue	Green	Total
Male	30	10	10	50
Female	20	10	20	50
Total	50	20	30	100

Note that the row marginal totals (50, 50) of the contingency table are fixed by the sampling design, but the column marginal totals (50, 20, 30) are random. There are six probabilities of interest for this table, and they are estimated by the sample proportions

$$p_{ij} = \frac{n_{ij}}{n_i}$$

where n_{ij} denotes the frequency for the ith population and the jth response, and n_i is the total frequency for the ith population. For this contingency table, the sample proportions are shown in Table 5.3.

Table 5.3. Table of Sample Proportions by Sex

	Favorite Color			
Sex	Red	Blue	Green	Total
Male	0.60	0.20	0. 20	1.00
Female	0.40	0. 20	0.40	1.00

The probability distribution of the six frequencies is the *product multinomial distribution*

$$\Pr(n_{11}, n_{12}, n_{13}, n_{21}, n_{22}, n_{23}) = \frac{n_1! n_2! \pi_{11}^{n_{11}} \pi_{12}^{n_{12}} \pi_{13}^{n_{13}} \pi_{21}^{n_{21}} \pi_{22}^{n_{22}} \pi_{23}^{n_{23}}}{n_{11}! n_{12}! n_{13}! n_{21}! n_{22}! n_{23}!}$$

where π_{ij} is the true probability of observing the jth response level in the ith population. The product multinomial distribution is simply the product of two or more individual multinomial distributions since the populations are independent. This distribution can be generalized to any number of populations and response levels.

Stratified simple random sampling is the type of sampling required by PROC CATMOD when there is more than one population. PROC CATMOD uses the product multinomial distribution to estimate a probability vector and its covariance matrix. If the sample sizes are sufficiently large, then the probability vector is approximately normally distributed as a result of central limit theory, and PROC CATMOD uses this result to compute appropriate test statistics for the specified statistical model. The statistics are known as Wald statistics, and they are approximately distributed as chi-square when the null hypothesis is true.

Observational Data: Analyzing the Entire Population

Sometimes the observed data do not come from a random sample but instead represent a complete set of observations on some population. For example, suppose a class of 100 students is classified according to sex and favorite color. The results are shown in Table 5.4.

In this case, you could argue that all of the frequencies are fixed since the entire population is observed; therefore, there is no sampling error. On the other hand, you could hypothesize that the observed table has only fixed marginals and that the cell frequencies represent one realization of a conceptual process of assigning color preferences to individuals. The assignment process is open to hypothesis, which means that you can hypothesize restrictions on the joint probabilities.

Table 5.4. Two-Way Contingency Table: Sex by Color

	Favorite Color			
Sex	Red	Blue	Green	Total
Male	16	21	20	57
Female	12	20	11	43
Total	28	41	31	100

The usual hypothesis (sometimes called *randomness*) is that the distribution of the column variable (Favorite Color) does not depend on the row variable (Sex). This implies that, for each row of the table, the assignment process corresponds to a simple random sample (without replacement) from the finite population represented by the column marginal totals (or by the column marginal subtotals that remain after sampling other rows). The hypothesis of randomness induces a probability distribution on the frequencies in the table; it is called the *hypergeometric distribution*.

If the same row and column variables are observed for each of several populations, then the probability distribution of all the frequencies can be called the *multiple hypergeometric distribution*. Each population is called a *stratum*, and an analysis that draws information from each stratum and then summarizes across them is called a *stratified analysis* (or a *blocked analysis* or a *matched analysis*). PROC FREQ does such a stratified analysis, computing test statistics and measures of association.

In general, the populations are formed on the basis of cross-classifications of independent variables. Stratified analysis is a method of adjusting for the effect of these variables without being forced to estimate parameters for them.

The multiple hypergeometric distribution is the one used by PROC FREQ for the computation of Cochran-Mantel-Haenszel statistics. These statistics are in the class of *randomization model test statistics*, which require minimal assumptions for their validity. PROC FREQ uses the multiple hypergeometric distribution to compute the mean and the covariance matrix of a function vector in order to measure the deviation between the observed and expected frequencies with respect to a particular type of alternative hypothesis. If the cell frequencies are sufficiently large, then the function vector is approximately normally distributed as a result of central limit theory, and FREQ uses this result to compute a quadratic form that has a chi-square distribution when the null hypothesis is true.

Randomized Experiments

Consider a *randomized experiment* in which patients are assigned to one of two treatment groups according to a randomization process that allocates fifty patients to each group. After a specified period of time, each patient's status (cured or uncured) is recorded. Suppose the data shown in Table 5.5 give the results of the experiment. The null hypothesis is that the two treatments are equally effective. Under this hypothesis, treatment is a randomly assigned label that has no effect on the cure rate of the patients. But this implies that each row of the table represents a simple random sample from the finite population whose cure rate is described by the column marginal totals. Therefore, the column marginals (58, 42) are fixed under the hypothesis. Since the row marginals (50, 50) are fixed by the allocation process, the hypergeometric distribution is induced on the cell frequencies. Randomized experiments can also be specified in a stratified framework, and Cochran-Mantel-Haenszel statistics can be computed relative to the corresponding multiple hypergeometric distribution.

Table 5.5. Two-Way Contingency Table: Treatment by Status

	Status		
Treatment	Cured	Uncured	Total
1	36	14	50
2	22	28	50
Total	58	42	100

Relaxation of Sampling Assumptions

As indicated above, the CATMOD procedure assumes that the data are from a stratified simple random sample, so it uses the product multinomial distribution. If the data are not from such a sample, then in many cases it is still possible to use PROC CATMOD by arguing that each row of the contingency table *does* represent a simple random sample from some hypothetical population. The extent to which the inferences are generalizable depends on the extent to which the hypothetical population is perceived to resemble the target population.

Similarly, the Cochran-Mantel-Haenszel statistics use the multiple hypergeometric distribution, which requires fixed row and column marginal totals in each contingency table. If the sampling process does not yield a table with fixed margins, then it is usually possible to fix the margins through conditioning arguments similar to the ones used by Fisher when he developed the Exact Test for 2×2 tables. In other words, if you want fixed marginal totals, you can generally make your analysis conditional on those observed totals.

For more information on sampling models for categorical data, see Bishop, Fienberg, and Holland (1975, Chapter 13).

Comparison of FREQ and CATMOD Procedures

PROC FREQ is used primarily to investigate the relationship between two variables; any confounding variables are taken into account by stratification rather than by parameter estimation. PROC CATMOD is used to investigate the relationship among many variables, all of which are integrated into a parametric model.

When PROC CATMOD estimates the covariance matrix of the frequencies, it assumes that the frequencies were obtained by a stratified simple random sampling procedure. However, PROC CATMOD can also analyze input data that consist of a function vector and a covariance matrix. Therefore, if the sampling procedure is different, you can estimate the covariance matrix of the frequencies in the appropriate manner before submitting the data to PROC CATMOD.

For the FREQ procedure, Fisher's Exact Test and Cochran-Mantel-Haenszel statistics are based on the hypergeometric distribution, which corresponds to fixed marginal totals. However, by conditioning arguments, these tests are generally applicable to a wide range of sampling procedures. Similarly, the Pearson and likelihood-ratio chi-square statistics can be derived under a variety of sampling situations.

PROC FREQ can do some traditional nonparametric analysis (such as the Kruskal-Wallis test and Spearman's correlation) since it can generate rank scores internally. Fisher's Exact Test and the Cochran-Mantel-Haenszel statistics are also inherently nonparametric. However, the main vehicle for nonparametric analyses in the SAS System is the NPAR1WAY procedure.

A large sample size is required for the validity of the chi-square distributions, the standard errors, and the covariance matrices for both PROC FREQ and PROC CATMOD. If sample size is a problem, then PROC FREQ has the advantage with its CMH statistics because it does not use any degrees of freedom to estimate parameters for confounding variables. In addition, PROC FREQ can compute exact p values for any two-way table, provided that the sample size is sufficiently small in relation to the size of the table. It can also produce exact p-values for the test of binomial proportions, the Cochran-Armitage test for trend, and the Jonckheere-Terpstra test for ordered differences among classes.

See the chapters on the FREQ and CATMOD procedures for more information. In addition, some well-known texts that deal with analyzing categorical data are listed in "References."

Comparison of CATMOD, GENMOD, LOGISTIC, and PROBIT Procedures

The LOGISTIC, GENMOD, PROBIT, and CATMOD procedures can all be used for statistical modeling of categorical data. The CATMOD procedure provides maximum likelihood estimation for logistic regression, including the analysis of logits for dichotomous outcomes and the analysis of generalized logits for polychotomous outcomes. It provides weighted least squares estimation of many other response functions, such as means, cumulative logits, and proportions, and you can also compute and analyze other response functions that can be formed from the proportions corresponding to the rows of a contingency table. In addition, a user can input and analyze a set of response functions and user-supplied covariance matrix with weighted least squares. With the CATMOD procedure, by default, all explanatory (independent) variables are treated as classification variables.

The GENMOD procedure is also a general statistical modeling tool which fits generalized linear models to data: it fits several useful models to categorical data including logistic regression, the proportional odds model, and Poisson regression. The GENMOD procedures also provides a facility for fitting generalized estimating equations to correlated response data that are categorical, such as repeated dichotomous outcomes. The GENMOD procedure fits models using maximum likelihood estimation, and you include classification variables in your models with a CLASS statement. PROC GENMOD can perform type I and type III tests, and it provides predicted values and residuals.

The LOGISTIC procedure is specifically designed for logistic regression. For dichotomous outcomes, it performs the usual logistic regression and for ordinal outcomes, it fits the proportional odds model. Note that any polychotomous response variable will be treated as an ordinal outcome by PROC LOGISTIC. This procedure has capabilities for a variety of model-building techniques, including stepwise, forward, and backwards selection. It produces predicted values and can create output data sets containing these values and other statistics including ROC, and it produces a number of regression diagnostics. The current version does not contain a CLASS statement, so that you have to code classification effects using indicator variables.

The PROBIT procedure is designed for quantal assay or other discrete event data. It performs logistic regression. This procedure includes a CLASS statement.

Stokes, Davis, and Koch (1995) provide substantial discussion of these procedures, particularly the use of the LOGISTIC and CATMOD procedures for statistical modeling.

Logistic Regression

Dichotomous Response

You have many options for performing logistic regression in the SAS System. For the dichotomous outcome, most of the time you would use the LOGISTIC procedure or the GENMOD procedure; you will need to code indicator variables for classification effects in PROC LOGISTIC but can use the CLASS statement in PROC GENMOD. The LOGISTIC procedure provides model-building, so you may choose to use it for that reason. (Note that a future release of PROC LOGISTIC will include a CLASS statement).

You may want to consider the CATMOD procedure for logistic regression since it handles classification variables; however it isn't efficient for this purpose when you have continuous variables with a large number of different values. For a continuous variable with a very limited number of values, PROC CATMOD may be useful. You list the continuous variables in the DIRECT statement.

The PROBIT procedure also performs logistic regression, and the LOGISTIC, GENMOD, and PROBIT procedures allow you to use events/trials input for the responses; the ratio of events to trials must be between 0 and 1.

Ordinal Response

The LOGISTIC and PROBIT procedures treat all response variables with more than two levels as ordinal responses and fit the proportional odds model. The GENMOD procedure fits this model with a link function of CLOGIT and the specification of the multinomial distribution.

Nominal Response

When the response variable is nominal, that is, there is no concept of ordering of the values, you can fit a logistic model to response functions called generalized logits. Only the CATMOD procedure presently performs a generalized logits analysis.

Parameterization

There are some differences in the way that models are parameterized, which means that you might get different parameter estimates if you were to perform logistic regression in each of these procedures.

- Parameter estimates from the procedures may differ in sign, depending on the ordering of response levels, which you can change if you want.
- The parameter estimates associated with a categorical independent variable may differ among the procedures since the estimates depend on the coding of the indicator variables in the design matrix. By default, the design matrix column produced by PROC CATMOD for a binary independent variable is coded using the values 1 and -1 . The same column produced by the CLASS statement of PROC GENMOD and PROC PROBIT is coded 1 and 0. PROC CATMOD uses fullrank parameterization using differential effects. As a result, the parameter estimate printed by PROC CATMOD is one-half of the estimate produced by the others. PROC LOGISTIC does not automatically create indicator variables for categorical independent variables. So, the parameterization

depends on how you code the indicator variables $(1, 0$ versus $-1, 1)$. See the "Details" sections in the chapters on the CATMOD, GENMOD, and PROBIT procedures for more information on the generation of the design matrices used by these procedures.

- The maximum-likelihood algorithm used differs among the procedures. PROC LOGISTIC uses Fisher's scoring method while PROC PROBIT, PROC GENMOD, and PROC CATMOD use the Newton-Raphson method (the PROC PROBIT algorithm is ridge stabilized and is a modified Newton-Raphson algorithm.) The parameter estimates should be the same for all three procedures and the standard errors should be the same for the logistic model. For the normal and extreme-value (Gompertz) distributions (handled by the PROBIT, GENMOD, and LOGISTIC procedures), the standard errors may differ. In general, tests computed using the standard errors from the Newton-Raphson method will be more conservative.
- The LOGISTIC, GENMOD, and PROBIT procedures can fit logistic regression models for ordinal response data using maximum-likelihood estimation. PROC LOGISTIC and PROC GENMOD use a different parameterization from that of PROC PROBIT, which results in different intercept parameters. Estimates of the slope parameters, however, should be the same for both procedures. The estimated standard errors of the slope estimates are slightly different between the two procedures because of the different computational algorithms used.

References

Agresti, A. (1984),, *Analysis of Ordinal Categorical Data*, New York: John Wiley & Sons, Inc.

Agresti, A. (1990), *Categorical Data Analysis,* New York: John Wiley & Sons, Inc.

Bishop, Y., Fienberg, S.E., and Holland, P.W. (1975), *Discrete Multivariate Analysis: Theory and Practice*, Cambridge, MA: MIT Press.

Collett, D. (1991), *Modelling Binary Data*, London: Chapman and Hall.

Cox, D.R. and Snell, E.J. (1989), *The Analysis of Binary Data*, Second Edition, London: Chapman and Hall.

Dobson, A. (1990), *An Introduction To Generalized Linear Models*, London: Chapman and Hall.

Fleiss, J.L. (1981), *Statistical Methods for Rates and Proportions*, Second Edition, New York: John Wiley & Sons, Inc.

Freeman, D.H., (1987), *Applied Categorical Data Analysis*, New York: Marcel-Dekker.

Grizzle, J.E., Starmer, C.F., and Koch, G.G. (1969), "Analysis of Categorical Data by Linear Models," *Biometrics*, 25, 489–504.

Hosmer, D.W, Jr. and Lemeshow, S. (1989), *Applied Logistic Regression*, New York: John Wiley & Sons, Inc.

McCullagh, P. and Nelder, J.A. (1989), *Generalized Linear Models*, London: Chapman and Hall.

Stokes, M.E., Davis, C.S., and Koch, G.G (1995), *Categorical Data Analysis Using the SAS System*, Cary NC: SAS Institute Inc.

Chapter 6
Introduction to Multivariate Procedures

Chapter Table of Contents

Chapter 6
Introduction to Multivariate Procedures

Overview

The procedures discussed in this chapter investigate relationships among variables without designating some as independent and others as dependent. Principal component analysis and common factor analysis examine relationships within a single set of variables, whereas canonical correlation looks at the relationship between two sets of variables. The following is a brief description of SAS/STAT multivariate procedures:

CORRESP	performs simple and multiple correspondence analyses, using a contingency table, Burt table, binary table, or raw categorical data as input. Correspondence analysis is a weighted form of principal component analysis that is appropriate for frequency data.
PRINCOMP	performs a principal component analysis and outputs standardized or unstandardized principal component scores.
PRINQUAL	performs a principal component analysis of qualitative data and multidimensional preference analysis.
FACTOR	performs principal component and common factor analyses with rotations and outputs component scores or estimates of common factor scores.
CANCORR	performs a canonical correlation analysis and outputs canonical variable scores.

Many other SAS/STAT procedures can also analyze multivariate data, for example, the CATMOD, GLM, REG, CALIS, and TRANSREG procedures as well as the procedures for clustering and discriminant analysis.

The purpose of *principal component analysis* (Rao 1964) is to derive a small number of linear combinations (principal components) of a set of variables that retain as much of the information in the original variables as possible. Often a small number of principal components can be used in place of the original variables for plotting, regression, clustering, and so on. Principal component analysis can also be viewed as an attempt to uncover approximate linear dependencies among variables.

The purpose of *common factor analysis* (Mulaik 1972) is to explain the correlations or covariances among a set of variables in terms of a limited number of unobservable, latent variables. The latent variables are not generally computable as linear combinations of the original variables. In common factor analysis, it is assumed that the variables are linearly related if not for uncorrelated random error or *unique variation* in each variable; both the linear relations and the amount of unique variation can be estimated.

Principal component and common factor analysis are often followed by rotation of the components or factors. *Rotation* is the application of a nonsingular linear transformation to components or common factors to aid interpretation.

The purpose of *canonical correlation analysis* (Mardia, Kent, and Bibby 1979) is to explain or summarize the relationship between two sets of variables by finding a small number of linear combinations from each set of variables that have the highest possible between-set correlations. Plots of the canonical variables can be useful in examining multivariate dependencies. If one of the two sets of variables consists of dummy variables generated from a classification variable, the canonical correlation is equivalent to canonical discriminant analysis (see Chapter 21, "The CANDISC Procedure"). If both sets of variables are dummy variables, canonical correlation is equivalent to simple correspondence analysis.

The purpose of *correspondence analysis* (Lebart, Morineau, and Warwick 1984; Greenacre 1984; Nishisato 1980) is to summarize the associations between a set of categorical variables in a small number of dimensions. Correspondence analysis computes scores on each dimension for each row and column category in a contingency table. Plots of these scores show the relationships among the categories.

The PRINQUAL procedure obtains linear and nonlinear transformations of variables using the method of alternating least squares (Young 1981) to optimize properties of the transformed variables' covariance or correlation matrix. PROC PRINQUAL nonlinearly transforms variables, improving their fit to a principal component model. The name, PRINQUAL, for principal components of qualitative data, comes from the special case analysis of fitting a principal component model to nominal and ordinal scale of measurement variables (Young, Takane, and de Leeuw 1978). However, PROC PRINQUAL also has facilities for smoothly transforming continuous variables. All of PROC PRINQUAL's transformations are also available in the TRANSREG procedure, which fits regression models with nonlinear transformations. PROC PRINQUAL can also perform metric and nonmetric multidimensional preference (MDPREF) analyses (Carroll 1972). The PRINQUAL procedure produces very little displayed output; the results are available in an output data set.

Comparison of the PRINCOMP and FACTOR Procedures

Although PROC FACTOR can be used for common factor analysis, the default method is principal components. PROC FACTOR produces the same results as PROC PRINCOMP except that scoring coefficients from PROC FACTOR are normalized to give principal component scores with unit variance, whereas PROC PRINCOMP by default produces principal component scores with variance equal to the corresponding eigenvalue. PROC PRINCOMP can also compute scores standardized to unit variance.

PROC PRINCOMP has the following advantages over PROC FACTOR:

- PROC PRINCOMP is slightly faster if a small number of components is requested.
- PROC PRINCOMP can analyze somewhat larger problems in a fixed amount of memory.
- PROC PRINCOMP can output scores from an analysis of a partial correlation or covariance matrix.
- PROC PRINCOMP is simpler to use.

PROC FACTOR has the following advantages over PROC PRINCOMP for principal component analysis:

- PROC FACTOR produces more output, including the scree (eigenvalue) plot, pattern matrix, and residual correlations.
- PROC FACTOR does rotations.

If you want to perform a common factor analysis, you must use PROC FACTOR instead of PROC PRINCOMP. Principal component analysis should never be used if a common factor solution is desired (Dziuban and Harris 1973; Lee and Comrey 1979).

Comparison of the PRINCOMP and PRINQUAL Procedures

The PRINCOMP procedure performs principal component analysis. The PRINQUAL procedure finds linear and nonlinear transformations of variables to optimize properties of the transformed variables' covariance or correlation matrix. One property is the sum of the first n eigenvalues, which is a measure of the fit of a principal component model with n components. Use PROC PRINQUAL to find nonlinear transformations of your variables or to perform a multidimensional preference analysis. Use PROC PRINCOMP to fit a principal component model to your data or to PROC PRINQUAL's output data set. PROC PRINCOMP produces a report of the principal component analysis and output data sets. PROC PRINQUAL produces only an output data set and an iteration history table.

Comparison of the PRINCOMP and CORRESP Procedures

As summarized previously, PROC PRINCOMP performs a principal component analysis of interval-scaled data. PROC CORRESP performs correspondence analysis, which is a weighted form of principal component analysis that is appropriate for frequency data. If your data are categorical, use PROC CORRESP instead of PROC

PRINCOMP. Both procedures produce an output data set that can be used with the %PLOTIT macro. The plots produced from the PROC CORRESP output data set graphically show relationships among the categories of the categorical variables.

Comparison of the PRINQUAL and CORRESP Procedures

Both PROC PRINQUAL and PROC CORRESP can be used to summarize associations among variables measured on a nominal scale. PROC PRINQUAL searches for a single nonlinear transformation of the original scoring of each nominal variable that optimizes some aspect of the covariance matrix of the transformed variables. For example, PROC PRINQUAL could be used to find scorings that maximize the fit of a principal component model with one component. PROC CORRESP uses the crosstabulations of nominal variables, not covariances, and produces multiple scores for each category of each nominal variable. The main conceptual difference between PROC PRINQUAL and PROC CORRESP is that PROC PRINQUAL assumes that the categories of a nominal variable correspond to values of a single underlying interval variable, whereas PROC CORRESP assumes that there are multiple underlying interval variables and therefore uses different category scores for each dimension of the correspondence analysis. PROC CORRESP scores on the first dimension match the single set of PROC PRINQUAL scores (with appropriate standardizations for both analyses).

Comparison of the TRANSREG and PRINQUAL Procedures

Both the TRANSREG and PRINQUAL procedures are data transformation procedures that have many of the same transformations. These procedures can either directly perform the specified transformation (such as taking the logarithm of the variable) or search for an optimal transformation (such as a spline with a specified number of knots). Both procedures can use an iterative, alternating-least-squares analysis. Both procedures create an output data set that can be used as input to other procedures. PROC PRINQUAL displays very little output, whereas PROC TRANSREG displays many results. PROC TRANSREG has two sets of variables, usually dependent and independent, and it fits linear models such as ordinary regression and ANOVA, multiple and multivariate regression, metric and nonmetric conjoint analysis, metric and nonmetric vector and ideal point preference mapping, redundancy analysis, canonical correlation, and response surface regression. In contrast, PROC PRINQUAL has one set of variables, fits a principal component model or multidimensional preference analysis, and can also optimize other properties of a correlation or covariance matrix. PROC TRANSREG performs hypothesis testing and can be used to code experimental designs prior to their use in other analyses.

See Chapter 3, "Introduction to Regression Procedures," for more comparisons of the TRANSREG and REG procedures.

References

Carroll J.D. (1972), "Individual Differences and Multidimensional Scaling," in R.N. Shepard, A.K. Romney, and S.B. Nerlove (eds.), *Multidimensional Scaling: Theory and Applications in the Behavioral Sciences (Volume 1)*, New York: Seminar Press.

Dziuban, C.D. and Harris, C.W. (1973), "On the Extraction of Components and the Applicability of the Factor Model," *American Educational Research Journal*, 10, 93–99.

Greenacre, M.J. (1984), *Theory and Applications of Correspondence Analysis*, London: Academic Press.

Hanson, R.J. and Norris, M.J. (1981), "Analysis of Measurements Based on the Singular Value Decomposition," *SIAM Journal on Scientific and Statistical Computing*, 2, 363–373.

Kshirsagar, A.M. (1972), *Multivariate Analysis*, New York: Marcel Dekker, Inc.

Lebart, L., Morineau, A., and Warwick, K.M. (1984), *Multivariate Descriptive Statistical Analysis: Correspondence Analysis and Related Techniques for Large Matrices*, New York: John Wiley & Sons, Inc.

Lee, H.B. and Comrey, A.L. (1979), "Distortions in a Commonly Used Factor Analytic Procedure," *Multivariate Behavioral Research*, 14, 301–321.

Mardia, K.V., Kent, J.T., and Bibby, J.M. (1979), *Multivariate Analysis*, London: Academic Press.

Mulaik, S.A. (1972), *The Foundations of Factor Analysis*, New York: McGraw-Hill Book Co.

Nishisato, S. (1980), *Analysis of Categorical Data: Dual Scaling and Its Applications*, Toronto: University of Toronto Press.

Rao, C.R. (1964), "The Use and Interpretation of Principal Component Analysis in Applied Research," *Sankhya A*, 26, 329–358.

Van den Wollenberg, A.L. (1977), "Redundancy Analysis—An Alternative to Canonical Correlation Analysis," *Psychometrika*, 42, 207–219.

Young, F.W. (1981), "Quantitative Analysis of Qualitative Data," *Psychometrika*, 46, 357–388.

Young, F.W., Takane, Y., and de Leeuw, J. (1978), "The Principal Components of Mixed Measurement Level Multivariate Data: An Alternating Least Squares Method with Optimal Scaling Features," *Psychometrika*, 43, 279–281.

Chapter 7
Introduction to Discriminant Procedures

Chapter Table of Contents

Chapter 7
Introduction to Discriminant Procedures

Overview

The SAS procedures for discriminant analysis treat data with one classification variable and several quantitative variables. The purpose of discriminant analysis can be to find one or more of the following:

- a mathematical rule, or *discriminant function*, for guessing to which class an observation belongs, based on knowledge of the quantitative variables only
- a set of linear combinations of the quantitative variables that best reveals the differences among the classes
- a subset of the quantitative variables that best reveals the differences among the classes

The SAS discriminant procedures are as follows:

DISCRIM computes various discriminant functions for classifying observations. Linear or quadratic discriminant functions can be used for data with approximately multivariate normal within-class distributions. Nonparametric methods can be used without making any assumptions about these distributions.

CANDISC performs a canonical analysis to find linear combinations of the quantitative variables that best summarize the differences among the classes.

STEPDISC uses forward selection, backward elimination, or stepwise selection to try to find a subset of quantitative variables that best reveals differences among the classes.

Background

The term *discriminant analysis* (Fisher 1936; Cooley and Lohnes 1971; Tatsuoka 1971; Kshirsagar 1972; Lachenbruch 1975, 1979; Gnanadesikan 1977; Klecka 1980; Hand 1981,1982; Silverman, 1986) refers to several different types of analysis. Classificatory discriminant analysis is used to classify observations into two or more known groups on the basis of one or more quantitative variables. Classification can be done by either a parametric method or a nonparametric method in the DISCRIM procedure. A parametric method is appropriate only for approximately normal within-class distributions. The method generates either a linear discriminant function (the within-class covariance matrices are assumed to be equal) or a quadratic discriminant function (the within-class covariance matrices are assumed to be unequal).

When the distribution within each group is not assumed to have any specific distribution or is assumed to have a distribution different from the multivariate normal distribution, nonparametric methods can be used to derive classification criteria. These methods include the kernel method and nearest-neighbor methods. The kernel method uses uniform, normal, Epanechnikov, biweight, or triweight kernels in estimating the group-specific density at each observation. The within-group covariance matrices or the pooled covariance matrix can be used to scale the data.

The performance of a discriminant function can be evaluated by estimating error rates (probabilities of misclassification). Error count estimates and posterior probability error rate estimates can be evaluated with PROC DISCRIM. When the input data set is an ordinary SAS data set, the error rates can also be estimated by cross validation.

In multivariate statistical applications, the data collected are largely from distributions different from the normal distribution. Various forms of nonnormality can arise, such as qualitative variables or variables with underlying continuous but nonnormal distributions. If the multivariate normality assumption is violated, the use of parametric discriminant analysis may not be appropriate. When a parametric classification criterion (linear or quadratic discriminant function) is derived from a nonnormal population, the resulting error rate estimates may be biased.

If your quantitative variables are not normally distributed, or if you want to classify observations on the basis of categorical variables, you should consider using the CATMOD or LOGISTIC procedure to fit a categorical linear model with the classification variable as the dependent variable. Press and Wilson (1978) compare logistic regression and parametric discriminant analysis and conclude that logistic regression is preferable to parametric discriminant analysis in cases for which the variables do not have multivariate normal distributions within classes. However, if you do have normal within-class distributions, logistic regression is less efficient than parametric discriminant analysis. Efron (1975) shows that with two normal populations having a common covariance matrix, logistic regression is between one half and two thirds as effective as the linear discriminant function in achieving asymptotically the same error rate.

Do not confuse discriminant analysis with cluster analysis. All varieties of discriminant analysis require prior knowledge of the classes, usually in the form of a sample from each class. In cluster analysis, the data do not include information on class membership; the purpose is to construct a classification. See Chapter 8, "Introduction to Clustering Procedures."

Canonical discriminant analysis is a dimension-reduction technique related to principal components and canonical correlation, and it can be performed by both the CANDISC and DISCRIM procedures. A discriminant criterion is always derived in PROC DISCRIM. If you want canonical discriminant analysis without the use of a discriminant criterion, you should use PROC CANDISC. Stepwise discriminant analysis is a variable-selection technique implemented by the STEPDISC procedure. After selecting a subset of variables with PROC STEPDISC, use any of the other discriminant procedures to obtain more detailed analyses. PROC CANDISC and PROC STEPDISC perform hypothesis tests that require the within-class distributions to be approximately normal, but these procedures can be used descriptively with nonnormal data.

Another alternative to discriminant analysis is to perform a series of univariate one-way ANOVAs. All three discriminant procedures provide summaries of the univariate ANOVAs. The advantage of the multivariate approach is that two or more classes that overlap considerably when each variable is viewed separately may be more distinct when examined from a multivariate point of view.

Example: Contrasting Univariate and Multivariate Analyses

Consider the two classes indicated by 'H' and 'O' in Figure 7.1. The results are shown in Figure 7.2.

```
data random;
   drop n;

   Group = 'H';
   do n = 1 to 20;
      X = 4.5 + 2 * normal(57391);
      Y = X + .5 + normal(57391);
      output;
   end;

   Group = 'O';
   do n = 1 to 20;
      X = 6.25 + 2 * normal(57391);
      Y = X - 1 + normal(57391);
      output;
   end;

run;

symbol1 v='H' c=blue;
symbol2 v='O' c=yellow;
proc gplot;
   plot Y*X=Group / cframe=ligr nolegend;
run;

proc candisc anova;
   class Group;
   var X Y;
run;
```

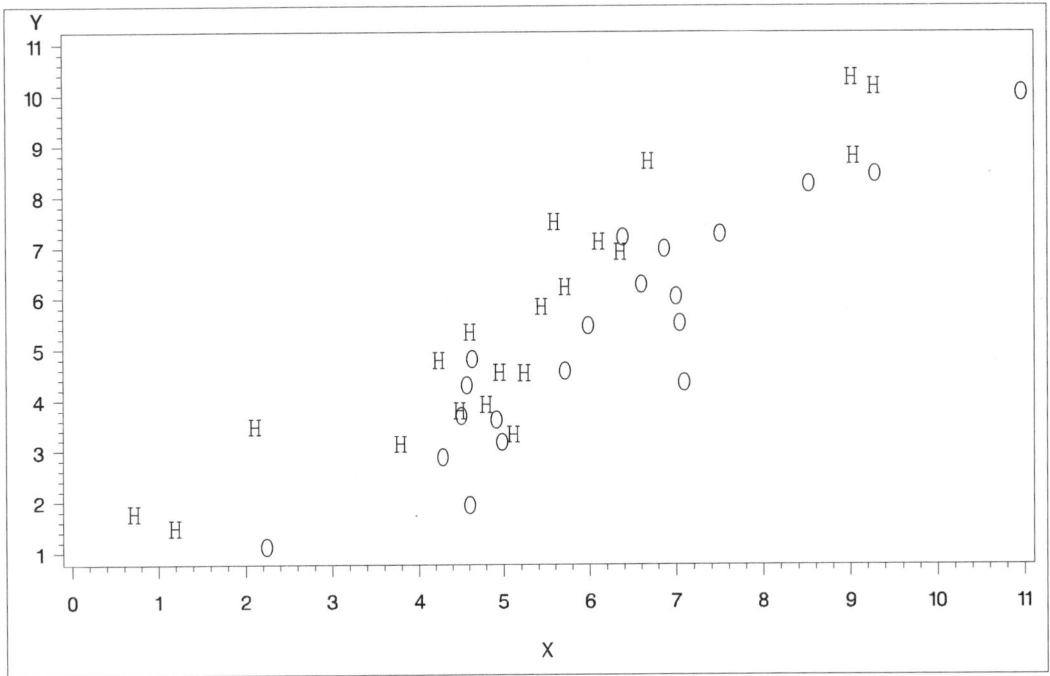

Figure 7.1. Groups for Contrasting Univariate and Multivariate Analyses

```
                         The CANDISC Procedure

     Observations        40          DF Total                    39
     Variables            2          DF Within Classes           38
     Classes              2          DF Between Classes           1


                       Class Level Information

              Variable
    Group     Name          Frequency       Weight     Proportion

    H         H                    20      20.0000       0.500000
    O         O                    20      20.0000       0.500000
```

Figure 7.2. Contrasting Univariate and Multivariate Analyses

```
                         The CANDISC Procedure

                      Univariate Test Statistics

                F Statistics,    Num DF=1,   Den DF=38

              Total     Pooled    Between
           Standard   Standard   Standard              R-Square
Variable  Deviation  Deviation  Deviation  R-Square  / (1-RSq)  F Value  Pr > F

X            2.1776     2.1498     0.6820    0.0503     0.0530     2.01  0.1641
Y            2.4215     2.4486     0.2047    0.0037     0.0037     0.14  0.7105


                          Average R-Square

                   Unweighted               0.0269868
                   Weighted by Variance     0.0245201


            Multivariate Statistics and Exact F Statistics

                         S=1    M=0    N=17.5

Statistic                      Value    F Value    Num DF    Den DF    Pr > F

Wilks' Lambda             0.64203704      10.31         2        37    0.0003
Pillai's Trace            0.35796296      10.31         2        37    0.0003
Hotelling-Lawley Trace    0.55754252      10.31         2        37    0.0003
Roy's Greatest Root       0.55754252      10.31         2        37    0.0003
```

```
                         The CANDISC Procedure

                            Adjusted    Approximate        Squared
              Canonical    Canonical       Standard      Canonical
            Correlation  Correlation          Error    Correlation

        1      0.598300     0.589467       0.102808       0.357963

                           Eigenvalues of Inv(E)*H
                             = CanRsq/(1-CanRsq)

              Eigenvalue    Difference    Proportion    Cumulative

         1        0.5575                      1.0000        1.0000

            Test of H0: The canonical correlations in the
              current row and all that follow are zero

            Likelihood    Approximate
                 Ratio        F Value    Num DF    Den DF    Pr > F

        1   0.64203704          10.31         2        37    0.0003

                  NOTE: The F statistic is exact.
```

```
                    The CANDISC Procedure

                 Total Canonical Structure

                 Variable              Can1

                 X                -0.374883
                 Y                 0.101206


                 Between Canonical Structure

                 Variable              Can1

                 X                -1.000000
                 Y                 1.000000


              Pooled Within Canonical Structure

                 Variable              Can1

                 X                -0.308237
                 Y                 0.081243
```

```
                    The CANDISC Procedure

       Total-Sample Standardized Canonical Coefficients

                 Variable              Can1

                 X             -2.625596855
                 Y              2.446680169


    Pooled Within-Class Standardized Canonical Coefficients

                 Variable              Can1

                 X             -2.592150014
                 Y              2.474116072


                 Raw Canonical Coefficients

                 Variable              Can1

                 X             -1.205756217
                 Y              1.010412967


              Class Means on Canonical Variables

                  Group              Can1

                  H          0.7277811475
                  O          -.7277811475
```

The univariate R^2s are very small, 0.0503 for X and 0.0037 for Y, and neither variable shows a significant difference between the classes at the 0.10 level.

The multivariate test for differences between the classes is significant at the 0.0003 level. Thus, the multivariate analysis has found a highly significant difference, whereas the univariate analyses failed to achieve even the 0.10 level. The Raw Canonical Coefficients for the first canonical variable, Can1, show that the classes differ most widely on the linear combination -1.205756217 X + 1.010412967 Y or approximately Y - 1.2 X. The R^2 between Can1 and the class variable is 0.357963 as given by the Squared Canonical Correlation, which is much higher than either univariate R^2.

In this example, the variables are highly correlated within classes. If the within-class correlation were smaller, there would be greater agreement between the univariate and multivariate analyses.

References

Cooley, W.W. and Lohnes, P.R. (1971), *Multivariate Data Analysis*, New York: John Wiley & Sons, Inc.

Dillion, W. and Goldstein, M. (1984), *Multivariate Analysis: Methods and Applications*, New York: John Wiley & Sons, Inc.

Efron, B. (1975), "The Efficiency of Logistic Regression Compared to Normal Discriminant Analysis," *Journal of the American Statistical Association*, 70, 892–898.

Fisher, R.A. (1936), "The Use of Multiple Measurements in Taxonomic Problems," *Annals of Eugenics*, 7, 179–188.

Gnanadesikan, R. (1977), *Methods for Statistical Data Analysis of Multivariate Observations*, New York: John Wiley & Sons, Inc.

Hand, D.J. (1981), *Discrimination and Classification*, New York: John Wiley & Sons, Inc.

Hand, D.J. (1982), *Kernel Discriminant Analysis*, New York: Research Studies Press.

Hora, S.C. and Wilcox, J.B. (1982), "Estimation of Error Rates in Several-Population Discriminant Analysis," *Journal of Marketing Research*, XIX, 57–61.

Klecka, W.R. (1980), *Discriminant Analysis*, Sage University Paper Series on Quantitative Applications in the Social Sciences, 07-019. Beverly Hills, CA: Sage Publications.

Kshirsagar, A.M. (1972), *Multivariate Analysis*, New York: Marcel Dekker, Inc.

Lachenbruch, P.A. (1975), *Discriminant Analysis*, New York: Hafner.

Lachenbruch, P.A. (1979), "Discriminant Analysis," *Biometrics*, 35, 69–85.

Press, S.J. and Wilson, S. (1978), "Choosing Between Logistic Regression and Discriminant Analysis," *Journal of the American Statistical Association*, 73, 699–705.

Silverman, B.W. (1986), *Density Estimation for Statistics and Data Analysis*, New York: Chapman and Hall.

Tatsuoka, M.M. (1971), *Multivariate Analysis*, New York: John Wiley & Sons, Inc.

Chapter 8

Introduction to Clustering Procedures

Chapter Table of Contents

Chapter 8
Introduction to Clustering Procedures

Overview

You can use SAS clustering procedures to cluster the observations or the variables in a SAS data set. Both hierarchical and disjoint clusters can be obtained. Only numeric variables can be analyzed directly by the procedures, although the %DISTANCE macro can compute a distance matrix using character or numeric variables.

The purpose of cluster analysis is to place objects into groups or clusters suggested by the data, not defined a priori, such that objects in a given cluster tend to be similar to each other in some sense, and objects in different clusters tend to be dissimilar. You can also use cluster analysis for summarizing data rather than for finding "natural" or "real" clusters; this use of clustering is sometimes called *dissection* (Everitt 1980).

Any generalization about cluster analysis must be vague because a vast number of clustering methods have been developed in several different fields, with different definitions of clusters and similarity among objects. The variety of clustering techniques is reflected by the variety of terms used for cluster analysis: botryology, classification, clumping, competitive learning, morphometrics, nosography, nosology, numerical taxonomy, partitioning, Q-analysis, systematics, taximetrics, taxonorics, typology, unsupervised pattern recognition, vector quantization, and winner-take-all learning. Good (1977) has also suggested aciniformics and agminatics.

Several types of clusters are possible:

- Disjoint clusters place each object in one and only one cluster.
- Hierarchical clusters are organized so that one cluster may be entirely contained within another cluster, but no other kind of overlap between clusters is allowed.
- Overlapping clusters can be constrained to limit the number of objects that belong simultaneously to two clusters, or they can be unconstrained, allowing any degree of overlap in cluster membership.
- Fuzzy clusters are defined by a probability or grade of membership of each object in each cluster. Fuzzy clusters can be disjoint, hierarchical, or overlapping.

The data representations of objects to be clustered also take many forms. The most common are

- a square distance or similarity matrix, in which both rows and columns correspond to the objects to be clustered. A correlation matrix is an example of a similarity matrix.
- a coordinate matrix, in which the rows are observations and the columns are variables, as in the usual SAS multivariate data set. The observations, the variables, or both may be clustered.

The SAS procedures for clustering are oriented toward disjoint or hierarchical clusters from coordinate data, distance data, or a correlation or covariance matrix. The following procedures are used for clustering:

CLUSTER — performs hierarchical clustering of observations using eleven agglomerative methods applied to coordinate data or distance data.

FASTCLUS — finds disjoint clusters of observations using a k-means method applied to coordinate data. PROC FASTCLUS is especially suitable for large data sets.

MODECLUS — finds disjoint clusters of observations with coordinate or distance data using nonparametric density estimation. It can also perform approximate nonparametric significance tests for the number of clusters.

VARCLUS — performs both hierarchical and disjoint clustering of variables by oblique multiple-group component analysis.

TREE — draws tree diagrams, also called *dendrograms* or *phenograms*, using output from the CLUSTER or VARCLUS procedures. PROC TREE can also create a data set indicating cluster membership at any specified level of the cluster tree.

The following procedures are useful for processing data prior to the actual cluster analysis:

ACECLUS — attempts to estimate the pooled within-cluster covariance matrix from coordinate data without knowledge of the number or the membership of the clusters (Art, Gnanadesikan, and Kettenring 1982). PROC ACECLUS outputs a data set containing canonical variable scores to be used in the cluster analysis proper.

PRINCOMP — performs a principal component analysis and outputs principal component scores.

STDIZE — standardizes variables using any of a variety of location and scale measures, including mean and standard deviation, minimum and range, median and absolute deviation from the median, various m estimators and a estimators, and some scale estimators designed specifically for cluster analysis.

Massart and Kaufman (1983) is the best elementary introduction to cluster analysis. Other important texts are Anderberg (1973), Sneath and Sokal (1973), Duran and Odell (1974), Hartigan (1975), Titterington, Smith, and Makov (1985), McLachlan and Basford (1988), and Kaufmann and Rousseeuw (1990). Hartigan (1975) and Spath (1980) give numerous FORTRAN programs for clustering. Any prospective user of cluster analysis should study the Monte Carlo results of Milligan (1980), Milligan and Cooper (1985), and Cooper and Milligan (1984). Important references on the statistical aspects of clustering include MacQueen (1967), Wolfe (1970), Scott and Symons (1971), Hartigan (1977; 1978; 1981; 1985), Symons (1981), Everitt (1981), Sarle (1983), Bock (1985), and Thode et al. (1988). Bayesian methods have important advantages over maximum likelihood; refer to Binder (1978; 1981), Banfield and Raftery (1993), and Bensmail et al, (1997). For fuzzy clustering, refer to Bezdek (1981) and Bezdek and Pal (1992). The signal-processing perspective is provided by Gersho and Gray (1992). Refer to Blashfield and Aldenderfer (1978) for a discussion of the fragmented state of the literature on cluster analysis.

Clustering Variables

Factor rotation is often used to cluster variables, but the resulting clusters are fuzzy. It is preferable to use PROC VARCLUS if you want hard (nonfuzzy), disjoint clusters. Factor rotation is better if you want to be able to find overlapping clusters. It is often a good idea to try both PROC VARCLUS and PROC FACTOR with an oblique rotation, compare the amount of variance explained by each, and see how fuzzy the factor loadings are and whether there seem to be overlapping clusters.

You can use PROC VARCLUS to harden a fuzzy factor rotation; use PROC FACTOR to create an output data set containing scoring coefficients and initialize PROC VARCLUS with this data set:

```
proc factor rotate=promax score outstat=fact;
run;

proc varclus initial=input proportion=0;
run;
```

You can use any rotation method instead of the PROMAX method. The SCORE and OUTSTAT= options are necessary in the PROC FACTOR statement. PROC VARCLUS reads the correlation matrix from the data set created by PROC FACTOR. The INITIAL=INPUT option tells PROC VARCLUS to read initial scoring coefficients from the data set. The option PROPORTION=0 keeps PROC VARCLUS from splitting any of the clusters.

Clustering Observations

PROC CLUSTER is easier to use than PROC FASTCLUS because one run produces results from one cluster up to as many as you like. You must run PROC FASTCLUS once for each number of clusters.

The time required by PROC FASTCLUS is roughly proportional to the number of observations, whereas the time required by PROC CLUSTER with most methods varies with the square or cube of the number of observations. Therefore, you can use PROC FASTCLUS with much larger data sets than PROC CLUSTER.

If you want to hierarchically cluster a data set that is too large to use with PROC CLUSTER directly, you can have PROC FASTCLUS produce, for example, 50 clusters, and let PROC CLUSTER analyze these 50 clusters instead of the entire data set. The MEAN= data set produced by PROC FASTCLUS contains two special variables:

- The variable _FREQ_ gives the number of observations in the cluster.
- The variable _RMSSTD_ gives the root-mean-square across variables of the cluster standard deviations.

These variables are automatically used by PROC CLUSTER to give the correct results when clustering clusters. For example, you could specify Ward's minimum variance method (Ward 1963),

```
proc fastclus maxclusters=50 mean=temp;
   var x y z;
run;

proc cluster method=ward outtree=tree;
   var x y z;
run;
```

or Wong's hybrid method (Wong 1982):

```
proc fastclus maxclusters=50 mean=temp;
   var x y z;
run;

proc cluster method=density hybrid outtree=tree;
   var x y z;
run;
```

More detailed examples are given in Chapter 23, "The CLUSTER Procedure."

Characteristics of Methods for Clustering Observations

Many simulation studies comparing various methods of cluster analysis have been performed. In these studies, artificial data sets containing known clusters are produced using pseudo-random-number generators. The data sets are analyzed by a variety of clustering methods, and the degree to which each clustering method recovers the known cluster structure is evaluated. Refer to Milligan (1981) for a review of such studies. In most of these studies, the clustering method with the best overall performance has been either average linkage or Ward's minimum variance method. The method with the poorest overall performance has almost invariably been single linkage. However, in many respects, the results of simulation studies are inconsistent and confusing.

When you attempt to evaluate clustering methods, it is essential to realize that most methods are biased toward finding clusters possessing certain characteristics related to size (number of members), shape, or dispersion. Methods based on the least-squares criterion (Sarle 1982), such as k-means and Ward's minimum variance method, tend to find clusters with roughly the same number of observations in each cluster. Average linkage is somewhat biased toward finding clusters of equal variance. Many clustering methods tend to produce compact, roughly hyperspherical clusters and are incapable of detecting clusters with highly elongated or irregular shapes. The methods with the least bias are those based on nonparametric density estimation such as single linkage and density linkage.

Most simulation studies have generated compact (often multivariate normal) clusters of roughly equal size or dispersion. Such studies naturally favor average linkage and Ward's method over most other hierarchical methods, especially single linkage. It would be easy, however, to design a study using elongated or irregular clusters in which single linkage would perform much better than average linkage or Ward's method (see some of the following examples). Even studies that compare clustering methods using "realistic" data may unfairly favor particular methods. For example, in all the data sets used by Mezzich and Solomon (1980), the clusters established by field experts are of equal size. When interpreting simulation or other comparative studies, you must, therefore, decide whether the artificially generated clusters in the study resemble the clusters you suspect may exist in your data in terms of size, shape, and dispersion. If, like many people doing exploratory cluster analysis, you have no idea what kinds of clusters to expect, you should include at least one of the relatively unbiased methods, such as density linkage, in your analysis.

The rest of this section consists of a series of examples that illustrate the performance of various clustering methods under various conditions. The first, and simplest example, shows a case of well-separated clusters. The other examples show cases of poorly separated clusters, clusters of unequal size, parallel elongated clusters, and nonconvex clusters.

Well-Separated Clusters

If the population clusters are sufficiently well separated, almost any clustering method performs well, as demonstrated in the following example using single linkage. In this and subsequent examples, the output from the clustering procedures is not shown, but cluster membership is displayed in scatter plots. The following SAS statements produce Figure 8.1:

```
data compact;
   keep x y;
   n=50; scale=1;
   mx=0; my=0; link generate;
   mx=8; my=0; link generate;
   mx=4; my=8; link generate;
   stop;
generate:
   do i=1 to n;
      x=rannor(1)*scale+mx;
      y=rannor(1)*scale+my;
      output;
   end;
   return;
run;

proc cluster data=compact outtree=tree
             method=single noprint;
run;

proc tree noprint out=out n=3;
   copy x y;
run;

legend1 frame cframe=ligr  cborder=black
        position=center value=(justify=center);
axis1 minor=none label=(angle=90 rotate=0);
axis2 minor=none;
proc gplot;
   plot y*x=cluster/frame cframe=ligr
        vaxis=axis1 haxis=axis2 legend=legend1;
   title 'Single Linkage Cluster Analysis';
   title2 'of Data Containing Well-Separated,
           Compact Clusters';
run;
```

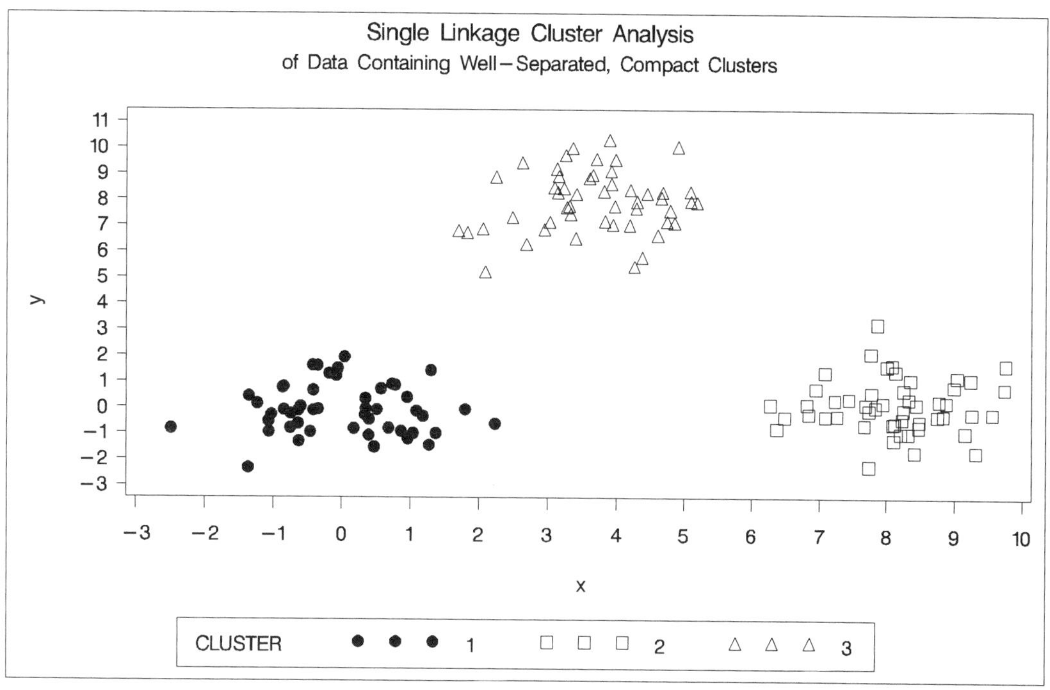

Figure 8.1. Data Containing Well-Separated, Compact Clusters: PROC CLUSTER with METHOD=SINGLE and PROC GPLOT

Poorly Separated Clusters

To see how various clustering methods differ, you must examine a more difficult problem than that of the previous example.

The following data set is similar to the first except that the three clusters are much closer together. This example demonstrates the use of PROC FASTCLUS and five hierarchical methods available in PROC CLUSTER. To help you compare methods, this example plots true, generated clusters. Also included is a bubble plot of the density estimates obtained in conjunction with two-stage density linkage in PROC CLUSTER. The following SAS statements produce Figure 8.2:

```
data closer;
   keep x y c;
   n=50; scale=1;
   mx=0; my=0; c=3; link generate;
   mx=3; my=0; c=1; link generate;
   mx=1; my=2; c=2; link generate;
   stop;
generate:
   do i=1 to n;
      x=rannor(9)*scale+mx;
      y=rannor(9)*scale+my;
      output;
   end;
   return;
run;
```

```
title 'True Clusters for Data Containing Poorly Separated,
       Compact Clusters';
proc gplot;
    plot y*x=c/frame cframe=ligr
        vaxis=axis1 haxis=axis2 legend=legend1;
run;
```

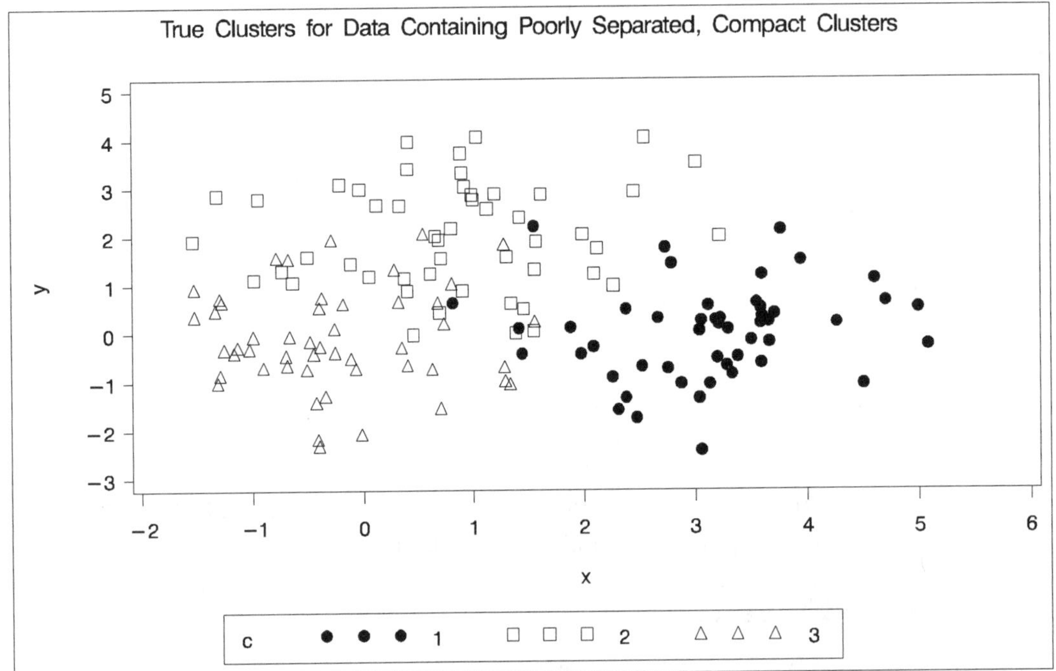

Figure 8.2. Data Containing Poorly Separated, Compact Clusters: Plot of True Clusters

The following statements use the FASTCLUS procedure to find three clusters and the GPLOT procedure to plot the clusters. Since the GPLOT step is repeated several times in this example, it is contained in the PLOTCLUS macro. The following statements produce Figure 8.3.

```
%macro plotclus;
   legend1 frame cframe=ligr  cborder=black
           position=center value=(justify=center);
   axis1 minor=none label=(angle=90 rotate=0);
   axis2 minor=none;
   proc gplot;
      plot y*x=cluster/frame cframe=ligr
           vaxis=axis1 haxis=axis2 legend=legend1;
   run;
%mend plotclus;

proc fastclus data=closer out=out maxc=3 noprint;
   var x y;
   title 'FASTCLUS Analysis';
   title2 'of Data Containing Poorly Separated,
           Compact Clusters';
run;
%plotclus;
```

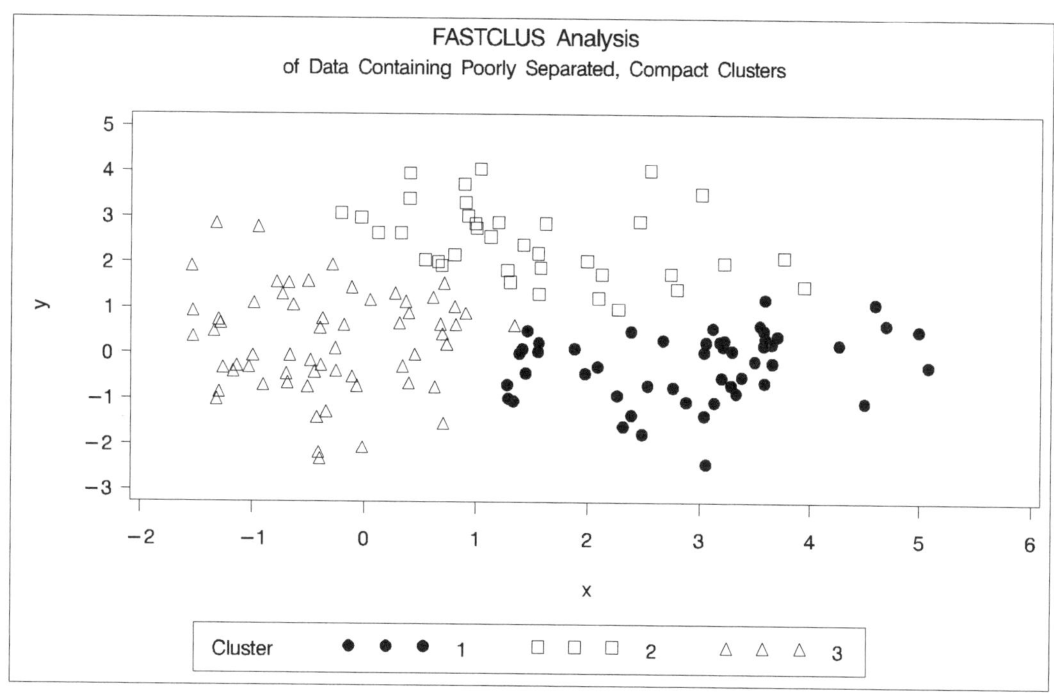

Figure 8.3. Data Containing Poorly Separated, Compact Clusters: PROC FASTCLUS

The following SAS statements produce Figure 8.4:

```
proc cluster data=closer outtree=tree method=ward noprint;
   var x y;
run;

proc tree noprint out=out n=3;
   copy x y;
   title 'Ward''s Minimum Variance Cluster Analysis';
   title2 'of Data Containing Poorly Separated,
           Compact Clusters';
run;

%plotclus;
```

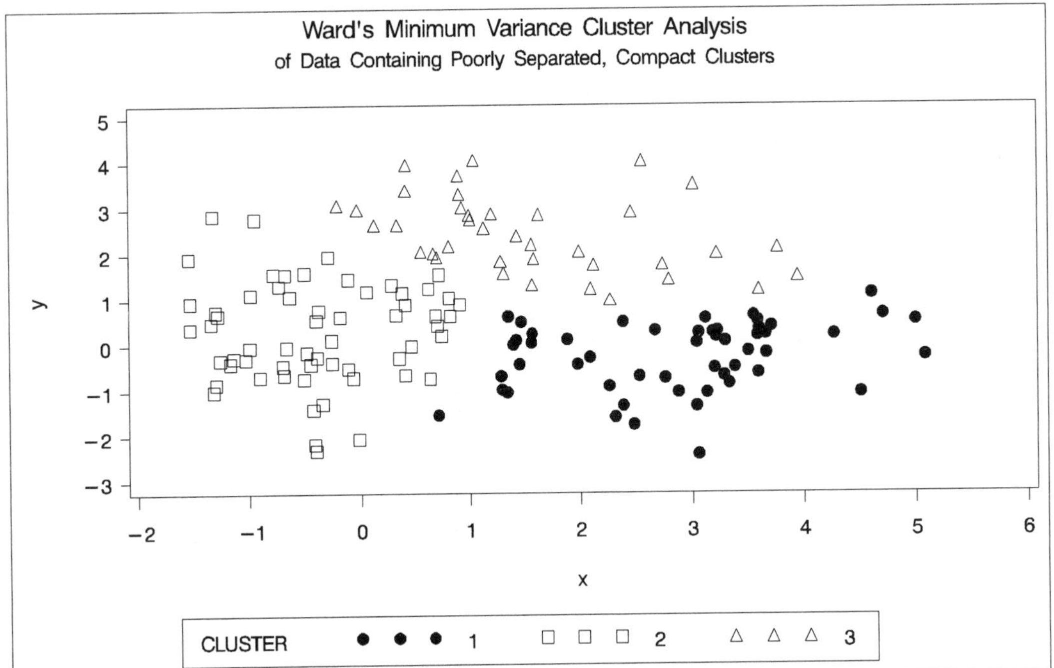

Figure 8.4. Data Containing Poorly Separated, Compact Clusters: PROC CLUSTER with METHOD=WARD

The following SAS statements produce Figure 8.5:

```
proc cluster data=closer outtree=tree method=average noprint;
   var x y;
run;

proc tree noprint out=out n=3 dock=5;
   copy x y;
   title 'Average Linkage Cluster Analysis';
   title2 'of Data Containing Poorly Separated,
           Compact Clusters';
run;

%plotclus;
```

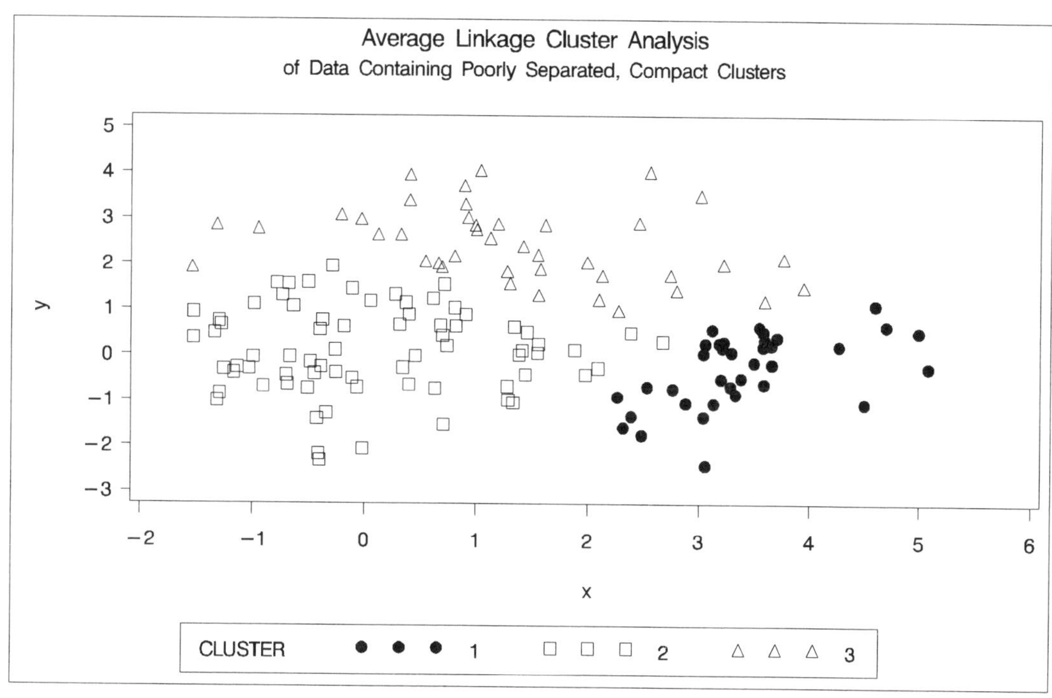

Figure 8.5. Data Containing Poorly Separated, Compact Clusters: PROC CLUSTER with METHOD=AVERAGE

The following SAS statements produce Figure 8.6:

```
proc cluster data=closer outtree=tree
             method=centroid noprint;
   var x y;
run;

proc tree noprint out=out n=3 dock=5;
   copy x y;
   title 'Centroid Cluster Analysis';
   title2 'of Data Containing Poorly Separated,
           Compact Clusters';
run;

%plotclus;
```

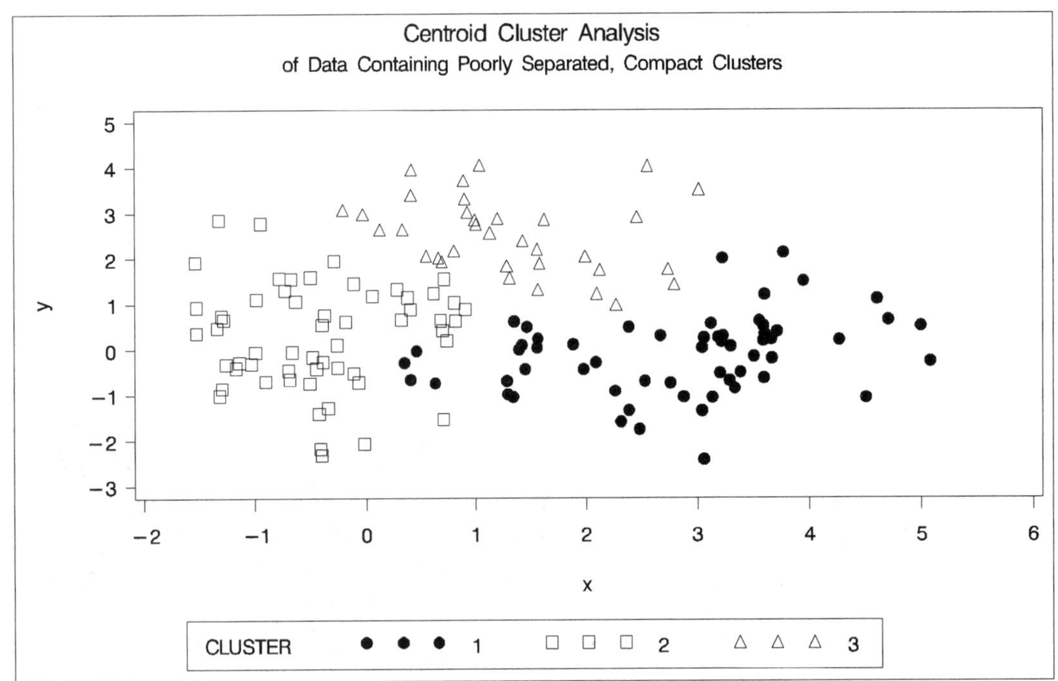

Figure 8.6. Data Containing Poorly Separated, Compact Clusters: PROC CLUSTER with METHOD=CENTROID

The following SAS statements produce Figure 8.7:

```
proc cluster data=closer outtree=tree
             method=twostage k=10 noprint;
   var x y;
run;

proc tree noprint out=out n=3;
   copy x y _dens_;
   title 'Two-Stage Density Linkage Cluster Analysis';
   title2 'of Data Containing Poorly Separated,
           Compact Clusters';
run;

%plotclus;

proc gplot;
   bubble y*x=_dens_/frame cframe=ligr
          vaxis=axis1 haxis=axis2;
   title 'Estimated Densities';
   title2 'for Data Containing Poorly Separated,
           Compact Clusters';
run;
```

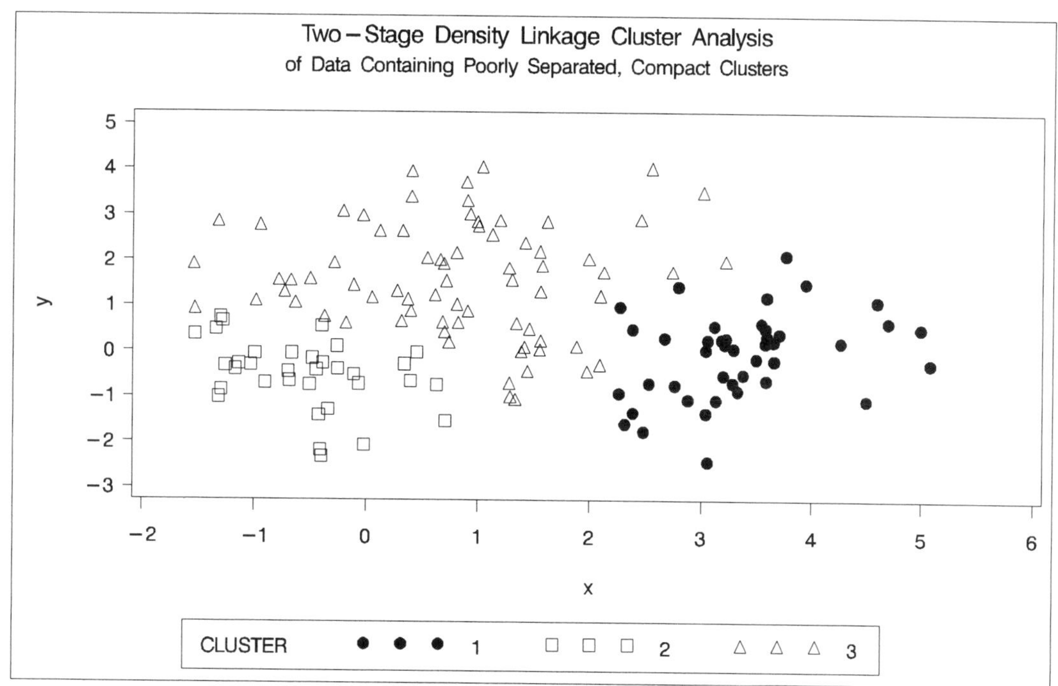

Figure 8.7. Data Containing Poorly Separated, Compact Clusters: PROC CLUSTER with METHOD=TWOSTAGE

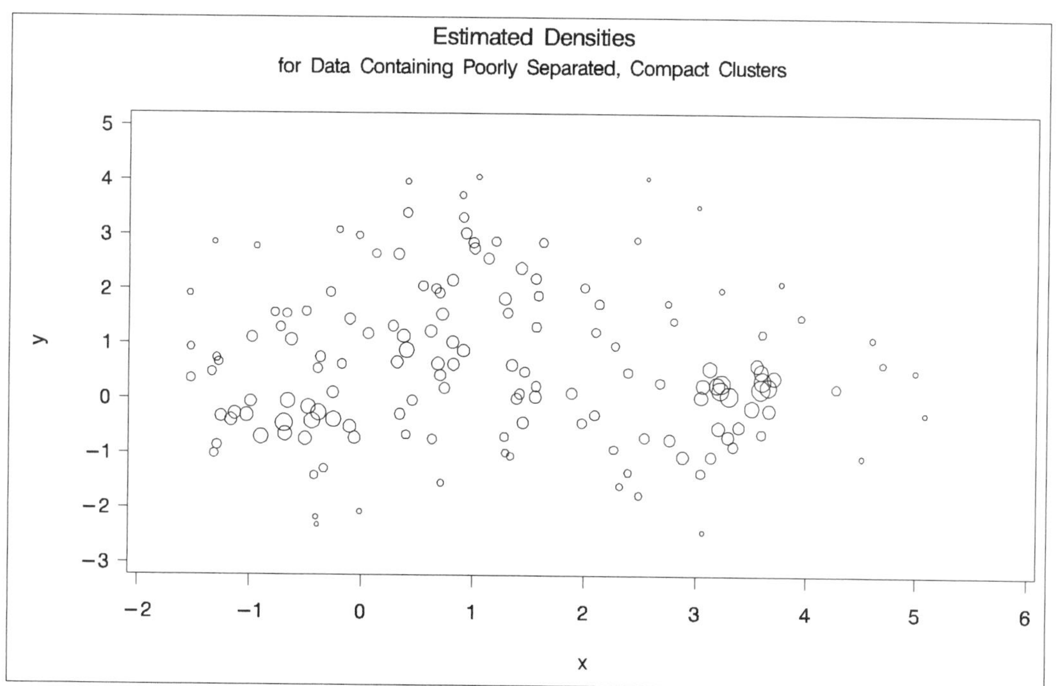

In two-stage density linkage, each cluster is a region surrounding a local maximum of the estimated probability density function. If you think of the estimated density function as a landscape with mountains and valleys, each mountain is a cluster, and the boundaries between clusters are placed near the bottoms of the valleys.

The following SAS statements produce Figure 8.8:

```
proc cluster data=closer outtree=tree
             method=single noprint;
   var x y;
run;

proc tree data=tree noprint out=out n=3 dock=5;
   copy x y;
   title 'Single Linkage Cluster Analysis';
   title2 'of Data Containing Poorly Separated,
          Compact Clusters';
run;

%plotclus;
```

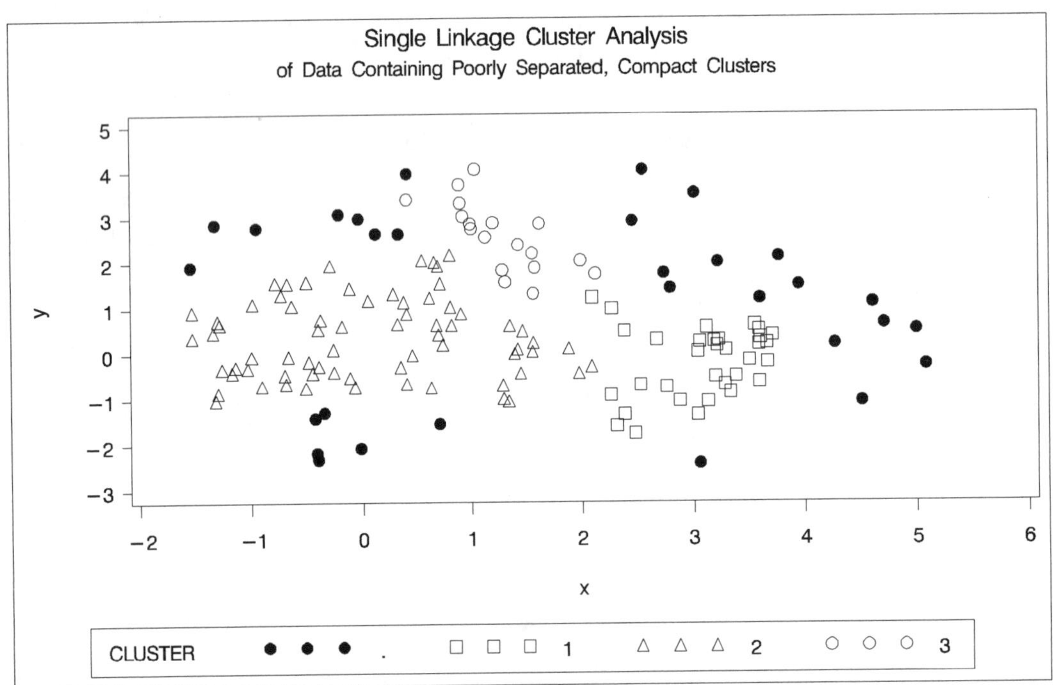

Figure 8.8. Data Containing Poorly Separated, Compact Clusters: PROC CLUSTER with METHOD=SINGLE

The two least-squares methods, PROC FASTCLUS and Ward's, yield the most uniform cluster sizes and the best recovery of the true clusters. This result is expected since these two methods are biased toward recovering compact clusters of equal size. With average linkage, the lower-left cluster is too large; with the centroid method, the lower-right cluster is too large; and with two-stage density linkage, the top cluster is too large. The single linkage analysis resembles average linkage except for the large number of outliers resulting from the DOCK= option in the PROC TREE statement; the outliers are plotted as dots (missing values).

Multinormal Clusters of Unequal Size and Dispersion

In this example, there are three multinormal clusters that differ in size and dispersion. PROC FASTCLUS and five of the hierarchical methods available in PROC CLUSTER are used. To help you compare methods, the true, generated clusters are plotted. The following SAS statements produce Figure 8.9:

```
data unequal;
   keep x y c;
   mx=1; my=0; n=20; scale=.5; c=1; link generate;
   mx=6; my=0; n=80; scale=2.; c=3; link generate;
   mx=3; my=4; n=40; scale=1.; c=2; link generate;
   stop;
generate:
   do i=1 to n;
      x=rannor(1)*scale+mx;
      y=rannor(1)*scale+my;
      output;
   end;
   return;
run;

title 'True Clusters for Data Containing Multinormal
       Clusters';
title2 'of Unequal Size';
proc gplot;
   plot y*x=c/frame cframe=ligr
        vaxis=axis1 haxis=axis2 legend=legend1;
run;
```

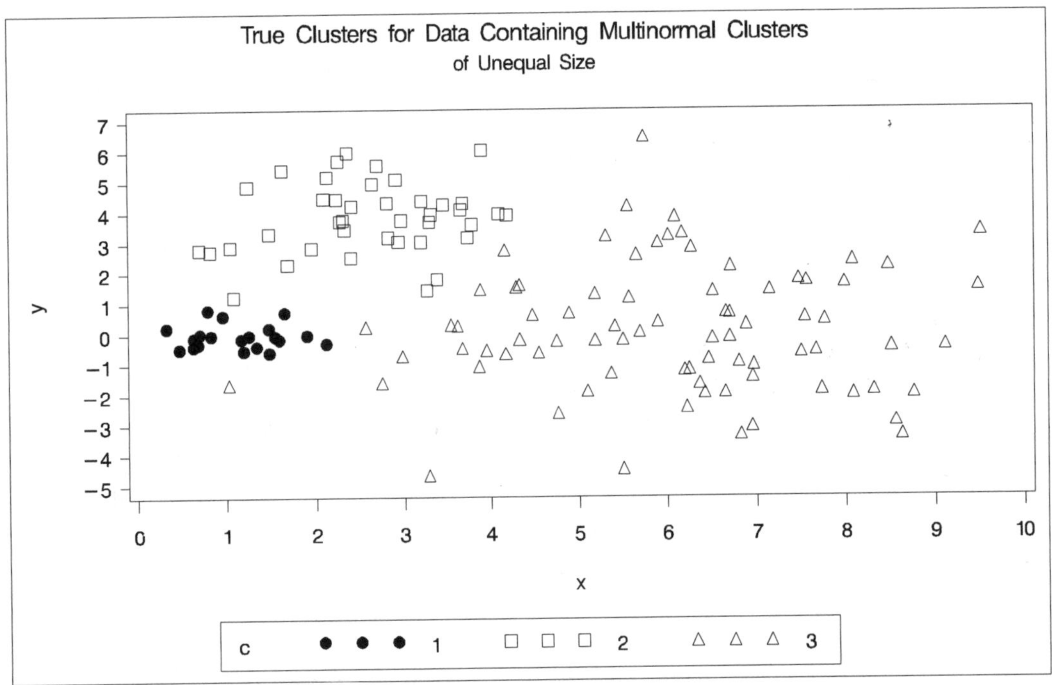

Figure 8.9. Data Containing Generated Clusters of Unequal Size

The following statements use the FASTCLUS procedure to find three clusters and the PLOTCLUS macro to plot the clusters. The statements produce Figure 8.10.

```
proc fastclus data=unequal out=out maxc=3 noprint;
   var x y;
   title 'FASTCLUS Analysis';
   title2 'of Data Containing Compact Clusters of
           Unequal Size';
run;

%plotclus;
```

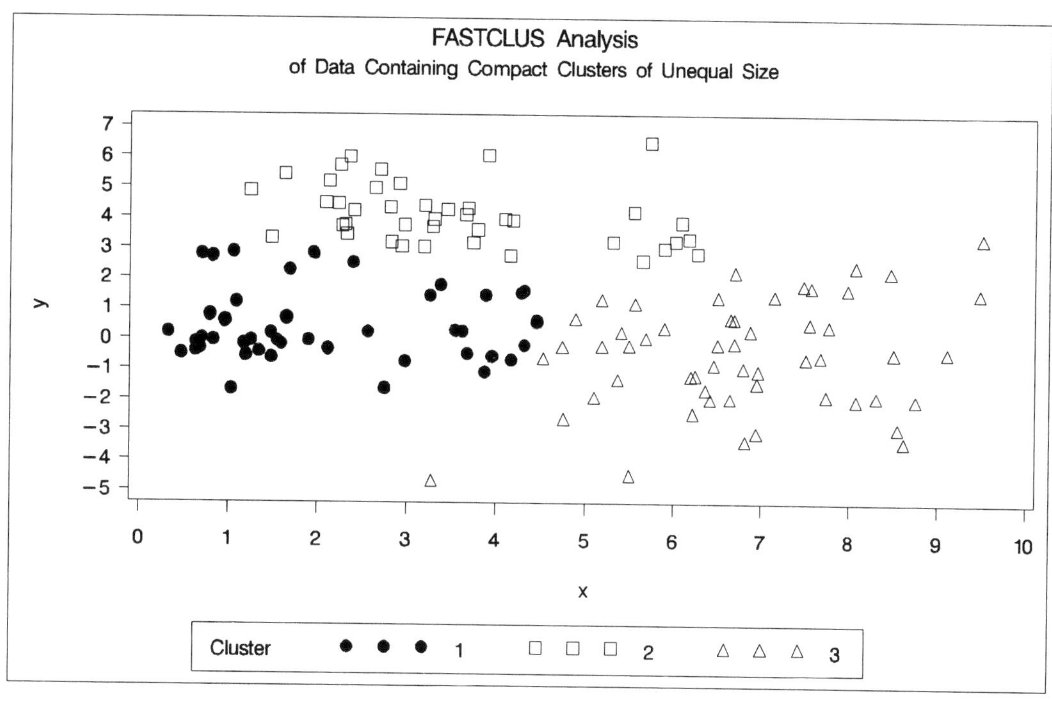

Figure 8.10. Data Containing Compact Clusters of Unequal Size: PROC FASTCLUS

The following SAS statements produce Figure 8.11:

```
proc cluster data=unequal outtree=tree
             method=ward noprint;
   var x y;
run;

proc tree noprint out=out n=3;
   copy x y;
   title 'Ward''s Minimum Variance Cluster Analysis';
   title2 'of Data Containing Compact Clusters of
           Unequal Size';
run;

%plotclus;
```

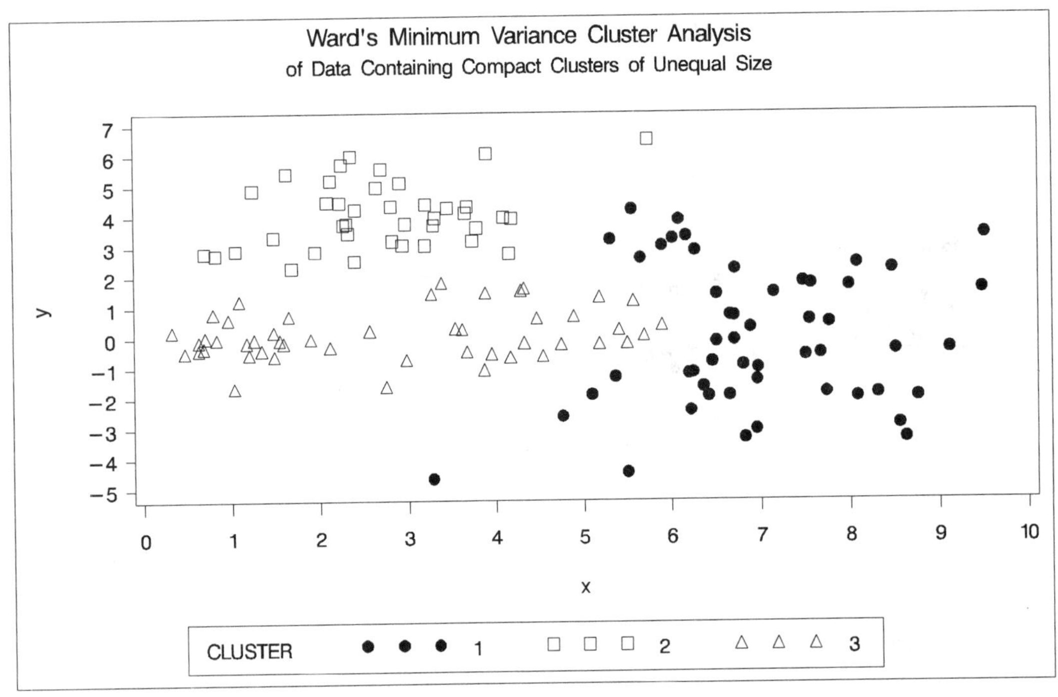

Figure 8.11. Data Containing Compact Clusters of Unequal Size: PROC CLUSTER with METHOD=WARD

The following SAS statements produce Figure 8.12:

```
proc cluster data=unequal outtree=tree method=average
             noprint;
   var x y;
run;

proc tree noprint out=out n=3 dock=5;
   copy x y;
   title 'Average Linkage Cluster Analysis';
   title2 'of Data Containing Compact Clusters of
           Unequal Size';
run;

%plotclus;
```

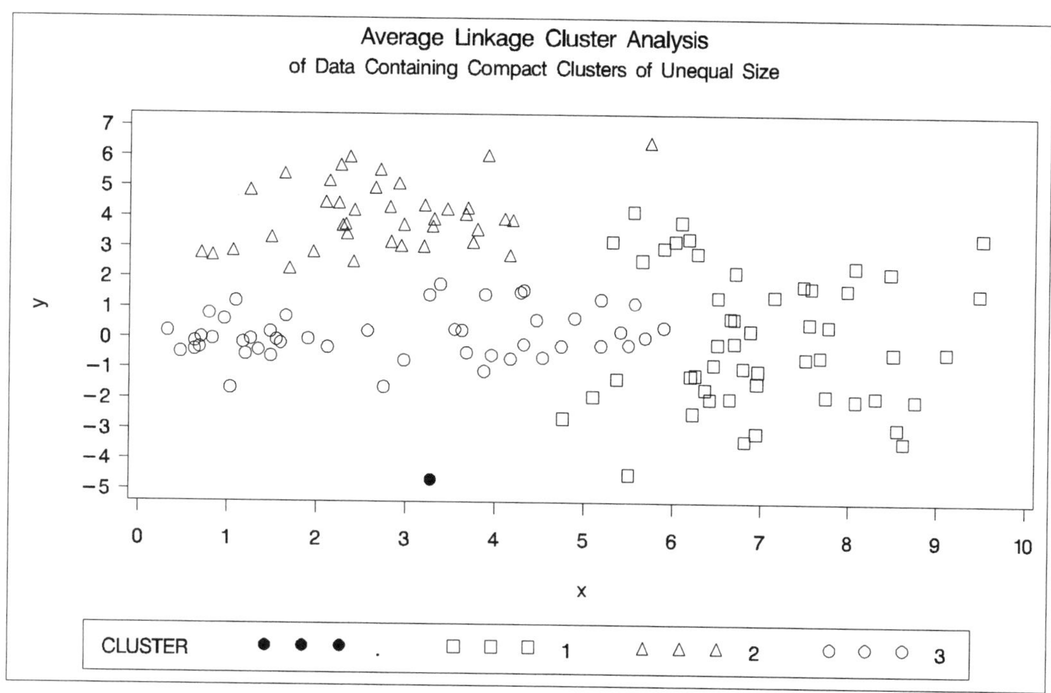

Figure 8.12. Data Containing Compact Clusters of Unequal Size: PROC CLUSTER with METHOD=AVERAGE

The following SAS statements produce Figure 8.13:

```
proc cluster data=unequal outtree=tree
             method=centroid noprint;
   var x y;
run;

proc tree noprint out=out n=3 dock=5;
   copy x y;
   title 'Centroid Cluster Analysis';
   title2 'of Data Containing Compact Clusters of
           Unequal Size';
run;

%plotclus;
```

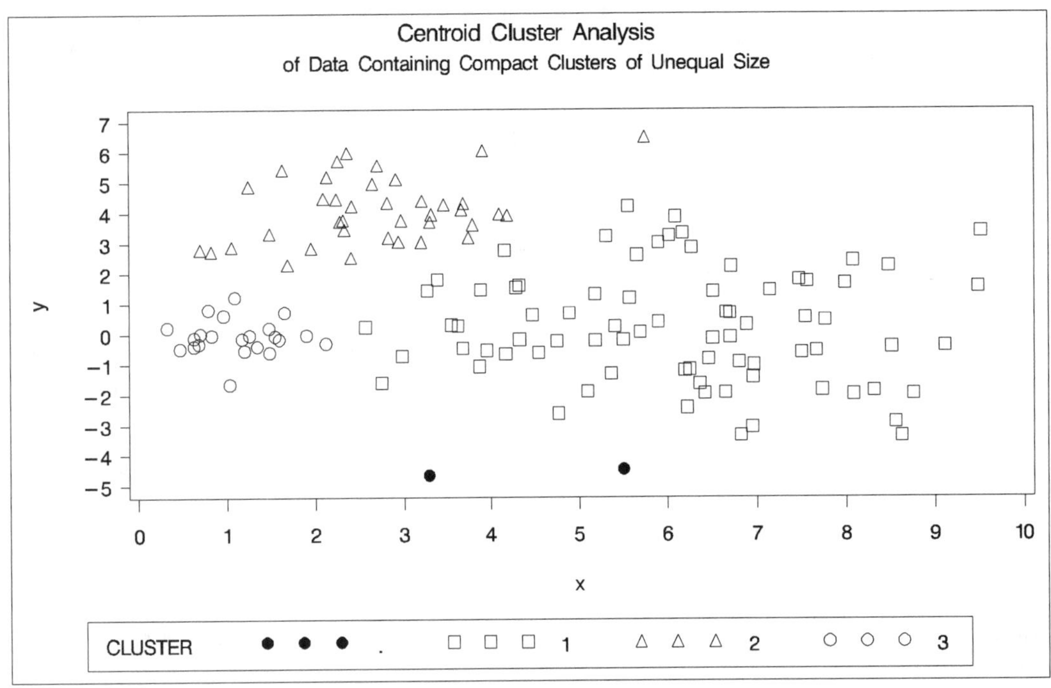

Figure 8.13. Data Containing Compact Clusters of Unequal Size: PROC CLUSTER with METHOD=CENTROID

The following SAS statements produce Figure 8.14:

```
proc cluster data=unequal outtree=tree method=twostage
             k=10 noprint;
   var x y;
run;

proc tree noprint out=out n=3;
   copy x y _dens_;
   title 'Two-Stage Density Linkage Cluster Analysis';
   title2 'of Data Containing Compact Clusters of
           Unequal Size';
run;

%plotclus;

proc gplot;
   bubble y*x=_dens_/frame cframe=ligr
          vaxis=axis1 haxis=axis2 ;
   title 'Estimated Densities';
   title2 'for Data Containing Compact Clusters of
           Unequal Size';
run;
```

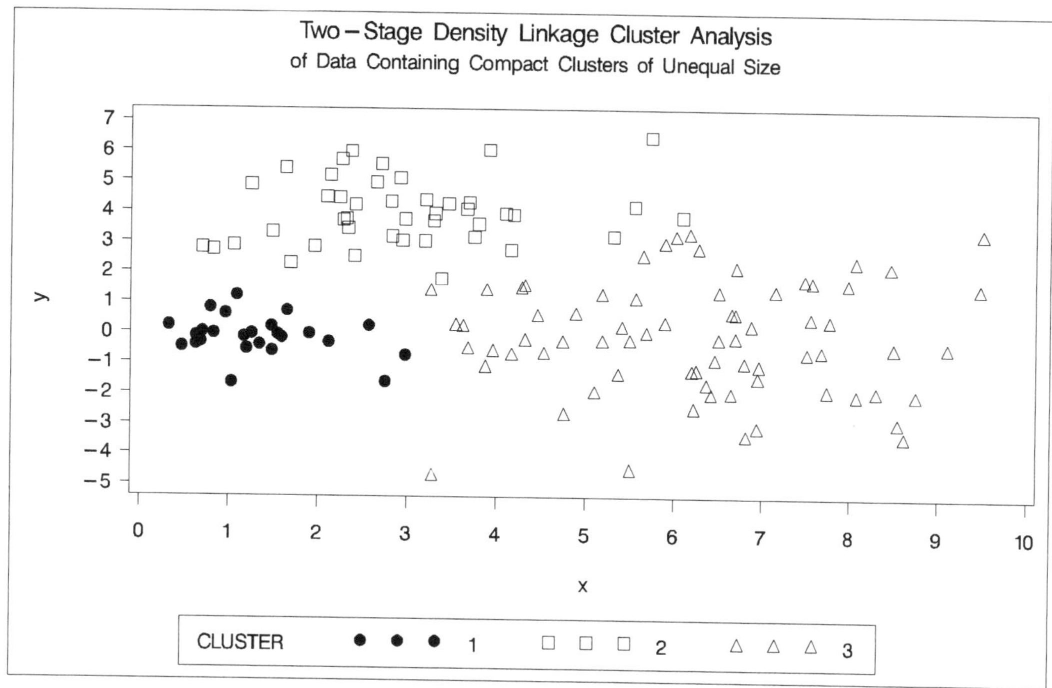

Figure 8.14. Data Containing Compact Clusters of Unequal Size: PROC CLUSTER with METHOD=TWOSTAGE

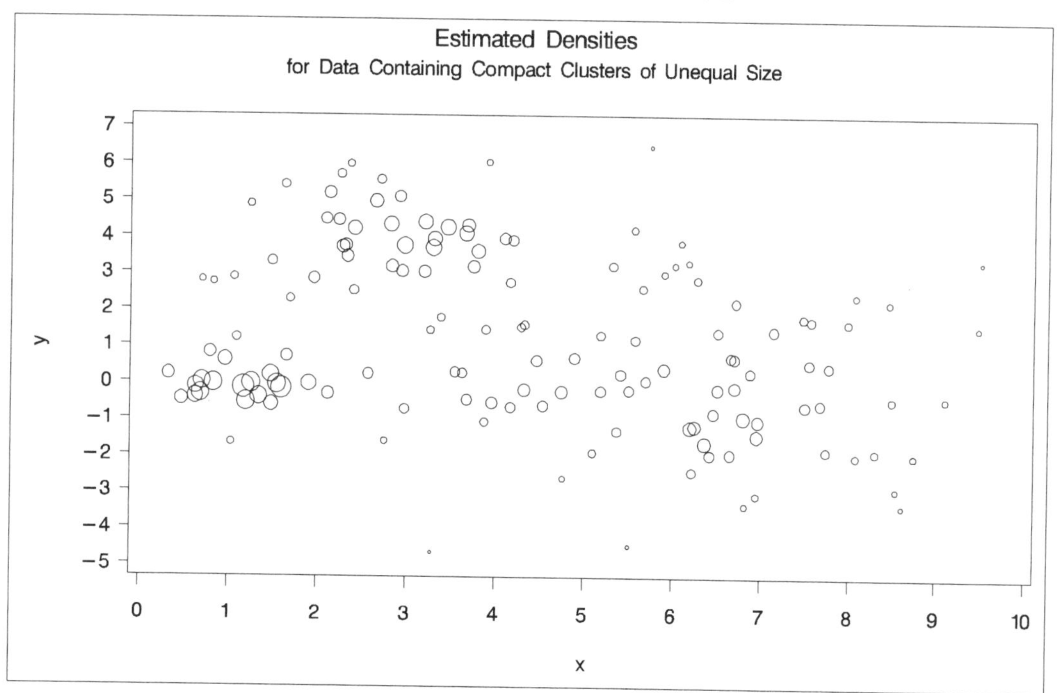

The following SAS statements produce Figure 8.15:

```
proc cluster data=unequal outtree=tree
             method=single noprint;
   var x y;
run;

proc tree data=tree noprint out=out n=3 dock=5;
   copy x y;
   title 'Single Linkage Cluster Analysis';
   title2 'of Data Containing Compact Clusters of
           Unequal Size';
run;

%plotclus;
```

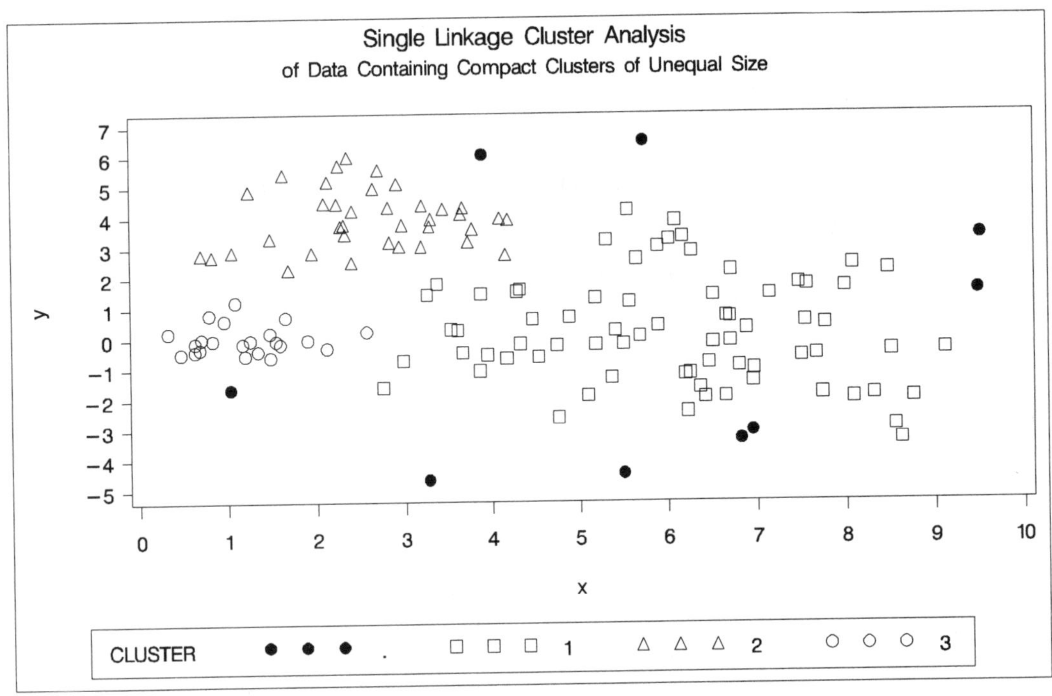

Figure 8.15. Data Containing Compact Clusters of Unequal Size: PROC CLUSTER with METHOD=SINGLE

In the PROC FASTCLUS analysis, the smallest cluster, in the bottom left of the plot, has stolen members from the other two clusters, and the upper-left cluster has also acquired some observations that rightfully belong to the larger, lower-right cluster. With Ward's method, the upper-left cluster is separated correctly, but the lower-left cluster has taken a large bite out of the lower-right cluster. For both of these methods, the clustering errors are in accord with the biases of the methods to produce clusters of equal size. In the average linkage analysis, both the upper- and lower-left clusters have encroached on the lower-right cluster, thereby making the variances more nearly equal than in the true clusters. The centroid method, which lacks the size and dispersion biases of the previous methods, obtains an essentially correct partition.

Two-stage density linkage does almost as well even though the compact shapes of these clusters favor the traditional methods. Single linkage also produces excellent results.

Elongated Multinormal Clusters

In this example, the data are sampled from two highly elongated multinormal distributions with equal covariance matrices. The following SAS statements produce Figure 8.16:

```
data elongate;
   keep x y;
   ma=8; mb=0; link generate;
   ma=6; mb=8; link generate;
   stop;
generate:
   do i=1 to 50;
      a=rannor(7)*6+ma;
      b=rannor(7)+mb;
      x=a-b;
      y=a+b;
      output;
   end;
   return;
run;

proc fastclus data=elongate out=out maxc=2 noprint;
run;

proc gplot;
   plot y*x=cluster/frame cframe=ligr
        vaxis=axis1 haxis=axis2 legend=legend1;
   title 'FASTCLUS Analysis';
   title2 'of Data Containing Parallel Elongated Clusters';
run;
```

Notice that PROC FASTCLUS found two clusters, as requested by the MAXC= option. However, it attempted to form spherical clusters, which are obviously inappropriate for this data.

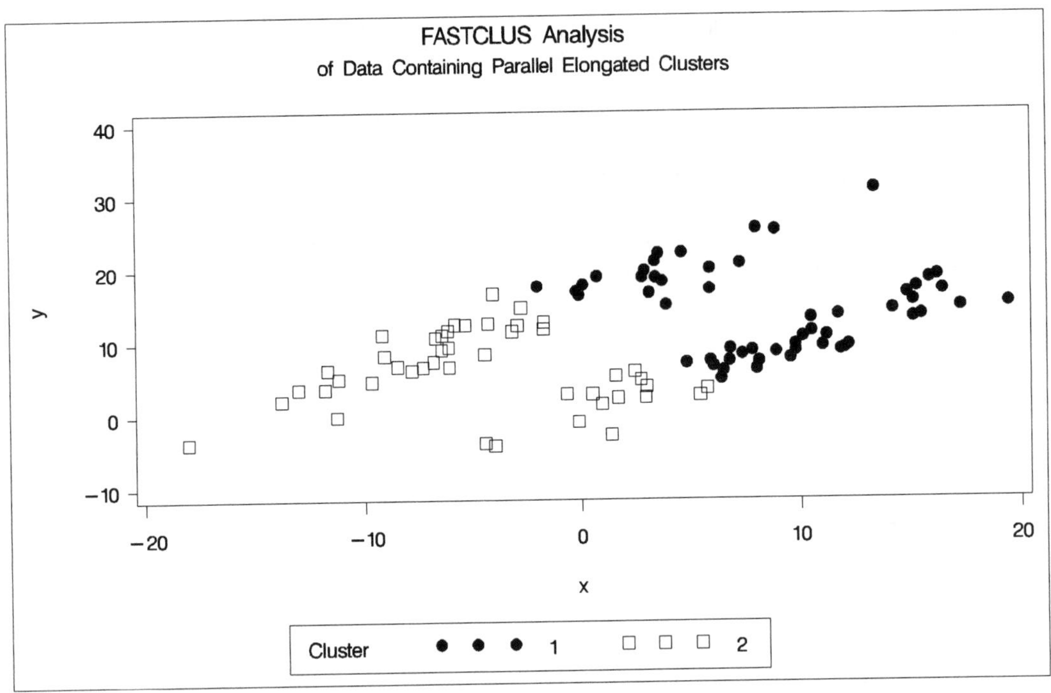

Figure 8.16. Data Containing Parallel Elongated Clusters: PROC FASTCLUS

The following SAS statements produce Figure 8.17:

```
proc cluster data=elongate outtree=tree
             method=average noprint;
run;

proc tree noprint out=out n=2 dock=5;
   copy x y;
run;

proc gplot;
   plot y*x=cluster/frame cframe=ligr
        vaxis=axis1 haxis=axis2 legend=legend1;
   title 'Average Linkage Cluster Analysis';
   title2 'of Data Containing Parallel Elongated Clusters';
run;
```

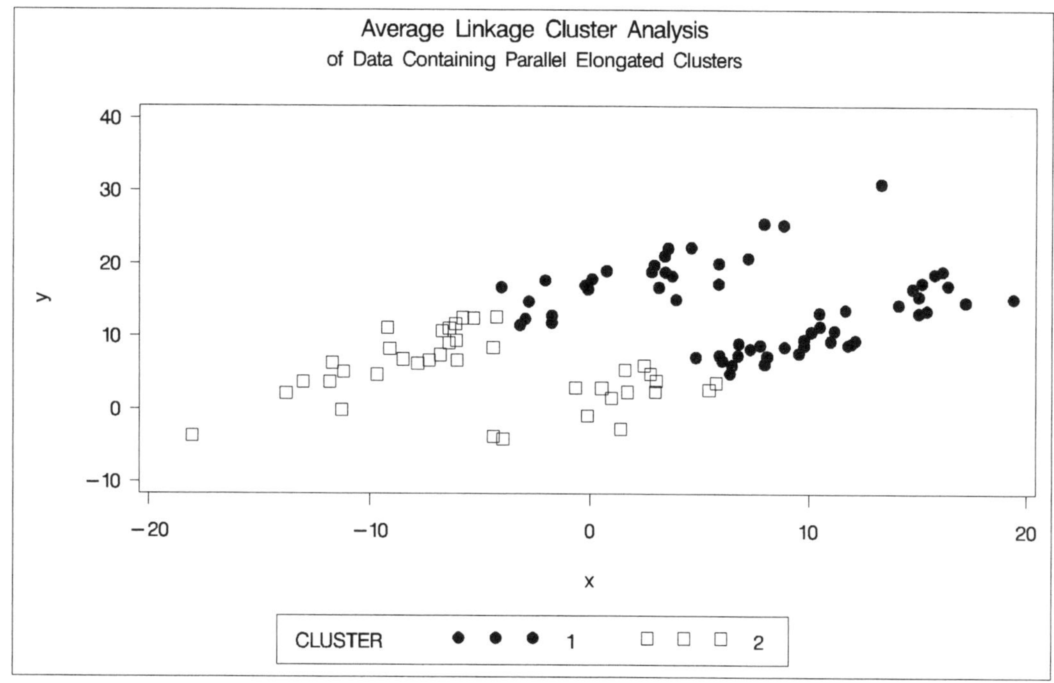

Figure 8.17. Data Containing Parallel Elongated Clusters: PROC CLUSTER with METHOD=AVERAGE

The following SAS statements produce Figure 8.18:

```
proc cluster data=elongate outtree=tree
             method=twostage k=10 noprint;
run;

proc tree noprint out=out n=2;
   copy x y;
run;

proc gplot;
   plot y*x=cluster/frame cframe=ligr
        vaxis=axis1 haxis=axis2 legend=legend1;
   title 'Two-Stage Density Linkage Cluster Analysis';
   title2 'of Data Containing Parallel Elongated Clusters';
run;
```

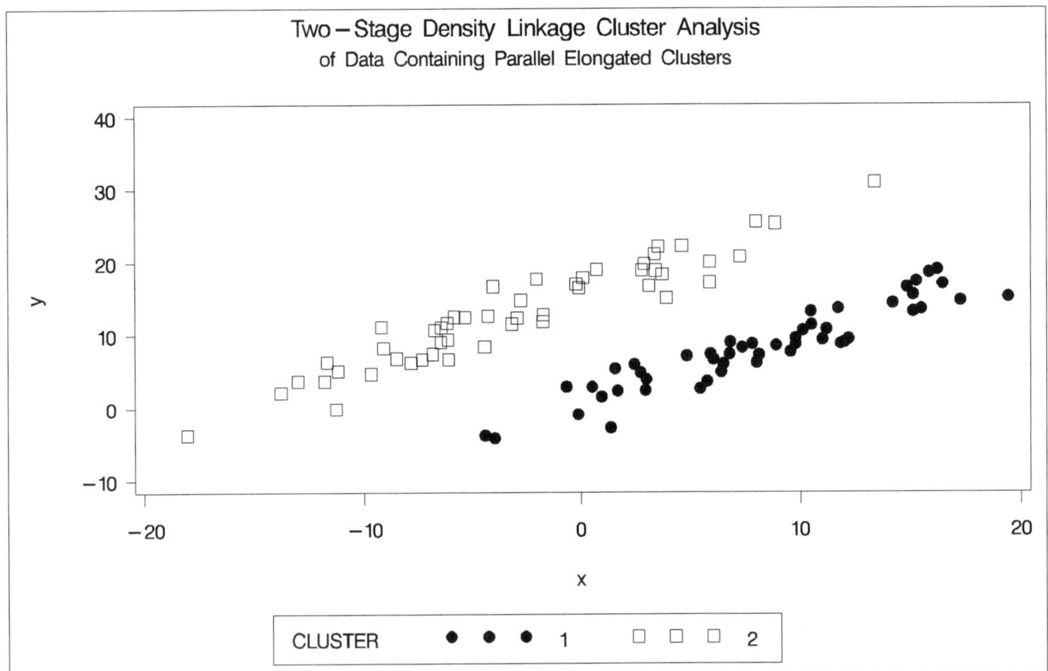

Figure 8.18. Data Containing Parallel Elongated Clusters: PROC CLUSTER with METHOD=TWOSTAGE

PROC FASTCLUS and average linkage fail miserably. Ward's method and the centroid method, not shown, produce almost the same results. Two-stage density linkage, however, recovers the correct clusters. Single linkage, not shown, finds the same clusters as two-stage density linkage except for some outliers.

In this example, the population clusters have equal covariance matrices. If the within-cluster covariances are known, the data can be transformed to make the clusters spherical so that any of the clustering methods can find the correct clusters. But when you are doing a cluster analysis, you do not know what the true clusters are, so you cannot calculate the within-cluster covariance matrix. Nevertheless, it is sometimes possible to estimate the within-cluster covariance matrix without knowing the cluster membership or even the number of clusters, using an approach invented by Art, Gnanadesikan, and Kettenring (1982). A method for obtaining such an estimate is available in the ACECLUS procedure.

In the following analysis, PROC ACECLUS transforms the variables X and Y into canonical variables CAN1 and CAN2. The latter are plotted and then used in a cluster analysis by Ward's method. The clusters are then plotted with the original variables X and Y. The following SAS statements produce Figure 8.19:

```
proc aceclus data=elongate out=ace p=.1;
   var x y;
   title 'ACECLUS Analysis';
   title2 'of Data Containing Parallel Elongated Clusters';
run;
```

```
proc gplot;
   plot can2*can1/frame cframe=ligr;
   title 'Data Containing Parallel Elongated Clusters';
   title2 'After Transformation by PROC ACECLUS';
run;
```

```
                    ACECLUS Analysis
         of Data Containing Parallel Elongated Clusters

                  The ACECLUS Procedure

       Approximate Covariance Estimation for Cluster Analysis


         Observations          100    Proportion      0.1000
         Variables               2    Converge       0.00100


                Means and Standard Deviations
                                         Standard
              Variable          Mean    Deviation

              x               2.6406       8.3494
              y              10.6488       6.8420


                COV: Total Sample Covariances

                               x                 y

            x       69.71314819       24.24268934
            y       24.24268934       46.81324861

 Initial Within-Cluster Covariance Estimate = Full Covariance Matrix


                 Threshold =      0.328478


                      Iteration History

                                               Pairs
                   RMS        Distance        Within     Convergence
    Iteration   Distance        Cutoff        Cutoff         Measure
    ------------------------------------------------------------
            1      2.000         0.657         672.0        0.673685
            2      9.382         3.082         716.0        0.006963
            3      9.339         3.068         760.0        0.008362
            4      9.437         3.100         824.0        0.009656
            5      9.359         3.074         889.0        0.010269
            6      9.267         3.044         955.0        0.011276
            7      9.208         3.025         999.0        0.009230
            8      9.230         3.032        1052.0        0.011394
            9      9.226         3.030        1091.0        0.007924
           10      9.173         3.013        1121.0        0.007993


 ERROR: Iteration limit exceeded.
```

Figure 8.19. Data Containing Parallel Elongated Clusters: PROC ACECLUS

```
                    ACECLUS Analysis
      of Data Containing Parallel Elongated Clusters

                  The ACECLUS Procedure

   ACE: Approximate Covariance Estimate Within Clusters

                             x                  y

           x       9.299329632        8.215362614
           y       8.215362614        8.937753936


          Eigenvalues of Inv(ACE)*(COV-ACE)

        Eigenvalue    Difference    Proportion    Cumulative

   1       36.7091       33.1672        0.9120        0.9120
   2        3.5420                      0.0880        1.0000


        Eigenvectors (Raw Canonical Coefficients)

                          Can1           Can2

               x       -.748392       0.109547
               y       0.736349       0.230272


           Standardized Canonical Coefficients

                          Can1           Can2

               x       -6.24866        0.91466
               y        5.03812        1.57553
```

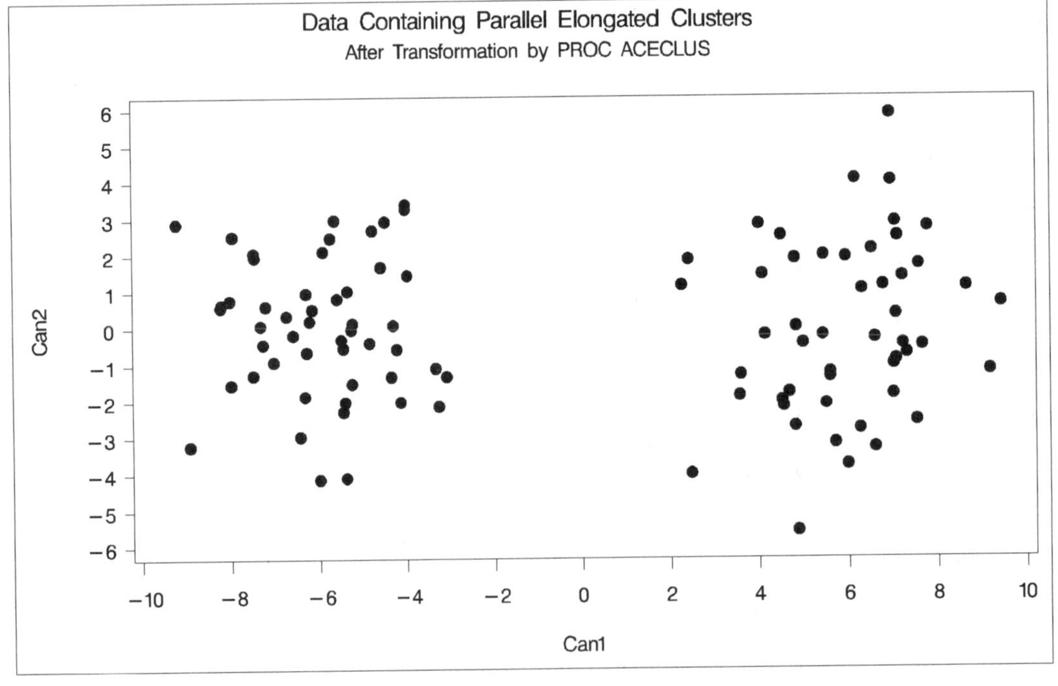

Figure 8.20. Data Containing Parallel Elongated Clusters After Transformation by PROC ACECLUS

The following SAS statements produce Figure 8.21:

```
proc cluster data=ace outtree=tree method=ward noprint;
   var can1 can2;
   copy x y;
run;

proc tree noprint out=out n=2;
   copy x y;
run;

proc gplot;
   plot y*x=cluster/frame cframe=ligr
        vaxis=axis1 haxis=axis2 legend=legend1;
   title 'Ward''s Minimum Variance Cluster Analysis';
   title2 'of Data Containing Parallel Elongated Clusters';
   title3 'After Transformation by PROC ACECLUS';
run;
```

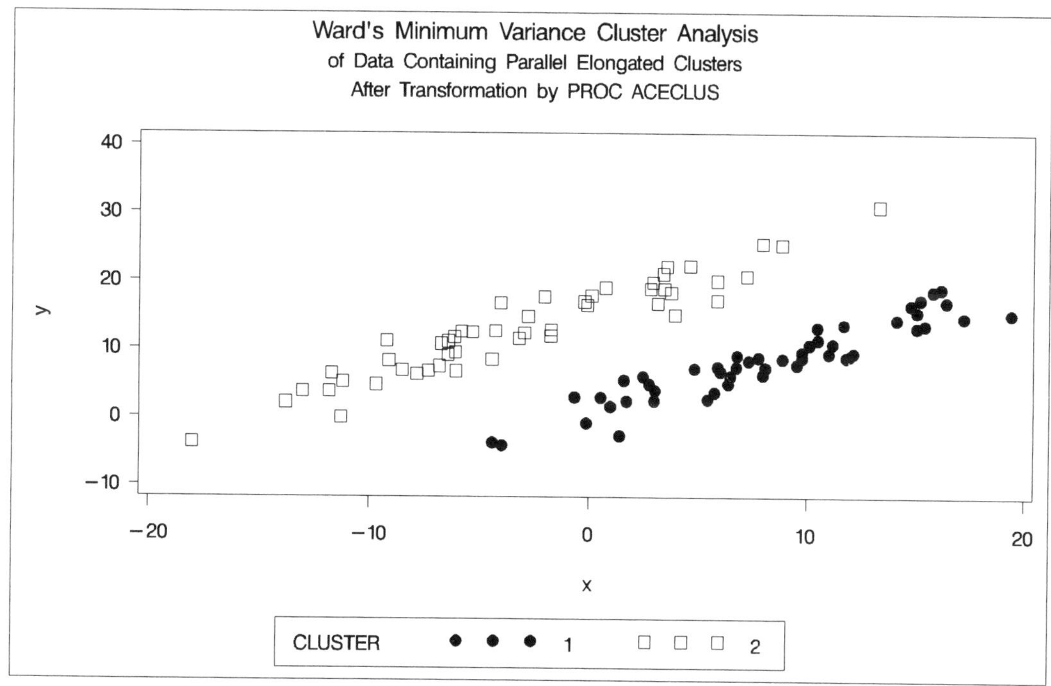

Figure 8.21. Transformed Data Containing Parallel Elongated Clusters: PROC CLUSTER with METHOD=WARD

Nonconvex Clusters

If the population clusters have very different covariance matrices, using PROC ACECLUS is of no avail. Although methods exist for estimating multinormal clusters with unequal covariance matrices (Wolfe 1970; Symons 1981; Everitt and Hand 1981; Titterington, Smith, and Makov 1985; McLachlan and Basford 1988, these methods tend to have serious problems with initialization and may converge to degenerate solutions. For unequal covariance matrices or radically nonnormal distributions, the best approach to cluster analysis is through nonparametric density estimation, as in density linkage. The next example illustrates population clusters with nonconvex density contours. The following SAS statements produce Figure 8.22.

```
data noncon;
   keep x y;
   do i=1 to 100;
      a=i*.0628319;
      x=cos(a)+(i>50)+rannor(7)*.1;
      y=sin(a)+(i>50)*.3+rannor(7)*.1;
      output;
   end;
run;

proc fastclus data=noncon out=out maxc=2 noprint;
run;

proc gplot;
   plot y*x=cluster/frame cframe=ligr
        vaxis=axis1 haxis=axis2 legend=legend1;
   title 'FASTCLUS Analysis';
   title2 'of Data Containing Nonconvex Clusters';
run;
```

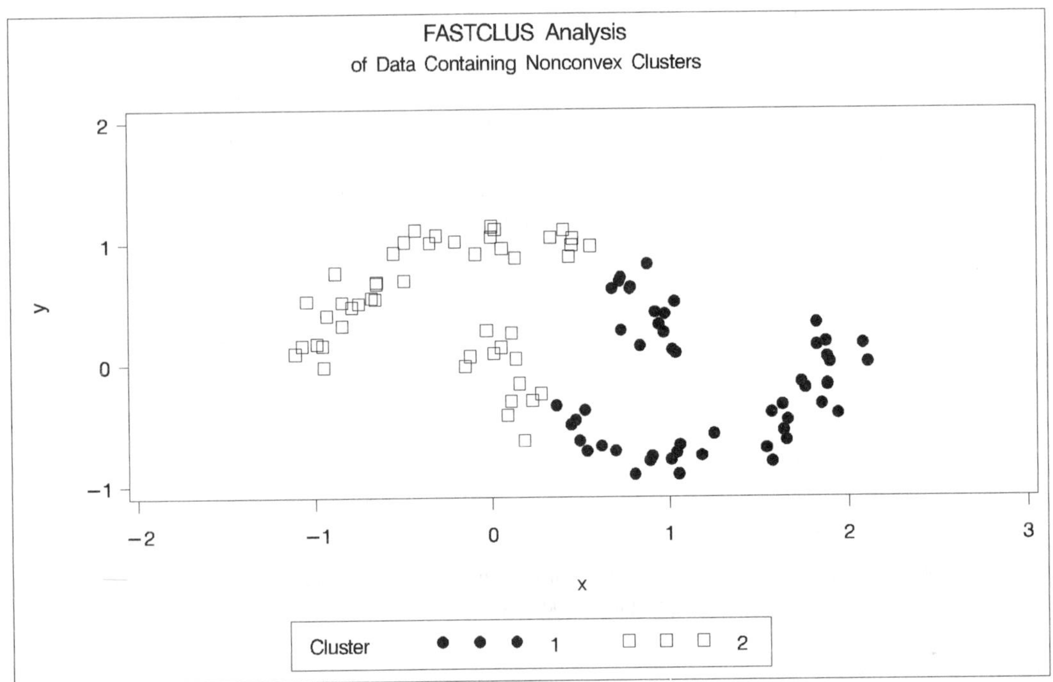

Figure 8.22. Data Containing Nonconvex Clusters: PROC FASTCLUS

The following SAS statements produce Figure 8.23.

```
proc cluster data=noncon outtree=tree
             method=centroid noprint;
run;
```

```
proc tree noprint out=out n=2 dock=5;
   copy x y;
run;

proc gplot;
   plot y*x=cluster/frame cframe=ligr
        vaxis=axis1 haxis=axis2 legend=legend1;
   title 'Centroid Cluster Analysis';
   title2 'of Data Containing Nonconvex Clusters';
run;
```

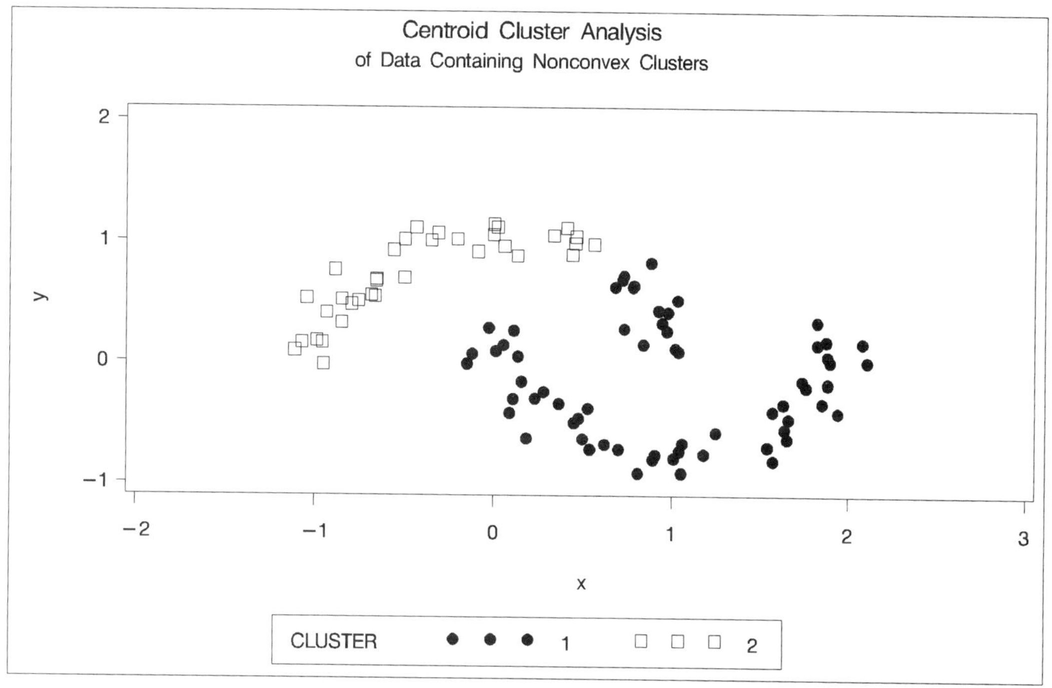

Figure 8.23. Data Containing Nonconvex Clusters: PROC CLUSTER with METHOD=CENTROID

The following SAS statements produce Figure 8.24.

```
proc cluster data=noncon outtree=tree
             method=twostage k=10 noprint;
run;

proc tree noprint out=out n=2;
   copy x y;
run;

proc gplot;
   plot y*x=cluster/frame cframe=ligr
        vaxis=axis1 haxis=axis2 legend=legend1;
   title 'Two-Stage Density Linkage Cluster Analysis';
   title2 'of Data Containing Nonconvex Clusters';
run;
```

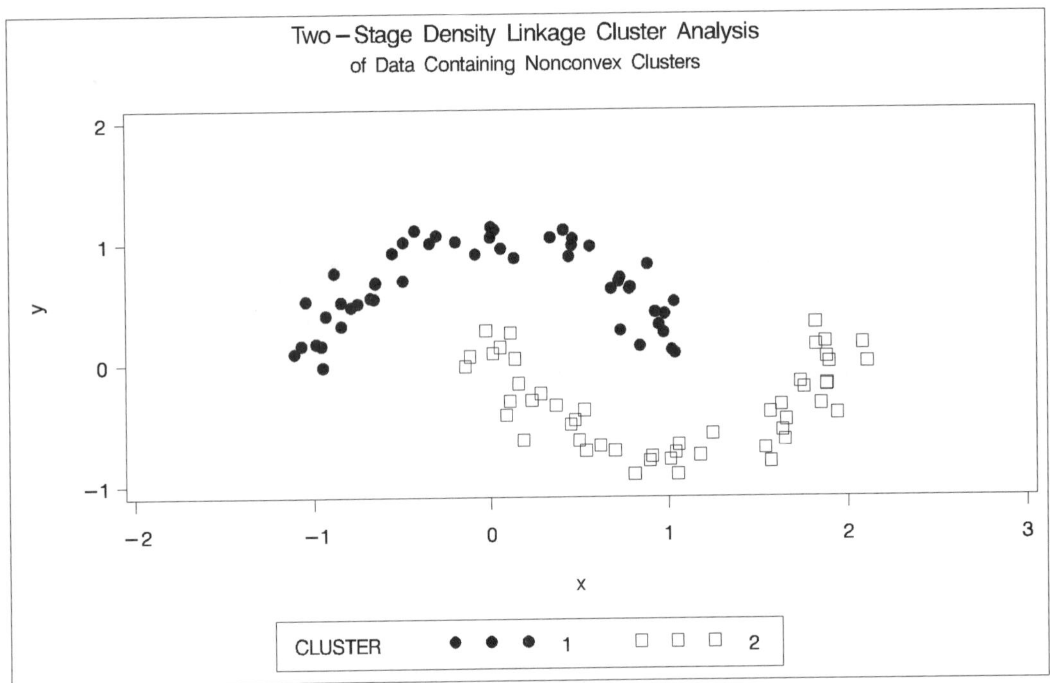

Figure 8.24. Data Containing Nonconvex Clusters: PROC CLUSTER with METHOD=TWOSTAGE

Ward's method and average linkage, not shown, do better than PROC FASTCLUS but not as well as the centroid method. Two-stage density linkage recovers the correct clusters, as does single linkage, which is not shown.

The preceding examples are intended merely to illustrate some of the properties of clustering methods in common use. If you intend to perform a cluster analysis, you should consult more systematic and rigorous studies of the properties of clustering methods, such as Milligan (1980).

The Number of Clusters

There are no completely satisfactory methods for determining the number of population clusters for any type of cluster analysis (Everitt 1979; Hartigan 1985; Bock 1985).

If your purpose in clustering is dissection, that is, to summarize the data without trying to uncover real clusters, it may suffice to look at R^2 for each variable and pooled over all variables. Plots of R^2 against the number of clusters are useful.

It is always a good idea to look at your data graphically. If you have only two or three variables, use PROC GPLOT to make scatter plots identifying the clusters. With more variables, use PROC CANDISC to compute canonical variables for plotting.

Ordinary significance tests, such as analysis of variance F tests, are not valid for testing differences between clusters. Since clustering methods attempt to maximize the separation between clusters, the assumptions of the usual significance tests, parametric or nonparametric, are drastically violated. For example, if you take a sample of 100 observations from a single univariate normal distribution, have PROC FASTCLUS divide it into two clusters, and run a t test between the clusters, you usually obtain a p-value of less than 0.0001. For the same reason, methods that purport to test for clusters against the null hypothesis that objects are assigned randomly to clusters (such as McClain and Rao 1975; Klastorin 1983) are useless.

Most valid tests for clusters either have intractable sampling distributions or involve null hypotheses for which rejection is uninformative. For clustering methods based on distance matrices, a popular null hypothesis is that all permutations of the values in the distance matrix are equally likely (Ling 1973; Hubert 1974). Using this null hypothesis, you can do a permutation test or a rank test. The trouble with the permutation hypothesis is that, with any real data, the null hypothesis is implausible even if the data do not contain clusters. Rejecting the null hypothesis does not provide any useful information (Hubert and Baker 1977).

Another common null hypothesis is that the data are a random sample from a multivariate normal distribution (Wolfe 1970, 1978; Duda and Hart 1973; Lee 1979). The multivariate normal null hypothesis arises naturally in normal mixture models (Titterington, Smith, and Makov 1985; McLachlan and Basford 1988). Unfortunately, the likelihood ratio test statistic does not have the usual asymptotic chi-squared distribution because the regularity conditions do not hold. Approximations to the asymptotic distribution of the likelihood ratio have been suggested (Wolfe 1978), but the adequacy of these approximations is debatable (Everitt 1981; Thode, Mendell, and Finch 1988). For small samples, bootstrapping seems preferable (McLachlan and Basford 1988). Bayesian inference provides a promising alternative to likelihood ratio tests for the number of mixture components for both normal mixtures and other types of distributions (Binder 1978, 1981; Banfield and Raftery 1993; Bensmail et al. 1997).

The multivariate normal null hypothesis is better than the permutation null hypothesis, but it is not satisfactory because there is typically a high probability of rejection if the data are sampled from a distribution with lower kurtosis than a normal distribution, such as a uniform distribution. The tables in Englemann and Hartigan (1969), for example, generally lead to rejection of the null hypothesis when the data are sampled from a uniform distribution. Hawkins, Muller, and ten Krooden (1982, pp. 337–340) discuss a highly conservative Bonferroni method for hypothesis testing. The conservativeness of this approach may compensate to some extent for the liberalness exhibited by tests based on normal distributions when the population is uniform.

Perhaps a better null hypothesis is that the data are sampled from a uniform distribution (Hartigan 1978; Arnold 1979; Sarle 1983). The uniform null hypothesis leads to conservative error rates when the data are sampled from a strongly unimodal distribution such as the normal. However, in two or more dimensions and depending on the test statistic, the results can be very sensitive to the shape of the region of support of the uniform distribution. Sarle (1983) suggests using a hyperbox with sides proportional in length to the singular values of the centered coordinate matrix.

Given that the uniform distribution provides an appropriate null hypothesis, there are still serious difficulties in obtaining sampling distributions. Some asymptotic results are available (Hartigan 1978, 1985; Pollard 1981; Bock 1985) for the within-cluster sum of squares, the criterion that PROC FASTCLUS and Ward's minimum variance method attempt to optimize. No distributional theory for finite sample sizes has yet appeared. Currently, the only practical way to obtain sampling distributions for realistic sample sizes is by computer simulation.

Arnold (1979) used simulation to derive tables of the distribution of a criterion based on the determinant of the within-cluster sum of squares matrix $|\mathbf{W}|$. Both normal and uniform null distributions were used. Having obtained clusters with either PROC FASTCLUS or PROC CLUSTER, you can compute Arnold's criterion with the ANOVA or CANDISC procedure. Arnold's tables provide a conservative test because PROC FASTCLUS and PROC CLUSTER attempt to minimize the trace of $\mathbf{W}$ rather than the determinant. Marriott (1971, 1975) also provides useful information on $|\mathbf{W}|$ as a criterion for the number of clusters.

Sarle (1983) used extensive simulations to develop the cubic clustering criterion (CCC), which can be used for crude hypothesis testing and estimating the number of population clusters. The CCC is based on the assumption that a uniform distribution on a hyperrectangle will be divided into clusters shaped roughly like hypercubes. In large samples that can be divided into the appropriate number of hypercubes, this assumption gives very accurate results. In other cases the approximation is generally conservative. For details about the interpretation of the CCC, consult Sarle (1983).

Milligan and Cooper (1985) and Cooper and Milligan (1988) compared thirty methods for estimating the number of population clusters using four hierarchical clustering methods. The three criteria that performed best in these simulation studies with a high degree of error in the data were a pseudo F statistic developed by Calinski and Harabasz (1974), a statistic referred to as $J_e(2)/J_e(1)$ by Duda and Hart (1973) that can be transformed into a pseudo t^2 statistic, and the cubic clustering criterion. The pseudo F statistic and the CCC are displayed by PROC FASTCLUS; these two statistics and the pseudo t^2 statistic, which can be applied only to hierarchical methods, are displayed by PROC CLUSTER. It may be advisable to look for consensus among the three statistics, that is, local peaks of the CCC and pseudo F statistic combined with a small value of the pseudo t^2 statistic and a larger pseudo t^2 for the next cluster fusion. It must be emphasized that these criteria are appropriate only for compact or slightly elongated clusters, preferably clusters that are roughly multivariate normal.

Recent research has tended to de-emphasize mixture models in favor of nonparametric models in which clusters correspond to modes in the probability density function. Hartigan and Hartigan (1985) and Hartigan (1985) developed a test of unimodality versus bimodality in the univariate case.

Nonparametric tests for the number of clusters can also be based on nonparametric density estimates. This approach requires much weaker assumptions than mixture models, namely, that the observations are sampled independently and that the distribution can be estimated nonparametrically. Silverman (1986) describes a bootstrap test for the number of modes using a Gaussian kernel density estimate, but problems have been reported with this method under the uniform null distribution. Further developments in nonparametric methods are given by Mueller and Sawitzki (1991), Minnotte (1992), and Polonik (1993). All of these methods suffer from heavy computational requirements.

One useful descriptive approach to the number-of-clusters problem is provided by Wong and Schaack (1982), based on a kth-nearest-neighbor density estimate. The kth-nearest-neighbor clustering method developed by Wong and Lane (1983) is applied with varying values of k. Each value of k yields an estimate of the number of modal clusters. If the estimated number of modal clusters is constant for a wide range of k values, there is strong evidence of at least that many modes in the population. A plot of the estimated number of modes against k can be highly informative. Attempts to derive a formal hypothesis test from this diagnostic plot have met with difficulties, but a simulation approach similar to Silverman's (1986) does seem to work (Girman 1994). The simulation, of course, requires considerable computer time.

Sarle and Kuo (1993) document a less expensive approximate nonparametric test for the number of clusters that has been implemented in the MODECLUS procedure. This test sacrifices statistical efficiency for computational efficiency. The method for conducting significance tests is described in the chapter on the MODECLUS procedure. This method has the following useful features:

- No distributional assumptions are required.
- The choice of smoothing parameter is not critical since you can try any number of different values.
- The data can be coordinates or distances.
- Time and space requirements for the significance tests are no worse than those for obtaining the clusters.
- The power is high enough to be useful for practical purposes.

The method for computing the p-values is based on a series of plausible approximations. There are as yet no rigorous proofs that the method is infallible. Neither are there any asymptotic results. However, simulations for sample sizes ranging from 20 to 2000 indicate that the p-values are almost always conservative. The only case discovered so far in which the p-values are liberal is a uniform distribution in one dimension for which the simulated error rates exceed the nominal significance level only slightly for a limited range of sample sizes.

References

Anderberg, M.R. (1973), *Cluster Analysis for Applications*, New York: Academic Press, Inc.

Arnold, S.J. (1979), "A Test for Clusters," *Journal of Marketing Research,* 16, 545–551.

Art, D., Gnanadesikan, R., and Kettenring, R. (1982), "Data-based Metrics for Cluster Analysis," *Utilitas Mathematica*, 21A, 75–99.

Banfield, J.D. and Raftery, A.E. (1993), "Model-Based Gaussian and Non-Gaussian Clustering," *Biometrics*, 49, 803–821.

Bensmail, H., Celeux, G., Raftery, A.E., and Robert, C.P. (1997), "Inference in Model-Based Cluster Analysis," *Statistics and Computing*, 7, 1–10.

Binder, D.A. (1978), "Bayesian Cluster Analysis," *Biometrika,* 65, 31–38.

Binder, D.A. (1981), "Approximations to Bayesian Clustering Rules," *Biometrika*, 68, 275–285.

Blashfield, R.K. and Aldenderfer, M.S. (1978), "The Literature on Cluster Analysis," *Multivariate Behavioral Research*, 13, 271–295.

Bock, H.H. (1985), "On Some Significance Tests in Cluster Analysis," *Journal of Classification*, 2, 77–108.

Calinski, T. and Harabasz, J. (1974), "A Dendrite Method for Cluster Analysis," *Communications in Statistics*, 3, 1–27.

Cooper, M.C. and Milligan, G.W. (1988), "The Effect of Error on Determining the Number of Clusters," *Proceedings of the International Workshop on Data Analysis, Decision Support and Expert Knowledge Representation in Marketing and Related Areas of Research,* 319–328.

Duda, R.O. and Hart, P.E. (1973), *Pattern Classification and Scene Analysis*, New York: John Wiley & Sons, Inc.

Duran, B.S. and Odell, P.L. (1974), *Cluster Analysis*, New York: Springer-Verlag.

Englemann, L. and Hartigan, J.A. (1969), "Percentage Points of a Test for Clusters," *Journal of the American Statistical Association,* 64, 1647–1648.

Everitt, B.S. (1979), "Unresolved Problems in Cluster Analysis," *Biometrics*, 35, 169–181.

Everitt, B.S. (1980), *Cluster Analysis*, Second Edition, London: Heineman Educational Books Ltd.

Everitt, B.S. (1981), "A Monte Carlo Investigation of the Likelihood Ratio Test for the Number of Components in a Mixture of Normal Distributions," *Multivariate Behavioral Research*, 16, 171–80.

Everitt, B.S. and Hand, D.J. (1981), *Finite Mixture Distributions*, New York: Chapman and Hall.

Girman, C.J. (1994), "Cluster Analysis and Classification Tree Methodology as an Aid to Improve Understanding of Benign Prostatic Hyperplasia," Ph.D. thesis, Chapel Hill, NC: Department of Biostatistics, University of North Carolina.

Good, I.J. (1977), "The Botryology of Botryology," in *Classification and Clustering,* ed. J. Van Ryzin, New York: Academic Press, Inc.

Harman, H.H. (1976), *Modern Factor Analysis*, Third Edition, Chicago: University of Chicago Press.

Hartigan, J.A. (1975), *Clustering Algorithms*, New York: John Wiley & Sons, Inc.

Hartigan, J.A. (1977), "Distribution Problems in Clustering," in *Classification and Clustering*, ed. J. Van Ryzin, New York: Academic Press, Inc.

Hartigan, J.A. (1978), "Asymptotic Distributions for Clustering Criteria," *Annals of Statistics*, 6, 117–131.

Hartigan, J.A. (1981), "Consistency of Single Linkage for High-Density Clusters," *Journal of the American Statistical Association*, 76, 388–394.

Hartigan, J.A. (1985), "Statistical Theory in Clustering," *Journal of Classification*, 2, 63–76.

Hartigan, J.A. and Hartigan, P.M. (1985), "The Dip Test of Unimodality," *Annals of Statistics*, 13, 70–84.

Hartigan, P.M. (1985), "Computation of the Dip Statistic to Test for Unimodality," *Applied Statistics*, 34, 320–325.

Hawkins, D.M., Muller, M.W., and ten Krooden, J.A. (1982), "Cluster Analysis," in *Topics in Applied Multivariate Analysis*, ed. D.M. Hawkins, Cambridge: Cambridge University Press.

Hubert, L. (1974), "Approximate Evaluation Techniques for the Single-Link and Complete-Link Hierarchical Clustering Procedures," *Journal of the American Statistical Association*, 69, 698–704.

Hubert, L.J. and Baker, F.B. (1977), "An Empirical Comparison of Baseline Models for Goodness-of-Fit in r-Diameter Hierarchical Clustering," in *Classification and Clustering*, ed. J. Van Ryzin, New York: Academic Press, Inc.

Klastorin, T.D. (1983), "Assessing Cluster Analysis Results," *Journal of Marketing Research*, 20, 92–98.

Lee, K.L. (1979), "Multivariate Tests for Clusters," *Journal of the American Statistical Association*, 74, 708–714.

Ling, R.F (1973), "A Probability Theory of Cluster Analysis," *Journal of the American Statistical Association*, 68, 159–169.

MacQueen, J.B. (1967), "Some Methods for Classification and Analysis of Multivariate Observations," *Proceedings of the Fifth Berkeley Symposium on Mathematical Statistics and Probability*, 1, 281–297.

Marriott, F.H.C. (1971), "Practical Problems in a Method of Cluster Analysis," *Biometrics*, 27, 501–514.

Marriott, F.H.C. (1975), "Separating Mixtures of Normal Distributions," *Biometrics*, 31, 767–769.

Massart, D.L. and Kaufman, L. (1983), *The Interpretation of Analytical Chemical Data by the Use of Cluster Analysis*, New York: John Wiley & Sons, Inc.

McClain, J.O. and Rao, V.R. (1975), "CLUSTISZ: A Program to Test for the Quality of Clustering of a Set of Objects," *Journal of Marketing Research*, 12, 456–460.

McLachlan, G.J. and Basford, K.E. (1988), *Mixture Models*, New York: Marcel Dekker, Inc.

Mezzich, J.E and Solomon, H. (1980), *Taxonomy and Behavioral Science*, New York: Academic Press, Inc.

Milligan, G.W. (1980), "An Examination of the Effect of Six Types of Error Perturbation on Fifteen Clustering Algorithms," *Psychometrika*, 45, 325–342.

Milligan, G.W. (1981), "A Review of Monte Carlo Tests of Cluster Analysis," *Multivariate Behavioral Research*, 16, 379–407.

Milligan, G.W. and Cooper, M.C. (1985), "An Examination of Procedures for Determining the Number of Clusters in a Data Set," *Psychometrika*, 50, 159–179.

Minnotte, M.C. (1992), "A Test of Mode Existence with Applications to Multimodality," Ph.D. thesis, Rice University, Department of Statistics.

Mueller, D.W. and Sawitzki, G. (1991), "Excess Mass Estimates and Tests for Multimodality," JASA 86, 738–746.

Pollard, D. (1981), "Strong Consistency of k-Means Clustering," *Annals of Statistics*, 9, 135–140.

Polonik, W. (1993), "Measuring Mass Concentrations and Estimating Density Contour Clusters—An Excess Mass Approach," Technical Report, Beitraege zur Statistik Nr. 7, Universitaet Heidelberg.

Sarle, W.S. (1982), "Cluster Analysis by Least Squares," *Proceedings of the Seventh Annual SAS Users Group International Conference*, 651–653.

Sarle, W.S. (1983), *Cubic Clustering Criterion*, SAS Technical Report A-108, Cary, NC: SAS Institute Inc.

Sarle, W.S and Kuo, An-Hsiang (1993), *The MODECLUS Procedure*, SAS Technical Report P-256, Cary, NC: SAS Institute Inc.

Scott, A.J. and Symons, M.J. (1971), "Clustering Methods Based on Likelihood Ratio Criteria," *Biometrics*, 27, 387–397.

Silverman, B.W. (1986), *Density Estimation*, New York: Chapman and Hall.

Sneath, P.H.A. and Sokal, R.R. (1973), *Numerical Taxonomy*, San Francisco: W.H. Freeman.

Spath, H. (1980), *Cluster Analysis Algorithms*, Chichester, England: Ellis Horwood.

Symons, M.J. (1981), "Clustering Criteria and Multivariate Normal Mixtures," *Biometrics*, 37, 35–43.

Thode, H.C. Jr., Mendell, N.R., and Finch, S.J. (1988), "Simulated Percentage Points for the Null Distribution of the Likelihood Ratio Test for a Mixture of Two Normals," *Biometrics*, 44, 1195–1201.

Titterington, D.M., Smith, A.F.M., and Makov, U.E. (1985), *Statistical Analysis of Finite Mixture Distributions*, New York: John Wiley & Sons, Inc.

Ward, J.H. (1963), "Hierarchical Grouping to Optimize an Objective Function," *Journal of the American Statistical Association*, 58, 236–244.

Wolfe, J.H. (1970), "Pattern Clustering by Multivariate Mixture Analysis," *Multivariate Behavioral Research*, 5, 329–350.

Wolfe, J.H. (1978), "Comparative Cluster Analysis of Patterns of Vocational Interest," *Multivariate Behavioral Research*, 13, 33–44.

Wong, M.A. (1982), "A Hybrid Clustering Method for Identifying High-Density Clusters," *Journal of the American Statistical Association*, 77, 841–847.

Wong, M.A. and Lane, T. (1983), "A *k*th Nearest Neighbor Clustering Procedure," *Journal of the Royal Statistical Society*, Series B, 45, 362–368.

Wong, M.A. and Schaack, C. (1982), "Using the *k*th Nearest Neighbor Clustering Procedure to Determine the Number of Subpopulations," *American Statistical Association 1982 Proceedings of the Statistical Computing Section*, 40–48.

Chapter 9
Introduction to Scoring, Standardization, and Ranking Procedures

Chapter Table of Contents

Chapter 9
Introduction to Scoring, Standardization, and Ranking Procedures

Overview

Several SAS/STAT procedures are utilities that produce an output data set with new variables that are transformations of data in the input data set. SAS/STAT software includes four of these procedures. The RANK procedure produces rank scores across observations, the SCORE procedure constructs functions across the variables, and the STANDARD and STDIZE procedures transform each variable individually.

RANK
: ranks the observations of each numeric variable from low to high and outputs ranks or rank scores. For a complete discussion of the RANK procedure, refer to the *SAS Procedures Guide*.

SCORE
: constructs new variables that are linear combinations of old variables according to a scoring data set. This procedure is used with the FACTOR procedure and other procedures that output scoring coefficients.

STANDARD
: standardizes variables to a given mean and standard deviation. For a complete discussion of PROC STANDARD, refer to the *SAS Procedures Guide*.

STDIZE
: standardizes variables by subtracting a location measure and dividing by a scale measure. A variety of location and scale measures are provided. Such measures include the mean, median, Huber's estimate, Tukey's biweight estimate, and Andrew's wave estimate.

Chapter 10
Introduction to Survival Analysis Procedures

Chapter Table of Contents

Chapter 10
Introduction to Survival Analysis Procedures

Overview

Data that measure lifetime or the length of time until the occurrence of an event are called lifetime, failure time, or survival data. For example, variables of interest might be the lifetime of diesel engines, the length of time a person stayed on a job, or the survival time for heart transplant patients. Such data have special considerations that must be incorporated into any analysis.

Background

Survival data consist of a response variable that measures the duration of time until a specified event occurs (event time, failure time, or survival time) and possibly a set of independent variables thought to be associated with the failure time variable. These independent variables (concomitant variables, covariates, or prognostic factors) can be either discrete, such as sex or race, or continuous, such as age or temperature. The system that gives rise to the event of interest can be biological, as for most medical data, or physical, as for engineering data. The purpose of survival analysis is to model the underlying distribution of the failure time variable and to assess the dependence of the failure time variable on the independent variables.

An intrinsic characteristic of survival data is the possibility for censoring of observations, that is, the actual time until the event is not observed. Such censoring can arise from withdrawal from the experiment or termination of the experiment. Because the response is usually a duration, some of the possible events may not yet have occurred when the period for data collection has terminated. For example, clinical trials are conducted over a finite period of time with staggered entry of patients. That is, patients enter a clinical trial over time and thus the length of follow-up varies by individuals; consequently, the time to the event may not be ascertained on all patients in the study. Additionally, some of the responses may be lost to follow-up (for example, a participant may move or refuse to continue to participate) before termination of data collection. In either case, only a lower bound on the failure time of the censored observations is known. These observations are said to be *right censored*. Thus, an additional variable is incorporated into the analysis indicating which responses are observed event times and which are censored times. More generally, the failure time may only be known to be smaller than a given value (*left censored*) or known to be within a given interval (*interval censored*). There are numerous possible censoring schemes that arise in survival analyses. The monograph by Maddala (1983) discusses several related types of censoring situations, and the text by Kalbfleisch and Prentice (1980) also discusses several censoring schemes. Data with censored observations cannot be analyzed by ignoring the censored observations because, among other considerations, the longer-lived individuals are generally more likely to be censored. The method of analysis must take the censoring into account and correctly use the censored observations as well as the uncensored observations.

Another characteristic of survival data is that the response cannot be negative. This suggests that a transformation of the survival time such as a log transformation may be necessary or that specialized methods may be more appropriate than those that assume a normal distribution for the error term. It is especially important to check any underlying assumptions as a part of the analysis because some of the models used are very sensitive to these assumptions.

Survival Analysis Procedures

There are three SAS procedures for analyzing survival data: LIFEREG, LIFETEST and PHREG. PROC LIFETEST is a nonparametric procedure for estimating the distribution of survival time and testing the association of survival time with other variables. PROC LIFEREG and PROC PHREG are regression procedures for modeling the distribution of survival time with a set of concomitant variables.

The LIFEREG Procedure

The LIFEREG procedure fits parametric accelerated failure time models to survival data that may be left, right, or interval censored. The parametric model is of the form

$$y = \mathbf{x}'\beta + \sigma\epsilon$$

where y is usually the log of the failure time variable, $\mathbf{x}$ is a vector of covariate values, β is a vector of unknown regression parameters to be fit, σ is an unknown scale parameter, and ϵ is an error term. The baseline distribution of the error term can be specified as one of several possible distributions, including, but not limited to, the log normal, log logistic, and Weibull distributions. Several texts that discuss these parametric models are Nelson (1990), Lawless (1982), and Kalbfleish and Prentice (1980).

The LIFETEST Procedure

The LIFETEST procedure computes nonparametric estimates of the survival distribution function. You can request either the product-limit (Kaplan-Meier) or the life table (actuarial) estimate of the distribution. The texts by Cox and Oakes (1984) and Kalbfleisch and Prentice (1980) provide good discussions of the product-limit estimator, and the texts by Lee (1992) and Elandt-Johnson and Johnson (1980) include detailed discussions of the life table estimator. The procedure also computes rank tests of association of the survival time variable with other concomitant variables as given in Kalbfleish and Prentice (1980, Chapter 6).

The PHREG Procedure

The PHREG procedure fits the proportional hazards model of Cox (1972, 1975) to survival data that may be right censored. The Cox model is a semiparametric model in which the hazard function of the survival time is given by

$$h(t|x) = h_0(t)\exp(\beta'\mathbf{x}(t))$$

where $h_0(t)$ is an unspecified baseline hazard function, $\mathbf{x}(t)$ is a vectors of covariate values, possibly time-dependent, and β is a vector of unknown regression parameters. The model is referred to as a semiparametric model since part of the model involves the unspecified baseline function over time (which is infinite dimensional) and the other part involves a finite number of regression parameters. Several texts that discuss the Cox regression models are Collett (1994), Cox and Oaks (1984), Lawless (1982), Kalbfleish and Prentice (1980).

Survival Analysis with SAS/STAT Procedures

The typical goal in survival analysis is to characterize the distribution of the survival time for a given population, to compare this survival time among different groups, or to study the relationship between the survival time and some concomitant variables.

A first step in the analysis of a set of survival data is to use PROC LIFETEST to compute and plot the estimate of the distribution of the survival time. The association between covariates and the survival time variable can be investigated by computing estimates of the survival distribution function within strata defined by the covariates. In particular, if the proportional hazards model is appropriate, the estimates of the log(-log(SURVIVAL)) plotted against the log(TIME) variable should give approximately parallel lines, where SURVIVAL is the survival distribution estimate and TIME is the failure time variable. Additionally, these lines should be approximately straight if the Weibull model is appropriate.

Statistics that test for association between failure time and covariates can be used to select covariates for further investigation. The LIFETEST procedure computes linear rank statistics using either Wilcoxon or log-rank scores. These statistics and their estimated covariance matrix can be used with the REG procedure with the option METHOD=RSQUARE to find the subset of variables that produce the largest joint test statistic for association. An example of this method of variable selection is given in the "Examples" section of Chapter 37, "The LIFETEST Procedure."

Another approach to examine the relationship between the concomitant variables and survival time is through a regression model in which the survival time has a distribution that depends on the concomitant variables. The regression coefficients may be interpreted as describing the direction and strength of the relationship of each explanatory variable on the effect of the survival time.

In many biological systems, the Cox model may be a reasonable description of the relationship between the distribution of the survival time and the prognostic factors. You use PROC PHREG to fit the Cox regression model. The regression coefficient is interpreted as the increase of the log hazard ratio resulting in the increase of one unit in the covariate. However, the underlying hazard function is left unspecified and, as in any other model, the results can be misleading if the proportional hazards assumptions do not hold.

Accelerated failure time models are popular for survival data of physical systems. In many cases, the underlying survival distribution is known empirically. You use PROC LIFEREG to fit these parametric models. Also, PROC LIFEREG can accommodate data with interval-censored observations, which are not allowed in PROC PHREG.

A common technique for checking the validity of a regression model is to embed it in a larger model and use the likelihood ratio test to check whether the reduction to the actual model is valid. Other techniques include examining the residuals. Both PROC LIFEREG and PROC PHREG produce predicted values, residuals, and other computed values that can be used to assess the model adequacy.

References

Collett, D. (1994), *Modelling Survival Data in Medical Research,* London: Chapman and Hall.

Cox, D.R. (1972), "Regression Models and Life-Tables (with Discussions)," *Journal of Royal Statistical Society. Series B,* 34, 187–220.

Cox, D.R. (1975), "Partial Likelihoods," *Biometrika,* 62, 269–276.

Cox, D.R. and Oakes, D. (1984), *Analysis of Survival Data*, London: Chapman and Hall.

Elandt-Johnson, R.C. and Johnson, N.L. (1980), *Survival Models and Data Analysis,* New York: John Wiley & Sons, Inc.

Gross, A.J. and Clark, V.A. (1975), *Survival Distributions: Reliability Applications in the Biomedical Sciences*, New York: John Wiley & Sons, Inc.

Kalbfleisch, J.D. and Prentice, R.L. (1980), *The Statistical Analysis of Failure Time Data*, New York: John Wiley & Sons, Inc.

Lawless, J.E. (1982), *Statistical Models and Methods for Lifetime Data*, New York: John Wiley & Sons, Inc.

Lee, E.T. (1992), *Statistical Methods for Survival Data Analysis*, Second Edition, New York: John Wiley & Sons, Inc..

Maddala, G.S. (1983) *Limited-Dependent and Qualitative Variables in Econometrics,* New York: Cambridge University Press.

Nelson, W. (1990) *Accelerated Testing: Statistical Models, Test Plans, and Data Analyses,* New York: John Wiley & Sons, Inc.

Chapter 11
Introduction to Survey Sampling and Analysis Procedures

Chapter Table of Contents

Chapter 11
Introduction to Survey Sampling and Analysis Procedures

Overview

This chapter introduces the SAS/STAT procedures for survey sampling and describes how you can use these procedures to analyze survey data.

Researchers often use sample survey methodology to obtain information about a large population by selecting and measuring a sample from that population. Due to variability among items, researchers apply scientific probability-based designs to select the sample. This reduces the risk of a distorted view of the population and allows statistically valid inferences to be made from the sample. Refer to Cochran (1977), Kalton (1983), and Kish (1965) for more information on statistical sampling. You can use the SURVEYSELECT procedure to select probability-based samples from a study population.

Many SAS/STAT procedures, such as the MEANS and GLM procedures, can compute sample means and estimate regression relationships. However, in most of these procedures, statistical inference is based on the assumption that the sample is drawn from an infinite population by simple random sampling. If the sample is actually selected from a finite population using a complex design, these procedures generally do not calculate the estimates and their variances correctly. The SURVEYMEANS and SURVEYREG procedures do properly analyze survey data, taking into account the sample design. These procedures use the Taylor expansion method to estimate sampling errors of estimators based on complex sample designs.

The following table briefly describes the sampling and analysis procedures in SAS/STAT software.

SURVEYSELECT	
Design Accommodated	stratification clustering replication multistage sampling unequal probabilities of selection

Sampling Methods	simple random sampling unrestricted random sampling (with replacement) systematic sequential selection probability proportional to size (PPS) with and without replacement PPS systematic PPS for two units per stratum sequential PPS with minimum replacement
SURVEYMEANS	
Design Accommodated	stratification clustering unequal weighting
Available Statistics	population total population mean proportion standard error confident limit *t* test
SURVEYREG	
Design Accommodated	stratification clustering unequal weighting
Available Analysis	fit linear regression model regression coefficients covariance matrix significance tests estimable functions contrasts

The following sections contain brief descriptions of these procedures.

Survey Sampling

The SURVEYSELECT procedure provides a variety of methods for selecting probability-based random samples. The procedure can select a simple random sample or a sample according to a complex multistage sample design that includes stratification, clustering, and unequal probabilities of selection. With probability sampling, each unit in the survey population has a known, positive probability of selection. This property of probability sampling avoids selection bias and enables you to use statistical theory to make valid inferences from the sample to the survey population.

PROC SURVEYSELECT provides methods for both equal probability sampling and sampling with probability proportional to size (PPS). In PPS sampling, a unit's selection probability is proportional to its size measure. PPS sampling is often used in cluster sampling, where you select clusters (groups of sampling units) of varying size in the first stage of selection. Available PPS methods include without replacement, with replacement, systematic, and sequential with minimum replacement. The procedure can apply these methods for stratified and replicated sample designs. See Chapter 63, "The SURVEYSELECT Procedure," for more information.

Survey Data Analysis

The SURVEYMEANS and SURVEYREG procedures perform statistical analysis for survey data. These analytical procedures take into account the design used to select the sample. The sample design can be a complex sample design with stratification, clustering, and unequal weighting.

You can use the SURVEYMEANS procedure to compute the following statistics:

- population total estimate and its standard deviation and corresponding *t* test
- population mean estimate and its standard error and corresponding *t* test
- proportion estimate for a categorical variable and corresponding *t* test
- $(1 - \alpha)\%$ confidence limits for the population total estimates, the population mean estimates, and the proportion estimates
- data summary information

PROC SURVEYREG fits linear models for survey data and computes regression coefficients and their variance-covariance matrix. The procedure also provides significance tests for the model effects and for any specified estimable linear functions of the model parameters.

PROC SURVEYMEANS presently does not perform domain analysis (subgroup analysis). However, note that you can produce a domain analysis with PROC SURVEYREG (see Example 62.7 on page 3269). This capability will be available in a future release of the SURVEYMEANS procedure.

Variance Estimation

The SURVEYMEANS and SURVEYREG procedures use the Taylor expansion method to estimate sampling errors of estimators based on complex sample designs. This method obtains a linear approximation for the estimator and then uses the variance estimate for this approximation to estimate the variance of the estimate itself (Woodruff 1971, Fuller 1975). When there are clusters, or primary sampling units (PSUs), in the sample design, the procedures estimate the variance from the variation among the PSUs. When the design is stratified, the procedures pool stratum variance estimates to compute the overall variance estimate.

For a multistage sample design, the variance estimation method depends only on the first stage of the sample design. Thus, the required input includes only first-stage cluster (PSU) and first-stage stratum identification. You do not need to input design information about any additional stages of sampling. This variance estimation method assumes that the first-stage sampling fraction is small or that the first-stage sample is drawn with replacement, as it often is in practice.

For more information on variance estimation for sample survey data, refer to Lee, Forthoffer, and Lorimor (1989), Cochran (1977), Kish (1965), Särndal, Swenson, and Wretman (1992), Wolter (1985), and Hansen, Hurwitz, and Madow (1953).

In addition to the traditional Taylor expansion method, other methods for variance estimation for survey data include balanced repeated replication and jackknife repeated replication. These methods usually give similar, satisfactory results (Wolter 1985, Särndal, Swenson, and Wretman 1992); the SURVEYMEANS and SURVEYREG procedures currently provide only the Taylor expansion method.

See Chapter 61, "The SURVEYMEANS Procedure," and Chapter 62, "The SURVEYREG Procedure," for complete details.

Design Information for Survey Procedures

Survey sampling is the process of selecting a probability-based sample from a finite population according to a sample design. You then collect data from these selected units and use them to estimate characteristics of the entire population.

A *sample design* encompasses the rules and operations by which you select sampling units from the population and the computation of sample statistics, which are estimates of the population values of interest. The objective of your survey often determines appropriate sample designs and valid data collection methodology. A complex sample design often includes stratification, clustering, multiple stages of selection, and unequal weighting.

For more detailed information, refer to Cochran (1977), Kalton (1983), Kish (1965), and Hansen, Hurwitz, and Madow (1953).

To select a sample with the SURVEYSELECT procedure and analyze your survey data with the SURVEYMEANS and SURVEYREG procedures, you need to specify sample design information to those procedures. This information includes design strata, clusters, and sampling weights.

Population

Population refers to the target population or group of individuals of interest for study. Often, the primary objective is to estimate certain characteristics of this population, called *population values*. A *sampling unit* is an element or an individual in the target population. A sample is a subset of the population that is selected for the study.

Before you use the survey procedures, you should have a well-defined target population, sampling units, and an appropriate sample design.

In order to select a sample according to your sample design, you need to have a list of sampling units in the population. This is called a *sampling frame*. PROC SURVEYSELECT selects a sample using this sampling frame.

Stratification

Stratified sampling involves selecting samples independently within strata, which are nonoverlapping subgroups of the survey population. Stratification controls the distribution of the sample size in the strata. It is widely used in practice to meet a variety of survey objectives. For example, with stratification you can ensure adequate sample sizes for subgroups of interest, including small subgroups, or you can use stratification to improve the precision of overall estimates. To improve precision, units within strata should be as homogeneous as possible for the characteristics of interest.

Clustering

Cluster sampling involves selecting clusters, which are groups of sampling units. For example, clusters may be schools, hospitals, or geographical areas, and sampling units may be students, patients, or citizens. Cluster sampling can provide efficiency in frame construction and other survey operations. However, it can also result in a loss in precision of your estimates, compared to a nonclustered sample of the same size. To minimize this effect, units within clusters should be as heterogeneous as possible for the characteristics of interest.

Multistage Sampling

In *multistage sampling*, you select an initial or first-stage sample based on groups of elements in the population, called *primary sampling units* or *PSUs*.

Then you create a second-stage sample by drawing a subsample from each selected PSU in the first-stage sample. By repeating this operation, you can select a higher-stage sample.

If you include all the elements from a selected primary sampling unit, then the two-stage sampling is a cluster sampling.

Sampling Weights

Sampling weights, or *survey weights*, are positive values associated with each unit in your sample. Ideally, the weight of a sampling unit should be the "frequency" that the sampling unit represents in the target population. Therefore, the sum of the weights over the sample should estimate the population size N. If you normalize the weights such that the sum of the weights over the sample equals the population size N, then the weighted sum of a characteristic y estimates the population total value Y.

Often, sampling weights are the reciprocals of the selection probabilities for the sampling units. When you use PROC SURVEYSELECT, the procedure generates the sampling weight component for each stage of the design, and you can multiply these sampling weight components to obtain the final sampling weights. Sometimes, sampling weights also include nonresponse adjustments, post-sampling stratification, or regression adjustments using supplemental information.

When the sampling units have unequal weights, you must provide the weights to the survey analysis procedures. If you do not specify sampling weights, the procedures use equal weights in the analysis.

Population Totals and Sampling Rates

The ratio of the sample size (the number of sampling units in the sample) n and the population size (the total number of sampling units in the target population) N is written as

$$f = \frac{n}{N}$$

This ratio is called the *sampling rate* or the *sampling fraction*. If you select a sample without replacement, the extra efficiency compared to selecting a sample with replacement can be measured by the *finite population correction* (fpc) factor, $(1 - f)$.

If your analysis should include a finite population correction factor, you can input either the sampling rate or the population total. Otherwise, the procedures do not use the fpc when computing variance estimates. For fairly small sampling fractions, it is appropriate to ignore this correction. Refer to Cochran (1977) and Kish (1965).

As stated in the section "Variance Estimation" on page 151, for a multistage sample design, the variance estimation method depends only on the first stage of the sample design. Therefore, if you are specifying the sampling rate, you should input the first-stage sampling rate, which is the ratio of the number of PSUs in the sample to the total number of PSUs in the target population.

An Example of Using the Survey Procedures

This section demonstrates how you can use the survey procedures to select a probability-based sample, compute descriptive statistics from the sample, perform regression analysis, and make inferences about income and expenditures of a group of households in North Carolina and South Carolina. The goals of the survey are to

- estimate total income and total basic living expenses
- investigate the linear relationship between income and living expenses

Sample Selection

To select a sample with PROC SURVEYSELECT, you input a SAS data set that contains the sampling frame, or list of units from which the sample is to be selected. You also specify the selection method, the desired sample size or sampling rate, and other selection parameters.

In this example, the sample design is a stratified simple random sampling design, with households as the sampling units. The sampling frame (the list of the group of the households) is stratified by State and Region. Within strata, households are selected by simple random sampling. Using this design, the following PROC SURVEYSELECT statements select a probability sample of households from the HHSample data set.

```
proc surveyselect data=HHSample out=Sample
                  method=srs n=(3, 5, 3, 6, 2);
   strata State Region;
run;
```

The STRATA statement names the stratification variables State and Region. In the PROC SURVEYSELECT statement, the DATA= option names the SAS data set HHSample as the input data set (the sampling frame) from which to select the sample. The OUT= option stores the sample in the SAS data set named Sample. The METHOD=SRS option specifies simple random sampling as the sample selection method. The N= option specifies the stratum sample sizes.

The SURVEYSELECT procedure then selects a stratified random sample of households and produces the output data set Sample, which contains the selected households together with their selection probabilities and sampling weights. The data set Sample also contains the sampling unit identification variable Id and the stratification variables State and Region from the data set HHSample.

Survey Data Analysis

You can use the SURVEYMEANS and SURVEYREG procedures to estimate population values and to perform regression analyses for survey data. The following example briefly shows the capabilities of each procedure. See Chapter 61, "The SURVEYMEANS Procedure," and Chapter 62, "The SURVEYREG Procedure," for more detailed information.

To estimate the total income and expenditure in the population from the sample, you specify the input data set containing the sample, the statistics to be computed, the variables to be analyzed, and any stratification variables. The statements to compute the descriptive statistics are as follows:

```
proc surveymeans data=Sample sum clm;
   var Income Expense;
   strata State Region;
   weight Weight;
run;
```

The PROC SURVEYMEANS statement invokes the procedure, specifies the input data set, and requests estimates of population totals and their standard deviations for the analysis variables (SUM), and confidence limits for the estimates (CLM).

The VAR statement specifies the two analysis variables, Income and Expense. The STRATA statement identifies State and Region as the stratification variables in the sample design. The WEIGHT statement specifies the sampling weight variable Weight.

You can also use the SURVEYREG procedure to perform regression analysis for sample survey data. Suppose that, in order to explore the relationship between the total income and the total basic living expenses of a household in the survey population, you choose the following linear model to describe the relationship.

$$\text{Expense} = \alpha + \beta * \text{Income} + \text{error}$$

The following statements fit this linear model.

```
proc surveyreg data=Sample;
   strata State Region ;
   model  Expense = Income;
   weight Weight;
run;
```

In the PROC SURVEYREG statement, the DATA= option specifies the input sample survey data as Sample. The STRATA statement identifies the stratification variables as State and Region . The MODEL statement specifies the model, with Expense as the dependent variable and Income as the independent variable. The WEIGHT statement specifies the sampling weight variable Weight.

References

Cochran, W. G. (1977), *Sampling Techniques*, Third Edition, New York: John Wiley & Sons, Inc.

Fuller, W. A. (1975), "Regression Analysis for Sample Survey," *Sankhyā*, 37 (3), Series C, 117–132.

Hansen, M. H., Hurwitz, W. N., and Madow, W. G. (1953), *Sample Survey Methods and Theory*, Volumes I and II, New York: John Wiley & Sons, Inc.

Kalton, G. (1983), *Introduction to Survey Sampling*, SAGE University Paper series on Quantitative Applications in the Social Sciences, series no. 07-035, Beverly Hills and London: SAGE Publications, Inc.

Kish, L. (1965), *Survey Sampling*, New York: John Wiley & Sons, Inc.

Lee, E. S., Forthoffer, R. N., and Lorimor, R. J. (1989), *Analyzing Complex Survey Data*, Sage University Paper series on Quantitative Applications in the Social Sciences, series no. 07-071, Beverly Hills and London: Sage Publications, Inc.

Särndal, C.E., Swenson, B., and Wretman, J. (1992), *Model Assisted Survey Sampling*, New York: Springer-Verlag Inc.

Wolter, K. M. (1985), *Introduction to Variance Estimation*, New York: Springer-Verlag Inc.

Woodruff, R. S. (1971), "A Simple Method for Approximating the Variance of a Complicated Estimate," *Journal of the American Statistical Association*, 66, 411–414.

Chapter 12

The Four Types of Estimable Functions

Chapter Table of Contents

Chapter 12
The Four Types of Estimable Functions

Overview

The GLM, VARCOMP, and other SAS/STAT procedures label the Sums of Squares (SS) associated with the various effects in the model as Type I, Type II, Type III, and Type IV. These four types of hypotheses may not always be sufficient for a statistician to perform all desired hypothesis tests, but they should suffice for the vast majority of analyses. This chapter explains the hypotheses tested by each of the four types of SS. For additional discussion, see Freund, Littell, and Spector (1991) or Milliken and Johnson (1984).

Estimability

For linear models such as

$$\mathbf{Y} = \mathbf{X}\boldsymbol{\beta} + \epsilon$$

with $E(\mathbf{Y}) = \mathbf{X}\beta$, a primary analytical goal is to estimate or test for the significance of certain linear combinations of the elements of $\boldsymbol{\beta}$. This is accomplished by computing linear combinations of the observed $\mathbf{Y}$s. An unbiased linear estimate of a specific linear function of the individual βs, say $\mathbf{L}\boldsymbol{\beta}$, is a linear combination of the $\mathbf{Y}$s that has an expected value of $\mathbf{L}\boldsymbol{\beta}$. Hence, the following definition:

> A linear combination of the parameters $\mathbf{L}\boldsymbol{\beta}$ is estimable if and only if a linear combination of the $\mathbf{Y}$s exists that has expected value $\mathbf{L}\boldsymbol{\beta}$.

Any linear combination of the $\mathbf{Y}$s, for instance $\mathbf{KY}$, will have expectation $E(\mathbf{KY}) = \mathbf{KX}\boldsymbol{\beta}$. Thus, the expected value of any linear combination of the $\mathbf{Y}$s is equal to that same linear combination of the rows of $\mathbf{X}$ multiplied by $\boldsymbol{\beta}$. Therefore,

> $\mathbf{L}\boldsymbol{\beta}$ is estimable if and only if there is a linear combination of the rows of $\mathbf{X}$ that is equal to $\mathbf{L}$—that is, if and only if there is a $\mathbf{K}$ such that $\mathbf{L} = \mathbf{KX}$.

Thus, the rows of $\mathbf{X}$ form a generating set from which any estimable $\mathbf{L}$ can be constructed. Since the row space of $\mathbf{X}$ is the same as the row space of $\mathbf{X'X}$, the rows of $\mathbf{X'X}$ also form a generating set from which all estimable $\mathbf{L}$s can be constructed. Similarly, the rows of $(\mathbf{X'X})^{-}\mathbf{X'X}$ also form a generating set for $\mathbf{L}$.

Therefore, if $\mathbf{L}$ can be written as a linear combination of the rows of $\mathbf{X}$, $\mathbf{X}'\mathbf{X}$, or $(\mathbf{X}'\mathbf{X})^{-}\mathbf{X}'\mathbf{X}$, then $\mathbf{L}\boldsymbol{\beta}$ is estimable.

Once an estimable $\mathbf{L}$ has been formed, $\mathbf{L}\boldsymbol{\beta}$ can be estimated by computing $\mathbf{Lb}$, where $\mathbf{b} = (\mathbf{X}'\mathbf{X})^{-}\mathbf{X}'\mathbf{Y}$. From the general theory of linear models, the unbiased estimator $\mathbf{Lb}$ is, in fact, the *best* linear unbiased estimator of $\mathbf{L}\boldsymbol{\beta}$ in the sense of having minimum variance as well as maximum likelihood when the residuals are normal. To test the hypothesis that $\mathbf{L}\boldsymbol{\beta} = 0$, compute SS $(H_0\colon\ \mathbf{L}\boldsymbol{\beta} = 0) = (\mathbf{Lb})'(\mathbf{L}(\mathbf{X}'\mathbf{X})^{-}\mathbf{L}')^{-1}\mathbf{Lb}$ and form an F test using the appropriate error term.

General Form of an Estimable Function

This section demonstrates a shorthand technique for displaying the generating set for any estimable $\mathbf{L}$. Suppose

$$\mathbf{X} = \begin{bmatrix} 1 & 1 & 0 & 0 \\ 1 & 1 & 0 & 0 \\ 1 & 0 & 1 & 0 \\ 1 & 0 & 1 & 0 \\ 1 & 0 & 0 & 1 \\ 1 & 0 & 0 & 1 \end{bmatrix} \quad \text{and} \quad \boldsymbol{\beta} = \begin{bmatrix} \mu \\ A_1 \\ A_2 \\ A_3 \end{bmatrix}$$

$\mathbf{X}$ is a generating set for $\mathbf{L}$, but so is the smaller set

$$\mathbf{X}^* = \begin{bmatrix} 1 & 1 & 0 & 0 \\ 1 & 0 & 1 & 0 \\ 1 & 0 & 0 & 1 \end{bmatrix}$$

$\mathbf{X}^*$ is formed from $\mathbf{X}$ by deleting duplicate rows.

Since all estimable $\mathbf{L}$s must be linear functions of the rows of $\mathbf{X}^*$ for $\mathbf{L}\boldsymbol{\beta}$ to be estimable, an $\mathbf{L}$ for a single-degree-of-freedom estimate can be represented symbolically as

$$L1 \times (1\,1\,0\,0) + L2 \times (1\,0\,1\,0) + L3 \times (1\,0\,0\,1)$$

or

$$\mathbf{L} = (L1 + L2 + L3,\ L1,\ L2,\ L3)$$

For this example, $\mathbf{L}\boldsymbol{\beta}$ is estimable if and only if the first element of $\mathbf{L}$ is equal to the sum of the other elements of $\mathbf{L}$ or if

$$\mathbf{L}\boldsymbol{\beta} = (L1 + L2 + L3) \times \mu + L1 \times A_1 + L2 \times A_2 + L3 \times A_3$$

is estimable for any values of $L1$, $L2$, and $L3$.

If other generating sets for $\mathbf{L}$ are represented symbolically, the symbolic notation looks different. However, the inherent nature of the rules is the same. For example, if row operations are performed on $\mathbf{X}^*$ to produce an identity matrix in the first 3×3 submatrix of the resulting matrix

$$\mathbf{X}^{**} = \begin{bmatrix} 1 & 0 & 0 & 1 \\ 0 & 1 & 0 & -1 \\ 0 & 0 & 1 & -1 \end{bmatrix}$$

then $\mathbf{X}^{**}$ is also a generating set for $\mathbf{L}$. An estimable $\mathbf{L}$ generated from $\mathbf{X}^{**}$ can be represented symbolically as

$$\mathbf{L} = (L1,\ L2,\ L3,\ L1 - L2 - L3)$$

Note that, again, the first element of $\mathbf{L}$ is equal to the sum of the other elements.

With the thousands of generating sets available, the question arises as to which one is the best to represent $\mathbf{L}$ symbolically. Clearly, a generating set containing a minimum of rows (of full row rank) and a maximum of zero elements is desirable. The generalized inverse of $\mathbf{X}'\mathbf{X}$ computed by the GLM procedure has the property that $(\mathbf{X}'\mathbf{X})^{-}\mathbf{X}'\mathbf{X}$ usually contains numerous zeros. For this reason, PROC GLM uses the nonzero rows of $(\mathbf{X}'\mathbf{X})^{-}\mathbf{X}'\mathbf{X}$ to represent $\mathbf{L}$ symbolically.

If the generating set represented symbolically is of full row rank, the number of symbols $(L1, L2, \ldots)$ represents the maximum rank of any testable hypothesis (in other words, the maximum number of linearly independent rows for any $\mathbf{L}$ matrix that can be constructed). By letting each symbol in turn take on the value of 1 while the others are set to 0, the original generating set can be reconstructed.

Introduction to Reduction Notation

Reduction notation can be used to represent differences in Sums of Squares for two models. The notation $R(\mu, A, B, C)$ denotes the complete main effects model for effects A, B, and C. The notation

$$R(A \mid \mu, B, C)$$

denotes the difference between the model SS for the complete main effects model containing A, B, and C and the model SS for the reduced model containing only B and C.

In other words, this notation represents the differences in Model SS produced by

```
proc glm;
   class a b c;
   model y=a b c;
run;
```

and

```
proc glm;
   class b c;
   model y=b c;
run;
```

As another example, consider a regression equation with four independent variables. The notation $R(\beta_3, \beta_4|\beta_1, \beta_2)$ denotes the differences in Model SS between

$$y = \beta_0 + \beta_1 x_1 + \beta_2 x_2 + \beta_3 x_3 + \beta_4 x_4 + \epsilon$$

and

$$y = \beta_0 + \beta_1 x_1 + \beta_2 x_2 + \epsilon$$

With PROC REG, this is the difference in Model SS for the models produced by

```
model y=x1 x2 x3 x4;
```

and

```
model y=x1 x2;
```

Examples

A One-Way Classification Model

For the model

$$Y = \mu + A_i + \epsilon \qquad i = 1, 2, 3$$

the general form of estimable functions $\mathbf{Lb}$ is (from the previous example)

$$\mathbf{L}\boldsymbol{\beta} = L1 \times \mu + L2 \times A_1 + L3 \times A_2 + (L1 - L2 - L3) \times A_3$$

Thus,

$$\mathbf{L} = (L1, L2, L3, L1 - L2 - L3)$$

Tests involving only the parameters A_1, A_2, and A_3 must have an $\mathbf{L}$ of the form

$$\mathbf{L} = (0, L2, L3, -L2 - L3)$$

Since the preceding $\mathbf{L}$ involves only two symbols, hypotheses with at most two degrees-of-freedom can be constructed. For example, let $L2 = 1$ and $L3 = 0$; then let $L2 = 0$ and $L3 = 1$:

$$\mathbf{L} = \begin{bmatrix} 0 & 1 & 0 & -1 \\ 0 & 0 & 1 & -1 \end{bmatrix}$$

The preceding $\mathbf{L}$ can be used to test the hypothesis that $A_1 = A_2 = A_3$. For this example, any $\mathbf{L}$ with two linearly independent rows with column 1 equal to zero produces the same Sum of Squares. For example, a pooled linear quadratic

$$\mathbf{L} = \begin{bmatrix} 0 & 1 & 0 & -1 \\ 0 & 1 & -2 & 1 \end{bmatrix}$$

gives the same SS. In fact, for any $\mathbf{L}$ of full row rank and any nonsingular matrix $\mathbf{K}$ of conformable dimensions,

$$\mathrm{SS}(H_0\colon \mathbf{L}\boldsymbol{\beta} = 0) = \mathrm{SS}(H_0\colon \mathbf{KL}\boldsymbol{\beta} = 0)$$

A Three-Factor Main Effects Model

Consider a three-factor main effects model involving the CLASS variables A, B, and C, as shown in Table 12.1.

Table 12.1. Three-Factor Main Effects Model

Obs	A	B	C
1	1	2	1
2	1	1	2
3	2	1	3
4	2	2	2
5	2	2	2

The general form of an estimable function is shown in Table 12.2.

Table 12.2. General Form of an Estimable Function for Three-Factor Main Effects Model

Parameter	Coefficient
μ (Intercept)	$L1$
$A1$	$L2$
$A2$	$L1 - L2$
$B1$	$L4$
$B2$	$L1 - L4$
$C1$	$L6$
$C2$	$L1 + L2 - L4 - 2 \times L6$
$C3$	$-L2 + L4 + L6$

Since only four symbols ($L1$, $L2$, $L4$, and $L6$) are involved, any testable hypothesis will have at most four degrees of freedom. If you form an $\mathbf{L}$ matrix with four linearly independent rows according to the preceding rules, then

$$\mathrm{SS}(H_0\text{: } \mathbf{L}\boldsymbol{\beta} = 0) = R(\mu, A, B, C)$$

In a main effects model, the usual hypothesis of interest for a main effect is the equality of all the parameters. In this example, it is not possible to test such a hypothesis because of confounding. One way to proceed is to construct a maximum rank hypothesis (MRH) involving only the parameters of the main effect in question. This can be done using the general form of estimable functions. Note the following:

- To get an MRH involving only the parameters of A, the coefficients of $\mathbf{L}$ associated with μ, $B1$, $B2$, $C1$, $C2$, and $C3$ must be equated to zero. Starting at the top of the general form, let $L1 = 0$, then $L4 = 0$, then $L6 = 0$. If $C2$ and $C3$ are not to be involved, then $L2$ must also be zero. Thus, $A1 - A2$ is not estimable; that is, the MRH involving only the A parameters has zero rank and $R(A \mid \mu, B, C) = 0$.
- To obtain the MRH involving only the B parameters, let $L1 = L2 = L6 = 0$. But then to remove $C2$ and $C3$ from the comparison, $L4$ must also be set to 0. Thus, $B1 - B2$ is not estimable and $R(B \mid \mu, A, C) = 0$.
- To obtain the MRH involving only the C parameters, let $L1 = L2 = L4 = 0$. Thus, the MRH involving only C parameters is

  $$C1 - 2 \times C2 + C3 = K \qquad \text{(for any } K\text{)}$$

  or any multiple of the left-hand side equal to K. Furthermore,

  $$\mathrm{SS}(H_0\text{: } C1 = 2 \times C2 - C3 = 0) = R(C \mid \mu, A, B)$$

A Multiple Regression Model

Suppose

$$E(Y) = \beta_0 + \beta_1 \times X1 + \beta_2 \times X2 + \beta_3 \times X3$$

If the $\mathbf{X}'\mathbf{X}$ matrix is of full rank, the general form of estimable functions is as shown in Table 12.3.

Table 12.3. General Form of Estimable Functions for a Multiple Regression Model When $\mathbf{X}'\mathbf{X}$ Matrix Is of Full Rank

Parameter	Coefficient
β_0	$L1$
β_1	$L2$
β_2	$L3$
β_3	$L4$

To test, for example, the hypothesis that $\beta_2 = 0$, let $L1 = L2 = L4 = 0$ and let $L3 = 1$. Then $\text{SS}(\mathbf{L}\boldsymbol{\beta} = 0) = R(\beta_2 \mid \beta_0, \beta_1, \beta_3)$. In the full-rank case, all parameters, as well as any linear combination of parameters, are estimable.

Suppose, however, that $X3 = 2 \times X1 + 3 \times X2$. The general form of estimable functions is shown in Table 12.4.

Table 12.4. General Form of Estimable Functions for a Multiple Regression Model When $\mathbf{X}'\mathbf{X}$ Matrix Is Not of Full Rank

Parameter	Coefficient
β_0	$L1$
β_1	$L2$
β_2	$L3$
β_3	$2 \times L2 + 3 \times L3$

For this example, it is possible to test H_0: $\beta_0 = 0$. However, β_1, β_2, and β_3 are not jointly estimable; that is,

$$\begin{aligned} R(\beta_1 \mid \beta_0, \beta_2, \beta_3) &= 0 \\ R(\beta_2 \mid \beta_0, \beta_1, \beta_3) &= 0 \\ R(\beta_3 \mid \beta_0, \beta_1, \beta_2) &= 0 \end{aligned}$$

Using Symbolic Notation

The preceding examples demonstrate the ability to manipulate the symbolic representation of a generating set. Note that any operations performed on the symbolic notation have corresponding row operations that are performed on the generating set itself.

Estimable Functions

Type I SS and Estimable Functions

The Type I SS and the associated hypotheses they test are by-products of the modified sweep operator used to compute a generalized inverse of $\mathbf{X}'\mathbf{X}$ and a solution to the normal equations. For the model $E(Y) = X1 \times B1 + X2 \times B2 + X3 \times B3$, the Type I SS for each effect correspond to

Effect	Type I SS
$B1$	$R(B1)$
$B2$	$R(B2\|B1)$
$B3$	$R(B3\|B1, B2)$

The Type I SS are model-order dependent; each effect is adjusted only for the preceding effects in the model.

There are numerous ways to obtain a Type I hypothesis matrix $\mathbf{L}$ for each effect. One way is to form the $\mathbf{X}'\mathbf{X}$ matrix and then reduce $\mathbf{X}'\mathbf{X}$ to an upper triangular matrix by row operations, skipping over any rows with a zero diagonal. The nonzero rows of the resulting matrix associated with $X1$ provide an $\mathbf{L}$ such that

$$\text{SS}(H_0\colon\ \mathbf{L}\boldsymbol{\beta} = 0) = R(B1)$$

The nonzero rows of the resulting matrix associated with $X2$ provide an $\mathbf{L}$ such that

$$\text{SS}(H_0\colon\ \mathbf{L}\boldsymbol{\beta} = 0) = R(B1|B2)$$

The last set of nonzero rows (associated with $X3$) provide an $\mathbf{L}$ such that

$$\text{SS}(H_0\colon\ \mathbf{L}\boldsymbol{\beta} = 0) = R(B3|B1, B2)$$

Another more formalized representation of Type I generating sets for $B1$, $B2$, and $B3$, respectively, is

$$\begin{array}{lcl} \mathbf{G}_1 & = & (\ \mathbf{X}_1'\mathbf{X}_1 \mid \mathbf{X}_1'\mathbf{X}_2 \mid \mathbf{X}_1'\mathbf{X}_3\ ) \\ \mathbf{G}_2 & = & (\ 0 \mid \mathbf{X}_2'\mathbf{M}_2\mathbf{X}_2 \mid \mathbf{X}_2'\mathbf{M}_2\mathbf{X}_3\ ) \\ \mathbf{G}_3 & = & (\ 0 \mid 0 \mid \mathbf{X}_3'\mathbf{M}_3\mathbf{X}_3\ ) \end{array}$$

where

$$\mathbf{M}_1 = \mathbf{I} - \mathbf{X}_1(\mathbf{X}_1'\mathbf{X}_1)^{-}\mathbf{X}_1'$$

and

$$\mathbf{M}_2 = \mathbf{M}_1 - \mathbf{M}_1\mathbf{X}_2(\mathbf{X}_2'\mathbf{M}_1\mathbf{X}_2)^{-}\mathbf{X}_2'\mathbf{M}_1$$

Using the Type I generating set $\mathbf{G}_2$ (for example), if an $\mathbf{L}$ is formed from linear combinations of the rows of $\mathbf{G}_2$ such that $\mathbf{L}$ is of full row rank and of the same row rank as $\mathbf{G}_2$, then $\mathrm{SS}(H_0: \mathbf{L}\boldsymbol{\beta} = 0) = R(B2|B1)$.

In the GLM procedure, the Type I estimable functions displayed symbolically when the E1 option is requested are

$$\begin{aligned} \mathbf{G}_1^* &= (\mathbf{X}_1'\mathbf{X}_1)^-\mathbf{G}_1 \\ \mathbf{G}_2^* &= (\mathbf{X}_2'\mathbf{M}_1\mathbf{X}_2)^-\mathbf{G}_2 \\ \mathbf{G}_3^* &= (\mathbf{X}_3'\mathbf{M}_2\mathbf{X}_3)^-\mathbf{G}_3 \end{aligned}$$

As can be seen from the nature of the generating sets $\mathbf{G}_1$, $\mathbf{G}_2$, and $\mathbf{G}_3$, only the Type I estimable functions for $B3$ are guaranteed not to involve the $B1$ and $B2$ parameters. The Type I hypothesis for $B2$ can (and usually does) involve $B3$ parameters. The Type I hypothesis for $B1$ usually involves $B2$ and $B3$ parameters.

There are, however, a number of models for which the Type I hypotheses are considered appropriate. These are

- balanced ANOVA models specified in proper sequence (that is, interactions do not precede main effects in the MODEL statement and so forth)
- purely nested models (specified in the proper sequence)
- polynomial regression models (in the proper sequence).

Type II SS and Estimable Functions

For main effects models and regression models, the general form of estimable functions can be manipulated to provide tests of hypotheses involving only the parameters of the effect in question. The same result can also be obtained by entering each effect in turn as the last effect in the model and obtaining the Type I SS for that effect. These are the *Type II SS*. Using a modified reversible sweep operator, it is possible to obtain the Type II SS without actually rerunning the model.

Thus, the **Type II SS correspond to the R notation in which each effect is adjusted for all other effects possible**. For a regression model such as

$$E(Y) = X1 \times B1 + X2 \times B2 + X3 \times B3$$

the Type II SS correspond to

Effect	Type II SS
$B1$	$R(B1 \mid B2, B3)$
$B2$	$R(B2 \mid B1, B3)$
$B3$	$R(B3 \mid B1, B2)$

For a main effects model (A, B, and C as classification variables), the Type II SS correspond to

Effect	Type II SS
A	$R(A \mid B, C)$
B	$R(B \mid A, C)$
C	$R(C \mid A, B)$

As the discussion in the section "A Three-Factor Main Effects Model" on page 163 indicates, for regression and main effects models the Type II SS provide an MRH for each effect that does not involve the parameters of the other effects.

For models involving interactions and nested effects, in the absence of a priori parametric restrictions, it is not possible to obtain a test of a hypothesis for a main effect free of parameters of higher-level effects with which the main effect is involved.

It is reasonable to assume, then, that any test of a hypothesis concerning an effect should involve the parameters of that effect and only those other parameters with which that effect is involved.

Contained Effect

Given two effects $F1$ and $F2$, $F1$ is said to be *contained in* $F2$ provided that

- both effects involve the same continuous variables (if any)
- $F2$ has more CLASS variables than does $F1$, and if $F1$ has CLASS variables, they all appear in $F2$

Note that the interaction effect μ is contained in all pure CLASS effects, but it is not contained in any effect involving a continuous variable. No effect is contained by μ.

Type II, Type III, and Type IV estimable functions rely on this definition, and they all have one thing in common: the estimable functions involving an effect $F1$ also involve the parameters of all effects that contain $F1$, and they do not involve the parameters of effects that do not contain $F1$ (other than $F1$).

Hypothesis Matrix for Type II Estimable Functions

The Type II estimable functions for an effect $F1$ have an $\mathbf{L}$ (before reduction to full row rank) of the following form:

- All columns of $\mathbf{L}$ associated with effects not containing $F1$ (except $F1$) are zero.
- The submatrix of $\mathbf{L}$ associated with effect $F1$ is $(\mathbf{X}_1'\mathbf{M}\mathbf{X}_1)^{-}(\mathbf{X}_1'\mathbf{M}\mathbf{X}_1)$.
- Each of the remaining submatrices of $\mathbf{L}$ associated with an effect $F2$ that contains $F1$ is $(\mathbf{X}_1'\mathbf{M}\mathbf{X}_1)^{-}(\mathbf{X}_1'\mathbf{M}\mathbf{X}_2)$.

In these submatrices,

$$\begin{aligned}
\mathbf{X}_0 &= \text{the columns of } \mathbf{X} \text{ whose associated effects do not contain } F1. \\
\mathbf{X}_1 &= \text{the columns of } \mathbf{X} \text{ associated with } F1. \\
\mathbf{X}_2 &= \text{the columns of } \mathbf{X} \text{ associated with an } F2 \text{ effect that contains } F1. \\
\mathbf{M} &= \mathbf{I} - \mathbf{X}_0(\mathbf{X}_0'\mathbf{X}_0)^{-}\mathbf{X}_0'.
\end{aligned}$$

For the model $Y = A\ B\ A*B$, the Type II SS correspond to

$$R(A \mid \mu, B), \quad R(B \mid \mu, A), \quad R(A*B \mid \mu, A, B)$$

for effects A, B, and $A*B$, respectively. For the model $Y = A\ B(A)\ C(A\ B)$, the Type II SS correspond to

$$R(A \mid \mu), \quad R(B(A) \mid \mu, A), \quad R(C(AB) \mid \mu, A, B(A))$$

for effects A, $B(A)$ and $C(AB)$, respectively. For the model $Y = X\ X*X$, the Type II SS correspond to

$$R(X \mid \mu, X*X) \text{ and } R(X*X \mid \mu, X)$$

for X and $X*X$, respectively.

Example of Type II Estimable Functions

For a 2×2 factorial with w observations per cell, the general form of estimable functions is shown in Table 12.5. Any nonzero values for $L2$, $L4$, and $L6$ can be used to construct **L** vectors for computing the Type II SS for A, B, and $A*B$, respectively.

Table 12.5. General Form of Estimable Functions for 2×2 Factorial

Effect	Coefficient
μ	$L1$
$A1$	$L2$
$A2$	$L1 - L2$
$B1$	$L4$
$B2$	$L1 - L4$
$AB11$	$L6$
$AB12$	$L2 - L6$
$AB21$	$L4 - L6$
$AB22$	$L1 - L2 - L4 + L6$

For a balanced 2×2 factorial with the same number of observations in every cell, the Type II estimable functions are shown in Table 12.6.

Table 12.6. Type II Estimable Functions for Balanced 2×2 Factorial

Effect	Coefficients for Effect		
	A	B	$A * B$
μ	0	0	0
$A1$	$L2$	0	0
$A2$	$-L2$	0	0
$B1$	0	$L4$	0
$B2$	0	$-L4$	0
$AB11$	$0.5 * L2$	$0.5 * L4$	$L6$
$AB12$	$0.5 * L2$	$-0.5 * L4$	$-L6$
$AB21$	$-0.5 * L2$	$0.5 * L4$	$-L6$
$AB22$	$-0.5 * L2$	$-0.5 * L4$	$L6$

For an unbalanced 2×2 factorial (with two observations in every cell except the $AB22$ cell, which contains only one observation), the general form of estimable functions is the same as if it were balanced since the same effects are still estimable. However, the Type II estimable functions for A and B are not the same as they were for the balanced design. The Type II estimable functions for this unbalanced 2×2 factorial are shown in Table 12.7.

Table 12.7. Type II Estimable Functions for Unbalanced 2×2 Factorial

Effect	Coefficients for Effect		
	A	B	$A * B$
μ	0	0	0
$A1$	$L2$	0	0
$A2$	$-L2$	0	0
$B1$	0	$L4$	0
$B2$	0	$-L4$	0
$AB11$	$0.6 * L2$	$0.6 * L4$	$L6$
$AB12$	$0.4 * L2$	$-0.6 * L4$	$-L6$
$AB21$	$-0.6 * L2$	$0.4 * L4$	$-L6$
$AB22$	$-0.4 * L2$	$-0.4 * L4$	$L6$

By comparing the hypothesis being tested in the balanced case to the hypothesis being tested in the unbalanced case for effects A and B, you can note that the Type II hypotheses for A and B are dependent on the cell frequencies in the design. For unbalanced designs in which the cell frequencies are not proportional to the background population, the Type II hypotheses for effects that are contained in other effects are of questionable merit.

However, if an effect is not contained in any other effect, the Type II hypothesis for that effect is an MRH that does not involve any parameters except those associated with the effect in question.

Thus, Type II SS are appropriate for

- any balanced model
- any main effects model

- any pure regression model
- an effect not contained in any other effect (regardless of the model)

In addition to the preceding, the Type II SS is generally accepted by most statisticians for purely nested models.

Type III and IV SS and Estimable Functions

When an effect is contained in another effect, the Type II hypotheses for that effect are dependent on the cell frequencies. The philosophy behind both the Type III and Type IV hypotheses is that the hypotheses tested for any given effect should be the same for all designs with the same general form of estimable functions.

To demonstrate this concept, recall the hypotheses being tested by the Type II SS in the balanced 2×2 factorial shown in Table 12.6. Those hypotheses are precisely the ones that the Type III and Type IV hypotheses employ for all 2×2 factorials that have at least one observation per cell. The Type III and Type IV hypotheses for a design without missing cells usually differ from the hypothesis employed for the same design with missing cells since the general form of estimable functions usually differs.

Type III Estimable Functions

Type III hypotheses are constructed by working directly with the general form of estimable functions. The following steps are used to construct a hypothesis for an effect $F1$:

1. For every effect in the model except $F1$ and those effects that contain $F1$, equate the coefficients in the general form of estimable functions to zero.

   If $F1$ is not contained in any other effect, this step defines the Type III hypothesis (as well as the Type II and Type IV hypotheses). If $F1$ is contained in other effects, go on to step 2. (See the section "Type II SS and Estimable Functions" on page 167 for a definition of when effect $F1$ is contained in another effect.)

2. If necessary, equate new symbols to compound expressions in the $F1$ block in order to obtain the simplest form for the $F1$ coefficients.

3. Equate all symbolic coefficients outside of the $F1$ block to a linear function of the symbols in the $F1$ block in order to make the $F1$ hypothesis orthogonal to hypotheses associated with effects that contain $F1$.

By once again observing the Type II hypotheses being tested in the balanced 2×2 factorial, it is possible to verify that the A and $A * B$ hypotheses are orthogonal and also that the B and $A * B$ hypotheses are orthogonal. This principle of orthogonality between an effect and any effect that contains it holds for all balanced designs. Thus, construction of Type III hypotheses for any design is a logical extension of a process that is used for balanced designs.

The Type III hypotheses are precisely the hypotheses being tested by programs that reparameterize using the usual assumptions (for example, all parameters for an effect summing to zero). When no missing cells exist in a factorial model, Type III SS coincide with Yates' weighted squares-of-means technique. When cells are missing in factorial models, the Type III SS coincide with those discussed in Harvey (1960) and Henderson (1953).

The following steps illustrate the construction of Type III estimable functions for a 2×2 factorial with no missing cells.

To obtain the $A * B$ interaction hypothesis, start with the general form and equate the coefficients for effects μ, A, and B to zero, as shown in Table 12.8.

Table 12.8. Type III Hypothesis for $A * B$ Interaction

Effect	General Form	$L1 = L2 = L4 = 0$
μ	$L1$	0
$A1$	$L2$	0
$A2$	$L1 - L2$	0
$B1$	$L4$	0
$B2$	$L1 - L4$	0
$AB11$	$L6$	$L6$
$AB12$	$L2 - L6$	$-L6$
$AB21$	$L4 - L6$	$-L6$
$AB22$	$L1 - L2 - L4 + L6$	$L6$

The last column in Table 12.8 represents the form of the MRH for $A * B$.

To obtain the Type III hypothesis for A, first start with the general form and equate the coefficients for effects μ and B to zero (let $L1 = L4 = 0$). Next let $L6 = K * L2$, and find the value of K that makes the A hypothesis orthogonal to the A*B hypothesis. In this case, K=0.5. Each of these steps is shown in Table 12.9.

In Table 12.9, the fourth column (under $L6 = K * L2$) represents the form of all estimable functions not involving μ, $B1$, or $B2$. The prime difference between the Type II and Type III hypotheses for A is the way K is determined. Type II chooses K as a function of the cell frequencies, whereas Type III chooses K such that the estimable functions for A are orthogonal to the estimable functions for $A * B$.

Table 12.9. Type III Hypothesis for A

Effect	General Form	$L1 = L4 = 0$	$L6 = K * L2$	$K = 0.5$
μ	$L1$	0	0	0
$A1$	$L2$	$L2$	$L2$	$L2$
$A2$	$L1 - L2$	$-L2$	$-L2$	$-L2$
$B1$	$L4$	0	0	0
$B2$	$L1 - L4$	0	0	0
$AB11$	$L6$	$L6$	$K * L2$	$0.5 * L2$
$AB12$	$L2 - L6$	$L2 - L6$	$(1 - K) * L2$	$0.5 * L2$
$AB21$	$L4 - L6$	$-L6$	$-K * L2$	$-0.5 * L2$
$AB22$	$L1 - L2 - L4 + L6$	$-L2 + L6$	$(K - 1) * L2$	$-0.5 * L2$

An example of Type III estimable functions in a 3×3 factorial with unequal cell frequencies and missing diagonals is given in Table 12.10 (N_1 through N_6 represent the nonzero cell frequencies).

Table 12.10. A 3×3 Factorial Design with Unequal Cell Frequencies and Missing Diagonals

		B 1	B 2	B 3
A	1		N_1	N_2
	2	N_3		N_4
	3	N_5	N_6	

For any nonzero values of N_1 through N_6, the Type III estimable functions for each effect are shown in Table 12.11.

Table 12.11. Type III Estimable Functions for 3×3 Factorial Design with Unequal Cell Frequencies and Missing Diagonals

Effect	A	B	$A*B$
μ	0	0	0
$A1$	$L2$	0	0
$A2$	$L3$	0	0
$A3$	$-L2 - L3$	0	0
$B1$	0	$L5$	0
$B2$	0	$L6$	0
$B3$	0	$-L5 - L6$	0
$AB12$	$0.667 * L2 + 0.333 * L3$	$0.333 * L5 + 0.667 * L6$	$L8$
$AB13$	$0.333 * L2 - 0.333 * L3$	$-0.333 * L5 - 0.667 * L6$	$-L8$
$AB21$	$0.333 * L2 + 0.667 * L3$	$0.667 * L5 + 0.333 * L6$	$-L8$
$AB23$	$-0.333 * L2 + 0.333 * L3$	$-0.667 * L5 - 0.333 * L6$	$L8$
$AB31$	$-0.333 * L2 - 0.667 * L3$	$0.333 * L5 - 0.333 * L6$	$L8$
$AB32$	$-0.667 * L2 - 0.333 * L3$	$-0.333 * L5 + 0.333 * L6$	$-L8$

Type IV Estimable Functions

By once again looking at the Type II hypotheses being tested in the balanced 2×2 factorial (see Table 12.6), you can see another characteristic of the hypotheses employed for balanced designs: the coefficients of lower-order effects are averaged across each higher-level effect involving the same subscripts. For example, in the A hypothesis, the coefficients of $AB11$ and $AB12$ are equal to one-half the coefficient of $A1$, and the coefficients of $AB21$ and $AB22$ are equal to one-half the coefficient of $A2$. With this in mind then, the basic concept used to construct Type IV hypotheses is that the coefficients of any effect, say $F1$, are distributed equitably across higher-level effects that contain $F1$. When missing cells occur, this same general philosophy is adhered to, but care must be taken in the way the distributive concept is applied.

Construction of Type IV hypotheses begins as does the construction of the Type III hypotheses. That is, for an effect $F1$, equate to zero all coefficients in the general form that do not belong to $F1$ or to any other effect containing $F1$. If $F1$ is not contained in any other effect, then the Type IV hypothesis (and Type II and III) has been found. If $F1$ is contained in other effects, then simplify, if necessary, the coefficients associated with $F1$ so that they are all free coefficients or functions of other free coefficients in the $F1$ block.

To illustrate the method of resolving the free coefficients outside of the $F1$ block, suppose that you are interested in the estimable functions for an effect A and that A is contained in AB, AC, and ABC. (In other words, the main effects in the model are A, B, and C.)

With missing cells, the coefficients of intermediate effects (here they are AB and AC) do not always have an equal distribution of the lower-order coefficients, so the coefficients of the highest-order effects are determined first (here it is ABC). Once the highest-order coefficients are determined, the coefficients of intermediate effects are automatically determined.

The following process is performed for each free coefficient of A in turn. The resulting symbolic vectors are then added together to give the Type IV estimable functions for A.

1. Select a free coefficient of A, and set all other free coefficients of A to zero.

2. If any of the levels of A have zero as a coefficient, equate all of the coefficients of higher-level effects involving that level of A to zero. This step alone usually resolves most of the free coefficients remaining.

3. Check to see if any higher-level coefficients are now zero when the coefficient of the associated level of A is not zero. If this situation occurs, the Type IV estimable functions for A are not unique.

4. For each level of A in turn, if the A coefficient for that level is nonzero, count the number of times that level occurs in the higher-level effect. Then equate each of the higher-level coefficients to the coefficient of that level of A divided by the count.

An example of a 3×3 factorial with four missing cells (N_1 through N_5 represent positive cell frequencies) is shown in Table 12.12.

Table 12.12. 3×3 Factorial Design with Four Missing Cells

		B		
		1	2	3
A	1	N_1	N_2	
	2	N_3	N_4	
	3			N_5

The Type IV estimable functions are shown in Table 12.13.

Table 12.13. Type IV Estimable Functions for 3×3 Factorial Design with Four Missing Cells

Effect	A	B	$A * B$
μ	0	0	0
$A1$	$-L3$	0	0
$A2$	$L3$	0	0
$A3$	0	0	0
$B1$	0	$L5$	0
$B2$	0	$-L5$	0
$B3$	0	0	0
$AB11$	$-0.5 * L3$	$0.5 * L5$	$L8$
$AB12$	$-0.5 * L3$	$-0.5 * L5$	$-L8$
$AB21$	$0.5 * L3$	$0.5 * L5$	$-L8$
$AB22$	$0.5 * L3$	$-0.5 * L5$	$L8$
$AB33$	0	0	0

A Comparison of Type III and Type IV Hypotheses

For the vast majority of designs, Type III and Type IV hypotheses for a given effect are the same. Specifically, they are the same for any effect $F1$ that is not contained in other effects for any design (with or without missing cells). For factorial designs with no missing cells, the Type III and Type IV hypotheses coincide for all effects. When there are missing cells, the hypotheses can differ. By using the GLM procedure, you can study the differences in the hypotheses and then decide on the appropriateness of the hypotheses for a particular model.

The Type III hypotheses for three-factor and higher completely nested designs with unequal Ns in the lowest level differ from the Type II hypotheses; however, the Type IV hypotheses do correspond to the Type II hypotheses in this case.

When missing cells occur in a design, the Type IV hypotheses may not be unique. If this occurs in PROC GLM, you are notified, and you may need to consider defining your own specific comparisons.

References

Freund, R.J., Littell, R.C., and Spector, P.C. (1991), *SAS System for Linear Models*, Cary, NC: SAS Institute Inc.

Harvey, W. R. (1960),"Least-Squares Analysis of Data with Unequal Subclass Frequencies," USDA, *Agriculture Research Service*, ARS 20-8, reprinted with corrections as ARS H-4, 1975, also reprinted 1979.

Henderson, C. R. (1953), "Estimation of Variance and Covariance Components," *Biometrics*, 9, 226–252.

Goodnight, J.H. (1978), *Tests of Hypotheses in Fixed Effects Linear Models*, SAS Technical Report R-101, Cary, NC: SAS Institute Inc.

Milliken, G.A. and Johnson, D.E. (1984), *Analysis of Messy Data, Volume I: Designed Experiments*, Belmont, CA: Lifetime Learning Publications.

Chapter 13
Introduction to Nonparametric Analysis

Chapter Table of Contents

Chapter 13
Introduction to Nonparametric Analysis

Overview

In statistical inference, or hypothesis testing, the traditional tests are called *parametric tests* because they depend on the specification of a probability distribution (such as the normal) except for a set of free parameters. Parametric tests are said to depend on distributional assumptions. *Nonparametric tests*, on the other hand, do not require any strict distributional assumptions. Even if the data are distributed normally, nonparametric methods are often almost as powerful as parametric methods.

Many nonparametric methods analyze the ranks of a variable rather than the original values. Procedures such as PROC NPAR1WAY calculate the ranks for you and then perform appropriate nonparametric tests. However, there are some situations in which you use a procedure such as PROC RANK to calculate ranks and then use another procedure to perform the appropriate test. See the section "Obtaining Ranks" on page 184 for details.

Although the NPAR1WAY procedure is specifically targeted for nonparametric analysis, many other procedures also perform nonparametric analyses. Some general references on nonparametrics include Lehman (1975), Conover (1980), Hollander and Wolfe (1973), Hettmansperger (1984), and Gibbons and Chakraborti (1992).

Testing for Normality

Many parametric tests assume an underlying normal distribution for the population. If your data do not meet this assumption, you may prefer to use a nonparametric analysis.

Base SAS software provides several tests for normality in the UNIVARIATE procedure. Depending on your sample size, PROC UNIVARIATE performs the Kolmogorov-Smirnov, Shapiro-Wilk, Anderson-Darling, and Cramér-von Mises tests. For more on PROC UNIVARIATE, see the *SAS Procedures Guide*.

Comparing Distributions

To test the hypothesis that two or more groups of observations have identical distributions, use the NPAR1WAY procedure. The procedure calculates the Kolmogorov-Smirnov statistic, an asymptotic Kolmogorov-Smirnov statistic, and the Cramér-von Mises statistic. In addition, for data with only two groups of observations, the procedure calculates the two-sample Kolmogorov statistic and the Kuiper statistic. To obtain these tests, use the EDF option in the PROC NPAR1WAY statement. For details, see Chapter 47, "The NPAR1WAY Procedure."

One-Sample Tests

Base SAS software provides two one-sample tests in the UNIVARIATE procedure: a sign test and the Wilcoxon signed rank test. Both tests are designed for situations where you want to make an inference about the location (median) of a population. For example, suppose you want to test if the median resting pulse rate of marathon runners differs from a specified value.

By default, both of these tests examine the hypothesis that the median of the population from which the sample is drawn is equal to a specified value, which is zero by default. The Wilcoxon signed rank test requires that the distribution be symmetric; the sign test does not require this assumption. These tests can also be used for the case of two related samples; see the section "Comparing Two Independent Samples" for more information.

The two tests are automatically provided by the UNIVARIATE procedure. For details, formulas, and examples, see the chapter on the UNIVARIATE procedure in the *SAS Procedures Guide*.

Two-Sample Tests

This section describes tests appropriate for two independent samples (for example, two groups of subjects given different treatments) and for two related samples (for example, before-and-after measurements on a single group of subjects). Related samples are also referred to as paired samples or matched pairs.

Comparing Two Independent Samples

SAS/STAT software provides several nonparametric tests for location and scale differences.

When you perform these tests, your data should consist of a random sample of observations from two different populations. Your goal is either to compare the location parameters (medians) or the scale parameters of the two populations. For example, suppose your data consist of the number of days in the hospital for two groups of patients: those who received a standard surgical procedure and those who received a new, experimental surgical procedure. These patients are a random sample from the population of patients who have received the two types of surgery. Your goal is to decide whether the median hospital stays differ for the two populations.

Tests in the NPAR1WAY Procedure

The NPAR1WAY procedure provides the following location tests: Wilcoxon rank sum test (Mann-Whitney U test), Median test, Savage test, and Van der Waerden test. Also note that the Wilcoxon rank sum test can be obtained from the FREQ procedure. In addition, PROC NPAR1WAY produces the following tests for scale differences: Siegel-Tukey test, Ansari-Bradley test, Klotz test, and Mood test.

When data are sparse, skewed, or heavily tied, the usual asymptotic tests may not be appropriate. In these situations, exact tests may be suitable for analyzing your data. The NPAR1WAY procedure can produce exact p-values for all of the two-sample tests for location and scale differences.

Chapter 47, "The NPAR1WAY Procedure," provides detailed statistical formulas for these statistics, as well as examples of their use.

Tests in the FREQ Procedure

This procedure provides a test for comparing the location of two groups and for testing for independence between two variables.

The situation in which you want to compare the location of two groups of observations corresponds to a table with two rows. In this case, the asymptotic Wilcoxon rank sum test can be obtained by using SCORES=RANK in the TABLES statement and by looking at either of the following:

- the Mantel-Haenszel statistic in the list of tests for no association. This is labeled as "Mantel Haenszel Chi-square" and PROC FREQ displays the statistic, the degrees of freedom, and the p-value.
- the CMH statistic 2 in the section on Cochran-Mantel-Haenszel statistics. PROC FREQ displays the statistic, the degrees of freedom, and the p-value. To obtain this statistic, specify the CMH2 option in the TABLES statement.

When you test for independence, the question being answered is whether the two variables of interest are related in some way. For example, you might want to know if student scores on a standard test are related to whether students attended a public or private school. One way to think of this situation is to consider the data as a two-way table; the hypothesis of interest is whether the rows and columns are independent. In the preceding example, the groups of students would form the two rows, and the scores would form the columns. The special case of a two-category response (Pass/Fail) leads to a 2×2 table; the case of more than two categories for the response (A/B/C/D/F) leads to a $2 \times c$ table, where c is the number of response categories.

For testing whether two variables are independent, PROC FREQ provides Fisher's exact test. For a 2×2 table, PROC FREQ automatically provides Fisher's exact test when you use the CHISQ option in the TABLES statement. For a $2 \times c$ table, use the EXACT option in the TABLES statement to obtain the test.

Comparing Two Related Samples

SAS/STAT software provides the following nonparametric tests for comparing the locations of two related samples:

- Wilcoxon signed rank test
- sign test
- McNemar's test

The first two tests are available in the UNIVARIATE procedure, and the last test is available in the FREQ procedure. When you perform these tests, your data should consist of pairs of measurements for a random sample from a single population. For example, suppose your data consist of SAT scores for students before and after attending a course on how to prepare for the SAT. The pairs of measurements are the scores before and after the course, and the students should be a random sample of students who attended the course. Your goal in analysis is to decide if the median change in scores is significantly different from zero.

Tests in the UNIVARIATE Procedure

By default, PROC UNIVARIATE performs a Wilcoxon signed rank test and a sign test. To use these tests on two related samples, perform the following steps:

1. In the DATA step, create a new variable that contains the differences between the two related variables.
2. Run PROC UNIVARIATE, using the new variable in the VAR statement.

For discussion of the tests, formulas, and examples, see the chapter on the UNIVARIATE procedure in the *SAS Procedures Guide*.

Tests in the FREQ Procedure

The FREQ procedure can be used to obtain McNemar's test, which is simply another special case of a Cochran-Mantel-Haenszel statistic (and also of the sign test). The AGREE option in the TABLES statement produces this test for 2×2 tables, and exact p-values are available for this test.

Tests for k Samples

Comparing k Independent Samples

One goal in comparing k independent samples is to determine whether the location parameters (medians) of the populations are different. Another goal is to determine whether the scale parameters for the populations are different. For example, suppose new employees are randomly assigned to one of three training programs. At the end of the program, the employees receive a standard test that gives a rating score of their job ability. The goal of analysis is to compare the median scores for the three groups and decide whether the differences are real or due to chance alone.

To compare k independent samples, either the NPAR1WAY or the FREQ procedure provides a Kruskal-Wallis test. PROC NPAR1WAY also provides the Savage, median, and Van der Waerden tests. In addition, PROC NPAR1WAY produces the following tests for scale differences: Siegel-Tukey test, Ansari-Bradley test, Klotz test, and Mood test. Note that you can obtain exact p-values for all of these tests.

In addition, you can specify the SCORES=DATA option to use the input data observations as scores. This enables you to produce a very wide variety of tests. You can construct any scores using the DATA step, and then PROC NPAR1WAY computes the corresponding linear rank and one-way ANOVA tests. You can also analyze the raw data with the SCORES=DATA option; for two-sample data, this permutation test is known as Pitman's test.

See Chapter 47, "The NPAR1WAY Procedure," for details, formulas, and examples.

To produce a Kruskal-Wallis test in the FREQ procedure, use SCORES=RANK and the CMH2 option in the TABLES statement. Then, look at the second Cochran-Mantel-Haenszel statistic (labeled "Row Mean Scores Differ") to obtain the Kruskal-Wallis test. The FREQ procedure also provides the Jonckheere-Terpstra test, which is more powerful than the Kruskal-Wallis test for comparing k samples against ordered alternatives. The exact test is also available. In addition, you can obtain a ridit analysis, developed by Bross (1958), by specifying SCORES=RIDIT or SCORES=MODRIDIT in the TABLES statement in the FREQ procedure.

Comparing k Dependent Samples

Friedman's test enables you to compare the locations of three or more dependent samples. You can obtain Friedman's Chi-square with the FREQ procedure by using the CMH2 option and SCORES=RANK and looking at the second CMH statistic in the output. For an example, see Chapter 28, "The FREQ Procedure"; this chapter also contains formulas and other details on the CMH statistics. For a discussion of how to use the RANK and GLM procedures to obtain Friedman's test, see Ipe (1987).

Measures of Correlation and Associated Tests

The CORR procedure in base SAS software provides several nonparametric measures of association and associated tests. It computes Spearman's rank-order correlation, Kendall's tau-b, and Hoeffding's measure of dependence, and it provides tests for each of these statistics. PROC CORR also computes Spearman's partial rank-order correlation and Kendall's partial tau-b. Finally, PROC CORR computes Cronbach's coefficient alpha for raw and standardized variables. This statistic can be used to estimate the reliability coefficient. For a general discussion of correlations, formulas, interpretation, and examples, see the chapter on the CORR procedure in the *SAS Procedures Guide*.

The FREQ procedure also provides some nonparametric measures of association: gamma, Kendall's tau-b, Stuart's tau-c, Somer's D, and the Spearman rank correlation. The output includes the measure, the asymptotic standard error, confidence limits, and the asymptotic test that the measure equals zero. For the Spearman rank correlation, you can optionally request an exact p-value that the correlation is equal to zero.

Obtaining Ranks

The primary procedure for obtaining ranks is the RANK procedure in base SAS software. Note that the PRINQUAL and TRANSREG procedures also provide rank transformations. With all three of these procedures, you can create an output data set and use it as input to another SAS/STAT procedure or to the IML procedure. See the *SAS Procedures Guide* for information on the RANK procedure, and see the chapters in this book for information on the PRINQUAL and TRANSREG procedures.

In addition, you can specify SCORES=RANK in the TABLES statement in the FREQ procedure. PROC FREQ then uses ranks to perform the analyses requested and generates nonparametric analyses.

For more discussion of using the rank transform, see Iman and Conover (1979), Conover and Iman (1981), Hora and Conover (1984), Iman, Hora, and Conover (1984), Hora and Iman (1988), and Iman (1988).

Kernel Density Estimation

The KDE procedure performs either univariate or bivariate kernel density estimation. Statistical *density estimation* involves approximating a hypothesized probability density function from observed data. *Kernel density estimation* is a nonparametric technique for density estimation in which a known density function (the kernel) is averaged across the observed data points to create a smooth approximation.

PROC KDE uses a Gaussian density as the kernel, and its assumed variance determines the smoothness of the resulting estimate. PROC KDE outputs the kernel density estimate to a SAS data set, which you can then use with other procedures for plotting or analysis. PROC KDE also computes a variety of common statistics, including estimates of the percentiles of the hypothesized probability density function.

References

Bross, I.D.J. (1958), "How to Use Ridit Analysis," *Biometrics*, 14, 18–38.

Conover, W.J. (1980), *Practical Nonparametric Statistics*, Second Edition, New York: John Wiley & Sons, Inc.

Conover, W.J. and Iman, R.L. (1981), "Rank Transformations as a Bridge between Parametric and Nonparametric Statistics," *The American Statistician*, 35, 124–129.

Gibbons, J.D. and Chakraborti, S. (1992), *Nonparametric Statistical Inference*, Third Edition, New York: Marcel Dekker, Inc.

Hettmansperger, T.P. (1984), *Statistical Inference Based on Ranks*, New York: John Wiley & Sons, Inc.

Hollander, M. and Wolfe, D.A. (1973), *Nonparametric Statistical Methods*, New York: John Wiley & Sons, Inc.

Hora, S.C. and Conover, W.J. (1984), "The *F* Statistic in the Two-Way Layout with Rank-Score Transformed Data," *Journal of the American Statistical Association*, 79, 668–673.

Hora, S.C. and Iman, R.L. (1988), "Asymptotic Relative Efficiencies of the Rank-Transformation Procedure in Randomized Complete Block Designs," *Journal of the American Statistical Association*, 83, 462–470.

Iman, R.L. and Conover, W.J. (1979), "The Use of the Rank Transform in Regression," *Technometrics*, 21, 499–509.

Iman, R.L., Hora, S.C., and Conover, W.J. (1984), "Comparison of Asymptotically Distribution-Free Procedures for the Analysis of Complete Blocks," *Journal of the American Statistical Association*, 79, 674–685.

Iman, R.L. (1988), "The Analysis of Complete Blocks Using Methods Based on Ranks," *Proceedings of the Thirteenth Annual SAS Users Group International Conference*, 13, 970–978.

Ipe, D. (1987), "Performing the Friedman Test and the Associated Multiple Comparison Test Using PROC GLM," *Proceedings of the Twelfth Annual SAS Users Group International Conference*, 12, 1146–1148.

Lehmann, E.L. (1975), *Nonparametrics: Statistical Methods Based on Ranks*, San Francisco: Holden-Day.

Chapter 14
Introduction to Structural Equations with Latent Variables

Chapter Table of Contents

Chapter 14
Introduction to Structural Equations with Latent Variables

Overview

You can use the CALIS procedure for analysis of covariance structures, fitting systems of linear structural equations, and path analysis. These terms are more or less interchangeable, but they emphasize different aspects of the analysis. The analysis of covariance structures refers to the formulation of a model for the variances and covariances among a set of variables and the fitting of the model to an observed covariance matrix. In linear structural equations, the model is formulated as a system of equations relating several random variables with assumptions about the variances and covariances of the random variables. In path analysis, the model is formulated as a path diagram, in which arrows connecting variables represent (co)variances and regression coefficients. Path models and linear structural equation models can be converted to models of the covariance matrix and can, therefore, be fitted by the methods of covariance structure analysis. All of these methods allow the use of hypothetical latent variables or measurement errors in the models.

Loehlin (1987) provides an excellent introduction to latent variable models using path diagrams and structural equations. A more advanced treatment of structural equation models with latent variables is given by Bollen (1989). Fuller (1987) provides a highly technical statistical treatment of measurement-error models.

Comparison of the CALIS and SYSLIN Procedures

The SYSLIN procedure in the SAS/ETS product can also fit certain kinds of path models and linear structural equation models. PROC CALIS differs from PROC SYSLIN in that PROC CALIS allows more generality in the use of latent variables in the models. Latent variables are unobserved, hypothetical variables, as distinct from manifest variables, which are the observed data. PROC SYSLIN allows at most one latent variable, the error term, in each equation. PROC CALIS allows several latent variables to appear in an equation—in fact, all the variables in an equation can be latent as long as there are other equations that relate the latent variables to manifest variables.

Both the CALIS and SYSLIN procedures enable you to specify a model as a system of linear equations. When there are several equations, a given variable may be a dependent variable in one equation and an independent variable in other equations. Therefore, additional terminology is needed to describe unambiguously the roles of variables in the system. Variables with values that are determined jointly and simultaneously by the system of equations are called *endogenous variables*. Variables with values that are determined outside the system, that is, in a manner separate from the process described by the system of equations, are called exogenous variables. The purpose of the system of equations is to explain the variation of each endogenous variable in terms of exogenous variables or other endogenous variables or both. Refer to Loehlin (1987, p. 4) for further discussion of endogenous and exogenous variables. In the econometric literature, error and disturbance terms are usually distinguished from exogenous variables, but in systems with more than one latent variable in an equation, the distinction is not always clear.

In PROC SYSLIN, endogenous variables are identified by the ENDOGENOUS statement. When you specify structural equations in PROC CALIS, endogenous variables are assumed to be those that appear on the left-hand sides of the equations; a given variable may appear on the left-hand side of at most one equation.

PROC SYSLIN provides many methods of estimation, some of which are applicable only in special cases. For example, ordinary least-squares estimates are suitable in certain kinds of systems but may be statistically biased and inconsistent in other kinds. PROC CALIS provides three methods of estimation that can be used with most models. Both the CALIS and SYSLIN procedures can do maximum likelihood estimation, which PROC CALIS calls ML and PROC SYSLIN calls FIML. PROC SYSLIN can be much faster than PROC CALIS in those special cases for which it provides computationally efficient estimation methods. However, PROC CALIS has a variety of sophisticated algorithms for maximum likelihood estimation that may be much faster than FIML in PROC SYSLIN.

PROC CALIS can impose a wider variety of constraints on the parameters, including nonlinear constraints, than can PROC SYSLIN. For example, PROC CALIS can constrain error variances or covariances to equal specified constants, or it can constrain two error variances to have a specified ratio.

Model Specification

PROC CALIS provides several ways to specify a model. Structural equations can be transcribed directly in the LINEQS statement. A path diagram can be described in the RAM statement. You can specify a first-order factor model in the FACTOR and MATRIX statements. Higher-order factor models and other complicated models can be expressed in the COSAN and MATRIX statements. For most applications, the LINEQS and RAM statements are easiest to use; the choice between these two statements is a matter of personal preference.

You can save a model specification in an OUTRAM= data set, which can then be used with the INRAM= option to specify the model in a subsequent analysis.

Estimation Methods

The CALIS procedure provides three methods of estimation specified by the METHOD= option:

ULS	unweighted least squares
GLS	generalized least squares
ML	maximum likelihood for multivariate normal distributions

Each estimation method is based on finding parameter estimates that minimize a badness-of-fit function that measures the difference between the observed sample covariance matrix and the predicted covariance matrix given the model and the parameter estimates. See the section "Estimation Methods" on page 462 in Chapter 19, "The CALIS Procedure," for formulas, or refer to Loehlin (1987, pp. 54–62) and Bollen (1989, pp. 104–123) for further discussion.

The default is METHOD=ML, which is the preferred method for most applications with respect to statistical considerations. The option METHOD=GLS usually produces very similar results to METHOD=ML. Both methods are suitable regardless of the scaling of the covariance matrix. The ULS method is appropriate for a covariance matrix only if the variables are measured on comparable scales; otherwise, METHOD=ULS should be applied to the correlation matrix. PROC CALIS cannot compute standard errors or test statistics with the ULS method.

You should not specify METHOD=ML or METHOD=GLS if the observed or predicted covariance matrix is singular—you should either remove variables involved in the linear dependencies or specify METHOD=ULS.

PROC CALIS should not be used if your data are extremely nonnormal data, especially if they have high kurtosis. You should remove outliers and try to transform variables that are skewed or heavy-tailed. This applies to all three estimation methods, since all the estimation methods depend on the sample covariance matrix, and the sample covariance matrix is a poor estimator for distributions with high kurtosis (Bollen 1989, pp. 415–418; Huber 1981; Hampel et. al 1986). PROC CALIS displays estimates of univariate and multivariate kurtosis (Bollen 1989, pp. 418–425) if you specify the KURTOSIS option in the PROC CALIS statement.

Statistical Inference

When you specify the ML or GLS estimates with appropriate models, PROC CALIS can compute

- a chi-square goodness-of-fit test of the specified model versus the alternative that the data are from a multivariate normal distribution with unconstrained covariance matrix (Loehlin 1987, pp. 62–64; Bollen 1989, pp. 110, 115, 263–269)

- approximate standard errors of the parameter estimates (Bollen 1989, pp. 109, 114, 286), displayed with the STDERR option
- various modification indices, requested via the MODIFICATION or MOD option, that give the approximate change in the chi-square statistic that would result from removing constraints on the parameters or constraining additional parameters to zero (Bollen 1989, pp. 293–303)

If you have two models such that one model results from imposing constraints on the parameters of the other, you can test the constrained model against the more general model by fitting both models with PROC CALIS. If the constrained model is correct, the difference between the chi-square goodness-of-fit statistics for the two models has an approximate chi-square distribution with degrees of freedom equal to the difference between the degrees of freedom for the two models (Loehlin 1987, pp. 62–67; Bollen 1989, pp. 291–292).

All of the test statistics and standard errors computed by PROC CALIS depend on the assumption of multivariate normality. Normality is a much more important requirement for data with random independent variables than it is for fixed independent variables. If the independent variables are random, distributions with high kurtosis tend to give liberal tests and excessively small standard errors, while low kurtosis tends to produce the opposite effects (Bollen 1989, pp. 266–267, 415–432).

The test statistics and standard errors computed by PROC CALIS are also based on asymptotic theory and should not be trusted in small samples. There are no firm guidelines on how large a sample must be for the asymptotic theory to apply with reasonable accuracy. Some simulation studies have indicated that problems are likely to occur with sample sizes less than 100 (Loehlin 1987, pp. 60–61; Bollen 1989, pp. 267–268). Extrapolating from experience with multiple regression would suggest that the sample size should be at least five to twenty times the number of parameters to be estimated in order to get reliable and interpretable results.

The asymptotic theory requires that the parameter estimates be in the interior of the parameter space. If you do an analysis with inequality constraints and one or more constraints are active at the solution (for example, if you constrain a variance to be nonnegative and the estimate turns out to be zero), the chi-square test and standard errors may not provide good approximations to the actual sampling distributions.

Standard errors may be inaccurate if you analyze a correlation matrix rather than a covariance matrix even for sample sizes as large as 400 (Boomsma 1983). The chi-square statistic is generally the same regardless of which matrix is analyzed provided that the model involves no scale-dependent constraints.

If you fit a model to a correlation matrix and the model constrains one or more elements of the predicted matrix to equal 1.0, the degrees of freedom of the chi-square statistic must be reduced by the number of such constraints. PROC CALIS attempts to determine which diagonal elements of the predicted correlation matrix are constrained to a constant, but it may fail to detect such constraints in complicated models, particularly when programming statements are used. If this happens, you should add parameters to the model to release the constraints on the diagonal elements.

Goodness-of-fit Statistics

In addition to the chi-square test, there are many other statistics for assessing the goodness of fit of the predicted correlation or covariance matrix to the observed matrix.

Akaike's (1987) information criterion (AIC) and Schwarz's (1978) Bayesian criterion (SBC) are useful for comparing models with different numbers of parameters—the model with the smallest value of AIC or SBC is considered best. Based on both theoretical considerations and various simulation studies, SBC seems to work better, since AIC tends to select models with too many parameters when the sample size is large.

There are many descriptive measures of goodness of fit that are scaled to range approximately from zero to one: the goodness of fit index (GFI) and GFI adjusted for degrees of freedom (AGFI) (Jöreskog and Sörbom 1988), centrality (McDonald 1989), and the parsimonious fit index (James, Mulaik, and Brett 1982). Bentler and Bonett (1980) and Bollen (1986) have proposed measures for comparing the goodness of fit of one model with another in a descriptive rather than inferential sense.

None of these measures of goodness of fit are related to the goodness of prediction of the structural equations. Goodness of fit is assessed by comparing the observed correlation or covariance matrix with the matrix computed from the model and parameter estimates. Goodness of prediction is assessed by comparing the actual values of the endogenous variables with their predicted values, usually in terms of root mean squared error or proportion of variance accounted for (R^2). For latent endogenous variables, root mean squared error and R^2 can be estimated from the fitted model.

Optimization Methods

PROC CALIS uses a variety of nonlinear optimization algorithms for computing parameter estimates. These algorithms are very complicated and do not always work. PROC CALIS will generally inform you when the computations fail, usually by displaying an error message about the iteration limit being exceeded. When this happens, you may be able to correct the problem simply by increasing the iteration limit (MAXITER= and MAXFUNC=). However, it is often more effective to change the optimization method (OMETHOD=) or initial values. For more details, see the section "Use of Optimization Techniques" on page 551 in Chapter 19, "The CALIS Procedure," and refer to Bollen (1989, pp. 254–256).

PROC CALIS may sometimes converge to a local optimum rather than the global optimum. To gain some protection against local optima, you can run the analysis several times with different initial estimates. The RANDOM= option in the PROC CALIS statement is useful for generating a variety of initial estimates.

Specifying Structural Equation Models

Consider fitting a linear equation to two observed variables, Y and X. Simple linear regression uses the model of a particular form, labeled for purposes of discussion, as Model Form A.

Model Form A

$$Y = \alpha + \beta X + E_Y$$

where α and β are coefficients to be estimated and E_Y is an error term. If the values of X are fixed, the values of E_Y are assumed to be independent and identically distributed realizations of a normally distributed random variable with mean zero and variance Var(E_Y). If X is a random variable, X and E_Y are assumed to have a bivariate normal distribution with zero correlation and variances Var(X) and Var(E_Y), respectively. Under either set of assumptions, the usual formulas hold for the estimates of the coefficients and their standard errors (see Chapter 3, "Introduction to Regression Procedures").

In the REG or SYSLIN procedure, you would fit a simple linear regression model with a MODEL statement listing only the names of the manifest variables:

```
proc reg;
   model y=x;
run;
```

You can also fit this model with PROC CALIS, but you must explicitly specify the names of the parameters and the error terms (except for the intercept, which is assumed to be present in each equation). The linear equation is given in the LINEQS statement, and the error variance is specified in the STD statement.

```
proc calis cov;
   lineqs y=beta x + ex;
   std ex=vex;
run;
```

The parameters are the regression coefficient BETA and the variance VEX of the error term EX. You do not need to type an * between BETA and X to indicate the multiplication of the variable by the coefficient.

The LINEQS statement uses the convention that the names of error terms begin with the letter E, disturbances (errors terms for latent variables) in equations begin with D, and other latent variables begin with F for "factor." Names of variables in the input SAS data set can, of course, begin with any letter.

If you leave out the name of a coefficient, the value of the coefficient is assumed to be 1. If you leave out the name of a variance, the variance is assumed to be 0. So if you tried to write the model the same way you would in PROC REG, for example,

```
proc calis cov;
   lineqs y=x;
```

you would be fitting a model that says Y is equal to X plus an intercept, with no error.

The COV option is used because PROC CALIS, like PROC FACTOR, analyzes the correlation matrix by default, yielding standardized regression coefficients. The COV option causes the covariance matrix to be analyzed, producing raw regression coefficients. See Chapter 3, "Introduction to Regression Procedures," for a discussion of the interpretation of raw and standardized regression coefficients.

Since the analysis of covariance structures is based on modeling the covariance matrix and the covariance matrix contains no information about means, PROC CALIS neglects the intercept parameter by default. To estimate the intercept, change the COV option to UCOV, which analyzes the uncorrected covariance matrix, and use the AUGMENT option, which adds a row and column for the intercept, called INTERCEP, to the matrix being analyzed. The model can then be specified as

```
proc calis ucov augment;
   lineqs y=alpha intercep + beta x + ex;
   std ex=vex;
run;
```

In the LINEQS statement, intercep represents a variable with a constant value of 1; hence, the coefficient alpha is the intercept parameter.

Other commonly used options in the PROC CALIS statement include

- MODIFICATION to display model modification indices
- RESIDUAL to display residual correlations or covariances
- STDERR to display approximate standard errors
- TOTEFF to display total effects

For ordinary unconstrained regression models, there is no reason to use PROC CALIS instead of PROC REG. But suppose that the observed variables Y and X are contaminated by error, and you want to estimate the linear relationship between their true, error-free scores. The model can be written in several forms. A model of Form B is as follows.

Model Form B

$$
\begin{aligned}
Y &= \alpha + \beta F_X + E_Y \\
X &= F_X + E_X \\
\mathrm{Cov}(F_X, E_X) &= \mathrm{Cov}(F_X, E_Y) = \mathrm{Cov}(E_X, E_Y) = 0
\end{aligned}
$$

This model has two error terms, E_Y and E_X, as well as another latent variable F_X representing the true value corresponding to the manifest variable X. The true value corresponding to Y does not appear explicitly in this form of the model.

The assumption in Model Form B is that the error terms and the latent variable F_X are jointly uncorrelated is of critical importance. This assumption must be justified on substantive grounds such as the physical properties of the measurement process. If this assumption is violated, the estimators may be severely biased and inconsistent.

You can express Model Form B in PROC CALIS as follows:

```
proc calis cov;
   lineqs y=beta fx + ey,
          x=fx + ex;
   std fx=vfx,
       ey=vey,
       ex=vex;
run;
```

You must specify a variance for each of the latent variables in this model using the STD statement. You can specify either a name, in which case the variance is considered a parameter to be estimated, or a number, in which case the variance is constrained to equal that numeric value. In general, you must specify a variance for each latent exogenous variable in the model, including error and disturbance terms. The variance of a manifest exogenous variable is set equal to its sample variance by default. The variances of endogenous variables are predicted from the model and are not parameters. Covariances involving latent exogenous variables are assumed to be zero by default. Covariances between manifest exogenous variables are set equal to the sample covariances by default.

Fuller (1987, pp. 18–19) analyzes a data set from Voss (1969) involving corn yields (Y) and available soil nitrogen (X) for which there is a prior estimate of the measurement error for soil nitrogen Var(E_X) of 57. You can fit Model Form B with this constraint using the following SAS statements.

```
data corn(type=cov);
   input _type_ $ _name_ $ y x;
   datalines;
n    . 11       11
mean . 97.4545  70.6364
cov  y 87.6727  .
cov  x 104.8818 304.8545
;

proc calis data=corn cov stderr;
   lineqs y=beta fx + ey,
          x=fx + ex;
   std ex=57,
       fx=vfx,
       ey=vey;
run;
```

In the STD statement, the variance of EX is given as the constant value 57. PROC CALIS produces the following estimates.

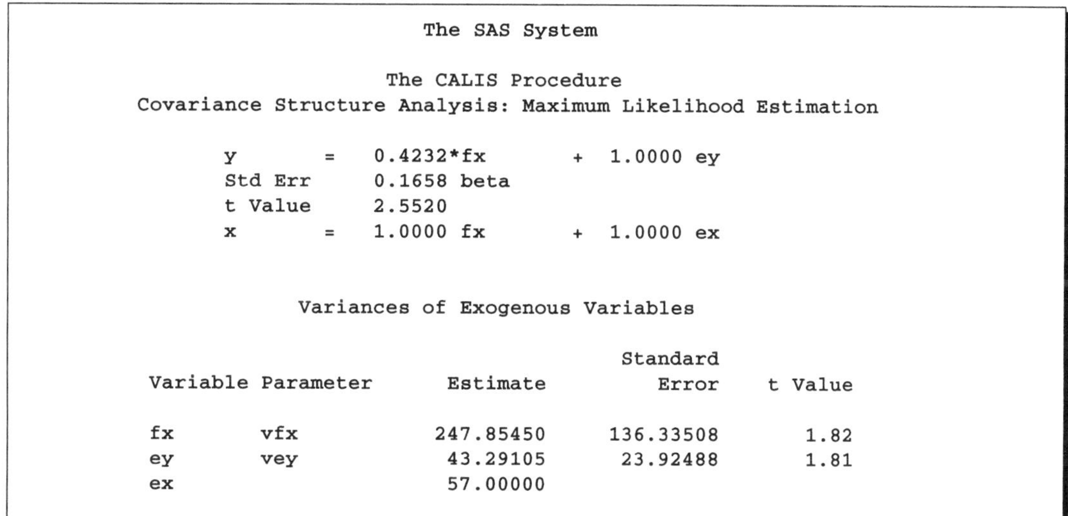

```
                              The SAS System

                           The CALIS Procedure
        Covariance Structure Analysis: Maximum Likelihood Estimation

              y        =    0.4232*fx        +  1.0000 ey
              Std Err       0.1658 beta
              t Value       2.5520
              x        =    1.0000 fx        +  1.0000 ex


                    Variances of Exogenous Variables

                                                    Standard
         Variable Parameter       Estimate             Error    t Value

         fx       vfx            247.85450         136.33508       1.82
         ey       vey             43.29105          23.92488       1.81
         ex                       57.00000
```

Figure 14.1. Measurement Error Model for Corn Data

PROC CALIS also displays information about the initial estimates that can be useful if there are optimization problems. If there are no optimization problems, the initial estimates are usually not of interest; they are not be reproduced in the examples in this chapter.

You can write an equivalent model (labeled here as Model Form C) using a latent variable F_Y to represent the true value corresponding to Y.

Model Form C

$$\begin{aligned} Y &= F_Y + E_Y \\ X &= F_X + E_X \\ F_Y &= \alpha + \beta F_X \\ \mathrm{Cov}(F_X, E_X) &= \mathrm{Cov}(F_X, E_X) = \mathrm{Cov}(E_X, E_Y) = 0 \end{aligned}$$

The first two of the three equations express the observed variables in terms of a true score plus error; these equations are called the measurement model. The third equation, expressing the relationship between the latent true-score variables, is called the structural or causal model. The decomposition of a model into a measurement model and a structural model (Keesling 1972; Wiley 1973; Jöreskog 1973) has been popularized by the program LISREL (Jöreskog and Sörbom 1988). The statements for fitting this model are

```
proc calis cov;
   lineqs y=fy + ey,
          x=fx + ex,
          fy=beta fx;
   std fx=vfx,
       ey=vey,
       ex=vex;
run;
```

You do not need to include the variance of F_Y in the STD statement because the variance of F_Y is determined by the structural model in terms of the variance of F_X, that is, Var(F_Y)=β^2 Var(F_X).

Correlations involving endogenous variables are derived from the model. For example, the structural equation in Model Form C implies that F_Y and F_X are correlated unless β is zero. In all of the models discussed so far, the latent exogenous variables are assumed to be jointly uncorrelated. For example, in Model Form C, E_Y, E_X, and F_X are assumed to be uncorrelated. If you want to specify a model in which E_Y and E_X, say, are correlated, you can use the COV statement to specify the numeric value of the covariance Cov(E_Y, E_X) between E_Y and E_X, or you can specify a name to make the covariance a parameter to be estimated. For example,

```
proc calis cov;
   lineqs y=fy + ey,
          x=fx + ex,
          fy=beta fx;
   std fy=vfy,
       fx=vfx,
       ey=vey,
       ex=vex;
   cov ey ex=ceyex;
run;
```

This COV statement specifies that the covariance between EY and EX is a parameter named CEYEX. All covariances that are not listed in the COV statement and that are not determined by the model are assumed to be zero. If the model contained two or more manifest exogenous variables, their covariances would be set to the observed sample values by default.

Identification of Models

Unfortunately, if you try to fit models of Form B or Form C without additional constraints, you cannot obtain unique estimates of the parameters. These models have four parameters (one coefficient and three variances). The covariance matrix of the observed variables Y and X has only three elements that are free to vary, since Cov(Y,X)=Cov(X,Y). The covariance structure can, therefore, be expressed as three equations in four unknown parameters. Since there are fewer equations than unknowns, there are many different sets of values for the parameters that provide a solution for the equations. Such a model is said to be underidentified.

If the number of parameters equals the number of free elements in the covariance matrix, then there may exist a unique set of parameter estimates that exactly reproduce the observed covariance matrix. In this case, the model is said to be just identified or saturated.

If the number of parameters is less than the number of free elements in the covariance matrix, there may exist no set of parameter estimates that reproduces the observed covariance matrix. In this case, the model is said to be overidentified. Various statistical criteria, such as maximum likelihood, can be used to choose parameter estimates that approximately reproduce the observed covariance matrix. If you use ML or GLS estimation, PROC CALIS can perform a statistical test of the goodness of fit of the model under the assumption of multivariate normality of all variables and independence of the observations.

If the model is just identified or overidentified, it is said to be identified. If you use ML or GLS estimation for an identified model, PROC CALIS can compute approximate standard errors for the parameter estimates. For underidentified models, PROC CALIS obtains approximate standard errors by imposing additional constraints resulting from the use of a generalized inverse of the Hessian matrix.

You cannot guarantee that a model is identified simply by counting the parameters. For example, for any latent variable, you must specify a numeric value for the variance, or for some covariance involving the variable, or for a coefficient of the variable in at least one equation. Otherwise, the scale of the latent variable is indeterminate, and the model will be underidentified regardless of the number of parameters and the size of the covariance matrix. As another example, an exploratory factor analysis with two or more common factors is always underidentified because you can rotate the common factors without affecting the fit of the model.

PROC CALIS can usually detect an underidentified model by computing the approximate covariance matrix of the parameter estimates and checking whether any estimate is linearly related to other estimates (Bollen 1989, pp. 248–250), in which case PROC CALIS displays equations showing the linear relationships among the estimates. Another way to obtain empirical evidence regarding the identification of a model is to run the analysis several times with different initial estimates to see if the same final estimates are obtained.

Bollen (1989) provides detailed discussions of conditions for identification in a variety of models.

The following example is inspired by Fuller (1987, pp. 40–41). The hypothetical data are counts of two types of cells, cells forming rosettes and nucleated cells, in spleen samples. It is reasonable to assume that counts have a Poisson distribution; hence, the square roots of the counts should have a constant error variance of 0.25.

You can use PROC CALIS to fit a model of Form C to the square roots of the counts without constraints on the parameters, as displayed in following statements. The option OMETHOD=QUANEW is used in the PROC CALIS statement because in this case it produces more rapid convergence than the default optimization method.

```
data spleen;
   input rosette nucleate;
   sqrtrose=sqrt(rosette);
   sqrtnucl=sqrt(nucleate);
   datalines;
4 62
5 87
5 117
6 142
8 212
9 120
12 254
13 179
15 125
19 182
28 301
51 357
;

proc calis data=spleen cov omethod=quanew;
   lineqs sqrtrose=factrose + err_rose,
          sqrtnucl=factnucl + err_nucl,
          factrose=beta factnucl;
   std err_rose=v_rose,
       err_nucl=v_nucl,
       factnucl=v_factnu;
run;
```

This model is underidentified. PROC CALIS displays the following warning:

```
WARNING: Problem not identified: More parameters to estimate ( 4 )
         than given values in data matrix ( 3 ).
```

and diagnoses the indeterminacy as follows:

```
NOTE: Hessian matrix is not full rank. Not all parameters are identified.
      Some parameter estimates are linearly related to other parameter
      estimates as shown in the following equations:

v_nucl   =   -10.554977 - 0.036438 * beta + 1.00000 * v_factnu
             + 0.149564 * v_rose
```

The constraint that the error variances equal 0.25 can be imposed by modifying the STD statement:

```
proc calis data=spleen cov stderr;
   lineqs sqrtrose=factrose + err_rose,
          sqrtnucl=factnucl + err_nucl,
          factrose=beta factnucl;
   std err_rose=.25,
       err_nucl=.25,
       factnucl=v_factnu;
run;
```

The resulting parameter estimates are displayed in Figure 14.2.

```
                         The CALIS Procedure
   Covariance Structure Analysis: Maximum Likelihood Estimation

                  factrose =    0.4034*factnucl
                  Std Err       0.0508 beta
                  t Value       7.9439


              Variances of Exogenous Variables

                                                 Standard
   Variable Parameter        Estimate               Error     t Value

   factnucl v_factnu         10.45846             4.56608        2.29
   err_rose                   0.25000
   err_nucl                   0.25000
```

Figure 14.2. Spleen Data: Parameter Estimates for Overidentified Model

This model is overidentified and the chi-square goodness-of-fit test yields a p-value of 0.0219, as displayed in Figure 14.3.

```
                         The CALIS Procedure
     Covariance Structure Analysis: Maximum Likelihood Estimation

     Fit Function                                              0.4775
     Goodness of Fit Index (GFI)                               0.7274
     GFI Adjusted for Degrees of Freedom (AGFI)                0.1821
     Root Mean Square Residual (RMR)                           0.1785
     Parsimonious GFI (Mulaik, 1989)                           0.7274
     Chi-Square                                                5.2522
     Chi-Square DF                                                  1
     Pr > Chi-Square                                           0.0219
     Independence Model Chi-Square                             13.273
     Independence Model Chi-Square DF                               1
     RMSEA Estimate                                            0.6217
     RMSEA 90% Lower Confidence Limit                          0.1899
     RMSEA 90% Upper Confidence Limit                          1.1869
     ECVI Estimate                                             0.9775
     ECVI 90% Lower Confidence Limit                                .
     ECVI 90% Upper Confidence Limit                           2.2444
     Probability of Close Fit                                  0.0237
     Bentler's Comparative Fit Index                           0.6535
     Normal Theory Reweighted LS Chi-Square                    9.5588
     Akaike's Information Criterion                            3.2522
     Bozdogan's (1987) CAIC                                    1.7673
     Schwarz's Bayesian Criterion                              2.7673
     McDonald's (1989) Centrality                              0.8376
     Bentler & Bonett's (1980) Non-normed Index                0.6535
     Bentler & Bonett's (1980) NFI                             0.6043
     James, Mulaik, & Brett (1982) Parsimonious NFI            0.6043
     Z-Test of Wilson & Hilferty (1931)                        2.0375
     Bollen (1986) Normed Index Rho1                           0.6043
     Bollen (1988) Non-normed Index Delta2                     0.6535
     Hoelter's (1983) Critical N                                   10
```

Figure 14.3. Spleen Data: Fit Statistics for Overidentified Model

The sample size is so small that the *p*-value should not be taken to be accurate, but to get a small *p*-value with such a small sample indicates it is possible that the model is seriously deficient. The deficiency could be due to any of the following:

- The error variances are not both equal to 0.25.
- The error terms are correlated with each other or with the true scores.
- The observations are not independent.
- There is a disturbance in the linear relation between factrose and factnucl.
- The relation between factrose and factnucl is not linear.
- The actual distributions are not adequately approximated by the multivariate normal distribution.

A simple and plausible modification to the model is to add a "disturbance term" or "error in the equation" to the structural model, as follows.

```
proc calis data=spleen cov stderr;
   lineqs sqrtrose=factrose + err_rose,
          sqrtnucl=factnucl + err_nucl,
          factrose=beta factnucl + disturb;
   std err_rose=.25,
       err_nucl=.25,
       factnucl=v_factnu,
       disturb=v_dist;
run;
```

The following parameter estimates are produced.

```
                    The CALIS Procedure
   Covariance Structure Analysis: Maximum Likelihood Estimation

         factrose =   0.3907*factnucl +  1.0000 disturb
         Std Err      0.0771 beta
         t Value      5.0692


              Variances of Exogenous Variables

                                            Standard
    Variable Parameter        Estimate         Error    t Value

    factnucl v_factnu         10.50458       4.58577       2.29
    err_rose                   0.25000
    err_nucl                   0.25000
    disturb  v_dist            0.38153       0.28556       1.34
```

Figure 14.4. Spleen Data: Parameter Estimated for Just Identified Model

This model is just identified, so there are no degrees of freedom for the chi-square goodness-of-fit test.

Path Diagrams and the RAM Model

Complicated models are often easier to understand when they are expressed as path diagrams. One advantage of path diagrams over equations is that variances and covariances can be shown directly in the path diagram. Loehlin (1987) provides a detailed discussion of path diagrams.

It is customary to write the names of manifest variables in rectangles and names of latent variables in ovals. The coefficients in each equation are indicated by drawing arrows from the independent variables to the dependent variable. Covariances between exogenous variables are drawn as two-headed arrows. The variance of an exogenous variable can be displayed as a two-headed arrow with both heads pointing to the exogenous variable, since the variance of a variable is the covariance of the variable with itself. Here is a path diagram for the spleen data, explicitly showing all latent variables and variances of exogenous variables.

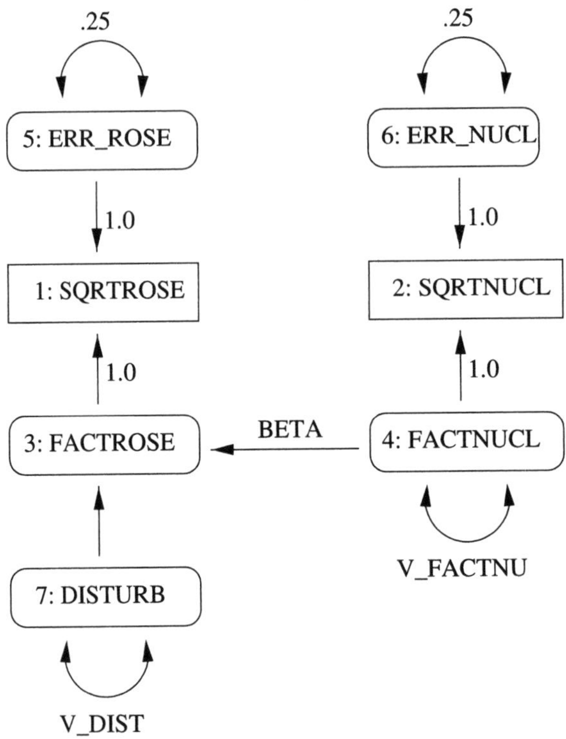

Figure 14.5. Path Diagram: Spleen

There is an easier way to draw the path diagram based on McArdle's reticular action model (RAM) (McArdle and McDonald 1984). McArdle uses the convention that a two-headed arrow that points to an endogenous variable actually refers to the error or disturbance term associated with that variable. A two-headed arrow with both heads pointing to the same endogenous variable represents the error or disturbance variance for the equation that determines the endogenous variable; there is no need to draw a separate oval for the error or disturbance term. Similarly, a two-headed arrow connecting two endogenous variables represents the covariance between the error of disturbance terms associated with the endogenous variables. The RAM conventions allow the previous path diagram to be simplified, as follows.

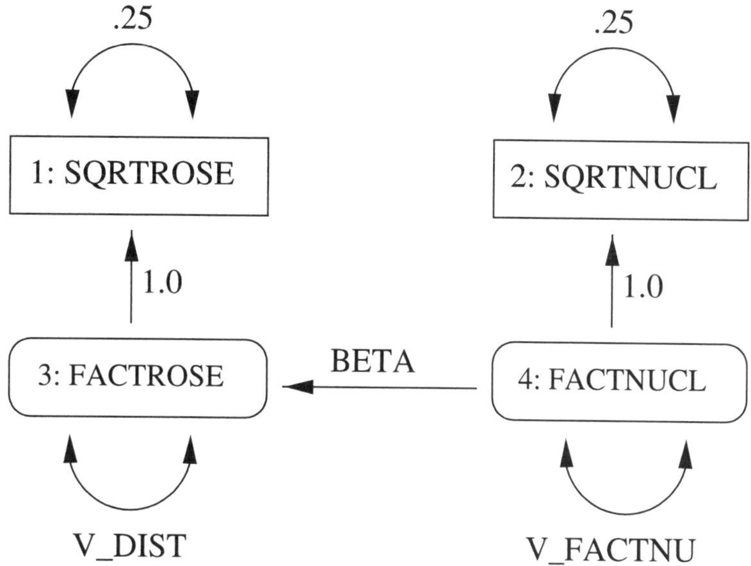

Figure 14.6. Path Diagram: Spleen

The RAM statement in PROC CALIS provides a simple way to transcribe a path diagram based on the reticular action model. Assign the integers 1, 2, 3,. . . to the variables in the order in which they appear in the SAS data set or in the VAR statement, if you use one. Assign subsequent consecutive integers to the latent variables displayed explicitly in the path diagram (excluding the error and disturbance terms implied by two-headed arrows) in any order. Each arrow in the path diagram can then be identified by two numbers indicating the variables connected by the path. The RAM statement consists of a list of descriptions of all the arrows in the path diagram. The descriptions are separated by commas. Each arrow description consists of three or four numbers and, optionally, a name in the following order:

1. The number of heads the arrow has.
2. The number of the variable the arrow points to, or either variable if the arrow is two-headed.
3. The number of the variable the arrow comes from, or the other variable if the arrow is two-headed.
4. The value of the coefficient or (co)variance that the arrow represents.

5. A name if the arrow represents a parameter to be estimated, in which case the previous number is taken to be the initial estimate of the parameter. Omit the name if the arrow represents a constant. If you specify a name, the fourth number may be omitted.

The model for the spleen data can be specified with the RAM statement, as follows:

```
      /* 1 sqrtrose   */
      /* 2 sqrtnucl   */
      /* 3 factrose   */
      /* 4 factnucl   */
proc calis data=spleen cov stderr method=ml outram=splram1;
   var sqrtrose sqrtnucl;
   ram 1 1 3 1,          /* sqrtrose <- factrose */
       1 2 4 1,          /* sqrtnucl <- factnucl */
       1 3 4 beta,       /* factrose <- factnucl */
       2 1 1 .25,        /* error variance for sqrtrose */
       2 2 2 .25,        /* error variance for sqrtnucl */
       2 3 3 v_dist,   /* disturbance variance for factrose */
       2 4 4 v_factnu;     /* variance of factnucl */
run;
```

The resulting output in RAM form is displayed in Figure 14.7.

```
                          The CALIS Procedure
        Covariance Structure Analysis: Maximum Likelihood Estimation

                             RAM Estimates

                                                                Standard
Term Matrix ----Row----- ---Column--- Parameter   Estimate        Error t Value

  1      2 sqrtrose    1 F1          3 .            1.00000
  1      2 sqrtnucl    2 F2          4 .            1.00000
  1      2 F1          3 F2          4 beta         0.39074      0.07708    5.07
  1      3 E1          1 E1          1 .            0.25000
  1      3 E2          2 E2          2 .            0.25000
  1      3 D1          3 D1          3 v_dist       0.38153      0.28556    1.34
  1      3 D2          4 D2          4 v_factnu    10.50458      4.58577    2.29
```

Figure 14.7. Spleen Data: RAM Model

You can request an output data set containing the model specification by using the OUTRAM= option in the PROC CALIS statement. Names for the latent variables can be specified in a VNAMES statement.

```
proc calis data=spleen cov stderr method=ml outram=splram1;
   var sqrtrose sqrtnucl;
   vnames 1 factrose factnucl,
          2 err_rose err_nucl disturb factnucl;
   ram 1 1 3 1,         /* sqrtrose <- factrose */
       1 2 4 1,         /* sqrtnucl <- factnucl */
       1 3 4 beta,      /* factrose <- factnucl */
       2 1 1 .25,       /* error variance for sqrtrose */


       2 2 2 .25,       /* error variance for sqrtnucl */
       2 3 3 v_dist,    /* disturbance variance for factrose */
       2 4 4 v_factnu;  /* variance of factnucl */
run;

proc print;
run;
```

The RAM output is displayed in Figure 14.8.

```
                         The CALIS Procedure
      Covariance Structure Analysis: Maximum Likelihood Estimation

                              RAM Estimates

                                                                Standard
Term Matrix ----Row----- ---Column--- Parameter   Estimate        Error t Value

   1      2 sqrtrose    1 factrose   3 .            1.00000
   1      2 sqrtnucl    2 factnucl   4 .            1.00000
   1      2 factrose    3 factnucl   4 beta         0.39074     0.07708    5.07
   1      3 err_rose    1 err_rose   1 .            0.25000
   1      3 err_nucl    2 err_nucl   2 .            0.25000
   1      3 disturb     3 disturb    3 v_dist       0.38153     0.28556    1.34
   1      3 factnucl    4 factnucl   4 v_factnu    10.50458     4.58577    2.29
```

Figure 14.8. Spleen Data: RAM Model with Names for Latent Variables

The OUTRAM= data set contains the RAM model as you specified it in the RAM statement, but it contains the final parameter estimates and standard errors instead of the initial values.

Obs	_TYPE_	_NAME_	_MATNR_	_ROW_	_COL_	_ESTIM_	_STDERR_
1	MODEL	_IDE_	1	2	4	1.0000	0.00000
2	MODEL	_A_	2	4	4	6.0000	2.00000
3	MODEL	_P_	3	4	4	3.0000	0.00000
4	VARNAME	sqrtrose	2	.	1	.	.
5	VARNAME	sqrtnucl	2	.	2	.	.
6	VARNAME	factrose	2	.	3	.	.
7	VARNAME	factnucl	2	.	4	.	.
8	VARNAME	err_rose	3	.	1	.	.
9	VARNAME	err_nucl	3	.	2	.	.
10	VARNAME	disturb	3	.	3	.	.
11	VARNAME	factnucl	3	.	4	.	.
12	METHOD	ML	.	.	.	.	.
13	STAT	N	.	.	.	12.0000	.
14	STAT	FIT	.	.	.	0.0000	.
15	STAT	GFI	.	.	.	1.0000	.
16	STAT	AGFI	.	.	.	.	.
17	STAT	RMR	.	.	.	0.0000	.
18	STAT	PGFI	.	.	.	0.0000	.
19	STAT	NPARM	.	.	.	3.0000	.
20	STAT	DF	.	.	.	0.0000	.
21	STAT	N_ACT	.	.	.	0.0000	.
22	STAT	CHISQUAR	.	.	.	0.0000	.
23	STAT	P_CHISQ	.	.	.	0.0000	.
24	STAT	CHISQNUL	.	.	.	13.2732	.
25	STAT	RMSEAEST	.	.	.	0.0000	.
26	STAT	RMSEALOB	.	.	.	.	.
27	STAT	RMSEAUPB	.	.	.	.	.
28	STAT	P_CLOSFT	.	.	.	.	.
29	STAT	ECVI_EST	.	.	.	0.7500	.
30	STAT	ECVI_LOB	.	.	.	.	.
31	STAT	ECVI_UPB	.	.	.	.	.
32	STAT	COMPFITI	.	.	.	1.0000	.
33	STAT	ADJCHISQ	.	.	.	.	.
34	STAT	P_ACHISQ	.	.	.	.	.
35	STAT	RLSCHISQ	.	.	.	0.0000	.
36	STAT	AIC	.	.	.	0.0000	.
37	STAT	CAIC	.	.	.	0.0000	.
38	STAT	SBC	.	.	.	0.0000	.
39	STAT	CENTRALI	.	.	.	1.0000	.
40	STAT	BB_NONOR	.	.	.	.	.
41	STAT	BB_NORMD	.	.	.	1.0000	.
42	STAT	PARSIMON	.	.	.	0.0000	.
43	STAT	ZTESTWH	.	.	.	.	.
44	STAT	BOL_RHO1	.	.	.	.	.
45	STAT	BOL_DEL2	.	.	.	1.0000	.
46	STAT	CNHOELT	.	.	.	.	.
47	ESTIM		2	1	3	1.0000	0.00000
48	ESTIM		2	2	4	1.0000	0.00000
49	ESTIM	beta	2	3	4	0.3907	0.07708
50	ESTIM		3	1	1	0.2500	0.00000
51	ESTIM		3	2	2	0.2500	0.00000
52	ESTIM	v_dist	3	3	3	0.3815	0.28556
53	ESTIM	v_factnu	3	4	4	10.5046	4.58577

Figure 14.9. Spleen Data: OUTRAM= Data Set with Final Parameter Estimates

This data set can be used as input to another run of PROC CALIS with the INRAM= option in the PROC CALIS statement. For example, if the iteration limit is exceeded, you can use the RAM data set to start a new run that begins with the final estimates from the last run. Or you can change the data set to add or remove constraints or modify the model in various other ways. The easiest way to change a RAM data set is to use the FSEDIT procedure, but you can also use a DATA step. For example, you could set the variance of the disturbance term to zero, effectively removing the disturbance from the equation, by removing the parameter name v_dist in the _NAME_ variable and setting the value of the estimate to zero in the _ESTIM_ variable:

```
data splram2(type=ram);
   set splram1;
   if _name_='v_dist' then
      do;
         _name_=' ';
         _estim_=0;
      end;
run;

proc calis data=spleen inram=splram2 cov stderr;
run;
```

The resulting RAM output is displayed in Figure 14.10.

```
                         The CALIS Procedure
      Covariance Structure Analysis: Maximum Likelihood Estimation

                            RAM Estimates

                                                              Standard
Term Matrix ----Row----- ---Column--- Parameter   Estimate      Error t Value

   1      2 sqrtrose    1 factrose    3 .          1.00000
   1      2 sqrtnucl    2 factnucl    4 .          1.00000
   1      2 factrose    3 factnucl    4 beta       0.40340    0.05078    7.94
   1      3 err_rose    1 err_rose    1 .          0.25000
   1      3 err_nucl    2 err_nucl    2 .          0.25000
   1      3 disturb     3 disturb     3 .                0
   1      3 factnucl    4 factnucl    4 v_factnu  10.45846    4.56608    2.29
```

Figure 14.10. Spleen Data: RAM Model with INRAM= Data Set

Some Measurement Models

Psychometric test theory involves many kinds of models relating scores on psychological and educational tests to latent variables representing intelligence or various underlying abilities. The following example uses data on four vocabulary tests from Lord (1957). Tests W and X have 15 items each and are administered with very liberal time limits. Tests Y and Z have 75 items and are administered under time pressure. The covariance matrix is read by the following DATA step:

```
data lord(type=cov);
   input _type_ $ _name_ $ w x y z;
   datalines;
n   . 649      .       .       .
cov w 86.3979  .       .       .
cov x 57.7751 86.2632  .       .
cov y 56.8651 59.3177 97.2850  .
cov z 58.8986 59.6683 73.8201 97.8192
;
```

The psychometric model of interest states that W and X are determined by a single common factor F_{WX}, and Y and Z are determined by a single common factor F_{YZ}. The two common factors are expected to have a positive correlation, and it is desired to estimate this correlation. It is convenient to assume that the common factors have unit variance, so their correlation will be equal to their covariance. The error terms for all the manifest variables are assumed to be uncorrelated with each other and with the common factors. The model (labeled here as Model Form D) is as follows.

Model Form D

$$
\begin{aligned}
W &= \beta_W F_{WX} + E_W \\
X &= \beta_X F_{WX} + E_X \\
Y &= \beta_Y F_{YZ} + E_Y \\
Z &= \beta_Z F_{YZ} + E_Z \\
\text{Var}(F_{WX}) &= \text{Var}(F_{YZ}) = 1 \\
\text{Cov}(F_{WX}, F_{YZ}) &= \rho \\
\text{Cov}(E_W, E_X) &= \text{Cov}(E_W, E_Y) = \text{Cov}(E_W, E_Z) = \text{Cov}(E_X, E_Y) \\
&= \text{Cov}(E_X, E_Z) = \text{Cov}(E_Y, E_Z) = \text{Cov}(E_W, F_{WX}) \\
&= \text{Cov}(E_W, F_{YZ}) = \text{Cov}(E_X, F_{WX}) = \text{Cov}(E_X, F_{YZ}) \\
&= \text{Cov}(E_Y, F_{WX}) = \text{Cov}(E_Y, F_{YZ}) = \text{Cov}(E_Z, F_{WX}) \\
&= \text{Cov}(E_Z, F_{YZ}) = 0
\end{aligned}
$$

The corresponding path diagram is as follows.

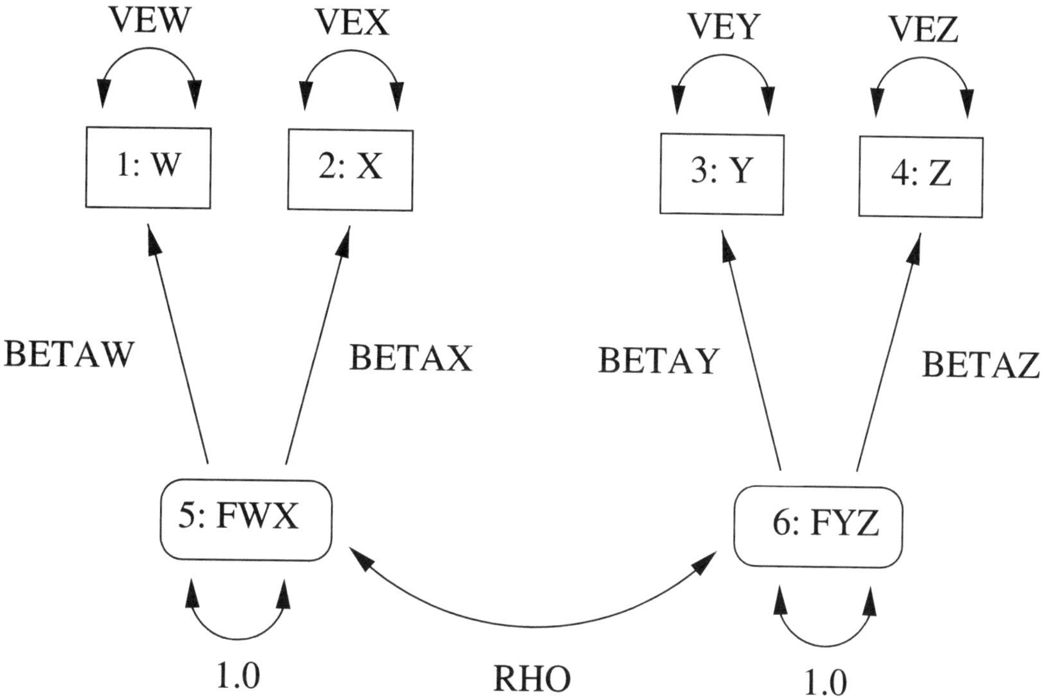

Figure 14.11. Path Diagram: Lord

This path diagram can be converted to a RAM model as follows:

```
   /* 1=w 2=x 3=y 4=z 5=fwx 6=fyz */
title 'H4: unconstrained';
proc calis data=lord cov;
   ram 1 1 5 betaw,
       1 2 5 betax,
       1 3 6 betay,
       1 4 6 betaz,
       2 1 1 vew,
       2 2 2 vex,
       2 3 3 vey,
       2 4 4 vez,
       2 5 5 1,
       2 6 6 1,
       2 5 6 rho;
run;
```

Here are the major results.

```
                    H4: unconstrained

                   The CALIS Procedure
  Covariance Structure Analysis: Maximum Likelihood Estimation

  Fit Function                                          0.0011
  Goodness of Fit Index (GFI)                           0.9995
  GFI Adjusted for Degrees of Freedom (AGFI)            0.9946
  Root Mean Square Residual (RMR)                       0.2720
  Parsimonious GFI (Mulaik, 1989)                       0.1666
  Chi-Square                                            0.7030
  Chi-Square DF                                              1
  Pr > Chi-Square                                       0.4018
  Independence Model Chi-Square                         1466.6
  Independence Model Chi-Square DF                           6
  RMSEA Estimate                                        0.0000
  RMSEA 90% Lower Confidence Limit                           .
  RMSEA 90% Upper Confidence Limit                      0.0974
  ECVI Estimate                                         0.0291
  ECVI 90% Lower Confidence Limit                            .
  ECVI 90% Upper Confidence Limit                       0.0391
  Probability of Close Fit                              0.6854
  Bentler's Comparative Fit Index                       1.0000
  Normal Theory Reweighted LS Chi-Square                0.7026
  Akaike's Information Criterion                       -1.2970
  Bozdogan's (1987) CAIC                               -6.7725
  Schwarz's Bayesian Criterion                         -5.7725
  McDonald's (1989) Centrality                          1.0002
  Bentler & Bonett's (1980) Non-normed Index            1.0012
  Bentler & Bonett's (1980) NFI                         0.9995
  James, Mulaik, & Brett (1982) Parsimonious NFI        0.1666
  Z-Test of Wilson & Hilferty (1931)                    0.2363
  Bollen (1986) Normed Index Rho1                       0.9971
  Bollen (1988) Non-normed Index Delta2                 1.0002
  Hoelter's (1983) Critical N                             3543
```

Figure 14.12. Lord Data: Major Results for RAM Model, Hypothesis H4

```
                          H4: unconstrained

                         The CALIS Procedure
        Covariance Structure Analysis: Maximum Likelihood Estimation

                            RAM Estimates

                                                                Standard
Term  Matrix  --Row--   -Column-   Parameter    Estimate        Error   t Value

   1       2  w      1  F1      5  betaw         7.50066      0.32339     23.19
   1       2  x      2  F1      5  betax         7.70266      0.32063     24.02
   1       2  y      3  F2      6  betay         8.50947      0.32694     26.03
   1       2  z      4  F2      6  betaz         8.67505      0.32560     26.64
   1       3  E1     1  E1      1  vew          30.13796      2.47037     12.20
   1       3  E2     2  E2      2  vex          26.93217      2.43065     11.08
   1       3  E3     3  E3      3  vey          24.87396      2.35986     10.54
   1       3  E4     4  E4      4  vez          22.56264      2.35028      9.60
   1       3  D1     5  D1      5  .             1.00000
   1       3  D2     6  D1      5  rho           0.89855      0.01865     48.18
   1       3  D2     6  D2      6  .             1.00000
```

The same analysis can be performed with the LINEQS statement. Subsequent analyses are illustrated with the LINEQS statement rather than the RAM statement because it is slightly easier to understand the constraints as written in the LINEQS statement without constantly referring to the path diagram. The LINEQS and RAM statements may yield slightly different results due to the inexactness of the numerical optimization; the discrepancies can be reduced by specifying a more stringent convergence criterion such as GCONV=1E-4 or GCONV=1E-6. It is convenient to create an OUTRAM= data set for use in fitting other models with additional constraints.

```
title 'H4: unconstrained';
proc calis data=lord cov outram=ram4;
   lineqs w=betaw fwx + ew,
          x=betax fwx + ex,
          y=betay fyz + ey,
          z=betaz fyz + ez;
   std fwx fyz=1,
       ew ex ey ez=vew vex vey vez;
   cov fwx fyz=rho;
run;
```

The LINEQS displayed output is as follows.

```
                    H4: unconstrained

                  The CALIS Procedure
  Covariance Structure Analysis: Maximum Likelihood Estimation

        w          =    7.5007*fwx      +  1.0000 ew
        Std Err         0.3234 betaw
        t Value        23.1939
        x          =    7.7027*fwx      +  1.0000 ex
        Std Err         0.3206 betax
        t Value        24.0235
        y          =    8.5095*fyz      +  1.0000 ey
        Std Err         0.3269 betay
        t Value        26.0273
        z          =    8.6751*fyz      +  1.0000 ez
        Std Err         0.3256 betaz
        t Value        26.6430


              Variances of Exogenous Variables

                                              Standard
   Variable Parameter        Estimate            Error     t Value

   fwx                        1.00000
   fyz                        1.00000
   ew        vew             30.13796          2.47037       12.20
   ex        vex             26.93217          2.43065       11.08
   ey        vey             24.87396          2.35986       10.54
   ez        vez             22.56264          2.35028        9.60


             Covariances Among Exogenous Variables

                                              Standard
   Var1 Var2 Parameter         Estimate          Error     t Value

   fwx  fyz  rho                0.89855        0.01865       48.18
```

Figure 14.13. Lord Data: Using LINEQS Statement for RAM Model, Hypothesis H4

In an analysis of these data by Jöreskog and Sörbom (1979, pp. 54–56; Loehlin 1987, pp. 84–87), four hypotheses are considered:

H_1: $\rho = 1$,
$\beta_W = \beta_X$, $\text{Var}(E_W) = \text{Var}(E_X)$,
$\beta_Y = \beta_Z$, $\text{Var}(E_Y) = \text{Var}(E_Z)$

H_2: same as H_1: except ρ is unconstrained

H_3: $\rho = 1$

H_4: Model Form D without any additional constraints

The hypothesis H_3 says that there is really just one common factor instead of two; in the terminology of test theory, W, X, Y, and Z are said to be congeneric. The hypothesis H_2 says that W and X have the same true-scores and have equal error variance; such tests are said to be parallel. The hypothesis H_2 also requires Y and Z to be parallel. The hypothesis H_1 says that W and X are parallel tests, Y and Z are parallel tests, and all four tests are congeneric.

It is most convenient to fit the models in the opposite order from that in which they are numbered. The previous analysis fit the model for H_4 and created an OUTRAM= data set called ram4. The hypothesis H_3 can be fitted directly or by modifying the ram4 data set. Since H_3 differs from H_4 only in that ρ is constrained to equal 1, the ram4 data set can be modified by finding the observation for which _NAME_='rho' and changing the variable _NAME_ to a blank value (meaning that the observation represents a constant rather than a parameter to be fitted) and setting the variable _ESTIM_ to the value 1. Both of the following analyses produce the same results:

```
title 'H3: W, X, Y, and Z are congeneric';
proc calis data=lord cov;
   lineqs w=betaw f + ew,
          x=betax f + ex,
          y=betay f + ey,
          z=betaz f + ez;
   std f=1,
       ew ex ey ez=vew vex vey vez;
run;

data ram3(type=ram);
   set ram4;
   if _name_='rho' then
      do;
         _name_=' ';
         _estim_=1;
      end;
run;

proc calis data=lord inram=ram3 cov;
run;
```

The resulting output from either of these analyses is displayed in Figure 14.14.

```
                 H3: W, X, Y, and Z are congeneric

                        The CALIS Procedure
      Covariance Structure Analysis: Maximum Likelihood Estimation

      Fit Function                                            0.0559
      Goodness of Fit Index (GFI)                             0.9714
      GFI Adjusted for Degrees of Freedom (AGFI)              0.8570
      Root Mean Square Residual (RMR)                         2.4636
      Parsimonious GFI (Mulaik, 1989)                         0.3238
      Chi-Square                                             36.2095
      Chi-Square DF                                                2
      Pr > Chi-Square                                         <.0001
      Independence Model Chi-Square                           1466.6
      Independence Model Chi-Square DF                             6
      RMSEA Estimate                                          0.1625
      RMSEA 90% Lower Confidence Limit                        0.1187
      RMSEA 90% Upper Confidence Limit                        0.2108
      ECVI Estimate                                           0.0808
      ECVI 90% Lower Confidence Limit                         0.0561
      ECVI 90% Upper Confidence Limit                         0.1170
      Probability of Close Fit                                0.0000
      Bentler's Comparative Fit Index                         0.9766
      Normal Theory Reweighted LS Chi-Square                 38.1432
      Akaike's Information Criterion                         32.2095
      Bozdogan's (1987) CAIC                                 21.2586
      Schwarz's Bayesian Criterion                           23.2586
      McDonald's (1989) Centrality                            0.9740
      Bentler & Bonett's (1980) Non-normed Index              0.9297
      Bentler & Bonett's (1980) NFI                           0.9753
      James, Mulaik, & Brett (1982) Parsimonious NFI          0.3251
      Z-Test of Wilson & Hilferty (1931)                      5.2108
      Bollen (1986) Normed Index Rho1                         0.9259
      Bollen (1988) Non-normed Index Delta2                   0.9766
      Hoelter's (1983) Critical N                                109
```

Figure 14.14. Lord Data: Major Results for Hypothesis H3

```
                H3: W, X, Y, and Z are congeneric

                       The CALIS Procedure
   Covariance Structure Analysis: Maximum Likelihood Estimation

          w         =    7.1047*fwx      +  1.0000 ew
          Std Err        0.3218 betaw
          t Value       22.0802
          x         =    7.2691*fwx      +  1.0000 ex
          Std Err        0.3183 betax
          t Value       22.8397
          y         =    8.3735*fyz      +  1.0000 ey
          Std Err        0.3254 betay
          t Value       25.7316
          z         =    8.5106*fyz      +  1.0000 ez
          Std Err        0.3241 betaz
          t Value       26.2598


                Variances of Exogenous Variables

                                                Standard
   Variable Parameter        Estimate              Error     t Value

   fwx                        1.00000
   fyz                        1.00000
   ew        vew             35.92087            2.41466       14.88
   ex        vex             33.42397            2.31038       14.47
   ey        vey             27.16980            2.24619       12.10
   ez        vez             25.38948            2.20839       11.50
```

The hypothesis H_2 requires that several pairs of parameters be constrained to have equal estimates. With PROC CALIS, you can impose this constraint by giving the same name to parameters that are constrained to be equal. This can be done directly in the LINEQS and STD statements or by using PROC FSEDIT or a DATA step to change the values in the ram4 data set:

```
title 'H2: W and X parallel, Y and Z parallel';
proc calis data=lord cov;
   lineqs w=betawx fwx + ew,
          x=betawx fwx + ex,
          y=betayz fyz + ey,
          z=betayz fyz + ez;
   std fwx fyz=1,
       ew ex ey ez=vewx vewx veyz veyz;
   cov fwx fyz=rho;
run;

data ram2(type=ram);
   set ram4;
   if _name_= 'betaw' then _name_='betawx';
   if _name_='betax' then _name_='betawx';
   if _name_='betay' then _name_='betayz';
   if _name_='betaz' then _name_='betayz';
   if _name_='vew' then _name_='vewx';
```

```
   if _name_='vex' then _name_='vewx';
   if _name_='vey' then _name_='veyz';
   if _name_='vez' then _name_='veyz';
run;

proc calis data=lord inram=ram2 cov;
run;
```

The resulting output from either of these analyses is displayed in Figure 14.15.

```
              H2: W and X parallel, Y and Z parallel

                        The CALIS Procedure
      Covariance Structure Analysis: Maximum Likelihood Estimation

      Fit Function                                           0.0030
      Goodness of Fit Index (GFI)                            0.9985
      GFI Adjusted for Degrees of Freedom (AGFI)             0.9970
      Root Mean Square Residual (RMR)                        0.6983
      Parsimonious GFI (Mulaik, 1989)                        0.8321
      Chi-Square                                             1.9335
      Chi-Square DF                                               5
      Pr > Chi-Square                                        0.8583
      Independence Model Chi-Square                          1466.6
      Independence Model Chi-Square DF                            6
      RMSEA Estimate                                         0.0000
      RMSEA 90% Lower Confidence Limit                            .
      RMSEA 90% Upper Confidence Limit                       0.0293
      ECVI Estimate                                          0.0185
      ECVI 90% Lower Confidence Limit                             .
      ECVI 90% Upper Confidence Limit                        0.0276
      Probability of Close Fit                               0.9936
      Bentler's Comparative Fit Index                        1.0000
      Normal Theory Reweighted LS Chi-Square                 1.9568
      Akaike's Information Criterion                        -8.0665
      Bozdogan's (1987) CAIC                               -35.4436
      Schwarz's Bayesian Criterion                         -30.4436
      McDonald's (1989) Centrality                           1.0024
      Bentler & Bonett's (1980) Non-normed Index             1.0025
      Bentler & Bonett's (1980) NFI                          0.9987
      James, Mulaik, & Brett (1982) Parsimonious NFI         0.8322
      Z-Test of Wilson & Hilferty (1931)                    -1.0768
      Bollen (1986) Normed Index Rho1                        0.9984
      Bollen (1988) Non-normed Index Delta2                  1.0021
      Hoelter's (1983) Critical N                              3712
```

Figure 14.15. Lord Data: Major Results for Hypothesis H2

```
              H2: W and X parallel, Y and Z parallel

                      The CALIS Procedure
  Covariance Structure Analysis: Maximum Likelihood Estimation

         w        =    7.6010*fwx      +  1.0000 ew
         Std Err       0.2684 betawx
         t Value      28.3158
         x        =    7.6010*fwx      +  1.0000 ex
         Std Err       0.2684 betawx
         t Value      28.3158
         y        =    8.5919*fyz      +  1.0000 ey
         Std Err       0.2797 betayz
         t Value      30.7215
         z        =    8.5919*fyz      +  1.0000 ez
         Std Err       0.2797 betayz
         t Value      30.7215


               Variances of Exogenous Variables

                                                Standard
  Variable Parameter        Estimate              Error     t Value

  fwx                        1.00000
  fyz                        1.00000
  ew        vewx            28.55545            1.58641       18.00
  ex        vewx            28.55545            1.58641       18.00
  ey        veyz            23.73200            1.31844       18.00
  ez        veyz            23.73200            1.31844       18.00


             Covariances Among Exogenous Variables

                                                Standard
  Var1 Var2 Parameter        Estimate             Error     t Value

  fwx   fyz   rho             0.89864           0.01865       48.18
```

The hypothesis H_1 requires one more constraint in addition to those in H_2:

```
title 'H1: W and X parallel, Y and Z parallel, all congeneric';
proc calis data=lord cov;
   lineqs w=betawx f + ew,
          x=betawx f + ex,
          y=betayz f + ey,
          z=betayz f + ez;
   std f=1,
       ew ex ey ez=vewx vewx veyz veyz;
run;

data ram1(type=ram);
   set ram2;
   if _name_='rho' then
      do;
         _name_=' ';
         _estim_=1;
      end;
run;
```

```
proc calis data=lord inram=ram1 cov;
run;
```

The resulting output from either of these analyses is displayed in Figure 14.16.

```
       H1: W and X parallel, Y and Z parallel, all congeneric

                     The CALIS Procedure
Covariance Structure Analysis: Maximum Likelihood Estimation

Fit Function                                            0.0576
Goodness of Fit Index (GFI)                             0.9705
GFI Adjusted for Degrees of Freedom (AGFI)              0.9509
Root Mean Square Residual (RMR)                         2.5430
Parsimonious GFI (Mulaik, 1989)                         0.9705
Chi-Square                                             37.3337
Chi-Square DF                                                6
Pr > Chi-Square                                         <.0001
Independence Model Chi-Square                           1466.6
Independence Model Chi-Square DF                             6
RMSEA Estimate                                          0.0898
RMSEA 90% Lower Confidence Limit                        0.0635
RMSEA 90% Upper Confidence Limit                        0.1184
ECVI Estimate                                           0.0701
ECVI 90% Lower Confidence Limit                         0.0458
ECVI 90% Upper Confidence Limit                         0.1059
Probability of Close Fit                                0.0076
Bentler's Comparative Fit Index                         0.9785
Normal Theory Reweighted LS Chi-Square                 39.3380
Akaike's Information Criterion                         25.3337
Bozdogan's (1987) CAIC                                 -7.5189
Schwarz's Bayesian Criterion                           -1.5189
McDonald's (1989) Centrality                            0.9761
Bentler & Bonett's (1980) Non-normed Index              0.9785
Bentler & Bonett's (1980) NFI                           0.9745
James, Mulaik, & Brett (1982) Parsimonious NFI          0.9745
Z-Test of Wilson & Hilferty (1931)                      4.5535
Bollen (1986) Normed Index Rho1                         0.9745
Bollen (1988) Non-normed Index Delta2                   0.9785
Hoelter's (1983) Critical N                                220
```

Figure 14.16. Lord Data: Major Results for Hypothesis H1

```
     H1: W and X parallel, Y and Z parallel, all congeneric

                            The CALIS Procedure
   Covariance Structure Analysis: Maximum Likelihood Estimation

         w          =    7.1862*fwx       +  1.0000 ew
         Std Err         0.2660 betawx
         t Value        27.0180
         x          =    7.1862*fwx       +  1.0000 ex
         Std Err         0.2660 betawx
         t Value        27.0180
         y          =    8.4420*fyz       +  1.0000 ey
         Std Err         0.2800 betayz
         t Value        30.1494
         z          =    8.4420*fyz       +  1.0000 ez
         Std Err         0.2800 betayz
         t Value        30.1494


                  Variances of Exogenous Variables

                                                    Standard
   Variable Parameter         Estimate                 Error      t Value

   fwx                         1.00000
   fyz                         1.00000
   ew        vewx             34.68865               1.64634        21.07
   ex        vewx             34.68865               1.64634        21.07
   ey        veyz             26.28513               1.39955        18.78
   ez        veyz             26.28513               1.39955        18.78


                Covariances Among Exogenous Variables

                                                      Standard
   Var1 Var2 Parameter         Estimate                  Error      t Value

   fwx  fyz                     1.00000
```

The goodness-of-fit tests for the four hypotheses are summarized in the following table.

Hypothesis	Number of Parameters	χ^2	Degrees of Freedom	p-value	$\hat{\rho}$
H_1	4	37.33	6	0.0000	1.0
H_2	5	1.93	5	0.8583	0.8986
H_3	8	36.21	2	0.0000	1.0
H_4	9	0.70	1	0.4018	0.8986

The hypotheses H_1 and H_3, which posit $\rho = 1$, can be rejected. Hypotheses H_2 and H_4 seem to be consistent with the available data. Since H_2 is obtained by adding four constraints to H_4, you can test H_2 versus H_4 by computing the differences of the chi-square statistics and their degrees of freedom, yielding a chi-square of 1.23 with four degrees of freedom, which is obviously not significant. So hypothesis H_2 is consistent with the available data.

The estimates of ρ for H_2 and H_4 are almost identical, about 0.90, indicating that the speeded and unspeeded tests are measuring almost the same latent variable, even though the hypotheses that stated they measured exactly the same latent variable are rejected.

A Combined Measurement-Structural Model with Reciprocal Influence and Correlated Residuals

To illustrate a more complex model, this example uses some well-known data from Haller and Butterworth (1960). Various models and analyses of these data are given by Duncan, Haller, and Portes (1968), Jöreskog and Sörbom (1988), and Loehlin (1987).

The study is concerned with the career aspirations of high-school students and how these aspirations are affected by close friends. The data are collected from 442 seventeen-year-old boys in Michigan. There are 329 boys in the sample who named another boy in the sample as a best friend. The observations to be analyzed consist of the data from these 329 boys paired with the data from their best friends.

The method of data collection introduces two statistical problems. First, restricting the analysis to boys whose best friends are in the original sample causes the reduced sample to be biased. Second, since the data from a given boy may appear in two or more observations, the observations are not independent. Therefore, any statistical conclusions should be considered tentative. It is difficult to accurately assess the effects of the dependence of the observations on the analysis, but it could be argued on intuitive grounds that since each observation has data from two boys and since it seems likely that many of the boys will appear in the data set at least twice, the effective sample size may be as small as half of the reported 329 observations.

The correlation matrix is taken from Jöreskog and Sörbom (1988).

```
title 'Peer Influences on Aspiration: Haller & Butterworth (1960)';
data aspire(type=corr);
   _type_='corr';
   input _name_ $ riq rpa rses roa rea fiq fpa fses foa fea;
   label riq='Respondent: Intelligence'
         rpa='Respondent: Parental Aspiration'
         rses='Respondent: Family SES'
         roa='Respondent: Occupational Aspiration'
         rea='Respondent: Educational Aspiration'
         fiq='Friend: Intelligence'
         fpa='Friend: Parental Aspiration'
         fses='Friend: Family SES'
         foa='Friend: Occupational Aspiration'
         fea='Friend: Educational Aspiration';
   datalines;
riq   1.     .      .      .      .      .      .       .      .     .
rpa   .1839  1.     .      .      .      .      .       .      .     .
rses  .2220  .0489  1.     .      .      .      .       .      .     .
roa   .4105  .2137  .3240  1.     .      .      .       .      .     .
rea   .4043  .2742  .4047  .6247  1.     .      .       .      .     .
fiq   .3355  .0782  .2302  .2995  .2863  1.     .       .      .     .
fpa   .1021  .1147  .0931  .0760  .0702  .2087  1.      .      .     .
fses  .1861  .0186  .2707  .2930  .2407  .2950  -.0438  1.     .     .
```

```
foa    .2598  .0839  .2786  .4216  .3275  .5007   .1988  .3607  1.     .
fea    .2903  .1124  .3054  .3269  .3669  .5191   .2784  .4105  .6404  1.
;
```

The model analyzed by Jöreskog and Sörbom (1988) is displayed in the following path diagram:

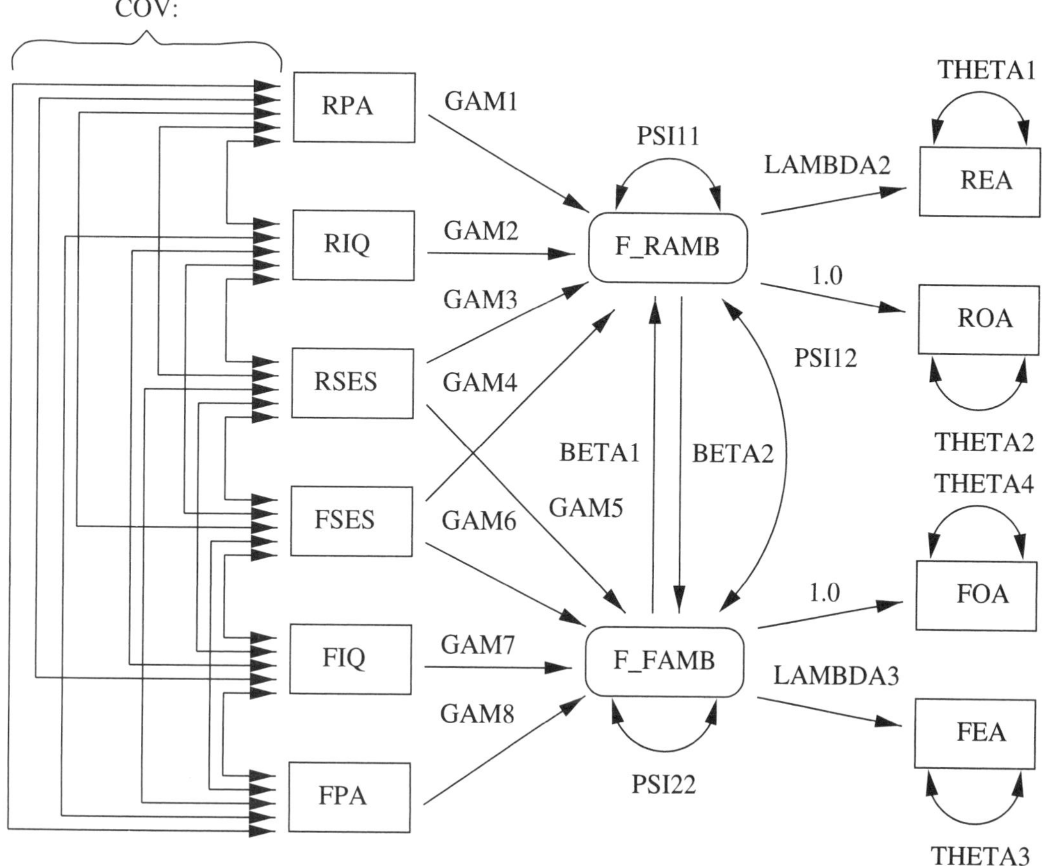

Figure 14.17. Path Diagram: Career Aspiration, Jöreskog and Sörbom

Two latent variables, f_ramb and f_famb, represent the respondent's level of ambition and his best friend's level of ambition, respectively. The model states that the respondent's ambition is determined by his intelligence and socioeconomic status, his perception of his parents' aspiration for him, and his friend's socioeconomic status and ambition. It is assumed that his friend's intelligence and socioeconomic status affect the respondent's ambition only indirectly through his friend's ambition. Ambition is indexed by the manifest variables of occupational and educational aspiration, which are assumed to have uncorrelated residuals. The path coefficient from ambition to occupational aspiration is set to 1.0 to determine the scale of the ambition latent variable.

This model can be analyzed with PROC CALIS using the LINEQS statement as follows, where the names of the parameters correspond to those used by Jöreskog and Sörbom (1988). Since this TYPE=CORR data set does not contain an observation with _TYPE_='N' giving the sample size, it is necessary to specify the degrees of freedom (sample size minus one) with the EDF= option in the PROC CALIS statement.

```
title2 'Joreskog-Sorbom (1988) analysis 1';
proc calis data=aspire edf=328;
   lineqs    /* measurement model for aspiration */
          rea=lambda2 f_ramb + e_rea,
          roa=f_ramb + e_roa,
          fea=lambda3 f_famb + e_fea,
          foa=f_famb + e_foa,
             /* structural model of influences */
          f_ramb=gam1 rpa + gam2 riq + gam3 rses +
             gam4 fses + beta1 f_famb + d_ramb,
          f_famb=gam8 fpa + gam7 fiq + gam6 fses +
             gam5 rses + beta2 f_ramb + d_famb;
   std d_ramb=psi11,
       d_famb=psi22,
       e_rea e_roa e_fea e_foa=theta:;
   cov d_ramb d_famb=psi12,
       rpa riq rses fpa fiq fses=cov:;
run;
```

Specify a name followed by a colon to represent a list of names formed by appending numbers to the specified name. For example, in the COV statement, the line

```
rpa riq rses fpa fiq fses=cov:;
```

is equivalent to

```
rpa riq rses fpa fiq fses=cov1-cov15;
```

The results from this analysis are as follows.

```
Peer Influences on Aspiration: Haller & Butterworth (1960)
          Joreskog-Sorbom (1988) analysis 1

                 The CALIS Procedure
Covariance Structure Analysis: Maximum Likelihood Estimation

Fit Function                                          0.0814
Goodness of Fit Index (GFI)                           0.9844
GFI Adjusted for Degrees of Freedom (AGFI)            0.9428
Root Mean Square Residual (RMR)                       0.0202
Parsimonious GFI (Mulaik, 1989)                       0.3281
Chi-Square                                           26.6972
Chi-Square DF                                             15
Pr > Chi-Square                                       0.0313
Independence Model Chi-Square                         872.00
Independence Model Chi-Square DF                          45
RMSEA Estimate                                        0.0488
RMSEA 90% Lower Confidence Limit                      0.0145
RMSEA 90% Upper Confidence Limit                      0.0783
ECVI Estimate                                         0.2959
ECVI 90% Lower Confidence Limit                       0.2823
ECVI 90% Upper Confidence Limit                       0.3721
Probability of Close Fit                              0.4876
Bentler's Comparative Fit Index                       0.9859
Normal Theory Reweighted LS Chi-Square               26.0113
Akaike's Information Criterion                       -3.3028
Bozdogan's (1987) CAIC                              -75.2437
Schwarz's Bayesian Criterion                        -60.2437
McDonald's (1989) Centrality                          0.9824
Bentler & Bonett's (1980) Non-normed Index            0.9576
Bentler & Bonett's (1980) NFI                         0.9694
James, Mulaik, & Brett (1982) Parsimonious NFI        0.3231
Z-Test of Wilson & Hilferty (1931)                    1.8625
Bollen (1986) Normed Index Rho1                       0.9082
Bollen (1988) Non-normed Index Delta2                 0.9864
Hoelter's (1983) Critical N                              309
```

Figure 14.18. Career Aspiration Data: J&S Analysis 1

Jöreskog and Sörbom (1988) present more detailed results from a second analysis in which two constraints are imposed:

- The coefficents connecting the latent ambition variables are equal.
- The covariance of the disturbances of the ambition variables is zero.

This analysis can be performed by changing the names beta1 and beta2 to beta and omitting the line from the COV statement for psi12:

```
title2 'Joreskog-Sorbom (1988) analysis 2';
proc calis data=aspire edf=328;
   lineqs     /* measurement model for aspiration */
          rea=lambda2 f_ramb + e_rea,
          roa=f_ramb + e_roa,
          fea=lambda3 f_famb + e_fea,
          foa=f_famb + e_foa,
             /* structural model of influences */
          f_ramb=gam1 rpa + gam2 riq + gam3 rses +
             gam4 fses + beta f_famb + d_ramb,
```

```
            f_famb=gam8 fpa + gam7 fiq + gam6 fses +
               gam5 rses + beta f_ramb + d_famb;
   std d_ramb=psi11,
       d_famb=psi22,
       e_rea e_roa e_fea e_foa=theta:;
   cov rpa riq rses fpa fiq fses=cov:;
run;
```

The results are displayed in Figure 14.19.

```
         Peer Influences on Aspiration: Haller & Butterworth (1960)
                    Joreskog-Sorbom (1988) analysis 2

                          The CALIS Procedure
        Covariance Structure Analysis: Maximum Likelihood Estimation

        Fit Function                                              0.0820
        Goodness of Fit Index (GFI)                               0.9843
        GFI Adjusted for Degrees of Freedom (AGFI)                0.9492
        Root Mean Square Residual (RMR)                           0.0203
        Parsimonious GFI (Mulaik, 1989)                           0.3718
        Chi-Square                                               26.8987
        Chi-Square DF                                                 17
        Pr > Chi-Square                                           0.0596
        Independence Model Chi-Square                             872.00
        Independence Model Chi-Square DF                              45
        RMSEA Estimate                                            0.0421
        RMSEA 90% Lower Confidence Limit                               .
        RMSEA 90% Upper Confidence Limit                          0.0710
        ECVI Estimate                                             0.2839
        ECVI 90% Lower Confidence Limit                                .
        ECVI 90% Upper Confidence Limit                           0.3592
        Probability of Close Fit                                  0.6367
        Bentler's Comparative Fit Index                           0.9880
        Normal Theory Reweighted LS Chi-Square                   26.1595
        Akaike's Information Criterion                           -7.1013
        Bozdogan's (1987) CAIC                                  -88.6343
        Schwarz's Bayesian Criterion                            -71.6343
        McDonald's (1989) Centrality                              0.9851
        Bentler & Bonett's (1980) Non-normed Index                0.9683
        Bentler & Bonett's (1980) NFI                             0.9692
        James, Mulaik, & Brett (1982) Parsimonious NFI            0.3661
        Z-Test of Wilson & Hilferty (1931)                        1.5599
        Bollen (1986) Normed Index Rho1                           0.9183
        Bollen (1988) Non-normed Index Delta2                     0.9884
        Hoelter's (1983) Critical N                                  338
```

Figure 14.19. Career Aspiration Data: J&S Analysis 2

```
        Peer Influences on Aspiration: Haller & Butterworth (1960)
                  Joreskog-Sorbom (1988) analysis 2

                          The CALIS Procedure
      Covariance Structure Analysis: Maximum Likelihood Estimation

          roa      =   1.0000 f_ramb   +  1.0000 e_roa
          rea      =   1.0610*f_ramb   +  1.0000 e_rea
          Std Err      0.0892 lambda2
          t Value     11.8923
          foa      =   1.0000 f_famb   +  1.0000 e_foa
          fea      =   1.0736*f_famb   +  1.0000 e_fea
          Std Err      0.0806 lambda3
          t Value     13.3150


        Peer Influences on Aspiration: Haller & Butterworth (1960)
                  Joreskog-Sorbom (1988) analysis 2

                          The CALIS Procedure
      Covariance Structure Analysis: Maximum Likelihood Estimation

   f_ramb  =    0.1801*f_famb   +  0.2540*riq      +  0.1637*rpa
   Std Err      0.0391 beta        0.0419 gam2        0.0387 gam1
   t Value      4.6031             6.0673             4.2274

        +  0.2211*rses     +  0.0773*fses     +  1.0000 d_ramb
           0.0419 gam3        0.0415 gam4
           5.2822             1.8626

   f_famb  =    0.1801*f_ramb   +  0.0684*rses     +  0.3306*fiq
   Std Err      0.0391 beta        0.0387 gam5        0.0412 gam7
   t Value      4.6031             1.7681             8.0331

        +  0.1520*fpa      +  0.2184*fses     +  1.0000 d_famb
           0.0364 gam8        0.0395 gam6
           4.1817             5.5320
```

```
          Peer Influences on Aspiration: Haller & Butterworth (1960)
                       Joreskog-Sorbom (1988) analysis 2

                              The CALIS Procedure
         Covariance Structure Analysis: Maximum Likelihood Estimation

                       Variances of Exogenous Variables

                                                  Standard
          Variable Parameter        Estimate         Error     t Value

          riq                        1.00000
          rpa                        1.00000
          rses                       1.00000
          fiq                        1.00000
          fpa                        1.00000
          fses                       1.00000
          e_rea     theta1           0.33764       0.05178        6.52
          e_roa     theta2           0.41205       0.05103        8.07
          e_fea     theta3           0.31337       0.04574        6.85
          e_foa     theta4           0.40381       0.04608        8.76
          d_ramb    psi11            0.28113       0.04640        6.06
          d_famb    psi22            0.22924       0.03889        5.89


                     Covariances Among Exogenous Variables

                                                       Standard
        Var1     Var2     Parameter       Estimate         Error     t Value

        riq      rpa      cov1             0.18390       0.05246        3.51
        riq      rses     cov3             0.22200       0.05110        4.34
        rpa      rses     cov2             0.04890       0.05493        0.89
        riq      fiq      cov8             0.33550       0.04641        7.23
        rpa      fiq      cov7             0.07820       0.05455        1.43
        rses     fiq      cov9             0.23020       0.05074        4.54
        riq      fpa      cov5             0.10210       0.05415        1.89
        rpa      fpa      cov4             0.11470       0.05412        2.12
        rses     fpa      cov6             0.09310       0.05438        1.71
        fiq      fpa      cov10            0.20870       0.05163        4.04
        riq      fses     cov12            0.18610       0.05209        3.57
        rpa      fses     cov11            0.01860       0.05510        0.34
        rses     fses     cov13            0.27070       0.04930        5.49
        fiq      fses     cov15            0.29500       0.04824        6.12
        fpa      fses     cov14           -0.04380       0.05476       -0.80
```

The difference between the chi-square values for the two preceding models is 26.8987 - 26.6972= 0.2015 with 2 degrees of freedom, which is far from significant. However, the chi-square test of the restricted model (analysis 2) against the alternative of a completely unrestricted covariance matrix yields a p-value of 0.0596, which indicates that the model may not be entirely satisfactory (p-values from these data are probably too small because of the dependence of the observations).

Loehlin (1987) points out that the models considered are unrealistic in at least two aspects. First, the variables of parental aspiration, intelligence, and socioeconomic status are assumed to be measured without error. Loehlin adds uncorrelated measurement errors to the model and assumes, for illustrative purposes, that the reliabilities of these variables are known to be 0.7, 0.8, and 0.9, respectively. In practice, these reliabilities would need to be obtained from a separate study of the same or a very similar population. If these constraints are omitted, the model is not identified. However, constraining parameters to a constant in an analysis of a correlation matrix may make the chi-square goodness-of-fit test inaccurate, so there is more reason to be skeptical of the *p*-values. Second, the error terms for the respondent's aspiration are assumed to be uncorrelated with the corresponding terms for his friend. Loehlin introduces a correlation between the two educational aspiration error terms and between the two occupational aspiration error terms. These additions produce the following path diagram for Loehlin's model 1.

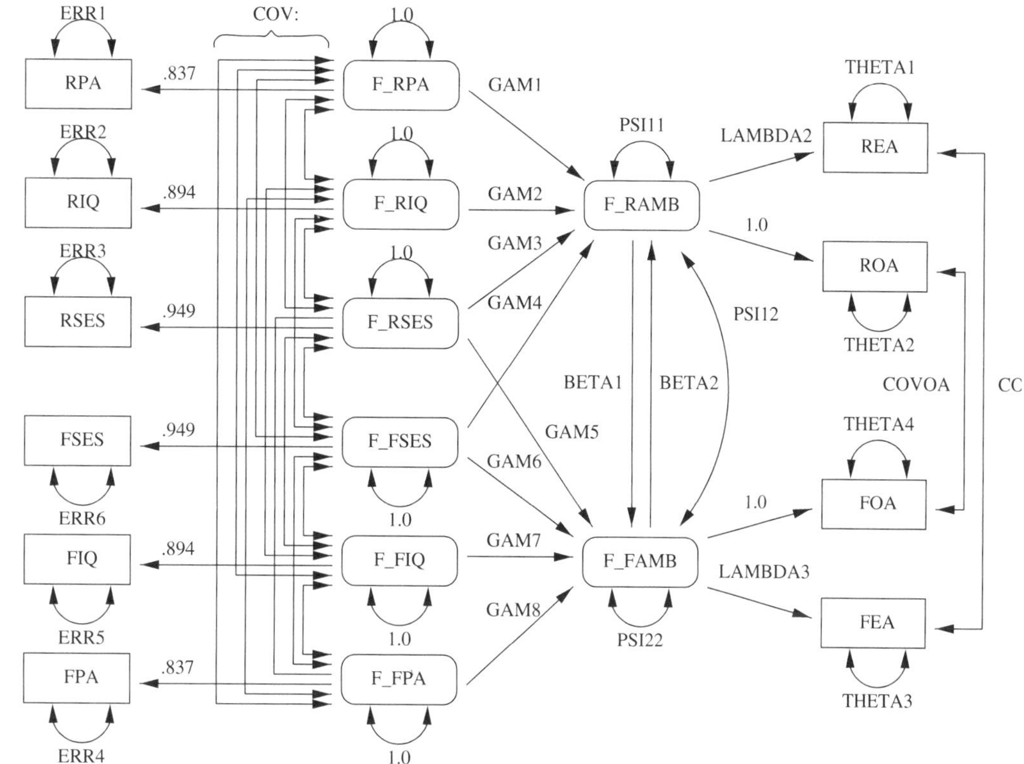

Figure 14.20. Path Diagram: Carrer Aspiration – Loehlin

The statements for fitting this model are as follows:

```
title2 'Loehlin (1987) analysis: Model 1';
proc calis data=aspire edf=328;
   lineqs    /* measurement model for aspiration */
          rea=lambda2 f_ramb + e_rea,
          roa=f_ramb + e_roa,
          fea=lambda3 f_famb + e_fea,
          foa=f_famb + e_foa,
          /* measurement model for intelligence and environment */
          rpa=.837 f_rpa + e_rpa,
          riq=.894 f_riq + e_riq,
          rses=.949 f_rses + e_rses,
          fpa=.837 f_fpa + e_fpa,
          fiq=.894 f_fiq + e_fiq,
          fses=.949 f_fses + e_fses,
```

```
              /* structural model of influences */
           f_ramb=gam1 f_rpa + gam2 f_riq + gam3 f_rses +
              gam4 f_fses + bet1 f_famb + d_ramb,
           f_famb=gam8 f_fpa + gam7 f_fiq + gam6 f_fses +
              gam5 f_rses + bet2 f_ramb + d_famb;
   std d_ramb=psi11,
       d_famb=psi22,
       f_rpa f_riq f_rses f_fpa f_fiq f_fses=1,
       e_rea e_roa e_fea e_foa=theta:,
       e_rpa e_riq e_rses e_fpa e_fiq e_fses=err:;
   cov d_ramb d_famb=psi12,
       e_rea e_fea=covea,
       e_roa e_foa=covoa,
       f_rpa f_riq f_rses f_fpa f_fiq f_fses=cov:;
run;
```

The results are displayed in Figure 14.21.

```
         Peer Influences on Aspiration: Haller & Butterworth (1960)
                    Loehlin (1987) analysis: Model 1

                          The CALIS Procedure
       Covariance Structure Analysis: Maximum Likelihood Estimation

       Fit Function                                              0.0366
       Goodness of Fit Index (GFI)                               0.9927
       GFI Adjusted for Degrees of Freedom (AGFI)                0.9692
       Root Mean Square Residual (RMR)                           0.0149
       Parsimonious GFI (Mulaik, 1989)                           0.2868
       Chi-Square                                               12.0132
       Chi-Square DF                                                 13
       Pr > Chi-Square                                           0.5266
       Independence Model Chi-Square                             872.00
       Independence Model Chi-Square DF                              45
       RMSEA Estimate                                            0.0000
       RMSEA 90% Lower Confidence Limit                               .
       RMSEA 90% Upper Confidence Limit                          0.0512
       ECVI Estimate                                             0.3016
       ECVI 90% Lower Confidence Limit                                .
       ECVI 90% Upper Confidence Limit                           0.3392
       Probability of Close Fit                                  0.9435
       Bentler's Comparative Fit Index                           1.0000
       Normal Theory Reweighted LS Chi-Square                   12.0168
       Akaike's Information Criterion                          -13.9868
       Bozdogan's (1987) CAIC                                  -76.3356
       Schwarz's Bayesian Criterion                            -63.3356
       McDonald's (1989) Centrality                              1.0015
       Bentler & Bonett's (1980) Non-normed Index                1.0041
       Bentler & Bonett's (1980) NFI                             0.9862
       James, Mulaik, & Brett (1982) Parsimonious NFI            0.2849
       Z-Test of Wilson & Hilferty (1931)                       -0.0679
       Bollen (1986) Normed Index Rho1                           0.9523
       Bollen (1988) Non-normed Index Delta2                     1.0011
       Hoelter's (1983) Critical N                                  612
```

Figure 14.21. Career Aspiration Data: Loehlin Model 1

```
          Peer Influences on Aspiration: Haller & Butterworth (1960)
                  Loehlin (1987) analysis: Model 1

                         The CALIS Procedure
      Covariance Structure Analysis: Maximum Likelihood Estimation

             riq      =   0.8940 f_riq    +  1.0000 e_riq
             rpa      =   0.8370 f_rpa    +  1.0000 e_rpa
             rses     =   0.9490 f_rses   +  1.0000 e_rses
             roa      =   1.0000 f_ramb   +  1.0000 e_roa
             rea      =   1.0840*f_ramb   +  1.0000 e_rea
             Std Err      0.0942 lambda2
             t Value     11.5105
             fiq      =   0.8940 f_fiq    +  1.0000 e_fiq
             fpa      =   0.8370 f_fpa    +  1.0000 e_fpa
             fses     =   0.9490 f_fses   +  1.0000 e_fses
             foa      =   1.0000 f_famb   +  1.0000 e_foa
             fea      =   1.1163*f_famb   +  1.0000 e_fea
             Std Err      0.0863 lambda3
             t Value     12.9394


          Peer Influences on Aspiration: Haller & Butterworth (1960)
                  Loehlin (1987) analysis: Model 1

                         The CALIS Procedure
      Covariance Structure Analysis: Maximum Likelihood Estimation

  f_ramb  =   0.1190*f_famb   +  0.1837*f_rpa    +  0.2800*f_riq
  Std Err     0.1140 bet1        0.0504 gam1        0.0614 gam2
  t Value     1.0440             3.6420             4.5618

       +  0.2262*f_rses   +  0.0870*f_fses   +  1.0000 d_ramb
          0.0522 gam3        0.0548 gam4
          4.3300             1.5884

  f_famb  =   0.1302*f_ramb   +  0.0633*f_rses   +  0.1688*f_fpa
  Std Err     0.1207 bet2        0.0522 gam5        0.0493 gam8
  t Value     1.0792             1.2124             3.4205

       +  0.3539*f_fiq    +  0.2154*f_fses   +  1.0000 d_famb
          0.0674 gam7        0.0512 gam6
          5.2497             4.2060
```

```
Peer Influences on Aspiration: Haller & Butterworth (1960)
             Loehlin (1987) analysis: Model 1

                   The CALIS Procedure
Covariance Structure Analysis: Maximum Likelihood Estimation

            Variances of Exogenous Variables

                                           Standard
Variable Parameter       Estimate            Error     t Value

f_rpa                     1.00000
f_riq                     1.00000
f_rses                    1.00000
f_fpa                     1.00000
f_fiq                     1.00000
f_fses                    1.00000
e_rea     theta1          0.32707          0.05452        6.00
e_roa     theta2          0.42307          0.05243        8.07
e_fea     theta3          0.28715          0.04804        5.98
e_foa     theta4          0.42240          0.04730        8.93
e_rpa     err1            0.29584          0.07774        3.81
e_riq     err2            0.20874          0.07832        2.67
e_rses    err3            0.09887          0.07803        1.27
e_fpa     err4            0.29987          0.07807        3.84
e_fiq     err5            0.19988          0.07674        2.60
e_fses    err6            0.10324          0.07824        1.32
d_ramb    psi11           0.25418          0.04469        5.69
d_famb    psi22           0.19698          0.03814        5.17


          Covariances Among Exogenous Variables

                                               Standard
Var1    Var2    Parameter         Estimate        Error     t Value

f_rpa   f_riq   cov1               0.24677      0.07519        3.28
f_rpa   f_rses  cov2               0.06184      0.06945        0.89
f_riq   f_rses  cov3               0.26351      0.06687        3.94
f_rpa   f_fpa   cov4               0.15789      0.07873        2.01
f_riq   f_fpa   cov5               0.13085      0.07418        1.76
f_rses  f_fpa   cov6               0.11517      0.06978        1.65
f_rpa   f_fiq   cov7               0.10853      0.07362        1.47
f_riq   f_fiq   cov8               0.42476      0.07219        5.88
f_rses  f_fiq   cov9               0.27250      0.06660        4.09
f_fpa   f_fiq   cov10              0.27867      0.07530        3.70
f_rpa   f_fses  cov11              0.02383      0.06952        0.34
f_riq   f_fses  cov12              0.22135      0.06648        3.33
f_rses  f_fses  cov13              0.30156      0.06359        4.74
f_fpa   f_fses  cov14             -0.05623      0.06971       -0.81
f_fiq   f_fses  cov15              0.34922      0.06771        5.16
e_rea   e_fea   covea              0.02308      0.03139        0.74
e_roa   e_foa   covoa              0.11206      0.03258        3.44
d_ramb  d_famb  psi12             -0.00935      0.05010       -0.19
```

Since the p-value for the chi-square test is 0.5266, this model clearly cannot be rejected. However, Schwarz's Bayesian Criterion for this model (SBC = -63.3356) is somewhat larger than for Jöreskog and Sörbom's (1988) analysis 2 (SBC =-71.6343), suggesting that a more parsimonious model would be desirable.

Since it is assumed that the same model applies to all the boys in the sample, the path diagram should be symmetric with respect to the respondent and friend. In particular, the corresponding coefficients should be equal. By imposing equality constraints on the 15 pairs of corresponding coefficents, this example obtains Loehlin's model 2. The LINEQS model is as follows, where an OUTRAM= data set is created to facilitate subsequent hypothesis tests:

```
title2 'Loehlin (1987) analysis: Model 2';
proc calis data=aspire edf=328 outram=ram2;
   lineqs    /* measurement model for aspiration */
          rea=lambda f_ramb + e_rea,            /* 1 ec! */
          roa=f_ramb + e_roa,
          fea=lambda f_famb + e_fea,
          foa=f_famb + e_foa,
          /* measurement model for intelligence and environment */
          rpa=.837 f_rpa + e_rpa,
          riq=.894 f_riq + e_riq,
          rses=.949 f_rses + e_rses,
          fpa=.837 f_fpa + e_fpa,
          fiq=.894 f_fiq + e_fiq,
          fses=.949 f_fses + e_fses,
             /* structural model of influences */     /* 5 ec! */
          f_ramb=gam1 f_rpa + gam2 f_riq + gam3 f_rses +
             gam4 f_fses + beta f_famb + d_ramb,
          f_famb=gam1 f_fpa + gam2 f_fiq + gam3 f_fses +
             gam4 f_rses + beta f_ramb + d_famb;
   std d_ramb=psi,                                 /* 1 ec! */
       d_famb=psi,
       f_rpa f_riq f_rses f_fpa f_fiq f_fses=1,
       e_rea e_fea=thetaea thetaea,                /* 2 ec! */
       e_roa e_foa=thetaoa thetaoa,
       e_rpa e_fpa=errpa1 errpa2,
       e_riq e_fiq=erriq1 erriq2,
       e_rses e_fses=errses1 errses2;
   cov d_ramb d_famb=psi12,
       e_rea e_fea=covea,
       e_roa e_foa = covoa,
       f_rpa f_riq f_rses=cov1-cov3,               /* 3 ec! */
       f_fpa f_fiq f_fses=cov1-cov3,
       f_rpa f_riq f_rses * f_fpa f_fiq f_fses =   /* 3 ec! */
          cov4 cov5 cov6
          cov5 cov7 cov8
          cov6 cov8 cov9;
run;
```

The results are displayed in Figure 14.22.

```
   Peer Influences on Aspiration: Haller & Butterworth (1960)
                Loehlin (1987) analysis: Model 2

                      The CALIS Procedure
 Covariance Structure Analysis: Maximum Likelihood Estimation

 Fit Function                                              0.0581
 Goodness of Fit Index (GFI)                               0.9884
 GFI Adjusted for Degrees of Freedom (AGFI)                0.9772
 Root Mean Square Residual (RMR)                           0.0276
 Parsimonious GFI (Mulaik, 1989)                           0.6150
 Chi-Square                                               19.0697
 Chi-Square DF                                                 28
 Pr > Chi-Square                                           0.8960
 Independence Model Chi-Square                             872.00
 Independence Model Chi-Square DF                              45
 RMSEA Estimate                                            0.0000
 RMSEA 90% Lower Confidence Limit                               .
 RMSEA 90% Upper Confidence Limit                          0.0194
 ECVI Estimate                                             0.2285
 ECVI 90% Lower Confidence Limit                                .
 ECVI 90% Upper Confidence Limit                           0.2664
 Probability of Close Fit                                  0.9996
 Bentler's Comparative Fit Index                           1.0000
 Normal Theory Reweighted LS Chi-Square                   19.2372
 Akaike's Information Criterion                          -36.9303
 Bozdogan's (1987) CAIC                                 -171.2200
 Schwarz's Bayesian Criterion                           -143.2200
 McDonald's (1989) Centrality                              1.0137
 Bentler & Bonett's (1980) Non-normed Index                1.0174
 Bentler & Bonett's (1980) NFI                             0.9781
 James, Mulaik, & Brett (1982) Parsimonious NFI            0.6086
 Z-Test of Wilson & Hilferty (1931)                       -1.2599
 Bollen (1986) Normed Index Rho1                           0.9649
 Bollen (1988) Non-normed Index Delta2                     1.0106
 Hoelter's (1983) Critical N                                  713
```

Figure 14.22. Career Aspiration Data: Loehlin Model 2

```
        Peer Influences on Aspiration: Haller & Butterworth (1960)
                   Loehlin (1987) analysis: Model 2

                          The CALIS Procedure
      Covariance Structure Analysis: Maximum Likelihood Estimation

           riq      =   0.8940 f_riq     +  1.0000 e_riq
           rpa      =   0.8370 f_rpa     +  1.0000 e_rpa
           rses     =   0.9490 f_rses    +  1.0000 e_rses
           roa      =   1.0000 f_ramb    +  1.0000 e_roa
           rea      =   1.1007*f_ramb    +  1.0000 e_rea
           Std Err      0.0684 lambda
           t Value     16.0879
           fiq      =   0.8940 f_fiq     +  1.0000 e_fiq
           fpa      =   0.8370 f_fpa     +  1.0000 e_fpa
           fses     =   0.9490 f_fses    +  1.0000 e_fses
           foa      =   1.0000 f_famb    +  1.0000 e_foa
           fea      =   1.1007*f_famb    +  1.0000 e_fea
           Std Err      0.0684 lambda
           t Value     16.0879



        Peer Influences on Aspiration: Haller & Butterworth (1960)
                   Loehlin (1987) analysis: Model 2

                          The CALIS Procedure
      Covariance Structure Analysis: Maximum Likelihood Estimation

  f_ramb  =    0.1158*f_famb   +  0.1758*f_rpa    +  0.3223*f_riq
  Std Err      0.0839 beta        0.0351 gam1        0.0470 gam2
  t Value      1.3801             5.0130             6.8557

       +  0.2227*f_rses   +  0.0756*f_fses   +  1.0000 d_ramb
          0.0363 gam3        0.0375 gam4
          6.1373             2.0170

  f_famb  =    0.1158*f_ramb   +  0.0756*f_rses   +  0.1758*f_fpa
  Std Err      0.0839 beta        0.0375 gam4        0.0351 gam1
  t Value      1.3801             2.0170             5.0130

       +  0.3223*f_fiq    +  0.2227*f_fses   +  1.0000 d_famb
          0.0470 gam2        0.0363 gam3
          6.8557             6.1373
```

```
            Peer Influences on Aspiration: Haller & Butterworth (1960)
                         Loehlin (1987) analysis: Model 2

                               The CALIS Procedure
          Covariance Structure Analysis: Maximum Likelihood Estimation

                         Variances of Exogenous Variables

                                                    Standard
            Variable Parameter       Estimate          Error     t Value

            f_rpa                     1.00000
            f_riq                     1.00000
            f_rses                    1.00000
            f_fpa                     1.00000
            f_fiq                     1.00000
            f_fses                    1.00000
            e_rea     thetaea         0.30662        0.03726        8.23
            e_roa     thetaoa         0.42295        0.03651       11.58
            e_fea     thetaea         0.30662        0.03726        8.23
            e_foa     thetaoa         0.42295        0.03651       11.58
            e_rpa     errpa1          0.30758        0.07511        4.09
            e_riq     erriq1          0.26656        0.07389        3.61
            e_rses    errses1         0.11467        0.07267        1.58
            e_fpa     errpa2          0.28834        0.07369        3.91
            e_fiq     erriq2          0.15573        0.06700        2.32
            e_fses    errses2         0.08814        0.07089        1.24
            d_ramb    psi             0.22456        0.02971        7.56
            d_famb    psi             0.22456        0.02971        7.56


                       Covariances Among Exogenous Variables

                                                         Standard
          Var1    Var2    Parameter        Estimate         Error     t Value

          f_rpa   f_riq   cov1              0.26470       0.05442        4.86
          f_rpa   f_rses  cov2              0.00176       0.04996        0.04
          f_riq   f_rses  cov3              0.31129       0.05057        6.16
          f_rpa   f_fpa   cov4              0.15784       0.07872        2.01
          f_riq   f_fpa   cov5              0.11837       0.05447        2.17
          f_rses  f_fpa   cov6              0.06910       0.04996        1.38
          f_rpa   f_fiq   cov5              0.11837       0.05447        2.17
          f_riq   f_fiq   cov7              0.43061       0.07258        5.93
          f_rses  f_fiq   cov8              0.24967       0.05060        4.93
          f_fpa   f_fiq   cov1              0.26470       0.05442        4.86
          f_rpa   f_fses  cov6              0.06910       0.04996        1.38
          f_riq   f_fses  cov8              0.24967       0.05060        4.93
          f_rses  f_fses  cov9              0.30190       0.06362        4.75
          f_fpa   f_fses  cov2              0.00176       0.04996        0.04
          f_fiq   f_fses  cov3              0.31129       0.05057        6.16
          e_rea   e_fea   covea             0.02160       0.03144        0.69
          e_roa   e_foa   covoa             0.11208       0.03257        3.44
          d_ramb  d_famb  psi12            -0.00344       0.04931       -0.07
```

The test of Loehlin's model 2 against model 1 yields a chi-square of 19.0697 - 12.0132 = 7.0565 with 15 degrees of freedom, which is clearly not significant. Schwarz's Bayesizn Criterion (SBC) is also much lower for model 2 (-143.2200) than model 1 (-63.3356). Hence, model 2 seems preferable on both substantive and statistical grounds.

A question of substantive interest is whether the friend's socioeconomic status (SES) has a significant direct influence on a boy's ambition. This can be addressed by omitting the paths from f_fses to f_ramb and from f_rses to f_famb designated by the parameter name gam4, yielding Loehlin's model 3:

```
title2 'Loehlin (1987) analysis: Model 3';
data ram3(type=ram);
   set ram2;
   if _name_='gam4' then
      do;
         _name_=' ';
         _estim_=0;
      end;
run;
proc calis data=aspire edf=328 inram=ram3;
run;
```

The output is displayed in Figure 14.23.

```
           Peer Influences on Aspiration: Haller & Butterworth (1960)
                      Loehlin (1987) analysis: Model 3

                            The CALIS Procedure
          Covariance Structure Analysis: Maximum Likelihood Estimation

          Fit Function                                              0.0702
          Goodness of Fit Index (GFI)                               0.9858
          GFI Adjusted for Degrees of Freedom (AGFI)                0.9731
          Root Mean Square Residual (RMR)                           0.0304
          Parsimonious GFI (Mulaik, 1989)                           0.6353
          Chi-Square                                               23.0365
          Chi-Square DF                                                 29
          Pr > Chi-Square                                           0.7749
          Independence Model Chi-Square                             872.00
          Independence Model Chi-Square DF                              45
          RMSEA Estimate                                            0.0000
          RMSEA 90% Lower Confidence Limit                               .
          RMSEA 90% Upper Confidence Limit                          0.0295
          ECVI Estimate                                             0.2343
          ECVI 90% Lower Confidence Limit                                .
          ECVI 90% Upper Confidence Limit                           0.2780
          Probability of Close Fit                                  0.9984
          Bentler's Comparative Fit Index                           1.0000
          Normal Theory Reweighted LS Chi-Square                   23.5027
          Akaike's Information Criterion                          -34.9635
          Bozdogan's (1987) CAIC                                 -174.0492
          Schwarz's Bayesian Criterion                           -145.0492
          McDonald's (1989) Centrality                              1.0091
          Bentler & Bonett's (1980) Non-normed Index                1.0112
          Bentler & Bonett's (1980) NFI                             0.9736
          James, Mulaik, & Brett (1982) Parsimonious NFI            0.6274
          Z-Test of Wilson & Hilferty (1931)                       -0.7563
          Bollen (1986) Normed Index Rho1                           0.9590
          Bollen (1988) Non-normed Index Delta2                     1.0071
          Hoelter's (1983) Critical N                                  607
```

Figure 14.23. Career Aspiration Data: Loehlin Model 3

The chi-square value for testing model 3 versus model 2 is 23.0365 - 19.0697 = 3.9668 with 1 degree of freedom and a p-value of 0.0464. Although the parameter is of marginal significance, the estimate in model 2 (0.0756) is small compared to the other coefficients, and SBC indicates that model 3 is preferable to model 2.

Another important question is whether the reciprocal influences between the respondent's and friend's ambitions are needed in the model. To test whether these paths are zero, set the parameter beta for the paths linking f_ramb and f_famb to zero to obtain Loehlin's model 4:

```
title2 'Loehlin (1987) analysis: Model 4';
data ram4(type=ram);
   set ram2;
   if _name_='beta' then
      do;
         _name_=' ';
         _estim_=0;
      end;
run;

proc calis data=aspire edf=328 inram=ram4;
run;
```

The output is displayed in Figure 14.24.

```
        Peer Influences on Aspiration: Haller & Butterworth (1960)
                     Loehlin (1987) analysis: Model 4

                          The CALIS Procedure
   Covariance Structure Analysis: Maximum Likelihood Estimation

   Fit Function                                                0.0640
   Goodness of Fit Index (GFI)                                 0.9873
   GFI Adjusted for Degrees of Freedom (AGFI)                  0.9760
   Root Mean Square Residual (RMR)                             0.0304
   Parsimonious GFI (Mulaik, 1989)                             0.6363
   Chi-Square                                                 20.9981
   Chi-Square DF                                                   29
   Pr > Chi-Square                                             0.8592
   Independence Model Chi-Square                               872.00
   Independence Model Chi-Square DF                                45
   RMSEA Estimate                                              0.0000
   RMSEA 90% Lower Confidence Limit                                 .
   RMSEA 90% Upper Confidence Limit                            0.0234
   ECVI Estimate                                               0.2281
   ECVI 90% Lower Confidence Limit                                  .
   ECVI 90% Upper Confidence Limit                             0.2685
   Probability of Close Fit                                    0.9994
   Bentler's Comparative Fit Index                             1.0000
   Normal Theory Reweighted LS Chi-Square                     20.8040
   Akaike's Information Criterion                            -37.0019
   Bozdogan's (1987) CAIC                                   -176.0876
   Schwarz's Bayesian Criterion                             -147.0876
   McDonald's (1989) Centrality                                1.0122
   Bentler & Bonett's (1980) Non-normed Index                  1.0150
   Bentler & Bonett's (1980) NFI                               0.9759
   James, Mulaik, & Brett (1982) Parsimonious NFI              0.6289
   Z-Test of Wilson & Hilferty (1931)                         -1.0780
   Bollen (1986) Normed Index Rho1                             0.9626
   Bollen (1988) Non-normed Index Delta2                       1.0095
   Hoelter's (1983) Critical N                                    666
```

Figure 14.24. Career Aspiration Data: Loehlin Model 4

```
        Peer Influences on Aspiration: Haller & Butterworth (1960)
                   Loehlin (1987) analysis: Model 4

                          The CALIS Procedure
       Covariance Structure Analysis: Maximum Likelihood Estimation

             riq      =   0.8940 f_riq    +  1.0000 e_riq
             rpa      =   0.8370 f_rpa    +  1.0000 e_rpa
             rses     =   0.9490 f_rses   +  1.0000 e_rses
             roa      =   1.0000 f_ramb   +  1.0000 e_roa
             rea      =   1.1051*f_ramb   +  1.0000 e_rea
             Std Err      0.0680 lambda
             t Value     16.2416
             fiq      =   0.8940 f_fiq    +  1.0000 e_fiq
             fpa      =   0.8370 f_fpa    +  1.0000 e_fpa
             fses     =   0.9490 f_fses   +  1.0000 e_fses
             foa      =   1.0000 f_famb   +  1.0000 e_foa
             fea      =   1.1051*f_famb   +  1.0000 e_fea
             Std Err      0.0680 lambda
             t Value     16.2416


        Peer Influences on Aspiration: Haller & Butterworth (1960)
                   Loehlin (1987) analysis: Model 4

                          The CALIS Procedure
       Covariance Structure Analysis: Maximum Likelihood Estimation

    f_ramb  =        0 f_famb   +  0.1776*f_rpa    +  0.3486*f_riq
    Std Err                        0.0361 gam1        0.0463 gam2
    t Value                        4.9195             7.5362

         +  0.2383*f_rses   +  0.1081*f_fses   +  1.0000 d_ramb
            0.0355 gam3        0.0299 gam4
            6.7158             3.6134

    f_famb  =        0 f_ramb   +  0.1081*f_rses   +  0.1776*f_fpa
    Std Err                        0.0299 gam4        0.0361 gam1
    t Value                        3.6134             4.9195

         +  0.3486*f_fiq    +  0.2383*f_fses   +  1.0000 d_famb
            0.0463 gam2        0.0355 gam3
            7.5362             6.7158
```

```
            Peer Influences on Aspiration: Haller & Butterworth (1960)
                         Loehlin (1987) analysis: Model 4

                               The CALIS Procedure
           Covariance Structure Analysis: Maximum Likelihood Estimation

                        Variances of Exogenous Variables

                                                     Standard
            Variable Parameter      Estimate            Error    t Value

            f_rpa                    1.00000
            f_riq                    1.00000
            f_rses                   1.00000
            f_fpa                    1.00000
            f_fiq                    1.00000
            f_fses                   1.00000
            e_rea    thetaea         0.30502          0.03728       8.18
            e_roa    thetaoa         0.42429          0.03645      11.64
            e_fea    thetaea         0.30502          0.03728       8.18
            e_foa    thetaoa         0.42429          0.03645      11.64
            e_rpa    errpa1          0.31354          0.07543       4.16
            e_riq    erriq1          0.29611          0.07299       4.06
            e_rses   errses1         0.12320          0.07273       1.69
            e_fpa    errpa2          0.29051          0.07374       3.94
            e_fiq    erriq2          0.18181          0.06611       2.75
            e_fses   errses2         0.09873          0.07109       1.39
            d_ramb   psi             0.22738          0.03140       7.24
            d_famb   psi             0.22738          0.03140       7.24
```

```
            Peer Influences on Aspiration: Haller & Butterworth (1960)
                         Loehlin (1987) analysis: Model 4

                               The CALIS Procedure
           Covariance Structure Analysis: Maximum Likelihood Estimation

                      Covariances Among Exogenous Variables

                                                        Standard
          Var1   Var2   Parameter      Estimate            Error    t Value

          f_rpa  f_riq  cov1            0.27241          0.05520       4.94
          f_rpa  f_rses cov2            0.00476          0.05032       0.09
          f_riq  f_rses cov3            0.32463          0.05089       6.38
          f_rpa  f_fpa  cov4            0.16949          0.07863       2.16
          f_riq  f_fpa  cov5            0.13539          0.05407       2.50
          f_rses f_fpa  cov6            0.07362          0.05027       1.46
          f_rpa  f_fiq  cov5            0.13539          0.05407       2.50
          f_riq  f_fiq  cov7            0.46893          0.06980       6.72
          f_rses f_fiq  cov8            0.26289          0.05093       5.16
          f_fpa  f_fiq  cov1            0.27241          0.05520       4.94
          f_rpa  f_fses cov6            0.07362          0.05027       1.46
          f_riq  f_fses cov8            0.26289          0.05093       5.16
          f_rses f_fses cov9            0.30880          0.06409       4.82
          f_fpa  f_fses cov2            0.00476          0.05032       0.09
          f_fiq  f_fses cov3            0.32463          0.05089       6.38
          e_rea  e_fea  covea           0.02127          0.03150       0.68
          e_roa  e_foa  covoa           0.11245          0.03258       3.45
          d_ramb d_famb psi12           0.05479          0.02699       2.03
```

The chi-square value for testing model 4 versus model 2 is 20.9981 - 19.0697 = 1.9284 with 1 degree of freedom and a *p*-value of 0.1649. Hence, there is little evidence of reciprocal influence.

Loehlin's model 2 has not only the direct paths connecting the latent ambition variables f_ramb and f_famb but also a covariance between the disturbance terms d_ramb and d_famb to allow for other variables omitted from the model that might jointly influence the respondent and his friend. To test the hypothesis that this covariance is zero, set the parameter psi12 to zero, yielding Loehlin's model 5:

```
title2 'Loehlin (1987) analysis: Model 5';
data ram5(type=ram);
   set ram2;
   if _name_='psi12' then
      do;
         _name_=' ';
         _estim_=0;
      end;
run;

proc calis data=aspire edf=328 inram=ram5;
run;
```

The output is displayed in Figure 14.25.

```
          Peer Influences on Aspiration: Haller & Butterworth (1960)
                       Loehlin (1987) analysis: Model 5

                             The CALIS Procedure
         Covariance Structure Analysis: Maximum Likelihood Estimation

         Fit Function                                              0.0582
         Goodness of Fit Index (GFI)                               0.9884
         GFI Adjusted for Degrees of Freedom (AGFI)                0.9780
         Root Mean Square Residual (RMR)                           0.0276
         Parsimonious GFI (Mulaik, 1989)                           0.6370
         Chi-Square                                               19.0745
         Chi-Square DF                                                 29
         Pr > Chi-Square                                           0.9194
         Independence Model Chi-Square                             872.00
         Independence Model Chi-Square DF                              45
         RMSEA Estimate                                            0.0000
         RMSEA 90% Lower Confidence Limit                               .
         RMSEA 90% Upper Confidence Limit                          0.0152
         ECVI Estimate                                             0.2222
         ECVI 90% Lower Confidence Limit                                .
         ECVI 90% Upper Confidence Limit                           0.2592
         Probability of Close Fit                                  0.9998
         Bentler's Comparative Fit Index                           1.0000
         Normal Theory Reweighted LS Chi-Square                   19.2269
         Akaike's Information Criterion                          -38.9255
         Bozdogan's (1987) CAIC                                 -178.0111
         Schwarz's Bayesian Criterion                           -149.0111
         McDonald's (1989) Centrality                              1.0152
         Bentler & Bonett's (1980) Non-normed Index                1.0186
         Bentler & Bonett's (1980) NFI                             0.9781
         James, Mulaik, & Brett (1982) Parsimonious NFI            0.6303
         Z-Test of Wilson & Hilferty (1931)                       -1.4014
         Bollen (1986) Normed Index Rho1                           0.9661
         Bollen (1988) Non-normed Index Delta2                     1.0118
         Hoelter's (1983) Critical N                                  733
```

Figure 14.25. Career Aspiration Data: Loehlin Model 5

```
        Peer Influences on Aspiration: Haller & Butterworth (1960)
                    Loehlin (1987) analysis: Model 5

                          The CALIS Procedure
       Covariance Structure Analysis: Maximum Likelihood Estimation

             riq      =   0.8940 f_riq    +  1.0000 e_riq
             rpa      =   0.8370 f_rpa    +  1.0000 e_rpa
             rses     =   0.9490 f_rses   +  1.0000 e_rses
             roa      =   1.0000 f_ramb   +  1.0000 e_roa
             rea      =   1.1009*f_ramb   +  1.0000 e_rea
             Std Err      0.0684 lambda
             t Value     16.1041
             fiq      =   0.8940 f_fiq    +  1.0000 e_fiq
             fpa      =   0.8370 f_fpa    +  1.0000 e_fpa
             fses     =   0.9490 f_fses   +  1.0000 e_fses
             foa      =   1.0000 f_famb   +  1.0000 e_foa
             fea      =   1.1009*f_famb   +  1.0000 e_fea
             Std Err      0.0684 lambda
             t Value     16.1041


        Peer Influences on Aspiration: Haller & Butterworth (1960)
                    Loehlin (1987) analysis: Model 5

                          The CALIS Procedure
       Covariance Structure Analysis: Maximum Likelihood Estimation

   f_ramb  =    0.1107*f_famb   +  0.1762*f_rpa    +  0.3235*f_riq
   Std Err      0.0428 beta        0.0350 gam1        0.0435 gam2
   t Value      2.5854             5.0308             7.4435

        +  0.2233*f_rses   +  0.0770*f_fses   +  1.0000 d_ramb
           0.0353 gam3        0.0323 gam4
           6.3215             2.3870

   f_famb  =    0.1107*f_ramb   +  0.0770*f_rses   +  0.1762*f_fpa
   Std Err      0.0428 beta        0.0323 gam4        0.0350 gam1
   t Value      2.5854             2.3870             5.0308

        +  0.3235*f_fiq    +  0.2233*f_fses   +  1.0000 d_famb
           0.0435 gam2        0.0353 gam3
           7.4435             6.3215
```

```
     Peer Influences on Aspiration: Haller & Butterworth (1960)
                  Loehlin (1987) analysis: Model 5

                          The CALIS Procedure
    Covariance Structure Analysis: Maximum Likelihood Estimation

                  Variances of Exogenous Variables

                                                  Standard
     Variable Parameter        Estimate              Error     t Value

     f_rpa                      1.00000
     f_riq                      1.00000
     f_rses                     1.00000
     f_fpa                      1.00000
     f_fiq                      1.00000
     f_fses                     1.00000
     e_rea      thetaea         0.30645            0.03721        8.24
     e_roa      thetaoa         0.42304            0.03650       11.59
     e_fea      thetaea         0.30645            0.03721        8.24
     e_foa      thetaoa         0.42304            0.03650       11.59
     e_rpa      errpa1          0.30781            0.07510        4.10
     e_riq      erriq1          0.26748            0.07295        3.67
     e_rses     errses1         0.11477            0.07265        1.58
     e_fpa      errpa2          0.28837            0.07366        3.91
     e_fiq      erriq2          0.15653            0.06614        2.37
     e_fses     errses2         0.08832            0.07088        1.25
     d_ramb     psi             0.22453            0.02973        7.55
     d_famb     psi             0.22453            0.02973        7.55


                 Covariances Among Exogenous Variables

                                                       Standard
   Var1     Var2     Parameter         Estimate           Error     t Value

   f_rpa   f_riq   cov1                 0.26494         0.05436        4.87
   f_rpa   f_rses  cov2                 0.00185         0.04995        0.04
   f_riq   f_rses  cov3                 0.31164         0.05039        6.18
   f_rpa   f_fpa   cov4                 0.15828         0.07846        2.02
   f_riq   f_fpa   cov5                 0.11895         0.05383        2.21
   f_rses  f_fpa   cov6                 0.06924         0.04993        1.39
   f_rpa   f_fiq   cov5                 0.11895         0.05383        2.21
   f_riq   f_fiq   cov7                 0.43180         0.07084        6.10
   f_rses  f_fiq   cov8                 0.25004         0.05039        4.96
   f_fpa   f_fiq   cov1                 0.26494         0.05436        4.87
   f_rpa   f_fses  cov6                 0.06924         0.04993        1.39
   f_riq   f_fses  cov8                 0.25004         0.05039        4.96
   f_rses  f_fses  cov9                 0.30203         0.06360        4.75
   f_fpa   f_fses  cov2                 0.00185         0.04995        0.04
   f_fiq   f_fses  cov3                 0.31164         0.05039        6.18
   e_rea   e_fea   covea                0.02120         0.03094        0.69
   e_roa   e_foa   covoa                0.11197         0.03254        3.44
   d_ramb  d_famb                             0
```

The chi-square value for testing model 5 versus model 2 is 19.0745 - 19.0697 = 0.0048 with 1 degree of freedom. Omitting the covariance between the disturbance terms, therefore, causes hardly any deterioration in the fit of the model.

These data fail to provide evidence of direct reciprocal influence between the respondent's and friend's ambitions or of a covariance between the disturbance terms when these hypotheses are considered separately. Notice, however, that the covariance psi12 between the disturbance terms increases from -0.003344 for model 2 to

0.05479 for model 4. Before you conclude that all of these paths can be omitted from the model, it is important to test both hypotheses together by setting both beta and psi12 to zero as in Loehlin's model 7:

```
title2 'Loehlin (1987) analysis: Model 7';
data ram7(type=ram);
   set ram2;
   if _name_='psi12'|_name_='beta' then
      do;
         _name_=' ';
         _estim_=0;
      end;
run;

proc calis data=aspire edf=328 inram=ram7;
run;
```

The relevant output is displayed in Figure 14.26.

```
       Peer Influences on Aspiration: Haller & Butterworth (1960)
                 Loehlin (1987) analysis: Model 7

                       The CALIS Procedure
     Covariance Structure Analysis: Maximum Likelihood Estimation

     Fit Function                                            0.0773
     Goodness of Fit Index (GFI)                             0.9846
     GFI Adjusted for Degrees of Freedom (AGFI)              0.9718
     Root Mean Square Residual (RMR)                         0.0363
     Parsimonious GFI (Mulaik, 1989)                         0.6564
     Chi-Square                                             25.3466
     Chi-Square DF                                               30
     Pr > Chi-Square                                         0.7080
     Independence Model Chi-Square                           872.00
     Independence Model Chi-Square DF                            45
     RMSEA Estimate                                          0.0000
     RMSEA 90% Lower Confidence Limit                             .
     RMSEA 90% Upper Confidence Limit                        0.0326
     ECVI Estimate                                           0.2350
     ECVI 90% Lower Confidence Limit                              .
     ECVI 90% Upper Confidence Limit                         0.2815
     Probability of Close Fit                                0.9975
     Bentler's Comparative Fit Index                         1.0000
     Normal Theory Reweighted LS Chi-Square                 25.1291
     Akaike's Information Criterion                        -34.6534
     Bozdogan's (1987) CAIC                               -178.5351
     Schwarz's Bayesian Criterion                         -148.5351
     McDonald's (1989) Centrality                            1.0071
     Bentler & Bonett's (1980) Non-normed Index              1.0084
     Bentler & Bonett's (1980) NFI                           0.9709
     James, Mulaik, & Brett (1982) Parsimonious NFI          0.6473
     Z-Test of Wilson & Hilferty (1931)                     -0.5487
     Bollen (1986) Normed Index Rho1                         0.9564
     Bollen (1988) Non-normed Index Delta2                   1.0055
     Hoelter's (1983) Critical N                                568
```

Figure 14.26. Career Aspiration Data: Loehlin Model 7

```
        Peer Influences on Aspiration: Haller & Butterworth (1960)
                    Loehlin (1987) analysis: Model 7

                          The CALIS Procedure
      Covariance Structure Analysis: Maximum Likelihood Estimation

             riq      =   0.8940 f_riq    +  1.0000 e_riq
             rpa      =   0.8370 f_rpa    +  1.0000 e_rpa
             rses     =   0.9490 f_rses   +  1.0000 e_rses
             roa      =   1.0000 f_ramb   +  1.0000 e_roa
             rea      =   1.1037*f_ramb   +  1.0000 e_rea
             Std Err      0.0678 lambda
             t Value     16.2701
             fiq      =   0.8940 f_fiq    +  1.0000 e_fiq
             fpa      =   0.8370 f_fpa    +  1.0000 e_fpa
             fses     =   0.9490 f_fses   +  1.0000 e_fses
             foa      =   1.0000 f_famb   +  1.0000 e_foa
             fea      =   1.1037*f_famb   +  1.0000 e_fea
             Std Err      0.0678 lambda
             t Value     16.2701



        Peer Influences on Aspiration: Haller & Butterworth (1960)
                    Loehlin (1987) analysis: Model 7

                          The CALIS Procedure
      Covariance Structure Analysis: Maximum Likelihood Estimation

  f_ramb  =        0 f_famb   +  0.1765*f_rpa    +  0.3573*f_riq
  Std Err                        0.0360 gam1        0.0461 gam2
  t Value                        4.8981             7.7520

       +  0.2419*f_rses   +  0.1109*f_fses   +  1.0000 d_ramb
          0.0363 gam3        0.0306 gam4
          6.6671             3.6280

  f_famb  =        0 f_ramb   +  0.1109*f_rses   +  0.1765*f_fpa
  Std Err                        0.0306 gam4        0.0360 gam1
  t Value                        3.6280             4.8981

       +  0.3573*f_fiq    +  0.2419*f_fses   +  1.0000 d_famb
          0.0461 gam2        0.0363 gam3
          7.7520             6.6671
```

```
Peer Influences on Aspiration: Haller & Butterworth (1960)
          Loehlin (1987) analysis: Model 7

                The CALIS Procedure
Covariance Structure Analysis: Maximum Likelihood Estimation

          Variances of Exogenous Variables

                                          Standard
Variable Parameter      Estimate             Error    t Value

f_rpa                    1.00000
f_riq                    1.00000
f_rses                   1.00000
f_fpa                    1.00000
f_fiq                    1.00000
f_fses                   1.00000
e_rea    thetaea         0.31633           0.03648       8.67
e_roa    thetaoa         0.42656           0.03610      11.82
e_fea    thetaea         0.31633           0.03648       8.67
e_foa    thetaoa         0.42656           0.03610      11.82
e_rpa    errpa1          0.31329           0.07538       4.16
e_riq    erriq1          0.30776           0.07307       4.21
e_rses   errses1         0.14303           0.07313       1.96
e_fpa    errpa2          0.29286           0.07389       3.96
e_fiq    erriq2          0.19193           0.06613       2.90
e_fses   errses2         0.11804           0.07147       1.65
d_ramb   psi             0.21011           0.02940       7.15
d_famb   psi             0.21011           0.02940       7.15


          Covariances Among Exogenous Variables

                                             Standard
Var1    Var2    Parameter        Estimate       Error    t Value

f_rpa   f_riq   cov1              0.27533     0.05552       4.96
f_rpa   f_rses  cov2              0.00611     0.05085       0.12
f_riq   f_rses  cov3              0.33510     0.05150       6.51
f_rpa   f_fpa   cov4              0.17099     0.07872       2.17
f_riq   f_fpa   cov5              0.13859     0.05431       2.55
f_rses  f_fpa   cov6              0.07563     0.05077       1.49
f_rpa   f_fiq   cov5              0.13859     0.05431       2.55
f_riq   f_fiq   cov7              0.48105     0.06993       6.88
f_rses  f_fiq   cov8              0.27235     0.05157       5.28
f_fpa   f_fiq   cov1              0.27533     0.05552       4.96
f_rpa   f_fses  cov6              0.07563     0.05077       1.49
f_riq   f_fses  cov8              0.27235     0.05157       5.28
f_rses  f_fses  cov9              0.32046     0.06517       4.92
f_fpa   f_fses  cov2              0.00611     0.05085       0.12
f_fiq   f_fses  cov3              0.33510     0.05150       6.51
e_rea   e_fea   covea             0.04535     0.02918       1.55
e_roa   e_foa   covoa             0.12085     0.03214       3.76
d_ramb  d_famb                          0
```

When model 7 is tested against models 2, 4, and 5, the p-values are respectively 0.0433, 0.0370, and 0.0123, indicating that the combined effect of the reciprocal influence and the covariance of the disturbance terms is statistically significant. Thus, the hypothesis tests indicate that it is acceptable to omit either the reciprocal influences or the covariance of the disturbances but not both.

It is also of interest to test the covariances between the error terms for educational (COVEA) and occupational aspiration (COVOA), since these terms are omitted from

Jöreskog and Sörbom's models. Constraining COVEA and COVOA to zero produces Loehlin's model 6:

```
title2 'Loehlin (1987) analysis: Model 6';
data ram6(type=ram);
   set ram2;
   if _name_='covea'|_name_='covoa' then
      do;
         _name_=' ';
         _estim_=0;
      end;
run;

proc calis data=aspire edf=328 inram=ram6;
run;
```

The relevant output is displayed in Figure 14.27.

```
          Peer Influences on Aspiration: Haller & Butterworth (1960)
                       Loehlin (1987) analysis: Model 6

                            The CALIS Procedure
        Covariance Structure Analysis: Maximum Likelihood Estimation

        Fit Function                                              0.1020
        Goodness of Fit Index (GFI)                               0.9802
        GFI Adjusted for Degrees of Freedom (AGFI)                0.9638
        Root Mean Square Residual (RMR)                           0.0306
        Parsimonious GFI (Mulaik, 1989)                           0.6535
        Chi-Square                                               33.4475
        Chi-Square DF                                                 30
        Pr > Chi-Square                                           0.3035
        Independence Model Chi-Square                             872.00
        Independence Model Chi-Square DF                              45
        RMSEA Estimate                                            0.0187
        RMSEA 90% Lower Confidence Limit                               .
        RMSEA 90% Upper Confidence Limit                          0.0471
        ECVI Estimate                                             0.2597
        ECVI 90% Lower Confidence Limit                                .
        ECVI 90% Upper Confidence Limit                           0.3164
        Probability of Close Fit                                  0.9686
        Bentler's Comparative Fit Index                           0.9958
        Normal Theory Reweighted LS Chi-Square                   32.9974
        Akaike's Information Criterion                          -26.5525
        Bozdogan's (1987) CAIC                                 -170.4342
        Schwarz's Bayesian Criterion                           -140.4342
        McDonald's (1989) Centrality                              0.9948
        Bentler & Bonett's (1980) Non-normed Index                0.9937
        Bentler & Bonett's (1980) NFI                             0.9616
        James, Mulaik, & Brett (1982) Parsimonious NFI            0.6411
        Z-Test of Wilson & Hilferty (1931)                        0.5151
        Bollen (1986) Normed Index Rho1                           0.9425
        Bollen (1988) Non-normed Index Delta2                     0.9959
        Hoelter's (1983) Critical N                                  431
```

Figure 14.27. Career Aspiration Data: Loehlin Model 6

The chi-square value for testing model 6 versus model 2 is 33.4476 - 19.0697 = 14.3779 with 2 degrees of freedom and a p-value of 0.0008, indicating that there is considerable evidence of correlation between the error terms.

The following table summarizes the results from Loehlin's seven models.

Model	χ^2	df	*p*-value	SBC
1. Full model	12.0132	13	0.5266	-63.3356
2. Equality constraints	19.0697	28	0.8960	-143.2200
3. No SES path	23.0365	29	0.7749	-145.0492
4. No reciprocal influence	20.9981	29	0.8592	-147.0876
5. No disturbance correlation	19.0745	29	0.9194	-149.0111
6. No error correlation	33.4475	30	0.3035	-140.4342
7. Constraints from both 4 & 5	25.3466	30	0.7080	-148.5351

For comparing models, you can use a DATA step to compute the differences of the chi-square statistics and *p*-values.

```
title 'Comparisons among Loehlin''s models';
data _null_;
   array achisq[7] _temporary_
      (12.0132 19.0697 23.0365 20.9981 19.0745 33.4475 25.3466);
   array adf[7] _temporary_
      (13 28 29 29 29 30 30);
   retain indent 16;
   file print;
   input ho ha @@;
   chisq = achisq[ho] - achisq[ha];
   df = adf[ho] - adf[ha];
   p = 1 - probchi( chisq, df);
   if _n_ = 1 then put
      / +indent 'model comparison   chi**2   df   p-value'
      / +indent '---------------------------------------';
   put +indent +3 ho ' versus ' ha @18 +indent chisq 8.4 df 5. p 9.4;
datalines;
2 1    3 2    4 2    5 2    7 2    7 4    7 5    6 2
;
```

The DATA step displays the following table.

```
   Comparisons among Loehlin's models

model comparison    chi**2   df  p-value
----------------------------------------
   2  versus 1      7.0565   15   0.9561
   3  versus 2      3.9668    1   0.0464
   4  versus 2      1.9284    1   0.1649
   5  versus 2      0.0048    1   0.9448
   7  versus 2      6.2769    2   0.0433
   7  versus 4      4.3485    1   0.0370
   7  versus 5      6.2721    1   0.0123
   6  versus 2     14.3778    2   0.0008
```

Although none of the seven models can be rejected when tested against the alternative of an unrestricted covariance matrix, the model comparisons make it clear that there are important differences among the models. Schwarz's Bayesian Criterion indicates model 5 as the model of choice. The constraints added to model 5 in model 7 can be rejected (p=0.0123), while model 5 cannot be rejected when tested against the less-constrained model 2 (p=0.9448). Hence, among the small number of models considered, model 5 has strong statistical support. However, as Loehlin (1987, p. 106) points out, many other models for these data could be constructed. Further analysis should consider, in addition to simple modifications of the models, the possibility that more than one friend could influence a boy's aspirations, and that a boy's ambition might have some effect on his choice of friends. Pursuing such theories would be statistically challenging.

References

Akaike, H. (1987), "Factor Analysis and AIC," *Psychometrika*, 52, 317–332.

Bentler, P.M. amd Bonett, D.G. (1980), "Significance Tests and Goodness of Fit in the Analysis of Covariance Structures," *Psychological Bulletin*, 88, 588–606.

Bollen, K.A. (1986), "Sample Size and Bentler and Bonett's Nonnormed Fit Index," *Psychometrika*, 51, 375–377.

Bollen, K.A. (1989), *Structural Equations with Latent Variables*, New York: John Wiley & Sons, Inc.

Boomsma, A. (1983), *On the Robustness of LISREL (Maximum Likelihood Estimation) against Small Sample Size and Nonnormality*, Amsterdam: Sociometric Research Foundation.

Duncan, O.D., Haller, A.O., and Portes, A. (1968), "Peer Influences on Aspirations: A Reinterpretation," *American Journal of Sociology*, 74, 119–137.

Fuller, W.A. (1987), *Measurement Error Models*, New York: John Wiley & Sons, Inc.

Haller, A.O., and Butterworth, C.E. (1960), "Peer Influences on Levels of Occupational and Educational Aspiration," *Social Forces*, 38, 289–295.

Hampel F.R., Ronchetti E.M., Rousseeuw P.J. and Stahel W.A. (1986), *Robust Statistics*, New York: John Wiley & Sons, Inc.

Hoelter, J.W. (1983), "The Analysis of Covariance Structures: Goodness-of-Fit Indices," *Sociological Methods and Research*, 11, 325–344.

Huber, P.J. (1981), *Robust Statistics*, New York: John Wiley & Sons, Inc.

James, L.R., Mulaik, S.A., and Brett, J.M. (1982), *Causal Analysis*, Beverly Hills: Sage Publications.

Jöreskog, K.G. (1973), "A General Method for Estimating a Linear Structural Equation System," in Goldberger, A.S. and Duncan, O.D., eds., *Structural Equation Models in the Social Sciences*, New York: Academic Press.

Jöreskog, K.G. and Sörbom, D. (1979), *Advances in Factor Analysis and Structural Equation Models*, Cambridge, MA: Abt Books.

Jöreskog, K.G. and Sörbom, D. (1988), *LISREL 7: A Guide to the Program and Applications*, Chicago: SPSS.

Keesling, J.W. (1972), "Maximum Likelihood Approaches to Causal Analysis," Ph.D. dissertation, Chicago: University of Chicago.

Lee. S.Y. (1985), "Analysis of Covariance and Correlation Structures," *Computational Statistics and Data Analysis*, 2, 279–295.

Loehlin, J.C. (1987), *Latent Variable Models*, Hillsdale, NJ: Lawrence Erlbaum Associates.

Lord, F.M. (1957), "A Significance Test for the Hypothesis that Two Variables Measure the Same Trait Except for Errors of Measurement," *Psychometrika*, 22, 207–220.

McArdle, J.J. and McDonald, R.P. (1984), "Some Algebraic Properties of the Reticular Action Model," *British Journal of Mathematical and Statistical Psychology*, 37, 234–251.

McDonald, R.P. (1989), "An Index of Goodness-of-Fit Based on Noncentrality," *Journal of Classification*, 6, 97–103.

Schwarz, G. (1978), "Estimating the Dimension of a Model," *Annals of Statistics*, 6, 461–464.

Voss, R.E. (1969), "Response by Corn to NPK Fertilization on Marshall and Monona Soils as Influenced by Management and Meteorological Factors," Ph.D. dissertation, Ames, Iowa: Iowa State University.

Wiley, D.E. (1973), "The Identification Problem for Structural Equation Models with Unmeasured Variables," in Goldberger, A.S. and Duncan, O.D., eds., *Structural Equation Models in the Social Sciences*, New York: Academic Press.

Wilson, E.B. and Hilferty, M.M. (1931), "The Distribution of Chi-Square," *Proceedings of the National Academy of Sciences*, 17, 694.

Chapter 15

Using the Output Delivery System

Chapter Table of Contents

Chapter 15
Using the Output Delivery System

Overview

In the latest version of SAS software, all SAS/STAT procedures use the Output Delivery System (ODS) to manage their output. This includes managing the form in which the output appears as well as its organization and format. The default for SAS/STAT procedures is to produce the usual SAS listing file. However, by using the features of the Output Delivery System, you can make changes to the format and appearance of your SAS output. In particular, you can

- display your output in hypertext markup language (HTML)
- display your output in Rich-Text-Format (RTF)*
- create SAS data sets directly from output tables
- select or exclude individual output tables
- customize the layout, format, and headers of your output

ODS features can provide you with a powerful tool for managing your output. This chapter provides background material and illustrates typical applications of ODS with SAS/STAT software.

For complete documentation on the Output Delivery System, refer to *The Complete Guide to the SAS Output Delivery System*.

Output Objects and ODS Destinations

All SAS procedures produce *output objects* that the Output Delivery System delivers to various *ODS destinations*, according to the default specifications for the procedure or to your own specifications.

All output objects (for example, a table of parameter estimates) consist of two component parts:

- the data component, which consists of the results computed by a SAS procedure
- the template, which contains rules for formatting and displaying the results

When you invoke a SAS procedure, the procedure sends all output to the Output Delivery System. ODS then routes the output to all open destinations. You define the

*experimental in Version 8

form that the output should take when you specify an ODS destination. Supported destinations are as follows:

- listing destination (the standard SAS listing), which is the default
- HTML destination, hypertext markup language
- output destination, SAS data set
- postscript and PCL for high fidelity printers

Future versions of ODS will support the following additional destinations:

- ODS Output Document for modifying and replaying output without rerunning the procedure that created it
- Rich Text Format (RTF) for inclusion in Microsoft Word

You can activate multiple ODS destinations at the same time, so that a single procedure step can route output to multiple destinations. If you do not supply any ODS statements, ODS delivers all output to the SAS listing, which is the default.

Each output object has an associated template that defines its presentation format. You can modify the presentation of the output by using the TEMPLATE procedure to alter these templates or to create new templates. You can also specify stylistic elements for ODS destinations, such as cell formats and headers, column ordering, colors, and fonts. For detailed information, refer to the chapter titled "The Template Procedure" in *The Complete Guide to the SAS Output Delivery System*.

Using the Output Delivery System

The ODS statement is a global statement that enables you to provide instructions to the Output Delivery System. You can use ODS statements to specify options for different ODS destinations, select templates to format your output, and select and exclude output. You can also display the names of individual output tables as they are generated.

In order to select, exclude, or modify a table, you must first know its name. You can obtain the table names in several ways:

- For any SAS/STAT procedure, you can obtain table names from the individual procedure chapter or from the individual procedure section of the SAS online Help system.
- For any SAS procedure, you can use the SAS Explorer window to view the names of the tables created in your SAS run (see the section "Using ODS with the SAS Explorer" on page 259 for more information).
- For any SAS procedure, you can use the ODS TRACE statement to find the names of tables created in your SAS run. The ODS TRACE statement writes identifying information to the SAS log (or, optionally, to the SAS listing) for each generated output table.

Specify the ODS TRACE ON statement prior to the procedure statements that create the output for which you want information. For example, the following statements write the trace record for the specific tables created in this REG procedure step.

```
ods trace on;
proc reg;
   model y=x;
   model z=x;
run;
ods trace off;
```

By default, the trace record is written to the SAS log, as displayed in Figure 15.1. Alternatively, you can specify the LISTING option, which writes the information, interleaved with the procedure output, to the SAS listing (see Example 15.3).

```
   ods trace on;
   proc reg;
      model y=x;
      model z=x;
   run;

    .
    .
    .

Output Added:
-------------
Name:       ParameterEstimates
Label:      Parameter Estimates
Template:   Stat.REG.ParameterEstimates
Path:       Reg.MODEL1.Fit.y.ParameterEstimates
-------------
    .
    .
    .

Output Added:
-------------
Name:       ParameterEstimates
Label:      Parameter Estimates
Template:   Stat.REG.ParameterEstimates
Path:       Reg.MODEL2.Fit.z.ParameterEstimates
-------------
```

Figure 15.1. Partial Contents of the SAS Log: Result of the ODS TRACE ON Statement

Figure 15.1 displays the trace record, which contains the name of each created table and its associated label, template, and path. The label provides a description of the table. The template name displays the name of the template used to format the table. The path shows the output hierarchy to which the table belongs.

The fully qualified path is given in the trace record. A partially qualified path consists of any part of the full path that begins immediately after a period (.) and continues to the end of the full path.

For example, the full path for the parameter estimates for the first model in the preceding regression analysis is

```
Reg.Model1.Fit.y.ParameterEstimates
```

Therefore, partially qualified paths for the table are

```
Model1.fit.y.ParameterEstimates
fit.y.ParameterEstimates
y.ParameterEstimates
```

To refer to a table (in order to select or exclude it from display, for example), specify either the table name or the table's fully or partially qualified path. You may want to use qualified paths when your SAS program creates several tables that have the same name, as in the preceding example. In such a case, you can use a partially qualified path to select a subset of tables, or you can use a fully qualified path to select a particular table.

You specify the tables that ODS selects or excludes with the ODS SELECT or ODS EXCLUDE statement. Suppose that you want to display only the tables of parameter estimates from the preceding regression analysis. You can give any of the following statements (before invoking the REG procedure) to display both tables of parameter estimates. For this example, these statements are equivalent:

```
ods select Reg.Model1.Fit.y.ParameterEstimates
           Reg.Model1.Fit.z.ParameterEstimates;

ods select y.ParameterEstimates z.ParameterEstimates;

ods select ParameterEstimates;
```

The first ODS SELECT statement specifies the full path for both tables. The second statement specifies the partially qualified path for both tables. The third statement specifies the single name "ParameterEstimates," which is shared by both tables.

The Output Delivery System records the specified table names in its internal selection or exclusion list. ODS then processes the output it receives. Note that ODS maintains an overall selection or exclusion list that pertains to all ODS destinations, and it maintains a separate selection or exclusion list for each ODS destination. The list for a specific destination provides the primary filtering step. Restrictions you specify in the overall list are added to the destination-specific lists.

Suppose, for example, that your listing exclusion list (that is, the list of tables you want to exclude from the SAS listing) contains the "FitStatistics" table, which you specify with the statement

```
ods listing exclude FitStatistics;
```

Suppose also that your overall selection list (that is, the list of tables you want to select for all destinations) contains the tables "FitStatistics" and "ParameterEstimates," which you specify with the statement

```
ods select ParameterEstimates FitStatistics;
```

The Output Delivery System then sends only the "ParameterEstimates" and "FitStatistics" tables to all open destinations except the SAS listing. It sends only the "ParameterEstimates" table to the SAS listing because the table "FitStatistics" is excluded from that destination.

Some SAS procedures, such as the REG or the GLM procedure, support run-group processing, which means that a RUN statement does not end the procedure. A QUIT statement explicitly ends such procedures; if you omit the QUIT statement, a PROC or a DATA statement implicitly ends such procedures. When you use the Output Delivery System with procedures that support run-group processing, it is good programming practice to specify a QUIT statement at the end of the procedure. This causes ODS to clear the selection or exclusion list, and you are less likely to encounter unexpected results.

Using ODS with the SAS Explorer

The SAS Explorer is a new feature that enables you to examine the various parts of the SAS System. Figure 15.2 displays the Results window from the SAS Explorer. The Results node retains a running record of your output as it is generated during your SAS session. Figure 15.2 displays the output hierarchy when the preceding statements are executed.

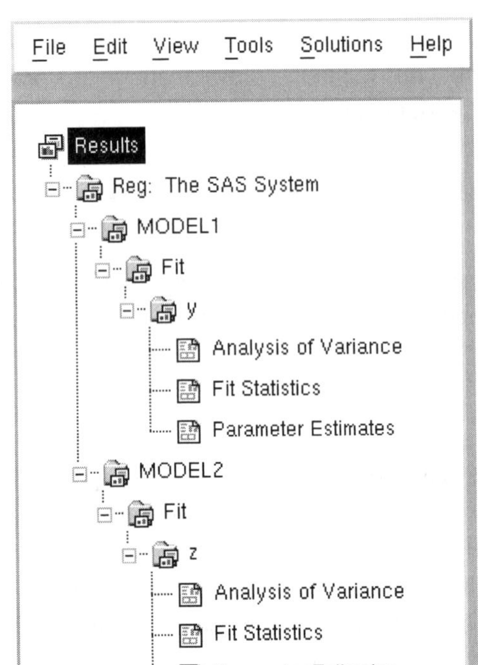

Figure 15.2. The Results Window from the SAS Explorer

When you click on the output table names in the Results window, you link directly to the output in the output window or, if you specify the HTML destination, in an HTML browser. The items on the left-hand side of the Results node are output directories. The items on the right-hand side of the Results node are the names of the actual output objects. You can also use the Explorer to determine names of the templates associated with each output table.

Controlling Output Appearance with Templates

A template is an abstract description of how output should appear when it is formatted. Templates describe several characteristics of the output, including headers, column ordering, style information, justification, and formats. All SAS/STAT procedures have templates, which are stored in the SASHELP library.

You can create or modify a template with the TEMPLATE procedure. For example, you can specify different column headings or different orderings of columns in a table. You can find the template associated with a particular output table or column by using the ODS TRACE statement or the SAS Explorer.

You can display the contents of a template by executing the following statements:

```
proc template;
   source  templatename;
run;
```

where *templatename* is the name of the template.

Suppose you want to change the way all of the analysis of variance tests are displayed by the GLM procedure. You can redefine the templates that the procedure uses with PROC TEMPLATE. For example, in order to have the SS and MS columns always displayed with more digits, you can redefine the columns used by the procedure to display them:

```
proc template;
   edit Stat.GLM.SS;
      format=Best16.;
   end;
   edit Stat.GLM.MS;
      format=Best16.;
   end;
run;
```

The BEST*w*. format enables you to display the most information about a value, according to the available field width. The BEST16. format specifies a field width of 16. Refer to the chapter on formats in *SAS Language Reference: Dictionary* for detailed information.

When you run PROC TEMPLATE to modify or edit a template, the template is stored in your SASUSER library (see Example 15.11). You can then modify the path that ODS uses to look up templates with the ODS PATH statement in order to access these new templates in a later SAS session. This means that you can create a default set of templates to modify the presentation format for all your SAS output. (Note that you can specify the SHOW option in the ODS PATH statement to determine the current path.)

It is important to note the difference between a style template and a column or table template. A column or table template applies to the specific columns or tables that reference the template. For example, the preceding statements that modify the "Stat.GLM.SS" and "Stat.GLM.MS" templates provide an example of modifying specific column templates.

A style template applies to an entire SAS job and can be specified only in the ODS HTML statement. You can specify a style as follows:

```
ods html style=Styles.Brown;
```

A style template controls stylistic elements such as colors, fonts, and presentation attributes. When you use a style template, you ensure that all your output shares a consistent presentation style.

You can also reference style information in table templates for individual headers and data cells. You can modify either type of template with the TEMPLATE procedure. For information on creating your own styles, refer to *The Complete Guide to the SAS Output Delivery System*.

Interaction Between ODS and the NOPRINT Option

Most SAS/STAT procedures support a NOPRINT option that you can use when you want to create an output data set but do not want any displayed output. Typically, you use an OUTPUT statement in addition to the procedure's NOPRINT option to create a data set and suppress displayed output.

You can also use the Output Delivery System to create output data sets by using the ODS OUTPUT statement. However, if you specify the NOPRINT option, the procedure may not send any output to the Output Delivery System. Therefore, when you want to create output data sets through ODS (using the ODS OUTPUT statement), and you want to suppress the display of all output, specify

```
ODS SELECT NONE;
```

or close the active ODS destinations by entering the command

```
ODS  destinationname CLOSE;
```

where *destinationname* is the name of the active ODS destination (for example, ODS HTML CLOSE).

Note: The ODS statement does not instruct a procedure to generate output: instead, it specifies how the Output Delivery System should manage the table once it is created. You must ensure that the proper options are in effect. For example, the following code does not create the requested data set Parms.

```
proc glm;
   ods output ParameterEstimates=Parms;
   class x;
   model y=x;
   run;
quit;
```

When you execute these statements, the following message is displayed in the log:

```
WARNING: Output 'ParameterEstimates' was not created.
```

The data set Parms is not created because the table of parameter estimates is generated only when the SOLUTION option is specified in the MODEL statement in the GLM procedure.

Compatibility Issues with Version 6 Prototypes

- In Version 6, the MIXED and GENMOD procedures use a prototype of the Output Delivery System. This prototype provides the MAKE statement in order to create data sets from output tables, and this statement remains supported in these procedures. However, the new mechanism to create SAS data sets from output tables is the ODS OUTPUT statement for all procedures.
- The Version 6 prototype of the ODS output hierarchy is stored in a SAS catalog. The latest version of SAS software has a more flexible item-store file type used to store templates and ODS output.
- The Version 6 prototype ODS uses two macro variables (_DISK_ and _PRINT_) to regulate the saving of an output hierarchy. The latest version of SAS software uses the global ODS statement to accomplish this task.
- The Version 6 PROC TEMPLATE and PROC OUTPUT syntax is not compatible with the latest version of SAS software.

Examples

The following examples display typical uses of the Output Delivery System.

Example 15.1. Creating HTML Output with ODS

This example demonstrates how you can use the ODS HTML statement to display your output in hypertext markup language (HTML).

The following statements create the data set scores, which contains the golf scores for boys and girls in a physical education class. The TTEST procedure is then invoked to compare the scores.

The ODS HTML statement specifies the name of the file to contain the HTML output.

```
data scores;
   input Gender $ Score @@;
   datalines;
f 75  f 76  f 80  f 77  f 80  f 77  f 73
m 82  m 80  m 85  m 85  m 78  m 87  m 82
;
run;

ods html body='ttest.htm';

title 'Comparing Group Means';
proc ttest ;
   class Gender;
   var Score;
run;
ods html close;
```

By default, the SAS listing receives all output generated during your SAS run. In this example, the ODS HTML statement opens the HTML destination, and both destinations receive the generated output. Output 15.1.1 displays the results as they are rendered in the SAS listing.

Note that you must specify the following statement before you can view your output in a browser.

```
ods html close;
```

If you do not close the HTML destination, your HTML file may contain no output, or you may experience other unexpected results.

Output 15.1.2 displays the file 'ttest.htm', which is specified in the preceding ODS HTML statement.

Output 15.1.1. Results for PROC TTEST: SAS Listing Procedure Output

```
                                        Comparing Group Means

                                         The TTEST Procedure

                                             Statistics

                              Lower CL            Upper CL  Lower CL            Upper CL
Variable  Class          N        Mean      Mean      Mean   Std Dev   Std Dev   Std Dev   Std Err   Minimum   Maximum

Score     f              7      74.504    76.857    79.211    1.6399    2.5448    5.6039    0.9619        73        80
Score     m              7      79.804    82.714    85.625     2.028    3.1472    6.9303    1.1895        78        87
Score     Diff (1-2)             -9.19    -5.857    -2.524    2.0522    2.8619    4.7242    1.5298

                                               T-Tests

                   Variable    Method           Variances        DF    t Value    Pr > |t|

                   Score       Pooled           Equal            12      -3.83      0.0024
                   Score       Satterthwaite    Unequal        11.5      -3.83      0.0026

                                       Equality of Variances

                      Variable    Method       Num DF    Den DF    F Value    Pr > F

                      Score       Folded F          6         6       1.53    0.6189
```

Output 15.1.2. Results for PROC TTEST: HTML Procedure Output

Comparing Group Means

The TTEST Procedure

Statistics												
Variable	Class	N	Lower CL Mean	Mean	Upper CL Mean	Lower CL Std Dev	Std Dev	Upper CL Std Dev	Std Err	Minimum	Maximum
Score	f	7	74.504	76.857	79.211	1.6399	2.5448	5.6039	0.9619	73	80
Score	m	7	79.804	82.714	85.625	2.028	3.1472	6.9303	1.1895	78	87
Score	Diff (1-2)		-9.19	-5.857	-2.524	2.0522	2.8619	4.7242	1.5298		

T-Tests					
Variable	Method	Variances	DF	t Value	Pr > |t|
Score	Pooled	Equal	12	-3.83	0.0024

Example 15.2. Creating HTML Output with a Table of Contents

The following example uses ODS to display the output in HTML with a table of contents.

The data are from Pothoff and Roy (1964) and consist of growth measurements for 11 girls and 16 boys at ages 8, 10, 12, and 14.

```
data pr;
   input Person Gender $ y1 y2 y3 y4;
   y=y1; Age=8;  output;
   y=y2; Age=10; output;
   y=y3; Age=12; output;
   y=y4; Age=14; output;
   drop y1-y4;
   datalines;
 1   F   21.0    20.0    21.5    23.0
 2   F   21.0    21.5    24.0    25.5
 3   F   20.5    24.0    24.5    26.0
 4   F   23.5    24.5    25.0    26.5
 5   F   21.5    23.0    22.5    23.5
 6   F   20.0    21.0    21.0    22.5
 7   F   21.5    22.5    23.0    25.0
 8   F   23.0    23.0    23.5    24.0
 9   F   20.0    21.0    22.0    21.5
10   F   16.5    19.0    19.0    19.5
11   F   24.5    25.0    28.0    28.0
12   M   26.0    25.0    29.0    31.0
13   M   21.5    22.5    23.0    26.5
14   M   23.0    22.5    24.0    27.5
15   M   25.5    27.5    26.5    27.0
16   M   20.0    23.5    22.5    26.0
```

```
17   M   24.5    25.5    27.0    28.5
18   M   22.0    22.0    24.5    26.5
19   M   24.0    21.5    24.5    25.5
20   M   23.0    20.5    31.0    26.0
21   M   27.5    28.0    31.0    31.5
22   M   23.0    23.0    23.5    25.0
23   M   21.5    23.5    24.0    28.0
24   M   17.0    24.5    26.0    29.5
25   M   22.5    25.5    25.5    26.0
26   M   23.0    24.5    26.0    30.0
27   M   22.0    21.5    23.5    25.0
run;

ods html body='mixed.htm'
         contents='mixedc.htm'
         frame='mixedf.htm';

proc mixed data=pr method=ml covtest asycov;
   class Person Gender;
   model y = Gender Age Gender*Age / s;
   repeated / type=un subject=Person r;
run;
ods html close;
```

The ODS HTML statement specifies three files. The BODY= argument specifies the file to contain the output generated from the statements that follow. The BODY= argument is required.

The CONTENTS= option specifies a file to contain the table of contents. The FRAME= option specifies a file to contain both the table of contents and the output. You open the FRAME= file in your browser to view the table of contents together with the generated output (see Output 15.2.1). Note that, if you specify the ODS HTML statement with only the BODY= argument, no table of contents is created.

The MIXED procedure is invoked to fit the specified model. The resulting output is displayed in Output 15.2.1.

Output 15.2.1. HTML Output from the MIXED Procedure

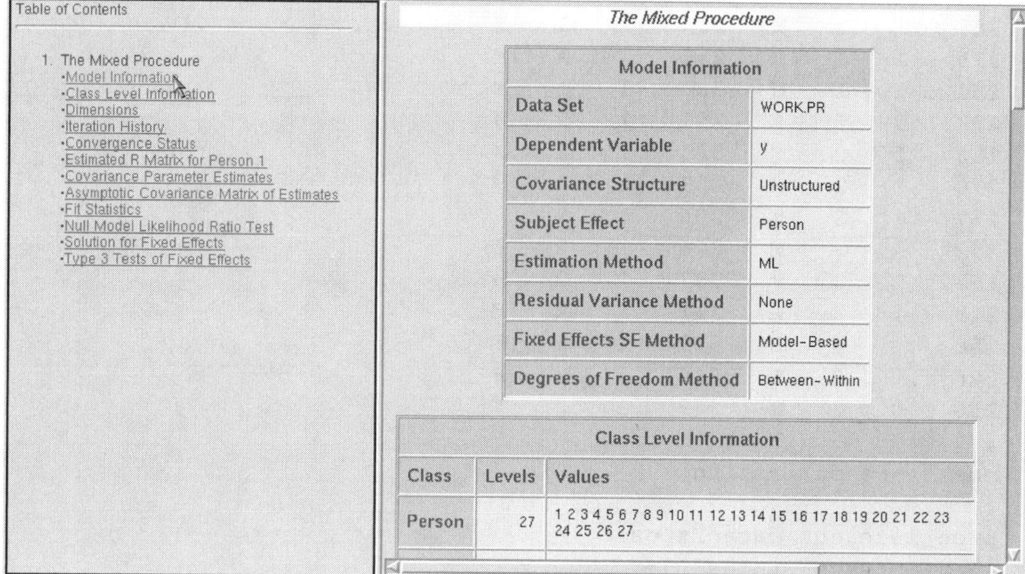

The table of contents displayed in Output 15.2.1 contains the descriptive label for each output table produced in the MIXED procedure step. You can select any label in the table of contents and the corresponding output will be displayed in the right-hand side of the browser window.

Example 15.3. Determining the Names of ODS Tables

In order to select or exclude a table, or to render it as a SAS data set, you must first know its name. You can obtain the table names in several ways (see the section "Using the Output Delivery System" beginning on page 256 for more information).

This example uses the ODS TRACE statement with the LISTING option to obtain the names of the created output objects. By default, the ODS TRACE statement writes its information to the SAS log. However, you can specify the LISTING option to have the information interleaved with the procedure output in the SAS listing.

Suppose that you perform a randomized trial on rats that have been exposed to a carcinogen. You divide them into two groups and give each group a different treatment. In the following example, interest lies in whether the survival distributions differ between the two treatments. The data set Exposed contains four variables: Days (survival time in days from treatment to death), Status (censoring indicator variable: 0 if censored and 1 if not censored), Treatment (treatment indicator), and Sex (gender: F if female and M if male).

```
data Exposed;
  input Days Status Treatment Sex $ @@;
  datalines;
179   1   1   F   378   0   1   M
256   1   1   F   355   1   1   M
262   1   1   M   319   1   1   M
256   1   1   F   256   1   1   M
255   1   1   M   171   1   1   F
224   0   1   F   325   1   1   M
```

```
225   1   1   F   325   1   1   M
287   1   1   M   217   1   1   F
319   1   1   M   255   1   1   F
264   1   1   M   256   1   1   F
237   0   2   F   291   1   2   M
156   1   2   F   323   1   2   M
270   1   2   M   253   1   2   M
257   1   2   M   206   1   2   F
242   1   2   M   206   1   2   F
157   1   2   F   237   1   2   M
249   1   2   M   211   1   2   F
180   1   2   F   229   1   2   F
226   1   2   F   234   1   2   F
268   0   2   M   209   1   2   F
;
ods trace on/listing;

proc lifetest data=Exposed;
   time Days*Status(0);
   strata Treatment;
run;

ods trace off;
```

The purpose of these statements is to obtain the names of the ODS tables produced in this PROC LIFETEST run. The ODS TRACE ON statement writes the trace record of ODS output tables. The LISTING option specifies that the information is interleaved with the output and written to the SAS listing.

The LIFETEST procedure is invoked to perform the analysis, the SAS listing receives the procedure output and the trace record, and the trace is then disabled with the OFF option.

Output 15.3.1. The ODS Trace, Interleaved with LIFETEST Results: Partial Results

```
                          The LIFETEST Procedure

Output Added:
-------------
Name:       ProductLimitEstimates
Label:      Product-Limit Estimates
Template:   Stat.Lifetest.ProductLimitEstimates
Path:       Lifetest.Stratum1.ProductLimitEstimates
-------------


                         Stratum 1: Treatment = 1

                      Product-Limit Survival Estimates

                                              Survival
                                              Standard      Number      Number
              Days      Survival    Failure     Error       Failed       Left

             0.000       1.0000           0          0          0         20
           171.000       0.9500      0.0500     0.0487          1         19
           179.000       0.9000      0.1000     0.0671          2         18
           217.000       0.8500      0.1500     0.0798          3         17
           224.000*           .           .          .          3         16
           225.000       0.7969      0.2031     0.0908          4         15
           255.000            .           .          .          5         14
           255.000       0.6906      0.3094     0.1053          6         13
           256.000            .           .          .          7         12
           256.000            .           .          .          8         11
           256.000            .           .          .          9         10
           256.000       0.4781      0.5219     0.1146         10          9
           262.000       0.4250      0.5750     0.1135         11          8
           264.000       0.3719      0.6281     0.1111         12          7
           287.000       0.3188      0.6813     0.1071         13          6
           319.000            .           .          .         14          5
           319.000       0.2125      0.7875     0.0942         15          4
           325.000            .           .          .         16          3
           325.000       0.1063      0.8938     0.0710         17          2
           355.000       0.0531      0.9469     0.0517         18          1
           378.000*           .           .          .         18          0

              NOTE: The marked survival times are censored observations.


                   Summary Statistics for Time Variable Days

Output Added:
-------------
Name:       Quartiles
Label:      Quartiles
Template:   Stat.Lifetest.Quartiles
Path:       Lifetest.Stratum1.TimeSummary.Quartiles
-------------


                            Quartile Estimates

                              Point      95% Confidence Interval
                 Percent    Estimate      [Lower        Upper)

                      75     319.000      262.000      325.000
                      50     256.000      255.000      319.000
                      25     255.000      217.000      256.000
```

As you can see in Output 15.3.1, the ODS TRACE ON statement writes the name, label, template, and path name of each generated ODS table. For more information on names, labels, and qualified path names, see the discussion in the section "Using the Output Delivery System" beginning on page 256.

The information obtained with the ODS TRACE ON statement enables you to request output tables by name. The examples that follow demonstrate how you can use this information to select, exclude, or create data sets from particular output tables.

Example 15.4. Selecting ODS Tables for Display

You can use the ODS SELECT statement to deliver only the desired tables to ODS destinations. In the following example, the GLM procedure is used to perform an analysis on an unbalanced two-way experimental design.

```
data twoway;
title "Unbalanced Two-way Design";
   input Treatment Block y @@;
   datalines;
1 1 17   1 1 28   1 1 19   1 1 21   1 1 19
1 2 43   1 2 30   1 2 39   1 2 44   1 2 44
1 3 16
2 1 21   2 1 21   2 1 24   2 1 25
2 2 39   2 2 45   2 2 42   2 2 47
2 3 19   2 3 22   2 3 16
3 1 22   3 1 30   3 1 33   3 1 31
3 2 46
3 3 26   3 3 31   3 3 26   3 3 33   3 3 29   3 3 25
;

proc glm data=twoway;
   class Treatment Block;
   model y = Treatment|Block;
   means Treatment;
   lsmeans Treatment;

ods select ModelANOVA Means;
ods trace on;
ods show;
run;
```

In the preceding statements, the GLM procedure is invoked to produce the output. The ODS SELECT statement specifies that only the two tables "ModelANOVA" and "Means" are to be delivered to the ODS destinations. In this example, no ODS destinations are explicitly opened. Therefore, only the default SAS listing receives the procedure output. The ODS SHOW statement displays the current overall selection list in the SAS log. The ODS TRACE statement writes the trace record of the ODS output objects to the SAS log.

Output 15.4.1 displays the results of the ODS SHOW statement, which writes the current overall selection list to the SAS log.

Output 15.4.1. Results of the ODS SHOW Statement

```
    ods select ModelANOVA Means;
    ods show;
Current OVERALL select list is:
1. ModelANOVA
2. Means
```

Partial results of the ODS TRACE statement, which are written to the SAS log, are displayed in Output 15.4.2. Note that there are two tables having the name "ModelANOVA," which are the Type I Model Anova and the Type III Model Anova tables. Similarly, there are two ODS tables having the name "Means," which are the Means and the LS-means tables.

Output 15.4.2. The ODS TRACE: Partial Contents of the SAS Log

```
Output Added:
-------------
Name:       ClassLevels
Label:      Class Levels
Template:   STAT.GLM.ClassLevels
Path:       GLM.Data.ClassLevels
-------------
            .
            .
            .
            .
Output Added:
-------------
Name:       ModelANOVA
Label:      Type I Model ANOVA
Template:   stat.GLM.Tests
Path:       GLM.ANOVA.y.ModelANOVA
-------------

Output Added:
-------------
Name:       ModelANOVA
Label:      Type III Model ANOVA
Template:   stat.GLM.Tests
Path:       GLM.ANOVA.y.ModelANOVA
-------------
NOTE: Means from the MEANS statement are not adjusted for other
terms in the model.  For adjusted means, use the LSMEANS statement.

Output Added:
-------------
Name:       Means
Label:      Means
Template:   stat.GLM.Means
Path:       GLM.Means.Treatment.Means
-------------

Output Added:
-------------
Name:       Means
Label:      Means
Template:   stat.GLM.LSMeans
Path:       GLM.LSMEANS.Treatment.Means
```

In the following statements, the ODS SHOW statement writes the current overall selection list to the SAS log. The QUIT statement ends the GLM procedure. The second ODS SHOW statement writes the selection list to the log after PROC GLM terminates. The ODS selection list is reset to 'ALL,' by default, when a procedure terminates. For more information on ODS exclusion and selection lists, see the section "Using the Output Delivery System" beginning on page 256.

```
ods show;
quit;
ods show;
```

The results of the statements are displayed in Output 15.4.3. Before the GLM procedure terminates, the ODS selection list includes only the two tables, "ModelANOVA" and "Means."

Output 15.4.3. The ODS Selection List, Before and After PROC GLM Terminates

```
     ods show;

  Current OVERALL select list is:
  1. ModelANOVA
  2. Means


     quit;

NOTE: There were 33 observations read from the dataset WORK.TWOWAY.

     ods show;

  Current OVERALL select list is: ALL
```

The GLM procedure supports interactive run-group processing. Before the QUIT statement is executed, PROC GLM is active and the ODS selection list remains at its previous setting before PROC GLM was invoked. After the QUIT statement, when PROC GLM is no longer active, the selection list is reset to deliver all output tables.

The entire displayed output consists of the four selected tables (two "ModelANOVA" tables and two "Means" tables), as displayed in Output 15.4.4 and Output 15.4.5.

Output 15.4.4. The ModelANOVA Tables from PROC GLM

```
                                           Unbalanced Two-way Design

                                              The GLM Procedure

Dependent Variable: y

        Source                                DF        Type I SS     Mean Square    F Value    Pr > F

        Treatment                              2         8.060606        4.030303       0.24    0.7888
        Block                                  2      2621.864124     1310.932062      77.95    <.0001
        Treatment*Block                        4        32.684361        8.171090       0.49    0.7460


        Source                                DF      Type III SS     Mean Square    F Value    Pr > F

        Treatment                              2       266.130682      133.065341       7.91    0.0023
        Block                                  2      1883.729465      941.864732      56.00    <.0001
        Treatment*Block                        4        32.684361        8.171090       0.49    0.7460
```

Output 15.4.5. The Means Tables from PROC GLM

```
                    Unbalanced Two-way Design

                       The GLM Procedure

          Level of           --------------y--------------
          Treatment     N            Mean          Std Dev

          1            11      29.0909091       11.5104695
          2            11      29.1818182       11.5569735
          3            11      30.1818182        6.3058414


                    Unbalanced Two-way Design

                       The GLM Procedure
                      Least Squares Means

                    Treatment          y LSMEAN

                    1                25.6000000
                    2                28.3333333
                    3                34.4444444
```

Example 15.5. Excluding ODS Tables from Display

The following example demonstrates how you can use the ODS EXCLUDE statement to exclude particular tables from ODS destinations. This example also creates a SAS data set from the excluded table.

The data are from Hemmerle and Hartley (1973). The response variable consists of measurements from an oven experiment, and the model contains a fixed effect A and random effects B and A*B.

```
data hh;
   input a b y @@;
   datalines;
1 1 237   1 1 254    1 1 246
1 2 178   1 2 179
2 1 208   2 1 178    2 1 187
2 2 146   2 2 145    2 2 141
3 1 186   3 1 183
3 2 142   3 2 125    3 2 136
;
ods html body='mixed.htm'
         contents='mixedc.htm'
         frame='mixedf.htm';

ods exclude ParmSearch(persist);
ods show;
```

The ODS HTML statement specifies the filenames to contain the output generated from the statements that follow.

The ODS EXCLUDE statement excludes the table "ParmSearch" from display. Although the table is excluded from the displayed output, the information contained in the "ParmSearch" table is graphically summarized in a later step.

The PERSIST option in the ODS EXCLUDE statement excludes the table for the entire SAS session or until you execute an ODS SELECT statement or an ODS EXCLUDE NONE statement. If you omit the PERSIST option, the exclusion list is cleared when the procedure terminates.

The resulting exclusion list is displayed in Output 15.5.1.

Output 15.5.1. Results of the ODS SHOW Statement, Before PROC MIXED

```
      ods exclude ParmSearch(persist);
      ods show;
Current OVERALL exclude list is:
1. ParmSearch(PERSIST)
```

The following ODS OUTPUT statement outputs the table "ParmSearch" to a SAS data set called parms. The MIXED procedure is invoked and the model is fit. All output from the MIXED procedure, except the "ParmSearch" table, is delivered to the HTML destination and the SAS listing. The ODS SHOW statement again displays the overall current exclusion list.

```
ods output ParmSearch=parms;
proc mixed data=hh asycov mmeq mmeqsol covtest;
   class a b;
   model y = a / outp=predicted;
   random b a*b;
   lsmeans a;
   parms (17 to 20 by 0.1) (.3 to .4 by .005) (1.0);
run;

ods show;
```

The results of the ODS SHOW statement, given after the MIXED procedure has terminated, are displayed in Output 15.5.2.

Output 15.5.2. Results of the ODS SHOW Statement, After PROC MIXED

```
   proc mixed data=hh asycov mmeq mmeqsol covtest;
      class a b;
      model y = a / outp=predicted;
      random b a*b;
      lsmeans a;
      parms (17 to 20 by 0.1) (.3 to .4 by .005) (1.0);
   run;

   ods show;

Current OVERALL exclude list is:
1. ParmSearch(PERSIST)
```

Normally the ODS exclusion list is cleared at the conclusion of a procedure (for more information on ODS exclusion and selection lists, see the section "Using the

Output Delivery System" on page 256). However, the PERSIST option in the preceding ODS EXCLUDE statement specifies that the "ParmSearch" table should remain in the exclusion list until the list is explicitly cleared (that is, when the ODS EXCLUDE NONE statement or an ODS SELECT statement is encountered). Output 15.5.2 shows that the exclusion list remains in effect after PROC MIXED terminates.

The PERSIST option is useful when you want to exclude the same table in further analyses during your SAS session.

The "ParmSearch" table is contained in the parms data set (as specified in the ODS OUTPUT statement). The information is plotted with the G3D procedure in the following step:

```
proc g3d data=parms;
   plot CovP1*CovP2 = ResLogLike /
              ctop=red cbottom=blue caxis=black;
run;

ods html close;
```

The MIXED procedure output resulting from the preceding statements is displayed in Output 15.5.3. The table of contents shows the names for all of the output tables. The "ParmSearch" table is not listed in the table of contents because of the preceding ODS EXCLUDE statement.

Output 15.5.3. HTML Output from the Mixed Procedure

Table of Contents

1. The Mixed Procedure
   - Model Information
   - Class Level Information
   - Dimensions
   - Iteration History
   - Convergence Status
   - Covariance Parameter Estimates
   - Asymptotic Covariance Matrix of Estimates
   - Fit Statistics
   - PARMS Model Likelihood Ratio Test
   - Mixed Model Equations
   - Mixed Model Equations Solution
   - Type 3 Tests of Fixed Effects
   - Least Squares Means
2. The G3d Procedure
   - Plot CovP1 * CovP2 = Res Log Like

The Mixed Procedure

Model Information	
Data Set	WORK.HH
Dependent Variable	y
Covariance Structure	Variance Components
Estimation Method	REML
Residual Variance Method	Profile
Fixed Effects SE Method	Model-Based
Degrees of Freedom Method	Containment

Class Level Information

Class	Levels	Values
a	3	1 2 3
b	2	1 2

The results of the G3D procedure is displayed in Output 15.5.4. The large amount of information contained in the table, which is excluded from display, can be summarized with a single plot.

Output 15.5.4. Plot of the ParmSearch Data Set

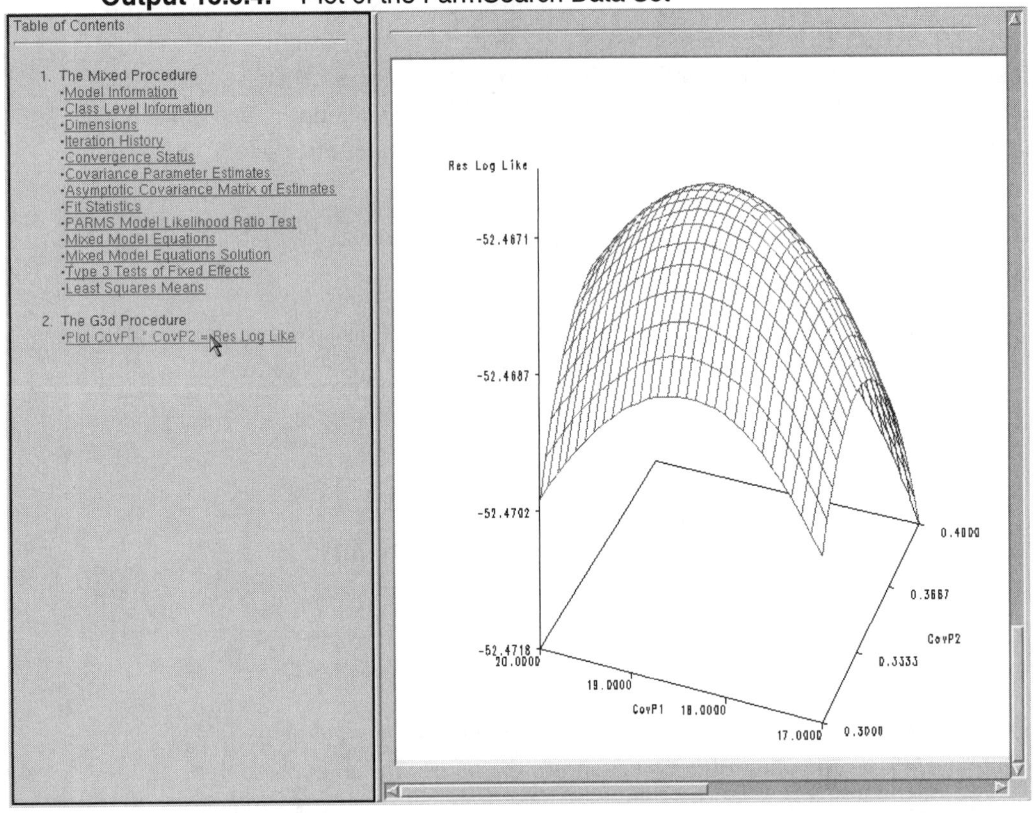

Example 15.6. Creating an Output Data Set from an ODS Table

The ODS OUTPUT statement creates SAS data sets from ODS tables. In the following example, the GENMOD procedure is invoked to perform Poisson regression and part of the resulting procedure output is written to a SAS data set.

Suppose the following insurance claims data are classified by two factors: age group (with two levels) and car type (with three levels).

```
data insure;
   input n c car$ age;
   ln = log(n);
   datalines;
500    42   small  1
1200   37   medium 1
100     1   large  1
400   101   small  2
500    73   medium 2
300    14   large  2
;
```

In the data set insure, the variable n represents the number of insurance policyholders and the variable c represents the number of insurance claims. The variable car represents the type of car involved (classified into three groups) and the variable age is the age group of a policyholder (classified into two groups).

In the statements that follow, PROC GENMOD performs a Poisson regression analysis of these data with a log link function. Assume that the number of claims c has a Poisson probability distribution and that its mean, μ_i, is related to the factors car and age.

Determining the Names of the ODS Tables

The purpose of the following statements is to obtain the names of the output tables produced in this PROC GENMOD run. The ODS TRACE statement lists the trace record, and the SAS listing destination is closed so that no output is displayed.

```
ods trace on;
ods listing close;

proc genmod data=insure;
   class car age;
   model c = car age / dist   = poisson
                       link   = log
                       offset = ln
                       obstats;
run;
ods trace off;
```

Output 15.6.1. The ODS TRACE: Partial Contents of the SAS Log

```
   ods trace on;
   ods listing close;

   proc genmod data=insure;
      class car age;
      model c = car age / dist   = poisson
                          link   = log
                          offset = ln
                          obstats;
   run;


Output Added:
-------------
Name:       ModelInfo
Label:      Model Information
Template:   Stat.Genmod.ModelInfo
Path:       Genmod.ModelInfo
-------------
         .
         .
         .
         .

NOTE: Algorithm converged.

Output Added:
-------------
Name:       ParameterEstimates
Label:      Analysis Of Parameter Estimates
Template:   stat.genmod.parameterestimates
Path:       Genmod.ParameterEstimates
-------------
NOTE: The scale parameter was held fixed.

Output Added:
-------------
Name:       ObStats
Label:      Observation Statistics
Template:   Stat.Genmod.Obstats
Path:       Genmod.ObStats
-------------
```

By default, the trace record is written to the SAS log, as displayed in Output 15.6.1. Note that you can alternatively specify that the information be interleaved with the procedure output in the SAS listing (see Example 15.3).

Creating the Output Data Set

In the statements that follow, the ODS OUTPUT statement writes the ODS table "ObStats" to a SAS data set called myObStats. All of the usual data set options, such as the KEEP= or RENAME= option, can be used in the ODS OUTPUT statement. Thus, to modify the ObStats data set so that it contains only certain variables, you can use the data set options as follows.

```
ods output ObStats=myObStats
                  (keep=Car Age Pred
                   rename=(Pred=PredictedValue));
```

```
proc genmod data=insure;
   class car age;
   model c = car age / dist   = poisson
                       link   = log
                       offset = ln
                       obstats;
run;
```

The KEEP= option in the ODS OUTPUT statement specifies that only the variables Car, Age, and Pred are written to the data set, and the Pred variable is renamed to PredictedValue. The GENMOD procedure is again invoked. In order to limit the amount of displayed output, the SAS listing destination remains closed. When a destination is closed, it remains closed until it is explicitly reopened.

In the following statements, the output data set myObStats is sorted, and the SAS listing is reopened for output. The results are displayed in Output 15.6.2.

```
proc sort data=myObStats;
   by descending PredictedValue;
run;

ods listing;
proc print data=myObStats noobs;
title 'Values of Car, Age, and the Predicted Values';
run;
```

Output 15.6.2. The ObStats Table, Created as a SAS Data Set

```
                Values of Car, Age, and the Predicted Values

                                         Predicted
                     car       age         Value

                    small       2        107.2011
                    medium      2       67.025444
                    medium      1       42.974556
                    small       1       35.798902
                    large       2       13.773459
                    large       1       1.2265414
```

Example 15.7. Creating an Output Data Set: Subsetting the Data

This example demonstrates how you can create an output data set with the ODS OUTPUT statement and also use data set selection keywords to limit the output that ODS writes to a SAS data set.

The following data set, called Color, contains the eye and hair color of children from two different regions of Europe. The data are recorded as cell counts, where the variable Count contains the number of children exhibiting each of the 15 eye and hair color combinations.

```
data Color;
   input Region Eyes $ Hair $ Count @@;
      label Eyes  ='Eye Color'
            Hair  ='Hair Color'
            Region='Geographic Region';
datalines;
1 blue  fair   23  1 blue  red     7  1 blue  medium 24
1 blue  dark   11  1 green fair   19  1 green red     7
1 green medium 18  1 green dark   14  1 brown fair   34
1 brown red     5  1 brown medium 41  1 brown dark   40
1 brown black   3  2 blue  fair   46  2 blue  red    21
2 blue  medium 44  2 blue  dark   40  2 blue  black   6
2 green fair   50  2 green red    31  2 green medium 37
2 green dark   23  2 brown fair   56  2 brown red    42
2 brown medium 53  2 brown dark   54  2 brown black  13
;
```

In the statements that follow, the SAS listing is closed. The ODS OUTPUT statement creates the "ChiSq" table as a SAS data set called myStats. Note that you can obtain the names of the tables created by any SAS/STAT procedure in the individual procedure chapter or from the individual procedure section of the SAS online Help system. You can also determine the names of tables with the ODS TRACE statement (see Example 15.3 and Example 15.6).

The DROP= data set option excludes variables from the new data set. The WHERE= data set option selects particular observations for output to the new data set myStats.

```
ods listing close;

ods output ChiSq=myStats
           (drop=Table
            where=(Statistic='Chi-Square' or
                   Statistic='Likelihood Ratio Chi-Square'));
```

In the following statements, the Color data set is first sorted by the Region variable. The FREQ procedure is invoked to create and analyze a crosstabulation table from the two categorical variables Eyes and Hair, for each value of the variable Region.

No ODS destinations are open until the ODS LISTING statement is encountered just prior to the invocation of the PRINT procedure.

```
proc sort data=Color;
   by Region;
run;
```

```
proc freq data=Color order=data;
   weight Count;
   tables Eyes*Hair/testp=(30 12 30 25 3);
   by Region;
   title 'Hair Color of European Children';
run;

ods listing;
proc print data=myStats;
run;
```

Output 15.7.1 displays the output resulting from the previous statements.

Output 15.7.1. Output Data Set from PROC FREQ and ODS

```
                    Hair Color of European Children

 Obs    Region    Statistic                      DF       Value      Prob

  1        1      Chi-Square                      8     12.6331    0.1251
  2        1      Likelihood Ratio Chi-Square     8     14.1503    0.0779
  3        2      Chi-Square                      8     18.2839    0.0192
  4        2      Likelihood Ratio Chi-Square     8     23.3021    0.0030
```

Example 15.8. Concatenating Output Data Sets: BY-Group Processing

Your data may be structured in such a way that the columns of an output table change over BY groups or from one section of output to another. This can occur in analyses that contain CLASS variables with differing values for some BY groups. This example demonstrates how you can write multiple ODS tables (possibly with different columns) to a single data set by using the MATCH_ALL option in the ODS OUTPUT statement.

Suppose that you want to analyze the following hypothetical data, which record the cell counts resulting from six types of blood tests administered at three laboratories. The values of method are not the same for each of the three laboratories. In the first laboratory, method = 1, 2, 3, 4; in the second laboratory, method = 2, 3, 4, 5; and in the third laboratory, method = 3, 4, 5, 6.

```
data Tests;
   input lab method count @@;
   datalines;
1 1 3  1 1 8  1 1 8  1 2 9  1 2 5  1 2 8
1 3 9  1 3 8  1 3 4  1 4 5  1 4 8  1 4 7
2 2 0  2 2 5  2 2 7  2 3 1  2 3 0  2 3 9
2 4 9  2 4 6  2 4 9  2 5 9  2 5 0  2 5 1
3 3 4  3 3 0  3 3 5  3 4 2  3 4 1  3 4 7
3 5 1  3 5 6  3 5 6  3 6 6  3 6 2  3 6 1
;
proc sort data=Tests;
   by lab;
run;
```

In the following analysis, the MATCH_ALL option is omitted and the $\mathbf{X'X}$ matrix for each of the BY groups is output to a SAS data set. The columns of $\mathbf{X'X}$ depend on the levels of the CLASS variable. Therefore, the structure of the $\mathbf{X'X}$ matrix differs according to the level of the CLASS variable (method).

```
ods output XpX=my1XpX;     /* Incorrect for this example */

proc glm data=Tests ;
   class method;
   model count = method / xpx;
   by lab;
quit;

proc print data=my1XpX;
title 'X''X Data Set, Omitting the MATCH_ALL Option';
run;
```

The GLM procedure produces the following warning:

```
WARNING: Output object 'XPX' contains 1 column(s) that cannot be
         mapped to data set WORK.MY1XPX (there is no corresponding
         variable on the output data set). Use the MATCH_ALL option
         to send each table to a separate data set.

NOTE: The above message was for the following by-group:
      lab=2
```

The PRINT procedure results, displayed in Output 15.8.1, show that the data set is missing columns for method=5 and method=6, which are in the second and third BY groups (methods performed in laboratories 2 and 3).

Output 15.8.1. PRINT Procedure: Omitting the MATCH_ALL Option

X'X Data Set, Omitting the MATCH_ALL Option

Obs	lab	Parameter	Intercept	method_1	method_2	method_3	method_4	count
1	1	Intercept	12	3	3	3	3	82
2	1	method 1	3	3	0	0	0	19
3	1	method 2	3	0	3	0	0	22
4	1	method 3	3	0	0	3	0	21
5	1	method 4	3	0	0	0	3	20
6	1	count	82	19	22	21	20	606
7	2	Intercept	12	.	3	3	3	56
8	2	method 2	3	.	3	0	0	12
9	2	method 3	3	.	0	3	0	10
10	2	method 4	3	.	0	0	3	24
11	2	method 5	3	.	0	0	0	10
12	2	count	56	.	12	10	24	436
13	3	Intercept	12	.	.	3	3	41
14	3	method 3	3	.	.	3	0	9
15	3	method 4	3	.	.	0	3	10
16	3	method 5	3	.	.	0	0	13
17	3	method 6	3	.	.	0	0	9
18	3	count	41	.	.	9	10	209

When multiple tables with different columns have the same name, as in this case, you can use the MATCH_ALL option to obtain correct results. The MATCH_ALL option creates a separate data set for each table. The initial data set name is specified after the equal sign, *outside* the parentheses, as follows:

```
ods output XpX(match_all=list)=matrix;   /* Correct */

proc glm data=Tests;
   class method;
   model count = method / xpx;
   by lab;
quit;
```

In the ODS OUTPUT statement, the specified data set name is matrix. When a second output table is generated, the corresponding data set name is created by appending a '1' to the specified data set name. In this case, the second data set name is matrix1. Subsequent data sets are named matrix2 and so on.

The macro variable list (specified as MATCH_ALL=list) contains the list of data set names. Thus, ODS creates the macro variable &list = matrix matrix1 matrix2. Note that the use of a macro variable name with MATCH_ALL is optional.

The set of values contained in the macro variable list is used in the following DATA step to combine all of the individual data sets into one data set. Note that, when you refer to a macro variable, an ampersand (&) always precedes a macro variable name but is not part of the name.

```
data my2XpX;
   set &list;
run;

proc print data=my2XpX;
title 'X''X Data Set, Specifying the MATCH_ALL Option';
run;
```

The final data set contains all of the results, including the results for method=5 and method=6 from the second and third laboratories. Output 15.8.2 displays the new data set.

Output 15.8.2. Print Procedure: Specifying the MATCH_ALL Option

X'X Data Set, Specifying the MATCH_ALL Option

Obs	Model	Parameter	Intercept	method_1	method_2	method_3	method_4	count	method_5	method_6
1	1	Intercept	12	3	3	3	3	82	.	.
2	1	method 1	3	3	0	0	0	19	.	.
3	1	method 2	3	0	3	0	0	22	.	.
4	1	method 3	3	0	0	3	0	21	.	.
5	1	method 4	3	0	0	0	3	20	.	.
6	1	count	82	19	22	21	20	606	.	.
7	2	Intercept	12	.	3	3	3	56	3	.
8	2	method 2	3	.	3	0	0	12	0	.
9	2	method 3	3	.	0	3	0	10	0	.
10	2	method 4	3	.	0	0	3	24	0	.
11	2	method 5	3	.	0	0	0	10	3	.
12	2	count	56	.	12	10	24	436	10	.
13	3	Intercept	12	.	.	3	3	41	3	3
14	3	method 3	3	.	.	3	0	9	0	0
15	3	method 4	3	.	.	0	3	10	0	0
16	3	method 5	3	.	.	0	0	13	3	0
17	3	method 6	3	.	.	0	0	9	0	3
18	3	count	41	.	.	9	10	209	13	9

Example 15.9. Concatenating Output Data Sets: RUN Group Processing

This example demonstrates how you can write multiple tables to a single data set using the MATCH_ALL= and PERSIST= options in the ODS OUTPUT statement. The PERSIST= option maintains ODS settings across RUN statements for procedures that support run-group processing. In the following analysis, the REG procedure is invoked and the covariance matrix of the estimates is output for two different models. The flexibility of the ODS OUTPUT statement enables you to create a single data set that contains both of the resulting covariance matrices.

Consider the following population growth trends. The population of the United States from 1790 to 1970 is fit to linear and quadratic functions of time. Note that the quadratic term, YearSq, is created in the DATA step; this is done since polynomial effects such as Year*Year cannot be specified in the MODEL statement in PROC REG. The data are as follows:

```
title1 'Concatenating Two Tables into One Data Set';
title2 'US Population Study';
data USPopulation;
   input Population @@;
   retain Year 1780;
   Year=Year+10;
   YearSq=Year*Year;
   Population=Population/1000;
   datalines;
3929 5308 7239 9638 12866 17069 23191 31443 39818 50155
62947 75994 91972 105710 122775 131669 151325 179323 203211
;
```

In the following statements, the REG procedure is invoked and the ODS statement requests that a data set be created to contain the COVB matrix (the covariance matrix of the estimates).

The ODS statement uses the MATCH_ALL= and PERSIST= options. The effect of these options is to create a separate data set for each COVB matrix encountered in the entire procedure step.

```
proc reg data=USPopulation;
   ods output covb(match_all=Bname           /* correct */
                   persist=run)=Bmatrix;
   var YearSq;
   model Population=Year / covb ;
run;
```

The MODEL statement defines the regression model, and the COVB matrix is requested. The RUN statement executes the REG procedure and the model is fit, producing a covariance matrix of the estimates with 2 rows and 2 columns.

Output 15.9.1. Regression Results for the Model Population=Year

```
                    Concatenating Two Output Tables into One Data Set
                                   US Population Study

                                    The REG Procedure
                                     Model: MODEL1
                             Dependent Variable: Population

                                  Analysis of Variance

                                         Sum of           Mean
Source                    DF            Squares         Square    F Value    Pr > F

Model                      1              66336          66336     201.87    <.0001
Error                     17         5586.29253      328.60544
Corrected Total           18              71923


             Root MSE             18.12748    R-Square     0.9223
             Dependent Mean       69.76747    Adj R-Sq     0.9178
             Coeff Var            25.98271


                                  Parameter Estimates

                          Parameter        Standard
    Variable      DF       Estimate           Error    t Value    Pr > |t|

    Intercept      1    -1958.36630       142.80455     -13.71      <.0001
    Year           1        1.07879         0.07593      14.21      <.0001
```

Output 15.9.2. CovB Matrix for the Model Population=Year

```
             Concatenating Two Output Tables into One Data Set
                           US Population Study

                            The REG Procedure
                             Model: MODEL1
                    Dependent Variable: Population

                        Covariance of Estimates

              Variable           Intercept                Year

              Intercept       20393.138485        -10.83821461
              Year            -10.83821461        0.0057650078
```

In the next step, the YearSq variable is added to the model and the model is again fit, producing a covariance matrix of the estimates with three rows and three columns.

```
add YearSq;
print;
run;
```

The results of the regression are displayed in Output 15.9.3.

Output 15.9.3. Regression Results for the Model Population=Year YearSq

```
             Concatenating Two Output Tables into One Data Set
                           US Population Study

                            The REG Procedure
                             Model: MODEL1.1
                    Dependent Variable: Population

                          Analysis of Variance

                                   Sum of           Mean
Source                   DF       Squares         Square    F Value    Pr > F

Model                     2         71799          35900    4641.72    <.0001
Error                    16     123.74557        7.73410
Corrected Total          18         71923


             Root MSE              2.78102    R-Square     0.9983
             Dependent Mean       69.76747    Adj R-Sq     0.9981
             Coeff Var             3.98613


                          Parameter Estimates

                          Parameter       Standard
    Variable      DF       Estimate          Error    t Value    Pr > |t|

    Intercept      1          20450      843.47533      24.25      <.0001
    Year           1      -22.78061        0.89785     -25.37      <.0001
    YearSq         1        0.00635     0.00023877      26.58      <.0001
```

Output 15.9.4. CovB Matrix for the Model Population=Year YearSq

```
          Concatenating Two Output Tables into One Data Set
                         US Population Study

                          The REG Procedure
                          Model: MODEL1.1
                 Dependent Variable: Population

                      Covariance of Estimates

Variable          Intercept                 Year             YearSq

Intercept      711450.62602         -757.2493826       0.2013282694
Year           -757.2493826         0.8061328943       -0.000214361
YearSq         0.2013282694         -0.000214361       5.7010894E-8
```

In the preceding analysis, two COVB matrices are generated, corresponding to the two fitted models. When you select two output tables that have the same name but different structures, specify the MATCH_ALL option to create a new data set for each table.

When you specify MATCH_ALL=*name*, a macro variable called *name* is created that contains the names of all the generated data sets. Thus, in this example, ODS creates two data sets (one for each model fit in the PROC REG run) and the macro variable Bname is created to contain the names of the two data sets.

The PERSIST=RUN option maintains the ODS selection list across RUN statements for procedures that support run-group processing. If the PERSIST=RUN option is omitted, the selection list is cleared when the RUN statement is encountered and only the first COVB matrix is selected. Because the PERSIST=RUN option is specified, the selection list remains in effect throughout the REG procedure step. This ensures that each of the COVB matrices is selected and output.

The first output data set has the specified name BMatrix. Subsequent data set names are automatically created by appending the numerals $1, 2, 3, \ldots$, as needed. In this case, the names of the data sets are BMatrix and BMatrix1. The names are contained in the macro variable Bname.

The result of the ODS OUTPUT statement is displayed with the following statements. The SET &BName statement reads observations from all data sets listed by the macro variable Bname. The variable Bname contains the two values (BMatrix and BMatrix1). Thus, the SET statement reads observations from these two data sets. Note that, when you refer to a macro variable, an ampersand (&) always precedes a macro variable name but is not part of the name.

```
data new2;
   title 'The COVB Matrix Data Set, Using the PERSIST option';
   title2 'Concatenating Two Tables into One Data Set';
   set &Bname;
run;
proc print;
run;
```

The data set new2 contains the two data sets created from the two COVB matrices.

Output 15.9.5. Results of the ODS OUTPUT Statement, Specifying the PERSIST Option

The COVB Matrix Data Set, Using the PERSIST option
Concatenating Two Output Tables into One Data Set

Obs	_Run_	Model	Dependent	Variable	Intercept	Year	YearSq
1	1	MODEL1	Population	Intercept	20393.138485	-10.83821461	.
2	1	MODEL1	Population	Year	-10.83821461	0.0057650078	.
3	2	MODEL1.1	Population	Intercept	711450.62602	-757.2493826	0.2013282694
4	2	MODEL1.1	Population	Year	-757.2493826	0.8061328943	-0.000214361
5	2	MODEL1.1	Population	YearSq	0.2013282694	-0.000214361	5.7010894E-8

Example 15.10. Using the TEMPLATE Procedure to Customize Output

You can use the TEMPLATE procedure to modify the appearance of your displayed ODS tables. The following example, similar to that given in Olinger and Tobias (1998), creates output data sets using the ODS OUTPUT statement, modifies a template using PROC TEMPLATE, and displays the output data sets using the modified template.

The data set comes from a preclinical drug experiment (Cole and Grizzle 1966). In order to study the effect of two different drugs on histamine levels in the blood, researchers administer the drugs to 13 animals, and the levels of histamine in the animals' blood is measured after 0, 1, 3, and 5 minutes. The response variable is the logarithm of the histamine level. The following statements create a SAS data set named Histamine that contains the experimental data.

```
title1 "Histamine Study";
data Histamine;
   input Drug $12. Depleted $ hist0 hist1 hist3 hist5;
   logHist0 = log(hist0); logHist1 = log(Hist1);
   logHist3 = log(hist3); logHist5 = log(Hist5);
   datalines;
Morphine      N  .04  .20  .10  .08
Morphine      N  .02  .06  .02  .02
Morphine      N  .07 1.40  .48  .24
Morphine      N  .17  .57  .35  .24
Morphine      Y  .10  .09  .13  .14
Morphine      Y  .07  .07  .06  .07
Morphine      Y  .05  .07  .06  .07
Trimethaphan  N  .03  .62  .31  .22
Trimethaphan  N  .03 1.05  .73  .60
Trimethaphan  N  .07  .83 1.07  .80
Trimethaphan  N  .09 3.13 2.06 1.23
Trimethaphan  Y  .10  .09  .09  .08
Trimethaphan  Y  .08  .09  .09  .10
Trimethaphan  Y  .13  .10  .12  .12
Trimethaphan  Y  .06  .05  .05  .05
;
```

In the analysis that follows, the GLM procedure is invoked to perform a repeated measures analysis, naming the drug and depletion status as between-subject factors in the MODEL statement and naming post-administration measurement time as the within-subject factor (for more information on this study and its analysis, see Example 7 in Chapter 30, "The GLM Procedure").

The following ODS statement requests that two ODS tables be written to SAS data sets called HistWithin and HistBetween. The SAS listing is closed so that no output is displayed. The GLM procedure is invoked and the model is fit.

```
ods output MultStat                        = HistWithin
           BetweenSubjects.ModelANOVA      = HistBetween;

ods listing close;

proc glm data=Histamine;
   class Drug Depleted;
   model LogHist0--LogHist5 = Drug Depleted Drug*Depleted / nouni;
   repeated Time 4 (0 1 3 5) polynomial / summary printe;
run;
quit;
```

All of the multivariate test results appear in the HistWithin data set. This is because all multivariate test tables are named "MultStat," although they occur in different directories in the output directory hierarchy.

Note that, even though there are also other tables named "ModelANOVA," the preceding ODS OUTPUT statement ensures that only the between-subject ANOVA appears in the HistBetween data set. The specific table is selected because of the additional specification of the partial path ("BetweenSubjects") in which it occurs. For more information on names and qualified path names, see the discussion in the section "Using the Output Delivery System" beginning on page 256.

In the following statements, a new data set, temp1, is created to contain the two data sets output in the preceding GLM run. They are displayed with no further processing.

```
ods listing;
title2 'Listing of Raw Data Sets';
data temp1;
   set HistBetween HistWithin;
run;
proc print;
run;
```

Output 15.10.1. Listing of the Raw Data Sets: Histamine Study

Histamine Study
Listing of Raw Data Sets

Obs	Dependent	Hypothesis Type	Source	DF	SS	MS	FValue	ProbF
1	BetweenSubjects	3	Drug	1	5.99336243	5.99336243	2.71	0.1281
2	BetweenSubjects	3	Depleted	1	15.44840703	15.44840703	6.98	0.0229
3	BetweenSubjects	3	Drug*Depleted	1	4.69087508	4.69087508	2.12	0.1734
4	BetweenSubjects	3	Error	11	24.34683348	2.21334850	_	_
5		.		.	.	.	24.03	0.0001
6		.		.	.	.	24.03	0.0001
7		.		.	.	.	24.03	0.0001
8		.		.	.	.	24.03	0.0001
9		.		.	.	.	5.78	0.0175
10		.		.	.	.	5.78	0.0175
11		.		.	.	.	5.78	0.0175
12		.		.	.	.	5.78	0.0175
13		.		.	.	.	21.31	0.0002
14		.		.	.	.	21.31	0.0002
15		.		.	.	.	21.31	0.0002
16		.		.	.	.	21.31	0.0002
17		.		.	.	.	12.48	0.0015
18		.		.	.	.	12.48	0.0015
19		.		.	.	.	12.48	0.0015
20		.		.	.	.	12.48	0.0015

Obs	Hypothesis	Error	Statistic	Value	NumDF	DenDF
1				.	.	.
2				.	.	.
3				.	.	.
4				.	.	.
5	Time	Error SSCP Matrix	Wilks' Lambda	0.11097706	3	9
6	Time	Error SSCP Matrix	Pillai's Trace	0.88902294	3	9
7	Time	Error SSCP Matrix	Hotelling-Lawley Trace	8.01087137	3	9
8	Time	Error SSCP Matrix	Roy's Greatest Root	8.01087137	3	9
9	Time_Drug	Error SSCP Matrix	Wilks' Lambda	0.34155984	3	9
10	Time_Drug	Error SSCP Matrix	Pillai's Trace	0.65844016	3	9
11	Time_Drug	Error SSCP Matrix	Hotelling-Lawley Trace	1.92774470	3	9
12	Time_Drug	Error SSCP Matrix	Roy's Greatest Root	1.92774470	3	9
13	Time_Depleted	Error SSCP Matrix	Wilks' Lambda	0.12339988	3	9
14	Time_Depleted	Error SSCP Matrix	Pillai's Trace	0.87660012	3	9
15	Time_Depleted	Error SSCP Matrix	Hotelling-Lawley Trace	7.10373567	3	9
16	Time_Depleted	Error SSCP Matrix	Roy's Greatest Root	7.10373567	3	9
17	Time_Drug_Depleted	Error SSCP Matrix	Wilks' Lambda	0.19383010	3	9
18	Time_Drug_Depleted	Error SSCP Matrix	Pillai's Trace	0.80616990	3	9
19	Time_Drug_Depleted	Error SSCP Matrix	Hotelling-Lawley Trace	4.15915732	3	9
20	Time_Drug_Depleted	Error SSCP Matrix	Roy's Greatest Root	4.15915732	3	9

In order to reduce the amount of information displayed in Output 15.10.1, this example creates the following data set, HistTests. Only the observations from the raw data sets that are needed for interpretation are included. The variable Hypothesis in the HistWithin data set is renamed to Source, and the NumDF variable is renamed DF.

The renamed variables correspond to the variable names found in the HistBetween data set.

```
data HistTests;
   set HistBetween(where =(Source    ^= "Error"))
       HistWithin (rename=(Hypothesis =  Source NumDF=DF)
                   where =(Statistic  =  "Hotelling-Lawley Trace"));
run;
proc print ;
title2 'Listing of Selections from the Raw Data Sets';
run;
```

Output 15.10.2. Listing of Selections from the Raw Data Sets: Histamine Study

Listing of Selections from the Raw Data Sets

Obs	Dependent	Hypothesis Type	Source	DF	SS	MS
1	BetweenSubjects	3	Drug	1	5.99336243	5.99336243
2	BetweenSubjects	3	Depleted	1	15.44840703	15.44840703
3	BetweenSubjects	3	Drug*Depleted	1	4.69087508	4.69087508
4		.	Time	3	.	.
5		.	Time_Drug	3	.	.
6		.	Time_Depleted	3	.	.
7		.	Time_Drug_Depleted	3	.	.

Obs	FValue	ProbF	Error	Statistic	Value	DenDF
1	2.71	0.1281			.	.
2	6.98	0.0229			.	.
3	2.12	0.1734			.	.
4	24.03	0.0001	Error SSCP Matrix	Hotelling-Lawley Trace	8.01087137	9
5	5.78	0.0175	Error SSCP Matrix	Hotelling-Lawley Trace	1.92774470	9
6	21.31	0.0002	Error SSCP Matrix	Hotelling-Lawley Trace	7.10373567	9
7	12.48	0.0015	Error SSCP Matrix	Hotelling-Lawley Trace	4.15915732	9

The amount of information contained in the HistTests is appropriate for interpreting the analysis (Output 15.10.2). However, you can further modify the presentation of the data by applying a template to this combined test data. A template specifies how data should be displayed. The output from previous ODS TRACE ON statements (for example, Output 15.4.2) shows that each table has an associated template as well as a name. In particular, the template associated with PROC GLM's ANOVA table is called 'Stat.GLM.Tests'.

You can use the 'Stat.GLM.Tests' template to display the SAS data set HistTests, as follows:

```
data _null_ ;
title2 'Listing of the Selections, Using a Standard Template';
   set HistTests;
   file print ods=(template='Stat.GLM.Tests');
   put _ods_;
run;
```

The ODS= option in the FILE statement enables you to use the DATA step to display a data set as a table. You do this by specifying data columns and associated attributes, such as the template specification.

The PUT statement contains the _ODS_ keyword. The keyword instructs the PUT statement to send the data values for all columns (as defined in the ODS= option in the FILE statement) to the open ODS destinations. For more information on using ODS in the DATA step, refer to *The Complete Guide to the SAS Output Delivery System*.

Output 15.10.3. Listing of the Data Sets Using a Standard Template

```
                          Histamine Study
          Listing of the Selections, Using a Standard Template
Source                  DF           SS     Mean Square    F Value     Pr > F

Drug                     1   5.99336243      5.99336243       2.71     0.1281
Depleted                 1  15.44840703     15.44840703       6.98     0.0229
Drug*Depleted            1   4.69087508      4.69087508       2.12     0.1734
Time                     3            .               .      24.03     0.0001
Time_Drug                3            .               .       5.78     0.0175
Time_Depleted            3            .               .      21.31     0.0002
Time_Drug_Depleted       3            .               .      12.48     0.0015
```

The data set contains the appropriate information, and it is presented in an easily understandable format, using the 'Stat.GLM.Tests' template.

Customizing Your Output

Suppose that you now want to modify the template used to format the ANOVA tables in order to emphasize significant effects. The following statements provide an example of how you can use the TEMPLATE procedure to

- redefine the format for the SS and Mean Square columns
- include the table title and footnote in the body of the table
- translate the missing values for SS and Mean Square in the rows corresponding to multivariate tests to asterisks (to refer to the footnote)
- add a column depicting the level of significance

For detailed information on using the TEMPLATE procedure, refer to the chapter titled "The Template Procedure" in *The Complete Guide to the SAS Output Delivery System.*

```
proc template;
   define table CombinedTests;
      parent=Stat.GLM.Tests;

      header "#Histamine Study##";
      footer "#* - Test computed using Hotelling-Lawley trace";

      column Source DF SS MS FValue ProbF Star;

      define SS;
         parent = Stat.GLM.SS;
         format = D7.3;
         translate _val_ = . into '    *';
      end;
      define MS;
         parent = Stat.GLM.MS;
         format = D7.3;
         translate _val_ = . into '    *';
      end;
      define Star;
         compute as ProbF;
         translate _val_ >  0.05  into "",
                   _val_ >  0.01  into "*",
                   _val_ >  0.001 into "**",
```

```
                _val_ <= 0.001 into "***";
          pre_space=1 width=3 just=l;
        end;
      end;
   run;
```

The D*w.s* format, used in the preceding statements to redefine the SS and Mean Square columns, writes numbers in similar ranges with the same number of decimal places. In the format specification, *w* represents the width of the field and *s* represents the number of significant digits. Refer to the chapter on formats in *SAS Language Reference: Dictionary* for detailed information.

The following statements display the HistTests data set using the customized template. The results are displayed in Output 15.10.4.

```
data _null_;
title2 'Listing of the Selections, Using a Customized Template';
   set HistTests;
   file print ods=(template='CombinedTests');
   put _ods_;
run;
```

Output 15.10.4. Listing of the Data Sets Using a Customized Template: Histamine Study

```
                              Histamine Study

                                   Sum of         Mean
Source                    DF      Squares       Square     F Value     Pr > F

Drug                       1        5.993        5.993        2.71     0.1281
Depleted                   1       15.448       15.448        6.98     0.0229 *
Drug*Depleted              1        4.691        4.691        2.12     0.1734
Time                       3          *            *         24.03     0.0001 ***
Time_Drug                  3          *            *          5.78     0.0175 *
Time_Depleted              3          *            *         21.31     0.0002 ***
Time_Drug_Depleted         3          *            *         12.48     0.0015 **

               * - Test computed using Hotelling-Lawley trace
```

Example 15.11. Creating HTML Output, Linked Within a Single Analysis

This example demonstrates how you can use ODS to provide links between different parts of your HTML procedure output.

Suppose that you are analyzing a 4x4 factorial experiment for an industrial process, testing for differences in the number of defective products manufactured by different machines using different sources of raw material. The data set Experiment is created as follows.

```
data Experiment;
   do Supplier = 'A','B','C','D';
      do Machine = 1 to 4;
         do rep = 1 to 5;
            input Defects @@;
            output;
            end;
         end;
      end;
   datalines;
 2  6  3  3  6  8  6  6  4  4  4  2  4  0  4  5  5  7  8  5
13 12 12 11 12 16 15 14 14 13 11 10 12 12 10 13 13 14 15 12
 2  6  3  6  6  6  4  4  6  6  0  3  2  0  2  4  6  7  6  4
20 19 18 21 22 22 24 23 20 20 17 19 18 16 17 23 20 20 22 21
;
```

Suppose that you are interested in fitting a model to determine the effect that the supplier of raw material and machine type have on the number of defects in the products. If the F test for a factor is significant, you would like to follow up with a multiple comparisons procedure. Thus, the tables of interest are the model ANOVA and the multiple comparisons output.

The following statements demonstrate how you can link a row of the ANOVA table to the corresponding multiple comparisons table. This is done by altering the display of values (inserting links) in the Source column of the ANOVA table. The links are inserted by using the TEMPLATE procedure.

```
proc template;
   edit Stat.GLM.Tests;
      edit Source;
         translate _val_ = "Supplier" into
              ('<a href="#IDX7">' || _val_ || '</a>'),
                   _val_ = "Machine"  into
              ('<a href="#IDX10">' || _val_ || '</a>');
         end;
      end;
run;
```

In order to determine the value to use in the HTML anchor link (<a href="">), you can run the analysis once and view information on your output in the Results node of the SAS Explorer. The anchor name '#IDX7' is given to the table "ANOVA.Means.Supplier.Defects.MCLines.Tukey.MCLines" (the anchor name is automatically generated in the SAS run). The statements create the Supplier label as a link that, when clicked, opens the table of means from the "Tukey's Studentized Range Test for Defects" associated with the Supplier variable.

The '#IDX10' anchor name is given to the table "ANOVA.Means.Machine.Defects.MCLines.Tukey.MCLines". The statements create the Machine label as a link that, when clicked, opens the table of means from the "Tukey's Studentized Range Test for Defects" associated with the Machine variable.

The following statements specify that ODS close the SAS listing destination and open the HTML destination. ODS writes the HTML output to the file 'anovab.htm'.

```
ods listing close;
ods html body='anovab.htm' ;
```

Since this is a balanced experiment, the ANOVA procedure computes the appropriate analysis, performed with the following statements:

```
proc anova data=Experiment;
   class Supplier Machine;
   model Defects = Supplier Machine;
   means Supplier Machine / tukey;
quit;

ods html close;
```

The output from the ANOVA procedure is displayed in Output 15.11.1.

Output 15.11.1. HTML Output from the ANOVA Procedure: Linked Output

Dependent Variable: Defects

Source	DF	Sum of Squares	Mean Square	F Value	Pr > F
Model	6	3604.775000	600.795833	304.12	<.0001
Error	73	144.212500	1.975514		
Corrected Total	79	3748.987500			

R-Square	Coeff Var	Root MSE	Defects Mean
0.961533	13.53097	1.405530	10.38750

Source	DF	Anova SS	Mean Square	F Value	Pr > F
Supplier	3	3441.637500	1147.212500	580.72	<.0001
Machine	3	163.137500	54.379167	27.53	<.0001

The ANOVA procedure uses the "Stat.GLM.Tests" template to format the ANOVA table. The underlined text displayed in Output 15.11.1 shows the links in the table cells labeled as 'Supplier' and 'Machine.' Because of the modifications in the preceding statements, the Supplier table listing contains the HTML anchor reference to the tag 'IDX7.' When you click on the 'Supplier' link, the appropriate multiple comparison table opens in your browser (Output 15.11.2). The links corresponding to the Machine variable operate similarly.

Output 15.11.2. Linked Output: Multiple Comparison Table from PROC ANOVA

Means with the same letter are not significantly different.			
Tukey Grouping	Mean	N	Supplier
A	20.1000	20	D
B	12.7000	20	B
C	4.6000	20	A
C			
C	4.1500	20	C

Example 15.12. Creating HTML Output, Linked Between Analyses

The following example demonstrates how you can use ODS to create links between different types of analyses.

The data in the following example are selected from a larger experiment on the use of drugs in the treatment of leprosy (Snedecor and Cochran 1967, p. 422).

Variables in the study are

Drug	- two antibiotics (A and D) and a control (F)
PreTreatment	- a pretreatment score of leprosy bacilli
PostTreatment	- a posttreatment score of leprosy bacilli

The data set is created as follows:

```
data drugtest;
   input drug $ PreTreatment PostTreatment @@;
   datalines;
a 11  6  a  8  0  a  5  2  a 14  8  a 19 11
a  6  4  a 10 13  a  6  1  a 11  8  a  3  0
```

```
d  6  0  d  6  2  d  7  3  d  8  1  d 18 18
d  8  4  d 19 14  d  8  9  d  5  1  d 15  9
f 16 13  f 13 10  f 11 18  f  9  5  f 21 23
f 16 12  f 12  5  f 12 16  f  7  1  f 12 20
;
```

The ODS HTML statement opens the HTML destination, specifies the body file name, requests that a table of contents be generated for the output, and specifies the file name of the frame to contain the body and table of contents. The NOGTITLE option in the ODS HTML statement specifies that titles are not to be included as an integral part of any generated graphics. For all graphics contained in the specified body file, titles appear in the body file and are external to graphics.

```
ods html body='glmb.htm'
         contents='glmc.htm'
         frame='glmf.htm'
         nogtitle;

ods output LSMeans=lsmeans;
```

The ODS OUTPUT statement writes the table of LS-means to the data set called lsmeans.

The GLM procedure is invoked to perform an analysis of covariance and compute LS-means for the variable Drug.

```
proc glm;
   class drug;
   model PostTreatment = Drug|PreTreatment / solution;
   lsmeans drug / stderr pdiff;
quit;
```

The following steps demonstrate how you can create links to connect the results of different analyses. In this example, the table of LS-means is graphically summarized with the GCHART procedure. In the steps that follow, each part of the resulting chart is linked to a plot that displays the relationship between the PostTreatment response variable and the PreTreatment variable.

The following DATA step creates a new variable called drugclick that matches each drug value with an HTML file. The variable drugclick is used in the subsequent GCHART procedure run. The variable provides the connection information for linking the two parts of the analysis together. The files referred to in these statements are created in a later step.

```
data lsmeans;
   set lsmeans;
   if Drug='a' then drugclick='HREF=drug1.htm';
   if Drug='d' then drugclick='HREF=drug2.htm';
   if Drug='f' then drugclick='HREF=drug3.htm';
run;
```

The following GOPTIONS and AXIS statements specify settings for the GCHART procedure. PROC GCHART is invoked, and the HBAR statement requests a horizontal bar chart for the variable drug. The length of the bars represent the value of the lsmean variable. The HTML option specifies the variable drugclick as the html linking variable to use. The FOOTNOTE1 and FOOTNOTE2 statements provide text that indicates how to use the links on the graph.

```
goptions ftext=swissb hsize=5.5in vsize=3.5in
         border cback=white;
axis1 minor=none label=(angle=90 rotate=0);
axis2 minor=none;

title f=swiss 'Chart of LS-means for Drug Type';
proc gchart data=lsmeans;
   hbar Drug/sumvar=lsmean type=mean
             frame cframe=ligr
             gaxis=axis1 raxis=axis2
             html=drugclick;
footnote1 j=l 'click on the bar to see a plot of PostTreatment';
footnote2 j=l 'versus PreTreatment for the corresponding drug';
format lsmean 6.3;
run;

footnote;
ods html close;
run;
```

The preceding statements create a chart that summarizes the information from PROC GLM and that contains links to a second graphic analysis (using the variable drugclick and the HTML option in PROC GCHART).

The following statements provide that second analysis. The three files referred to by the drugclick variable are created as follows.

```
ods html body='drug1.htm' newfile=page;
symbol1 c=white v=dot i=r ;
title 'Plot of PostTreatment versus PreTreatment';
proc gplot data=drugtest uniform;
   plot PostTreatment*PreTreatment/frame cframe=ligr;
by Drug notsorted;
footnote;
run;
ods html close;
```

The NEWFILE option in the ODS HTML statement specifies that a new HTML file be created for each page of output. Note that page breaks occur only when a procedure explicitly starts a new page. The NEWFILE option also increments the filename for each new HTML file created, with the first filename corresponding to that given in the BODY= option, 'drug1.htm'.

The GPLOT procedure is invoked, producing a plot of the variable PostTreatment versus the variable PreTreatment for each value of the Drug variable. Thus, three plots are created, and each plot is contained in a separate html file. The files are named 'drug1.htm', 'drug2.htm', and 'drug3.htm'. The filenames match those filenames specified as values of the **drugclick** variable.

Output 15.12.1. Output from PROC GLM

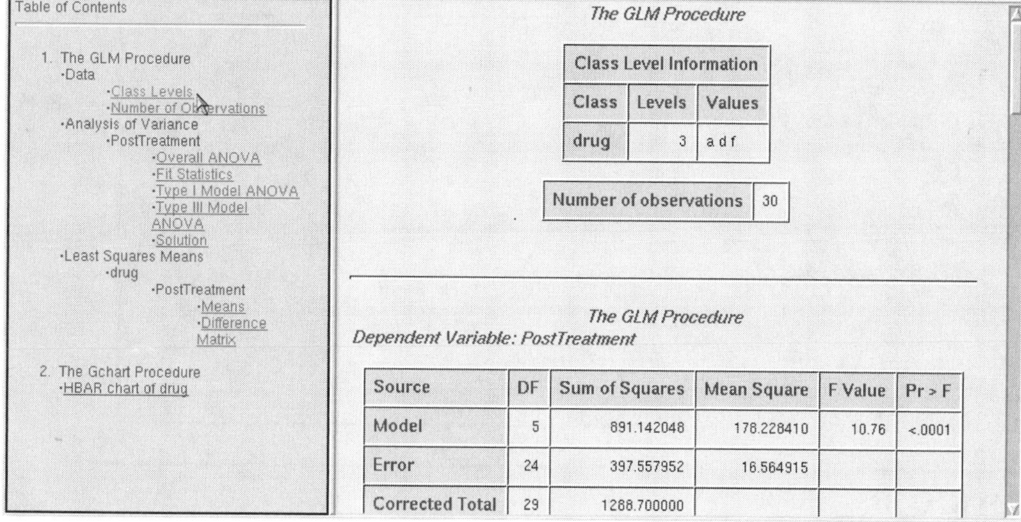

Table of Contents

1. The GLM Procedure
   - Data
     - Class Levels
     - Number of Observations
   - Analysis of Variance
     - PostTreatment
       - Overall ANOVA
       - Fit Statistics
       - Type I Model ANOVA
       - Type III Model ANOVA
       - Solution
   - Least Squares Means
     - drug
       - PostTreatment
         - Means
         - Difference Matrix
2. The Gchart Procedure
   - HBAR chart of drug

The GLM Procedure

Class Level Information		
Class	Levels	Values
drug	3	a d f

Number of observations	30

The GLM Procedure

Dependent Variable: PostTreatment

Source	DF	Sum of Squares	Mean Square	F Value	Pr > F
Model	5	891.142048	178.228410	10.76	<.0001
Error	24	397.557952	16.564915		
Corrected Total	29	1288.700000			

Output 15.12.2. Bar Chart of LS-means by Drug Type: Linked Output

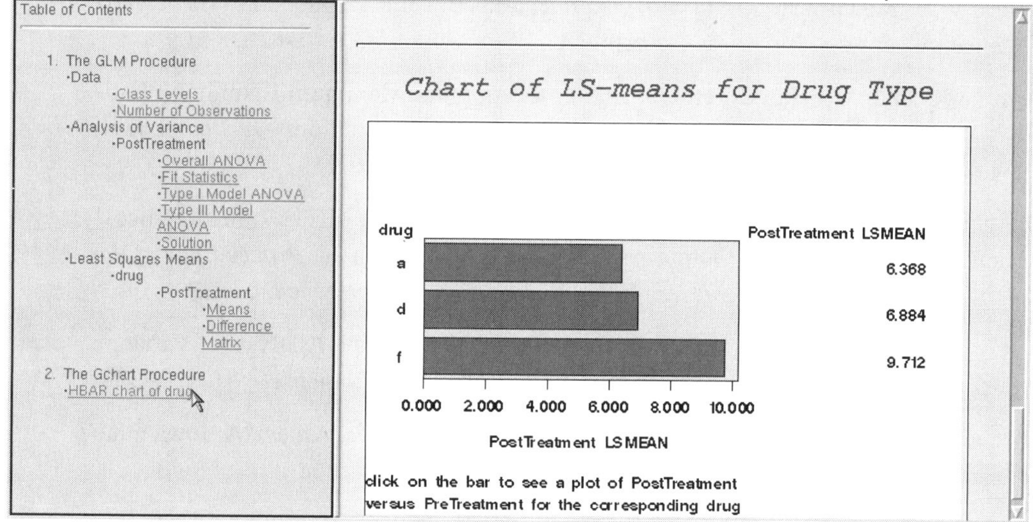

The graphic in Output 15.12.2 displays the difference in **lsmeans** for each drug type. When you click on a bar that represents a value of the variable **drug**, the browser opens the plot of **PostTreatment** versus **PostTreatment** that corresponds to that value of the variable **Drug**. Output 15.12.3 displays the plot corresponding to the drug type 'f'. You can view this graphic by clicking on the bottom bar in the bar chart in Output 15.12.2.

Output 15.12.3. Plot of PostTreatment versus PreTreatment for Drug Type 'f': Linked Output

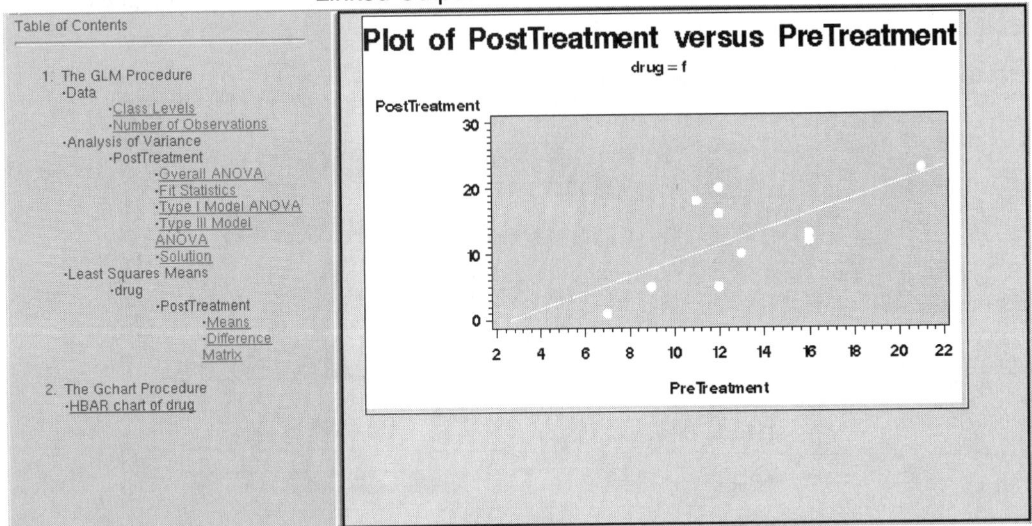

References

Cole, J.W.L. and Grizzle, J.E. (1966), "Applications of Multivariate Analysis of Variance to Repeated Measures Experiments," *Biometrics*, 22, 810–828.

Hemmerle, W.J. and Hartley, H. O. (1973), "Computing Maximum Likelihood Estimates for the Mixed AOV Model Using the W-Transformation," *Technometrics*, 15, 819–831.

Olinger, C. R. and Tobias, R. D. (1998), "It Chops, It Dices, It Makes Julienne Slices! ODS for Data Analysis Output As-You-Like-It in Version 7," *Proceedings of the Twenty-third Annual SAS Users Group International Conference*, 23.

Pothoff, R.F. and Roy, S.N. (1964), "A Generalized Multivariate Analysis of Variance Model Useful Especially for Growth Curve Problems," *Biometrika*, 51, 313–326.

Snedecor, G.W. and Cochran, W.G. (1967), *Statistical Methods*, Ames, IA: Iowa State University Press.

Chapter 16

The ACECLUS Procedure

Chapter Table of Contents

Chapter 16
The ACECLUS Procedure

Overview

The ACECLUS (Approximate Covariance Estimation for CLUStering) procedure obtains approximate estimates of the pooled within-cluster covariance matrix when the clusters are assumed to be multivariate normal with equal covariance matrices. Neither cluster membership nor the number of clusters need be known. PROC ACECLUS is useful for preprocessing data to be subsequently clustered by the CLUSTER or the FASTCLUS procedure.

Many clustering methods perform well with spherical clusters but poorly with elongated elliptical clusters (Everitt 1980, 77–97). If the elliptical clusters have roughly the same orientation and eccentricity, you can apply a linear transformation to the data to yield a spherical within-cluster covariance matrix, that is, a covariance matrix proportional to the identity. Equivalently, the distance between observations can be measured in the metric of the inverse of the pooled within-cluster covariance matrix. The remedy is difficult to apply, however, because you need to know what the clusters are in order to compute the sample within-cluster covariance matrix. One approach is to estimate iteratively both cluster membership and within-cluster covariance (Wolfe 1970; Hartigan 1975). Another approach is provided by Art, Gnanadesikan, and Kettenring (1982). They have devised an ingenious method for estimating the within-cluster covariance matrix without knowledge of the clusters. The method can be applied before any of the usual clustering techniques, including hierarchical clustering methods.

First, Art, Gnanadesikan, and Kettenring (1982) obtain a decomposition of the total-sample sum-of-squares-and-cross-products (SSCP) matrix into within-cluster and between-cluster SSCP matrices computed from pairwise differences between observations, rather than differences between observations and means. Then, they show how the within-cluster SSCP matrix based on pairwise differences can be approximated without knowing the number or the membership of the clusters. The approximate within-cluster SSCP matrix can be used to compute distances for cluster analysis, or it can be used in a canonical analysis similar to canonical discriminant analysis. For more information, see Chapter 21, "The CANDISC Procedure."

Art, Gnanadesikan, and Kettenring demonstrate by Monte Carlo calculations that their method can produce better clusters than the Euclidean metric even when the approximation to the within-cluster SSCP matrix is poor or the within-cluster covariances are moderately heterogeneous. The algorithm used by the ACECLUS procedure differs slightly from the algorithm used by Art, Gnanadesikan, and Kettenring. In the following sections, the PROC ACECLUS algorithm is described first; then, differences between PROC ACECLUS and the method used by Art, Gnanadesikan, and Kettenring are summarized.

Background

It is well known from the literature on nonparametric statistics that variances and, hence, covariances can be computed from pairwise differences instead of deviations from means. (For example, Puri and Sen (1971, pp. 51–52) show that the variance is a U statistic of degree 2.) Let $\mathbf{X} = (x_{ij})$ be the data matrix with n observations (rows) and v variables (columns), and let $\bar{x}_j$ be the mean of the jth variable. The sample covariance matrix $\mathbf{S} = (s_{jk})$ is usually defined as

$$s_{jk} = \frac{1}{n-1} \sum_{i=1}^{n} (x_{ij} - \bar{x}_j)(x_{ik} - \bar{x}_k)$$

The matrix $\mathbf{S}$ can also be computed as

$$s_{jk} = \frac{1}{n(n-1)} \sum_{i=2}^{n} \sum_{h=1}^{i-1} (x_{ij} - x_{hj})(x_{ik} - x_{hk})$$

Let $\mathbf{W} = (w_{jk})$ be the pooled within-cluster covariance matrix, q be the number of clusters, n_c be the number of observations in the cth cluster, and

$$d''_{ic} = \begin{cases} 1 & \text{if observation } i \text{ is in cluster } c \\ 0 & \text{otherwise} \end{cases}$$

The matrix $\mathbf{W}$ is normally defined as

$$w_{jk} = \frac{1}{n-q} \sum_{c=1}^{q} \sum_{i=1}^{n} d''_{ic} (x_{ij} - \bar{x}_{cj})(x_{ik} - \bar{x}_{ck})$$

where $\bar{x}_{cj}$ is the mean of the jth variable in cluster c. Let

$$d'_{ih} = \begin{cases} \frac{1}{n_c} & \text{if observations } i \text{ and } h \text{ are in cluster } c \\ 0 & \text{otherwise} \end{cases}$$

The matrix $\mathbf{W}$ can also be computed as

$$w_{jk} = \frac{1}{n-q} \sum_{i=2}^{n} \sum_{h=1}^{i-1} d'_{ih} (x_{ij} - x_{hj})(x_{ik} - x_{hk})$$

If the clusters are not known, d'_{ih} cannot be determined. However, an approximation to $\mathbf{W}$ can be obtained by using instead

$$d'_{ih} = \begin{cases} 1 & \text{if } \sum_{j=1}^{v} \sum_{k=1}^{v} m_{jk} (x_{ij} - x_{hj})(x_{ik} - x_{hk}) \le u^2 \\ 0 & \text{otherwise} \end{cases}$$

where u is an appropriately chosen value and $\mathbf{M} = (m_{jk})$ is an appropriate metric. Let $\mathbf{A} = (a_{jk})$ be defined as

$$a_{jk} = \frac{\sum_{i=2}^{n} \sum_{h=1}^{i-1} d_{ih}(x_{ij} - x_{hj})(x_{ik} - x_{hk})}{2\sum_{i=2}^{n} \sum_{h=1}^{i-1} d_{ih}}$$

If all of the following conditions hold, $\mathbf{A}$ equals $\mathbf{W}$:

- all within-cluster distances in the metric $\mathbf{M}$ are less than or equal to u
- all between-cluster distances in the metric $\mathbf{M}$ are greater than u
- all clusters have the same number of members n_c

If the clusters are of unequal size, $\mathbf{A}$ gives more weight to large clusters than $\mathbf{W}$ does, but this discrepancy should be of little importance if the population within-cluster covariance matrices are equal. There may be large differences between $\mathbf{A}$ and $\mathbf{W}$ if the cutoff u does not discriminate between pairs in the same cluster and pairs in different clusters. Lack of discrimination may occur for one of the following reasons:

- The clusters are not well separated.
- The metric $\mathbf{M}$ or the cutoff u is not chosen appropriately.

In the former case, little can be done to remedy the problem. The remaining question concerns how to choose $\mathbf{M}$ and u. Consider $\mathbf{M}$ first. The best choice for $\mathbf{M}$ is $\mathbf{W}^{-1}$, but $\mathbf{W}$ is not known. The solution is to use an iterative algorithm:

1. Obtain an initial estimate of $\mathbf{A}$, such as the identity or the total-sample covariance matrix. (See the INITIAL= option in the PROC ACECLUS statement for more information.)
2. Let $\mathbf{M}$ equal $\mathbf{A}^{-1}$.
3. Recompute $\mathbf{A}$ using the preceding formula.
4. Repeat steps 2 and 3 until the estimate stabilizes.

Convergence is assessed by comparing values of $\mathbf{A}$ on successive iterations. Let $\mathbf{A}_i$ be the value of $\mathbf{A}$ on the ith iteration and $\mathbf{A}_0$ be the initial estimate of $\mathbf{A}$. Let $\mathbf{Z}$ be a user-specified $v \times v$ matrix. (See the METRIC= option in the PROC ACECLUS statement for more information.) The convergence measure is

$$e_i = \frac{1}{v} \parallel \mathbf{Z}'(\mathbf{A}_i - \mathbf{A}_{i-1})\mathbf{Z} \parallel$$

where $\parallel \cdots \parallel$ indicates the Euclidean norm, that is, the square root of the sum of the squares of the elements of the matrix. In PROC ACECLUS, $\mathbf{Z}$ can be the identity or an inverse factor of **S** or diag(**S**). Iteration stops when e_i falls below a user-specified value. (See the CONVERGE= option or the MAXITER= option in the PROC ACECLUS statement for more information.)

The remaining question of how to choose u has no simple answer. In practice, you must try several different values. PROC ACECLUS provides four different ways of specifying u:

- You can specify a constant value for u. This method is useful if the initial estimate of **A** is quite good. (See the ABSOLUTE option and the THRESHOLD= option in the PROC ACECLUS statement for more information.)
- You can specify a threshold value $t > 0$ that is multiplied by the root mean square distance between observations in the current metric on each iteration to give u. Thus, the value of u changes from iteration to iteration. This method is appropriate if the initial estimate of **A** is poor. (See the THRESHOLD= option in the PROC ACECLUS statement for more information)
- You can specify a value p, $0 < p < 1$, to be transformed into a distance u such that approximately a proportion p of the pairwise Mahalanobis distances between observations in a random sample from a multivariate normal distribution will be less than u in repeated sampling. The transformation can be computed only if the number of observations exceeds the number of variables, preferably by at least 10 percent. This method also requires a good initial estimate of **A**. (See the PROPORTION= option and the ABSOLUTE option in the PROC ACECLUS statement for more information.)
- You can specify a value p, $0 < p < 1$, to be transformed into a value t that is then multiplied by $1/\sqrt{2v}$ times the root mean square distance between observations in the current metric on each iteration to yield u. The value of u changes from iteration to iteration. This method can be used with a poor initial estimate of **A**. (See the PROPORTION= option in the PROC ACECLUS statement for more information.)

In most cases, the analysis should begin with the last method using values of p between 0.5 and 0.01 and using the full covariance matrix as the initial estimate of **A**.

Proportions p are transformed to distances t using the formula

$$t^2 = 2v \left\{ \left[F^{-1}_{v,n-v}(p)\right]^{\frac{n-v}{n-1}} \right\}$$

where $F^{-1}_{v,n-v}$ is the quantile (inverse cumulative distribution) function of an F random variable with v and $n-v$ degrees of freedom. The squared Mahalanobis distance between a single pair of observations sampled from a multivariate normal distribution is distributed as $2v$ times an F random variable with v and $n-v$ degrees of freedom. The distances between two pairs of observations are correlated if the pairs have an observation in common. The quantile function is raised to the power given in the preceding formula to compensate approximately for the correlations among distances between pairs of observations that share a member. Monte Carlo studies indicate that the approximation is acceptable if the number of observations exceeds the number of variables by at least 10 percent.

If $\mathbf{A}$ becomes singular, step 2 in the iterative algorithm cannot be performed because $\mathbf{A}$ cannot be inverted. In this case, let $\mathbf{Z}$ be the matrix as defined in discussing the convergence measure, and let $\mathbf{Z}'\mathbf{A}\mathbf{Z} = \mathbf{R}'\mathbf{\Lambda}\mathbf{R}$ where $\mathbf{R}'\mathbf{R} = \mathbf{R}\mathbf{R}' = \mathbf{I}$ and $\mathbf{\Lambda} = (\lambda_{jk})$ is diagonal. Let $\mathbf{\Lambda}^* = (\lambda^*_{jk})$ be a diagonal matrix where $\lambda^*_{jj} = \max(\lambda_{jj}, g\ \text{trace}(\mathbf{\Lambda}))$, and $0 < g < 1$ is a user-specified singularity criterion (see the SINGULAR= option in the PROC ACECLUS statement for more information). Then $\mathbf{M}$ is computed as $\mathbf{Z}\mathbf{R}'(\mathbf{\Lambda}^*)^{-1}\mathbf{R}\mathbf{Z}'$.

The ACECLUS procedure differs from the method used by Art, Gnanadesikan, and Kettenring (1982) in several respects.

- The Art, Gnanadesikan, and Kettenring method uses the identity matrix as the initial estimate, whereas the ACECLUS procedure enables you to specify any symmetric matrix as the initial estimate and defaults to the total-sample covariance matrix. The default initial estimate in PROC ACECLUS is chosen to yield invariance under nonsingular linear transformations of the data but may sometimes obscure clusters that become apparent if the identity matrix is used.
- The Art, Gnanadesikan, and Kettenring method carries out all computations with SSCP matrices, whereas the ACECLUS procedure uses estimated covariance matrices because covariances are easier to interpret than crossproducts.
- The Art, Gnanadesikan, and Kettenring method uses the m pairs with the smallest distances to form the new estimate at each iteration, where m is specified by the user, whereas the ACECLUS procedure uses all pairs closer than a given cutoff value. Kettenring (1984) says that the m-closest-pairs method seems to give the user more direct control. PROC ACECLUS uses a distance cutoff because it yields a slight decrease in computer time and because in some cases, such as widely separated spherical clusters, the results are less sensitive to the choice of distance cutoff than to the choice of m. Much research remains to be done on this issue.
- The Art, Gnanadesikan, and Kettenring method uses a different convergence measure. Let $\mathbf{A}_i$ be computed on each iteration using the m-closest-pairs method, and let $\mathbf{B}_i = \mathbf{A}_{i-1}^{-1}\mathbf{A}_i - \mathbf{I}$ where $\mathbf{I}$ is the identity matrix. The convergence measure is equivalent to trace$(\mathbf{B}_i^2)$.

Analyses of Fisher's (1936) iris data, consisting of measurements of petal and sepal length and width for fifty specimens from each of three iris species, are summarized in Table 16.1. The number of misclassified observations out of 150 is given for four clustering methods:

- k-means as implemented in PROC FASTCLUS with MAXC=3, MAXITER=99, and CONV=0
- Ward's minimum variance method as implemented in PROC CLUSTER

- average linkage on Euclidean distances as implemented in PROC CLUSTER
- the centroid method as implemented in PROC CLUSTER

Each hierarchical analysis is followed by the TREE procedure with NCL=3 to determine cluster assignments at the three-cluster level. Clusters with twenty or fewer observations are discarded by using the DOCK=20 option. The observations in a discarded cluster are considered unclassified.

Each method is applied to

- the raw data
- the data standardized to unit variance by the STANDARD procedure
- two standardized principal components accounting for 95 percent of the standardized variance and having an identity total-sample covariance matrix, computed by the PRINCOMP procedure with the STD option
- four standardized principal components having an identity total-sample covariance matrix, computed by PROC PRINCOMP with the STD option
- the data transformed by PROC ACECLUS using seven different settings of the PROPORTION= (P=) option
- four canonical variables having an identity pooled within-species covariance matrix, computed using the CANDISC procedure

Theoretically, the best results should be obtained by using the canonical variables from PROC CANDISC. PROC ACECLUS yields results comparable to PROC CANDISC for values of the PROPORTION= option ranging from 0.005 to 0.02. At PROPORTION=0.04, average linkage and the centroid method show some deterioration, but k-means and Ward's method continue to produce excellent classifications. At larger values of the PROPORTION= option, all methods perform poorly, although no worse than with four standardized principal components.

Table 16.1. Number of Misclassified and Unclassified Observations Using Fisher's (1936) Iris Data

Data	Clustering Method			
	k-means	Ward's	Average Linkage	Centroid
raw data	16*	16*	25 + 12**	14*
standardized data	25	26	33+4	33+4
two standardized principal components	29	31	30+9	27+32
four standardized principal components	39	27	32+7	45+11
transformed by ACECLUS P=0.32	39	10+9	7+25	
transformed by ACECLUS P=0.16	39	18+9	7+19	7+26
transformed by ACECLUS P=0.08	19	9	3+13	5+16
transformed by ACECLUS P=0.04	4	5	1+19	3+12
transformed by ACECLUS P=0.02	4	3	3	3
transformed by ACECLUS P=0.01	4	4	3	4
transformed by ACECLUS P=0.005	4	4	4	4
canonical variables	3	5	4	4+1

* A single number represents misclassified observations with no unclassified observations.

** Where two numbers are separated by a plus sign, the first is the number of misclassified observations; the second is the number of unclassified observations.

This example demonstrates the following:

- PROC ACECLUS can produce results as good as those from the optimal transformation.
- PROC ACECLUS can be useful even when the within-cluster covariance matrices are moderately heterogeneous.
- The choice of the distance cutoff as specified by the PROPORTION= or the THRESHOLD= option is important, and several values should be tried.
- Commonly used transformations such as standardization and principal components can produce poor classifications.

Although experience with the Art, Gnanadesikan, and Kettenring and PROC ACECLUS methods is limited, the results so far suggest that these methods help considerably more often than they hinder the subsequent cluster analysis, especially with normal-mixture techniques such as k-means and Ward's minimum variance method.

Getting Started

The following example demonstrates how you can use the ACECLUS procedure to obtain approximate estimates of the pooled within-cluster covariance matrix and to compute canonical variables for subsequent analysis. You use PROC ACECLUS to preprocess data before you cluster it using the FASTCLUS or CLUSTER procedure.

Suppose you want to determine whether national figures for birth rates, death rates, and infant death rates can be used to determine certain types or categories of countries. You want to perform a cluster analysis to determine whether the observations can be formed into groups suggested by the data. Previous studies indicate that the clusters computed from this type of data can be elongated and elliptical. Thus, you need to perform a linear transformation on the raw data before the cluster analysis.

The following data* from Rouncefield (1995) are the birth rates, death rates, and infant death rates for 97 countries. The following statements create the SAS data set Poverty:

```
data poverty;
   input Birth Death InfantDeath Country $15. @@;
   datalines;
24.7  5.7  30.8 Albania         12.5 11.9  14.4 Bulgaria
13.4 11.7  11.3 Czechoslovakia  12   12.4   7.6 Former_E._Germa
11.6 13.4  14.8 Hungary         14.3 10.2    16 Poland
13.6 10.7  26.9 Romania           14    9  20.2 Yugoslavia
17.7   10    23 USSR            15.2  9.5  13.1 Byelorussia
13.4 11.6    13 Ukrainian_SSR   20.7  8.4  25.7 Argentina
46.6   18   111 Bolivia         28.6  7.9    63 Brazil
23.4  5.8  17.1 Chile           27.4  6.1    40 Columbia
```

*These data have been compiled from the United Nations Demographic Yearbook 1990 (United Nations publications, Sales No. E/F.91.XII.1, copyright 1991, United Nations, New York) and are reproduced with the permission of the United Nations.

```
32.9  7.4    63 Ecuador        28.3  7.3    56 Guyana
34.8  6.6    42 Paraguay       32.9  8.3 109.9 Peru
  18  9.6  21.9 Uruguay        27.5  4.4  23.3 Venezuela
  29 23.2    43 Mexico           12 10.6   7.9 Belgium
13.2 10.1   5.8 Finland        12.4 11.9   7.5 Denmark
13.6  9.4   7.4 France         11.4 11.2   7.4 Germany
10.1  9.2    11 Greece         15.1  9.1   7.5 Ireland
 9.7  9.1   8.8 Italy          13.2  8.6   7.1 Netherlands
14.3 10.7   7.8 Norway         11.9  9.5  13.1 Portugal
10.7  8.2   8.1 Spain          14.5 11.1   5.6 Sweden
12.5  9.5   7.1 Switzerland    13.6 11.5   8.4 U.K.
14.9  7.4     8 Austria         9.9  6.7   4.5 Japan
14.5  7.3   7.2 Canada         16.7  8.1   9.1 U.S.A.
40.4 18.7 181.6 Afghanistan    28.4  3.8    16 Bahrain
42.5 11.5 108.1 Iran           42.6  7.8    69 Iraq
22.3  6.3   9.7 Israel         38.9  6.4    44 Jordan
26.8  2.2  15.6 Kuwait         31.7  8.7    48 Lebanon
45.6  7.8    40 Oman           42.1  7.6    71 Saudi_Arabia
29.2  8.4    76 Turkey         22.8  3.8    26 United_Arab_Emr
42.2 15.5   119 Bangladesh     41.4 16.6   130 Cambodia
21.2  6.7    32 China          11.7  4.9   6.1 Hong_Kong
30.5 10.2    91 India          28.6  9.4    75 Indonesia
23.5 18.1    25 Korea          31.6  5.6    24 Malaysia
36.1  8.8    68 Mongolia       39.6 14.8   128 Nepal
30.3  8.1 107.7 Pakistan       33.2  7.7    45 Philippines
17.8  5.2   7.5 Singapore      21.3  6.2  19.4 Sri_Lanka
22.3  7.7    28 Thailand       31.8  9.5    64 Vietnam
35.5  8.3    74 Algeria        47.2 20.2   137 Angola
48.5 11.6    67 Botswana       46.1 14.6    73 Congo
38.8  9.5  49.4 Egypt          48.6 20.7   137 Ethiopia
39.4 16.8   103 Gabon          47.4 21.4   143 Gambia
44.4 13.1    90 Ghana            47 11.3    72 Kenya
  44  9.4    82 Libya        48.3   25   130 Malawi
35.5  9.8    82 Morocco          45 18.5   141 Mozambique
  44 12.1   135 Namibia        48.5 15.6   105 Nigeria
48.2 23.4   154 Sierra_Leone   50.1 20.2   132 Somalia
32.1  9.9    72 South_Africa   44.6 15.8   108 Sudan
46.8 12.5   118 Swaziland      31.1  7.3    52 Tunisia
52.2 15.6   103 Uganda         50.5   14   106 Tanzania
45.6 14.2    83 Zaire          51.1 13.7    80 Zambia
41.7 10.3    66 Zimbabwe
;
```

The data set Poverty contains the character variable Country and the numeric variables Birth, Death, and InfantDeath, which represent the birth rate per thousand, death rate per thousand, and infant death rate per thousand. The $15. in the INPUT statement specifies that the variable Country is a character variable with a length of 15. The double trailing at sign (@@) in the INPUT statement specifies that observations are input from each line until all values have been read.

It is often useful when beginning a cluster analysis to look at the data graphically. The following statements use the GPLOT procedure to make a scatter plot of the variables Birth and Death.

```
axis1 label=(angle=90 rotate=0) minor=none;
axis2 minor=none;
proc gplot data=poverty;
   plot Birth*Death/
   frame cframe=ligr vaxis=axis1 haxis=axis2;
run;
```

The plot, displayed in Figure 16.1, indicates the difficulty of dividing the points into clusters. Plots of the other variable pairs (not shown) display similar characteristics. The clusters that comprise these data may be poorly separated and elongated. Data with poorly separated or elongated clusters must be transformed.

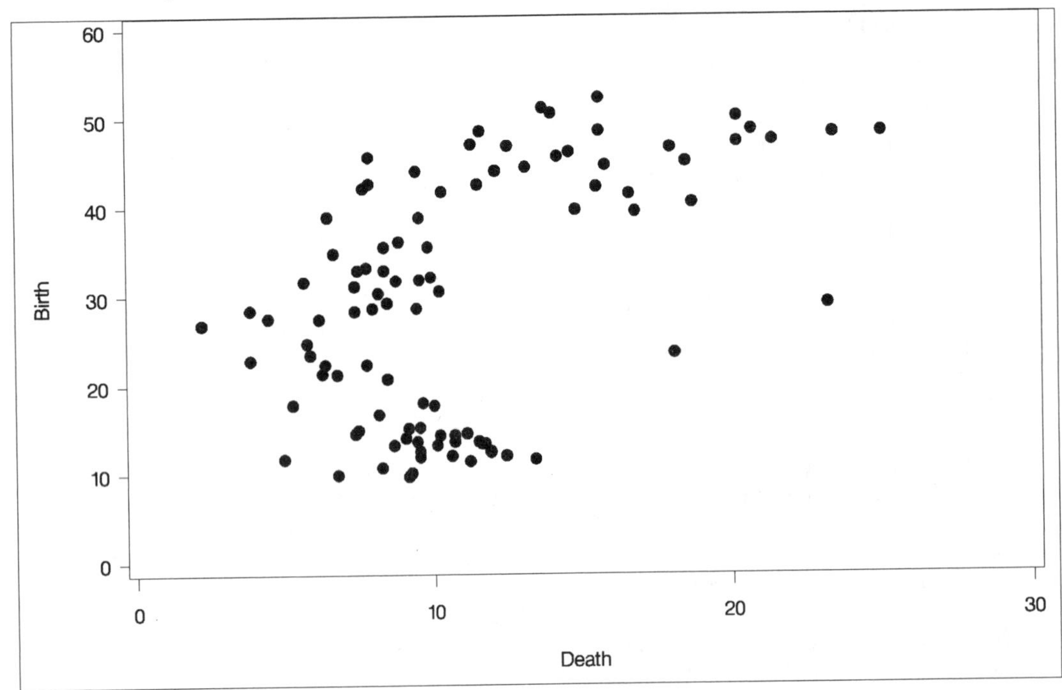

Figure 16.1. Scatter Plot of Original Poverty Data: Birth Rate versus Death Rate

If you know the within-cluster covariances, you can transform the data to make the clusters spherical. However, since you do not know what the clusters are, you cannot calculate exactly the within-cluster covariance matrix. The ACECLUS procedure estimates the within-cluster covariance matrix to transform the data, even when you have no knowledge of cluster membership or the number of clusters.

The following statements perform the ACECLUS procedure transformation using the SAS data set Poverty.

```
proc aceclus data=poverty out=ace proportion=.03;
   var Birth Death InfantDeath;
run;
```

The OUT= option creates an output data set called Ace to contain the canonical variable scores. The PROPORTION= option specifies that approximately three percent of the pairs are included in the estimation of the within-cluster covariance matrix. The VAR statement specifies that the variables Birth, Death, and InfantDeath are used in computing the canonical variables.

The results of this analysis are displayed in the following figures.

Figure 16.2 displays the number of observations, the number of variables, and the settings for the PROPORTION and CONVERGE options. The PROPORTION option is set at 0.03, as specified in the previous statements. The CONVERGE parameter is set at its default value of 0.001.

```
                     The ACECLUS Procedure

        Approximate Covariance Estimation for Cluster Analysis


         Observations            97    Proportion        0.0300
         Variables                3    Converge         0.00100


                 Means and Standard Deviations
                                                 Standard
                Variable               Mean     Deviation

                Birth               29.2299       13.5467
                Death               10.8361        4.6475
                InfantDeath         54.9010       45.9926


                 COV: Total Sample Covariances

                            Birth                 Death          InfantDeath

 Birth                 183.512951             30.610056           534.794969
 Death                  30.610056             21.599205           139.925900
 InfantDeath           534.794969            139.925900          2115.317811

Initial Within-Cluster Covariance Estimate = Full Covariance Matrix


                   Threshold =      0.292815
```

Figure 16.2. Means, Standard Deviations, and Covariance Matrix from the ACECLUS Procedure

Figure 16.2 next displays the means, standard deviations, and sample covariance matrix of the analytical variables.

The type of matrix used for the initial within-cluster covariance estimate is displayed in Figure 16.3. In this example, that initial estimate is the full covariance matrix. The threshold value that corresponds to the PROPORTION=0.03 setting is given as 0.292815.

```
                         The ACECLUS Procedure

          Approximate Covariance Estimation for Cluster Analysis

    Initial Within-Cluster Covariance Estimate = Full Covariance Matrix


                           Iteration History

                                                 Pairs
                       RMS        Distance      Within     Convergence
     Iteration      Distance       Cutoff       Cutoff       Measure
     ------------------------------------------------------------------
             1         2.449        0.717        385.0      0.552025
             2        12.534        3.670        446.0      0.008406
             3        12.851        3.763        521.0      0.009655
             4        12.882        3.772        591.0      0.011193
             5        12.716        3.723        628.0      0.008784
             6        12.821        3.754        658.0      0.005553
             7        12.774        3.740        680.0      0.003010
             8        12.631        3.699        683.0      0.000676


    Algorithm converged.
```

Figure 16.3. Table of Iteration History from the ACECLUS Procedure

Figure 16.3 displays the iteration history. For each iteration, PROC ACECLUS displays the following measures:

- root mean square distance between all pairs of observations
- distance cutoff for including pairs of observations in the estimate of within-cluster covariances (equal to RMS*Threshold)
- number of pairs within the cutoff
- convergence measure

Figure 16.4 displays the approximate within-cluster covariance matrix and the table of eigenvalues from the canonical analysis. The first column of the eigenvalues table contains numbers for the eigenvectors. The next column of the table lists the eigenvalues of Inv(ACE)*(COV-ACE).

```
                    The ACECLUS Procedure

       Approximate Covariance Estimation for Cluster Analysis

  Initial Within-Cluster Covariance Estimate = Full Covariance Matrix


       ACE: Approximate Covariance Estimate Within Clusters

                        Birth            Death      InfantDeath

 Birth             5.94644949      -0.63235725       6.28151537
 Death            -0.63235725       2.33464129       1.59005857
 InfantDeath       6.28151537       1.59005857      35.10327233


              Eigenvalues of Inv(ACE)*(COV-ACE)

             Eigenvalue    Difference    Proportion    Cumulative

        1       63.5500       54.7313        0.8277        0.8277
        2        8.8187        4.4038        0.1149        0.9425
        3        4.4149                      0.0575        1.0000
```

Figure 16.4. Approximate Within–Cluster Covariance Estimates

The next three columns of the eigenvalue table (Figure 16.4) display measures of the relative size and importance of the eigenvalues. The first column lists the difference between each eigenvalue and its successor. The last two columns display the individual and cumulative proportions that each eigenvalue contributes to the total sum of eigenvalues.

The raw and standardized canonical coefficients are displayed in Figure 16.5. The coefficients are standardized by multiplying the raw coefficients with the standard deviation of the associated variable. The ACECLUS procedure uses these standardized canonical coefficients to create the transformed canonical variables, which are the linear transformations of the original input variables, Birth, Death, and InfantDeath.

```
                    The ACECLUS Procedure

      Approximate Covariance Estimation for Cluster Analysis

Initial Within-Cluster Covariance Estimate = Full Covariance Matrix


          Eigenvectors (Raw Canonical Coefficients)

                           Can1           Can2           Can3

      Birth            0.125610       0.457037       0.003875
      Death            0.108402       0.163792       0.663538
      InfantDeath      0.134704       -.133620       -.046266

             Standardized Canonical Coefficients

                           Can1           Can2           Can3

      Birth             1.70160        6.19134        0.05249
      Death             0.50380        0.76122        3.08379
      InfantDeath       6.19540       -6.14553       -2.12790
```

Figure 16.5. Raw and Standardized Canonical Coefficients from the ACECLUS Procedure

The following statements invoke the CLUSTER procedure, using the SAS data set Ace created in the previous ACECLUS procedure.

```
proc cluster data=ace outtree=tree noprint method=ward;
   var can1 can2 can3 ;
   copy Birth--Country;
run;
```

The OUTTREE= option creates the output SAS data set Tree that is used in subsequent statements to draw a tree diagram. The NOPRINT option suppresses the display of the output. The METHOD= option specifies Ward's minimum-variance clustering method.

The VAR statement specifies that the canonical variables computed in the ACECLUS procedure are used in the cluster analysis. The COPY statement specifies that all the variables from the SAS data set Poverty (Birth—Country) are added to the output data set Tree.

The following statements use the TREE procedure to create an output SAS data set called New. The NCLUSTERS= option specifies the number of clusters desired in the SAS data set New. The NOPRINT option suppresses the display of the output.

```
proc tree data=tree out=new nclusters=3 noprint;
   copy Birth Death InfantDeath can1 can2 ;
   id Country;
run;
```

The COPY statement copies the canonical variables CAN1 and CAN2 (computed in the preceding ACECLUS procedure) and the original analytical variables Birth, Death, and InfantDeath into the output SAS data set New.

The following statements invoke the GPLOT procedure, using the SAS data set created by PROC TREE:

```
legend1 frame cframe=ligr cborder=black
        position=center value=(justify=center);
axis1 label=(angle=90 rotate=0) minor=none;
axis2 minor=none;
proc gplot data=new;
   plot Birth*Death=cluster/
        frame cframe=ligr legend=legend1 vaxis=axis1 haxis=axis2;
   plot can2*can1=cluster/
        frame cframe=ligr legend=legend1 vaxis=axis1 haxis=axis2;
run;
```

The first plot statement requests a scatter plot of the two variables Birth and Death, using the variable CLUSTER as the identification variable.

The second PLOT statement requests a plot of the two canonical variables, using the value of the variable CLUSTER as the identification variable.

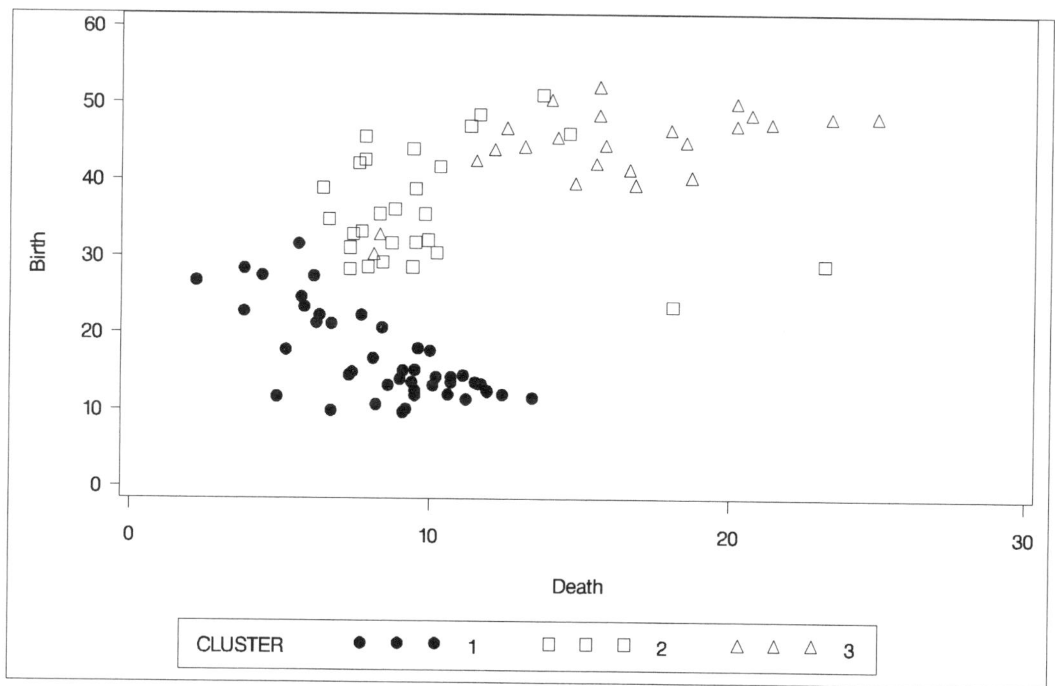

Figure 16.6. Scatter Plot of Poverty Data, Identified by Cluster

Figure 16.6 and Figure 16.7 display the separation of the clusters when three clusters are calculated.

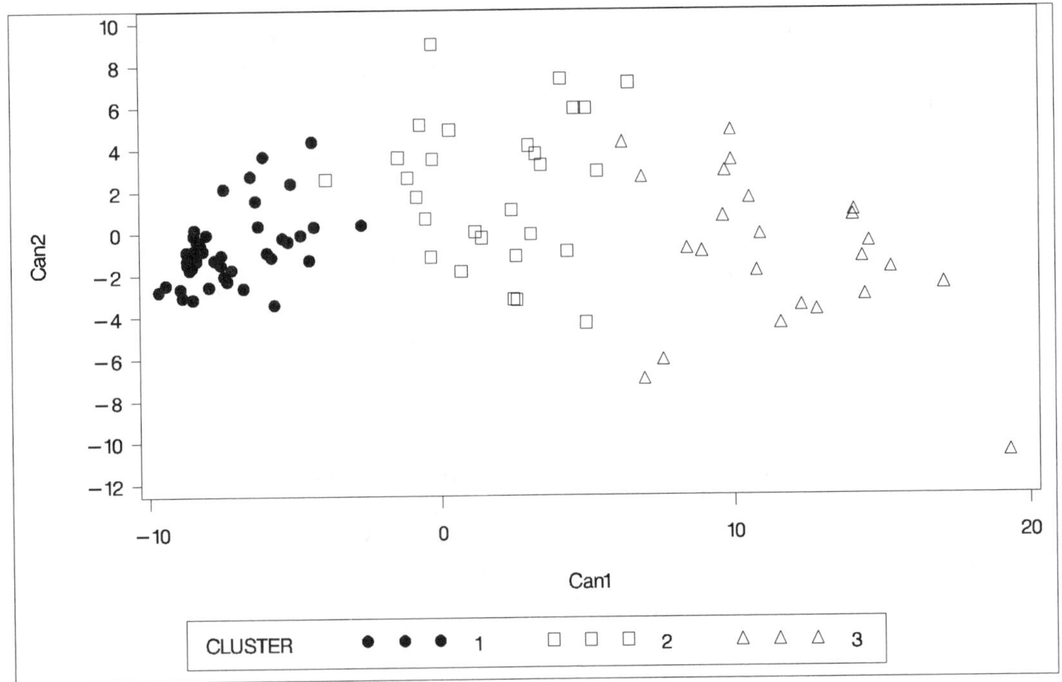

Figure 16.7. Scatter Plot of Canonical Variables

Syntax

The following statements are available in the ACECLUS procedure.

PROC ACECLUS *PROPORTION=p* | *THRESHOLD=t* < *options* > ;
  BY *variables* ;
  FREQ *variable* ;
  VAR *variables* ;
  WEIGHT *variable* ;

Usually you need only the VAR statement in addition to the required PROC ACECLUS statement. The optional BY, FREQ, VAR, and WEIGHT statements are described in alphabetical order after the PROC ACECLUS statement.

PROC ACECLUS Statement

PROC ACECLUS *PROPORTION=p / THRESHOLD=t* < *options* > ;

The PROC ACECLUS statement starts the ACECLUS procedure. The options available with the PROC ACECLUS statement are summarized in Table 16.2 and discussed in the following sections. Note that, if you specify the METHOD=COUNT option, you must specify either the PROPORTION= or the MPAIRS= option. Otherwise, you must specify either the PROPORTION= or THRESHOLD= option.

Table 16.2. Summary of PROC ACECLUS Statement Options

Task	Options	Description
Specify clustering options		
	METHOD=	specify the clustering method
	MPAIRS=	specify number of pairs for estimating within-cluster covariance (when you specify the option METHOD=COUNT)
	PROPORTION=	specify proportion of pairs for estimating within-cluster covariance
	THRESHOLD=	specify the threshold for including pairs in the estimation of the within-cluster covariance
Specify input and output data sets		
	DATA=	specify input data set name
	OUT=	specify output data set name
	OUTSTAT=	specify output data set name containing various statistics
Specify iteration options		
	ABSOLUTE	use absolute instead of relative threshold
	CONVERGE=	specify convergence criterion
	INITIAL=	specify initial estimate of within-cluster covariance matrix
	MAXITER=	specify maximum number of iterations
	METRIC=	specify metric in which computations are performed
	SINGULAR=	specify singularity criterion
Specify canonical analysis options		
	N=	specify number of canonical variables
	PREFIX=	specify prefix for naming canonical variables
Control displayed output		
	NOPRINT	suppress the display of the output
	PP	produce PP-plot of distances between pairs from last iteration
	QQ	produce QQ-plot of power transformation of distances between pairs from last iteration
	SHORT	omit all output except for iteration history and eigenvalue table

The following list provides details on the options. The list is in alphabetical order.

ABSOLUTE

causes the THRESHOLD= value or the threshold computed from the PROPORTION= option to be treated absolutely rather than relative to the root mean square distance between observations. Use the ABSOLUTE option only when you are confident that the initial estimate of the within-cluster covariance matrix is close to the final estimate, such as when the INITIAL= option specifies a data set created by a previous execution of PROC ACECLUS using the OUTSTAT= option.

CONVERGE=*c*

specifies the convergence criterion. By default, CONVERGE= 0.001. Iteration stops when the convergence measure falls below the value specified by the CONVERGE= option or when the iteration limit as specified by the MAXITER= option is exceeded, whichever happens first.

DATA=*SAS-data-set*

specifies the SAS data set to be analyzed. By default, PROC ACECLUS uses the most recently created SAS data set.

INITIAL=*name*

specifies the matrix for the initial estimate of the within-cluster covariance matrix. Valid values for *name* are as follows:

DIAGONAL | D	uses the diagonal matrix of sample variances as the initial estimate of the within-cluster covariance matrix.
FULL | F	uses the total-sample covariance matrix as the initial estimate of the within-cluster covariance matrix.
IDENTITY | I	uses the identity matrix as the initial estimate of the within-cluster covariance matrix.
INPUT=*SAS-data-set*	specifies a SAS data set from which to obtain the initial estimate of the within-cluster covariance matrix. The data set can be TYPE=CORR, COV, UCORR, UCOV, SSCP, or ACE, or it can be an ordinary SAS data set. (See Appendix 1, "Special SAS Data Sets," for descriptions of CORR, COV, UCORR, UCOV, and SSCP data sets. See the section "Output Data Sets" on page 325 for a description of ACE data sets.)

If you do not specify the INITIAL= option, the default is the matrix specified by the METRIC= option. If neither the INITIAL= nor the METRIC= option is specified, INITIAL=FULL is used if there are enough observations to obtain a nonsingular total-sample covariance matrix; otherwise, INITIAL=DIAGONAL is used.

MAXITER=*n*

specifies the maximum number of iterations. By default, MAXITER=10.

METHOD= COUNT | C
METHOD= THRESHOLD | T

specifies the clustering method. The METHOD=THRESHOLD option requests a method (also the default) that uses all pairs closer than a given cutoff value to form the estimate at each iteration. The METHOD=COUNT option requests a method that uses a number of pairs, m, with the smallest distances to form the estimate at each iteration.

METRIC=*name*

specifies the metric in which the computations are performed, implies the default value for the INITIAL= option, and specifies the matrix $\mathbf{Z}$ used in the formula for the convergence measure e_i and for checking singularity of the $\mathbf{A}$ matrix. Valid values for *name* are as follows:

DIAGONAL | D	uses the diagonal matrix of sample variances $\text{diag}(\mathbf{S})$ and sets $\mathbf{Z} = \text{diag}(\mathbf{S})^{-\frac{1}{2}}$, where the superscript $-\frac{1}{2}$ indicates an inverse factor.
FULL | F	uses the total-sample covariance matrix $\mathbf{S}$ and sets $\mathbf{Z} = \mathbf{S}^{-\frac{1}{2}}$.
IDENTITY | I	uses the identity matrix $\mathbf{I}$ and sets $\mathbf{Z} = \mathbf{I}$.

If you do not specify the METRIC= option, METRIC=FULL is used if there are enough observations to obtain a nonsingular total-sample covariance matrix; otherwise, METRIC=DIAGONAL is used.

The option METRIC= is rather technical. It affects the computations in a variety of ways, but for well-conditioned data the effects are subtle. For most data sets, the METRIC= option is not needed.

MPAIRS=*m*

specifies the number of pairs to be included in the estimation of the within-cluster covariance matrix when METHOD=COUNT is requested. The values of m must be greater than 0 but less than or equal to $(totfq \times (totfq - 1))/2$, where *totfq* is the sum of nonmissing frequencies specified in the FREQ statement. If there is no FREQ statement, *totfq* equals the number of total nonmissing observations.

N=*n*

specifies the number of canonical variables to be computed. The default is the number of variables analyzed. N=0 suppresses the canonical analysis.

NOPRINT

suppresses the display of all output. Note that this option temporarily disables the Output Delivery System (ODS). For more information, see Chapter 15, "Using the Output Delivery System."

OUT=*SAS-data-set*

creates an output SAS data set that contains all the original data as well as the canonical variables having an estimated within-cluster covariance matrix equal to the identity matrix. If you want to create a permanent SAS data set, you must specify a two-level name. See Chapter 16, “SAS Data Files” in *SAS Language Reference: Concepts* for information on permanent SAS data sets.

OUTSTAT=*SAS-data-set*

specifies a TYPE=ACE output SAS data set that contains means, standard deviations, number of observations, covariances, estimated within-cluster covariances, eigenvalues, and canonical coefficients. If you want to create a permanent SAS data set, you must specify a two-level name. See Chapter 16, “SAS Data Files” in *SAS Language Reference: Concepts* for information on permanent SAS data sets.

PROPORTION=*p*
PERCENT=*p*
P=*p*

specifies the percentage of pairs to be included in the estimation of the within-cluster covariance matrix. The value of p must be greater than 0. If p is greater than or equal to 1, it is interpreted as a percentage and divided by 100; PROPORTION=0.02 and PROPORTION=2 are equivalent. When you specify METHOD=THRESHOLD, a threshold value is computed from the PROPORTION= option under the assumption that the observations are sampled from a multivariate normal distribution.

When you specify METHOD=COUNT, the number of pairs, m, is computed from PROPORTION=p as

$$m = \text{floor}\left(\frac{p}{2} \times \mathit{totfq} \times (\mathit{totfq} - 1)\right)$$

where *totfq* is the number of total non-missing observations.

PP

produces a PP probability plot of distances between pairs of observations computed in the last iteration.

PREFIX=*name*

specifies a prefix for naming the canonical variables. By default the names are CAN1, CAN2, . . . , CANn. If you specify PREFIX=ABC, the variables are named ABC1, ABC2, ABC3, and so on. The number of characters in the prefix plus the number of digits required to designate the variables should not exceed the name length defined by the VALIDVARNAME= system option. For more information on the VALIDVARNAME= system option, refer to *SAS Language Reference: Dictionary*.

QQ

produces a QQ probability plot of a power transformation of the distances between pairs of observations computed in the last iteration. **Caution:** The QQ plot may require an enormous amount of computer time.

SHORT

omits all items from the standard output except for the iteration history and the eigenvalue table.

SINGULAR=*g*
SING=*g*

specifies a singularity criterion $0 < g < 1$ for the total-sample covariance matrix $\mathbf{S}$ and the approximate within-cluster covariance estimate $\mathbf{A}$. The default is SINGULAR=1E−4.

THRESHOLD=*t*
T=*t*

specifies the threshold for including pairs of observations in the estimation of the within-cluster covariance matrix. A pair of observations is included if the Euclidean distance between them is less than or equal to t times the root mean square distance computed over all pairs of observations.

BY Statement

BY *variables* **;**

You can specify a BY statement with PROC ACECLUS to obtain separate analyses on observations in groups defined by the BY variables. When a BY statement appears, the procedure expects the input data set to be sorted in order of the BY variables.

If your input data set is not sorted in ascending order, use one of the following alternatives:

- Sort the data using the SORT procedure with a similar BY statement.
- Specify the BY statement option NOTSORTED or DESCENDING in the BY statement for the ACECLUS procedure. The NOTSORTED option does not mean that the data are unsorted but rather that the data are arranged in groups (according to values of the BY variables) and that these groups are not necessarily in alphabetical or increasing numeric order.
- Create an index on the BY variables using the DATASETS procedure.

If you specify the INITIAL=INPUT= option and the INITIAL=INPUT= data set does not contain any of the BY variables, the entire INITIAL=INPUT= data set provides the initial value for the matrix **A** for each BY group in the DATA= data set.

If the INITIAL=INPUT= data set contains some but not all of the BY variables, or if some BY variables do not have the same type or length in the INITIAL=INPUT= data set as in the DATA= data set, then PROC ACECLUS displays an error message and stops.

If all the BY variables appear in the INITIAL=INPUT= data set with the same type and length as in the DATA= data set, then each BY group in the INITIAL=INPUT= data set provides the initial value for **A** for the corresponding BY group in the DATA= data set. All BY groups in the DATA= data set must also appear in the INITIAL= INPUT= data set. The BY groups in the INITIAL=INPUT= data set must be in the same order as in the DATA= data set. If you specify NOTSORTED in the BY statement, identical BY groups must occur in the same order in both data sets. If you do not specify NOTSORTED, some BY groups can appear in the INITIAL= INPUT= data set, but not in the DATA= data set; such BY groups are not used in the analysis.

For more information on the BY statement, refer to the discussion in *SAS Language Reference: Concepts*. For more information on the DATASETS procedure, refer to the discussion in the *SAS Procedures Guide*.

FREQ Statement

FREQ *variable* ;

If a variable in your data set represents the frequency of occurrence for the observation, include the name of that variable in the FREQ statement. The procedure then treats the data set as if each observation appears n times, where n is the value of the FREQ variable for the observation. If a value of the FREQ variable is not integral, it is truncated to the largest integer not exceeding the given value. Observations with FREQ values less than one are not included in the analysis. The total number of observations is considered equal to the sum of the FREQ variable.

VAR Statement

VAR *variables* ;

The VAR statement specifies the numeric variables to be analyzed. If the VAR statement is omitted, all numeric variables not specified in other statements are analyzed.

WEIGHT Statement

WEIGHT *variable* ;

If you want to specify relative weights for each observation in the input data set, place the weights in a variable in the data set and specify that variable name in a WEIGHT statement. This is often done when the variance associated with each observation is different and the values of the weight variable are proportional to the reciprocals of the variances. The values of the WEIGHT variable can be non-integral and are not truncated. An observation is used in the analysis only if the value of the WEIGHT variable is greater than zero.

The WEIGHT and FREQ statements have a similar effect, except in calculating the divisor of the **A** matrix.

Details

Missing Values

Observations with missing values are omitted from the analysis and are given missing values for canonical variable scores in the OUT= data set.

Output Data Sets

OUT= Data Set

The OUT= data set contains all the variables in the original data set plus new variables containing the canonical variable scores. The N= option determines the number of new variables. The OUT= data set is not created if N=0. The names of the new variables are formed by concatenating the value given by the PREFIX= option (or the prefix CAN if the PREFIX= option is not specified) and the numbers 1, 2, 3, and so on. The OUT= data set can be used as input to PROC CLUSTER or PROC FASTCLUS. The cluster analysis should be performed on the canonical variables, not on the original variables.

OUTSTAT= Data Set

The OUTSTAT= data set is a TYPE=ACE data set containing the following variables.

- the BY variables, if any
- the two new character variables, _TYPE_ and _NAME_
- the variables analyzed, that is, those in the VAR statement, or, if there is no VAR statement, all numeric variables not listed in any other statement

Each observation in the new data set contains some type of statistic as indicated by the _TYPE_ variable. The values of the _TYPE_ variable are as follows:

TYPE	**Contents**
MEAN	mean of each variable
STD	standard deviation of each variable
N	number of observations on which the analysis is based. This value is the same for each variable.
SUMWGT	sum of the weights if a WEIGHT statement is used. This value is the same for each variable.
COV	covariances between each variable and the variable named by the _NAME_ variable. The number of observations with _TYPE_=COV is equal to the number of variables being analyzed.
ACE	estimated within-cluster covariances between each variable and the variable named by the _NAME_ variable. The number of observations with _TYPE_=ACE is equal to the number of variables being analyzed.

EIGENVAL	eigenvalues of INV(ACE)*(COV−ACE). If the N= option requests fewer than the maximum number of canonical variables, only the specified number of eigenvalues are produced, with missing values filling out the observation.
SCORE	standardized canonical coefficients. The _NAME_ variable contains the name of the corresponding canonical variable as constructed from the PREFIX= option. The number of observations with _TYPE_=SCORE equals the number of canonical variables computed. To obtain the canonical variable scores, these coefficients should be multiplied by the standardized data.
RAWSCORE	raw canonical coefficients. To obtain the canonical variable scores, these coefficients should be multiplied by the raw (centered) data.

The OUTSTAT= data set can be used

- to initialize another execution of PROC ACECLUS
- to compute canonical variable scores with the SCORE procedure
- as input to the FACTOR procedure, specifying METHOD=SCORE, to rotate the canonical variables

Computational Resources

Let

$$n = \text{number of observations}$$
$$v = \text{number of variables}$$
$$i = \text{number of iterations}$$

Memory

The memory in bytes required by PROC ACECLUS is approximately

$$8(2n(v+1) + 21v + 5v^2)$$

bytes. If you request the PP or QQ option, an additional $4n(n-1)$ bytes are needed.

Time

The time required by PROC ACECLUS is roughly proportional to

$$2nv^2 + 10v^3 + i\left(\frac{n^2v}{2} + nv^2 + 5v^3\right)$$

Displayed Output

Unless the SHORT option is specified, the ACECLUS procedure displays the following items:

- Means and Standard Deviations of the input variables
- the **S** matrix, labeled COV: Total Sample Covariances
- the name or value of the matrix used for the Initial Within-Cluster Covariance Estimate
- the Threshold value if the PROPORTION= option is specified

For each iteration, PROC ACECLUS displays

- the Iteration number
- RMS Distance, the root mean square distance between all pairs of observations
- the Distance Cutoff (u) for including pairs of observations in the estimate of the within-cluster covariances, which equals the RMS distance times the threshold
- the number of Pairs Within Cutoff
- the Convergence Measure (e_i) as specified by the METRIC= option

If the SHORT option is not specified, PROC ACECLUS also displays the **A** matrix, labeled ACE: Approximate Covariance Estimate Within Clusters.

The ACECLUS procedure displays a table of eigenvalues from the canonical analysis containing the following items:

- Eigenvalues of Inv(ACE)*(COV−ACE)
- the Difference between successive eigenvalues
- the Proportion of variance explained by each eigenvalue
- the Cumulative proportion of variance explained

If the SHORT option is not specified, PROC ACECLUS displays

- the Eigenvectors or raw canonical coefficients
- the standardized eigenvectors or standard canonical coefficients

ODS Table Names

PROC ACECLUS assigns a name to each table it creates. You can use these names to reference the table when using the Output Delivery System (ODS) to select tables and create output data sets. These names are listed in the following table. For more information on ODS, see Chapter 15, "Using the Output Delivery System."

Table 16.3. ODS Tables Produced in PROC ACECLUS

ODS Table Name	Description	Statement	Option
ConvergenceStatus	Convergence status	PROC	default
DataOptionInfo	Data and option information	PROC	default
Eigenvalues	Eigenvalues of Inv(ACE)*(COV-ACE)	PROC	default
Eigenvectors	Eigenvectors (raw canonical coefficients)	PROC	default
InitWithin	Initial within-cluster covariance estimate	PROC	INITIAL=INPUT
IterHistory	Iteration history	PROC	default
SimpleStatistics	Simple statistics	PROC	default
StdCanCoef	Standardized canonical coefficients	PROC	default
Threshold	Threshold value	PROC	PROPORTION=
TotSampleCov	Total sample covariances	PROC	default
Within	Approximate covariance estimate within clusters	PROC	default

Example

Example 16.1. Transformation and Cluster Analysis of Fisher Iris Data

The iris data published by Fisher (1936) have been widely used for examples in discriminant analysis and cluster analysis. The sepal length, sepal width, petal length, and petal width are measured in millimeters on fifty iris specimens from each of three species, *Iris setosa, I. versicolor,* and *I. virginica*. Mezzich and Solomon (1980) discuss a variety of cluster analyses of the iris data.

In this example PROC ACECLUS is used to transform the data, and the clustering is performed by PROC FASTCLUS. Compare this with the example in Chapter 27, "The FASTCLUS Procedure." The results from the FREQ procedure display fewer misclassifications when PROC ACECLUS is used. The following statements produce Output 16.1.1 through Output 16.1.5.

```
proc format;
   value specname
      1='Setosa    '
      2='Versicolor'
      3='Virginica ';
run;

data iris;
   title 'Fisher (1936) Iris Data';
   input SepalLength SepalWidth PetalLength PetalWidth Species @@;
   format Species specname.;
```

```
   label SepalLength='Sepal Length in mm.'
         SepalWidth ='Sepal Width in mm.'
         PetalLength='Petal Length in mm.'
         PetalWidth ='Petal Width in mm.';
   symbol = put(species, specname10.);
   datalines;
50 33 14 02 1 64 28 56 22 3 65 28 46 15 2 67 31 56 24 3
63 28 51 15 3 46 34 14 03 1 69 31 51 23 3 62 22 45 15 2
59 32 48 18 2 46 36 10 02 1 61 30 46 14 2 60 27 51 16 2
65 30 52 20 3 56 25 39 11 2 65 30 55 18 3 58 27 51 19 3
68 32 59 23 3 51 33 17 05 1 57 28 45 13 2 62 34 54 23 3
77 38 67 22 3 63 33 47 16 2 67 33 57 25 3 76 30 66 21 3
49 25 45 17 3 55 35 13 02 1 67 30 52 23 3 70 32 47 14 2
64 32 45 15 2 61 28 40 13 2 48 31 16 02 1 59 30 51 18 3
55 24 38 11 2 63 25 50 19 3 64 32 53 23 3 52 34 14 02 1
49 36 14 01 1 54 30 45 15 2 79 38 64 20 3 44 32 13 02 1
67 33 57 21 3 50 35 16 06 1 58 26 40 12 2 44 30 13 02 1
77 28 67 20 3 63 27 49 18 3 47 32 16 02 1 55 26 44 12 2
50 23 33 10 2 72 32 60 18 3 48 30 14 03 1 51 38 16 02 1
61 30 49 18 3 48 34 19 02 1 50 30 16 02 1 50 32 12 02 1
61 26 56 14 3 64 28 56 21 3 43 30 11 01 1 58 40 12 02 1
51 38 19 04 1 67 31 44 14 2 62 28 48 18 3 49 30 14 02 1
51 35 14 02 1 56 30 45 15 2 58 27 41 10 2 50 34 16 04 1
46 32 14 02 1 60 29 45 15 2 57 26 35 10 2 57 44 15 04 1
50 36 14 02 1 77 30 61 23 3 63 34 56 24 3 58 27 51 19 3
57 29 42 13 2 72 30 58 16 3 54 34 15 04 1 52 41 15 01 1
71 30 59 21 3 64 31 55 18 3 60 30 48 18 3 63 29 56 18 3
49 24 33 10 2 56 27 42 13 2 57 30 42 12 2 55 42 14 02 1
49 31 15 02 1 77 26 69 23 3 60 22 50 15 3 54 39 17 04 1
66 29 46 13 2 52 27 39 14 2 60 34 45 16 2 50 34 15 02 1
44 29 14 02 1 50 20 35 10 2 55 24 37 10 2 58 27 39 12 2
47 32 13 02 1 46 31 15 02 1 69 32 57 23 3 62 29 43 13 2
74 28 61 19 3 59 30 42 15 2 51 34 15 02 1 50 35 13 03 1
56 28 49 20 3 60 22 40 10 2 73 29 63 18 3 67 25 58 18 3
49 31 15 01 1 67 31 47 15 2 63 23 44 13 2 54 37 15 02 1
56 30 41 13 2 63 25 49 15 2 61 28 47 12 2 64 29 43 13 2
51 25 30 11 2 57 28 41 13 2 65 30 58 22 3 69 31 54 21 3
54 39 13 04 1 51 35 14 03 1 72 36 61 25 3 65 32 51 20 3
61 29 47 14 2 56 29 36 13 2 69 31 49 15 2 64 27 53 19 3
68 30 55 21 3 55 25 40 13 2 48 34 16 02 1 48 30 14 01 1
45 23 13 03 1 57 25 50 20 3 57 38 17 03 1 51 38 15 03 1
55 23 40 13 2 66 30 44 14 2 68 28 48 14 2 54 34 17 02 1
51 37 15 04 1 52 35 15 02 1 58 28 51 24 3 67 30 50 17 2
63 33 60 25 3 53 37 15 02 1
;

proc aceclus data=iris out=ace p=.02 outstat=score;
   var SepalLength SepalWidth PetalLength PetalWidth ;
run;

legend1 frame cframe=ligr cborder=black position=center
        value=(justify=center);
axis1 label=(angle=90 rotate=0) minor=none;
axis2 minor=none;
```

```
proc gplot data=ace;
   plot can2*can1=Species/
      frame cframe=ligr legend=legend1 vaxis=axis1 haxis=axis2;
   format Species specname. ;
run;
proc fastclus data=ace maxc=3 maxiter=10 conv=0 out=clus;
   var can:;
run;
proc freq;
   tables cluster*Species;
run;
```

Output 16.1.1. Using PROC ACECLUS to Transform Fisher's Iris Data

```
                        Fisher (1936) Iris Data

                        The ACECLUS Procedure

          Approximate Covariance Estimation for Cluster Analysis


            Observations         150     Proportion       0.0200
            Variables              4     Converge        0.00100


                    Means and Standard Deviations
                                     Standard
        Variable            Mean     Deviation     Label

        SepalLength      58.4333        8.2807     Sepal Length in mm.
        SepalWidth       30.5733        4.3587     Sepal Width in mm.
        PetalLength      37.5800       17.6530     Petal Length in mm.
        PetalWidth       11.9933        7.6224     Petal Width in mm.

    Initial Within-Cluster Covariance Estimate = Full Covariance Matrix
```

The ACECLUS Procedure

Approximate Covariance Estimation for Cluster Analysis

COV: Total Sample Covariances

	SepalLength	SepalWidth	PetalLength	PetalWidth
SepalLength	68.5693512	-4.2434004	127.4315436	51.6270694
SepalWidth	-4.2434004	18.9979418	-32.9656376	-12.1639374
PetalLength	127.4315436	-32.9656376	311.6277852	129.5609396
PetalWidth	51.6270694	-12.1639374	129.5609396	58.1006264

Initial Within-Cluster Covariance Estimate = Full Covariance Matrix

Threshold = 0.334211

Iteration History

Iteration	RMS Distance	Distance Cutoff	Pairs Within Cutoff	Convergence Measure
1	2.828	0.945	408.0	0.465775
2	11.905	3.979	559.0	0.013487
3	13.152	4.396	940.0	0.029499
4	13.439	4.491	1506.0	0.046846
5	13.271	4.435	2036.0	0.046859
6	12.591	4.208	2285.0	0.025027
7	12.199	4.077	2366.0	0.009559
8	12.121	4.051	2402.0	0.003895
9	12.064	4.032	2417.0	0.002051
10	12.047	4.026	2429.0	0.000971

Algorithm converged.

ACE: Approximate Covariance Estimate Within Clusters

	SepalLength	SepalWidth	PetalLength	PetalWidth
SepalLength	11.73342939	5.47550432	4.95389049	2.02902429
SepalWidth	5.47550432	6.91992590	2.42177851	1.74125154
PetalLength	4.95389049	2.42177851	6.53746398	2.35302594
PetalWidth	2.02902429	1.74125154	2.35302594	2.05166735

Output 16.1.2. Eigenvalues, Raw Canonical Coefficients, and Standardized Canonical Coefficients

```
                              The ACECLUS Procedure

                Approximate Covariance Estimation for Cluster Analysis

        Initial Within-Cluster Covariance Estimate = Full Covariance Matrix


                         Eigenvalues of Inv(ACE)*(COV-ACE)

                     Eigenvalue    Difference    Proportion    Cumulative

                1       63.7716       61.1593        0.9367        0.9367
                2        2.6123        1.5561        0.0384        0.9751
                3        1.0562        0.4167        0.0155        0.9906
                4        0.6395                     0.00939        1.0000


                    Eigenvectors (Raw Canonical Coefficients)

                                              Can1        Can2        Can3        Can4

SepalLength    Sepal Length in mm.      -.012009    -.098074    -.059852    0.402352
SepalWidth     Sepal Width in mm.       -.211068    -.000072    0.402391    -.225993
PetalLength    Petal Length in mm.      0.324705    -.328583    0.110383    -.321069
PetalWidth     Petal Width in mm.       0.266239    0.870434    -.085215    0.320286


                       Standardized Canonical Coefficients

                                              Can1        Can2        Can3        Can4

SepalLength    Sepal Length in mm.      -0.09944    -0.81211    -0.49562     3.33174
SepalWidth     Sepal Width in mm.       -0.91998    -0.00031     1.75389    -0.98503
PetalLength    Petal Length in mm.       5.73200    -5.80047     1.94859    -5.66782
PetalWidth     Petal Width in mm.        2.02937     6.63478    -0.64954     2.44134
```

Output 16.1.3. Plot of Transformed Iris Data: PROC PLOT

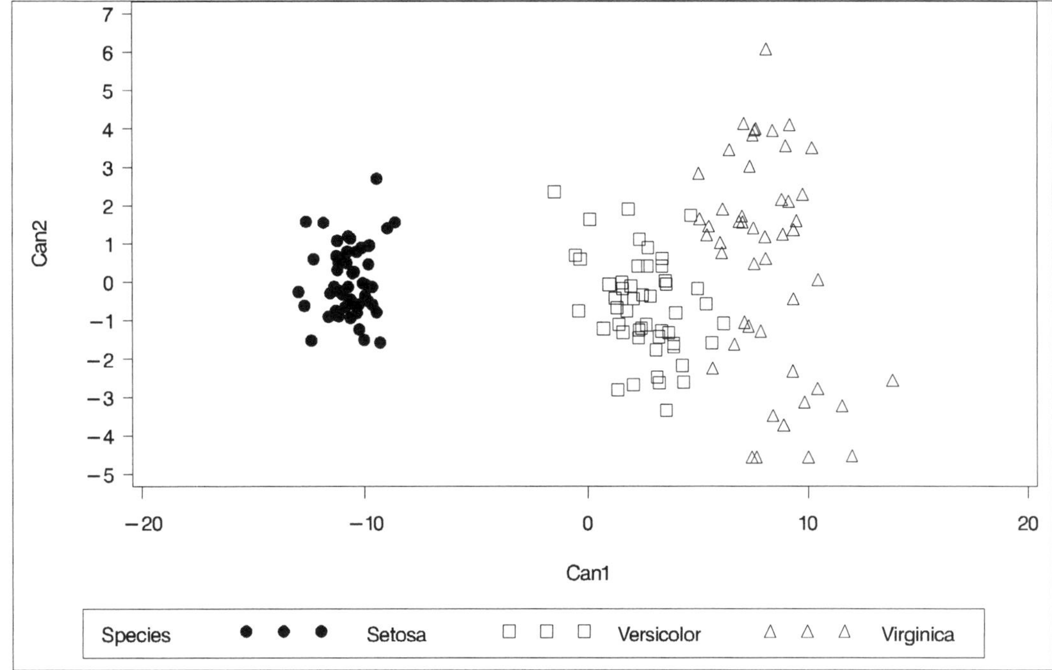

Output 16.1.4. Clustering of Transformed Iris Data: Partial Output from PROC FASTCLUS

```
                     The FASTCLUS Procedure
      Replace=FULL  Radius=0  Maxclusters=3 Maxiter=10  Converge=0

                         Cluster Summary

                                Maximum Distance
                     RMS Std           from Seed      Radius     Nearest
Cluster    Frequency  Deviation      to Observation    Exceeded    Cluster
---------------------------------------------------------------------------
   1             50     1.1016              5.2768                      3
   2             50     1.8880              6.8298                      3
   3             50     1.4138              5.3152                      2

                         Cluster Summary

                               Distance Between
                     Cluster   Cluster Centroids
                     ----------------------------
                        1               13.2845
                        2                5.8580
                        3                5.8580


                     Statistics for Variables

      Variable     Total STD    Within STD       R-Square     RSQ/(1-RSQ)
      -------------------------------------------------------------------
      Can1           8.04808       1.48537       0.966394       28.756658
      Can2           1.90061       1.85646       0.058725        0.062389
      Can3           1.43395       1.32518       0.157417        0.186826
      Can4           1.28044       1.27550       0.021025        0.021477
      OVER-ALL       4.24499       1.50298       0.876324        7.085666

                     Pseudo F Statistic =    520.80

          Approximate Expected Over-All R-Squared =    0.80391

                 Cubic Clustering Criterion =     5.179

     WARNING: The two above values are invalid for correlated variables.

                          Cluster Means

Cluster               Can1              Can2              Can3              Can4
-------------------------------------------------------------------------------
   1          -10.67516964        0.06706906        0.27068819        0.11164209
   2            8.12988211        0.52566663        0.51836499        0.14915404
   3            2.54528754       -0.59273569       -0.78905317       -0.26079612

                   Cluster Standard Deviations

Cluster               Can1              Can2              Can3              Can4
-------------------------------------------------------------------------------
   1           0.953761025       0.931943571       1.398456061       1.058217627
   2           1.799159552       2.743869556       1.270344142       1.370523175
   3           1.572366584       1.393565864       1.303411851       1.372050319
```

Output 16.1.5. Crosstabulation of Cluster by Species for Fisher's Iris Data: PROC FREQ

```
                 The FREQ Procedure

             Table of CLUSTER by Species

    CLUSTER(Cluster)     Species

    Frequency|
    Percent  |
    Row Pct  |
    Col Pct  |Setosa  |Versicol|Virginic|  Total
             |        |or      |a       |
    ---------+--------+--------+--------+
           1 |     50 |      0 |      0 |     50
             |  33.33 |   0.00 |   0.00 |  33.33
             | 100.00 |   0.00 |   0.00 |
             | 100.00 |   0.00 |   0.00 |
    ---------+--------+--------+--------+
           2 |      0 |      2 |     48 |     50
             |   0.00 |   1.33 |  32.00 |  33.33
             |   0.00 |   4.00 |  96.00 |
             |   0.00 |   4.00 |  96.00 |
    ---------+--------+--------+--------+
           3 |      0 |     48 |      2 |     50
             |   0.00 |  32.00 |   1.33 |  33.33
             |   0.00 |  96.00 |   4.00 |
             |   0.00 |  96.00 |   4.00 |
    ---------+--------+--------+--------+
    Total          50       50       50      150
                33.33    33.33    33.33   100.00
```

References

Art, D., Gnanadesikan, R., and Kettenring, R. (1982), "Data-based Metrics for Cluster Analysis," *Utilitas Mathematica*, 21A, 75–99.

Everitt, B.S. (1980), *Cluster Analysis*, Second Edition, London: Heineman Educational Books Ltd.

Fisher, R.A. (1936), "The Use of Multiple Measurements in Taxonomic Problems," *Annals of Eugenics*, 7, 179–188.

Hartigan, J.A. (1975), *Clustering Algorithms*, New York: John Wiley & Sons, Inc.

Kettenring, R. (1984), personal communication.

Mezzich, J.E and Solomon, H. (1980), *Taxonomy and Behavioral Science*, New York: Academic Press, Inc.

Puri, M.L. and Sen, P.K. (1971), *Nonparametric Methods in Multivariate Analysis,* New York: John Wiley & Sons, Inc.

Rouncefield, M. (1995), "The Statistics of Poverty and Inequality," *Journal of Statistics Education*, 3(2). [Online]: [http://www.stat.ncsu.edu/info/jse], accessed Dec. 19, 1997.

Wolfe, J.H. (1970),"Pattern Clustering by Multivariate Mixture Analysis," *Multivariate Behavioral Research*, 5, 329–350.

Chapter 17
The ANOVA Procedure

Chapter Table of Contents

Chapter 17
The ANOVA Procedure

Overview

The ANOVA procedure performs *analysis of variance* (ANOVA) for balanced data from a wide variety of experimental designs. In analysis of variance, a continuous response variable, known as a *dependent variable*, is measured under experimental conditions identified by classification variables, known as *independent variables*. The variation in the response is assumed to be due to effects in the classification, with random error accounting for the remaining variation.

The ANOVA procedure is one of several procedures available in SAS/STAT software for analysis of variance. The ANOVA procedure is designed to handle balanced data (that is, data with equal numbers of observations for every combination of the classification factors), whereas the GLM procedure can analyze both balanced and unbalanced data. Because PROC ANOVA takes into account the special structure of a balanced design, it is faster and uses less storage than PROC GLM for balanced data.

Use PROC ANOVA for the analysis of balanced data only, with the following exceptions: one-way analysis of variance, Latin square designs, certain partially balanced incomplete block designs, completely nested (hierarchical) designs, and designs with cell frequencies that are proportional to each other and are also proportional to the background population. These exceptions have designs in which the factors are all orthogonal to each other. For further discussion, refer to Searle (1971, p. 138). PROC ANOVA works for designs with block diagonal $\mathbf{X}'\mathbf{X}$ matrices where the elements of each block all have the same value. The procedure partially tests this requirement by checking for equal cell means. However, this test is imperfect: some designs that cannot be analyzed correctly may pass the test, and designs that can be analyzed correctly may not pass. If your design does not pass the test, PROC ANOVA produces a warning message to tell you that the design is unbalanced and that the ANOVA analyses may not be valid; if your design is not one of the special cases described here, then you should use PROC GLM instead. Complete validation of designs is not performed in PROC ANOVA since this would require the whole $\mathbf{X}'\mathbf{X}$ matrix; if you're unsure about the validity of PROC ANOVA for your design, you should use PROC GLM.

Caution: If you use PROC ANOVA for analysis of unbalanced data, you must assume responsibility for the validity of the results.

Getting Started

The following examples demonstrate how you can use the ANOVA procedure to perform analyses of variance for a one-way layout and a randomized complete block design.

One-Way Layout with Means Comparisons

A one-way analysis of variance considers one treatment factor with two or more treatment levels. The goal of the analysis is to test for differences among the means of the levels and to quantify these differences. If there are two treatment levels, this analysis is equivalent to a t test comparing two group means.

The assumptions of analysis of variance (Steel and Torrie 1980) are

- treatment effects are additive
- experimental errors
  - are random
  - are independently distributed
  - follow a normal distribution
  - have mean zero and constant variance

The following example studies the effect of bacteria on the nitrogen content of red clover plants. The treatment factor is bacteria strain, and it has six levels. Five of the six levels consist of five different *Rhizobium trifolii* bacteria cultures combined with a composite of five *Rhizobium meliloti* strains. The sixth level is a composite of the five *Rhizobium trifolii* strains with the composite of the *Rhizobium meliloti*. Red clover plants are inoculated with the treatments, and nitrogen content is later measured in milligrams. The data are derived from an experiment by Erdman (1946) and are analyzed in Chapters 7 and 8 of Steel and Torrie (1980). The following DATA step creates the SAS data set Clover:

```
title 'Nitrogen Content of Red Clover Plants';
data Clover;
   input Strain $ Nitrogen @@;
   datalines;
3DOK1  19.4 3DOK1  32.6 3DOK1  27.0 3DOK1  32.1 3DOK1  33.0
3DOK5  17.7 3DOK5  24.8 3DOK5  27.9 3DOK5  25.2 3DOK5  24.3
3DOK4  17.0 3DOK4  19.4 3DOK4   9.1 3DOK4  11.9 3DOK4  15.8
3DOK7  20.7 3DOK7  21.0 3DOK7  20.5 3DOK7  18.8 3DOK7  18.6
3DOK13 14.3 3DOK13 14.4 3DOK13 11.8 3DOK13 11.6 3DOK13 14.2
COMPOS 17.3 COMPOS 19.4 COMPOS 19.1 COMPOS 16.9 COMPOS 20.8
;
```

The variable Strain contains the treatment levels, and the variable Nitrogen contains the response. The following statements produce the analysis.

```
proc anova;
   class Strain;
   model Nitrogen = Strain;
run;
```

The classification variable is specified in the CLASS statement. Note that, unlike the GLM procedure, PROC ANOVA does not allow continuous variables on the right-hand side of the model. Figure 17.1 and Figure 17.2 display the output produced by these statements.

```
                     Nitrogen Content of Red Clover Plants

                            The ANOVA Procedure

                          Class Level Information

     Class         Levels    Values

     Strain             6    3DOK1 3DOK13 3DOK4 3DOK5 3DOK7 COMPOS


                        Number of observations    30
```

Figure 17.1. Class Level Information

The "Class Level Information" table shown in Figure 17.1 lists the variables that appear in the CLASS statement, their levels, and the number of observations in the data set.

Figure 17.2 displays the ANOVA table, followed by some simple statistics and tests of effects.

```
                     Nitrogen Content of Red Clover Plants

                            The ANOVA Procedure

Dependent Variable: Nitrogen

                                        Sum of
 Source                      DF        Squares    Mean Square   F Value   Pr > F

 Model                        5     847.046667     169.409333     14.37   <.0001

 Error                       24     282.928000      11.788667

 Corrected Total             29    1129.974667


            R-Square     Coeff Var      Root MSE    Nitrogen Mean

            0.749616      17.26515      3.433463         19.88667


 Source                      DF       Anova SS    Mean Square   F Value   Pr > F

 Strain                       5    847.0466667    169.4093333     14.37   <.0001
```

Figure 17.2. ANOVA Table

The degrees of freedom (DF) column should be used to check the analysis results. The model degrees of freedom for a one-way analysis of variance are the number of levels minus 1; in this case, $6 - 1 = 5$. The Corrected Total degrees of freedom are always the total number of observations minus one; in this case $30 - 1 = 29$. The sum of Model and Error degrees of freedom equal the Corrected Total.

The overall F test is significant ($F = 14.37, p < 0.0001$), indicating that the model as a whole accounts for a significant portion of the variability in the dependent variable. The F test for Strain is significant, indicating that some contrast between the means for the different strains is different from zero. Notice that the Model and Strain F tests are identical, since Strain is the only term in the model.

The F test for Strain ($F = 14.37, p < 0.0001$) suggests that there are differences among the bacterial strains, but it does not reveal any information about the nature of the differences. Mean comparison methods can be used to gather further information. The interactivity of PROC ANOVA enables you to do this without re-running the entire analysis. After you specify a model with a MODEL statement and execute the ANOVA procedure with a RUN statement, you can execute a variety of statements (such as MEANS, MANOVA, TEST, and REPEATED) without PROC ANOVA recalculating the model sum of squares.

The following command requests means of the Strain levels with Tukey's studentized range procedure.

```
   means Strain / tukey;
run;
```

Results of Tukey's procedure are shown in Figure 17.3.

```
                    Nitrogen Content of Red Clover Plants

                            The ANOVA Procedure

              Tukey's Studentized Range (HSD) Test for Nitrogen

NOTE: This test controls the Type I experimentwise error rate, but it generally
                  has a higher Type II error rate than REGWQ.


                  Alpha                                     0.05
                  Error Degrees of Freedom                    24
                  Error Mean Square                     11.78867
                  Critical Value of Studentized Range    4.37265
                  Minimum Significant Difference          6.7142


          Means with the same letter are not significantly different.


             Tukey Grouping          Mean       N    Strain

                          A        28.820       5    3DOK1
                          A
                     B    A        23.980       5    3DOK5
                     B
                     B    C        19.920       5    3DOK7
                     B    C
                     B    C        18.700       5    COMPOS
                          C
                          C        14.640       5    3DOK4
                          C
                          C        13.260       5    3DOK13
```

Figure 17.3. Tukey's Multiple Comparisons Procedure

The multiple comparisons results indicate, for example, that

- strain 3DOK1 fixes significantly more nitrogen than all but 3DOK5
- even though 3DOK5 is not significantly different from 3DOK1, it is also not significantly better than all the rest

Although the experiment has succeeded in separating the best strains from the worst, clearly distinguishing the very best strain requires more experimentation.

Randomized Complete Block with One Factor

This example illustrates the use of PROC ANOVA in analyzing a randomized complete block design. Researchers are interested in whether three treatments have different effects on the yield and worth of a particular crop. They believe that the experimental units are not homogeneous. So, a blocking factor is introduced that allows the experimental units to be homogeneous within each block. The three treatments are then randomly assigned within each block.

The data from this study are input into the SAS data set RCB:

```
title 'Randomized Complete Block';
data RCB;
   input Block Treatment $ Yield Worth @@;
   datalines;
1 A 32.6 112   1 B 36.4 130   1 C 29.5 106
2 A 42.7 139   2 B 47.1 143   2 C 32.9 112
3 A 35.3 124   3 B 40.1 134   3 C 33.6 116
;
```

The variables Yield and Worth are continuous response variables, and the variables Block and Treatment are the classification variables. Because the data for the analysis are balanced, you can use PROC ANOVA to run the analysis.

The statements for the analysis are

```
proc anova;
   class Block Treatment;
   model Yield Worth=Block Treatment;
run;
```

The Block and Treatment effects appear in the CLASS statement. The MODEL statement requests an analysis for each of the two dependent variables, Yield and Worth.

Figure 17.4 shows the "Class Level Information" table.

```
                    Randomized Complete Block

                       The ANOVA Procedure

                     Class Level Information

               Class           Levels    Values

               Block                3    1 2 3

               Treatment            3    A B C


                 Number of observations    9
```

Figure 17.4. Class Level Information

The "Class Level Information" table lists the number of levels and their values for all effects specified in the CLASS statement. The number of observations in the data set are also displayed. Use this information to make sure that the data have been read correctly.

The overall ANOVA table for Yield in Figure 17.5 appears first in the output because it is the first response variable listed on the left side in the MODEL statement.

```
                        Randomized Complete Block

                          The ANOVA Procedure

Dependent Variable: Yield

                                       Sum of
 Source                    DF         Squares     Mean Square    F Value    Pr > F

 Model                      4     225.2777778      56.3194444       8.94    0.0283

 Error                      4      25.1911111       6.2977778

 Corrected Total            8     250.4688889


              R-Square     Coeff Var      Root MSE    Yield Mean

              0.899424      6.840047      2.509537      36.68889
```

Figure 17.5. Overall ANOVA Table for Yield

The overall F statistic is significant ($F = 8.94, p = 0.02583$), indicating that the model as a whole accounts for a significant portion of the variation in Yield and that you may proceed to tests of effects.

The degrees of freedom (DF) are used to ensure correctness of the data and model. The Corrected Total degrees of freedom are one less than the total number of observations in the data set; in this case, $9 - 1 = 8$. The Model degrees of freedom for a randomized complete block are $(b - 1) + (t - 1)$, where b =number of block levels and t =number of treatment levels. In this case, $(3 - 1) + (3 - 1) = 4$.

Several simple statistics follow the ANOVA table. The R-Square indicates that the model accounts for nearly 90% of the variation in the variable Yield. The coefficient of variation (C.V.) is listed along with the Root MSE and the mean of the dependent variable. The Root MSE is an estimate of the standard deviation of the dependent variable. The C.V. is a unitless measure of variability.

The tests of the effects shown in Figure 17.6 are displayed after the simple statistics.

Randomized Complete Block

The ANOVA Procedure

Dependent Variable: Yield

Source	DF	Anova SS	Mean Square	F Value	Pr > F
Block	2	98.1755556	49.0877778	7.79	0.0417
Treatment	2	127.1022222	63.5511111	10.09	0.0274

Figure 17.6. Tests of Effects for Yield

For Yield, both the Block and Treatment effects are significant ($F = 7.79, p = 0.0417$ and $F = 10.09, p = 0.0274$, respectively) at the 95% level. From this you can conclude that blocking is useful for this variable and that some contrast between the treatment means is significantly different from zero.

Figure 17.7 shows the ANOVA table, simple statistics, and tests of effects for the variable Worth.

Randomized Complete Block

The ANOVA Procedure

Dependent Variable: Worth

Source	DF	Sum of Squares	Mean Square	F Value	Pr > F
Model	4	1247.333333	311.833333	8.28	0.0323
Error	4	150.666667	37.666667		
Corrected Total	8	1398.000000			

R-Square	Coeff Var	Root MSE	Worth Mean
0.892227	4.949450	6.137318	124.0000

Source	DF	Anova SS	Mean Square	F Value	Pr > F
Block	2	354.6666667	177.3333333	4.71	0.0889
Treatment	2	892.6666667	446.3333333	11.85	0.0209

Figure 17.7. ANOVA Table for Worth

The overall F test is significant $(F = 8.28, p = 0.0323)$ at the 95% level for the variable Worth. The Block effect is not significant at the 0.05 level but is significant at the 0.10 confidence level $(F = 4.71, p = 0.0889)$. Generally, the usefulness of blocking should be determined before the analysis. However, since there are two dependent variables of interest, and Block is significant for one of them (Yield), blocking appears to be generally useful. For Worth, as with Yield, the effect of Treatment is significant $(F = 11.85, p = 0.0209)$.

Issuing the following command produces the Treatment means.

```
   means Treatment;
run;
```

Figure 17.8 displays the treatment means and their standard deviations for both dependent variables.

Randomized Complete Block

The ANOVA Procedure

Level of Treatment	N	Yield Mean	Yield Std Dev	Worth Mean	Worth Std Dev
A	3	36.8666667	5.22908532	125.000000	13.5277493
B	3	41.2000000	5.43415127	135.666667	6.6583281
C	3	32.0000000	2.19317122	111.333333	5.0332230

Figure 17.8. Means of Yield and Worth

Syntax

The following statements are available in PROC ANOVA.

PROC ANOVA < *options* > **;**
CLASS *variables* **;**
MODEL *dependents=effects* < */ options* > **;**
ABSORB *variables* **;**
BY *variables* **;**
FREQ *variable* **;**
MANOVA < *test-options* >< */ detail-options* > **;**
MEANS *effects* < */ options* > **;**
REPEATED *factor-specification* < */ options* > **;**
TEST < **H=***effects* > **E=***effect* **;**

The PROC ANOVA, CLASS, and MODEL statements are required, and they must precede the first RUN statement. The CLASS statement must precede the MODEL statement. If you use the ABSORB, FREQ, or BY statement, it must precede the first RUN statement. The MANOVA, MEANS, REPEATED, and TEST statements must follow the MODEL statement, and they can be specified in any order. These four statements can also appear after the first RUN statement.

The following table summarizes the function of each statement (other than the PROC statement) in the ANOVA procedure:

Table 17.1. Statements in the ANOVA Procedure

Statement	Description
ABSORB	absorbs classification effects in a model
BY	specifies variables to define subgroups for the analysis
CLASS	declares classification variables
FREQ	specifies a frequency variable
MANOVA	performs a multivariate analysis of variance
MEANS	computes and compares means
MODEL	defines the model to be fit
REPEATED	performs multivariate and univariate repeated measures analysis of variance
TEST	constructs tests using the sums of squares for effects and the error term you specify

PROC ANOVA Statement

PROC ANOVA < *options* > **;**

The PROC ANOVA statement starts the ANOVA procedure.

You can specify the following options in the PROC ANOVA statement:

DATA=*SAS-data-set*
names the SAS data set used by the ANOVA procedure. By default, PROC ANOVA uses the most recently created SAS data set.

MANOVA
requests the multivariate mode of eliminating observations with missing values. If any of the dependent variables have missing values, the procedure eliminates that observation from the analysis. The MANOVA option is useful if you use PROC ANOVA in interactive mode and plan to perform a multivariate analysis.

MULTIPASS
requests that PROC ANOVA reread the input data set, when necessary, instead of writing the values of dependent variables to a utility file. This option decreases disk space usage at the expense of increased execution times and is useful only in rare situations where disk space is at an absolute premium.

NAMELEN=n
specifies the length of effect names to be n characters long, where n is a value between 20 and 200 characters. The default length is 20 characters.

NOPRINT
suppresses the normal display of results. The NOPRINT option is useful when you want to create only the output data set with the procedure. Note that this option temporarily disables the Output Delivery System (ODS); see Chapter 15, "Using the Output Delivery System," for more information.

ORDER=DATA | FORMATTED | FREQ | INTERNAL
specifies the sorting order for the levels of the classification variables (specified in the CLASS statement). This ordering determines which parameters in the model correspond to each level in the data. Note that the ORDER= option applies to the levels for all classification variables. The exception is ORDER=FORMATTED (the default) for numeric variables for which you have supplied no explicit format (that is, for which there is no corresponding FORMAT statement in the current PROC ANOVA run or in the DATA step that created the data set). In this case, the levels are ordered by their internal (numeric) value. Note that this represents a change from previous releases for how class levels are ordered. In releases previous to Version 8, numeric class levels with no explicit format were ordered by their BEST12. formatted values, and in order to revert to the previous ordering you can specify this format explicitly for the affected classification variables. The change was implemented because the former default behavior for ORDER=FORMATTED often resulted in levels not being ordered numerically and usually required the user to intervene with an explicit format or ORDER=INTERNAL to get the more natural ordering.

The following table shows how PROC ANOVA interprets values of the ORDER= option.

Value of ORDER=	Levels Sorted By
DATA	order of appearance in the input data set
FORMATTED	external formatted value, except for numeric variables with no explicit format, which are sorted by their unformatted (internal) value
FREQ	descending frequency count; levels with the most observations come first in the order
INTERNAL	unformatted value

OUTSTAT=*SAS-data-set*

names an output data set that contains sums of squares, degrees of freedom, F statistics, and probability levels for each effect in the model. If you use the CANONICAL option in the MANOVA statement and do not use an M= specification in the MANOVA statement, the data set also contains results of the canonical analysis. See the "Output Data Set" section on page 370 for more information.

ABSORB Statement

ABSORB *variables* ;

Absorption is a computational technique that provides a large reduction in time and memory requirements for certain types of models. The *variables* are one or more variables in the input data set.

For a main effect variable that does not participate in interactions, you can absorb the effect by naming it in an ABSORB statement. This means that the effect can be adjusted out before the construction and solution of the rest of the model. This is particularly useful when the effect has a large number of levels.

Several variables can be specified, in which case each one is assumed to be nested in the preceding variable in the ABSORB statement.

Note: When you use the ABSORB statement, the data set (or each BY group, if a BY statement appears) must be sorted by the variables in the ABSORB statement. Including an absorbed variable in the CLASS list or in the MODEL statement may produce erroneous sums of squares. If the ABSORB statement is used, it must appear before the first RUN statement or it is ignored.

When you use an ABSORB statement and also use the INT option in the MODEL statement, the procedure ignores the option but produces the uncorrected total sum of squares (SS) instead of the corrected total SS.

See the "Absorption" section on page 1532 in Chapter 30, "The GLM Procedure," for more information.

BY Statement

BY *variables* ;

You can specify a BY statement with PROC ANOVA to obtain separate analyses on observations in groups defined by the BY variables. When a BY statement appears, the procedure expects the input data set to be sorted in order of the BY variables. The *variables* are one or more variables in the input data set.

If your input data set is not sorted in ascending order, use one of the following alternatives:

- Sort the data using the SORT procedure with a similar BY statement.
- Specify the BY statement option NOTSORTED or DESCENDING in the BY statement for the ANOVA procedure. The NOTSORTED option does not mean that the data are unsorted but rather that the data are arranged in groups (according to values of the BY variables) and that these groups are not necessarily in alphabetical or increasing numeric order.
- Create an index on the BY variables using the DATASETS procedure (in base SAS software).

Since sorting the data changes the order in which PROC ANOVA reads observations, the sorting order for the levels of the classification variables may be affected if you have also specified the ORDER=DATA option in the PROC ANOVA statement.

If the BY statement is used, it must appear before the first RUN statement or it is ignored. When you use a BY statement, the interactive features of PROC ANOVA are disabled.

When both a BY and an ABSORB statement are used, observations must be sorted first by the variables in the BY statement, and then by the variables in the ABSORB statement.

For more information on the BY statement, refer to the discussion in *SAS Language Reference: Concepts*. For more information on the DATASETS procedure, refer to the discussion in the *SAS Procedures Guide*.

CLASS Statement

CLASS *variables* ;

The CLASS statement names the classification variables to be used in the model. Typical class variables are TREATMENT, SEX, RACE, GROUP, and REPLICATION. The CLASS statement is required, and it must appear before the MODEL statement.

Class levels are determined from up to the first 16 characters of the formatted values of the CLASS variables. Thus, you can use formats to group values into levels. Refer to the discussion of the FORMAT procedure in the *SAS Procedures Guide* and the discussions for the FORMAT statement and SAS formats in *SAS Language Reference: Concepts*.

FREQ Statement

FREQ *variable* ;

The FREQ statement names a variable that provides frequencies for each observation in the DATA= data set. Specifically, if n is the value of the FREQ variable for a given observation, then that observation is used n times.

The analysis produced using a FREQ statement reflects the expanded number of observations. For example, means and total degrees of freedom reflect the expanded number of observations. You can produce the same analysis (without the FREQ statement) by first creating a new data set that contains the expanded number of observations. For example, if the value of the FREQ variable is 5 for the first observation, the first 5 observations in the new data set would be identical. Each observation in the old data set would be replicated n_i times in the new data set, where n_i is the value of the FREQ variable for that observation.

If the value of the FREQ variable is missing or is less than 1, the observation is not used in the analysis. If the value is not an integer, only the integer portion is used.

If the FREQ statement is used, it must appear before the first RUN statement or it is ignored.

MANOVA Statement

MANOVA < *test-options* >< / *detail-options* > ;

If the MODEL statement includes more than one dependent variable, you can perform multivariate analysis of variance with the MANOVA statement. The *test-options* define which effects to test, while the *detail-options* specify how to execute the tests and what results to display.

When a MANOVA statement appears before the first RUN statement, PROC ANOVA enters a multivariate mode with respect to the handling of missing values; in addition to observations with missing independent variables, observations with *any* missing dependent variables are excluded from the analysis. If you want to use this mode of handling missing values but do not need any multivariate analyses, specify the MANOVA option in the PROC ANOVA statement.

Test-Options

You can specify the following options in the MANOVA statement as *test-options* in order to define which multivariate tests to perform.

H=*effects* | **INTERCEPT** | **_ALL_**

specifies effects in the preceding model to use as hypothesis matrices. for multivariate tests For each SSCP matrix $\mathbf{H}$ associated with an effect, the H= specification computes an analysis based on the characteristic roots of $\mathbf{E}^{-1}\mathbf{H}$, where $\mathbf{E}$ is the matrix associated with the error effect. The characteristic roots and vectors are displayed, along with the Hotelling-Lawley trace, Pillai's trace, Wilks' criterion, and Roy's maximum root criterion with approximate F statistics. Use the keyword INTERCEPT to produce tests for the intercept. To produce tests for all effects listed in the MODEL statement, use the keyword _ALL_ in place of a list of effects. For background and further details, see the "Multivariate Analysis of Variance" section on page 1558 in Chapter 30, "The GLM Procedure."

E=*effect*

specifies the error effect. If you omit the E= specification, the ANOVA procedure uses the error SSCP (residual) matrix from the analysis.

M=*equation,. . .,equation* | **(***row-of-matrix,. . .,row-of-matrix***)**

specifies a transformation matrix for the dependent variables listed in the MODEL statement. The equations in the M= specification are of the form

$$\begin{aligned} c_1 \times \textit{dependent-variable} \quad &\pm \quad c_2 \times \textit{dependent-variable} \\ \cdots \quad &\pm \quad c_n \times \textit{dependent-variable} \end{aligned}$$

where the c_i values are coefficients for the various *dependent-variables*. If the value of a given c_i is 1, it may be omitted; in other words $1 \times Y$ is the same as Y. Equations should involve two or more dependent variables. For sample syntax, see the "Examples" section on page 354.

Alternatively, you can input the transformation matrix directly by entering the elements of the matrix with commas separating the rows, and parentheses surrounding the matrix. When this alternate form of input is used, the number of elements in each row must equal the number of dependent variables. Although these combinations actually represent the columns of the $\mathbf{M}$ matrix, they are displayed by rows.

When you include an M= specification, the analysis requested in the MANOVA statement is carried out for the variables defined by the equations in the specification, not the original dependent variables. If you omit the M= option, the analysis is performed for the original dependent variables in the MODEL statement.

If an M= specification is included without either the MNAMES= or the PREFIX= option, the variables are labeled MVAR1, MVAR2, and so forth by default. For further information, see the section "Multivariate Analysis of Variance" on page 1558 in Chapter 30, "The GLM Procedure."

MNAMES=*names*

provides names for the variables defined by the equations in the M= specification. Names in the list correspond to the M= equations or the rows of the **M** matrix (as it is entered).

PREFIX=*name*

is an alternative means of identifying the transformed variables defined by the M= specification. For example, if you specify PREFIX=DIFF, the transformed variables are labeled DIFF1, DIFF2, and so forth.

Detail-Options

You can specify the following options in the MANOVA statement after a slash as *detail-options*:

CANONICAL

produces a canonical analysis of the **H** and **E** matrices (transformed by the **M** matrix, if specified) instead of the default display of characteristic roots and vectors.

ORTH

requests that the transformation matrix in the M= specification of the MANOVA statement be orthonormalized by rows before the analysis.

PRINTE

displays the error SSCP matrix **E**. If the **E** matrix is the error SSCP (residual) matrix from the analysis, the partial correlations of the dependent variables given the independent variables are also produced.

For example, the statement

```
manova / printe;
```

displays the error SSCP matrix and the partial correlation matrix computed from the error SSCP matrix.

PRINTH

displays the hypothesis SSCP matrix **H** associated with each effect specified by the H= specification.

SUMMARY

produces analysis-of-variance tables for each dependent variable. When no **M** matrix is specified, a table is produced for each original dependent variable from the MODEL statement; with an **M** matrix other than the identity, a table is produced for each transformed variable defined by the **M** matrix.

Examples

The following statements give several examples of using a MANOVA statement.

```
proc anova;
   class A B;
   model Y1-Y5=A B(A);
   manova h=A e=B(A) / printh printe;
   manova h=B(A) / printe;
   manova h=A e=B(A) m=Y1-Y2,Y2-Y3,Y3-Y4,Y4-Y5
          prefix=diff;
```

```
      manova h=A e=B(A) m=(1 -1  0  0  0,
                           0  1 -1  0  0,
                           0  0  1 -1  0,
                           0  0  0  1 -1) prefix=diff;
   run;
```

The first MANOVA statement specifies A as the hypothesis effect and B(A) as the error effect. As a result of the PRINTH option, the procedure displays the hypothesis SSCP matrix associated with the A effect; and, as a result of the PRINTE option, the procedure displays the error SSCP matrix associated with the B(A) effect.

The second MANOVA statement specifies B(A) as the hypothesis effect. Since no error effect is specified, PROC ANOVA uses the error SSCP matrix from the analysis as the **E** matrix. The PRINTE option displays this **E** matrix. Since the **E** matrix is the error SSCP matrix from the analysis, the partial correlation matrix computed from this matrix is also produced.

The third MANOVA statement requests the same analysis as the first MANOVA statement, but the analysis is carried out for variables transformed to be successive differences between the original dependent variables. The PREFIX=DIFF specification labels the transformed variables as DIFF1, DIFF2, DIFF3, and DIFF4.

Finally, the fourth MANOVA statement has the identical effect as the third, but it uses an alternative form of the M= specification. Instead of specifying a set of equations, the fourth MANOVA statement specifies rows of a matrix of coefficients for the five dependent variables.

As a second example of the use of the M= specification, consider the following:

```
proc anova;
   class group;
   model dose1-dose4=group / nouni;
   manova h = group
          m = -3*dose1 -   dose2 +   dose3 + 3*dose4,
                 dose1 -   dose2 -   dose3 +   dose4,
                -dose1 + 3*dose2 - 3*dose3 +   dose4
          mnames = Linear Quadratic Cubic
          / printe;
run;
```

The M= specification gives a transformation of the dependent variables dose1 through dose4 into orthogonal polynomial components, and the MNAMES= option labels the transformed variables as LINEAR, QUADRATIC, and CUBIC, respectively. Since the PRINTE option is specified and the default residual matrix is used as an error term, the partial correlation matrix of the orthogonal polynomial components is also produced.

For further information, see the "Multivariate Analysis of Variance" section on page 1558 in Chapter 30, "The GLM Procedure."

MEANS Statement

MEANS *effects* < */ options* > **;**

PROC ANOVA can compute means of the dependent variables for any effect that appears on the right-hand side in the MODEL statement.

You can use any number of MEANS statements, provided that they appear after the MODEL statement. For example, suppose A and B each have two levels. Then, if you use the following statements

```
proc anova;
   class A B;
   model Y=A B A*B;
   means A B / tukey;
   means A*B;
run;
```

means, standard deviations, and Tukey's multiple comparison tests are produced for each level of the main effects A and B, and just the means and standard deviations for each of the four combinations of levels for A*B. Since multiple comparisons options apply only to main effects, the single MEANS statement

```
means A B A*B / tukey;
```

produces the same results.

Options are provided to perform multiple comparison tests for only main effects in the model. PROC ANOVA does not perform multiple comparison tests for interaction terms in the model; for multiple comparisons of interaction terms, see the LSMEANS statement in Chapter 30, "The GLM Procedure." The following table summarizes categories of options available in the MEANS statement.

Table 17.2. Options Available in the MEANS Statement

Task	Available options
Perform multiple comparison tests	BON
	DUNCAN
	DUNNETT
	DUNNETTL
	DUNNETTU
	GABRIEL
	GT2
	LSD
	REGWQ
	SCHEFFE
	SIDAK

Table 17.2. (continued)

Task	Available options
	SMM
Perform multiple comparison tests	SNK
	T
	TUKEY
	WALLER
Specify additional details for multiple comparison tests	ALPHA=
	CLDIFF
	CLM
	E=
	KRATIO=
	LINES
	NOSORT
Test for homogeneity of variances	HOVTEST
Compensate for heterogeneous variances	WELCH

Descriptions of these options follow. For a further discussion of these options, see the section "Multiple Comparisons" on page 1540 in Chapter 30, "The GLM Procedure."

ALPHA=*p*

specifies the level of significance for comparisons among the means. By default, ALPHA=0.05. You can specify any value greater than 0 and less than 1.

BON

performs Bonferroni t tests of differences between means for all main effect means in the MEANS statement. See the CLDIFF and LINES options, which follow, for a discussion of how the procedure displays results.

CLDIFF

presents results of the BON, GABRIEL, SCHEFFE, SIDAK, SMM, GT2, T, LSD, and TUKEY options as confidence intervals for all pairwise differences between means, and the results of the DUNNETT, DUNNETTU, and DUNNETTL options as confidence intervals for differences with the control. The CLDIFF option is the default for unequal cell sizes unless the DUNCAN, REGWQ, SNK, or WALLER option is specified.

CLM

presents results of the BON, GABRIEL, SCHEFFE, SIDAK, SMM, T, and LSD options as intervals for the mean of each level of the variables specified in the MEANS statement. For all options except GABRIEL, the intervals are confidence intervals for the true means. For the GABRIEL option, they are *comparison intervals* for comparing means pairwise: in this case, if the intervals corresponding to two means overlap, the difference between them is insignificant according to Gabriel's method.

DUNCAN

performs Duncan's multiple range test on all main effect means given in the MEANS statement. See the LINES option for a discussion of how the procedure displays results.

DUNNETT < **(*formatted-control-values*)** >

performs Dunnett's two-tailed t test, testing if any treatments are significantly different from a single control for all main effects means in the MEANS statement.

To specify which level of the effect is the control, enclose the formatted value in quotes in parentheses after the keyword. If more than one effect is specified in the MEANS statement, you can use a list of control values within the parentheses. By default, the first level of the effect is used as the control. For example,

```
means a / dunnett('CONTROL');
```

where CONTROL is the formatted control value of A. As another example,

```
means a b c / dunnett('CNTLA' 'CNTLB' 'CNTLC');
```

where CNTLA, CNTLB, and CNTLC are the formatted control values for A, B, and C, respectively.

DUNNETTL < **(*formatted-control-value*)** >

performs Dunnett's one-tailed t test, testing if any treatment is significantly less than the control. Control level information is specified as described previously for the DUNNETT option.

DUNNETTU < **(*formatted-control-value*)** >

performs Dunnett's one-tailed t test, testing if any treatment is significantly greater than the control. Control level information is specified as described previously for the DUNNETT option.

E=*effect*

specifies the error mean square used in the multiple comparisons. By default, PROC ANOVA uses the residual Mean Square (MS). The effect specified with the E= option must be a term in the model; otherwise, the procedure uses the residual MS.

GABRIEL

performs Gabriel's multiple-comparison procedure on all main effect means in the MEANS statement. See the CLDIFF and LINES options for discussions of how the procedure displays results.

GT2

see the SMM option.

HOVTEST
HOVTEST=BARTLETT
HOVTEST=BF
HOVTEST=LEVENE <**(TYPE=ABS | SQUARE)**>
HOVTEST=OBRIEN <**(W=*number*)**>

requests a homogeneity of variance test for the groups defined by the MEANS effect. You can optionally specify a particular test; if you do not specify a test, Levene's test (Levene 1960) with TYPE=SQUARE is computed. Note that this option is ignored unless your MODEL statement specifies a simple one-way model.

The HOVTEST=BARTLETT option specifies Bartlett's test (Bartlett 1937), a modification of the normal-theory likelihood ratio test.

The HOVTEST=BF option specifies Brown and Forsythe's variation of Levene's test (Brown and Forsythe 1974).

The HOVTEST=LEVENE option specifies Levene's test (Levene 1960), which is widely considered to be the standard homogeneity of variance test. You can use the TYPE= option in parentheses to specify whether to use the absolute residuals (TYPE=ABS) or the squared residuals (TYPE=SQUARE) in Levene's test. The default is TYPE=SQUARE.

The HOVTEST=OBRIEN option specifies O'Brien's test (O'Brien 1979), which is basically a modification of HOVTEST=LEVENE(TYPE=SQUARE). You can use the W= option in parentheses to tune the variable to match the suspected kurtosis of the underlying distribution. By default, W=0.5, as suggested by O'Brien (1979, 1981).

See the section "Homogeneity of Variance in One-Way Models" on page 1553 in Chapter 30, "The GLM Procedure," for more details on these methods. Example 30.10 on page 1623 in the same chapter illustrates the use of the HOVTEST and WELCH options in the MEANS statement in testing for equal group variances.

KRATIO=*value*

specifies the Type 1/Type 2 error seriousness ratio for the Waller-Duncan test. Reasonable values for KRATIO are 50, 100, and 500, which roughly correspond for the two-level case to ALPHA levels of 0.1, 0.05, and 0.01. By default, the procedure uses the default value of 100.

LINES

presents results of the BON, DUNCAN, GABRIEL, REGWQ, SCHEFFE, SIDAK, SMM, GT2, SNK, T, LSD, TUKEY, and WALLER options by listing the means in descending order and indicating nonsignificant subsets by line segments beside the corresponding means. The LINES option is appropriate for equal cell sizes, for which it is the default. The LINES option is also the default if the DUNCAN, REGWQ, SNK, or WALLER option is specified, or if there are only two cells of unequal size. If the cell sizes are unequal, the harmonic mean of the cell sizes is used, which may lead to somewhat liberal tests if the cell sizes are highly disparate. The LINES option cannot be used in combination with the DUNNETT, DUNNETTL, or DUNNETTU option. In addition, the procedure has a restriction that no more than 24 overlapping groups of means can exist. If a mean belongs to more than 24 groups, the procedure issues an error message. You can either reduce the number of levels of the variable or use a multiple comparison test that allows the CLDIFF option rather than the LINES option.

LSD

see the T option.

NOSORT

prevents the means from being sorted into descending order when the CLDIFF or CLM option is specified.

REGWQ
performs the Ryan-Einot-Gabriel-Welsch multiple range test on all main effect means in the MEANS statement. See the LINES option for a discussion of how the procedure displays results.

SCHEFFE
performs Scheffé's multiple-comparison procedure on all main effect means in the MEANS statement. See the CLDIFF and LINES options for discussions of how the procedure displays results.

SIDAK
performs pairwise t tests on differences between means with levels adjusted according to Sidak's inequality for all main effect means in the MEANS statement. See the CLDIFF and LINES options for discussions of how the procedure displays results.

SMM
GT2
performs pairwise comparisons based on the studentized maximum modulus and Sidak's uncorrelated-t inequality, yielding Hochberg's GT2 method when sample sizes are unequal, for all main effect means in the MEANS statement. See the CLDIFF and LINES options for discussions of how the procedure displays results.

SNK
performs the Student-Newman-Keuls multiple range test on all main effect means in the MEANS statement. See the LINES option for a discussion of how the procedure displays results.

T
LSD
performs pairwise t tests, equivalent to Fisher's least-significant-difference test in the case of equal cell sizes, for all main effect means in the MEANS statement. See the CLDIFF and LINES options for discussions of how the procedure displays results.

TUKEY
performs Tukey's studentized range test (HSD) on all main effect means in the MEANS statement. (When the group sizes are different, this is the Tukey-Kramer test.) See the CLDIFF and LINES options for discussions of how the procedure displays results.

WALLER
performs the Waller-Duncan k-ratio t test on all main effect means in the MEANS statement. See the KRATIO= option for information on controlling details of the test, and see the LINES option for a discussion of how the procedure displays results.

WELCH
requests Welch's (1951) variance-weighted one-way ANOVA. This alternative to the usual analysis of variance for a one-way model is robust to the assumption of equal within-group variances. This option is ignored unless your MODEL statement specifies a simple one-way model.

Note that using the WELCH option merely produces one additional table consisting of Welch's ANOVA. It does not affect all of the other tests displayed by the ANOVA procedure, which still require the assumption of equal variance for exact validity.

See the "Homogeneity of Variance in One-Way Models" section on page 1553 in Chapter 30, "The GLM Procedure," for more details on Welch's ANOVA. Example 30.10 on page 1623 in the same chapter illustrates the use of the HOVTEST and WELCH options in the MEANS statement in testing for equal group variances.

MODEL Statement

MODEL *dependents=effects* < / *options* > **;**

The MODEL statement names the dependent variables and independent effects. The syntax of effects is described in the section "Specification of Effects" on page 366. If no independent effects are specified, only an intercept term is fit. This tests the hypothesis that the mean of the dependent variable is zero. All variables in effects that you specify in the MODEL statement must appear in the CLASS statement because PROC ANOVA does not allow for continuous effects.

You can specify the following options in the MODEL statement; they must be separated from the list of independent effects by a slash.

INTERCEPT
INT

displays the hypothesis tests associated with the intercept as an effect in the model. By default, the procedure includes the intercept in the model but does not display associated tests of hypotheses. Except for producing the uncorrected total SS instead of the corrected total SS, the INT option is ignored when you use an ABSORB statement.

NOUNI

suppresses the display of univariate statistics. You typically use the NOUNI option with a multivariate or repeated measures analysis of variance when you do not need the standard univariate output. The NOUNI option in a MODEL statement does not affect the univariate output produced by the REPEATED statement.

REPEATED Statement

REPEATED *factor-specification* < **/** *options* > **;**

When values of the dependent variables in the MODEL statement represent repeated measurements on the same experimental unit, the REPEATED statement enables you to test hypotheses about the measurement factors (often called *within-subject factors*), as well as the interactions of within-subject factors with independent variables in the MODEL statement (often called *between-subject factors*). The REPEATED statement provides multivariate and univariate tests as well as hypothesis tests for a variety of single-degree-of-freedom contrasts. There is no limit to the number of within-subject factors that can be specified. For more details, see the "Repeated Measures Analysis of Variance" section on page 1560 in Chapter 30, "The GLM Procedure."

The REPEATED statement is typically used for handling repeated measures designs with one repeated response variable. Usually, the variables on the left-hand side of the equation in the MODEL statement represent one repeated response variable. This does not mean that only one factor can be listed in the REPEATED statement. For example, one repeated response variable (hemoglobin count) might be measured 12 times (implying variables Y1 to Y12 on the left-hand side of the equal sign in the MODEL statement), with the associated within-subject factors treatment and time (implying two factors listed in the REPEATED statement). See the "Examples" section on page 365 for an example of how PROC ANOVA handles this case. Designs with two or more repeated response variables can, however, be handled with the IDENTITY transformation; see Example 30.9 on page 1618 in Chapter 30, "The GLM Procedure," for an example of analyzing a doubly-multivariate repeated measures design.

When a REPEATED statement appears, the ANOVA procedure enters a multivariate mode of handling missing values. If any values for variables corresponding to each combination of the within-subject factors are missing, the observation is excluded from the analysis.

The simplest form of the REPEATED statement requires only a *factor-name*. With two repeated factors, you must specify the *factor-name* and number of levels (*levels*) for each factor. Optionally, you can specify the actual values for the levels (*level-values*), a *transformation* that defines single-degree-of freedom contrasts, and *options* for additional analyses and output. When more than one within-subject factor is specified, *factor-names* (and associated level and transformation information) must be separated by a comma in the REPEATED statement. These terms are described in the following section, "Syntax Details."

Syntax Details

You can specify the following terms in the REPEATED statement.

factor-specification

The *factor-specification* for the REPEATED statement can include any number of individual factor specifications, separated by commas, of the following form:

factor-name levels < **(***level-values***)** > < *transformation* >

where

factor-name names a factor to be associated with the dependent variables. The name should not be the same as any variable name that already exists in the data set being analyzed and should conform to the usual conventions of SAS variable names.

When specifying more than one factor, list the dependent variables in the MODEL statement so that the within-subject factors defined in the REPEATED statement are nested; that is, the first factor defined in the REPEATED statement should be the one with values that change least frequently.

levels
: specifies the number of levels associated with the factor being defined. When there is only one within-subject factor, the number of levels is equal to the number of dependent variables. In this case, *levels* is optional. When more than one within-subject factor is defined, however, *levels* is required, and the product of the number of levels of all the factors must equal the number of dependent variables in the MODEL statement.

(level-values)
: specifies values that correspond to levels of a repeated-measures factor. These values are used to label output; they are also used as spacings for constructing orthogonal polynomial contrasts if you specify a POLYNOMIAL transformation. The number of level values specified must correspond to the number of levels for that factor in the REPEATED statement. Enclose the *level-values* in parentheses.

The following *transformation* keywords define single-degree-of-freedom contrasts for factors specified in the REPEATED statement. Since the number of contrasts generated is always one less than the number of levels of the factor, you have some control over which contrast is omitted from the analysis by which transformation you select. The only exception is the IDENTITY transformation; this transformation is not composed of contrasts, and it has the same degrees of freedom as the factor has levels. By default, the procedure uses the CONTRAST transformation.

CONTRAST < **(***ordinal-reference-level***)** > generates contrasts between levels of the factor and a reference level. By default, the procedure uses the last level; you can optionally specify a reference level in parentheses after the keyword CONTRAST. The reference level corresponds to the ordinal value of the level rather than the level value specified. For example, to generate contrasts between the first level of a factor and the other levels, use

```
contrast(1)
```

HELMERT
: generates contrasts between each level of the factor and the mean of subsequent levels.

IDENTITY
: generates an identity transformation corresponding to the associated factor. This transformation is *not* composed of contrasts; it has n degrees of freedom for an n-level factor, instead of $n - 1$. This can be used for doubly-multivariate repeated measures.

MEAN < **(***ordinal-reference-level***)** > generates contrasts between levels of the factor and the mean of all other levels of the factor. Specifying a reference level eliminates the contrast between that level and the mean. Without a reference level, the contrast involving the last level is omitted. See the CONTRAST transformation for an example.

POLYNOMIAL generates orthogonal polynomial contrasts. Level values, if provided, are used as spacings in the construction of the polynomials; otherwise, equal spacing is assumed.

PROFILE generates contrasts between adjacent levels of the factor.

For examples of the transformation matrices generated by these contrast transformations, see the section "Repeated Measures Analysis of Variance" on page 1560 in Chapter 30, "The GLM Procedure."

You can specify the following options in the REPEATED statement after a slash:

CANONICAL
performs a canonical analysis of the $\mathbf{H}$ and $\mathbf{E}$ matrices corresponding to the transformed variables specified in the REPEATED statement.

NOM
displays only the results of the univariate analyses.

NOU
displays only the results of the multivariate analyses.

PRINTE
displays the $\mathbf{E}$ matrix for each combination of within-subject factors, as well as partial correlation matrices for both the original dependent variables and the variables defined by the transformations specified in the REPEATED statement. In addition, the PRINTE option provides sphericity tests for each set of transformed variables. If the requested transformations are not orthogonal, the PRINTE option also provides a sphericity test for a set of orthogonal contrasts.

PRINTH
displays the $\mathbf{H}$ (SSCP) matrix associated with each multivariate test.

PRINTM
displays the transformation matrices that define the contrasts in the analysis. PROC ANOVA always displays the $\mathbf{M}$ matrix so that the transformed variables are defined by the rows, not the columns, of the displayed $\mathbf{M}$ matrix. In other words, PROC ANOVA actually displays $\mathbf{M}'$.

PRINTRV
produces the characteristic roots and vectors for each multivariate test.

SUMMARY
produces analysis-of-variance tables for each contrast defined by the within-subjects factors. Along with tests for the effects of the independent variables specified in the MODEL statement, a term labeled MEAN tests the hypothesis that the overall mean of the contrast is zero.

Examples

When specifying more than one factor, list the dependent variables in the MODEL statement so that the within-subject factors defined in the REPEATED statement are nested; that is, the first factor defined in the REPEATED statement should be the one with values that change least frequently. For example, assume that three treatments are administered at each of four times, for a total of twelve dependent variables on each experimental unit. If the variables are listed in the MODEL statement as Y1 through Y12, then the following REPEATED statement

```
repeated trt 3, time 4;
```

implies the following structure:

	Dependent Variables											
	Y1	Y2	Y3	Y4	Y5	Y6	Y7	Y8	Y9	Y10	Y11	Y12
Value of trt	1	1	1	1	2	2	2	2	3	3	3	3
Value of time	1	2	3	4	1	2	3	4	1	2	3	4

The REPEATED statement always produces a table like the preceding one. For more information on repeated measures analysis and on using the REPEATED statement, see the section "Repeated Measures Analysis of Variance" on page 1560 in Chapter 30, "The GLM Procedure."

TEST Statement

TEST < **H=** *effects* > **E=** *effect* **;**

Although an F value is computed for all SS in the analysis using the residual MS as an error term, you can request additional F tests using other effects as error terms. You need a TEST statement when a nonstandard error structure (as in a split plot) exists.

Caution: The ANOVA procedure does not check any of the assumptions underlying the F statistic. When you specify a TEST statement, you assume sole responsibility for the validity of the F statistic produced. To help validate a test, you may want to use the GLM procedure with the RANDOM statement and inspect the expected mean squares. In the GLM procedure, you can also use the TEST option in the RANDOM statement.

You can use as many TEST statements as you want, provided that they appear after the MODEL statement.

You can specify the following terms in the TEST statement.

H=*effects* specifies which effects in the preceding model are to be used as hypothesis (numerator) effects.

E=*effect* specifies one, and only one, effect to use as the error (denominator) term. The E= specification is required.

The following example uses two TEST statements and is appropriate for analyzing a split-plot design.

```
proc anova;
   class a b c;
   model y=a|b(a)|c;
   test h=a e=b(a);
   test h=c a*c e=b*c(a);
run;
```

Details

Specification of Effects

In SAS analysis-of-variance procedures, the variables that identify levels of the classifications are called *classification variables*, and they are declared in the CLASS statement. Classification variables are also called *categorical*, *qualitative*, *discrete*, or *nominal variables*. The values of a class variable are called *levels*. Class variables can be either numeric or character. This is in contrast to the *response* (or *dependent*) *variables*, which are continuous. Response variables must be numeric.

The analysis-of-variance model specifies *effects*, which are combinations of classification variables used to explain the variability of the dependent variables in the following manner:

- Main effects are specified by writing the variables by themselves in the CLASS statement: A B C. Main effects used as independent variables test the hypothesis that the mean of the dependent variable is the same for each level of the factor in question, ignoring the other independent variables in the model.
- Crossed effects (interactions) are specified by joining the class variables with asterisks in the MODEL statement: A*B A*C A*B*C. Interaction terms in a model test the hypothesis that the effect of a factor does not depend on the levels of the other factors in the interaction.
- Nested effects are specified by following a main effect or crossed effect with a class variable or list of class variables enclosed in parentheses in the MODEL statement. The main effect or crossed effect is nested within the effects listed in parentheses: B(A) C*D(A B). Nested effects test hypotheses similar to interactions, but the levels of the nested variables are not the same for every combination within which they are nested.

The general form of an effect can be illustrated using the class variables A, B, C, D, E, and F:

$$A * B * C(D\ E\ F)$$

The crossed list should come first, followed by the nested list in parentheses. Note that no asterisks appear within the nested list or immediately before the left parenthesis.

Main Effects Models

For a three-factor main effects model with A, B, and C as the factors and Y as the dependent variable, the necessary statements are

```
proc anova;
   class A B C;
   model Y=A B C;
run;
```

Models with Crossed Factors

To specify interactions in a factorial model, join effects with asterisks as described previously. For example, these statements specify a complete factorial model, which includes all the interactions:

```
proc anova;
   class A B C;
   model Y=A B C A*B A*C B*C A*B*C;
run;
```

Bar Notation

You can shorten the specifications of a full factorial model by using bar notation. For example, the preceding statements can also be written

```
proc anova;
   class A B C;
   model Y=A|B|C;
run;
```

When the bar (|) is used, the expression on the right side of the equal sign is expanded from left to right using the equivalents of rules 2–4 given in Searle (1971, p. 390). The variables on the right- and left-hand sides of the bar become effects, and the cross of them becomes an effect. Multiple bars are permitted. For instance, A | B | C is evaluated as follows:

$$
\begin{aligned}
\text{A | B | C} &\rightarrow \{\text{A | B}\} \text{ | C} \\
&\rightarrow \{\text{A B A*B}\} \text{ | C} \\
&\rightarrow \text{A B A*B A*C B*C A*B*C}
\end{aligned}
$$

You can also specify the maximum number of variables involved in any effect that results from bar evaluation by specifying that maximum number, preceded by an @ sign, at the end of the bar effect. For example, the specification A | B | C@2 results in only those effects that contain two or fewer variables; in this case, A B A*B C A*C and B*C.

The following table gives more examples of using the bar and at operators.

A | C(B)	is equivalent to	A C(B) A*C(B)
A(B) | C(B)	is equivalent to	A(B) C(B) A*C(B)
A(B) | B(D E)	is equivalent to	A(B) B(D E)
A | B(A) | C	is equivalent to	A B(A) C A*C B*C(A)
A | B(A) | C@2	is equivalent to	A B(A) C A*C
A | B | C | D@2	is equivalent to	A B A*B C A*C B*C D A*D B*D C*D

Consult the "Specification of Effects" section on page 1517 in Chapter 30, "The GLM Procedure," for further details on bar notation.

Nested Models

Write the effect that is nested within another effect first, followed by the other effect in parentheses. For example, if A and B are main effects and C is nested within A and B (that is, the levels of C that are observed are not the same for each combination of A and B), the statements for PROC ANOVA are

```
proc anova;
   class A B C;
   model y=A B C(A B);
run;
```

The identity of a level is viewed within the context of the level of the containing effects. For example, if City is nested within State, then the identity of City is viewed within the context of State.

The distinguishing feature of a nested specification is that nested effects never appear as main effects. Another way of viewing nested effects is that they are effects that pool the main effect with the interaction of the nesting variable. See the "Automatic Pooling" section, which follows.

Models Involving Nested, Crossed, and Main Effects

Asterisks and parentheses can be combined in the MODEL statement for models involving nested and crossed effects:

```
proc anova;
   class A B C;
   model Y=A B(A) C(A) B*C(A);
run;
```

Automatic Pooling

In line with the general philosophy of the GLM procedure, there is no difference between the statements

```
model Y=A B(A);
```

and

```
model Y=A A*B;
```

The effect B becomes a nested effect by virtue of the fact that it does not occur as a main effect. If B is not written as a main effect in addition to participating in A*B, then the sum of squares that is associated with B is pooled into A*B.

This feature allows the automatic pooling of sums of squares. If an effect is omitted from the model, it is automatically pooled with all the higher-level effects containing the class variables in the omitted effect (or within-error). This feature is most useful in split-plot designs.

Using PROC ANOVA Interactively

PROC ANOVA can be used interactively. After you specify a model in a MODEL statement and run PROC ANOVA with a RUN statement, a variety of statements (such as MEANS, MANOVA, TEST, and REPEATED) can be executed without PROC ANOVA recalculating the model sum of squares.

The "Syntax" section (page 348) describes which statements can be used interactively. You can execute these interactive statements individually or in groups by following the single statement or group of statements with a RUN statement. Note that the MODEL statement cannot be repeated; the ANOVA procedure allows only one MODEL statement.

If you use PROC ANOVA interactively, you can end the procedure with a DATA step, another PROC step, an ENDSAS statement, or a QUIT statement. The syntax of the QUIT statement is

```
quit;
```

When you use PROC ANOVA interactively, additional RUN statements do not end the procedure but tell PROC ANOVA to execute additional statements.

When a WHERE statement is used with PROC ANOVA, it should appear before the first RUN statement. The WHERE statement enables you to select only certain observations for analysis without using a subsetting DATA step. For example, the statement `where group ne 5` omits observations with GROUP=5 from the analysis. Refer to *SAS Language Reference: Dictionary* for details on this statement.

When a BY statement is used with PROC ANOVA, interactive processing is not possible; that is, once the first RUN statement is encountered, processing proceeds for each BY group in the data set, and no further statements are accepted by the procedure.

Interactivity is also disabled when there are different patterns of missing values among the dependent variables. For details, see the section "Missing Values," which follows.

Missing Values

For an analysis involving one dependent variable, PROC ANOVA uses an observation if values are nonmissing for that dependent variable and for all the variables used in independent effects.

For an analysis involving multiple dependent variables without the MANOVA or REPEATED statement, or without the MANOVA option in the PROC ANOVA statement, a missing value in one dependent variable does not eliminate the observation from the analysis of other nonmissing dependent variables. For an analysis with the MANOVA or REPEATED statement, or with the MANOVA option in the PROC ANOVA statement, the ANOVA procedure requires values for all dependent variables to be nonmissing for an observation before the observation can be used in the analysis.

During processing, PROC ANOVA groups the dependent variables by their pattern of missing values across observations so that sums and cross products can be collected in the most efficient manner.

If your data have different patterns of missing values among the dependent variables, interactivity is disabled. This could occur when some of the variables in your data set have missing values and

- you do not use the MANOVA option in the PROC ANOVA statement
- you do not use a MANOVA or REPEATED statement before the first RUN statement

Output Data Set

The OUTSTAT= option in the PROC ANOVA statement produces an output data set that contains the following:

- the BY variables, if any
- _TYPE_, a new character variable. This variable has the value 'ANOVA' for observations corresponding to sums of squares; it has the value 'CANCORR', 'STRUCTUR', or 'SCORE' if a canonical analysis is performed through the MANOVA statement and no M= matrix is specified.
- _SOURCE_, a new character variable. For each observation in the data set, _SOURCE_ contains the name of the model effect from which the corresponding statistics are generated.

- _NAME_, a new character variable. The variable _NAME_ contains the name of one of the dependent variables in the model or, in the case of canonical statistics, the name of one of the canonical variables (CAN1, CAN2, and so on).
- four new numeric variables, SS, DF, F, and PROB, containing sums of squares, degrees of freedom, F values, and probabilities, respectively, for each model or contrast sum of squares generated in the analysis. For observations resulting from canonical analyses, these variables have missing values.
- if there is more than one dependent variable, then variables with the same names as the dependent variables represent
  - for _TYPE_='ANOVA', the crossproducts of the hypothesis matrices
  - for _TYPE_='CANCORR', canonical correlations for each variable
  - for _TYPE_='STRUCTUR', coefficients of the total structure matrix
  - for _TYPE_='SCORE', raw canonical score coefficients

The output data set can be used to perform special hypothesis tests (for example, with the IML procedure in SAS/IML software), to reformat output, to produce canonical variates (through the SCORE procedure), or to rotate structure matrices (through the FACTOR procedure).

Computational Method

Let $\mathbf{X}$ represent the $n \times p$ design matrix. The columns of $\mathbf{X}$ contain only 0s and 1s. Let $\mathbf{Y}$ represent the $n \times 1$ vector of dependent variables.

In the GLM procedure, $\mathbf{X}'\mathbf{X}$, $\mathbf{X}'\mathbf{Y}$, and $\mathbf{Y}'\mathbf{Y}$ are formed in main storage. However, in the ANOVA procedure, only the diagonals of $\mathbf{X}'\mathbf{X}$ are computed, along with $\mathbf{X}'\mathbf{Y}$ and $\mathbf{Y}'\mathbf{Y}$. Thus, PROC ANOVA saves a considerable amount of storage as well as time. The memory requirements for PROC ANOVA are asymptotically linear functions of n^2 and nr, where n is the number of dependent variables and r the number of independent parameters.

The elements of $\mathbf{X}'\mathbf{Y}$ are cell totals, and the diagonal elements of $\mathbf{X}'\mathbf{X}$ are cell frequencies. Since PROC ANOVA automatically pools omitted effects into the next higher-level effect containing the names of the omitted effect (or within-error), a slight modification to the rules given by Searle (1971, p. 389) is used.

1. PROC ANOVA computes the sum of squares for each effect as if it is a main effect. In other words, for each effect, PROC ANOVA squares each cell total and divides by its cell frequency. The procedure then adds these quantities together and subtracts the correction factor for the mean (total squared over N).
2. For each effect involving two class names, PROC ANOVA subtracts the SS for any main effect with a name that is contained in the two-factor effect.
3. For each effect involving three class names, PROC ANOVA subtracts the SS for all main effects and two-factor effects with names that are contained in the three-factor effect. If effects involving four or more class names are present, the procedure continues this process.

Displayed Output

PROC ANOVA first displays a table that includes the following:

- the name of each variable in the CLASS statement
- the number of different values or Levels of the Class variables
- the Values of the Class variables
- the Number of observations in the data set and the number of observations excluded from the analysis because of missing values, if any

PROC ANOVA then displays an analysis-of-variance table for each dependent variable in the MODEL statement. This table breaks down

- the Total Sum of Squares for the dependent variable into the portion attributed to the Model and the portion attributed to Error
- the Mean Square term, which is the Sum of Squares divided by the degrees of freedom (DF)

The analysis-of-variance table also lists the following:

- the Mean Square for Error (MSE), which is an estimate of σ^2, the variance of the true errors
- the F Value, which is the ratio produced by dividing the Mean Square for the Model by the Mean Square for Error. It tests how well the model as a whole (adjusted for the mean) accounts for the dependent variable's behavior. This F test is a test of the null hypothesis that all parameters except the intercept are zero.
- the significance probability associated with the F statistic, labeled "Pr > F"
- R-Square, R^2, which measures how much variation in the dependent variable can be accounted for by the model. The R^2 statistic, which can range from 0 to 1, is the ratio of the sum of squares for the model divided by the sum of squares for the corrected total. In general, the larger the R^2 value, the better the model fits the data.
- C.V., the coefficient of variation, which is often used to describe the amount of variation in the population. The C.V. is 100 times the standard deviation of the dependent variable divided by the Mean. The coefficient of variation is often a preferred measure because it is unitless.
- Root MSE, which estimates the standard deviation of the dependent variable. Root MSE is computed as the square root of Mean Square for Error, the mean square of the error term.
- the Mean of the dependent variable

For each effect (or source of variation) in the model, PROC ANOVA then displays the following:

- DF, degrees of freedom
- Anova SS, the sum of squares, and the associated Mean Square
- the F Value for testing the hypothesis that the group means for that effect are equal
- Pr > F, the significance probability value associated with the F Value

When you specify a TEST statement, PROC ANOVA displays the results of the requested tests. When you specify a MANOVA statement and the model includes more than one dependent variable, PROC ANOVA produces these additional statistics:

- the characteristic roots and vectors of $\mathbf{E}^{-1}\mathbf{H}$ for each $\mathbf{H}$ matrix
- the Hotelling-Lawley trace
- Pillai's trace
- Wilks' criterion
- Roy's maximum root criterion

See Example 30.6 on page 1600 in Chapter 30, "The GLM Procedure," for an example of the MANOVA results. These MANOVA tests are discussed in Chapter 3, "Introduction to Regression Procedures."

ODS Table Names

PROC ANOVA assigns a name to each table it creates. You can use these names to reference the table when using the Output Delivery System (ODS) to select tables and create output data sets. These names are listed in the following table. For more information on ODS, see Chapter 15, "Using the Output Delivery System."

Table 17.3. ODS Tables Produced in PROC ANOVA

ODS Table Name	Description	Statement / Option
AltErrTests	Anova tests with error other than MSE	TEST /E=
Bartlett	Bartlett's homogeneity of variance test	MEANS / HOVTEST=BARTLETT
CLDiffs	Multiple comparisons of pairwise differences	MEANS / CLDIFF or DUNNETT or (Unequal cells and not LINES)
CLDiffsInfo	Information for multiple comparisons of pairwise differences	MEANS / CLDIFF or DUNNETT or (Unequal cells and not LINES)
CLMeans	Multiple comparisons of means with confidence/comparison interval	MEANS / CLM with (BON or GABRIEL or SCHEFFE or SIDAK or SMM or T or LSD)
CLMeansInfo	Information for multiple comparisons of means with confidence/comparison interval	MEANS / CLM

Table 17.3. (continued)

ODS Table Name	Description	Statement / Option
CanAnalysis	Canonical analysis	(MANOVA or REPEATED) / CANONICAL
CanCoefficients	Canonical coefficients	(MANOVA or REPEATED) / CANONICAL
CanStructure	Canonical structure	(MANOVA or REPEATED) / CANONICAL
CharStruct	Characteristic roots and vectors	(MANOVA / not CANONICAL) or (REPEATED / PRINTRV)
ClassLevels	Classification variable levels	CLASS statement
DependentInfo	Simultaneously analyzed dependent variables	default when there are multiple dependent variables with different patterns of missing values
Epsilons	Greenhouse-Geisser and Huynh-Feldt epsilons	REPEATED statement
ErrorSSCP	Error SSCP matrix	(MANOVA or REPEATED) / PRINTE
FitStatistics	R-Square, C.V., Root MSE, and dependent mean	default
HOVFTest	Homogeneity of variance ANOVA	MEANS / HOVTEST
HypothesisSSCP	Hypothesis SSCP matrix	(MANOVA or REPEATED) / PRINTE
MANOVATransform	Multivariate transformation matrix	MANOVA / M=
MCLines	Multiple comparisons LINES output	MEANS / LINES or ((DUNCAN or WALLER or SNK or REGWQ) and not(CLDIFF or CLM)) or (Equal cells and not CLDIFF)
MCLinesInfo	Information for multiple comparison LINES output	MEANS / LINES or ((DUNCAN or WALLER or SNK or REGWQ) and not (CLDIFF or CLM)) or (Equal cells and not CLDIFF)
MCLinesRange	Ranges for multiple range MC tests	MEANS / LINES or ((DUNCAN or WALLER or SNK or REGWQ) and not (CLDIFF or CLM)) or (Equal cells and not CLDIFF)
MTests	Multivariate tests	MANOVA statement
Means	Group means	MEANS statement
ModelANOVA	ANOVA for model terms	default
NObs	Number of observations	default
OverallANOVA	Over-all ANOVA	default
PartialCorr	Partial correlation matrix	(MANOVA or REPEATED) / PRINTE
RepTransform	Repeated transformation matrix	REPEATED (CONTRAST or HELMERT or MEAN or POLYNOMIAL or PROFILE)

Table 17.3. (continued)

ODS Table Name	Description	Statement / Option
RepeatedLevelInfo	Correspondence between dependents and repeated measures levels	REPEATED statement
Sphericity	Sphericity tests	REPEATED / PRINTE
Tests	Summary ANOVA for specified MANOVA H= effects	MANOVA / H= SUMMARY
Welch	Welch's ANOVA	MEANS / WELCH

Examples

Example 17.1. Randomized Complete Block With Factorial Treatment Structure

This example uses statements for the analysis of a randomized block with two treatment factors occuring in a factorial structure. The data, from Neter, Wasserman, and Kutner (1990, p. 941), are from an experiment examining the effects of codeine and acupuncture on post-operative dental pain in male subjects. Both treatment factors have two levels. The codeine levels are a codeine capsule or a sugar capsule. The acupuncture levels are two inactive acupuncture points or two active acupuncture points. There are four distinct treatment combinations due to the factorial treatment structure. The 32 subjects are assigned to eight blocks of four subjects each based on an assessment of pain tolerance.

The data for the analysis are balanced, so PROC ANOVA is used. The data are as follows:

```
title 'Randomized Complete Block With Two Factors';
data PainRelief;
   input PainLevel Codeine Acupuncture Relief @@;
   datalines;
1 1 1 0.0  1 2 1 0.5  1 1 2 0.6  1 2 2 1.2
2 1 1 0.3  2 2 1 0.6  2 1 2 0.7  2 2 2 1.3
3 1 1 0.4  3 2 1 0.8  3 1 2 0.8  3 2 2 1.6
4 1 1 0.4  4 2 1 0.7  4 1 2 0.9  4 2 2 1.5
5 1 1 0.6  5 2 1 1.0  5 1 2 1.5  5 2 2 1.9
6 1 1 0.9  6 2 1 1.4  6 1 2 1.6  6 2 2 2.3
7 1 1 1.0  7 2 1 1.8  7 1 2 1.7  7 2 2 2.1
8 1 1 1.2  8 2 1 1.7  8 1 2 1.6  8 2 2 2.4
;
```

The variable PainLevel is the blocking variable, and Codeine and Acupuncture represent the levels of the two treatment factors. The variable Relief is the pain relief score (the higher the score, the more relief the patient has).

The following code invokes PROC ANOVA. The blocking variable and treatment factors appear in the CLASS statement. The bar between the treatment factors Codeine and Acupuncture adds their main effects as well as their interaction Codeine*Acupuncture to the model.

```
proc anova;
   class PainLevel Codeine Acupuncture;
   model Relief = PainLevel Codeine|Acupuncture;
run;
```

The results from the analysis are shown in Output 17.1.1 and Output 17.1.2.

Output 17.1.1. Class Level Information and ANOVA Table

```
                 Randomized Complete Block With Two Factors

                           The ANOVA Procedure

                         Class Level Information

                Class             Levels    Values

                PainLevel              8    1 2 3 4 5 6 7 8

                Codeine                2    1 2

                Acupuncture            2    1 2


                     Number of observations    32
```

```
                 Randomized Complete Block With Two Factors

                           The ANOVA Procedure

Dependent Variable: Relief

                                            Sum of
 Source                      DF          Squares     Mean Square    F Value    Pr > F

 Model                       10      11.33500000      1.13350000      78.37    <.0001

 Error                       21       0.30375000      0.01446429

 Corrected Total             31      11.63875000


              R-Square     Coeff Var      Root MSE    Relief Mean

              0.973902      10.40152      0.120268       1.156250
```

The Class Level Information and ANOVA table are shown in Output 17.1.1. The class level information summarizes the structure of the design. It is good to check these consistently in search of errors in the data step. The overall F test is significant, indicating that the model accounts for a significant amount of variation in the dependent variable.

Output 17.1.2. Tests of Effects

```
                 Randomized Complete Block With Two Factors

                            The ANOVA Procedure

Dependent Variable: Relief

 Source                     DF         Anova SS     Mean Square    F Value    Pr > F

 PainLevel                   7       5.59875000      0.79982143      55.30    <.0001
 Codeine                     1       2.31125000      2.31125000     159.79    <.0001
 Acupuncture                 1       3.38000000      3.38000000     233.68    <.0001
 Codeine*Acupuncture         1       0.04500000      0.04500000       3.11    0.0923
```

Output 17.1.2 shows tests of the effects. The blocking effect is significant; hence, it is useful. The interaction between codeine and acupuncture is significant at the 90% level but not at the 95% level. The significance level of this test should be determined before the analysis. The main effects of both treatment factors are highly significant.

Example 17.2. Alternative Multiple Comparison Procedures

The following is a continuation of the first example in the the "One-Way Layout with Means Comparisons" section on page 340. You are studying the effect of bacteria on the nitrogen content of red clover plants, and the analysis of variance shows a highly significant effect. The following statements create the data set and compute the analysis of variance as well as Tukey's multiple comparisons test for pairwise differences between bacteria strains; the results are shown in Figure 17.1, Figure 17.2, and Figure 17.3

```
title 'Nitrogen Content of Red Clover Plants';
data Clover;
   input Strain $ Nitrogen @@;
   datalines;
3DOK1  19.4 3DOK1  32.6 3DOK1  27.0 3DOK1  32.1 3DOK1  33.0
3DOK5  17.7 3DOK5  24.8 3DOK5  27.9 3DOK5  25.2 3DOK5  24.3
3DOK4  17.0 3DOK4  19.4 3DOK4   9.1 3DOK4  11.9 3DOK4  15.8
3DOK7  20.7 3DOK7  21.0 3DOK7  20.5 3DOK7  18.8 3DOK7  18.6
3DOK13 14.3 3DOK13 14.4 3DOK13 11.8 3DOK13 11.6 3DOK13 14.2
COMPOS 17.3 COMPOS 19.4 COMPOS 19.1 COMPOS 16.9 COMPOS 20.8
;

proc anova;
   class Strain;
   model Nitrogen = Strain;
   means Strain / tukey;
run;
```

The interactivity of PROC ANOVA enables you to submit further MEANS statements without re-running the entire analysis. For example, the following command requests means of the Strain levels with Duncan's multiple range test and the Waller-Duncan k-ratio t test.

```
      means Strain / duncan waller;
   run;
```

Results of the Waller-Duncan k-ratio t test are shown in Output 17.2.1.

Output 17.2.1. Waller-Duncan K-ratio t Test

```
                    Nitrogen Content of Red Clover Plants

                            The ANOVA Procedure

                  Waller-Duncan K-ratio t Test for Nitrogen

NOTE: This test minimizes the Bayes risk under additive loss and certain other
                                 assumptions.


                  Kratio                                 100
                  Error Degrees of Freedom                24
                  Error Mean Square                 11.78867
                  F Value                              14.37
                  Critical Value of t                1.91873
                  Minimum Significant Difference      4.1665


          Means with the same letter are not significantly different.


            Waller Grouping          Mean      N    Strain

                          A        28.820      5    3DOK1

                          B        23.980      5    3DOK5
                          B
                     C    B        19.920      5    3DOK7
                     C
                     C    D        18.700      5    COMPOS
                          D
                     E    D        14.640      5    3DOK4
                     E
                     E             13.260      5    3DOK13
```

The Waller-Duncan k-ratio t test is a multiple range test. Unlike Tukey's test, this test does not operate on the principle of controlling Type I error. Instead, it compares the Type I and Type II error rates based on Bayesian principles (Steel and Torrie 1980).

The Waller Grouping column in Output 17.2.1 shows which means are significantly different. From this test, you can conclude the following:

- The mean nitrogen content for strain 3DOK1 is higher than the means for all other strains.
- The mean nitrogen content for strain 3DOK5 is higher than the means for COMPOS, 3DOK4, and 3DOK13.
- The mean nitrogen content for strain 3DOK7 is higher than the means for 3DOK4 and 3DOK13.
- The mean nitrogen content for strain COMPOS is higher than the mean for 3DOK13.

- Differences between all other means are not significant based on this sample size.

Output 17.2.2 shows the results of Duncan's multiple range test. Duncan's test is a result-guided test that compares the treatment means while controlling the comparison-wise error rate. You should use this test for planned comparisons only (Steel and Torrie 1980). The results and conclusions for this example are the same as for the Waller-Duncan k-ratio t test. This is not always the case.

Output 17.2.2. Duncan's Multiple Range Test

```
                 Nitrogen Content of Red Clover Plants

                          The ANOVA Procedure

                Duncan's Multiple Range Test for Nitrogen

NOTE: This test controls the Type I comparisonwise error rate, not the
                        experimentwise error rate.


                  Alpha                            0.05
                  Error Degrees of Freedom           24
                  Error Mean Square            11.78867


Number of Means            2          3          4          5          6
Critical Range         4.482      4.707      4.852      4.954      5.031


     Means with the same letter are not significantly different.


       Duncan Grouping            Mean      N    Strain

                     A          28.820      5    3DOK1

                     B          23.980      5    3DOK5
                     B
                C    B          19.920      5    3DOK7
                C
                C    D          18.700      5    COMPOS
                     D
                E    D          14.640      5    3DOK4
                E
                E               13.260      5    3DOK13
```

Tukey and Least Significant Difference (LSD) tests are requested with the following MEANS statement. The CLDIFF option requests confidence intervals for both tests.

```
   means Strain / lsd tukey cldiff;
run;
```

The LSD tests for this example are shown in Output 17.2.3, and they give the same results as the previous two multiple comparison tests. Again, this is not always the case.

Output 17.2.3. T Tests (LSD)

```
                 Nitrogen Content of Red Clover Plants

                          The ANOVA Procedure

                       t Tests (LSD) for Nitrogen

NOTE: This test controls the Type I comparisonwise error rate, not the
                       experimentwise error rate.


                 Alpha                               0.05
                 Error Degrees of Freedom              24
                 Error Mean Square               11.78867
                 Critical Value of t              2.06390
                 Least Significant Difference      4.4818


    Comparisons significant at the 0.05 level are indicated by ***.


                            Difference
            Strain            Between        95% Confidence
          Comparison           Means             Limits

        3DOK1  - 3DOK5         4.840       0.358     9.322  ***
        3DOK1  - 3DOK7         8.900       4.418    13.382  ***
        3DOK1  - COMPOS       10.120       5.638    14.602  ***
        3DOK1  - 3DOK4        14.180       9.698    18.662  ***
        3DOK1  - 3DOK13       15.560      11.078    20.042  ***
        3DOK5  - 3DOK1        -4.840      -9.322    -0.358  ***
        3DOK5  - 3DOK7         4.060      -0.422     8.542
        3DOK5  - COMPOS        5.280       0.798     9.762  ***
        3DOK5  - 3DOK4         9.340       4.858    13.822  ***
        3DOK5  - 3DOK13       10.720       6.238    15.202  ***
        3DOK7  - 3DOK1        -8.900     -13.382    -4.418  ***
        3DOK7  - 3DOK5        -4.060      -8.542     0.422
        3DOK7  - COMPOS        1.220      -3.262     5.702
        3DOK7  - 3DOK4         5.280       0.798     9.762  ***
        3DOK7  - 3DOK13        6.660       2.178    11.142  ***
        COMPOS - 3DOK1       -10.120     -14.602    -5.638  ***
        COMPOS - 3DOK5        -5.280      -9.762    -0.798  ***
        COMPOS - 3DOK7        -1.220      -5.702     3.262
        COMPOS - 3DOK4         4.060      -0.422     8.542
        COMPOS - 3DOK13        5.440       0.958     9.922  ***
        3DOK4  - 3DOK1       -14.180     -18.662    -9.698  ***
        3DOK4  - 3DOK5        -9.340     -13.822    -4.858  ***
        3DOK4  - 3DOK7        -5.280      -9.762    -0.798  ***
        3DOK4  - COMPOS       -4.060      -8.542     0.422
        3DOK4  - 3DOK13        1.380      -3.102     5.862
        3DOK13 - 3DOK1       -15.560     -20.042   -11.078  ***
        3DOK13 - 3DOK5       -10.720     -15.202    -6.238  ***
        3DOK13 - 3DOK7        -6.660     -11.142    -2.178  ***
        3DOK13 - COMPOS       -5.440      -9.922    -0.958  ***
        3DOK13 - 3DOK4        -1.380      -5.862     3.102
```

If you only perform the LSD tests when the overall model F-test is significant, then this is called Fisher's protected LSD test. Note that the LSD tests should be used for planned comparisons.

The TUKEY tests shown in Output 17.2.4 find fewer significant differences than the other three tests. This is not unexpected, as the TUKEY test controls the Type I experimentwise error rate. For a complete discussion of multiple comparison methods, see the "Multiple Comparisons" section on page 1540 in Chapter 30, "The GLM Procedure."

Output 17.2.4. Tukey's Studentized Range Test

```
                 Nitrogen Content of Red Clover Plants

                         The ANOVA Procedure

           Tukey's Studentized Range (HSD) Test for Nitrogen

     NOTE: This test controls the Type I experimentwise error rate.


            Alpha                                      0.05
            Error Degrees of Freedom                     24
            Error Mean Square                      11.78867
            Critical Value of Studentized Range     4.37265
            Minimum Significant Difference           6.7142


    Comparisons significant at the 0.05 level are indicated by ***.


                              Difference
             Strain              Between     Simultaneous 95%
           Comparison              Means    Confidence Limits

        3DOK1  - 3DOK5             4.840       -1.874   11.554
        3DOK1  - 3DOK7             8.900        2.186   15.614  ***
        3DOK1  - COMPOS           10.120        3.406   16.834  ***
        3DOK1  - 3DOK4            14.180        7.466   20.894  ***
        3DOK1  - 3DOK13           15.560        8.846   22.274  ***
        3DOK5  - 3DOK1            -4.840      -11.554    1.874
        3DOK5  - 3DOK7             4.060       -2.654   10.774
        3DOK5  - COMPOS            5.280       -1.434   11.994
        3DOK5  - 3DOK4             9.340        2.626   16.054  ***
        3DOK5  - 3DOK13           10.720        4.006   17.434  ***
        3DOK7  - 3DOK1            -8.900      -15.614   -2.186  ***
        3DOK7  - 3DOK5            -4.060      -10.774    2.654
        3DOK7  - COMPOS            1.220       -5.494    7.934
        3DOK7  - 3DOK4             5.280       -1.434   11.994
        3DOK7  - 3DOK13            6.660       -0.054   13.374
        COMPOS - 3DOK1           -10.120      -16.834   -3.406  ***
        COMPOS - 3DOK5            -5.280      -11.994    1.434
        COMPOS - 3DOK7            -1.220       -7.934    5.494
        COMPOS - 3DOK4             4.060       -2.654   10.774
        COMPOS - 3DOK13            5.440       -1.274   12.154
        3DOK4  - 3DOK1           -14.180      -20.894   -7.466  ***
        3DOK4  - 3DOK5            -9.340      -16.054   -2.626  ***
        3DOK4  - 3DOK7            -5.280      -11.994    1.434
        3DOK4  - COMPOS           -4.060      -10.774    2.654
        3DOK4  - 3DOK13            1.380       -5.334    8.094
        3DOK13 - 3DOK1           -15.560      -22.274   -8.846  ***
        3DOK13 - 3DOK5           -10.720      -17.434   -4.006  ***
        3DOK13 - 3DOK7            -6.660      -13.374    0.054
        3DOK13 - COMPOS           -5.440      -12.154    1.274
        3DOK13 - 3DOK4            -1.380       -8.094    5.334
```

Example 17.3. Split Plot

In some experiments, treatments can be applied only to groups of experimental observations rather than separately to each observation. When there are two nested groupings of the observations on the basis of treatment application, this is known as a *split plot design*. For example, in integrated circuit fabrication it is of interest to see how different manufacturing methods affect the characteristics of individual chips. However, much of the manufacturing process is applied to a relatively large wafer of material, from which many chips are made. Additionally, a chip's position within a wafer may also affect chip performance. These two groupings of chips—by wafer and by position-within-wafer—might form the *whole plots* and the *subplots*, respectively, of a split plot design for integrated circuits.

The following statements produce an analysis for a split-plot design. The CLASS statement includes the variables Block, A, and B, where B defines subplots within BLOCK*A whole plots. The MODEL statement includes the independent effects Block, A, Block*A, B, and A*B. The TEST statement asks for an F test of the A effect, using the Block*A effect as the error term. The following statements produce Output 17.3.1 and Output 17.3.2:

```
title 'Split Plot Design';
data Split;
   input Block 1 A 2 B 3 Response;
   datalines;
142 40.0
141 39.5
112 37.9
111 35.4
121 36.7
122 38.2
132 36.4
131 34.8
221 42.7
222 41.6
212 40.3
211 41.6
241 44.5
242 47.6
231 43.6
232 42.8
;

proc anova;
   class Block A B;
   model Response = Block A Block*A B A*B;
   test h=A e=Block*A;
run;
```

Output 17.3.1. Class Level Information and ANOVA Table

```
                    Split Plot Design

                   The ANOVA Procedure

                 Class Level Information

             Class         Levels    Values

             Block              2    1 2

             A                  4    1 2 3 4

             B                  2    1 2


               Number of observations    16
```

```
                    Split Plot Design

                   The ANOVA Procedure

Dependent Variable: Response

                                       Sum of
 Source                      DF       Squares    Mean Square   F Value   Pr > F

 Model                       11   182.0200000     16.5472727      7.85   0.0306

 Error                        4     8.4300000      2.1075000

 Corrected Total             15   190.4500000


             R-Square     Coeff Var      Root MSE    Response Mean

             0.955736      3.609007      1.451723         40.22500
```

First, notice that the overall F test for the model is significant.

Output 17.3.2. Tests of Effects

```
                              Split Plot Design

                            The ANOVA Procedure

Dependent Variable: Response

 Source                      DF        Anova SS     Mean Square    F Value    Pr > F

 Block                        1     131.1025000     131.1025000      62.21    0.0014
 A                            3      40.1900000      13.3966667       6.36    0.0530
 Block*A                      3       6.9275000       2.3091667       1.10    0.4476
 B                            1       2.2500000       2.2500000       1.07    0.3599
 A*B                          3       1.5500000       0.5166667       0.25    0.8612


      Tests of Hypotheses Using the Anova MS for Block*A as an Error Term

 Source                      DF        Anova SS     Mean Square    F Value    Pr > F

 A                            3     40.19000000     13.39666667       5.80    0.0914
```

The effect of Block is significant. The effect of A is not significant: look at the F test produced by the TEST statement, not at the F test produced by default. Neither the B nor A*B effects are significant. The test for Block*A is irrelevant, as this is simply the main-plot error.

Example 17.4. Latin Square Split Plot

The data for this example is taken from Smith (1951). A Latin square design is used to evaluate six different sugar beet varieties arranged in a six-row (Rep) by six-column (Column) square. The data are collected over two harvests. The variable Harvest then becomes a split plot on the original Latin square design for whole plots. The following statements produce Output 17.4.1 and Output 17.4.2:

```
title 'Sugar Beet Varieties';
title3 'Latin Square Split-Plot Design';
data Beets;
   do Harvest=1 to 2;
      do Rep=1 to 6;
         do Column=1 to 6;
            input Variety Y @;
            output;
            end;
         end;
      end;
   datalines;
3 19.1 6 18.3 5 19.6 1 18.6 2 18.2 4 18.5
6 18.1 2 19.5 4 17.6 3 18.7 1 18.7 5 19.9
1 18.1 5 20.2 6 18.5 4 20.1 3 18.6 2 19.2
2 19.1 3 18.8 1 18.7 5 20.2 4 18.6 6 18.5
4 17.5 1 18.1 2 18.7 6 18.2 5 20.4 3 18.5
5 17.7 4 17.8 3 17.4 2 17.0 6 17.6 1 17.6
3 16.2 6 17.0 5 18.1 1 16.6 2 17.7 4 16.3
```

```
6 16.0 2 15.3 4 16.0 3 17.1 1 16.5 5 17.6
1 16.5 5 18.1 6 16.7 4 16.2 3 16.7 2 17.3
2 17.5 3 16.0 1 16.4 5 18.0 4 16.6 6 16.1
4 15.7 1 16.1 2 16.7 6 16.3 5 17.8 3 16.2
5 18.3 4 16.6 3 16.4 2 17.6 6 17.1 1 16.5
;

proc anova;
   class Column Rep Variety Harvest;
   model Y=Rep Column Variety Rep*Column*Variety
           Harvest Harvest*Rep
           Harvest*Variety;
   test h=Rep Column Variety e=Rep*Column*Variety;
   test h=Harvest            e=Harvest*Rep;
run;
```

Output 17.4.1. Class Level Information and ANOVA Table

```
                    Sugar Beet Varieties

                Latin Square Split-Plot Design

                    The ANOVA Procedure

                  Class Level Information

          Class          Levels    Values

          Column              6    1 2 3 4 5 6

          Rep                 6    1 2 3 4 5 6

          Variety             6    1 2 3 4 5 6

          Harvest             2    1 2


              Number of observations    72
```

```
                           Sugar Beet Varieties

                      Latin Square Split-Plot Design

                           The ANOVA Procedure

Dependent Variable: Y

                                            Sum of
 Source                      DF            Squares    Mean Square   F Value   Pr > F

 Model                       46         98.9147222      2.1503200      7.22   <.0001

 Error                       25          7.4484722      0.2979389

 Corrected Total             71        106.3631944


              R-Square     Coeff Var      Root MSE        Y Mean

              0.929971      3.085524      0.545838      17.69028


 Source                      DF           Anova SS    Mean Square   F Value   Pr > F

 Rep                          5         4.32069444     0.86413889      2.90   0.0337
 Column                       5         1.57402778     0.31480556      1.06   0.4075
 Variety                      5        20.61902778     4.12380556     13.84   <.0001
 Column*Rep*Variety          20         3.25444444     0.16272222      0.55   0.9144
 Harvest                      1        60.68347222    60.68347222    203.68   <.0001
 Rep*Harvest                  5         7.71736111     1.54347222      5.18   0.0021
 Variety*Harvest              5         0.74569444     0.14913889      0.50   0.7729
```

First, note from Output 17.4.1 that the overall model is significant.

Output 17.4.2. Tests of Effects

```
                              Sugar Beet Varieties

                         Latin Square Split-Plot Design

                              The ANOVA Procedure

Dependent Variable: Y

 Tests of Hypotheses Using the Anova MS for Column*Rep*Variety as an Error Term

 Source                     DF        Anova SS     Mean Square    F Value    Pr > F

 Rep                         5      4.32069444      0.86413889       5.31    0.0029
 Column                      5      1.57402778      0.31480556       1.93    0.1333
 Variety                     5     20.61902778      4.12380556      25.34    <.0001


    Tests of Hypotheses Using the Anova MS for Rep*Harvest as an Error Term

 Source                     DF        Anova SS     Mean Square    F Value    Pr > F

 Harvest                     1     60.68347222     60.68347222      39.32    0.0015
```

Output 17.4.2 shows that the effects for Rep and Harvest are significant, while the Column effect is not. The average Ys for the six different Varietys are significantly different. For these four tests, look at the output produced by the two TEST statements, not at the usual ANOVA procedure output. The Variety*Harvest interaction is not significant. All other effects in the default output should either be tested using the results from the TEST statements or are irrelevant as they are only error terms for portions of the model.

Example 17.5. Strip-Split Plot

In this example, four different fertilizer treatments are laid out in vertical strips, which are then split into subplots with different levels of calcium. Soil type is stripped across the split-plot experiment, and the entire experiment is then replicated three times. The dependent variable is the yield of winter barley. The data come from the notes of G. Cox and A. Rotti.

The input data are the 96 values of Y, arranged so that the calcium value (Calcium) changes most rapidly, then the fertilizer value (Fertilizer), then the Soil value, and, finally, the Rep value. Values are shown for Calcium (0 and 1); Fertilizer (0, 1, 2, 3); Soil (1, 2, 3); and Rep (1, 2, 3, 4). The following example produces Output 17.5.1, Output 17.5.2, and Output 17.5.3.

```
title 'Strip-split Plot';
data Barley;
   do Rep=1 to 4;
      do Soil=1 to 3;                    /* 1=d 2=h 3=p */
         do Fertilizer=0 to 3;
            do Calcium=0,1;
               input Yield @;
               output;
            end;
         end;
      end;
   end;
   datalines;
4.91 4.63 4.76 5.04 5.38 6.21 5.60 5.08
4.94 3.98 4.64 5.26 5.28 5.01 5.45 5.62
5.20 4.45 5.05 5.03 5.01 4.63 5.80 5.90
6.00 5.39 4.95 5.39 6.18 5.94 6.58 6.25
5.86 5.41 5.54 5.41 5.28 6.67 6.65 5.94
5.45 5.12 4.73 4.62 5.06 5.75 6.39 5.62
4.96 5.63 5.47 5.31 6.18 6.31 5.95 6.14
5.71 5.37 6.21 5.83 6.28 6.55 6.39 5.57
4.60 4.90 4.88 4.73 5.89 6.20 5.68 5.72
5.79 5.33 5.13 5.18 5.86 5.98 5.55 4.32
5.61 5.15 4.82 5.06 5.67 5.54 5.19 4.46
5.13 4.90 4.88 5.18 5.45 5.80 5.12 4.42
;

proc anova;
   class Rep Soil Calcium Fertilizer;
   model Yield =
           Rep
           Fertilizer Fertilizer*Rep
           Calcium Calcium*Fertilizer
                   Calcium*Rep(Fertilizer)
           Soil Soil*Rep
           Soil*Fertilizer Soil*Rep*Fertilizer
           Soil*Calcium Soil*Fertilizer*Calcium
           Soil*Calcium*Rep(Fertilizer);
   test h=Fertilizer          e=Fertilizer*Rep;
   test h=Calcium
          Calcium*Fertilizer e=Calcium*Rep(Fertilizer);
   test h=Soil                e=Soil*Rep;
   test h=Soil*Fertilizer     e=Soil*Rep*Fertilizer;
   test h=Soil*Calcium
          Soil*Fertilizer*Calcium
                              e=Soil*Calcium*Rep(Fertilizer);
   means Fertilizer Calcium Soil Calcium*Fertilizer;
run;
```

Output 17.5.1. Class Level Information and ANOVA Table

```
                         Strip-split Plot

                       The ANOVA Procedure

                     Class Level Information

              Class          Levels    Values

              Rep                 4    1 2 3 4

              Soil                3    1 2 3

              Calcium             2    0 1

              Fertilizer          4    0 1 2 3


                 Number of observations    96
```

```
                         Strip-split Plot

                       The ANOVA Procedure

Dependent Variable: Yield

                                       Sum of
 Source                     DF        Squares    Mean Square   F Value    Pr > F

 Model                      95    31.89149583     0.33569996         .         .

 Error                       0     0.00000000              .

 Corrected Total            95    31.89149583


              R-Square     Coeff Var      Root MSE    Yield Mean

              1.000000             .             .      5.427292


 Source                     DF        Anova SS    Mean Square   F Value    Pr > F

 Rep                         3     6.27974583     2.09324861         .         .
 Fertilizer                  3     7.22127083     2.40709028         .         .
 Rep*Fertilizer              9     6.08211250     0.67579028         .         .
 Calcium                     1     0.27735000     0.27735000         .         .
 Calcium*Fertilizer          3     1.96395833     0.65465278         .         .
 Rep*Calcium(Fertili)       12     1.76705833     0.14725486         .         .
 Soil                        2     1.92658958     0.96329479         .         .
 Rep*Soil                    6     1.66761042     0.27793507         .         .
 Soil*Fertilizer             6     0.68828542     0.11471424         .         .
 Rep*Soil*Fertilizer        18     1.58698125     0.08816563         .         .
 Soil*Calcium                2     0.04493125     0.02246562         .         .
 Soil*Calcium*Fertili        6     0.18936042     0.03156007         .         .
 Rep*Soil*Calc(Ferti)       24     2.19624167     0.09151007         .         .
```

As the model is completely specified by the MODEL statement, the entire top portion of output (Output 17.5.1) should be ignored. Look at the following output produced by the various TEST statements.

Output 17.5.2. Tests of Effects

```
                              Strip-split Plot

                            The ANOVA Procedure

Dependent Variable: Yield

   Tests of Hypotheses Using the Anova MS for Rep*Fertilizer as an Error Term

 Source                      DF        Anova SS     Mean Square    F Value    Pr > F

 Fertilizer                   3      7.22127083      2.40709028       3.56    0.0604


                 Tests of Hypotheses Using the Anova MS for
                   Rep*Calcium(Fertili) as an Error Term

 Source                      DF        Anova SS     Mean Square    F Value    Pr > F

 Calcium                      1      0.27735000      0.27735000       1.88    0.1950
 Calcium*Fertilizer           3      1.96395833      0.65465278       4.45    0.0255


      Tests of Hypotheses Using the Anova MS for Rep*Soil as an Error Term

 Source                      DF        Anova SS     Mean Square    F Value    Pr > F

 Soil                         2      1.92658958      0.96329479       3.47    0.0999


                 Tests of Hypotheses Using the Anova MS for
                    Rep*Soil*Fertilizer as an Error Term

 Source                      DF        Anova SS     Mean Square    F Value    Pr > F

 Soil*Fertilizer              6      0.68828542      0.11471424       1.30    0.3063


                 Tests of Hypotheses Using the Anova MS for
                   Rep*Soil*Calc(Ferti) as an Error Term

 Source                      DF        Anova SS     Mean Square    F Value    Pr > F

 Soil*Calcium                 2      0.04493125      0.02246562       0.25    0.7843
 Soil*Calcium*Fertili         6      0.18936042      0.03156007       0.34    0.9059
```

The only significant effect is the Calcium*Fertilizer interaction.

Output 17.5.3. Results of MEANS statement

```
                        Strip-split Plot

                      The ANOVA Procedure

      Level of              ------------Yield------------
      Fertilizer      N            Mean          Std Dev

      0              24      5.18416667       0.48266395
      1              24      5.12916667       0.38337082
      2              24      5.75458333       0.53293265
      3              24      5.64125000       0.63926801


      Level of              ------------Yield------------
      Calcium        N            Mean          Std Dev

      0              48      5.48104167       0.54186141
      1              48      5.37354167       0.61565219


      Level of              ------------Yield------------
      Soil           N            Mean          Std Dev

      1              32      5.54312500       0.55806369
      2              32      5.51093750       0.62176315
      3              32      5.22781250       0.51825224


Level of     Level of                ------------Yield------------
Calcium      Fertilizer      N            Mean          Std Dev

0            0              12      5.34666667       0.45029956
0            1              12      5.08833333       0.44986530
0            2              12      5.62666667       0.44707806
0            3              12      5.86250000       0.52886027
1            0              12      5.02166667       0.47615569
1            1              12      5.17000000       0.31826233
1            2              12      5.88250000       0.59856077
1            3              12      5.42000000       0.68409197
```

The final portion of output shows the results of the MEANS statement. This portion shows means for various effects and combinations of effects, as requested. Because no multiple comparison procedures are requested, none are performed. You can examine the Calcium*Fertilizer means to understand the interaction better.

In this example, you could reduce memory requirements by omitting the Soil*Calcium*Rep(Fertilizer) effect from the model in the MODEL statement. This effect then becomes the ERROR effect, and you can omit the last TEST statement (in the code shown earlier). The test for the Soil*Calcium effect is then given in the Analysis of Variance table in the top portion of output. However, for all other tests, you should look at the results from the TEST statement. In large models, this method may lead to significant reductions in memory requirements.

References

Bartlett, M.S. (1937), "Properties of Sufficiency and Statistical Tests," *Proceedings of the Royal Society of London, Series A* 160, 268–282.

Brown, M.B. and Forsythe, A.B. (1974), "Robust Tests for Equality of Variances," *Journal of the American Statistical Association,* 69, 364–367.

Erdman, L.W. (1946), "Studies to Determine if Antibiosis Occurs among Rhizobia," *Journal of the American Society of Agronomy*, 38, 251–258.

Fisher, R.A. (1942), *The Design of Experiments,* Third Edition, Edinburgh: Oliver & Boyd.

Freund, R.J., Littell, R.C., and Spector, P.C. (1986), *SAS System for Linear Models, 1986 Edition*, Cary, NC: SAS Institute Inc.

Graybill, F.A. (1961), *An Introduction to Linear Statistical Models,* Volume I, New York: McGraw-Hill Book Co.

Henderson, C.R. (1953), "Estimation of Variance and Covariance Components," *Biometrics*, 9, 226–252.

Levene, H. (1960), "Robust Tests for the Equality of Variance," in *Contributions to Probability and Statistics,* ed. I. Olkin, Palo Alto, CA: Stanford University Press, 278–292.

Neter, J., Wasserman, W., and Kutner, M.H. (1990), *Applied Linear Statistical Models: Regression, Analysis of Variance, and Experimental Designs*, Homewood, IL: Richard D. Irwin, Inc.

O'Brien, R.G. (1979), "A General ANOVA Method for Robust Tests of Additive Models for Variances," *Journal of the American Statistical Association,* 74, 877–880.

O'Brien, R.G. (1981), "A Simple Test for Variance Effects in Experimental Designs," *Psychological Bulletin,* 89(3), 570–574.

Remington, R.D. and Schork, M.A. (1970), *Statistics with Applications to the Biological and Health Sciences*, Englewood Cliffs, NJ: Prentice-Hall, Inc.

Scheffé, H. (1959), *The Analysis of Variance*, New York: John Wiley & Sons, Inc.

Schlotzhauer, S.D. and Littell, R.C. (1987), *SAS System for Elementary Statistical Analysis*, Cary, NC: SAS Institute Inc.

Searle, S.R. (1971), *Linear Models*, New York: John Wiley & Sons, Inc.

Smith, W.G. (1951), Dissertation Notes on Canadian Sugar Factories, Ltd., Alberta, Canada: Taber.

Snedecor, G.W. and Cochran, W.G. (1967), *Statistical Methods,* Sixth Edition, Ames, IA: Iowa State University Press.

Steel, R.G.D. and Torrie, J.H. (1980), *Principles and Procedures of Statistics*, New York: McGraw-Hill Book Co.

Chapter 18
The BOXPLOT Procedure

Chapter Table of Contents

Chapter 18
The BOXPLOT Procedure

Overview

The BOXPLOT procedure creates side-by-side box-and-whisker plots of measurements organized in groups. A box-and-whisker plot displays the mean, quartiles, and minimum and maximum observations for a group. Throughout this chapter, this type of plot, which can contain one or more box-and-whisker plots, is referred to as a *box plot*.

The PLOT statement of the BOXPLOT procedure produces a box plot. You can specify more than one PLOT statement to produce multiple box plots.

You can use options in the PLOT statement to

- control the style of the box-and-whisker plots
- specify one of several methods for calculating quantile statistics (percentiles)
- add block legends and symbol markers to reveal stratification in data
- display vertical and horizontal reference lines
- control axis values and labels
- control the layout and appearance of the plot

Getting Started

This section demonstrates how you can use the BOXPLOT procedure to produce box plots for your data.

Suppose that a petroleum company uses a turbine to heat water into steam that is pumped into the ground to make oil more viscous and easier to extract. This process occurs 20 times daily, and the amount of power (in kilowatts) used to heat the water to the desired temperature is recorded. The following statements create a SAS data set called Turbine that contains the power output measurements for 20 work days.

```
data Turbine;
   informat day date7.;
   format day date5.;
   label kwatts='Average Power Output';
   input day @;
   do i=1 to 10;
      input kwatts @;
      output;
      end;
```

```
   drop i;
datalines;
05JUL94 3196 3507 4050 3215 3583 3617 3789 3180 3505 3454
05JUL94 3417 3199 3613 3384 3475 3316 3556 3607 3364 3721
06JUL94 3390 3562 3413 3193 3635 3179 3348 3199 3413 3562
06JUL94 3428 3320 3745 3426 3849 3256 3841 3575 3752 3347
07JUL94 3478 3465 3445 3383 3684 3304 3398 3578 3348 3369
07JUL94 3670 3614 3307 3595 3448 3304 3385 3499 3781 3711
08JUL94 3448 3045 3446 3620 3466 3533 3590 3070 3499 3457
08JUL94 3411 3350 3417 3629 3400 3381 3309 3608 3438 3567
11JUL94 3568 2968 3514 3465 3175 3358 3460 3851 3845 2983
11JUL94 3410 3274 3590 3527 3509 3284 3457 3729 3916 3633
12JUL94 3153 3408 3741 3203 3047 3580 3571 3579 3602 3335
12JUL94 3494 3662 3586 3628 3881 3443 3456 3593 3827 3573
13JUL94 3594 3711 3369 3341 3611 3496 3554 3400 3295 3002
13JUL94 3495 3368 3726 3738 3250 3632 3415 3591 3787 3478
14JUL94 3482 3546 3196 3379 3559 3235 3549 3445 3413 3859
14JUL94 3330 3465 3994 3362 3309 3781 3211 3550 3637 3626
15JUL94 3152 3269 3431 3438 3575 3476 3115 3146 3731 3171
15JUL94 3206 3140 3562 3592 3722 3421 3471 3621 3361 3370
18JUL94 3421 3381 4040 3467 3475 3285 3619 3325 3317 3472
18JUL94 3296 3501 3366 3492 3367 3619 3550 3263 3355 3510
19JUL94 3795 3872 3559 3432 3322 3587 3336 3732 3451 3215
19JUL94 3594 3410 3335 3216 3336 3638 3419 3515 3399 3709
20JUL94 3850 3431 3460 3623 3516 3810 3671 3602 3480 3388
20JUL94 3365 3845 3520 3708 3202 3365 3731 3840 3182 3677
21JUL94 3711 3648 3212 3664 3281 3371 3416 3636 3701 3385
21JUL94 3769 3586 3540 3703 3320 3323 3480 3750 3490 3395
22JUL94 3596 3436 3757 3288 3417 3331 3475 3600 3690 3534
22JUL94 3306 3077 3357 3528 3530 3327 3113 3812 3711 3599
25JUL94 3428 3760 3641 3393 3182 3381 3425 3467 3451 3189
25JUL94 3588 3484 3759 3292 3063 3442 3712 3061 3815 3339
26JUL94 3746 3426 3320 3819 3584 3877 3779 3506 3787 3676
26JUL94 3727 3366 3288 3684 3500 3501 3427 3508 3392 3814
27JUL94 3676 3475 3595 3122 3429 3474 3125 3307 3467 3832
27JUL94 3383 3114 3431 3693 3363 3486 3928 3753 3552 3524
28JUL94 3349 3422 3674 3501 3639 3682 3354 3595 3407 3400
28JUL94 3401 3359 3167 3524 3561 3801 3496 3476 3480 3570
29JUL94 3618 3324 3475 3621 3376 3540 3585 3320 3256 3443
29JUL94 3415 3445 3561 3494 3140 3090 3561 3800 3056 3536
01AUG94 3421 3787 3454 3699 3307 3917 3292 3310 3283 3536
01AUG94 3756 3145 3571 3331 3725 3605 3547 3421 3257 3574
;
run;
```

In the data set Turbine, each observation contains the date and the power output for a single heating. The first 20 observations contain the outputs for the first day, the second 20 observations contain the outputs for the second day, and so on. Because the variable day classifies the observations into rational groups, it is referred to as the *group variable*. The variable kwatts contains the output measurements and is referred to as the *analysis variable*.

You can create a box plot to examine the distribution of power output for each day. The following statements create the box plot shown in Figure 18.1.

```
symbol color = salmon h = .8;
goptions ftext=swiss;
axis1 minor=none color=black label=(angle=90 rotate=0);
title 'Box Plot for Power Output';

proc boxplot data=Turbine;
   plot kwatts*day/ cframe    = vligb
                    cboxes    = dagr
                    cboxfill  = ywh
                    vaxis     = axis1;
run;
```

The input data set Turbine is specified with the DATA= option in the PROC BOXPLOT statement. The PLOT statement requests a box-and-whisker plot for each group of data. After the keyword PLOT, you specify the analysis variable (in this case, kwatts), followed by an asterisk and the group variable (day).

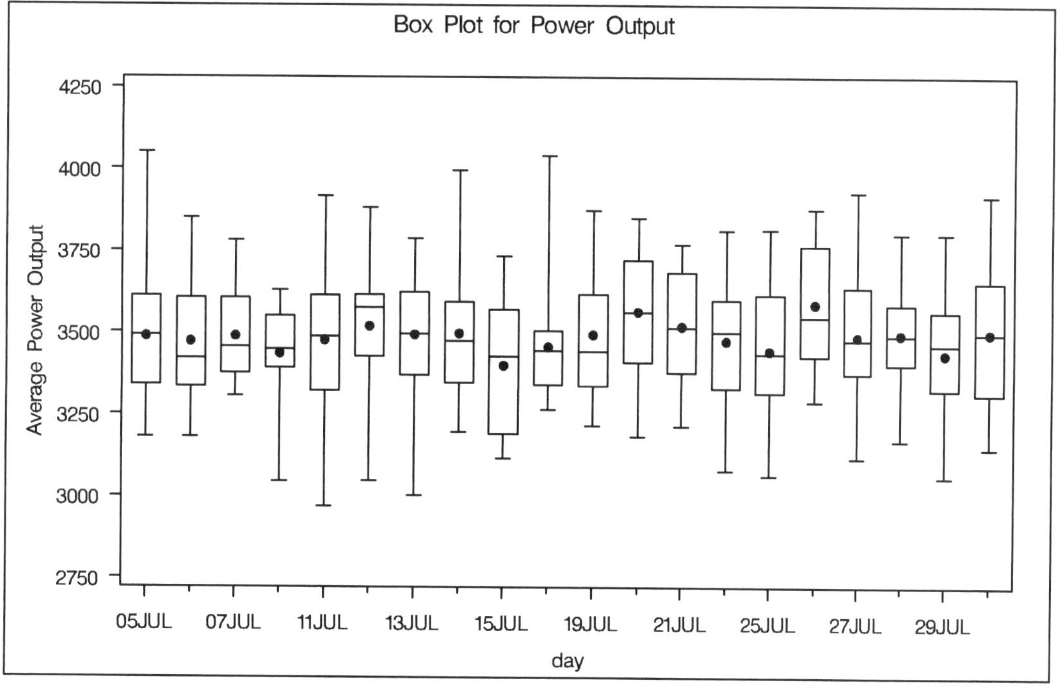

Figure 18.1. Box Plot for Power Output Data

The box plot displayed in Figure 18.1 represents summary statistics for the analysis variable kwatts; each of the 20 box-and-whisker plots describes the variable kwatts for a particular day. The plot elements and the statistics they represent are as follows.

- the length of the box represents the interquartile range (the distance between the 25th and the 75th percentiles)

- the dot in the box interior represents the mean
- the horizontal line in the box interior represents the median
- the vertical lines issuing from the box extend to the minimum and maximum values of the analysis variable

Syntax

The syntax for the BOXPLOT procedure is as follows:

PROC BOXPLOT < *options* > ;
  PLOT *analysis-variable*group-variable* < *(block-variables)* >
    < *=symbol-variable* > < */ options* > ;
  BY *variables*;
  ID *variables*;

Both the PROC BOXPLOT and PLOT statements are required. You can specify any number of PLOT statements within a single PROC BOXPLOT invocation.

PROC BOXPLOT Statement

PROC BOXPLOT < *options* > ;

The PROC BOXPLOT statement starts the BOXPLOT procedure. The following options can appear in the PROC BOXPLOT statement.

ANNOTATE=*SAS-data-set*
specifies an ANNOTATE= type data set, as described in *SAS/GRAPH Software: Reference*, that enhances all box plots requested in subsequent PLOT statements.

DATA=*SAS-data-set*
names the SAS data set containing the data to be analyzed. If you omit the DATA= option, the procedure uses the most recently created SAS data set.

GOUT=<*libref.*>*output catalog*
specifies the SAS catalog in which to save the graphics output that is produced by the BOXPLOT procedure. If you omit the libref, PROC BOXPLOT looks for the catalog in the temporary library called WORK and creates the catalog if it does not exist.

PLOT Statement

PLOT *(analysis-variables)*group-variable* <*(block-variables)*>
< *=symbol-variable* > < */ options* >*;*

You can specify multiple PLOT statements after the PROC BOXPLOT statement. The components of the PLOT statement are as follows.

analysis-variables
: identify one or more variables to be analyzed. An analysis variable is required. If you specify more than one analysis variable, enclose the list in parentheses. For example, the following statements request distinct box plots for the variables weight, length, and width:

```
proc boxplot data=summary;
   plot (weight length width)*day;
run;
```

group-variable
: specifies the variable that identifies groups in the data. The group variable is required. In the preceding PLOT statement, day is the group variable.

block-variables
: specify optional variables that group the data into blocks of consecutive groups. These blocks are labeled in a legend, and each block variable provides one level of labels in the legend.

symbol-variable
: specifies an optional variable whose levels (unique values) determine the symbol marker used to plot the means. Distinct symbol markers are displayed for points corresponding to the various levels of the symbol variable. You can specify the symbol markers with SYMBOL*n* statements (refer to *SAS/GRAPH Software: Reference* for complete details).

options
: enhance the appearance of the box plot, request additional analyses, save results in data sets, and so on. Complete descriptions for each option follow.

Table 18.1 lists all options in the PLOT statement by function.

Table 18.1. PLOT Statement Options

Option	Description
Options for Controlling Box Appearance	
BOXCONNECT	connects group means in box-and-whisker plots
BOXCONNECT=	connects group means, medians, maximum values, minimum values, or quartiles in box-and-whisker plots
BOXSTYLE=	specifies style of box-and-whisker plots
BOXWIDTH=	specifies width of box-and-whisker plots

Table 18.1. (continued)

Option	Description
BOXWIDTHSCALE=	specifies that widths of box-and-whisker plots vary proportionately to group size
CBOXES=	specifies color for outlines of box-and-whisker plots
CBOXFILL=	specifies fill color for interior of box-and-whisker plots
IDCOLOR=	specifies outlier symbol color in schematic box-and-whisker plots
IDCTEXT=	specifies outlier label color in schematic box-and-whisker plots
IDFONT=	specifies outlier label font in schematic box-and-whisker plots
IDHEIGHT=	specifies outlier label height in schematic box-and-whisker plots
IDSYMBOL=	specifies outlier symbol in schematic box-and-whisker plots
LBOXES=	specifies line types for outlines of box-and-whisker plots
NOSERIFS	eliminates serifs from the whiskers of box-and-whisker plots
NOTCHES	specifies that box-and-whisker plots are to be notched
PCTLDEF=	specifies percentile definition used for box-and-whisker plots
Options for Plotting and Labeling Points	
CCONNECT=	specifies color for line segments that connect points on plot
SYMBOLLEGEND=	specifies LEGEND statement for levels of the symbol variable
SYMBOLORDER=	specifies order in which symbols are assigned for levels of the symbol variable
Reference Line Options	
CHREF=	specifies color for lines requested by HREF= option
CVREF=	specifies color for lines requested by VREF= option
HREF=	specifies position of reference lines perpendicular to horizontal axis on box plot
HREFLABELS=	specifies labels for HREF= lines
HREFLABPOS=	specifies position of HREFLABELS= labels
LHREF=	specifies line type for HREF= lines
LVREF=	specifies line type for VREF= lines
NOBYREF	specifies that reference line information in a data set is to be applied uniformly to plots created for all BY groups
VREF=	specifies position of reference lines perpendicular to vertical axis on box plot
VREFLABELS=	specifies labels for VREF= lines
VREFLABPOS=	specifies position of VREFLABELS= labels
Block Variable Legend Options	
BLOCKLABELPOS=	specifies position of label for the block variable legend
BLOCKLABTYPE=	specifies text size of the block variable legend
BLOCKPOS=	specifies vertical position of the block variable legend

Table 18.1. (continued)

Option	Description
BLOCKREP	repeats identical consecutive labels in the block variable legend
CBLOCKLAB=	specifies color for filling background in the block variable legend
CBLOCKVAR=	specifies one or more variables whose values are colors for filling background of the block variable legend
Axis and Axis Label Options	
CAXIS=	specifies color for axis lines and tick marks
CFRAME=	specifies fill colors for frame for plot area
CONTINUOUS	produces horizontal axis for continuous group variable values
CTEXT=	specifies color for tick mark values and axis labels
HAXIS=	specifies major tick mark values for horizontal axis
HEIGHT=	specifies height of axis label and axis legend text
HMINOR=	specifies number of minor tick marks between major tick marks on horizontal axis
HOFFSET=	specifies length of offset at both ends of horizontal axis
NOHLABEL	suppresses label for horizontal axis
NOTICKREP	specifies that only the first occurrence of repeated, adjacent group values is to be labeled on horizontal axis
NOVANGLE	requests vertical axis labels that are strung out vertically
SKIPHLABELS=	specifies thinning factor for tick mark labels on horizontal axis
TURNHLABELS	requests horizontal axis labels that are strung out vertically
VAXIS=	specifies major tick mark values for vertical axis of box plot
VMINOR=	specifies number of minor tick marks between major tick marks on vertical axis
VOFFSET=	specifies length of offset at both ends of vertical axis
VZERO	forces origin to be included in vertical axis
WAXIS=	specifies width of axis lines
Input Data Set Options	
MISSBREAK	specifies that missing values between identical character group values signify the start of a new group
Graphical Enhancement Options	
ANNOTATE=	specifies annotate data set that adds features to box plot
BWSLEGEND	displays a legend identifying the function of group size specified with the BOXWIDTHSCALE= option
DESCRIPTION=	specifies string that appears in the description field of the PROC GREPLAY master menu for box plot
FONT=	specifies software font for labels and legends on plots
NAME=	specifies name that appears in the name field of the PROC GREPLAY master menu for box plot

Table 18.1. (continued)

Option	Description
NLEGEND	requests a legend displaying group sample sizes
PAGENUM=	specifies the form of the label used in pagination
PAGENUMPOS=	specifies the position of the page number requested with the PAGENUM= option
Grid Options	
ENDGRID	adds grid after last box-and-whisker plot
GRID	adds grid to box plot
LENDGRID=	specifies line type for grid requested with the ENDGRID option
LGRID=	specifies line type for grid requested with the GRID option
WGRID=	specifies width of grid lines
Plot Layout Options	
INTERVAL=	specifies natural time interval between consecutive group positions when time, date, or datetime format is associated with a numeric group variable
MAXPANELS=	specifies maximum number of pages or screens for plot
NOFRAME	suppresses frame for plot area
NPANELPOS=	specifies number of group positions per panel on each plot
REPEAT	repeats last group position on panel as first group position of next panel
TOTPANELS=	specifies number of pages or screens to be used to display plot

Following are explanations of the options that you can specify in the PLOT statement after a slash (/).

ANNOTATE=*SAS-data-set*

specifies an ANNOTATE= type data set, as described in *SAS/GRAPH Software: Reference*.

BLOCKLABELPOS=ABOVE | LEFT

specifies the position of a block variable label in the block legend. The keyword ABOVE places the label immediately above the legend, and LEFT places the label to the left of the legend. Use the keyword LEFT with labels that are short enough to fit in the margin of the plot; otherwise, they are truncated. The default keyword is ABOVE.

BLOCKLABTYPE=SCALED | TRUNCATED
BLOCKLABTYPE=*height*

specifies how lengthy block variable values are to be treated when there is insufficient space to display them in the block legend. If you specify the BLOCKLABTYPE=SCALED option, the values are uniformly reduced in height so that they fit. If you specify the BLOCKLABTYPE=TRUNCATED option, lengthy values are truncated on the right until they fit. You can also specify a text height in vertical percent screen units for the values. By default, lengthy values are not displayed. For more information, see the section "Displaying Blocks of Data" on page 422.

BLOCKPOS=*n*

specifies the vertical position of the legend for the values of the block variables. Values of n and the corresponding positions are as follows. By default, BLOCKPOS=1.

n	Legend Position
1	top of plot, offset from axis frame
2	top of plot, immediately above axis frame
3	bottom of plot, immediately above horizontal axis
4	bottom of plot, below horizontal axis label

BLOCKREP

specifies that block variable values for all groups are to be displayed. By default, only the first block variable value in any block is displayed, and repeated block variable values are not displayed.

BOXCONNECT
BOXCONNECT=MEAN | MEDIAN | MAX | MIN | Q1 | Q3

specifies that the points representing group means, medians, maximum values, minimum values, first quartiles, or third quartiles are to be connected with line segments. If the BOXCONNECT option is specified without a keyword identifying the points to be connected, group means are connected. By default, no points are connected.

BOXSTYLE=*keyword*

specifies the style of the box-and-whisker plots displayed. If you specify BOXSTYLE=SKELETAL, the whiskers are drawn from the edges of the box to the extreme values of the group. This plot is sometimes referred to as a skeletal box-and-whisker plot. By default, the whiskers are drawn with serifs: you can specify the NOSERIFS option to draw the whiskers without serifs.

In the following descriptions, the terms *fence* and *far fence* refer to the distance from the first and third quartiles (25th and 75th percentiles, respectively), expressed in terms of the interquartile range (IQR). For example, the lower fence is located at $1.5 \times$ IQR below the 25th percentile; the upper fence is located at $1.5 \times$ IQR above the 75th percentile. Similarly, the lower far fence is located at $3 \times$ IQR below the 25th percentile; the upper far fence is located at $3 \times$ IQR above the 75th percentile.

If you specify BOXSTYLE=SCHEMATIC, a whisker is drawn from the upper edge of the box to the largest value within the upper fence and from the lower edge of the box to the smallest value within the lower fence. Serifs are added to the whiskers by default. Observations outside the fences are identified with a special symbol; you can specify the shape and color for this symbol with the IDSYMBOL= and IDCOLOR= options. The default symbol is a square. This type of plot corresponds to the schematic box-and-whisker plot described in Chapter 2 of Tukey (1977). See Figure 18.4 and the discussion in the section "Styles of Box Plots" on page 418 for more information.

If you specify BOXSTYLE=SCHEMATICID, a schematic box-and-whisker plot is displayed in which the value of the first variable listed in the ID statement is used to label the symbol marking each observation outside the upper and lower fences.

If you specify BOXSTYLE=SCHEMATICIDFAR, a schematic box-and-whisker plot is displayed in which the value of the first variable listed in the ID statement is used to label the symbol marking each observation outside the lower and upper far fences. Observations between the fences and the far fences are identified with a symbol but are not labeled with the ID variable.

Figure 18.2 illustrates the elements of a skeletal box-and-whisker plot.

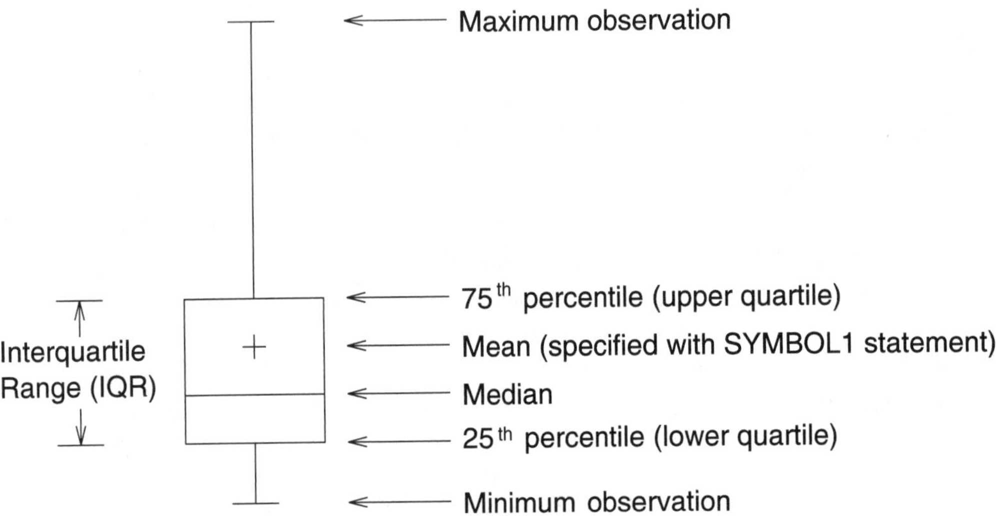

Figure 18.2. Skeletal Box-and-Whisker Plot

The skeletal style of the box-and-whisker plot shown in Figure 18.2 is the default.

BOXWIDTH=*value*
specifies the width (in horizontal percent screen units) of the box-and-whisker plots.

BOXWIDTHSCALE=*value*
specifies that the box-and-whisker plot width is to vary proportionately to a particular function of the group size n. The function is determined by the *value*.

If you specify a positive value, the widths are proportional to n^{value}. In particular, if you specify BOXWIDTHSCALE=1, the widths are proportional to the group size. If you specify BOXWIDTHSCALE=0.5, the widths are proportional to $\sqrt{n}$, as described by McGill, Tukey, and Larsen (1978). If you specify BOXWIDTHSCALE=0, the widths are proportional to $\log(n)$. See Example 18.4 on page 432 for an illustration of the BOXWIDTHSCALE= option.

You can specify the BWSLEGEND option to display a legend identifying the function of n used to determine the box-and-whisker plot widths.

By default, the box widths are constant.

BWSLEGEND

displays a legend identifying the function of group size n specified with the BOXWIDTHSCALE= option. No legend is displayed if all group sizes are equal. The BWSLEGEND option is not applicable unless you also specify the BOXWIDTHSCALE= option.

CAXIS=*color*
CAXES=*color*
CA=*color*

specifies the color for the axes and tick marks. This option overrides any COLOR= specifications in an AXIS statement. The default value is the first color in the device color list.

CBLOCKLAB=*color*

specifies a fill color for the frame that encloses the block variable label in a block legend. By default, this area is not filled.

CBLOCKVAR=*variable | (variable-list)*

specifies variables whose values are colors for filling the background of the legend associated with block variables. Each CBLOCKVAR= variable must be a character variable of no more than eight characters in the input data set, and its values must be valid SAS/GRAPH color names (refer to *SAS/GRAPH Software: Reference* for complete details). A list of CBLOCKVAR= variables must be enclosed in parentheses.

The procedure matches the CBLOCKVAR= variables with block variables in the order specified. That is, each block legend is filled with the color value of the CBLOCKVAR= variable of the first observation in each block. In general, values of the *i*th CBLOCKVAR= variable are used to fill the block of the legend corresponding to the *i*th block variable.

By default, fill colors are not used for the block variable legend. The CBLOCKVAR= option is available only when block variables are used in the PLOT statement.

CBOXES=*color*
CBOXES=*(variable)*

specifies the colors for the outlines of the box-and-whisker plots created with the PLOT statement. You can use one of the following approaches:

- You can specify CBOXES=*color* to provide a single outline color for all the box-and-whisker plots.
- You can specify CBOXES=*(variable)* to provide a distinct outline color for each box-and-whisker plot as the value of the variable. The variable must be a character variable of length 8 or less in the input data set, and its values must be valid SAS/GRAPH color names (refer to *SAS/GRAPH Software: Reference* for complete details). The outline color of the plot displayed for a particular group is the value of the variable in the observations corresponding to this group. Note that, if there are multiple observations per group in the input data set, the values of the variable should be identical for all the observations in a given group.

The default color is the second color in the device color list.

CBOXFILL=*color*
CBOXFILL=*(variable)*
specifies the interior fill colors for the box-and-whisker plots. You can use one of the following approaches:

- You can specify CBOXFILL=*color* to provide a single color for all of the box-and-whisker plots.
- You can specify CBOXFILL=*(variable)* to provide a distinct color for each box-and-whisker plot as the value of the variable. The variable must be a character variable of length 8 or less in the input data set, and its values must be valid SAS/GRAPH color names (or the value EMPTY, which you can use to suppress color filling). Refer to *SAS/GRAPH Software: Reference* for complete details. The interior color of the box displayed for a particular group is the value of the variable in the observations corresponding to this group. Note that if there are multiple observations per group in the input data set, the values of the variable should be identical for all the observations in a given group.

By default, the interiors are not filled.

CCONNECT=*color*
specifies the color for the line segments connecting points on the plot. The default color is the color specified in the COLOR= option in the SYMBOL1 statement. This option is not applicable unless you also specify the BOXCONNECT option.

CFRAME=*color*
CFRAME=*(color-list)*
specifies the colors for filling the rectangle enclosed by the axes and the frame. By default, this area is not filled. The CFRAME= option cannot be used in conjunction with the NOFRAME option. You can specify a single color to fill the entire area.

CHREF=*color*
specifies the color for the lines requested by the HREF= option. The default value is the first color in the device color list.

CONTINUOUS
specifies that numeric group variable values are to be treated as continuous values. By default, the values of a numeric group variable are considered discrete values unless the HAXIS= option is specified. For more information, see the discussion in the section "Continuous Group Variables" on page 420.

CTEXT=*color*
specifies the color for tick mark values and axis labels. The default color is the color specified in the CTEXT= option in the most recent GOPTIONS statement.

CVREF=*color*
specifies the color for the lines requested by the VREF= option. The default value is the first color in the device color list.

DESCRIPTION=*'string'*
DES=*'string'*

specifies a description of the box plot, not longer than 40 characters, that appears in the PROC GREPLAY master menu. The default string is the variable name.

ENDGRID

adds a grid to the rightmost portion of the plot, beginning with the first labeled major tick mark position that follows the box-and-whisker plot. You can use the HAXIS= option to force space to be added to the horizontal axis.

FONT=*font*

specifies a software font for labels and legends. You can also specify fonts for axis labels in an AXIS statement. The FONT= font takes precedence over the FTEXT= font specified in the GOPTIONS statement. Hardware characters are used by default. Refer to *SAS/GRAPH Software: Reference* for more information on the GOPTIONS statement.

GRID

adds a grid to the box plot. Grid lines are horizontal lines positioned at labeled major tick marks, and they cover the length and height of the plotting area.

HAXIS=*values*
HAXIS=AXIS*n*

specifies tick mark values for the horizontal (group) axis. If the group variable is numeric, the values must be numeric and equally spaced. Optionally, you can specify an axis name defined in a previous AXIS statement. Refer to *SAS/GRAPH Software: Reference* for more information on the AXIS statement.

Specifying the HAXIS= option with a numeric group variable causes the group variable values to be treated as continuous values. For more information, see the description of the CONTINUOUS option and the discussion in the section "Continuous Group Variables" on page 420. Numeric values can be given in an explicit or implicit list. If the group variable is character, values must be quoted strings of length 16 or less. If a date, time, or datetime format is associated with a numeric group variable, SAS datetime literals can be used. Examples of HAXIS= lists follow:

- haxis=0 2 4 6 8 10
- haxis=0 to 10 by 2
- haxis='LT12A' 'LT12B' 'LT12C' 'LT15A' 'LT15B' 'LT15C'
- haxis='20MAY88'D to '20AUG88'D by 7
- haxis='01JAN88'D to '31DEC88'D by 30

If the group variable is numeric, the HAXIS= list must span the group variable values, and if the group variable is character, the HAXIS= list must include all of the group variable values. You can add group positions to the box plot by specifying HAXIS= values that are not group variable values.

If you specify a large number of HAXIS= values, some of these may be thinned to avoid collisions between tick mark labels. To avoid thinning, use one of the following methods.

- Shorten values of the group variable by eliminating redundant characters. For example, if your group variable has values LOT1, LOT2, LOT3, and so on, you can use the SUBSTR function in a DATA step to eliminate LOT from each value, and you can modify the horizontal axis label to indicate that the values refer to lots.
- Use the TURNHLABELS option to turn the labels vertically.
- Use the NPANELPOS= option to force fewer group positions per panel.

HEIGHT=*value*

specifies the height (in vertical screen percent units) of the text for axis labels and legends. This value takes precedence over the HTEXT= value specified in the GOPTIONS statement. This option is recommended for use with software fonts specified with the FONT= option or with the FTEXT= option in the GOPTIONS statement. Refer to *SAS/GRAPH Software: Reference* for complete information on the GOPTIONS statement.

HMINOR=*n*
HM=*n*

specifies the number of minor tick marks between each major tick mark on the horizontal axis. Minor tick marks are not labeled. The default is HMINOR=0.

HOFFSET=*value*

specifies the length (in percent screen units) of the offset at both ends of the horizontal axis. You can eliminate the offset by specifying HOFFSET=0.

HREF=*values*
HREF=*SAS-data-set*

draws reference lines perpendicular to the horizontal (group) axis on the box plot. You can use this option in the following ways:

- You can specify the values for the lines with an HREF=list. If the group variable is numeric, the values must be numeric. If the group variable is character, the values must be quoted strings of up to 16 characters. If the group variable is formatted, the values must be given as internal values. Examples of HREF=values follow:

  ```
  href=5
  href=5 10 15 20 25 30
  href='Shift 1' 'Shift 2' 'Shift 3'
  ```

- You can specify reference line values as the values of a variable named _REF_ in an HREF= data set. The type and length of _REF_ must match those of the group variable specified in the PLOT statement. Optionally, you can provide labels for the lines as values of a variable named _REFLAB_, which must be a character variable of length 16 or less. If you want distinct reference lines to be displayed in plots for different analysis variables specified in the PLOT statement, you must include a character variable named _VAR_, whose values are the analysis variable names. If you do not include the variable _VAR_, all of the lines are displayed in all of the plots.

Each observation in an HREF= data set corresponds to a reference line. If BY variables are used in the input data set, the same BY variable structure must be used in the reference line data set unless you specify the NOBYREF option.

Unless the CONTINUOUS or HAXIS= option is specified, numeric group variable values are treated as discrete values, and only HREF= values matching these discrete values are valid. Other values are ignored.

HREFLABELS=*'label$_1$' ... 'label$_n$'*
HREFLABEL=*'label$_1$' ... 'label$_n$'*
HREFLAB=*'label$_1$' ... 'label$_n$'*

specifies labels for the reference lines requested by the HREF=option. The number of labels must equal the number of lines. Enclose each label in quotes. Labels can be up to 16 characters.

HREFLABPOS=*n*

specifies the vertical position of the HREFLABEL= label, as described in the following table. By default, n=2.

HREFLABPOS=	Label Position
1	along top of plot area
2	staggered from top to bottom of plot area
3	along bottom of plot area
4	staggered from bottom to top of plot area

IDCOLOR=*color*

specifies the color of the symbol marker used to identify outliers in schematic box-and-whisker plots (that is, when you also specify one of the following options: BOXSTYLE=SCHEMATIC, BOXSTYLE=SCHEMATICID, and BOXSTYLE=SCHEMATICIDFAR). The default color is the color specified with the CBOXES= option; otherwise, the second color in the device color list is used.

IDCTEXT=*color*

specifies the color for the text used to label outliers when you specify one of the keywords SCHEMATICID or SCHEMATICIDFAR with the BOXSTYLE= option. The default value is the color specified with the CTEXT= option.

IDFONT=*font*

specifies the font for the text used to label outliers when you specify one of the keywords SCHEMATICID or SCHEMATICIDFAR with the BOXSTYLE= option. The default font is SIMPLEX.

IDHEIGHT=*value*

specifies the height for the text used to label outliers when you specify one of the keywords SCHEMATICID or SCHEMATICIDFAR with the BOXSTYLE= option. The default value is the height specified with the HTEXT= option in the GOPTIONS statement. Refer to *SAS/GRAPH Software: Reference* for complete information on the GOPTIONS statement.

IDSYMBOL=*symbol*

specifies the symbol marker used to identify outliers in schematic box plots when you also specify one of the following options: BOXSTYLE=SCHEMATIC, BOXSTYLE=SCHEMATICID, and BOXSTYLE=SCHEMATICIDFAR. The default symbol is SQUARE.

INTERVAL=DAY | DTDAY | HOUR | MINUTE | MONTH | QTR | SECOND

specifies the natural time interval between consecutive group positions when a time, date, or datetime format is associated with a numeric group variable. By default, the INTERVAL= option uses the number of group positions per panel that you specify with the NPANELPOS= option. The default time interval keywords for various time formats are shown in the following table.

Format	Default Keyword	Format	Default Keyword
DATE	DAY	MONYY	MONTH
DATETIME	DTDAY	TIME	SECOND
DDMMYY	DAY	TOD	SECOND
HHMM	HOUR	WEEKDATE	DAY
HOUR	HOUR	WORDDATE	DAY
MMDDYY	DAY	YYMMDD	DAY
MMSS	MINUTE	YYQ	QTR

You can use the INTERVAL= option to modify the effect of the NPANELPOS= option, which specifies the number of group positions per panel (screen or page). The INTERVAL= option enables you to match the scale of the horizontal axis to the scale of the group variable without having to associate a different format with the group variable.

For example, suppose that your formatted group values span an overall time interval of 100 days and a DATETIME format is associated with the group variable. Since the default interval for the DATETIME format is DTDAY and since NPANELPOS=20 by default, the plot is displayed with two panels (screens or pages).

Now, suppose that your data span an overall time interval of 100 hours and a DATETIME format is associated with the group variable. The plot for these data is created in a single panel, but the data occupy only a small fraction of the plot since the scale of the data (hours) does not match that of the horizontal axis (days). If you specify INTERVAL=HOUR, the horizontal axis is scaled for 50 hours, matching the scale of the data, and the plot is displayed with two panels.

You should use the INTERVAL= option only in conjunction with the CONTINUOUS or HAXIS= option, which produces a horizontal axis of continuous group variable values. For more information, see the descriptions of the CONTINUOUS and HAXIS= options, and the discussion in the section “Continuous Group Variables” on page 420.

LBOXES=*linetype*
LBOXES=*(variable)*

specifies the line types for the outlines of the box-and-whisker plots. You can use one of the following approaches:

- You can specify LBOXES=*linetype* to provide a single linetype for all of the box-and-whisker plots.
- You can specify LBOXES=*(variable)* to provide a distinct line type for each box-and-whisker plot. The variable must be a numeric variable in the input data set, and its values must be valid SAS/GRAPH linetype values (numbers ranging from 1 to 46). The line type for the plot displayed for a particular group is the value of the variable in the observations corresponding to this group. Note that if there are multiple observations per group in the input data set, the values of the variable should be identical for all of the observations in a given group.

The default value is 1, which produces solid lines. Refer to the description of the SYMBOL statement in *SAS/GRAPH Software: Reference* for more information on valid linetypes.

LENDGRID=*n*

specifies the line type for the grid requested with the ENDGRID option. The default value is *n=1*, which produces a solid line. If you use the LENDGRID= option, you do not need to specify the ENDGRID option. Refer to the description of the SYMBOL statement in *SAS/GRAPH Software: Reference* for more information on valid linetypes.

LGRID=*n*

specifies the line type for the grid requested with the GRID option. The default value is *n=1*, which produces a solid line. If you use the LGRID= option, you do not need to specify the GRID option. Refer to the description of the SYMBOL statement in *SAS/GRAPH Software: Reference* for more information on valid linetypes.

LHREF=*linetype*
LH=*linetype*

specifies the line type for reference lines requested with the HREF= option. The default value is 2, which produces a dashed line. Refer to the description of the SYMBOL statement in *SAS/GRAPH Software: Reference* for more information on valid linetypes.

LVREF=*linetype*
LV=*linetype*

specifies the line type for reference lines requested by the VREF= option. The default value is 2, which produces a dashed line. Refer to the description of the SYMBOL statement in *SAS/GRAPH Software: Reference* for more information on valid linetypes.

MAXPANELS=*n*

specifies the maximum number of pages or screens for a plot. By default, $n = 20$.

MISSBREAK

determines how groups are formed when observations are read from a DATA= data set and a character group variable is provided. When you specify the MISSBREAK option, observations with missing values of the group variable are not processed. Furthermore, the next observation with a nonmissing value of the group variable is treated as the beginning observation of a new group even if this value is identical to the most recent nonmissing group value. In other words, by specifying the option MISSBREAK and by inserting an observation with a missing group variable value into a group of consecutive observations with the same group variable value, you can split the group into two distinct groups of observations.

By default (that is, when you omit the MISSBREAK option), observations with missing values of the group variable are not processed, and all remaining observations with the same consecutive value of the group variable are treated as a single group.

NAME=*'string'*

specifies a name for the box plot, not more than 8 characters, that appears in the PROC GREPLAY master menu.

NLEGEND

requests a legend displaying group sample sizes. If the sample size is the same for each group, that number is displayed. Otherwise, the minimum and maximum group sample sizes are displayed.

NOBYREF

specifies that the reference line information in an HREF= or VREF= data set is to be applied uniformly to box plots created for all the BY groups in the input data set. If you specify the NOBYREF option, you do not need to provide BY variables in the reference line data set. By default, you must provide BY variables.

NOFRAME

suppresses the default frame drawn around the plot.

NOHLABEL

suppresses the label for the horizontal (group) axis. Use the NOHLABEL option when the meaning of the axis is evident from the tick mark labels, such as when a date format is associated with the group variable.

NOSERIFS

eliminates serifs from the whiskers of box-and-whisker plots.

NOTCHES

specifies that box-and-whisker plots are to be notched. The endpoints of the notches are located at the median plus and minus $1.58(\mathrm{IQR}/\sqrt{n})$, where IQR is the interquartile range and n is the group sample size. The medians (central lines) of two box-and-whisker plots are significantly different at approximately the 0.05 level if the corresponding notches do not overlap. Refer to McGill, Tukey, and Larsen (1978) for more information. Figure 18.3 illustrates the NOTCHES option. Notice the folding effect at the bottom, which happens when the endpoint of a notch is beyond its corresponding quartile. This situation typically occurs when the group sample size is small.

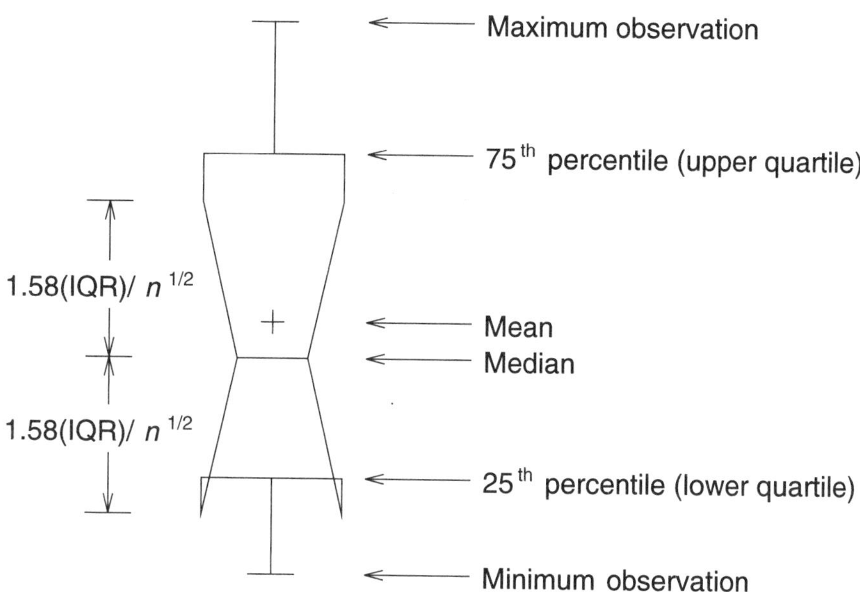

Figure 18.3. Box Plot: the NOTCHES Option

NOTICKREP

applies to character-valued group variables and specifies that only the first occurrence of repeated, adjacent group values is to be labeled on the horizontal axis.

NOVANGLE

requests vertical axis labels that are oriented vertically. By default, the labels are drawn at an angle of 90 degrees if a software font is used.

NPANELPOS=*n*
NPANEL=*n*

specifies the number of group positions per panel. A panel is defined as a screen or page. You typically specify the NPANELPOS= option to display more box-and-whisker plots on a panel than the default number, which is $n = 20$.

You can specify a positive or negative number for n. The absolute value of n must be at least 5. If n is positive, the number of positions is adjusted so that it is approximately equal to n and so that all panels display approximately the same number of group positions. If n is negative, no balancing is done, and each panel (except possibly the last) displays approximately $|n|$ positions. In this case, the approximation is due only to axis scaling.

You can use the INTERVAL= option to change the effect of the NPANELPOS= option when a date or time format is associated with the group variable. The INTERVAL= option enables you to match the scale of the horizontal axis to the scale of the group variable without having to associate a different format with the group variable.

PAGENUM=*'string'*

specifies the form of the label used for pagination. The string must be no longer than 16 characters, and it must include one or two occurrences of the substitution character '#'. The first '#' is replaced with the page number, and the optional second '#' is replaced with the total number of pages.

The PAGENUM= option is useful when you are working with a large number of groups, resulting in multiple pages of output. For example, suppose that each of the following PLOT statements produces multiple pages:

```
proc boxplot data=pistons;
   plot diameter*hour / pagenum='Page #';
   plot diameter*hour / pagenum='Page # of #';
   plot diameter*hour / pagenum='#/#';
run;
```

The third page produced by the first statement would be labeled *Page 3*. The third page produced by the second statement would be labeled *Page 3 of 5*. The third page produced by the third statement would be labeled *3/5*.

By default, no page number is displayed.

PAGENUMPOS=TL | TR | BL | BR | TL100 | TR100 | BL0 | BR0

specifies where to position the page number requested with the PAGENUM= option. The keywords TL, TR, BL, and BR correspond to the positions top left, top right, bottom left, and bottom right, respectively. You can use the TL100 and TR100 keywords to ensure that the page number appears at the very top of a page when a title is displayed. The BL0 and BR0 keywords ensure that the page number appears at the very bottom of a page when footnotes are displayed.

The default keyword is BR.

PCTLDEF=*index*

specifies one of five definitions used to calculate percentiles in the construction of box-and-whisker plots. The index can be 1, 2, 3, 4, or 5. The five corresponding percentile definitions are discussed in the section "Percentile Definitions" on page 419. The default index is 5.

REPEAT
REP

specifies that the horizontal axis of a plot that spans multiple pages is to be arranged so that the last group position on a page is repeated as the first group position on the next page. The REPEAT option facilitates cutting and pasting panels together. When a SAS DATETIME format is associated with the group variable, the REPEAT option is the default.

SKIPHLABELS=*n*
SKIPHLABEL=*n*

specifies the number n of consecutive tick mark labels, beginning with the second tick mark label, that are thinned (not displayed) on the horizontal (group) axis. For example, specifying SKIPHLABEL=1 causes every other label to be skipped. Specifying SKIPHLABEL=2 causes the second and third labels to be skipped, the fifth and sixth labels to be skipped, and so forth.

The default value of the SKIPHLABELS= option is the smallest value n for which tick mark labels do not collide. A specified n will be overridden to avoid collision. To reduce thinning, you can use the TURNHLABELS option.

SYMBOLLEGEND=LEGEND*n*
SYMBOLLEGEND=NONE

controls the legend for the levels of a symbol variable (see Example 18.1). You can specify SYMBOLLEGEND=LEGEND*n*, where *n* is the number of a LEGEND statement defined previously. You can specify SYMBOLLEGEND=NONE to suppress the default legend. Refer to *SAS/GRAPH Software: Reference* for more information on the LEGEND statement.

SYMBOLORDER=DATA | INTERNAL | FORMATTED
SYMORD=DATA | INTERNAL | FORMATTED

specifies the order in which symbols are assigned for levels of the symbol variable. The DATA keyword assigns symbols to values in the order in which values appear in the input data. The INTERNAL keyword assigns symbols based on sorted order of internal values of the symbol variable, and the FORMATTED keyword assigns them based on sorted formatted values. The default value is FORMATTED.

TOTPANELS=*n*

specifies the total number of panels to be used to display the plot. This option overrides the NPANEL= option.

TURNHLABELS
TURNHLABEL

turns the major tick mark labels for the horizontal (group) axis so that they are arranged vertically. By default, labels are arranged horizontally. You should specify a software font (using the FONT= option) in conjunction with the TURNHLABELS option. Otherwise, the labels may be displayed with a mixture of hardware and software fonts.

Note that arranging the labels vertically may leave insufficient room on the screen or page for a plot.

VAXIS=*value-list*
VAXIS=AXIS*n*

specifies major tick mark values for the vertical axis of a box plot. The values must be listed in increasing order, must be evenly spaced, and must span the range of values displayed on the plot. You can specify the values with an explicit list or with an implicit list, as shown in the following example:

```
proc boxplot;
   plot width*hour / vaxis=0 2 4 6 8;
   plot width*hour / vaxis=0 to 8 by 2;
run;
```

You can also specify a previously defined AXIS statement with the VAXIS= option.

VMINOR=*n*
VM=*n*

specifies the number of minor tick marks between each major tick mark on the vertical axis. Minor tick marks are not labeled. By default, VMINOR=0.

VOFFSET=*value*

specifies the length in percent screen units of the offset at the ends of the vertical axis.

VREF=*value-list*
VREF=*SAS-data-set*

draws reference lines perpendicular to the vertical axis on the box plot. You can use this option in the following ways:

- Specify the values for the lines with a VREF= list. Examples of the VREF= option follow:

```
vref=20
vref=20 40 80
```

- Specify the values for the lines as the values of a numeric variable named _REF_ in a VREF= data set. Optionally, you can provide labels for the lines as values of a variable named _REFLAB_, which must be a character variable of length 16 or less. If you want distinct reference lines to be displayed in plots for different analysis variables specified in the PLOT statement, you must include a character variable named _VAR_, whose values are the names of the analysis variables. If you do not include the variable _VAR_, all of the lines are displayed in all of the plots.

  Each observation in the VREF= data set corresponds to a reference line. If BY variables are used in the input data set, the same BY variable structure must be used in the VREF= data set unless you specify the NOBYREF option.

VREFLABELS=*'label1' ... 'labeln'*

specifies labels for the reference lines requested by the VREF= option. The number of labels must equal the number of lines. Enclose each label in quotes. Labels can be up to 16 characters.

VREFLABPOS=*n*

specifies the horizontal position of the VREFLABEL= label, as described in the following table. By default, *n=1*.

n	Label Position
1	left-justified in plot area
2	right-justified in plot area
3	left-justified in right margin

VZERO

forces the origin to be included in the vertical axis for a box plot.

WAXIS=*n*
specifies the width in pixels for the axis and frame lines. By default, $n=1$.

WGRID=*n*
specifies the width in pixels for grid lines requested with the ENDGRID and GRID options. By default, $n=1$.

BY Statement

BY *variables* ;

You can specify a BY statement with PROC BOXPLOT to obtain separate box plots for each group defined by the levels of the BY variables. When a BY statement appears, the procedure expects the input data set to be sorted in order of the BY variables.

If your input data set is not sorted in ascending order, use one of the following alternatives:

- Sort the data using the SORT procedure with a similar BY statement.
- Specify the BY statement option NOTSORTED or DESCENDING in the BY statement for the BOXPLOT procedure. The NOTSORTED option does not mean that the data are unsorted but rather that the data are arranged in groups (according to values of the BY variables) and that these groups are not necessarily in alphabetical or increasing numeric order.
- Create an index on the BY variables using the DATASETS procedure.

For more information on the BY statement, refer to the discussion in *SAS Language Reference: Concepts*. For more information on the DATASETS procedure, refer to the discussion in the *SAS Procedures Guide*.

ID Statement

ID *variables* ;

The ID statement specifies variables used to identify observations. The ID variables must be variables in the DATA= data set.

If you specify either the BOXSTYLE=SCHEMATICID option or the BOXSTYLE=SCHEMATICIDFAR option, the value of the first variable listed in the ID statement is used to label each extreme observation. For an example illustrating the use of the ID statement, see Example 18.2 or Example 18.3.

Details

Summary Statistics Represented by Box Plots

Table 18.2 lists the summary statistics represented in each box-and-whisker plot.

Table 18.2. Summary Statistics Represented by Box Plots

Group Summary Statistic	Feature of Box-and-Whisker Plot
Maximum	Endpoint of upper whisker
Third quartile (75th percentile)	Upper edge of box
Median (50th percentile)	Line inside box
Mean	Symbol marker
First quartile (25th percentile)	Lower edge of box
Minimum	Endpoint of lower whisker

Note that you can request different box plot styles, as discussed in the section "Styles of Box Plots," which follows, and as illustrated in Example 18.2 on page 427.

Input Data Set

You can read data (analysis variable measurements) from a data set specified with the DATA= option in the PROC BOXPLOT statement. Each analysis variable specified in the PLOT statement must be a SAS variable in the data set. This variable provides measurements that are organized into groups indexed by the group variable. The group variable, specified in the PLOT statement, must also be a SAS variable in the DATA= data set. Each observation in a DATA= data set must contain a value for each analysis variable and a value for the group variable. If the *i*th group contains n_i measurements, there should be n_i consecutive observations for which the value of the group variable is the index of the *i*th group. For example, if each group contains 20 items and there are 30 groups, the DATA= data set should contain 600 observations. Other variables that can be read from a DATA= data set include

- *block-variables*
- *symbol-variable*
- BY variables
- ID variables

Styles of Box Plots

A box-and-whisker plot is displayed for the measurements in each group on the box plot. The skeletal style of the box-and-whisker plot shown in Figure 18.2 is the default. Figure 18.4 illustrates a typical schematic box plot and the locations of the fences (which are not displayed in actual output). See the description of the BOXSTYLE= option on page 403 for complete details.

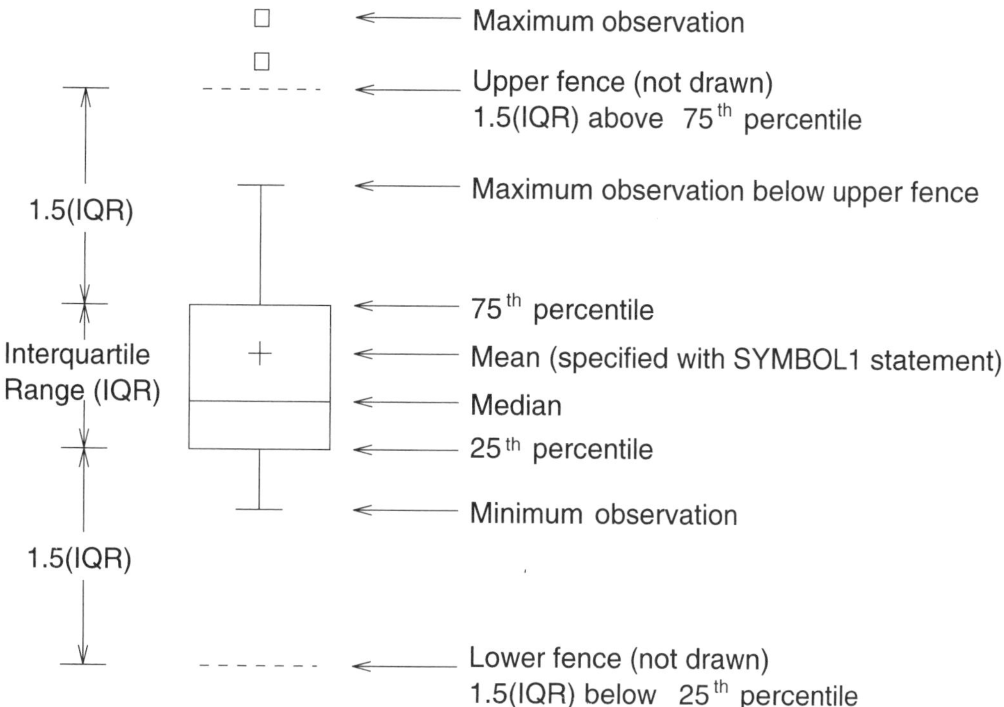

Figure 18.4. BOXSTYLE= SCHEMATIC

You can draw connecting lines between adjacent box-and-whisker plots using the BOXCONNECT=*keyword* option. For example, BOXCONNECT=MEAN connects the points representing the means of adjacent groups. Other available keywords are MIN, Q1, MEDIAN, Q3, and MAX. Specifying BOXCONNECT without a keyword is equivalent to specifying BOXCONNECT=MEAN. You can specify the color for the connecting lines with the CCONNECT= option.

Percentile Definitions

You can use the PCTLDEF= option to specify one of five definitions for computing quantile statistics (percentiles). Suppose that n equals the number of nonmissing values for a variable and that $x_1, x_2, \ldots, x_n$ represents the ordered values of the analysis variable. For the *t*th percentile, set $p = t/100$.

For the following definitions numbered 1, 2, 3, and 5, express np as

$$np = j + g$$

where j is the integer part of np, and g is the fractional part of np. For definition 4, let

$$(n + 1)p = j + g$$

The *t*th percentile (call it y) can be defined as follows:

PCTLDEF=1 weighted average at x_{np}

$$y = (1 - g)x_j + gx_{j+1}$$

where x_0 is taken to be x_1

PCTLDEF=2 observation numbered closest to np

$$y = x_i$$

where i is the integer part of $np + 1/2$ if $g \neq 1/2$. If $g = 1/2$, then $y = x_j$ if j is even, or $y = x_{j+1}$ if j is odd.

PCTLDEF=3 empirical distribution function

$$y = x_j \text{ if } g = 0$$

$$y = x_{j+1} \text{ if } g > 0$$

PCTLDEF=4 weighted average aimed at $x_{p(n+1)}$

$$y = (1 - g)x_j + gx_{j+1}$$

where x_{n+1} is taken to be x_n

PCTLDEF=5 empirical distribution function with averaging

$$y = (x_j + x_{j+1})/2 \text{ if } g = 0$$

$$y = x_{j+1} \text{ if } g > 0$$

Missing Values

An observation read from a DATA= data set is not analyzed if the value of the group variable is missing. For a particular analysis variable, an observation read from a DATA= data set is not analyzed if the value of the analysis variable is missing.

Missing values of analysis variables generally lead to unequal group sizes.

Continuous Group Variables

By default, the PLOT statement treats numerical group variable values as *discrete* values and spaces the boxes evenly on the plot. The following statements produce the plot shown in Figure 18.5:

```
symbol v=dot c=salmon;
goptions ftext=swiss;
axis1 minor=none color=black label=(angle=90 rotate=0);
title 'Box Plot for Power Output';

proc boxplot data=turbine;
   plot kwatts*day / turnhlabel
                     cframe   = vligb
                     cboxes   = dagr
                     cboxfill = ywh
                     vaxis    = axis1;
run;
```

The labels on the horizontal axis in Figure 18.5 do not represent 20 consecutive days, but the box-and-whisker plots are evenly spaced (note that the TURNHLABEL option orients the horizontal axis labels vertically so there is room to display them all).

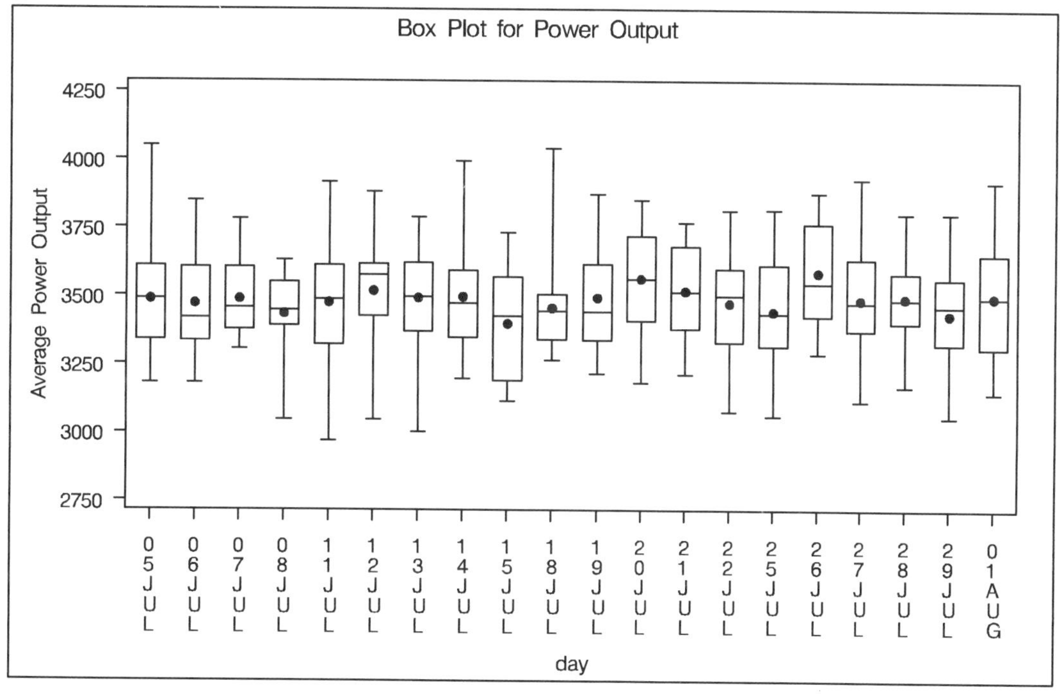

Figure 18.5. Box Plot with Discrete Group Variable

In order to treat the group variable as *continuous*, you can specify the CONTINUOUS or HAXIS= option. Either option produces a box plot with a horizontal axis scaled for continuous group variable values.

The following statements produce the plot shown in Figure 18.6. Note that the values on the horizontal axis represent consecutive days. Box-and-whisker plots are not produced for days when no turbine data was collected. The TOTPANELS= option is specified to display the entire box plot on one panel.

```
symbol v=dot c=salmon;
title 'Box Plot for Power Output';
axis1 minor=none color=black label=(angle=90 rotate=0);

proc boxplot data=turbine;
   plot kwatts*day / turnhlabel
                     cframe    = vligb
                     cboxes    = dagr
                     cboxfill  = ywh
                     totpanels = 1
                     vaxis     = axis1
                     continuous;

run;
```

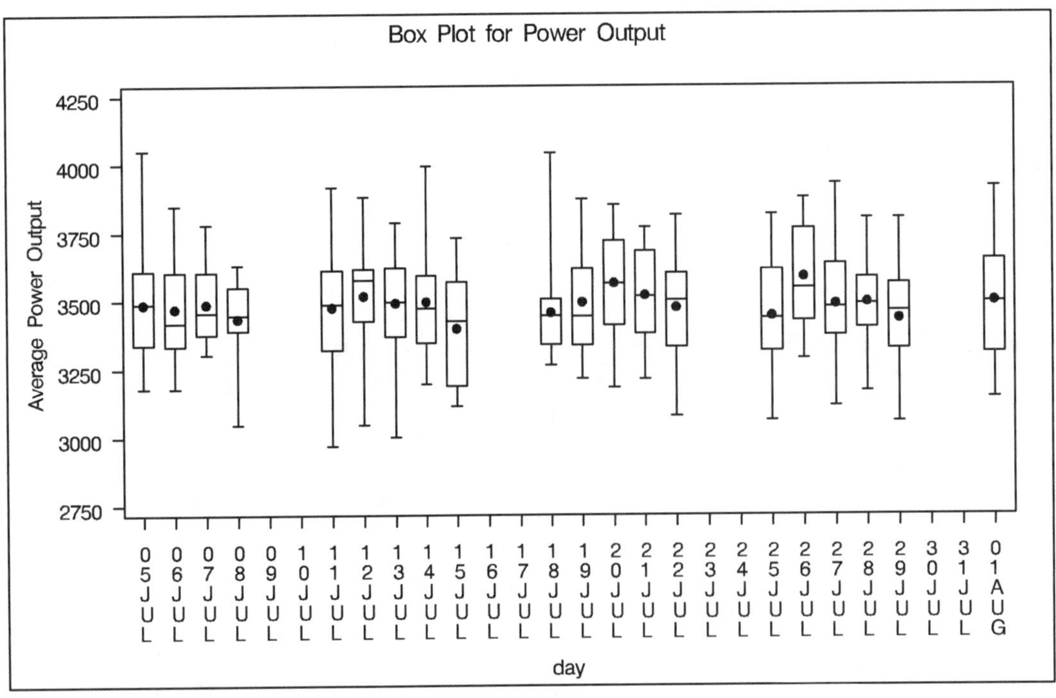

Figure 18.6. Box Plot with Continuous Group Variable

Displaying Blocks of Data

To display data organized in blocks of consecutive observations, specify one or more *block-variables* in parentheses after the *group-variable* in the PLOT statement. The block variables must be variables in the input data set. The procedure displays a legend identifying blocks of consecutive observations with identical values of the block variables. The legend displays one track of values for each block variable containing formatted values of the block variable.

The values of a block variable must be the same for all observations with the same value of the group variable. In other words, groups must be nested within blocks determined by block variables.

The following statements create a SAS data set containing diameter measurements for a part produced on three different machines:

```
data Parts;
   length Machine $ 4;
   input Sample Machine $ @;
   do i= 1 to 4;
      input Diam @;
      output;
   end;
   drop i;
datalines;
1  A386  4.32 4.55 4.16 4.44
2  A386  4.49 4.30 4.52 4.61
3  A386  4.44 4.32 4.25 4.50
4  A386  4.55 4.15 4.42 4.49
5  A386  4.21 4.30 4.29 4.63
6  A386  4.56 4.61 4.29 4.56
7  A386  4.63 4.30 4.41 4.58
8  A386  4.38 4.65 4.43 4.44
9  A386  4.12 4.49 4.30 4.36
10  A455  4.45 4.56 4.38 4.51
11  A455  4.62 4.67 4.70 4.58
12  A455  4.33 4.23 4.34 4.58
13  A455  4.29 4.38 4.28 4.41
14  A455  4.15 4.35 4.28 4.23
15  A455  4.21 4.30 4.32 4.38
16  C334  4.16 4.28 4.31 4.59
17  C334  4.14 4.18 4.08 4.21
18  C334  4.51 4.20 4.28 4.19
19  C334  4.10 4.33 4.37 4.47
20  C334  3.99 4.09 4.47 4.25
21  C334  4.24 4.54 4.43 4.38
22  C334  4.23 4.48 4.31 4.57
23  C334  4.27 4.40 4.32 4.56
24  C334  4.70 4.65 4.49 4.38
;
```

The following statements create a box plot for the data in the Parts data set grouped into blocks by the *block-variable* Machine. The plot is shown in Figure 18.7.

```
symbol v=dot c=salmon;
goptions ftext=swiss;
axis1 minor=none color=black label=(angle=90 rotate=0);
title 'Box Plot for Diameter Grouped By Machine';

proc boxplot data=Parts;
   plot Diam*Sample (Machine) / cframe = vligb vaxis = axis1;
```

```
      label Sample  = 'Sample Number'
            Machine = 'Machine'
            Diam    = 'Diameter' ;
   run;
```

The unique consecutive values of Machine (A386, A455, and C334) are displayed in a legend above the plot. Note the LABEL statement used to provide labels for the axes and for the block legend.

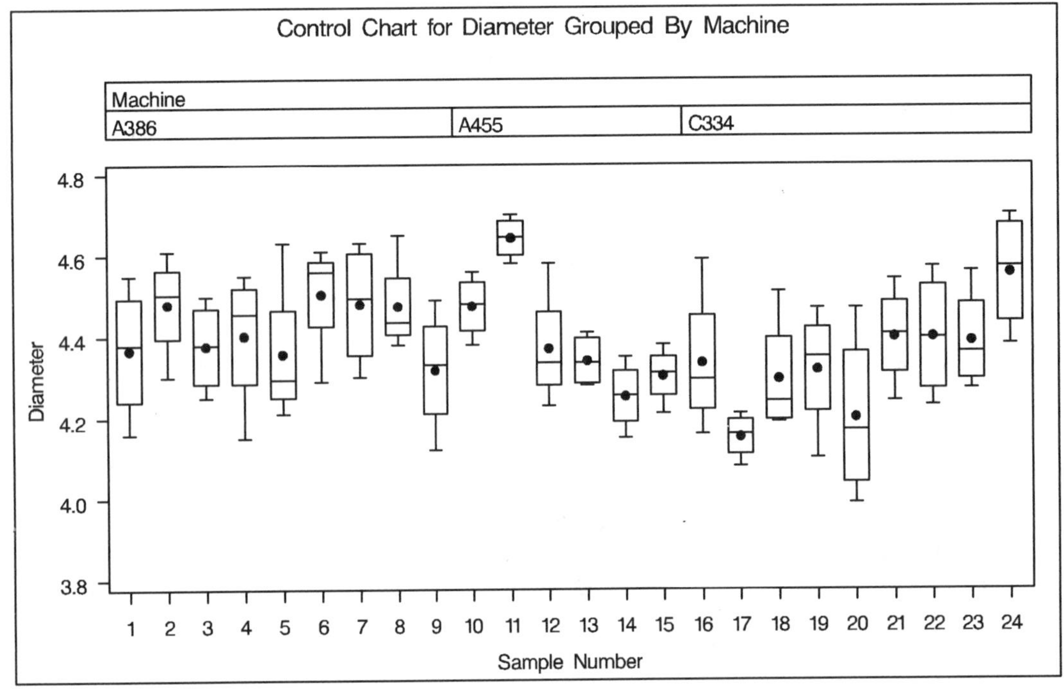

Figure 18.7. Box Plot Using a Block Variable

By default, the block legend is placed above the plot, as in Figure 18.7. You can control the position of the legend with the BLOCKPOS=*n* option; see the BLOCKPOS= option on page 403.

By default, block variable values that are too long to fit into the available space in a block legend are not displayed. You can specify the BLOCKLABTYPE= option to display lengthy labels. Specify BLOCKLABTYPE=SCALED to scale down the text size of the values so they all fit. Choose BLOCKLABTYPE=TRUNCATED to truncate lengthy values. You can also use BLOCKLABTYPE=*height* to specify a text height in vertical percent screen units for the values.

You can control the position of legend labels with the BLOCKLABELPOS=*keyword* option. The valid keywords are ABOVE (the default, as shown in Figure 18.7) and LEFT.

Examples

This section provides advanced examples of the PLOT statement.

Example 18.1. Using Box Plots to Compare Groups

In the following example, a box plot is used to compare the delay times for airline flights during the Christmas holidays with the delay times prior to the holiday period. The following statements create a data set named Times with the delay times in minutes for 25 flights each day. When a flight is canceled, the delay is recorded as a missing value.

```
data Times;
   informat day date7. ;
   format   day date7. ;
   input day @ ;
   do flight=1 to 25;
      input delay @ ;
      output;
      end;
datalines;
16DEC88   4  12   2   2  18   5   6  21   0   0   0  14   3
          .   2   3   5   0   6  19   7   4   9   5  10
17DEC88   1  10   3   3   0   1   5   0   .   .   1   5   7
          1   7   2   2  16   2   1   3   1  31   5   0
18DEC88   7   8   4   2   3   2   7   6  11   3   2   7   0
          1  10   2   3  12   8   6   2   7   2   4   5
19DEC88  15   6   9   0  15   7   1   1   0   2   5   6   5
         14   7  20   8   1  14   3  10   0   1  11   7
20DEC88   2   1   0   4   4   6   2   2   1   4   1  11   .
          1   0   6   5   5   4   2   2   6   6   4   0
21DEC88   2   6   6   2   7   7   5   2   5   0   9   2   4
          2   5   1   4   7   5   6   5   0   4  36  28
22DEC88   3   7  22   1  11  11  39  46   7  33  19  21   1
          3  43  23   9   0  17  35  50   0   2   1   0
23DEC88   6  11   8  35  36  19  21   .   .   4   6  63  35
          3  12  34   9   0  46   0   0  36   3   0  14
24DEC88  13   2  10   4   5  22  21  44  66  13   8   3   4
         27   2  12  17  22  19  36   9  72   2   4   4
25DEC88   4  33  35   0  11  11  10  28  34   3  24   6  17
          0   8   5   7  19   9   7  21  17  17   2   6
26DEC88   3   8   8   2   7   7   8   2   5   9   2   8   2
         10  16   9   5  14  15   1  12   2   2  14  18
;
```

In the following statements, the MEANS procedure is used to count the number of canceled flights for each day. This information is then added to the data set Times.

```
proc means data=Times noprint;
   var delay;
   by day ;
   output out=cancel nmiss=ncancel;

data Times;
   merge Times cancel;
   by day;
run;
```

The following statements create a data set named Weather that contains information about possible causes for delays. This data set is merged with the data set Times.

```
data Weather;
   informat day date7. ;
   format   day date7. ;
   length reason $ 16 ;
input day flight reason & ;
datalines;
16DEC88  8   Fog
17DEC88  18  Snow Storm
17DEC88  23  Sleet
21DEC88  24  Rain
21DEC88  25  Rain
22DEC88  7   Mechanical
22DEC88  15  Late Arrival
24DEC88  9   Late Arrival
24DEC88  22  Late Arrival
;

data times;
   merge Times Weather;
   by day flight;
run;
```

The following statements create a box plot for the complete set of data.

```
symbol1 v=plus     c=salmon;
symbol2 v=square   c=vigb;
symbol3 v=triangle c=vig;
goptions ftext=swiss;
axis1 minor=none color=black label=(angle=90 rotate=0);
title 'Box Plot for Airline Delays';

proc boxplot data=times;
   plot delay * day = ncancel /
                      nohlabel
                      symbollegend = legend1
                      cboxes       = dagr
                      cboxfill     = ywh
                      cframe       = vligb
                      vaxis        = axis1;
```

```
   legend1 label=('Cancellations:')
           cborder=black cframe=ligr;
   label delay = 'Delay in Minutes';
run;
```

The box plot is shown in Output 18.1.1. The level of the *symbol-variable* ncancel determines the symbol marker for each group mean, and the SYMBOLLEGEND= option controls the appearance of the legend for the symbols. The NOHLABEL option suppresses the label for the horizontal axis.

Output 18.1.1. Box Plot for Airline Data

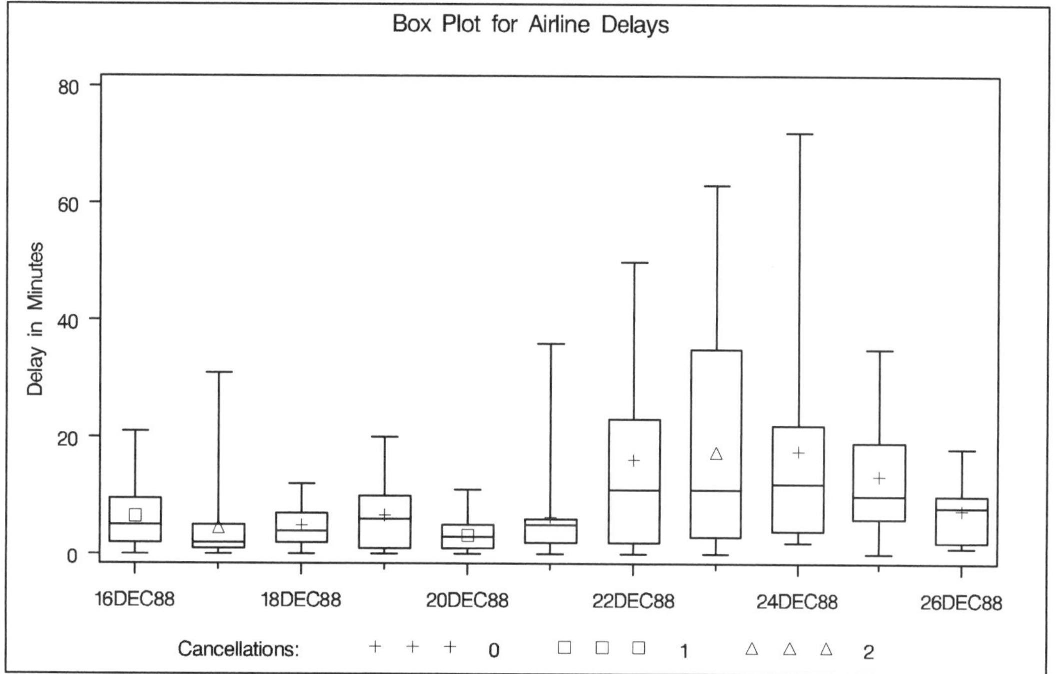

The delay distributions from December 22 through December 25 are drastically different from the delay distributions during the pre-holiday period. Both the mean delay and the variability of the delays are much greater during the holiday period.

Example 18.2. Creating Various Styles of Box-and-Whisker Plots

The following example uses the flight delay data of the preceding example to illustrate how you can create box plots with various styles of box-and-whisker plots. The following statements create a plot, shown in Output 18.2.1, that displays skeletal box-and-whisker plots:

```
symbol v=plus c=salmon;
axis1 minor=none color=black label=(angle=90 rotate=0);
title 'Analysis of Airline Departure Delays';
title2 'BOXSTYLE=SKELETAL';

proc boxplot data=times;
```

```
      plot delay * day /
                   boxstyle = skeletal
                   nohlabel
                   cframe   = vligb
                   cboxes   = dagr
                   cboxfill = ywh
                   vaxis    = axis1;
         label delay = 'Delay in Minutes';
run;
```

In a skeletal box-and-whisker plot, the whiskers are drawn from the quartiles to the extreme values of the group. The skeletal box-and-whisker plot is the default style; consequently, you can also request this style by omitting the BOXSTYLE= option.

Output 18.2.1. BOXSTYLE=SKELETAL

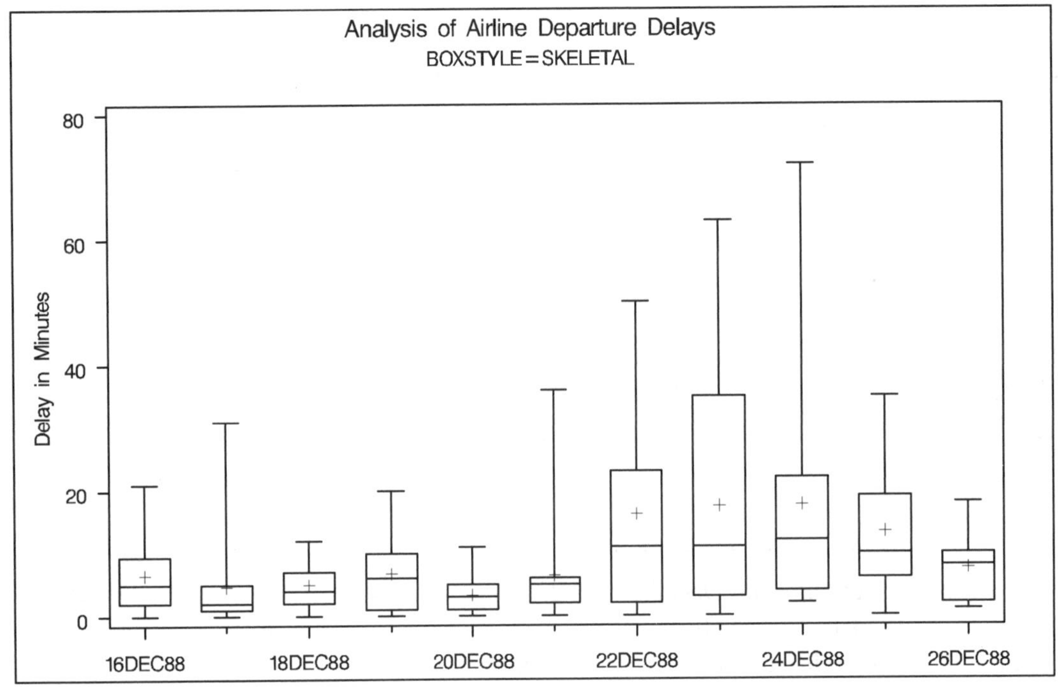

The following statements request a box plot with schematic box-and-whisker plots:

```
title2 'BOXSTYLE=SCHEMATIC';
proc boxplot data=times;
   plot delay * day /
                boxstyle  = schematic
                nohlabel
                cframe   = vligb
                cboxes   = dagr
                cboxfill = ywh
                idcolor  = salmon
                vaxis    = axis1;
   label delay = 'Delay in Minutes';
run;
```

The plot is shown in Output 18.2.2. When BOXSTYLE=SCHEMATIC is specified, the whiskers are drawn to the most extreme points in the group that lie within the *fences*. The *upper fence* is defined as the third quartile (represented by the upper edge of the box) plus 1.5 times the interquartile range (IQR). The *lower fence* is defined as the first quartile (represented by the lower edge of the box) minus 1.5 times the interquartile range. Observations outside the fences are identified with a special symbol. The default symbol is a square, and you can specify the shape and color for this symbol with the IDSYMBOL= and IDCOLOR= options. Serifs are added to the whiskers by default. For further details, see the entry for the BOXSTYLE= option on page 403.

Output 18.2.2. BOXSTYLE=SCHEMATIC

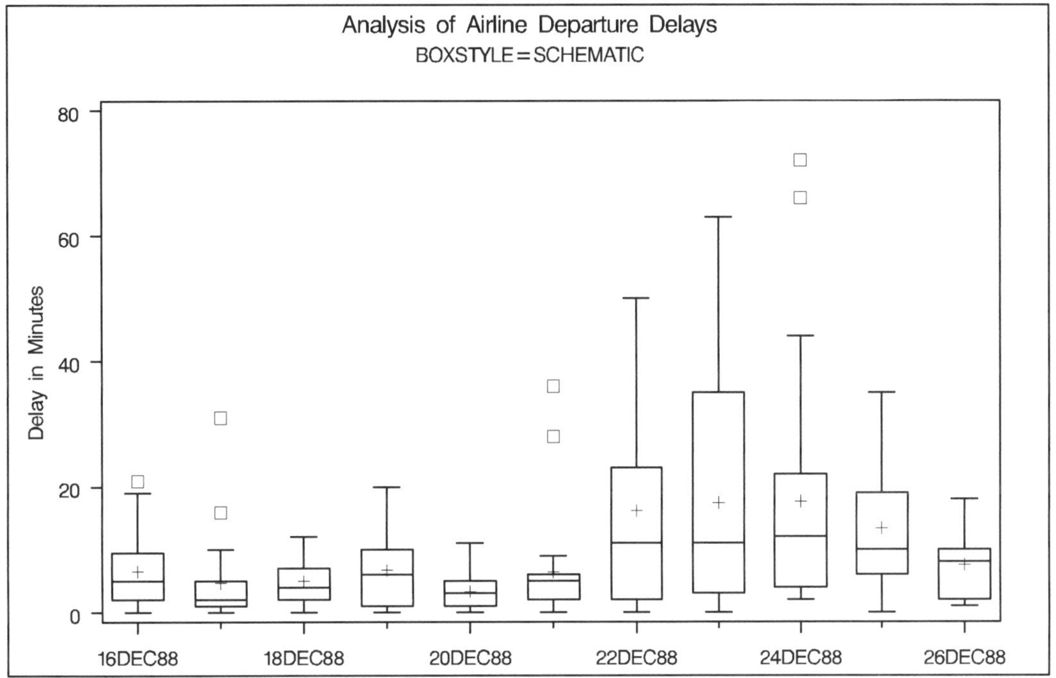

The following statements create a box plot with schematic box-and-whisker plots in which the observations outside the fences are labeled:

```
title2 'BOXSTYLE=SCHEMATICID';
proc boxplot data=times;
   plot delay * day /
                 boxstyle = schematicid
                 nohlabel
                 cboxes   = dagr
                 cboxfill = ywh
                 cframe   = vligb
                 idcolor  = salmon
                 vaxis    = axis1;
   id reason;
   label delay = 'Delay in Minutes';
run;
```

The plot is shown in Output 18.2.3. If you specify BOXSTYLE=SCHEMATICID, schematic box-and-whisker plots are displayed in which the value of the first ID variable (in this case, reason) is used to label each observation outside the fences.

Output 18.2.3. BOXSTYLE=SCHEMATICID

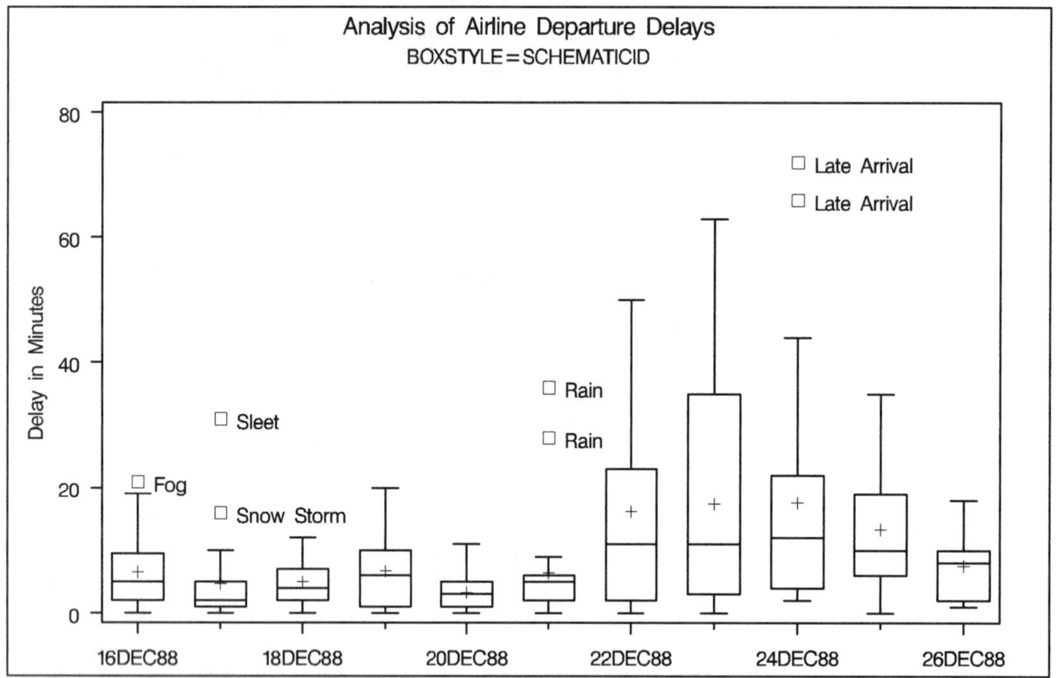

The following statements create a box plot with schematic box-and-whisker plots in which only the extreme observations outside the fences are labeled:

```
title2 'BOXSTYLE=SCHEMATICIDFAR';
proc boxplot data=times;
   plot delay * day /
                 boxstyle = schematicidfar
                 nohlabel
                 cframe   = vligb
                 cboxes   = dagr
                 cboxfill = ywh
                 idcolor  = salmon
                 vaxis    = axis1;
   id reason;
   label delay    = 'Delay in Minutes';
run;
```

The plot is shown in Output 18.2.4. If you specify BOXSTYLE=SCHEMATICIDFAR, schematic plots are displayed in which the value of the first ID variable is used to label each observation outside the *lower* and *upper far fences*. The lower and upper far fences are located $3 \times \text{IQR}$ below the 25th percentile and above the 75th percentile, respectively. Observations between the fences and the far fences are identified with a symbol but are not labeled.

Output 18.2.4. BOXSTYLE=SCHEMATICIDFAR

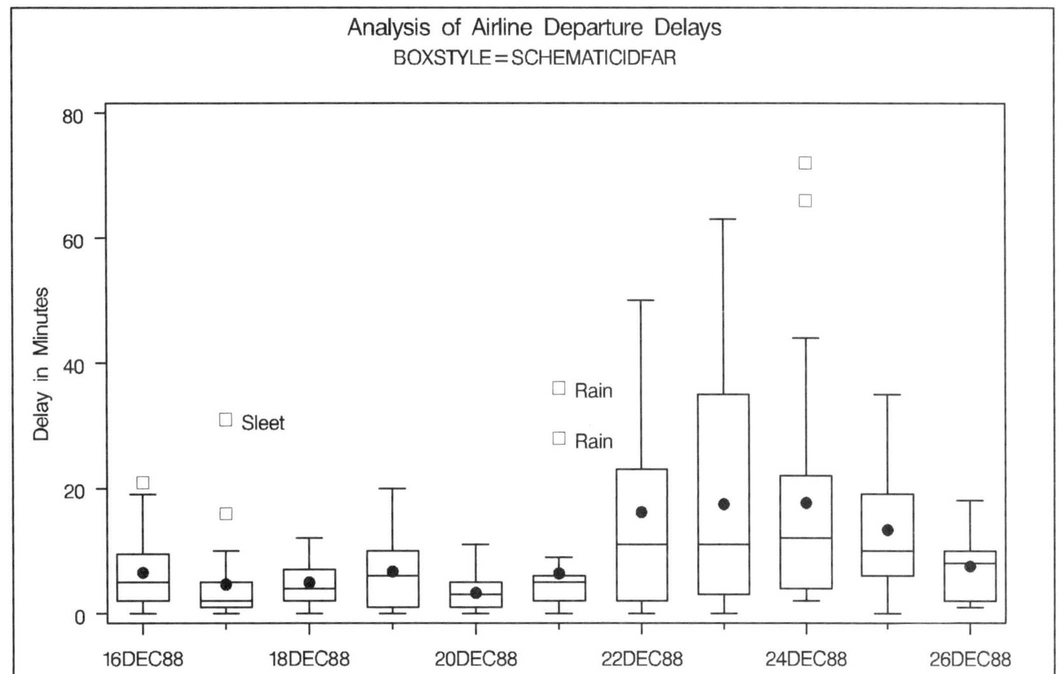

Other options for controlling the display of box-and-whisker plots include the BOXWIDTH=, BOXWIDTHSCALE=, CBOXES=, CBOXFILL=, and LBOXES= options.

Example 18.3. Creating Notched Box-and-Whisker Plots

The following statements use the flight delay data of Example 18.1 to illustrate how to create side-by-side box-and-whisker plots with notches:

```
title 'Analysis of Airline Departure Delays';
title2 'Using the NOTCHES Option';
proc boxplot data=times;
   plot delay * day /
               boxstyle = schematicid
               cboxfill = ywh
               nohlabel
               notches
               cboxes   = dagr
               cframe   = vligb
               idcolor  = salmon
               vaxis    = axis1;
   id reason;
   label delay = 'Delay in Minutes';
run;
```

The notches, requested with the NOTCHES option, measure the significance of the difference between two medians. The medians of two box plots are significantly different at approximately the 0.05 level if the corresponding notches do not overlap.

For example, in Output 18.3.1, the median for December 20 is significantly different from the median for December 24.

Output 18.3.1. Notched Side-by-Side Box-and-Whisker Plots

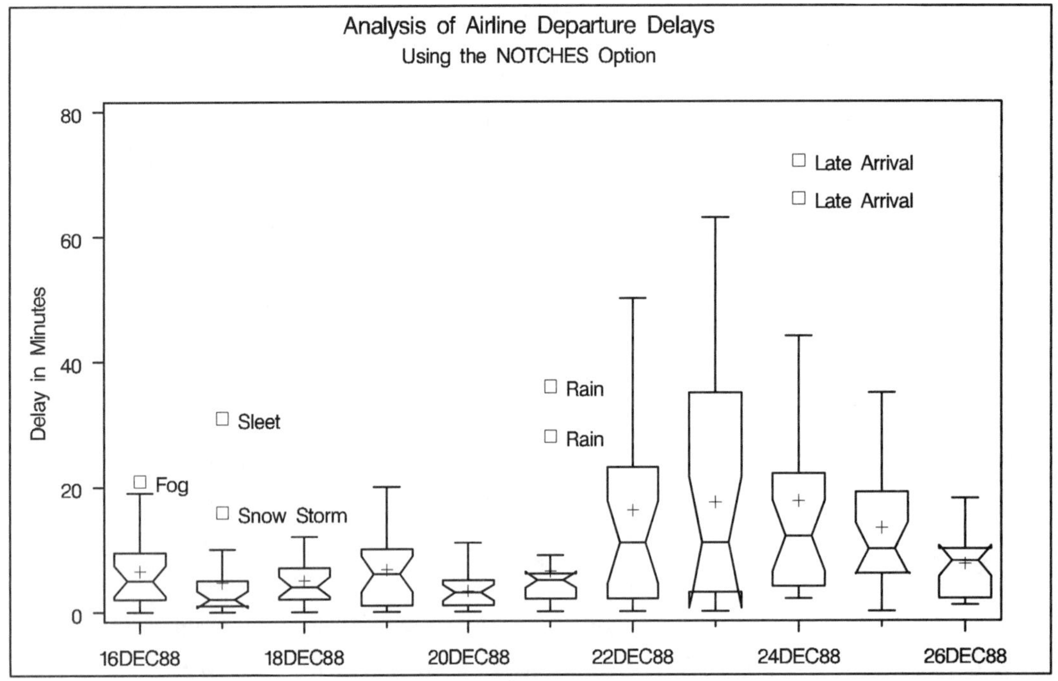

Example 18.4. Creating Box-and-Whisker Plots with Varying Widths

The following example shows how to create a box plot with box-and-whisker plots whose widths vary proportionately with the group size. The following statements create a SAS data set named Times2 that contains flight departure delays (in minutes) recorded daily for eight consecutive days:

```
data Times2;
   label delay = 'Delay in Minutes';
   informat day date7. ;
   format   day date7. ;
   input day @ ;
   do flight=1 to 25;
      input delay @ ;
      output;
      end;
datalines;
01MAR90  12   4   2   2  15   8   0  11   0   0   0  12   3
          .   2   3   5   0   6  25   7   4   9   5  10
02MAR90   1   .   3   .   0   1   5   0   .   .   1   5   7
          .   7   2   2  16   2   1   3   1  31   .   0
03MAR90   6   8   4   2   3   2   7   6  11   3   2   7   0
          1  10   2   5  12   8   6   2   7   2   4   5
04MAR90  12   6   9   0  15   7   1   1   0   2   5   6   5
         14   7  21   8   1  14   3  11   0   1  11   7
```

```
05MAR90   2   1   0   4   .   6   2   2   1   4   1  11   .
          1   0   .   5   5   .   2   3   6   6   4   0
06MAR90   8   6   5   2   9   7   4   2   5   1   2   2   4
          2   5   1   3   9   7   8   1   0   4  26  27
07MAR90   9   6   6   2   7   8   .   .  10   8   0   2   4
          3   .   .   .   7   .   6   4   0   .   .   .
08MAR90   1   6   6   2   8   8   5   3   5   0   8   2   4
          2   5   1   6   4   5  10   2   0   4   1   1
;
```

The following statements create the box plot shown in Output 18.4.1:

```
goptions ftext=swiss;
title 'Analysis of Airline Departure Delays';
title2 'Using the BOXWIDTHSCALE= Option';

proc boxplot data=Times2;
   plot delay * day /
                boxwidthscale = 1
                boxstyle      = schematic
                nohlabel
                cframe        = vligb
                cboxes        = dagr
                cboxfill      = ywh
                idcolor       = salmon
                vaxis         = axis1;
run;
```

The BOXWIDTHSCALE=*value* option specifies that the width of box plots is to vary proportionately to a particular function of the group size n. The function is determined by the *value* and is identified on the plot with a legend if the BWSLEGEND option is specified. The BOXWIDTHSCALE= option is useful in situations where the group sizes vary widely.

Output 18.4.1. Box Plot with Box-and-Whisker Plots of Varying Widths

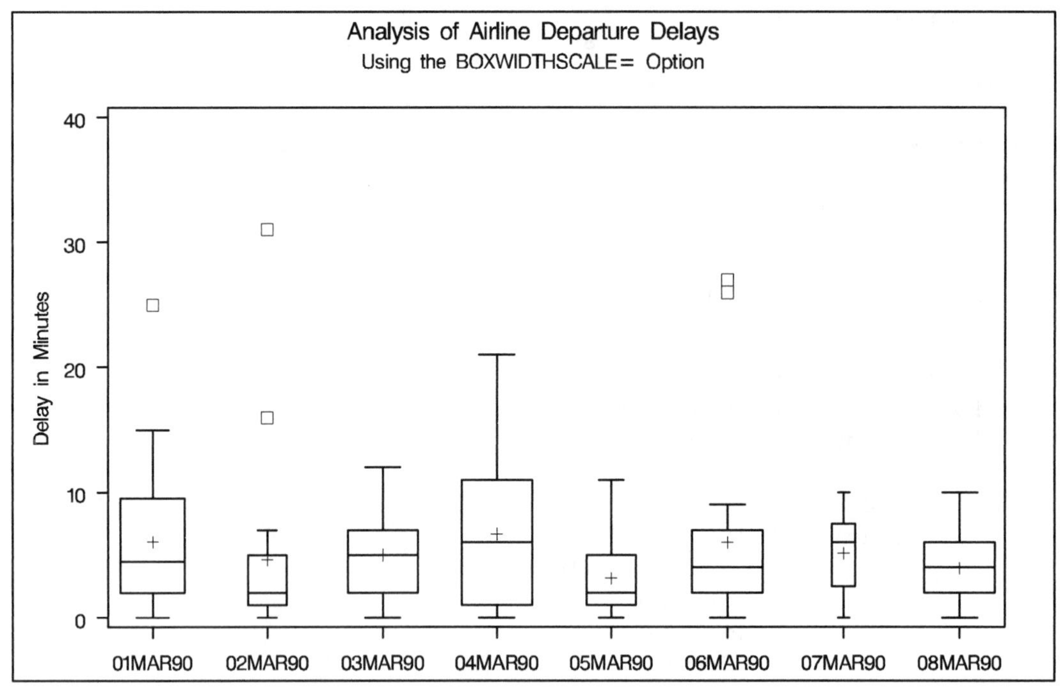

References

McGill, R., Tukey, J. W., and Larsen, W. A. (1978), "Variations of Box Plots," *The American Statistician,* 32, 12–16.

Tukey, J. W. (1977), *Exploratory Data Analysis*, Reading, MA: Addison-Wesley.

Chapter 19
The CALIS Procedure

Chapter Table of Contents

Chapter 19
The CALIS Procedure

Overview

Structural equation modeling using covariance analysis is an important statistical tool in economics and behavioral sciences. Structural equations express relationships among several variables that can be either directly observed variables (manifest variables) or unobserved hypothetical variables (latent variables). For an introduction to latent variable models, refer to Loehlin (1987), Bollen (1989b), Everitt (1984), or Long (1983); and for manifest variables, refer to Fuller (1987).

In structural models, as opposed to functional models, all variables are taken to be random rather than having fixed levels. For maximum likelihood (default) and generalized least-squares estimation in PROC CALIS, the random variables are assumed to have an approximately multivariate normal distribution. Nonnormality, especially high kurtosis, can produce poor estimates and grossly incorrect standard errors and hypothesis tests, even in large samples. Consequently, the assumption of normality is much more important than in models with nonstochastic exogenous variables. You should remove outliers and consider transformations of nonnormal variables before using PROC CALIS with maximum likelihood (default) or generalized least-squares estimation. If the number of observations is sufficiently large, Browne's asymptotically distribution-free (ADF) estimation method can be used.

You can use the CALIS procedure to estimate parameters and test hypotheses for constrained and unconstrained problems in

- multiple and multivariate linear regression
- linear measurement-error models
- path analysis and causal modeling
- simultaneous equation models with reciprocal causation
- exploratory and confirmatory factor analysis of any order
- canonical correlation
- a wide variety of other (non)linear latent variable models

The parameters are estimated using the criteria of

- unweighted least squares (ULS)
- generalized least squares (GLS, with optional weight matrix input)
- maximum likelihood (ML, for multivariate normal data)

- weighted least squares (WLS, ADF, with optional weight matrix input)
- diagonally weighted least squares (DWLS, with optional weight matrix input)

The default weight matrix for generalized least-squares estimation is the sample covariance or correlation matrix. The default weight matrix for weighted least-squares estimation is an estimate of the asymptotic covariance matrix of the sample covariance or correlation matrix. In this case, weighted least-squares estimation is equivalent to Browne's (1982, 1984) asymptotic distribution-free estimation. The default weight matrix for diagonally weighted least-squares estimation is an estimate of the asymptotic variances of the input sample covariance or correlation matrix. You can also use an input data set to specify the weight matrix in GLS, WLS, and DWLS estimation.

You can specify the model in several ways:

- You can do a constrained (confirmatory) first-order factor analysis or component analysis using the FACTOR statement.
- You can specify simple path models using an easily formulated list-type RAM statement similar to that originally developed by J. McArdle (McArdle and McDonald 1984).
- If you have a set of structural equations to describe the model, you can use an equation-type LINEQS statement similar to that originally developed by P. Bentler (1985).
- You can analyze a broad family of matrix models using COSAN and MATRIX statements that are similar to the COSAN program of R. McDonald and C. Fraser (McDonald 1978, 1980). It enables you to specify complex matrix models including nonlinear equation models and higher-order factor models.

You can specify linear and nonlinear equality and inequality constraints on the parameters with several different statements, depending on the type of input. Lagrange multiplier test indices are computed for simple constant and equality parameter constraints and for active boundary constraints. General equality and inequality constraints can be formulated using program statements. For more information, see the "SAS Program Statements" section on page 514.

PROC CALIS offers a variety of methods for the automatic generation of initial values for the optimization process:

- two-stage least-squares estimation
- instrumental variable factor analysis
- approximate factor analysis
- ordinary least-squares estimation
- McDonald's (McDonald and Hartmann 1992) method

In many common applications, these initial values prevent computational problems and save computer time.

Because numerical problems can occur in the (non)linearly constrained optimization process, the CALIS procedure offers several optimization algorithms:

- Levenberg-Marquardt algorithm (Moré, 1978)
- trust region algorithm (Gay 1983)
- Newton-Raphson algorithm with line search
- ridge-stabilized Newton-Raphson algorithm
- various quasi-Newton and dual quasi-Newton algorithms: Broyden-Fletcher-Goldfarb-Shanno and Davidon-Fletcher-Powell, including a sequential quadratic programming algorithm for processing nonlinear equality and inequality constraints
- various conjugate gradient algorithms: automatic restart algorithm of Powell (1977), Fletcher-Reeves, Polak-Ribiere, and conjugate descent algorithm of Fletcher (1980)

The quasi-Newton and conjugate gradient algorithms can be modified by several line-search methods. All of the optimization techniques can impose simple boundary and general linear constraints on the parameters. Only the dual quasi-Newton algorithm is able to impose general nonlinear equality and inequality constraints.

The procedure creates an OUTRAM= output data set that completely describes the model (except for program statements) and also contains parameter estimates. This data set can be used as input for another execution of PROC CALIS. Small model changes can be made by editing this data set, so you can exploit the old parameter estimates as starting values in a subsequent analysis. An OUTEST= data set contains information on the optimal parameter estimates (parameter estimates, gradient, Hessian, projected Hessian and Hessian of Lagrange function for constrained optimization, the information matrix, and standard errors). The OUTEST= data set can be used as an INEST= data set to provide starting values and boundary and linear constraints for the parameters. An OUTSTAT= data set contains residuals and, for exploratory factor analysis, the rotated and unrotated factor loadings.

Automatic variable selection (using only those variables from the input data set that are used in the model specification) is performed in connection with the RAM and LINEQS input statements or when these models are recognized in an input model file. Also in these cases, the covariances of the exogenous manifest variables are recognized as given constants. With the PREDET option, you can display the predetermined pattern of constant and variable elements in the predicted model matrix before the minimization process starts. For more information, see the section "Automatic Variable Selection" on page 548 and the section "Exogenous Manifest Variables" on page 549.

PROC CALIS offers an analysis of linear dependencies in the information matrix (approximate Hessian matrix) that may be helpful in detecting unidentified models. You also can save the information matrix and the approximate covariance matrix of the parameter estimates (inverse of the information matrix), together with parameter estimates, gradient, and approximate standard errors, in an output data set for further analysis.

PROC CALIS does not provide the analysis of multiple samples with different sample size or a generalized algorithm for missing values in the data. However, the analysis of multiple samples with equal sample size can be performed by the analysis of a moment supermatrix containing the individual moment matrices as block diagonal submatrices.

Structural Equation Models

The Generalized COSAN Model

PROC CALIS can analyze matrix models of the form

$$\mathbf{C} = \mathbf{F}_1\mathbf{P}_1\mathbf{F}_1' + \cdots + \mathbf{F}_m\mathbf{P}_m\mathbf{F}_m'$$

where $\mathbf{C}$ is a symmetric correlation or covariance matrix, each matrix $\mathbf{F}_k$, $k = 1, \ldots, m$, is the product of $n(k)$ matrices $\mathbf{F}_{k_1}, \ldots, \mathbf{F}_{k_{n(k)}}$, and each matrix $\mathbf{P}_k$ is symmetric, that is,

$$\mathbf{F}_k = \mathbf{F}_{k_1} \cdots \mathbf{F}_{k_{n(k)}} \quad \text{and} \quad \mathbf{P}_k = \mathbf{P}_k', \quad k = 1, \ldots, m$$

The matrices $\mathbf{F}_{k_j}$ and $\mathbf{P}_k$ in the model are parameterized by the matrices $\mathbf{G}_{k_j}$ and $\mathbf{Q}_k$

$$\mathbf{F}_{k_j} = \left\{ \begin{array}{c} \mathbf{G}_{k_j} \\ \mathbf{G}_{k_j}^{-1} \\ (\mathbf{I} - \mathbf{G}_{k_j})^{-1} \end{array} \right. \quad j = 1, \ldots, n(k) \qquad \text{and} \qquad \mathbf{P}_k = \left\{ \begin{array}{c} \mathbf{Q}_k \\ \mathbf{Q}_k^{-1} \end{array} \right.$$

where you can specify the type of matrix desired.

The matrices $\mathbf{G}_{k_j}$ and $\mathbf{Q}_k$ can contain

- constant values
- parameters to be estimated
- values computed from parameters via programming statements

The parameters can be summarized in a parameter vector $\mathbf{X} = (x_1, \ldots, x_t)$. For a given covariance or correlation matrix $\mathbf{C}$, PROC CALIS computes the unweighted least-squares (ULS), generalized least-squares (GLS), maximum likelihood (ML), weighted least-squares (WLS), or diagonally weighted least-squares (DWLS) estimates of the vector $\mathbf{X}$.

Some Special Cases of the Generalized COSAN Model

Original COSAN (Covariance Structure Analysis) Model (McDonald 1978, 1980)

Covariance Structure:

$$\mathbf{C} = \mathbf{F}_1 \cdots \mathbf{F}_n \mathbf{P} \mathbf{F}'_n \cdots \mathbf{F}'_1$$

RAM (Reticular Action) Model (McArdle 1980; McArdle and McDonald 1984)

Structural Equation Model:

$$\mathbf{v} = \mathbf{A}\mathbf{v} + \mathbf{u}$$

where $\mathbf{A}$ is a matrix of coefficients, and $\mathbf{v}$ and $\mathbf{u}$ are vectors of random variables. The variables in $\mathbf{v}$ and $\mathbf{u}$ can be manifest or latent variables. The endogenous variables corresponding to the components in $\mathbf{v}$ are expressed as a linear combination of the remaining variables and a residual component in $\mathbf{u}$ with covariance matrix $\mathbf{P}$.

Covariance Structure:

$$\mathbf{C} = \mathbf{J}(\mathbf{I} - \mathbf{A})^{-1}\mathbf{P}((\mathbf{I} - \mathbf{A})^{-1})'\mathbf{J}'$$

with selection matrix $\mathbf{J}$ and

$$\mathbf{C} = \mathcal{E}\{\mathbf{J}\mathbf{v}\mathbf{v}'\mathbf{J}'\} \qquad \text{and} \qquad \mathbf{P} = \mathcal{E}\{\mathbf{u}\mathbf{u}'\}$$

LINEQS (Linear Equations) Model (Bentler and Weeks 1980)

Structural Equation Model:

$$\eta = \beta\eta + \gamma\xi$$

where β and γ are coefficient matrices, and η and ξ are vectors of random variables. The components of η correspond to the endogenous variables; the components of ξ correspond to the exogenous variables and to error variables. The variables in η and ξ can be manifest or latent variables. The endogenous variables in η are expressed as a linear combination of the remaining endogenous variables, of the exogenous variables of ξ, and of a residual component in ξ. The coefficient matrix β describes the relationships among the endogenous variables of η, and $I - \beta$ should be nonsingular. The coefficient matrix γ describes the relationships between the endogenous variables of η and the exogenous and error variables of ξ.

Covariance Structure:

$$\mathbf{C} = \mathbf{J}(\mathbf{I}-\mathbf{B})^{-1}\mathbf{\Gamma\Phi\Gamma}'((\mathbf{I}-\mathbf{B})^{-1})'\mathbf{J}'$$

with selection matrix $\mathbf{J}$, $\mathbf{\Phi} = \mathcal{E}\{\xi\xi'\}$, and

$$\mathbf{B} = \begin{pmatrix} \beta & 0 \\ 0 & 0 \end{pmatrix} \quad \text{and} \quad \mathbf{\Gamma} = \begin{pmatrix} \gamma \\ \mathbf{I} \end{pmatrix}$$

Keesling - Wiley - Jöreskog LISREL (Linear Structural Relationship) Model

Structural Equation Model and Measurement Models:

$$\eta = \mathbf{B}\eta + \mathbf{\Gamma}\xi + \zeta \quad , \qquad \mathbf{y} = \mathbf{\Lambda}_y\eta + \varepsilon \quad , \qquad \mathbf{x} = \mathbf{\Lambda}_x\xi + \delta$$

where η and ξ are vectors of latent variables (factors), and $\mathbf{x}$ and $\mathbf{y}$ are vectors of manifest variables. The components of η correspond to endogenous latent variables; the components of ξ correspond to exogenous latent variables. The endogenous and exogenous latent variables are connected by a system of linear equations (the structural model) with coefficient matrices $\mathbf{B}$ and $\mathbf{\Gamma}$ and an error vector ζ. It is assumed that matrix $\mathbf{I}-\mathbf{B}$ is nonsingular. The random vectors $\mathbf{y}$ and $\mathbf{x}$ correspond to manifest variables that are related to the latent variables η and ξ by two systems of linear equations (the measurement model) with coefficients $\mathbf{\Lambda}_y$ and $\mathbf{\Lambda}_x$ and with measurement errors ε and δ.

Covariance Structure:

$$\begin{aligned} \mathbf{C} &= \mathbf{J}(\mathbf{I}-\mathbf{A})^{-1}\mathbf{P}((\mathbf{I}-\mathbf{A})^{-1})'\mathbf{J}' \\ A &= \begin{pmatrix} 0 & 0 & \mathbf{\Lambda}_y & 0 \\ 0 & 0 & 0 & \mathbf{\Lambda}_x \\ 0 & 0 & \mathbf{B} & \mathbf{\Gamma} \\ 0 & 0 & 0 & 0 \end{pmatrix} \quad \text{and} \quad P = \begin{pmatrix} \mathbf{\Theta}_\varepsilon & & & \\ & \mathbf{\Theta}_\delta & & \\ & & \mathbf{\Psi} & \\ & & & \mathbf{\Phi} \end{pmatrix} \end{aligned}$$

with selection matrix $\mathbf{J}$, $\mathbf{\Phi} = \mathcal{E}\{\xi\xi'\}$, $\mathbf{\Psi} = \mathcal{E}\{\zeta\zeta'\}$, $\mathbf{\Theta}_\delta = \mathcal{E}\{\delta\delta'\}$, and $\mathbf{\Theta}_\varepsilon = \mathcal{E}\{\varepsilon\varepsilon'\}$.

Higher-Order Factor Analysis Models

First-order model:

$$\mathbf{C} = \mathbf{F}_1\mathbf{P}_1\mathbf{F}_1' + \mathbf{U}_1^2$$

Second-order model:

$$\mathbf{C} = \mathbf{F}_1\mathbf{F}_2\mathbf{P}_2\mathbf{F}_2'\mathbf{F}_1' + \mathbf{F}_1\mathbf{U}_2^2\mathbf{F}_1' + \mathbf{U}_1^2$$

First-Order Autoregressive Longitudinal Factor Model

Example of McDonald (1980): k=3: Occasions of Measurement; n=3: Variables (Tests); m=2: Common Factors

$$\mathbf{C} = \mathbf{F}_1\mathbf{F}_2\mathbf{F}_3\mathbf{L}\mathbf{F}_3^{-1}\mathbf{F}_2^{-1}\mathbf{P}(\mathbf{F}_2^{-1})'(\mathbf{F}_3^{-1})'\mathbf{L}'\mathbf{F}_3'\mathbf{F}_2'\mathbf{F}_1' + \mathbf{U}^2$$

$$F_1 = \begin{pmatrix} B_1 & & \\ & B_2 & \\ & & B_3 \end{pmatrix}, \quad F_2 = \begin{pmatrix} I_2 & & \\ & D_2 & \\ & & D_2 \end{pmatrix}, \quad F_3 = \begin{pmatrix} I_2 & & \\ & I_2 & \\ & & D_3 \end{pmatrix}$$

$$L = \begin{pmatrix} I_2 & o & o \\ I_2 & I_2 & o \\ I_2 & I_2 & I_2 \end{pmatrix}, \quad P = \begin{pmatrix} I_2 & & \\ & S_2 & \\ & & S_3 \end{pmatrix}, \quad U = \begin{pmatrix} U_{11} & U_{12} & U_{13} \\ U_{21} & U_{22} & U_{23} \\ U_{31} & U_{32} & U_{33} \end{pmatrix}$$

$$S_2 = I_2 - D_2^2 \ , \qquad S_3 = I_2 - D_3^2$$

For more information on this model, see Example 19.6 on page 623.

A Structural Equation Example

This example from Wheaton et al. (1977) illustrates the relationships among the RAM, LINEQS, and LISREL models. Different structural models for these data are in Jöreskog and Sörbom (1985) and in Bentler (1985, p. 28). The data set contains covariances among six (manifest) variables collected from 932 people in rural regions of Illinois:

Variable 1: $V1, y_1$: Anomia 1967

Variable 2: $V2, y_2$: Powerlessness 1967

Variable 3: $V3, y_3$: Anomia 1971

Variable 4: $V4, y_4$: Powerlessness 1971

Variable 5: $V5, x_1$: Education (years of schooling)

Variable 6: $V6, x_2$: Duncan's Socioeconomic Index (SEI)

It is assumed that anomia and powerlessness are indicators of an alienation factor and that education and SEI are indicators for a socioeconomic status (SES) factor. Hence, the analysis contains three latent variables:

Variable 7: $F1, \eta_1$: Alienation 1967

Variable 8: $F2, \eta_2$: Alienation 1971

Variable 9: $F3, \xi_1$: Socioeconomic Status (SES)

The following path diagram shows the structural model used in Bentler (1985, p. 29) and slightly modified in Jöreskog and Sörbom (1985, p. 56). In this notation for the path diagram, regression coefficients between the variables are indicated as one-headed arrows. Variances and covariances among the variables are indicated as two-headed arrows. Indicating error variances and covariances as two-headed arrows with the same source and destination (McArdle 1988; McDonald 1985) is helpful in transforming the path diagram to RAM model list input for the CALIS procedure.

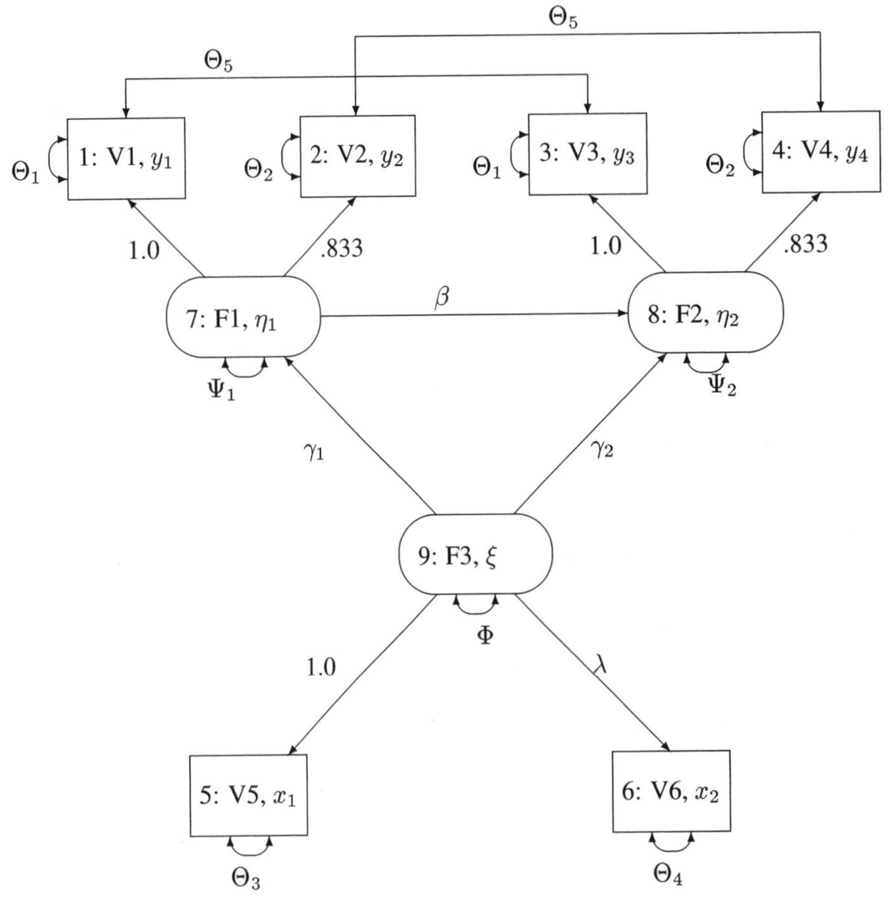

Figure 19.1. Path Diagram of Stability and Alienation Example

Variables in Figure 19.1 are as follows:

Variable 1:	$V1, y_1$: Anomia 1967
Variable 2:	$V2, y_2$: Powerlessness 1967
Variable 3:	$V3, y_3$: Anomia 1971
Variable 4:	$V4, y_4$: Powerlessness 1971
Variable 5:	$V5, x_1$: Education (years of schooling)
Variable 6:	$V6, x_2$: Duncan's Socioeconomic Index (SEI)
Variable 7:	$F1, \eta_1$: Alienation 1967
Variable 8:	$F2, \eta_2$: Alienation 1971
Variable 9:	$F3, \xi_1$: Socioeconomic Status (SES)

RAM Model

The vector $\mathbf{v}$ contains the six manifest variables $v_1 = V1, \ldots, v_6 = V6$ and the three latent variables $v_7 = F1, v_8 = F2, v_9 = F3$. The vector $\mathbf{u}$ contains the corresponding error variables $u_1 = E1, \ldots, u_6 = E6$ and $u_7 = D1, u_8 = D2, u_9 = D3$. The path diagram corresponds to the following set of structural equations of the RAM model:

$$\begin{aligned}
v_1 &= 1.000 v_7 + u_1 \\
v_2 &= 0.833 v_7 + u_2 \\
v_3 &= 1.000 v_8 + u_3 \\
v_4 &= 0.833 v_8 + u_4 \\
v_5 &= 1.000 v_9 + u_5 \\
v_6 &= \lambda v_9 + u_6 \\
v_7 &= \gamma_1 v_9 + u_7 \\
v_8 &= \beta v_7 + \gamma_2 v_9 + u_8 \\
v_9 &= u_9
\end{aligned}$$

This gives the matrices $\mathbf{A}$ and $\mathbf{P}$ in the RAM model:

$$\mathbf{A} = \begin{pmatrix}
o & o & o & o & o & o & 1.000 & o & o \\
o & o & o & o & o & o & 0.833 & o & o \\
o & o & o & o & o & o & o & 1.000 & o \\
o & o & o & o & o & o & o & 0.833 & o \\
o & o & o & o & o & o & o & o & 1.000 \\
o & o & o & o & o & o & o & o & \lambda \\
o & o & o & o & o & o & o & o & \gamma_1 \\
o & o & o & o & o & o & \beta & o & \gamma_2 \\
o & o & o & o & o & o & o & o & o
\end{pmatrix}$$

$$\mathbf{P} = \begin{pmatrix}
\theta_1 & o & \theta_5 & o & o & o & o & o & o \\
o & \theta_2 & o & \theta_5 & o & o & o & o & o \\
\theta_5 & o & \theta_1 & o & o & o & o & o & o \\
o & \theta_5 & o & \theta_2 & o & o & o & o & o \\
o & o & o & o & \theta_3 & o & o & o & o \\
o & o & o & o & o & \theta_4 & o & o & o \\
o & o & o & o & o & o & \psi_1 & o & o \\
o & o & o & o & o & o & o & \psi_2 & o \\
o & o & o & o & o & o & o & o & \phi
\end{pmatrix}$$

The RAM model input specification of this example for the CALIS procedure is in the "RAM Model Specification" section on page 451.

LINEQS Model

The vector η contains the six endogenous manifest variables $V1, \ldots, V6$ and the two endogenous latent variables $F1$ and $F2$. The vector ξ contains the exogenous error variables $E1, \ldots, E6$, $D1$, and $D2$ and the exogenous latent variable $F3$. The path diagram corresponds to the following set of structural equations of the LINEQS model:

$$\begin{aligned}
V1 &= 1.0F1 + E1 \\
V2 &= .833F1 + E2 \\
V3 &= 1.0F2 + E3 \\
V4 &= .833F2 + E4 \\
V5 &= 1.0F3 + E5 \\
V6 &= \lambda F3 + E6 \\
F1 &= \gamma_1 F3 + D1 \\
F2 &= \beta F1 + \gamma_2 F3 + D2
\end{aligned}$$

This gives the matrices $\boldsymbol{\beta}$, γ and $\boldsymbol{\Phi}$ in the LINEQS model:

$$\boldsymbol{\beta} = \begin{pmatrix}
o & o & o & o & o & o & 1. & o \\
o & o & o & o & o & o & .833 & o \\
o & o & o & o & o & o & o & 1. \\
o & o & o & o & o & o & o & .833 \\
o & o & o & o & o & o & o & o \\
o & o & o & o & o & o & o & o \\
o & o & o & o & o & o & o & o \\
o & o & o & o & o & o & \beta & o
\end{pmatrix}, \quad \gamma = \begin{pmatrix}
1 & o & o & o & o & o & o & o & o \\
o & 1 & o & o & o & o & o & o & o \\
o & o & 1 & o & o & o & o & o & o \\
o & o & o & 1 & o & o & o & o & o \\
o & o & o & o & 1 & o & o & o & 1. \\
o & o & o & o & o & 1 & o & o & \lambda \\
o & o & o & o & o & o & 1 & o & \gamma_1 \\
o & o & o & o & o & o & o & 1 & \gamma_2
\end{pmatrix}$$

$$\boldsymbol{\Phi} = \begin{pmatrix}
\theta_1 & o & \theta_5 & o & o & o & o & o & o \\
o & \theta_2 & o & \theta_5 & o & o & o & o & o \\
\theta_5 & o & \theta_1 & o & o & o & o & o & o \\
o & \theta_5 & o & \theta_2 & o & o & o & o & o \\
o & o & o & o & \theta_3 & o & o & o & o \\
o & o & o & o & o & \theta_4 & o & o & o \\
o & o & o & o & o & o & \psi_1 & o & o \\
o & o & o & o & o & o & o & \psi_2 & o \\
o & o & o & o & o & o & o & o & \phi
\end{pmatrix}$$

The LINEQS model input specification of this example for the CALIS procedure is in the section "LINEQS Model Specification" on page 450.

LISREL Model

The vector $\mathbf{y}$ contains the four endogenous manifest variables $y_1 = V1, \ldots, y_4 = V4$, and the vector $\mathbf{x}$ contains the exogenous manifest variables $x_1 = V5$ and $x_2 = V6$. The vector $\boldsymbol{\varepsilon}$ contains the error variables $\varepsilon_1 = E1, \ldots, \varepsilon_4 = E4$ corresponding to $\mathbf{y}$, and the vector $\boldsymbol{\delta}$ contains the error variables $\delta_1 = E5$ and $\delta_2 = E6$ corresponding to $\mathbf{x}$. The vector $\boldsymbol{\eta}$ contains the endogenous latent variables (factors) $\eta_1 = F1$ and $\eta_2 = F2$, while the vector $\boldsymbol{\xi}$ contains the exogenous latent variable (factor) $\xi_1 = F3$. The vector $\boldsymbol{\zeta}$ contains the errors $\zeta_1 = D1$ and $\zeta_2 = D2$ in the equations (disturbance terms) corresponding to $\boldsymbol{\eta}$. The path diagram corresponds to the following set of structural equations of the LISREL model:

$$\begin{aligned}
y_1 &= 1.0\eta_1 + \epsilon_1 \\
y_2 &= .833\eta_1 + \epsilon_2 \\
y_3 &= 1.0\eta_2 + \epsilon_3 \\
y_4 &= .833\eta_2 + \epsilon_4 \\
x_1 &= 1.0\xi_1 + \delta_1 \\
x_2 &= \lambda\xi_1 + \delta_2 \\
\eta_1 &= \gamma_1\xi_1 + \zeta_1 \\
\eta_2 &= \beta\eta_1 + \gamma_2\xi_1 + \zeta_2
\end{aligned}$$

This gives the matrices $\mathbf{\Lambda}_y$, $\mathbf{\Lambda}_x$, $\mathbf{B}$, $\mathbf{\Gamma}$, and $\mathbf{\Phi}$ in the LISREL model:

$$\mathbf{\Lambda}_y = \begin{pmatrix} 1. & o \\ .833 & o \\ o & 1. \\ o & .833 \end{pmatrix}, \mathbf{\Lambda}_x = \begin{pmatrix} 1. \\ \lambda \end{pmatrix}, \mathbf{B} = \begin{pmatrix} o & o \\ \beta & o \end{pmatrix}, \mathbf{\Gamma} = \begin{pmatrix} \gamma_1 \\ \gamma_2 \end{pmatrix}$$

$$\mathbf{\Theta}_\varepsilon^2 = \begin{pmatrix} \theta_1 & o & \theta_5 & o \\ o & \theta_2 & o & \theta_5 \\ \theta_5 & o & \theta_1 & o \\ o & \theta_5 & o & \theta_2 \end{pmatrix}, \mathbf{\Theta}_\delta^2 = \begin{pmatrix} \theta_3 & o \\ \theta_4 & o \end{pmatrix}, \mathbf{\Psi} = \begin{pmatrix} \psi_1 & o \\ o & \psi_2 \end{pmatrix}, \mathbf{\Phi} = (\phi)$$

The CALIS procedure does not provide a LISREL model input specification. However, any model that can be specified by the LISREL model can also be specified by using the COSAN, LINEQS, or RAM model specifications in PROC CALIS.

Getting Started

There are four sets of statements available in the CALIS procedure to specify a model. Since a LISREL analysis can be performed easily by using a RAM, COSAN, or LINEQS statement, there is no specific LISREL input form available in the CALIS procedure.

For COSAN-style input, you can specify the following statements:

COSAN *analysis model in matrix notation* ;
    MATRIX *definition of matrix elements* ;
    VARNAMES *names of additional variables* ;
    BOUNDS *boundary constraints* ;
    PARAMETERS *parameter names from program statements* ;

For linear equations input, you can specify the following statements:

LINEQS *analysis model in equations notation* ;
    STD *variance pattern* ;
    COV *covariance pattern* ;
    BOUNDS *boundary constraints* ;
    PARAMETERS *parameter names from program statements* ;

For RAM-style input, you can specify the following statements:

RAM *analysis model in list notation* ;
    VARNAMES *names of latent and error variables* ;
    BOUNDS *boundary constraints* ;
    PARAMETERS *parameter names from program statements* ;

For (confirmatory) factor analysis input, you can specify the following statements:

FACTOR *options* ;
    MATRIX *definition of matrix elements* ;
    VARNAMES *names of latent and residual variables* ;
    BOUNDS *boundary constraints* ;
    PARAMETERS *parameter names from program statements* ;

The model can also be obtained from an INRAM= data set, which is usually a version of an OUTRAM= data set produced by a previous PROC CALIS analysis (and possibly modified).

If no INRAM= data set is specified, you must use one of the four statements that defines the input form of the analysis model: COSAN, RAM, LINEQS, or FACTOR.

COSAN Model Specification

You specify the model for a generalized COSAN analysis with a COSAN statement and one or more MATRIX statements. The COSAN statement determines the name, dimension, and type (identity, diagonal, symmetric, upper, lower, general, inverse, and so forth) of each matrix in the model. You can specify the values of the constant elements in each matrix and give names and initial values to the elements that are to be estimated as parameters or functions of parameters using MATRIX statements. The resulting displayed output is in matrix form.

The following statements define the structural model of the alienation example as a COSAN model:

```
Cosan J(9, Ide) * A(9, Gen, Imi) * P(9, Sym);
Matrix A
            [ ,7] = 1. .833  5 * 0. Beta (.5) ,
            [ ,8] = 2 * 0.  1.   .833 ,
            [ ,9] = 4 * 0.  1.  Lamb Gam1-Gam2 (.5 2 * -.5);
Matrix P
            [1,1] = The1-The2 The1-The4 (6 * 3.) ,
            [7,7] = Psi1-Psi2 Phi (2 * 4. 6.) ,
            [3,1] = The5 (.2) ,
            [4,2] = The5 (.2) ;
```

The matrix model specified in the COSAN statement is the RAM model

$$\mathbf{C} = \mathbf{J}(\mathbf{I} - \mathbf{A})^{-1}\mathbf{P}((\mathbf{I} - \mathbf{A})^{-1})'\mathbf{J}'$$

with selection matrix $\mathbf{J}$ and

$$\mathbf{C} = \mathcal{E}\{\mathbf{J}\mathbf{v}\mathbf{v}'\mathbf{J}'\}, \qquad \mathbf{P} = \mathcal{E}\{\mathbf{u}\mathbf{u}'\}$$

The COSAN statement must contain only the matrices up to the central matrix $\mathbf{P}$ because of the symmetry of each matrix term in a COSAN model. Each matrix name is followed by one to three arguments in parentheses. The first argument is the number of columns. The second and third arguments are optional, and they specify the form of the matrix. The selection matrix $\mathbf{J}$ in the RAM model is specified by the 6×9 identity (IDE) (sub)matrix $\mathbf{J}$ because the first six variables in vector $\mathbf{v}$ correspond to the six manifest variables in the data set. The 9×9 parameter matrix $\mathbf{A}$ has a general (GEN) form and is used as $(\mathbf{I} - \mathbf{A})^{-1}$ in the analysis, as indicated by the identity-minus-inverse (IMI) argument. The central 9×9 matrix P is specified as a symmetric (SYM) matrix.

The MATRIX statement for matrix $\mathbf{A}$ specifies the values in columns 7, 8, and 9, which correspond to the three latent variables $F1$, $F2$, and $F3$, in accordance with the RAM model. The other columns of $\mathbf{A}$ are assumed to be zero. The initial values for the parameter elements in $\mathbf{A}$ are chosen as in the path diagram to be

$$\lambda = \beta = .5, \qquad \gamma_1 = \gamma_2 = -.5$$

In accordance with matrix **P** of the RAM model and the path model, the nine diagonal elements of matrix **P** are parameters with initial values

$$\theta_1 = \theta_2 = \theta_3 = \theta_4 = 3, \quad \psi_1 = \psi_2 = 4, \quad \phi = 6$$

There are also two off-diagonal elements in each triangle of **P** that are constrained to be equal, and they have an initial value of 0.2.

See the section "COSAN Model Statement" on page 479 for more information about the COSAN statement.

LINEQS Model Specification

You can also describe the model by a set of linear equations combined with variance and covariance specifications, using notation similar to that originally developed by P. Bentler for his EQS program. The displayed output can be in either equation form or matrix form.

The following statements define the structural model of the alienation example as a LINEQS model:

```
Lineqs
     V1  =          F1                     + E1,
     V2  =      .833 F1                    + E2,
     V3  =          F2                     + E3,
     V4  =      .833 F2                    + E4,
     V5  =          F3                     + E5,
     V6  = Lamb (.5) F3                    + E6,
     F1  = Gam1(-.5) F3                    + D1,
     F2  = Beta (.5) F1 + Gam2(-.5) F3     + D2;
Std
     E1-E6  = The1-The2 The1-The4 (6 * 3.),
     D1-D2  = Psi1-Psi2 (2 * 4.),
     F3     = Phi (6.) ;
Cov
     E1 E3  = The5 (.2),
     E4 E2  = The5 (.2);
```

The LINEQS statement shows the equations in the section "LINEQS Model" on page 446, except that in this case the coefficients to be estimated can be followed (optionally) by the initial value to use in the optimization process. If you do not specify initial values for the parameters in a LINEQS statement, PROC CALIS tries to assign these values automatically. The endogenous variables used on the left side can be manifest variables (with names that must be defined by the input data set) or latent variables (which must have names starting with F). The variables used on the right side can be manifest variables, latent variables (with names that must start with F), or error variables (which must have names starting with an E or D). Commas separate the equations. The coefficients to be estimated are indicated by names. If no name is used, the coefficient is constant, either equal to a specified number or, if no number is used, equal to 1. The VAR statement in Bentler's notation is replaced here by the STD statement, because the VAR statement in PROC CALIS defines the subset of manifest variables in the data set to be analyzed. The variable names used in the STD or COV statement must be exogenous (that is, they should not occur on the left side of any equation). The STD and COV statements define the diagonal and off-diagonal elements in the **Φ** matrix. The parameter specifications in the STD and COV statements are separated by commas. Using k variable names on the left of an equal sign in a COV statement means that the parameter list on the right side refers to all $k(k-1)/2$ distinct variable pairs in the **Φ** matrix. Identical coefficient names indicate parameters constrained to be equal. You can also use prefix names to specify those parameters for which you do not need a precise name in any parameter constraint.

See the section "LINEQS Model Statement" on page 488 for more information about the precise syntax rules for a LINEQS statement.

RAM Model Specification

The RAM model allows a path diagram to be transcribed into a RAM statement in list form. The displayed output from the RAM statement is in matrix or list form.

The following statement defines the structural model of the alienation example as a RAM model:

```
Ram
        1  1  7  1.           ,
        1  2  7  .833         ,
        1  3  8  1.           ,
        1  4  8  .833         ,
        1  5  9  1.           ,
        1  6  9  .5     Lamb ,
        1  7  9  -.5    Gam1 ,
        1  8  7  .5     Beta ,
        1  8  9  -.5    Gam2 ,
        2  1  1  3.     The1 ,
        2  2  2  3.     The2 ,
        2  3  3  3.     The1 ,
        2  4  4  3.     The2 ,
        2  5  5  3.     The3 ,
        2  6  6  3.     The4 ,
        2  1  3  .2     The5 ,
        2  2  4  .2     The5 ,
        2  7  7  4.     Psi1 ,
        2  8  8  4.     Psi2 ,
        2  9  9  6.     Phi  ;
```

You must assign numbers to the nodes in the path diagram. In the path diagram of Figure 19.1, the boxes corresponding to the six manifest variables $V1, \ldots, V6$ are assigned the number of the variable in the covariance matrix (1, ... ,6); the circles corresponding to the three latent variables $F1$, $F2$, and $F3$ are given the numbers 7, 8, and 9. The path diagram contains 20 paths between the nine nodes; nine of the paths are one-headed arrows and eleven are two-headed arrows.

The RAM statement contains a list of items separated by commas. Each item corresponds to an arrow in the path diagram. The first entry in each item is the number of arrow heads (matrix number), the second entry shows where the arrow points to (row number), the third entry shows where the arrow comes from (column number), the fourth entry gives the (initial) value of the coefficient, and the fifth entry assigns a name if the path represents a parameter rather than a constant. If you specify the fifth entry as a parameter name, then the fourth list entry can be omitted, since PROC CALIS tries to assign an initial value to this parameter.

See the section "RAM Model Statement" on page 484 for more information about the RAM statement.

FACTOR Model Specification

You can specify the FACTOR statement to compute factor loadings $\mathbf{F}$ and unique variances $\mathbf{U}$ of an exploratory or confirmatory first-order factor (or component) analysis. By default, the factor correlation matrix $\mathbf{P}$ is an identity matrix.

$$\mathbf{C} = \mathbf{F}\mathbf{F}' + \mathbf{U}, \quad \mathbf{U} = diag$$

For a first-order confirmatory factor analysis, you can use MATRIX statements to define elements in the matrices $\mathbf{F}$, $\mathbf{P}$, and $\mathbf{U}$ of the more general model

$$\mathbf{C} = \mathbf{F}\mathbf{P}\mathbf{F}' + \mathbf{U}, \quad \mathbf{P} = \mathbf{P}', \quad \mathbf{U} = diag$$

To perform a component analysis, specify the COMPONENT option to constrain the matrix $\mathbf{U}$ to a zero matrix; that is, the model is replaced by

$$\mathbf{C} = \mathbf{F}\mathbf{F}'$$

Note that the rank of $\mathbf{F}\mathbf{F}'$ is equal to the number m of components in $\mathbf{F}$, and if m is smaller than the number of variables in the moment matrix $\mathbf{C}$, the matrix of predicted model values is singular and maximum likelihood estimates for $\mathbf{F}$ cannot be computed. You should compute ULS estimates in this case.

The HEYWOOD option constrains the diagonal elements of $\mathbf{U}$ to be nonnegative; that is, the model is replaced by

$$\mathbf{C} = \mathbf{F}\mathbf{F}' + \mathbf{U}^2, \quad \mathbf{U} = diag$$

If the factor loadings are unconstrained, they can be orthogonally rotated by one of the following methods:

- principal axes rotation
- quartimax
- varimax
- equamax
- parsimax

The most common approach to factor analysis consists of two steps:

1. Obtain estimates for factor loadings and unique variances.
2. Apply an orthogonal or oblique rotation method.

Most programs of factor analysis do not provide standard errors for the rotated factor loadings. PROC CALIS enables you to specify general linear and nonlinear equality and inequality constraints using the LINCON and NLINCON statements. You can specify the NLINCON statement to estimate orthogonal or oblique rotated factor loadings; refer to Browne and Du Toit (1992).

For default (exploratory) factor analysis, PROC CALIS computes initial estimates. If you use a MATRIX statement together with a FACTOR model specification, initial values are generally computed by McDonald's (McDonald and Hartmann 1992) method or are set by the START= option. See the section "FACTOR Model Statement" on page 493 and Example 19.3 for more information about the FACTOR statement.

Constrained Estimation

- Simple equality constraints, $x_i = c_i,\ c_i = const,$ and $x_i = x_j,$ can be defined in each model by specifying constants or using the same name for parameters constrained to be equal.
- BOUNDS statement: You can specify boundary constraints, $l_i \leq x_i \leq u_i,\ l_i,\ u_i = const,$ with the BOUNDS statement for the COSAN, LINEQS, and RAM models and in connection with an INRAM= data set. There may be serious convergence problems if negative values appear in the diagonal locations (variances) of the central model matrices during the minimization process. You can use the BOUNDS statement to constrain these parameters to have nonnegative values.
- LINCON statement: You can specify general linear equality and inequality constraints of the parameter estimates with the LINCON statement or by using an INEST= data set. The variables listed in the LINCON statements must be (a subset of) the model parameters. All optimization methods can be used with linear constraints.
- NLINCON statement: You can specify general nonlinear equality and inequality constraints of the parameter estimates with the NLINCON statement. The syntax of the NLINCON statement is almost the same as that for the BOUNDS statement with the exception that the BOUNDS statement can contain only names of the model parameters. However, the variables listed in the NLINCON statement can be defined by program statements. Only the quasi-Newton optimization method can be used when there are nonlinear constraints.
- Reparameterizing the Model: Complex linear equality and inequality constraints can be defined by means of program statements similar to those used in the DATA step. In this case, some of the parameters x_i are not elements of the matrices $\mathbf{G}_{kj}$ and $\mathbf{Q}_k$ but are instead defined in a PARAMETERS statement. Elements of the model matrices can then be computed by program statements as functions of parameters in the PARAMETERS statement. This approach is

similar to the classical COSAN program of R. McDonald, implemented by C. Fraser (McDonald 1978, 1980). One advantage of the CALIS procedure is that you need not supply code for the derivatives of the specified functions. The analytic derivatives of the user-written functions are computed automatically by PROC CALIS. The specified functions must be continuous and have continuous first-order partial derivatives. See the "SAS Program Statements" section on page 514 and the "Constrained Estimation Using Program Code" section on page 561 for more information about imposing linear and nonlinear restrictions on parameters by using program statements.

Although much effort has been made to implement reliable and numerically stable optimization methods, no practical algorithm exists that can always find the global optimum of a nonlinear function, especially when there are nonlinear constraints.

Syntax

PROC CALIS < *options* > ;
    COSAN *matrix model* ;
        MATRIX *matrix elements* ;
        VARNAMES *variables* ;
    LINEQS *model equations* ;
        STD *variance pattern* ;
        COV *covariance pattern* ;
    RAM *model list* ;
        VARNAMES *variables* ;
    FACTOR < *options* > ;
        MATRIX *matrix elements* ;
        VARNAMES *variables* ;
    BOUNDS *boundary constraints* ;
    BY *variables* ;
    FREQ *variable* ;
    LINCON *linear constraints* ;
    NLINCON *nonlinear constraints* ;
    NLOPTIONS *optimization options* ;
    PARAMETERS *parameters* ;
    PARTIAL *variables* ;
    STRUCTEQ *variables* ;
    VAR *variables* ;
    WEIGHT *variable* ;
    program statements

- If no INRAM= data set is specified, one of the four statements that defines the input form of the analysis model, COSAN, LINEQS, RAM, or FACTOR, must be used.
- The MATRIX statement can be used multiple times for the same or different matrices along with a COSAN or FACTOR statement. If the MATRIX

statement is used multiple times for the same matrix, later definitions override earlier ones.

- The STD and COV statements can be used only with the LINEQS model statement.
- You can formulate a generalized COSAN model using a COSAN statement. MATRIX statements can be used to define the elements of a matrix used in the COSAN statement. The input notation resembles the COSAN program of R. McDonald and C. Fraser (McDonald 1978, 1980).
- The RAM statement uses a simple list input that is especially suitable for describing J. McArdle's RAM analysis model (McArdle 1980, McArdle and McDonald 1984) for causal and path analysis problems.
- The LINEQS statement formulates the analysis model by means of a system of linear equations similar to P. Bentler's (1989) EQS program notation. The STD and COV statements can be used to define the variances and covariances corresponding to elements of matrix $\mathbf{\Phi}$ in the LINEQS model.
- A FACTOR statement can be used to compute a first-order exploratory or confirmatory factor (or component) analysis. The analysis of a simple exploratory factor analysis model performed by PROC CALIS is not as efficient as one performed by the FACTOR procedure. The CALIS procedure is designed for more general structural problems, and it needs significantly more computation time for a simple unrestricted factor or component analysis than does PROC FACTOR.
- You can add program statements to impose linear or nonlinear constraints on the parameters if you specify the model by means of a COSAN, LINEQS, or RAM statement. The PARAMETERS statement defines additional parameters that are needed as independent variables in your program code and that belong to the set of parameters to be estimated. Variable names used in the program code should differ from the preceding statement names. The code should respect the syntax rules of SAS statements usually used in the DATA step. See the "SAS Program Statements" section on page 514 for more information.
- The BOUNDS statement can be used to specify simple lower and upper boundary constraints for the parameters.
- You can specify general linear equality and inequality constraints with the LINCON statement (or via an INEST= data set). The NLINCON statement can be used to specify general nonlinear equality and inequality constraints by referring to nonlinear functions defined by program statements.
- The VAR, PARTIAL, WEIGHT, FREQ, and BY statements can be used in the same way as in other procedures, for example, the FACTOR or PRINCOMP procedure. You can select a subset of the input variables to analyze with the VAR statement. The PARTIAL statement defines a set of input variables that are chosen as partial variables for the analysis of a matrix of partial correlations or covariances. The BY statement specifies groups in which separate covariance structure analyses are performed.

PROC CALIS Statement

PROC CALIS < *options* > **;**

This statement invokes the procedure. The options available with the PROC CALIS statement are summarized in Table 19.1 and discussed in the following six sections.

Table 19.1. PROC CALIS Statement Options

Data Set Options	Short Description
DATA=	input data set
INEST=	input initial values, constraints
INRAM=	input model
INWGT=	input weight matrix
OUTEST=	covariance matrix of estimates
OUTJAC	Jacobian into OUTEST= data set
OUTRAM=	output model
OUTSTAT=	output statistic
OUTWGT=	output weight matrix

Data Processing	Short Description
AUGMENT	analyzes augmented moment matrix
COVARIANCE	analyzes covariance matrix
EDF=	defines nobs by number error df
NOBS=	defines number of observations nobs
NOINT	analyzes uncorrected moments
RDF=	defines nobs by number regression df
RIDGE	specifies ridge factor for moment matrix
UCORR	analyzes uncorrected CORR matrix
UCOV	analyzes uncorrected COV matrix
VARDEF=	specifies variance divisor

Estimation Methods	Short Description
METHOD=	estimation method
ASYCOV=	formula of asymptotic covariances
DFREDUCE=	reduces degrees of freedom
G4=	algorithm for STDERR
NODIAG	excludes diagonal elements from fit
WPENALTY=	penalty weight to fit correlations
WRIDGE=	ridge factor for weight matrix

Optimization Techniques	Short Description
TECHNIQUE=	minimization method
UPDATE=	update technique
LINESEARCH=	line-search method
FCONV=	function convergence criterion

Table 19.1. (continued)

Optimization Techniques	Short Description
GCONV=	gradient convergence criterion
INSTEP=	initial step length (RADIUS=, SALPHA=)
LSPRECISION=	line-search precision (SPRECISION=)
MAXFUNC=	max number function calls
MAXITER=	max number iterations

Displayed Output Options	Short Description
KURTOSIS	compute and display kurtosis
MODIFICATION	modification indices
NOMOD	no modification indices
NOPRINT	suppresses the displayed output
PALL	all displayed output (ALL)
PCORR	analyzed and estimated moment matrix
PCOVES	covariance matrix of estimates
PDETERM	determination coefficients
PESTIM	parameter estimates
PINITIAL	pattern and initial values
PJACPAT	displays structure of variable and constant elements of the Jacobian matrix
PLATCOV	latent variable covariances, scores
PREDET	displays predetermined moment matrix
PRIMAT	displays output in matrix form
PRINT	adds default displayed output
PRIVEC	displays output in vector form
PSHORT	reduces default output (SHORT)
PSUMMARY	displays only fit summary (SUMMARY)
PWEIGHT	weight matrix
RESIDUAL=	residual matrix and distribution
SIMPLE	univariate statistics
STDERR	standard errors
NOSTDERR	computes no standard errors
TOTEFF	displays total and indirect effects

Miscellaneous Options	Short Description
ALPHAECV=	probability Browne & Cudeck ECV
ALPHARMS=	probability Steiger & Lind RMSEA
BIASKUR	biased skewness and kurtosis
DEMPHAS=	emphasizes diagonal entries
FDCODE	uses numeric derivatives for code
HESSALG=	algorithm for Hessian
NOADJDF	no adjustment of df for active constraints
RANDOM=	randomly generated initial values
SINGULAR=	singularity criterion
ASINGULAR=	absolute singularity information matrix

Table 19.1. (continued)

Miscellaneous Options	Short Description
COVSING=	singularity tolerance of information matrix
MSINGULAR=	relative M singularity of information matrix
VSINGULAR=	relative V singularity of information matrix
SLMW=	probability limit for Wald test
START=	constant initial values

Data Set Options

DATA=*SAS-data-set*

specifies an input data set that can be an ordinary SAS data set or a specially structured TYPE=CORR, TYPE=COV, TYPE=UCORR, TYPE=UCOV, TYPE=SSCP, or TYPE=FACTOR SAS data set, as described in the section "Input Data Sets" on page 517. If the DATA= option is omitted, the most recently created SAS data set is used.

INEST | INVAR | ESTDATA=*SAS-data-set*

specifies an input data set that contains initial estimates for the parameters used in the optimization process and can also contain boundary and general linear constraints on the parameters. If the model did not change too much, you can specify an OUTEST= data set from a previous PROC CALIS analysis. The initial estimates are taken from the values of the PARMS observation.

INRAM=*SAS-data-set*

specifies an input data set that contains in RAM list form all information needed to specify an analysis model. The INRAM= data set is described in the section "Input Data Sets" on page 517. Typically, this input data set is an OUTRAM= data set (possibly modified) from a previous PROC CALIS analysis. If you use an INRAM= data set to specify the analysis model, you cannot use the model specification statements COSAN, MATRIX, RAM, LINEQS, STD, COV, FACTOR, or VARNAMES, but you can use the BOUNDS and PARAMETERS statements and program statements. If the INRAM= option is omitted, you must define the analysis model with a COSAN, RAM, LINEQS, or FACTOR statement.

INWGT=*SAS-data-set*

specifies an input data set that contains the weight matrix **W** used in generalized least-squares (GLS), weighted least-squares (WLS, ADF), or diagonally weighted least-squares (DWLS) estimation. If the weight matrix **W** defined by an INWGT= data set is not positive definite, it can be ridged using the WRIDGE= option. See the section "Estimation Criteria" on page 531 for more information. If no INWGT= data set is specified, default settings for the weight matrices are used in the estimation process. The INWGT= data set is described in the section "Input Data Sets" on page 517. Typically, this input data set is an OUTWGT= data set from a previous PROC CALIS analysis.

OUTEST | OUTVAR=*SAS-data-set*

creates an output data set containing the parameter estimates, their gradient, Hessian matrix, and boundary and linear constraints. For METHOD=ML, METHOD=GLS, and METHOD=WLS, the OUTEST= data set also contains the information matrix, the approximate covariance matrix of the parameter estimates ((generalized) inverse of information matrix), and approximate standard errors. If linear or nonlinear equality or active inequality constraints are present, the Lagrange multiplier estimates of the active constraints, the projected Hessian, and the Hessian of the Lagrange function are written to the data set. The OUTEST= data set also contains the Jacobian if the OUTJAC option is used.

The OUTEST= data set is described in the section "OUTEST= SAS-data-set" on page 521. If you want to create a permanent SAS data set, you must specify a two-level name. Refer to the chapter titled "SAS Data Files" in *SAS Language Reference: Concepts* for more information on permanent data sets.

OUTJAC

writes the Jacobian matrix, if it has been computed, to the OUTEST= data set. This is useful when the information and Jacobian matrices need to be computed for other analyses.

OUTSTAT=*SAS-data-set*

creates an output data set containing the BY group variables, the analyzed covariance or correlation matrices, and the predicted and residual covariance or correlation matrices of the analysis. You can specify the correlation or covariance matrix in an OUTSTAT= data set as an input DATA= data set in a subsequent analysis by PROC CALIS. The OUTSTAT= data set is described in the section "OUTSTAT= SAS-data-set" on page 528. If the model contains latent variables, this data set also contains the predicted covariances between latent and manifest variables and the latent variables scores regression coefficients (see the PLATCOV option on page 473). If the FACTOR statement is used, the OUTSTAT= data set also contains the rotated and unrotated factor loadings, the unique variances, the matrix of factor correlations, the transformation matrix of the rotation, and the matrix of standardized factor loadings.

You can specify the latent variable score regression coefficients with PROC SCORE to compute factor scores.

If you want to create a permanent SAS data set, you must specify a two-level name. Refer to the chapter titled "SAS Data Files" in *SAS Language Reference: Concepts* for more information on permanent data sets.

OUTRAM=*SAS-data-set*

creates an output data set containing the model information for the analysis, the parameter estimates, and their standard errors. An OUTRAM= data set can be used as an input INRAM= data set in a subsequent analysis by PROC CALIS. The OUTRAM= data set also contains a set of fit indices; it is described in more detail in the section "OUTRAM= SAS-data-set" on page 525. If you want to create a permanent SAS data set, you must specify a two-level name. Refer to the chapter titled "SAS Data Files" in *SAS Language Reference: Concepts* for more information on permanent data sets.

OUTWGT=*SAS-data-set*

creates an output data set containing the weight matrix **W** used in the estimation process. You cannot create an OUTWGT= data set with an unweighted least-squares or maximum likelihood estimation. The fit function in GLS, WLS (ADF), and DWLS estimation contain the inverse of the (Cholesky factor of the) weight matrix **W** written in the OUTWGT= data set. The OUTWGT= data set contains the weight matrix on which the WRIDGE= and the WPENALTY= options are applied. An OUTWGT= data set can be used as an input INWGT= data set in a subsequent analysis by PROC CALIS. The OUTWGT= data set is described in the section "OUTWGT= SAS-data-set" on page 530. If you want to create a permanent SAS data set, you must specify a two-level name. Refer to the chapter titled "SAS Data Files" in *SAS Language Reference: Concepts* for more information on permanent data sets.

Data Processing Options

AUGMENT | AUG

analyzes the augmented correlation or covariance matrix. Using the AUG option is equivalent to specifying UCORR (NOINT but not COV) or UCOV (NOINT and COV) for a data set that is augmented by an intercept variable INTERCEPT that has constant values equal to 1. The variable INTERCEP can be used instead of the default INTERCEPT only if you specify the SAS option OPTIONS VALIDVARNAME=V6. The dimension of an augmented matrix is one higher than that of the corresponding correlation or covariance matrix. The AUGMENT option is effective only if the data set does not contain a variable called INTERCEPT and if you specify the UCOV, UCORR, or NOINT option.

Caution: The INTERCEPT variable is included in the moment matrix as the variable with number $n+1$. Using the RAM model statement assumes that the first n variable numbers correspond to the n manifest variables in the input data set. Therefore, specifying the AUGMENT option assumes that the numbers of the latent variables used in the RAM or path model have to start with number $n+2$.

COVARIANCE | COV

analyzes the covariance matrix instead of the correlation matrix. By default, PROC CALIS (like the FACTOR procedure) analyzes a correlation matrix. If the DATA= input data set is a valid TYPE=CORR data set (containing a correlation matrix and standard deviations), using the COV option means that the covariance matrix is computed and analyzed.

DFE | EDF=*n*

makes the effective number of observations $n+i$, where i is 0 if the NOINT, UCORR, or UCOV option is specified without the AUGMENT option or where i is 1 otherwise. You can also use the NOBS= option to specify the number of observations.

DFR | RDF=*n*

makes the effective number of observations the actual number of observations minus the RDF= value. The degree of freedom for the intercept should not be included in the RDF= option. If you use PROC CALIS to compute a regression model, you can specify RDF= *number-of-regressor-variables* to get approximate standard errors equal to those computed by PROC REG.

NOBS= *nobs*

specifies the number of observations. If the DATA= input data set is a raw data set, *nobs* is defined by default to be the number of observations in the raw data set. The NOBS= and EDF= options override this default definition. You can use the

RDF= option to modify the *nobs* specification. If the DATA= input data set contains a covariance, correlation, or scalar product matrix, you can specify the number of observations either by using the NOBS=, EDF=, and RDF= options in the PROC CALIS statement or by including a _TYPE_='N' observation in the DATA= input data set.

NOINT

specifies that no intercept be used in computing covariances and correlations; that is, covariances or correlations are not corrected for the mean. You can specify this option (or UCOV or UCORR) to analyze mean structures in an uncorrected moment matrix, that is, to compute intercepts in systems of structured linear equations (see Example 19.2). The term NOINT is misleading in this case because an uncorrected covariance or correlation matrix is analyzed containing a constant (intercept) variable that is used in the analysis model. The degrees of freedom used in the variance divisor (specified by the VARDEF= option) and some of the assessment of the fit function (see the section "Assessment of Fit" on page 536) depend on whether an intercept variable is included in the model (the intercept is used in computing the corrected covariance or correlation matrix or is used as a variable in the uncorrected covariance or correlation matrix to estimate mean structures) or not included (an uncorrected covariance or correlation matrix is used that does not contain a constant variable).

RIDGE<=*r*>

defines a ridge factor r for the diagonal of the moment matrix $\mathbf{S}$ that is analyzed. The matrix $\mathbf{S}$ is transformed to

$$\mathbf{S} \longrightarrow \tilde{\mathbf{S}} = \mathbf{S} + r(diag(\mathbf{S}))$$

If you do not specify r in the RIDGE option, PROC CALIS tries to ridge the moment matrix $\mathbf{S}$ so that the smallest eigenvalue is about 10^{-3}.

Caution: The moment matrix in the OUTSTAT= output data set does not contain the ridged diagonal.

UCORR

analyzes the uncorrected correlation matrix instead of the correlation matrix corrected for the mean. Using the UCORR option is equivalent to specifying the NOINT option but not the COV option.

UCOV

analyzes the uncorrected covariance matrix instead of the covariance matrix corrected for the mean. Using the UCOV option is equivalent to specifying both the COV and NOINT options. You can specify this option to analyze mean structures in an uncorrected covariance matrix, that is, to compute intercepts in systems of linear structural equations (see Example 19.2).

VARDEF= DF | N | WDF | WEIGHT | WGT

specifies the divisor used in the calculation of covariances and standard deviations. The default value is VARDEF=DF. The values and associated divisors are displayed in the following table, where $i = 0$ if the NOINT option is used and $i = 1$ otherwise and where k is the number of partial variables specified in the PARTIAL statement. Using an intercept variable in a mean structure analysis, by specifying the AUG-

MENT option, includes the intercept variable in the analysis. In this case, $i = 1$. When a WEIGHT statement is used, w_j is the value of the WEIGHT variable in the jth observation, and the summation is performed only over observations with positive weight.

Value	Description	Divisor
DF	degrees of freedom	$N - k - i$
N	number of observations	N
WDF	sum of weights DF	$\sum_j^N w_j - k - i$
WEIGHT | WGT	sum of weights	$\sum_j^N w_j$

Estimation Methods

The default estimation method is maximum likelihood (METHOD=ML), assuming a multivariate normal distribution of the observed variables. The two-stage estimation methods METHOD=LSML, METHOD=LSGLS, METHOD=LSWLS, and METHOD=LSDWLS first compute unweighted least-squares estimates of the model parameters and their residuals. Afterward, these estimates are used as initial values for the optimization process to compute maximum likelihood, generalized least-squares, weighted least-squares, or diagonally weighted least-squares parameter estimates. You can do the same thing by using an OUTRAM= data set with least-squares estimates as an INRAM= data set for a further analysis to obtain the second set of parameter estimates. This strategy is also discussed in the section "Use of Optimization Techniques" on page 551. For more details, see the "Estimation Criteria" section on page 531.

METHOD | MET=*name*

specifies the method of parameter estimation. The default is METHOD=ML. Valid values for *name* are as follows:

ML | M | MAX
: performs normal-theory maximum likelihood parameter estimation. The ML method requires a nonsingular covariance or correlation matrix.

GLS | G
: performs generalized least-squares parameter estimation. If no INWGT= data set is specified, the GLS method uses the inverse sample covariance or correlation matrix as weight matrix **W**. Therefore, METHOD=GLS requires a nonsingular covariance or correlation matrix.

WLS | W | ADF
: performs weighted least-squares parameter estimation. If no INWGT= data set is specified, the WLS method uses the inverse matrix of estimated asymptotic covariances of the sample covariance or correlation matrix as the weight matrix **W**. In this case, the WLS estimation method is equivalent to Browne's (1982, 1984) asymptotically distribution-free estimation. The WLS method requires a nonsingular weight matrix.

DWLS | D
: performs diagonally weighted least-squares parameter estimation. If no INWGT= data set is specified, the DWLS method uses the inverse diagonal matrix of asymptotic

	variances of the input sample covariance or correlation matrix as the weight matrix **W**. The DWLS method requires a nonsingular diagonal weight matrix.
ULS | LS | U	performs unweighted least-squares parameter estimation.
LSML | LSM | LSMAX	performs unweighted least-squares followed by normal-theory maximum likelihood parameter estimation.
LSGLS | LSG	performs unweighted least-squares followed by generalized least-squares parameter estimation.
LSWLS | LSW | LSADF	performs unweighted least-squares followed by weighted least-squares parameter estimation.
LSDWLS | LSD	performs unweighted least-squares followed by diagonally weighted least-squares parameter estimation.
NONE | NO	uses no estimation method. This option is suitable for checking the validity of the input information and for displaying the model matrices and initial values.

ASYCOV | ASC=*name*

specifies the formula for asymptotic covariances used in the weight matrix **W** for WLS and DWLS estimation. The ASYCOV option is effective only if METHOD= WLS or METHOD=DWLS and no INWGT= input data set is specified. The following formulas are implemented:

BIASED:	Browne's (1984) formula (3.4) biased asymptotic covariance estimates; the resulting weight matrix is at least positive semidefinite. This is the default for analyzing a covariance matrix.
UNBIASED:	Browne's (1984) formula (3.8) asymptotic covariance estimates corrected for bias; the resulting weight matrix can be indefinite (that is, can have negative eigenvalues), especially for small N.
CORR:	Browne and Shapiro's (1986) formula (3.2) (identical to DeLeeuw's (1983) formulas (2,3,4)) the asymptotic variances of the diagonal elements are set to the reciprocal of the value r specified by the WPENALTY= option (default: $r = 100$). This formula is the default for analyzing a correlation matrix.

Caution: Using the WLS and DWLS methods with the ASYCOV=CORR option means that you are fitting a correlation (rather than a covariance) structure. Since the fixed diagonal of a correlation matrix for some models does not contribute to the model's degrees of freedom, you can specify the DFREDUCE=i option to reduce the degrees of freedom by the number of manifest variables used in the model. See the section "Counting the Degrees of Freedom" on page 563 for more information.

DFREDUCE | DFRED=*i*

reduces the degrees of freedom of the χ^2 test by i. In general, the number of degrees of freedom is the number of elements of the lower triangle of the predicted model matrix $\mathbf{C}$, $n(n+1)/2$, minus the number of parameters, t. If the NODIAG option is used, the number of degrees of freedom is additionally reduced by n. Because negative values of i are allowed, you can also increase the number of degrees of freedom by using this option. If the DFREDUCE= or NODIAG option is used in a correlation structure analysis, PROC CALIS does not additionally reduce the degrees of freedom by the number of constant elements in the diagonal of the predicted model matrix, which is otherwise done automatically. See the section "Counting the Degrees of Freedom" on page 563 for more information.

G4=*i*

specifies the algorithm to compute the approximate covariance matrix of parameter estimates used for computing the approximate standard errors and modification indices when the information matrix is singular. If the number of parameters t used in the model you analyze is smaller than the value of i, the time-expensive Moore-Penrose (G4) inverse of the singular information matrix is computed by eigenvalue decomposition. Otherwise, an inexpensive pseudo (G1) inverse is computed by sweeping. By default, $i = 60$. For more details, see the section "Estimation Criteria" on page 531.

NODIAG | NODI

omits the diagonal elements of the analyzed correlation or covariance matrix from the fit function. This option is useful only for special models with constant error variables. The NODIAG option does not allow fitting those parameters that contribute to the diagonal of the estimated moment matrix. The degrees of freedom are automatically reduced by n. A simple example for the usefulness of the NODIAG option is the fit of the first-order factor model, $\mathbf{S} = \mathbf{F}\mathbf{F}' + \mathbf{U}^2$. In this case, you do not have to estimate the diagonal matrix of unique variances $\mathbf{U}^2$ that are fully determined by $diag(\mathbf{S} - \mathbf{F}\mathbf{F}')$.

WPENALTY | WPEN=*r*

specifies the penalty weight $r \geq 0$ for the WLS and DWLS fit of the diagonal elements of a correlation matrix (constant 1s). The criterion for weighted least-squares estimation of a correlation structure is

$$\mathbf{F}_{WLS} = \sum_{i=2}^{n}\sum_{j=1}^{i-1}\sum_{k=2}^{n}\sum_{l=1}^{k-1} w^{ij,kl}(s_{ij} - c_{ij})(s_{kl} - c_{kl}) + r\sum_{i}^{n}(s_{ii} - c_{ii})^2$$

where r is the penalty weight specified by the WPENALTY=r option and the $w^{ij,kl}$ are the elements of the inverse of the reduced $(n(n-1)/2) \times (n(n-1)/2)$ weight matrix that contains only the nonzero rows and columns of the full weight matrix $\mathbf{W}$. The second term is a penalty term to fit the diagonal elements of the correlation matrix. The default value is 100. The reciprocal of this value replaces the asymptotic variance corresponding to the diagonal elements of a correlation matrix in the weight matrix $\mathbf{W}$, and it is effective only with the ASYCOV=CORR option. The often used value $r = 1$ seems to be too small in many cases to fit the diagonal elements of a correlation matrix properly. The default WPENALTY= value emphasizes the importance of the fit of the diagonal elements in the correlation matrix. You can decrease or increase the value of r if you want to decrease or increase the importance of the diagonal elements fit. This option is effective only with the WLS or DWLS estimation method and the analysis of a correlation matrix. See the section "Estimation Criteria" on page 531 for more details.

WRIDGE=*r*

defines a ridge factor r for the diagonal of the weight matrix $\mathbf{W}$ used in GLS, WLS, or DWLS estimation. The weight matrix $\mathbf{W}$ is transformed to

$$\mathbf{W} \longrightarrow \tilde{\mathbf{W}} = \mathbf{W} + r(diag(\mathbf{W}))$$

The WRIDGE= option is applied on the weight matrix

- before the WPENALTY= option is applied on it
- before the weight matrix is written to the OUTWGT= data set
- before the weight matrix is displayed

Optimization Techniques

Since there is no single nonlinear optimization algorithm available that is clearly superior (in terms of stability, speed, and memory) for all applications, different types of optimization techniques are provided in the CALIS procedure. Each technique can be modified in various ways. The default optimization technique for less than 40 parameters ($t < 40$) is TECHNIQUE=LEVMAR. For $40 \leq t < 400$, TECHNIQUE=QUANEW is the default method, and for $t \geq 400$, TECHNIQUE=CONGRA is the default method. For more details, see the section "Use of Optimization Techniques" on page 551. You can specify the following set of options in the PROC CALIS statement or in the NLOPTIONS statement.

TECHNIQUE | TECH=*name*
OMETHOD | OM=*name*

specifies the optimization technique. Valid values for *name* are as follows:

CONGRA | CG — chooses one of four different conjugate-gradient optimization algorithms, which can be more precisely defined with the UPDATE= option and modified with the LINESEARCH= option. The conjugate-gradient techniques need only $O(t)$ memory compared to the $O(t^2)$ memory for the other three techniques, where t is the number of parameters. On the other hand, the conjugate-gradient techniques are significantly slower than other optimization techniques and should be used only when memory is insufficient for more efficient techniques. When you choose this option, UPDATE=PB by default. This is the default optimization technique if there are more than 400 parameters to estimate.

DBLDOG | DD performs a version of double dogleg optimization, which uses the gradient to update an approximation of the Cholesky factor of the Hessian. This technique is, in many aspects, very similar to the dual quasi-Newton method, but it does not use line search. The implementation is based on Dennis and Mei (1979) and Gay (1983).

LEVMAR | LM | MARQUARDT performs a highly stable but, for large problems, memory- and time-consuming Levenberg-Marquardt optimization technique, a slightly improved variant of the Moré (1978) implementation. This is the default optimization technique if there are fewer than 40 parameters to estimate.

NEWRAP | NR | NEWTON performs a usually stable but, for large problems, memory- and time-consuming Newton-Raphson optimization technique. The algorithm combines a line-search algorithm with ridging, and it can be modified with the LINESEARCH= option. In releases prior to Release 6.11, this option invokes the NRRIDG option.

NRRIDG | NRR | NR performs a usually stable but, for large problems, memory- and time-consuming Newton-Raphson optimization technique. This algorithm does not perform a line search. Since TECH=NRRIDG uses an orthogonal decomposition of the approximate Hessian, each iteration of TECH=NRRIDG can be slower than that of TECH=NEWRAP, which works with Cholesky decomposition. However, usually TECH=NRRIDG needs less iterations than TECH=NEWRAP.

QUANEW | QN chooses one of four different quasi-Newton optimization algorithms that can be more precisely defined with the UPDATE= option and modified with the LINESEARCH= option. If boundary constraints are used, these techniques sometimes converge slowly. When you choose this option, UPDATE=DBFGS by default. If nonlinear constraints are specified in the NLINCON statement, a modification of Powell's (1982a, 1982b) VMCWD algorithm is used, which is a sequential quadratic programming (SQP) method. This algorithm can be modified by specifying VERSION=1, which replaces the update of the Lagrange multiplier estimate vector μ to the original update of Powell (1978a, 1978b) that is used in the VF02AD algorithm. This can be helpful for applications with linearly dependent active constraints. The QUANEW technique is the default optimization technique if there are nonlinear constraints specified or if there are more than 40 and fewer than 400 parameters to estimate. The QUANEW algorithm uses only first-order derivatives of the objective function and, if available, of the nonlinear constraint functions.

TRUREG | TR — performs a usually very stable but, for large problems, memory- and time-consuming trust region optimization technique. The algorithm is implemented similar to Gay (1983) and Moré and Sorensen (1983).

NONE | NO — does not perform any optimization. This option is similar to METHOD=NONE, but TECH=NONE also computes and displays residuals and goodness-of-fit statistics. If you specify METHOD=ML, METHOD=LSML, METHOD=GLS, METHOD=LSGLS, METHOD=WLS, or METHOD=LSWLS, this option allows computing and displaying (if the display options are specified) of the standard error estimates and modification indices corresponding to the input parameter estimates.

UPDATE | UPD=*name*

specifies the update method for the quasi-Newton or conjugate-gradient optimization technique.

For TECHNIQUE=CONGRA, the following updates can be used:

PB — performs the automatic restart update methodof Powell (1977) and Beale (1972). This is the default.

FR — performs the Fletcher-Reeves update (Fletcher 1980, p. 63).

PR — performs the Polak-Ribiere update (Fletcher 1980, p. 66).

CD — performs a conjugate-descent update of Fletcher (1987).

For TECHNIQUE=DBLDOG, the following updates (Fletcher 1987) can be used:

DBFGS — performs the dual Broyden, Fletcher, Goldfarb, and Shanno (BFGS) update of the Cholesky factor of the Hessian matrix. This is the default.

DDFP — performs the dual Davidon, Fletcher, and Powell (DFP) update of the Cholesky factor of the Hessian matrix.

For TECHNIQUE=QUANEW, the following updates (Fletcher 1987) can be used:

BFGS — performs original BFGS update of the inverse Hessian matrix. This is the default for earlier releases.

DFP — performs the original DFP update of the inverse Hessian matrix.

DBFGS — performs the dual BFGS update of the Cholesky factor of the Hessian matrix. This is the default.

DDFP — performs the dual DFP update of the Cholesky factor of the Hessian matrix.

LINESEARCH | LIS | SMETHOD | SM=*i*

specifies the line-search method for the CONGRA, QUANEW, and NEWRAP optimization techniques. Refer to Fletcher (1980) for an introduction to line-search techniques. The value of i can be $1, \ldots, 8$; the default is $i = 2$.

LIS=1 specifies a line-search method that needs the same number of function and gradient calls for cubic interpolation and cubic extrapolation; this method is similar to one used by the Harwell subroutine library.

LIS=2 specifies a line-search method that needs more function calls than gradient calls for quadratic and cubic interpolation and cubic extrapolation; this method is implemented as shown in Fletcher (1987) and can be modified to an exact line search by using the LSPRECISION= option.

LIS=3 specifies a line-search method that needs the same number of function and gradient calls for cubic interpolation and cubic extrapolation; this method is implemented as shown in Fletcher (1987) and can be modified to an exact line search by using the LSPRECISION= option.

LIS=4 specifies a line-search method that needs the same number of function and gradient calls for stepwise extrapolation and cubic interpolation.

LIS=5 specifies a line-search method that is a modified version of LIS=4.

LIS=6 specifies golden section line search (Polak 1971), which uses only function values for linear approximation.

LIS=7 specifies bisection line search (Polak 1971), which uses only function values for linear approximation.

LIS=8 specifies Armijo line-search technique (Polak 1971), which uses only function values for linear approximation.

FCONV | FTOL=*r*

specifies the relative function convergence criterion. The optimization process is terminated when the relative difference of the function values of two consecutive iterations is smaller than the specified value of r, that is

$$\frac{|f(x^{(k)}) - f(x^{(k-1)})|}{\max(|f(x^{(k-1)})|, FSIZE)} \leq r$$

where $FSIZE$ can be defined by the FSIZE= option in the NLOPTIONS statement. The default value is $r = 10^{-FDIGITS}$, where $FDIGITS$ either can be specified in the NLOPTIONS statement or is set by default to $-\log_{10}(\epsilon)$, where ϵ is the machine precision.

GCONV | GTOL=*r*

specifies the relative gradient convergence criterion (see the ABSGCONV= option on page 504 for the absolute gradient convergence criterion).

Termination of all techniques (except the CONGRA technique) requires the normalized predicted function reduction to be small,

$$\frac{[g(x^{(k)})]'[\mathbf{G}^{(k)}]^{-1}g(x^{(k)})}{\max(|f(x^{(k)})|, FSIZE)} \leq r$$

where $FSIZE$ can be defined by the FSIZE= option in the NLOPTIONS statement. For the CONGRA technique (where a reliable Hessian estimate **G** is not available),

$$\frac{\| g(x^{(k)}) \|_2^2 \ \ \| s(x^{(k)}) \|_2}{\| g(x^{(k)}) - g(x^{(k-1)}) \|_2 \max(|f(x^{(k)})|, FSIZE)} \leq r$$

is used. The default value is $r = 10^{-8}$.

Note that for releases prior to Release 6.11, the GCONV= option specified the absolute gradient convergence criterion.

INSTEP=*r*

For highly nonlinear objective functions, such as the EXP function, the default initial radius of the trust-region algorithms TRUREG, DBLDOG, and LEVMAR or the default step length of the line-search algorithms can produce arithmetic overflows. If this occurs, specify decreasing values of $0 < r < 1$ such as INSTEP=1E−1, INSTEP=1E−2, INSTEP=1E−4, . . ., until the iteration starts successfully.

- For trust-region algorithms (TRUREG, DBLDOG, and LEVMAR), the INSTEP option specifies a positive factor for the initial radius of the trust region. The default initial trust-region radius is the length of the scaled gradient, and it corresponds to the default radius factor of $r = 1$.
- For line-search algorithms (NEWRAP, CONGRA, and QUANEW), INSTEP specifies an upper bound for the initial step length for the line search during the first five iterations. The default initial step length is $r = 1$.

For releases prior to Release 6.11, specify the SALPHA= and RADIUS= options. For more details, see the section "Computational Problems" on page 564.

LSPRECISION | LSP=*r*
SPRECISION | SP=*r*

specifies the degree of accuracy that should be obtained by the line-search algorithms LIS=2 and LIS=3. Usually an imprecise line search is inexpensive and successful. For more difficult optimization problems, a more precise and more expensive line search may be necessary (Fletcher 1980, p.22). The second (default for NEWRAP, QUANEW, and CONGRA) and third line-search methods approach exact line search for small LSPRECISION= values. If you have numerical problems, you should decrease the LSPRECISION= value to obtain a more precise line search. The default LSPRECISION= values are displayed in the following table.

TECH=	UPDATE=	LSP default
QUANEW	DBFGS, BFGS	$r = 0.4$
QUANEW	DDFP, DFP	$r = 0.06$
CONGRA	all	$r = 0.1$
NEWRAP	no update	$r = 0.9$

For more details, refer to Fletcher (1980, pp. 25–29).

MAXFUNC | MAXFU=*i*

specifies the maximum number i of function calls in the optimization process. The default values are displayed in the following table.

TECH=	MAXFUNC default
LEVMAR, NEWRAP, NRRIDG, TRUREG	i=125
DBLDOG, QUANEW	i=500
CONGRA	i=1000

The default is used if you specify MAXFUNC=0. The optimization can be terminated only after completing a full iteration. Therefore, the number of function calls that is actually performed can exceed the number that is specified by the MAXFUNC= option.

MAXITER | MAXIT=*i* <*n*>

specifies the maximum number i of iterations in the optimization process. The default values are displayed in the following table.

TECH=	MAXITER default
LEVMAR, NEWRAP, NRRIDG, TRUREG	i=50
DBLDOG, QUANEW	i=200
CONGRA	i=400

The default is used if you specify MAXITER=0 or if you omit the MAXITER option.

The optional second value n is valid only for TECH=QUANEW with nonlinear constraints. It specifies an upper bound n for the number of iterations of an algorithm and reduces the violation of nonlinear constraints at a starting point. The default is n=20. For example, specifying

```
maxiter= . 0
```

means that you do not want to exceed the default number of iterations during the main optimization process and that you want to suppress the feasible point algorithm for nonlinear constraints.

RADIUS=*r*

is an alias for the INSTEP= option for Levenberg-Marquardt minimization.

SALPHA=*r*

is an alias for the INSTEP= option for line-search algorithms.

SPRECISION | SP=*r*
is an alias for the LSPRECISION= option.

Displayed Output Options

There are three kinds of options to control the displayed output:

- The PCORR, KURTOSIS, MODIFICATION, NOMOD, PCOVES, PDETERM, PESTIM, PINITIAL, PJACPAT, PLATCOV, PREDET, PWEIGHT, RESIDUAL, SIMPLE, STDERR, and TOTEFF options refer to specific parts of displayed output.
- The PALL, PRINT, PSHORT, PSUMMARY, and NOPRINT options refer to special subsets of the displayed output options mentioned in the first item. If the NOPRINT option is not specified, a default set of output is displayed. The PRINT and PALL options add other output options to the default output, and the PSHORT and PSUMMARY options reduce the default displayed output.
- The PRIMAT and PRIVEC options describe the form in which some of the output is displayed (the only nonredundant information displayed by PRIVEC is the gradient).

Output Options	PALL	PRINT	default	PSHORT	PSUMMARY
fit indices	*	*	*	*	*
linear dependencies	*	*	*	*	*
PREDET	*	(*)	(*)	(*)	
model matrices	*	*	*	*	
PESTIM	*	*	*	*	
iteration history	*	*	*	*	
PINITIAL	*	*	*		
SIMPLE	*	*	*		
STDERR	*	*	*		
RESIDUAL	*	*			
KURTOSIS	*	*			
PLATCOV	*	*			
TOTEFF	*	*			
PCORR	*				
MODIFICATION	*				
PWEIGHT	*				
PCOVES					
PDETERM					
PJACPAT					
PRIMAT					
PRIVEC					

KURTOSIS | KU
computes and displays univariate kurtosis and skewness, various coefficients of multivariate kurtosis, and the numbers of observations that contribute most to the normalized multivariate kurtosis. See the section "Measures of Multivariate Kurtosis" on page 544 for more information. Using the KURTOSIS option implies the SIMPLE display option. This information is computed only if the DATA= data set is a

raw data set, and it is displayed by default if the PRINT option is specified. The multivariate LS kappa and the multivariate mean kappa are displayed only if you specify METHOD=WLS and the weight matrix is computed from an input raw data set. All measures of skewness and kurtosis are corrected for the mean. If an intercept variable is included in the analysis, the measures of multivariate kurtosis do not include the intercept variable in the corrected covariance matrix, as indicated by a displayed message. Using the BIASKUR option displays the biased values of univariate skewness and kurtosis.

MODIFICATION | MOD

computes and displays Lagrange multiplier test indices for constant parameter constraints, equality parameter constraints, and active boundary constraints, as well as univariate and multivariate Wald test indices. The modification indices are not computed in the case of unweighted or diagonally weighted least-squares estimation.

The Lagrange multiplier test (Bentler 1986; Lee 1985; Buse 1982) provides an estimate of the χ^2 reduction that results from dropping the constraint. For constant parameter constraints and active boundary constraints, the approximate change of the parameter value is displayed also. You can use this value to obtain an initial value if the parameter is allowed to vary in a modified model. For more information, see the section "Modification Indices" on page 560.

NOMOD

does not compute modification indices. The NOMOD option is useful in connection with the PALL option because it saves computing time.

NOPRINT | NOP

suppresses the displayed output. Note that this option temporarily disables the Output Delivery System (ODS). For more information, see Chapter 15, "Using the Output Delivery System."

PALL | ALL

displays all optional output except the output generated by the PCOVES, PDETERM, PJACPAT, and PRIVEC options.

Caution: The PALL option includes the very expensive computation of the modification indices. If you do not really need modification indices, you can save computing time by specifying the NOMOD option in addition to the PALL option.

PCORR | CORR

displays the (corrected or uncorrected) covariance or correlation matrix that is analyzed and the predicted model covariance or correlation matrix.

PCOVES | PCE

displays the following:

- the information matrix (crossproduct Jacobian)
- the approximate covariance matrix of the parameter estimates (generalized inverse of the information matrix)
- the approximate correlation matrix of the parameter estimates

The covariance matrix of the parameter estimates is not computed for estimation methods ULS and DWLS. This displayed output is not included in the output generated by the PALL option.

PDETERM | PDE

displays three coefficients of determination: the determination of all equations (DETAE), the determination of the structural equations (DETSE), and the determination of the manifest variable equations (DETMV). These determination coefficients are intended to be global means of the squared multiple correlations for different subsets of model equations and variables. The coefficients are displayed only when you specify a RAM or LINEQS model, but they are displayed for all five estimation methods: ULS, GLS, ML, WLS, and DWLS.

You can use the STRUCTEQ statement to define which equations are structural equations. If you don't use the STRUCTEQ statement, PROC CALIS uses its own default definition to identify structural equations.

The term "structural equation" is not defined in a unique way. The LISREL program defines the structural equations by the user-defined BETA matrix. In PROC CALIS, the default definition of a structural equation is an equation that has a dependent left side variable that appears at least once on the right side of another equation, or an equation that has at least one right side variable that is the left side variable of another equation. Therefore, PROC CALIS sometimes identifies more equations as structural equations than the LISREL program does.

If the model contains structural equations, PROC CALIS also displays the "Stability Coefficient of Reciprocal Causation," that is, the largest eigenvalue of the $\mathbf{BB}'$ matrix, where $\mathbf{B}$ is the causal coefficient matrix of the structural equations. These coefficients are computed as in the LISREL VI program of Jöreskog and Sörbom (1985). This displayed output is not included in the output generated by the PALL option.

PESTIM | PES

displays the parameter estimates. In some cases, this includes displaying the standard errors and t values.

PINITIAL | PIN

displays the input model matrices and the vector of initial values.

PJACPAT | PJP

displays the structure of variable and constant elements of the Jacobian matrix. This displayed output is not included in the output generated by the PALL option.

PLATCOV | PLC

displays the following:

- the estimates of the covariances among the latent variables
- the estimates of the covariances between latent and manifest variables
- the latent variable score regression coefficients

The estimated covariances between latent and manifest variables and the latent variable score regression coefficients are written to the OUTSTAT= data set. You can use the score coefficients with PROC SCORE to compute factor scores.

PREDET | PRE
displays the pattern of variable and constant elements of the predicted moment matrix that is predetermined by the analysis model. It is especially helpful in finding manifest variables that are not used or that are used as exogenous variables in a complex model specified in the COSAN statement. Those entries of the predicted moment matrix for which the model generates variable (rather than constant) elements are displayed as missing values. This output is displayed even without specifying the PREDET option if the model generates constant elements in the predicted model matrix different from those in the analysis moment matrix and if you specify at least the PSHORT amount of displayed output.

If the analyzed matrix is a correlation matrix (containing constant elements of 1s in the diagonal) and the model generates a predicted model matrix with q constant (rather than variable) elements in the diagonal, the degrees of freedom are automatically reduced by q. The output generated by the PREDET option displays those constant diagonal positions. If you specify the DFREDUCE= or NODIAG option, this automatic reduction of the degrees of freedom is suppressed. See the section "Counting the Degrees of Freedom" on page 563 for more information.

PRIMAT | PMAT
displays parameter estimates, approximate standard errors, and t values in matrix form if you specify the analysis model in the RAM or LINEQS statement. When a COSAN statement is used, this occurs by default.

PRINT | PRI
adds the options KURTOSIS, RESIDUAL, PLATCOV, and TOTEFF to the default output.

PRIVEC | PVEC
displays parameter estimates, approximate standard errors, the gradient, and t values in vector form. The values are displayed with more decimal places. This displayed output is not included in the output generated by the PALL option.

PSHORT | SHORT | PSH
excludes the output produced by the PINITIAL, SIMPLE, and STDERR options from the default output.

PSUMMARY | SUMMARY | PSUM
displays the fit assessment table and the ERROR, WARNING, and NOTE messages.

PWEIGHT | PW
displays the weight matrix **W** used in the estimation. The weight matrix is displayed after the WRIDGE= and the WPENALTY= options are applied to it.

RESIDUAL | RES < = NORM | VARSTAND | ASYSTAND >
displays the absolute and normalized residual covariance matrix, the rank order of the largest residuals, and a bar chart of the residuals. This information is displayed by default when you specify the PRINT option.

Three types of normalized or standardized residual matrices can be chosen with the RESIDUAL= specification.

RESIDUAL= NORM	Normalized Residuals
RESIDUAL= VARSTAND	Variance Standardized Residuals
RESIDUAL= ASYSTAND	Asymptotically Standardized Residuals

For more details, see the section "Assessment of Fit" on page 536.

SIMPLE | S
displays means, standard deviations, skewness, and univariate kurtosis if available. This information is displayed when you specify the PRINT option. If you specify the UCOV, UCORR, or NOINT option, the standard deviations are not corrected for the mean. If the KURTOSIS option is specified, the SIMPLE option is set by default.

STDERR | SE
displays approximate standard errors if estimation methods other than unweighted least squares (ULS) or diagonally weighted least squares (DWLS) are used (and the NOSTDERR option is not specified). If you specify neither the STDERR nor the NOSTDERR option, the standard errors are computed for the OUTRAM= data set. This information is displayed by default when you specify the PRINT option.

NOSTDERR | NOSE
specifies that standard errors should not be computed. Standard errors are not computed for unweighted least-squares (ULS) or diagonally weighted least-squares (DWLS) estimation. In general, standard errors are computed even if the STDERR display option is not used (for file output).

TOTEFF | TE
computes and displays total effects and indirect effects.

Miscellaneous Options

ALPHAECV=α
specifies the significance level for a $1 - \alpha$ confidence interval, $0 \leq \alpha \leq 1$, for the Browne & Cudeck (1993) expected cross validation index (ECVI) . The default value is $\alpha = 0.1$, which corresponds to a 90% confidence interval for the ECVI.

ALPHARMS=α
specifies the significance level for a $1 - \alpha$ confidence interval, $0 \leq \alpha \leq 1$, for the Steiger & Lind (1980) root mean squared error of approximation (RMSEA) coefficient (refer to Browne and Du Toit 1992). The default value is $\alpha = 0.1$, which corresponds to a 90% confidence interval for the RMSEA.

ASINGULAR | ASING=*r*
specifies an absolute singularity criterion r, $r > 0$, for the inversion of the information matrix, which is needed to compute the covariance matrix. The following singularity criterion is used:

$$|d_{j,j}| \leq \max(ASING, VSING * |H_{j,j}|, MSING * \max(|H_{1,1}|, \ldots, |H_{n,n}|))$$

In the preceding criterion, $d_{j,j}$ is the diagonal pivot of the matrix, and *VSING* and *MSING* are the specified values of the VSINGULAR= and MSINGULAR= options. The default value for *ASING* is the square root of the smallest positive double precision value. Note that, in many cases, a normalized matrix $\mathbf{D}^{-1}\mathbf{H}\mathbf{D}^{-1}$ is decomposed, and the singularity criteria are modified correspondingly.

BIASKUR

computes univariate skewness and kurtosis by formulas uncorrected for bias. See the section "Measures of Multivariate Kurtosis" on page 544 for more information.

COVSING=*r*

specifies a nonnegative threshold r, which determines whether the eigenvalues of the information matrix are considered to be zero. If the inverse of the information matrix is found to be singular (depending on the VSINGULAR=, MSINGULAR=, ASINGULAR=, or SINGULAR= option), a generalized inverse is computed using the eigenvalue decomposition of the singular matrix. Those eigenvalues smaller than r are considered to be zero. If a generalized inverse is computed and you do not specify the NOPRINT option, the distribution of eigenvalues is displayed.

DEMPHAS | DE=*r*

changes the initial values of all parameters that are located on the diagonals of the central model matrices by the relationship

$$diag_{new} = r(|diag_{old}| + 1)$$

The initial values of the diagonal elements of the central matrices should always be nonnegative to generate positive definite predicted model matrices in the first iteration. By using values of $r > 1$, for example, $r = 2$, $r = 10$, ..., you can increase these initial values to produce predicted model matrices with high positive eigenvalues in the first iteration. The DEMPHAS= option is effective independent of the way the initial values are set; that is, it changes the initial values set in the model specification as well as those set by an INRAM= data set and those automatically generated for RAM, LINEQS, or FACTOR model statements. It also affects the initial values set by the START= option, which uses, by default, DEMPHAS=100 if a covariance matrix is analyzed and DEMPHAS=10 for a correlation matrix.

FDCODE

replaces the analytic derivatives of the program statements by numeric derivatives (finite difference approximations). In general, this option is needed only when you have program statements that are too difficult for the built-in function compiler to differentiate analytically. For example, if the program code for the nonlinear constraints contains many arrays and many DO loops with array processing, the built-in function compiler can require too much time and memory to compute derivatives of the constraints with respect to the parameters. In this case, the Jacobian matrix of constraints is computed numerically by using finite difference approximations. The FDCODE option does not modify the kind of derivatives specified with the HESSALG= option.

HESSALG | HA = 1 | 2 | 3 | 4 | 5 | 6 | 11

specifies the algorithm used to compute the (approximate) Hessian matrix when TECHNIQUE=LEVMAR and NEWRAP, to compute approximate standard errors of the parameter estimates, and to compute Lagrange multipliers. There are different groups of algorithms available.

- analytic formulas: HA=*1,2,3,4,11*
- finite difference approximation: HA=*5,6*
- dense storage: HA=*1,2,3,4,5,6*
- sparse storage: HA=*11*

If the Jacobian is more than 25% dense, the dense analytic algorithm, HA= 1, is used by default. The HA= 1 algorithm is faster than the other dense algorithms, but it needs considerably more memory for large problems than HA= 2,3,4. If the Jacobian is more than 75% sparse, the sparse analytic algorithm, HA= 11, is used by default. The dense analytic algorithm HA= 4 corresponds to the original COSAN algorithm; you are advised not to specify HA= 4 due to its very slow performance. If there is not enough memory available for the dense analytic algorithm HA= 1 and you must specify HA= 2 or HA= 3, it may be more efficient to use one of the quasi-Newton or conjugate-gradient optimization techniques since Levenberg-Marquardt and Newton-Raphson optimization techniques need to compute the Hessian matrix in each iteration. For approximate standard errors and modification indices, the Hessian matrix has to be computed at least once, regardless of the optimization technique.

The algorithms HA= 5 and HA= 6 compute approximate derivatives by using forward difference formulas. The HA= 5 algorithm corresponds to the analytic HA= 1: it is faster than HA= 6, however it needs much more memory. The HA= 6 algorithm corresponds to the analytic HA= 2: it is slower than HA= 5, however it needs much less memory.

Test computations of large sparse problems show that the sparse algorithm HA= 11 can be up to ten times faster than HA= 1 (and needs much less memory).

MSINGULAR | MSING=*r*

specifies a relative singularity criterion r, $r > 0$, for the inversion of the information matrix, which is needed to compute the covariance matrix. The following singularity criterion is used:

$$|d_{j,j}| \leq \max(\mathit{ASING}, \mathit{VSING} * |H_{j,j}|, \mathit{MSING} * \max(|H_{1,1}|, \ldots, |H_{n,n}|))$$

where $d_{j,j}$ is the diagonal pivot of the matrix, and *ASING* and *VSING* are the specified values of the ASINGULAR= and VSINGULAR= options. If you do not specify the SINGULAR= option, the default value for *MSING* is 1E−12; otherwise, the default value is 1E−4 * SINGULAR. Note that, in many cases, a normalized matrix $\mathbf{D}^{-1}\mathbf{H}\mathbf{D}^{-1}$ is decomposed, and the singularity criteria are modified correspondingly.

NOADJDF

turns off the automatic adjustment of degrees of freedom when there are active constraints in the analysis. When the adjustment is in effect, most fit statistics and the associated probability levels will be affected. This option should be used when the researcher believes that the active constraints observed in the current sample will have little chance to occur in repeated sampling.

RANDOM =*i*

specifies a positive integer as a seed value for the pseudo-random number generator to generate initial values for the parameter estimates for which no other initial value assignments in the model definitions are made. Except for the parameters in the diagonal locations of the central matrices in the model, the initial values are set to random numbers in the range $0 \leq r \leq 1$. The values for parameters in the diagonals of the central matrices are random numbers multiplied by 10 or 100. For more information, see the section "Initial Estimates" on page 547.

SINGULAR | SING =*r*

specifies the singularity criterion r, $0 < r < 1$, used, for example, for matrix inversion. The default value is the square root of the relative machine precision or, equivalently, the square root of the largest double precision value that, when added to 1, results in 1.

SLMW=*r*

specifies the probability limit used for computing the stepwise multivariate Wald test. The process stops when the univariate probability is smaller than r. The default value is $r = 0.05$.

START =*r*

In general, this option is needed only in connection with the COSAN model statement, and it specifies a constant r as an initial value for all the parameter estimates for which no other initial value assignments in the pattern definitions are made. Start values in the diagonal locations of the central matrices are set to $100|r|$ if a COV or UCOV matrix is analyzed and $10|r|$ if a CORR or UCORR matrix is analyzed. The default value is $r = .5$. Unspecified initial values in a FACTOR, RAM, or LINEQS model are usually computed by PROC CALIS. If none of the initialization methods are able to compute all starting values for a model specified by a FACTOR, RAM, or LINEQS statement, then the start values of parameters that could not be computed are set to r, $10|r|$, or $100|r|$. If the DEMPHAS= option is used, the initial values of the diagonal elements of the central model matrices are multiplied by the value specified in the DEMPHAS= option. For more information, see the section "Initial Estimates" on page 547.

VSINGULAR | VSING=*r*

specifies a relative singularity criterion r, $r > 0$, for the inversion of the information matrix, which is needed to compute the covariance matrix. The following singularity criterion is used:

$$|d_{j,j}| \leq \max(ASING, VSING * |H_{j,j}|, MSING * \max(|H_{1,1}|, \ldots, |H_{n,n}|))$$

where $d_{j,j}$ is the diagonal pivot of the matrix, and *ASING* and *MSING* are the specified values of the ASINGULAR= and MSINGULAR= options. If you do not specify the SINGULAR= option, the default value for *VSING* is 1E−8; otherwise, the default value is SINGULAR. Note that in many cases a normalized matrix $\mathbf{D}^{-1}\mathbf{H}\mathbf{D}^{-1}$ is decomposed, and the singularity criteria are modified correspondingly.

COSAN Model Statement

COSAN *matrix_term* < *+ matrix_term...* > **;**
where *matrix_term* represents
matrix_definition < ∗ *matrix_definition* ... >
and *matrix_definition* represents
matrix_name (column_number < *,general_form* < *,transformation* >> *)*

The COSAN statement constructs the symmetric matrix model for the covariance analysis mentioned earlier (see the section "The Generalized COSAN Model" on page 440):

$$\mathbf{C} = \mathbf{F}_1\mathbf{P}_1\mathbf{F}_1' + \cdots + \mathbf{F}_m\mathbf{P}_m\mathbf{F}_m',$$

$$\mathbf{F}_k = \mathbf{F}_{k_1} \cdots \mathbf{F}_{k_{n(k)}}, \qquad \text{and} \quad \mathbf{P}_k = \mathbf{P}_k', \quad k = 1, \ldots, m$$

$$\mathbf{F}_{k_j} = \begin{cases} \mathbf{G}_{k_j} \\ \mathbf{G}_{k_j}^{-1} \\ (\mathbf{I} - \mathbf{G}_{k_j})^{-1} \end{cases} \quad j = 1, \ldots, n(k), \qquad \text{and} \quad \mathbf{P}_k = \begin{cases} \mathbf{Q}_k \\ \mathbf{Q}_k^{-1} \end{cases}$$

You can specify only one COSAN statement with each PROC CALIS statement. The COSAN statement contains m *matrix_terms* corresponding to the generalized COSAN formula. The *matrix_terms* are separated by plus signs (+) according to the addition of the terms within the model.

Each *matrix_term* of the COSAN statement contains the definitions of the first $n(k)+1$ matrices, $\mathbf{F}_{k_j}$ and $\mathbf{P}_k$, separated by asterisks (*) according to the multiplication of the matrices within the term. The matrices $\mathbf{F}_k'$ of the right-hand-side product are redundant and are not specified within the COSAN statement.

Each *matrix_definition* consists of the name of the matrix (*matrix_name*), followed in parentheses by the number of columns of the matrix (*column_number*) and, optionally, one or two matrix properties, separated by commas, describing the form of the matrix.

The number of rows of the first matrix in each term is defined by the input correlation or covariance matrix. You can reorder and reduce the variables in the input moment matrix using the VAR statement. The number of rows of the other matrices within the term is defined by the number of columns of the preceding matrix.

The first matrix property describes the general form of the matrix in the model. You can choose one of the following specifications of the first matrix property. The default first matrix property is GEN.

Code	**Description**
IDE	specifies an identity matrix; if the matrix is not square, this specification describes an identity submatrix followed by a rectangular zero submatrix.
ZID	specifies an identity matrix; if the matrix is not square, this specification describes a rectangular zero submatrix followed by an identity submatrix.
DIA	specifies a diagonal matrix; if the matrix is not square, this specification describes a diagonal submatrix followed by a rectangular zero submatrix.
ZDI	specifies a diagonal matrix; if the matrix is not square, this specification describes a rectangular zero submatrix followed by a diagonal submatrix.
LOW	specifies a lower triangular matrix; the matrix can be rectangular.
UPP	specifies an upper triangular matrix; the matrix can be rectangular.
SYM	specifies a symmetric matrix; the matrix cannot be rectangular.
GEN	specifies a general rectangular matrix (default).

The second matrix property describes the kind of inverse matrix transformation. If the second matrix property is omitted, no transformation is applied to the matrix.

Code	**Description**
INV	uses the inverse of the matrix.
IMI	uses the inverse of the difference between the identity and the matrix.

You cannot specify a nonsquare parameter matrix as an INV or IMI model matrix. Specifying a matrix of type DIA, ZDI, UPP, LOW, or GEN is not necessary if you do not use the *unspecified location* list in the corresponding MATRIX statements. After PROC CALIS processes the corresponding MATRIX statements, the matrix type DIA, ZDI, UPP, LOW, or GEN is recognized from the pattern of possibly nonzero elements. If you do not specify the first matrix property and you use the *unspecified location* list in a corresponding MATRIX statement, the matrix is recognized as a GEN matrix. You can also generate an IDE or ZID matrix by specifying a DIA, ZDI, or IMI matrix and by using MATRIX statements that define the pattern structure. However, PROC CALIS would be unable to take advantage of the fast algorithms that are available for IDE and ZID matrices in this case.

For example, to specify a second-order factor analysis model

$$\mathbf{S} = \mathbf{F}_1\mathbf{F}_2\mathbf{P}_2\mathbf{F}_2'\mathbf{F}_1' + \mathbf{F}_1\mathbf{U}_2^2\mathbf{F}_1' + \mathbf{U}_1^2$$

with $m_1 = 3$ first-order factors and $m_2 = 2$ second-order factors and with $n = 9$ variables, you can use the following COSAN statement:

```
cosan F1(3) * F2(2) * P2(2,SYM)+F1(3) * U2(3,DIA) * I1(3,IDE)
      +U1(9,DIA) * I2(9,IDE)
```

MATRIX Statement

MATRIX *matrix-name* < *location* > = *list* < , *location* = *list* . . . > ;

You can specify one or more MATRIX statements with a COSAN or FACTOR statement. A MATRIX statement specifies which elements of the matrix are constant and which are parameters. You can also assign values to the constant elements and initial values for the parameters. The input notation resembles that used in the COSAN program of R. McDonald and C. Fraser (personal communication), except that in PROC CALIS, parameters are distinguished from constants by giving parameters names instead of by using positive and negative integers.

A MATRIX statement cannot be used for an IDE or ZID matrix. For all other types of matrices, each element is assumed to be a constant of 0 unless a MATRIX statement specifies otherwise. Hence, there must be at least one MATRIX statement for each matrix mentioned in the COSAN statement except for IDE and ZID matrices. There can be more than one MATRIX statement for a given matrix. If the same matrix element is given different definitions, later definitions override earlier definitions.

At the start, all elements of each model matrix, except IDE or ZID matrices, are set equal to 0.

Description of *location*:

There are several ways to specify the starting *location* and continuation direction of a *list* with $n + 1$, $n \geq 0$, elements within the parameter matrix.

[*i* , *j*] The *list* elements correspond to the diagonally continued matrix elements [*i,j*] , [*i*+1,*j*+1] , ... , [*i*+*n*,*j*+*n*]. The number of elements is defined by the length of the list and eventually terminated by the matrix boundaries. If the list contains just one element (constant or variable), then it is assigned to the matrix element [*i,j*].

[*i* ,] The *list* elements correspond to the horizontally continued matrix elements [*i,j*], [*i,j*+1] , ... , [*i,j*+*n*], where the starting column *j* is the diagonal position for a DIA, ZDI, or UPP matrix and is the first column for all other matrix types. For a SYM matrix, the list elements refer only to the matrix elements in the lower triangle. For a DIA or ZDI matrix, only one list element is accepted.

[, *j*] The *list* elements correspond to the vertically continued matrix elements [*i,j*], [*i*+1,*j*] , ... , [*i*+*n*,*j*], where the starting row *i* is equal to the diagonal position for a DIA, ZDI, SYM, or LOW matrix and is the first row for each other matrix type. For a SYM matrix, the list elements refer only to the matrix elements in the lower triangle. For a DIA or ZDI matrix, only one list element is accepted.

[,] unspecified location: The *list* is allocated to all valid matrix positions (except for a ZDI matrix) starting at the element [1,1] and continuing rowwise. The only valid matrix positions for a DIA or ZDI matrix are the diagonal

elements; for an UPP or LOW matrix, the valid positions are the elements above or below the diagonal; and for a symmetric matrix, the valid positions are the elements in the lower triangle since the other triangle receives the symmetric allocation automatically. This *location* definition differs from the definitions with specified pattern locations in one important respect: if the number of elements in the *list* is smaller than the number of valid matrix elements, the list is repeated in the allocation process until all valid matrix elements are filled.

Omitting the left-hand-side term is equivalent to using [,] for an *unspecified location*.

Description of *list*:

The *list* contains numeric values or parameter names, or both, that are assigned to a list of matrix elements starting at a specified position and proceeding in a specified direction. A real number r in the list defines the corresponding matrix element as a constant element with this value. The notation $n * r$ generates n values of r in the list. A name in the list defines the corresponding matrix element as a parameter to be estimated. You can use numbered name lists (X1-X10) or the asterisk notation (5 *X means five occurrences of the parameter X). If a sublist of n_1 names inside a *list* is followed by a list of $n_2 \leq n_1$ real values inside parentheses, the last n_2 parameters in the name sublist are given the initial values mentioned inside the parenthesis. For example, the following *list*

```
0. 1. A2-A5 (1.4 1.9 2.5) 5.
```

specifies that the first two matrix elements (specified by the *location* to the left of the equal sign) are constants with values 0 and 1. The next element is parameter A2 with no specified initial value. The next three matrix elements are the variable parameters A3, A4, and A5 with initial values 1.4, 1.9, and 2.5, respectively. The next matrix element is specified by the seventh list element to be the constant 5.

If your model contains many unconstrained parameters and it is too cumbersome to find different parameter names, you can specify all those parameters by the same prefix name. A prefix is a short name followed by a colon. The CALIS procedure generates a parameter name by appending an integer suffix to this prefix name. The prefix name should have no more than five or six characters so that the generated parameter name is not longer than eight characters. For example, if the prefix A (the parameter A1) is already used once in a *list*, the previous example would be identical to

```
0. 1. 4 * A: (1.4 1.9 2.5) 5.
```

To avoid unintentional equality constraints, the prefix names should not coincide with explicitly defined parameter names.

If you do not assign initial values to the parameters (listed in parentheses following a name sublist within the pattern list), PROC CALIS assigns initial values as follows:

- If the PROC CALIS statement contains a START=r option, each uninitialized parameter is given the initial value r. The uninitialized parameters in the diagonals of the central model matrices are given the initial value $10|r|$, $100|r|$, or $|r|$ multiplied by the value specified in the DEMPHAS= option.

- If the PROC CALIS statement contains a RANDOM=i option, each uninitialized parameter is given a random initial value $0 \leq r \leq 1$. The uninitialized parameters in the diagonals of the central model matrices are given the random values multiplied by 10, 100, or the value specified in the DEMPHAS= option.
- Otherwise, the initial value is set corresponding to START=0.5.

For example, to specify a confirmatory second-order factor analysis model

$$\mathbf{S} = \mathbf{F}_1\mathbf{F}_2\mathbf{P}_2\mathbf{F}_2'\mathbf{F}_1' + \mathbf{F}_1\mathbf{U}_2^2\mathbf{F}_1' + \mathbf{U}_1^2$$

with $m_1 = 3$ first-order factors, $m_2 = 2$ second-order factors, and $n = 9$ variables and the following matrix pattern,

$$\mathbf{F}_1 = \begin{pmatrix} X_1 & 0 & 0 \\ X_2 & 0 & 0 \\ X_3 & 0 & 0 \\ 0 & X_4 & 0 \\ 0 & X_5 & 0 \\ 0 & X_6 & 0 \\ 0 & 0 & X_7 \\ 0 & 0 & X_8 \\ 0 & 0 & X_9 \end{pmatrix}, \quad \mathbf{U}_1 = \begin{pmatrix} U_1 & & & & & & & & \\ & U_2 & & & & & & & \\ & & U_3 & & & & & & \\ & & & U_4 & & & & & \\ & & & & U_5 & & & & \\ & & & & & U_6 & & & \\ & & & & & & U_7 & & \\ & & & & & & & U_8 & \\ & & & & & & & & U_9 \end{pmatrix}$$

$$\mathbf{F}_2 = \begin{pmatrix} Y_1 & 0 \\ Y_1 & Y_2 \\ 0 & Y_2 \end{pmatrix}, \quad \mathbf{P}_2 = \begin{pmatrix} P & 0 \\ 0 & P \end{pmatrix}, \quad \mathbf{U}_2 = \begin{pmatrix} V_1 & & \\ & V_2 & \\ & & V_3 \end{pmatrix}$$

you can specify the following COSAN and MATRIX statements:

```
cosan f1(3) * f2(2) * p2(2,dia) + f1(3) * u2(3,dia) * i1(3,ide)
      + u1(9,dia) * i2(9,ide);
matrix f1
         [ ,1]= x1-x3,
         [ ,2]= 3 * 0 x4-x6,
         [ ,3]= 6 * 0 x7-x9;
matrix u1
         [1,1]=u1-u9;


matrix f2
         [ ,1]= 2 * y1,
         [ ,2]= 0. 2 * y2;
matrix u2 = 3 * v:;
matrix p2 = 2 * p;
run;
```

The matrix pattern includes several equality constraints. Two loadings in the first and second factor of $\mathbf{F}_2$ (parameter names Y1 and Y2) and the two factor correlations in the diagonal of matrix $\mathbf{P}_2$ (parameter name P) are constrained to be equal. There are many other ways to specify the same model. See Figure 19.2 for the path diagram of this model.

The MATRIX statment can also be used with the FACTOR model statement. See "Using the FACTOR and MATRIX Statements" on page 494 for the usage.

RAM Model Statement

RAM *list-entry* < , *list-entry* . . . > ;
where *list-entry* represents
matrix-number row-number column-number <*value*><*parameter-name*>

The RAM statement defines the elements of the symmetric RAM matrix model

$$\mathbf{v} = \mathbf{A}\mathbf{v} + \mathbf{u}$$

in the form of a list type input (McArdle and McDonald 1984).

The covariance structure is given by

$$\mathbf{C} = \mathbf{J}(\mathbf{I} - \mathbf{A})^{-1}\mathbf{P}((\mathbf{I} - \mathbf{A})^{-1})'\mathbf{J}'$$

with selection matrix $\mathbf{J}$ and

$$\mathbf{C} = \mathcal{E}\{\mathbf{J}\mathbf{v}\mathbf{v}'\mathbf{J}'\}, \qquad \mathbf{P} = \mathcal{E}\{\mathbf{u}\mathbf{u}'\}$$

You can specify only one RAM statement with each PROC CALIS statement. Using the RAM statement requires that the first n variable numbers in the path diagram and in the vector v correspond to the numbers of the n manifest variables of the given covariance or correlation matrix. If you are not sure what the order of the manifest variables in the DATA= data set is, use a VAR statement to specify the order of these observed variables. Using the AUGMENT option includes the INTERCEPT variable as a manifest variable with number $n + 1$ in the RAM model. In this case, latent variables have to start with $n + 2$. The box of each manifest variable in the path diagram is assigned the number of the variable in the covariance or correlation matrix.

The selection matrix $\mathbf{J}$ is always a rectangular identity (IDE) matrix, and it does not have to be specified in the RAM statement. A constant matrix element is defined in a RAM statement by a *list-entry* with four numbers. You define a parameter element by three or four numbers followed by a name for the parameter. Separate the list entries with a comma. Each *list-entry* in the RAM statement corresponds to a path in the diagram, as follows:

- The first number in each list entry (*matrix-number*) is the number of arrow heads of the path, which is the same as the number of the matrix in the RAM model (1 := $\mathbf{A}$, 2 := $\mathbf{P}$).

- The second number in each list entry (*row-number*) is the number of the node in the diagram to which the path points, which is the same as the row number of the matrix element.
- The third number in each list entry (*column-number*) is the number of the node in the diagram from which the path originates, which is the same as the column number of the matrix element.
- The fourth number (*value*) gives the (initial) value of the path coefficient. If you do not specify a fifth *list-entry*, this number specifies a constant coefficient; otherwise, this number specifies the initial value of this parameter. It is not necessary to specify the fourth item. If you specify neither the fourth nor the fifth item, the constant is set to 1 by default. If the fourth item (*value*) is not specified for a parameter, PROC CALIS tries to compute an initial value for this parameter.
- If the path coefficient is a parameter rather than a constant, then a fifth item in the list entry (*parameter-name*) is required to assign a name to the parameter. Using the same name for different paths constrains the corresponding coefficients to be equal.

If the initial value of a parameter is not specified in the list, the initial value is chosen in one of the following ways:

- If the PROC CALIS statement contains a RANDOM=i option, then the parameter obtains a randomly generated initial value r, such that $0 \leq r \leq 1$. The uninitialized parameters in the diagonals of the central model matrices are given the random values r multiplied by 10, 100, or the value specified in the DEMPHAS= option.
- If the RANDOM= option is not used, PROC CALIS tries to estimate the initial values.
- If the initial values cannot be estimated, the value of the START= option is used as an initial value.

If your model contains many unconstrained parameters and it is too cumbersome to find different parameter names, you can specify all those parameters by the same prefix name. A prefix is a short name followed by a colon. The CALIS procedure then generates a parameter name by appending an integer suffix to this prefix name. The prefix name should have no more than five or six characters so that the generated parameter name is not longer than eight characters. To avoid unintentional equality constraints, the prefix names should not coincide with explicitly defined parameter names.

For example, you can specify the confirmatory second-order factor analysis model (mentioned on page 483)

$$\mathbf{S} = \mathbf{F}_1\mathbf{F}_2\mathbf{P}_2\mathbf{F}_2'\mathbf{F}_1' + \mathbf{F}_1\mathbf{U}_2^2\mathbf{F}_1' + \mathbf{U}_1^2$$

using the following RAM model statement.

```
ram
   1  1 10    x1,
   1  2 10    x2,
   1  3 10    x3,
   1  4 11    x4,
   1  5 11    x5,
   1  6 11    x6,
   1  7 12    x7,
   1  8 12    x8,
   1  9 12    x9,
   1 10 13    y1,
   1 11 13    y1,
   1 11 14    y2,
   1 12 14    y2,
   2  1  1    u:,
   2  2  2    u:,
   2  3  3    u:,
   2  4  4    u:,
   2  5  5    u:,
   2  6  6    u:,
   2  7  7    u:,
   2  8  8    u:,
   2  9  9    u:,
   2 10 10    v:,
   2 11 11    v:,
   2 12 12    v:,
   2 13 13    p ,
   2 14 14    p ;
run;
```

The confirmatory second-order factor analysis model corresponds to the path diagram displayed in Figure 19.2.

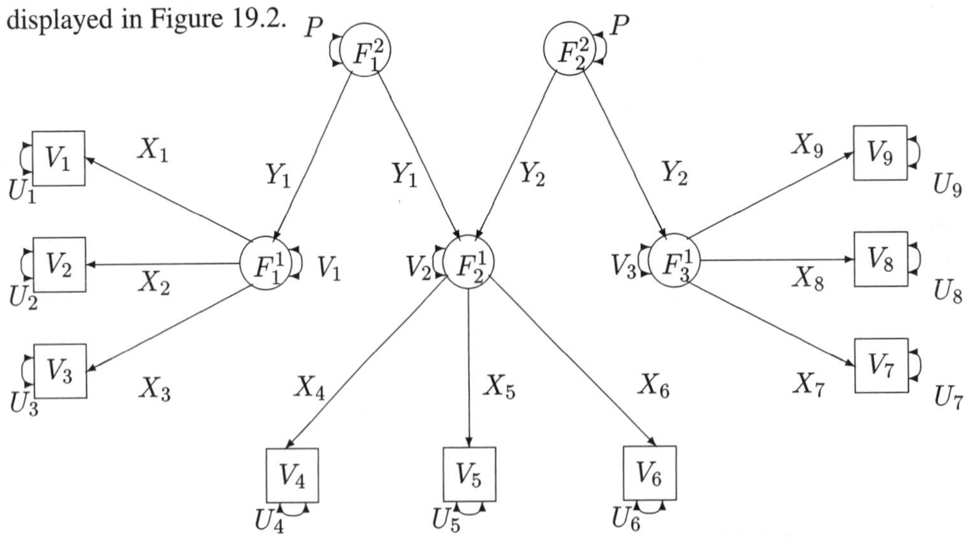

Figure 19.2. Path Diagram of Second-Order Factor Analysis Model

There is a very close relationship between the RAM model algebra and the specification of structural linear models by path diagrams. See Figure 19.3 for an example.

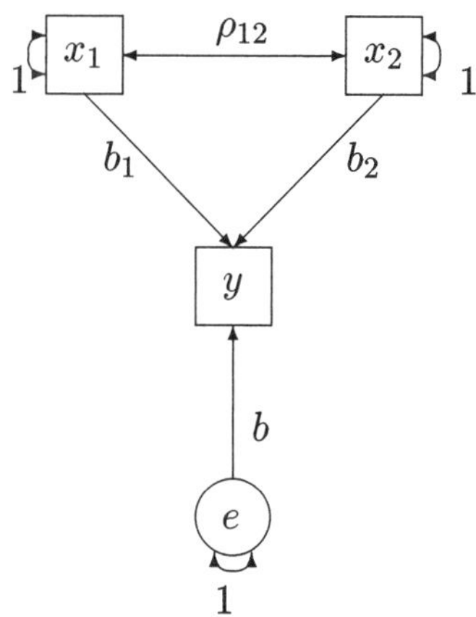

1. Multiple Regression

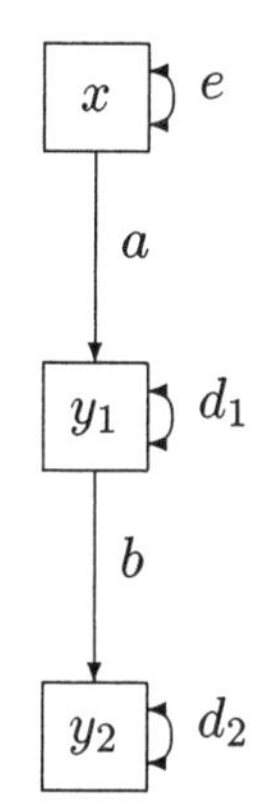

2. Chain Simplex

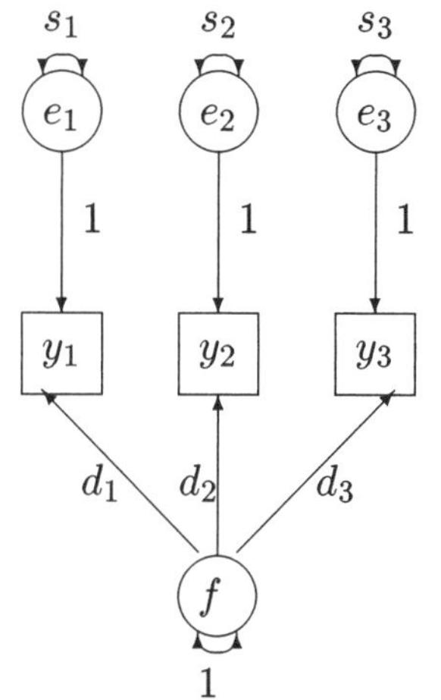

3. First-Order Factor Analysis

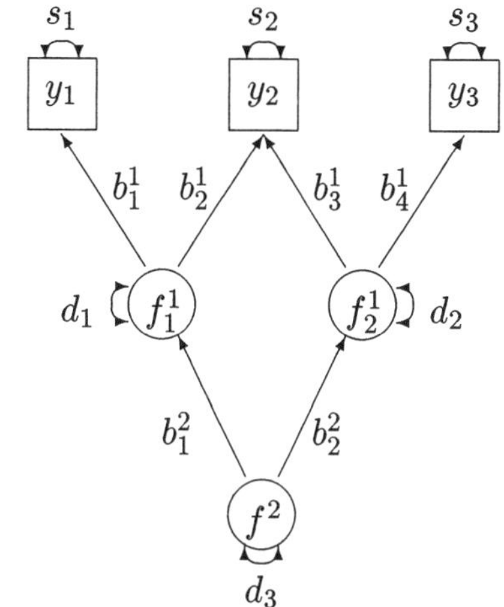

4. Second-Order Factor Analysis

Figure 19.3. Examples of RAM Nomography

Refer to McArdle (1980) for the interpretation of the models displayed in Figure 19.3.

LINEQS Model Statement

LINEQS *equation* < , *equation* ... > **;**

where *equation* represents *dependent* = *term* < + *term* ... >

and where *term* represents one of the following:

- *coefficient-name* < *(number)* > *variable-name*
- *prefix-name* < *(number)* > *variable-name*
- < *number* > *variable-name*

The LINEQS statement defines the LINEQS model

$$
\begin{aligned}
\eta &= \beta\eta + \gamma\xi \\
\mathbf{C} &= \mathbf{J}(\mathbf{I}-\mathbf{B})^{-1}\mathbf{\Gamma}\mathbf{\Phi}\mathbf{\Gamma}'((\mathbf{I}-\mathbf{B})^{-1})'\mathbf{J}'
\end{aligned}
$$

You can specify only one LINEQS statement with each PROC CALIS statement. There are some differences from Bentler's notation in choosing the variable names. The length of each variable name is restricted to eight characters. The names of the manifest variables are defined in the DATA= input data set. The VAR statement can be used to select a subset of manifest variables in the DATA= input data set to analyze. You do not need to use a V prefix for manifest variables in the LINEQS statement nor do you need to use a numerical suffix in any variable name. The names of the latent variables must start with the prefix letter F (for Factor); the names of the residuals must start with the prefix letters E (for Error) or D (for Disturbance). The trailing part of the variable name can contain letters or digits. The prefix letter E is used for the errors of the manifest variables, and the prefix letter D is used for the disturbances of the latent variables. The names of the manifest variables in the DATA= input data set can start with F, E, or D, but these names should not coincide with the names of latent or error variables used in the model. The left-hand side (that is, endogenous *dependent* variable) of each equation should be either a manifest variable of the data set or a latent variable with prefix letter F. The left-hand-side variable should not appear on the right-hand side of the same equation; this means that matrix $\boldsymbol{\beta}$ should not have a nonzero diagonal element. Each equation should contain, at most, one E or D variable.

The equations must be separated by a comma. The order of the equations is arbitrary. The displayed output generally contains equations and terms in an order different from the input.

Coefficients to estimate are indicated in the equations by a name preceding the independent variable's name. The coefficient's name can be followed by a number inside parentheses indicating the initial value for this coefficient. A number preceding the independent variable's name indicates a constant coefficient. If neither a coefficient name nor a number precedes the independent variable's name, a constant coefficient of 1 is assumed.

If the initial value of a parameter is not specified in the equation, the initial value is chosen in one of the following ways:

- If you specify the RANDOM= option in the PROC CALIS statement, the variable obtains a randomly generated initial value r, such that $0 \leq r \leq 1$. The uninitialized parameters in the diagonals of the central model matrices are given the nonnegative random values r multiplied by 10, 100, or the value specified in the DEMPHAS= option.
- If the RANDOM= option is not used, PROC CALIS tries to estimate the initial values.
- If the initial values cannot be estimated, the value of the START= option is used as an initial value.

In Bentler's notation, estimated coefficients are indicated by asterisks. Referring to a parameter in Bentler's notation requires the specification of two variable names that correspond to the row and column of the position of the parameter in the matrix. Specifying the estimated coefficients by parameter names makes it easier to impose additional constraints with code. You do not need any additional statements to express equality constraints. Simply specify the same name for parameters that should have equal values.

If your model contains many unconstrained parameters and it is too cumbersome to find different parameter names, you can specify all those parameters by the same prefix name. A prefix is a short name followed by a colon. The CALIS procedure then generates a parameter name by appending an integer suffix to this prefix name. The prefix name should have no more than five or six characters so that the generated parameter name is not longer than eight characters. To avoid unintentional equality constraints, the prefix names should not coincide with explicitly defined parameter names.

For example, you can specify confirmatory second-order factor analysis model (mentioned on page 483)

$$\mathbf{S} = \mathbf{F}_1\mathbf{F}_2\mathbf{P}_2\mathbf{F}_2'\mathbf{F}_1' + \mathbf{F}_1\mathbf{U}_2^2\mathbf{F}_1' + \mathbf{U}_1^2$$

by using the LINEQS and STD statements:

```
lineqs
        V1  = X1 F1 + E1,
        V2  = X2 F1 + E2,
        V3  = X3 F1 + E3,
        V4  = X4 F2 + E4,
        V5  = X5 F2 + E5,
        V6  = X6 F2 + E6,
        V7  = X7 F3 + E7,
        V8  = X8 F3 + E8,
        V9  = X9 F3 + E9,
        F1  = Y1 F4 + D1,
        F2  = Y1 F4 + Y2 F5 + D2,
        F3  = Y2 F5 + D3;
```

```
std
        E1-E9 = 9 * U:,
        D1-D3 = 3 * V:,
        F4 F5 = 2 * P;
run;
```

STD Statement

STD *assignment* < , *assignment* ... > ;

where *assignment* represents *variables = pattern-definition*

The STD statement tells which variances are parameters to estimate and which are fixed. The STD statement can be used only with the LINEQS statement. You can specify only one STD statement with each LINEQS model statement. The STD statement defines the diagonal elements of the central model matrix $\mathbf{\Phi}$. These elements correspond to the variances of the exogenous variables and to the error variances of the endogenous variables. Elements that are not defined are assumed to be 0.

Each *assignment* consists of a variable list (*variables*) on the left-hand side and a pattern list (*pattern-definition*) on the right-hand side of an equal sign. The *assignments* in the STD statement must be separated by commas. The *variables* list on the left-hand side of the equal sign should contain only names of variables that do not appear on the left-hand side of an equation in the LINEQS statement, that is, exogenous, error, and disturbance variables.

The *pattern-definition* on the right-hand side is similar to that used in the MATRIX statement. Each list element on the right-hand side defines the variance of the variable on the left-hand side in the same list position. A name on the right-hand side means that the corresponding variance is a parameter to estimate. A name on the right-hand side can be followed by a number inside parentheses that gives the initial value. A number on the right-hand side means that the corresponding variance of the variable on the left-hand side is fixed. If the right-hand-side list is longer than the left-hand-side variable list, the right-hand-side list is shortened to the length of the variable list. If the right-hand-side list is shorter than the variable list, the right-hand-side list is filled with repetitions of the last item in the list.

The right-hand side can also contain prefixes. A prefix is a short name followed by a colon. The CALIS procedure then generates a parameter name by appending an integer suffix to this prefix name. The prefix name should have no more than five or six characters so that the generated parameter name is not longer than eight characters. To avoid unintentional equality constraints, the prefix names should not coincide with explicitly defined parameter names. For example, if the prefix A is not used in any previous statement, this STD statement

```
std E1-E6=6 * A: (6 * 3.) ;
```

defines the six error variances as free parameters $A1,\ldots,A6$, all with starting values of 3.

COV Statement

COV *assignment* < , *assignment* . . . > ;

where *assignment* represents *variables* < ∗ *variables2* > = *pattern-definition*

The COV statement tells which covariances are parameters to estimate and which are fixed. The COV statement can be used only with the LINEQS statement. The COV statement differs from the STD statement only in the meaning of the left-hand-side *variables* list. You can specify only one COV statement with each LINEQS statement. The COV statement defines the off-diagonal elements of the central model matrix $\mathbf{\Phi}$. These elements correspond to the covariances of the exogenous variables and to the error covariances of the endogenous variables. Elements that are not defined are assumed to be 0. The *assignment*s in the COV statement must be separated by commas.

The *variables* list on the left-hand side of the equal sign should contain only names of variables that do not appear on the left-hand side of an equation in the LINEQS statement, that is, exogenous, error, and disturbance variables.

The *pattern-definition* on the right-hand side is similar to that used in the MATRIX statement. Each list element on the right-hand side defines the covariance of a pair of variables in the list on the left-hand side. A name on the right-hand side can be followed by a number inside parentheses that gives the initial value. A number on the right-hand side means that the corresponding covariance of the variable on the left-hand side is fixed. If the right-hand-side list is longer than the left-hand-side variable list, the right-hand-side list is shortened to the length of the variable list. If the right-hand-side list is shorter than the variable list, the right-hand-side list is filled with repetitions of the last item in the list.

You can use one of two alternatives to refer to parts of $\mathbf{\Phi}$. The first alternative uses only one variable list and refers to all distinct pairs of variables within the list. The second alternative uses two variable lists separated by an asterisk and refers to all pairs of variables among the two lists.

Within-List Covariances

Using k variable names in the *variables* list on the left-hand side of an equal sign in a COV statement means that the parameter list (*pattern-definition*) on the right-hand side refers to all $k(k-1)/2$ distinct variable pairs in the below-diagonal part of the $\mathbf{\Phi}$ matrix. Order is very important. The order relation between the left-hand-side variable pairs and the right-hand-side parameter list is illustrated by the following example:

```
COV E1-E4 = PHI1-PHI6 ;
```

This is equivalent to the following specification:

```
COV E2 E1 = PHI1,
    E3 E1 = PHI2, E3 E2 = PHI3,
    E4 E1 = PHI4, E4 E2 = PHI5, E4 E3 = PHI6;
```

The symmetric elements are generated automatically. When you use prefix names on the right-hand sides, you do not have to count the exact number of parameters. For example,

```
COV E1-E4 = PHI: ;
```

generates the same list of parameter names if the prefix PHI is not used in a previous statement.

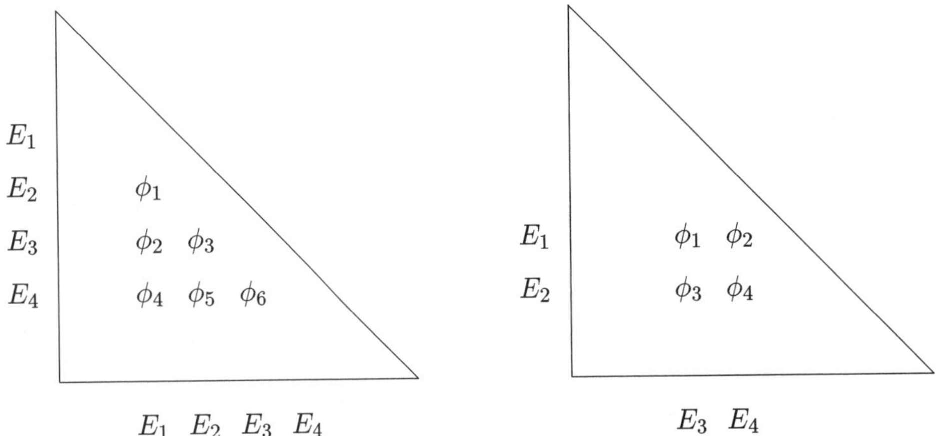

Figure 19.4. Within-List and Between-List Covariances

Between-List Covariances

Using k_1 and k_2 variable names in the two lists (separated by an asterisk) on the left-hand side of an equal sign in a COV statement means that the parameter list on the right-hand side refers to all $k_1 \times k_2$ distinct variable pairs in the $\mathbf{\Phi}$ matrix. Order is very important. The order relation between the left-hand-side variable pairs and the right-hand-side parameter list is illustrated by the following example:

```
COV E1 E2 * E3 E4 = PHI1-PHI4 ;
```

This is equivalent to the following specification:

```
COV   E1 E3 = PHI1, E1 E4 = PHI2,
      E2 E3 = PHI3, E2 E4 = PHI4;
```

The symmetric elements are generated automatically.

Using prefix names on the right-hand sides lets you achieve the same purpose without counting the number of parameters. That is,

```
COV   E1 E2 * E3 E4 = PHI: ;
```

FACTOR Model Statement

FACTOR < *options* > **;**

You can use the FACTOR statement to specify an exploratory or confirmatory first-order factor analysis of the given covariance or correlation matrix $\mathbf{C}$,

$$\mathbf{C} = \mathbf{F}\mathbf{F}' + \mathbf{U}, \quad \mathbf{U} = diag$$

or

$$\mathbf{C} = \mathbf{F}\mathbf{P}\mathbf{F}' + \mathbf{U}, \quad \mathbf{P} = \mathbf{P}'$$

where $\mathbf{U}$ is a diagonal matrix and $\mathbf{P}$ is symmetric. Within this section, n denotes the number of manifest variables corresponding to the rows and columns of matrix $\mathbf{C}$, and m denotes the number of latent variables (factors or components) corresponding to the columns of the loading matrix $\mathbf{F}$.

You can specify only one FACTOR statement with each PROC CALIS statement. You can specify higher-order factor analysis problems using a COSAN model specification. PROC CALIS requires more computing time and memory than PROC FACTOR because it is designed for more general structural estimation problems and is unable to exploit the special properties of the unconstrained factor analysis model.

For default (exploratory) factor analysis, PROC CALIS computes initial estimates for factor loadings and unique variances by an algebraic method of approximate factor analysis. If you use a MATRIX statement together with a FACTOR model specification, initial values are computed by McDonald's (McDonald and Hartmann 1992) method (if possible). For details, see "Using the FACTOR and MATRIX Statements" on page 494. If neither of the two methods are appropriate, the initial values are set by the START= option.

The unrestricted factor analysis model is not identified because any orthogonal rotated factor loading matrix $\tilde{\mathbf{F}} = \mathbf{F}\mathbf{\Theta}$ is equivalent to the result $\mathbf{F}$,

$$\mathbf{C} = \tilde{\mathbf{F}}\tilde{\mathbf{F}}' + \mathbf{U}, \qquad \tilde{\mathbf{F}} = \mathbf{F}\mathbf{\Theta}, \quad \text{where} \quad \mathbf{\Theta}'\mathbf{\Theta} = \mathbf{\Theta}\mathbf{\Theta}' = \mathbf{I}$$

To obtain an identified factor solution, the FACTOR statement imposes zero constraints on the $m(m-1)/2$ elements in the upper triangle of $\mathbf{F}$ by default.

The following options are available in the FACTOR statement.

COMPONENT | COMP

computes a component analysis instead of a factor analysis (the diagonal matrix $\mathbf{U}$ in the model is set to 0). Note that the rank of $\mathbf{F}\mathbf{F}'$ is equal to the number m of components in $\mathbf{F}$. If m is smaller than the number of variables in the moment matrix $\mathbf{C}$, the matrix of predicted model values is singular and maximum likelihood estimates for $\mathbf{F}$ cannot be computed. You should compute ULS estimates in this case.

HEYWOOD | HEY

constrains the diagonal elements of $\mathbf{U}$ to be nonnegative; in other words, the model is replaced by

$$\mathbf{C} = \mathbf{FF}' + \mathbf{U}^2, \quad \mathbf{U} = diag$$

N = *m*

specifies the number of first-order factors or components. The number m of factors should not exceed the number n of variables in the covariance or correlation matrix analyzed. For the saturated model, $m = n$, the COMP option should generally be specified for $\mathbf{U} = 0$; otherwise, $df < 0$. For $m = 0$ no factor loadings are estimated, and the model is $\mathbf{C} = \mathbf{U}$, with $\mathbf{U} = diag$. By default, $m = 1$.

NORM

normalizes the rows of the factor pattern for rotation using Kaiser's normalization.

ROTATE | R = *name*

specifies an orthogonal rotation. By default, ROTATE=NONE. The possible values for *name* are as follows:

PRINCIPAL | PC — specifies a principal axis rotation. If ROTATE=PRINCIPAL is used with a factor rather than a component model, the following rotation is performed:

$$\mathbf{F}_{new} = \mathbf{F}_{old}\mathbf{T}, \quad \text{with} \quad \mathbf{F}'_{old}\mathbf{F}_{old} = \mathbf{T}\mathbf{\Lambda}\mathbf{T}'$$

where the columns of matrix $\mathbf{T}$ contain the eigenvectors of $\mathbf{F}'_{old}\mathbf{F}_{old}$.

QUARTIMAX | Q — specifies quartimax rotation.

VARIMAX | V — specifies varimax rotation.

EQUAMAX | E — specifies equamax rotation.

PARSIMAX | P — specifies parsimax rotation.

NONE — performs no rotation (default).

Using the FACTOR and MATRIX Statements

You can specify the MATRIX statement and the FACTOR statement to compute a confirmatory first-order factor or component analysis. You can define the elements of the matrices $\mathbf{F}$, $\mathbf{P}$, and $\mathbf{U}$ of the oblique model,

$$\mathbf{C} = \mathbf{FPF}' + \mathbf{U}^2, \quad \mathbf{P} = \mathbf{P}', \quad \mathbf{U} = diag$$

To specify the structure for matrix $\mathbf{F}$, $\mathbf{P}$, or $\mathbf{U}$, you have to refer to the matrix _F_, _P_, or _U_ in the MATRIX statement. Matrix names automatically set by PROC CALIS always start with an underscore. As you name your own matrices or variables, you should avoid leading underscores.

The default matrix forms are as follows.

_F_ lower triangular matrix (0 upper triangle for problem identification, removing rotational invariance)

_P_ identity matrix (constant)

_U_ diagonal matrix

For details about specifying the elements in matrices, see the section "MATRIX Statement" on page 481. If you are using at least one MATRIX statement in connection with a FACTOR model statement, you can also use the BOUNDS or PARAMETERS statement and program statements to constrain the parameters named in the MATRIX statement. Initial estimates are computed by McDonald's (McDonald and Hartmann 1992) method. McDonald's method of computing initial values works better if you scale the factors by setting the factor variances to 1 rather than by setting the loadings of the reference variables equal to 1.

BOUNDS Statement

BOUNDS *constraint* < , *constraint* ... > ;
where *constraint* represents
< *number operator* > *parameter-list* < *operator number* >

You can use the BOUNDS statement to define boundary constraints for any parameter that has its name specified in a MATRIX, LINEQS, STD, COV, or RAM statement or that is used in the model of an INRAM= data set. Valid operators are <=, <, >=, >, and = or, equivalently, LE, LT, GE, GT, and EQ. The following is an example of the BOUNDS statement:

```
bounds         0.   <= a1-a9 x    <= 1. ,
              -1.   <= c2-c5           ,
                       b1-b10 y   >= 0. ;
```

You must separate boundary constraints with a comma, and you can specify more than one BOUNDS statement. The feasible region for a parameter is the intersection of all boundary constraints specified for that parameter; if a parameter has a maximum lower boundary constraint larger than its minimum upper bound, the parameter is set equal to the minimum of the upper bounds.

If you need to compute the values of the upper or lower bounds, create a TYPE=EST data set containing _TYPE_='UPPERBD' or _TYPE_='LOWERBD' observations and use it as an INEST= or INVAR= input data set in a later PROC CALIS run.

The BOUNDS statement can contain only parameter names and numerical constants. You cannot use the names of variables created in program statements.

The active set strategies made available in PROC CALIS cannot realize the strict inequality constraints < or >. For example, you cannot specify `BOUNDS x > 0;` to prevent infinite values for $y = log(x)$. Use `BOUNDS x > 1E-8;` instead.

If the CALIS procedure encounters negative diagonal elements in the central model matrices during the minimization process, serious convergence problems can occur.

You can use the BOUNDS statement to constrain these parameters to nonnegative values. Using negative values in these locations can lead to a smaller χ^2 value but uninterpretable estimates.

LINCON Statement

LINCON *constraint* < , *constraint* . . . > ;

where *constraint* represents

number operator linear-term or

linear-term operator number ,

and *linear-term* is

<+|-><*coefficient*∗ >*parameter* <<+|-><*coefficient*∗ >*parameter*. . . >

The LINCON statement specifies a set of linear equality or inequality constraints of the form

$$\sum_{j=1}^{n} a_{ij} x_j \le b_i, \quad i = 1, \ldots, m$$

The constraints must be separated by commas. Each linear constraint i in the statement consists of a linear combination $\sum_j a_{ij} x_j$ of a subset of the n parameters $x_j, j = 1, \ldots, n$, and a constant value b_i separated by a comparison operator. Valid operators are <=, <, >=, >, and = or, equivalently, LE, LT, GE, GT, and EQ. PROC CALIS cannot enforce the strict inequalities < or >. Note that the coefficients a_{ij} in the linear combination must be constant numbers and must be followed by an asterisk and the name of a parameter (for example, listed in the PARMS, STD or COV statement). The following is an example of the LINCON statement that sets a linear constraint on parameters x1 and x2:

```
lincon        x1 + 3 * x2 <= 1;
```

Although you can easily express boundary constraints in LINCON statements, for many applications it is much more convenient to specify both the BOUNDS and the LINCON statements in the same PROC CALIS call.

The LINCON statement can contain only parameter names, operators, and numerical constants. If you need to compute the values of the coefficients a_{ij} or right-hand sides b_i, you can run a preliminary DATA step and create a TYPE=EST data set containing _TYPE_='LE', _TYPE_='GE', or _TYPE_='EQ' observations, then specify this data set as an INEST= or INVAR= data set in a following PROC CALIS run.

NLINCON Statement

NLINCON | NLC *constraint* < *, constraint . . .* > **;**

where *constraint* represents

number operator variable-list number operator or
variable-list operator number or
number operator variable-list

You can specify nonlinear equality and inequality constraints with the NLINCON or NLC statement. The QUANEW optimization subroutine is used when you specify nonlinear constraints using the NLINCON statement.

The syntax of the NLINCON statement is similar to that of the BOUNDS statement, except that the NLINCON statement must contain the names of variables that are defined in the program statements and are defined as continuous functions of parameters in the model. They must not be confused with the variables in the data set.

As with the BOUNDS statement, one- or two-sided constraints are allowed in the NLINCON statement; equality constraints must be one sided. Valid operators are $<=$, $<$, $>=$, $>$, and $=$ or, equivalently, LE, LT, GE, GT, and EQ.

PROC CALIS cannot enforce the strict inequalities $<$ or $>$ but instead treats them as $<=$ and $>=$, respectively. The listed nonlinear constraints must be separated by commas. The following is an example of the NLINCON statement that constrains the nonlinear parametric function $x_1 * x_1 + u_1$, which is defined below in a program statement, to a fixed value of 1:

```
nlincon    xx = 1;
xx = x1 * x1 + u1;
```

Note that x1 and u1 are parameters defined in the model. The following three NLINCON statements, which require xx1, xx2, and xx3 to be between zero and ten, are equivalent:

```
nlincon  0. <= xx1-xx3,
                xx1-xx3 <= 10;
nlincon 0. <= xx1-xx3 <= 10.;
nlincon 10. >= xx1-xx3 >= 0.;
```

NLOPTIONS Statement

NLOPTIONS *option(s)* ;

Many options that are available in PROC NLP can now be specified for the optimization subroutines in PROC CALIS using the NLOPTIONS statement. The NLOPTIONS statement provides more displayed and file output on the results of the optimization process, and it permits the same set of termination criteria as in PROC NLP. These are more technical options that you may not need to specify in most cases. The available options are summarized in Table 19.2 through Table 19.4, and the options are described in detail in the following three sections.

Table 19.2. Options Documented in the PROC CALIS Statement

Option	Short Description
Estimation Methods	
G4=*i*	algorithm for computing STDERR
Optimization Techniques	
TECHNIQUE=*name*	minimization method
UPDATE=*name*	update technique
LINESEARCH=*i*	line-search method
FCONV=*r*	relative change function convergence criterion
GCONV=*r*	relative gradient convergence criterion
INSTEP=*r*	initial step length (SALPHA=, RADIUS=)
LSPRECISION=*r*	line-search precision
MAXFUNC=*i*	maximum number of function calls
MAXITER=*i* <*n*>	maximum number of iterations
Miscellaneous Options	
ASINGULAR=*r*	absolute singularity criterion for inversion of the information matrix
COVSING=*r*	singularity tolerance of the information matrix
MSINGULAR=*r*	relative M singularity criterion for inversion of the information matrix
SINGULAR=*r*	singularity criterion for inversion of the Hessian
VSINGULAR=*r*	relative V singularity criterion for inversion of the information matrix

Table 19.3. Termination Criteria Options

Option	Short Description
Options Used by All Techniques	
ABSCONV=*r*	absolute function convergence criterion
MAXFUNC=*i*	maximum number of function calls
MAXITER=*i* <*n*>	maximum number of iterations
MAXTIME=*r*	maximum CPU time
MINITER=*i*	minimum number of iterations
Options for Unconstrained and Linearly Constrained Techniques	
ABSFCONV=*r* <*n*>	absolute change function convergence criterion
ABSGCONV=*r* <*n*>	absolute gradient convergence criterion
ABSXCONV=*r* <*n*>	absolute change parameter convergence criterion
FCONV=*r* <*n*>	relative change function convergence criterion
FCONV2=*r* <*n*>	function convergence criterion
FDIGITS=*r*	precision in computation of the objective function
FSIZE=*r*	parameter for FCONV= and GCONV=
GCONV=*r* <*n*>	relative gradient convergence criterion
GCONV2=*r* <*n*>	relative gradient convergence criterion
XCONV=*r* <*n*>	relative change parameter convergence criterion
XSIZE=*r*	parameter for XCONV=
Options for Nonlinearly Constrained Techniques	
ABSGCONV=*r* <*n*>	maximum absolute gradient of Lagrange function criterion
FCONV2=*r* <*n*>	predicted objective function reduction criterion
GCONV=*r* <*n*>	normalized predicted objective function reduction criterion

Table 19.4. Miscellaneous Options

Option	Short Description
Options for the Approximate Covariance Matrix of Parameter Estimates	
CFACTOR=*r*	scalar factor for STDERR
NOHLF	use Hessian of the objective function for STDERR
Options for Additional Displayed Output	
PALL	display initial and final optimization values
PCRPJAC	display approximate Hessian matrix
PHESSIAN	display Hessian matrix
PHISTORY	display optimization history
PINIT	display initial values and derivatives (PALL)
PNLCJAC	display Jacobian matrix of nonlinear constraints (PALL)
PRINT	display results of the optimization process
Additional Options for Optimization Techniques	
DAMPSTEP< =*r* >	controls initial line-search step size
HESCAL=*n*	scaling version of Hessian or Jacobian
LCDEACT=*r*	Lagrange multiplier threshold of constraint
LCEPSILON=*r*	range for boundary and linear constraints
LCSINGULAR=*r*	QR decomposition linear dependence criterion
NOEIGNUM	suppress computation of matrices
RESTART=*i*	restart algorithm with a steepest descent direction
VERSION=1 | 2	quasi-Newton optimization technique version

Options Documented in the PROC CALIS Statement

The following options are the same as in the PROC CALIS statement and are documented in the section "PROC CALIS Statement" on page 456.

Estimation Method Option

G4=*i*

specifies the method for computing the generalized (G2 or G4) inverse of a singular matrix needed for the approximate covariance matrix of parameter estimates. This option is valid only for applications where the approximate covariance matrix of parameter estimates is found to be singular.

Optimization Technique Options

TECHNIQUE | TECH=*name*

OMETHOD | OM=*name*

specifies the optimization technique.

UPDATE | UPD=*name*

specifies the update method for the quasi-Newton or conjugate-gradient optimization technique.

LINESEARCH | LIS=*i*

specifies the line-search method for the CONGRA, QUANEW, and NEWRAP optimization techniques.

FCONV | FTOL=*r*

specifies the relative function convergence criterion. For more details, see the section "Termination Criteria Options" on page 502.

GCONV | GTOL=*r*

specifies the relative gradient convergence criterion. For more details, see the section "Termination Criteria Options" on page 502.

INSTEP | SALPHA | RADIUS=*r*

restricts the step length of an optimization algorithm during the first iterations.

LSPRECISION | LSP=*r*

specifies the degree of accuracy that should be obtained by the line-search algorithms LIS=2 and LIS=3.

MAXFUNC | MAXFU=*i*

specifies the maximum number i of function calls in the optimization process. For more details, see the section "Termination Criteria Options" on page 502.

MAXITER | MAXIT=*i* <*n*>

specifies the maximum number i of iterations in the optimization process. For more details, see the section "Termination Criteria Options" on page 502.

Miscellaneous Options

ASINGULAR | ASING=*r*

specifies an absolute singularity criterion r, $r > 0$, for the inversion of the information matrix, which is needed to compute the approximate covariance matrix of parameter estimates.

COVSING=*r*

specifies a nonnegative threshold r, $r > 0$, that decides whether the eigenvalues of the information matrix are considered to be zero. This option is valid only for applications where the approximate covariance matrix of parameter estimates is found to be singular.

MSINGULAR | MSING=*r*

specifies a relative singularity criterion r, $r > 0$, for the inversion of the information matrix, which is needed to compute the approximate covariance matrix of parameter estimates.

SINGULAR | SING =*r*

specifies the singularity criterion r, $0 \leq r \leq 1$, that is used for the inversion of the Hessian matrix. The default value is 1E−8.

VSINGULAR | VSING=*r*

specifies a relative singularity criterion r, $r > 0$, for the inversion of the information matrix, which is needed to compute the approximate covariance matrix of parameter estimates.

Termination Criteria Options

Let x^* be the point at which the objective function $f(\cdot)$ is optimized, and let $x^{(k)}$ be the parameter values attained at the kth iteration. All optimization techniques stop at the kth iteration if at least one of a set of termination criteria is satisfied. The specified termination criteria should allow termination in an area of sufficient size around x^*. You can avoid termination respective to any of the following function, gradient, or parameter criteria by setting the corresponding option to zero. There is a default set of termination criteria for each optimization technique; most of these default settings make the criteria ineffective for termination. PROC CALIS may have problems due to rounding errors (especially in derivative evaluations) that prevent an optimizer from satisfying strong termination criteria.

Note that PROC CALIS also terminates if the point $x^{(k)}$ is fully constrained by linearly independent active linear or boundary constraints, and all Lagrange multiplier estimates of active inequality constraints are greater than a small negative tolerance.

The following options are available only in the NLOPTIONS statement (except for FCONV, GCONV, MAXFUNC, and MAXITER), and they affect the termination criteria.

Options Used by All Techniques

The following five criteria are used by all optimization techniques.

ABSCONV | ABSTOL=*r*

specifies an absolute function convergence criterion.

- For minimization, termination requires

$$f^{(k)} = f(x^{(k)}) \leq ABSCONV$$

- For maximization, termination requires

$$f^{(k)} = f(x^{(k)}) \geq ABSCONV$$

The default value of ABSCONV is

- for minimization, the negative square root of the largest double precision value
- for maximization, the positive square root of the largest double precision value

MAXFUNC | MAXFU=*i*

requires the number of function calls to be no larger than i. The default values are listed in the following table.

TECH=	MAXFUNC default
LEVMAR, NEWRAP, NRRIDG, TRUREG	i=125
DBLDOG, QUANEW	i=500
CONGRA	i=1000

The default is used if you specify MAXFUNC=0. The optimization can be terminated only after completing a full iteration. Therefore, the number of function calls that is actually performed can exceed the number that is specified by the MAXFUNC= option.

MAXITER | MAXIT= *i* <*n*>

requires the number of iterations to be no larger than i. The default values are listed in the following table.

TECH=	MAXITER default
LEVMAR, NEWRAP, NRRIDG, TRUREG	i=50
DBLDOG, QUANEW	i=200
CONGRA	i=400

The default is used if you specify MAXITER=0 or you omit the MAXITER option.

The optional second value n is valid only for TECH=QUANEW with nonlinear constraints. It specifies an upper bound n for the number of iterations of an algorithm and reduces the violation of nonlinear constraints at a starting point. The default value is n=20. For example, specifying `MAXITER= .  0` means that you do not want to exceed the default number of iterations during the main optimization process and that you want to suppress the feasible point algorithm for nonlinear constraints.

MAXTIME=*r*

requires the CPU time to be no larger than r. The default value of the MAXTIME= option is the largest double floating point number on your computer.

MINITER | MINIT=*i*

specifies the minimum number of iterations. The default value is $i = 0$.

The ABSCONV=, MAXITER=, MAXFUNC=, and MAXTIME= options are useful for dividing a time-consuming optimization problem into a series of smaller problems by using the OUTEST= and INEST= data sets.

Options for Unconstrained and Linearly Constrained Techniques

This section contains additional termination criteria for all unconstrained, boundary, or linearly constrained optimization techniques.

ABSFCONV | ABSFTOL=*r* <*n*>

specifies the absolute function convergence criterion. Termination requires a small change of the function value in successive iterations,

$$|f(x^{(k-1)}) - f(x^{(k)})| \leq r$$

The default value is $r = 0$. The optional integer value n determines the number of successive iterations for which the criterion must be satisfied before the process can be terminated.

ABSGCONV | ABSGTOL=*r* <*n*>

specifies the absolute gradient convergence criterion. Termination requires the maximum absolute gradient element to be small,

$$\max_j |g_j^{(k)}| \leq r$$

The default value is r=1E−5. The optional integer value n determines the number of successive iterations for which the criterion must be satisfied before the process can be terminated.

Note: In some applications, the small default value of the ABSGCONV= criterion is too difficult to satisfy for some of the optimization techniques.

ABSXCONV | ABSXTOL=*r* <*n*>

specifies the absolute parameter convergence criterion. Termination requires a small Euclidean distance between successive parameter vectors,

$$\| x^{(k)} - x^{(k-1)} \|_2 \leq r$$

The default value is $r = 0$. The optional integer value n determines the number of successive iterations for which the criterion must be satisfied before the process can be terminated.

FCONV | FTOL=*r* <*n*>

specifies the relative function convergence criterion. Termination requires a small relative change of the function value in successive iterations,

$$\frac{|f(x^{(k)}) - f(x^{(k-1)})|}{\max(|f(x^{(k-1)})|, FSIZE)} \leq r$$

where $FSIZE$ is defined by the FSIZE= option. The default value is $r = 10^{-FDIGITS}$, where $FDIGITS$ either is specified or is set by default to $-log_{10}(\epsilon)$, where ϵ is the machine precision. The optional integer value n determines the number of successive iterations for which the criterion must be satisfied before the process can be terminated.

FCONV2 | FTOL2=*r* <*n*>

specifies another function convergence criterion. For least-squares problems, termination requires a small predicted reduction

$$df^{(k)} \approx f(x^{(k)}) - f(x^{(k)} + s^{(k)})$$

of the objective function.

The predicted reduction

$$\begin{aligned} df^{(k)} &= -g^{(k)\prime} s^{(k)} - \frac{1}{2} s^{(k)\prime} G^{(k)} s^{(k)} \\ &= -\frac{1}{2} s^{(k)\prime} g^{(k)} \\ &\leq r \end{aligned}$$

is computed by approximating the objective function f by the first two terms of the Taylor series and substituting the Newton step

$$s^{(k)} = -G^{(k)-1} g^{(k)}$$

The FCONV2 criterion is the unscaled version of the GCONV criterion. The default value is $r = 0$. The optional integer value n determines the number of successive iterations for which the criterion must be satisfied before the process can be terminated.

FDIGITS=*r*

specifies the number of accurate digits in evaluations of the objective function. Fractional values such as FDIGITS=4.7 are allowed. The default value is $r = -log_{10}\epsilon$, where ϵ is the machine precision. The value of r is used for the specification of the default value of the FCONV= option.

FSIZE=*r*

specifies the $FSIZE$ parameter of the relative function and relative gradient termination criteria. The default value is $r = 0$. See the FCONV= and GCONV= options.

GCONV | GTOL=*r* <*n*>

specifies the relative gradient convergence criterion. For all techniques except the CONGRA technique, termination requires that the normalized predicted function reduction is small,

$$\frac{[g^{(k)}]'[G^{(k)}]^{-1} g^{(k)}}{\max(|f(x^{(k)})|, FSIZE)} \leq r$$

where $FSIZE$ is defined by the FSIZE= option. For the CONGRA technique (where a reliable Hessian estimate **G** is not available),

$$\frac{\| g^{(k)} \|_2^2 \quad \| s^{(k)} \|_2}{\| g^{(k)} - g^{(k-1)} \|_2 \max(|f(x^{(k)})|, FSIZE)} \leq r$$

is used. The default value is r=1E−8. The optional integer value n determines the number of successive iterations for which the criterion must be satisfied before the process can be terminated.

Note: The default setting for the GCONV= option sometimes leads to early termination far from the location of the optimum. This is especially true for the special form of this criterion used in the CONGRA optimization.

GCONV2 | GTOL2=*r* <*n*>

specifies another relative gradient convergence criterion. For least-squares problems and the TRUREG, LEVMAR, NRRIDG, and NEWRAP techniques, the criterion of Browne (1982) is used,

$$\max_j \frac{|g_j^{(k)}|}{\sqrt{f(x^{(k)})G_{j,j}^{(k)}}} \leq r$$

This criterion is not used by the other techniques. The default value is $r = 0$. The optional integer value n determines the number of successive iterations for which the criterion must be satisfied before the process can be terminated.

XCONV | XTOL=*r* <*n*>

specifies the relative parameter convergence criterion. Termination requires a small relative parameter change in subsequent iterations,

$$\frac{\max_j |x_j^{(k)} - x_j^{(k-1)}|}{\max(|x_j^{(k)}|, |x_j^{(k-1)}|, XSIZE)} \leq r$$

The default value is $r = 0$. The optional integer value n determines the number of successive iterations for which the criterion must be satisfied before the process can be terminated.

XSIZE=*r*

specifies the $XSIZE$ parameter of the relative function and relative gradient termination criteria. The default value is $r = 0$. See the XCONV= option.

Options for Nonlinearly Constrained Techniques

The non-NMSIMP algorithms available for nonlinearly constrained optimization (currently only TECH=QUANEW) do not monotonically reduce either the value of the objective function or some kind of merit function that combines objective and constraint functions. Furthermore, the algorithm uses the watchdog technique with backtracking (Chamberlain et al., 1982). Therefore, no termination criteria are implemented that are based on the values (x or f) of successive iterations. In addition to the criteria used by all optimization techniques, only three more termination criteria are currently available, and they are based on the Lagrange function

$$L(x, \lambda) = f(x) - \sum_{i=1}^{m} \lambda_i c_i(x)$$

and its gradient

$$\nabla_x L(x, \lambda) = g(x) - \sum_{i=1}^{m} \lambda_i \nabla_x c_i(x)$$

Here, m denotes the total number of constraints, $g = g(x)$ denotes the gradient of the objective function, and λ denotes the m vector of Lagrange multipliers. The Kuhn-

Tucker conditions require that the gradient of the Lagrange function is zero at the optimal point (x^*, λ^*):

$$\nabla_x L(x^*, \lambda^*) = 0$$

The termination criteria available for nonlinearly constrained optimization follow.

ABSGCONV | ABSGTOL=*r* <*n*>
specifies that termination requires the maximum absolute gradient element of the Lagrange function to be small,

$$\max_j |\{\nabla_x L(x^{(k)}, \lambda^{(k)})\}_j| \leq r$$

The default value is r=1E−5. The optional integer value n determines the number of successive iterations for which the criterion must be satisfied before the process can be terminated.

FCONV2 | FTOL2=*r* <*n*>
specifies that termination requires the predicted objective function reduction to be small:

$$|g(x^{(k)})s(x^{(k)})| + \sum_{i=1}^{m} |\lambda_i c_i| \leq r$$

The default value is r=1E−6. This is the criterion used by the programs VMCWD and VF02AD (Powell 1982b). The optional integer value n determines the number of successive iterations for which the criterion must be satisfied before the process can be terminated.

GCONV | GTOL=*r* <*n*>
specifies that termination requires the normalized predicted objective function reduction to be small:

$$\frac{|g(x^{(k)})s(x^{(k)})| + \sum_{i=1}^{m} |\lambda_i c_i(x^{(k)})|}{\max(|f(x^{(k)})|, FSIZE)} \leq r$$

where $FSIZE$ is defined by the FSIZE= option. The default value is r=1E−8. The optional integer value n determines the number of successive iterations for which the criterion must be satisfied before the process can be terminated.

Miscellaneous Options

Options for the Approximate Covariance Matrix of Parameter Estimates

You can specify the following options to modify the approximate covariance matrix of parameter estimates.

CFACTOR=*r*
specifies the scalar factor for the covariance matrix of parameter estimates. The scalar $r \geq 0$ replaces the default value c/NM. For more details, see the section "Approximate Standard Errors" on page 535.

NOHLF

specifies that the Hessian matrix of the objective function (rather than the Hessian matrix of the Lagrange function) is used for computing the approximate covariance matrix of parameter estimates and, therefore, the approximate standard errors.

It is theoretically not correct to use the NOHLF option. However, since most implementations use the Hessian matrix of the objective function and not the Hessian matrix of the Lagrange function for computing approximate standard errors, the NOHLF option can be used to compare the results.

Options for Additional Displayed Output

You can specify the following options to obtain additional displayed output.

PALL | ALL

displays information on the starting values and final values of the optimization process.

PCRPJAC | PJTJ

displays the approximate Hessian matrix. If general linear or nonlinear constraints are active at the solution, the projected approximate Hessian matrix is also displayed.

PHESSIAN | PHES

displays the Hessian matrix. If general linear or nonlinear constraints are active at the solution, the projected Hessian matrix is also displayed.

PHISTORY | PHIS

displays the optimization history. The PHISTORY option is set automatically if the PALL or PRINT option is set.

PINIT | PIN

displays the initial values and derivatives (if available). The PINIT option is set automatically if the PALL option is set.

PNLCJAC

displays the Jacobian matrix of nonlinear constraints specified by the NLINCON statement. The PNLCJAC option is set automatically if the PALL option is set.

PRINT | PRI

displays the results of the optimization process, such as parameter estimates and constraints.

More Options for Optimization Techniques

You can specify the following options, in addition to the options already listed, to fine-tune the optimization process. These options should not be necessary in most applications of PROC CALIS.

DAMPSTEP | DS *<=r>*

specifies that the initial step-size value $\alpha^{(0)}$ for each line search (used by the QUANEW, CONGRA, or NEWRAP techniques) cannot be larger than r times the step-size value used in the former iteration. If the factor r is not specified, the default value is $r = 2$. The DAMPSTEP option can prevent the line-search algorithm from repeatedly stepping into regions where some objective functions are difficult to compute or where they can lead to floating point overflows during the computation of objective functions and their derivatives. The DAMPSTEP<=r> option can prevent time-costly function calls during line searches with very small step sizes α of objective functions. For more information on setting the start values of each line search, see the section "Restricting the Step Length" on page 558.

HESCAL | HS = 0 | 1 | 2 | 3

specifies the scaling version of the Hessian or crossproduct Jacobian matrix used in NRRIDG, TRUREG, LEVMAR, NEWRAP, or DBLDOG optimization. If HS is not equal to zero, the first iteration and each restart iteration sets the diagonal scaling matrix $\mathbf{D}^{(0)} = diag(d_i^{(0)})$:

$$d_i^{(0)} = \sqrt{\max(|\mathbf{G}_{i,i}^{(0)}|, \epsilon)}$$

where $\mathbf{G}_{i,i}^{(0)}$ are the diagonal elements of the Hessian or crossproduct Jacobian matrix. In every other iteration, the diagonal scaling matrix $\mathbf{D}^{(0)} = diag(d_i^{(0)})$ is updated depending on the HS option:

HS=0 specifies that no scaling is done.

HS=1 specifies the Moré (1978) scaling update:

$$d_i^{(k+1)} = \max(d_i^{(k)}, \sqrt{\max(|\mathbf{G}_{i,i}^{(k)}|, \epsilon)})$$

HS=2 specifies the Dennis, Gay, and Welsch (1981) scaling update:

$$d_i^{(k+1)} = \max(0.6 * d_i^{(k)}, \sqrt{\max(|\mathbf{G}_{i,i}^{(k)}|, \epsilon)})$$

HS=3 specifies that d_i is reset in each iteration:

$$d_i^{(k+1)} = \sqrt{\max(|\mathbf{G}_{i,i}^{(k)}|, \epsilon)}$$

In the preceding equations, ϵ is the relative machine precision. The default is HS=1 for LEVMAR minimization and HS=0 otherwise. Scaling of the Hessian or crossproduct Jacobian can be time-consuming in the case where general linear constraints are active.

LCDEACT | LCD = *r*

specifies a threshold r for the Lagrange multiplier that decides whether an active inequality constraint remains active or can be deactivated. For maximization, r must be greater than zero; for minimization, r must be smaller than zero. The default is

$$r = \pm \min(0.01, \max(0.1 * ABSGCONV, 0.001 * gmax^{(k)}))$$

where "+" stands for maximization, "−" stands for minimization, $ABSGCONV$ is the value of the absolute gradient criterion, and $gmax^{(k)}$ is the maximum absolute element of the (projected) gradient $g^{(k)}$ or $Z'g^{(k)}$.

LCEPSILON | LCEPS | LCE = ***r***

specifies the range r, $r \geq 0$, for active and violated boundary and linear constraints. If the point $x^{(k)}$ satisfies the condition

$$|\sum_{j=1}^{n} a_{ij} x_j^{(k)} - b_i| \leq r * (|b_i| + 1)$$

the constraint i is recognized as an active constraint. Otherwise, the constraint i is either an inactive inequality or a violated inequality or equality constraint. The default value is r=1E−8. During the optimization process, the introduction of rounding errors can force PROC NLP to increase the value of r by factors of 10. If this happens, it is indicated by a message displayed in the log.

LCSINGULAR | LCSING | LCS = ***r***

specifies a criterion r, $r \geq 0$, used in the update of the QR decomposition that decides whether an active constraint is linearly dependent on a set of other active constraints. The default is r=1E−8. The larger r becomes, the more the active constraints are recognized as being linearly dependent.

NOEIGNUM

suppresses the computation and displayed output of the determinant and the inertia of the Hessian, crossproduct Jacobian, and covariance matrices. The inertia of a symmetric matrix are the numbers of negative, positive, and zero eigenvalues. For large applications, the NOEIGNUM option can save computer time.

RESTART | REST = ***i***

specifies that the QUANEW or CONGRA algorithm is restarted with a steepest descent/ascent search direction after at most i iterations, $i > 0$. Default values are as follows:

- CONGRA: UPDATE=PB: restart is done automatically so specification of i is not used.
- CONGRA: UPDATE≠PB: $i = \min(10n, 80)$, where n is the number of parameters.
- QUANEW: i is the largest integer available.

VERSION | VS = 1 | 2

specifies the version of the quasi-Newton optimization technique with nonlinear constraints.

VS=1 specifies the update of the μ vector as in Powell (1978a, 1978b) (update like VF02AD).

VS=2 specifies the update of the μ vector as in Powell (1982a, 1982b) (update like VMCWD).

The default is VS=2.

PARAMETERS Statement

PARAMETERS | PARMS *parameter(s)* << = > *number(s)* >
<< , > *parameter(s)* << = > *number(s)* > . . . > **;**

The PARAMETERS statement defines additional parameters that are not elements of a model matrix to use in your own program statements. You can specify more than one PARAMETERS statement with each PROC CALIS statement. The *parameters* can be followed by an equal sign and a number list. The values of the *numbers* list are assigned as initial values to the preceding parameters in the *parameters* list. For example, each of the following statements assigns the initial values ALPHA=.5 and BETA=-.5 for the parameters used in program statements:

```
parameters alfa beta=.5 -.5;
parameters alfa beta (.5 -.5);
parameters alfa beta .5 -.5;
parameters alfa=.5 beta (-.5);
```

The number of parameters and the number of values does not have to match. When there are fewer values than parameter names, either the RANDOM= or START= option is used. When there are more values than parameter names, the extra values are dropped. Parameters listed in the PARAMETERS statement can be assigned initial values by program statements or by the START= or RANDOM= option in the PROC CALIS statement.

Caution: The OUTRAM= and INRAM= data sets do not contain any information about the PARAMETERS statement or additional program statements.

STRUCTEQ Statement

STRUCTEQ *variable* < *variable* . . . > **;**

The STRUCTEQ statement is used to list the dependent variables of the structural equations. This statement is ignored if you omit the PDETERM option. This statement is useful because the term *structural equation* is not defined in a unique way, and PROC CALIS has difficulty identifying the structural equations.

If LINEQS statements are used, the names of the left-hand-side (dependent) variables of those equations to be treated as structural equations should be listed in the STRUCTEQ statement.

If the RAM statement is used, variable names in the STRUCTEQ statements depend on the VARNAMES statement:

- If the VARNAMES statement is used, variable names must correspond to those in the VARNAMES statement.

- If the VARNAMES statement is not used, variable names must correspond to the names of manifest variables or latent (F) variables.

The STRUCTEQ statement also defines the names of variables used in the causal coefficient matrix of the structural equations, $\mathbf{B}$, for computing the *Stability Coefficient of Reciprocal Causation* (the largest eigenvalue of the $\mathbf{BB}'$ matrix). If the PROC CALIS option PDETERM is used without the STRUCTEQ statement, the structural equations are defined as described in the PDETERM option. See the PROC CALIS option PDETERM on page 473 for more details.

VARNAMES Statement

VARNAMES | VNAMES *assignment* < *, assignment* ... > **;**

where *assignment* represents

matrix-id variable-names or *matrix-name* = *matrix-name*

Use the VARNAMES statement in connection with the RAM, COSAN, or FACTOR model statement to allocate names to latent variables including error and disturbance terms. This statement is not needed if you are using the LINEQS statement.

In connection with the RAM model statement, the *matrix-id* must be specified by the integer number as it is used in the RAM list input (1 for matrix $\mathbf{A}$, 2 for matrix $\mathbf{P}$). Because the first variables of matrix $\mathbf{A}$ correspond to the manifest variables in the input data set, you can specify names only for the latent variables following the manifest variables in the rows of $\mathbf{A}$. For example, in the RAM notation of the alienation example, you can specify the latent variables by names F1, F2, F3 and the error variables by names E1, ... , E6, D1, D2, D3 with the following statement:

```
vnames 1  F1-F3,
       2  E1-E6 D1-D3;
```

If the RAM model statement is not accompanied by a VNAMES statement, default variable names are assigned using the prefixes F, E, and D with numerical suffixes: latent variables are F1, F2, ... , and error variables are E1, E2, ...

The *matrix-id* must be specified by its name when used with the COSAN or FACTOR statement. The *variable-names* following the matrix name correspond to the columns of this matrix. The variable names corresponding to the rows of this matrix are set automatically by

- the names of the manifest variables for the first matrix in each term
- the column variable names of the same matrix for the central symmetric matrix in each term
- the column variable names of the preceding matrix for each other matrix

You also can use the second kind of name assignment in connection with a COSAN statement. Two matrix names separated by an equal sign allocate the column names of one matrix to the column names of the other matrix. This assignment assumes that the column names of at least one of the two matrices are already allocated. For example, in the COSAN notation of the alienation example, you can specify the variable names by using the following statements to allocate names to the columns of **J**, **A**, and **P**:

```
vnames  J  V1-V6 F1-F3 ,
        A =J ,
        P  E1-E6 D1-D3 ;
```

BY Statement

BY *variables* ;

You can specify a BY statement with PROC CALIS to obtain separate analyses on observations in groups defined by the BY variables. When a BY statement appears, the procedure expects the input data set to be sorted in order of the BY variables.

If your input data set is not sorted in ascending order, use one of the following alternatives:

- Sort the data using the SORT procedure with a similar BY statement.
- Specify the BY statement option NOTSORTED or DESCENDING in the BY statement for the CALIS procedure. The NOTSORTED option does not mean that the data are unsorted but rather that the data are arranged in groups (according to values of the BY variables) and that these groups are not necessarily in alphabetical or increasing numeric order.
- Create an index on the BY variables using the DATASETS procedure.

For more information on the BY statement, refer to the discussion in *SAS Language Reference: Concepts*. For more information on the DATASETS procedure, refer to the discussion in the *SAS Procedures Guide*.

VAR Statement

VAR *variables* ;

The VAR statement lists the numeric variables to be analyzed. If the VAR statement is omitted, all numeric variables not mentioned in other statements are analyzed. You can use the VAR statement to ensure that the manifest variables appear in correct order for use in the RAM statement. Only one VAR statement can be used with each PROC CALIS statement. If you do not use all manifest variables when you specify the model with a RAM or LINEQS statement, PROC CALIS does automatic variable selection. For more information, see the section "Automatic Variable Selection" on page 548.

PARTIAL Statement

PARTIAL *variables* ;

If you want the analysis to be based on a partial correlation or covariance matrix, use the PARTIAL statement to list the variables used to partial out the variables in the analysis. You can specify only one PARTIAL statement with each PROC CALIS statement.

FREQ Statement

FREQ *variable* ;

If one variable in your data set represents the frequency of occurrence for the other values in the observation, specify the variable's name in a FREQ statement. PROC CALIS then treats the data set as if each observation appears n_i times, where n_i is the value of the FREQ variable for observation i. Only the integer portion of the value is used. If the value of the FREQ variable is less than 1 or is missing, that observation is not included in the analysis. The total number of observations is considered to be the sum of the FREQ values when the procedure computes significance probabilities. You can use only one FREQ statement with each PROC CALIS statement.

WEIGHT Statement

WEIGHT *variable* ;

To compute weighted covariances or correlations, specify the name of the weighting variable in a WEIGHT statement. This is often done when the error variance associated with each observation is different and the values of the weight variable are proportional to the reciprocals of the variances. You can use only one WEIGHT statement with each PROC CALIS statement. The WEIGHT and FREQ statements have a similar effect, except the WEIGHT statement does not alter the number of observations unless VARDEF=WGT or VARDEF=WDF. An observation is used in the analysis only if the WEIGHT variable is greater than 0 and is not missing.

SAS Program Statements

This section lists the program statements used to express the linear and nonlinear constraints on the parameters and documents the differences between program statements in PROC CALIS and program statements in the DATA step. The very different use of the ARRAY statement by PROC CALIS is also discussed. Most of the program statements that can be used in the SAS DATA step also can be used in PROC CALIS. Refer to *SAS Language Reference: Dictionary* for a description of the SAS program statements. You can specify the following SAS program statements to compute parameter constraints with the CALIS procedure:

ABORT ;

CALL *name* < (*expression* < , *expression* . . . >) > ;

DELETE;

DO < *variable* = *expression* < **TO** *expression*> < **BY** *expression*>
    <, *expression* < **TO** *expression*> < **BY** *expression*> . . . > >
    < **WHILE** *expression*>
    < **UNTIL** *expression*> ;

END;

GOTO *statement-label* ;

IF *expression*;

IF *expression* **THEN** *program-statement* ;
    ELSE *program-statement* ;

variable = *expression* ;

variable+*expression* ;

LINK *statement-label* ;

PUT <*variable*> <=> < . . . > ;

RETURN ;

SELECT < (*expression*) > ;

STOP;

SUBSTR (*variable*, *index*, *length*) = *expression* ;

WHEN (*expression*) *program-statement* ;
    OTHERWISE *program-statement* ;

For the most part, the SAS program statements work the same as they do in the SAS DATA step as documented in *SAS Language Reference: Concepts*. However, there are several differences that should be noted.

- The ABORT statement does not allow any arguments.
- The DO statement does not allow a character index variable. Thus,

  ```
  do I=1,2,3;
  ```

  is supported; however,

  ```
  do I='A','B','C';
  ```

  is not valid in PROC CALIS, although it is supported in the DATA step.
- The PUT statement, used mostly for program debugging in PROC CALIS, supports only some of the features of the DATA step PUT statement, and it has some new features that the DATA step PUT statement does not have:
  - The CALIS procedure PUT statement does not support line pointers, factored lists, iteration factors, overprinting, _INFILE_, the colon (:) format modifier, or $.

– The CALIS procedure PUT statement does support expressions enclosed in parentheses. For example, the following statement displays the square root of x:

```
put (sqrt(x));
```

– The CALIS procedure PUT statement supports the print item _PDV_ to display a formatted listing of all variables in the program. For example, the following statement displays a much more readable listing of the variables than the _ALL_ print item:

```
put _pdv_ ;
```

- The WHEN and OTHERWISE statements allow more than one target statement. That is, DO/END groups are not necessary for multiple WHEN statements. For example, the following syntax is valid:

```
select;
   when ( expression1 ) statement1;
                        statement2;
   when ( expression2 ) statement3;
                        statement4;
end;
```

You can specify one or more PARMS statements to define parameters used in the program statements that are not defined in the model matrices (MATRIX, RAM, LINEQS, STD, or COV statement).

Parameters that are used only on the right-hand side of your program statements are called independent, and parameters that are used at least once on the left-hand side of an equation in the program code are called dependent parameters. The dependent parameters are used only indirectly in the minimization process. They should be fully defined as functions of the independent parameters. The independent parameters are included in the set **X** of parameters used in the minimization. Be sure that all independent parameters used in your program statements are somehow connected to elements of the model matrices. Otherwise the minimization function does not depend on those independent parameters, and the parameters vary without control (since the corresponding derivative is the constant 0). You also can specify the PARMS statement to set the initial values of all independent parameters used in the program statements that are not defined as elements of model matrices.

ARRAY Statement

ARRAY *arrayname* <*(dimensions)*>< *$* ><*variables and constants*> **;**

The ARRAY statement is similar to, but not the same as, the ARRAY statement in the DATA step. The ARRAY statement is used to associate a name with a list of variables and constants. The array name can then be used with subscripts in the program to refer to the items in the list.

The ARRAY statement supported by PROC CALIS does not support all the features of the DATA step ARRAY statement. With PROC CALIS, the ARRAY statement cannot be used to give initial values to array elements. Implicit indexing variables cannot be used; all array references must have explicit subscript expressions. Only exact array dimensions are allowed; lower-bound specifications are not supported. A maximum of six dimensions is allowed.

On the other hand, the ARRAY statement supported by PROC CALIS does allow both variables and constants to be used as array elements. Constant array elements cannot be changed. Both the dimension specification and the list of elements are optional, but at least one must be given. When the list of elements is not given or fewer elements than the size of the array are listed, array variables are created by suffixing element numbers to the array name to complete the element list.

Details

Input Data Sets

You can use four different kinds of input data sets in the CALIS procedure, and you can use them simultaneously. The DATA= data set contains the data to be analyzed, and it can be an ordinary SAS data set containing raw data or a special TYPE=COV, TYPE=UCOV, TYPE=CORR, TYPE=UCORR, TYPE=SYMATRIX, TYPE=SSCP, or TYPE=FACTOR data set containing previously computed statistics. The INEST= data set specifies an input data set that contains initial estimates for the parameters used in the optimization process, and it can also contain boundary and general linear constraints on the parameters. If the model does not change too much, you can use an OUTEST= data set from a previous PROC CALIS analysis; the initial estimates are taken from the values of the PARMS observation. The INRAM= data set names a third input data set that contains all information needed to specify the analysis model in RAM list form (except for user-written program statements). Often the INRAM= data set can be the OUTRAM= data set from a previous PROC CALIS analysis. See the section "OUTRAM= SAS-data-set" on page 525 for the structure of both OUTRAM= and INRAM= data sets. Using the INWGT= data set enables you to read in the weight matrix $\mathbf{W}$ that can be used in generalized least-squares, weighted least-squares, or diagonally weighted least-squares estimation.

DATA= SAS-data-set

A TYPE=COV, TYPE=UCOV, TYPE=CORR, or TYPE=UCORR data set can be created by the CORR procedure or various other procedures. It contains means, standard deviations, the sample size, the covariance or correlation matrix, and possibly other statistics depending on which procedure is used.

If your data set has many observations and you plan to run PROC CALIS several times, you can save computer time by first creating a TYPE=COV, TYPE=UCOV, TYPE=CORR, or TYPE=UCORR data set and using it as input to PROC CALIS. For example, assuming that PROC CALIS is first run with an OUTRAM=MOD option, you can run

```
* create TYPE=COV data set;
proc corr cov nocorr data=raw outp=cov(type=cov);
run;
* analysis using correlations;
proc calis data=cov inram=mod;
run;
* analysis using covariances;
proc calis cov data=cov inram=mod;
run;
```

Most procedures automatically set the TYPE= option of an output data set appropriately. However, the CORR procedure sets TYPE=CORR unless an explicit TYPE= option is used. Thus, `(TYPE=COV)` is needed in the preceding PROC CORR request, since the output data set is a covariance matrix. If you use a DATA step with a SET statement to modify this data set, you must declare the TYPE=COV, TYPE=UCOV, TYPE=CORR, or TYPE=UCORR attribute in the new data set.

You can use a VAR statement with PROC CALIS when reading a TYPE=COV, TYPE=UCOV, TYPE=CORR, TYPE=UCORR, or TYPE=SSCP data set to select a subset of the variables or change the order of the variables.

Caution: Problems can arise from using the CORR procedure when there are missing data. By default, PROC CORR computes each covariance or correlation from all observations that have values present for the pair of variables involved ("pairwise deletion"). The resulting covariance or correlation matrix can have negative eigenvalues. A correlation or covariance matrix with negative eigenvalues is recognized as a singular matrix in PROC CALIS, and you cannot compute (default) generalized least-squares or maximum likelihood estimates. You can specify the RIDGE option to ridge the diagonal of such a matrix to obtain a positive definite data matrix. If the NOMISS option is used with the CORR procedure, observations with any missing values are completely omitted from the calculations ("listwise deletion"), and there is no possibility of negative eigenvalues (but still a chance for a singular matrix).

PROC CALIS can also create a TYPE=COV, TYPE=UCOV, TYPE=CORR, or TYPE=UCORR data set that includes all the information needed for repeated analyses. If the data set DATA=RAW does not contain missing values, the following statements should give the same PROC CALIS results as the previous example.

```
* using correlations;
proc calis data=raw outstat=cov inram=mod;
run;
* using covariances;
proc calis cov data=cov inram=mod;
run;
```

You can create a TYPE=COV, TYPE=UCOV, TYPE=CORR, TYPE=UCORR, or TYPE=SSCP data set in a DATA step. Be sure to specify the TYPE= option in parentheses after the data set name in the DATA statement, and include the _TYPE_ and _NAME_ variables. If you want to analyze the covariance matrix but your DATA= data set is a TYPE=CORR or TYPE=UCORR data set, you should include an observation with _TYPE_=STD giving the standard deviation of each variable. If you specify the COV option, PROC CALIS analyzes the recomputed covariance matrix:

```
data correl(type=corr);
   input _type_ $ _name_ $ X1-X3;
   datalines;
std   .   4.  2.  8.
corr  X1  1.0  .   .
corr  X2   .7 1.0  .
corr  X3   .5  .4 1.0
;
proc calis cov inram=model;
run;
```

If you want to analyze the UCOV or UCORR matrix but your DATA= data set is a TYPE=COV or TYPE=CORR data set, you should include observations with _TYPE_=STD and _TYPE_=MEAN giving the standard deviation and mean of each variable.

INEST= SAS-data-set

You can use the INEST= (or INVAR= or ESTDATA=) input data set to specify the initial values of the parameters used in the optimization and to specify boundary constraints and the more general linear constraints that can be imposed on these parameters.

The variables of the INEST= data set must correspond to

- a character variable _TYPE_ that indicates the type of the observation
- n numeric variables with the parameter names used in the specified PROC CALIS model
- the BY variables that are used in a DATA= input data set
- a numeric variable _RHS_ (right-hand side) (needed only if linear constraints are used)
- additional variables with names corresponding to constants used in the program statements

The content of the _TYPE_ variable defines the meaning of the observation of the INEST= data set. PROC CALIS recognizes observations with the following _TYPE_ specifications.

PARMS
: specifies initial values for parameters that are defined in the model statements of PROC CALIS. The _RHS_ variable is not used. Additional variables can contain the values of constants that are referred to in program statements. At the beginning of each run of PROC CALIS, the values of the constants are read from the PARMS observation initializing the constants in the program statements.

UPPERBD | UB
: specifies upper bounds with nonmissing values. The use of a missing value indicates that no upper bound is specified for the parameter. The _RHS_ variable is not used.

LOWERBD | LB
: specifies lower bounds with nonmissing values. The use of a missing value indicates that no lower bound is specified for the parameter. The _RHS_ variable is not used.

LE | <= | <
: specifies the linear constraint $\sum_j a_{ij} x_j \leq b_i$. The n parameter values contain the coefficients a_{ij}, and the _RHS_ variable contains the right-hand-side b_i. The use of a missing value indicates a zero coefficient a_{ij}.

GE | >= | >
: specifies the linear constraint $\sum_j a_{ij} x_j \geq b_i$. The n parameter values contain the coefficients a_{ij}, and the _RHS_ variable contains the right-hand-side b_i. The use of a missing value indicates a zero coefficient a_{ij}.

EQ | =
: specifies the linear constraint $\sum_j a_{ij} x_j = b_i$. The n parameter values contain the coefficients a_{ij}, and the _RHS_ variable contains the right-hand-side b_i. The use of a missing value indicates a zero coefficient a_{ij}.

The constraints specified in the INEST=, INVAR=, or ESTDATA= data set are added to the constraints specified in BOUNDS and LINCON statements.

You can use an OUTEST= data set from a PROC CALIS run as an INEST= data set in a new run. However, be aware that the OUTEST= data set also contains the boundary and general linear constraints specified in the previous run of PROC CALIS. When you are using this OUTEST= data set without changes as an INEST= data set, PROC CALIS adds the constraints from the data set to the constraints specified by a BOUNDS and LINCON statement. Although PROC CALIS automatically eliminates multiple identical constraints, you should avoid specifying the same constraint a second time.

INRAM= SAS-data-set

This data set is usually created in a previous run of PROC CALIS. It is useful if you want to reanalyze a problem in a different way such as using a different estimation method. You can alter an existing OUTRAM= data set, either in the DATA step or using the FSEDIT procedure, to create the INRAM= data set describing a modified model. For more details on the INRAM= data set, see the section "OUTRAM= SAS-data-set" on page 525.

In the case of a RAM or LINEQS analysis of linear structural equations, the OUTRAM= data set always contains the variable names of the model specified. These variable names and the model specified in the INRAM= data set are the basis of the automatic variable selection algorithm performed after reading the INRAM= data set.

INWGT= SAS-data-set

This data set enables you to specify a weight matrix other than the default matrix for the generalized, weighted, and diagonally weighted least-squares estimation methods. The specification of any INWGT= data set for unweighted least-squares or maximum likelihood estimation is ignored. For generalized and diagonally weighted least-squares estimation, the INWGT= data set must contain a _TYPE_ and a _NAME_ variable as well as the manifest variables used in the analysis. The value of the _NAME_ variable indicates the row index i of the weight w_{ij}. For weighted least squares, the INWGT= data set must contain _TYPE_, _NAME_, _NAM2_, and _NAM3_ variables as well as the manifest variables used in the analysis. The values of the _NAME_, _NAM2_, and _NAM3_ variables indicate the three indices i, j, k of the weight $w_{ij,kl}$. You can store information other than the weight matrix in the INWGT= data set, but only observations with _TYPE_=WEIGHT are used to specify the weight matrix $\mathbf{W}$. This property enables you to store more than one weight matrix in the INWGT= data set. You can then run PROC CALIS with each of the weight matrices by changing only the _TYPE_ observation in the INWGT= data set with an intermediate DATA step.

For more details on the INWGT= data set, see the section "OUTWGT= SAS-data-set" on page 530.

Output Data Sets

OUTEST= SAS-data-set

The OUTEST= (or OUTVAR=) data set is of TYPE=EST and contains the final parameter estimates, the gradient, the Hessian, and boundary and linear constraints. For METHOD=ML, METHOD=GLS, and METHOD=WLS, the OUTEST= data set also contains the approximate standard errors, the information matrix (crossproduct Jacobian), and the approximate covariance matrix of the parameter estimates ((generalized) inverse of the information matrix). If there are linear or nonlinear equality or active inequality constraints at the solution, the OUTEST= data set also contains Lagrange multipliers, the projected Hessian matrix, and the Hessian matrix of the Lagrange function.

The OUTEST= data set can be used to save the results of an optimization by PROC CALIS for another analysis with either PROC CALIS or another SAS procedure. Saving results to an OUTEST= data set is advised for expensive applications that cannot be repeated without considerable effort.

The OUTEST= data set contains the BY variables, two character variables _TYPE_ and _NAME_, t numeric variables corresponding to the parameters used in the model, a numeric variable _RHS_ (right-hand side) that is used for the right-hand-side value b_i of a linear constraint or for the value $f = f(x)$ of the objective function at the final point x^* of the parameter space, and a numeric variable _ITER_ that is set to zero for initial values, set to the iteration number for the OUTITER output, and set to missing for the result output.

The _TYPE_ observations in Table 19.5 are available in the OUTEST= data set, depending on the request.

Table 19.5. _TYPE_ Observations in the OUTEST= data set

TYPE	Description
ACTBC	If there are active boundary constraints at the solution x^*, three observations indicate which of the parameters are actively constrained, as follows. **_NAME_** **Description** GE indicates the active lower bounds LE indicates the active upper bounds EQ indicates the active masks
COV	contains the approximate covariance matrix of the parameter estimates; used in computing the approximate standard errors.
COVRANK	contains the rank of the covariance matrix of the parameter estimates.
CRPJ_LF	contains the Hessian matrix of the Lagrange function (based on CRPJAC).
CRPJAC	contains the approximate Hessian matrix used in the optimization process. This is the inverse of the information matrix.
EQ	If linear constraints are used, this observation contains the ith linear constraint $\sum_j a_{ij}x_j = b_i$. The parameter variables contain the coefficients a_{ij}, $j = 1, \ldots, n$, the _RHS_ variable contains b_i, and _NAME_=ACTLC or _NAME_=LDACTLC.
GE	If linear constraints are used, this observation contains the ith linear constraint $\sum_j a_{ij}x_j \geq b_i$. The parameter variables contain the coefficients a_{ij}, $j = 1, \ldots, n$, and the _RHS_ variable contains b_i. If the constraint i is active at the solution x^*, then _NAME_=ACTLC or _NAME_=LDACTLC.
GRAD	contains the gradient of the estimates.
GRAD_LF	contains the gradient of the Lagrange function. The _RHS_ variable contains the value of the Lagrange function.
HESSIAN	contains the Hessian matrix.
HESS_LF	contains the Hessian matrix of the Lagrange function (based on HESSIAN).

Table 19.5. _TYPE_ Observations in the OUTEST= data set (continued)

TYPE	Description
INFORMAT	contains the information matrix of the parameter estimates (only for METHOD=ML, METHOD=GLS, or METHOD=WLS).
INITIAL	contains the starting values of the parameter estimates.
JACNLC	contains the Jacobian of the nonlinear constraints evaluated at the final estimates.
JACOBIAN	contains the Jacobian matrix (only if the OUTJAC option is used).
LAGM BC	contains Lagrange multipliers for masks and active boundary constraints. _NAME_ — **Description** GE — indicates the active lower bounds LE — indicates the active upper bounds EQ — indicates the active masks
LAGM LC	contains Lagrange multipliers for linear equality and active inequality constraints in pairs of observations containing the constraint number and the value of the Lagrange multiplier. _NAME_ — **Description** LEC_NUM — number of the linear equality constraint LEC_VAL — corresponding Lagrange multiplier value LIC_NUM — number of the linear inequality constraint LIC_VAL — corresponding Lagrange multiplier value
LAGM NLC	contains Lagrange multipliers for nonlinear equality and active inequality constraints in pairs of observations containing the constraint number and the value of the Lagrange multiplier. _NAME_ — **Description** NLEC_NUM — number of the nonlinear equality constraint NLEC_VAL — corresponding Lagrange multiplier value NLIC_NUM — number of the linear inequality constraint NLIC_VAL — corresponding Lagrange multiplier value
LE	If linear constraints are used, this observation contains the ith linear constraint $\sum_j a_{ij}x_j \leq b_i$. The parameter variables contain the coefficients a_{ij}, $j = 1, \ldots, n$, and the _RHS_ variable contains b_i. If the constraint i is active at the solution x^*, then _NAME_=ACTLC or _NAME_=LDACTLC.
LOWERBD | LB	If boundary constraints are used, this observation contains the lower bounds. Those parameters not subjected to lower bounds contain missing values. The _RHS_ variable contains a missing value, and the _NAME_ variable is blank.

Table 19.5. _TYPE_ Observations in the OUTEST= data set (continued)

TYPE	Description
NACTBC	All parameter variables contain the number n_{abc} of active boundary constraints at the solution x^*. The _RHS_ variable contains a missing value, and the _NAME_ variable is blank.
NACTLC	All parameter variables contain the number n_{alc} of active linear constraints at the solution x^* that are recognized as linearly independent. The _RHS_ variable contains a missing value, and the _NAME_ variable is blank.
NLC_EQ NLC_GE NLC_LE	contains values and residuals of nonlinear constraints. The _NAME_ variable is described as follows. _NAME_ — Description NLC — inactive nonlinear constraint NLCACT — linear independent active nonlinear constr. NLCACTLD — linear dependent active nonlinear constr.
NLDACTBC	contains the number of active boundary constraints at the solution x^* that are recognized as linearly dependent. The _RHS_ variable contains a missing value, and the _NAME_ variable is blank.
NLDACTLC	contains the number of active linear constraints at the solution x^* that are recognized as linearly dependent. The _RHS_ variable contains a missing value, and the _NAME_ variable is blank.
NOBS	contains the number of observations.
PARMS	contains the final parameter estimates. The _RHS_ variable contains the value of the objective function.
PCRPJ_LF	contains the projected Hessian matrix of the Lagrange function (based on CRPJAC).
PHESS_LF	contains the projected Hessian matrix of the Lagrange function (based on HESSIAN).
PROJCRPJ	contains the projected Hessian matrix (based on CRPJAC).
PROJGRAD	If linear constraints are used in the estimation, this observation contains the $n - n_{act}$ values of the projected gradient $g_Z = Z'g$ in the variables corresponding to the first $n - n_{act}$ parameters. The _RHS_ variable contains a missing value, and the _NAME_ variable is blank.
PROJHESS	contains the projected Hessian matrix (based on HESSIAN).
SIGSQ	contains the scalar factor of the covariance matrix of the parameter estimates.
STDERR	contains approximate standard errors (only for METHOD=ML, METHOD=GLS, or METHOD=WLS).

Table 19.5. _TYPE_ Observations in the OUTEST= data set (continued)

TYPE	**Description**
TERMINAT	The _NAME_ variable contains the name of the termination criterion.
UPPERBD | UB	If boundary constraints are used, this observation contains the upper bounds. Those parameters not subjected to upper bounds contain missing values. The _RHS_ variable contains a missing value, and the _NAME_ variable is blank.

If the technique specified by the TECH= option cannot be performed (for example, no feasible initial values can be computed, or the function value or derivatives cannot be evaluated at the starting point), the OUTEST= data set may contain only some of the observations (usually only the PARMS and GRAD observations).

OUTRAM= SAS-data-set

The OUTRAM= data set is of TYPE=RAM and contains the model specification and the computed parameter estimates. This data set is intended to be reused as an INRAM= data set to specify good initial values in a subsequent analysis by PROC CALIS. For a structural equation model, after some alterations, this data set can be used for plotting a path diagram by the NETDRAW procedure, a SAS/OR procedure.

The OUTRAM= data set contains the following variables:

- the BY variables, if any
- the character variable _TYPE_, which takes the values MODEL, ESTIM, VARNAME, METHOD, and STAT
- six additional variables whose meaning depends on the _TYPE_ of the observation

Each observation with _TYPE_ =MODEL defines one matrix in the generalized COSAN model. The additional variables are as follows.

Table 19.6. Additional Variables when _TYPE_=MODEL

Variable	**Contents**
NAME	name of the matrix (character)
MATNR	number for the term and matrix in the model (numeric)
ROW	matrix row number (numeric)
COL	matrix column number (numeric)
ESTIM	first matrix type (numeric)
STDERR	second matrix type (numeric)

If the generalized COSAN model has only one matrix term, the _MATNR_ variable contains only the number of the matrix in the term. If there is more than one term, then it is the term number multiplied by 10,000 plus the matrix number (assuming that there are no more than 9,999 matrices specified in the COSAN model statement).

Each observation with _TYPE_ =ESTIM defines one element of a matrix in the generalized COSAN model. The variables are used as follows.

Table 19.7. Additional Variables when _TYPE_=ESTIM

Variable	Contents
NAME	name of the parameter (character)
MATNR	term and matrix location of parameter (numeric)
ROW	row location of parameter (numeric)
COL	column location of parameter (numeric)
ESTIM	parameter estimate or constant value (numeric)
STDERR	standard error of estimate (numeric)

For constants rather than estimates, the _STDERR_ variable is 0. The _STDERR_ variable is missing for ULS and DWLS estimates if NOSTDERR is specified or if the approximate standard errors are not computed.

Each observation with _TYPE_ =VARNAME defines a column variable name of a matrix in the generalized COSAN model.

The observations with _TYPE_=METHOD and _TYPE_=STAT are not used to build the model. The _TYPE_=METHOD observation contains the name of the estimation method used to compute the parameter estimates in the _NAME_ variable. If METHOD=NONE is not specified, the _ESTIM_ variable of the _TYPE_=STAT observations contains the information summarized in Table 19.8 (described in the section "Assessment of Fit" on page 536).

Table 19.8. _ESTIM_ Contents for _TYPE_=STAT

NAME	_ESTIM_
N	sample size
NPARM	number of parameters used in the model
DF	degrees of freedom
N_ACT	number of active boundary constraints for ML, GLS, and WLS estimation
FIT	fit function
GFI	goodness-of-fit index (GFI)
AGFI	adjusted GFI for degrees of freedom
RMR	root mean square residual
PGFI	parsimonious GFI of Mulaik et al. (1989)
CHISQUAR	overall χ^2
P_CHISQ	probability > χ^2
CHISQNUL	null (baseline) model χ^2
RMSEAEST	Steiger & Lind's (1980) RMSEA index estimate
RMSEALOB	lower range of RMSEA confidence interval
RMSEAUPB	upper range of RMSEA confidence interval
P_CLOSFT	Browne & Cudeck's (1993) probability of close fit
ECVI_EST	Browne & Cudeck's (1993) ECV index estimate
ECVI_LOB	lower range of ECVI confidence interval
ECVI_UPB	upper range of ECVI confidence interval
COMPFITI	Bentler's (1989) comparative fit index

Table 19.8. _ESTIM_ Contents for _TYPE_=STAT (continued)

NAME	_ESTIM_
ADJCHISQ	adjusted χ^2 for elliptic distribution
P_ACHISQ	probability corresponding adjusted χ^2
RLSCHISQ	reweighted least-squares χ^2 (only ML estimation)
AIC	Akaike's information criterion
CAIC	Bozdogan's consistent information criterion
SBC	Schwarz's Bayesian criterion
CENTRALI	McDonald's centrality criterion
PARSIMON	Parsimonious index of James, Mulaik, and Brett
ZTESTWH	z test of Wilson and Hilferty
BB_NONOR	Bentler-Bonett (1980) nonnormed index ρ
BB_NORMD	Bentler-Bonett (1980) normed index Δ
BOL_RHO1	Bollen's (1986) normed index ρ_1
BOL_DEL2	Bollen's (1989a) nonnormed index Δ_2
CNHOELT	Hoelter's critical N index

You can edit the OUTRAM= data set to use its contents for initial estimates in a subsequent analysis by PROC CALIS, perhaps with a slightly changed model. But you should be especially careful for _TYPE_=MODEL when changing matrix types. The codes for the two matrix types are listed in Table 19.9.

Table 19.9. Matrix Type Codes

Code	First Matrix Type	Description
1:	IDE	identity matrix
2:	ZID	zero:identity matrix
3:	DIA	diagonal matrix
4:	ZDI	zero:diagonal matrix
5:	LOW	lower triangular matrix
6:	UPP	upper triangular matrix
7:		temporarily not used
8:	SYM	symmetric matrix
9:	GEN	general-type matrix
10:	BET	identity minus general-type matrix
11:	PER	selection matrix
12:		first matrix (**J**) in LINEQS model statement
13:		second matrix ($\boldsymbol{\beta}$) in LINEQS model statement
14:		third matrix (γ) in LINEQS model statement
Code	**Second Matrix Type**	**Description**
0:		noninverse model matrix
1:	INV	inverse model matrix
2:	IMI	'identity minus inverse' model matrix

OUTSTAT= SAS-data-set

The OUTSTAT= data set is similar to the TYPE=COV, TYPE=UCOV, TYPE=CORR, or TYPE=UCORR data set produced by the CORR procedure. The OUTSTAT= data set contains the following variables:

- the BY variables, if any
- two character variables, _TYPE_ and _NAME_
- the variables analyzed, that is, those in the VAR statement, or if there is no VAR statement, all numeric variables not listed in any other statement but used in the analysis. (**Caution**: Using the LINEQS or RAM model statements selects variables automatically.)

The OUTSTAT= data set contains the following information (when available):

- the mean and standard deviation
- the skewness and kurtosis (if the DATA= data set is a raw data set and the KURTOSIS option is specified)
- the number of observations
- if the WEIGHT statement is used, sum of the weights
- the correlation or covariance matrix to be analyzed
- the predicted correlation or covariance matrix
- the standardized or normalized residual correlation or covariance matrix
- if the model contains latent variables, the predicted covariances between latent and manifest variables, and the latent variable (or factor) score regression coefficients (see the PLATCOV display option on page 473)

In addition, if the FACTOR model statement is used, the OUTSTAT= data set contains:

- the unrotated factor loadings, the unique variances, and the matrix of factor correlations
- the rotated factor loadings and the transformation matrix of the rotation
- the matrix of standardized factor loadings

Each observation in the OUTSTAT= data set contains some type of statistic as indicated by the _TYPE_ variable. The values of the _TYPE_ variable are given in Table 19.10.

Table 19.10. _TYPE_ Observations in the OUTSTAT= data set

TYPE	**Contents**
MEAN	means
STD	standard deviations
USTD	uncorrected standard deviations
SKEWNESS	univariate skewness
KURTOSIS	univariate kurtosis
N	sample size
SUMWGT	sum of weights (if WEIGHT statement is used)
COV	covariances analyzed
CORR	correlations analyzed
UCOV	uncorrected covariances analyzed
UCORR	uncorrected correlations analyzed
ULSPRED	ULS predicted model values
GLSPRED	GLS predicted model values
MAXPRED	ML predicted model values
WLSPRED	WLS predicted model values
DWLSPRED	DWLS predicted model values
ULSNRES	ULS normalized residuals
GLSNRES	GLS normalized residuals
MAXNRES	ML normalized residuals
WLSNRES	WLS normalized residuals
DWLSNRES	DWLS normalized residuals
ULSSRES	ULS variance standardized residuals
GLSSRES	GLS variance standardized residuals
MAXSRES	ML variance standardized residuals
WLSSRES	WLS variance standardized residuals
DWLSSRES	DWLS variance standardized residuals
ULSASRES	ULS asymptotically standardized residuals
GLSASRES	GLS asymptotically standardized residuals
MAXASRES	ML asymptotically standardized residuals
WLSASRES	WLS asymptotically standardized residuals
DWLSASRS	DWLS asymptotically standardized residuals
UNROTATE	unrotated factor loadings
FCORR	matrix of factor correlations
UNIQUE_V	unique variances
TRANSFOR	transformation matrix of rotation
LOADINGS	rotated factor loadings
STD_LOAD	standardized factor loadings
LSSCORE	latent variable (or factor) score regression coefficients for ULS method
SCORE	latent variable (or factor) score regression coefficients other than ULS method

The _NAME_ variable contains the name of the manifest variable corresponding to each row for the covariance, correlation, predicted, and residual matrices and contains the name of the latent variable in case of factor regression scores. For other observations, _NAME_ is blank.

The unique variances and rotated loadings can be used as starting values in more difficult and constrained analyses.

If the model contains latent variables, the OUTSTAT= data set also contains the latent variable score regression coefficients and the predicted covariances between latent and manifest variables. You can use the latent variable score regression coefficients with PROC SCORE to compute factor scores.

If the analyzed matrix is a (corrected or uncorrected) covariance rather than a correlation matrix, the _TYPE_=STD or _TYPE_=USTD observation is not included in the OUTSTAT= data set. In this case, the standard deviations can be obtained from the diagonal elements of the covariance matrix. Dropping the _TYPE_=STD or _TYPE_=USTD observation prevents PROC SCORE from standardizing the observations before computing the factor scores.

OUTWGT= SAS-data-set

You can create an OUTWGT= data set that is of TYPE=WEIGHT and contains the weight matrix used in generalized, weighted, or diagonally weighted least-squares estimation. The *inverse* of the weight matrix is used in the corresponding fit function. The OUTWGT= data set contains the weight matrix on which the WRIDGE= and the WPENALTY= options are applied. For unweighted least-squares or maximum likelihood estimation, no OUTWGT= data set can be written. The last weight matrix used in maximum likelihood estimation is the predicted model matrix (observations with _TYPE_ =MAXPRED) that is included in the OUTSTAT= data set.

For generalized and diagonally weighted least-squares estimation, the weight matrices **W** of the OUTWGT= data set contain all elements w_{ij}, where the indices i and j correspond to all manifest variables used in the analysis. Let $varnam_i$ be the name of the ith variable in the analysis. In this case, the OUTWGT= data set contains n observations with variables as displayed in the following table.

Table 19.11. Contents of OUTWGT= data set for GLS and DWLS Estimation

Variable	Contents
TYPE	WEIGHT (character)
NAME	name of variable $varnam_i$ (character)
$varnam_1$	weight w_{i1} for variable $varnam_1$ (numeric)
$\vdots$	$\vdots$
$varnam_n$	weight w_{in} for variable $varnam_n$ (numeric)

For weighted least-squares estimation, the weight matrix **W** of the OUTWGT= data set contains only the nonredundant elements $w_{ij,kl}$. In this case, the OUTWGT= data set contains $n(n+1)(2n+1)/6$ observations with variables as follows.

Table 19.12. Contents of OUTWGT= data set for WLS Estimation

Variable	Contents
TYPE	WEIGHT (character)
NAME	name of variable $varnam_i$ (character)
NAM2	name of variable $varnam_j$ (character)
NAM3	name of variable $varnam_k$ (character)
$varnam_1$	weight $w_{ij,k1}$ for variable $varnam_1$ (numeric)
⋮	⋮
$varnam_n$	weight $w_{ij,kn}$ for variable $varnam_n$ (numeric)

Symmetric redundant elements are set to missing values.

Missing Values

If the DATA= data set contains raw data (rather than a covariance or correlation matrix), observations with missing values for any variables in the analysis are omitted from the computations. If a covariance or correlation matrix is read, missing values are allowed as long as every pair of variables has at least one nonmissing value.

Estimation Criteria

The following five estimation methods are available in PROC CALIS:

- unweighted least squares (ULS)
- generalized least squares (GLS)
- normal-theory maximum likelihood (ML)
- weighted least squares (WLS, ADF)
- diagonally weighted least squares (DWLS)

An INWGT= data set can be used to specify other than the default weight matrices $\mathbf{W}$ for GLS, WLS, and DWLS estimation.

In each case, the parameter vector is estimated iteratively by a nonlinear optimization algorithm that optimizes a goodness-of-fit function F. When n denotes the number of manifest variables, $\mathbf{S}$ denotes the given sample covariance or correlation matrix for a sample with size N, and $\mathbf{C}$ denotes the predicted moment matrix, then the fit function for unweighted least-squares estimation is

$$F_{ULS} = .5Tr[(\mathbf{S} - \mathbf{C})^2]$$

For normal-theory generalized least-squares estimation, the function is

$$F_{GLS} = .5Tr[(\mathbf{S}^{-1}(\mathbf{S} - \mathbf{C}))^2]$$

For normal-theory maximum likelihood estimation, the function is

$$F_{ML} = Tr(\mathbf{S}\mathbf{C}^{-1}) - n + ln(det(\mathbf{C})) - ln(det(\mathbf{S}))$$

The first three functions can be expressed by the generally weighted least-squares criterion (Browne 1982):

$$F_{GWLS} = .5Tr[(\mathbf{W}^{-1}(\mathbf{S} - \mathbf{C}))^2]$$

For unweighted least squares, the weight matrix $\mathbf{W}$ is chosen as the identity matrix $\mathbf{I}$; for generalized least squares, the default weight matrix $\mathbf{W}$ is the sample covariance matrix $\mathbf{S}$; and for normal-theory maximum likelihood, $\mathbf{W}$ is the iteratively updated predicted moment matrix $\mathbf{C}$. The values of the normal-theory maximum likelihood function F_{ML} and the generally weighted least-squares criterion F_{GWLS} with $\mathbf{W} = \mathbf{C}$ are asymptotically equivalent.

The goodness-of-fit function that is minimized in weighted least-squares estimation is

$$F_{WLS} = Vec(s_{ij} - c_{ij})'\mathbf{W}^{-1}Vec(s_{ij} - c_{ij})$$

where $Vec(s_{ij} - c_{ij})$ denotes the vector of the $n(n+1)/2$ elements of the lower triangle of the symmetric matrix $\mathbf{S} - \mathbf{C}$, and $\mathbf{W} = (w_{ij,kl})$ is a positive definite symmetric matrix with $n(n+1)/2$ rows and columns.

If the moment matrix $\mathbf{S}$ is considered as a covariance rather than a correlation matrix, the default setting of $\mathbf{W} = (w_{ij,kl})$ is the consistent but biased estimators of the asymptotic covariances $\sigma_{ij,kl}$ of the sample covariance s_{ij} with the sample covariance s_{kl}

$$w_{ij,kl} = s_{ij,kl} - s_{ij}s_{kl}$$

where

$$s_{ij,kl} = \frac{1}{N}\sum_{r=1}^{N}(z_{ri} - \overline{z_i})(z_{rj} - \overline{z_j})(z_{rk} - \overline{z_k})(z_{rl} - \overline{z_l})$$

The formula of the asymptotic covariances of uncorrected covariances (using the UCOV or NOINT option) is a straightforward generalization of this expression.

The resulting weight matrix $\mathbf{W}$ is at least positive semidefinite (except for rounding errors). Using the ASYCOV option, you can use Browne's (1984, formula (3.8)) unbiased estimators

$$\begin{aligned} w_{ij,kl} &= \frac{N(N-1)}{(N-2)(N-3)}(s_{ij,kl} - s_{ij}s_{kl}) \\ &\quad - \frac{N}{(N-2)(N-3)}(s_{ik}s_{jl} + s_{il}s_{jk} - \frac{2}{N-1}s_{ij}s_{kl}) \end{aligned}$$

There is no guarantee that this weight matrix is positive semidefinite. However, the second part is of order $O(N^{-1})$ and does not destroy the positive semidefinite first part for sufficiently large N. For a large number of independent observations, default settings of the weight matrix $\mathbf{W}$ result in asymptotically distribution-free parameter estimates with unbiased standard errors and a correct χ^2 test statistic (Browne 1982, 1984).

If the moment matrix $\mathbf{S}$ is a correlation (rather than a covariance) matrix, the default setting of $\mathbf{W} = (w_{ij,kl})$ is the estimators of the asymptotic covariances $\sigma_{ij,kl}$ of the correlations $\mathbf{S} = (s_{ij})$ (Browne and Shapiro 1986; DeLeeuw 1983)

$$\begin{aligned} w_{ij,kl} &= r_{ij,kl} - \frac{1}{2} r_{ij}(r_{ii,kl} + r_{jj,kl}) - \frac{1}{2} r_{kl}(r_{kk,ij} + r_{ll,ij}) \\ &\quad + \frac{1}{4} r_{ij} r_{kl}(r_{ii,kk} + r_{ii,ll} + r_{jj,kk} + r_{jj,ll}) \end{aligned}$$

where

$$r_{ij,kl} = \frac{s_{ij,kl}}{\sqrt{s_{ii}s_{jj}s_{kk}s_{ll}}}$$

The asymptotic variances of the diagonal elements of a correlation matrix are 0. Therefore, the weight matrix computed by Browne and Shapiro's formula is always singular. In this case the goodness-of-fit function for weighted least-squares estimation is modified to

$$F_{WLS} = \sum_{i=2}^{n} \sum_{j=1}^{i-1} \sum_{k=2}^{n} \sum_{l=1}^{k-1} w^{ij,kl}(s_{ij} - c_{ij})(s_{kl} - c_{kl}) + r \sum_{i}^{n} (s_{ii} - c_{ii})^2$$

where r is the penalty weight specified by the WPENALTY=r option and the $w^{ij,kl}$ are the elements of the inverse of the reduced $(n(n-1)/2) \times (n(n-1)/2)$ weight matrix that contains only the nonzero rows and columns of the full weight matrix $\mathbf{W}$. The second term is a penalty term to fit the diagonal elements of the moment matrix $\mathbf{S}$. The default value of $r = 100$ can be decreased or increased by the WPENALTY= option. The often used value of $r = 1$ seems to be too small in many cases to fit the diagonal elements of a correlation matrix properly. If your model does not fit the diagonal of the moment matrix $\mathbf{S}$, you can specify the NODIAG option to exclude the diagonal elements from the fit function.

Storing and inverting the huge weight matrix $\mathbf{W}$ in WLS estimation needs considerable computer resources. A compromise is found by implementing the DWLS method that uses only the diagonal of the weight matrix $\mathbf{W}$ from the WLS estimation in the minimization function

$$F_{DWLS} = Vec(s_{ij} - c_{ij})' diag(\mathbf{W})^{-1} Vec(s_{ij} - c_{ij})$$

The statistical properties of DWLS estimates are still not known.

In generalized, weighted, or diagonally weighted least-squares estimation, you can change from the default settings of weight matrices $\mathbf{W}$ by using an INWGT= data set. Because the diagonal elements $w_{ii,kk}$ of the weight matrix $\mathbf{W}$ are interpreted as asymptotic variances of the sample covariances or correlations, they cannot be negative. The CALIS procedure requires a positive definite weight matrix that has positive diagonal elements.

Relationships among Estimation Criteria

The five estimation functions, F_{ULS}, F_{GLS}, F_{ML}, F_{WLS}, and F_{DWLS}, belong to the following two groups:

- The functions F_{ULS}, F_{GLS}, and F_{ML} take into account all n^2 elements of the symmetric residual matrix $\mathbf{S} - \mathbf{C}$. This means that the off-diagonal residuals contribute twice to F, as lower and as upper triangle elements.
- The functions F_{WLS} and F_{DWLS} take into account only the $n(n+1)/2$ lower triangular elements of the symmetric residual matrix $\mathbf{S} - \mathbf{C}$. This means that the off-diagonal residuals contribute to F only once.

The F_{DWLS} function used in PROC CALIS differs from that used by the LISREL 7 program. Formula (1.25) of the LISREL 7 manual (Jöreskog and Sörbom 1988, p. 23) shows that LISREL groups the F_{DWLS} function in the first group by taking into account all n^2 elements of the symmetric residual matrix $\mathbf{S} - \mathbf{C}$.

- Relationship between DWLS and WLS:
  PROC CALIS: The F_{DWLS} and F_{WLS} estimation functions deliver the same results for the special case that the weight matrix $\mathbf{W}$ used by WLS estimation is a diagonal matrix.
  LISREL 7: This is not the case.
- Relationship between DWLS and ULS:
  LISREL 7: The F_{DWLS} and F_{ULS} estimation functions deliver the same results for the special case that the diagonal weight matrix $\mathbf{W}$ used by DWLS estimation is an identity matrix (contains only 1s).
  PROC CALIS: To obtain the same results with F_{DWLS} and F_{ULS} estimation, set the diagonal weight matrix $\mathbf{W}$ used in DWLS estimation to

  $$w_{ii,kk} = \begin{cases} 1. & \text{if } i = k \\ 0.5 & \text{otherwise} \end{cases}$$

  Because the reciprocal elements of the weight matrix are used in the goodness-of-fit function, the off-diagonal residuals are weighted by a factor of 2.

Testing Rank Deficiency in the Approximate Covariance Matrix

The inverse of the information matrix (or approximate Hessian matrix) is used for the covariance matrix of the parameter estimates, which is needed for the computation of approximate standard errors and modification indices. The numerical condition of the information matrix (computed as the crossproduct $\mathbf{J}'\mathbf{J}$ of the Jacobian matrix $\mathbf{J}$) can be very poor in many practical applications, especially for the analysis of unscaled covariance data. The following four-step strategy is used for the inversion of the information matrix.

1. The inversion (usually of a normalized matrix $\mathbf{D}^{-1}\mathbf{H}\mathbf{D}^{-1}$) is tried using a modified form of the Bunch and Kaufman (1977) algorithm, which allows the

specification of a different singularity criterion for each pivot. The following three criteria for the detection of rank loss in the information matrix are used to specify thresholds:

- *ASING* specifies absolute singularity.
- *MSING* specifies relative singularity depending on the whole matrix norm.
- *VSING* specifies relative singularity depending on the column matrix norm.

If no rank loss is detected, the inverse of the information matrix is used for the covariance matrix of parameter estimates, and the next two steps are skipped.

2. The linear dependencies among the parameter subsets are displayed based on the singularity criteria.
3. If the number of parameters t is smaller than the value specified by the G4= option (the default value is 60), the Moore-Penrose inverse is computed based on the eigenvalue decomposition of the information matrix. If you do not specify the NOPRINT option, the distribution of eigenvalues is displayed, and those eigenvalues that are set to zero in the Moore-Penrose inverse are indicated. You should inspect this eigenvalue distribution carefully.
4. If PROC CALIS did not set the right subset of eigenvalues to zero, you can specify the COVSING= option to set a larger or smaller subset of eigenvalues to zero in a further run of PROC CALIS.

Approximate Standard Errors

Except for unweighted and diagonally weighted least-squares estimation, approximate standard errors can be computed as the diagonal elements of the matrix

$$\frac{c}{NM}\mathbf{H}^{-1}, \quad \text{where}$$

$$NM = \begin{cases} (N-1) & \text{if the CORR or COV matrix is analyzed} \\ & \text{or the intercept variable is not used in the model} \\ N & \text{if the UCORR or UCOV matrix is analyzed} \\ & \text{and the intercept variable is not used in the model} \end{cases}$$

The matrix $\mathbf{H}$ is the approximate Hessian matrix of F evaluated at the final estimates, $c = 1$ for the WLS estimation method, $c = 2$ for the GLS and ML method, and N is the sample size. If a given correlation or covariance matrix is singular, PROC CALIS offers two ways to compute a generalized inverse of the information matrix and, therefore, two ways to compute approximate standard errors of implicitly constrained parameter estimates, t values, and modification indices. Depending on the G4= specification, either a Moore-Penrose inverse or a G2 inverse is computed. The expensive Moore-Penrose inverse computes an estimate of the null space using an eigenvalue decomposition. The cheaper G2 inverse is produced by sweeping the linearly independent rows and columns and zeroing out the dependent ones. The information matrix, the approximate covariance matrix of the parameter estimates, and the approximate standard errors are not computed in the cases of unweighted or diagonally weighted least-squares estimation.

Assessment of Fit

This section contains a collection of formulas used in computing indices to assess the goodness of fit by PROC CALIS. The following notation is used:

- N for the sample size
- n for the number of manifest variables
- t for the number of parameters to estimate
- $NM = \begin{cases} (N-1) & \text{if the CORR or COV matrix is analyzed} \\ & \text{or the intercept variable is not used in the model} \\ N & \text{if the UCORR or UCOV matrix is analyzed} \\ & \text{and the intercept variable is not used in the model} \end{cases}$
- df for the degrees of freedom
- $\gamma = \mathbf{X}$ for the t vector of optimal parameter estimates
- $\mathbf{S} = (s_{ij})$ for the $n \times n$ input COV, CORR, UCOV, or UCORR matrix
- $\mathbf{C} = (c_{ij}) = \hat{\mathbf{\Sigma}} = \mathbf{\Sigma}(\hat{\gamma})$ for the predicted model matrix
- $\mathbf{W}$ for the weight matrix ($\mathbf{W} = \mathbf{I}$ for ULS, $\mathbf{W} = \mathbf{S}$ for default GLS, and $\mathbf{W} = \mathbf{C}$ for ML estimates)
- $\mathbf{U}$ for the $n^2 \times n^2$ asymptotic covariance matrix of sample covariances
- $\Phi(x|\lambda, df)$ for the cumulative distribution function of the noncentral chi-squared distribution with noncentrality parameter λ

The following notation is for indices that allow testing nested models by a χ^2 difference test:

- f_0 for the function value of the independence model
- df_0 for the degrees of freedom of the independence model
- $f_{min} = F$ for the function value of the fitted model
- $df_{min} = df$ for the degrees of freedom of the fitted model

The degrees of freedom df_{min} and the number of parameters t are adjusted automatically when there are active constraints in the analysis. The computation of many fit statistics and indices are affected. You can turn off the automatic adjustment using the NOADJDF option. See the section “Counting the Degrees of Freedom” on page 563 for more information.

Residuals

PROC CALIS computes four types of residuals and writes them to the OUTSTAT= data set.

- **Raw Residuals**

$$Res = \mathbf{S} - \mathbf{C}, Res_{ij} = s_{ij} - c_{ij}$$

The raw residuals are displayed whenever the PALL, the PRINT, or the RESIDUAL option is specified.

- **Variance Standardized Residuals**

$$VSRes_{ij} = \frac{s_{ij} - c_{ij}}{\sqrt{s_{ii}s_{jj}}}$$

The variance standardized residuals are displayed when you specify

  - the PALL, the PRINT, or the RESIDUAL option and METHOD=NONE, METHOD=ULS, or METHOD=DWLS
  - RESIDUAL=VARSTAND

The variance standardized residuals are equal to those computed by the EQS 3 program (Bentler 1989).

- **Asymptotically Standardized Residuals**

$$ASRes_{ij} = \frac{s_{ij} - c_{ij}}{\sqrt{c_{ij,ij}}}, \quad \text{where}$$

$$c_{ij,ij} = diag(\mathbf{U} - \mathbf{J}Cov(\gamma)\mathbf{J}')_{ij}$$

The matrix $\mathbf{J}$ is the $n^2 \times t$ Jacobian matrix $d\mathbf{\Sigma}/d\gamma$, and $Cov(\gamma)$ is the $t \times t$ asymptotic covariance matrix of parameter estimates (the inverse of the information matrix). Asymptotically standardized residuals are displayed when one of the following conditions is met:

  - The PALL, the PRINT, or the RESIDUAL option is specified, and METHOD=ML, METHOD=GLS, or METHOD=WLS, and the expensive information and Jacobian matrices are computed for some other reason.
  - RESIDUAL= ASYSTAND is specified.

The asymptotically standardized residuals are equal to those computed by the LISREL 7 program (Jöreskog and Sörbom 1988) except for the denominator NM in the definition of matrix $\mathbf{U}$.

- **Normalized Residuals**

$$NRes_{ij} = \frac{s_{ij} - c_{ij}}{\sqrt{u_{ij,ij}}}$$

where the diagonal elements $u_{ij,ij}$ of the $n^2 \times n^2$ asymptotic covariance matrix $\mathbf{U}$ of sample covariances are defined for the following methods.

- **GLS** as $u_{ij,ij} = \frac{1}{NM}(s_{ii}s_{jj} + s_{ij}^2)$
- **ML** as $u_{ij,ij} = \frac{1}{NM}(c_{ii}c_{jj} + c_{ij}^2)$
- **WLS** as $u_{ij,ij} = w_{ij,ij}$

Normalized residuals are displayed when one of the following conditions is met:

- The PALL, the PRINT, or the RESIDUAL option is specified, and METHOD=ML, METHOD=GLS, or METHOD=WLS, and the expensive information and Jacobian matrices are **not** computed for some other reason.
- RESIDUAL=NORM is specified.

The normalized residuals are equal to those computed by the LISREL VI program (Jöreskog and Sörbom 1985) except for the definition of the denominator NM in matrix $\mathbf{U}$.

For estimation methods that are not BGLS estimation methods (Browne 1982, 1984), such as METHOD=NONE, METHOD=ULS, or METHOD=DWLS, the assumption of an asymptotic covariance matrix $\mathbf{U}$ of sample covariances does not seem to be appropriate. In this case, the normalized residuals should be replaced by the more relaxed variance standardized residuals. Computation of asymptotically standardized residuals requires computing the Jacobian and information matrices. This is computationally very expensive and is done only if the Jacobian matrix has to be computed for some other reason, that is, if at least one of the following items is true:

- The default, PRINT, or PALL displayed output is requested, and neither the NOMOD nor NOSTDERR option is specified.
- Either the MODIFICATION (included in PALL), PCOVES, or STDERR (included in default, PRINT, and PALL output) option is requested or RESIDUAL=ASYSTAND is specified.
- The LEVMAR or NEWRAP optimization technique is used.
- An OUTRAM= data set is specified without using the NOSTDERR option.
- An OUTEST= data set is specified without using the NOSTDERR option.

Since normalized residuals use an overestimate of the asymptotic covariance matrix of residuals (the diagonal of $\mathbf{U}$), the normalized residuals cannot be larger than the asymptotically standardized residuals (which use the diagonal of $\mathbf{U} - \mathbf{J}Cov(\gamma)\mathbf{J}'$).

Together with the residual matrices, the values of the average residual, the average off-diagonal residual, and the rank order of the largest values are displayed. The distribution of the normalized and standardized residuals is displayed also.

Goodness-of-Fit Indices Based on Residuals

The following items are computed for all five kinds of estimation:ULS, GLS, ML, WLS, and DWLS. All these indices are written to the OUTRAM= data set. The goodness of fit (GFI), adjusted goodness of fit (AGFI), and root mean square residual (RMR) are computed as in the LISREL VI program of Jöreskog and Sörbom (1985).

- **Goodness-of-Fit Index**
  The goodness-of-fit index for the ULS, GLS, and ML estimation methods is

$$GFI = 1 - \frac{Tr((\mathbf{W}^{-1}(\mathbf{S} - \mathbf{C}))^2)}{Tr((\mathbf{W}^{-1}\mathbf{S})^2)}$$

  but for WLS and DWLS estimation, it is

$$GFI = 1 - \frac{Vec(s_{ij} - c_{ij})'\mathbf{W}^{-1}Vec(s_{ij} - c_{ij})}{Vec(s_{ij})'\mathbf{W}^{-1}Vec(s_{ij})}$$

  where $\mathbf{W} = diag$ for DWLS estimation, and $Vec(s_{ij} - c_{ij})$ denotes the vector of the $n(n+1)/2$ elements of the lower triangle of the symmetric matrix $\mathbf{S} - \mathbf{C}$. For a constant weight matrix $\mathbf{W}$, the goodness-of-fit index is 1 minus the ratio of the minimum function value and the function value before any model has been fitted. The GFI should be between 0 and 1. The data probably do not fit the model if the GFI is negative or much larger than 1.

- **Adjusted Goodness-of-Fit Index**
  The AGFI is the GFI adjusted for the degrees of freedom of the model

$$AGFI = 1 - \frac{n(n+1)}{2df}(1 - GFI)$$

  The AGFI corresponds to the GFI in replacing the total sum of squares by the mean sum of squares.

  Caution:

  - Large n and small *df* can result in a negative AGFI. For example, GFI=0.90, n=19, and df=2 result in an AGFI of -8.5.
  - AGFI is not defined for a saturated model, due to division by $df = 0$.
  - AGFI is not sensitive to losses in *df*.

  The AGFI should be between 0 and 1. The data probably do not fit the model if the AGFI is negative or much larger than 1. For more information, refer to Mulaik et al. (1989).

- **Root Mean Square Residual**
  The RMR is the mean of the squared residuals:

$$RMR = \sqrt{\frac{2}{n(n+1)} \sum_{i}^{n} \sum_{j}^{i} (s_{ij} - c_{ij})^2}$$

- **Parsimonious Goodness-of-Fit Index**
  The PGFI (Mulaik et al. 1989) is a modification of the GFI that takes the parsimony of the model into account:

$$PGFI = \frac{df_{min}}{df_0} GFI$$

  The PGFI uses the same parsimonious factor as the parsimonious normed Bentler-Bonett index (James, Mulaik, and Brett 1982).

Goodness-of-Fit Indices Based on the χ^2

The following items are transformations of the overall χ^2 value and in general depend on the sample size N. These indices are not computed for ULS or DWLS estimates.

- **Uncorrected χ^2**
  The overall χ^2 measure is the optimum function value F multiplied by $N-1$ if a CORR or COV matrix is analyzed, or multiplied by N if a UCORR or UCOV matrix is analyzed. This gives the likelihood ratio test statistic for the null hypothesis that the predicted matrix **C** has the specified model structure against the alternative that **C** is unconstrained. The χ^2 test is valid only if the observations are independent and identically distributed, the analysis is based on the nonstandardized sample covariance matrix **S**, and the sample size N is sufficiently large (Browne 1982; Bollen 1989b; Jöreskog and Sörbom 1985). For ML and GLS estimates, the variables must also have an approximately multivariate normal distribution. The notation Prob>Chi**2 means "the probability under the null hypothesis of obtaining a greater χ^2 statistic than that observed."

  $$\chi^2 = NM * F$$

  where F is the function value at the minimum.

- **χ_0^2 Value of the Independence Model**
  The χ_0^2 value of the independence model

  $$\chi_0^2 = NM * f_0$$

  and the corresponding degrees of freedom df_0 can be used (in large samples) to evaluate the gain of explanation by fitting the specific model (Bentler 1989).

- **RMSEA Index (Steiger and Lind 1980)**
  The Steiger and Lind (1980) root mean squared error approximation (RMSEA) coefficient is

  $$\epsilon_\alpha = \sqrt{\max(\frac{F}{df} - \frac{1}{NM}, 0)}$$

  The lower and upper limits of the confidence interval are computed using the cumulative distribution function of the noncentral chi-squared distribution $\Phi(x|\lambda, df) = \alpha$, with $x = NM * F$, λ_L satisfying $\Phi(x|\lambda_L, df) = 1 - \frac{\alpha}{2}$, and λ_U satisfying $\Phi(x|\lambda_U, df) = \frac{\alpha}{2}$:

  $$(\epsilon_{\alpha_L}; \epsilon_{\alpha_U}) = (\sqrt{\frac{\lambda_L}{NM * df}}; \sqrt{\frac{\lambda_U}{NM * df}})$$

  Refer to Browne and Du Toit (1992) for more details. The size of the confidence interval is defined by the option ALPHARMS=α, $0 \le \alpha \le 1$. The default is $\alpha = 0.1$, which corresponds to the 90% confidence interval for the RMSEA.

- **Probability for Test of Close Fit (Browne and Cudeck 1993)**
  The traditional exact χ^2 test hypothesis $H_0: \epsilon_\alpha = 0$ is replaced by the null hypothesis of close fit $H_0: \epsilon_\alpha \leq 0.05$ and the exceedance probability P is computed as

$$P = 1 - \Phi(x|\lambda^*, df)$$

  where $x = NM * F$ and $\lambda^* = 0.05^2 * NM * df$. The null hypothesis of close fit is rejected if P is smaller than a prespecified level (for example, $P < 0.05$).

- **Expected Cross Validation Index (Browne and Cudeck 1993)**
  For GLS and WLS, the estimator c of the ECVI is linearly related to AIC:

$$c = F(\mathbf{S}, \mathbf{C}) + \frac{2t}{NM}$$

  For ML estimation, c_{ML} is used.

$$c_{ML} = F_{ML}(\mathbf{S}, \mathbf{C}) + \frac{2t}{NM - n - 1}$$

  The confidence interval $(c_L; c_U)$ for c is computed using the cumulative distribution function $\Phi(x|\lambda, df)$ of the noncentral chi-squared distribution,

$$(c_L; c_U) = (\frac{\lambda_L + nnt}{NM}; \frac{\lambda_U + nnt}{NM})$$

  with $nnt = n(n+1)/2 + t$, $x = NM * F$, $\Phi(x|\lambda_U, df) = 1 - \frac{\alpha}{2}$, and $\Phi(x|\lambda_L, df) = \frac{\alpha}{2}$. The confidence interval $(c_L^*; c_U^*)$ for c_{ML} is

$$(c_L^*; c_U^*) = (\frac{\lambda_L^* + nnt}{NM - n - 1}; \frac{\lambda_U^* + nnt}{NM - n - 1})$$

  where $nnt = n(n+1)/2 + t$, $x = (NM - n - 1) * F$, $\Phi(x|\lambda_U^*, df) = 1 - \frac{\alpha}{2}$ and $\Phi(x|\lambda_L^*, df) = \frac{\alpha}{2}$. Refer to Browne and Cudeck (1993). The size of the confidence interval is defined by the option ALPHAECV=α, $0 \leq \alpha \leq 1$. The default is $\alpha = 0.1$, which corresponds to the 90% confidence interval for the ECVI.

- **Comparative Fit Index (Bentler 1989)**

$$CFI = 1 - \frac{\max(NM * f_{min} - df_{min}, 0)}{\max(NM * f_0 - df_0, 0)}$$

- **Adjusted χ^2 Value (Browne 1982)**
  If the variables are n-variate elliptic rather than normal and have significant amounts of multivariate kurtosis (leptokurtic or platykurtic), the χ^2 value can be adjusted to

$$\chi^2_{ell} = \frac{\chi^2}{\eta_2}$$

  where η_2 is the multivariate relative kurtosis coefficient.

- **Normal Theory Reweighted LS χ^2 Value**
  This index is displayed only if METHOD=ML. Instead of the function value F_{ML}, the reweighted goodness-of-fit function F_{GWLS} is used,

  $$\chi^2_{GWLS} = NM * F_{GWLS}$$

  where F_{GWLS} is the value of the function at the minimum.

- **Akaike's Information Criterion (AIC) (Akaike 1974; Akaike 1987)**
  This is a criterion for selecting the best model among a number of candidate models. The model that yields the smallest value of AIC is considered the best.

  $$AIC = \chi^2 - 2df$$

- **Consistent Akaike's Information Criterion (CAIC) (Bozdogan 1987)**
  This is another criterion, similar to AIC, for selecting the best model among alternatives. The model that yields the smallest value of CAIC is considered the best. CAIC is preferred by some people to AIC or the χ^2 test.

  $$CAIC = \chi^2 - (ln(N) + 1)df$$

- **Schwarz's Bayesian Criterion (SBC) (Schwarz 1978; Sclove 1987)**
  This is another criterion, similar to AIC, for selecting the best model. The model that yields the smallest value of SBC is considered the best. SBC is preferred by some people to AIC or the χ^2 test.

  $$SBC = \chi^2 - ln(N)df$$

- **McDonald's Measure of Centrality (McDonald and Hartmann 1992)**

  $$CENT = exp(-\frac{(\chi^2 - df)}{2N})$$

- **Parsimonious Normed Fit Index (James, Mulaik, and Brett 1982)**
  The PNFI is a modification of Bentler-Bonett's normed fit index that takes parsimony of the model into account,

  $$PNFI = \frac{df_{min}}{df_0} \frac{(f_0 - f_{min})}{f_0}$$

  The PNFI uses the same parsimonious factor as the parsimonious GFI of Mulaik et al. (1989).

- **Z-Test (Wilson and Hilferty 1931)**
  The Z-Test of Wilson and Hilferty assumes an n-variate normal distribution:

  $$Z = \frac{\sqrt[3]{\frac{\chi^2}{df}} - (1 - \frac{2}{9df})}{\sqrt{\frac{2}{9df}}}$$

  Refer to McArdle (1988) and Bishop, Fienberg, and Holland (1977, p. 527) for an application of the Z-Test.

- **Nonnormed Coefficient (Bentler and Bonett 1980)**

$$\rho = \frac{f_0/df_0 - f_{min}/df_{min}}{f_0/df_0 - 1/NM}$$

Refer to Tucker and Lewis (1973).

- **Normed Coefficient (Bentler and Bonett 1980)**

$$\Delta = \frac{f_0 - f_{min}}{f_0}$$

Mulaik et al. (1989) recommend the parsimonious weighted form PNFI.

- **Normed Index ρ_1 (Bollen 1986)**

$$\rho_1 = \frac{f_0/df_0 - f_{min}/df_{min}}{f_0/df_0}$$

ρ_1 is always less than or equal to 1; $\rho_1 < 0$ is unlikely in practice. Refer to the discussion in Bollen (1989a).

- **Nonnormed Index Δ_2 (Bollen 1989a)**

$$\Delta_2 = \frac{f_0 - f_{min}}{f_0 - \frac{df}{NM}}$$

is a modification of Bentler & Bonett's Δ that uses *df* and "lessens the dependence" on N. Refer to the discussion in Bollen (1989b). Δ_2 is identical to Mulaik et al.'s (1989) IFI2 index.

- **Critical N Index (Hoelter 1983)**

$$CN = \frac{\chi^2_{crit}}{F} + 1$$

where χ^2_{crit} is the critical chi-square value for the given *df* degrees of freedom and probability $\alpha = 0.05$, and F is the value of the estimation criterion (minimization function). Refer to Bollen (1989b, p. 277). Hoelter (1983) suggests that CN should be at least 200; however, Bollen (1989b) notes that the CN value may lead to an overly pessimistic assessment of fit for small samples.

Squared Multiple Correlation

The following are measures of the squared multiple correlation for manifest and endogenous variables and are computed for all five estimation methods: ULS, GLS, ML, WLS, and DWLS. These coefficients are computed as in the LISREL VI program of Jöreskog and Sörbom (1985). The DETAE, DETSE, and DETMV determination coefficients are intended to be global means of the squared multiple correlations for different subsets of model equations and variables. These coefficients are displayed only when you specify the PDETERM option with a RAM or LINEQS model.

- **R^2 Values Corresponding to Endogenous Variables**

$$R_i^2 = 1 - \frac{\widehat{var}(\zeta_i)}{\widehat{var}(\eta_i)}$$

- **Total Determination of All Equations**

$$DETAE = 1 - \frac{det(\hat{\Theta}, \hat{\Psi})}{det(\widehat{Cov}(y, x, \eta))}$$

- **Total Determination of the Structural Equations**

$$DETSE = 1 - \frac{det(\hat{\Psi})}{det(\widehat{Cov}(\eta))}$$

- **Total Determination of the Manifest Variables**

$$DETMV = 1 - \frac{det(\hat{\Theta})}{det(\mathbf{S})}$$

Caution: In the LISREL program, the structural equations are defined by specifying the BETA matrix. In PROC CALIS, a structural equation has a dependent left-hand-side variable that appears at least once on the right-hand side of another equation, or the equation has at least one right-hand-side variable that is the left-hand-side variable of another equation. Therefore, PROC CALIS sometimes identifies more equations as structural equations than the LISREL program does.

Measures of Multivariate Kurtosis

In many applications, the manifest variables are not even approximately multivariate normal. If this happens to be the case with your data set, the default generalized least-squares and maximum likelihood estimation methods are not appropriate, and you should compute the parameter estimates and their standard errors by an asymptotically distribution-free method, such as the WLS estimation method. If your manifest variables are multivariate normal, then they have a zero relative multivariate kurtosis, and all marginal distributions have zero kurtosis (Browne 1982). If your DATA= data set contains raw data, PROC CALIS computes univariate skewness and kurtosis and a set of multivariate kurtosis values. By default, the values of univariate skewness and kurtosis are corrected for bias (as in PROC UNIVARIATE), but using the BIASKUR option enables you to compute the uncorrected values also. The values are displayed when you specify the PROC CALIS statement option KURTOSIS.

- **Corrected Variance for Variable** z_j

$$\sigma_j^2 = \frac{1}{N-1}\sum_i^N (z_{ij} - \overline{z_j})^2$$

- **Corrected Univariate Skewness for Variable** z_j

$$\gamma_{1(j)} = \frac{N}{(N-1)(N-2)} \frac{\sum_i^N (z_{ij} - \overline{z_j})^3}{\sigma_j^3}$$

- **Uncorrected Univariate Skewness for Variable** z_j

$$\gamma_{1(j)} = \frac{N \sum_i^N (z_{ij} - \overline{z_j})^3}{\sqrt{N[\sum_i^N (z_{ij} - \overline{z_j})^2]^3}}$$

- **Corrected Univariate Kurtosis for Variable** z_j

$$\gamma_{2(j)} = \frac{N(N+1)}{(N-1)(N-2)(N-3)} \frac{\sum_i^N (z_{ij} - \overline{z_j})^4}{\sigma_j^4} - \frac{3(N-1)^2}{(N-2)(N-3)}$$

- **Uncorrected Univariate Kurtosis for Variable** z_j

$$\gamma_{2(j)} = \frac{N \sum_i^N (z_{ij} - \overline{z_j})^4}{[\sum_i^N (z_{ij} - \overline{z_j})^2]^2} - 3$$

- **Mardia's Multivariate Kurtosis**

$$\gamma_2 = \frac{1}{N}\sum_i^N [(z_i - \overline{z})' S^{-1} (z_i - \overline{z})]^2 - n(n+2)$$

- **Relative Multivariate Kurtosis**

$$\eta_2 = \frac{\gamma_2 + n(n+2)}{n(n+2)}$$

- **Normalized Multivariate Kurtosis**

$$\kappa_0 = \frac{\gamma_2}{\sqrt{8n(n+2)/N}}$$

- **Mardia Based Kappa**

$$\kappa_1 = \frac{\gamma_2}{n(n+2)}$$

- **Mean Scaled Univariate Kurtosis**

$$\kappa_2 = \frac{1}{3n}\sum_{j}^{n} \gamma_{2(j)}$$

- **Adjusted Mean Scaled Univariate Kurtosis**

$$\kappa_3 = \frac{1}{3n}\sum_{j}^{n} \gamma_{2(j)}^{*}$$

with

$$\gamma_{2(j)}^{*} = \begin{cases} \gamma_{2(j)} \quad , & if \quad \gamma_{2(j)} > \frac{-6}{n+2} \\ \frac{-6}{n+2} \quad , & \text{otherwise} \end{cases}$$

If variable Z_j is normally distributed, the uncorrected univariate kurtosis $\gamma_{2(j)}$ is equal to 0. If Z has an n-variate normal distribution, Mardia's multivariate kurtosis γ_2 is equal to 0. A variable Z_j is called *leptokurtic* if it has a positive value of $\gamma_{2(j)}$ and is called *platykurtic* if it has a negative value of $\gamma_{2(j)}$. The values of κ_1, κ_2, and κ_3 should not be smaller than a lower bound (Bentler 1985):

$$\hat{\kappa} \geq \frac{-2}{n+2}$$

PROC CALIS displays a message if this happens.

If weighted least-squares estimates (METHOD=WLS or METHOD=ADF) are specified and the weight matrix is computed from an input raw data set, the CALIS procedure computes two further measures of multivariate kurtosis.

- **Multivariate Mean Kappa**

$$\kappa_4 = \frac{1}{m}\sum_{i}^{n}\sum_{j}^{i}\sum_{k}^{j}\sum_{l}^{k} \hat{\kappa}_{ij,kl} - 1$$

where

$$\hat{\kappa}_{ij,kl} = \frac{s_{ij,kl}}{s_{ij}s_{kl} + s_{ik}s_{jl} + s_{il}s_{jk}}$$

and $m = n(n+1)(n+2)(n+3)/24$ is the number of elements in the vector $s_{ij,kl}$ (Bentler 1985).

- **Multivariate Least-Squares Kappa**

  $$\kappa_5 = \frac{s_4' s_2}{s_2' s_2} - 1$$

  where

  $$s_{ij,kl} = \frac{1}{N} \sum_{r=1}^{N} (z_{ri} - \overline{z_i})(z_{rj} - \overline{z_j})(z_{rk} - \overline{z_k})(z_{rl} - \overline{z_l})$$

  s_4 is the vector of the $s_{ij,kl}$, and s_2 is the vector of the elements in the denominator of $\hat{\kappa}$ (Bentler 1985).

The occurrence of significant nonzero values of Mardia's multivariate kurtosis γ_2 and significant amounts of some of the univariate kurtosis values $\gamma_{2(j)}$ indicate that your variables are not multivariate normal distributed. Violating the multivariate normality assumption in (default) generalized least-squares and maximum likelihood estimation usually leads to the wrong approximate standard errors and incorrect fit statistics based on the χ^2 value. In general, the parameter estimates are more stable against violation of the normal distribution assumption. For more details, refer to Browne (1974, 1982, 1984).

Initial Estimates

Each optimization technique requires a set of initial values for the parameters. To avoid local optima, the initial values should be as close as possible to the globally optimal solution. You can check for local optima by running the analysis with several different sets of initial values; the RANDOM= option in the PROC CALIS statement is useful in this regard.

- RAM and LINEQS: There are several default estimation methods available in PROC CALIS for initial values of parameters in a linear structural equation model specified by a RAM or LINEQS model statement, depending on the form of the specified model.

  - two-stage least-squares estimation
  - instrumental variable method (Hägglund 1982; Jennrich 1987)
  - approximative factor analysis method
  - ordinary least-squares estimation
  - estimation method of McDonald (McDonald and Hartmann 1992)

- FACTOR: For default (exploratory) factor analysis, PROC CALIS computes initial estimates for factor loadings and unique variances by an algebraic method of approximate factor analysis. If you use a MATRIX statement together with a FACTOR model specification, initial values are computed by McDonald's (McDonald and Hartmann 1992) method if possible. McDonald's method of computing initial values works better if you scale the factors by setting the factor variances to 1 rather than setting the loadings of the reference variables equal to 1. If none of the two methods seems to be appropriate, the initial values are set by the START= option.

- COSAN: For the more general COSAN model, there is no default estimation method for the initial values. In this case, the START= or RANDOM= option can be used to set otherwise unassigned initial values.

Poor initial values can cause convergence problems, especially with maximum likelihood estimation. You should not specify a constant initial value for all parameters since this would produce a singular predicted model matrix in the first iteration. Sufficiently large positive diagonal elements in the central matrices of each model matrix term provide a nonnegative definite initial predicted model matrix. If maximum likelihood estimation fails to converge, it may help to use METHOD=LSML, which uses the final estimates from an unweighted least-squares analysis as initial estimates for maximum likelihood. Or you can fit a slightly different but better-behaved model and produce an OUTRAM= data set, which can then be modified in accordance with the original model and used as an INRAM= data set to provide initial values for another analysis.

If you are analyzing a covariance or scalar product matrix, be sure to take into account the scales of the variables. The default initial values may be inappropriate when some variables have extremely large or small variances.

Automatic Variable Selection

You can use the VAR statement to reorder the variables in the model and to delete the variables not used. Using the VAR statement saves memory and computation time. If a linear structural equation model using the RAM or LINEQS statement (or an INRAM= data set specifying a RAM or LINEQS model) does not use all the manifest variables given in the input DATA= data set, PROC CALIS automatically deletes those manifest variables not used in the model.

In some special circumstances, the automatic variable selection performed for the RAM and LINEQS statements may be inappropriate, for example, if you are interested in modification indices connected to some of the variables that are not used in the model. You can include such manifest variables as exogenous variables in the analysis by specifying constant zero coefficients.

For example, the first three steps in a stepwise regression analysis of the Werner Blood Chemistry data (Jöreskog and Sörbom 1988, p. 111) can be performed as follows:

```
proc calis data=dixon method=gls nobs=180 print mod;
   lineqs y=0 x1+0 x2+0 x3+0 x4+0 x5+0 x6+0 x7+e;
   std    e=var;
run;
proc calis data=dixon method=gls nobs=180 print mod;
   lineqs y=g1 x1+0 x2+0 x3+0 x4+0 x5+0 x6+0 x7+e;
   std    e=var;
```

```
run;
proc calis data=dixon method=gls nobs=180 print mod;
   lineqs y=g1 x1+0 x2+0 x3+0 x4+0 x5+g6 x6+0 x7+e;
   std    e=var;
run;
```

Using the COSAN statement does not automatically delete those variables from the analysis that are not used in the model. You can use the output of the predetermined values in the predicted model matrix (PREDET option) to detect unused variables. Variables that are not used in the model are indicated by 0 in the rows and columns of the predetermined predicted model matrix.

Exogenous Manifest Variables

If there are exogenous manifest variables in the linear structural equation model, then there is a one-to-one relationship between the given covariances and corresponding estimates in the central model matrix ($\mathbf{P}$ or $\mathbf{\Phi}$). In general, using exogenous manifest variables reduces the degrees of freedom since the corresponding sample correlations or covariances are not part of the exogenous information provided for the parameter estimation. See the section "Counting the Degrees of Freedom" on page 563 for more information.

If you specify a RAM or LINEQS model statement, or if such a model is recognized in an INRAM= data set, those elements in the central model matrices that correspond to the exogenous manifest variables are reset to the sample values after computing covariances or correlations within the current BY group.

The COSAN statement does not automatically set the covariances in the central model matrices that correspond to manifest exogenous variables.

You can use the output of the predetermined values in the predicted model matrix (PREDET option) that correspond to manifest exogenous variables to see which of the manifest variables are exogenous variables and to help you set the corresponding locations of the central model matrices with their covariances.

The following two examples show how different the results of PROC CALIS can be if manifest variables are considered either as endogenous or as exogenous variables. (See Figure 19.5.) In both examples, a correlation matrix $\mathbf{S}$ is tested against an identity model matrix $\mathbf{C}$; that is, no parameter is estimated. The three runs of the first example (specified by the COSAN, LINEQS, and RAM statements) consider the two variables y and x as endogenous variables.

```
title2 'Data: FULLER (1987, p.18)';
data corn;
   input y x;
   datalines;
 86  70
115  97
 90  53
 86  64
110  95
```

```
 91   64
 99   50
 96   70
 99   94
104   69
 96   51
;

title3 'Endogenous Y and X';
proc calis data=corn;
   cosal corr(2,ide);
run;
proc calis data=corn;
   lineqs
            y=ey,
            x=ex;
   std      ey ex=2 * 1;
run;
proc calis data=corn;
   ram
        1  1  3  1.,
        1  2  4  1.,
        2  3  3  1.,
        2  4  4  1.;
run;
```

The two runs of the second example (specified by the LINEQS and RAM statements) consider y and x as exogenous variables.

```
title3 'Exogenous Y and X';
proc calis data=corn;
   std y x=2 * 1;
run;
proc calis data=corn;
   ram
        2  1  1  1.,
        2  2  2  1.;
run;
```

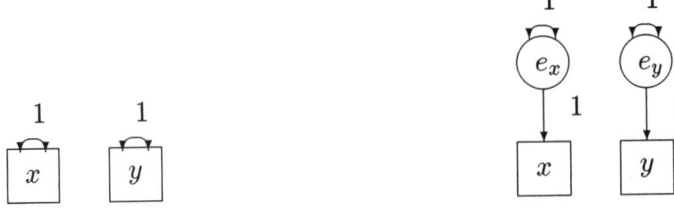

Figure 19.5. Exogenous and Endogenous Variables

The LINEQS and the RAM model statements set the covariances (correlations) of exogenous manifest variables in the estimated model matrix and automatically reduce the degrees of freedom.

Use of Optimization Techniques

No algorithm for optimizing general nonlinear functions exists that will always find the global optimum for a general nonlinear minimization problem in a reasonable amount of time. Since no single optimization technique is invariably superior to others, PROC CALIS provides a variety of optimization techniques that work well in various circumstances. However, you can devise problems for which none of the techniques in PROC CALIS will find the correct solution. All optimization techniques in PROC CALIS use $O(n^2)$ memory except the conjugate gradient methods, which use only $O(n)$ of memory and are designed to optimize problems with many parameters.

The PROC CALIS statement NLOPTIONS can be especially helpful for tuning applications with nonlinear equality and inequality constraints on the parameter estimates. Some of the options available in NLOPTIONS may also be invoked as PROC CALIS options. The NLOPTIONS statement can specify almost the same options as the SAS/OR NLP procedure.

Nonlinear optimization requires the repeated computation of

- the function value (optimization criterion)
- the gradient vector (first-order partial derivatives)
- for some techniques, the (approximate) Hessian matrix (second-order partial derivatives)
- values of linear and nonlinear constraints
- the first-order partial derivatives (Jacobian) of nonlinear constraints

For the criteria used by PROC CALIS, computing the gradient takes more computer time than computing the function value, and computing the Hessian takes *much* more computer time and memory than computing the gradient, especially when there are many parameters to estimate. Unfortunately, optimization techniques that do not use the Hessian usually require many more iterations than techniques that do use the (approximate) Hessian, and so they are often slower. Techniques that do not use the Hessian also tend to be less reliable (for example, they may terminate at local rather than global optima).

The available optimization techniques are displayed in Table 19.13 and can be chosen by the TECH=*name* option.

Table 19.13. Optimization Techniques

TECH=	Optimization Technique
LEVMAR	Levenberg-Marquardt Method
TRUREG	Trust-Region Method
NEWRAP	Newton-Raphson Method with Line Search
NRRIDG	Newton-Raphson Method with Ridging
QUANEW	Quasi-Newton Methods (DBFGS, DDFP, BFGS, DFP)
DBLDOG	Double-Dogleg Method (DBFGS, DDFP)
CONGRA	Conjugate Gradient Methods (PB, FR, PR, CD)

Table 19.14 shows, for each optimization technique, which derivatives are needed (first-order or second-order) and what kind of constraints (boundary, linear, or nonlinear) can be imposed on the parameters.

Table 19.14. Derivatives Needed and Constraints Allowed

	Derivatives		Constraints		
TECH=	First Order	Second Order	Boundary	Linear	Nonlinear
LEVMAR	x	x	x	x	-
TRUREG	x	x	x	x	-
NEWRAP	x	x	x	x	-
NRRIDG	x	x	x	x	-
QUANEW	x	-	x	x	x
DBLDOG	x	-	x	x	-
CONGRA	x	-	x	x	-

The Levenberg-Marquardt, trust-region, and Newton-Raphson techniques are usually the most reliable, work well with boundary and general linear constraints, and generally converge after a few iterations to a precise solution. However, these techniques need to compute a Hessian matrix in each iteration. For HESSALG=1, this means that you need about $4(n(n+1)/2)t$ bytes of work memory ($n =$ the number of manifest variables, $t =$ the number of parameters to estimate) to store the Jacobian and its cross product. With HESSALG=2 or HESSALG=3, you do not need this work memory, but the use of a utility file increases execution time. Computing the approximate Hessian in each iteration can be very time- and memory-consuming, especially for large problems (more than 60 or 100 parameters, depending on the computer used). For large problems, a quasi-Newton technique, especially with the BFGS update, can be far more efficient.

For a poor choice of initial values, the Levenberg-Marquardt method seems to be more reliable.

If memory problems occur, you can use one of the conjugate gradient techniques, but they are generally slower and less reliable than the methods that use second-order information.

There are several options to control the optimization process. First of all, you can specify various termination criteria. You can specify the GCONV= option to specify a relative gradient termination criterion. If there are active boundary constraints, only those gradient components that correspond to inactive constraints contribute to the criterion. When you want very precise parameter estimates, the GCONV= option is useful. Other criteria that use relative changes in function values or parameter estimates in consecutive iterations can lead to early termination when active constraints cause small steps to occur. The small default value for the FCONV= option helps prevent early termination. Using the MAXITER= and MAXFUNC= options enables you to specify the maximum number of iterations and function calls in the optimization process. These limits are especially useful in combination with the INRAM= and OUTRAM= options; you can run a few iterations at a time, inspect the results, and decide whether to continue iterating.

Nonlinearly Constrained QN Optimization

The algorithm used for nonlinearly constrained quasi-Newton optimization is an efficient modification of Powell's (1978a, 1978b, 1982a, 1982b) *Variable Metric Constrained WatchDog* (VMCWD) algorithm. A similar but older algorithm (VF02AD) is part of the Harwell library. Both VMCWD and VF02AD use Fletcher's VE02AD algorithm (also part of the Harwell library) for positive definite quadratic programming. The PROC CALIS QUANEW implementation uses a quadratic programming subroutine that updates and downdates the approximation of the Cholesky factor when the active set changes. The nonlinear QUANEW algorithm is not a feasible point algorithm, and the value of the objective function need not decrease (minimization) or increase (maximization) monotonically. Instead, the algorithm tries to reduce a linear combination of the objective function and constraint violations, called the *merit function*.

The following are similarities and differences between this algorithm and VMCWD:

- A modification of this algorithm can be performed by specifying VERSION=1, which replaces the update of the Lagrange vector μ with the original update of Powell (1978a, 1978b), which is used in VF02AD. This can be helpful for some applications with linearly dependent active constraints.
- If the VERSION= option is not specified or VERSION=2 is specified, the evaluation of the Lagrange vector μ is performed in the same way as Powell (1982a, 1982b) describes.
- Instead of updating an approximate Hessian matrix, this algorithm uses the dual BFGS (or DFP) update that updates the Cholesky factor of an approximate Hessian. If the condition of the updated matrix gets too bad, a restart is done with a positive diagonal matrix. At the end of the first iteration after each restart, the Cholesky factor is scaled.
- The Cholesky factor is loaded into the quadratic programming subroutine, automatically ensuring positive definiteness of the problem. During the quadratic programming step, the Cholesky factor of the projected Hessian matrix $\mathbf{Z}_k'\mathbf{G}\mathbf{Z}_k$ and the QT decomposition are updated simultaneously when the active set changes. Refer to Gill et al. (1984) for more information.
- The line-search strategy is very similar to that of Powell (1982a, 1982b). However, this algorithm does not call for derivatives during the line search; hence, it generally needs fewer derivative calls than function calls. The VMCWD algorithm always requires the same number of derivative and function calls. It was also found in several applications of VMCWD that Powell's line-search method sometimes uses steps that are too long during the first iterations. In

those cases, you can use the INSTEP= option specification to restrict the step length α of the first iterations.

- Also the watchdog strategy is similar to that of Powell (1982a, 1982b). However, this algorithm doesn't return automatically after a fixed number of iterations to a former better point. A return here is further delayed if the observed function reduction is close to the expected function reduction of the quadratic model.
- Although Powell's termination criterion still is used (as FCONV2), the QUANEW implementation uses two additional termination criteria (GCONV and ABSGCONV).

This algorithm is automatically invoked when you specify the NLINCON statement. The nonlinear QUANEW algorithm needs the Jacobian matrix of the first-order derivatives (constraints normals) of the constraints

$$(\nabla c_i) = (\frac{\partial c_i}{\partial x_j}), \quad i = 1, \ldots, nc, j = 1, \ldots, n$$

where nc is the number of nonlinear constraints for a given point x.

You can specify two update formulas with the UPDATE= option:

- UPDATE=DBFGS performs the dual BFGS update of the Cholesky factor of the Hessian matrix. This is the default.
- UPDATE=DDFP performs the dual DFP update of the Cholesky factor of the Hessian matrix.

This algorithm uses its own line-search technique. All options and parameters (except the INSTEP= option) controlling the line search in the other algorithms do not apply here. In several applications, large steps in the first iterations are troublesome. You can specify the INSTEP= option to impose an upper bound for the step size α during the first five iterations. The values of the LCSINGULAR=, LCEPSILON=, and LCDEACT= options, which control the processing of linear and boundary constraints, are valid only for the quadratic programming subroutine used in each iteration of the nonlinear constraints QUANEW algorithm.

Optimization and Iteration History

The optimization and iteration histories are displayed by default because it is important to check for possible convergence problems.

The optimization history includes the following summary of information about the initial state of the optimization.

- the number of constraints that are active at the starting point, or more precisely, the number of constraints that are currently members of the working set. If this number is followed by a plus sign, there are more active constraints, of which at least one is temporarily released from the working set due to negative Lagrange multipliers.
- the value of the objective function at the starting point

- if the (projected) gradient is available, the value of the largest absolute (projected) gradient element
- for the TRUREG and LEVMAR subroutines, the initial radius of the trust region around the starting point

The optimization history ends with some information concerning the optimization result:

- the number of constraints that are active at the final point, or more precisely, the number of constraints that are currently members of the working set. If this number is followed by a plus sign, there are more active constraints, of which at least one is temporarily released from the working set due to negative Lagrange multipliers.
- the value of the objective function at the final point
- if the (projected) gradient is available, the value of the largest absolute (projected) gradient element
- other information specific to the optimization technique

The iteration history generally consists of one line of displayed output containing the most important information for each iteration. The _LIST_ variable (see the "SAS Program Statements" section on page 514) also enables you to display the parameter estimates and the gradient in some or all iterations.

The iteration history always includes the following (the words in parentheses are the column header output):

- the iteration number (Iter)
- the number of iteration restarts (rest)
- the number of function calls (nfun)
- the number of active constraints (act)
- the value of the optimization criterion (optcrit)
- the difference between adjacent function values (difcrit)
- the maximum of the absolute gradient components corresponding to inactive boundary constraints (maxgrad)

An apostrophe trailing the number of active constraints indicates that at least one of the active constraints is released from the active set due to a significant Lagrange multiplier.

For the Levenberg-Marquardt technique (LEVMAR), the iteration history also includes the following information:

- An asterisk trailing the iteration number means that the computed Hessian approximation is singular and consequently ridged with a positive lambda value. If all or the last several iterations show a singular Hessian approximation, the problem is not sufficiently identified. Thus, there are other locally optimal solutions that lead to the same optimum function value for different parameter values. This implies that standard errors for the parameter estimates are not computable without the addition of further constraints.

- the value of the Lagrange multiplier (lambda); this is 0 if the optimum of the quadratic function approximation is inside the trust region (a trust-region-scaled Newton step can be performed) and is greater than 0 when the optimum of the quadratic function approximation is located at the boundary of the trust region (the scaled Newton step is too long to fit in the trust region and a quadratic constraint optimization is performed). Large values indicate optimization difficulties. For a nonsingular Hessian matrix, the value of lambda should go to 0 during the last iterations, indicating that the objective function can be well approximated by a quadratic function in a small neighborhood of the optimum point. An increasing lambda value often indicates problems in the optimization process.
- the value of the ratio ρ (rho) between the actually achieved difference in function values and the predicted difference in the function values on the basis of the quadratic function approximation. Values much less than 1 indicate optimization difficulties. The value of the ratio ρ indicates the goodness of the quadratic function approximation; in other words, $\rho << 1$ means that the radius of the trust region has to be reduced. A fairly large value of ρ means that the radius of the trust region need not be changed. And a value close to or larger than 1 means that the radius can be increased, indicating a good quadratic function approximation.

For the Newton-Raphson technique (NRRIDG), the iteration history also includes the following information:

- the value of the ridge parameter. This is 0 when a Newton step can be performed, and it is greater than 0 when either the Hessian approximation is singular or a Newton step fails to reduce the optimization criterion. Large values indicate optimization difficulties.
- the value of the ratio ρ (rho) between the actually achieved difference in function values and the predicted difference in the function values on the basis of the quadratic function approximation. Values much less than 1.0 indicate optimization difficulties.

For the Newton-Raphson with line-search technique (NEWRAP), the iteration history also includes

- the step size α (alpha) computed with one of the line-search algorithms
- the slope of the search direction at the current parameter iterate. For minimization, this value should be significantly negative. Otherwise, the line-search algorithm has difficulty reducing the function value sufficiently.

For the Trust-Region technique (TRUREG), the iteration history also includes the following information.

- An asterisk after the iteration number means that the computed Hessian approximation is singular and consequently ridged with a positive lambda value.
- the value of the Lagrange multiplier (lambda). This value is zero when the optimum of the quadratic function approximation is inside the trust region (a trust-region-scaled Newton step can be performed) and is greater than zero when the optimum of the quadratic function approximation is located at the boundary of the trust region (the scaled Newton step is too long to fit in the trust region and a quadratically constrained optimization is performed). Large values indicate optimization difficulties. As in Gay (1983), a negative lambda value indicates the special case of an indefinite Hessian matrix (the smallest eigenvalue is negative in minimization).
- the value of the radius Δ of the trust region. Small trust region radius values combined with large lambda values in subsequent iterations indicate optimization problems.

For the quasi-Newton (QUANEW) and conjugate gradient (CONGRA) techniques, the iteration history also includes the following information:

- the step size (alpha) computed with one of the line-search algorithms
- the descent of the search direction at the current parameter iterate. This value should be significantly smaller than 0. Otherwise, the line-search algorithm has difficulty reducing the function value sufficiently.

Frequent update restarts (rest) of a quasi-Newton algorithm often indicate numerical problems related to required properties of the approximate Hessian update, and they decrease the speed of convergence. This can happen particularly if the ABSGCONV= termination criterion is too small, that is, when the requested precision cannot be obtained by quasi-Newton optimization. Generally, the number of automatic restarts used by conjugate gradient methods are much higher.

For the nonlinearly constrained quasi-Newton technique, the iteration history also includes the following information:

- the maximum value of all constraint violations,

$$\text{conmax} = \max(|c_i(x)| : c_i(x) < 0)$$

- the value of the predicted function reduction used with the GCONV and FCONV2 termination criteria,

$$\text{pred} = |g(x^{(k)})s(x^{(k)})| + \sum_{i=1}^{m} |\lambda_i c_i(x^{(k)})|$$

- the step size α of the quasi-Newton step. Note that this algorithm works with a special line-search algorithm.

- the maximum element of the gradient of the Lagrange function,

$$\begin{aligned} \text{lfgmax} &= \nabla_x L(x^{(k)}, \lambda^{(k)}) \\ &= \nabla_x f(x^{(k)}) - \sum_{i=1}^{m} \lambda_i^{(k)} \nabla_x c_i(x^{(k)}) \end{aligned}$$

For the double dogleg technique, the iteration history also includes the following information:

- the parameter λ of the double-dogleg step. A value $\lambda = 0$ corresponds to the full (quasi) Newton step.
- the slope of the search direction at the current parameter iterate. For minimization, this value should be significantly negative.

Line-Search Methods

In each iteration k, the (dual) quasi-Newton, hybrid quasi-Newton, conjugate gradient, and Newton-Raphson minimization techniques use iterative line-search algorithms that try to optimize a linear, quadratic, or cubic approximation of the nonlinear objective function f of n parameters x along a feasible descent search direction $s^{(k)}$

$$f(x^{(k+1)}) = f(x^{(k)} + \alpha^{(k)} s^{(k)})$$

by computing an approximately optimal scalar $\alpha^{(k)} > 0$. Since the outside iteration process is based only on the approximation of the objective function, the inside iteration of the line-search algorithm does not have to be perfect. Usually, it is satisfactory that the choice of α significantly reduces (in a minimization) the objective function. Criteria often used for termination of line-search algorithms are the Goldstein conditions (Fletcher 1987).

Various line-search algorithms can be selected by using the LIS= option (page 468). The line-search methods LIS=1, LIS=2, and LIS=3 satisfy the left-hand-side and right-hand-side Goldstein conditions (refer to Fletcher 1987). When derivatives are available, the line-search methods LIS=6, LIS=7, and LIS=8 try to satisfy the right-hand-side Goldstein condition; if derivatives are not available, these line-search algorithms use only function calls.

The line-search method LIS=2 seems to be superior when function evaluation consumes significantly less computation time than gradient evaluation. Therefore, LIS=2 is the default value for Newton-Raphson, (dual) quasi-Newton, and conjugate gradient optimizations.

Restricting the Step Length

Almost all line-search algorithms use iterative extrapolation techniques that can easily lead to feasible points where the objective function f is no longer defined (resulting in indefinite matrices for ML estimation) or is difficult to compute (resulting in floating point overflows). Therefore, PROC CALIS provides options that restrict the step length or trust region radius, especially during the first main iterations.

The inner product $g's$ of the gradient g and the search direction s is the slope of $f(\alpha) = f(x + \alpha s)$ along the search direction s with step length α. The default starting value $\alpha^{(0)} = \alpha^{(k,0)}$ in each line-search algorithm ($\min_{\alpha>0} f(x+\alpha s)$) during the main iteration k is computed in three steps.

1. Use either the difference $df = |f^{(k)} - f^{(k-1)}|$ of the function values during the last two consecutive iterations or the final stepsize value $\alpha-$ of the previous iteration $k-1$ to compute a first value $\alpha_1^{(0)}$.
   - Using the DAMPSTEP<=*r*> option:

     $$\alpha_1^{(0)} = \min(1, r\alpha-)$$

     The initial value for the new step length can be no larger than r times the final step length $\alpha-$ of the previous iteration. The default is $r = 2$.
   - Not using the DAMPSTEP option:

     $$\alpha_1^{(0)} = \begin{cases} step & \text{if } 0.1 \le step \le 10 \\ 10 & \text{if } step > 10 \\ 0.1 & \text{if } step < 0.1 \end{cases}$$

     with

     $$step = \begin{cases} df/|g's| & \text{if } |g's| \ge \epsilon \max(100df, 1) \\ 1 & \text{otherwise} \end{cases}$$

     This value of $\alpha_1^{(0)}$ can be too large and can lead to a difficult or impossible function evaluation, especially for highly nonlinear functions such as the EXP function.

2. During the first five iterations, the second step enables you to reduce $\alpha_1^{(0)}$ to a smaller starting value $\alpha_2^{(0)}$ using the INSTEP=r option:

   $$\alpha_2^{(0)} = \min(\alpha_1^{(0)}, r)$$

   After more than five iterations, $\alpha_2^{(0)}$ is set to $\alpha_1^{(0)}$.

3. The third step can further reduce the step length by

   $$\alpha_3^{(0)} = \min(\alpha_2^{(0)}, \min(10, u))$$

   where u is the maximum length of a step inside the feasible region.

The INSTEP=r option lets you specify a smaller or larger radius of the trust region used in the first iteration by the trust-region, double-dogleg, and Levenberg-Marquardt algorithm. The default initial trust region radius is the length of the scaled gradient (Moré 1978). This step corresponds to the default radius factor of $r = 1$. This choice is successful in most practical applications of the TRUREG, DBLDOG, and LEVMAR algorithms. However, for bad initial values used in the analysis of a covariance matrix with high variances, or for highly nonlinear constraints (such as using the EXP function) in your programming code, the default start radius can result in arithmetic overflows. If this happens, you can try decreasing values of INSTEP=r, $0 < r < 1$, until the iteration starts successfully. A small factor r also affects the trust region radius of the next steps because the radius is changed in each iteration by a factor $0 < c \le 4$ depending on the ρ ratio. Reducing the radius corresponds to increasing the ridge parameter λ that produces smaller steps directed closer toward the gradient direction.

Modification Indices

While fitting structural models, you may want to modify the specified model in order to

- reduce the χ^2 value significantly
- reduce the number of parameters to estimate without increasing the χ^2 value too much

If you specify the MODIFICATION or MOD option, PROC CALIS computes and displays a default set of modification indices:

- **Univariate Lagrange multiplier test indices** for most elements in the model matrices that are constrained to *equal constants*. These are second-order approximations of the decrease in the χ^2 value that would result from allowing the constant matrix element to vary. Besides the value of the Lagrange multiplier, the corresponding probability ($df = 1$) and the approximate change of the parameter value (should the constant be changed to a parameter) are displayed. If allowing the constant to be a free estimated parameter would result in a singular information matrix, the string 'sing' is displayed instead of the Lagrange multiplier index. Not all elements in the model matrices should be allowed to vary; the diagonal elements of the inverse matrices in the RAM or LINEQS model must be constant ones. The univariate Lagrange multipliers are displayed at the constant locations of the model matrices.
- **Univariate Wald test indices** for those matrix elements that correspond to *parameter estimates* in the model. These are second-order approximations of the increase in the χ^2 value that would result from constraining the parameter to a 0 constant. The univariate Wald test indices are the same as the t values that are displayed together with the parameter estimates and standard errors. The univariate Wald test indices are displayed at the parameter locations of the model matrices.
- **Univariate Lagrange multiplier test indices** that are second-order approximations of the decrease in the χ^2 value that would result from the release of *equality constraints*. Multiple equality constraints containing $n > 2$ parameters are tested successively in n steps, each assuming the release of one of the equality-constrained parameters. The expected change of the parameter values of the separated parameter and the remaining parameter cluster are displayed, too.
- **Univariate Lagrange multiplier test indices** for releasing *active boundary constraints* specified by the BOUNDS statement
- **Stepwise multivariate Wald test indices** for constraining estimated parameters to 0 are computed and displayed. In each step, the parameter that would lead to the smallest increase in the multivariate χ^2 value is set to 0. Besides the multivariate χ^2 value and its probability, the univariate increments are also displayed. The process stops when the univariate probability is smaller than the specified value in the SLMW= option.

All of the preceding tests are approximations. You can often get more accurate tests by actually fitting different models and computing likelihood ratio tests. For more details about the Wald and the Lagrange multiplier test, refer to MacCallum (1986), Buse (1982), Bentler (1986), or Lee (1985).

Note that, for large model matrices, the computation time for the default modification indices can considerably exceed the time needed for the minimization process.

The modification indices are not computed for unweighted least-squares or diagonally weighted least-squares estimation.

Caution: Modification indices are not computed if the model matrix is an identity matrix (IDE or ZID), a selection matrix (PER), or the first matrix **J** in the LINEQS model. If you want to display the modification indices for such a matrix, you should specify the matrix as another type; for example, specify an identity matrix used in the COSAN statement as a diagonal matrix with constant diagonal elements of 1.

Constrained Estimation Using Program Code

The CALIS procedure offers a very flexible way to constrain parameter estimates. You can use your own programming statements to express special properties of the parameter estimates. This tool is also present in McDonald's COSAN implementation but is considerably easier to use in the CALIS procedure. PROC CALIS is able to compute analytic first- and second-order derivatives that you would have to specify using the COSAN program. There are also three PROC CALIS statements you can use:

- the BOUNDS statement, to specify simple bounds on the parameters used in the optimization process
- the LINCON statement, to specify general linear equality and inequality constraints on the parameters used in the optimization process
- the NLINCON statement, to specify general nonlinear equality and inequality constraints on the parameters used in the optimization process. The variables listed in the NLINCON statement must be specified in the program code.

There are some traditional ways to enforce parameter constraints by using parameter transformations (McDonald 1980).

- **One-sided boundary constraints:** For example, the parameter q_k should be at least as large (or at most as small) as a given constant value a (or b),

  $$q_k \geq a \qquad \text{or} \qquad q_k \leq b$$

  This inequality constraint can be expressed as an equality constraint

  $$q_k = a + x_j^2 \qquad \text{or} \qquad q_k = b - x_j^2$$

  in which the fundamental parameter x_j is unconstrained.

- **Two-sided boundary constraints:** For example, the parameter q_k should be located between two given constant values a and b, $a < b$,

  $$a \leq q_k \leq b$$

  This inequality constraint can be expressed as an equality constraint

  $$q_k = a + b\frac{exp(x_j)}{1 + exp(x_j)}$$

  in which the fundamental parameter x_j is unconstrained.

- **One-sided order constraints:** For example, the parameters $q_1, \ldots, q_k$ should be ordered in the form

  $$q_1 \leq q_2, \quad q_1 \leq q_3, \quad \ldots, \quad q_1 \leq q_k$$

  These inequality constraints can be expressed as a set of equality constraints

  $$q_1 = x_1, \quad q_2 = x_1 + x_2^2, \quad \ldots, \quad q_k = x_1 + x_k^2$$

  in which the fundamental parameters $x_1, \ldots, x_k$ are unconstrained.

- **Two-sided order constraints:** For example, the parameters $q_1, \ldots, q_k$ should be ordered in the form

  $$q_1 \leq q_2 \leq q_3 \leq \ldots \leq q_k$$

  These inequality constraints can be expressed as a set of equality constraints

  $$q_1 = x_1, \quad q_2 = q_1 + x_2^2, \quad \ldots, \quad q_k = q_{k-1} + x_k^2$$

  in which the fundamental parameters $x_1, \ldots, x_k$ are unconstrained.

- **Linear equation constraints:** For example, the parameters q_1, q_2, q_3 should be linearly constrained in the form

  $$q_1 + q_2 + q_3 = a$$

  which can be expressed in the form of three explicit equations in which the fundamental parameters x_1 and x_2 are unconstrained:

  $$q_1 = x_1, \quad q_2 = x_2, \quad q_3 = a - x_1 - x_2$$

Refer to McDonald (1980) and Browne (1982) for further notes on reparameterizing techniques. If the optimization problem is not too large to apply the Levenberg-Marquardt or Newton-Raphson algorithm, boundary constraints should be requested by the BOUNDS statement rather than by reparameterizing code. If the problem is so large that you must use a quasi-Newton or conjugate gradient algorithm, reparameterizing techniques may be more efficient than the BOUNDS statement.

Counting the Degrees of Freedom

In a regression problem, the number of degrees of freedom for the error estimate is the number of observations in the data set minus the number of parameters. The NOBS=, DFR= (RDF=), and DFE= (EDF=) options refer to degrees of freedom in this sense. However, these values are not related to the degrees of freedom of a test statistic used in a covariance or correlation structure analysis. The NOBS=, DFR=, and DFE= options should be used in PROC CALIS to specify only the effective number of observations in the input DATA= data set.

In general, the number of degrees of freedom in a covariance or correlation structure analysis is defined as the difference between the number of nonredundant values q in the observed $n \times n$ correlation or covariance matrix $\mathbf{S}$ and the number t of free parameters $\mathbf{X}$ used in the fit of the specified model, $df = q - t$. Both values, q and t, are counted differently in different situations by PROC CALIS.

The number of nonredundant values q is generally equal to the number of lower triangular elements in the $n \times n$ moment matrix $\mathbf{S}$ including all diagonal elements, minus a constant c dependent upon special circumstances,

$$q = n(n + 1)/2 - c$$

The number c is evaluated by adding the following quantities:

- If you specify a linear structural equation model containing exogenous manifest variables by using the RAM or LINEQS statement, PROC CALIS adds to c the number of variances and covariances among these manifest exogenous variables, which are automatically set in the corresponding locations of the central model matrices (see the section "Exogenous Manifest Variables" on page 549).
- If you specify the DFREDUCE=i option, PROC CALIS adds the specified number i to c. The number i can be a negative integer.
- If you specify the NODIAG option to exclude the fit of the diagonal elements of the data matrix $\mathbf{S}$, PROC CALIS adds the number n of diagonal elements to c.
- If all the following conditions hold, then PROC CALIS adds to c the number of the diagonal locations:
  - NODIAG and DFREDUC= options are not specified.
  - A correlation structure is being fitted.
  - The predicted correlation matrix contains constants on the diagonal.

In some complicated models, especially those using programming statements, PROC CALIS may not be able to detect all the constant predicted values. In such cases, you must specify the DFREDUCE= option to get the correct degrees of freedom.

The number t is the number of different parameter names used in constructing the model if you do not use programming statements to impose constraints on the parameters. Using programming statements in general introduces two kinds of parameters:

- independent parameters, which are used only at the right-hand side of the expressions
- dependent parameters, which are used at least once at the left-hand side of the expressions

The independent parameters belong to the parameters involved in the estimation process, whereas the dependent parameters are fully defined by the programming statements and can be computed from the independent parameters. In this case, the number t is the number of different parameter names used in the model specification, but not used in the programming statements, plus the number of independent parameters. The independent parameters and their initial values can be defined in a model specification statement or in a PARMS statement.

The degrees of freedom are automatically increased by the number of active constraints in the solution. Similarly, the number of parameters are decreased by the number of active constraints. This affects the computation of many fit statistics and indices. Refer to Dijkstra (1992) for a discussion of the validity of statistical inferences with active boundary constraints. If the researcher believes that the active constraints will have a small chance of occurrence in repeated sampling, it may be more suitable to turn off the automatic adjustment using the NOADJDF option.

Computational Problems

First Iteration Overflows

Analyzing a covariance matrix including high variances in the diagonal and using bad initial estimates for the parameters can easily lead to arithmetic overflows in the first iterations of the minimization algorithm. The line-search algorithms that work with cubic extrapolation are especially sensitive to arithmetic overflows. If this occurs with quasi-Newton or conjugate gradient minimization, you can specify the INSTEP= option to reduce the length of the first step. If an arithmetic overflow occurs in the first iteration of the Levenberg-Marquardt algorithm, you can specify the INSTEP= option to reduce the trust region radius of the first iteration. You also can change the minimization technique or the line-search method. If none of these help, you should consider

- scaling the covariance matrix
- providing better initial values
- changing the model

No Convergence of Minimization Process

If convergence does not occur during the minimization process, perform the following tasks:

- If there are *negative variance estimates* in the diagonal locations of the central model matrices, you can
  - specify the BOUNDS statement to obtain nonnegative variance estimates
  - specify the HEYWOOD option, if the FACTOR model statement is specified
- Change the estimation method to obtain a better set of initial estimates. For example, if you use METHOD=ML, you can
  - change to METHOD=LSML
  - run some iterations with METHOD=DWLS or METHOD=GLS, write the results in an OUTRAM= data set, and use the results as initial values specified by an INRAM= data set in a second run with METHOD=ML
- Change the optimization technique. For example, if you use the default TECH=LEVMAR, you can
  - change to TECH=QUANEW or to TECH=NEWRAP
  - run some iterations with TECH=CONGRA, write the results in an OUTRAM= data set, and use the results as initial values specified by an INRAM= data set in a second run with a different TECH= technique
- Change or modify the update technique or the line-search algorithm, or both, when using TECH=QUANEW or TECH=CONGRA. For example, if you use the default update formula and the default line-search algorithm, you can
  - change the update formula with the UPDATE= option
  - change the line-search algorithm with the LIS= option
  - specify a more precise line search with the LSPRECISION= option, if you use LIS=2 or LIS=3
- You can allow more iterations and function calls by using the MAXIT= and MAXFU= options.
- Change the initial values. For many categories of model specifications done by the LINEQS, RAM, or FACTOR model, PROC CALIS computes an appropriate set of initial values automatically. However, for some of the model specifications (for example, structural equations with latent variables on the left-hand side and manifest variables on the right-hand side), PROC CALIS can generate very obscure initial values. In these cases, you have to set the initial values yourself.
  - Increase the initial values of the parameters located at the diagonal of central matrices
    - manually, by setting the values in the model specification
    - automatically, by using the DEMPHAS= option

  - Use a slightly different, but more stable, model to obtain preliminary estimates.
  - Use additional information to specify initial values, for example, by using other SAS software like the FACTOR, REG, SYSLIN, and MODEL (SYSNLIN) procedures for the modified, unrestricted model case.

- Change the optimization technique. For example, if you use the default TECH=LEVMAR, you can
  - change to TECH=QUANEW or to TECH=NEWRAP
  - run some iterations with TECH=CONGRA, write the results in an OUTRAM= data set, and use the results as initial values specified by an INRAM= data set in a second run with a different TECH= technique
- Change or modify the update technique or the line-search algorithm, or both, when using TECH=QUANEW or TECH=CONGRA. For example, if you use the default update formula and the default line-search algorithm, you can
  - change the update formula with the UPDATE= option
  - change the line-search algorithm with the LIS= option
  - specify a more precise line search with the LSPRECISION= option, if you use LIS=2 or LIS=3
- Temporarily change the estimation method to obtain a better set of initial estimates. For example, if you use METHOD=ML, you can
  - change to METHOD=LSML
  - run some iterations with METHOD=DWLS or GLS, write the results in an OUTRAM= data set, and use the results as initial values specified by an INRAM= data set in a second run with METHOD=ML
- You can allow more iterations and function calls by using the MAXIT= and MAXFU= options.

Unidentified Model

The parameter vector $\mathbf{x}$ in the covariance structure model

$$\mathbf{C} = \mathbf{C}(\mathbf{x})$$

is said to be identified in a parameter space G, if

$$\mathbf{C}(\mathbf{x}) = \mathbf{C}(\tilde{\mathbf{x}}), \quad \tilde{\mathbf{x}} \in G$$

implies $\mathbf{x} = \tilde{\mathbf{x}}$. The parameter estimates that result from an unidentified model can be very far from the parameter estimates of a very similar but identified model. They are usually machine dependent. Don't use parameter estimates of an unidentified model as initial values for another run of PROC CALIS.

Singular Predicted Model Matrix

You can easily specify models with singular predicted model matrices, for example, by fixing diagonal elements of central matrices to 0. In such cases, you cannot compute maximum likelihood estimates (the ML function value F is not defined). Since singular predicted model matrices can also occur temporarily in the minimization process, PROC CALIS tries in such cases to change the parameter estimates so that the predicted model matrix becomes positive definite. In such cases, the following message is displayed:

```
NOTE: Parameter set changed.
```

This process does not always work well, especially if there are fixed instead of variable diagonal elements in the central model matrices. A famous example where you cannot compute ML estimates is a component analysis with fewer components than given manifest variables. See the section "FACTOR Model Statement" on page 493 for more details. If you continue to get a singular predicted model matrix after changing initial values and optimization techniques, then your model is perhaps specified so that ML estimates cannot be computed.

Saving Computing Time

For large models, the most computing time is needed to compute the modification indices. If you don't really need the Lagrange multipliers or multiple Wald test indices (the univariate Wald test indices are the same as the t values), using the NOMOD option can save a considerable amount of computing time.

Central Matrices with Negative Eigenvalues

A covariance matrix cannot have negative eigenvalues, since a negative eigenvalue means that some linear combination of the variables has negative variance. PROC CALIS displays a warning if a central model matrix has negative eigenvalues but does not actually compute the eigenvalues. Sometimes this warning can be triggered by 0 or very small positive eigenvalues that appear negative because of numerical error. If you want to be sure that the central model matrix you are fitting can be considered to be a variance-covariance matrix, you can use the SAS/IML command *VAL=EIGVAL(U)* to compute the vector *VAL* of eigenvalues of matrix **U**.

Negative R^2 Values

The estimated squared multiple correlations R^2 of the endogenous variables are computed using the estimated error variances

$$R_i^2 = 1 - \frac{\widehat{var(\zeta_i)}}{\widehat{var(\eta_i)}}$$

If the model is a poor fit, it is possible that $\widehat{var(\zeta_i)} > \widehat{var(\eta_i)}$, which results in $R_i^2 < 0$.

Displayed Output

The output displayed by PROC CALIS depends on the statement used to specify the model. Since an analysis requested by the LINEQS or RAM statement implies the analysis of a structural equation model, more statistics can be computed and displayed than for a covariance structure analysis following the generalized COSAN model requested by the COSAN statement. The displayed output resulting from use of the FACTOR statement includes all the COSAN displayed output as well as more statistics displayed only when you specify the FACTOR statement. Since the displayed output using the RAM statement differs only in its form from that generated by the LINEQS statement, in this section distinctions are made between COSAN and LINEQS output only.

The unweighted least-squares and diagonally weighted least-squares estimation methods do not provide a sufficient statistical basis to provide the following output (neither displayed nor written to an OUTEST= data set):

- most of the fit indices
- approximate standard errors
- normalized or asymptotically standardized residuals
- modification indices
- information matrix
- covariance matrix of parameter estimates

The notation $\mathbf{S} = (s_{ij})$ is used for the analyzed covariance or correlation matrix, $\mathbf{C} = (c_{ij})$ for the predicted model matrix, $\mathbf{W}$ for the weight matrix (for example, $\mathbf{W} = \mathbf{I}$ for ULS, $\mathbf{W} = \mathbf{S}$ for GLS, $\mathbf{W} = \mathbf{C}$ for ML estimates), $\mathbf{X}$ for the vector of optimal parameter estimates, n for the number of manifest variables, t for the number of parameter estimates, and N for the sample size.

The output of PROC CALIS includes the following:

- COSAN and LINEQS: List of the matrices and their properties specified by the generalized COSAN model if you specify at least the PSHORT option.
- LINEQS: List of manifest variables that are not used in the specified model and that are automatically omitted from the analysis. Note that there is no automatic variable reduction with the COSAN or FACTOR statement. If necessary, you should use the VAR statement in these cases.
- LINEQS: List of the endogenous and exogenous variables specified by the LINEQS, STD, and COV statements if you specify at least the PSHORT option.
- COSAN: Initial values of the parameter matrices indicating positions of constants and parameters. The output, or at least the default output, is displayed if you specify the PINITIAL option.

- LINEQS: The set of structural equations containing the initial values and indicating constants and parameters, and output of the initial error variances and covariances. The output, or at least the default output, is displayed if you specify the PINITIAL option.
- COSAN and LINEQS: The weight matrix **W** is displayed if GLS, WLS, or DWLS estimation is used and you specify the PWEIGHT or PALL option.
- COSAN and LINEQS: General information about the estimation problem: number of observations (N), number of manifest variables (n), amount of independent information in the data matrix (information, $n(n+1)/2$), number of terms and matrices in the specified generalized COSAN model, and number of parameters to be estimated (parameters, t). If there are no exogenous manifest variables, the difference between the amount of independent information ($n(n+1)/2$) and the number of requested estimates (t) is equal to the degrees of freedom (df). A necessary condition for a model to be identified is that the degrees of freedom are nonnegative. The output, or at least the default output, is displayed if you specify the SIMPLE option.
- COSAN and LINEQS: Mean and Std Dev (standard deviation) of each variable if you specify the SIMPLE option, as well as skewness and kurtosis if the DATA= data set is a raw data set and you specify the KURTOSIS option.
- COSAN and LINEQS: Various coefficients of multivariate kurtosis and the numbers of observations that contribute most to the normalized multivariate kurtosis if the DATA= data set is a raw data set and the KURTOSIS option, or you specify at least the PRINT option. See the section "Measures of Multivariate Kurtosis" on page 544 for more information.
- COSAN and LINEQS: Covariance or correlation matrix to be analyzed and the value of its determinant if you specify the output option PCORR or PALL. A 0 determinant indicates a singular data matrix. In this case, the generalized least-squares estimates with default weight matrix **S** and maximum likelihood estimates cannot be computed.
- LINEQS: If exogenous manifest variables in the linear structural equation model are specified, then there is a one-to-one relationship between the given covariances and corresponding estimates in the central model matrix Φ or P. The output indicates which manifest variables are recognized as exogenous, that is, for which variables the entries in the central model matrix are set to fixed parameters. The output, or at least the default output, is displayed if you specify the PINITIAL option.
- COSAN and LINEQS: Vector of parameter names, initial values, and corresponding matrix locations, also indicating dependent parameter names used in your program statements that are not allocated to matrix locations and have no influence on the fit function. The output, or at least the default output, is displayed if you specify the PINITIAL option.
- COSAN and LINEQS: The pattern of variable and constant elements of the predicted moment matrix that is predetermined by the analysis model is displayed if there are significant differences between constant elements in the predicted model matrix and the data matrix and you specify at least the PSHORT option.

It is also displayed if you specify the PREDET option. The output indicates the differences between constant values in the predicted model matrix and the data matrix that is analyzed.

- COSAN and LINEQS: Special features of the optimization technique chosen if you specify at least the PSHORT option.
- COSAN and LINEQS: Optimization history if at least the PSHORT option is specified. For more details, see the section "Use of Optimization Techniques" on page 551.
- COSAN and LINEQS: Specific output requested by options in the NLOPTIONS statement; for example, parameter estimates, gradient, gradient of Lagrange function, constraints, Lagrange multipliers, projected gradient, Hessian, projected Hessian, Hessian of Lagrange function, Jacobian of nonlinear constraints.
- COSAN and LINEQS: The predicted model matrix and its determinant, if you specify the output option PCORR or PALL.
- COSAN and LINEQS: Residual and normalized residual matrix if you specify the RESIDUAL, or at least the PRINT option. The variance standardized or asymptotically standardized residual matrix can be displayed also. The average residual and the average off-diagonal residual are also displayed. See the section "Assessment of Fit" on page 536 for more details.
- COSAN and LINEQS: Rank order of the largest normalized residuals if you specify the RESIDUAL, or at least the PRINT option.
- COSAN and LINEQS: Bar chart of the normalized residuals if you specify the RESIDUAL, or at least the PRINT option.
- COSAN and LINEQS: Value of the fit function F. See the section "Estimation Criteria" on page 531 for more details. This output can be suppressed only by the NOPRINT option.
- COSAN and LINEQS: Goodness-of-fit index (GFI), adjusted goodness-of-fit index (AGFI), and root mean square residual (RMR) (Jöreskog and Sörbom 1985). See the section "Assessment of Fit" on page 536 for more details. This output can be suppressed only by the NOPRINT option.
- COSAN and LINEQS: Parsimonious goodness-of-fit index (PGFI) of Mulaik et al. (1989). See the section "Assessment of Fit" on page 536 for more detail. This output can be suppressed only by the NOPRINT option.
- COSAN and LINEQS: Overall χ^2, df, and Prob>Chi**2 if the METHOD= option is not ULS or DWLS. The χ^2 measure is the optimum function value F multiplied by $(N-1)$ if a CORR or COV matrix is analyzed or multiplied by N if a UCORR or UCOV matrix is analyzed; χ^2 measures the likelihood ratio test statistic for the null hypothesis that the predicted matrix **C** has the specified model structure against the alternative that **C** is unconstrained. The notation Prob>Chi**2 means "the probability under the null hypothesis of obtaining a greater χ^2 statistic than that observed." This output can be suppressed only by the NOPRINT option.

- COSAN and LINEQS: If METHOD= is not ULS or DWLS, the χ_0^2 value of the independence model and the corresponding degrees of freedom can be used (in large samples) to evaluate the gain of explanation by fitting the specific model (Bentler 1989). See the section "Assessment of Fit" on page 536 for more detail. This output can be suppressed only by the NOPRINT option.
- COSAN and LINEQS: If METHOD= is not ULS or DWLS, the value of the Steiger & Lind (1980) root mean squared error of approximation (RMSEA) coefficient and the lower and upper limits of the confidence interval. The size of the confidence interval is defined by the option ALPHARMS=α, $0 \leq \alpha \leq 1$. The default is $\alpha = 0.1$, which corresponds to a 90% confidence interval. See the section "Assessment of Fit" on page 536 for more detail. This output can be suppressed only by the NOPRINT option.
- COSAN and LINEQS: If the value of the METHOD= option is not ULS or DWLS, the value of the *probability of close fit* (Browne and Cudeck 1993). See the section "Assessment of Fit" on page 536 for more detail. This output can be suppressed only by the NOPRINT option.
- COSAN and LINEQS: If the value of the METHOD= option is not ULS or DWLS, the value of the Browne & Cudeck (1993) expected cross validation (ECVI) index and the lower and upper limits of the confidence interval. The size of the confidence interval is defined by the option ALPHAECV=α, $0 \leq \alpha \leq 1$. The default is $\alpha = 0.1$, which corresponds to a 90% confidence interval. See the section "Assessment of Fit" on page 536 for more detail. This output can be suppressed only by the NOPRINT option.
- COSAN and LINEQS: If the value of the METHOD= option is not ULS or DWLS, Bentler's (1989) Comparative Fit Index. See the section "Assessment of Fit" on page 536 for more detail. This output can be suppressed only by the NOPRINT option.
- COSAN and LINEQS: If you specify METHOD=ML or METHOD=GLS, the χ^2 value and corresponding probability adjusted by the relative kurtosis coefficient η_2, which should be a close approximation of the χ^2 value for elliptically distributed data (Browne 1982). See the section "Assessment of Fit" on page 536 for more detail. This output can be suppressed only by the NOPRINT option.
- COSAN and LINEQS: The Normal Theory Reweighted LS χ^2 Value is displayed if METHOD= ML. Instead of the function value F_{ML}, the reweighted goodness-of-fit function F_{GWLS} is used. See the section "Assessment of Fit" on page 536 for more detail.
- COSAN and LINEQS: Akaike's Information Criterion if the value of the METHOD= option is not ULS or DWLS. See the section "Assessment of Fit" on page 536. This output can be suppressed only by the NOPRINT option.
- COSAN and LINEQS: Bozdogan's (1987) Consistent Information Criterion, CAIC. See the section "Assessment of Fit" on page 536. This output can be suppressed only by the NOPRINT option.
- COSAN and LINEQS: Schwarz's Bayesian Criterion (SBC) if the value of the METHOD= option is not ULS or DWLS (Schwarz 1978). See the section

"Assessment of Fit" on page 536. This output can be suppressed only by the NOPRINT option.

- COSAN and LINEQS: If the value of the METHOD= option is not ULS or DWLS, the following fit indices based on the overall χ^2 value are displayed:
  - McDonald's (McDonald and Hartmann 1992) measure of centrality
  - Parsimonious index of James, Mulaik, and Brett (1982)
  - Z-Test of Wilson and Hilferty (1931)
  - Bentler and Bonett's (1980) nonnormed coefficient
  - Bentler and Bonett's (1980) normed coefficient
  - Bollen's (1986) normed index ρ_1
  - Bollen's (1989a) nonnormed index Δ_2

  See the section "Assessment of Fit" on page 536 for more detail. This output can be suppressed only by the NOPRINT option.
- COSAN and LINEQS: Hoelter's (1983) Critical N Index is displayed (Bollen 1989b, p. 277). See the section "Assessment of Fit" on page 536 for more detail. This output can be suppressed only by the NOPRINT option.
- COSAN and LINEQS: Equations of linear dependencies among the parameters used in the model specification if the information matrix is recognized as singular at the final solution.
- COSAN: Model matrices containing the parameter estimates. Except for ULS or DWLS estimates, the approximate standard errors and *t* values are also displayed. This output is displayed if you specify the PESTIM option or at least the PSHORT option.
- LINEQS: Linear equations containing the parameter estimates. Except for ULS and DWLS estimates, the approximate standard errors and *t* values are also displayed. This output is displayed if you specify the PESTIM option, or at least the PSHORT option.
- LINEQS: Variances and covariances of the exogenous variables. This output is displayed if you specify the PESTIM option, or at least the PSHORT.
- LINEQS: Linear equations containing the standardized parameter estimates. This output is displayed if you specify the PESTIM option, or at least the PSHORT option.
- LINEQS: Table of correlations among the exogenous variables. This output is displayed if you specify the PESTIM option, or at least the PSHORT option.
- LINEQS: Correlations among the exogenous variables. This output is displayed if you specify the PESTIM option, or at least the PSHORT option.
- LINEQS: Squared Multiple Correlations table, which displays the error variances of the endogenous variables. These are the diagonal elements of the predicted model matrix. Also displayed is the Total Variance and the R^2 values corresponding to all endogenous variables. See the section "Assessment of Fit" on page 536 for more detail. This output is displayed if you specify the PESTIM option, or at least the PSHORT option.

- LINEQS: If you specify the PDETERM or the PALL option, the total determination of all equations (DETAE), the total determination of the structural equations (DETSE), and the total determination of the manifest variables (DETMV) are displayed. See the section "Assessment of Fit" on page 536 for more details. If one of the determinants in the formulas is 0, the corresponding coefficient is displayed as a missing value. If there are structural equations, PROC CALIS also displays the Stability Coefficient of Reciprocal Causation, that is, the largest eigenvalue of the $\mathbf{BB}'$ matrix, where $\mathbf{B}$ is the causal coefficient matrix of the structural equations.
- LINEQS: The matrix of estimated covariances among the latent variables if you specify the PLATCOV option, or at least the PRINT option.
- LINEQS: The matrix of estimated covariances between latent and manifest variables used in the model if you specify the PLATCOV option, or at least the PRINT option.
- LINEQS and FACTOR: The matrix $\mathbf{FSR}$ of latent variable scores regression coefficients if you specify the PLATCOV option, or at least the PRINT option. The $\mathbf{FSR}$ matrix is a generalization of Lawley and Maxwell's (1971, p.109) factor scores regression matrix,

  $$\mathbf{FSR} = \mathbf{C}_{yx}\mathbf{C}_{xx}^{-1}$$

  where $\mathbf{C}_{xx}$ is the $n \times n$ predicted model matrix (predicted covariances among manifest variables) and $\mathbf{C}_{yx}$ is the $n_{lat} \times n$ matrix of the predicted covariances between latent and manifest variables. You can multiply the manifest observations by this matrix to estimate the scores of the latent variables used in your model.
- LINEQS: The matrix $\mathbf{TEF}$ of total effects if you specify the TOTEFF option, or at least the PRINT option. For the LINEQS model, the matrix of total effects is

  $$\mathbf{TEF} = (\mathbf{I} - \boldsymbol{\beta})^{-1}\boldsymbol{\gamma} - (\mathbf{O} : I)$$

  (For the LISREL model, refer to Jöreskog and Sörbom 1985) The matrix of indirect effects is displayed also.
- FACTOR: The matrix of rotated factor loadings and the orthogonal transformation matrix if you specify the ROTATE= and PESTIM options, or at least the PSHORT options.
- FACTOR: Standardized (rotated) factor loadings, variance estimates of endogenous variables, R^2 values, correlations among factors, and factor scores regression matrix, if you specify the PESTIM option, or at least the PSHORT option. The determination of manifest variables is displayed only if you specify the PDETERM option.
- COSAN and LINEQS: Univariate Lagrange multiplier and Wald test indices are displayed in matrix form if you specify the MODIFICATION (or MOD) or the PALL option. Those matrix locations that correspond to constants in the model in general contain three values: the value of the Lagrange multiplier, the

corresponding probability ($df = 1$), and the estimated change of the parameter value should the constant be changed to a parameter. If allowing the constant to be an estimated parameter would result in a singular information matrix, the string 'sing' is displayed instead of the Lagrange multiplier index. Those matrix locations that correspond to parameter estimates in the model contain the Wald test index and the name of the parameter in the model. See the section "Modification Indices" on page 560 for more detail.

- COSAN and LINEQS: Univariate Lagrange multiplier test indices for releasing equality constraints if you specify the MODIFICATION (or MOD) or the PALL option. See the section "Modification Indices" on page 560 for more detail.
- COSAN and LINEQS: Univariate Lagrange multiplier test indices for releasing active boundary constraints specified by the BOUNDS statement if you specify the MODIFICATION (or MOD) or the PALL option. See the section "Modification Indices" on page 560 for more detail.
- COSAN and LINEQS: If the MODIFICATION (or MOD) or the PALL option is specified, the stepwise multivariate Wald test for constraining estimated parameters to zero constants is performed as long as the univariate probability is larger than the value specified in the PMW= option (default PMW=0.05). See the section "Modification Indices" on page 560 for more details.

ODS Table Names

PROC CALIS assigns a name to each table it creates. You can use these names to reference the table when using the Output Delivery System (ODS) to select tables and create output data sets. These names are listed in the following table. For more information on ODS, see Chapter 15, "Using the Output Delivery System."

Table 19.15. ODS Tables Created in PROC CALIS

ODS Table Name	Model[1]	Description	Option[2]
AddParms	C, F, L, R	Additional parameters in the PARAMETERS statement	PINITIAL, or default
AsymStdRes	C, F, L, R	Asymptotically standardized residual matrix	RESIDUAL=, or PRINT
AveAsymStdRes	C, F, L, R	Average absolute asymptotically standardized residuals	RESIDUAL=, or PRINT
AveNormRes	C, F, L, R	Average absolute normalized residuals	RESIDUAL=, or PRINT
AveRawRes	C, F, L, R	Average absolute raw residuals	RESIDUAL=, or PRINT
AveVarStdRes	C, F, L, R	Average absolute variance standardized residuals	RESIDUAL=, or PRINT
CholeskyWeights	C, F, L, R	Cholesky factor of weights	PWEIGHT, or PALL
ContKurtosis	C, F, L, R	Contributions to kurtosis	KURTOSIS, or PRINT
ConvergenceStatus	C, F, L, R	Convergence status	PSHORT
CorrExog	L	Correlations among exogenous variables	PESTIM, or PSHORT
CorrParm	C, F, L, R	Correlations among parameter estimates	PCOVES, and default
CovMat	C, F, L, R	Assorted cov matrices	PCOVES, and default

Table 19.15. (continued)

ODS Table Name	Model[1]	Description	Option[2]
DependParms	C, F, L, R	Dependent parameters (if specified by program statements)	PRIVEC, and default
Determination	L, F, R	Coefficients of determination	PDETERM, and default
DistAsymStdRes	C, F, L, R	Distribution of asymptotically standardized residuals	RESIDUAL=, or PRINT
DistNormRes	C, F, L, R	Distribution of normalized residuals	RESIDUAL=, or PRINT
DistRawRes	C, F, L, R	Distribution of residuals	RESIDUAL=, or PRINT
DistVarStdRes	C, F, L, R	Distribution of variance standardized residuals	RESIDUAL=, or PRINT
EndogenousVar	L	Endogenous variables	PESTIM, or PSHORT
EstCovExog	L	Estimated covariances among exogenous variables	PESTIM, or PSHORT
Estimates	C, F, L, R	Vector of estimates	PRIVEC
EstLatentEq	L	Estimated latent variable equations	PESTIM, or PSHORT
EstManifestEq	L	Estimated manifest variable equations	PESTIM, or PSHORT
EstParms	C, F	Estimated parameter matrix	PESTIM, or PSHORT
EstVarExog	L	Estimated variances of exogenous variables	PESTIM, or PSHORT
ExogenousVar	L	List of exogenous variables	PESTIM, or PSHORT
FACTCorrExog	F	Correlations among factors	PESTIM, or PSHORT
FactScoreCoef	F	Factor score regression coefficients	PESTIM, or PSHORT
FirstDer	C, F, L, R	Vector of the first partial derivatives	PRIVEC, and default
Fit	C, F, L, R	Fit statistics	PSUMMARY
GenModInfo	C, F, L, R	General modeling information	PSIMPLE, or default
Gradient	C, F, L, R	First partial derivatives (Gradient)	PRIVEC, and default
InCorr	C, F, L, R	Input correlation matrix	PCORR, or PALL
InCorrDet	C, F, L, R	Determinant of the input correlation matrix	PCORR, or PALL
InCov	C, F, L, R	Input covariance matrix	PCORR, or PALL
InCovDet	C, F, L, R	Determinant of the input covariance matrix	PCORR, or PALL
InCovExog	L	Input covariances among exogenous variables	PESTIM, or PSHORT
Indirect Effects	L, R	Indirect effects	TOTEFF, or PRINT
Information	C, F, L, R	Information matrix	PCOVES, and default
InitEstimates	C, F, L, R	Initial vector of parameter estimates	PINITIAL, or default
InitParms	C, F	Initial matrix of parameter estimates	PINITIAL, or default
InitParms	L, R	Initial matrix of parameter estimates	PRIMAT, and default
InitRAMEstimates	R	Initial RAM estimates	PESTIM, or PSHORT
InLatentEq	L	Input latent variable equations	PESTIM, or PSHORT
InManifestEq	L	Input manifest variable equations	PESTIM, or PSHORT
InSymmetric	C, F, L, R	Input symmetric matrix	PCORR, or PALL
InVarExog	L	Input variances of exogenous variables	PESTIM, or PSHORT
InvDiagWeights	C, F, L, R	Inverse of diagonal of weights	PWEIGHT, or PALL
IterHist	C, F, L, R	Iteration history	PSHORT

Table 19.15. (continued)

ODS Table Name	Model[1]	Description	Option[2]
IterStart	C, F, L, R	Iteration start	PSHORT
IterStop	C, F, L, R	Iteration stop	PSHORT
Jacobian	C, F, L, R	Jacobi column pattern	PJACPAT
Kurtosis	C, F, L, R	Kurtosis, with raw data input	KURTOSIS, or PRINT
LagrangeBoundary	C, F, L, R	Lagrange, releasing active boundary constraints	MODIFICATION, or PALL
LagrangeEquality	C, F, L, R	Lagrange, releasing equality constraints	MODIFICATION, or PALL
LatentScoreCoef	L, R	Latent variable regression score coefficients	PLATCOV, or PRINT
ModelStatement	C, F, L, R	Model summary	PSHORT
ModIndices	C, F, L, R	Lagrange multiplier and Wald test statistics	MODIFICATION, or PALL
NormRes	C, F, L, R	Normalized residual matrix	RESIDUAL=, or PRINT
PredetElements	C, F, L, R	Predetermined elements	PREDET, or PALL
PredModel	C, F, L, R	Predicted model matrix	PCORR, or PALL
PredModelDet	C, F, L, R	Predicted model determinant	PCORR, or PALL
PredMomentLatent	L, R	Predicted latent variable moments	PLATCOV, or PRINT
PredMomentManLat	L, R	Predicted manifest and latent variable moments	PLATCOV, or PRINT
ProblemDescription	C, F, L, R	Problem description	PSHORT
RAMCorrExog	R	Correlations among exogenous variables	PESTIM, or PSHORT
RAMEstimates	R	RAM Final Estimates	PESTIM, or PSHORT
RAMStdEstimates	R	Standardized estimates	PESTIM, or PSHORT
RankAsymStdRes	C, F, L, R	Ranking of the largest asymptotically standardized residuals	RESIDUAL=, or PRINT
RankLagrange	C, F, L, R	Ranking of the largest Lagrange indices	RESIDUAL=, or PRINT
RankNormRes	C, F, L, R	Ranking of the largest normalized residuals	RESIDUAL=, or PRINT
RankRawRes	C, F, L, R	Ranking of the largest raw residuals	RESIDUAL=, or PRINT
RankVarStdRes	C, F, L, R	Ranking of the largest variance standardized residuals	RESIDUAL=, or PRINT
RawRes	C, F, L, R	Raw residual matrix	RESIDUAL=, or PRINT
RotatedLoadings	F	Rotated loadings, with ROTATE= option in FACTOR statement	PESTIM, or PSHORT
Rotation	F	Rotation Matrix, with ROTATE= option in FACTOR statement	PESTIM, or PSHORT
SetCovExog	L, R	Set covariance parameters for manifest exogenous variables	PINITIAL, or default
SimpleStatistics	C, F, L, R	Simple statistics, with raw data input	SIMPLE, or default
SqMultCorr	F, L, R	Squared multiple correlations	PESTIM, or PSHORT
Stability	L, R	Stability of reciprocal causation	PDETERM, and default
StdErrs	C, F, L, R	Vector of standard errors	PRIVEC, and default
StdLatentEq	L	Standardized latent variable equations	PESTIM, or PSHORT
StdLoadings	F	Standardized factor loadings	PESTIM, or PSHORT
StdManifestEq	L	Standardized manifest variable equations	PESTIM, or PSHORT

Table 19.15. (continued)

ODS Table Name	Model[1]	Description	Option[2]
StructEq	L, R	Variables in the structural equations	PDETERM, and default
SumSqDif	C, F, L, R	Sum of squared differences of pre-determined elements	PREDET, or PALL
TotalEffects	L, R	Total effects	TOTEFF, or PRINT
tValues	C, F, L, R	Vector of t values	PRIVEC, and default
VarSelection	L, R	Manifest variables, if not all are used, selected for Modeling	default
VarStdRes	C, F, L, R	Variance standardized residual matrix	RESIDUAL=, or PRINT
WaldTest	C, F, L, R	Wald test	MODIFICATION, or PALL
Weights	C, F, L, R	Weight matrix	PWEIGHT, or PALL
WeightsDet	C, F, L, R	Determinant of the weight matrix	PWEIGHT, or PALL

1. Most CALIS output tables are specific to the model statement used. Keys: C: COSAN model, F: FACTOR model, L: LINEQS model, R: RAM model.

2. The printing options PALL, PRINT, "default", PSHORT, and PSUMM form hierarchical levels of output control, with PALL including all the output enabled by the options at the lower levels, and so on. The "default" option means that NOPRINT is not specified. Therefore, in the table, for example, if PSHORT is the printing option for an output, PALL, PRINT, or "default" will also enable the same output printing.

Examples

Example 19.1. Path Analysis: Stability of Alienation

The following covariance matrix from Wheaton, Muthen, Alwin, and Summers (1977) has served to illustrate the performance of several implementations for the analysis of structural equation models. Two different models have been analyzed by an early implementation of LISREL and are mentioned in Jöreskog (1978). You also can find a more detailed discussion of these models in the LISREL VI manual (Jöreskog and Sörbom 1985). A slightly modified model for this covariance matrix is included in the EQS 2.0 manual (Bentler 1985, p. 28). The path diagram of this model is displayed in Figure 19.1. The same model is reanalyzed here by PROC CALIS. However, for the analysis with the EQS implementation, the last variable (V6) is rescaled by a factor of 0.1 to make the matrix less ill-conditioned. Since the Levenberg-Marquardt or Newton-Raphson optimization techniques are used with PROC CALIS, rescaling the data matrix is not necessary and, therefore, is not done here. The results reported here reflect the estimates based on the original covariance matrix.

```
data Wheaton(TYPE=COV);
title "Stability of Alienation";
title2 "Data Matrix of WHEATON, MUTHEN, ALWIN & SUMMERS (1977)";
   _type_ = 'cov'; input _name_ $ v1-v6;
   label v1='Anomia (1967)' v2='Anomia (1971)' v3='Education'
         v4='Powerlessness (1967)' v5='Powerlessness (1971)'
```

```
         v6='Occupational Status Index';
   datalines;
v1   11.834      .         .         .         .        .
v2    6.947     9.364      .         .         .        .
v3    6.819     5.091    12.532      .         .        .
v4    4.783     5.028     7.495     9.986      .        .
v5   -3.839    -3.889    -3.841    -3.625    9.610      .
v6  -21.899   -18.831   -21.748   -18.775   35.522   450.288
;

proc calis cov data=Wheaton tech=nr edf=931 pall;
   Lineqs
      V1 =          F1                        + E1,
      V2 =     .833 F1                        + E2,
      V3 =          F2                        + E3,
      V4 =     .833 F2                        + E4,
      V5 =          F3                        + E5,
      V6 = Lamb (.5) F3                       + E6,
      F1 = Gam1(-.5) F3                       + D1,
      F2 = Beta (.5) F1 + Gam2(-.5) F3 + D2;
   Std
      E1-E6 = The1-The2 The1-The4 (6 * 3.),
      D1-D2 = Psi1-Psi2 (2 * 4.),
      F3    = Phi (6.) ;
   Cov
      E1 E3 = The5 (.2),
      E4 E2 = The5 (.2);
run;
```

The COV option in the PROC CALIS statement requests the analysis of the covariance matrix. Without the COV option, the correlation matrix would be computed and analyzed. Since no METHOD= option has been used, maximum likelihood estimates are computed by default. The TECH=NR option requests the Newton-Raphson optimization method. The PALL option produces the almost complete set of displayed output, as displayed in Output 19.1.1 through Output 19.1.11. Note that, when you specify the PALL option, you can produce large amounts of output. The PALL option is used in this example to show how you can get a wide spectrum of useful information from PROC CALIS.

Output 19.1.1 displays the model specification in matrix terms, followed by the lists of endogenous and exogenous variables. Equations and initial parameter estimates are also displayed. You can use this information to ensure that the desired model is the model being analyzed.

Output 19.1.1. Model Specification

```
                              Stability of Alienation
               Data Matrix of WHEATON, MUTHEN, ALWIN & SUMMERS (1977)

                                The CALIS Procedure
             Covariance Structure Analysis: Pattern and Initial Values

                               LINEQS Model Statement


                         Matrix      Rows    Columns    ------Matrix Type-------

Term 1              1    _SEL_          6         17    SELECTION
                    2    _BETA_        17         17    EQSBETA        IMINUSINV
                    3    _GAMMA_       17          9    EQSGAMMA
                    4    _PHI_          9          9    SYMMETRIC


                          The 8 Endogenous Variables

    Manifest        v1  v2  v3  v4  v5  v6
    Latent          F1  F2


                          The 9 Exogenous Variables

    Manifest
    Latent          F3
    Error           E1  E2  E3  E4  E5  E6  D1  D2
```

```
                              Stability of Alienation
               Data Matrix of WHEATON, MUTHEN, ALWIN & SUMMERS (1977)

                                The CALIS Procedure
             Covariance Structure Analysis: Pattern and Initial Values

                    v1      =   1.0000 F1    +   1.0000 E1
                    v2      =   0.8330 F1    +   1.0000 E2
                    v3      =   1.0000 F2    +   1.0000 E3
                    v4      =   0.8330 F2    +   1.0000 E4
                    v5      =   1.0000 F3    +   1.0000 E5
                    v6      =   0.5000*F3    +   1.0000 E6
                                       Lamb



                              Stability of Alienation
               Data Matrix of WHEATON, MUTHEN, ALWIN & SUMMERS (1977)

                                The CALIS Procedure
             Covariance Structure Analysis: Pattern and Initial Values

           F1       =  -0.5000*F3    +  1.0000 D1
                               Gam1
           F2       =   0.5000*F1    + -0.5000*F3    +  1.0000 D2
                               Beta          Gam2
```

```
                    Stability of Alienation
       Data Matrix of WHEATON, MUTHEN, ALWIN & SUMMERS (1977)

                     The CALIS Procedure
     Covariance Structure Analysis: Pattern and Initial Values

                 Variances of Exogenous Variables

                 Variable Parameter      Estimate

                 F3       Phi             6.00000
                 E1       The1            3.00000
                 E2       The2            3.00000
                 E3       The1            3.00000
                 E4       The2            3.00000
                 E5       The3            3.00000
                 E6       The4            3.00000
                 D1       Psi1            4.00000
                 D2       Psi2            4.00000


              Covariances Among Exogenous Variables

                Var1 Var2 Parameter       Estimate

                E1   E3   The5             0.20000
                E2   E4   The5             0.20000
```

General modeling information and simple descriptive statistics are displayed in Output 19.1.2. Because the input data set contains only the covariance matrix, the means of the manifest variables are assumed to be zero. Note that this has no impact on the estimation, unless a mean structure model is being analyzed. The twelve parameter estimates in the model and their respective locations in the parameter matrices are also displayed. Each of the parameters, The1, The2, and The5, is specified for two elements in the parameter matrix _PHI_.

Output 19.1.2. Modeling Information, Simple Statistics and Parameter Vector

```
                    Stability of Alienation
       Data Matrix of WHEATON, MUTHEN, ALWIN & SUMMERS (1977)

                     The CALIS Procedure
     Covariance Structure Analysis: Maximum Likelihood Estimation

       Observations          932    Model Terms            1
       Variables               6    Model Matrices         4
       Informations           21    Parameters            12


               Variable                         Mean        Std Dev

     v1     Anomia (1967)                          0        3.44006
     v2     Anomia (1971)                          0        3.06007
     v3     Education                              0        3.54006
     v4     Powerlessness (1967)                   0        3.16006
     v5     Powerlessness (1971)                   0        3.10000
     v6     Occupational Status Index              0       21.21999
```

```
                                 Stability of Alienation
                    Data Matrix of WHEATON, MUTHEN, ALWIN & SUMMERS (1977)

                                   The CALIS Procedure
                 Covariance Structure Analysis: Maximum Likelihood Estimation

                                       Covariances

                                            v1            v2            v3            v4            v5            v6

v1   Anomia (1967)                 11.83400000    6.94700000    6.81900000    4.78300000   -3.83900000   -21.8990000
v2   Anomia (1971)                  6.94700000    9.36400000    5.09100000    5.02800000   -3.88900000   -18.8310000
v3   Education                      6.81900000    5.09100000   12.53200000    7.49500000   -3.84100000   -21.7480000
v4   Powerlessness (1967)           4.78300000    5.02800000    7.49500000    9.98600000   -3.62500000   -18.7750000
v5   Powerlessness (1971)          -3.83900000   -3.88900000   -3.84100000   -3.62500000    9.61000000    35.5220000
v6   Occupational Status Index    -21.89900000  -18.83100000  -21.74800000  -18.77500000   35.52200000   450.2880000

                              Determinant       6080570     Ln      15.620609
```

```
                     Stability of Alienation
      Data Matrix of WHEATON, MUTHEN, ALWIN & SUMMERS (1977)

                      The CALIS Procedure
   Covariance Structure Analysis: Maximum Likelihood Estimation

                  Vector of Initial Estimates

       Parameter       Estimate     Type

  1    Beta             0.50000     Matrix Entry: _BETA_[8:7]
  2    Lamb             0.50000     Matrix Entry: _GAMMA_[6:1]
  3    Gam1            -0.50000     Matrix Entry: _GAMMA_[7:1]
  4    Gam2            -0.50000     Matrix Entry: _GAMMA_[8:1]
  5    Phi              6.00000     Matrix Entry: _PHI_[1:1]
  6    The1             3.00000     Matrix Entry: _PHI_[2:2]  _PHI_[4:4]
  7    The2             3.00000     Matrix Entry: _PHI_[3:3]  _PHI_[5:5]
  8    The5             0.20000     Matrix Entry: _PHI_[4:2]  _PHI_[5:3]
  9    The3             3.00000     Matrix Entry: _PHI_[6:6]
 10    The4             3.00000     Matrix Entry: _PHI_[7:7]
 11    Psi1             4.00000     Matrix Entry: _PHI_[8:8]
 12    Psi2             4.00000     Matrix Entry: _PHI_[9:9]
```

PROC CALIS examines whether each element in the moment matrix is modeled by the parameters defined in the model. If an element is not structured by the model parameters, it is predetermined by its observed value. This occurs, for example, when there are exogenous manifest variables in the model. If present, the predetermined values of the elements will be displayed. In the current example, the '.' displayed for all elements in the predicted moment matrix (Output 19.1.3) indicates that there are no predetermined elements in the model.

Output 19.1.3. Predetermined Elements

```
                         Stability of Alienation
              Data Matrix of WHEATON, MUTHEN, ALWIN & SUMMERS (1977)

                           The CALIS Procedure
          Covariance Structure Analysis: Maximum Likelihood Estimation

              Predetermined Elements of the Predicted Moment Matrix

                              v1          v2          v3          v4          v5          v6

v1   Anomia (1967)             .           .           .           .           .           .
v2   Anomia (1971)             .           .           .           .           .           .
v3   Education                 .           .           .           .           .           .
v4   Powerlessness (1967)      .           .           .           .           .           .
v5   Powerlessness (1971)      .           .           .           .           .           .
v6   Occupational Status Index .           .           .           .           .           .

                    Sum of Squared Differences                0
```

Output 19.1.4 displays the optimization information. You can check this table to determine whether the convergence criterion is satisfied. PROC CALIS displays an error message when problematic solutions are encountered.

Output 19.1.4. Optimization

```
                         Stability of Alienation
              Data Matrix of WHEATON, MUTHEN, ALWIN & SUMMERS (1977)

                           The CALIS Procedure
          Covariance Structure Analysis: Maximum Likelihood Estimation

                  Parameter Estimates                     12
                  Functions (Observations)                21

                           Optimization Start

 Active Constraints                         0  Objective Function                   119.33282242
 Max Abs Gradient Element        74.016932345

                                                                                         Ratio
                                                                                       Between
                                                                                        Actual
                                                       Objective    Max Abs                and
                     Function       Active    Objective   Function   Gradient          Predicted
 Iter    Restarts       Calls  Constraints     Function     Change    Element   Ridge     Change

    1           0           2            0      0.82689      118.5     1.3507       0     0.0154
    2           0           3            0      0.09859     0.7283     0.2330       0      0.716
    3           0           4            0      0.01581     0.0828    0.00684       0      1.285
    4           0           5            0      0.01449    0.00132   0.000286       0      1.042
    5           0           6            0      0.01448  9.936E-7   0.000045       0      1.053
    6           0           7            0      0.01448  4.227E-9   1.685E-6       0      1.056

                           Optimization Results

 Iterations                                 6  Function Calls                                  8
 Jacobian Calls                             7  Active Constraints                              0
 Objective Function              0.0144844811  Max Abs Gradient Element             1.6847829E-6
 Ridge                                      0  Actual Over Pred Change              1.0563187228

     ABSGCONV convergence criterion satisfied.
```

The predicted model matrix is displayed next, followed by a list of model test statistics or fit indices (Output 19.1.5). Depending on your modeling philosophy, some indices may be preferred to others. In this example, all indices and test statistics point to a good fit of the model.

Output 19.1.5. Predicted Model Matrix and Fit Statistics

```
                              Stability of Alienation
                 Data Matrix of WHEATON, MUTHEN, ALWIN & SUMMERS (1977)

                               The CALIS Procedure
               Covariance Structure Analysis: Maximum Likelihood Estimation

                              Predicted Model Matrix

                                       v1            v2            v3            v4            v5            v6

v1   Anomia (1967)                11.90390632    6.91059048    6.83016211    4.93499582   -4.16791157   -22.3768816
v2   Anomia (1971)                 6.91059048    9.35145064    4.93499582    5.01664889   -3.47187034   -18.6399424
v3   Education                     6.83016211    4.93499582   12.61574998    7.50355625   -4.06565606   -21.8278873
v4   Powerlessness (1967)          4.93499582    5.01664889    7.50355625    9.84539112   -3.38669150   -18.1826302
v5   Powerlessness (1971)         -4.16791157   -3.47187034   -4.06565606   -3.38669150    9.61000000    35.5219999
v6   Occupational Status Index   -22.37688158  -18.63994236  -21.82788734  -18.18263015   35.52199986   450.2879993

                          Determinant        6169285      Ln        15.635094
```

```
                    Stability of Alienation
       Data Matrix of WHEATON, MUTHEN, ALWIN & SUMMERS (1977)

                      The CALIS Procedure
   Covariance Structure Analysis: Maximum Likelihood Estimation

   Fit Function                                               0.0145
   Goodness of Fit Index (GFI)                                0.9953
   GFI Adjusted for Degrees of Freedom (AGFI)                 0.9890
   Root Mean Square Residual (RMR)                            0.2281
   Parsimonious GFI (Mulaik, 1989)                            0.5972
   Chi-Square                                                13.4851
   Chi-Square DF                                                   9
   Pr > Chi-Square                                            0.1419
   Independence Model Chi-Square                              2131.4
   Independence Model Chi-Square DF                               15
   RMSEA Estimate                                             0.0231
   RMSEA 90% Lower Confidence Limit                                .
   RMSEA 90% Upper Confidence Limit                           0.0470
   ECVI Estimate                                              0.0405
   ECVI 90% Lower Confidence Limit                                 .
   ECVI 90% Upper Confidence Limit                            0.0556
   Probability of Close Fit                                   0.9705
   Bentler's Comparative Fit Index                            0.9979
   Normal Theory Reweighted LS Chi-Square                    13.2804
   Akaike's Information Criterion                            -4.5149
   Bozdogan's (1987) CAIC                                   -57.0509
   Schwarz's Bayesian Criterion                             -48.0509
   McDonald's (1989) Centrality                               0.9976
   Bentler & Bonett's (1980) Non-normed Index                 0.9965
   Bentler & Bonett's (1980) NFI                              0.9937
   James, Mulaik, & Brett (1982) Parsimonious NFI             0.5962
   Z-Test of Wilson & Hilferty (1931)                         1.0754
   Bollen (1986) Normed Index Rho1                            0.9895
   Bollen (1988) Non-normed Index Delta2                      0.9979
   Hoelter's (1983) Critical N                                  1170
```

PROC CALIS can perform a detailed residual analysis. Large residuals may indicate misspecification of the model. In Output 19.1.6 for example, note the table for the 10 largest asymptotically standardized residuals. As the table shows, the specified model performs the poorest concerning the variable V5 and its covariance with V2, V1, and V3. This may be the result of a misspecification of the model equation for

V5. However, because the model fit is quite good, such a possible misspecification may have no practical significance and is not a serious concern in the analysis.

Output 19.1.6. Residual Analysis

```
                                 Stability of Alienation
                    Data Matrix of WHEATON, MUTHEN, ALWIN & SUMMERS (1977)

                                  The CALIS Procedure
                  Covariance Structure Analysis: Maximum Likelihood Estimation

                                  Raw Residual Matrix

                                        v1           v2           v3           v4           v5           v6

v1  Anomia (1967)               -.0699063150 0.0364095216 -.0111621061 -.1519958205 0.3289115712 0.4778815840
v2  Anomia (1971)               0.0364095216 0.0125493646 0.1560041795 0.0113511059 -.4171296612 -.1910576405
v3  Education                   -.0111621061 0.1560041795 -.0837499788 -.0085562504 0.2246560598 0.0798873380
v4  Powerlessness (1967)        -.1519958205 0.0113511059 -.0085562504 0.1406088766 -.2383085022 -.5923698474
v5  Powerlessness (1971)        0.3289115712 -.4171296612 0.2246560598 -.2383085022 0.0000000000 0.0000000000
v6  Occupational Status Index   0.4778815840 -.1910576405 0.0798873380 -.5923698474 0.0000000000 0.0000000000

                               Average Absolute Residual                  0.153928
                               Average Off-diagonal Absolute Residual     0.195045
```

```
                        Stability of Alienation
           Data Matrix of WHEATON, MUTHEN, ALWIN & SUMMERS (1977)

                          The CALIS Procedure
         Covariance Structure Analysis: Maximum Likelihood Estimation

                 Rank Order of the 10 Largest Raw Residuals

                     Row          Column          Residual

                     v6           v4              -0.59237
                     v6           v1               0.47788
                     v5           v2              -0.41713
                     v5           v1               0.32891
                     v5           v4              -0.23831
                     v5           v3               0.22466
                     v6           v2              -0.19106
                     v3           v2               0.15600
                     v4           v1              -0.15200
                     v4           v4               0.14061
```

```
                                 Stability of Alienation
                    Data Matrix of WHEATON, MUTHEN, ALWIN & SUMMERS (1977)

                                  The CALIS Procedure
                  Covariance Structure Analysis: Maximum Likelihood Estimation

                        Asymptotically Standardized Residual Matrix

                                        v1           v2           v3           v4           v5           v6

v1  Anomia (1967)               -0.308548787  0.526654452 -0.056188826 -0.865070455  2.553366366  0.464866661
v2  Anomia (1971)                0.526654452  0.054363484  0.876120855  0.057354415 -2.763708659 -0.170127806
v3  Education                   -0.056188826  0.876120855 -0.354347092 -0.121874301  1.697931678  0.070202664
v4  Powerlessness (1967)        -0.865070455  0.057354415 -0.121874301  0.584930625 -1.557412695 -0.495982427
v5  Powerlessness (1971)         2.553366366 -2.763708659  1.697931678 -1.557412695  0.000000000  0.000000000
v6  Occupational Status Index    0.464866661 -0.170127806  0.070202664 -0.495982427  0.000000000  0.000000000

                               Average Standardized Residual                  0.646622
                               Average Off-diagonal Standardized Residual     0.818457
```

```
                        Stability of Alienation
          Data Matrix of WHEATON, MUTHEN, ALWIN & SUMMERS (1977)

                          The CALIS Procedure
       Covariance Structure Analysis: Maximum Likelihood Estimation

    Rank Order of the 10 Largest Asymptotically Standardized Residuals

                    Row          Column         Residual

                    v5           v2             -2.76371
                    v5           v1              2.55337
                    v5           v3              1.69793
                    v5           v4             -1.55741
                    v3           v2              0.87612
                    v4           v1             -0.86507
                    v4           v4              0.58493
                    v2           v1              0.52665
                    v6           v4             -0.49598
                    v6           v1              0.46487
```

```
                        Stability of Alienation
          Data Matrix of WHEATON, MUTHEN, ALWIN & SUMMERS (1977)

                          The CALIS Procedure
       Covariance Structure Analysis: Maximum Likelihood Estimation

          Distribution of Asymptotically Standardized Residuals

                    Each * Represents 1 Residuals

----------Range---------      Freq     Percent

  -3.00000      -2.75000         1        4.76     *
  -2.75000      -2.50000         0        0.00
  -2.50000      -2.25000         0        0.00
  -2.25000      -2.00000         0        0.00
  -2.00000      -1.75000         0        0.00
  -1.75000      -1.50000         1        4.76     *
  -1.50000      -1.25000         0        0.00
  -1.25000      -1.00000         0        0.00
  -1.00000      -0.75000         1        4.76     *
  -0.75000      -0.50000         0        0.00
  -0.50000      -0.25000         3       14.29     ***
  -0.25000             0         3       14.29     ***
         0       0.25000         6       28.57     ******
   0.25000       0.50000         1        4.76     *
   0.50000       0.75000         2        9.52     **
   0.75000       1.00000         1        4.76     *
   1.00000       1.25000         0        0.00
   1.25000       1.50000         0        0.00
   1.50000       1.75000         1        4.76     *
   1.75000       2.00000         0        0.00
   2.00000       2.25000         0        0.00
   2.25000       2.50000         0        0.00
   2.50000       2.75000         1        4.76     *
```

Output 19.1.7 displays the equations and parameter estimates. Each parameter estimate is displayed with its standard error and the corresponding *t* ratio. As a general rule, a *t* ratio larger than 2 represents a statistically significant departure from 0. From these results, it is observed that both F1 (Alienation 1967) and F2 (Alienation 1971) are regressed negatively on F3 (Socioeconomic Status), and F1 has a positive effect on F2. The estimates and significance tests for the variance and covariance of the exogenous variables are also displayed.

Output 19.1.7. Equations and Parameter Estimates

```
                        Stability of Alienation
           Data Matrix of WHEATON, MUTHEN, ALWIN & SUMMERS (1977)

                          The CALIS Procedure
        Covariance Structure Analysis: Maximum Likelihood Estimation

               v1        =     1.0000 F1        +  1.0000 E1
               v2        =     0.8330 F1        +  1.0000 E2
               v3        =     1.0000 F2        +  1.0000 E3
               v4        =     0.8330 F2        +  1.0000 E4
               v5        =     1.0000 F3        +  1.0000 E5
               v6        =     5.3688*F3        +  1.0000 E6
               Std Err         0.4337 Lamb
               t Value        12.3788


                        Stability of Alienation
           Data Matrix of WHEATON, MUTHEN, ALWIN & SUMMERS (1977)

                          The CALIS Procedure
        Covariance Structure Analysis: Maximum Likelihood Estimation

     F1        =  -0.6299*F3        +  1.0000 D1
     Std Err       0.0563 Gam1
     t Value     -11.1809
     F2        =   0.5931*F1        + -0.2409*F3        +  1.0000 D2
     Std Err       0.0468 Beta          0.0549 Gam2
     t Value      12.6788              -4.3885
```

```
                    Stability of Alienation
      Data Matrix of WHEATON, MUTHEN, ALWIN & SUMMERS (1977)

                      The CALIS Procedure
    Covariance Structure Analysis: Maximum Likelihood Estimation

                 Variances of Exogenous Variables

                                               Standard
     Variable Parameter        Estimate           Error    t Value

     F3        Phi              6.61632         0.63914      10.35
     E1        The1             3.60788         0.20092      17.96
     E2        The2             3.59493         0.16448      21.86
     E3        The1             3.60788         0.20092      17.96
     E4        The2             3.59493         0.16448      21.86
     E5        The3             2.99368         0.49861       6.00
     E6        The4           259.57580        18.31150      14.18
     D1        Psi1             5.67047         0.42301      13.41
     D2        Psi2             4.51480         0.33532      13.46


               Covariances Among Exogenous Variables

                                               Standard
     Var1 Var2 Parameter        Estimate          Error    t Value

     E1   E3   The5              0.90580        0.12167       7.44
     E2   E4   The5              0.90580        0.12167       7.44
```

The measurement scale of variables is often arbitrary. Therefore, it can be useful to look at the standardized equations produced by PROC CALIS. Output 19.1.8 displays the standardized equations and predicted moments. From the standardized structural equations for F1 and F2, you can conclude that SES (F3) has a larger impact on earlier Alienation (F1) than on later Alienation (F3).

The squared multiple correlation for each equation, the correlation among the exogenous variables, and the covariance matrices among the latent variables and between the observed and the latent variables help to describe the relationships among all variables.

Output 19.1.8. Standardized Equations and Predicted Moments

```
                      Stability of Alienation
        Data Matrix of WHEATON, MUTHEN, ALWIN & SUMMERS (1977)

                        The CALIS Procedure
     Covariance Structure Analysis: Maximum Likelihood Estimation

              v1       =   0.8348 F1    +  0.5505 E1
              v2       =   0.7846 F1    +  0.6200 E2
              v3       =   0.8450 F2    +  0.5348 E3
              v4       =   0.7968 F2    +  0.6043 E4
              v5       =   0.8297 F3    +  0.5581 E5
              v6       =   0.6508*F3    +  0.7593 E6
                                  Lamb



                      Stability of Alienation
        Data Matrix of WHEATON, MUTHEN, ALWIN & SUMMERS (1977)

                        The CALIS Procedure
     Covariance Structure Analysis: Maximum Likelihood Estimation

        F1       =  -0.5626*F3    +  0.8268 D1
                            Gam1
        F2       =   0.5692*F1    + -0.2064*F3    +  0.7080 D2
                            Beta          Gam2
```

```
                      Stability of Alienation
        Data Matrix of WHEATON, MUTHEN, ALWIN & SUMMERS (1977)

                        The CALIS Procedure
     Covariance Structure Analysis: Maximum Likelihood Estimation

                   Squared Multiple Correlations

                               Error          Total
            Variable        Variance       Variance    R-Square

       1    v1               3.60788       11.90391      0.6969
       2    v2               3.59493        9.35145      0.6156
       3    v3               3.60788       12.61575      0.7140
       4    v4               3.59493        9.84539      0.6349
       5    v5               2.99368        9.61000      0.6885
       6    v6             259.57580      450.28800      0.4235
       7    F1               5.67047        8.29603      0.3165
       8    F2               4.51480        9.00787      0.4988


                Correlations Among Exogenous Variables

                  Var1 Var2 Parameter       Estimate

                  E1   E3   The5             0.25106
                  E2   E4   The5             0.25197
```

```
                     Stability of Alienation
      Data Matrix of WHEATON, MUTHEN, ALWIN & SUMMERS (1977)

                       The CALIS Procedure
   Covariance Structure Analysis: Maximum Likelihood Estimation

              Predicted Moments of Latent Variables

                         F1                 F2                 F3

  F1            8.296026985        5.924364730       -4.167911571
  F2            5.924364730        9.007870649       -4.065656060
  F3           -4.167911571       -4.065656060        6.616317547

      Predicted Moments between Manifest and Latent Variables

                         F1                 F2                 F3

  v1             8.29602698         5.92436473        -4.16791157
  v2             6.91059048         4.93499582        -3.47187034
  v3             5.92436473         9.00787065        -4.06565606
  v4             4.93499582         7.50355625        -3.38669150
  v5            -4.16791157        -4.06565606         6.61631755
  v6           -22.37688158       -21.82788734        35.52199986
```

Output 19.1.9 displays the latent variable score regression coefficients that produce the latent variable scores. Each latent variable is expressed as a linear combination of the observed variables. See Chapter 57, "The SCORE Procedure," for more information on the creation of latent variable scores. Note that the total effects and indirect effects of the exogenous variables are also displayed.

Output 19.1.9. Latent Variable Score Regression, Direct and Indirect Effects

```
                              Stability of Alienation
                Data Matrix of WHEATON, MUTHEN, ALWIN & SUMMERS (1977)

                               The CALIS Procedure
             Covariance Structure Analysis: Maximum Likelihood Estimation

                     Latent Variable Score Regression Coefficients

                                               F1               F2               F3

v1     Anomia (1967)                  0.4131113567     0.0482681051     -.0521264408
v2     Anomia (1971)                  0.3454029627     0.0400143300     -.0435560637
v3     Education                      0.0526632293     0.4306175653     -.0399927539
v4     Powerlessness (1967)           0.0437036855     0.3600452776     -.0334000265
v5     Powerlessness (1971)           -.0749215200     -.0639697183     0.5057060770
v6     Occupational Status Index      -.0046390513     -.0039609288     0.0313127184

                                    Total Effects

                         F3                  F1                  F2

            v1     -0.629944307         1.000000000         0.000000000
            v2     -0.524743608         0.833000000         0.000000000
            v3     -0.614489258         0.593112208         1.000000000
            v4     -0.511869552         0.494062469         0.833000000
            v5      1.000000000         0.000000000         0.000000000
            v6      5.368847492         0.000000000         0.000000000
            F1     -0.629944307         0.000000000         0.000000000
            F2     -0.614489258         0.593112208         0.000000000

                                   Indirect Effects

                         F3                  F1                  F2

            v1     -.6299443069        0.0000000000                 0
            v2     -.5247436076        0.0000000000                 0
            v3     -.6144892580        0.5931122083                 0
            v4     -.5118695519        0.4940624695                 0
            v5     0.0000000000        0.0000000000                 0
            v6     0.0000000000        0.0000000000                 0
            F1     0.0000000000        0.0000000000                 0
            F2     -.3736276589        0.0000000000                 0
```

PROC CALIS can display Lagrange multiplier and Wald statistics for model modifications. Modification indices are displayed for each parameter matrix. Only the Lagrange multiplier statistics have significance levels and approximate changes of values displayed. The significance level of the Wald statistic for a given parameter is the same as that shown in the equation output. An insignificant *p*-value for a Wald statistic means that the corresponding parameter can be dropped from the model without significantly worsening the fit of the model.

A significant *p*-value for a Lagrange multiplier test indicates that the model would achieve a better fit if the corresponding parameter is free. To aid in determining significant results, PROC CALIS displays the rank order of the ten largest Lagrange multiplier statistics. For example, [E5:E2] in the _PHI_ matrix is associated with the largest Lagrange multiplier statistic; the associated *p*-value is 0.0067. This means that adding a parameter for the covariance between E5 and E2 will lead to a significantly better fit of the model. However, adding parameters indiscriminately can result in specification errors. An over-fitted model may not perform well with future samples. As always, the decision to add parameters should be accompanied with consideration and knowledge of the application area.

Output 19.1.10. Lagrange Multiplier and Wald Tests

Stability of Alienation
Data Matrix of WHEATON, MUTHEN, ALWIN & SUMMERS (1977)

The CALIS Procedure
Covariance Structure Analysis: Maximum Likelihood Estimation

Lagrange Multiplier and Wald Test Indices _PHI_[9:9]
Symmetric Matrix
Univariate Tests for Constant Constraints
Lagrange Multiplier or Wald Index / Probability / Approx Change of Value

	F3	E1	E2	E3	E4	E5	E6	D1	D2
F3	107.1619 . . [Phi]	3.3903 0.0656 0.5079	3.3901 0.0656 -0.4231	0.5752 0.4482 0.2090	0.5753 0.4482 -0.1741	. . . Sing	. . . Sing	. . . Sing	. . . Sing
E1	3.3903 0.0656 0.5079	322.4501 . . [The1]	0.1529 0.6958 0.0900	55.4237 . . [The5]	1.2037 0.2726 -0.3262	5.8025 0.0160 0.5193	0.7398 0.3897 -1.2587	0.4840 0.4866 0.2276	0.0000 0.9961 0.0014
E2	3.3901 0.0656 -0.4231	0.1529 0.6958 0.0900	477.6768 . . [The2]	0.5946 0.4406 0.2328	55.4237 . . [The5]	7.3649 0.0067 -0.5060	1.4168 0.2339 1.5431	0.4840 0.4866 -0.1896	0.0000 0.9961 -0.0011
E3	0.5752 0.4482 0.2090	55.4237 . . [The5]	0.5946 0.4406 0.2328	322.4501 . . [The1]	0.1528 0.6958 -0.0900	1.5982 0.2062 0.2709	0.0991 0.7529 -0.4579	1.1825 0.2768 0.2984	0.5942 0.4408 -0.2806
E4	0.5753 0.4482 -0.1741	1.2037 0.2726 -0.3262	55.4237 . . [The5]	0.1528 0.6958 -0.0900	477.6768 . . [The2]	1.2044 0.2724 -0.2037	0.0029 0.9568 0.0700	1.1825 0.2768 -0.2486	0.5942 0.4408 0.2338
E5	. . . Sing	5.8025 0.0160 0.5193	7.3649 0.0067 -0.5060	1.5982 0.2062 0.2709	1.2044 0.2724 -0.2037	36.0486 . . [The3]	. . . Sing	0.1033 0.7479 -0.2776	0.1035 0.7477 0.1062
E6	. . . Sing	0.7398 0.3897 -1.2587	1.4168 0.2339 1.5431	0.0991 0.7529 -0.4579	0.0029 0.9568 0.0700	. . . Sing	200.9466 . . [The4]	0.1034 0.7478 1.4906	0.1035 0.7477 -0.5700
D1	. . . Sing	0.4840 0.4866 0.2276	0.4840 0.4866 -0.1896	1.1825 0.2768 0.2984	1.1825 0.2768 -0.2486	0.1033 0.7479 -0.2776	0.1034 0.7478 1.4906	179.6950 . . [Psi1]	. . . Sing
D2	. . . Sing	0.0000 0.9961 0.0014	0.0000 0.9961 -0.0011	0.5942 0.4408 -0.2806	0.5942 0.4408 0.2338	0.1035 0.7477 0.1062	0.1035 0.7477 -0.5700	. . . Sing	181.2787 . . [Psi2]

```
                    Stability of Alienation
       Data Matrix of WHEATON, MUTHEN, ALWIN & SUMMERS (1977)

                      The CALIS Procedure
    Covariance Structure Analysis: Maximum Likelihood Estimation

     Rank Order of the 10 Largest Lagrange Multipliers in _PHI_

          Row          Column       Chi-Square     Pr > ChiSq

          E5           E2              7.36486         0.0067
          E5           E1              5.80246         0.0160
          E1           F3              3.39030         0.0656
          E2           F3              3.39013         0.0656
          E5           E3              1.59820         0.2062
          E6           E2              1.41677         0.2339
          E5           E4              1.20437         0.2724
          E4           E1              1.20367         0.2726
          D1           E3              1.18251         0.2768
          D1           E4              1.18249         0.2768
```

```
                      Stability of Alienation
          Data Matrix of WHEATON, MUTHEN, ALWIN & SUMMERS (1977)

                         The CALIS Procedure
       Covariance Structure Analysis: Maximum Likelihood Estimation

          Lagrange Multiplier and Wald Test Indices _GAMMA_[8:1]
                            General Matrix
                Univariate Tests for Constant Constraints
  Lagrange Multiplier or Wald Index / Probability / Approx Change of Value

                                   F3

                    v1        3.3903
                              0.0656
                              0.0768


                    v2        3.3901
                              0.0656
                             -0.0639


                    v3        0.5752
                              0.4482
                              0.0316


                    v4        0.5753
                              0.4482
                             -0.0263


                    v5           .
                                 .
                                 .
                                Sing

                    v6      153.2354
                                 .
                                 .
                              [Lamb]

                    F1      125.0132
                                 .
                                 .
                              [Gam1]

                    F2       19.2585
                                 .
                                 .
                              [Gam2]
```

Stability of Alienation
Data Matrix of WHEATON, MUTHEN, ALWIN & SUMMERS (1977)

The CALIS Procedure
Covariance Structure Analysis: Maximum Likelihood Estimation

Rank Order of the 4 Largest Lagrange Multipliers in _GAMMA_

Row	Column	Chi-Square	Pr > ChiSq
v1	F3	3.39030	0.0656
v2	F3	3.39013	0.0656
v4	F3	0.57526	0.4482
v3	F3	0.57523	0.4482

Stability of Alienation
Data Matrix of WHEATON, MUTHEN, ALWIN & SUMMERS (1977)

The CALIS Procedure
Covariance Structure Analysis: Maximum Likelihood Estimation

Lagrange Multiplier and Wald Test Indices _BETA_[8:8]
General Matrix
Identity-Minus-Inverse Model Matrix
Univariate Tests for Constant Constraints
Lagrange Multiplier or Wald Index / Probability / Approx Change of Value

	v1	v2	v3	v4	v5	v6	F1	F2
v1	. . . Sing	0.1647 0.6849 -0.0159	0.0511 0.8212 -0.0063	0.8029 0.3702 -0.0284	5.4083 0.0200 0.0697	0.1233 0.7255 0.0015	0.4047 0.5247 -0.0257	0.4750 0.4907 -0.0239
v2	0.5957 0.4402 0.0218	. . . Sing	0.6406 0.4235 0.0185	0.0135 0.9076 0.0032	5.8858 0.0153 -0.0609	0.0274 0.8686 -0.0006	0.4047 0.5247 0.0214	0.4750 0.4907 0.0199
v3	0.3839 0.5355 0.0178	0.3027 0.5822 0.0180	. . . Sing	0.1446 0.7038 -0.0145	1.1537 0.2828 0.0322	0.0296 0.8634 0.0007	0.1588 0.6902 0.0144	0.0817 0.7750 -0.0110
v4	0.4487 0.5030 -0.0160	0.2519 0.6157 -0.0144	0.0002 0.9877 -0.0004	. . . Sing	0.9867 0.3206 -0.0249	0.1442 0.7041 -0.0014	0.1588 0.6903 -0.0120	0.0817 0.7750 0.0092
v5	5.4085 0.0200 0.1242	8.6455 0.0033 -0.1454	2.7123 0.0996 0.0785	2.1457 0.1430 -0.0674	. . . Sing	. . . Sing	0.1033 0.7479 -0.0490	0.1035 0.7476 0.0329
v6	0.4209 0.5165 -0.2189	1.4387 0.2304 0.3924	0.3044 0.5811 -0.1602	0.0213 0.8841 0.0431	. . . Sing	. . . Sing	0.1034 0.7478 0.2629	0.1035 0.7477 -0.1765
F1	1.0998 0.2943 0.0977	1.1021 0.2938 -0.0817	1.6114 0.2043 0.0993	1.6128 0.2041 -0.0831	0.1032 0.7480 -0.0927	0.1035 0.7477 0.0057	. . . Sing	. . . Sing
F2	0.0193 0.8896 -0.0104	0.0194 0.8892 0.0087	0.4765 0.4900 -0.0625	0.4760 0.4902 0.0522	0.1034 0.7477 0.0355	0.1035 0.7477 -0.0022	160.7520 . . [Beta]	. . . Sing

```
                    Stability of Alienation
       Data Matrix of WHEATON, MUTHEN, ALWIN & SUMMERS (1977)

                      The CALIS Procedure
    Covariance Structure Analysis: Maximum Likelihood Estimation

     Rank Order of the 10 Largest Lagrange Multipliers in _BETA_

          Row           Column        Chi-Square     Pr > ChiSq

          v5            v2               8.64546         0.0033
          v2            v5               5.88576         0.0153
          v5            v1               5.40848         0.0200
          v1            v5               5.40832         0.0200
          v5            v3               2.71233         0.0996
          v5            v4               2.14572         0.1430
          F1            v4               1.61279         0.2041
          F1            v3               1.61137         0.2043
          v6            v2               1.43867         0.2304
          v3            v5               1.15372         0.2828
```

When you specify equality constraints, PROC CALIS displays Lagrange multiplier tests for releasing the constraints. In the current example, none of the three constraints achieve a p-value smaller than 0.05. This means that releasing the constraints may not lead to a significantly better fit of the model. Therefore, all constraints are retained in the model.

Output 19.1.11. Tests for Equality Constraints

```
                    Stability of Alienation
       Data Matrix of WHEATON, MUTHEN, ALWIN & SUMMERS (1977)

                      The CALIS Procedure
    Covariance Structure Analysis: Maximum Likelihood Estimation

 Univariate Lagrange Multiplier Test for Releasing Equality Constraints

  Equality Constraint     -----Changes-----     Chi-Square     Pr > ChiSq

  [E1:E1] = [E3:E3]        0.0293   -0.0308       0.02106         0.8846
  [E2:E2] = [E4:E4]       -0.1342    0.1388       0.69488         0.4045
  [E3:E1] = [E4:E2]        0.2468   -0.1710       1.29124         0.2558
```

The model is specified using the LINEQS, STD, and COV statements. The section "Getting Started" on page 448 also contains the COSAN and RAM specifications of this model. These model specifications would give essentially the same results.

```
proc calis cov data=Wheaton tech=nr edf=931;
   Cosan J(9, Ide) * A(9, Gen, Imi) * P(9, Sym);
   Matrix A
           [ ,7] = 1. .833  5 * 0. Beta (.5) ,
           [ ,8] = 2 * 0.  1.  .833 ,
           [ ,9] = 4 * 0.  1.  Lamb Gam1-Gam2 (.5 2 * -.5);
   Matrix P
           [1,1] = The1-The2 The1-The4 (6 * 3.) ,
           [7,7] = Psi1-Psi2 Phi (2 * 4. 6.) ,
           [3,1] = The5 (.2) ,
```

```
                [4,2] = The5 (.2) ;
      Vnames J V1-V6 F1-F3 ,
             A = J ,
             P E1-E6 D1-D3 ;
   run;

   proc calis cov data=Wheaton tech=nr edf=931;
      Ram
         1   1  7   1.        ,
         1   2  7   .833      ,
         1   3  8   1.        ,
         1   4  8   .833      ,
         1   5  9   1.        ,
         1   6  9   .5    Lamb ,
         1   7  9   -.5   Gam1 ,
         1   8  7   .5    Beta ,
         1   8  9   -.5   Gam2 ,
         2   1  1   3.    The1 ,
         2   2  2   3.    The2 ,
         2   3  3   3.    The1 ,
         2   4  4   3.    The2 ,
         2   5  5   3.    The3 ,
         2   6  6   3.    The4 ,
         2   1  3   .2    The5 ,
         2   2  4   .2    The5 ,
         2   7  7   4.    Psi1 ,
         2   8  8   4.    Psi2 ,
         2   9  9   6.    Phi  ;
      Vnames 1 F1-F3,
             2 E1-E6 D1-D3;
   run;
```

Example 19.2. Simultaneous Equations with Intercept

The demand-and-supply food example of Kmenta (1971, pp. 565, 582) is used to illustrate the use of PROC CALIS for the estimation of intercepts and coefficients of simultaneous equations. The model is specified by two simultaneous equations containing two endogenous variables Q and P and three exogenous variables D, F, and Y,

$$Q_t(demand) = \alpha_1 + \beta_1 P_t + \gamma_1 D_t$$

$$Q_t(supply) = \alpha_2 + \beta_2 P_t + \gamma_2 F_t + \gamma_3 Y_t$$

for $t = 1, \ldots, 20$.

The LINEQS statement requires that each endogenous variable appear on the left-hand side of exactly one equation. Instead of analyzing the system

$$\mathbf{B}^* \eta = \mathbf{\Gamma} \xi + \zeta$$

PROC CALIS analyzes the equivalent system

$$\eta = \mathbf{B}\eta + \mathbf{\Gamma}\xi + \zeta$$

with $\mathbf{B}^* = \mathbf{I} - \mathbf{B}$. This requires that one of the preceding equations be solved for P_t. Solving the second equation for P_t yields

$$P_t = \frac{1}{\beta_2} Q_t - \frac{\alpha_2}{\beta_2} - \frac{\gamma_2}{\beta_2} F_t - \frac{\gamma_3}{\beta_2} Y_t$$

You can estimate the intercepts of a system of simultaneous equations by applying PROC CALIS on the uncorrected covariance (UCOV) matrix of the data set that is augmented by an additional constant variable with the value 1. In the following example, the uncorrected covariance matrix is augmented by an additional variable INTERCEPT by using the AUGMENT option. The PROC CALIS statement contains the options UCOV and AUG to compute and analyze an augmented UCOV matrix from the input data set FOOD.

```
data food;
Title 'Food example of KMENTA(1971, p.565 & 582)';
   Input Q P D F Y;
   Label Q='Food Consumption per Head'
         P='Ratio of Food Prices to General Price'
         D='Disposable Income in Constant Prices'
         F='Ratio of Preceding Years Prices'
         Y='Time in Years 1922-1941';
   datalines;
  98.485  100.323    87.4    98.0   1
  99.187  104.264    97.6    99.1   2
 102.163  103.435    96.7    99.1   3
 101.504  104.506    98.2    98.1   4
 104.240   98.001    99.8   110.8   5
 103.243   99.456   100.5   108.2   6
 103.993  101.066   103.2   105.6   7
  99.900  104.763   107.8   109.8   8
 100.350   96.446    96.6   108.7   9
 102.820   91.228    88.9   100.6  10
  95.435   93.085    75.1    81.0  11
  92.424   98.801    76.9    68.6  12
  94.535  102.908    84.6    70.9  13
  98.757   98.756    90.6    81.4  14
 105.797   95.119   103.1   102.3  15
 100.225   98.451   105.1   105.0  16
 103.522   86.498    96.4   110.5  17
  99.929  104.016   104.4    92.5  18
 105.223  105.769   110.7    89.3  19
 106.232  113.490   127.1    93.0  20
;
```

```
proc calis ucov aug data=food pshort;
   Title2 'Compute ML Estimates With Intercept';
   Lineqs
      Q = alf1 Intercept + alf2 P + alf3 D + E1,
      P = gam1 Intercept + gam2 Q + gam3 F + gam4 Y + E2;
   Std
      E1-E2 = eps1-eps2;
   Cov
      E1-E2 = eps3;
   Bounds
      eps1-eps2 >= 0. ;
run;
```

The following, essentially equivalent model definition uses program code to reparameterize the model in terms of the original equations; the output is displayed in Output 19.2.1.

```
proc calis data=food ucov aug pshort;
   Lineqs
      Q = alpha1 Intercept + beta1 P + gamma1 D + E1,
      P = alpha2_b Intercept + gamma2_b F + gamma3_b Y + _b Q + E2;
   Std
      E1-E2 = eps1-eps2;
   Cov
      E1-E2 = eps3;

   Parameters alpha2 (50.) beta2 gamma2 gamma3 (3*.25);
      alpha2_b = -alpha2 / beta2;
      gamma2_b = -gamma2 / beta2;
      gamma3_b = -gamma3 / beta2;
      _b       = 1 / beta2;

   Bounds
      eps1-eps2 >= 0. ;
run;
```

Output 19.2.1. Food Example of Kmenta

```
                 Food example of KMENTA(1971, p.565 & 582)

                            The CALIS Procedure
          Covariance Structure Analysis: Pattern and Initial Values

                           LINEQS Model Statement


                     Matrix       Rows    Columns    ------Matrix Type-------

Term 1          1    _SEL_           6          8    SELECTION
                2    _BETA_          8          8    EQSBETA           IMINUSINV
                3    _GAMMA_         8          6    EQSGAMMA
                4    _PHI_           6          6    SYMMETRIC


                       The 2 Endogenous Variables

    Manifest        Q          P
    Latent


                       The 6 Exogenous Variables

    Manifest        D          F          Y          Intercept
    Latent
    Error           E1         E2
```

Food example of KMENTA(1971, p.565 & 582)

The CALIS Procedure

Covariance Structure Analysis: Maximum Likelihood Estimation

Parameter Estimates	10
Functions (Observations)	21
Lower Bounds	2
Upper Bounds	0

Optimization Start

Active Constraints	0	Objective Function	2.3500065042
Max Abs Gradient Element	203.9741437	Radius	62167.829174

Iter	Restarts	Function Calls	Active Constraints	Objective Function	Objective Function Change	Max Abs Gradient Element	Lambda	Ratio Between Actual and Predicted Change
1	0	2	0	1.19094	1.1591	3.9410	0	0.688
2	0	5	0	0.32678	0.8642	9.9864	0.00127	2.356
3	0	7	0	0.19108	0.1357	5.5100	0.00006	0.685
4	0	10	0	0.16682	0.0243	2.0513	0.00005	0.867
5	0	12	0	0.16288	0.00393	1.0570	0.00014	0.828
6	0	13	0	0.16132	0.00156	0.3643	0.00004	0.864
7	0	15	0	0.16077	0.000557	0.2176	0.00006	0.984
8	0	16	0	0.16052	0.000250	0.1819	0.00001	0.618
9	0	17	0	0.16032	0.000201	0.0662	0	0.971
10	0	18	0	0.16030	0.000011	0.0195	0	1.108
11	0	19	0	0.16030	6.116E-7	0.00763	0	1.389
12	0	20	0	0.16030	9.454E-8	0.00301	0	1.389
13	0	21	0	0.16030	1.461E-8	0.00118	0	1.388
14	0	22	0	0.16030	2.269E-9	0.000465	0	1.395
15	0	23	0	0.16030	3.59E-10	0.000182	0	1.427

Optimization Results

Iterations	15	Function Calls	24
Jacobian Calls	16	Active Constraints	0
Objective Function	0.1603035477	Max Abs Gradient Element	0.0001820805
Lambda	0	Actual Over Pred Change	1.4266532872
Radius	0.0010322573		

GCONV convergence criterion satisfied.

```
            Food example of KMENTA(1971, p.565 & 582)

                       The CALIS Procedure
          Covariance Structure Analysis: Maximum Likelihood Estimation

          Fit Function                                           0.1603
          Goodness of Fit Index (GFI)                            0.9530
          GFI Adjusted for Degrees of Freedom (AGFI)             0.0120
          Root Mean Square Residual (RMR)                        2.0653
          Parsimonious GFI (Mulaik, 1989)                        0.0635
          Chi-Square                                             3.0458
          Chi-Square DF                                               1
          Pr > Chi-Square                                        0.0809
          Independence Model Chi-Square                          534.27
          Independence Model Chi-Square DF                           15
          RMSEA Estimate                                         0.3281
          RMSEA 90% Lower Confidence Limit                            .
          RMSEA 90% Upper Confidence Limit                       0.7777
          ECVI Estimate                                          1.8270
          ECVI 90% Lower Confidence Limit                             .
          ECVI 90% Upper Confidence Limit                        3.3493
          Probability of Close Fit                               0.0882
          Bentler's Comparative Fit Index                        0.9961
          Normal Theory Reweighted LS Chi-Square                 2.8142
          Akaike's Information Criterion                         1.0458
          Bozdogan's (1987) CAIC                                -0.9500
          Schwarz's Bayesian Criterion                           0.0500
          McDonald's (1989) Centrality                           0.9501
          Bentler & Bonett's (1980) Non-normed Index             0.9409
          Bentler & Bonett's (1980) NFI                          0.9943
          James, Mulaik, & Brett (1982) Parsimonious NFI         0.0663
          Z-Test of Wilson & Hilferty (1931)                     1.4250
          Bollen (1986) Normed Index Rho1                        0.9145
          Bollen (1988) Non-normed Index Delta2                  0.9962
          Hoelter's (1983) Critical N                                25
```

```
                            Food example of KMENTA(1971, p.565 & 582)

                                       The CALIS Procedure
                     Covariance Structure Analysis: Maximum Likelihood Estimation

Q          =  -0.2295*P        +  0.3100*D       + 93.6193*Intercept +  1.0000 E1
                beta1                gamma1            alpha1
P          =   4.2140*Q        + -0.9305*F       + -1.5579*Y          +  -218.9*Intercept +  1.0000 E2
                _b                   gamma2_b          gamma3_b              alpha2_b
```

```
                Food example of KMENTA(1971, p.565 & 582)

                         The CALIS Procedure
      Covariance Structure Analysis: Maximum Likelihood Estimation

                  Variances of Exogenous Variables

                  Variable  Parameter       Estimate

                  D                            10154
                  F                             9989
                  Y                        151.05263
                  Intercept                  1.05263
                  E1         eps1            3.51274
                  E2         eps2          105.06746


                 Covariances Among Exogenous Variables

             Var1       Var2       Parameter        Estimate

             D          F                               9994
             D          Y                               1101
             F          Y                               1046
             D          Intercept                  102.66842
             F          Intercept                  101.71053
             Y          Intercept                   11.05263
             E1         E2         eps3            -18.87270
```

```
                    Food example of KMENTA(1971, p.565 & 582)

                              The CALIS Procedure
          Covariance Structure Analysis: Maximum Likelihood Estimation

Q        =  -0.2278*P       +  0.3016*D       +  0.9272*Intercept +  0.0181 E1
                beta1             gamma1            alpha1
P        =   4.2467*Q       + -0.9048*F       + -0.1863*Y         + -2.1849*Intercept +  0.0997 E2
                _b                gamma2_b          gamma3_b            alpha2_b


                        Squared Multiple Correlations

                                  Error          Total
             Variable           Variance       Variance      R-Square

         1   Q                   3.51274          10730        0.9997
         2   P                 105.06746          10565        0.9901


                   Correlations Among Exogenous Variables

           Var1       Var2       Parameter        Estimate

           D          F                            0.99237
           D          Y                            0.88903
           F          Y                            0.85184
           D          Intercept                    0.99308
           F          Intercept                    0.99188
           Y          Intercept                    0.87652
           E1         E2         eps3             -0.98237


                 Additional PARMS and Dependent Parameters

                  The Number of Dependent Parameters is 4

                                           Standard
         Parameter        Estimate           Error     t Value

         alpha2           51.94453              .           .
         beta2             0.23731              .           .
         gamma2            0.22082              .           .
         gamma3            0.36971              .           .
         _b                4.21397              .           .
         gamma2_b         -0.93053              .           .
         gamma3_b         -1.55794              .           .
         alpha2_b       -218.89288              .           .
```

You can obtain almost equivalent results by applying the SAS/ETS procedure SYSLIN on this problem.

Example 19.3. Second-Order Confirmatory Factor Analysis

A second-order confirmatory factor analysis model is applied to a correlation matrix of Thurstone reported by McDonald (1985). Using the LINEQS statement, the three-term second-order factor analysis model is specified in equations notation. The first-order loadings for the three factors, F1, F2, and F3, each refer to three variables, X1-X3, X4-X6, and X7-X9. One second-order factor, F4, reflects the correlations among the three first-order factors. The second-order factor correlation matrix P is defined as a 1×1 identity matrix. Choosing the second-order uniqueness matrix U2 as a diagonal matrix with parameters U21-U23 gives an unidentified model. To compute identified maximum likelihood estimates, the matrix U2 is defined as a 3×3 identity matrix. The following code generates results that are partially displayed in Output 19.3.1.

```
data Thurst(TYPE=CORR);
Title "Example of THURSTONE resp. McDONALD (1985, p.57, p.105)";
   _TYPE_ = 'CORR'; Input _NAME_ $ Obs1-Obs9;
   Label Obs1='Sentences' Obs2='Vocabulary' Obs3='Sentence Completion'
         Obs4='First Letters' Obs5='Four-letter Words' Obs6='Suffices'
         Obs7='Letter series' Obs8='Pedigrees' Obs9='Letter Grouping';
   datalines;
Obs1  1.      .      .      .      .      .      .      .      .
Obs2   .828   1.     .      .      .      .      .      .      .
Obs3   .776   .779   1.     .      .      .      .      .      .
Obs4   .439   .493    .460  1.     .      .      .      .      .
Obs5   .432   .464    .425   .674  1.     .      .      .      .
Obs6   .447   .489    .443   .590   .541  1.     .      .      .
Obs7   .447   .432    .401   .381   .402   .288  1.     .      .
Obs8   .541   .537    .534   .350   .367   .320   .555  1.     .
Obs9   .380   .358    .359   .424   .446   .325   .598   .452  1.
;

proc calis data=Thurst method=max edf=212 pestim se;
Title2 "Identified Second Order Confirmatory Factor Analysis";
Title3 "C = F1 * F2 * P * F2' * F1' + F1 * U2 * F1' + U1, With P=U2=Ide";
Lineqs
   Obs1 = X1 F1 + E1,
   Obs2 = X2 F1 + E2,
   Obs3 = X3 F1 + E3,
   Obs4 = X4 F2 + E4,
   Obs5 = X5 F2 + E5,
   Obs6 = X6 F2 + E6,
   Obs7 = X7 F3 + E7,
   Obs8 = X8 F3 + E8,
   Obs9 = X9 F3 + E9,
   F1   = X10 F4 + E10,
   F2   = X11 F4 + E11,
   F3   = X12 F4 + E12;
Std
   F4      = 1. ,
   E1-E9   = U11-U19 ,
   E10-E12 = 3 * 1.;
Bounds
   0. <= U11-U19;
run;
```

Output 19.3.1. Second-Order Confirmatory Factor Analysis

```
              Example of THURSTONE resp. McDONALD (1985, p.57, p.105)
                 Identified Second Order Confirmatory Factor Analysis
          C = F1 * F2 * P * F2' * F1' + F1 * U2 * F1' + U1, With P=U2=Ide

                              The CALIS Procedure
             Covariance Structure Analysis: Maximum Likelihood Estimation

                     Parameter Estimates                   21
                     Functions (Observations)              45
                     Lower Bounds                           9
                     Upper Bounds                           0

                              Optimization Start

Active Constraints                            0  Objective Function            0.7151823452
Max Abs Gradient Element           0.4067179803  Radius                        2.2578762496
```

Iter	Restarts	Function Calls	Active Constraints	Objective Function	Objective Function Change	Max Abs Gradient Element	Lambda	Ratio Between Actual and Predicted Change
1	0	2	0	0.23113	0.4840	0.1299	0	1.363
2	0	3	0	0.18322	0.0479	0.0721	0	1.078
3	0	4	0	0.18051	0.00271	0.0200	0	1.006
4	0	5	0	0.18022	0.000289	0.00834	0	1.093
5	0	6	0	0.18018	0.000041	0.00251	0	1.201
6	0	7	0	0.18017	6.523E-6	0.00114	0	1.289
7	0	8	0	0.18017	1.085E-6	0.000388	0	1.347
8	0	9	0	0.18017	1.853E-7	0.000173	0	1.380
9	0	10	0	0.18017	3.208E-8	0.000063	0	1.399
10	0	11	0	0.18017	5.593E-9	0.000028	0	1.408
11	0	12	0	0.18017	9.79E-10	0.000011	0	1.414

```
                             Optimization Results

Iterations                                   11  Function Calls                          13
Jacobian Calls                               12  Active Constraints                       0
Objective Function                 0.1801712147  Max Abs Gradient Element      0.0000105805
Lambda                                        0  Actual Over Pred Change       1.4135857595
Radius                             0.0002026368

      GCONV convergence criterion satisfied.
```

```
        Example of THURSTONE resp. McDONALD (1985, p.57, p.105)
          Identified Second Order Confirmatory Factor Analysis
C = F1 * F2 * P * F2' * F1' + F1 * U2 * F1' + U1, With P=U2=Ide

                         The CALIS Procedure
  Covariance Structure Analysis: Maximum Likelihood Estimation

  Fit Function                                                  0.1802
  Goodness of Fit Index (GFI)                                   0.9596
  GFI Adjusted for Degrees of Freedom (AGFI)                    0.9242
  Root Mean Square Residual (RMR)                               0.0436
  Parsimonious GFI (Mulaik, 1989)                               0.6397
  Chi-Square                                                   38.1963
  Chi-Square DF                                                     24
  Pr > Chi-Square                                               0.0331
  Independence Model Chi-Square                                 1101.9
  Independence Model Chi-Square DF                                  36
  RMSEA Estimate                                                0.0528
  RMSEA 90% Lower Confidence Limit                              0.0153
  RMSEA 90% Upper Confidence Limit                              0.0831
  ECVI Estimate                                                 0.3881
  ECVI 90% Lower Confidence Limit                                    .
  ECVI 90% Upper Confidence Limit                               0.4888
  Probability of Close Fit                                      0.4088
  Bentler's Comparative Fit Index                               0.9867
  Normal Theory Reweighted LS Chi-Square                       40.1947
  Akaike's Information Criterion                               -9.8037
  Bozdogan's (1987) CAIC                                     -114.4747
  Schwarz's Bayesian Criterion                                -90.4747
  McDonald's (1989) Centrality                                  0.9672
  Bentler & Bonett's (1980) Non-normed Index                    0.9800
  Bentler & Bonett's (1980) NFI                                 0.9653
  James, Mulaik, & Brett (1982) Parsimonious NFI                0.6436
  Z-Test of Wilson & Hilferty (1931)                            1.8373
  Bollen (1986) Normed Index Rho1                               0.9480
  Bollen (1988) Non-normed Index Delta2                         0.9868
  Hoelter's (1983) Critical N                                      204
```

```
      Example of THURSTONE resp. McDONALD (1985, p.57, p.105)
        Identified Second Order Confirmatory Factor Analysis
C = F1 * F2 * P * F2' * F1' + F1 * U2 * F1' + U1, With P=U2=Ide

                        The CALIS Procedure
   Covariance Structure Analysis: Maximum Likelihood Estimation

            Obs1     =   0.5151*F1      +  1.0000 E1
            Std Err      0.0629 X1
            t Value      8.1868
            Obs2     =   0.5203*F1      +  1.0000 E2
            Std Err      0.0634 X2
            t Value      8.2090
            Obs3     =   0.4874*F1      +  1.0000 E3
            Std Err      0.0608 X3
            t Value      8.0151
            Obs4     =   0.5211*F2      +  1.0000 E4
            Std Err      0.0611 X4
            t Value      8.5342
            Obs5     =   0.4971*F2      +  1.0000 E5
            Std Err      0.0590 X5
            t Value      8.4213
            Obs6     =   0.4381*F2      +  1.0000 E6
            Std Err      0.0560 X6
            t Value      7.8283
            Obs7     =   0.4524*F3      +  1.0000 E7
            Std Err      0.0660 X7
            t Value      6.8584
            Obs8     =   0.4173*F3      +  1.0000 E8
            Std Err      0.0622 X8
            t Value      6.7135
            Obs9     =   0.4076*F3      +  1.0000 E9
            Std Err      0.0613 X9
            t Value      6.6484


      Example of THURSTONE resp. McDONALD (1985, p.57, p.105)
        Identified Second Order Confirmatory Factor Analysis
C = F1 * F2 * P * F2' * F1' + F1 * U2 * F1' + U1, With P=U2=Ide

                        The CALIS Procedure
   Covariance Structure Analysis: Maximum Likelihood Estimation

            F1       =   1.4438*F4      +  1.0000 E10
            Std Err      0.2565 X10
            t Value      5.6282
            F2       =   1.2538*F4      +  1.0000 E11
            Std Err      0.2114 X11
            t Value      5.9320
            F3       =   1.4065*F4      +  1.0000 E12
            Std Err      0.2689 X12
            t Value      5.2307
```

Example of THURSTONE resp. McDONALD (1985, p.57, p.105)
Identified Second Order Confirmatory Factor Analysis
C = F1 * F2 * P * F2' * F1' + F1 * U2 * F1' + U1, With P=U2=Ide

The CALIS Procedure
Covariance Structure Analysis: Maximum Likelihood Estimation

Variances of Exogenous Variables

Variable	Parameter	Estimate	Standard Error	t Value
F4		1.00000		
E1	U11	0.18150	0.02848	6.37
E2	U12	0.16493	0.02777	5.94
E3	U13	0.26713	0.03336	8.01
E4	U14	0.30150	0.05102	5.91
E5	U15	0.36450	0.05264	6.93
E6	U16	0.50642	0.05963	8.49
E7	U17	0.39032	0.05934	6.58
E8	U18	0.48138	0.06225	7.73
E9	U19	0.50509	0.06333	7.98
E10		1.00000		
E11		1.00000		
E12		1.00000		

```
      Example of THURSTONE resp. McDONALD (1985, p.57, p.105)
        Identified Second Order Confirmatory Factor Analysis
 C = F1 * F2 * P * F2' * F1' + F1 * U2 * F1' + U1, With P=U2=Ide

                         The CALIS Procedure
   Covariance Structure Analysis: Maximum Likelihood Estimation

                Obs1     =    0.9047*F1    +  0.4260 E1
                                 X1
                Obs2     =    0.9138*F1    +  0.4061 E2
                                 X2
                Obs3     =    0.8561*F1    +  0.5168 E3
                                 X3
                Obs4     =    0.8358*F2    +  0.5491 E4
                                 X4
                Obs5     =    0.7972*F2    +  0.6037 E5
                                 X5
                Obs6     =    0.7026*F2    +  0.7116 E6
                                 X6
                Obs7     =    0.7808*F3    +  0.6248 E7
                                 X7
                Obs8     =    0.7202*F3    +  0.6938 E8
                                 X8
                Obs9     =    0.7035*F3    +  0.7107 E9
                                 X9



      Example of THURSTONE resp. McDONALD (1985, p.57, p.105)
        Identified Second Order Confirmatory Factor Analysis
 C = F1 * F2 * P * F2' * F1' + F1 * U2 * F1' + U1, With P=U2=Ide

                         The CALIS Procedure
   Covariance Structure Analysis: Maximum Likelihood Estimation

                F1       =    0.8221*F4    +  0.5694 E10
                                 X10
                F2       =    0.7818*F4    +  0.6235 E11
                                 X11
                F3       =    0.8150*F4    +  0.5794 E12
                                 X12
```

```
          Example of THURSTONE resp. McDONALD (1985, p.57, p.105)
            Identified Second Order Confirmatory Factor Analysis
      C = F1 * F2 * P * F2' * F1' + F1 * U2 * F1' + U1, With P=U2=Ide

                            The CALIS Procedure
        Covariance Structure Analysis: Maximum Likelihood Estimation

                      Squared Multiple Correlations

                                   Error          Total
              Variable          Variance       Variance       R-Square

         1    Obs1               0.18150        1.00000         0.8185
         2    Obs2               0.16493        1.00000         0.8351
         3    Obs3               0.26713        1.00000         0.7329
         4    Obs4               0.30150        1.00000         0.6985
         5    Obs5               0.36450        1.00000         0.6355
         6    Obs6               0.50642        1.00000         0.4936
         7    Obs7               0.39032        1.00000         0.6097
         8    Obs8               0.48138        1.00000         0.5186
         9    Obs9               0.50509        1.00000         0.4949
        10    F1                 1.00000        3.08452         0.6758
        11    F2                 1.00000        2.57213         0.6112
        12    F3                 1.00000        2.97832         0.6642
```

To compute McDonald's unidentified model, you would have to change the STD and BOUNDS statements to include three more parameters:

```
Std
   F4       = 1. ,
   E1-E9    = U11-U19 ,
   E10-E12  = U21-U23 ;
Bounds
   0. <= U11-U19,
   0. <= U21-U23;
```

The unidentified model is indicated in the output by an analysis of the linear dependencies in the approximate Hessian matrix (not shown). Because the information matrix is singular, standard errors are computed based on a Moore-Penrose inverse. The results computed by PROC CALIS differ from those reported by McDonald (1985). In the case of an unidentified model, the parameter estimates are not unique.

To specify the identified model using the COSAN model statement, you can use the following statements:

```
Title2 "Identified Second Order Confirmatory Factor Analysis Using COSAN";
Title3 "C = F1*F2*P*F2'*F1' + F1*U2*F1' + U1, With P=U2=Ide";
proc calis data=Thurst method=max edf=212 pestim se;
   Cosan F1(3) * F2(1) * P(1,Ide) + F1(3) * U2(3,Ide) + U1(9,Dia);
   Matrix F1
          [ ,1] = X1-X3,
          [ ,2] = 3 * 0. X4-X6,
          [ ,3] = 6 * 0. X7-X9;
   Matrix F2
          [ ,1] = X10-X12;
```

```
    Matrix U1
           [1,1] = U11-U19;
    Bounds
           0. <= U11-U19;
run;
```

Because PROC CALIS cannot compute initial estimates for a model specified by the general COSAN statement, this analysis may require more iterations than one using the LINEQS statement, depending on the precision of the processor.

Example 19.4. Linear Relations Among Factor Loadings

The correlation matrix from Kinzer and Kinzer (N=326) is used by Guttman (1957) as an example that yields an approximate simplex. McDonald (1980) uses this data set as an example of factor analysis where he supposes that the loadings of the second factor are a linear function of the loadings on the first factor, for example

$$b_{j2} = \alpha + \beta b_{j1}, \quad j = 1, \ldots, n$$

This example is also discussed in Browne (1982). The matrix specification of the model is

$$\mathbf{C} = \mathbf{F}_1 \mathbf{F}_1'$$

with

$$F_1 = \begin{pmatrix} b_{11} & \alpha + \beta b_{11} & u_{11} & & & & & \\ b_{21} & \alpha + \beta b_{21} & & u_{22} & & & & \\ b_{31} & \alpha + \beta b_{31} & & & u_{33} & & & \\ b_{41} & \alpha + \beta b_{41} & & & & u_{44} & & \\ b_{51} & \alpha + \beta b_{51} & & & & & u_{55} & \\ b_{61} & \alpha + \beta b_{61} & & & & & & u_{66} \end{pmatrix}$$

This example is recomputed by PROC CALIS to illustrate a simple application of the COSAN model statement combined with program statements. This example also serves to illustrate the identification problem.

```
data Kinzer(TYPE=CORR);
Title "Data Matrix of Kinzer & Kinzer, see GUTTMAN (1957)";
   _TYPE_ = 'CORR'; INPUT _NAME_ $ Obs1-Obs6;
   datalines;
Obs1  1.00    .     .     .     .     .
Obs2   .51  1.00    .     .     .     .
Obs3   .46   .51  1.00    .     .     .
Obs4   .46   .47   .54  1.00    .     .
Obs5   .40   .39   .49   .57  1.00    .
Obs6   .33   .39   .47   .45   .56  1.00
;
```

In a first test run of PROC CALIS, the same model is used as reported in McDonald (1980). Using the Levenberg-Marquardt optimization algorithm, this example specifies maximum likelihood estimation in the following code:

```
proc calis data=Kinzer method=max outram=ram nobs=326;
   Title2 "Linearly Related Factor Analysis, (Mcdonald,1980)";
   Title3 "Identification Problem";
   Cosan F(8,Gen) * I(8,Ide);
   Matrix F
          [ ,1]= X1-X6,
          [ ,2]= X7-X12,
          [1,3]= X13-X18;
   Parms Alfa = .5 Beta = -.5;
      X7  = Alfa + Beta * X1;
      X8  = Alfa + Beta * X2;
      X9  = Alfa + Beta * X3;
      X10 = Alfa + Beta * X4;
      X11 = Alfa + Beta * X5;
      X12 = Alfa + Beta * X6;
   Bounds X13-X18 >= 0.;
   Vnames F Fact1 Fact2 Uvar1-Uvar6;
run;
```

The pattern of the initial values is displayed in vector and in matrix form. You should always read this output very carefully, particularly when you use your own programming statements to constrain the matrix elements. The vector form shows the mapping of the model parameters to indices of the vector X that is optimized. The matrix form indicates parameter elements that are constrained by program statements by indices of X in angle brackets (< >). An asterisk trailing the iteration number in the displayed optimization history of the Levenberg-Marquardt algorithm indicates that the optimization process encountered a singular Hessian matrix. When this happens, especially in the last iterations, the model may not be properly identified. The computed χ^2 value of 10.337 for 7 degrees of freedom and the computed unique loadings agree with those reported by McDonald (1980), but the maximum likelihood estimates for the common factor loadings differ to some degree. The common factor loadings can be subjected to transformations that do not increase the value of the optimization criterion because the problem is not identified. An estimation problem that is not fully identified can lead to different solutions caused only by different initial values, different optimization techniques, or computers with different machine precision or floating-point arithmetic.

To overcome the identification problem in the first model, restart PROC CALIS with a simple modification to the model in which the former parameter X1 is fixed to 0. This leads to 8 instead of 7 degrees of freedom. The following code produces results that are partially displayed in Output 19.4.1.

```
data ram2(TYPE=RAM); set ram;
   if _type_ = 'ESTIM' then
      if _name_ = 'X1' then do;
         _name_ = ' '; _estim_ = 0.;
      end;
run;

proc calis data=Kinzer method=max inram=ram2 nobs=326;
   Title2 "Linearly Related Factor Analysis, (Mcdonald,1980)";
   Title3 "Identified Model";
   Parms Alfa = .5 Beta = -.5;
      X7  = Alfa;
      X8  = Alfa + Beta * X2;
      X9  = Alfa + Beta * X3;
      X10 = Alfa + Beta * X4;
      X11 = Alfa + Beta * X5;
      X12 = Alfa + Beta * X6;
   Bounds X13-X18 >= 0.;
run;
```

Output 19.4.1. Linearly Related Factor Analysis: Identification Problem

```
                     Data Matrix of Kinzer & Kinzer, see GUTTMAN (1957)
                     Linearly Related Factor Analysis, (Mcdonald,1980)
                                      Identified Model

                                    The CALIS Procedure
                 Covariance Structure Analysis: Pattern and Initial Values

                                   COSAN Model Statement


                             Matrix     Rows    Columns     ------Matrix Type-------

        Term 1          1    F             6          8     GENERAL
                        2    I             8          8     IDENTITY


                     Data Matrix of Kinzer & Kinzer, see GUTTMAN (1957)
                     Linearly Related Factor Analysis, (Mcdonald,1980)
                                      Identified Model

                                    The CALIS Procedure
                Covariance Structure Analysis: Maximum Likelihood Estimation

                        Parameter Estimates                  13
                        Functions (Observations)             21
                        Lower Bounds                          6
                        Upper Bounds                          0

                                   Optimization Start

Active Constraints                          0  Objective Function              0.3234289189
Max Abs Gradient Element         2.2633860283  Radius                          5.8468569273
```

Data Matrix of Kinzer & Kinzer, see GUTTMAN (1957)
Linearly Related Factor Analysis, (Mcdonald,1980)
Identified Model

The CALIS Procedure
Covariance Structure Analysis: Maximum Likelihood Estimation

Iter	Restarts	Function Calls	Active Constraints	Objective Function	Objective Function Change	Max Abs Gradient Element	Lambda	Ratio Between Actual and Predicted Change
1	0	2	0	0.07994	0.2435	0.3984	0	0.557
2	0	3	0	0.03334	0.0466	0.0672	0	1.202
3	0	4	0	0.03185	0.00150	0.00439	0	1.058
4	0	5	0	0.03181	0.000034	0.00236	0	0.811
5	0	6	0	0.03181	3.982E-6	0.000775	0	0.591
6	0	7	0	0.03181	9.275E-7	0.000490	0	0.543
7	0	8	0	0.03181	2.402E-7	0.000206	0	0.526
8	0	9	0	0.03181	6.336E-8	0.000129	0	0.514
9	0	10	0	0.03181	1.687E-8	0.000054	0	0.505
10	0	11	0	0.03181	4.521E-9	0.000034	0	0.498
11	0	12	0	0.03181	1.217E-9	0.000014	0	0.493
12	0	13	0	0.03181	3.29E-10	8.971E-6	0	0.489

Optimization Results

Iterations	12	Function Calls	14
Jacobian Calls	13	Active Constraints	0
Objective Function	0.0318073951	Max Abs Gradient Element	8.9711916E-6
Lambda	0	Actual Over Pred Change	0.4888109559
Radius	0.0002016088		

ABSGCONV convergence criterion satisfied.

```
Data Matrix of Kinzer & Kinzer, see GUTTMAN (1957)
Linearly Related Factor Analysis, (Mcdonald,1980)
Identified Model

The CALIS Procedure
Covariance Structure Analysis: Maximum Likelihood Estimation

Fit Function                                              0.0318
Goodness of Fit Index (GFI)                               0.9897
GFI Adjusted for Degrees of Freedom (AGFI)                0.9730
Root Mean Square Residual (RMR)                           0.0409
Parsimonious GFI (Mulaik, 1989)                           0.5278
Chi-Square                                               10.3374
Chi-Square DF                                                  8
Pr > Chi-Square                                           0.2421
Independence Model Chi-Square                             682.87
Independence Model Chi-Square DF                              15
RMSEA Estimate                                            0.0300
RMSEA 90% Lower Confidence Limit                               .
RMSEA 90% Upper Confidence Limit                          0.0756
ECVI Estimate                                             0.1136
ECVI 90% Lower Confidence Limit                                .
ECVI 90% Upper Confidence Limit                           0.1525
Probability of Close Fit                                  0.7137
Bentler's Comparative Fit Index                           0.9965
Normal Theory Reweighted LS Chi-Square                   10.1441
Akaike's Information Criterion                           -5.6626
Bozdogan's (1987) CAIC                                  -43.9578
Schwarz's Bayesian Criterion                            -35.9578
McDonald's (1989) Centrality                              0.9964
Bentler & Bonett's (1980) Non-normed Index                0.9934
Bentler & Bonett's (1980) NFI                             0.9849
James, Mulaik, & Brett (1982) Parsimonious NFI            0.5253
Z-Test of Wilson & Hilferty (1931)                        0.7019
Bollen (1986) Normed Index Rho1                           0.9716
Bollen (1988) Non-normed Index Delta2                     0.9965
Hoelter's (1983) Critical N                                  489
```

Data Matrix of Kinzer & Kinzer, see GUTTMAN (1957)
Linearly Related Factor Analysis, (Mcdonald,1980)
Identified Model

The CALIS Procedure
Covariance Structure Analysis: Maximum Likelihood Estimation

Estimated Parameter Matrix F[6:8]
Standard Errors and t Values
General Matrix

	Fact1	Fact2	Uvar1	Uvar2	Uvar3	Uvar4	Uvar5	Uvar6
Obs1	0	0.7151	0.7283	0	0	0	0	0
	0	0.0405	0.0408	0	0	0	0	0
	0	17.6382	17.8276	0	0	0	0	0
		<X7>	[X13]					
Obs2	-0.0543	0.7294	0	0.6707	0	0	0	0
	0.1042	0.0438	0	0.0472	0	0	0	0
	-0.5215	16.6655	0	14.2059	0	0	0	0
	[X2]	<X8>		[X14]				
Obs3	0.1710	0.6703	0	0	0.6983	0	0	0
	0.0845	0.0396	0	0	0.0324	0	0	0
	2.0249	16.9077	0	0	21.5473	0	0	0
	[X3]	<X9>			[X15]			
Obs4	0.2922	0.6385	0	0	0	0.6876	0	0
	0.0829	0.0462	0	0	0	0.0319	0	0
	3.5224	13.8352	0	0	0	21.5791	0	0
	[X4]	<X10>				[X16]		
Obs5	0.5987	0.5582	0	0	0	0	0.5579	0
	0.1003	0.0730	0	0	0	0	0.0798	0
	5.9665	7.6504	0	0	0	0	6.9938	0
	[X5]	<X11>					[X17]	
Obs6	0.4278	0.6029	0	0	0	0	0	0.7336
	0.0913	0.0586	0	0	0	0	0	0.0400
	4.6844	10.2928	0	0	0	0	0	18.3580
	[X6]	<X12>						[X18]

Data Matrix of Kinzer & Kinzer, see GUTTMAN (1957)
Linearly Related Factor Analysis, (Mcdonald,1980)
Identified Model

The CALIS Procedure
Covariance Structure Analysis: Maximum Likelihood Estimation

Additional PARMS and Dependent Parameters

The Number of Dependent Parameters is 6

Parameter	Estimate	Standard Error	t Value
Alfa	0.71511	0.04054	17.64
Beta	-0.26217	0.12966	-2.02
X7	0.71511	0.04054	17.64
X8	0.72936	0.04376	16.67
X9	0.67027	0.03964	16.91
X10	0.63851	0.04615	13.84
X11	0.55815	0.07296	7.65
X12	0.60295	0.05858	10.29

The lambda value of the iteration history indicates that Newton steps can always be performed. Because no singular Hessian matrices (which can slow down the convergence rate considerably) are computed, this example needs just 12 iterations compared to the 17 needed in the previous example. Note that the number of iterations may be machine-dependent. The value of the fit funciton, the residuals, and the χ^2 value agree with the values obtained in fitting the first model. This indicates that this second model is better identified than the first one. It is fully identified, as indicated by the fact that the Hessian matrix is nonsingular.

Example 19.5. Ordinal Relations Among Factor Loadings

McDonald (1980) uses the same data set to compute a factor analysis with ordinally constrained factor loadings. The results of the linearly constrained factor analysis show that the loadings of the two factors are ordered as 2, 1, 3, 4, 6, 5. McDonald (1980) then tests the hypothesis that the factor loadings are all nonnegative and can be ordered in the following manner:

$$b_{11} \leq b_{21} \leq b_{31} \leq b_{41} \leq b_{51} \leq b_{61}$$

$$b_{12} \geq b_{22} \geq b_{32} \geq b_{42} \geq b_{52} \geq b_{62}$$

This example is recomputed by PROC CALIS to illustrate a further application of the COSAN model statement combined with program statements. The same identification problem as in Example 19.4 on page 611 occurs here. The following model specification describes an unidentified model:

```
proc calis data=Kinzer method=max outram=ram tech=nr nobs=326;
Title2 "Ordinally Related Factor Analysis, (Mcdonald,1980)";
Title3 "Identification Problem";
Cosan F(8,Gen) * I(8,Ide);
   MATRIX F
      [,1]  = x1-x6,
      [,2]  = x7-x12,
      [1,3] = x13-x18;
   PARAMETERS t1-t10=1.;
      x2  = x1  + t1  * t1;
      x3  = x2  + t2  * t2;
      x4  = x3  + t3  * t3;
      x5  = x4  + t4  * t4;
      x6  = x5  + t5  * t5;
      x11 = x12 + t6  * t6;
      x10 = x11 + t7  * t7;
      x9  = x10 + t8  * t8;
      x8  = x9  + t9  * t9;
      x7  = x8  + t10 * t10;
   Bounds x13-x18 >= 0.;
   Vnames F Fact1 Fact2 Uvar1-Uvar6;
run;
```

You can specify the same model with the LINCON statement:

```
proc calis data=Kinzer method=max tech=lm edf=325;
   Title3 "Identified Problem 2";
   cosan f(8,gen)*I(8,ide);
   matrix F
      [,1]   = x1-x6,
      [,2]   = x7-x12,
      [1,3]  = x13-x18;
   lincon  x1   <= x2,
           x2   <= x3,
           x3   <= x4,
           x4   <= x5,
           x5   <= x6,
           x7   >= x8,
           x8   >= x9,
           x9   >= x10,
           x10  >= x11,
           x11  >= x12;
   Bounds x13-x18 >= 0.;
   Vnames F Fact1 Fact2 Uvar1-Uvar6;
run;
```

To have an identified model, the loading, b_{11} (x1), is fixed at 0. The information in the OUTRAM= data set (the data set ram), produced by the unidentified model, can be used to specify the identified model. However, because x1 is now a fixed constant in the identified model, it should not have a parameter name in the new analysis. Thus, the data set ram is modified as follows:

```
data ram2(type=ram); set ram;
   if _name_ = 'x1' then do;
      _name_ = ' '; _estim_ = 0.;
   end;
run;
```

The data set ram2 is now an OUTRAM= data set in which x1 is no longer a parameter. PROC CALIS reads the information (that is, the set of parameters and the model specification) in the data set ram2 for the identified model. As displayed in the following code, you can use the PARMS statement to specify the desired ordinal relationships between the parameters.

```
proc calis data=Kinzer method=max inram=ram2 tech=nr nobs=326;
   title2 "Ordinally Related Factor Analysis, (Mcdonald,1980)";
   title3 "Identified Model with X1=0";
   parms t1-t10= 10 * 1.;
      x2   =      + t1   * t1;
      x3   = x2   + t2   * t2;
      x4   = x3   + t3   * t3;
      x5   = x4   + t4   * t4;
      x6   = x5   + t5   * t5;
```

```
         x11 = x12 + t6  * t6;
         x10 = x11 + t7  * t7;
         x9  = x10 + t8  * t8;
         x8  = x9  + t9  * t9;
         x7  = x8  + t10 * t10;
      bounds x13-x18 >= 0.;
   run;
```

Selected output for the identified model is displayed in Output 19.5.1.

Output 19.5.1. Factor Analysis with Ordinal Constraints

```
                    Data Matrix of Kinzer & Kinzer, see GUTTMAN (1957)
                    Ordinally Related Factor Analysis, (Mcdonald,1980)
                             Identified Model with X1=0

                                 The CALIS Procedure
                 Covariance Structure Analysis: Maximum Likelihood Estimation

                         Parameter Estimates                  17
                         Functions (Observations)             21
                         Lower Bounds                          6
                         Upper Bounds                          0

                                 Optimization Start

 Active Constraints                             0  Objective Function                   5.2552270182
 Max Abs Gradient Element              0.8821788922
```

Iter	Restarts	Function Calls	Active Constraints	Objective Function	Objective Function Change	Max Abs Gradient Element	Ridge	Ratio Between Actual and Predicted Change
1	0	2	0	3.14901	2.1062	1.0712	0	2.226
2	0	3	0	1.42725	1.7218	1.0902	0	2.064
3	0	4	0	0.41661	1.0106	0.7472	0	1.731
4	0	5	0	0.09260	0.3240	0.3365	0	1.314
5	0	6	0	0.09186	0.000731	0.3880	0	0.0123
6	0	8	0	0.04570	0.0462	0.2870	0.0313	0.797
7	0	10	0	0.03269	0.0130	0.0909	0.0031	0.739
8	0	16	0	0.02771	0.00498	0.0890	0.0800	0.682
9	0	17	0	0.02602	0.00168	0.0174	0.0400	0.776
10	0	19	0	0.02570	0.000323	0.0141	0.0800	0.630
11	0	21	0	0.02560	0.000103	0.00179	0.160	1.170
12	0	23	0	0.02559	7.587E-6	0.000670	0.160	1.423
13	0	24	0	0.02559	2.993E-6	0.000402	0.0400	1.010
14	0	27	0	0.02559	1.013E-6	0.000206	0.160	1.388
15	0	28	0	0.02559	1.889E-7	0.000202	0.0400	0.530
16	0	30	0	0.02559	1.803E-7	0.000097	0.0800	0.630
17	0	32	0	0.02559	4.845E-8	0.000035	0.160	1.340
18	0	33	0	0.02559	1.837E-9	0.000049	0.0400	0.125
19	0	35	0	0.02559	9.39E-9	0.000024	0.0800	0.579
20	0	37	0	0.02559	2.558E-9	6.176E-6	0.160	1.305

```
                                Optimization Results

 Iterations                                    20  Function Calls                               38
 Jacobian Calls                                21  Active Constraints                            0
 Objective Function                  0.0255871615  Max Abs Gradient Element           6.1764582E-6
 Ridge                                       0.04  Actual Over Pred Change            1.3054374955

     ABSGCONV convergence criterion satisfied.
```

```
        Data Matrix of Kinzer & Kinzer, see GUTTMAN (1957)
        Ordinally Related Factor Analysis, (Mcdonald,1980)
                    Identified Model with X1=0

                       The CALIS Procedure
   Covariance Structure Analysis: Maximum Likelihood Estimation

   Fit Function                                             0.0256
   Goodness of Fit Index (GFI)                              0.9916
   GFI Adjusted for Degrees of Freedom (AGFI)               0.9557
   Root Mean Square Residual (RMR)                          0.0180
   Parsimonious GFI (Mulaik, 1989)                          0.2644
   Chi-Square                                               8.3158
   Chi-Square DF                                                 4
   Pr > Chi-Square                                          0.0807
   Independence Model Chi-Square                            682.87
   Independence Model Chi-Square DF                             15
   RMSEA Estimate                                           0.0576
   RMSEA 90% Lower Confidence Limit                              .
   RMSEA 90% Upper Confidence Limit                         0.1133
   ECVI Estimate                                            0.1325
   ECVI 90% Lower Confidence Limit                               .
   ECVI 90% Upper Confidence Limit                          0.1711
   Probability of Close Fit                                 0.3399
   Bentler's Comparative Fit Index                          0.9935
   Normal Theory Reweighted LS Chi-Square                   8.2901
   Akaike's Information Criterion                           0.3158
   Bozdogan's (1987) CAIC                                 -18.8318
   Schwarz's Bayesian Criterion                           -14.8318
   McDonald's (1989) Centrality                             0.9934
   Bentler & Bonett's (1980) Non-normed Index               0.9758
   Bentler & Bonett's (1980) NFI                            0.9878
   James, Mulaik, & Brett (1982) Parsimonious NFI           0.2634
   Z-Test of Wilson & Hilferty (1931)                       1.4079
   Bollen (1986) Normed Index Rho1                          0.9543
   Bollen (1988) Non-normed Index Delta2                    0.9936
   Hoelter's (1983) Critical N                                 372
```

Data Matrix of Kinzer & Kinzer, see GUTTMAN (1957)
Ordinally Related Factor Analysis, (Mcdonald,1980)
Identified Model with X1=0

The CALIS Procedure
Covariance Structure Analysis: Maximum Likelihood Estimation

Estimated Parameter Matrix F[6:8]
Standard Errors and t Values
General Matrix

	Fact1	Fact2	Uvar1	Uvar2	Uvar3	Uvar4	Uvar5	Uvar6
Obs1	0	0.7101	0.7131	0	0	0	0	0
	0	0.0435	0.0404	0	0	0	0	0
	0	16.3317	17.6427	0	0	0	0	0
		<x7>	[x13]					
Obs2	0.0261	0.7101	0	0.6950	0	0	0	0
	0.0875	0.0435	0	0.0391	0	0	0	0
	0.2977	16.3317	0	17.7571	0	0	0	0
	<x2>	<x8>		[x14]				
Obs3	0.2382	0.6827	0	0	0.6907	0	0	0
	0.0851	0.0604	0	0	0.0338	0	0	0
	2.7998	11.3110	0	0	20.4239	0	0	0
	<x3>	<x9>			[x15]			
Obs4	0.3252	0.6580	0	0	0	0.6790	0	0
	0.0823	0.0621	0	0	0	0.0331	0	0
	3.9504	10.5950	0	0	0	20.5361	0	0
	<x4>	<x10>				[x16]		
Obs5	0.5395	0.5528	0	0	0	0	0.6249	0
	0.0901	0.0705	0	0	0	0	0.0534	0
	5.9887	7.8359	0	0	0	0	11.7052	0
	<x5>	<x11>					[x17]	
Obs6	0.5395	0.4834	0	0	0	0	0	0.7005
	0.0918	0.0726	0	0	0	0	0	0.0524
	5.8776	6.6560	0	0	0	0	0	13.3749
	<x6>	[x12]						[x18]

```
                Data Matrix of Kinzer & Kinzer, see GUTTMAN (1957)
                Ordinally Related Factor Analysis, (Mcdonald,1980)
                            Identified Model with X1=0

                               The CALIS Procedure
           Covariance Structure Analysis: Maximum Likelihood Estimation

                    Additional PARMS and Dependent Parameters

                     The Number of Dependent Parameters is 10

                                                 Standard
                 Parameter        Estimate          Error     t Value

                 t1                0.16143        0.27111        0.60
                 t2                0.46060        0.09289        4.96
                 t3                0.29496        0.13702        2.15
                 t4                0.46297        0.10756        4.30
                 t5              0.0000522           1311        0.00
                 t6                0.26347        0.12203        2.16
                 t7                0.32430        0.09965        3.25
                 t8                0.15721        0.21134        0.74
                 t9                0.16543        0.20537        0.81
                 t10             -4.2528E-7       0.47736       -0.00
                 x7                0.71007        0.04348       16.33
                 x2                0.02606        0.08753        0.30
                 x8                0.71007        0.04348       16.33
                 x3                0.23821        0.08508        2.80
                 x9                0.68270        0.06036       11.31
                 x4                0.32521        0.08232        3.95
                 x10               0.65799        0.06210       10.60
                 x5                0.53955        0.09009        5.99
                 x11               0.55282        0.07055        7.84
                 x6                0.53955        0.09180        5.88
```

By fixing the loading b_{11} (x1) to constant 0, you obtain $\chi^2 = 8.316$ on $df = 4$ ($p < .09$). McDonald reports the same χ^2 value, but on $df = 3$, and thus, he obtains a smaller p-value. An analysis without the fixed loading shows typical signs of an unidentified problem: after more iterations it leads to a parameter set with a χ^2 value of 8.174 on $df = 3$. A singular Hessian matrix occurs.

The singular Hessian matrix of the unidentified problem slows down the convergence rate of the Levenberg-Marquardt algorithm considerably. Compared to the unidentified problem with 30 iterations, the identified problem needs only 20 iterations. Note that the number of iterations may depend on the precision of the processor.

The same model can also be specified using the LINCON statement for linear constraints:

```
proc calis data=Kinzer method=max tech=lm edf=325;
   Title3 "Identified Model 2";
   cosan f(8,gen)*I(8,ide);
   matrix f
      [,1]  = 0. x2-x6,
      [,2]  = x7-x12,
      [1,3] = x13-x18;
```

```
   lincon  x2  <= x3,
           x3  <= x4,
           x4  <= x5,
           x5  <= x6,
           x7  >= x8,
           x8  >= x9,
           x9  >= x10,
           x10 >= x11,
           x11 >= x12;
   bounds x2 x13-x18 >= 0.;
run;
```

Example 19.6. Longitudinal Factor Analysis

The following example (McDonald 1980) illustrates both the ability of PROC CALIS to formulate complex covariance structure analysis problems by the generalized COSAN matrix model and the use of program statements to impose nonlinear constraints on the parameters. The example is a longitudinal factor analysis using the Swaminathan (1974) model. For $m = 3$ tests, $k = 3$ occasions, and $r = 2$ factors the matrix model is formulated in the section "First-Order Autoregressive Longitudinal Factor Model" on page 443 as follows:

$$\mathbf{C} = \mathbf{F}_1\mathbf{F}_2\mathbf{F}_3\mathbf{L}\mathbf{F}_3^{-1}\mathbf{F}_2^{-1}\mathbf{P}(\mathbf{F}_2^{-1})'(\mathbf{F}_3^{-1})'\mathbf{L}'\mathbf{F}_3'\mathbf{F}_2'\mathbf{F}_1' + \mathbf{U}^2$$

$$F_1 = \begin{pmatrix} B_1 & & \\ & B_2 & \\ & & B_3 \end{pmatrix}, \quad F_2 = \begin{pmatrix} I_2 & & \\ & D_2 & \\ & & D_2 \end{pmatrix}, \quad F_3 = \begin{pmatrix} I_2 & & \\ & I_2 & \\ & & D_3 \end{pmatrix}$$

$$L = \begin{pmatrix} I_2 & o & o \\ I_2 & I_2 & o \\ I_2 & I_2 & I_2 \end{pmatrix}, \quad P = \begin{pmatrix} I_2 & & \\ & S_2 & \\ & & S_3 \end{pmatrix}, \quad U = \begin{pmatrix} U_{11} & U_{12} & U_{13} \\ U_{21} & U_{22} & U_{23} \\ U_{31} & U_{32} & U_{33} \end{pmatrix}$$

$$S_2 = I_2 - D_2^2, \qquad S_3 = I_2 - D_3^2$$

The Swaminathan longitudinal factor model assumes that the factor scores for each (m) common factor change from occasion to occasion (k) according to a first-order autoregressive scheme. The matrix $\mathbf{F}_1$ contains the k factor loading matrices $\mathbf{B}_1, \mathbf{B}_2, \mathbf{B}_3$ (each is $n \times m$). The matrices $\mathbf{D}_2, \mathbf{D}_3, \mathbf{S}_2, \mathbf{S}_3$ and $\mathbf{U}_{ij}, i, j = 1, \ldots, k$, are diagonal, and the matrices $\mathbf{D}_i$ and $\mathbf{S}_i, i = 2, \ldots, k$, are subjected to the constraint

$$\mathbf{S}_i + \mathbf{D}_i^2 = \mathbf{I}$$

Since the constructed correlation matrix given in McDonald's (1980) paper is singular, only unweighted least-squares estimates can be computed.

```
data Mcdon(TYPE=CORR);
Title "Swaminathan's Longitudinal Factor Model, Data: McDONALD(1980)";
Title2 "Constructed Singular Correlation Matrix, GLS & ML not possible";
   _TYPE_ = 'CORR'; INPUT _NAME_ $ Obs1-Obs9;
   datalines;
Obs1  1.000    .      .      .      .      .      .      .      .
Obs2   .100  1.000    .      .      .      .      .      .      .
Obs3   .250   .400  1.000    .      .      .      .      .      .
Obs4   .720   .108   .270  1.000    .      .      .      .      .
Obs5   .135   .740   .380   .180  1.000    .      .      .      .
Obs6   .270   .318   .800   .360   .530  1.000    .      .      .
Obs7   .650   .054   .135   .730   .090   .180  1.000    .      .
Obs8   .108   .690   .196   .144   .700   .269   .200  1.000    .
Obs9   .189   .202   .710   .252   .336   .760   .350   .580  1.000
  ;

proc calis data=Mcdon method=ls tech=nr nobs=100;
cosan B(6,Gen) * D1(6,Dia) * D2(6,Dia) * T(6,Low) * D3(6,Dia,Inv) *
                 D4(6,Dia,Inv) * P(6,Dia) + U(9,Sym);
   Matrix B
            [ ,1]= X1-X3,
            [ ,2]= 0. X4-X5,
            [ ,3]= 3 * 0. X6-X8,
            [ ,4]= 4 * 0. X9-X10,
            [ ,5]= 6 * 0. X11-X13,
            [ ,6]= 7 * 0. X14-X15;
   Matrix D1
            [1,1]= 2 * 1. X16 X17 X16 X17;
   Matrix D2
            [1,1]= 4 * 1. X18 X19;
   Matrix T
            [1,1]= 6 * 1.,
            [3,1]= 4 * 1.,
            [5,1]= 2 * 1.;
   Matrix D3
            [1,1]= 4 * 1. X18 X19;
   Matrix D4
            [1,1]= 2 * 1. X16 X17 X16 X17;
   Matrix P
            [1,1]= 2 * 1. X20-X23;
   Matrix U
            [1,1]= X24-X32,
            [4,1]= X33-X38,
            [7,1]= X39-X41;
   Bounds 0. <= X24-X32,
         -1. <= X16-X19 <= 1.;
   X20 = 1. - X16 * X16;
   X21 = 1. - X17 * X17;
   X22 = 1. - X18 * X18;
   X23 = 1. - X19 * X19;
run;
```

Because this formulation of Swaminathan's model in general leads to an unidentified problem, the results given here are different from those reported by McDonald (1980). The displayed output of PROC CALIS also indicates that the fitted central model matrices **P** and **U** are not positive definite. The BOUNDS statement constrains the diagonals of the matrices **P** and **U** to be nonnegative, but this cannot prevent **U** from having three negative eigenvalues. The fact that many of the published results for more complex models in covariance structure analysis are connected to unidentified problems implies that more theoretical work should be done to study the general features of such models.

References

Akaike, H. (1974), "A New Look at the Statistical Identification Model," *IEEE Transactions on Automatic Control*, 19, 716–723.

Akaike, H. (1987), "Factor Analysis and AIC," *Psychometrika*, 52, 317–332.

Al-Baali, M. and Fletcher, R. (1985), "Variational Methods for Nonlinear Least Squares," *J. Oper. Res. Soc.*, 36, 405–421.

Al-Baali, M. and Fletcher, R. (1986), "An Efficient Line Search for Nonlinear Least Squares," *J. Optimiz. Theory Appl.*, 48, 359–377.

Anderson, T.W. (1960), "Some Stochastic Process Models for Intelligence Test Scores," in *Mathematical Methods in the Social Sciences*, eds. K.J. Arrow, S. Karlin, and P. Suppes Stanford: Stanford University Press.

Beale, E.M.L. (1972), "A Derivation of Conjugate Gradients," in *Numerical Methods for Nonlinear Optimization*, ed. F.A. Lootsma, London: Academic Press.

Bentler, P.M. (1983), "Some Contributions to Efficient Statistics in Structural Models: Specification and Estimation of Moment Structures," *Psychometrika*, 48, 493–517.

Bentler, P.M. (1985), *Theory and Implementation of EQS: A Structural Equations Program*, Manual for Program Version 2.0, Los Angeles: BMDP Statistical Software, Inc.

Bentler, P.M. (1986), *Lagrange Multiplier and Wald Tests for EQS and EQS/PC*, Los Angeles: BMDP Statistical Software, Inc.

Bentler, P.M. (1989), *EQS, Structural Equations, Program Manual*, Program Version 3.0, Los Angeles: BMDP Statistical Software, Inc.

Bentler, P.M. and Bonett, D.G. (1980), "Significance Tests and Goodness of Fit in the Analysis of Covariance Structures," *Psychological Bulletin*, 88, 588–606.

Bentler, P.M. and Weeks, D.G. (1980), "Linear Structural Equations with Latent Variables," *Psychometrika*, 45, 289–308.

Bentler, P.M. and Weeks, D.G. (1982), "Multivariate Analysis with Latent Variables," in *Handbook of Statistics, Vol. 2*, eds. P.R. Krishnaiah and L.N. Kanal, Amsterdam: North Holland Publishing Company.

Bishop, Y.M.M., Fienberg, S.E., and Holland, P.W. (1977), *Discrete Multivariate Analysis: Theory and Practice*, Cambridge and London: MIT Press.

Bollen, K.A. (1986), "Sample Size and Bentler and Bonett's Nonnormed Fit Index," *Psychometrika*, 51, 375–377.

Bollen, K.A. (1989a), "A New Incremental Fit Index for General Structural Equation Models," *Sociological Methods and Research*, 17, 303–316.

Bollen, K.A. (1989b), *Structural Equations with Latent Variables*, New York: John Wiley & Sons, Inc.

Bozdogan, H. (1987), "Model Selection and Akaike's Information Criterion (AIC): The General Theory and its Analytical Extensions," *Psychometrika*, 52, 345–370.

Browne, M.W. (1974), "Generalized Least Squares Estimators in the Analysis of Covariance Structures," *South African Statistical Journal*, 8, 1–24.

Browne, M.W. (1982), "Covariance Structures," in *Topics in Multivariate Analyses*, ed. D.M. Hawkins, New York: Cambridge University Press.

Browne, M. W. (1984), "Asymptotically Distribution-Free Methods for the Analysis of Covariance Structures," *British Journal of Mathematical and Statistical Psychology*, 37, 62–83.

Browne, M. W. (1992), "Circumplex Models for Correlation Matrices," Psychometrika, 57, 469–497.

Browne, M. W. and Cudeck, R. (1993), "Alternative Ways of Assessing Model Fit," in *Testing Structural Equation Models*, eds. K. A. Bollen and S. Long, Newbury Park, CA: Sage Publications, Inc.

Browne, M. W. and Du Toit, S.H.C. (1992), "Automated Fitting of Nonstandard Models," *Multivariate Behavioral Research*, 27, 269–300.

Browne, M.W. and Shapiro, A. (1986), "The Asymptotic Covariance Matrix of Sample Correlation Coefficients under General Conditions," *Linear Algebra and its Applications*, 82, 169–176.

Bunch, J.R. and Kaufman, K. (1977), "Some Stable Methods for Calculating Inertia and Solving Symmetric Linear Systems," *Mathematics of Computation*, 31, 162–179.

Buse, A. (1982), "The Likelihood Ratio, Wald, and Lagrange Multiplier Tests: An Expository Note," *The American Statistician*, 36, 153–157.

Chamberlain, R.M., Powell, M.J.D., Lemarechal, C., and Pedersen, H.C. (1982), "The Watchdog Technique for Forcing Convergence in Algorithms for Constrained Optimization," *Mathematical Programming*, 16, 1–17.

Cramer, J.S. (1986), *Econometric Applications of Maximum Likelihood Methods*, Cambridge: Cambridge University Press.

DeLeeuw, J. (1983), "Models and Methods for the Analysis of Correlation Coefficients," *Journal of Econometrics*, 22, 113–137.

Dennis, J.E., Gay, D.M., and Welsch, R.E. (1981), "An Adaptive Nonlinear Least-Squares Algorithm," *ACM Trans. Math. Software*, 7, 348–368.

Dennis, J.E. and Mei, H.H.W. (1979), "Two New Unconstrained Optimization Algorithms which use Function and Gradient Values," *J. Optim. Theory Appl.*, 28, 453–482.

Dennis, J.E. and Schnabel, R.B. (1983), *Numerical Methods for Unconstrained Optimization and Nonlinear Equations*, New Jersey: Prentice-Hall.

Dijkstra, T. K. (1992), "On Statistical Inference with Parameter Estimates on the Boundary of the Parameter Space," *British Journal of Mathematical and Statistical Psychology*, 45, 289–309.

Everitt, B.S. (1984), *An Introduction to Latent Variable Methods*, London: Chapman & Hall.

Fletcher, R. (1980), *Practical Methods of Optimization*, Vol. 1, Chichester: John Wiley & Sons, Inc.

Fletcher, R. (1987), *Practical Methods of Optimization*, Second Edition, Chichester: John Wiley & Sons, Inc.

Fletcher, R. and Powell, M.J.D. (1963), "A Rapidly Convergent Descent Method for Minimization," *Comput.J.*, 6, 163–168.

Fletcher, R. and Xu, C. (1987), "Hybrid Methods for Nonlinear Least Squares," *J. Numerical Analysis*, 7, 371–389.

Fuller, A.W. (1987), *Measurement Error Models*, New York: John Wiley & Sons, Inc.

Gallant, A. R. (1987), *Nonlinear Statistical Models*, New York: John Wiley & Sons, Inc.

Gay, D.M. (1983), "Subroutines for Unconstrained Minimization," *ACM Trans. Math. Software*, 9, 503–524.

Gill, E.P., Murray, W., Saunders, M.A., and Wright, M.H. (1983), "Computing Forward-Difference Intervals for Numerical Optimization," *SIAM J. Sci. Stat. Comput.*, 4, 310–321.

Gill, E.P., Murray, W., and Wright, M.H. (1981), *Practical Optimization*, London: Academic Press.

Gill, E.P., Murray, W., Saunders, M.A., and Wright, M.H. (1984), "Procedures for Optimization Problems with a Mixture of Bounds and General Linear Constraints," *ACM Trans. Math. Software*, 10, 282–298.

Goldfeld, S.M., Quandt, R.E., and Trotter, H.F. (1966), "Maximization by Quadratic Hill-Climbing," *Econometrica*, 34, 541–551.

Guttman, L. (1953), "Image Theory for the Structure of Quantitative Variates," *Psychometrika*, 18, 277–296.

Guttman, L. (1957), "Empirical Verification of the Radex Structure of Mental Abilities and Personality Traits," *Educational and Psychological Measurement*, 17, 391–407.

Hägglund, G. (1982), "Factor Analysis by Instrumental Variable Methods," *Psychometrika*, 47, 209–222.

Hartmann, W.M. (1992), *The NLP Procedure: Extended User's Guide*, Cary: SAS Institute Inc.

Hartmann, W. M. and Hartwig, R. E. (1995), "Computing the Moore-Penrose Inverse for the Covariance Matrix in Constrained Nonlinear Estimation," accepted for publication in *SIAM Journal on Optimization*.

Hartmann, W. M. and So, Y. (1995), "Nonlinear Least-Squares and Maximum-Likelihood Estimation Using PROC NLP and SAS/IML," Computer Technology Workshop, American Statistical Association, Joint Statistical Meeting, Orlando, 1995.

Hoelter, J.W. (1983), "The Analysis of Covariance Structures: Goodness-of-Fit Indices," *Sociological Methods and Research*, 11, 325–344.

James, L.R., Mulaik, S.A., and Brett, J.M. (1982), *Causal Analysis: Assumptions, Models, and Data*, Beverly Hills: Sage Publications, Inc.

Jennrich, R.I. (1987), "Tableau Algorithms for Factor Analysis by Instrumental Variable Methods," *Psychometrika*, 52, 469–476.

Jöreskog, K.G. (1963), *Statistical Estimation in Factor Analysis*, Stockholm: Almqvist & Wicksell.

Jöreskog, K.G. (1969), "Efficient Estimation in Image Factor Analysis," *Psychometrika*, 34, 51–75.

Jöreskog, K.G. (1973), "A General Method for Estimating a Linear Structural Equation System," in *Structural Equation Models in the Social Sciences*, eds. A.S. Goldberger and O.D. Duncan, New York: Academic Press.

Jöreskog, K.G. (1978), "Structural Analysis of Covariance and Correlation Matrices," *Psychometrika*, 43, 443–477.

Jöreskog, K.G. (1982), "Analysis of Covariance Structures," in *A Second Generation of Multivariate Analysis*, ed. C. Fornell, New York: Praeger Publishers.

Jöreskog, K.G. and Sörbom, D. (1979), *Advances in Factor Analysis and Structural Equation Modeling*, Cambridge MA: Abt Books.

Jöreskog, K.G. and Sörbom, D. (1985), *LISREL VI; Analysis of Linear Structural Relationships by Maximum Likelihood, Instrumental Variables, and Least Squares*, Uppsala: University of Uppsala.

Jöreskog, K.G. and Sörbom, D. (1988), *LISREL 7: A Guide to the Program and Applications*, Chicago, Illinois: SPSS Inc.

Keesling, J.W. (1972), "Maximum Likelihood Approaches to Causal Analysis," Ph.D. dissertation, Chicago, 1972.

Kmenta, J. (1971), *Elements of Econometrics*, New York: Macmillan Publishing Co.

Krane, W.R. and McDonald, R.P. (1978), "Scale Invariance and the Factor Analysis of Correlation Matrices," *British Journal of Mathematical and Statistical Psychology*, 31, 218–228.

Lawley, D.N. and Maxwell, A.E. (1971), *Factor Analysis as a Statistical Method*, New York: American Elsevier Publishing Company.

Lee, S.Y. (1985), "On Testing Functional Constraints in Structural Equation Models," *Biometrika*, 72, 125–131.

Lee, S.Y. and Jennrich, R.I. (1979), "A Study of Algorithms for Covariance Structure Analysis with Specific Comparisons Using Factor Analysis," *Psychometrika*, 44, 99–113.

Loehlin, J.C. (1987), *Latent Variable Models, An Introduction to Factor, Path, and Structural Analysis*, Hillsdale, NJ: L. Erlbaum Associates.

Long, J.S. (1983), *Covariance Structure Models, an Introduction to LISREL*, Beverly Hills, CA: SAGE Publications, Inc.

MacCallum, R. (1986), "Specification Searches in Covariance Structure Modeling," *Psychological Bulletin*, 100, 107–120.

Marsh, H.W., Balla, J.R. and McDonald, R.P. (1988), "Goodness-of-Fit Indices in Confirmatory Factor Analysis. The Effect of Sample Size," *Psychological Bulletin*, 103, 391–410.

McArdle, J.J. (1980), "Causal Modeling Applied to Psychonomic Systems Simulation," *Behavior Research Methods & Instrumentation*, 12, 193–209.

McArdle, J.J. (1988), "Dynamic but Structural Equation Modeling of Repeated Measures Data," in *The Handbook of Multivariate Experimental Psychology*, eds. J.R. Nesselroade and R.B. Cattell, New York: Plenum Press.

McArdle, J.J. and Boker, S.M. (1986), *RAMpath - Path Diagram Software*, Denver: DATA Transforms, Inc.

McArdle, J.J. and McDonald, R.P. (1984), "Some Algebraic Properties of the Reticular Action Model," *British Journal of Mathematical and Statistical Psychology*, 37, 234–251.

McDonald, R.P. (1978), "A Simple Comprehensive Model for the Analysis of Covariance Structures," *British Journal of Mathematical and Statistical Psychology*, 31, 59–72.

McDonald, R.P. (1980), "A Simple Comprehensive Model for the Analysis of Covariance Structures: Some Remarks on Applications," *British Journal of Mathematical and Statistical Psychology*, 33, 161–183.

McDonald, R.P. (1984), "Confirmatory Models for Nonlinear Structural Analysis," in *Data Analysis and Informatics*, III, eds. E. Diday et al., North Holland: Elsevier Publishers.

McDonald, R.P. (1985), *Factor Analysis and Related Methods*, Hillsdale, NJ: Lawrence Erlbaum Associates.

McDonald, R.P. (1989), "An Index of Goodness-of-Fit Based on Noncentrality," *Journal of Classification*, 6, 97–103.

McDonald, R.P. and Hartmann, W. (1992), "A Procedure for Obtaining Initial Values of Parameters in the RAM Model," *Multivariate Behavioral Research*, 27, 57–176.

McDonald, R.P. and Marsh, H.W. (1988), "Choosing a Multivariate Model: Noncentrality and Goodness of Fit," distributed paper.

McDonald, R.P., Parker, P.M., and Ishizuka, T. (1993), "A Scale-Invariant Treatment of Recursive Path Models," *Psychometrika*, 58, 431–443.

Moré, J.J. (1978), "The Levenberg-Marquardt Algorithm: Implementation and Theory," in *Numerical Analysis–Dundee 1977*, ed. G.A. Watson, Lecture Notes in Mathematics 630, Berlin: Springer-Verlag.

Moré, J.J. and Sorensen, D.C. (1983), "Computing a Trust-Region Step," *SIAM J. Sci. Stat. Comput.*, 4, 553–572.

Mulaik, S.A., James, L.R., Van Alstine, J., Bennett, N., Lind, S. and Stilwell, C.D. (1989), "Evaluation of Goodness-of-Fit Indices for Structural Equation Models," *Psychological Bulletin*, 105, 430–445.

Muthèn, B.O. (1987), LISCOMP: *Analysis of Linear Structural Relations Using a Comprehensive Measurement Model*, Mooresville IN: Scientific Software, Inc.

Polak, E. (1971), *Computational Methods in Optimization*, New York: Academic Press, Inc.

Powell, J.M.D. (1977), "Restart Procedures for the Conjugate Gradient Method," *Math. Prog.*, 12, 241–254.

Powell, J.M.D. (1978a), "A Fast Algorithm for Nonlinearly Constraint Optimization Calculations," in *Numerical Analysis, Dundee 1977, Lecture Notes in Mathematics 630*, ed. G.A. Watson, Berlin: Springer Verlag, 144–175.

Powell, J.M.D. (1978b), "Algorithms for Nonlinear Constraints that Use Lagrangian Functions," *Mathematical Programming*, 14, 224–248.

Powell, M.J.D. (1982a), "Extensions to Subroutine VF02AD," in *Systems Modeling and Optimization, Lecture Notes In Control and Information Sciences 38*, eds. R.F. Drenick and F. Kozin, Berlin: Springer Verlag, 529–538.

Powell, J.M.D. (1982b), "VMCWD: A Fortran Subroutine for Constrained Optimization," *DAMTP 1982/NA4*, Cambridge, England.

Powell, J.M.D. (1992), "A Direct Search Optimization Method that Models the Objective and Constraint Functions by Linear Interpolation," *DAMTP/NA5*, Cambridge, England.

Saris, W. (1982), "Linear Structural Relationships," in *A Second Generation of Multivariate Analysis*, ed. C. Fornell, New York: Praeger Publishers.

Schmid, J. and Leiman, J.M. (1957), "The Development of Hierarchical Factor Solutions," *Psychometrika*, 22, 53–61.

Schwarz, G. (1978), "Estimating the Dimension of a Model," *Annals of Statistics*, 6, 461–464.

Sclove, L.S. (1987), "Application of Model-Selection Criteria to Some Problems in Multivariate Analysis," *Psychometrika*, 52, 333–343.

Steiger, J.H. and Lind, J.C. (1980), "Statistically Based Tests for the Number of Common Factors," paper presented at the annual meeting of the Psychometric Society, Iowa City, IA.

Swaminathan, H. (1974), "A General Factor Model for the Description of Change," Report LR-74-9, Laboratory of Psychometric and Evaluative Research, University of Massachusetts.

Tucker, L.R. and Lewis, C. (1973), "A Reliability Coefficient for Maximum Likelihood Factor Analysis," *Psychometrika*, 38, 1–10.

Wheaton, B., Muthèn, B., Alwin, D.F., and Summers, G.F. (1977), "Assessing Reliability and Stability in Panel Models," in *Sociological Methodology*, ed. D.R. Heise, San Francisco: Jossey Bass.

Wiley, D.E. (1973), "The Identification Problem for Structural Equation Models with Unmeasured Variables," in *Structural Equation Models in the Social Sciences*, eds. A.S. Goldberger and O.D. Duncan, New York: Academic Press.

Wilson, E.B. and Hilferty, M.M. (1931), "The Distribution of Chi-Square," *Proceeding of the National Academy of Science*, 17, 694.

Chapter 20
The CANCORR Procedure

Chapter Table of Contents

Chapter 20
The CANCORR Procedure

Overview

The CANCORR procedure performs canonical correlation, partial canonical correlation, and canonical redundancy analysis.

Canonical correlation is a technique for analyzing the relationship between two sets of variables—each set can contain several variables. Canonical correlation is a variation on the concept of multiple regression and correlation analysis. In multiple regression and correlation, you examine the relationship between a linear combination of a set of X variables and a single Y variable. In canonical correlation analysis, you examine the relationship between a linear combination of the set of X variables with a linear combination of a *set* of Y variables. Simple and multiple correlation are special cases of canonical correlation in which one or both sets contain a single variable.

The CANCORR procedure tests a series of hypotheses that each canonical correlation and all smaller canonical correlations are zero in the population. PROC CANCORR uses an F approximation (Rao 1973; Kshirsagar 1972) that gives better small sample results than the usual χ^2 approximation. At least one of the two sets of variables should have an approximate multivariate normal distribution in order for the probability levels to be valid.

Both standardized and unstandardized canonical coefficients are produced, as well as all correlations between canonical variables and the original variables. A canonical redundancy analysis (Stewart and Love 1968; Cooley and Lohnes 1971) can also be performed. PROC CANCORR provides multiple regression analysis options to aid in interpreting the canonical correlation analysis. You can examine the linear regression of each variable on the opposite set of variables. PROC CANCORR uses the least-squares criterion in linear regression analysis.

PROC CANCORR can produce a data set containing the scores of each observation on each canonical variable, and you can use the PRINT procedure to list these values. A plot of each canonical variable against its counterpart in the other group is often useful, and you can use PROC PLOT with the output data set to produce these plots. A second output data set contains the canonical correlations, coefficients, and most other statistics computed by the procedure.

Background

Canonical correlation was developed by Hotelling (1935, 1936). The application of canonical correlation is discussed by Cooley and Lohnes (1971), Tatsuoka (1971), and Mardia, Kent, and Bibby (1979). One of the best theoretical treatments is given by Kshirsagar (1972).

Consider the situation in which you have a set of p X variables and q Y variables. The CANCORR procedure finds the linear combinations

$$w_1 = a_1 x_1 + a_2 x_2 + \ldots + a_p x_p$$

$$v_1 = b_1 y_1 + b_2 y_2 + \cdots \ldots + b_q y_q$$

such that the correlation between the two canonical variables, w_1 and v_1, is maximized. This correlation between the two canonical variables is the first canonical correlation. The coefficients of the linear combinations are canonical coefficients or canonical weights. It is customary to normalize the canonical coefficients so that each canonical variable has a variance of 1.

PROC CANCORR continues by finding a second set of canonical variables, uncorrelated with the first pair, that produces the second highest correlation coefficient. The process of constructing canonical variables continues until the number of pairs of canonical variables equals the number of variables in the smaller group.

Each canonical variable is uncorrelated with all the other canonical variables of either set except for the one corresponding canonical variable in the opposite set. The canonical coefficients are not generally orthogonal, however, so the canonical variables do not represent jointly perpendicular directions through the space of the original variables.

The first canonical correlation is at least as large as the multiple correlation between any variable and the opposite set of variables. It is possible for the first canonical correlation to be very large while all the multiple correlations for predicting one of the original variables from the opposite set of canonical variables are small. Canonical redundancy analysis (Stewart and Love 1968; Cooley and Lohnes 1971; van den Wollenberg 1977), which is available with the CANCORR procedure, examines how well the original variables can be predicted from the canonical variables.

PROC CANCORR can also perform partial canonical correlation, which is a multivariate generalization of ordinary partial correlation (Cooley and Lohnes 1971; Timm 1975). Most commonly used parametric statistical methods, ranging from t tests to multivariate analysis of covariance, are special cases of partial canonical correlation.

Getting Started

The following example demonstrates how you can use the CANCORR procedure to calculate and test canonical correlations between two sets of variables.

Suppose you want to determine the degree of correspondence between a set of job characteristics and measures of employee satisfaction. Using a survey instrument for employees, you calculate three measures of job satisfaction. With another instrument designed for supervisors, you calculate the corresponding job characteristics profile.

Your three variables associated with job satisfaction are

- career track satisfaction: employee satisfaction with career direction and the possibility of future advancement, expressed as a percent
- management and supervisor satisfaction: employee satisfaction with supervisor's communication and management style, expressed as a percent
- financial satisfaction: employee satisfaction with salary and other benefits, using a scale measurement from 1 to 10 (1=unsatisfied, 10=satisfied)

The three variables associated with job characteristics are

- task variety: degree of variety involved in tasks, expressed as a percent
- feedback: degree of feedback required in job tasks, expressed as a percent
- autonomy: degree of autonomy required in job tasks, expressed as a percent

The following statements create the SAS data set Jobs and request a canonical correlation analysis:

```
options ls=120;
data Jobs;
   input Career Supervisor Finance Variety Feedback Autonomy;
   label
     Career    ='Career Satisfaction' Variety ='Task Variety'
     Supervisor='Supervisor Satisfaction' Feedback='Amount of Feedback'
     Finance   ='Financial Satisfaction' Autonomy='Degree of Autonomy';
   datalines;
72  26  9          10  11  70
63  76  7          85  22  93
96  31  7          83  63  73
96  98  6          82  75  97
84  94  6          36  77  97
66  10  5          28  24  75
31  40  9          64  23  75
45  14  2          19  15  50
42  18  6          33  13  70
79  74  4          23  14  90
39  12  2          37  13  70
54  35  3          23  74  53
60  75  5          45  58  83
63  45  5          22  67  53
;
```

```
proc cancorr data=Jobs
  vprefix=Satisfaction wprefix=Characteristics
  vname='Satisfaction Areas' wname='Job Characteristics';
  var  Career Supervisor Finance;
  with Variety Feedback Autonomy;
run;
```

The DATA= option in the PROC CANCORR statement specifies Jobs as the SAS data set to be analyzed. The VPREFIX and WPREFIX options specify the prefixes for naming the canonical variables from the VAR statement and the WITH statement, respectively. The VNAME option specifies 'Satisfaction Areas' to refer to the set of variables from the VAR statement. Similarly, the WNAME option specifies 'Job Characteristics' to refer to the set of variables from the WITH statement.

The VAR statement defines the first of the two sets of variables to be analyzed as Career, Supervisor and Finance. The WITH statement defines the second set of variables to be Variety, Feedback, and Autonomy. The results of this analysis are displayed in the following figures.

The SAS System

The CANCORR Procedure

Canonical Correlation Analysis

	Canonical Correlation	Adjusted Canonical Correlation	Approximate Standard Error	Squared Canonical Correlation
1	0.919412	0.898444	0.042901	0.845318
2	0.418649	0.276633	0.228740	0.175267
3	0.113366	.	0.273786	0.012852

Eigenvalues of Inv(E)*H = CanRsq/(1-CanRsq)

Test of H0: The canonical correlations in the current row and all that follow are zero

	Eigenvalue	Difference	Proportion	Cumulative	Likelihood Ratio	Approximate F Value	Num DF	Den DF	Pr > F
1	5.4649	5.2524	0.9604	0.9604	0.12593148	2.93	9	19.621	0.0223
2	0.2125	0.1995	0.0373	0.9977	0.81413359	0.49	4	18	0.7450
3	0.0130		0.0023	1.0000	0.98714819	0.13	1	10	0.7257

Figure 20.1. Canonical Correlations, Eigenvalues, and Likelihood Tests

Figure 20.1 displays the canonical correlation, adjusted canonical correlation, approximate standard error, and squared canonical correlation for each pair of canonical variables. The first canonical correlation (the correlation between the first pair of canonical variables) is 0.9194. This value represents the highest possible correlation between any linear combination of the job satisfaction variables and any linear combination of the job characteristics variables.

Figure 20.1 also lists the likelihood ratio and associated statistics for testing the hypothesis that the canonical correlations in the current row and all that follow are zero.

The first approximate F value of 2.93 corresponds to the test that all three canonical correlations are zero. Since the p-value is small (0.0223), you would reject the null hypothesis at the 0.05 level. The second approximate F value of 0.49 corresponds to the test that both the second and the third canonical correlations are zero. Since the p-value is large (0.7450), you would fail to reject the hypothesis and conclude that only the first canonical correlation is significant.

Figure 20.2 lists several multivariate statistics and F test approximations for the null hypothesis that all canonical correlations are zero. These statistics are described in the section "Multivariate Tests" in Chapter 3, "Introduction to Regression Procedures."

```
                         The CANCORR Procedure

                     Canonical Correlation Analysis

              Multivariate Statistics and F Approximations

                         S=3    M=-0.5    N=3

Statistic                        Value    F Value    Num DF    Den DF    Pr > F

Wilks' Lambda               0.12593148       2.93         9    19.621    0.0223
Pillai's Trace              1.03343732       1.75         9        30    0.1204
Hotelling-Lawley Trace      5.69042615       4.76         9    9.8113    0.0119
Roy's Greatest Root         5.46489324      18.22         3        10    0.0002

          NOTE: F Statistic for Roy's Greatest Root is an upper bound.
```

Figure 20.2. Multivariate Statistics and Approximate F Tests

The small p-values for these tests (< 0.05), except for Pillai's Trace, suggest rejecting the null hypothesis that all canonical correlations are zero in the population, confirming the results of the preceding likelihood ratio test (Figure 20.1). With only one of the tests resulting in a p-value larger than 0.05, you can assume that the first canonical correlation is significant. The next step is to interpret or identify the two canonical variables corresponding to this significant correlation.

Even though canonical variables are artificial, they can often be "identified" in terms of the original variables. This is done primarily by inspecting the standardized coefficients of the canonical variables and the correlations between the canonical variables and their original variables. Since only the first canonical correlation is significant, only the first pair of canonical variables (Satisfaction1 and Characteristics1) need to be identified.

PROC CANCORR calculates and displays the raw canonical coefficients for the job satisfaction variables and the job characteristic variables. However, since the original variables do not necessarily have equal variance and are not measured in the same units, the raw coefficients must be standardized to allow interpretation. The coefficients are standardized by multiplying the raw coefficients with the standard deviation of the associated variable.

The standardized canonical coefficients in Figure 20.3 show that the first canonical variable for the Satisfaction group is a weighted sum of the variables Supervisor (0.7854) and Career (0.3028), with the emphasis on Supervisor. The coefficient for the variable Finance is near 0. Thus, a person satisfied with his or her supervisor and with a large degree of career satisfaction would score high on the canonical variable Satisfaction1.

The CANCORR Procedure

Canonical Correlation Analysis

Standardized Canonical Coefficients for the Satisfaction Areas

		Satisfaction1	Satisfaction2	Satisfaction3
Career	Career Satisfaction	0.3028	-0.5416	1.0408
Supervisor	Supervisor Satisfaction	0.7854	0.1305	-0.9085
Finance	Financial Satisfaction	0.0538	0.9754	0.3329

Standardized Canonical Coefficients for the Job Characteristics

		Characteristics1	Characteristics2	Characteristics3
Variety	Task Variety	-0.1108	0.8095	0.9071
Feedback	Amount of Feedback	0.5520	-0.7722	0.4194
Autonomy	Degree of Autonomy	0.8403	0.1020	-0.8297

Figure 20.3. Standardized Canonical Coefficients from the CANCORR Procedure

The coefficients for the job characteristics variables show that degree of autonomy (Autonomy) and amount of feedback (Feedback) contribute heavily to the Characteristics1 canonical variable (0.8403 and 0.5520, respectively).

Figure 20.4 shows the table of correlations between the canonical variables and the original variables.

The CANCORR Procedure

Canonical Structure

Correlations Between the Satisfaction Areas and Their Canonical Variables

		Satisfaction1	Satisfaction2	Satisfaction3
Career	Career Satisfaction	0.7499	-0.2503	0.6123
Supervisor	Supervisor Satisfaction	0.9644	0.0362	-0.2618
Finance	Financial Satisfaction	0.2873	0.8814	0.3750

Correlations Between the Job Characteristics and Their Canonical Variables

		Characteristics1	Characteristics2	Characteristics3
Variety	Task Variety	0.4863	0.6592	0.5736
Feedback	Amount of Feedback	0.6216	-0.5452	0.5625
Autonomy	Degree of Autonomy	0.8459	0.4451	-0.2938

Correlations Between the Satisfaction Areas and the Canonical Variables of the Job Characteristics

		Characteristics1	Characteristics2	Characteristics3
Career	Career Satisfaction	0.6895	-0.1048	0.0694
Supervisor	Supervisor Satisfaction	0.8867	0.0152	-0.0297
Finance	Financial Satisfaction	0.2642	0.3690	0.0425

Correlations Between the Job Characteristics and the Canonical Variables of the Satisfaction Areas

		Satisfaction1	Satisfaction2	Satisfaction3
Variety	Task Variety	0.4471	0.2760	0.0650
Feedback	Amount of Feedback	0.5715	-0.2283	0.0638
Autonomy	Degree of Autonomy	0.7777	0.1863	-0.0333

Figure 20.4. Canonical Structure Correlations from the CANCORR Procedure

Although these univariate correlations must be interpreted with caution since they do not indicate how the original variables contribute *jointly* to the canonical analysis, they are often useful in the identification of the canonical variables.

Figure 20.4 shows that the supervisor satisfaction variable Supervisor is strongly associated with the Satisfaction1 canonical variable with a correlation of 0.9644. Slightly less influential is the variable Career, which has a correlation with the canonical variable of 0.7499. Thus, the canonical variable Satisfaction1 seems to represent satisfaction with supervisor and career track.

The correlations for the job characteristics variables show that the canonical variable Characteristics1 seems to represent all three measured variables, with degree of autonomy variable (Autonomy) being the most influential (0.8459).

Hence, you can interpret these results to mean that job characteristics and job satisfaction are related—jobs that possess a high degree of autonomy and level of feedback are associated with workers who are more satisfied with their supervisor and their career. While financial satisfaction is a factor in job satisfaction, it is not as important as the other measured satisfaction-related variables.

Syntax

The following statements are available in PROC CANCORR.

PROC CANCORR < *options* > ;
  WITH *variables* ;

  BY *variables* ;
  FREQ *variable* ;
  PARTIAL *variables* ;
  VAR *variables* ;
  WEIGHT *variable* ;

The PROC CANCORR statement and the WITH statement are required. The rest of this section provides detailed syntax information for each of the preceding statements, beginning with the PROC CANCORR statement. The remaining statements are covered in alphabetical order.

PROC CANCORR Statement

PROC CANCORR < *options* > ;

The PROC CANCORR statement starts the CANCORR procedure and optionally identifies input and output data sets, specifies the analyses performed, and controls displayed output. Table 20.1 summarizes the options.

Table 20.1. PROC CANCORR Statement Options

Task	Options	Description
Specify computational details	EDF=	specify error degrees of freedom if input observations are regression residuals
	NOINT	omit intercept from canonical correlation and regression models
	RDF=	specify regression degrees of freedom if input observations are regression residuals
	SINGULAR=	specify the singularity criterion
Specify input and output data sets	DATA=	specify input data set name
	OUT=	specify output data set name
	OUTSTAT=	specify output data set name containing various statistics
Specify labeling options	VNAME=	specify a name to refer to VAR statement variables
	VPREFIX=	specify a prefix for naming VAR statement canonical variables
	WNAME=	specify a name to refer to WITH statement variables
	WPREFIX=	specify a prefix for naming WITH statement canonical variables
Control amount of output	ALL	produce simple statistics, input variable correlations, and canonical redundancy analysis
	CORR	produce input variable correlations
	NCAN=	specify number of canonical variables for which full output is desired
	NOPRINT	suppress all displayed output
	REDUNDANCY	produce canonical redundancy analysis
	SHORT	suppress default output from canonical analysis
	SIMPLE	produce means and standard deviations
Request regression analyses	VDEP	request multiple regression analyses with the VAR variables as dependents and the WITH variables as regressors
	VREG	request multiple regression analyses with the VAR variables as regressors and the WITH variables as dependents
	WDEP	same as VREG
	WREG	same as VDEP

Table 20.1. (continued)

Task	Options	Description
Specify regression statistics	ALL	produce all regression statistics and includes these statistics in the OUTSTAT= data set
	B	produce raw regression coefficients
	CLB	produce 95% confidence interval limits for the regression coefficients
	CORRB	produce correlations among regression coefficients
	INT	request statistics for the intercept when you specify the B, CLB, SEB, T, or PROBT option
	PCORR	display partial correlations between regressors and dependents
	PROBT	display probability levels for t statistics
	SEB	display standard errors of regression coefficients
	SMC	display squared multiple correlations and F tests
	SPCORR	display semipartial correlations between regressors and dependents
	SQPCORR	display squared partial correlations between regressors and dependents
	SQSPCORR	display squared semipartial correlations between regressors and dependents
	STB	display standardized regression coefficients
	T	display t statistics for regression coefficients

Following are explanations of the options that can be used in the PROC CANCORR statement (in alphabetic order):

ALL

displays simple statistics, correlations among the input variables, the confidence limits for the regression coefficients, and the canonical redundancy analysis. If you specify the VDEP or WDEP option, the ALL option displays all related regression statistics (unless the NOPRINT option is specified) and includes these statistics in the OUTSTAT= data set.

B

produces raw regression coefficients from the regression analyses.

CLB

produces the 95% confidence limits for the regression coefficients from the regression analyses.

CORR

C

produces correlations among the original variables. If you include a PARTIAL statement, the CORR option produces a correlation matrix for all variables in the analysis, the regression statistics (R^2, RMSE), the standardized regression coefficients for both the VAR and WITH variables as predicted from the PARTIAL statement variables, and partial correlation matrices.

CORRB

produces correlations among the regression coefficient estimates.

DATA=*SAS-data-set*

names the SAS data set to be analyzed by PROC CANCORR. It can be an ordinary SAS data set or a TYPE=CORR, COV, FACTOR, SSCP, UCORR, or UCOV data set. By default, the procedure uses the most recently created SAS data set.

EDF=*error-df*

specifies the error degrees of freedom if the input observations are residuals from a regression analysis. The effective number of observations is the EDF= value plus one. If you have 100 observations, then specifying EDF=99 has the same effect as omitting the EDF= option.

INT

requests that statistics for the intercept be included when B, CLB, SEB, T, or PROBT is specified for the regression analyses.

NCAN=*number*

specifies the number of canonical variables for which full output is desired. The *number* must be less than or equal to the number of canonical variables in the analysis.

The value of the NCAN= option specifies the number of canonical variables for which canonical coefficients and canonical redundancy statistics are displayed, and the number of variables shown in the canonical structure matrices. The NCAN= option does not affect the number of displayed canonical correlations.

If an OUTSTAT= data set is requested, the NCAN= option controls the number of canonical variables for which statistics are output. If an OUT= data set is requested, the NCAN= option controls the number of canonical variables for which scores are output.

NOINT

omits the intercept from the canonical correlation and regression models. Standard deviations, variances, covariances, and correlations are not corrected for the mean. If you use a TYPE=SSCP data set as input to the CANCORR procedure and list the variable Intercept in the VAR or WITH statement, the procedure runs as if you also specified the NOINT option. If you use NOINT and also create an OUTSTAT= data set, the data set is TYPE=UCORR.

NOPRINT

suppresses the display of all output. Note that this option temporarily disables the Output Delivery System (ODS). For more information, see Chapter 15, "Using the Output Delivery System."

OUT=*SAS-data-set*

creates an output SAS data set to contain all the original data plus scores on the canonical variables. If you want to create a permanent SAS data set, you must specify a two-level name. The OUT= option cannot be used when the DATA= data set is TYPE=CORR, COV, FACTOR, SSCP, UCORR, or UCOV. For details on OUT= data sets, see the section "Output Data Sets" on page 649. Refer to *SAS Language Reference: Concepts* for more information on permanent SAS data sets.

OUTSTAT=*SAS-data-set*

creates an output SAS data set containing various statistics, including the canonical correlations and coefficients and the multiple regression statistics you request. If you want to create a permanent SAS data set, you must specify a two-level name. For details on OUTSTAT= data sets, see the section "Output Data Sets" on page 649. Refer to *SAS Language Reference: Concepts* for more information on permanent SAS data sets.

PCORR

produces partial correlations between regressors and dependent variables, removing from each dependent variable and regressor the effects of all other regressors.

PROBT

produces probability levels for the t statistics in the regression analyses.

RDF=*regression-df*

specifies the regression degrees of freedom if the input observations are residuals from a regression analysis. The effective number of observations is the actual number minus the RDF= value. The degrees of freedom for the intercept should not be included in the RDF= option.

REDUNDANCY
RED

produces canonical redundancy statistics.

SEB

produces standard errors of the regression coefficients.

SHORT

suppresses all default output from the canonical analysis except the tables of canonical correlations and multivariate statistics.

SIMPLE
S

produces means and standard deviations.

SINGULAR=*p*
SING=*p*

specifies the singularity criterion, where $0 < p < 1$. If a variable in the PARTIAL statement has an R^2 as large as $1-p$ (where p is the value of the SINGULAR= option) when predicted from the variables listed before it in the statement, the variable is assigned a standardized regression coefficient of 0, and the LOG generates a linear dependency warning message. By default, SINGULAR=1E−8.

SMC

produces squared multiple correlations and F tests for the regression analyses.

SPCORR

produces semipartial correlations between regressors and dependent variables, removing from each regressor the effects of all other regressors.

SQPCORR

produces squared partial correlations between regressors and dependent variables, removing from each dependent variable and regressor the effects of all other regressors.

SQSPCORR

produces squared semipartial correlations between regressors and dependent variables, removing from each regressor the effects of all other regressors.

STB

produces standardized regression coefficients.

T

produces t statistics for the regression coefficients.

VDEP
WREG

requests multiple regression analyses with the VAR variables as dependent variables and the WITH variables as regressors.

VNAME=*'label'*
VN=*'label'*

specifies a character constant to refer to variables from the VAR statement on the output. Enclose the constant in single quotes. If you omit the VNAME= option, these variables are referred to as the VAR Variables. The number of characters in the label should not exceed the label length defined by the VALIDVARNAME= system option. For more information on the VALIDVARNAME= system option, refer to *SAS Language Reference: Dictionary*.

VPREFIX=*name*
VP=*name*

specifies a prefix for naming canonical variables from the VAR statement. By default, these canonical variables are given the names V1, V2, and so on. If you specify VPREFIX=ABC, the names are ABC1, ABC2, and so forth. The number of characters in the prefix plus the number of digits required to designate the variables should not exceed the name length defined by the VALIDVARNAME= system option. For more information on the VALIDVARNAME= system option, refer to *SAS Language Reference: Dictionary*.

WDEP
VREG

requests multiple regression analyses with the WITH variables as dependent variables and the VAR variables as regressors.

WNAME='*label*'
WN='*label*'

specifies a character constant to refer to variables in the WITH statement on the output. Enclose the constant in quotes. If you omit the WNAME= option, these variables are referred to as the WITH Variables. The number of characters in the label should not exceed the label length defined by the VALIDVARNAME= system option. For more information, on the VALIDVARNAME= system option, refer to *SAS Language Reference: Dictionary*.

WPREFIX=*name*
WP=*name*

specifies a prefix for naming canonical variables from the WITH statement. By default, these canonical variables are given the names W1, W2, and so on. If you specify WPREFIX=XYZ, then the names are XYZ1, XYZ2, and so forth. The number of characters in the prefix plus the number of digits required to designate the variables should not exceed the label length defined by the VALIDVARNAME= system option. For more information, on the VALIDVARNAME= system option, refer to *SAS Language Reference: Dictionary*.

BY Statement

BY *variables* ;

You can specify a BY statement with PROC CANCORR to obtain separate analyses on observations in groups defined by the BY variables. When a BY statement appears, the procedure expects the input data set to be sorted in order of the BY variables.

If your input data set is not sorted in ascending order, use one of the following alternatives:

- Sort the data using the SORT procedure with a similar BY statement.
- Specify the BY statement option NOTSORTED or DESCENDING in the BY statement for the CANCORR procedure. The NOTSORTED option does not mean that the data are unsorted but rather that the data are arranged in groups (according to values of the BY variables) and that these groups are not necessarily in alphabetical or increasing numeric order.
- Create an index on the BY variables using the DATASETS procedure.

For more information on the BY statement, refer to the discussion in *SAS Language Reference: Concepts*. For more information on the DATASETS procedure, refer to the discussion in the *SAS Procedures Guide*.

FREQ Statement

FREQ *variable* ;

If one variable in your input data set represents the frequency of occurrence for other values in the observation, specify the variable's name in a FREQ statement. PROC CANCORR then treats the data set as if each observation appeared n times, where n is the value of the FREQ variable for the observation. If the value of the FREQ variable is less than one, the observation is not used in the analysis. Only the integer portion of the value is used. The total number of observations is considered to be equal to the sum of the FREQ variable when PROC CANCORR calculates significance probabilities.

PARTIAL Statement

PARTIAL *variables* ;

You can use the PARTIAL statement to base the canonical analysis on partial correlations. The variables in the PARTIAL statement are partialled out of the VAR and WITH variables.

VAR Statement

VAR *variables* ;

The VAR statement lists the variables in the first of the two sets of variables to be analyzed. The variables must be numeric. If you omit the VAR statement, all numeric variables not mentioned in other statements make up the first set of variables. If, however, the DATA= data set is TYPE=SSCP, the default set of variables used as VAR variables does not include the variable Intercept.

WEIGHT Statement

WEIGHT *variable* **;**

If you want to compute weighted product-moment correlation coefficients, specify the name of the weighting variable in a WEIGHT statement. The WEIGHT and FREQ statements have a similar effect, except the WEIGHT statement does not alter the degrees of freedom or number of observations. An observation is used in the analysis only if the WEIGHT variable is greater than zero.

WITH Statement

WITH *variables* **;**

The WITH statement lists the variables in the second set of variables to be analyzed. The variables must be numeric. The WITH statement is required.

Details

Missing Values

If an observation has a missing value for any of the variables in the analysis, that observation is omitted from the analysis.

Test Criterion

The CANCORR procedure uses an F approximation (Rao 1973; Kshirsagar 1972) that gives better small sample results than the usual χ^2 approximation. At least one of the two sets of variables should have an approximate multivariate normal distribution in order for the probability levels to be valid.

PROC CANCORR uses the least-squares criterion in linear regression analysis.

Output Data Sets

OUT= Data Set

The OUT= data set contains all the variables in the original data set plus new variables containing the canonical variable scores. The number of new variables is twice that specified by the NCAN= option. The names of the new variables are formed by concatenating the values given by the VPREFIX= and WPREFIX= options (the defaults are V and W) with the numbers 1, 2, 3, and so on. The new variables have mean 0 and variance equal to 1. An OUT= data set cannot be created if the DATA= data set is TYPE=CORR, COV, FACTOR, SSCP, UCORR, or UCOV or if a PARTIAL statement is used.

OUTSTAT= Data Set

The OUTSTAT= data set is similar to the TYPE=CORR or TYPE=UCORR data set produced by the CORR procedure, but it contains several results in addition to those produced by PROC CORR.

The new data set contains the following variables:

- the BY variables, if any
- two new character variables, _TYPE_ and _NAME_
- Intercept, if the INT option is used
- the variables analyzed (those in the VAR statement and the WITH statement)

Each observation in the new data set contains some type of statistic as indicated by the _TYPE_ variable. The values of the _TYPE_ variable are as follows:

TYPE	**Contents**
USTD	uncorrected standard deviations. When you specify the NOINT option in the PROC CANCORR statement, the OUTSTAT= data set contains standard deviations not corrected for the mean (_TYPE_='USTD').
N	number of observations on which the analysis is based. This value is the same for each variable.
SUMWGT	sum of the weights if a WEIGHT statement is used. This value is the same for each variable.
CORR	correlations. The _NAME_ variable contains the name of the variable corresponding to each row of the correlation matrix.
UCORR	uncorrected correlation matrix. When you specify the NOINT option in the PROC CANCORR statement, the OUTSTAT= data set contains a matrix of correlations not corrected for the means.
CANCORR	canonical correlations
SCORE	standardized canonical coefficients. The _NAME_ variable contains the name of the canonical variable.
RAWSCORE	raw canonical coefficients
USCORE	scoring coefficients to be applied without subtracting the mean from the raw variables. These are standardized canonical coefficients computed under a NOINT model.
STRUCTUR	canonical structure
RSQUARED	R^2s for the multiple regression analyses
ADJRSQ	adjusted R^2s
LCLRSQ	approximate 95% lower confidence limits for the R^2s
UCLRSQ	approximate 95% upper confidence limits for the R^2s

F	F statistics for the multiple regression analyses
PROBF	probability levels for the F statistics
CORRB	correlations among the regression coefficient estimates
STB	standardized regression coefficients. The _NAME_ variable contains the name of the dependent variable.
B	raw regression coefficients
SEB	standard errors of the regression coefficients
LCLB	95% lower confidence limits for the regression coefficients
MEAN	means
STD	standard deviations
UCLB	95% upper confidence limits for the regression coefficients
T	t statistics for the regression coefficients
PROBT	probability levels for the t statistics
SPCORR	semipartial correlations between regressors and dependent variables
SQSPCORR	squared semipartial correlations between regressors and dependent variables
PCORR	partial correlations between regressors and dependent variables
SQPCORR	squared partial correlations between regressors and dependent variables

Computational Resources

Notation

n = number of observations

v = number of variables

w = number of WITH variables

p = $\max(v, w)$

q = $\min(v, w)$

b = $v + w$

t = total number of variables (VAR, WITH, and PARTIAL)

Time Requirements

The time required to compute the correlation matrix is roughly proportional to

$$n(p+q)^2$$

The time required for the canonical analysis is roughly proportional to

$$\frac{1}{6}p^3 + p^2q + \frac{3}{2}pq^2 + 5q^3$$

but the coefficient for q^3 varies depending on the number of QR iterations in the singular value decomposition.

Memory Requirements

The minimum memory required is approximately

$$4(v^2 + w^2 + t^2)$$

bytes. Additional memory is required if you request the VDEP or WDEP option.

Displayed Output

If the SIMPLE option is specified, PROC CANCORR produces means and standard deviations for each input variable. If the CORR option is specified, PROC CANCORR produces correlations among the input variables. Unless the NOPRINT option is specified, PROC CANCORR displays a table of canonical correlations containing the following:

- Canonical Correlations. These are always nonnegative.
- Adjusted Canonical Correlations (Lawley 1959), which are asymptotically less biased than the raw correlations and may be negative. The adjusted canonical correlations may not be computable, and they are displayed as missing values if two canonical correlations are nearly equal or if some are close to zero. A missing value is also displayed if an adjusted canonical correlation is larger than a previous adjusted canonical correlation.
- Approx Standard Errors, which are the approximate standard errors of the canonical correlations
- Squared Canonical Correlations
- Eigenvalues of INV(E)*H, which are equal to CanRsq/(1−CanRsq), where CanRsq is the corresponding squared canonical correlation. Also displayed for each eigenvalue is the Difference from the next eigenvalue, the Proportion of the sum of the eigenvalues, and the Cumulative proportion.
- Likelihood Ratio for the hypothesis that the current canonical correlation and all smaller ones are 0 in the population. The likelihood ratio for all canonical correlations equals Wilks' lambda.
- Approx F statistic based on Rao's approximation to the distribution of the likelihood ratio (Rao 1973, p. 556; Kshirsagar 1972, p. 326)
- Num DF and Den DF (numerator and denominator degrees of freedom) and Pr $> F$ (probability level) associated with the F statistic

Unless you specify the NOPRINT option, PROC CANCORR produces a table of multivariate statistics for the null hypothesis that all canonical correlations are zero in the population. These statistics are described in the section "Multivariate Tests" in Chapter 3, "Introduction to Regression Procedures." The statistics are as follows.

- Wilks' Lambda
- Pillai's Trace
- Hotelling-Lawley Trace
- Roy's Greatest Root

For each of the preceding statistics, PROC CANCORR displays

- an F approximation or upper bound
- Num DF, the numerator degrees of freedom
- Den DF, the denominator degrees of freedom
- Pr $>$ F, the probability level

Unless you specify the SHORT or NOPRINT option, PROC CANCORR displays the following:

- both Raw (unstandardized) and Standardized Canonical Coefficients normalized to give canonical variables with unit variance. Standardized coefficients can be used to compute canonical variable scores from the standardized (zero mean and unit variance) input variables. Raw coefficients can be used to compute canonical variable scores from the input variables without standardizing them.
- all four Canonical Structure matrices, giving Correlations Between the canonical variables and the original variables

If you specify the REDUNDANCY option, PROC CANCORR displays

- the Canonical Redundancy Analysis (Stewart and Love 1968; Cooley and Lohnes 1971), including Raw (unstandardized) and Standardized Variance and Cumulative Proportion of the Variance of each set of variables Explained by Their Own Canonical Variables and Explained by The Opposite Canonical Variables
- the Squared Multiple Correlations of each variable with the first m canonical variables of the opposite set, where m varies from 1 to the number of canonical correlations

If you specify the VDEP option, PROC CANCORR performs multiple regression analyses with the VAR variables as dependent variables and the WITH variables as regressors. If you specify the WDEP option, PROC CANCORR performs multiple regression analyses with the WITH variables as dependent variables and the VAR variables as regressors. If you specify the VDEP or WDEP option and also specify the ALL option, PROC CANCORR displays the following items. You can also specify individual options to request a subset of the output generated by the ALL option; or you can suppress the output by specifying the NOPRINT option.

- if you specify the SMC option, Squared Multiple Correlations and F Tests. For each regression model, identified by its dependent variable name, PROC CANCORR displays the R-Squared, Adjusted R-Squared (Wherry 1931), F Statistic, and Pr $> F$. Also for each regression model, PROC CANCORR displays an Approximate 95% Confidence Interval for the population R^2 (Helland 1987). These confidence limits are valid only when the regressors are random and when the regressors and dependent variables are approximately distributed according to a multivariate normal distribution.

  The average R^2s for the models considered, unweighted and weighted by variance, are also given.
- if you specify the CORRB option, Correlations Among the Regression Coefficient Estimates
- if you specify the STB option, Standardized Regression Coefficients
- if you specify the B option, Raw Regression Coefficients
- if you specify the SEB option, Standard Errors of the Regression Coefficients
- if you specify the CLB option, 95% confidence limits for the regression coefficients
- if you specify the T option, T Statistics for the Regression Coefficients
- if you specify the PROBT option, Probability > |T| for the Regression Coefficients
- if you specify the SPCORR option, Semipartial Correlations between regressors and dependent variables, Removing from Each Regressor the Effects of All Other Regressors
- if you specify the SQSPCORR option, Squared Semipartial Correlations between regressors and dependent variables, Removing from Each Regressor the Effects of All Other Regressors
- if you specify the PCORR option, Partial Correlations between regressors and dependent variables, Removing the Effects of All Other Regressors from Both Regressor and Criterion
- if you specify the SQPCORR option, Squared Partial Correlations between regressors and dependent variables, Removing the Effects of All Other Regressors from Both Regressor and Criterion

ODS Table Names

PROC CANCORR assigns a name to each table it creates. You can use these names to reference the table when using the Output Delivery System (ODS) to select tables and create output data sets. These names are listed in the following table. For more information on ODS, see Chapter 15, "Using the Output Delivery System."

Table 20.2. ODS Tables Produced in PROC CANCORR

ODS Table Name	Description	Statement	Option
AvgRSquare	Average R-Squares (weighted and unweighted)	PROC CANCORR	VDEP (or WDEP) SMC (or ALL)
CanCorr	Canonical correlations	PROC CANCORR	default
CanStructureVCan	Correlations between the VAR canonical variables and the VAR and WITH variables	PROC CANCORR	default (unless SHORT)
CanStructureWCan	Correlations between the WITH canonical variables and the WITH and VAR variables	PROC CANCORR	default (unless SHORT)
ConfidenceLimits	95% Confidence limits for the regression coefficients	PROC CANCORR	VDEP (or WDEP) CLB (or ALL)
Corr	Correlations among the original variables	PROC CANCORR	CORR (or ALL)
CorrOnPartial	Partial correlations	PARTIAL	CORR (or ALL)
CorrRegCoefEst	Correlations among the regression coefficient estimates	PROC CANCORR	VDEP (or WDEP) CORRB (or ALL)
MultStat	Multivariate statistics	default	
NObsNVar	Number of observations and variables	PROC CANCORR	SIMPLE (or ALL)
ParCorr	Partial correlations	PROC CANCORR	VDEP (or WDEP) PCORR (or ALL)
ProbtRegCoef	Prob > |t| for the regression coefficients	PROC CANCORR	VDEP (or WDEP) PROBT (or ALL)
RawCanCoefV	Raw canonical coefficients for the var variables	PROC CANCORR	default (unless SHORT)
RawCanCoefW	Raw canonical coefficients for the with variables	PROC CANCORR	default (unless SHORT)
RawRegCoef	Raw regression coefficients	PROC CANCORR	VDEP (or WDEP) B (or ALL)
Redundancy	Canonical redundancy analysis	PROC CANCORR	REDUNDANCY (or ALL)
Regression	Squared multiple correlations and F tests	PROC CANCORR	VDEP (or WDEP) SMC (or ALL)
RSquareRMSEOnPartial	R-Squares and RMSEs on PARTIAL	PARTIAL	CORR (or ALL)
SemiParCorr	Semi-partial correlations	PROC CANCORR	VDEP (or WDEP) SPCORR (or ALL)
SimpleStatistics	Simple statistics	PROC CANCORR	SIMPLE (or ALL)
SqMultCorr	Canonical redundancy analysis: squared multiple correlations	PROC CANCORR	REDUNDANCY (or ALL)
SqParCorr	Squared partial correlations	PROC CANCORR	VDEP (or WDEP) SQPCORR (or ALL)

Table 20.2. (continued)

ODS Table Name	Description	Statement	Option
SqSemiParCorr	Squared semi-partial correlations	PROC CANCORR	VDEP (or WDEP) SQSPCORR (or ALL)
StdCanCoefV	Standardized Canonical coefficients for the VAR variables	PROC CANCORR	default (unless SHORT)
StdCanCoefW	Standardized Canonical coefficients for the WITH variables	PROC CANCORR	default (unless SHORT)
StdErrRawRegCoef	Standard errors of the raw regression coefficients	PROC CANCORR	VDEP (or WDEP) SEB (or ALL)
StdRegCoef	Standardized regression coefficients	PROC CANCORR	VDEP (or WDEP) STB (or ALL)
StdRegCoefOnPartial	Standardized regression coefficients on PARTIAL	PARTIAL	CORR (or ALL)
tValueRegCoef	t values for the regression coefficients	PROC CANCORR	VDEP (or WDEP) T (or ALL)

Example

Example 20.1. Canonical Correlation Analysis of Fitness Club Data

Three physiological and three exercise variables are measured on twenty middle-aged men in a fitness club. You can use the CANCORR procedure to determine whether the physiological variables are related in any way to the exercise variables. The following statements create the SAS data set Fit:

```
data Fit;
   input Weight Waist Pulse Chins Situps Jumps;
   datalines;
191  36  50   5  162   60
189  37  52   2  110   60
193  38  58  12  101  101
162  35  62  12  105   37
189  35  46  13  155   58
182  36  56   4  101   42
211  38  56   8  101   38
167  34  60   6  125   40
176  31  74  15  200   40
154  33  56  17  251  250
169  34  50  17  120   38
166  33  52  13  210  115
154  34  64  14  215  105
247  46  50   1   50   50
```

```
193  36  46   6   70   31
202  37  62  12  210  120
176  37  54   4   60   25
157  32  52  11  230   80
156  33  54  15  225   73
138  33  68   2  110   43
;
proc cancorr data=Fit all
     vprefix=Physiological vname='Physiological Measurements'
     wprefix=Exercises wname='Exercises';
   var Weight Waist Pulse;
   with Chins Situps Jumps;
   title 'Middle-Aged Men in a Health Fitness Club';
   title2 'Data Courtesy of Dr. A. C. Linnerud, NC State Univ';
run;
```

Output 20.1.1. Correlations among the Original Variables

```
                Middle-Aged Men in a Health Fitness Club
             Data Courtesy of Dr. A. C. Linnerud, NC State Univ

                        The CANCORR Procedure

               Correlations Among the Original Variables

          Correlations Among the Physiological Measurements

                      Weight            Waist             Pulse

    Weight            1.0000           0.8702           -0.3658
    Waist             0.8702           1.0000           -0.3529
    Pulse            -0.3658          -0.3529            1.0000

                  Correlations Among the Exercises

                       Chins           Situps             Jumps

    Chins             1.0000           0.6957            0.4958
    Situps            0.6957           1.0000            0.6692
    Jumps             0.4958           0.6692            1.0000

 Correlations Between the Physiological Measurements and the Exercises

                       Chins           Situps             Jumps

    Weight           -0.3897          -0.4931           -0.2263
    Waist            -0.5522          -0.6456           -0.1915
    Pulse             0.1506           0.2250            0.0349
```

Output 20.1.1 displays the correlations among the original variables. The correlations between the physiological and exercise variables are moderate, the largest being −0.6456 between Waist and Situps. There are larger within-set correlations: 0.8702 between Weight and Waist, 0.6957 between Chins and Situps, and 0.6692 between Situps and Jumps.

Output 20.1.2. Canonical Correlations and Multivariate Statistics

```
                  Middle-Aged Men in a Health Fitness Club
             Data Courtesy of Dr. A. C. Linnerud, NC State Univ

                           The CANCORR Procedure

                      Canonical Correlation Analysis

                                 Adjusted    Approximate        Squared
                  Canonical     Canonical       Standard      Canonical
                Correlation   Correlation          Error    Correlation

          1        0.795608      0.754056       0.084197       0.632992
          2        0.200556      -.076399       0.220188       0.040223
          3        0.072570       .             0.228208       0.005266

                                 Eigenvalues of Inv(E)*H
                                   = CanRsq/(1-CanRsq)

                 Eigenvalue    Difference    Proportion    Cumulative

            1        1.7247        1.6828        0.9734        0.9734
            2        0.0419        0.0366        0.0237        0.9970
            3        0.0053                      0.0030        1.0000

                Test of H0: The canonical correlations in the
                  current row and all that follow are zero

                Likelihood    Approximate
                     Ratio        F Value    Num DF    Den DF    Pr > F

          1     0.35039053           2.05         9    34.223    0.0635
          2     0.95472266           0.18         4        30    0.9491
          3     0.99473355           0.08         1        16    0.7748


               Multivariate Statistics and F Approximations

                           S=3    M=-0.5    N=6

Statistic                         Value    F Value    Num DF    Den DF    Pr > F

Wilks' Lambda                0.35039053       2.05         9    34.223    0.0635
Pillai's Trace               0.67848151       1.56         9        48    0.1551
Hotelling-Lawley Trace       1.77194146       2.64         9    19.053    0.0357
Roy's Greatest Root          1.72473874       9.20         3        16    0.0009

          NOTE: F Statistic for Roy's Greatest Root is an upper bound.
```

As Output 20.1.2 shows, the first canonical correlation is 0.7956, which would appear to be substantially larger than any of the between-set correlations. The probability level for the null hypothesis that all the canonical correlations are 0 in the population is only 0.0635, so no firm conclusions can be drawn. The remaining canonical correlations are not worthy of consideration, as can be seen from the probability levels and especially from the negative adjusted canonical correlations.

Because the variables are not measured in the same units, the standardized coefficients rather than the raw coefficients should be interpreted. The correlations given in the canonical structure matrices should also be examined.

Output 20.1.3. Raw and Standardized Canonical Coefficients

```
                 Middle-Aged Men in a Health Fitness Club
              Data Courtesy of Dr. A. C. Linnerud, NC State Univ

                          The CANCORR Procedure

                      Canonical Correlation Analysis

        Raw Canonical Coefficients for the Physiological Measurements

                  Physiological1      Physiological2       Physiological3

Weight            -0.031404688        -0.076319506         -0.007735047
Waist             0.4932416756        0.3687229894         0.1580336471
Pulse             -0.008199315        -0.032051994         0.1457322421

                  Raw Canonical Coefficients for the Exercises

                       Exercises1           Exercises2          Exercises3

   Chins            -0.066113986         -0.071041211        -0.245275347
   Situps           -0.016846231         0.0019737454        0.0197676373
   Jumps            0.0139715689         0.0207141063        -0.008167472


                 Middle-Aged Men in a Health Fitness Club
              Data Courtesy of Dr. A. C. Linnerud, NC State Univ

                          The CANCORR Procedure

                      Canonical Correlation Analysis

   Standardized Canonical Coefficients for the Physiological Measurements

                  Physiological1      Physiological2       Physiological3

Weight                 -0.7754             -1.8844              -0.1910
Waist                   1.5793              1.1806               0.5060
Pulse                  -0.0591             -0.2311               1.0508

            Standardized Canonical Coefficients for the Exercises

                        Exercises1       Exercises2       Exercises3

      Chins                -0.3495          -0.3755          -1.2966
      Situps               -1.0540           0.1235           1.2368
      Jumps                 0.7164           1.0622          -0.4188
```

The first canonical variable for the physiological variables, displayed in Output 20.1.3, is a weighted difference of Waist (1.5793) and Weight (−0.7754), with more emphasis on Waist. The coefficient for Pulse is near 0. The correlations between Waist and Weight and the first canonical variable are both positive, 0.9254 for Waist and 0.6206 for Weight. Weight is therefore a suppressor variable, meaning that its coefficient and its correlation have opposite signs.

The first canonical variable for the exercise variables also shows a mixture of signs, subtracting Situps (−1.0540) and Chins (−0.3495) from Jumps (0.7164), with the most weight on Situps. All the correlations are negative, indicating that Jumps is also a suppressor variable.

It may seem contradictory that a variable should have a coefficient of opposite sign from that of its correlation with the canonical variable. In order to understand how this can happen, consider a simplified situation: predicting Situps from Waist and Weight by multiple regression. In informal terms, it seems plausible that fat people should do fewer sit-ups than skinny people. Assume that the men in the sample do not vary much in height, so there is a strong correlation between Waist and Weight (0.8702). Examine the relationships between fatness and the independent variables:

- People with large waists tend to be fatter than people with small waists. Hence, the correlation between Waist and Situps should be negative.
- People with high weights tend to be fatter than people with low weights. Therefore, Weight should correlate negatively with Situps.
- For a fixed value of Weight, people with large waists tend to be shorter and fatter. Thus, the multiple regression coefficient for Waist should be negative.
- For a fixed value of Waist, people with higher weights tend to be taller and skinnier. The multiple regression coefficient for Weight should, therefore, be positive, of opposite sign from the correlation between Weight and Situps.

Therefore, the general interpretation of the first canonical correlation is that Weight and Jumps act as suppressor variables to enhance the correlation between Waist and Situps. This canonical correlation may be strong enough to be of practical interest, but the sample size is not large enough to draw definite conclusions.

The canonical redundancy analysis (Output 20.1.4) shows that neither of the first pair of canonical variables is a good overall predictor of the opposite set of variables, the proportions of variance explained being 0.2854 and 0.2584. The second and third canonical variables add virtually nothing, with cumulative proportions for all three canonical variables being 0.2969 and 0.2767.

Output 20.1.4. Canonical Redundancy Analysis

Middle-Aged Men in a Health Fitness Club
Data Courtesy of Dr. A. C. Linnerud, NC State Univ

The CANCORR Procedure

Canonical Redundancy Analysis

Standardized Variance of the Physiological Measurements Explained by

	Their Own Canonical Variables			The Opposite Canonical Variables	
Canonical Variable Number	Proportion	Cumulative Proportion	Canonical R-Square	Proportion	Cumulative Proportion
1	0.4508	0.4508	0.6330	0.2854	0.2854
2	0.2470	0.6978	0.0402	0.0099	0.2953
3	0.3022	1.0000	0.0053	0.0016	0.2969

Standardized Variance of the Exercises Explained by

	Their Own Canonical Variables			The Opposite Canonical Variables	
Canonical Variable Number	Proportion	Cumulative Proportion	Canonical R-Square	Proportion	Cumulative Proportion
1	0.4081	0.4081	0.6330	0.2584	0.2584
2	0.4345	0.8426	0.0402	0.0175	0.2758
3	0.1574	1.0000	0.0053	0.0008	0.2767

Middle-Aged Men in a Health Fitness Club
Data Courtesy of Dr. A. C. Linnerud, NC State Univ

The CANCORR Procedure

Canonical Redundancy Analysis

Squared Multiple Correlations Between the Physiological Measurements
and the First M Canonical Variables of the Exercises

M	1	2	3
Weight	0.2438	0.2678	0.2679
Waist	0.5421	0.5478	0.5478
Pulse	0.0701	0.0702	0.0749

Squared Multiple Correlations Between the Exercises and the First
M Canonical Variables of the Physiological Measurements

M	1	2	3
Chins	0.3351	0.3374	0.3396
Situps	0.4233	0.4365	0.4365
Jumps	0.0167	0.0536	0.0539

The squared multiple correlations indicate that the first canonical variable of the physiological measurements has some predictive power for Chins (0.3351) and Situps (0.4233) but almost none for Jumps (0.0167). The first canonical variable of the exercises is a fairly good predictor of Waist (0.5421), a poorer predictor of Weight (0.2438), and nearly useless for predicting Pulse (0.0701).

References

Cooley, W.W. and Lohnes, P.R. (1971), *Multivariate Data Analysis*, New York: John Wiley & Sons, Inc.

Fisher, R.A. (1938), *Statistical Methods for Research Workers*, Tenth Edition, Edinburgh: Oliver & Boyd.

Hanson, R.J. and Norris, M.J. (1981), "Analysis of Measurements Based on the Singular Value Decomposition," *SIAM Journal of Scientific and Statistical Computing*, 2, 363–373.

Helland, I.S. (1987), "On the Interpretation and Use of R^2 in Regression Analysis," *Biometrics*, 43, 61–69.

Hotelling, H. (1935), "The Most Predictable Criterion," *Journal of Educational Psychology*, 26, 139–142.

Hotelling, H. (1936), "Relations Between Two Sets of Variables," *Biometrika*, 28, 321–377.

Kshirsagar, A.M. (1972), *Multivariate Analysis*, New York: Marcel Dekker, Inc.

Lawley, D.N. (1959), "Tests of Significance in Canonical Analysis," *Biometrika*, 46, 59–66.

Mardia, K.V., Kent, J.T., and Bibby, J.M. (1979), *Multivariate Analysis*, London: Academic Press, Inc.

Mulaik, S.A. (1972), *The Foundations of Factor Analysis*, New York: McGraw-Hill Book Co.

Rao, C.R. (1964), "The Use and Interpretation of Principal Component Analysis in Applied Research," *Sankhya A*, 26, 329–358.

Rao, C.R. (1973), *Linear Statistical Inference*, New York: John Wiley & Sons, Inc.

Stewart, D.K. and Love, W.A. (1968), "A General Canonical Correlation Index," *Psychological Bulletin*, 70, 160–163.

Tatsuoka, M.M. (1971), *Multivariate Analysis*, New York: John Wiley & Sons, Inc.

Thompson, B. (1984), "Canonical Correlation Analysis," Sage University Paper series in Quantitative Applications in the Social Sciences, 07-047, Beverly Hills and London: Sage Publications.

Timm, N.H. (1975), *Multivariate Analysis*, Monterey, CA: Brooks-Cole Publishing Co.

van den Wollenberg, A.L. (1977), "Redundancy Analysis—An Alternative to Canonical Correlation Analysis," *Psychometrika*, 42, 207–219.

Wherry, R.J. (1931), "A New Formula for Predicting the Shrinkage of the Coefficient of Multiple Correlation," *Annals of Mathematical Statistics*, 2, 440–457.

Chapter 21
The CANDISC Procedure

Chapter Table of Contents

Chapter 21
The CANDISC Procedure

Overview

Canonical discriminant analysis is a dimension-reduction technique related to principal component analysis and canonical correlation. The methodology used in deriving the canonical coefficients parallels that of a one-way MANOVA. Whereas in MANOVA the goal is to test for equality of the mean vector across class levels, in a canonical discriminant analysis we find linear combinations of the quantitative variables that provide maximal separation between the classes or groups. Given a classification variable and several quantitative variables, the CANDISC procedure derives *canonical variables*, linear combinations of the quantitative variables that summarize between-class variation in much the same way that principal components summarize total variation.

The CANDISC procedure performs a canonical discriminant analysis, computes squared Mahalanobis distances between class means, and performs both univariate and multivariate one-way analyses of variance. Two output data sets can be produced: one containing the canonical coefficients and another containing, among other things, scored canonical variables. The canonical coefficients output data set can be rotated by the FACTOR procedure. It is customary to standardize the canonical coefficients so that the canonical variables have means that are equal to zero and pooled within-class variances that are equal to one. PROC CANDISC displays both standardized and unstandardized canonical coefficients. Correlations between the canonical variables and the original variables as well as the class means for the canonical variables are also displayed; these correlations, sometimes known as loadings, are called canonical structures. The scored canonical variables output data set can be used in conjunction with the PLOT procedure or the %PLOTIT macro to plot pairs of canonical variables to aid visual interpretation of group differences.

Given two or more groups of observations with measurements on several quantitative variables, canonical discriminant analysis derives a linear combination of the variables that has the highest possible multiple correlation with the groups. This maximal multiple correlation is called the *first canonical correlation*. The coefficients of the linear combination are the *canonical coefficients* or *canonical weights*. The variable defined by the linear combination is the *first canonical variable* or *canonical component*. The second canonical correlation is obtained by finding the linear combination uncorrelated with the first canonical variable that has the highest possible multiple correlation with the groups. The process of extracting canonical variables can be repeated until the number of canonical variables equals the number of original variables or the number of classes minus one, whichever is smaller.

The first canonical correlation is at least as large as the multiple correlation between the groups and any of the original variables. If the original variables have high within-group correlations, the first canonical correlation can be large even if all the multiple correlations are small. In other words, the first canonical variable can show substantial differences between the classes, even if none of the original variables do. Canonical variables are sometimes called *discriminant functions*, but this usage is ambiguous because the DISCRIM procedure produces very different functions for classification that are also called discriminant functions.

For each canonical correlation, PROC CANDISC tests the hypothesis that it and all smaller canonical correlations are zero in the population. An F approximation (Rao 1973; Kshirsagar 1972) is used that gives better small-sample results than the usual chi-square approximation. The variables should have an approximate multivariate normal distribution within each class, with a common covariance matrix in order for the probability levels to be valid.

Canonical discriminant analysis is equivalent to canonical correlation analysis between the quantitative variables and a set of dummy variables coded from the class variable. Canonical discriminant analysis is also equivalent to performing the following steps:

1. Transform the variables so that the pooled within-class covariance matrix is an identity matrix.
2. Compute class means on the transformed variables.
3. Perform a principal component analysis on the means, weighting each mean by the number of observations in the class. The eigenvalues are equal to the ratio of between-class variation to within-class variation in the direction of each principal component.
4. Back-transform the principal components into the space of the original variables, obtaining the canonical variables.

An interesting property of the canonical variables is that they are uncorrelated whether the correlation is calculated from the total sample or from the pooled within-class correlations. The canonical coefficients are not orthogonal, however, so the canonical variables do not represent perpendicular directions through the space of the original variables.

Getting Started

The data in this example are measurements on 159 fish caught off the coast of Finland. The species, weight, three different length measurements, height, and width of each fish is tallied. The complete data set is displayed in Chapter 60, "The STEPDISC Procedure"; the STEPDISC procedure identified all the variables as significant indicators of the differences among the seven fish species.

```
proc format;
   value specfmt
      1='Bream'
      2='Roach'
      3='Whitefish'
      4='Parkki'
      5='Perch'
      6='Pike'
      7='Smelt';
data fish (drop=HtPct WidthPct);
   title 'Fish Measurement Data';
   input Species Weight Length1 Length2 Length3 HtPct
         WidthPct @@;
   Height=HtPct*Length3/100;
   Width=WidthPct*Length3/100;
   format Species specfmt.;
   symbol = put(Species, specfmt2.);
   datalines;
1  242.0 23.2 25.4 30.0 38.4 13.4
1  290.0 24.0 26.3 31.2 40.0 13.8
1  340.0 23.9 26.5 31.1 39.8 15.1
1  363.0 26.3 29.0 33.5 38.0 13.3
 ...[155 more records]
;
```

The following program uses PROC CANDISC to find the three canonical variables that best separate the species of fish in the fish data and creates the output data set outcan. The NCAN= option is used to request that only the first three canonical variables are displayed. The %PLOTIT macro is invoked to create a plot of the first two canonical variables. See Appendix B, "Using the %PLOTIT Macro," for more information on the %PLOTIT macro.

```
proc candisc data=fish ncan=3 out=outcan;
   class Species;
   var Weight Length1 Length2 Length3 Height Width;
run;
%plotit(data=outcan, plotvars=Can2 Can1,
        labelvar=_blank_, symvar=symbol, typevar=symbol,
        symsize=1, symlen=4, tsize=1.5, exttypes=symbol, ls=100,
        plotopts=vaxis=-5 to 15 by 5, vtoh=, extend=close);
```

PROC CANDISC begins by displaying summary information about the variables in the analysis. This information includes the number of observations, the number of quantitative variables in the analysis (specified with the VAR statement), and the number of classes in the classification variable (specified with the CLASS statement). The frequency of each class is also displayed.

```
                         Fish Measurement Data

                         The CANDISC Procedure

     Observations     158            DF Total                 157
     Variables          6            DF Within Classes        151
     Classes            7            DF Between Classes         6


                       Class Level Information

                  Variable
  Species         Name            Frequency        Weight    Proportion

  Bream           Bream                  34       34.0000      0.215190
  Parkki          Parkki                 11       11.0000      0.069620
  Perch           Perch                  56       56.0000      0.354430
  Pike            Pike                   17       17.0000      0.107595
  Roach           Roach                  20       20.0000      0.126582
  Smelt           Smelt                  14       14.0000      0.088608
  Whitefish       Whitefish               6        6.0000      0.037975
```

Figure 21.1. Summary Information

PROC CANDISC performs a multivariate one-way analysis of variance (one-way MANOVA) and provides four multivariate tests of the hypothesis that the class mean vectors are equal. These tests, shown in Figure 21.2, indicate that not all of the mean vectors are equal ($p < .0001$).

```
                        Fish Measurement Data

                        The CANDISC Procedure

          Multivariate Statistics and F Approximations

                      S=6     M=-0.5     N=72

Statistic                        Value    F Value    Num DF    Den DF    Pr > F

Wilks' Lambda               0.00036325      90.71        36    643.89    <.0001
Pillai's Trace              3.10465132      26.99        36       906    <.0001
Hotelling-Lawley Trace     52.05799676     209.24        36    413.64    <.0001
Roy's Greatest Root        39.13499776     984.90         6       151    <.0001

        NOTE: F Statistic for Roy's Greatest Root is an upper bound.
```

Figure 21.2. MANOVA and Multivariate Tests

The first canonical correlation is the greatest possible multiple correlation with the classes that can be achieved using a linear combination of the quantitative variables. The first canonical correlation, displayed in Figure 21.3, is 0.987463.

```
                        Fish Measurement Data

                        The CANDISC Procedure

                          Adjusted    Approximate        Squared
             Canonical   Canonical       Standard      Canonical
           Correlation Correlation          Error    Correlation

      1       0.987463    0.986671       0.001989       0.975084
      2       0.952349    0.950095       0.007425       0.906969
      3       0.838637    0.832518       0.023678       0.703313
      4       0.633094    0.623649       0.047821       0.400809
      5       0.344157    0.334170       0.070356       0.118444
      6       0.005701     .             0.079806       0.000033
```

Figure 21.3. Canonical Correlations

A likelihood ratio test is displayed of the hypothesis that the current canonical correlation and all smaller ones are zero. The first line is equivalent to Wilks' Lambda multivariate test.

```
           Test of H0: The canonical correlations in the
             current row and all that follow are zero

           Likelihood   Approximate
                Ratio       F Value    Num DF    Den DF    Pr > F

      1    0.00036325         90.71        36    643.89    <.0001
      2    0.01457896         46.46        25    547.58    <.0001
      3    0.15671134         23.61        16    452.79    <.0001
      4    0.52820347         12.09         9    362.78    <.0001
      5    0.88152702          4.88         4       300    0.0008
      6    0.99996749          0.00         1       151    0.9442
```

Figure 21.4. Likelihood Ratio Test

The first canonical variable, Can1, shows that the linear combination of the centered variables Can1$= -0.0006\times$Weight $-$ $0.33\times$Length1 $-$ $2.49\times$Length2 $+$ $2.60\times$Length3 $+$ $1.12\times$Height $-$ $1.45\times$Width separates the species most effectively (see Figure 21.5).

Fish Measurement Data

The CANDISC Procedure

Raw Canonical Coefficients

Variable	Can1	Can2	Can3
Weight	-0.000648508	-0.005231659	-0.005596192
Length1	-0.329435762	-0.626598051	-2.934324102
Length2	-2.486133674	-0.690253987	4.045038893
Length3	2.595648437	1.803175454	-1.139264914
Height	1.121983854	-0.714749340	0.283202557
Width	-1.446386704	-0.907025481	0.741486686

Figure 21.5. Raw Canonical Coefficients

PROC CANDISC computes the means of the canonical variables for each class. The first canonical variable is the linear combination of the variables Weight, Length1, Length2, Length3, Height, and Width that provides the greatest difference (in terms of a univariate F-test) between the class means. The second canonical variable provides the greatest difference between class means while being uncorrelated with the first canonical variable.

Fish Measurement Data

The CANDISC Procedure

Class Means on Canonical Variables

Species	Can1	Can2	Can3
Bream	10.94142464	0.52078394	0.23496708
Parkki	2.58903743	-2.54722416	-0.49326158
Perch	-4.47181389	-1.70822715	1.29281314
Pike	-4.89689441	8.22140791	-0.16469132
Roach	-0.35837149	0.08733611	-1.10056438
Smelt	-4.09136653	-2.35805841	-4.03836098
Whitefish	-0.39541755	-0.42071778	1.06459242

Figure 21.6. Class Means for Canonical Variables

A plot of the first two canonical variables (Figure 21.7) shows that Can1 discriminates between three groups: 1) bream; 2) whitefish, roach, and parkki; and 3) smelt, pike, and perch. Can2 best discriminates between pike and the other species.

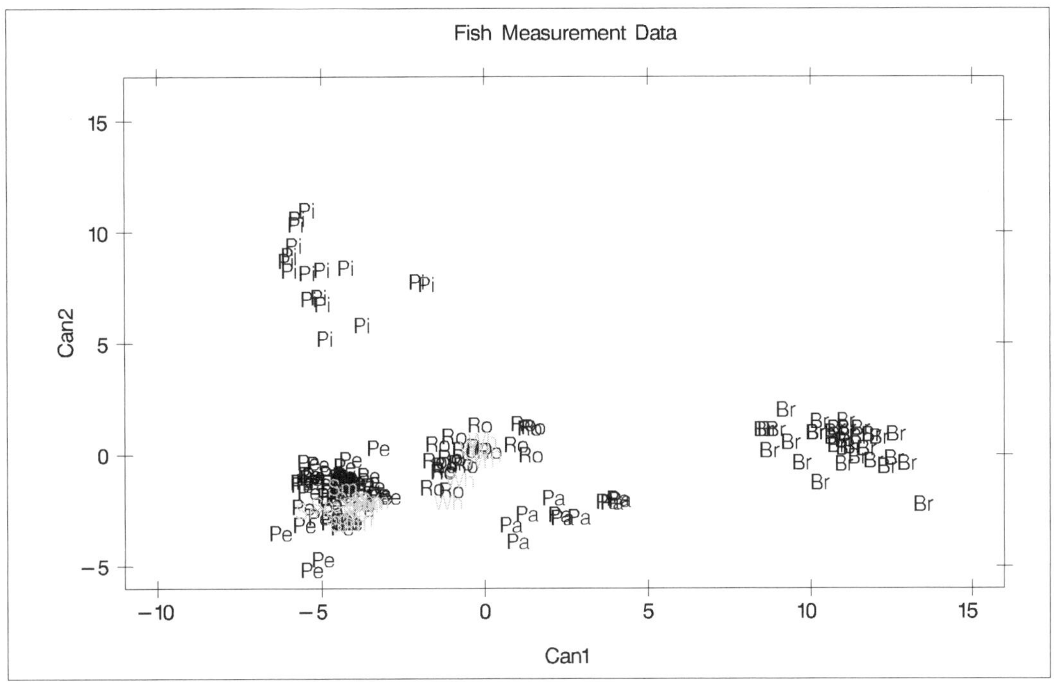

Figure 21.7. Plot of First Two Canonical Variables

Syntax

The following statements are available in PROC CANDISC.

PROC CANDISC < *options* > **;**
  CLASS *variable* **;**
  BY *variables* **;**
  FREQ *variable* **;**
  VAR *variables* **;**
  WEIGHT *variable* **;**

The BY, CLASS, FREQ, VAR, and WEIGHT statements are described after the PROC CANDISC statement.

PROC CANDISC Statement

PROC CANDISC < *options* > **;**

This statement invokes the CANDISC procedure. The options listed in the following table can appear in the PROC CANDISC statement.

Table 21.1. CANDISC Procedure Options

Task	Options
Specify Data Sets	DATA=
	OUT=
	OUTSTAT=
Control Canonical Variables	NCAN=
	PREFIX=
Determine Singularity	SINGULAR=
Control Displayed Correlations	BCORR
	PCORR
	TCORR
	WCORR
Control Displayed Covariances	BCOV
	PCOV
	TCOV
	WCOV
Control Displayed SSCP Matrices	BSSCP
	PSSCP
	TSSCP
	WSSCP
Suppress Output	NOPRINT
	SHORT
Miscellaneous	ALL
	ANOVA
	DISTANCE
	SIMPLE
	STDMEAN

ALL

activates all of the display options.

ANOVA

displays univariate statistics for testing the hypothesis that the class means are equal in the population for each variable.

BCORR

displays between-class correlations.

BCOV

displays between-class covariances. The between-class covariance matrix equals the between-class SSCP matrix divided by $n(c-1)/c$, where n is the number of observations and c is the number of classes. The between-class covariances should be interpreted in comparison with the total-sample and within-class covariances, not as formal estimates of population parameters.

BSSCP

displays the between-class SSCP matrix.

DATA=*SAS-data-set*

specifies the data set to be analyzed. The data set can be an ordinary SAS data set or one of several specially structured data sets created by SAS statistical procedures. These specially structured data sets include TYPE=CORR, COV, CSSCP, and SSCP. If you omit the DATA= option, the procedure uses the most recently created SAS data set.

DISTANCE

displays squared Mahalanobis distances between the group means, F statistics, and the corresponding probabilities of greater squared Mahalanobis distances between the group means.

NCAN=*n*

specifies the number of canonical variables to be computed. The value of n must be less than or equal to the number of variables. If you specify NCAN=0, the procedure displays the canonical correlations, but not the canonical coefficients, structures, or means. A negative value suppresses the canonical analysis entirely. Let v be the number of variables in the VAR statement and c be the number of classes. If you omit the NCAN= option, only $\min(v, c-1)$ canonical variables are generated; if you also specify an OUT= output data set, v canonical variables are generated, and the last $v-(c-1)$ canonical variables have missing values.

NOPRINT

suppresses the normal display of results. Note that this option temporarily disables the Output Delivery System (ODS); see Chapter 15, "Using the Output Delivery System," for more information.

OUT=*SAS-data-set*

creates an output SAS data set containing the original data and the canonical variable scores. To create a permanent SAS data set, specify a two-level name (refer to *SAS Language Reference: Concepts*, for more information on permanent SAS data sets).

OUTSTAT=*SAS-data-set*

creates a TYPE=CORR output SAS data set that contains various statistics including class means, standard deviations, correlations, canonical correlations, canonical structures, canonical coefficients, and means of canonical variables for each class. To create a permanent SAS data set, specify a two-level name (refer to *SAS Language Reference: Concepts*, for more information on permanent SAS data sets).

PCORR

displays pooled within-class correlations (partial correlations based on the pooled within-class covariances).

PCOV

displays pooled within-class covariances.

PREFIX=*name*

specifies a prefix for naming the canonical variables. By default the names are Can1, Can2, Can3 and so forth. If you specify PREFIX=Abc, the components are named Abc1, Abc2, and so on. The number of characters in the prefix, plus the number of digits required to designate the canonical variables, should not exceed 32. The prefix is truncated if the combined length exceeds 32.

PSSCP

displays the pooled within-class corrected SSCP matrix.

SHORT

suppresses the display of canonical structures, canonical coefficients, and class means on canonical variables; only tables of canonical correlations and multivariate test statistics are displayed.

SIMPLE

displays simple descriptive statistics for the total sample and within each class.

SINGULAR=*p*

specifies the criterion for determining the singularity of the total-sample correlation matrix and the pooled within-class covariance matrix, where $0 < p < 1$. The default is SINGULAR=1E−8.

Let **S** be the total-sample correlation matrix. If the R^2 for predicting a quantitative variable in the VAR statement from the variables preceding it exceeds $1 - p$, **S** is considered singular. If **S** is singular, the probability levels for the multivariate test statistics and canonical correlations are adjusted for the number of variables with R^2 exceeding $1 - p$.

If **S** is considered singular and the inverse of **S** (Squared Mahalanobis Distances) is required, a quasi-inverse is used instead. For details see the "Quasi-Inverse" section in Chapter 25, "The DISCRIM Procedure."

STDMEAN

displays total-sample and pooled within-class standardized class means.

TCORR

displays total-sample correlations.

TCOV

displays total-sample covariances.

TSSCP

displays the total-sample corrected SSCP matrix.

WCORR
displays within-class correlations for each class level.

WCOV
displays within-class covariances for each class level.

WSSCP
displays the within-class corrected SSCP matrix for each class level.

BY Statement

BY *variables* **;**

You can specify a BY statement with PROC CANDISC to obtain separate analyses on observations in groups defined by the BY variables. When a BY statement appears, the procedure expects the input data set to be sorted in order of the BY variables.

If your input data set is not sorted in ascending order, use one of the following alternatives:

- Sort the data using the SORT procedure with a similar BY statement.
- Specify the BY statement option NOTSORTED or DESCENDING in the BY statement for the CANDISC procedure. The NOTSORTED option does not mean that the data are unsorted but rather that the data are arranged in groups (according to values of the BY variables) and that these groups are not necessarily in alphabetical or increasing numeric order.
- Create an index on the BY variables using the DATASETS procedure (in base SAS software).

For more information on the BY statement, refer to the discussion in *SAS Language Reference: Concepts*. For more information on the DATASETS procedure, refer to the discussion in the *SAS Procedures Guide*.

CLASS Statement

CLASS *variable* **;**

The values of the CLASS variable define the groups for analysis. Class levels are determined by the formatted values of the CLASS variable. The CLASS variable can be numeric or character. A CLASS statement is required.

FREQ Statement

FREQ *variable* ;

If a variable in the data set represents the frequency of occurrence for the other values in the observation, include the name of the variable in a FREQ statement. The procedure then treats the data set as if each observation appears n times, where n is the value of the FREQ variable for the observation. The total number of observations is considered to be equal to the sum of the FREQ variable when the procedure determines degrees of freedom for significance probabilities.

If the value of the FREQ variable is missing or is less than one, the observation is not used in the analysis. If the value is not an integer, the value is truncated to an integer.

VAR Statement

VAR *variables* ;

You specify the quantitative variables to include in the analysis using a VAR statement. If you do not use a VAR statement, the analysis includes all numeric variables not listed in other statements.

WEIGHT Statement

WEIGHT *variable* ;

To use relative weights for each observation in the input data set, place the weights in a variable in the data set and specify the name in a WEIGHT statement. This is often done when the variance associated with each observation is different and the values of the WEIGHT variable are proportional to the reciprocals of the variances. If the value of the WEIGHT variable is missing or is less than zero, then a value of zero for the weight is assumed.

The WEIGHT and FREQ statements have a similar effect except that the WEIGHT statement does not alter the degrees of freedom.

Details

Missing Values

If an observation has a missing value for any of the quantitative variables, it is omitted from the analysis. If an observation has a missing CLASS value but is otherwise complete, it is not used in computing the canonical correlations and coefficients; however, canonical variable scores are computed for that observation for the OUT= data set.

Computational Details

General Formulas

Canonical discriminant analysis is equivalent to canonical correlation analysis between the quantitative variables and a set of dummy variables coded from the class variable. In the following notation the dummy variables will be denoted by $\mathbf{y}$ and the quantitative variables by $\mathbf{x}$. The total sample covariance matrix for the $\mathbf{x}$ and $\mathbf{y}$ variables is

$$\mathbf{S} = \begin{bmatrix} \mathbf{S}_{xx} & \mathbf{S}_{xy} \\ \mathbf{S}_{yx} & \mathbf{S}_{yy} \end{bmatrix}$$

When c is the number of groups, n_t is the number of observations in group t, and $\mathbf{S}_t$ is the sample covariance matrix for the $\mathbf{x}$ variables in group t, the within-class pooled covariance matrix for the $\mathbf{x}$ variables is

$$\mathbf{S}_p = \frac{1}{\sum n_t - c} \sum (n_t - 1)\mathbf{S}_t$$

The canonical correlations, ρ_i, are the square roots of the eigenvalues, λ_i, of the following matrix. The corresponding eigenvectors are $\mathbf{v}_i$.

$$\mathbf{S}_p{}^{-1/2}\mathbf{S}_{xy}\mathbf{S}_{yy}{}^{-1}\mathbf{S}_{yx}\mathbf{S}_p{}^{-1/2}$$

Let $\mathbf{V}$ be the matrix with the eigenvectors $\mathbf{v}_i$ that correspond to nonzero eigenvalues as columns. The raw canonical coefficients are calculated as follows

$$\mathbf{R} = \mathbf{S}_p{}^{-1/2}\mathbf{V}$$

The pooled within-class standardized canonical coefficients are

$$\mathbf{P} = \mathrm{diag}(\mathbf{S}_p)^{1/2}\mathbf{R}$$

And the total sample standardized canonical coefficients are

$$\mathbf{T} = \mathrm{diag}(\mathbf{S}_{xx})^{1/2}\mathbf{R}$$

Let $\mathbf{X}_c$ be the matrix with the centered $\mathbf{x}$ variables as columns. The canonical scores may be calculated by any of the following

$$\mathbf{X}_c\,\mathbf{R}$$

$$\mathbf{X}_c\,\mathrm{diag}(\mathbf{S}_p)^{-1/2}\mathbf{P}$$

$$\mathbf{X}_c\,\mathrm{diag}(\mathbf{S}_{xx})^{-1/2}\mathbf{T}$$

For the Multivariate tests based on $\mathbf{E}^{-1}\mathbf{H}$

$$\mathbf{E} = (n-1)(\mathbf{S}_{yy} - \mathbf{S}_{yx}\mathbf{S}_{xx}^{-1}\mathbf{S}_{xy})$$

$$\mathbf{H} = (n-1)\mathbf{S}_{yx}\mathbf{S}_{xx}^{-1}\mathbf{S}_{xy}$$

where n is the total number of observations.

Input Data Set

The input DATA= data set can be an ordinary SAS data set or one of several specially structured data sets created by statistical procedures available with SAS/STAT software. For more information on special types of data sets, see Appendix A, "Special SAS Data Sets." The BY variable in these data sets becomes the CLASS variable in PROC CANDISC. These specially structured data sets include

- TYPE=CORR data sets created by PROC CORR using a BY statement
- TYPE=COV data sets created by PROC PRINCOMP using both the COV option and a BY statement
- TYPE=CSSCP data sets created by PROC CORR using the CSSCP option and a BY statement, where the OUT= data set is assigned TYPE=CSSCP with the TYPE= data set option
- TYPE=SSCP data sets created by PROC REG using both the OUTSSCP= option and a BY statement.

When the input data set is TYPE=CORR, TYPE=COV, or TYPE=CSSCP, PROC CANDISC reads the number of observations for each class from the observations with _TYPE_='N' and the variable means in each class from the observations with _TYPE_='MEAN'. The CANDISC procedure then reads the within-class correlations from the observations with _TYPE_='CORR', the standard deviations from the observations with _TYPE_='STD' (data set TYPE=CORR), the within-class covariances from the observations with _TYPE_='COV' (data set TYPE=COV), or the within-class corrected sums of squares and crossproducts from the observations with _TYPE_='CSSCP' (data set TYPE=CSSCP).

When the data set does not include any observations with _TYPE_='CORR' (data set TYPE=CORR), _TYPE_='COV' (data set TYPE=COV), or _TYPE_='CSSCP' (data set TYPE=CSSCP) for each class, PROC CANDISC reads the pooled within-class information from the data set. In this case, PROC CANDISC reads the pooled within-class correlations from the observations with _TYPE_='PCORR', the pooled within-class standard deviations from the observations with _TYPE_='PSTD' (data set TYPE=CORR), the pooled within-class covariances from the observations with _TYPE_='PCOV' (data set TYPE=COV), or the pooled within-class corrected SSCP matrix from the observations with_TYPE_='PSSCP' (data set TYPE=CSSCP).

When the input data set is TYPE=SSCP, PROC CANDISC reads the number of observations for each class from the observations with _TYPE_='N', the sum of weights of observations from the variable INTERCEPT in observations with _TYPE_='SSCP' and _NAME_='INTERCEPT', the variable sums from the variable=*variablenames* in observations with _TYPE_='SSCP' and _NAME_='INTERCEPT', and the uncorrected sums of squares and crossproducts from the variable=*variablenames* in observations with _TYPE_='SSCP' and _NAME_=*variablenames*.

Output Data Sets

OUT= Data Set

The OUT= data set contains all the variables in the original data set plus new variables containing the canonical variable scores. You determine the number of new variables using the NCAN= option. The names of the new variables are formed as described in the PREFIX= option. The new variables have means equal to zero and pooled within-class variances equal to one. An OUT= data set cannot be created if the DATA= data set is not an ordinary SAS data set.

OUTSTAT= Data Set

The OUTSTAT= data set is similar to the TYPE=CORR data set produced by the CORR procedure but contains many results in addition to those produced by the CORR procedure.

The OUTSTAT= data set is TYPE=CORR, and it contains the following variables:

- the BY variables, if any
- the CLASS variable
- _TYPE_, a character variable of length 8 that identifies the type of statistic
- _NAME_, a character variable of length 32 that identifies the row of the matrix or the name of the canonical variable
- the quantitative variables (those in the VAR statement, or if there is no VAR statement, all numeric variables not listed in any other statement)

The observations, as identified by the variable _TYPE_, have the following _TYPE_ values:

TYPE	Contents
N	number of observations for both the total sample (CLASS variable missing) and within each class (CLASS variable present)
SUMWGT	sum of weights for both the total sample (CLASS variable missing) and within each class (CLASS variable present) if a WEIGHT statement is specified
MEAN	means for both the total sample (CLASS variable missing) and within each class (CLASS variable present)
STDMEAN	total-standardized class means
PSTDMEAN	pooled within-class standardized class means
STD	standard deviations for both the total sample (CLASS variable missing) and within each class (CLASS variable present)
PSTD	pooled within-class standard deviations
BSTD	between-class standard deviations
RSQUARED	univariate R^2s

The following kinds of observations are identified by the combination of the variables _TYPE_ and _NAME_. When the _TYPE_ variable has one of the following values, the _NAME_ variable identifies the row of the matrix.

TYPE	Contents
CSSCP	corrected SSCP matrix for the total sample (CLASS variable missing) and within each class (CLASS variable present)
PSSCP	pooled within-class corrected SSCP matrix
BSSCP	between-class SSCP matrix
COV	covariance matrix for the total sample (CLASS variable missing) and within each class (CLASS variable present)
PCOV	pooled within-class covariance matrix
BCOV	between-class covariance matrix
CORR	correlation matrix for the total sample (CLASS variable missing) and within each class (CLASS variable present)
PCORR	pooled within-class correlation matrix
BCORR	between-class correlation matrix

When the _TYPE_ variable has one of the following values, the _NAME_ variable identifies the canonical variable:

TYPE	**Contents**
CANCORR	canonical correlations
STRUCTUR	canonical structure
BSTRUCT	between canonical structure
PSTRUCT	pooled within-class canonical structure
SCORE	total sample standardized canonical coefficients
PSCORE	pooled within-class standardized canonical coefficients
RAWSCORE	raw canonical coefficients
CANMEAN	means of the canonical variables for each class

Computational Resources

In the following discussion, let

n = number of observations
c = number of class levels
v = number of variables in the VAR list
l = length of the CLASS variable

Memory Requirements

The amount of memory in bytes for temporary storage needed to process the data is

$$c(4v^2 + 28v + 4l + 68) + 16v^2 + 96v + 4l$$

With the ANOVA option, the temporary storage must be increased by 16v bytes. The DISTANCE option requires an additional temporary storage of $4v^2 + 4v$ bytes.

Time Requirements

The following factors determine the time requirements of the CANDISC procedure.

- The time needed for reading the data and computing covariance matrices is proportional to nv^2. PROC CANDISC must also look up each class level in the list. This is faster if the data are sorted by the CLASS variable. The time for looking up class levels is proportional to a value ranging from n to $n \log(c)$.
- The time for inverting a covariance matrix is proportional to v^3.
- The time required for the canonical discriminant analysis is proportional to v^3.

Each of the preceding factors has a different constant of proportionality.

Displayed Output

The output produced by PROC CANDISC includes

- Class Level Information, including the values of the classification variable, the Frequency and Weight of each value, and its Proportion in the total sample.

Optional output includes

- Within-Class SSCP Matrices for each group
- Pooled Within-Class SSCP Matrix
- Between-Class SSCP Matrix
- Total-Sample SSCP Matrix
- Within-Class Covariance Matrices for each group
- Pooled Within-Class Covariance Matrix
- Between-Class Covariance Matrix, equal to the between-class SSCP matrix divided by $n(c-1)/c$, where n is the number of observations and c is the number of classes
- Total-Sample Covariance Matrix
- Within-Class Correlation Coefficients and Pr $> |r|$ to test the hypothesis that the within-class population correlation coefficients are zero
- Pooled Within-Class Correlation Coefficients and Pr $> |r|$ to test the hypothesis that the partial population correlation coefficients are zero
- Between-Class Correlation Coefficients and Pr $> |r|$ to test the hypothesis that the between-class population correlation coefficients are zero
- Total-Sample Correlation Coefficients and Pr $> |r|$ to test the hypothesis that the total population correlation coefficients are zero
- Simple Statistics including N (the number of observations), Sum, Mean, Variance, and Standard Deviation both for the total sample and within each class
- Total-Sample Standardized Class Means, obtained by subtracting the grand mean from each class mean and dividing by the total sample standard deviation
- Pooled Within-Class Standardized Class Means, obtained by subtracting the grand mean from each class mean and dividing by the pooled within-class standard deviation
- Pairwise Squared Distances Between Groups
- Univariate Test Statistics, including Total-Sample Standard Deviations, Pooled Within-Class Standard Deviations, Between-Class Standard Deviations, R^2, $R^2/(1-R^2)$, F, and Pr $> F$ (univariate F values and probability levels for one-way analyses of variance)

By default, PROC CANDISC displays these statistics:

- Multivariate Statistics and F Approximations including Wilks' Lambda, Pillai's Trace, Hotelling-Lawley Trace, and Roy's Greatest Root with F approximations, degrees of freedom (Num DF and Den DF), and probability values ($\text{Pr} > F$). Each of these four multivariate statistics tests the hypothesis that the class means are equal in the population. See the "Multivariate Tests" section in Chapter 3, "Introduction to Regression Procedures," for more information.
- Canonical Correlations
- Adjusted Canonical Correlations (Lawley 1959). These are asymptotically less biased than the raw correlations and can be negative. The adjusted canonical correlations may not be computable and are displayed as missing values if two canonical correlations are nearly equal or if some are close to zero. A missing value is also displayed if an adjusted canonical correlation is larger than a previous adjusted canonical correlation.
- Approx Standard Error, approximate standard error of the canonical correlations
- Squared Canonical Correlations
- Eigenvalues of $\mathbf{E}^{-1}\mathbf{H}$. Each eigenvalue is equal to $\rho^2/(1-\rho^2)$, where ρ^2 is the corresponding squared canonical correlation and can be interpreted as the ratio of between-class variation to pooled within-class variation for the corresponding canonical variable. The table includes Eigenvalues, Differences between successive eigenvalues, the Proportion of the sum of the eigenvalues, and the Cumulative proportion.
- Likelihood Ratio for the hypothesis that the current canonical correlation and all smaller ones are zero in the population. The likelihood ratio for the hypothesis that all canonical correlations equal zero is Wilks' lambda.
- Approx F statistic based on Rao's approximation to the distribution of the likelihood ratio (Rao 1973, p. 556; Kshirsagar 1972, p. 326)
- Num DF (numerator degrees of freedom), Den DF (denominator degrees of freedom), and $\text{Pr} > F$, the probability level associated with the F statistic

The following statistics can be suppressed with the SHORT option:

- Total Canonical Structure, giving total-sample correlations between the canonical variables and the original variables
- Between Canonical Structure, giving between-class correlations between the canonical variables and the original variables
- Pooled Within Canonical Structure, giving pooled within-class correlations between the canonical variables and the original variables
- Total-Sample Standardized Canonical Coefficients, standardized to give canonical variables with zero mean and unit pooled within-class variance when applied to the total-sample standardized variables

- Pooled Within-Class Standardized Canonical Coefficients, standardized to give canonical variables with zero mean and unit pooled within-class variance when applied to the pooled within-class standardized variables
- Raw Canonical Coefficients, standardized to give canonical variables with zero mean and unit pooled within-class variance when applied to the centered variables
- Class Means on Canonical Variables

ODS Table Names

PROC CANDISC assigns a name to each table it creates. You can use these names to reference the table when using the Output Delivery System (ODS) to select tables and create output data sets. These names are listed in the following table. For more information on ODS, see Chapter 15, "Using the Output Delivery System."

Table 21.2. ODS Tables Produced in PROC CANDISC

ODS Table Name	Description	PROC CANDISC Option
ANOVA	Univariate statistics	ANOVA
AveRSquare	Average R-square	ANOVA
BCorr	Between-class correlations	BCORR
BCov	Between-class covariances	BCOV
BSSCP	Between-class SSCP matrix	BSSCP
BStruc	Between canonical structure	default
CanCorr	Canonical correlations	default
CanonicalMeans	Class means on canonical variables	default
Counts	Number of observations, variables, classes, df	default
CovDF	DF for covariance matrices, not printed	any *COV option
Dist	Squared distances	MAHALANOBIS
DistFValues	F statistics based on squared distances	MAHALANOBIS
DistProb	Probabilities for F statistics from squared distances	MAHALANOBIS
Levels	Class level information	default
MultStat	MANOVA	default
PCoef	Pooled standard canonical coefficients	default
PCorr	Pooled within-class correlations	PCORR
PCov	Pooled within-class covariances	PCOV
PSSCP	Pooled within-class SSCP matrix	PSSCP
PStdMeans	Pooled standardized class means	STDMEAN
PStruc	Pooled within canonical structure	default
RCoef	Raw canonical coefficients	default
SimpleStatistics	Simple statistics	SIMPLE
TCoef	Total-sample standard canonical coefficients	default
TCorr	Total-sample correlations	TCORR
TCov	Total-sample covariances	TCOV
TSSCP	Total-sample SSCP matrix	TSSCP

Table 21.2. (continued)

ODS Table Name	Description	PROC CANDISC Option
TStdMeans	Total standardized class means	STDMEAN
TStruc	Total canonical structure	default
WCorr	Within-class correlations	WCORR
WCov	Within-class covariances	WCOV
WSSCP	Within-class SSCP matrices	WSSCP

Example

Example 21.1. Analysis of Iris Data Using PROC CANDISC

The iris data published by Fisher (1936) have been widely used for examples in discriminant analysis and cluster analysis. The sepal length, sepal width, petal length, and petal width are measured in millimeters on fifty iris specimens from each of three species: *Iris setosa, I. versicolor, and I. virginica.*

This example is a canonical discriminant analysis that creates an output data set containing scores on the canonical variables and plots the canonical variables. The following statements produce Output 21.1.1 through Output 21.1.7:

```
proc format;
   value specname
      1='Setosa    '
      2='Versicolor'
      3='Virginica ';
run;

data iris;
   title 'Fisher (1936) Iris Data';
   input SepalLength SepalWidth PetalLength PetalWidth
         Species @@;
   format Species specname.;
   label SepalLength='Sepal Length in mm.'
         SepalWidth ='Sepal Width in mm.'
         PetalLength='Petal Length in mm.'
         PetalWidth ='Petal Width in mm.';
   symbol = put(Species, specname10.);
   datalines;
50 33 14 02 1 64 28 56 22 3 65 28 46 15 2 67 31 56 24 3
63 28 51 15 3 46 34 14 03 1 69 31 51 23 3 62 22 45 15 2
59 32 48 18 2 46 36 10 02 1 61 30 46 14 2 60 27 51 16 2
65 30 52 20 3 56 25 39 11 2 65 30 55 18 3 58 27 51 19 3
68 32 59 23 3 51 33 17 05 1 57 28 45 13 2 62 34 54 23 3
77 38 67 22 3 63 33 47 16 2 67 33 57 25 3 76 30 66 21 3
49 25 45 17 3 55 35 13 02 1 67 30 52 23 3 70 32 47 14 2
64 32 45 15 2 61 28 40 13 2 48 31 16 02 1 59 30 51 18 3
55 24 38 11 2 63 25 50 19 3 64 32 53 23 3 52 34 14 02 1
49 36 14 01 1 54 30 45 15 2 79 38 64 20 3 44 32 13 02 1
67 33 57 21 3 50 35 16 06 1 58 26 40 12 2 44 30 13 02 1
```

```
77 28 67 20 3 63 27 49 18 3 47 32 16 02 1 55 26 44 12 2
50 23 33 10 2 72 32 60 18 3 48 30 14 03 1 51 38 16 02 1
61 30 49 18 3 48 34 19 02 1 50 30 16 02 1 50 32 12 02 1
61 26 56 14 3 64 28 56 21 3 43 30 11 01 1 58 40 12 02 1
51 38 19 04 1 67 31 44 14 2 62 28 48 18 3 49 30 14 02 1
51 35 14 02 1 56 30 45 15 2 58 27 41 10 2 50 34 16 04 1
46 32 14 02 1 60 29 45 15 2 57 26 35 10 2 57 44 15 04 1
50 36 14 02 1 77 30 61 23 3 63 34 56 24 3 58 27 51 19 3
57 29 42 13 2 72 30 58 16 3 54 34 15 04 1 52 41 15 01 1
71 30 59 21 3 64 31 55 18 3 60 30 48 18 3 63 29 56 18 3
49 24 33 10 2 56 27 42 13 2 57 30 42 12 2 55 42 14 02 1
49 31 15 02 1 77 26 69 23 3 60 22 50 15 3 54 39 17 04 1
66 29 46 13 2 52 27 39 14 2 60 34 45 16 2 50 34 15 02 1
44 29 14 02 1 50 20 35 10 2 55 24 37 10 2 58 27 39 12 2
47 32 13 02 1 46 31 15 02 1 69 32 57 23 3 62 29 43 13 2
74 28 61 19 3 59 30 42 15 2 51 34 15 02 1 50 35 13 03 1
56 28 49 20 3 60 22 40 10 2 73 29 63 18 3 67 25 58 18 3
49 31 15 01 1 67 31 47 15 2 63 23 44 13 2 54 37 15 02 1
56 30 41 13 2 63 25 49 15 2 61 28 47 12 2 64 29 43 13 2
51 25 30 11 2 57 28 41 13 2 65 30 58 22 3 69 31 54 21 3
54 39 13 04 1 51 35 14 03 1 72 36 61 25 3 65 32 51 20 3
61 29 47 14 2 56 29 36 13 2 69 31 49 15 2 64 27 53 19 3
68 30 55 21 3 55 25 40 13 2 48 34 16 02 1 48 30 14 01 1
45 23 13 03 1 57 25 50 20 3 57 38 17 03 1 51 38 15 03 1
55 23 40 13 2 66 30 44 14 2 68 28 48 14 2 54 34 17 02 1
51 37 15 04 1 52 35 15 02 1 58 28 51 24 3 67 30 50 17 2
63 33 60 25 3 53 37 15 02 1
;
proc candisc data=iris out=outcan distance anova;
   class Species;
   var SepalLength SepalWidth PetalLength PetalWidth;
run;
```

PROC CANDISC first displays information about the observations and the classes in the data set in Output 21.1.1.

Output 21.1.1. Iris Data: Summary Information

```
                         Fisher (1936) Iris Data

                         The CANDISC Procedure

        Observations     150          DF Total                  149
        Variables          4          DF Within Classes         147
        Classes            3          DF Between Classes          2


                        Class Level Information

                    Variable
     Species        Name             Frequency        Weight    Proportion

     Setosa         Setosa                  50       50.0000      0.333333
     Versicolor     Versicolor              50       50.0000      0.333333
     Virginica      Virginica               50       50.0000      0.333333
```

The DISTANCE option in the PROC CANDISC statement displays squared Mahalanobis distances between class means. Results from the DISTANCE option is shown in Output 21.1.2 and Output 21.1.3.

Output 21.1.2. Iris Data: Squared Mahalanobis Distances

```
                    Fisher (1936) Iris Data

                    The CANDISC Procedure

           Pairwise Squared Distances Between Groups

               2              _   _       -1  _   _
              D (i|j) = (X - X )' COV   (X - X )
                          i   j           i   j


                  Squared Distance to Species

      From
      Species          Setosa    Versicolor     Virginica

      Setosa                0      89.86419     179.38471
      Versicolor     89.86419             0      17.20107
      Virginica     179.38471      17.20107             0
```

Output 21.1.3. Iris Data: Squared Mahalanobis Distance Statistics

```
                    Fisher (1936) Iris Data

                    The CANDISC Procedure

           Pairwise Squared Distances Between Groups

               2              _   _       -1  _   _
              D (i|j) = (X - X )' COV   (X - X )
                          i   j           i   j


  F Statistics, NDF=4, DDF=144 for Squared Distance to Species

      From
      Species          Setosa    Versicolor     Virginica

      Setosa                0     550.18889          1098
      Versicolor    550.18889             0     105.31265
      Virginica          1098     105.31265             0


   Prob > Mahalanobis Distance for Squared Distance to Species

      From
      Species          Setosa    Versicolor     Virginica

      Setosa           1.0000        <.0001        <.0001
      Versicolor       <.0001        1.0000        <.0001
      Virginica        <.0001        <.0001        1.0000
```

The ANOVA option specifies testing of the hypothesis that the class means are equal using univariate statistics. The resulting R^2 values (see Output 21.1.4) range from 0.4008 for SepalWidth to 0.9414 for PetalLength, and each variable is significant at the 0.0001 level. The multivariate test for differences between the classes (which is displayed by default) is also significant at the 0.0001 level; you would expect this from the highly significant univariate test results.

Output 21.1.4. Iris Data: Univariate and Multivariate Statistics

Fisher (1936) Iris Data

The CANDISC Procedure

Univariate Test Statistics

F Statistics, Num DF=2, Den DF=147

Variable	Label	Total Standard Deviation	Pooled Standard Deviation	Between Standard Deviation	R-Square	R-Square / (1-RSq)	F Value	Pr > F
SepalLength	Sepal Length in mm.	8.2807	5.1479	7.9506	0.6187	1.6226	119.26	<.0001
SepalWidth	Sepal Width in mm.	4.3587	3.3969	3.3682	0.4008	0.6688	49.16	<.0001
PetalLength	Petal Length in mm.	17.6530	4.3033	20.9070	0.9414	16.0566	1180.16	<.0001
PetalWidth	Petal Width in mm.	7.6224	2.0465	8.9673	0.9289	13.0613	960.01	<.0001

Average R-Square

Unweighted	0.7224358
Weighted by Variance	0.8689444

Multivariate Statistics and F Approximations

S=2 M=0.5 N=71

Statistic	Value	F Value	Num DF	Den DF	Pr > F
Wilks' Lambda	0.02343863	199.15	8	288	<.0001
Pillai's Trace	1.19189883	53.47	8	290	<.0001
Hotelling-Lawley Trace	32.47732024	582.20	8	203.4	<.0001
Roy's Greatest Root	32.19192920	1166.96	4	145	<.0001

NOTE: F Statistic for Roy's Greatest Root is an upper bound.
NOTE: F Statistic for Wilks' Lambda is exact.

The R^2 between Can1 and the class variable, 0.969872, is much larger than the corresponding R^2 for Can2, 0.222027. This is displayed in Output 21.1.5.

Output 21.1.5. Iris Data: Canonical Correlations and Eigenvalues

Fisher (1936) Iris Data

The CANDISC Procedure

	Canonical Correlation	Adjusted Canonical Correlation	Approximate Standard Error	Squared Canonical Correlation
1	0.984821	0.984508	0.002468	0.969872
2	0.471197	0.461445	0.063734	0.222027

Eigenvalues of Inv(E)*H = CanRsq/(1-CanRsq)

Test of H0: The canonical correlations in the current row and all that follow are zero

	Eigenvalue	Difference	Proportion	Cumulative	Likelihood Ratio	Approximate F Value	Num DF	Den DF	Pr > F
1	32.1919	31.9065	0.9912	0.9912	0.02343863	199.15	8	288	<.0001
2	0.2854		0.0088	1.0000	0.77797337	13.79	3	145	<.0001

Output 21.1.6. Iris Data: Correlations Between Canonical and Original Variables

```
                         Fisher (1936) Iris Data

                         The CANDISC Procedure

                       Total Canonical Structure

Variable        Label                           Can1            Can2

SepalLength     Sepal Length in mm.         0.791888        0.217593
SepalWidth      Sepal Width in mm.         -0.530759        0.757989
PetalLength     Petal Length in mm.         0.984951        0.046037
PetalWidth      Petal Width in mm.          0.972812        0.222902


                      Between Canonical Structure

Variable        Label                           Can1            Can2

SepalLength     Sepal Length in mm.         0.991468        0.130348
SepalWidth      Sepal Width in mm.         -0.825658        0.564171
PetalLength     Petal Length in mm.         0.999750        0.022358
PetalWidth      Petal Width in mm.          0.994044        0.108977


                   Pooled Within Canonical Structure

Variable        Label                           Can1            Can2

SepalLength     Sepal Length in mm.         0.222596        0.310812
SepalWidth      Sepal Width in mm.         -0.119012        0.863681
PetalLength     Petal Length in mm.         0.706065        0.167701
PetalWidth      Petal Width in mm.          0.633178        0.737242
```

The raw canonical coefficients (shown in Output 21.1.7) for the first canonical variable, Can1, show that the classes differ most widely on the linear combination of the centered variables $-0.0829378 \times$ SepalLength $- 0.153447 \times$ SepalWidth $+ 0.220121 \times$ PetalLength $+ 0.281046 \times$ PetalWidth.

Output 21.1.7. Iris Data: Canonical Coefficients

```
                         Fisher (1936) Iris Data

                         The CANDISC Procedure

           Total-Sample Standardized Canonical Coefficients

Variable        Label                           Can1            Can2

SepalLength     Sepal Length in mm.      -0.686779533     0.019958173
SepalWidth      Sepal Width in mm.       -0.668825075     0.943441829
PetalLength     Petal Length in mm.       3.885795047    -1.645118866
PetalWidth      Petal Width in mm.        2.142238715     2.164135931


        Pooled Within-Class Standardized Canonical Coefficients

Variable        Label                           Can1            Can2

SepalLength     Sepal Length in mm.      -.4269548486    0.0124075316
SepalWidth      Sepal Width in mm.       -.5212416758    0.7352613085
PetalLength     Petal Length in mm.      0.9472572487    -.4010378190
PetalWidth      Petal Width in mm.       0.5751607719    0.5810398645
```

```
                         Fisher (1936) Iris Data

                         The CANDISC Procedure

                       Raw Canonical Coefficients

Variable          Label                               Can1              Can2

SepalLength       Sepal Length in mm.         -.0829377642      0.0024102149
SepalWidth        Sepal Width in mm.          -.1534473068      0.2164521235
PetalLength       Petal Length in mm.         0.2201211656      -.0931921210
PetalWidth        Petal Width in mm.          0.2810460309      0.2839187853

                  Class Means on Canonical Variables

             Species                 Can1                Can2

             Setosa          -7.607599927         0.215133017
             Versicolor       1.825049490        -0.727899622
             Virginica        5.782550437         0.512766605
```

The plot of canonical variables in Output 21.1.8 shows that of the two canonical variables Can1 has the most discriminatory power. The following invocation of the %PLOTIT macro creates this plot:

```
%plotit(data=outcan, plotvars=Can2 Can1,
        labelvar=_blank_, symvar=symbol, typevar=symbol,
        symsize=1, symlen=4, exttypes=symbol, ls=100,
        tsize=1.5, extend=close);
```

Output 21.1.8. Iris Data: Plot of First Two Canonical Variables

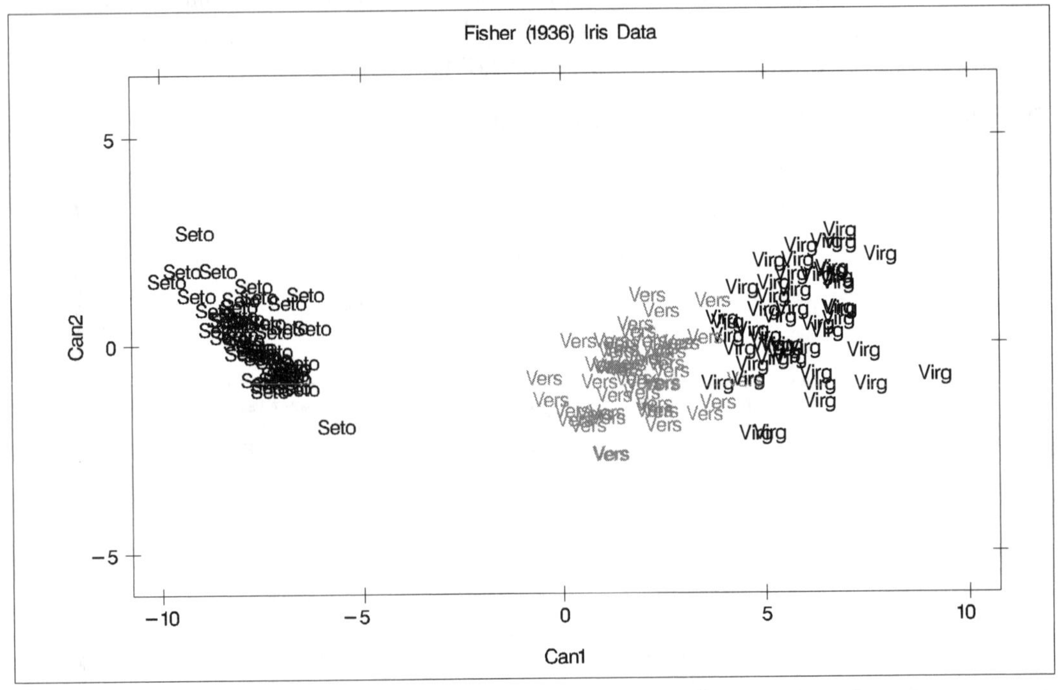

References

Fisher, R.A. (1936), "The Use of Multiple Measurements in Taxonomic Problems," *Annals of Eugenics*, 7, 179–188.

Kshirsagar, A.M. (1972), *Multivariate Analysis*, New York: Marcel Dekker, Inc.

Lawley, D.N. (1959), "Tests of Significance in Canonical Analysis," *Biometrika*, 46, 59–66.

Rao, C.R. (1973), *Linear Statistical Inference*, New York: John Wiley & Sons, Inc.

Chapter 22
The CATMOD Procedure

Chapter Table of Contents

Chapter 22
The CATMOD Procedure

Overview

The CATMOD procedure performs categorical data modeling of data that can be represented by a contingency table. PROC CATMOD fits linear models to functions of response frequencies, and it can be used for linear modeling, log-linear modeling, logistic regression, and repeated measurement analysis. PROC CATMOD uses

- maximum likelihood (ML) estimation of parameters for log-linear models and the analysis of generalized logits
- weighted least-squares (WLS) estimation of parameters for a wide range of general linear models

The CATMOD procedure provides a wide variety of categorical data analyses, many of which are generalizations of continuous data analysis methods. For example, analysis of variance, in the traditional sense, refers to the analysis of means and the partitioning of variation among the means into various sources. Here, the term *analysis of variance* is used in a generalized sense to denote the analysis of response functions and the partitioning of variation among those functions into various sources. The response functions might be mean scores if the dependent variables are ordinally scaled. But they can also be marginal probabilities, cumulative logits, or other functions that incorporate the essential information from the dependent variables.

Types of Input Data

The data that PROC CATMOD analyzes are usually supplied in one of two ways. First, you can supply raw data, where each observation is a subject. Second, you can supply cell count data, where each observation is a cell in a contingency table. (A third way, which uses direct input of the covariance matrix, is also available; details are given in the "Inputting Response Functions and Covariances Directly" section on page 743.)

Suppose detergent preference is related to three other categorical variables: water softness, water temperature, and previous use of a brand of detergent. In the raw data case, each observation in the input data set identifies a given respondent in the study and contains information on all four variables. The data set contains the same number of observations as the survey had respondents. In the cell count case, each observation identifies a given cell in the four-way table of water softness, water temperature, previous use of brand, and brand preference. A fifth variable contains the number of respondents in the cell. In the analysis, this fifth variable is identified in a WEIGHT statement. The data set contains the same number of observations as the number of cross-classifications formed by the four categorical variables. For more on this particular example, see Example 22.1 on page 780. For additional details, see the section "Input Data Sets" on page 742.

Most of the examples in this chapter use cell counts as input and use a WEIGHT statement.

Types of Statistical Analyses

This section illustrates, by example, the wide variety of categorical data analyses that PROC CATMOD provides. For each type of analysis, a brief description of the statistical problem and the SAS statements to provide the analysis are given. For each analysis, assume that the input data set consists of a set of cell counts from a contingency table. The variable specified in the WEIGHT statement contains these counts. In all these analyses, both the dependent and independent variables are categorical.

Linear Model Analysis

Suppose you want to analyze the relationship between the dependent variables (r1, r2) and the independent variables (a, b). Analyze the marginal probabilities of the dependent variables, and use a main-effects model.

```
proc catmod;
   weight wt;
   response marginals;
   model r1*r2=a b;
quit;
```

Log-Linear Model Analysis

Suppose you want to analyze the nominal dependent variables (r1, r2, r3) with a log-linear model. Use maximum likelihood analysis, and include the main effects and the r1*r2 interaction in the model. Obtain the predicted cell frequencies.

```
proc catmod;
   weight wt;
   model r1*r2*r3=_response_ / pred=freq;
   loglin r1|r2 r3;
quit;
```

Logistic Regression

Suppose you want to analyze the relationship between the nominal dependent variable (r) and the independent variables (x1, x2) with a logistic regression analysis. Use maximum likelihood estimation.

```
proc catmod;
   weight wt;
   direct x1 x2;
   model r=x1 x2;
quit;
```

If x1 and x2 are continuous so that each observation has a unique value of these two variables, then it may be more appropriate to use the LOGISTIC, GENMOD, or PROBIT procedure. See the "Logistic Regression" section on page 750.

Repeated Measures Analysis

Suppose the dependent variables (r1, r2, r3) represent the same type of measurement taken at three different times. Analyze the relationship among the dependent variables, the repeated measurement factor (time), and the independent variable (a).

```
proc catmod;
   weight wt;
   response marginals;
   model r1*r2*r3=_response_|a;
   repeated time 3 / _response_=time;
quit;
```

Analysis of Variance

Suppose you want to investigate the relationship between the dependent variable (r) and the independent variables (a, b). Analyze the mean of the dependent variable, and include all main effects and interactions in the model.

```
proc catmod;
   weight wt;
   response mean;
   model r=a|b;
quit;
```

Linear Regression

PROC CATMOD can analyze the relationship between the dependent variables (r1, r2) and the independent variables (x1, x2). Use a linear regression analysis to analyze the marginal probabilities of the dependent variables.

```
proc catmod;
   weight wt;
   direct x1 x2;
   response marginals;
   model r1*r2=x1 x2;
quit;
```

Logistic Analysis of Ordinal Data

Suppose you want to analyze the relationship between the ordinally scaled dependent variable (r) and the independent variable (a). Use cumulative logits to take into account the ordinal nature of the dependent variable. Use weighted least-squares estimation.

```
proc catmod;
   weight wt;
   response clogits;
   model r=_response_ a;
quit;
```

Sample Survey Analysis

Suppose the data set contains estimates of a vector of four functions and their covariance matrix, estimated in such a way as to correspond to the sampling process that is used. Analyze the functions with respect to the independent variables (a, b), and use a main-effects model.

```
proc catmod;
   response read b1-b10;
   model _f_=_response_;
   factors  a 2 , b 5 / _response_=a b;
quit;
```

Background: The Underlying Model

The CATMOD procedure analyzes data that can be represented by a two-dimensional contingency table. The rows of the table correspond to populations (or samples) formed on the basis of one or more independent variables. The columns of the table correspond to observed responses formed on the basis of one or more dependent variables. The frequency in the (i, j)th cell is the number of subjects in the ith population that have the jth response. The frequencies in the table are assumed to follow a product multinomial distribution, corresponding to a sampling design in which a simple random sample is taken for each population. The contingency table can be represented as shown in Table 22.1.

Table 22.1. Contingency Table Representation

	Response				
Sample	1	2	$\cdots$	r	**Total**
1	n_{11}	n_{12}	$\cdots$	n_{1r}	n_1
2	n_{21}	n_{22}	$\cdots$	n_{2r}	n_2
$\vdots$	$\vdots$	$\vdots$	$\ddots$	$\vdots$	$\vdots$
s	n_{s1}	n_{s2}	$\cdots$	n_{sr}	n_s

For each sample i, the probability of the jth response (π_{ij}) is estimated by the sample proportion, $p_{ij} = n_{ij}/n_i$. The vector (p) of all such proportions is then transformed into a vector of functions, denoted by $\mathbf{F} = \mathbf{F}(\mathbf{p})$. If π denotes the vector of true probabilities for the entire table, then the functions of the true probabilities, denoted by $\mathbf{F}(\pi)$, are assumed to follow a linear model

$$\mathbf{E_A}(\mathbf{F}) = \mathbf{F}(\pi) = \mathbf{X}\beta$$

where $\mathbf{E_A}$ denotes asymptotic expectation, $\mathbf{X}$ is the design matrix containing fixed constants, and β is a vector of parameters to be estimated.

PROC CATMOD provides two estimation methods:

- The maximum likelihood method estimates the parameters of the linear model so as to maximize the value of the joint multinomial likelihood function of the responses. Maximum likelihood estimation is available only for the standard response functions, logits and generalized logits, which are used for logistic regression analysis and log-linear model analysis. For details of the theory, refer to Bishop, Fienberg, and Holland (1975).
- The weighted least-squares method minimizes the weighted residual sum of squares for the model. The weights are contained in the inverse covariance matrix of the functions $\mathbf{F}(\mathbf{p})$. According to central limit theory, if the sample sizes within populations are sufficiently large, the elements of $\mathbf{F}$ and $\mathbf{b}$ (the estimate of $\boldsymbol{\beta}$) are distributed approximately as multivariate normal. This allows the computation of statistics for testing the goodness of fit of the model and the significance of other sources of variation. For details of the theory, refer to Grizzle, Starmer, and Koch (1969) or Koch et al. (1977, Appendix 1). Weighted least-squares estimation is available for all types of response functions.

Following parameter estimation, hypotheses about linear combinations of the parameters can be tested. For that purpose, PROC CATMOD computes generalized Wald (1943) statistics, which are approximately distributed as chi-square if the sample sizes are sufficiently large and the null hypotheses are true.

Linear Models Contrasted with Log-Linear Models

Linear model methods (as typified by the Grizzle, Starmer, Koch approach) make a very clear distinction between independent and dependent variables. The emphasis of these methods is estimation and hypothesis testing of the model parameters. Therefore, it is easy to test for differences among probabilities, perform repeated measurement analysis, and test for marginal homogeneity, but it is awkward to test independence and generalized independence. These methods are a natural extension of the usual ANOVA approach for continuous data.

In contrast, log-linear model methods (as typified by the Bishop, Fienberg, Holland approach) do not make an a priori distinction between independent and dependent variables, although model specifications that allow for the distinction can be made. The emphasis of these methods is on model building, goodness-of-fit tests, and estimation of cell frequencies or probabilities for the underlying contingency table. With these methods, it is easy to test independence and generalized independence, but it is awkward to test for differences among probabilities, do repeated measurement analysis, and test for marginal homogeneity.

Using PROC CATMOD Interactively

You can use the CATMOD procedure interactively. After specifying a model with a MODEL statement and running PROC CATMOD with a RUN statement, you can execute any statement without reinvoking PROC CATMOD. You can execute the statements singly or in groups by following the single statement or group of statements with a RUN statement. Note that you can use more than one MODEL statement; this is an important difference from the GLM procedure.

If you use PROC CATMOD interactively, you can end the CATMOD procedure with a DATA step, another PROC step, an ENDSAS statement, or a QUIT statement. The syntax of the QUIT statement is

```
quit;
```

When you are using PROC CATMOD interactively, additional RUN statements do not end the procedure but tell the procedure to execute additional statements.

When the CATMOD procedure detects a BY statement, it disables interactive processing; that is, once the BY statement and the next RUN statement are encountered, processing proceeds for each BY group in the data set, and no additional statements are accepted by the procedure. For example, the following statements tell PROC CATMOD to do three analyses: one for the entire data set, one for males, and one for females.

```
proc catmod;
   weight wt;
   response marginals;
   model r1*r2=a|b;
run;
   by sex;
run;
```

Note that the BY statement may appear after the first RUN statement; this is an important difference from PROC GLM, which requires that the BY statement appear before the first RUN statement.

Getting Started

The CATMOD procedure is a general modeling procedure for categorical data analysis, and it can be used for very sophisticated analyses that require matrix specification of the response function and the design matrix. It can be used to perform very basic analysis-of-variance-type analyses that require very few statements. The following is a basic example.

Weighted-Least-Squares Analysis of Mean Response

Consider the data in the following table (Stokes, Davis, and Koch 1995).

Table 22.2. Colds in Children

		Periods with Colds			
Sex	**Residence**	**0**	**1**	**2**	**Total**
Female	Rural	45	64	71	180
Female	Urban	80	104	116	300
Male	Rural	84	124	82	290
Male	Urban	106	117	87	310

For males and females in rural and urban counties, the number of periods (of two) in which subjects report cold symptoms are recorded. Thus, 45 subjects who were female and in rural counties report no cold symptoms, and 71 subjects who are female and from rural counties report colds in both periods.

The question of interest is whether the mean number of periods with colds reported is associated with gender or type of county. There is no reason to believe that the mean number of periods with colds is normally distributed, so a weighted least-squares analysis of these data is performed with PROC CATMOD instead of an analysis of variance with PROC ANOVA or PROC GLM.

The input data for categorical data is often recorded in frequency form, with the counts for each particular profile being the input values. Thus, for the colds data, the input SAS data set colds is created with the following statements. The variable count contains the frequency of observations that have the particular profile described by the values of the other variables on that input line.

```
data colds;
   input sex $ residence $ periods count @@;
datalines;
female rural 0  45  female rural 1  64  female rural 2  71
female urban 0  80  female urban 1 104  female urban 2 116
male   rural 0  84  male   rural 1 124  male   rural 2  82
male   urban 0 106  male   urban 1 117  male   urban 2  87
;
run;
```

In order to fit a model to the mean number of periods with colds, you have to specify the response function in PROC CATMOD. The default response function is the logit if the response variable has two values, and it is generalized logits if the response variable has more than two values. If you want a different response function, then you request that function in the RESPONSE statement. To request the mean number of periods with colds, you specify the MEANS option in the RESPONSE statement.

You can request a model consisting of the main effects and interaction of the variables sex and residence just as you would in the GLM procedure. Unlike the GLM procedure, you don't need to use a CLASS statement in PROC CATMOD to treat a variable as a classification variable. All variables in the MODEL statement in the CATMOD procedure are treated as classification variables unless you specify otherwise with a DIRECT statement.

Thus, the PROC CATMOD statements required to model mean periods of colds with a main effects and interaction model are

```
proc catmod data=colds;
   weight count;
   response means;
   model periods = sex residence sex*residence;
run;
```

The results of this analysis are shown in Figure 22.1 through Figure 22.3.

```
                    The CATMOD Procedure

Response              periods      Response Levels      3
Weight Variable       count        Populations          4
Data Set              COLDS        Total Frequency   1080
Frequency Missing     0            Observations        12


                    Population Profiles

     Sample     sex        residence     Sample Size
     ---------------------------------------------
        1       female     rural                180
        2       female     urban                300
        3       male       rural                290
        4       male       urban                310


                     Response Profiles

                   Response     periods
                   -------------------
                       1           0
                       2           1
                       3           2
```

Figure 22.1. Model Information and Profile Tables

The CATMOD procedure first displays a summary of the contingency table you are analyzing. The "Population Profiles" table lists the values of the explanatory variables that define each population, or row of the underlying contingency table, and labels each group with a sample number. The number of observations in each population is also displayed. The "Response Profiles" table lists the variable levels that define the response, or columns of the underlying contingency table.

The CATMOD Procedure

Sample	Response Function	Design Matrix 1	2	3	4
1	1.14444	1	1	1	1
2	1.12000	1	1	-1	-1
3	0.99310	1	-1	1	-1
4	0.93871	1	-1	-1	1

Figure 22.2. Observed Response Functions and Design Matrix

The "Design Matrix" table contains the observed response functions—in this case, the mean number of periods with colds for each of the populations—and the design matrix. The first column of the design matrix contains the coefficients for the intercept parameter, the second column coefficients are for the sex parameter (note that the sum-to-zero constraint of a full-rank parameterization implies that the coefficient for males is the negative of that for females. The parameter is called the *differential effect* for females), the third column is similarly set up for residence, and the last column is for the interaction.

The CATMOD Procedure

Analysis of Variance

Source	DF	Chi-Square	Pr > ChiSq
Intercept	1	1841.13	<.0001
sex	1	11.57	0.0007
residence	1	0.65	0.4202
sex*residence	1	0.09	0.7594
Residual	0	.	.

Figure 22.3. ANOVA Table for the Saturated Model

The model-fitting results are displayed in the "Analysis of Variance" table (Figure 22.3), which is similar to an ANOVA table. The effects from the right-hand side of the MODEL statement are listed under the "Source" column.

The interaction effect is nonsignificant, so the data is reanalyzed using a main-effects model. Since PROC CATMOD is an interactive procedure, you can analyze the main-effects model by simply submitting the new MODEL statement as follows. The resulting tables are displayed in Figure 22.4 through Figure 22.7.

```
model periods = sex residence;
run;
```

```
                    The CATMOD Procedure

       Response             periods     Response Levels      3
       Weight Variable      count       Populations          4
       Data Set             COLDS       Total Frequency   1080
       Frequency Missing    0           Observations        12


                    Population Profiles

           Sample     sex        residence     Sample Size
           -------------------------------------------------
              1       female     rural                 180
              2       female     urban                 300
              3       male       rural                 290
              4       male       urban                 310


                     Response Profiles

                    Response     periods
                    -------------------
                        1          0
                        2          1
                        3          2
```

Figure 22.4. Population and Response Profiles, Main-Effects Model

```
                    The CATMOD Procedure

                  Response          Design Matrix
       Sample     Function          1          2          3
       ------------------------------------------------------
          1        1.14444          1          1          1
          2        1.12000          1          1         -1
          3        0.99310          1         -1          1
          4        0.93871          1         -1         -1
```

Figure 22.5. Design Matrix for the Main-Effects Model

```
                    The CATMOD Procedure

                    Analysis of Variance

        Source          DF   Chi-Square    Pr > ChiSq
        ---------------------------------------------
        Intercept        1      1882.77        <.0001
        sex              1        12.08        0.0005
        residence        1         0.76        0.3839

        Residual         1         0.09        0.7594
```

Figure 22.6. ANOVA Table for the Main-Effects Model

The goodness-of-fit chi-square statistic is 0.09 with one degree of freedom and a *p*-value of 0.7594; hence, the model fits the data. Note that the chi-square tests in Figure 22.6 test whether all the parameters for a given effect are zero. In this model, each effect has only one parameter, and therefore only one degree of freedom.

```
                          The CATMOD Procedure

           Analysis of Weighted Least Squares Estimates

                                            Standard         Chi-
Effect         Parameter     Estimate          Error       Square     Pr > ChiSq
--------------------------------------------------------------------------------
Intercept              1       1.0501         0.0242      1882.77         <.0001
sex                    2       0.0842         0.0242        12.08         0.0005
residence              3       0.0210         0.0241         0.76         0.3839
```

Figure 22.7. Parameter Estimates for the Main-Effects Model

The "Analysis of Weighted-Least-Squares Estimates" table lists the parameters and their estimates for the model, as well as the standard errors, Wald statistics, and p-values. These chi-square tests are single degree-of-freedom tests that the individual parameter is equal to zero. They are equal to the tests shown in Figure 22.6 since each effect is composed of exactly one parameter.

You can compute the mean number of periods of colds for the first population (Sample 1, females in rural residences) from Table 22.2 as follows.

$$\text{mean colds} = 0 \times \frac{45}{180} + 1 \times \frac{64}{180} + 2 \times \frac{71}{180} = 1.1444$$

This is the same value as reported for the Response Function for Sample 1 in Figure 22.5.

PROC CATMOD is fitting a model to the mean number of colds in each population as follows:

$$\begin{bmatrix} \text{Expected number of colds for rural females} \\ \text{urban females} \\ \text{rural males} \\ \text{urban males} \end{bmatrix} = \begin{bmatrix} 1 & 1 & 1 \\ 1 & 1 & -1 \\ 1 & -1 & 1 \\ 1 & -1 & -1 \end{bmatrix} \begin{bmatrix} \beta_0 \\ \beta_1 \\ \beta_2 \end{bmatrix}$$

where the design matrix is the same one displayed in Figure 22.5, β_0 is the mean number of colds averaged over all the populations, β_1 is the differential effect for females, and β_2 is the differential effect for rural residences. The parameter estimates are shown in Figure 22.7; thus, the expected number of periods with colds for rural females from this model is

$$1 \times 1.0501 + 1 \times 0.0842 + 1 \times 0.0210 = 1.1553$$

and the expected number for rural males from this model is

$$1 \times 1.0501 - 1 \times 0.0842 + 1 \times 0.0210 = 0.9869$$

Notice also, in Figure 22.7, that the differential effect for residence is nonsignificant ($p = 0.3839$): If you continued the analysis by fitting a single effect model (sex), you would need to include a POPULATION statement to maintain the same underlying contingency table.

```
   population sex residence;
   model periods = sex;
run;
```

Generalized Logits Model

Over the course of one school year, third graders from three different schools are exposed to three different styles of mathematics instruction: a self-paced computer-learning style, a team approach, and a traditional class approach. The students are asked which style they prefer and their responses, classified by the type of program they are in (a regular school day versus a regular day supplemented with an afternoon school program) are displayed in Table 22.3. The data set is from Stokes, Davis, and Koch (1995).

Table 22.3. School Program Data

School	Program	Learning Style Preference		
		Self	Team	Class
1	Regular	10	17	26
1	Afternoon	5	12	50
2	Regular	21	17	26
2	Afternoon	16	12	36
3	Regular	15	15	16
3	Afternoon	12	12	20

The levels of the response variable (self, team, and class) have no essential ordering, hence a logistic regression is performed on the generalized logits. The model to be fit is

$$\log\left(\frac{\pi_{hij}}{\pi_{hir}}\right) = \alpha_j + \mathbf{x}'_{hi}\beta_j$$

where π_{hij} is the probability that a student in school h and program i prefers teaching style j, $j \neq r$, and style r is the class style. There are separate sets of intercept parameters α_j and regression parameters β_j for each logit, and the matrix $\mathbf{x}_{hi}$ is the set of explanatory variables for the hith population. Thus, two logits are modeled for each school and program combination (population): the logit comparing self to class and the logit comparing team to class.

The following statements create the data set school and request the analysis. Generalized logits are the default response functions, and maximum likelihood estimation is the default method for analyzing generalized logits, so only the WEIGHT and MODEL statements are required. The option ORDER=DATA means that the response variable levels are ordered as they exist in the data set: self, team, and class; thus the logits are formed by comparing self to class and by comparing team to class. The results of this analysis are shown in Figure 22.8 and Figure 22.9.

```
data school;
   length Program $ 9;
   input School Program $ Style $ Count @@;
   datalines;
1 regular   self 10  1 regular   team 17  1 regular   class 26
1 afternoon self  5  1 afternoon team 12  1 afternoon class 50
2 regular   self 21  2 regular   team 17  2 regular   class 26
2 afternoon self 16  2 afternoon team 12  2 afternoon class 36
3 regular   self 15  3 regular   team 15  3 regular   class 16
3 afternoon self 12  3 afternoon team 12  3 afternoon class 20
;
proc catmod order=data;
   weight Count;
   model Style=School Program School*Program;
run;
```

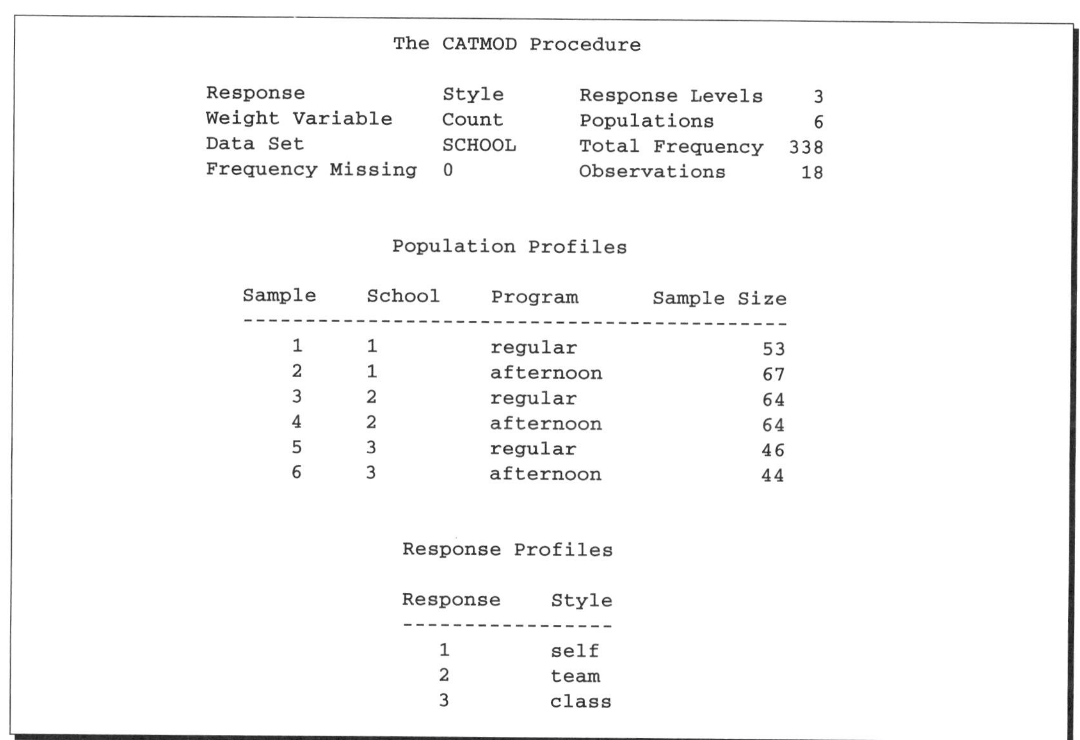

```
                    The CATMOD Procedure

       Response              Style       Response Levels     3
       Weight Variable       Count       Populations         6
       Data Set              SCHOOL      Total Frequency   338
       Frequency Missing     0           Observations       18


                    Population Profiles

          Sample     School     Program       Sample Size
          -------------------------------------------------
              1        1        regular               53
              2        1        afternoon             67
              3        2        regular               64
              4        2        afternoon             64
              5        3        regular               46
              6        3        afternoon             44


                     Response Profiles

                     Response     Style
                     -----------------
                         1        self
                         2        team
                         3        class
```

Figure 22.8. Model Information and Profile Tables

A summary of the data set is displayed in Figure 22.8; the variable levels that form the three responses and six populations are listed in the "Response Profiles" and "Population Profiles" table, respectively. A table containing the iteration history is also produced, but it is not displayed here.

```
                        The CATMOD Procedure

            Maximum Likelihood Analysis of Variance

     Source                DF   Chi-Square    Pr > ChiSq
     --------------------------------------------------
     Intercept              2        40.05        <.0001
     School                 4        14.55        0.0057
     Program                2        10.48        0.0053
     School*Program         4         1.74        0.7827

     Likelihood Ratio       0          .             .
```

Figure 22.9. ANOVA Table

The analysis of variance table is displayed in Figure 22.9. Since this is a saturated model, there are no degrees of freedom remaining for a likelihood ratio test, and missing values are displayed in the table. The interaction effect is clearly nonsignificant, so a main effects model is fit.

Since PROC CATMOD is an interactive procedure, you can analyze the main effects model by simply submitting the new MODEL statement as follows.

```
model Style=School Program;
run;
```

```
                        The CATMOD Procedure

            Maximum Likelihood Analysis of Variance

     Source                DF   Chi-Square    Pr > ChiSq
     --------------------------------------------------
     Intercept              2        39.88        <.0001
     School                 4        14.84        0.0050
     Program                2        10.92        0.0043

     Likelihood Ratio       4         1.78        0.7766
```

Figure 22.10. ANOVA Table

You can check the population and response profiles (not shown) to confirm that they are the same as those in Figure 22.8. The analysis of variance table is shown in Figure 22.10. The likelihood ratio chi-square statistic is 1.78 with a p-value of 0.7766, indicating a good fit; the Wald chi-square tests for the school and program effects are also significant. Since School has three levels, two parameters are estimated for each of the two logits they modeled, for a total of four degrees of freedom. Since Program has two levels, one parameter is estimated for each of the two logits, for a total of two degrees of freedom.

The CATMOD Procedure

Analysis of Maximum Likelihood Estimates

Effect	Parameter	Estimate	Standard Error	Chi-Square	Pr > ChiSq
Intercept	1	-0.7979	0.1465	29.65	<.0001
	2	-0.6589	0.1367	23.23	<.0001
School	3	-0.7992	0.2198	13.22	0.0003
	4	-0.2786	0.1867	2.23	0.1356
	5	0.2836	0.1899	2.23	0.1352
	6	-0.0985	0.1892	0.27	0.6028
Program	7	0.3737	0.1410	7.03	0.0080
	8	0.3713	0.1353	7.53	0.0061

Figure 22.11. Parameter Estimates

The parameter estimates and tests for individual parameters are displayed in Figure 22.11. The ordering of the parameters corresponds to the order of the population and response variables as shown in the profile tables (see Figure 22.8), with the levels of the response variables varying most rapidly. So, for the first response function, which is the logit that compares self to class, Parameter 1 is the intercept, Parameter 3 is the parameter for the differential effect for School=1, Parameter 5 is the parameter for the differential effect for School=2, and Parameter 7 is the parameter for the differential effect for Program=regular. The even parameters are interpreted similarly for the second logit, which compares team to class.

The Program variable (Parameters 7 and 8) has nearly the same effect on both logits, while School=1 (Parameters 3 and 4) has the largest effect of the schools.

Syntax

The following statements are available in PROC CATMOD.

PROC CATMOD < *options* > **;**
DIRECT < *variables* > **;**
MODEL *response-effect=design-effects* < */ options* > **;**
CONTRAST *'label' row-description* <, . . . , *row-description* >
< */ option* > **;**
BY *variables* **;**
FACTORS *factor-description* <, . . . , *factor-description* >
< */ options* > **;**
LOGLIN *effects* **;**
POPULATION *variables* **;**
REPEATED *factor-description* <, . . . , *factor-description* >
< */ options* > **;**
RESPONSE *function* <, . . . , *function* >< */ options* > **;**
RESTRICT *parameter=value* < . . . *parameter=value* > **;**
WEIGHT *variable* **;**

You can use all of the statements in PROC CATMOD interactively. The first RUN statement executes all of the previous statements. Any subsequent RUN statement executes only those statements that appear between the previous RUN statement and the current one. However, if you specify a BY statement, interactive processing is disabled. That is, all statements through the following RUN statement are processed for each BY group in the data set, but no additional statements are accepted by the procedure.

If more than one CONTRAST statement appears between two RUN statements, all the CONTRAST statements are processed. If more than one RESPONSE statement appears between two RUN statements, then analyses associated with each RESPONSE statement are produced. For all other statements, there can be only one occurrence of the statement between any two RUN statements. For example, if there are two LOGLIN statements between two RUN statements, the first LOGLIN statement is ignored.

The PROC CATMOD and MODEL statements are required. If specified, the DIRECT statement must precede the MODEL statement. As a result, if you use the DIRECT statement interactively, you need to specify a MODEL statement in the same RUN group. See the section "DIRECT Statement" on page 718 for an example.

The CONTRAST statements, if any, must follow the MODEL statement.

You can specify only one of the LOGLIN, REPEATED, and FACTORS statements between any two RUN statements, because they all specify the same information: how to partition the variation among the response functions within a population.

A QUIT statement executes any statements that have not been processed and then ends the CATMOD procedure.

The purpose of each statement, other than the PROC CATMOD statement, are summarized in the following list:

BY	determines groups in which data are to be processed separately.
CONTRAST	specifies a hypothesis to test.
DIRECT	specifies independent variables that are to be treated quantitatively (like continuous variables) rather than qualitatively (like class or discrete variables). These variables also help to determine the rows of the contingency table and distinguish response functions in one population from those in other populations.
FACTORS	specifies (1) the factors that distinguish response functions from others in the same population and (2) model effects, based on these factors, which help to determine the design matrix.
LOGLIN	specifies log-linear model effects.
MODEL	specifies (1) dependent variables, which determine the columns of the contingency table, (2) independent variables, which distinguish response functions in one population from those in other populations, and (3) model effects, which determine the design matrix

	and the way in which total variation among the response functions is partitioned.
POPULATION	specifies variables which determine the rows of the contingency table and distinguish response functions in one population from those in other populations.
REPEATED	specifies (1) the repeated measurement factors that distinguish response functions from others in the same population and (2) model effects, based on these factors, which help to determine the design matrix.
RESPONSE	determines the response functions that are to be modeled.
RESTRICT	restricts values of parameters to the values you specify.
WEIGHT	specifies a variable containing frequency counts.

PROC CATMOD Statement

PROC CATMOD < *options* > **;**

The PROC CATMOD statement invokes the procedure. You can specify the following options.

DATA=*SAS-data-set*

names the SAS data set containing the data to be analyzed. By default, the CATMOD procedure uses the most recently created SAS data set. For details, see the section "Input Data Sets" on page 742.

NAMELEN=*n*

specifies the length of effect names in tables and output data sets to be n characters long, where n is a value between 24 and 200 characters. The default length is 24 characters.

NOPRINT

suppresses the normal display of results. The NOPRINT option is useful when you only want to create output data sets with the OUT= or OUTEST= option in the RESPONSE statement. A NOPRINT option is also available in the MODEL statement. Note that this option temporarily disables the Output Delivery System (ODS); see Chapter 15, "Using the Output Delivery System," for more information.

ORDER=DATA

orders variable levels according to the sequence in which they appear in the input stream. This affects the ordering of the populations, responses, and parameters, as well as the definitions of the parameters. By default, the variable levels are ordered according to their internal sorting sequence (for example, numeric order or alphabetical order). See the section "Ordering of Populations and Responses" on page 744 for more information and examples.

BY Statement

BY *variables* **;**

You can specify a BY statement with PROC CATMOD to obtain separate analyses of groups determined by the BY variables. When a BY statement appears, the procedure expects the input data set to be sorted in order of the BY variables. The *variables* are one or more variables in the input data set.

If your input data set is not sorted in ascending order, use one of the following alternatives:

- Sort the data using the SORT procedure with a similar BY statement.
- Specify the BY statement option NOTSORTED or DESCENDING in the BY statement for the CATMOD procedure. The NOTSORTED option does not mean that the data are unsorted but rather that the data are arranged in groups (according to values of the BY variables) and that these groups are not necessarily in alphabetical or increasing numeric order.
- Create an index on the BY variables using the DATASETS procedure (in base SAS software).

For more information on the BY statement, refer to the discussion in *SAS Language Reference: Concepts*. For more information on the DATASETS procedure, refer to the discussion in the *SAS Procedures Guide*.

When you specify a BY statement with PROC CATMOD, no further interactive processing is possible. In other words, once the BY statement appears, all statements up to the associated RUN statement are executed for each BY group in the data set. After the RUN statement, no further statements are accepted by the procedure.

CONTRAST Statement

CONTRAST *'label' row-description* <,..., *row-description* ></ *option* >**;**

where a *row-description* is

< @*n* > *effect values* < ... < @*n* > *effect values*>

The CONTRAST statement constructs and tests linear functions of the parameters in the MODEL statement or effects listed in the LOGLIN statement. Each set of effects (separated by commas) specifies one row or set of rows of the matrix **C** that PROC CATMOD uses to test the hypothesis $\mathbf{C}\boldsymbol{\beta} = \mathbf{0}$.

CONTRAST statements must be preceded by the MODEL statement, and by the LOGLIN statement, if one is used. You can specify the following terms in the CONTRAST statement.

'label' specifies up to 256 characters of identifying information displayed with the test. The *'label'* is required.

effect is one of the effects specified in the MODEL or LOGLIN statement, INTERCEPT (for the intercept parameter), or ALL_PARMS (for the complete set of parameters).

The ALL_PARMS option is regarded as an effect with the same number of parameters as the number of columns in the design matrix. This is particularly useful when the design matrix is input directly, as in the following example:

```
model y=(1 0 0 0,
         1 0 1 0,
         1 1 0 0,
         1 1 1 1);
contrast 'Main Effect of B' all_parms 0 1 0 0;
contrast 'Main Effect of C' all_parms 0 0 1 0;
contrast 'B*C Interaction ' all_parms 0 0 0 1;
```

values are numbers that form the coefficients of the parameters associated with the given effect. If there are fewer values than parameters for an effect, the remaining coefficients become zero. For example, if you specify two values and the effect actually has five parameters, the final three are set to zero.

$@n$ points to the parameters in the nth set when the model has a separate set of parameters for each of the response functions. The $@n$ notation is seldom needed. It enables you to test the variation among response functions in the same population. However, it is usually easier to model and test such variation by using the _RESPONSE_ effect in the MODEL statement or by using the ALL_PARMS designation. Usually, contrasts are performed with respect to all of the response functions, and this is what the CONTRAST statement does by default (in this case, do not use the $@n$ notation).

For example, if there are three response functions per population, then

```
contrast 'Level 1 vs. Level 2' A 1 -1 0;
```

results in a three-degree-of-freedom test comparing the first two levels of A simultaneously on the three response functions.

If, however, you want to specify a contrast with respect to the parameters in the nth set only, then use a single $@n$ in a *row-description*. For example, to test that the first parameter of A and the first parameter of B are zero in the third response function, specify

```
contrast 'A=0, B=0, Function 3'  @3  A 1  B 1;
```

To specify a contrast with respect to parameters in two or more different sets of effects, use $@n$ with each effect. For example,

```
contrast 'Average over Functions' @1 A 1 0 -1
                                  @2 A 1 1 -2;
```

When the model does not have a separate set of parameters for each of the response functions, the $@n$ notation is invalid. This type of model is called AVERAGED. For details, see the description of the AVERAGED option on page 725 and the "Generation of the Design Matrix" section on page 757.

You can specify the following options in the CONTRAST statement after a slash.

ALPHA= *value*

specifies the significance level of the confidence interval for each contrast when the ESTIMATE= option is specified. The default is ALPHA=0.05, resulting in a 95% confidence interval for each contrast.

ESTIMATE=*keyword*

EST=*keyword*

requests that each individual contrast (that is, each row, $c_i\boldsymbol{\beta}$, of $\mathbf{C}\boldsymbol{\beta}$) or exponentiated contrast $(\exp(c_i\boldsymbol{\beta}))$ be estimated and tested. PROC CATMOD displays the point estimate, its standard error, a Wald confidence interval, and a Wald chi-square test for each contrast. The significance level of the confidence interval is controlled by the ALPHA= option.

You can estimate the contrast or the exponentiated contrast, or both, by specifying one of the following keywords:

PARM	specifies that the contrast itself be estimated.
EXP	specifies that the exponentiated contrast be estimated.
BOTH	specifies that both the contrast and the exponentiated contrast be estimated.

Specifying Contrasts

PROC CATMOD is parameterized differently than PROC GLM, so you must be careful not to use the same contrasts that you would with PROC GLM. Since PROC CATMOD uses a full-rank parameterization, all estimable parameters are directly estimable without involving other parameters.

For example, suppose a class variable A has four levels. Then there are four parameters $(\alpha_1, \alpha_2, \alpha_3, \alpha_4)$, of which PROC CATMOD uses only the first three. The fourth parameter is related to the others by the equation

$$\alpha_4 = -\alpha_1 - \alpha_2 - \alpha_3$$

To test the first versus the fourth level of A, you would test $\alpha_1 = \alpha_4$, which is

$$\alpha_1 = -\alpha_1 - \alpha_2 - \alpha_3$$

or, equivalently,

$$2\alpha_1 + \alpha_2 + \alpha_3 = 0$$

Therefore, you would use the following CONTRAST statement:

```
contrast '1 vs. 4' A 2 1 1;
```

To contrast the third level with the average of the first two levels, you would test

$$\frac{\alpha_1 + \alpha_2}{2} = \alpha_3$$

or, equivalently,

$$\alpha_1 + \alpha_2 - 2\alpha_3 = 0$$

Therefore, you would use the following CONTRAST statement:

```
contrast '1&2 vs. 3' A 1 1 -2;
```

Other CONTRAST statements are constructed similarly; for example,

```
contrast '1 vs. 2      '  A  1 -1  0;
contrast '1&2 vs. 4    '  A  3  3  2;
contrast '1&2 vs. 3&4'    A  2  2  0;
contrast 'Main Effect'    A  1  0  0,
                          A  0  1  0,
                          A  0  0  1;
```

The actual form of the **C** matrix depends on the effects in the model. The following examples assume a single response function for each population.

```
proc catmod;
   model y=a;
   contrast '1 vs. 4' A 2 1 1;
run;
```

The **C** matrix for the preceding statements is

$$\mathbf{C} = [\,0\;2\;1\;1\,]$$

since the first parameter corresponds to the intercept.

But if there is a variable B with three levels and you use the following statements,

```
proc catmod;
   model y=b a;
   contrast '1 vs. 4' A 2 1 1;
run;
```

then the CONTRAST statement induces the **C** matrix

$$\mathbf{C} = [\,0\;0\;0\;2\;1\;1\,]$$

since the first parameter corresponds to the intercept and the next two correspond to the B main effect.

You can also use the CONTRAST statement to test the joint effect of two or more effects in the MODEL statement. For example, the joint effect of A and B in the previous model has five degrees of freedom and is obtained by specifying

```
contrast 'Joint Effect of A&B' A 1 0 0,
                               A 0 1 0,
                               A 0 0 1,
                               B 1 0,
                               B 0 1;
```

The ordering of variable levels is determined by the ORDER= option in the PROC CATMOD statement. Whenever you specify a contrast that depends on the order of the variable levels, you should verify the order from the "Population Profiles" table, the "Response Profiles" table, or the "One-Way Frequencies" table.

DIRECT Statement

DIRECT *variables* ;

The DIRECT statement lists numeric independent variables to be treated in a quantitative, rather than qualitative, way. The DIRECT statement is useful for logistic regression, which is described in the "Logistic Regression" section on page 750. For limitations of models involving continuous variables, see the "Continuous Variables" section on page 751.

If specified, the DIRECT statement must precede the MODEL statement. For example,

```
proc catmod;
   direct X;
   model Y=X;
run;
```

Suppose X has five levels. Then the main effect X induces only one column in the design matrix, rather than four. The values inserted into the design matrix are the actual values of X.

You can interactively change the variables declared as DIRECT variables by using the statement without listing any variables. The following statements are valid:

```
proc catmod;
   direct X;
   model Y=X;
   weight wt;
run;
   direct;
   model Y=X;
run;
```

The first MODEL statement uses the actual values of X, and the second MODEL statement uses the four variables created when PROC CATMOD generates the design matrix. Note that the preceding statements can be run without a WEIGHT statement if the input data are raw data rather than cell counts.

For more details, see the discussions of main and direct effects in the section "Generation of the Design Matrix" on page 757.

FACTORS Statement

FACTORS *factor-description* <, . . . , *factor-description* >< / *options* > ;

where a *factor-description* is

factor-name < $ >< *levels* >

and *factor-descriptions* are separated from each other by a comma. The $ is required for character-valued factors. The value of *levels* provides the number of levels of the factor identified by a given *factor-name*. For only one factor, *levels* is optional; for two or more factors, it is required.

The FACTORS statement identifies factors that distinguish response functions from others in the same population. It also specifies how those factors are incorporated into the model. You can use the FACTORS statement whenever there is more than one response function per population and the keyword _RESPONSE_ is specified in the MODEL statement. You can specify the name, type, and number of levels of each factor and the identification of each level.

The FACTORS statement is most useful when the response functions and their covariance matrix are read directly from the input data set. In this case, PROC CATMOD reads the response functions as though they are from one population (this poses no problem in the multiple-population case because the appropriately constructed covariance matrix is also read directly). Thus, you can use the FACTORS statement to partition the variation among the response functions into appropriate sources, even when the functions actually represent separate populations.

The format of the FACTORS statement is identical to that of the REPEATED statement. In fact, repeated measurement factors are simply special cases of factors in which some of the response functions correspond to multiple dependent variables that are measurements on the same experimental (or sampling) units.

You cannot specify the FACTORS statement for an analysis that also contains the REPEATED or LOGLIN statement since all of them specify the same information: how to partition the variation among the response functions within a population.

In the FACTORS statement,

factor-name names a factor that corresponds to two or more response functions. This name must be a valid SAS variable name, and it should not be the same as the name of a variable that already exists in the data set being analyzed.

$ indicates that the factor is character-valued. If the $ is omitted, then PROC CATMOD assumes that the factor is numeric. The type of the factor is relevant only when you use the PROFILE= option or when the _RESPONSE_= option (described later in this section) specifies nested-by-value effects.

levels specifies the number of levels of the corresponding factor. If there is only one such factor, and the number is omitted, then PROC CATMOD assumes that the number of levels is equal to the number of response functions per population (q). Unless you specify the PROFILE= option, the number q must either be equal to or be a multiple of the product of the number of levels of all the factors.

You can specify the following options in the FACTORS statement after a slash.

PROFILE=(*matrix*)

specifies the values assumed by the factors for each response function. There should be one column for each factor, and the values in a given column (character or numeric) should match the type of the corresponding factor. Character values are restricted to 16 characters or less. If there are q response functions per population, then the matrix must have i rows, where q must either be equal to or be a multiple of i. Adjacent rows of the matrix should be separated by a comma.

The values in the PROFILE matrix are useful for specifying models in those situations where the study design is not a full factorial with respect to the factors. They can also be used to specify nested-by-value effects in the _RESPONSE_= option. If you specify character values in both places (the PROFILE= option and the _RESPONSE_= option), then the values must match with respect to whether or not they are enclosed in quotes (that is, enclosed in quotes in both places or in neither place).

For an example of using the PROFILE= option, see Example 22.10 on page 821.

RESPONSE=*effects*
specifies design effects. The variables named in the effects must be *factor-names* that appear in the FACTORS statement. If the _RESPONSE_= option is omitted, then PROC CATMOD builds a full factorial _RESPONSE_ effect with respect to the factors.

TITLE=*'title'*
displays the *title* at the top of certain pages of output that correspond to the current FACTORS statement.

For an example of how the FACTORS statement is useful, consider the case where the response functions and their covariance matrix are read directly from the input data set. The TYPE=EST data set might be created in the following manner:

```
data direct(type=est);
   input b1-b4 _type_ $ _name_ $8.;
   datalines;
0.590463    0.384720    0.273269    0.136458    parms     .
0.001690    0.000911    0.000474    0.000432    cov       b1
0.000911    0.001823    0.000031    0.000102    cov       b2
0.000474    0.000031    0.001056    0.000477    cov       b3
0.000432    0.000102    0.000477    0.000396    cov       b4
;
```

Suppose the response functions correspond to four populations that represent the cross-classification of age (two groups) by sex. You can use the FACTORS statement to identify these two factors and to name the effects in the model. The statements required to fit a main-effects model to these data are

```
proc catmod data=direct;
   response read b1-b4;
   model _f_=_response_;
   factors age 2, sex 2 / _response_=age sex;
run;
```

If you want to specify some nested-by-value effects, you can change the FACTORS statement to

```
factors age $ 2, sex $ 2 /
       _response_=age sex(age='under 30') sex(age='30 & over')
        profile=('under 30'   male,
                 'under 30'   female,
                 '30 & over'  male,
                 '30 & over'  female);
```

If, by design or by chance, the study contains no male subjects under 30 years of age, then there are only three response functions, and you can specify a main-effects model as

```
proc catmod data=direct;
   response read b2-b4;
   model _f_=_response_;
   factors age $ 2, sex $ 2 / _response_=age sex
           profile=('under 30'   female,
                    '30 & over'  male,
                    '30 & over'  female);
run;
```

When you specify two or more factors and omit the PROFILE= option, PROC CATMOD presumes that the response functions are ordered so that the levels of the rightmost factor change most rapidly. For the preceding example, the order implied by the FACTORS statement is as follows.

Response Function	Dependent Variable	Age	Sex
1	b1	1	1
2	b2	1	2
3	b3	2	1
4	b4	2	2

For additional examples of how to use the FACTORS statement, see the section "Repeated Measures Analysis" on page 754. All of the examples in that section are applicable, with the REPEATED statement replaced by the FACTORS statement.

LOGLIN Statement

LOGLIN *effects* < / *option* > **;**

The LOGLIN statement is used to define log-linear model effects. It can be used whenever the default response functions (generalized logits) are used.

In the LOGLIN statement, *effects* are design effects that contain dependent variables in the MODEL statement. You can use the bar (|) and at (@) operators as well. The following lists of effects are equivalent:

```
a b c a*b a*c b*c
```

and

```
a|b|c @2
```

When you use the LOGLIN statement, the keyword _RESPONSE_ should be specified in the MODEL statement. For further information on log-linear model analysis, see the "Log-Linear Model Analysis" section on page 751.

You cannot specify the LOGLIN statement for an analysis that also contains the REPEATED or FACTORS statement since all of them specify the same information: how to partition the variation among the response functions within a population.

You can specify the following option in the LOGLIN statement after a slash.

TITLE=*'title'*
displays the *title* at the top of certain pages of output that correspond to this LOGLIN statement.

The following statements give an example of how to use the LOGLIN statement.

```
proc catmod;
   model a*b*c=_response_;
   loglin a|b|c @ 2;
run;
```

These statements yield a log-linear model analysis that contains all main effects and two-variable interactions. For more examples of log-linear model analysis, see the "Log-Linear Model Analysis" section on page 751.

MODEL Statement

MODEL *response-effect=< design-effects >< / options >* **;**

PROC CATMOD requires a MODEL statement. You can specify the following in a MODEL statement:

response-effect can be either a single variable, a crossed effect with two or more variables joined by asterisks, or _F_. The _F_ specification indicates that the response functions and their estimated covariance matrix are to be read directly into the procedure. The *response-effect* indicates the dependent variables that determine the response categories (the columns of the underlying contingency table).

design-effects specify potential sources of variation (such as main effects and interactions) in the model. Thus, these effects determine the number of model parameters, as well as the interpretation of such parameters. In addition, if there is no POPULATION statement, PROC CATMOD uses these variables to determine the populations (the rows of the underlying contingency table). When fitting the model, PROC CATMOD adjusts the independent effects in the model for all other independent effects in the model.

Design-effects can be any of those described in the section "Specification of Effects" on page 745, or they can be defined by specifying the actual design matrix, enclosed in parentheses (see the "Specifying the Design Matrix Directly" section on page 727). In addition, you can use the keyword _RESPONSE_ alone or as part of an effect. Effects cannot be nested within _RESPONSE_, so effects of the form A(_RESPONSE_) are invalid.

For more information, see the "Log-Linear Model Analysis" section on page 751 and the "Repeated Measures Analysis" section on page 754.

Some examples of MODEL statements are

`model r=a b;`	main effects only
`model r=a b a*b;`	main effects with interaction
`model r=a b(a);`	nested effect
`model r=a|b;`	complete factorial
`model r=a b(a=1) b(a=2);`	nested-by-value effects
`model r*s=_response_;`	log-linear model
`model r*s=a _response_(a);`	nested repeated measurement factor
`model _f_=_response_;`	direct input of the response functions

The relationship between these specifications and the structure of the design matrix **X** is described in the "Generation of the Design Matrix" section on page 757.

The following table summarizes the options available in the MODEL statement.

Task	Options
Specify details of computation	
Generates maximum likelihood estimates	ML
Generates weighted least-squares estimates	GLS
	WLS
Omits intercept term from the model	NOINT
Adds a number to each cell frequency	ADDCELL=
Averages main effects across response functions	AVERAGED
Specifies the convergence criterion for maximum likelihood	EPSILON=
Specifies the number of iterations for maximum likelihood	MAXITER=
Request additional computation and tables	
Estimated correlation matrix of estimates	CORRB
Covariance matrix of response functions	COV
Estimated covariance matrix of estimates	COVB
Two-way frequency tables	FREQ
One-way frequency tables	ONEWAY
Predicted values	PRED=
	PREDICT
Probability estimates	PROB
Crossproducts matrix	XPX
Title	TITLE=
Suppress output	
Design matrix	NODESIGN
Iterations for maximum likelihood	NOITER
Parameter estimates	NOPARM
Population and response profiles	NOPROFILE
RESPONSE matrix	NORESPONSE

The following list describes these options in alphabetical order.

ADDCELL=*number*

adds *number* to the frequency count in each cell, where *number* is any positive number. This option has no effect on maximum likelihood analysis; it is used only for weighted least-squares analysis.

AVERAGED

specifies that dependent variable effects can be modeled and that independent variable main effects are averaged across the response functions in a population. For further information on the effect of using (or not using) the AVERAGED option, see the "Generation of the Design Matrix" section on page 757. Direct input of the design matrix or specification of the _RESPONSE_ keyword in the MODEL statement automatically induces an AVERAGED model type.

CORRB

displays the estimated correlation matrix of the parameter estimates.

COV

displays $\mathbf{S}_i$, which is the covariance matrix of the response functions for each population.

COVB

displays the estimated covariance matrix of the parameter estimates.

EPSILON=*number*

specifies the convergence criterion for the maximum likelihood estimation of the parameters. The iterative estimation process stops when the proportional change in the log likelihood is less than *number*, or after the number of iterations specified by the MAXITER= option, whichever comes first. By default, EPSILON=1E−8.

FREQ

produces the two-way frequency table for the cross-classification of populations by responses.

MAXITER=*number*

specifies the maximum number of iterations used for the maximum likelihood estimation of the parameters. By default, MAXITER=20.

ML

computes maximum likelihood estimates. This option is available when generalized logits are used, or for the special case of a single two-level dependent variable where cumulative logits or adjacent category logits are used. For generalized logits (the default response functions), ML is the default estimation method.

NODESIGN

suppresses the display of the design matrix $\mathbf{X}$.

NOINT

suppresses the intercept term in the model.

NOITER

suppresses the display of parameter estimates and other information at each iteration of a maximum likelihood analysis.

NOPARM

suppresses the display of the estimated parameters and the statistics for testing that each parameter is zero.

NOPREDVAR

suppresses the display of the variable levels in tables requested with the PRED= option.

NOPRINT

suppresses the normal display of results. The NOPRINT option is useful when you only want to create output data sets with the OUT= or OUTEST= option in the RESPONSE statement. A NOPRINT option is also available in the PROC CATMOD statement. Note that this option temporarily disables the Output Delivery System (ODS); see Chapter 15, "Using the Output Delivery System," for more information.

NOPROFILE

suppresses the display of the population profiles and the response profiles.

NORESPONSE

suppresses the display of the _RESPONSE_ matrix for log-linear models. For further information, see the "Log-Linear Model Design Matrices" section on page 764.

ONEWAY

produces a one-way table of frequencies for each variable used in the analysis. This table is useful in determining the order of the observed levels for each variable.

PREDICT

PRED=FREQ | PROB

displays the observed and predicted values of the response functions for each population, together with their standard errors and the residuals (observed − predicted). In addition, if the response functions are the standard ones (generalized logits), then the PRED=FREQ option specifies the computation and display of predicted cell frequencies, while PRED=PROB (or just PREDICT) specifies the computation and display of predicted cell probabilities.

The OUT= data set always contains the predicted probabilities. If the response functions are the generalized logits, the predicted cell probabilities are output unless the option PRED=FREQ is specified, in which case the predicted cell frequencies are output.

PROB

produces the two-way table of probability estimates for the cross-classification of populations by responses. These estimates sum to one across the response categories for each population.

TITLE=*'title'*

displays the *title* at the top of certain pages of output that correspond to this MODEL statement.

WLS

GLS

computes weighted least-squares estimates. This type of estimation is also called generalized-least-squares estimation. For response functions other than the default (of generalized logits), WLS is the default estimation method.

XPX

displays $\mathbf{X}'\mathbf{S}^{-1}\mathbf{X}$, the crossproducts matrix for the normal equations.

Specifying the Design Matrix Directly

If you specify the design matrix directly, adjacent rows of the matrix must be separated by a comma, and the matrix must have $q \times s$ rows, where s is the number of populations and q is the number of response functions per population. The first q rows correspond to the response functions for the first population, the second set of q rows corresponds to the functions for the second population, and so forth. The following is an example using direct specification of the design matrix.

```
proc catmod;
   model R=(1 0,
            1 1,
            1 2,
            1 3);
run;
```

These statements are appropriate for the case of one population and for R with five levels (generating four response functions), so that $4 \times 1 = 4$. These statements are also appropriate for a situation with two populations and two response functions per population; giving $2 \times 2 = 4$ rows of the design matrix. (To induce more than one population, the POPULATION statement is needed.)

When you input the design matrix directly, you also have the option of specifying that any subsets of the parameters be tested for equality to zero. Indicate each subset by specifying the appropriate column numbers of the design matrix, followed by an equal sign and a label (24 characters or less, in quotes) that describes the subset. Adjacent subsets are separated by a comma, and the entire specification is enclosed in parentheses and placed after the design matrix. For example,

```
proc catmod;
   population Group Time;
   model R=(1  1  0  0,
            1  1  0  1,
            1  1  0  2,
            1  0  1  0,
            1  0  1  1,
            1  0  1  2,
            1 -1 -1  0,
            1 -1 -1  1,
            1 -1 -1  2) (1  ='Intercept',
                         2 3='Group main effect',
                         4  ='Linear effect of Time');
run;
```

The preceding statements are appropriate when Group and Time each have three levels, and R is dichotomous. The POPULATION statement induces nine populations, and $q = 1$ (since R is dichotomous), so $q \times s = 1 \times 9 = 9$.

If you input the design matrix directly but do not specify any subsets of the parameters to be tested, then PROC CATMOD tests the effect of MODEL | MEAN, which represents the significance of the model beyond what is explained by an overall mean. For the previous example, the MODEL | MEAN effect is the same as that obtained by specifying

```
(2 3 4='model|mean');
```

at the end of the MODEL statement.

POPULATION Statement

POPULATION *variables* ;

The POPULATION statement specifies that populations are to be formed on the basis of cross-classifications of the specified variables. If you do not specify the POPULATION statement, then populations are formed on the basis of cross-classifications of the independent variables in the MODEL statement. The POPULATION statement has two major uses:

- When you enter the design matrix directly, there are no independent variables in the MODEL statement; therefore, the POPULATION statement is the only way of inducing more than one population.
- When you fit a reduced model, the POPULATION statement may be necessary if you want to induce the same number of populations as there are for the saturated model.

To illustrate the first use, suppose that you specify the following statements:

```
data one;
   input A $ B $ wt @@;
   datalines;
yes yes 23   yes no 31   no yes 47   no no 50
;

proc catmod;
   weight wt;
   population B;
   model A=(1 0,
            1 1);
run;
```

Since the dependent variable A has two levels, there is one response function per population. Since the variable B has two levels, there are two populations. Thus, the MODEL statement is valid since the number of rows in the design matrix (2) is the same as the total number of response functions. If the POPULATION statement is omitted, there would be only one population and one response function, and the MODEL statement would be invalid.

To illustrate the second use, suppose that you specify

```
data two;
   input A $ B $ Y wt @@;
   datalines;
yes  yes  1  23        yes  yes  2  63
yes  no   1  31        yes  no   2  70
no   yes  1  47        no   yes  2  80
no   no   1  50        no   no   2  84
;

proc catmod;
   weight wt;
   model Y=A B A*B / wls;
run;
```

These statements induce four populations and produce the following design matrix and analysis of variance table.

$$\mathbf{X} = \begin{bmatrix} 1 & 1 & 1 & 1 \\ 1 & 1 & -1 & -1 \\ 1 & -1 & 1 & -1 \\ 1 & -1 & -1 & 1 \end{bmatrix}$$

Source	DF	Chi-Square	Pr > ChiSq
Intercept	1	48.10	<.0001
A	1	3.47	0.0625
B	1	0.25	0.6186
A*B	1	0.19	0.6638
Residual	0		

Since the B and A*B effects are nonsignificant ($p > 0.10$), you may want to fit the reduced model that contains only the A effect. If your new statements are

```
proc catmod;
   weight wt;
   model Y=A / wls;
run;
```

then only two populations are induced, and the design matrix and the analysis of variance table are as follows.

$$\mathbf{X} = \begin{bmatrix} 1 & 1 \\ 1 & -1 \end{bmatrix}$$

Source	DF	Chi-Square	Pr > ChiSq
Intercept	1	47.94	<.0001
A	1	3.33	0.0678
Residual	0		

However, if the new statements are

```
proc catmod;
   weight wt;
   population A B;
   model Y=A / wls;
run;
```

then four populations are induced, and the design matrix and the analysis of variance table are as follows.

$$\mathbf{X} = \begin{bmatrix} 1 & 1 \\ 1 & 1 \\ 1 & -1 \\ 1 & -1 \end{bmatrix}$$

Source	DF	Chi-Square	Pr > ChiSq
Intercept	1	47.76	<.0001
A	1	3.30	0.0694
Residual	2	0.35	0.8374

The advantage of the latter analysis is that it retains four populations for the reduced model, thereby creating a built-in goodness-of-fit test: the residual chi-square. Such a test is important because the cumulative (or joint) effect of deleting two or more effects from the model may be significant, even if the individual effects are not.

The resulting differences between the two analyses are due to the fact that the latter analysis uses pure weighted least-squares estimates with respect to the four populations that are actually sampled. The former analysis pools populations and therefore uses parameter estimates that can be regarded as weighted least-squares estimates of maximum likelihood predicted cell frequencies. In any case, the estimation methods are asymptotically equivalent; therefore, the results are very similar. If you specify the ML option (instead of the WLS option) in the MODEL statements, then the parameter estimates are identical for the two analyses.

REPEATED Statement

REPEATED *factor-description* < *,... , factor-description* >< */ options* > **;**

where a *factor-description* is

factor-name < *$* >< *levels* >

and *factor-descriptions* are separated from each other by a comma. The $ is required for character-valued factors. The value of *levels* provides the number of levels of the repeated measurement factor identified by a given *factor-name*. For only one repeated measurement factor, *levels* is optional; for two or more repeated measurement factors, it is required.

The REPEATED statement incorporates repeated measurement factors into the model. You can use this statement whenever there is more than one dependent variable and the keyword _RESPONSE_ is specified in the MODEL statement. If the dependent variables correspond to one or more repeated measurement factors, you can use the REPEATED statement to define _RESPONSE_ in terms of those factors. You can specify the name, type, and number of levels of each factor, as well as the identification of each level.

You cannot specify the REPEATED statement for an analysis that also contains the FACTORS or LOGLIN statement since all of them specify the same information: how to partition the variation among the response functions within a population.

factor-name names a repeated measurement factor that corresponds to two or more response functions. This name must be a valid SAS variable name, and it should not be the same as the name of a variable that already exists in the data set being analyzed.

$ indicates that the factor is character-valued. If the $ is omitted, then PROC CATMOD assumes that the factor is numeric. The type of the factor is relevant only when you use the PROFILE= option or when the _RESPONSE_= option specifies nested-by-value effects.

levels specifies the number of levels of the corresponding repeated measurement factor. If there is only one such factor and the number is omitted, then PROC CATMOD assumes that the number of levels is equal to the number of response functions per population (q). Unless you specify the PROFILE= option, the number q must either be equal to or be a multiple of the product of the number of levels of all the factors.

You can specify the following options in the REPEATED statement after a slash.

PROFILE=(*matrix*)

specifies the values assumed by the factors for each response function. There should be one column for each factor, and the values in a given column should match the type (character or numeric) of the corresponding factor. Character values are restricted to 16 characters or less. If there are q response functions per population, then the matrix must have i rows, where q must either be equal to or be a multiple of i. Adjacent rows of the matrix should be separated by a comma.

The values in the PROFILE matrix are useful for specifying models in those situations where the study design is not a full factorial with respect to the factors. They can also be used to specify nested-with-value effects in the _RESPONSE_= option. If you specify character values in both the PROFILE= option and the _RESPONSE_= option, then the values must match with respect to whether or not they are enclosed in quotes (that is, enclosed in quotes in both places or in neither place).

RESPONSE=*effects*

specifies design effects. The variables named in the effects must be *factor-names* that appear in the REPEATED statement. If the _RESPONSE_= option is omitted, then PROC CATMOD builds a full factorial _RESPONSE_ effect with respect to the repeated measurement factors. For example, the following two statements are equivalent in that they produce the same parameter estimates.

```
repeated Time 2, Treatment 2;
repeated Time 2, Treatment 2 / _response_=Time|Treatment;
```

However, the second statement produces tests of the Time, Treatment, and Time*Treatment effects in the "Analysis of Variance" table, whereas the first statement produces a single test for the combined effects in _RESPONSE_.

TITLE=*'title'*

displays the *title* at the top of certain pages of output that correspond to this REPEATED statement.

For further information and numerous examples of the REPEATED statement, see the section "Repeated Measures Analysis" on page 754.

RESPONSE Statement

RESPONSE < *function* >< */ options* > **;**

The RESPONSE statement specifies functions of the response probabilities. The procedure models these response functions as linear combinations of the parameters.

By default, PROC CATMOD uses the standard response functions (generalized logits, which are explained in detail in the "Understanding the Standard Response Functions" section on page 740). With these standard response functions, the default estimation method is maximum likelihood, but you can use the WLS option in the MODEL statement to request weighted least-squares estimation. With other response functions (specified in the RESPONSE statement), the default (and only) estimation method is weighted least squares.

You can specify more than one RESPONSE statement, in which case each RESPONSE statement produces a separate analysis. If the computed response functions for any population are linearly dependent (yielding a singular covariance matrix), then PROC CATMOD displays an error message and stops processing. See the "Cautions" section on page 766 for methods of dealing with this.

The *function* specification can be any of the items in the following list. For an example of response functions generated and formulas for q (the number of response functions), see the "More on Response Functions" section on page 735.

ALOGIT
ALOGITS
specifies response functions as adjacent-category logits of the marginal probabilities for each of the dependent variables. For each dependent variable, the response functions are a set of linearly independent adjacent-category logits, obtained by taking the logarithms of the ratios of two probabilities. The denominator of the kth ratio is the marginal probability corresponding to the kth level of the variable, and the numerator is the marginal probability corresponding to the $(k+1)$th level. If a dependent variable has two levels, then the adjacent-category logit is the negative of the generalized logit.

CLOGIT
CLOGITS
specifies that the response functions are cumulative logits of the marginal probabilities for each of the dependent variables. For each dependent variable, the response functions are a set of linearly independent cumulative logits, obtained by taking the logarithms of the ratios of two probabilities. The denominator of the kth ratio is the cumulative probability, c_k, corresponding to the kth level of the variable, and the numerator is $1 - c_k$ (Agresti 1984, 113–114). If a dependent variable has two levels, then PROC CATMOD computes its cumulative logit as the negative of its generalized logit. You should use cumulative logits only when the dependent variables are ordinally scaled.

JOINT
specifies that the response functions are the joint response probabilities. A linearly independent set is created by deleting the last response probability. For the case of one dependent variable, the JOINT and MARGINALS specifications are equivalent.

LOGIT
LOGITS
specifies that the response functions are generalized logits of the marginal probabilities for each of the dependent variables. For each dependent variable, the response functions are a set of linearly independent generalized logits, obtained by taking the logarithms of the ratios of two probabilities. The denominator of each ratio is the marginal probability corresponding to the last observed level of the variable, and the numerators are the marginal probabilities corresponding to each of the other levels. If there is one dependent variable, then specifying LOGIT is equivalent to using the standard response functions.

MARGINAL
MARGINALS
specifies that the response functions are marginal probabilities for each of the dependent variables in the MODEL statement. For each dependent variable, the response functions are a set of linearly independent marginals, obtained by deleting the marginal probability corresponding to the last level.

MEAN
MEANS
specifies that the response functions are the means of the dependent variables in the MODEL statement. This specification requires that all of the dependent variables be numeric.

READ *variables* specifies that the response functions and their covariance matrix are to be read directly from the input data set with one response function for each variable named. See the section "Inputting Response Functions and Covariances Directly" on page 743 for more information.

transformation specifies response functions that can be expressed by using successive applications of the four operations: **LOG**, **EXP**, $*$ matrix literal, or $+$ matrix literal. The operations are described in detail in the "Using a Transformation to Specify Response Functions" section on page 738.

You can specify the following options in the RESPONSE statement after a slash.

OUT=*SAS-data-set*

produces a SAS data set that contains, for each population, the observed and predicted values of the response functions, their standard errors, and the residuals. Moreover, if you use the standard response functions, the data set also includes observed and predicted values of the cell frequencies or the cell probabilities. For further information, see the "Output Data Sets" section on page 747.

OUTEST=*SAS-data-set*

produces a SAS data set that contains the estimated parameter vector and its estimated covariance matrix. For further information, see the "Output Data Sets" section on page 747.

TITLE=*'title'*

displays the *title* at the top of certain pages of output that correspond to this RESPONSE statement.

More on Response Functions

Suppose the dependent variable A has 3 levels and is the only *response-effect* in the MODEL statement. The following table shows the proportions upon which the response functions are defined.

Value of A:	1	2	3
proportions:	p_1	p_2	p_3

Note that $\sum_j p_j = 1$. The following table shows the response functions generated for each population.

Function Specification	Value of q	Response Function
none*	2	$\ln\left(\frac{p_1}{p_3}\right),\ \ln\left(\frac{p_2}{p_3}\right)$
ALOGITS	2	$\ln\left(\frac{p_2}{p_1}\right),\ \ln\left(\frac{p_3}{p_2}\right)$
CLOGITS	2	$\ln\left(\frac{1-p_1}{p_1}\right),\ \ln\left(\frac{1-(p_1+p_2)}{p_1+p_2}\right)$
JOINT	2	$p_1,\ p_2$
LOGITS	2	$\ln\left(\frac{p_1}{p_3}\right),\ \ln\left(\frac{p_2}{p_3}\right)$
MARGINAL	2	$p_1,\ p_2$
MEAN	1	$1p_1 + 2p_2 + 3p_3$

*Without a function specification, the default response functions are generalized logits.

Now, suppose the dependent variables A and B each have 3 levels (valued 1, 2, and 3 each) and the *response-effect* in the MODEL statement is A*B. The following table shows the proportions upon which the response functions are defined.

Value of A:	1	1	1	2	2	2	3	3	3
Value of B:	1	2	3	1	2	3	1	2	3
proportions:	p_1	p_2	p_3	p_4	p_5	p_6	p_7	p_8	p_9

The marginal totals for the preceding table are defined as follows,

$$\begin{aligned} p_{1\cdot} &= p_1 + p_2 + p_3 & \qquad p_{\cdot 1} &= p_1 + p_4 + p_7 \\ p_{2\cdot} &= p_4 + p_5 + p_6 & p_{\cdot 2} &= p_2 + p_5 + p_8 \\ p_{3\cdot} &= p_7 + p_8 + p_9 & p_{\cdot 3} &= p_3 + p_6 + p_9 \end{aligned}$$

where $\sum_j p_j = 1$. The following table shows the response functions generated for each population.

Function Specification	Value of q	Response Function
none*	8	$\ln\left(\frac{p_1}{p_9}\right),\ \ln\left(\frac{p_2}{p_9}\right),\ \ln\left(\frac{p_3}{p_9}\right),\ldots,\ \ln\left(\frac{p_8}{p_9}\right)$
ALOGITS	4	$\ln\left(\frac{p_{2\cdot}}{p_{1\cdot}}\right),\ \ln\left(\frac{p_{3\cdot}}{p_{2\cdot}}\right),\ \ln\left(\frac{p_{\cdot 2}}{p_{\cdot 1}}\right),\ \ln\left(\frac{p_{\cdot 3}}{p_{\cdot 2}}\right)$
CLOGITS	4	$\ln\left(\frac{1-p_{1\cdot}}{p_{1\cdot}}\right),\ \ln\left(\frac{1-(p_{1\cdot}+p_{2\cdot})}{p_{1\cdot}+p_{2\cdot}}\right),\ \ln\left(\frac{1-p_{\cdot 1}}{p_{\cdot 1}}\right),\ \ln\left(\frac{1-(p_{\cdot 1}+p_{\cdot 2})}{p_{\cdot 1}+p_{\cdot 2}}\right)$
JOINT	8	$p_1,\ p_2,\ p_3,\ p_4,\ p_5,\ p_6,\ p_7,\ p_8$
LOGITS	4	$\ln\left(\frac{p_{1\cdot}}{p_{3\cdot}}\right),\ \ln\left(\frac{p_{2\cdot}}{p_{3\cdot}}\right),\ \ln\left(\frac{p_{\cdot 1}}{p_{\cdot 3}}\right),\ \ln\left(\frac{p_{\cdot 2}}{p_{\cdot 3}}\right)$
MARGINAL	4	$p_{1\cdot},\ p_{2\cdot},\ p_{\cdot 1},\ p_{\cdot 2}$
MEAN	2	$1p_{1\cdot} + 2p_{2\cdot} + 3p_{3\cdot},\ 1p_{\cdot 1} + 2p_{\cdot 2} + 3p_{\cdot 3}$

* Without a function specification, the default response functions are generalized logits.

The READ and *transformation* function specifications are not shown in the preceding table. For these two situations, there is not a general response function; the response functions generated depend on what you specify.

Another important aspect of the function specification is the number of response functions generated per population, q. Let m_i represent the number of levels for the ith dependent variable in the MODEL statement, and let d represent the number of dependent variables in the MODEL statement. Then, if the function specification is ALOGITS, CLOGITS, LOGITS, or MARGINALS, the number of response functions is

$$q = \sum_{i=1}^{d} (m_i - 1)$$

If the function specification is JOINT or the default (generalized logits), the number of response functions per population is

$$q = r - 1$$

where r is the number of response profiles. If every possible cross-classification of the dependent variables is observed in the samples, then

$$r = \prod_{i=1}^{d} m_i$$

Otherwise, r is the number of cross-classifications actually observed.

If the function specification is MEANS, the number of response functions per population is $q = d$.

Response Statement Examples

Some example response statements are shown in the following table.

Example	Result
`response marginals;`	marginals for each dependent variable
`response means;`	the mean of each dependent variable
`response logits;`	generalized logits of the marginal probabilities
`response clogits;`	cumulative logits of the marginal probabilities
`response alogits;`	adjacent-category logits of the marginal probabilities
`response joint;`	the joint probabilities
`response 1 -1 log;`	the logit
`response;`	generalized logits
`response 1 2 3;`	the mean score, with scores of 1, 2, and 3 corresponding to the three response levels
`response read b1-b4;`	four response functions and their covariance matrix, read directly from the input data set

Using a Transformation to Specify Response Functions

If you specify a *transformation*, it is applied to the vector that contains the sample proportions in each population. The *transformation* can be any combination of the following four operations.

Operation	Specification
linear combination	$*$ matrix literal matrix literal
logarithm	**LOG**
exponential	**EXP**
adding constant	$+$ matrix literal

If more than one operation is specified, then PROC CATMOD applies the operations consecutively from right to left.

A matrix literal is a matrix of numbers with each row of the matrix separated from the next by a comma. If you specify a linear combination, in most cases the $*$ is not needed. The following statement defines the response function $p_1 + 1$. The $*$ is needed to separate the two matrix literals '1' and '1 0'.

```
response + 1 * 1 0;
```

The **LOG** of a vector transforms each element of the vector into its natural logarithm; the **EXP** of a vector transforms each element into its exponential function (antilogarithm).

In order to specify a linear response function for data that have $r = 3$ response categories, you could specify either of the following RESPONSE statements:

```
response   * 1 0 0 , 0 1 0;
response     1 0 0 , 0 1 0;
```

The matrix literal in the preceding statements specifies a 2×3 matrix, which is applied to each population as follows:

$$\begin{bmatrix} F_1 \\ F_2 \end{bmatrix} = \begin{bmatrix} 1 & 0 & 0 \\ 0 & 1 & 0 \end{bmatrix} * \begin{bmatrix} p_1 \\ p_2 \\ p_3 \end{bmatrix}$$

where p_1, p_2, and p_3 are sample proportions for the three response categories in a population, and F_1 and F_2 are the two response functions computed for that population. This response function, therefore, sets $F1 = p_1$ and $F2 = p_2$ in each population.

As another example of the linear response function, suppose you have two dependent variables corresponding to two observers who evaluate the same subjects. If the observers grade on the same three-point scale and if all nine possible responses are observed, then the following RESPONSE statement would compute the probability that the observers agree on their assessments:

```
response 1 0 0 0 1 0 0 0 1;
```

This response function is then computed as

$$F = p_{11} + p_{22} + p_{33} = \begin{bmatrix} 1 & 0 & 0 & 0 & 1 & 0 & 0 & 0 & 1 \end{bmatrix} * \begin{bmatrix} p_{11} \\ p_{12} \\ p_{13} \\ p_{21} \\ p_{22} \\ p_{23} \\ p_{31} \\ p_{32} \\ p_{33} \end{bmatrix}$$

where p_{ij} denotes the probability that a subject gets a grade of i from the first observer and j from the second observer.

If the function is a compound function, requiring more than one operation to specify it, then the operations should be listed so that the first operation to be applied is on the right and the last operation to be applied is on the left. For example, if there are two response levels, the response function

```
response 1 -1 log;
```

is equivalent to the matrix expression:

$$F = \begin{bmatrix} 1 & -1 \end{bmatrix} * \begin{bmatrix} \log(p_1) \\ \log(p_2) \end{bmatrix} = \log(p_1) - \log(p_2) = \log\left(\frac{p_1}{p_2}\right)$$

which is the logit response function since $p_2 = 1 - p_1$ when there are only two response levels.

Another example of a compound response function is

```
response exp 1 -1 * 1 0 0 1, 0 1 1 0 log;
```

which is equivalent to the matrix expression

$$F = \mathbf{EXP}(\mathbf{A} * \mathbf{B} * \mathbf{LOG}(\mathbf{P}))$$

where $\mathbf{P}$ is the vector of sample proportions for some population,

$$\mathbf{A} = \begin{bmatrix} 1 & -1 \end{bmatrix} \text{ and } \mathbf{B} = \begin{bmatrix} 1 & 0 & 0 & 1 \\ 0 & 1 & 1 & 0 \end{bmatrix}$$

If the four responses are based on two dependent variables, each with two levels, then the function can also be written as

$$F = \frac{p_{11}p_{22}}{p_{12}p_{21}}$$

which is the odds (crossproduct) ratio for a 2×2 table.

Understanding the Standard Response Functions

If no RESPONSE statement is specified, PROC CATMOD computes the standard response functions, which contrast the log of each response probability with the log of the probability for the last response category. If there are r response categories, then there are $r - 1$ standard response functions. For example, if there are four response categories, using no RESPONSE statement is equivalent to specifying

```
response  1 0 0 -1,
          0 1 0 -1,
          0 0 1 -1  log;
```

This results in three response functions:

$$F = \begin{bmatrix} F_1 \\ F_2 \\ F_3 \end{bmatrix} = \begin{bmatrix} \log(p_1/p_4) \\ \log(p_2/p_4) \\ \log(p_3/p_4) \end{bmatrix}$$

If there are only two response levels, the resulting response function would be a logit. Thus, the standard response functions are called generalized logits. They are useful in dealing with the log-linear model:

$$\pi = \mathbf{EXP}(\mathbf{X}\boldsymbol{\beta})$$

If **C** denotes the matrix in the preceding RESPONSE statement, then because of the restriction that the probabilities sum to 1, it follows that an equivalent model is

$$\mathbf{C} * \mathbf{LOG}(\pi) = (\mathbf{CX})\boldsymbol{\beta}$$

But **C**∗**LOG**(**P**) is simply the vector of standard response functions. Thus, fitting a log-linear model on the cell probabilities is equivalent to fitting a linear model on the generalized logits.

RESTRICT Statement

RESTRICT *parameter=value* < . . . *parameter=value* > ;

where *parameter* is the letter B followed by a number; for example, B3 specifies the third parameter in the model. The *value* is the value to which the parameter is restricted. The RESTRICT statement restricts values of parameters to the values you specify, so that the estimation of the remaining parameters is subject to these restrictions. Consider the following statement:

```
restrict b1=1 b4=0 b6=0;
```

This restricts the values of three parameters. The first parameter is set to 1, and the fourth and sixth parameters are set to zero.

The RESTRICT statement is interactive. A new RESTRICT statement replaces any previous ones. In addition, if you submit two or more MODEL, LOGLIN, FACTORS, or REPEATED statements, then the subsequent occurrences of these statements also delete the previous RESTRICT statement.

WEIGHT Statement

WEIGHT *variable* ;

You can use a WEIGHT statement to refer to a variable containing the cell frequencies, which need not be integers. The WEIGHT statement lets you use summary data sets containing a count variable. See the "Input Data Sets" section on page 742 for further information concerning the WEIGHT statement.

Details

Missing Values

Observations with missing values for any variable listed in the MODEL, POPULATION, or WEIGHT statement are omitted from the analysis.

Input Data Sets

Data to be analyzed by PROC CATMOD must be in a SAS data set containing one of the following:

- raw data values (variable values for every subject)
- frequency counts and the corresponding variable values
- response function values and their covariance matrix

If you specify a WEIGHT statement, then PROC CATMOD uses the values of the WEIGHT variable as the frequency counts. If the READ function is specified in the RESPONSE statement, then the procedure expects the input data set to contain the values of response functions and their covariance matrix. Otherwise, PROC CATMOD assumes that the SAS data set contains raw data values.

Raw Data Values

If you use raw data, PROC CATMOD first counts the number of observations having each combination of values for all variables specified in the MODEL or POPULATION statements. For example, suppose the variables A and B each take on the values 1 and 2, and their frequencies can be represented as follows.

	A=1	A=2
B=1	2	1
B=2	3	1

The SAS data set Raw containing the raw data might be as follows.

Observation	A	B
1	1	1
2	1	1
3	1	2
4	1	2
5	1	2
6	2	1
7	2	2

And the statements for PROC CATMOD would be

```
proc catmod data=Raw;
   model A=B;
run;
```

For discussions of how to handle structural and random zeros with raw data as input data, see the "Zero Frequencies" section on page 767 and Example 22.5 on page 796.

Frequency Counts

If your data set contains frequency counts, then use the WEIGHT statement in PROC CATMOD to specify the variable containing the frequencies. For example, you could create the Summary data set as follows.

```
data Summary;
   input A B Count;
   datalines;
1 1 2
1 2 3
2 1 1
2 2 1
;
```

In this case, the corresponding statements would be

```
proc catmod data=Summary;
   weight Count;
   model A=B;
run;
```

The data set Summary can also be created from data set Raw by using the FREQ procedure:

```
proc freq data=Raw;
   tables A*B / out=Summary;
run;
```

Inputting Response Functions and Covariances Directly

If you want to read in the response functions and their covariance matrix, rather than have PROC CATMOD compute them, create a TYPE=EST data set. In addition to having one variable name for each function, the data set should have two additional variables: _TYPE_ and _NAME_, both character variables of length 8. The variable _TYPE_ should have the value 'PARMS' when the observation contains the response functions; it should have the value 'COV' when the observation contains elements of the covariance matrix of the response functions. The variable _NAME_ is used only when _TYPE_=COV, in which case it should contain the name of the variable that has its covariance elements stored in that observation. In the following data set, for example, the covariance between the second and fourth response functions is 0.000102.

```
data direct(type=est);
   input b1-b4 _type_ $ _name_ $8.;
   datalines;
0.590463    0.384720    0.273269    0.136458    PARMS      .
0.001690    0.000911    0.000474    0.000432    COV        B1
0.000911    0.001823    0.000031    0.000102    COV        B2
0.000474    0.000031    0.001056    0.000477    COV        B3
0.000432    0.000102    0.000477    0.000396    COV        B4
;
```

In order to tell PROC CATMOD that the input data set contains the values of response functions and their covariance matrix,

- specify the READ function in the RESPONSE statement
- specify _F_ as the dependent variable in the MODEL statement

For example, suppose the response functions correspond to four populations that represent the cross-classification of two age groups by two race groups. You can use the FACTORS statement to identify these two factors and to name the effects in the model. The statements required to fit a main-effects model to these data are

```
proc catmod data=direct;
   response read b1-b4;
   model _f_=_response_;
   factors age 2, race 2 / _response_=age race;
run;
```

Ordering of Populations and Responses

By default, populations and responses are sorted in standard SAS order as follows:

- alphabetic order for character variables
- increasing numeric order for numeric variables

Suppose you specify the following statements:

```
data one;
   length A B $ 6;
   input A $ B $ wt @@;
   datalines;
low        low   23  low     medium  31 low     high  38
medium     low   40  medium medium   42 medium high   50
high       low   52  high    medium  54 high    high  61
;

proc catmod;
   weight wt;
   model A=B / oneway;
run;
```

The ordering of populations and responses corresponds to the alphabetical order of the levels of the character variables. You can specify the ONEWAY option to display the ordering of the variables, while the "Population Profiles" and "Response Profiles" tables display the ordering of the populations and the responses, respectively.

Population Profiles		Response Profiles	
Sample	**B**	**Response**	**A**
1	high	1	high
2	low	2	low
3	medium	3	medium

However, in this example, you may want to have the levels ordered in the natural order of 'low,' 'medium,' 'high.' If you specify the ORDER=DATA option

```
proc catmod order=data;
   weight wt;
   model a=b / oneway;
run;
```

then the ordering of populations and responses is as follows.

Population Profiles		Response Profiles	
Sample	**B**	**Response**	**A**
1	low	1	low
2	medium	2	medium
3	high	3	high

Thus, you can use the ORDER=DATA option to ensure that populations and responses are ordered in a specific way. But since this also affects the definitions and the ordering of the parameters, you must exercise caution when using the _RESPONSE_ effect, the CONTRAST statement, or direct input of the design matrix.

An alternative method of ensuring that populations and responses are ordered in a specific way is to replace any character variables with numeric variables and to assign formatted values such as 'yes' and 'no' to the numeric levels. PROC CATMOD orders the populations and responses according to the numeric values but displays the formatted values.

Specification of Effects

By default, the CATMOD procedure treats all variables as classification variables. As a result, there is no CLASS statement in PROC CATMOD. The values of a classification variable can be numeric or character. PROC CATMOD builds a set of effects-coded variables to represent the levels of the classification variable and then uses these to fit the model (for details, see the "Generation of the Design Matrix" section on page 757). You can modify the default by using the DIRECT statement to treat numeric independent continuous variables as continuous variables. The classification variables, combinations of classification variables, and continuous variables are then used in fitting linear models to data.

The parameters of a linear model are generally divided into subsets that correspond to meaningful sources of variation in the response functions. These sources, called *effects*, can be specified in the MODEL, LOGLIN, FACTORS, REPEATED, and CONTRAST statements. Effects can be specified in any of the following ways:

- A main effect is a single class variable (that is, it induces classification levels): A B C.
- A crossed effect (or interaction) is two or more class variables joined by asterisks, for example: A*B A*B*C.
- A nested effect is a main effect or an interaction, followed by a parenthetical field containing a main effect or an interaction. Multiple variables within the parentheses are assumed to form a crossed effect even when the asterisk is absent. Thus, the last two effects are identical: B(A) C(A*B) A*B(C*D) A*B(C D).
- A nested-by-value effect is the same as a nested effect except that any variable in the parentheses can be followed by an equal sign and a value: B(A=1) C(A B=1) C*D(A=1 B=1) A(C='low').
- A direct effect is a variable specified in a DIRECT statement: X Y.
- Direct effects can be crossed with other effects: X*Y X*X*X X*A*B(C D=1).

The variables for crossed and nested effects remain in the order in which they are first encountered. For example, in the model

```
model R=B A A*B C(A B);
```

the effect A*B is reported as B*A since B appeared before A in the statement. Also, C(A B) is interpreted as C(A*B) and is therefore reported as C(B*A).

Bar Notation

You can shorten the specification of multiple effects by using bar notation. For example, two methods of writing a full three-way factorial model are

```
proc catmod;
   model y=a b c a*b a*c b*c a*b*c;
run;
```

and

```
proc catmod;
   model y=a|b|c;
run;
```

When you use the bar (|) notation, the right- and left-hand sides become effects, and the interaction between them becomes an effect. Multiple bars are permitted. The expressions are expanded from left to right, using rules 1 through 4 given in Searle (1971, p. 390):

- Multiple bars are evaluated left to right. For example, A|B|C is evaluated as follows:

```
A | B | C  →  {A | B} | C
           →  {A B A*B} | C
           →  A B A*B C A*C B*C A*B*C
```

- Crossed and nested groups of variables are combined. For example, A(B) | C(D) generates A*C(B D), among other terms.
- Duplicate variables are removed. For example, A(C) | B(C) generates A*B(C C), among other terms, and the extra C is removed.
- Effects are discarded if a variable occurs on both the crossed and nested sides of an effect. For instance, A(B) | B(D E) generates A*B(B D E), but this effect is deleted.

You can also specify the maximum number of variables involved in any effect that results from bar evaluation by specifying that maximum number, preceded by an @ sign, at the end of the bar effect. For example, the specification A | B | C @ 2 would result in only those effects that contain 2 or fewer variables; in this case, the effects A, B, A*B, C, A*C, and B*C are generated.

Other examples of the bar notation are

A | C(B)	is equivalent to	A C(B) A*C(B)
A(B) | C(B)	is equivalent to	A(B) C(B) A*C(B)
A(B) | B(D E)	is equivalent to	A(B) B(D E)
A | B(A) | C	is equivalent to	A B(A) C A*C B*C(A)
A | B(A) | C@2	is equivalent to	A B(A) C A*C
A | B | C | D@2	is equivalent to	A B A*B C A*C B*C D A*D B*D C*D

For details on how the effects specified lead to a design matrix, see the "Generation of the Design Matrix" section on page 757.

Output Data Sets

OUT= Data Set

For each population, the OUT= data set contains the observed and predicted values of the response functions, their standard errors, the residuals, and variables that describe the population and response profiles. In addition, if you use the standard response functions, the data set includes observed and predicted values for the cell frequencies or the cell probabilities, together with their standard errors and residuals. See Example 22.11 on page 826 for an example of creating an OUT= data set.

Number of Observations

For the standard response functions, there are $s \times (2q - 1)$ observations in the data set for each BY group, where s is the number of populations, and q is the number of response functions per population. Otherwise, there are $s \times q$ observations in the data set for each BY group.

Variables in the OUT= Data Set

The data set contains the following variables:

BY variables	If you use a BY statement, the BY variables are included in the OUT= data set.
dependent variables	If the response functions are the default ones (generalized logits), then the dependent variables, which describe the response profiles, are included in the OUT= data set. When _TYPE_=FUNCTION, the values of these variables are missing.
independent variables	The independent variables, which describe the population profiles, are included in the OUT= data set.
NUMBER	the sequence number of the response function or the cell probability or the cell frequency
OBS	the observed value
PRED	the predicted value
RESID	the residual (observed − predicted)
SAMPLE	the population number. This matches the sample number in the Population Profile section of the output.
SEOBS	the standard error of the observed value
SEPRED	the standard error of the predicted value
TYPE	specifies a character variable with three possible values. When _TYPE_=FUNCTION, the observed and predicted values are values of the response functions. When _TYPE_=PROB, they are values of the cell probabilities. When _TYPE_=FREQ, they are values of the cell frequencies. Cell probabilities or frequencies are provided only when the default response functions are modeled. In this case, cell probabilities are provided by default, and cell frequencies are provided if you specify the option PRED=FREQ.

OUTEST= Data Set

This TYPE=EST output data set contains the estimated parameter vector and its estimated covariance matrix. If you specify both the ML and WLS options in the MODEL statement, the OUTEST= data set contains both sets of estimates. For each BY group, there are $p + 1$ observations in the data set for each estimation method, where p is the number of estimated parameters. The data set contains the following variables.

B1, B2, and so on — variables for the estimated parameters. The OUTEST= data set contains one variable for each estimated parameter.

BY variables — If you use a BY statement, the BY variables are included in the OUT= data set.

METHOD — the method used to obtain parameter estimates. For weighted least-squares estimation, _METHOD_=WLS, and for maximum likelihood estimation, _METHOD_=ML.

NAME — identifies parameter names. When _TYPE_=PARMS, _NAME_ is blank, but when _TYPE_=COV, _NAME_ has one of the values B1, B2, and so on, corresponding to the parameter names.

STATUS — indicates whether the estimates have converged

TYPE — identifies the statistics contained in the variables for parameter estimates (B1, B2, and so on). When _TYPE_=PARMS, the variables contain parameter estimates; when _TYPE_=COV, they contain covariance estimates.

The variables _METHOD_, _NAME_, and _TYPE_ are character variables; the BY variables can be either character or numeric; and the variables for estimated parameters are numeric.

See Appendix A, "Special SAS Data Sets," for more information on special SAS data sets.

Logistic Analysis

In a logistic analysis, the response functions are the logits of the dependent variable.

PROC CATMOD can compute three different types of logits with the use of keywords in the RESPONSE statement. Other types of response functions can be generated by specifying appropriate transformations in the RESPONSE statement.

- Generalized logits are used primarily for nominally scaled dependent variables, but they can also be used for ordinal data modeling. Maximum likelihood estimation is available for the analysis of these logits.
- Cumulative logits are used for ordinally scaled dependent variables. Except for dependent variables with two response levels, only weighted least-squares estimation is available for the analysis of these logits.
- Adjacent-category logits are equivalent to generalized logits, but they have some advantages for ordinal data analysis because they automatically incorporate integer scores for the levels of the dependent variable. Except for dependent variables with two response levels, only weighted least-squares estimation is available for the analysis of these logits.

If the dependent variable has only two responses, then the cumulative logit and the adjacent-category logit are the negative of the generalized logit, as computed by PROC CATMOD. Consequently, parameter estimates obtained using these logits are the negative of those obtained using generalized logits. A simple logistic analysis of variance uses statements like the following:

```
proc catmod;
   model r=a|b;
run;
```

Logistic Regression

If the independent variables are treated quantitatively (like continuous variables), then a logistic analysis is known as a *logistic regression*. If you want PROC CATMOD to treat the independent variables as quantitative variables, specify them in both the DIRECT and MODEL statements, as follows.

```
proc catmod;
   direct x1 x2 x3;
   model r=x1 x2 x3;
run;
```

Since the preceding statements do not include a RESPONSE statement, generalized logits are computed. See Example 22.3 for another example.

When the dependent variable has two responses, the parameter estimates from the CATMOD procedure are the same as those from a logistic regression program such as PROC LOGISTIC (see Chapter 39, "The LOGISTIC Procedure"). The chi-square statistics and the predicted values are also identical. In the two-response case, PROC CATMOD can be made to model the probability of the maximum value by either (1) organizing the input data so that the maximum value occurs first and specifying ORDER=DATA in the PROC CATMOD statement or (2) specifying cumulative logits (CLOGITS) in the RESPONSE statement.

Caution: Computational difficulties may occur if you use a continuous variable with a large number of unique values in a DIRECT statement. See the "Continuous Variables" section on page 751 for more details.

Cumulative Logits

If your dependent variable is ordinally scaled, you can specify the analysis of cumulative logits that take into account the ordinal nature of the dependent variable:

```
proc catmod;
   response clogits;
   direct x;
   model r=a x;
run;
```

The preceding statements correspond to a simple analysis that addresses the question of existence of an association between the independent variables and the ordinal dependent variable. However, there are some commonly used models for the analysis of ordinal data (Agresti 1984) that address the structure of association (in terms of odds ratios), as well as its existence.

If the independent variables are class variables, a typical analysis for such a model uses the following statements:

```
proc catmod;
   weight wt;
   response clogits;
   model r=_response_ a b;
run;
```

On the other hand, if the independent variables are ordinally scaled, you might specify numeric scores in variables x1 and x2, and use the following statements:

```
proc catmod;
   weight wt;
   direct x1 x2;
   response clogits;
   model r=_response_ x1 x2;
run;
```

Refer to Agresti (1984) for additional details of estimation, testing, and interpretation.

Continuous Variables

Computational difficulties may occur if you have a continuous variable with a large number of unique values and you use this variable in a DIRECT statement, since an observation often represents a separate population of size one. At this extreme of sparseness, the weighted least-squares method is inappropriate since there are too many zero frequencies. Therefore, you should use the maximum likelihood method. PROC CATMOD is not designed optimally for continuous variables and therefore may be less efficient and may be unable to allocate sufficient memory to handle this problem, as compared with a procedure designed specifically to handle continuous data. In these situations, consider using the LOGISTIC, GENMOD, or PROBIT procedure to analyze your data.

Log-Linear Model Analysis

When the response functions are the default generalized logits, then inclusion of the keyword _RESPONSE_ in every effect in the right-hand side of the MODEL statement induces a log-linear model. The keyword _RESPONSE_ tells PROC CATMOD that you want to model the variation among the dependent variables. You then specify the actual model in the LOGLIN statement.

One word of caution about log-linear model analyses: sampling zeros in the input data set should be replaced by some positive number close to zero (such as 1E-20) to ensure that these sampling zeros are not treated as structural zeros. This can be performed in a DATA step that changes cell counts for sampling zeros to a very small number. Data containing sampling zeros should be analyzed with maximum likelihood estimation. See the “Cautions” section on page 766 and Example 22.5 on page 796 for further information and an illustration for both cell count data and raw data.

When you perform log-linear model analysis, you can request weighted least-squares estimates, maximum likelihood estimates, or both. By default, PROC CATMOD calculates maximum likelihood estimates when the default response functions are used. The following table provides appropriate MODEL statements for the combinations of types of estimates.

Estimation Desired	MODEL Statement
Maximum likelihood	`model a*b=_response_;`
Weighted least squares	`model a*b=_response_ / wls;`
Maximum likelihood and weighted least squares	`model a*b=_response_ / wls ml;`

One Population

The usual log-linear model analysis has one population, which means that all of the variables are dependent variables. For example, the statements

```
proc catmod;
   weight wt;
   model r1*r2=_response_;
   loglin r1|r2;
run;
```

yield a maximum likelihood analysis of a saturated log-linear model for the dependent variables r1 and r2.

If you want to fit a reduced model with respect to the dependent variables (for example, a model of independence or conditional independence), specify the reduced model in the LOGLIN statement. For example, the statements

```
proc catmod;
   weight wt;
   model r1*r2=_response_ / pred;
   loglin r1 r2;
run;
```

yield a main-effects log-linear model analysis of the factors r1 and r2. The output includes Wald statistics for the individual effects r1 and r2, as well as predicted cell probabilities. Moreover, the goodness-of-fit statistic is the likelihood ratio test for the hypothesis of independence between r1 and r2 or, equivalently, a test of r1*r2.

Multiple Populations

You can do log-linear model analysis with multiple populations by using a POPULATION statement or by including effects on the right-hand side of the MODEL statement that contain independent variables. Each effect must include the _RESPONSE_ keyword.

For example, suppose the dependent variables r1 and r2 are dichotomous, and the independent variable group has three levels. Then

```
proc catmod;
   weight wt;
   model r1*r2=_response_ group*_response_;
   loglin r1|r2;
run;
```

specifies a saturated model (three degrees of freedom for _RESPONSE_ and six degrees of freedom for the interaction between _RESPONSE_ and group). From another point of view, _RESPONSE_*group can be regarded as a main effect for group with respect to the three response functions, while _RESPONSE_ can be regarded as an intercept effect with respect to the functions. In other words, these statements give essentially the same results as the logistic analysis:

```
proc catmod;
   weight wt;
   model r1*r2=group;
run;
```

The ability to model the interaction between the independent and the dependent variables becomes particularly useful when a reduced model is specified for the dependent variables. For example,

```
proc catmod;
   weight wt;
   model r1*r2=_response_ group*_response_;
   loglin r1 r2;
run;
```

specifies a model with two degrees of freedom for _RESPONSE_ (one for r1 and one for r2) and four degrees of freedom for the interaction of _RESPONSE_*group. The likelihood ratio goodness-of-fit statistic (three degrees of freedom) tests the hypothesis that r1 and r2 are independent in each of the three groups.

Repeated Measures Analysis

If there are multiple dependent variables and the variables represent repeated measurements of the same observational unit, then the variation among the dependent variables can be attributed to one or more repeated measurement factors. The factors can be included in the model by specifying _RESPONSE_ on the right-hand side of the MODEL statement and using a REPEATED statement to identify the factors.

To perform a repeated measures analysis, you also need to specify a RESPONSE statement, since the standard response functions (generalized logits) cannot be used. Typically, the MEANS or MARGINALS response functions are specified in a repeated measures analysis, but other response functions may also be reasonable.

One Population

Consider an experiment in which each subject is measured at three times, and the response functions are marginal probabilities for each of the dependent variables. If the dependent variables each has k levels, then PROC CATMOD computes $k-1$ response functions for each time. Differences among the response functions with respect to these times could be attributed to the repeated measurement factor Time. To incorporate the Time variation into the model, specify

```
proc catmod;
   response marginals;
   model t1*t2*t3=_response_;
   repeated Time 3 / _response_=Time;
run;
```

These statements induce a Time effect that has $2(k-1)$ degrees of freedom since there are $k-1$ response functions at each time point. Thus, for a dichotomous variable, the Time effect has two degrees of freedom.

Now suppose that at each time point, each subject has X-rays taken, and the X-rays are read by two different radiologists. This creates six dependent variables that represent the 3×2 cross-classification of the repeated measurement factors Time and Reader. A saturated model with respect to these factors can be obtained by specifying

```
proc catmod;
   response marginals;
   model r11*r12*r21*r22*r31*r32=_response_;
   repeated Time 3, Reader 2
      / _response_=Time Reader Time*Reader;
run;
```

If you want to fit a main-effects model with respect to Time and Reader, then change the REPEATED statement to

```
repeated Time 3, Reader 2 / _response_=Time Reader;
```

If you want to fit a main-effects model for Time but for only one of the readers, the REPEATED statement might look like

```
repeated Time $ 3, Reader $ 2
         /_response_=Time(Reader=Smith)
           profile  =('1'  Smith,
                      '1'  Jones,
                      '2'  Smith,
                      '2'  Jones,
                      '3'  Smith,
                      '3'  Jones);
```

If Jones had been unavailable for a reading at time 3, then there would be only $5(k-1)$ response functions, even though PROC CATMOD would be expecting some multiple of 6 $(= 3 \times 2)$. In that case, the PROFILE= option would be necessary to indicate which repeated measurement profiles were actually represented:

```
repeated Time $ 3, Reader $ 2
         /_response_=Time(Reader=Smith)
           profile  =('1'  Smith,
                      '1'  Jones,
                      '2'  Smith,
                      '2'  Jones,
                      '3'  Smith);
```

When two or more repeated measurement factors are specified, PROC CATMOD presumes that the response functions are ordered so that the levels of the rightmost factor change most rapidly. This means that the dependent variables should be specified in the same order. For this example, the order implied by the REPEATED statement is as follows, where the variable r_{ij} corresponds to Time i and Reader j.

Response Function	Dependent Variable	Time	Reader
1	r_{11}	1	1
2	r_{12}	1	2
3	r_{21}	2	1
4	r_{22}	2	2
5	r_{31}	3	1
6	r_{32}	3	2

Thus, the order of dependent variables in the MODEL statement must agree with the order implied by the REPEATED statement.

Multiple Populations

When there are variables specified in the POPULATION statement or in the right-hand side of the MODEL statement, these variables induce multiple populations. PROC CATMOD can then model these independent variables, the repeated measurement factors, and the interactions between the two.

For example, suppose that there are five groups of subjects, that each subject in the study is measured at three different times, and that the dichotomous dependent variables are labeled t1, t2, and t3. The following statements induce the computation of three response functions for each population:

```
proc catmod;
   weight wt;
   population Group;
   response marginals;
   model t1*t2*t3=_response_;
   repeated Time / _response_=Time;
run;
```

PROC CATMOD then regards _RESPONSE_ as a variable with three levels corresponding to the three response functions in each population and forms an effect with two degrees of freedom. The MODEL and REPEATED statements tell PROC CATMOD to fit the main effect of Time.

In general, the MODEL statement tells PROC CATMOD how to integrate the independent variables and the repeated measurement factors into the model. For example, again suppose that there are five groups of subjects, that each subject is measured at three times, and that the dichotomous independent variables are labeled t1, t2, and t3. If you use the same WEIGHT, POPULATION, RESPONSE, and REPEATED statements as in the preceding program, the following MODEL statements result in the indicated analyses:

`model t1*t2*t3=Group / averaged;`	specifies the Group main effect (with four degrees of freedom).
`model t1*t2*t3=_response_;`	specifies the Time main effect (with two degrees of freedom).
`model t1*t2*t3=_response_*Group;`	specifies the interaction between Time and Group (with eight degrees of freedom).
`model t1*t2*t3=_response_|Group;`	specifies both main effects, and the interaction between Time and Group (with a total of fourteen degrees of freedom).
`model t1*t2*t3=_response_(Group);`	specifies a Time main effect within each Group (with ten degrees of freedom).

However, the following MODEL statement is invalid since effects cannot be nested within _RESPONSE_:

```
model t1*t2*t3=Group(_response_);
```

Generation of the Design Matrix

Each row of the design matrix (corresponding to a population) is generated by a unique combination of independent variable values. Each column of the design matrix corresponds to a model parameter. The columns are produced from the effect specifications in the MODEL, LOGLIN, FACTORS, and REPEATED statements. For details on effect specifications, see the "Specification of Effects" section on page 745. This section is divided into three parts:

- one response function per population
- two or more response functions per population (excluding log-linear models), beginning on page 760
- log-linear models, beginning on page 764

One Response Function Per Population

Intercept

When there is one response function per population, all design matrices start with a column of 1s for the intercept unless the NOINT option is specified or the design matrix is input directly.

Main Effects

If a class variable A has k levels, then its main effect has $k-1$ degrees of freedom, and the design matrix has $k-1$ columns that correspond to the first $k-1$ levels of A. The ith column contains a 1 in the ith row, a -1 in the last row, and 0s everywhere else. If α_i denotes the parameter that corresponds to the ith level of variable A, then the $k-1$ columns yield estimates of the independent parameters, $\alpha_1, \alpha_i, \ldots, \alpha_{k-1}$. The last parameter is not needed because PROC CATMOD constrains the k parameters to sum to zero. In other words, PROC CATMOD uses a full-rank center-point parameterization to build design matrices. Here are two examples.

Data Levels	**Design Columns**	
A	A	
1	1	0
2	0	1
3	−1	−1
B	B	
1	1	
2	−1	

For an effect with three levels, such as A, PROC CATMOD produces two parameter estimates for each response function. By default, the first (corresponding to the first row in the "Design Columns") estimates the effect of level 1 of A. The second (corresponding to the second row in the "Design Columns") estimates the effect of level 2 of A. The sum-to-zero constraint requires the effect of level 3 of A to be the negative of the sum of the level 1 and 2 effects (as shown by the third row in the "Design Columns").

Crossed Effects (Interactions)

Crossed effects (such as A*B) are formed by the horizontal direct products of main effects, as illustrated in the following table.

Data Levels		Design Matrix Columns				
A	B	A		B	A*B	
1	1	1	0	1	1	0
1	2	1	0	−1	−1	0
2	1	0	1	1	0	1
2	2	0	1	−1	0	−1
3	1	−1	−1	1	−1	−1
3	2	−1	−1	−1	1	1

The number of degrees of freedom for a crossed effect (that is, the number of design matrix columns) is equal to the product of the numbers of degrees of freedom for the separate effects.

Nested Effects

The effect A(B) is read "A within B" and is the same as specifying an A main effect for every value of B. If n_a and n_b are the number of levels in A and B, respectively, then the number of columns for A(B) is $(n_a - 1)n_b$ when every combination of levels exists in the data. The following table gives an example.

Data Levels		Design Matrix Columns			
B	A	A(B)			
1	1	1	0	0	0
1	2	0	1	0	0
1	3	−1	−1	0	0
2	1	0	0	1	0
2	2	0	0	0	1
2	3	0	0	−1	−1

PROC CATMOD actually allocates a column for all possible combinations of values even though some combinations may not be present in the data.

Nested-by-value Effects

Instead of nesting an effect within all values of the main effect, you can nest an effect within specified values of the nested variable (A(B=1), for example). The four degrees of freedom for the A(B) effect shown in the preceding section can also be obtained by specifying the two separate nested effects with values.

Data Levels		Design Matrix Columns			
B	A	A(B=1)		A(B=2)	
1	1	1	0	0	0
1	2	0	1	0	0
1	3	−1	−1	0	0
2	1	0	0	1	0
2	2	0	0	0	1
2	3	0	0	−1	−1

Each effect has $n_a - 1$ degrees of freedom, assuming a complete combination. Thus, for the example, each effect has two degrees of freedom.

The procedure compares nested values to data values on the basis of formatted values. If a format is not specified for the variable, the procedure formats internal data values to BEST16, left-justified. The nested values specified in nested-by-value effects are also converted to a BEST16 formatted value, left-justified.

For example, if the numeric variable B has internal data values 1 and 2, then A(B=1), A(B=1.0), and A(B=1E0) are all valid nested-by-value effects. However, if the data value 1 is formatted as 'one', then A(B='one') is a valid effect, but A(B=1) is not since the formatted nested value (1) does not match the formatted data value (one).

To ensure correct nested-by-value effects, look at the tables of population and response profiles. These are displayed by default, and they contain the formatted data values. In addition, the population and response profiles are displayed when you specify the ONEWAY option in the MODEL statement.

Direct Effects

To request that the actual values of a variable be inserted into the design matrix, declare the variable in a DIRECT statement, and specify the effect by the variable name. For example, specifying the effects X1 and X2 in both the MODEL and DIRECT statements results in the following.

Data Levels		Design Columns	
X1	X2	X1	X2
1	1	1	1
2	4	2	4
3	9	3	9

Unless there is a POPULATION statement that excludes the direct variables, the direct variables help to define the sample populations. In general, the variables should not be continuous in the sense that every subject has a different value because this would induce a separate population for each subject (note, however, that such a strategy is used purposely for logistic regression).

If there is a POPULATION statement that omits mention of the direct variables, then the values of the direct variables must be identical for all subjects in a given population since there can only be one independent variable profile for each population.

Two or More Response Functions Per Population

When there is more than one response function per population, the structure of the design matrix depends on whether or not the model type is AVERAGED (see the AVERAGED option on page 725). The model type is AVERAGED if independent variable effects are averaged over the multiple responses within a population, rather than being nested in them.

The following subsections illustrate the effect of specifying (or not specifying) an AVERAGED model type. This section does not apply to log-linear models; for these models, see the "Log-Linear Model Design Matrices" section on page 764.

Model Type Not AVERAGED

Suppose the variable A has two levels, and you specify

```
proc catmod;
   model Y=A;
run;
```

If the variable Y has two levels, then there is only one response function per population, and the design matrix is as follows.

	Design Matrix	
Sample	Intercept	A
1	1	1
2	1	−1

But if the variable Y has three levels, then there are two response functions per population, and the preceding design matrix is assumed to hold for each of the two response functions. The response functions are always ordered so that the multiple response functions within a population are grouped together. For this example, the design matrix would be as follows.

	Response Function	**Design Matrix**			
Sample	**Number**	Intercept		A	
1	1	1	0	1	0
1	2	0	1	0	1
2	1	1	0	−1	0
2	2	0	1	0	−1

Since the same submatrix applies to each of the multiple response functions, PROC CATMOD displays only the submatrix (that is, the one it would create if there were only one response function per population) rather than the entire design matrix. PROC CATMOD displays

$$\begin{bmatrix} 1 & 1 \\ 1 & -1 \end{bmatrix}$$

Ordering of Parameters

This grouping of multiple response functions within populations also has an effect in the table of parameter estimates displayed by PROC CATMOD. The following table shows some parameter estimates, where the four rows of the table correspond to the four columns in the preceding design matrix.

Effect	Parameter	Estimate
Intercept	1	1.4979
	2	0.8404
A	3	0.1116
	4	−0.3296

Notice that the intercept and the A effect each have two parameter estimates associated with them. The first estimate in each pair is associated with the first response function, and the second in each pair is associated with the second response function. Consequently, 0.1116 is the effect of the first level of A on the first response function. In any table of parameter estimates displayed by PROC CATMOD, as you read down the column of estimates, the response function level changes before levels of the variables making up the effect.

Model Type AVERAGED

When the model type is AVERAGED (for example, when the AVERAGED option is specified in the MODEL statement, when _RESPONSE_ is used in the MODEL statement, or when the design matrix is input directly in the MODEL statement), PROC CATMOD does not assume that the same submatrix applies to each of the q response functions per population. Rather, it averages any independent variable effects across the functions, and it enables you to study variation among the q functions. The first column of the design matrix is always a column of 1s corresponding to the intercept, unless the NOINT option is specified in the MODEL statement or the design matrix is input directly. Also, since the design matrix does not have any special submatrix structure, PROC CATMOD displays the entire matrix.

For example, suppose the dependent variable Y has three levels, the independent variable A has two levels, and you specify

```
proc catmod;
   response marginals;
   model y=a / averaged;
run;
```

Then there are two response functions per population, and the response functions are always ordered so that the multiple response functions within a population are grouped together. For this example, the design matrix would be as follows.

Sample	Response Function Number	Design Matrix	
		Intercept	A
1	1	1	1
1	2	1	1
2	1	1	−1
2	2	1	−1

Note that the model now has only two degrees of freedom. The remaining two degrees of freedom in the residual correspond to variation among the three levels of the dependent variable. Generally, that variation tends to be statistically significant and therefore should not be left out of the model. You can include it in the model by including the two effects, _RESPONSE_ and _RESPONSE_*A, but if the study is not a repeated measurement study, those sources of variation tend to be uninteresting. Thus, the usual solution for this type of study (one dependent variable) is to exclude the AVERAGED option from the MODEL statement.

An AVERAGED model type is automatically induced whenever you use the _RESPONSE_ keyword in the MODEL statement. The _RESPONSE_ effect models variation among the q response functions per population. If there is no REPEATED, FACTORS, or LOGLIN statement, then PROC CATMOD builds a main effect with $q - 1$ degrees of freedom. For example, three response functions would induce the following design columns.

Response Function Number	Design Columns	
	Response	
1	1	0
2	0	1
3	−1	−1

If there is more than one population, then the _RESPONSE_ effect is averaged over the populations. Also, the _RESPONSE_ effect can be crossed with any other effect, or it can be nested within an effect.

If there is a REPEATED statement that contains only one repeated measurement factor, then PROC CATMOD builds the design columns for _RESPONSE_ in the same way, except that the output labels the main effect with the factor name rather than with the word _RESPONSE_. For example, suppose an independent variable A has two levels, and the input statements are

```
proc catmod;
   response marginals;
   model Time1*Time2=A _response_ A*_response_;
   repeated Time 2 / _response_=Time;
run;
```

If Time1 and Time2 each have two levels (so that they each have one independent marginal probability), then the RESPONSE statement causes PROC CATMOD to compute two response functions per population. Thus, the design matrix is as follows.

Sample	Response Function Number	Design Matrix Intercept	A	Time	A*Time
1	1	1	1	1	1
1	2	1	1	−1	−1
2	1	1	−1	1	−1
2	2	1	−1	−1	1

However, if Time1 and Time2 each have three levels (so that they each have two independent marginal probabilities), then the RESPONSE statement causes PROC CATMOD to compute four response functions per population. In that case, since Time has two levels, PROC CATMOD groups the functions into sets of 2 $(= 4/2)$ and constructs the preceding submatrix for each function in the set. This results in the following design matrix, which is obtained from the previous one by multiplying each element by an identity matrix of order two.

Sample	Response Function	Design Matrix Intercept		A		Time		A*Time	
1	P(Time1=1)	1	0	1	0	1	0	1	0
1	P(Time1=2)	0	1	0	1	0	1	0	1
1	P(Time2=1)	1	0	1	0	−1	0	−1	0
1	P(Time2=2)	0	1	0	1	0	−1	0	−1
2	P(Time1=1)	1	0	−1	0	1	0	−1	0
2	P(Time1=2)	0	1	0	−1	0	1	0	−1
2	P(Time2=1)	1	0	−1	0	−1	0	1	0
2	P(Time2=2)	0	1	0	−1	0	−1	0	1

If there is a REPEATED statement that contains two or more repeated measurement factors, then PROC CATMOD builds the design columns for _RESPONSE_ according to the definition of _RESPONSE_ in the REPEATED statement. For example, suppose you specify

```
proc catmod;
   response marginals;
   model R11*R12*R21*R22=_response_;
   repeated Time 2, Place 2 / _response_=Time Place;
run;
```

If each of the dependent variables has two levels, then PROC CATMOD builds four response functions. The _RESPONSE_ effect generates a main effects model with respect to Time and Place.

Response Function Number	Variable	Time	Place	Design Matrix Intercept	_Response_	
1	R11	1	1	1	1	1
2	R12	1	2	1	1	−1
3	R21	2	1	1	−1	1
4	R22	2	2	1	−1	−1

Log-Linear Model Design Matrices

When the response functions are the standard ones (generalized logits), then inclusion of the keyword _RESPONSE_ in every design effect induces a log-linear model. The design matrix for a log-linear model looks different from a standard design matrix because the standard one is transformed by the same linear transformation that converts the r response probabilities to $r-1$ generalized logits. For example, suppose the dependent variables X and Y each have two levels, and you specify a saturated log-linear model analysis:

```
proc catmod;
   model X*Y=_response_;
   loglin X Y X*Y;
run;
```

Then the cross-classification of X and Y yields four response probabilities, p_{11}, p_{12}, p_{21}, and p_{22}, which are then reduced to three generalized logit response functions, $F_1 = \log(p_{11}/p_{22})$, $F_2 = \log(p_{12}/p_{22})$, and $F_3 = \log(p_{21}/p_{22})$.

Since the saturated log-linear model implies that

$$\begin{bmatrix} \log(p_{11}) \\ \log(p_{12}) \\ \log(p_{21}) \\ \log(p_{22}) \end{bmatrix} = \begin{bmatrix} 1 & 1 & 1 & 1 \\ 1 & 1 & -1 & -1 \\ 1 & -1 & 1 & -1 \\ 1 & -1 & -1 & 1 \end{bmatrix} \gamma - \lambda \begin{bmatrix} 1 \\ 1 \\ 1 \\ 1 \end{bmatrix}$$

$$= \begin{bmatrix} 1 & 1 & 1 \\ 1 & -1 & -1 \\ -1 & 1 & -1 \\ -1 & -1 & 1 \end{bmatrix} \boldsymbol{\beta} - \delta \begin{bmatrix} 1 \\ 1 \\ 1 \\ 1 \end{bmatrix}$$

where γ and $\boldsymbol{\beta}$ are parameter vectors, and λ and δ are normalizing constants required by the restriction that the probabilities sum to 1, it follows that the MODEL statement yields

$$\begin{bmatrix} F_1 \\ F_2 \\ F_3 \end{bmatrix} = \begin{bmatrix} 1 & 0 & 0 & -1 \\ 0 & 1 & 0 & -1 \\ 0 & 0 & 1 & -1 \end{bmatrix} \times \begin{bmatrix} \log(p_{11}) \\ \log(p_{12}) \\ \log(p_{21}) \\ \log(p_{22}) \end{bmatrix}$$

$$= \begin{bmatrix} 1 & 0 & 0 & -1 \\ 0 & 1 & 0 & -1 \\ 0 & 0 & 1 & -1 \end{bmatrix} \times \begin{bmatrix} 1 & 1 & 1 \\ 1 & -1 & -1 \\ -1 & 1 & -1 \\ -1 & -1 & 1 \end{bmatrix} \boldsymbol{\beta}$$

$$= \begin{bmatrix} 2 & 2 & 0 \\ 2 & 0 & -2 \\ 0 & 2 & -2 \end{bmatrix} \boldsymbol{\beta}$$

Thus, the design matrix is as follows.

	Response			
	Function	Design Matrix		
Sample	Number	X	Y	X*Y
1	1	2	2	0
1	2	2	0	−2
1	3	0	2	−2

Design matrices for reduced models are constructed similarly. For example, suppose you request a main-effects log-linear model analysis of the factors X and Y:

```
proc catmod;
   model X*Y=_response_;
   loglin X Y;
run;
```

Since the main-effects log-linear model implies that

$$\begin{bmatrix} \log(p_{11}) \\ \log(p_{12}) \\ \log(p_{21}) \\ \log(p_{22}) \end{bmatrix} = \begin{bmatrix} 1 & 1 & 1 \\ 1 & 1 & -1 \\ 1 & -1 & 1 \\ 1 & -1 & -1 \end{bmatrix} \gamma - \lambda \begin{bmatrix} 1 \\ 1 \\ 1 \\ 1 \end{bmatrix}$$

$$= \begin{bmatrix} 1 & 1 \\ 1 & -1 \\ -1 & 1 \\ -1 & -1 \end{bmatrix} \boldsymbol{\beta} - \delta \begin{bmatrix} 1 \\ 1 \\ 1 \\ 1 \end{bmatrix}$$

it follows that the MODEL statement yields

$$\begin{bmatrix} F_1 \\ F_2 \\ F_3 \end{bmatrix} = \begin{bmatrix} 1 & 0 & 0 & -1 \\ 0 & 1 & 0 & -1 \\ 0 & 0 & 1 & -1 \end{bmatrix} \times \begin{bmatrix} \log(p_{11}) \\ \log(p_{12}) \\ \log(p_{21}) \\ \log(p_{22}) \end{bmatrix}$$

$$= \begin{bmatrix} 1 & 0 & 0 & -1 \\ 0 & 1 & 0 & -1 \\ 0 & 0 & 1 & -1 \end{bmatrix} \times \begin{bmatrix} 1 & 1 \\ 1 & -1 \\ -1 & 1 \\ -1 & -1 \end{bmatrix} \boldsymbol{\beta}$$

$$= \begin{bmatrix} 2 & 2 \\ 2 & 0 \\ 0 & 2 \end{bmatrix} \boldsymbol{\beta}$$

Therefore, the corresponding design matrix is as follows.

Sample	Response Function Number	Design Matrix	
		X	Y
1	1	2	2
1	2	2	0
1	3	0	2

Since it is difficult to tell from the final design matrix whether PROC CATMOD used the parameterization that you intended, the procedure displays the untransformed _RESPONSE_ matrix for log-linear models. For example, the main-effects model in the preceding example induces the display of the following matrix.

Response Function Number	_Response_ Matrix	
	1	2
1	1	1
2	1	−1
3	−1	1
4	−1	−1

You can suppress the display of this matrix by specifying the NORESPONSE option in the MODEL statement.

Cautions

Effective Sample Size

Since the method depends on asymptotic approximations, you need to be careful that the sample sizes are sufficiently large to support the asymptotic normal distributions of the response functions. A general guideline is that you would like to have an effective sample size of at least 25 to 30 for each response function that is being analyzed. For example, if you have one dependent variable and $r = 4$ response levels, and you use the standard response functions to compute three generalized logits for each population, then you would like the sample size of each population to be at least 75. Moreover, the subjects should be dispersed throughout the table so that less than 20 percent of the response functions have an effective sample size less than 5. For example, if each population had less than 5 subjects in the first response category, then it would be wiser to pool this category with another category rather than to assume the asymptotic normality of the first response function. Or, if the dependent variable is ordinally scaled, an alternative is to request the mean score response function rather than three generalized logits.

If there is more than one dependent variable, and you specify RESPONSE MEANS, then the effective sample size for each response function is the same as the actual sample size. Thus, a sample size of 30 could be sufficient to support four response functions, provided that the functions are the means of four dependent variables.

A Singular Covariance Matrix

If there is a singular (noninvertible) covariance matrix for the response functions in any population, then PROC CATMOD writes an error message and stops processing. You have several options available to correct this situation:

- You can reduce the number of response functions according to how many can be supported by the populations with the smallest sample sizes.
- If there are three or more levels for any independent variable, you can pool the levels into a fewer number of categories, thereby reducing the number of populations. However, your interpretation of results must be done more cautiously since such pooling implies a different sampling scheme and masks any differences that existed among the pooled categories.
- If there are two or more independent variables, you can delete at least one of them from the model. However, this is just another form of pooling, and the same cautions that apply to the previous option also apply here.
- If there is one independent variable, then, in some situations, you might simply eliminate the populations that are causing the covariance matrices to be singular.
- You can use the ADDCELL option in the MODEL statement to add a small amount (for example, 0.5) to every cell frequency, but this can seriously bias the results if the cell frequencies are small.

Zero Frequencies

If you use the standard response functions and there are zero frequencies, you should use maximum likelihood estimation (the default) rather than weighted least-squares to analyze the data. For weighted least-squares analysis, the CATMOD procedure always computes the observed response functions. If PROC CATMOD needs to take the logarithm of a zero proportion, it issues a warning and then proceeds to take the log of a small value ($0.5/n_i$ for the probability) in order to continue. This can produce invalid results if the cells contain too few observations. The ML analysis, on the other hand, does not require computation of the observed response functions and therefore yields valid results for the parameter estimates and all of the predicted values.

For any log-linear model analysis, it is important to remember that PROC CATMOD creates response profiles only for those profiles that are actually observed. Thus, for any log-linear model analysis with one population (the usual case), there are no zeros in the contingency table, which means that the CATMOD procedure treats all zero frequencies as structural zeros. If there is more than one population, then a zero can appear in the body of the contingency table, in which case the zero is treated as a sampling zero (as long as some population has a nonzero count for that profile). If you want zero frequencies that PROC CATMOD would normally treat as structural zeros to be interpreted as sampling zeros, simply insert a one-line statement into the data step that changes each zero to a very small number (such as 1E−20). Refer to Bishop, Fienberg, and Holland (1975) for a discussion of the issues and Example 22.5 on page 796 for an illustration of a log-linear model analysis of data that contain both structural and sampling zeros.

If you perform a weighted least-squares analysis on a contingency table that contains zero cell frequencies, then avoid using the LOG transformation as the first transformation on the observed proportions. In general, it may be better to change the response functions or to pool some of the response categories than to settle for the 0.5 correction or to use the ADDCELL option.

Testing the Wrong Hypothesis

If you use the keyword _RESPONSE_ in the MODEL statement, and you specify MARGINALS, LOGITS, ALOGITS, or CLOGITS in your RESPONSE statement, you may receive the following warning message:

```
Warning: The _RESPONSE_ effect may be testing the wrong
         hypothesis since the marginal levels of the
         dependent variables do not coincide. Consult the
         response profiles and the CATMOD documentation.
```

The following examples illustrate situations in which the _RESPONSE_ effect tests the wrong hypothesis.

Zeros in the Marginal Frequencies

Suppose you specify the following statements:

```
data A1;
   input Time1 Time2 @@;
   datalines;
1 2    2 3    1 3
;

proc catmod;
   response marginals;
   model Time1*Time2=_response_;
   repeated Time 2 / _response_=Time;
run;
```

One marginal probability is computed for each dependent variable, resulting in two response functions. The model is a saturated one: one degree of freedom for the intercept and one for the main effect of Time. Except for the warning message, PROC CATMOD produces an analysis with no apparent errors, but the “Response Profiles” table displayed by PROC CATMOD is as follows.

Response Profiles		
Response	**Time1**	**Time2**
1	1	2
2	1	3
3	2	3

Since RESPONSE MARGINALS yields marginal probabilities for every level but the last, the two response functions being analyzed are Prob(Time1=1) and Prob(Time2=2). Thus, the Time effect is testing the hypothesis that Prob(Time1=1)=Prob(Time2=2). What it *should* be testing is the hypothesis that

```
Prob(Time1=1) = Prob(Time2=1)
Prob(Time1=2) = Prob(Time2=2)
Prob(Time1=3) = Prob(Time2=3)
```

but there are not enough data to support the test (assuming that none of the probabilities are structural zeros by the design of the study).

The ORDER=DATA Option

Suppose you specify

```
data a1;
   input Time1 Time2 @@;
   datalines;
2 1    2 2    1 1    1 2    2 1
;

proc catmod order=data;
   response marginals;
   model Time1*Time2=_response_;
   repeated Time 2 / _response_=Time;
run;
```

As in the preceding example, one marginal probability is computed for each dependent variable, resulting in two response functions. The model is also the same: one degree of freedom for the intercept and one for the main effect of Time. PROC CATMOD issues the warning message and displays the following "Response Profiles" table.

Response Profiles		
Response	**Time1**	**Time2**
1	2	1
2	2	2
3	1	1
4	1	2

Although the marginal levels are the same for the two dependent variables, they are not in the same order because the ORDER=DATA option specified that they be ordered according to their appearance in the input stream. Since RESPONSE MARGINALS yields marginal probabilities for every level except the last, the two response functions being analyzed are Prob(Time1=2) and Prob(Time2=1). Thus, the Time effect is testing the hypothesis that Prob(Time1=2)=Prob(Time2=1). What it *should* be testing is the hypothesis that

```
Prob(Time1=1) = Prob(Time2=1)
Prob(Time1=2) = Prob(Time2=2)
```

Whenever the warning message appears, look at the "Response Profiles" table or the "One-Way Frequencies" table to determine what hypothesis is actually being tested. For the latter example, a correct analysis can be obtained by deleting the ORDER=DATA option or by reordering the data so that the (1,1) observation is first.

Computational Method

The notation used in PROC CATMOD differs slightly from that used in other literature. The following table provides a summary of the basic dimensions and the notation for a contingency table. See the "Computational Formulas" section, which follows, for a complete description.

Summary of Basic Dimensions

s = number of populations or samples (= number of rows in the underlying contingency table)

r = number of response categories (= number of columns in the underlying contingency table)

q = number of response functions computed for each population

d = number of parameters

Notation

$\mathbf{j}$	denotes a column vector of 1s.
$\mathbf{J}$	denotes a square matrix of 1s.
$\sum_k$	is the sum over all the possible values of k.
n_i	denotes the row sum $\sum_j n_{ij}$.
$\mathbf{DIAG}_n(\mathbf{p})$	is the diagonal matrix formed from the first n elements of the vector $\mathbf{p}$.
$\mathbf{DIAG}_n^{-1}(\mathbf{p})$	is the inverse of $\mathbf{DIAG}_n(\mathbf{p})$.
$\mathbf{DIAG}(\mathbf{A}_1, \mathbf{A}_2, \ldots, \mathbf{A}_k)$	denotes a block diagonal matrix with the $\mathbf{A}$ matrices on the main diagonal.

Input data can be represented by a contingency table, as shown in Table 22.4.

Table 22.4. Input Data Represented by a Contingency Table

Population	**Response**				**Total**
	1	2	$\cdots$	r	
1	n_{11}	n_{12}	$\cdots$	n_{1r}	n_1
2	n_{21}	n_{22}	$\cdots$	n_{2r}	n_2
$\vdots$	$\vdots$	$\vdots$	$\ddots$	$\vdots$	$\vdots$
s	n_{s1}	n_{s2}	$\cdots$	n_{sr}	n_s

Computational Formulas

The following calculations are shown for each population and then for all populations combined.

Source	Formula	Dimension
Probability Estimates		
jth response	$p_{ij} = \frac{n_{ij}}{n_i}$	1×1
ith population	$\mathbf{p}_i = \begin{bmatrix} p_{i1} \\ p_{i2} \\ \vdots \\ p_{ir} \end{bmatrix}$	$r \times 1$
all populations	$\mathbf{p} = \begin{bmatrix} \mathbf{p}_1 \\ \mathbf{p}_2 \\ \vdots \\ \mathbf{p}_s \end{bmatrix}$	$sr \times 1$
Variance of Probability Estimates		
ith population	$\mathbf{V}_i = \frac{1}{n_i}(\mathbf{DIAG}(\mathbf{p}_i) - \mathbf{p}_i\mathbf{p}_i{}')$	$r \times r$
all populations	$\mathbf{V} = \mathbf{DIAG}(\mathbf{V}_1, \mathbf{V}_2, \ldots, \mathbf{V}_s)$	$sr \times sr$
Response Functions		
ith population	$\mathbf{F}_i = \mathbf{F}(\mathbf{p}_i)$	$q \times 1$
all populations	$\mathbf{F} = \begin{bmatrix} \mathbf{F}_1 \\ \mathbf{F}_2 \\ \vdots \\ \mathbf{F}_s \end{bmatrix}$	$sq \times 1$

Source	Formula	Dimension
Derivative of Function with Respect to Probability Estimates		
ith population	$\mathbf{H}_i = \dfrac{\partial \mathbf{F}(\mathbf{p}_i)}{\partial \mathbf{p}_i}$	$q \times r$
all populations	$\mathbf{H} = \mathbf{DIAG}(\mathbf{H}_1, \mathbf{H}_2, \ldots, \mathbf{H}_s)$	$sq \times sr$
Variance of Functions		
ith population	$\mathbf{S}_i = \mathbf{H}_i \mathbf{V}_i \mathbf{H}_i{}'$	$q \times q$
all populations	$\mathbf{S} = \mathbf{DIAG}(\mathbf{S}_1, \mathbf{S}_2, \ldots, \mathbf{S}_s)$	$sq \times sq$
Inverse Variance of Functions		
ith population	$\mathbf{S}^i = (\mathbf{S}_i)^{-1}$	$q \times q$
all populations	$\mathbf{S}^{-1} = \mathbf{DIAG}(\mathbf{S}^1, \mathbf{S}^2, \ldots, \mathbf{S}^s)$	$sq \times sq$

Derivative Table for Compound Functions: Y=F(G(p))

In the following table, let $\mathbf{G}(\mathbf{p})$ be a vector of functions of $\mathbf{p}$, and let $\mathbf{D}$ denote $\partial\mathbf{G}/\partial\mathbf{p}$, which is the first derivative matrix of $\mathbf{G}$ with respect to $\mathbf{p}$.

Function	$\mathbf{Y} = \mathbf{F}(\mathbf{G})$	Derivative $(\partial\mathbf{Y}/\partial\mathbf{p})$
Multiply matrix	$\mathbf{Y} = \mathbf{A} * \mathbf{G}$	$\mathbf{A} * \mathbf{D}$
Logarithm	$\mathbf{Y} = \mathbf{LOG}(\mathbf{G})$	$\mathbf{DIAG}^{-1}(\mathbf{G}) * \mathbf{D}$
Exponential	$\mathbf{Y} = \mathbf{EXP}(\mathbf{G})$	$\mathbf{DIAG}(\mathbf{Y}) * \mathbf{D}$
Add constant	$\mathbf{Y} = \mathbf{G} + \mathbf{A}$	$\mathbf{D}$

Default Response Functions: Generalized Logits

In the following table, subscripts i for the population are suppressed. Also denote $f_j = \log\left(\frac{p_j}{p_r}\right)$ for $j = 1, \ldots, r-1$ for each population $i = 1, \ldots, s$.

Inverse of Response Functions for a Population

$$p_j = \frac{\exp(f_j)}{1 + \sum_k \exp(f_k)} \quad \text{for } j = 1, \ldots, r-1$$

$$p_r = \frac{1}{1 + \sum_k \exp(f_k)}$$

Form of F and Derivative for a Population

$$\mathbf{F} = \mathbf{KLOG}(\mathbf{p}) = (\mathbf{I}_{r-1}, -\mathbf{j})\,\mathbf{LOG}(\mathbf{p})$$

$$\mathbf{H} = \frac{\partial \mathbf{F}}{\partial \mathbf{p}} = \left(\mathbf{DIAG}_{r-1}^{-1}(\mathbf{p}), \frac{-1}{p_r}\mathbf{j}\right)$$

Covariance Results for a Population

$$\mathbf{S} = \mathbf{HVH}'$$

$$= \frac{1}{n}\left(\mathbf{DIAG}_{r-1}^{-1}(\mathbf{p}) + \frac{1}{p_r}\mathbf{J}_{r-1}\right)$$

where $\mathbf{V}, \mathbf{H},$ and $\mathbf{J}$ are as previously defined.

$$\mathbf{S}^{-1} = n(\mathbf{DIAG}_{r-1}(\mathbf{p}) - \mathbf{qq}') \quad \text{where } \mathbf{q} = \mathbf{DIAG}_{r-1}(\mathbf{p})\,\mathbf{j}$$

$$\mathbf{S}^{-1}\mathbf{F} = n\mathbf{DIAG}_{r-1}(\mathbf{p})\mathbf{F} - (n\sum_j p_j f_j)\,\mathbf{q}$$

$$\mathbf{F}'\mathbf{S}^{-1}\mathbf{F} = n\sum_j p_j f_j^2 - n(\sum_j p_j f_j)^2$$

The following calculations are shown for each population and then for all populations combined.

Source	Formula	Dimension
Design Matrix		
ith population	$\mathbf{X}_i$	$q \times d$
all populations	$\mathbf{X} = \begin{bmatrix} \mathbf{X}_1 \\ \mathbf{X}_2 \\ \vdots \\ \mathbf{X}_s \end{bmatrix}$	$sq \times d$
Crossproduct of Design Matrix		
ith population	$\mathbf{C}_i = \mathbf{X}_i{}'\mathbf{S}^i\mathbf{X}_i$	$d \times d$
all populations	$\mathbf{C} = \mathbf{X}'\mathbf{S}^{-1}\mathbf{X} = \sum_i \mathbf{C}_i$	$d \times d$
Crossproduct of Design Matrix with Function		
	$\mathbf{R} = \mathbf{X}'\mathbf{S}^{-1}\mathbf{F} = \sum_i \mathbf{X}_i{}'\mathbf{S}^i\mathbf{F}_i$	$d \times 1$
Weighted Least-Squares Estimates		
	$\mathbf{b} = \mathbf{C}^{-1}\mathbf{R} = (\mathbf{X}'\mathbf{S}^{-1}\mathbf{X})^{-1}(\mathbf{X}'\mathbf{S}^{-1}\mathbf{F})$	$d \times 1$
Covariance of Weighted Least-Squares Estimates		
	$\mathbf{COV}(\mathbf{b}) = \mathbf{C}^{-1}$	$d \times d$
Predicted Response Functions		
	$\hat{\mathbf{F}} = \mathbf{Xb}$	$sq \times 1$

Source	Formula	Dimension
Covariance of Predicted Response Functions		
	$\mathbf{V}_{\hat{\mathbf{F}}} = \mathbf{X}\mathbf{C}^{-1}\mathbf{X}'$	$sq \times sq$
Residual Chi-Square		
	$\text{RSS} = \mathbf{F}'\mathbf{S}^{-1}\mathbf{F} - \hat{\mathbf{F}}'\mathbf{S}^{-1}\hat{\mathbf{F}}$	1×1
Chi-Square for H_0: $\mathbf{L}\boldsymbol{\beta} = \mathbf{0}$		
	$\text{Q} = (\mathbf{Lb})'(\mathbf{L}\mathbf{C}^{-1}\mathbf{L}')^{-1}(\mathbf{Lb})$	1×1

Maximum Likelihood Method

Let $\mathbf{C}$ be the Hessian matrix and $\mathbf{G}$ be the gradient of the log-likelihood function (both functions of π and the parameters $\boldsymbol{\beta}$). Let $\mathbf{p}_i^*$ denote the vector containing the first $r-1$ sample proportions from population i, and let π_i^* denote the corresponding vector of probability estimates from the current iteration. Starting with the least-squares estimates $\mathbf{b}_0$ of $\boldsymbol{\beta}$ (if you use the ML and WLS options; with the ML option alone, the procedure starts with $\mathbf{0}$), the probabilities $\pi(\mathbf{b})$ are computed, and $\mathbf{b}$ is calculated iteratively by the Newton-Raphson method until it converges (see the EPSILON= option on page 726). The factor λ is a step-halving factor that equals one at the start of each iteration. For any iteration in which the likelihood decreases, PROC CATMOD uses a series of subiterations in which λ is iteratively divided by two. The subiterations continue until the likelihood is greater than that of the previous iteration. If the likelihood has not reached that point after ten subiterations, then convergence is assumed, and a warning message is displayed.

Sometimes, infinite parameters may be present in the model, either because of the presence of one or more zero frequencies or because of a poorly specified model with collinearity among the estimates. If an estimate is tending toward infinity, then PROC CATMOD flags the parameter as infinite and holds the estimate fixed in subsequent iterations. PROC CATMOD regards a parameter to be infinite when two conditions apply:

- The absolute value of its estimate exceeds five divided by the range of the corresponding variable.
- The standard error of its estimate is at least three times greater than the estimate itself.

The estimator of the asymptotic covariance matrix of the maximum likelihood predicted probabilities is given by Imrey, Koch, and Stokes (1981, eq. 2.18).

The following equations summarize the method:

$$\mathbf{b}_{k+1} = \mathbf{b}_k - \lambda \mathbf{C}^{-1}\mathbf{G}$$

where

$$\begin{aligned}
\mathbf{C} &= \mathbf{X}'\mathbf{S}^{-1}(\pi)\mathbf{X} \\
\mathbf{N} &= \begin{bmatrix} n_1(\mathbf{p}_1^* - \pi_1^*) \\ \vdots \\ n_s(\mathbf{p}_s^* - \pi_s^*) \end{bmatrix} \\
\mathbf{G} &= \mathbf{X}'\mathbf{N}
\end{aligned}$$

Memory and Time Requirements

The memory and time required by PROC CATMOD are proportional to the number of parameters in the model.

Displayed Output

PROC CATMOD displays the following information in the "Data Summary" table:

- the Response effect
- the Weight Variable, if one is specified
- the Data Set name
- the number of Response Levels
- the number of samples or Populations
- the Total Frequency, which is the total sample size
- the number of Observations from the data set (the number of data records)
- the frequency of missing observations, labeled as "Frequency Missing"

Except for the analysis of variance table, all of the following items can be displayed or suppressed, depending on your specification of statements and options.

- The ONEWAY option produces the "One-Way Frequencies" table, which displays the frequencies of each variable value used in the analysis.
- The populations (or samples) are defined in a table labeled "Population Profiles." The Sample Size and the values of the defining variables are displayed for each Sample. This table is suppressed if the NOPROFILE option is specified.
- The observed responses are defined in a table labeled "Response Profiles." The values of the defining variables are displayed for each Response. This table is suppressed if the NOPROFILE option is specified.

- If the FREQ option is specified, then the "Response Frequencies" table is displayed, which shows the frequency of each response for each population.
- If the PROB option is specified, then the "Response Probabilities" table is produced. This table displays the probability of each response for each population.
- If the COV option is specified, the "Response Functions, Covariance Matrix" table, which shows the covariance matrix of the response functions for each Sample, is displayed.
- The Response Functions are displayed in the "Response Functions, Design Matrix" table, unless the COV option is specified, in which case they are displayed in the "Response Functions, Covariance Matrix" table.
- The design matrix is displayed in the "Response Functions, Design Matrix" table for weighted least-squares analyses, unless the NODESIGN option is specified. If the model type is AVERAGED, then the design matrix is displayed with $q * s$ rows, assuming q response functions for each of s populations. Otherwise, the design matrix is displayed with only s rows since the model is the same for each of the q response functions.
- The "X′*Inv(S)*X" matrix is displayed for weighted least-squares analyses if the XPX option is specified.
- The "Analysis of Variance" table for the weighted least-squares analysis reports the results of significance tests for each of the *design-effects* in the right-hand side of the MODEL statement. If _RESPONSE_ is a *design-effect* and is defined explicitly in the LOGLIN, FACTORS, or REPEATED statement, then the table contains test statistics for the individual effects constituting the _RESPONSE_ effect. If the design matrix is input directly, then the content of the displayed output depends on whether you specify any subsets of the parameters to be tested. If you specify one or more subsets, then the table contains one test for each subset. Otherwise, the table contains one test for the effect MODEL | MEAN. In every case, the table also contains the Residual goodness-of-fit test. Produced for each test of significance are the Source of variation, the number of degrees of freedom (DF), the Chi-Square value (which is a Wald statistic), and the significance probability (Pr > ChiSq).
- The "Analysis of Weighted Least-Squares Estimates" table lists the Effect in the model for which parameters are formed, the Parameter number, the least-squares Estimate, the estimated Standard Error of the parameter estimate, the Chi-Square value (a Wald statistic) for testing that the parameter is zero, and the significance probability (Pr > ChiSq) of the test. The statistic is calculated as $((\text{parameter estimate})/(\text{standard error}))^2$.
- The "Covariance Matrix of the Parameter Estimates" table for the weighted least-squares analysis displays the estimated covariance matrix of the least-squares estimates of the parameters, provided the COVB option is specified.
- The "Correlation Matrix of the Parameter Estimates" table for the weighted least-squares analysis displays the estimated correlation matrix of the least-squares estimates of the parameters, provided that the CORRB option is specified.

- The "Maximum Likelihood Analysis" table is produced when the ML option is specified for the standard response functions (generalized logits). It displays the Iteration number, the number of step-halving Sub-Iterations, -2 Log Likelihood for that iteration, the Convergence Criterion, and the Parameter Estimates for each iteration.
- The "Maximum Likelihood Analysis of Variance" table, displayed when the ML option is specified for the standard response functions, is similar to the table produced for the least-squares analysis. The Chi-Square test for each effect is a Wald test based on the information matrix from the likelihood calculations. The Likelihood Ratio statistic compares the specified model with the unrestricted (saturated) model and is an appropriate goodness-of-fit test for the model.
- The "Analysis of Maximum Likelihood Estimates" table, displayed when the ML option is specified for the standard response functions, is similar to the one produced for the least-squares analysis. The table includes the maximum likelihood estimates, the estimated Standard Errors based on the information matrix, and the Wald Statistics (Chi-Square) based on the estimated standard errors.
- The "Covariance Matrix of the Maximum Likelihood Estimates" table displays the estimated covariance matrix of the maximum likelihood estimates of the parameters, provided that the COVB and ML options are specified for the standard response functions.
- The "Correlation Matrix of the Maximum Likelihood Estimates" table displays the estimated correlation matrix of the maximum likelihood estimates of the parameters, provided that the CORRB and ML options are specified for the standard response functions.
- For each source of variation specified in a CONTRAST statement, the "Contrasts" table lists the label for the source (Contrast), the number of degrees of freedom (DF), the Chi-Square value (which is a Wald statistic), and the significance probability (Pr > ChiSq). If the ESTIMATE= option is specified, the "Analysis of Contrasts" table displays, for each row of the contrast, the label (Contrast), the Type (PARM or EXP), the Row of the contrast, the Estimate and its Standard Error, a Wald confidence interval, the Wald Chi-Square, and the p-value (Pr > ChiSq) for 1 degree of freedom.

- Specification of the PREDICT option in the MODEL statement has the following effect. Produced for each response function within each population are the Observed and Predicted Function values, their Standard Errors, and the Residual (Observed − Predicted). The displayed output also includes the values of the variables that define the populations unless the NOPREDVAR option is specified in the MODEL statement. If the response functions are the default ones (generalized logits), additional information displayed for each response within each population includes the Observed and Predicted cell probabilities, their Standard Errors, and the Residual. The first cell probability is labeled P1, the second P2, and so forth. However, specifying PRED=FREQ in the MODEL statement results in the display of the predicted cell frequencies, rather than the predicted cell probabilities. The first cell frequency is labeled F1, the second F2, and so forth.
- When there are multiple RESPONSE statements, the output for each statement starts on a new page. For each RESPONSE statement, the corresponding title, if specified, is displayed at the top of each page.
- If the ADDCELL= option is specified in the MODEL statement, and if there is a weighted least-squares analysis specified, the adjusted sample size for each population (with number added to each cell) is labeled Adjusted Sample Size in the "Population Profiles" table. Similarly, the adjusted response frequencies and probabilities are displayed in the "Adjusted Response Frequencies" and "Adjusted Response Probabilities" tables, respectively.
- If _RESPONSE_ is defined explicitly in the LOGLIN, FACTORS, or REPEATED statement, then the definition is displayed as a NOTE whenever _RESPONSE_ appears in the output.

ODS Table Names

PROC CATMOD assigns a name to each table it creates. You can use these names to reference the table when using the Output Delivery System (ODS) to select tables and create output data sets. These names are listed in the following table. For more information on ODS, see Chapter 15, "Using the Output Delivery System."

Table 22.5. ODS Tables Produced in PROC CATMOD

ODS Table Name	Description	Statement	Option
ANOVA	Analysis of variance	MODEL	default
Contrasts	Contrasts	CONTRAST	default
ContrastEstimates	Analysis of Contrasts	CONTRAST	ESTIMATE=
ConvergenceStatus	Convergence status	MODEL	ML
CorrB	Correlation matrix of the estimates	MODEL	CORRB
CovB	Covariance matrix of the estimates	MODEL	COVB
DataSummary	Data summary	PROC	default
Estimates	Analysis of estimates	MODEL	default, unless NOPARM
MaxLikelihood	Maximum likelihood analysis	MODEL	ML
OneWayFreqs	One-way frequencies	MODEL	ONEWAY
PopProfiles	Population profiles	MODEL	default, unless NOPROFILE
PredictedFreqs	Predicted frequencies	MODEL	PRED=FREQ
PredictedProbs	Predicted probabilities	MODEL	PREDICT or PRED=PROB
PredictedValues	Predicted values	MODEL	PREDICT or PRED=
ResponseCov	Response functions, covariance matrix	MODEL	COV
ResponseDesign	Response functions, design matrix	MODEL	WLS*, unless NODESIGN
ResponseFreqs	Response frequencies	MODEL	FREQ
ResponseMatrix	_RESPONSE_ matrix	MODEL & LOGLIN	unless NORESPONSE
ResponseProbs	Response probabilities	MODEL	PROB
ResponseProfiles	Response profiles	MODEL	default, unless NOPROFILE
XPX	**X**'*Inv(**S**)***X** matrix	MODEL	XPX, for WLS*

* WLS estimation is the default for response functions other than the default (generalized logits).

Examples

Example 22.1. Linear Response Function, r=2 Responses

In an example from Ries and Smith (1963), the choice of detergent brand (Brand= M or X) is related to three other categorical variables: the softness of the laundry water (Softness= soft, medium, or hard), the temperature of the water (Temperature= high or low), and whether the subject was a previous user of brand M (Previous= yes or no). The linear response function, which could also be specified as RESPONSE MARGINALS, yields one probability, Pr(brand preference=M), as the response function to be analyzed. Two models are fit in this example: the first model is a saturated one, containing all of the main effects and interactions, while the second is a reduced model containing only the main effects. The following statements produce Output 22.1.1 through Output 22.1.4:

```
title 'Detergent Preference Study';
data detergent;
   input Softness $ Brand $ Previous $ Temperature $ Count @@;
   datalines;
soft X yes high 19   soft X yes low 57
soft X no  high 29   soft X no  low 63
soft M yes high 29   soft M yes low 49
soft M no  high 27   soft M no  low 53
med  X yes high 23   med  X yes low 47
med  X no  high 33   med  X no  low 66
med  M yes high 47   med  M yes low 55
med  M no  high 23   med  M no  low 50
hard X yes high 24   hard X yes low 37
hard X no  high 42   hard X no  low 68
hard M yes high 43   hard M yes low 52
hard M no  high 30   hard M no  low 42
;

proc catmod data=detergent;
   response 1 0;
   weight Count;
   model Brand=Softness|Previous|Temperature
         / freq prob nodesign;
   title2 'Saturated Model';
run;
```

Output 22.1.1. Detergent Preference Study: Linear Model Analysis

```
                    Detergent Preference Study
                         Saturated Model

                      The CATMOD Procedure

Response               Brand          Response Levels      2
Weight Variable        Count          Populations         12
Data Set               DETERGENT      Total Frequency   1008
Frequency Missing      0              Observations        24
```

The "Data Summary" table (Output 22.1.1) indicates that you have two response levels and twelve populations.

Output 22.1.2. Population Profiles

```
                    Detergent Preference Study
                         Saturated Model

                      The CATMOD Procedure

                       Population Profiles

Sample    Softness    Previous    Temperature    Sample Size
-------------------------------------------------------------
     1    hard        no          high                    72
     2    hard        no          low                    110
     3    hard        yes         high                    67
     4    hard        yes         low                     89
     5    med         no          high                    56
     6    med         no          low                    116
     7    med         yes         high                    70
     8    med         yes         low                    102
     9    soft        no          high                    56
    10    soft        no          low                    116
    11    soft        yes         high                    48
    12    soft        yes         low                    106
```

The "Population Profiles" table in Output 22.1.2 displays the ordering of independent variable levels as used in the table of parameter estimates.

Output 22.1.3. Response Profiles, Frequencies, and Probabilities

```
                 Detergent Preference Study
                      Saturated Model

                   The CATMOD Procedure

                    Response Profiles

                    Response    Brand
                    -----------------
                       1          M
                       2          X


                  Response Frequencies

                      Response Number
              Sample       1        2
              ------------------------
                 1        30       42
                 2        42       68
                 3        43       24
                 4        52       37
                 5        23       33
                 6        50       66
                 7        47       23
                 8        55       47
                 9        27       29
                10        53       63
                11        29       19
                12        49       57


                 Response Probabilities

                        Response Number
            Sample           1           2
            ----------------------------
               1       0.41667     0.58333
               2       0.38182     0.61818
               3       0.64179     0.35821
               4       0.58427     0.41573
               5       0.41071     0.58929
               6       0.43103     0.56897
               7       0.67143     0.32857
               8       0.53922     0.46078
               9       0.48214     0.51786
              10       0.45690     0.54310
              11       0.60417     0.39583
              12       0.46226     0.53774
```

Since Brand M is the first level in the “Response Profiles” table (Output 22.1.3), the RESPONSE statement causes Pr(Brand=M) to be the single response function modeled.

Output 22.1.4. Analysis of Variance and WLS Estimates

```
                    Detergent Preference Study
                         Saturated Model

                      The CATMOD Procedure

                      Analysis of Variance

     Source                        DF   Chi-Square    Pr > ChiSq
     -----------------------------------------------------------
     Intercept                      1       983.13        <.0001
     Softness                       2         0.09        0.9575
     Previous                       1        22.68        <.0001
     Softness*Previous              2         3.85        0.1457
     Temperature                    1         3.67        0.0555
     Softness*Temperature           2         0.23        0.8914
     Previous*Temperature           1         2.26        0.1324
     Softnes*Previou*Temperat       2         0.76        0.6850

     Residual                       0          .             .


            Analysis of Weighted Least Squares Estimates

                                                Standard      Chi-
Effect                     Parameter  Estimate     Error    Square  Pr > ChiSq
------------------------------------------------------------------------------
Intercept                          1    0.5069    0.0162    983.13      <.0001
Softness                           2  -0.00073    0.0225      0.00      0.9740
                                   3   0.00623    0.0226      0.08      0.7830
Previous                           4   -0.0770    0.0162     22.68      <.0001
Softness*Previous                  5   -0.0299    0.0225      1.77      0.1831
                                   6   -0.0152    0.0226      0.45      0.5007
Temperature                        7    0.0310    0.0162      3.67      0.0555
Softness*Temperature               8  -0.00786    0.0225      0.12      0.7265
                                   9  -0.00298    0.0226      0.02      0.8953
Previous*Temperature              10   -0.0243    0.0162      2.26      0.1324
Softnes*Previou*Temperat          11    0.0187    0.0225      0.69      0.4064
                                  12   -0.0138    0.0226      0.37      0.5415
```

The "Analysis of Variance" table in Output 22.1.4 shows that all of the interactions are nonsignificant. Therefore, a main-effects model is fit with the following statements:

```
      model Brand=Softness Previous Temperature / noprofile;
      title2 'Main-Effects Model';
   run;
   quit;
```

The PROC CATMOD statement is not required due to the interactive capability of the CATMOD procedure. The NOPROFILE option suppresses the redisplay of the "Response Profiles" table. Output 22.1.5 through Output 22.1.7 are produced.

Output 22.1.5. Main-Effects Design Matrix

```
                    Detergent Preference Study
                        Main-Effects Model

                      The CATMOD Procedure

          Response            Brand         Response Levels      2
          Weight Variable     Count         Populations         12
          Data Set            DETERGENT     Total Frequency   1008
          Frequency Missing   0             Observations        24


               Response                        Design Matrix
Sample         Function           1          2          3          4          5
-------------------------------------------------------------------------------
     1          0.41667           1          1          0          1          1
     2          0.38182           1          1          0          1         -1
     3          0.64179           1          1          0         -1          1
     4          0.58427           1          1          0         -1         -1
     5          0.41071           1          0          1          1          1
     6          0.43103           1          0          1          1         -1
     7          0.67143           1          0          1         -1          1
     8          0.53922           1          0          1         -1         -1
     9          0.48214           1         -1         -1          1          1
    10          0.45690           1         -1         -1          1         -1
    11          0.60417           1         -1         -1         -1          1
    12          0.46226           1         -1         -1         -1         -1
```

The design matrix in Output 22.1.5 displays the results of the factor effects modeling used in PROC CATMOD.

Output 22.1.6. ANOVA Table for the Main-Effects Model

```
                    Detergent Preference Study
                        Main-Effects Model

                      The CATMOD Procedure

                      Analysis of Variance

          Source            DF    Chi-Square    Pr > ChiSq
          ------------------------------------------------
          Intercept          1       1004.93        <.0001
          Softness           2          0.24        0.8859
          Previous           1         20.96        <.0001
          Temperature        1          3.95        0.0468

          Residual           7          8.26        0.3100
```

The analysis of variance table in Output 22.1.6 shows that previous use of Brand M, together with the temperature of the laundry water, are significant factors in preferring Brand M laundry detergent. The table also shows that the additive model fits since the goodness-of-fit statistic (the Residual Chi-Square) is nonsignificant.

Output 22.1.7. WLS Estimates for the Main-Effects Model

```
                    Detergent Preference Study
                       Main-Effects Model

                     The CATMOD Procedure

          Analysis of Weighted Least Squares Estimates

                                           Standard        Chi-
Effect          Parameter    Estimate        Error        Square     Pr > ChiSq
--------------------------------------------------------------------------------
Intercept               1      0.5080       0.0160       1004.93         <.0001
Softness                2    -0.00256       0.0218          0.01         0.9066
                        3      0.0104       0.0218          0.23         0.6342
Previous                4     -0.0711       0.0155         20.96         <.0001
Temperature             5      0.0319       0.0161          3.95         0.0468
```

The negative coefficient for Previous (−0.0711) in Output 22.1.7 indicates that the first level of Previous (which, from the table of population profiles, is 'no') is associated with a smaller probability of preferring Brand M than the second level of Previous (with coefficient constrained to be 0.0711 since the parameter estimates for a given effect must sum to zero). In other words, previous users of Brand M are much more likely to prefer it than those who have never used it before.

Similarly, the positive coefficient for Temperature indicates that the first level of Temperature (which, from the "Population Profiles" table, is 'high') has a larger probability of preferring Brand M than the second level of Temperature. In other words, those who do their laundry in hot water are more likely to prefer Brand M than those who do their laundry in cold water.

Example 22.2. Mean Score Response Function, r=3 Responses

Four surgical operations for duodenal ulcers are compared in a clinical trial at four hospitals. The operations performed are: Treatment=a, drainage and vagotomy; Treatment=b, 25%resection and vagotomy; Treatment=c, 50%resection and vagotomy; and Treatment=d, 75%resection. The response is severity of an undesirable complication called "dumping syndrome." The data are from Grizzle, Starmer, and Koch (1969, pp. 489–504).

```
title 'Dumping Syndrome Data';
data operate;
   input Hospital Treatment $ Severity $ wt @@;
   datalines;
1 a none 23    1 a slight  7    1 a moderate 2
1 b none 23    1 b slight 10    1 b moderate 5
1 c none 20    1 c slight 13    1 c moderate 5
1 d none 24    1 d slight 10    1 d moderate 6
2 a none 18    2 a slight  6    2 a moderate 1
2 b none 18    2 b slight  6    2 b moderate 2
2 c none 13    2 c slight 13    2 c moderate 2
2 d none  9    2 d slight 15    2 d moderate 2
3 a none  8    3 a slight  6    3 a moderate 3
```

```
3 b none 12      3 b slight   4      3 b moderate 4
3 c none 11      3 c slight   6      3 c moderate 2
3 d none  7      3 d slight   7      3 d moderate 4
4 a none 12      4 a slight   9      4 a moderate 1
4 b none 15      4 b slight   3      4 b moderate 2
4 c none 14      4 c slight   8      4 c moderate 3
4 d none 13      4 d slight   6      4 d moderate 4
;
```

The response variable (Severity) is ordinally scaled with three levels, so assignment of scores is appropriate (0=none, 0.5=slight, 1=moderate). For these scores, the response function yields the mean score. The following statements produce Output 22.2.1 through Output 22.2.6.

```
proc catmod data=operate order=data ;
   weight wt;
   response 0  0.5  1;
   model Severity=Treatment Hospital / freq oneway;
   title2 'Main-Effects Model';
quit;
```

The ORDER= option is specified so that the levels of the response variable remain in the correct order. A main effects model is fit. The FREQ option displays the frequency of each response within each sample (Output 22.2.3), and the ONEWAY option produces a table of the number of subjects within each variable level (Output 22.2.1).

Output 22.2.1. Surgical Data: Analysis of Mean Scores

```
                         Dumping Syndrome Data
                          Main-Effects Model

                         The CATMOD Procedure

        Response             Severity     Response Levels     3
        Weight Variable      wt           Populations        16
        Data Set             OPERATE      Total Frequency   417
        Frequency Missing    0            Observations       48


                         One-Way Frequencies

                 Variable      Value       Frequency
                 --------------------------------
                 Severity      none              240
                               slight            129
                               moderate           48

                 Treatment     a                  96
                               b                 104
                               c                 110
                               d                 107

                 Hospital            1           148
                                     2           105
                                     3            74
                                     4            90
```

Output 22.2.2. Population Sizes

```
                    Dumping Syndrome Data
                     Main-Effects Model

                    The CATMOD Procedure

                    Population Profiles

Sample    Treatment    Hospital    Sample Size
----------------------------------------------
    1     a            1                    32
    2     a            2                    25
    3     a            3                    17
    4     a            4                    22
    5     b            1                    38
    6     b            2                    26
    7     b            3                    20
    8     b            4                    20
    9     c            1                    38
   10     c            2                    28
   11     c            3                    19
   12     c            4                    25
   13     d            1                    40
   14     d            2                    26
   15     d            3                    18
   16     d            4                    23
```

Output 22.2.3. Response Frequencies

```
                    Dumping Syndrome Data
                     Main-Effects Model

                    The CATMOD Procedure

                     Response Profiles

                   Response    Severity
                   --------------------
                       1       none
                       2       slight
                       3       moderate


                   Response Frequencies

                     Response Number
         Sample         1         2         3
         ---------------------------------
              1        23         7         2
              2        18         6         1
              3         8         6         3
              4        12         9         1
              5        23        10         5
              6        18         6         2
              7        12         4         4
              8        15         3         2
              9        20        13         5
             10        13        13         2
             11        11         6         2
             12        14         8         3
             13        24        10         6
             14         9        15         2
             15         7         7         4
             16        13         6         4
```

You can use the oneway frequencies (Output 22.2.1) and the response profiles (Output 22.2.3) to verify that the response levels are in the desired order (none, slight, moderate) so that the response scores (0, 0.5, 1.0) are applied appropriately. If the ORDER=DATA option had not been used, the levels would have been in a different order.

Output 22.2.4. Design Matrix

Dumping Syndrome Data
Main-Effects Model

The CATMOD Procedure

Sample	Response Function	Design Matrix 1	2	3	4	5	6	7
1	0.17188	1	1	0	0	1	0	0
2	0.16000	1	1	0	0	0	1	0
3	0.35294	1	1	0	0	0	0	1
4	0.25000	1	1	0	0	-1	-1	-1
5	0.26316	1	0	1	0	1	0	0
6	0.19231	1	0	1	0	0	1	0
7	0.30000	1	0	1	0	0	0	1
8	0.17500	1	0	1	0	-1	-1	-1
9	0.30263	1	0	0	1	1	0	0
10	0.30357	1	0	0	1	0	1	0
11	0.26316	1	0	0	1	0	0	1
12	0.28000	1	0	0	1	-1	-1	-1
13	0.27500	1	-1	-1	-1	1	0	0
14	0.36538	1	-1	-1	-1	0	1	0
15	0.41667	1	-1	-1	-1	0	0	1
16	0.30435	1	-1	-1	-1	-1	-1	-1

Output 22.2.5. ANOVA Table

Dumping Syndrome Data
Main-Effects Model

The CATMOD Procedure

Analysis of Variance

Source	DF	Chi-Square	Pr > ChiSq
Intercept	1	248.77	<.0001
Treatment	3	8.90	0.0307
Hospital	3	2.33	0.5065
Residual	9	6.33	0.7069

The analysis of variance table (Output 22.2.5) shows that the additive model fits (since the Residual Chi-Square is not significant), that the Treatment effect is significant, and that the Hospital effect is not significant.

Output 22.2.6. Parameter Estimates

```
                    Dumping Syndrome Data
                     Main-Effects Model

                    The CATMOD Procedure

        Analysis of Weighted Least Squares Estimates

                                         Standard        Chi-
Effect        Parameter    Estimate        Error       Square    Pr > ChiSq
----------------------------------------------------------------------------
Intercept         1          0.2724       0.0173       248.77        <.0001
Treatment         2         -0.0552       0.0270         4.17        0.0411
                  3         -0.0365       0.0289         1.59        0.2073
                  4          0.0248       0.0280         0.78        0.3757
Hospital          5         -0.0204       0.0264         0.60        0.4388
                  6         -0.0178       0.0268         0.44        0.5055
                  7          0.0531       0.0352         2.28        0.1312
```

The coefficients of Treatment in Output 22.2.6 show that the first two treatments (with negative coefficients) have lower mean scores than the last two treatments (the fourth coefficient, not shown, must be positive since the four coefficients must sum to zero). In other words, the less severe treatments (the first two) cause significantly less severe dumping syndrome complications.

Example 22.3. Logistic Regression, Standard Response Function

In this data set, from Cox and Snell (1989), ingots are prepared with different heating and soaking times and tested for their readiness to be rolled. The response variable Y has value 1 for ingots that are not ready and value 0 otherwise. The explanatory variables are Heat and Soak.

```
title 'Maximum Likelihood Logistic Regression';
data ingots;
   input Heat Soak nready ntotal @@;
   Count=nready;
   Y=1;
   output;
   Count=ntotal-nready;
   Y=0;
   output;
   drop nready ntotal;
   datalines;
7 1.0 0 10   14 1.0 0 31   27 1.0 1 56   51 1.0 3 13
7 1.7 0 17   14 1.7 0 43   27 1.7 4 44   51 1.7 0  1
7 2.2 0  7   14 2.2 2 33   27 2.2 0 21   51 2.2 0  1
7 2.8 0 12   14 2.8 0 31   27 2.8 1 22   51 4.0 0  1
7 4.0 0  9   14 4.0 0 19   27 4.0 1 16
;
```

Logistic regression analysis is often used to investigate the relationship between discrete response variables and continuous explanatory variables. For logistic regression, the continuous *design-effects* are declared in a DIRECT statement. The following statements produce Output 22.3.1 through Output 22.3.7.

```
proc catmod data=ingots;
   weight Count;
   direct Heat Soak;
   model Y=Heat Soak / freq covb corrb;
quit;
```

Output 22.3.1. Maximum Likelihood Logistic Regression

```
                Maximum Likelihood Logistic Regression

                        The CATMOD Procedure

Response            Y          Response Levels     2
Weight Variable     Count      Populations        19
Data Set            INGOTS     Total Frequency   387
Frequency Missing   0          Observations       25


                        Population Profiles

          Sample     Heat     Soak     Sample Size
          -------------------------------------
             1         7        1           10
             2         7      1.7           17
             3         7      2.2            7
             4         7      2.8           12
             5         7        4            9
             6        14        1           31
             7        14      1.7           43
             8        14      2.2           33
             9        14      2.8           31
            10        14        4           19
            11        27        1           56
            12        27      1.7           44
            13        27      2.2           21
            14        27      2.8           22
            15        27        4           16
            16        51        1           13
            17        51      1.7            1
            18        51      2.2            1
            19        51        4            1
```

You can verify that the populations are defined as you intended by looking at the "Population Profiles" table in Output 22.3.1.

Output 22.3.2. Response Summaries

```
                 Maximum Likelihood Logistic Regression

                         The CATMOD Procedure

                          Response Profiles

                            Response    Y
                            -------------
                               1        0
                               2        1


                        Response Frequencies

                              Response Number
                      Sample        1        2
                      ------------------------
                           1       10        0
                           2       17        0
                           3        7        0
                           4       12        0
                           5        9        0
                           6       31        0
                           7       43        0
                           8       31        2
                           9       31        0
                          10       19        0
                          11       55        1
                          12       40        4
                          13       21        0
                          14       21        1
                          15       15        1
                          16       10        3
                          17        1        0
                          18        1        0
                          19        1        0
```

Since the "Response Profiles" table shows the response level ordering as 0, 1, the default response function, the logit, is defined as $\log\left(\frac{p_{Y=0}}{p_{Y=1}}\right)$.

Output 22.3.3. Iteration History

```
                 Maximum Likelihood Logistic Regression

                         The CATMOD Procedure

                    Maximum Likelihood Analysis

             Sub       -2 Log  Convergence         Parameter Estimates
Iteration  Iteration  Likelihood   Criterion          1          2          3
-------------------------------------------------------------------------------
    0          0     536.49592      1.0000            0          0          0
    1          0     152.58961      0.7156       2.1594    -0.0139  -0.003733
    2          0     106.76066      0.3003       3.5334    -0.0363    -0.0120
    3          0     96.692171      0.0943       4.7489    -0.0640    -0.0299
    4          0     95.383825      0.0135       5.4138    -0.0790    -0.0498
    5          0     95.345659    0.000400       5.5539    -0.0819    -0.0564
    6          0     95.345613   4.8289E-7       5.5592    -0.0820    -0.0568
    7          0     95.345613    7.73E-13       5.5592    -0.0820    -0.0568

               Maximum likelihood computations converged.
```

Seven Newton-Raphson iterations are required to find the maximum likelihood estimates.

Output 22.3.4. Analysis of Variance Table

```
                Maximum Likelihood Logistic Regression

                        The CATMOD Procedure

               Maximum Likelihood Analysis of Variance

      Source                 DF    Chi-Square    Pr > ChiSq
      -----------------------------------------------------
      Intercept               1         24.65        <.0001
      Heat                    1         11.95        0.0005
      Soak                    1          0.03        0.8639

      Likelihood Ratio       16         13.75        0.6171
```

The analysis of variance table (Output 22.3.4) shows that the model fits since the likelihood ratio goodness-of-fit test is nonsignificant. It also shows that the length of heating time is a significant factor with respect to readiness but that length of soaking time is not.

Output 22.3.5. Maximum Likelihood Estimates

```
                Maximum Likelihood Logistic Regression

                        The CATMOD Procedure

              Analysis of Maximum Likelihood Estimates

                                          Standard        Chi-
Effect        Parameter     Estimate        Error       Square    Pr > ChiSq
----------------------------------------------------------------------------
Intercept             1       5.5592       1.1197        24.65        <.0001
Heat                  2      -0.0820       0.0237        11.95        0.0005
Soak                  3      -0.0568       0.3312         0.03        0.8639
```

Output 22.3.6. Covariance Matrix

```
                Maximum Likelihood Logistic Regression

                        The CATMOD Procedure

          Covariance Matrix of the Maximum Likelihood Estimates

                            1                2                3
        ---------------------------------------------------------
          1         1.2537133       -0.0215664       -0.2817648
          2        -0.0215664        0.0005633        0.0026243
          3        -0.2817648        0.0026243        0.1097020
```

Output 22.3.7. Correlation Matrix

```
                 Maximum Likelihood Logistic Regression

                          The CATMOD Procedure

         Correlation Matrix of the Maximum Likelihood Estimates

                         1                2                3
    ---------------------------------------------------------
     1             1.00000         -0.81152         -0.75977
     2            -0.81152          1.00000          0.33383
     3            -0.75977          0.33383          1.00000
```

From the table of maximum likelihood estimates (Output 22.3.5), the fitted model is

$$\mathrm{E}(\mathrm{logit}(p)) = 5.559 - 0.082(\textsf{Heat}) - 0.057(\textsf{Soak})$$

For example, for Sample 1 with Heat $= 7$ and Soak $= 1$, the estimate is

$$\mathrm{E}(\mathrm{logit}(p)) = 5.559 - 0.082(7) - 0.057(1) = 4.9284$$

Predicted values of the logits, as well as the probabilities of readiness, could be obtained by specifying PRED=PROB in the MODEL statement. For the example of Sample 1 with Heat $= 7$ and Soak $= 1$, PRED=PROB would give an estimate of the probability of readiness equal to 0.9928 since

$$4.9284 = \log\left(\frac{\hat{p}}{1-\hat{p}}\right)$$

implies that

$$\hat{p} = \frac{e^{4.9284}}{1+e^{4.9284}} = 0.9928$$

As another consideration, since soaking time is nonsignificant, you could fit another model that deleted the variable Soak.

Example 22.4. Log-Linear Model, Three Dependent Variables

This analysis reproduces the predicted cell frequencies for Bartlett's data using a log-linear model of no three-variable interaction (Bishop, Fienberg, and Holland 1975, p. 89). Cuttings of two different lengths (Length=short or long) are planted at one of two time points (Time=now or spring), and their survival status (Status=dead or alive) is recorded.

As in the text, the variable levels are simply labeled 1 and 2. The following statements produce Output 22.4.1 through Output 22.4.5:

```
title "Bartlett's Data";
data bartlett;
   input Length Time Status wt @@;
   datalines;
1 1 1 156     1 1 2  84     1 2 1 84     1 2 2 156
2 1 1 107     2 1 2 133     2 2 1 31     2 2 2 209
;

proc catmod data=bartlett;
   weight wt;
   model Length*Time*Status=_response_
         / noparm noresponse pred=freq;
   loglin Length|Time|Status @ 2;
   title2 'Model with No 3-Variable Interaction';
quit;
```

Output 22.4.1. Analysis of Bartlett's Data: Log-Linear Model

```
                         Bartlett's Data
              Model with No 3-Variable Interaction

                      The CATMOD Procedure

Response            Length*Time*Status      Response Levels     8
Weight Variable     wt                      Populations         1
Data Set            BARTLETT                Total Frequency   960
Frequency Missing   0                       Observations        8


                     Sample     Sample Size
                     ---------------------
                         1             960
```

Output 22.4.2. Response Profiles

```
                         Bartlett's Data
              Model with No 3-Variable Interaction

                      The CATMOD Procedure

                       Response Profiles

              Response    Length    Time    Status
              ------------------------------------
                  1          1        1        1
                  2          1        1        2
                  3          1        2        1
                  4          1        2        2
                  5          2        1        1
                  6          2        1        2
                  7          2        2        1
                  8          2        2        2
```

Output 22.4.3. Iteration History

```
                    Bartlett's Data
          Model with No 3-Variable Interaction

                 The CATMOD Procedure

            Maximum Likelihood Analysis

                 Sub          -2 Log    Convergence
  Iteration  Iteration    Likelihood      Criterion
  ---------------------------------------------------
          0          0     3992.5278         1.0000
          1          0     3812.5059         0.0451
          2          0     3800.2168       0.003223
          3          0       3800.12      0.0000255
          4          0       3800.12      3.6909E-9

            Maximum Likelihood Analysis

                          Parameter Estimates
Iteration          1          2          3          4          5          6
-------------------------------------------------------------------------------
     0             0          0          0          0          0          0
     1             0  2.961E-17  -2.96E-17    -0.2125     0.2125     0.3083
     2        0.0494     0.0752    -0.0752    -0.2486     0.2486     0.3502
     3        0.0555     0.0809    -0.0809    -0.2543     0.2543     0.3568
     4        0.0556     0.0810    -0.0810    -0.2544     0.2544     0.3569

         Maximum likelihood computations converged.
```

Output 22.4.4. Analysis of Variance Table

```
                    Bartlett's Data
          Model with No 3-Variable Interaction

                 The CATMOD Procedure

       Maximum Likelihood Analysis of Variance

  Source              DF   Chi-Square    Pr > ChiSq
  --------------------------------------------------
  Length               1         2.64        0.1041
  Time                 1         5.25        0.0220
  Length*Time          1         5.25        0.0220
  Status               1        48.94        <.0001
  Length*Status        1        48.94        <.0001
  Time*Status          1        95.01        <.0001

  Likelihood Ratio     1         2.29        0.1299
```

The analysis of variance table shows that the model fits since the likelihood ratio test for the three-variable interaction is nonsignificant. All of the two-variable interactions, however, are significant; this shows that there is mutual dependence among all three variables.

Output 22.4.5. Response Function Predicted Values

```
                              Bartlett's Data
                     Model with No 3-Variable Interaction

                            The CATMOD Procedure

          Maximum Likelihood Predicted Values for Response Functions

                             -------Observed-------     -------Predicted------
             Function                   Standard                   Standard
   Sample     Number       Function      Error        Function      Error        Residual
   ----------------------------------------------------------------------------------------
      1          1        -0.2924782    0.105806     -0.2356473    0.098486      -0.056831
                 2        -0.9115175    0.129188     -0.9494184    0.129948     0.03790099
                 3        -0.9115175    0.129188     -0.9494184    0.129948     0.03790099
                 4        -0.2924782    0.105806     -0.2356473    0.098486      -0.056831
                 5        -0.6695054    0.118872     -0.6936188    0.120172     0.02411336
                 6        -0.4519851    0.110921     -0.3896985    0.102267     -0.0622866
                 7         -1.908347    0.192465     -1.7314626    0.142969     -0.1768845
```

The predicted values table displays observed and predicted values for the generalized logits.

Output 22.4.6. Predicted Frequencies

```
                                  Bartlett's Data
                         Model with No 3-Variable Interaction

                                The CATMOD Procedure

                   Maximum Likelihood Predicted Values for Frequencies

                                                 -------Observed------    ------Predicted------
                                    Function                 Standard                 Standard
Sample   Length   Time   Status      Number     Frequency      Error      Frequency      Error       Residual
------------------------------------------------------------------------------------------------------------
   1       1        1      1          F1              156    11.43022    161.096138    11.07379    -5.0961381
           1        1      2          F2               84    8.754999    78.9038609    7.808613    5.09613909
           1        2      1          F3               84    8.754999    78.9038609    7.808613    5.09613909
           1        2      2          F4              156    11.43022    161.096138    11.07379    -5.0961381
           2        1      1          F5              107    9.750588    101.903861    8.924304    5.09613941
           2        1      2          F6              133    10.70392    138.096139    10.33434    -5.0961386
           2        2      1          F7               31     5.47713    36.0961431    4.826315    -5.0961431
           2        2      2          F8              209    12.78667     203.90386    12.21285    5.09614031
```

The predicted frequencies table displays observed and predicted cell frequencies, their standard errors, and residuals.

Example 22.5. Log-Linear Model, Structural and Sampling Zeros

This example illustrates a log-linear model of independence, using data that contain structural zero frequencies as well as sampling (random) zero frequencies.

In a population of six squirrel monkeys, the joint distribution of genital display with respect to active or passive role was observed. The data are from Fienberg (1980, Table 8-2). Since a monkey cannot have both the active and passive roles in the same interaction, the diagonal cells of the table are structural zeros. See Agresti (1990) for more information on the quasi-independence model.

Since there is only one population, the structural zeros are automatically deleted by PROC CATMOD. The sampling zeros are replaced in the DATA step by some positive number close to zero (1E−20). Also, the row for Monkey 't' is deleted since it contains all zeros; therefore, the cell frequencies predicted by a model of independence are also zero. In addition, the CONTRAST statement compares the behavior of the two monkeys labeled 'u' and 'v'. The following statements produce Output 22.5.1 through Output 22.5.8:

```
title 'Behavior of Squirrel Monkeys';
data Display;
   input Active $ Passive $ wt @@;
   if Active ne 't';
   if Active ne Passive then
      if wt=0 then wt=1e-20;
   datalines;
r r  0   r s  1   r t  5   r u  8   r v  9   r w  0
s r 29   s s  0   s t 14   s u 46   s v  4   s w  0
t r  0   t s  0   t t  0   t u  0   t v  0   t w  0
u r  2   u s  3   u t  1   u u  0   u v 38   u w  2
v r  0   v s  0   v t  0   v u  0   v v  0   v w  1
w r  9   w s 25   w t  4   w u  6   w v 13   w w  0
;

proc catmod data=Display;
   weight wt;
   model Active*Passive=_response_
         / freq pred=freq noparm noresponse oneway;
   loglin Active Passive;
   contrast 'Passive, U vs. V' Passive 0 0 0 1 -1;
   contrast 'Active,  U vs. V' Active  0 0 1 -1;
   title2 'Test Quasi-Independence for the Incomplete Table';
quit;
```

Output 22.5.1. Log-Linear Model Analysis with Zero Frequencies

```
                  Behavior of Squirrel Monkeys
          Test Quasi-Independence for the Incomplete Table

                      The CATMOD Procedure

Response             Active*Passive     Response Levels    25
Weight Variable      wt                 Populations         1
Data Set             DISPLAY            Total Frequency   220
Frequency Missing    0                  Observations       25
```

The results of the ONEWAY option are shown in Output 22.5.2. Monkey 't' does not show up as a value for the Active variable since that row was removed.

Output 22.5.2. Output from the ONEWAY option

```
                 Behavior of Squirrel Monkeys
       Test Quasi-Independence for the Incomplete Table

                     The CATMOD Procedure

                     One-Way Frequencies

                Variable    Value   Frequency
                -----------------------------
                Active      r              23
                            s              93
                            u              46
                            v               1
                            w              57

                Passive     r              40
                            s              29
                            t              24
                            u              60
                            v              64
                            w               3
```

Output 22.5.3. Profiles

```
                 Behavior of Squirrel Monkeys
       Test Quasi-Independence for the Incomplete Table

                     The CATMOD Procedure

                    Sample    Sample Size
                    ---------------------
                       1             220


                      Response Profiles

                 Response    Active    Passive
                 -----------------------------
                     1         r          s
                     2         r          t
                     3         r          u
                     4         r          v
                     5         r          w
                     6         s          r
                     7         s          t
                     8         s          u
                     9         s          v
                    10         s          w
                    11         u          r
                    12         u          s
                    13         u          t
                    14         u          v
                    15         u          w
                    16         v          r
                    17         v          s
                    18         v          t
                    19         v          u
                    20         v          w
                    21         w          r
                    22         w          s
                    23         w          t
                    24         w          u
                    25         w          v
```

Sampling zeros are displayed as 1E−20 in Output 22.5.4. The Response Number corresponds to the value displayed in Output 22.5.2.

Output 22.5.4. Frequency of Response by Response Number

```
                    Behavior of Squirrel Monkeys
          Test Quasi-Independence for the Incomplete Table

                        The CATMOD Procedure

                        Response Frequencies

                               Response Number
Sample        1         2         3         4         5         6         7         8
---------------------------------------------------------------------------------------
    1         1         5         8         9     1E-20        29        14        46

                        Response Frequencies

                               Response Number
Sample        9        10        11        12        13        14        15        16
---------------------------------------------------------------------------------------
    1         4     1E-20         2         3         1        38         2     1E-20

                        Response Frequencies

                               Response Number
Sample       17        18        19        20        21        22        23        24
---------------------------------------------------------------------------------------
    1     1E-20     1E-20     1E-20         1         9        25         4         6

                        Response Frequencies

                                Response
                                 Number
                          Sample      25
                          ---------------
                              1       13
```

Output 22.5.5. Iteration History

```
                      Behavior of Squirrel Monkeys
              Test Quasi-Independence for the Incomplete Table

                            The CATMOD Procedure

                        Maximum Likelihood Analysis

             Sub       -2 Log    Convergence                 Parameter Estimates
Iteration  Iteration  Likelihood    Criterion          1            2            3            4
-----------------------------------------------------------------------------------------------
    0          0      1416.3054        1.0000           0            0            0            0
    1          0      1238.2417        0.1257     -0.4976       1.1112       0.1722      -0.8804
    2          0      1205.1264        0.0267     -0.3420       1.0962       0.5612      -1.7549
    3          0      1199.5068      0.004663     -0.1570       1.2687       0.7058      -2.3992
    4          0      1198.6271      0.000733     -0.0466       1.3791       0.8170      -2.8422
    5          0      1198.5611     0.0000551   -0.002748       1.4230       0.8609      -3.0176
    6          0      1198.5603     6.5351E-7    0.002760       1.4285       0.8664      -3.0396
    7          0      1198.5603     1.217E-10    0.002837       1.4285       0.8665      -3.0399

                        Maximum Likelihood Analysis

                                Parameter Estimates
          Iteration            5            6            7            8            9
          ---------------------------------------------------------------------------
              0                0            0            0            0            0
              1        -0.006978       0.0827      -0.4735       0.7287       0.5791
              2           0.2233       0.3899      -0.4086       0.7875       0.5728
              3           0.3034       0.4360      -0.3162       0.8812       0.6703
              4           0.3309       0.4625      -0.2890       0.9085       0.6968
              5           0.3334       0.4649      -0.2866       0.9110       0.6992
              6           0.3334       0.4649      -0.2865       0.9110       0.6992
              7           0.3334       0.4649      -0.2865       0.9110       0.6992

                  Maximum likelihood computations converged.
```

Output 22.5.6. Analysis of Variance Table

```
                 Behavior of Squirrel Monkeys
        Test Quasi-Independence for the Incomplete Table

                     The CATMOD Procedure

           Maximum Likelihood Analysis of Variance

        Source              DF    Chi-Square    Pr > ChiSq
        --------------------------------------------------
        Active               4         56.58        <.0001
        Passive              5         47.94        <.0001

        Likelihood Ratio    15        135.17        <.0001
```

The analysis of variance table (Output 22.5.6) shows that the model of independence does not fit since the likelihood ratio test for the interaction is significant. In other words, active and passive behaviors of the squirrel monkeys are dependent behavior roles.

Output 22.5.7. Contrasts between Monkeys 'u' and 'v'

```
                    Behavior of Squirrel Monkeys
            Test Quasi-Independence for the Incomplete Table

                         The CATMOD Procedure

              Contrasts of Maximum Likelihood Estimates

          Contrast            DF     Chi-Square    Pr > ChiSq
          -------------------------------------------------
          Passive, U vs. V     1           1.31        0.2524
          Active,  U vs. V     1          14.87        0.0001
```

If the model fit these data, then the contrasts in Output 22.5.7 show that monkeys 'u' and 'v' appear to have similar passive behavior patterns but very different active behavior patterns.

Output 22.5.8. Response Function Predicted Values

```
                          Behavior of Squirrel Monkeys
                 Test Quasi-Independence for the Incomplete Table

                              The CATMOD Procedure

            Maximum Likelihood Predicted Values for Response Functions

                          -------Observed-------     -------Predicted------
          Function                    Standard                   Standard
Sample     Number        Function        Error       Function       Error       Residual
-----------------------------------------------------------------------------------------
   1          1         -2.5649494    1.037749     -0.973554     0.339019    -1.5913953
              2         -0.9555114    0.526235    -1.7250404     0.345438    0.76952896
              3         -0.4855078    0.449359    -0.5275144     0.309254     0.0420066
              4         -0.3677248    0.433629    -0.7392682     0.249006    0.37154345
              5         -48.616651        1E10     -3.560517     0.634104    -45.056134
              6         0.80234647    0.333775    0.32058886      0.26629    0.48175761
              7         0.07410797    0.385164    -0.2993416     0.295634    0.37344956
              8         1.26369204    0.314105    0.89818441     0.250857    0.36550763
              9          -1.178655    0.571772     0.6864306     0.173396    -1.8650856
             10         -48.616651        1E10    -2.1348182     0.608071    -46.481833
             11         -1.8718022    0.759555    -0.2414953     0.287218    -1.6303069
             12         -1.4663371    0.640513    -0.1099394     0.303568    -1.3563977
             13         -2.5649494    1.037749    -0.8614257     0.314794    -1.7035236
             14          1.0726368    0.321308    0.12434644     0.204345    0.94829036
             15         -1.8718022    0.759555    -2.6969023     0.617433    0.82510014
             16         -48.616651        1E10    -4.1478747     1.024508    -44.468777
             17         -48.616651        1E10    -4.0163187     1.030062    -44.600332
             18         -48.616651        1E10    -4.7678051     1.032457    -43.848846
             19         -48.616651        1E10    -3.5702791     1.020794    -45.046372
             20         -2.5649494    1.037749    -6.6032817     1.161289    4.03833233
             21         -0.3677248    0.433629    -0.3658417     0.202959     -0.001883
             22         0.65392647     0.34194    -0.2342858     0.232794    0.88821229
             23          -1.178655    0.571772    -0.9857722     0.239408    -0.1928828
             24         -0.7731899    0.493548    0.21175381     0.185007    -0.9849437
```

Output 22.5.9. Predicted Frequencies

Behavior of Squirrel Monkeys
Test Quasi-Independence for the Incomplete Table

The CATMOD Procedure

Maximum Likelihood Predicted Values for Frequencies

Sample	Active	Passive	Function Number	Observed Frequency	Observed Standard Error	Predicted Frequency	Predicted Standard Error	Residual
1	r	s	F1	1	0.997725	5.25950838	1.36156	-4.2595084
	r	t	F2	5	2.210512	2.48072585	0.691066	2.51927415
	r	u	F3	8	2.776525	8.21594841	1.855146	-0.2159484
	r	v	F4	9	2.937996	6.64804868	1.50932	2.35195132
	r	w	F5	1E-20	1E-10	0.39576868	0.240268	-0.3957687
	s	r	F6	29	5.017696	19.1859928	3.147915	9.81400723
	s	t	F7	14	3.620648	10.321716	2.169599	3.67828404
	s	u	F8	46	6.031734	34.1846262	4.428706	11.8153738
	s	v	F9	4	1.981735	27.6609647	3.722788	-23.660965
	s	w	F10	1E-20	1E-10	1.64670026	0.952712	-1.6467003
	u	r	F11	2	1.407771	10.936396	2.12322	-8.936396
	u	s	F12	3	1.720201	12.4740717	2.554336	-9.4740717
	u	t	F13	1	0.997725	5.8835826	1.380655	-4.8835826
	u	v	F14	38	5.606814	15.7672979	2.684692	22.2327021
	u	w	F15	2	1.407771	0.93865177	0.551645	1.06134823
	v	r	F16	1E-20	1E-10	0.21996583	0.221779	-0.2199658
	v	s	F17	1E-20	1E-10	0.2508934	0.253706	-0.2508934
	v	t	F18	1E-20	1E-10	0.11833763	0.120314	-0.1183376
	v	u	F19	1E-20	1E-10	0.39192393	0.393255	-0.3919239
	v	w	F20	1	0.997725	0.01887928	0.021728	0.98112072
	w	r	F21	9	2.937996	9.6576454	1.808656	-0.6576454
	w	s	F22	25	4.707344	11.0155266	2.275019	13.9844734
	w	t	F23	4	1.981735	5.19563797	1.184452	-1.195638
	w	u	F24	6	2.415857	17.2075014	2.772098	-11.207501
	w	v	F25	13	3.497402	13.9236886	2.24158	-0.9236886

Output 22.5.8 displays the predicted response functions and Output 22.5.9 displays predicted cell frequencies (from the PRED=FREQ option), but since the model does not fit, these should be ignored.

Structural and Sampling Zeros with Raw Data

The preceding PROC CATMOD step uses cell count data as input. Prior to invoking the CATMOD procedure, structural and sampling zeros are easily identified and manipulated in a single DATA step. For the situation where structural or sampling zeros (or both) may exist and the input data set is raw data, use the following steps:

1. Run PROC FREQ on the raw data. In the TABLES statement, list all dependent and independent variables separated by asterisks and use the SPARSE option and the OUT= option. This creates an output data set that contains all possible zero frequencies.

2. Use a DATA step to change the zero frequencies associated with sampling zeros to a small value, such as 1E−20.

3. Use the resulting data set as input to PROC CATMOD, and specify the statement WEIGHT COUNT to use adjusted frequencies.

For example, suppose the data set RawDisplay contains the raw data for the squirrel monkey data. The following statements show how to obtain the same analysis as shown previously:

```
proc freq data=RawDisplay;
   tables Active*Passive / sparse out=Combos noprint;
run;

data Combos2;
   set Combos;
   if Active ne 't';
   if Active ne Passive then
      if count=0 then count=1e-20;
run;

proc catmod data=Combos2;
   weight count;
   model Active*Passive=_response_
         / freq pred=freq noparm noresponse;
   loglin Active Passive;
quit;
```

The first IF statement in the DATA step is needed only for this particular example; since observations for Monkey 't' were deleted from the Display data set, they also need to be deleted from Combos2.

Example 22.6. Repeated Measures, 2 Response Levels, 3 Populations

In this multi-population repeated measures example, from Guthrie (1981), subjects from three groups have their responses (0 or 1) recorded in each of four trials. The analysis of the marginal probabilities is directed at assessing the main effects of the repeated measurement factor (Trial) and the independent variable (Group), as well as their interaction. Although the contingency table is incomplete (only thirteen of the sixteen possible responses are observed), this poses no problem in the computation of the marginal probabilities. The following statements produce Output 22.6.1 through Output 22.6.5:

```
title 'Multi-Population Repeated Measures';
data group;
   input a b c d Group wt @@;
   datalines;
1 1 1 1 2 2    0 0 0 0 2 2    0 0 1 0 1 2    0 0 1 0 2 2
0 0 0 1 1 4    0 0 0 1 2 1    0 0 0 1 3 3    1 0 0 1 2 1
0 0 1 1 1 1    0 0 1 1 2 2    0 0 1 1 3 5    0 1 0 0 1 4
0 1 0 0 2 1    0 1 0 1 2 1    0 1 0 1 3 2    0 1 1 0 3 1
1 0 0 0 1 3    1 0 0 0 2 1    0 1 1 1 2 1    0 1 1 1 3 2
1 0 1 0 1 1    1 0 1 1 2 1    1 0 1 1 3 2
;
```

```
proc catmod data=group;
   weight wt;
   response marginals;
   model a*b*c*d=Group _response_ Group*_response_
         / freq nodesign;
   repeated Trial 4;
   title2 'Saturated Model';
run;
```

Output 22.6.1. Analysis of Multiple-Population Repeated Measures

```
                    Multi-Population Repeated Measures
                             Saturated Model

                          The CATMOD Procedure

        Response            a*b*c*d      Response Levels  13
        Weight Variable     wt           Populations       3
        Data Set            GROUP        Total Frequency  45
        Frequency Missing   0            Observations     23


                          Population Profiles

                   Sample    Group    Sample Size
                   ------------------------------
                       1     1                 15
                       2     2                 15
                       3     3                 15
```

Output 22.6.2. Response Profiles

```
                    Multi-Population Repeated Measures
                             Saturated Model

                          The CATMOD Procedure

                           Response Profiles

                    Response     a     b     c     d
                    ----------------------------
                        1        0     0     0     0
                        2        0     0     0     1
                        3        0     0     1     0
                        4        0     0     1     1
                        5        0     1     0     0
                        6        0     1     0     1
                        7        0     1     1     0
                        8        0     1     1     1
                        9        1     0     0     0
                       10        1     0     0     1
                       11        1     0     1     0
                       12        1     0     1     1
                       13        1     1     1     1
```

Output 22.6.3. Response Frequencies

Multi-Population Repeated Measures
Saturated Model

The CATMOD Procedure

Response Frequencies

	Response Number							
Sample	1	2	3	4	5	6	7	8
1	0	4	2	1	4	0	0	0
2	2	1	2	2	1	1	0	1
3	0	3	0	5	0	2	1	2

Response Frequencies

	Response Number				
Sample	9	10	11	12	13
1	3	0	1	0	0
2	1	1	0	1	2
3	0	0	0	2	0

Output 22.6.4. Analysis of Variance Table

Multi-Population Repeated Measures
Saturated Model

The CATMOD Procedure

Analysis of Variance

Source	DF	Chi-Square	Pr > ChiSq
Intercept	1	354.88	<.0001
Group	2	24.79	<.0001
Trial	3	21.45	<.0001
Group*Trial	6	18.71	0.0047
Residual	0	.	.

Output 22.6.5. Parameter Estimates

```
                     Multi-Population Repeated Measures
                              Saturated Model

                           The CATMOD Procedure

                Analysis of Weighted Least Squares Estimates

                                                 Standard       Chi-
Effect                 Parameter     Estimate       Error      Square     Pr > ChiSq
-----------------------------------------------------------------------------------
Intercept                      1       0.5833      0.0310      354.88         <.0001
Group                          2       0.1333      0.0335       15.88         <.0001
                               3      -0.0333      0.0551        0.37         0.5450
Trial                          4       0.1722      0.0557        9.57         0.0020
                               5       0.1056      0.0647        2.66         0.1028
                               6      -0.0722      0.0577        1.57         0.2107
Group*Trial                    7      -0.1556      0.0852        3.33         0.0679
                               8      -0.0556      0.0800        0.48         0.4877
                               9      -0.0889      0.0953        0.87         0.3511
                              10       0.0111      0.0866        0.02         0.8979
                              11       0.0889      0.0822        1.17         0.2793
                              12      -0.0111      0.0824        0.02         0.8927
```

The analysis of variance table in Output 22.6.4 shows that there is a significant interaction between the independent variable Group and the repeated measurement factor Trial. Thus, an intermediate model (not shown) is fit in which the effects Trial and Group* Trial are replaced by Trial(Group=1), Trial(Group=2), and Trial(Group=3). Of these three effects, only the last is significant, so it is retained in the final model. The following statements produce Output 22.6.6 and Output 22.6.7:

```
      model a*b*c*d=Group _response_(Group=3)
            / noprofile noparm;
      title2 'Trial Nested within Group 3';
   quit;
```

Output 22.6.6. Final Model: Design Matrix

```
                    Multi-Population Repeated Measures
                       Trial Nested within Group 3

                           The CATMOD Procedure

            Response            a*b*c*d      Response Levels  13
            Weight Variable     wt           Populations       3
            Data Set            GROUP        Total Frequency  45
            Frequency Missing   0            Observations     23


         Function     Response                     Design Matrix
Sample    Number      Function        1        2        3        4        5        6
-----------------------------------------------------------------------------------
   1         1         0.73333        1        1        0        0        0        0
             2         0.73333        1        1        0        0        0        0
             3         0.73333        1        1        0        0        0        0
             4         0.66667        1        1        0        0        0        0

   2         1         0.66667        1        0        1        0        0        0
             2         0.66667        1        0        1        0        0        0
             3         0.46667        1        0        1        0        0        0
             4         0.40000        1        0        1        0        0        0

   3         1         0.86667        1       -1       -1        1        0        0
             2         0.66667        1       -1       -1        0        1        0
             3         0.33333        1       -1       -1        0        0        1
             4         0.06667        1       -1       -1       -1       -1       -1
```

Output 22.6.6 displays the design matrix resulting from retaining the nested effect.

Output 22.6.7. ANOVA Table

```
                    Multi-Population Repeated Measures
                       Trial Nested within Group 3

                           The CATMOD Procedure

                           Analysis of Variance

          Source                DF    Chi-Square    Pr > ChiSq
          ----------------------------------------------------
          Intercept              1        386.94        <.0001
          Group                  2         25.42        <.0001
          Trial(Group=3)         3         75.07        <.0001

          Residual               6          5.09        0.5319
```

The residual goodness-of-fit statistic tests the joint effect of Trial(Group=1) and Trial(Group=2). The analysis of variance table in Output 22.6.7 shows that the final model fits, that there is a significant Group effect, and that there is a significant Trial effect in Group 3.

Example 22.7. Repeated Measures, 4 Response Levels, 1 Population

This example illustrates a repeated measurement analysis in which there are more than two levels of response. In this study, from Grizzle, Starmer, and Koch (1969, p. 493), 7477 women aged 30–39 are tested for vision in both right and left eyes. Since there are four response levels for each dependent variable, the RESPONSE statement computes three marginal probabilities for each dependent variable, resulting in six response functions for analysis. Since the model contains a repeated measurement factor (Side) with two levels (Right, Left), PROC CATMOD groups the functions into sets of three (=6/2). Therefore, the Side effect has three degrees of freedom (one for each marginal probability), and it is the appropriate test of marginal homogeneity. The following statements produce Output 22.7.1 through Output 22.7.5:

```
title 'Vision Symmetry';
data vision;
   input Right Left count @@;
   datalines;
1 1 1520     1 2  266     1 3  124     1 4  66
2 1  234     2 2 1512     2 3  432     2 4  78
3 1  117     3 2  362     3 3 1772     3 4 205
4 1   36     4 2   82     4 3  179     4 4 492
;

proc catmod data=vision;
   weight count;
   response marginals;
   model Right*Left=_response_ / freq;
   repeated Side 2;
   title2 'Test of Marginal Homogeneity';
quit;
```

Output 22.7.1. Vision Study: Analysis of Marginal Homogeneity

```
                         Vision Symmetry
                  Test of Marginal Homogeneity

                       The CATMOD Procedure

 Response              Right*Left      Response Levels     16
 Weight Variable       count           Populations          1
 Data Set              VISION          Total Frequency   7477
 Frequency Missing     0               Observations        16


                      Sample     Sample Size
                      ---------------------
                         1           7477
```

Output 22.7.2. Response Profiles

Vision Symmetry
Test of Marginal Homogeneity

The CATMOD Procedure

Response Profiles

Response	Right	Left
1	1	1
2	1	2
3	1	3
4	1	4
5	2	1
6	2	2
7	2	3
8	2	4
9	3	1
10	3	2
11	3	3
12	3	4
13	4	1
14	4	2
15	4	3
16	4	4

Response Frequencies

	Response Number							
Sample	1	2	3	4	5	6	7	8
1	1520	266	124	66	234	1512	432	78

Response Frequencies

	Response Number							
Sample	9	10	11	12	13	14	15	16
1	117	362	1772	205	36	82	179	492

Output 22.7.3. Design Matrix

Vision Symmetry
Test of Marginal Homogeneity

The CATMOD Procedure

Sample	Function Number	Response Function	Design Matrix 1	2	3	4	5	6
1	1	0.26428	1	0	0	1	0	0
	2	0.30173	0	1	0	0	1	0
	3	0.32847	0	0	1	0	0	1
	4	0.25505	1	0	0	-1	0	0
	5	0.29718	0	1	0	0	-1	0
	6	0.33529	0	0	1	0	0	-1

Output 22.7.4. ANOVA Table

```
                    Vision Symmetry
             Test of Marginal Homogeneity

                  The CATMOD Procedure

                  Analysis of Variance

 Source          DF    Chi-Square     Pr > ChiSq
 --------------------------------------------
 Intercept        3      78744.17         <.0001
 Side             3         11.98         0.0075

 Residual         0             .              .
```

Output 22.7.5. Parameter Estimates

```
                                 Vision Symmetry
                          Test of Marginal Homogeneity

                              The CATMOD Procedure

                  Analysis of Weighted Least Squares Estimates

                                              Standard         Chi-
 Effect           Parameter      Estimate        Error       Square     Pr > ChiSq
 ---------------------------------------------------------------------------------
 Intercept               1         0.2597      0.00468      3073.03         <.0001
                         2         0.2995      0.00464      4160.17         <.0001
                         3         0.3319      0.00483      4725.25         <.0001
 Side                    4        0.00461      0.00194         5.65         0.0174
                         5        0.00227      0.00255         0.80         0.3726
                         6       -0.00341      0.00252         1.83         0.1757
```

The analysis of variance table in Output 22.7.4 shows that the Side effect is significant, so there is not marginal homogeneity between left-eye vision and right-eye vision. In other words, the distribution of the quality of right-eye vision differs significantly from the quality of left-eye vision in the same subjects. The test of the Side effect is equivalent to Bhapkar's test (Agresti 1990).

Example 22.8. Repeated Measures, Logistic Analysis of Growth Curve

The data, from a longitudinal study reported in Koch et al. (1977), are from patients in four populations (2 diagnostic groups × 2 treatments) who are measured at three times to assess their response (n=normal or a=abnormal) to treatment.

```
title 'Growth Curve Analysis';
data growth2;
   input Diagnosis $ Treatment $ week1 $ week2 $ week4
                   $ count @@;
   datalines;
mild std n n n 16    severe std n n n  2
mild std n n a 13    severe std n n a  2
mild std n a n  9    severe std n a n  8
mild std n a a  3    severe std n a a  9
```

```
mild std a n n 14     severe std a n n  9
mild std a n a  4     severe std a n a 15
mild std a a n 15     severe std a a n 27
mild std a a a  6     severe std a a a 28
mild new n n n 31     severe new n n n  7
mild new n n a  0     severe new n n a  2
mild new n a n  6     severe new n a n  5
mild new n a a  0     severe new n a a  2
mild new a n n 22     severe new a n n 31
mild new a n a  2     severe new a n a  5
mild new a a n  9     severe new a a n 32
mild new a a a  0     severe new a a a  6
;
```

The analysis is directed at assessing the effect of the repeated measurement factor, Time, as well as the independent variables, Diagnosis (mild or severe) and Treatment (std or new). The RESPONSE statement is used to compute the logits of the marginal probabilities. The times used in the design matrix (0, 1, 2) correspond to the logarithms (base 2) of the actual times (1, 2, 4). The following statements produce Output 22.8.1 through Output 22.8.7:

```
proc catmod order=data data=growth2;
   title2 'Reduced Logistic Model';
   weight count;
   population Diagnosis Treatment;
   response logit;
   model week1*week2*week4=(1 0 0 0,  /* mild, std */
                            1 0 1 0,
                            1 0 2 0,

                            1 0 0 0,  /* mild, new */
                            1 0 0 1,
                            1 0 0 2,

                            0 1 0 0,  /* severe, std */
                            0 1 1 0,
                            0 1 2 0,

                            0 1 0 0,  /* severe, new */
                            0 1 0 1,
                            0 1 0 2)
          (1='Mild diagnosis, week 1',
           2='Severe diagnosis, week 1',
           3='Time effect for std trt',
           4='Time effect for new trt')
           / freq;
   contrast 'Diagnosis effect, week 1' all_parms 1 -1 0 0;
   contrast 'Equal time effects' all_parms 0 0 1 -1;
quit;
```

Output 22.8.1. Logistic Analysis of Growth Curve

```
                         Growth Curve Analysis
                         Reduced Logistic Model

                          The CATMOD Procedure

Response            week1*week2*week4      Response Levels     8
Weight Variable     count                  Populations         4
Data Set            GROWTH2                Total Frequency   340
Frequency Missing   0                      Observations       29
```

Output 22.8.2. Population Profiles

```
                         Growth Curve Analysis
                         Reduced Logistic Model

                          The CATMOD Procedure

                          Population Profiles

       Sample    Diagnosis    Treatment    Sample Size
       -----------------------------------------------
            1    mild         std                   80
            2    mild         new                   70
            3    severe       std                  100
            4    severe       new                   90


                           Response Profiles

             Response    week1    week2    week4
             -----------------------------------
                    1    n        n        n
                    2    n        n        a
                    3    n        a        n
                    4    n        a        a
                    5    a        n        n
                    6    a        n        a
                    7    a        a        n
                    8    a        a        a
```

The samples and the response numbers are defined in Output 22.8.2.

Output 22.8.3. Response Frequencies

```
                          Growth Curve Analysis
                          Reduced Logistic Model

                           The CATMOD Procedure

                           Response Frequencies

                                  Response Number
Sample        1        2        3        4        5        6        7        8
-------------------------------------------------------------------------------
     1       16       13        9        3       14        4       15        6
     2       31        0        6        0       22        2        9        0
     3        2        2        8        9        9       15       27       28
     4        7        2        5        2       31        5       32        6
```

Output 22.8.4. Design Matrix

```
                        Growth Curve Analysis
                        Reduced Logistic Model

                         The CATMOD Procedure

             Function      Response                Design Matrix
Sample        Number       Function         1         2         3         4
-----------------------------------------------------------------------------
    1            1          0.05001         1         0         0         0
                 2          0.35364         1         0         1         0
                 3          0.73089         1         0         2         0

    2            1          0.11441         1         0         0         0
                 2          1.29928         1         0         0         1
                 3          3.52636         1         0         0         2

    3            1         -1.32493         0         1         0         0
                 2         -0.94446         0         1         1         0
                 3         -0.16034         0         1         2         0

    4            1         -1.53148         0         1         0         0
                 2          0.00000         0         1         0         1
                 3          1.60944         0         1         0         2
```

Output 22.8.5. Analysis of Variance

```
                        Growth Curve Analysis
                        Reduced Logistic Model

                         The CATMOD Procedure

                         Analysis of Variance

      Source                        DF   Chi-Square    Pr > ChiSq
      -----------------------------------------------------------
      Mild diagnosis, week 1         1         0.28        0.5955
      Severe diagnosis, week 1       1       100.48        <.0001
      Time effect for std trt        1        26.35        <.0001
      Time effect for new trt        1       125.09        <.0001

      Residual                       8         4.20        0.8387
```

The analysis of variance table (Output 22.8.5) shows that the data can be adequately modeled by two parameters that represent diagnosis effects at week 1 and two log-linear time effects (one for each treatment). Both of the time effects are significant.

Output 22.8.6. Parameter Estimates

```
                         Growth Curve Analysis
                         Reduced Logistic Model

                          The CATMOD Procedure

              Analysis of Weighted Least Squares Estimates

                                   Standard        Chi-
Effect     Parameter    Estimate      Error      Square     Pr > ChiSq
----------------------------------------------------------------------
Model              1     -0.0716     0.1348        0.28         0.5955
                   2     -1.3529     0.1350      100.48         <.0001
                   3      0.4944     0.0963       26.35         <.0001
                   4      1.4552     0.1301      125.09         <.0001
```

Output 22.8.7. Contrasts

```
                    Growth Curve Analysis
                    Reduced Logistic Model

                     The CATMOD Procedure

                    Analysis of Contrasts

Contrast                   DF    Chi-Square    Pr > ChiSq
---------------------------------------------------------
Diagnosis effect, week 1    1         77.02        <.0001
Equal time effects          1         59.12        <.0001
```

The analysis of contrasts (Output 22.8.7) shows that the diagnosis effect at week 1 is highly significant. In Output 22.8.6, since the estimate of the logit for the severe diagnosis effect (parameter 2) is more negative than it is for the mild diagnosis effect (parameter 1), there is a smaller predicted probability of the first response (normal) for the severe diagnosis group. In other words, those subjects with a severe diagnosis have a significantly higher probability of abnormal response at week 1 than those subjects with a mild diagnosis.

The analysis of contrasts also shows that the time effect for the standard treatment is significantly different than the one for the new treatment. The table of parameter estimates (Output 22.8.6) shows that the time effect for the new treatment (parameter 4) is stronger than it is for the standard treatment (parameter 3).

Example 22.9. Repeated Measures, Two Repeated Measurement Factors

This example, from MacMillan et al. (1981), illustrates a repeated measurement analysis in which there are two repeated measurement factors. Two diagnostic procedures (standard and test) are performed on each subject, and the results of both are evaluated at each of two times as being positive or negative.

```
title 'Diagnostic Procedure Comparison';
data a;
   input std1 $ test1 $ std2 $ test2 $ wt @@;
   datalines;
```

```
neg neg neg neg 509  neg neg neg pos  4  neg neg pos neg  17
neg neg pos pos   3  neg pos neg neg 13  neg pos neg pos   8
neg pos pos pos   8  pos neg neg neg 14  pos neg neg pos   1
pos neg pos neg  17  pos neg pos pos  9  pos pos neg neg   7
pos pos neg pos   4  pos pos pos neg  9  pos pos pos pos 170
;
```

For the initial model, the response functions are marginal probabilities, and the repeated measurement factors are Time and Treatment. The model is a saturated one, containing effects for Time, Treatment, and Time*Treatment. The following statements produce Output 22.9.1 through Output 22.9.5:

```
proc catmod data=a;
   title2 'Marginal Symmetry, Saturated Model';
   weight wt;
   response marginals;
   model std1*test1*std2*test2=_response_ / freq noparm;
   repeated Time 2, Treatment 2 / _response_=Time Treatment
            Time*Treatment;
run;
```

Output 22.9.1. Diagnosis Data: Two Repeated Measurement Factors

```
                    Diagnostic Procedure Comparison
                   Marginal Symmetry, Saturated Model

                         The CATMOD Procedure

Response            std1*test1*std2*test2     Response Levels   15
Weight Variable     wt                        Populations        1
Data Set            A                         Total Frequency  793
Frequency Missing   0                         Observations      15


                        Sample    Sample Size
                        ---------------------
                             1            793
```

Output 22.9.2. Response Profiles

```
                 Diagnostic Procedure Comparison
                 Marginal Symmetry, Saturated Model

                       The CATMOD Procedure

                        Response Profiles

             Response     std1     test1     std2     test2
             -----------------------------------------
                 1        neg      neg       neg      neg
                 2        neg      neg       neg      pos
                 3        neg      neg       pos      neg
                 4        neg      neg       pos      pos
                 5        neg      pos       neg      neg
                 6        neg      pos       neg      pos
                 7        neg      pos       pos      pos
                 8        pos      neg       neg      neg
                 9        pos      neg       neg      pos
                10        pos      neg       pos      neg
                11        pos      neg       pos      pos
                12        pos      pos       neg      neg
                13        pos      pos       neg      pos
                14        pos      pos       pos      neg
                15        pos      pos       pos      pos
```

Output 22.9.3. Response Frequencies

```
                 Diagnostic Procedure Comparison
                 Marginal Symmetry, Saturated Model

                       The CATMOD Procedure

                       Response Frequencies

                              Response Number
Sample        1         2         3         4         5         6         7         8
--------------------------------------------------------------------------------------
    1       509         4        17         3        13         8         8        14

                       Response Frequencies

                              Response Number
    Sample         9        10        11        12        13        14        15
    ----------------------------------------------------------------------
        1          1        17         9         7         4         9       170
```

Output 22.9.4. Design Matrix

```
                 Diagnostic Procedure Comparison
                 Marginal Symmetry, Saturated Model

                       The CATMOD Procedure

              Function      Response                Design Matrix
      Sample     Number      Function         1         2         3         4
      ----------------------------------------------------------------------
         1          1        0.70870         1         1         1         1
                    2        0.72383         1         1        -1        -1
                    3        0.70618         1        -1         1        -1
                    4        0.73897         1        -1        -1         1
```

Output 22.9.5. ANOVA Table

```
                  Diagnostic Procedure Comparison
                  Marginal Symmetry, Saturated Model

                        The CATMOD Procedure

                        Analysis of Variance

           Source              DF   Chi-Square    Pr > ChiSq
           ----------------------------------------------------
           Intercept            1      2385.34        <.0001
           Time                 1         0.85        0.3570
           Treatment            1         8.20        0.0042
           Time*Treatment       1         2.40        0.1215

           Residual             0          .             .
```

The analysis of variance table in Output 22.9.5 shows that there is no significant effect of Time, either by itself or in its interaction with Treatment. Thus, the second model includes only the Treatment effect. Again, the response functions are marginal probabilities, and the repeated measurement factors are Time and Treatment. A main effect model with respect to Treatment is fit. The following statements produce Output 22.9.6 through Output 22.9.9:

```
   title2 'Marginal Symmetry, Reduced Model';
   model std1*test1*std2*test2=_response_ / noprofile corrb;
   repeated Time 2, Treatment 2 / _response_=Treatment;
run;
```

Output 22.9.6. Diagnosis Data: Reduced Model

```
                  Diagnostic Procedure Comparison
                  Marginal Symmetry, Reduced Model

                        The CATMOD Procedure

Response            std1*test1*std2*test2     Response Levels   15
Weight Variable     wt                        Populations        1
Data Set            A                         Total Frequency  793
Frequency Missing   0                         Observations      15
```

Output 22.9.7. Design Matrix

```
                  Diagnostic Procedure Comparison
                  Marginal Symmetry, Reduced Model

                        The CATMOD Procedure

                   Function       Response      Design Matrix
          Sample    Number        Function        1        2
          -------------------------------------------------
             1         1           0.70870        1        1
                       2           0.72383        1       -1
                       3           0.70618        1        1
                       4           0.73897        1       -1
```

Output 22.9.8. ANOVA Table

```
                 Diagnostic Procedure Comparison
                 Marginal Symmetry, Reduced Model

                       The CATMOD Procedure

                       Analysis of Variance

           Source           DF    Chi-Square     Pr > ChiSq
           ---------------------------------------------
           Intercept         1       2386.97         <.0001
           Treatment         1          9.55         0.0020

           Residual          2          3.51         0.1731
```

Output 22.9.9. Parameter Estimates

```
                 Diagnostic Procedure Comparison
                 Marginal Symmetry, Reduced Model

                       The CATMOD Procedure

           Analysis of Weighted Least Squares Estimates

                                               Standard        Chi-
Effect           Parameter     Estimate          Error       Square    Pr > ChiSq
----------------------------------------------------------------------------------
Intercept                1       0.7196         0.0147      2386.97        <.0001
Treatment                2      -0.0128        0.00416         9.55        0.0020
```

Output 22.9.10. Correlation Matrix

```
                 Diagnostic Procedure Comparison
                 Marginal Symmetry, Reduced Model

                       The CATMOD Procedure

          Correlation Matrix of the Parameter Estimates

                               1                2
                 -----------------------------------
                 1       1.00000          0.04194
                 2       0.04194          1.00000
```

The analysis of variance table for the reduced model (Output 22.9.8) shows that the model fits (since the Residual is nonsignificant) and that the treatment effect is significant. The negative parameter estimate for Treatment in Output 22.9.9 shows that the first level of treatment (std) has a smaller probability of the first response level (neg) than the second level of treatment (test). In other words, the standard diagnostic procedure gives a significantly higher probability of a positive response than the test diagnostic procedure.

The next example illustrates a RESPONSE statement that, at each time, computes the sensitivity and specificity of the test diagnostic procedure with respect to the standard procedure. Since these are measures of the relative accuracy of the two diagnostic procedures, the repeated measurement factors in this case are labeled Time and Accuracy. Only fifteen of the sixteen possible responses are observed, so additional care must be taken in formulating the RESPONSE statement for computation of sensitivity and specificity.

The following statements produce Output 22.9.11 through Output 22.9.15:

```
   title2 'Sensitivity and Specificity Analysis, '
          'Main-Effects Model';
   model std1*test1*std2*test2=_response_ / covb noprofile;
   repeated Time 2, Accuracy 2 / _response_=Time Accuracy;
   response exp  1 -1  0  0  0  0  0  0,
                 0  0  1 -1  0  0  0  0,
                 0  0  0  0  1 -1  0  0,
                 0  0  0  0  0  0  1 -1

             log 0 0 0 0  0 0 0  0 0 0 0  1 1 1 1,
                 0 0 0 0  0 0 0  1 1 1 1  1 1 1 1,
                 1 1 1 1  0 0 0  0 0 0 0  0 0 0 0,
                 1 1 1 1  1 1 1  0 0 0 0  0 0 0 0,
                 0 0 0 1  0 0 1  0 0 0 1  0 0 0 1,
                 0 0 1 1  0 0 1  0 0 1 1  0 0 1 1,
                 1 0 0 0  1 0 0  1 0 0 0  1 0 0 0,
                 1 1 0 0  1 1 0  1 1 0 0  1 1 0 0;
quit;
```

Output 22.9.11. Diagnosis Data: Sensitivity and Specificity Analysis

```
                    Diagnostic Procedure Comparison
      Sensitivity and Specificity Analysis, Main-Effects Model

                          The CATMOD Procedure

Response            std1*test1*std2*test2      Response Levels   15
Weight Variable     wt                         Populations        1
Data Set            A                          Total Frequency  793
Frequency Missing   0                          Observations      15
```

Output 22.9.12. Design Matrix

```
                    Diagnostic Procedure Comparison
      Sensitivity and Specificity Analysis, Main-Effects Model

                          The CATMOD Procedure

              Function       Response          Design Matrix
   Sample      Number        Function         1        2        3
   -----------------------------------------------------------
      1           1          0.82251          1        1        1
                  2          0.94840          1        1       -1
                  3          0.81545          1       -1        1
                  4          0.96964          1       -1       -1
```

For the sensitivity and specificity analysis, the four response functions displayed next to the design matrix (Output 22.9.12) represent the following:

1. sensitivity, time 1
2. specificity, time 1
3. sensitivity, time 2
4. specificity, time 2

The sensitivities and specificities are for the test diagnostic procedure relative to the standard procedure.

Output 22.9.13. ANOVA Table

```
                   Diagnostic Procedure Comparison
        Sensitivity and Specificity Analysis, Main-Effects Model

                         The CATMOD Procedure

                         Analysis of Variance

              Source          DF    Chi-Square    Pr > ChiSq
              --------------------------------------------
              Intercept        1       6448.79        <.0001
              Time             1          4.10        0.0428
              Accuracy         1         38.81        <.0001

              Residual         1          1.00        0.3178
```

The ANOVA table shows that an additive model fits, that there is a significant effect of time, and that the sensitivity is significantly different from the specificity.

Output 22.9.14. Parameter Estimates

```
                   Diagnostic Procedure Comparison
        Sensitivity and Specificity Analysis, Main-Effects Model

                         The CATMOD Procedure

              Analysis of Weighted Least Squares Estimates

                                               Standard          Chi-
Effect          Parameter      Estimate          Error        Square    Pr > ChiSq
----------------------------------------------------------------------------------
Intercept               1        0.8892         0.0111       6448.79        <.0001
Time                    2      -0.00932        0.00460          4.10        0.0428
Accuracy                3       -0.0702         0.0113         38.81        <.0001
```

Output 22.9.15. Covariance Matrix

```
                 Diagnostic Procedure Comparison
     Sensitivity and Specificity Analysis, Main-Effects Model

                       The CATMOD Procedure

          Covariance Matrix of the Parameter Estimates

                      1                2                3
     ---------------------------------------------------
       1     0.00012260       0.00000229       0.00010137
       2     0.00000229       0.00002116       -.00000587
       3     0.00010137       -.00000587       0.00012697
```

Output 22.9.14 shows that the predicted sensitivities and specificities are lower for time 1 (since parameter 2 is negative). It also shows that the sensitivity is significantly less than the specificity.

Example 22.10. Direct Input of Response Functions and Covariance Matrix

This example illustrates the ability of PROC CATMOD to operate on an existing vector of functions and the corresponding covariance matrix. The estimates under investigation are composite indices summarizing the responses to eighteen psychological questions pertaining to general well-being. These estimates are computed for domains corresponding to an age by sex cross-classification, and the covariance matrix is calculated via the method of balanced repeated replications. The analysis is directed at obtaining a description of the variation among these domain estimates. The data are from Koch and Stokes (1979).

```
data fbeing(type=est);
   input  b1-b5   _type_ $  _name_ $  b6-b10 #2;
   datalines;
 7.93726   7.92509   7.82815   7.73696   8.16791  parms  .
 7.24978   7.18991   7.35960   7.31937   7.55184
 0.00739   0.00019   0.00146  -0.00082   0.00076  cov    b1
 0.00189   0.00118   0.00140  -0.00140   0.00039
 0.00019   0.01172   0.00183   0.00029   0.00083  cov    b2
-0.00123  -0.00629  -0.00088  -0.00232   0.00034
 0.00146   0.00183   0.01050  -0.00173   0.00011  cov    b3
 0.00434  -0.00059  -0.00055   0.00023  -0.00013
-0.00082   0.00029  -0.00173   0.01335   0.00140  cov    b4
 0.00158   0.00212   0.00211   0.00066   0.00240
 0.00076   0.00083   0.00011   0.00140   0.01430  cov    b5
-0.00050  -0.00098   0.00239  -0.00010   0.00213
 0.00189  -0.00123   0.00434   0.00158  -0.00050  cov    b6
 0.01110   0.00101   0.00177  -0.00018  -0.00082
 0.00118  -0.00629  -0.00059   0.00212  -0.00098  cov    b7
 0.00101   0.02342   0.00144   0.00369   0.25300
 0.00140  -0.00088  -0.00055   0.00211   0.00239  cov    b8
 0.00177   0.00144   0.01060   0.00157   0.00226
-0.00140  -0.00232   0.00023   0.00066  -0.00010  cov    b9
-0.00018   0.00369   0.00157   0.02298   0.00918
```

```
 0.00039   0.00034  -0.00013   0.00240   0.00213  cov   b10
-0.00082   0.00253   0.00226   0.00918   0.01921
;
```

The following statements produce Output 22.10.1 through Output 22.10.3:

```
proc catmod data=fbeing;
   title 'Complex Sample Survey Analysis';
   response read b1-b10;
   factors sex $ 2, age $ 5 / _response_=sex age
                              profile=(male     '25-34',
                                       male     '35-44',
                                       male     '45-54',
                                       male     '55-64',
                                       male     '65-74',
                                       female   '25-34',
                                       female   '35-44',
                                       female   '45-54',
                                       female   '55-64',
                                       female   '65-74');
   model _f_=_response_
         / title='Main Effects for Sex and Age';
run;
```

Output 22.10.1. Health Survey Data: Using Direct Input

Complex Sample Survey Analysis

Main Effects for Sex and Age

The CATMOD Procedure

Response Functions Directly Input from Data Set FBEING

Sample	Function Number	Response Function	Design Matrix 1	2	3	4	5	6
1	1	7.93726	1	1	1	0	0	0
	2	7.92509	1	1	0	1	0	0
	3	7.82815	1	1	0	0	1	0
	4	7.73696	1	1	0	0	0	1
	5	8.16791	1	1	-1	-1	-1	-1
	6	7.24978	1	-1	1	0	0	0
	7	7.18991	1	-1	0	1	0	0
	8	7.35960	1	-1	0	0	1	0
	9	7.31937	1	-1	0	0	0	1
	10	7.55184	1	-1	-1	-1	-1	-1

Output 22.10.2. ANOVA Table

```
                    Complex Sample Survey Analysis

                     Main Effects for Sex and Age

                        The CATMOD Procedure

       Response Functions Directly Input from Data Set FBEING


                        Analysis of Variance

             Source         DF   Chi-Square    Pr > ChiSq
             ------------------------------------------
             Intercept       1     28089.07        <.0001
             sex             1        65.84        <.0001
             age             4         9.21        0.0561

             Residual        4         2.92        0.5713
```

Output 22.10.3. Parameter Estimates

```
                    Complex Sample Survey Analysis

                     Main Effects for Sex and Age

                        The CATMOD Procedure

       Response Functions Directly Input from Data Set FBEING


             Analysis of Weighted Least Squares Estimates

                                         Standard        Chi-
Effect         Parameter    Estimate       Error       Square    Pr > ChiSq
------------------------------------------------------------------------
Intercept              1      7.6319      0.0455     28089.07        <.0001
sex                    2      0.2900      0.0357        65.84        <.0001
age                    3    -0.00780      0.0645         0.01        0.9037
                       4     -0.0465      0.0636         0.54        0.4642
                       5     -0.0343      0.0557         0.38        0.5387
                       6     -0.1098      0.0764         2.07        0.1506
```

The analysis of variance table (Output 22.10.2) shows that the additive model fits and that there is a significant effect of both sex and age. The following statements produce Output 22.10.4:

```
contrast 'No Age Effect for Age<65' all_parms 0 0 1 0 0 -1,
                                    all_parms 0 0 0 1 0 -1,
                                    all_parms 0 0 0 0 1 -1;
run;
```

Output 22.10.4. Age<65 Contrast

```
                    Complex Sample Survey Analysis

                     Main Effects for Sex and Age

                        The CATMOD Procedure

         Response Functions Directly Input from Data Set FBEING


                       Analysis of Contrasts

Contrast                      DF     Chi-Square     Pr > ChiSq
---------------------------------------------------------------
No Age Effect for Age<65       3           0.72         0.8678
```

The analysis of the contrast shows that there is no significant difference among the four age groups that are under age 65. Thus, the next model contains a binary age effect (less than 65 versus 65 and over). The following statements produce Output 22.10.5 through Output 22.10.7:

```
   model _f_=(1  1  1,
              1  1  1,
              1  1  1,
              1  1  1,
              1  1 -1,
              1 -1  1,
              1 -1  1,
              1 -1  1,
              1 -1  1,
              1 -1 -1)
                        (1='Intercept' ,
                         2='Sex'       ,
                         3='Age (25-64 vs. 65-74)')
          / title='Binary Age Effect (25-64 vs. 65-74)' ;
quit;
```

Output 22.10.5. Design Matrix

```
                     Complex Sample Survey Analysis

                     Main Effects for Sex and Age

                         The CATMOD Procedure

         Response Functions Directly Input from Data Set FBEING


                     Complex Sample Survey Analysis

                   Binary Age Effect (25-64 vs. 65-74)

                         The CATMOD Procedure

         Response Functions Directly Input from Data Set FBEING


              Function      Response          Design Matrix
    Sample     Number       Function         1        2        3
    ------------------------------------------------------------
       1          1          7.93726         1        1        1
                  2          7.92509         1        1        1
                  3          7.82815         1        1        1
                  4          7.73696         1        1        1
                  5          8.16791         1        1       -1
                  6          7.24978         1       -1        1
                  7          7.18991         1       -1        1
                  8          7.35960         1       -1        1
                  9          7.31937         1       -1        1
                 10          7.55184         1       -1       -1
```

Output 22.10.6. ANOVA Table

```
                     Complex Sample Survey Analysis

                     Main Effects for Sex and Age

                         The CATMOD Procedure

         Response Functions Directly Input from Data Set FBEING


                     Complex Sample Survey Analysis

                   Binary Age Effect (25-64 vs. 65-74)

                         The CATMOD Procedure

         Response Functions Directly Input from Data Set FBEING


                         Analysis of Variance

      Source                     DF   Chi-Square    Pr > ChiSq
      --------------------------------------------------------
      Intercept                   1     19087.16        <.0001
      Sex                         1        72.64        <.0001
      Age (25-64 vs. 65-74)       1         8.49        0.0036

      Residual                    7         3.64        0.8198
```

Output 22.10.7. Parameter Estimates

```
                     Complex Sample Survey Analysis

                      Main Effects for Sex and Age

                         The CATMOD Procedure

        Response Functions Directly Input from Data Set FBEING


                     Complex Sample Survey Analysis

                  Binary Age Effect (25-64 vs. 65-74)

                         The CATMOD Procedure

        Response Functions Directly Input from Data Set FBEING


             Analysis of Weighted Least Squares Estimates

                                      Standard        Chi-
Effect     Parameter     Estimate        Error      Square    Pr > ChiSq
------------------------------------------------------------------------
Model              1       7.7183       0.0559    19087.16        <.0001
                   2       0.2800       0.0329       72.64        <.0001
                   3      -0.1304       0.0448        8.49        0.0036
```

The analysis of variance table in Output 22.10.6 shows that the model fits (note that the goodness-of-fit statistic is the sum of the previous one (Output 22.10.2) plus the chi-square for the contrast matrix in Output 22.10.4). The age and sex effects are significant. Since the second parameter in the table of estimates is positive, males (the first level for the sex variable) have a higher predicted index of well-being than females. Since the third parameter estimate is negative, those younger than age 65 (the first level of age) have a lower predicted index of well-being than those 65 and older.

Example 22.11. Predicted Probabilities

Suppose you have collected marketing research data to examine the relationship between a prospect's likelihood of buying your product and their education and income. Specifically, the variables are as follows.

Variable	Levels	Interpretation
Education	high, low	prospect's education level
Income	high, low	prospect's income level
Purchase	yes, no	Did prospect purchase product?

The following statements first create a data set, loan, that contains the marketing research data, then they use the CATMOD procedure to fit a model, obtain the parameter estimates, and obtain the predicted probabilities of interest. These statements produce Output 22.11.1 through Output 22.11.5.

```
data loan;
   input Education $ Income $ Purchase $ wt;
   datalines;
high  high  yes   54
high  high  no    23
high  low   yes   41
high  low   no    12
low   high  yes   35
low   high  no    42
low   low   yes   19
low   low   no     8
;

ods output PredictedValues=Predicted
           (keep=Education Income PredFunction);

proc catmod data=loan order=data;
   weight wt;
   response marginals;
   model Purchase=Education Income / pred;
run;

proc sort data=Predicted;
   by descending PredFunction;
run;

proc print data=Predicted;
run;
```

Notice that the preceding statements use the Output Delivery system (ODS) to output the parameter estimates instead of the OUT= option, though either can be used.

Output 22.11.1. Marketing Research Data: Obtaining Predicted Probabilities

```
                          The CATMOD Procedure

       Response            Purchase     Response Levels     2
       Weight Variable     wt           Populations         4
       Data Set            LOAN         Total Frequency   234
       Frequency Missing   0            Observations        8
```

Output 22.11.2. Profiles and Design Matrix

```
                     The CATMOD Procedure

                     Population Profiles

         Sample     Education     Income    Sample Size
         ---------------------------------------------
            1       high          high               77
            2       high          low                53
            3       low           high               77
            4       low           low                27


                      Response Profiles

                     Response    Purchase
                     --------------------
                         1        yes
                         2        no


                 Response            Design Matrix
       Sample    Function          1         2         3
       -------------------------------------------------
          1       0.70130          1         1         1
          2       0.77358          1         1        -1
          3       0.45455          1        -1         1
          4       0.70370          1        -1        -1
```

Output 22.11.3. ANOVA Table and Parameter Estimates

```
                     The CATMOD Procedure

                     Analysis of Variance

         Source          DF   Chi-Square    Pr > ChiSq
         ---------------------------------------------
         Intercept        1       418.36        <.0001
         Education        1         8.85        0.0029
         Income           1         4.70        0.0302

         Residual         1         1.84        0.1745


        Analysis of Weighted Least Squares Estimates

                                            Standard        Chi-
Effect         Parameter     Estimate        Error        Square     Pr > ChiSq
-------------------------------------------------------------------------------
Intercept              1       0.6481       0.0317        418.36         <.0001
Education              2       0.0924       0.0311          8.85         0.0029
Income                 3      -0.0675       0.0312          4.70         0.0302
```

Output 22.11.4. Predicted Values and Residuals

The CATMOD Procedure

Predicted Values for Response Functions

Sample	Education	Income	Function Number	Observed Function	Observed Standard Error	Predicted Function	Predicted Standard Error	Residual
1	high	high	1	0.7012987	0.052158	0.67293982	0.047794	0.02835888
2	high	low	1	0.77358491	0.057487	0.80803395	0.051586	-0.034449
3	low	high	1	0.45454545	0.056744	0.48811031	0.051077	-0.0335649
4	low	low	1	0.7037037	0.087877	0.62320444	0.064867	0.08049927

Output 22.11.5. Predicted Probabilities Data Set

Obs	Education	Income	Pred Function
1	high	low	0.80803395
2	high	high	0.67293982
3	low	low	0.62320444
4	low	high	0.48811031

You can use the predicted values (values of PredFunction in Output 22.11.5) as scores representing the likelihood that a randomly chosen subject from one of these populations will purchase the product. Notice that the Response Profiles in Output 22.11.2 show you that the first sorted level of Purchase is "yes," indicating that the predicted probabilities are for Pr(Purchase='yes'). For example, someone with high education and low income has an estimated probability of purchase of 0.808. As with any response function estimate given by PROC CATMOD, this estimate can be obtained by cross-multiplying the row from the design matrix corresponding to the sample (sample number 2 in this case) with the vector of parameter estimates $((1 * 0.6481) + (1 * 0.0924) + (-1 * (-0.0675)))$.

This ranking of scores can help in decision making (for example, with respect to allocation of advertising dollars, choice of advertising media, choice of print media, and so on).

References

Agresti, A. (1984), *Analysis of Ordinal Categorical Data*, New York: John Wiley & Sons, Inc.

Agresti, A. (1990), *Categorical Data Analysis*, New York: John Wiley & Sons, Inc.

Agresti, A. (1996), *An Introduction to Categorical Data Analysis*, New York: John Wiley & Sons, Inc.

Bishop, Y.M.M., Fienberg, S.E., and Holland, P.W. (1975), *Discrete Multivariate Analysis: Theory and Practice*, Cambridge, MA: The MIT Press.

Breslow, N. (1982), "Covariance Adjustment of Relative-Risk Estimates in Matched Studies," *Biometrics*, 38, 661–672.

Cox, D.R. and Snell, E.J. (1989), *The Analysis of Binary Data*, Second Edition, London: Chapman and Hall.

Fienberg, S.E. (1980), *The Analysis of Cross-Classified Categorical Data*, Second Edition, Cambridge, MA: The MIT Press.

Forthofer, R.N. and Koch, G.G. (1973), "An Analysis of Compounded Functions of Categorical Data," *Biometrics*, 29, 143–157.

Forthofer, R.N. and Lehnen R.G. (1981), *Public Program Analysis: A New Categorical Data Approach*, Belmont, CA: Wadsworth.

Freeman, D. H. (1987), *Applied Categorical Data Analysis*, New York: Marcel Dekker Inc.

Grizzle, J.E., Starmer, C.F., and Koch, G.G. (1969), "Analysis of Categorical Data by Linear Models," *Biometrics*, 25, 489–504.

Guthrie, D. (1981), "Analysis of Dichotomous Variables in Repeated Measures Experiments," *Psychological Bulletin*, 90, 189–195.

Imrey, P.B., Koch, G.G., and Stokes, M.E. (1981), "Categorical Data Analysis: Some Reflections on the Log Linear Model and Logistic Regression. Part I: Historical and Methodological Overview," *International Statistical Review*, 49, 265–283.

Koch, G.G., Landis, J.R., Freeman, J.L., Freeman, D.H., and Lehnen, R.G. (1977), "A General Methodology for the Analysis of Experiments with Repeated Measurement of Categorical Data," *Biometrics*, 33, 133–158.

Koch, G.G. and Stokes, M.E. (1979), "Annotated Computer Applications of Weighted Least Squares Methods for Illustrative Analyses of Examples Involving Health Survey Data." Technical Report prepared for the U.S. National Center for Health Statistics.

Landis, J.R., Stanish, W.M., Freeman, J.L., and Koch, G.G. (1976), "A Computer Program for the Generalized Chi-Square Analysis of Categorical Data Using Weighted Least Squares (GENCAT)," *Computer Programs in Biomedicine*, 6, 196–231.

MacMillan, J., Becker, C., Koch, G.G., Stokes, M., and Vandiviere, H.M. (1981), "An Application of Weighted Least Squares Methods to the Analysis of Measurement Process Components of Variability in an Observational Study," *American Statistical Association Proceedings of Survey Research Methods*, 680–685.

Ries, P.N. and Smith, H. (1963), "The Use of Chi-Square for Preference Testing in Multidimensional Problems," *Chemical Engineering Progress*, 59, 39–43.

Searle, S.R. (1971), *Linear Models*, New York: John Wiley & Sons, Inc.

Stanish, W.M. and Koch, G.G. (1984), "The Use of CATMOD for Repeated Measurement Analysis of Categorical Data," *Proceedings of the Ninth Annual SAS Users Group International Conference*, 9, 761–770.

Stokes, M.E., Davis, C.S., and Koch, G.G. (1995), *Categorical Data Analysis Using the SAS System*, Cary, NC: SAS Institute Inc.

Wald, A. (1943), "Tests of Statistical Hypotheses Concerning General Parameters When the Number of Observations Is Large," *Transactions of the American Mathematical Society*, 54, 426–482.

Chapter 23
The CLUSTER Procedure

Chapter Table of Contents

Chapter 23
The CLUSTER Procedure

Overview

The CLUSTER procedure hierarchically clusters the observations in a SAS data set using one of eleven methods. The CLUSTER procedure finds hierarchical clusters of the observations in a SAS data set. The data can be coordinates or distances. If the data are coordinates, PROC CLUSTER computes (possibly squared) Euclidean distances. If you want to perform a cluster analysis on non-Euclidean distance data, it is possible to do so by using a TYPE=DISTANCE data set as input. The %DISTANCE macro in the SAS/STAT sample library can compute many kinds of distance matrices.

One situation where analyzing non-Euclidean distance data can be useful is when you have categorical data, where the distance data are calculated using an association measure. For more information, see Example 23.5 on page 916.

The clustering methods available are average linkage, the centroid method, complete linkage, density linkage (including Wong's hybrid and kth-nearest-neighbor methods), maximum likelihood for mixtures of spherical multivariate normal distributions with equal variances but possibly unequal mixing proportions, the flexible-beta method, McQuitty's similarity analysis, the median method, single linkage, two-stage density linkage, and Ward's minimum-variance method.

All methods are based on the usual agglomerative hierarchical clustering procedure. Each observation begins in a cluster by itself. The two closest clusters are merged to form a new cluster that replaces the two old clusters. Merging of the two closest clusters is repeated until only one cluster is left. The various clustering methods differ in how the distance between two clusters is computed. Each method is described in the section "Clustering Methods" on page 854.

The CLUSTER procedure is not practical for very large data sets because, with most methods, the CPU time varies as the square or cube of the number of observations. The FASTCLUS procedure requires time proportional to the number of observations and can, therefore, be used with much larger data sets than PROC CLUSTER. If you want to cluster a very large data set hierarchically, you can use PROC FASTCLUS for a preliminary cluster analysis producing a large number of clusters and then use PROC CLUSTER to cluster the preliminary clusters hierarchically. This method is used to find clusters for the Fisher Iris data in Example 23.3, later in this chapter.

PROC CLUSTER displays a history of the clustering process, giving statistics useful for estimating the number of clusters in the population from which the data are sampled. PROC CLUSTER also creates an output data set that can be used by the TREE procedure to draw a tree diagram of the cluster hierarchy or to output the cluster membership at any desired level. For example, to obtain the six-cluster solution, you could first use PROC CLUSTER with the OUTTREE= option then use this output data set as the input data set to the TREE procedure. With PROC TREE, specify NCLUSTERS=6 and the OUT= options to obtain the six-cluster solution and draw a tree diagram. For an example, see Example 66.1 in Chapter 66, "The TREE Procedure."

Before you perform a cluster analysis on coordinate data, it is necessary to consider scaling or transforming the variables since variables with large variances tend to have more effect on the resulting clusters than those with small variances. The ACECLUS procedure is useful for performing linear transformations of the variables. You can also use the PRINCOMP procedure with the STD option, although in some cases it tends to obscure clusters or magnify the effect of error in the data when all components are retained. The STD option in the CLUSTER procedure standardizes the variables to mean 0 and standard deviation 1. Standardization is not always appropriate. See Milligan and Cooper (1987) for a Monte Carlo study on various methods of variable standardization. You should remove outliers before using PROC PRINCOMP or before using PROC CLUSTER with the STD option unless you specify the TRIM= option.

Nonlinear transformations of the variables may change the number of population clusters and should, therefore, be approached with caution. For most applications, the variables should be transformed so that equal differences are of equal practical importance. An interval scale of measurement is required if raw data are used as input. Ordinal or ranked data are generally not appropriate.

Agglomerative hierarchical clustering is discussed in all standard references on cluster analysis, for example, Anderberg (1973), Sneath and Sokal (1973), Hartigan (1975), Everitt (1980), and Spath (1980). An especially good introduction is given by Massart and Kaufman (1983). Anyone considering doing a hierarchical cluster analysis should study the Monte Carlo results of Milligan (1980), Milligan and Cooper (1985), and Cooper and Milligan (1988). Other essential, though more advanced, references on hierarchical clustering include Hartigan (1977, pp. 60–68; 1981), Wong (1982), Wong and Schaack (1982), and Wong and Lane (1983). Refer to Blashfield and Aldenderfer (1978) for a discussion of the confusing terminology in hierarchical cluster analysis.

Getting Started

The following example demonstrates how you can use the CLUSTER procedure to compute hierarchical clusters of observations in a SAS data set.

Suppose you want to determine whether national figures for birth rates, death rates, and infant death rates can be used to determine certain types or categories of countries. You want to perform a cluster analysis to determine whether the observations can be formed into groups suggested by the data. Previous studies indicate that the clusters computed from this type of data can be elongated and elliptical. Thus, you need to perform some linear transformation on the raw data before the cluster analysis.

The following data* from Rouncefield (1995) are birth rates, death rates, and infant death rates for 97 countries. The DATA step creates the SAS data set Poverty:

```
data Poverty;
   input Birth Death InfantDeath Country $20. @@;
   datalines;
24.7  5.7  30.8 Albania               12.5 11.9  14.4 Bulgaria
13.4 11.7  11.3 Czechoslovakia        12   12.4   7.6 Former_E._Germany
11.6 13.4  14.8 Hungary               14.3 10.2    16 Poland
13.6 10.7  26.9 Romania                 14    9  20.2 Yugoslavia
17.7   10    23 USSR                  15.2  9.5  13.1 Byelorussia_SSR
13.4 11.6    13 Ukrainian_SSR         20.7  8.4  25.7 Argentina
46.6   18   111 Bolivia               28.6  7.9    63 Brazil
23.4  5.8  17.1 Chile                 27.4  6.1    40 Columbia
32.9  7.4    63 Ecuador               28.3  7.3    56 Guyana
34.8  6.6    42 Paraguay              32.9  8.3 109.9 Peru
  18  9.6  21.9 Uruguay               27.5  4.4  23.3 Venezuela
  29 23.2    43 Mexico                  12 10.6   7.9 Belgium
13.2 10.1   5.8 Finland               12.4 11.9   7.5 Denmark
13.6  9.4   7.4 France                11.4 11.2   7.4 Germany
10.1  9.2    11 Greece                15.1  9.1   7.5 Ireland
 9.7  9.1   8.8 Italy                 13.2  8.6   7.1 Netherlands
14.3 10.7   7.8 Norway                11.9  9.5  13.1 Portugal
10.7  8.2   8.1 Spain                 14.5 11.1   5.6 Sweden
12.5  9.5   7.1 Switzerland           13.6 11.5   8.4 U.K.
14.9  7.4     8 Austria                9.9  6.7   4.5 Japan
14.5  7.3   7.2 Canada                16.7  8.1   9.1 U.S.A.
40.4 18.7 181.6 Afghanistan           28.4  3.8    16 Bahrain
42.5 11.5 108.1 Iran                  42.6  7.8    69 Iraq
22.3  6.3   9.7 Israel                38.9  6.4    44 Jordan
26.8  2.2  15.6 Kuwait                31.7  8.7    48 Lebanon
45.6  7.8    40 Oman                  42.1  7.6    71 Saudi_Arabia
29.2  8.4    76 Turkey                22.8  3.8    26 United_Arab_Emirates
42.2 15.5   119 Bangladesh            41.4 16.6   130 Cambodia
21.2  6.7    32 China                 11.7  4.9   6.1 Hong_Kong
30.5 10.2    91 India                 28.6  9.4    75 Indonesia
23.5 18.1    25 Korea                 31.6  5.6    24 Malaysia
36.1  8.8    68 Mongolia              39.6 14.8   128 Nepal
```

*These data have been compiled from the United Nations Demographic Yearbook 1990 (United Nations publications, Sales No. E/F.91.XII.1, copyright 1991, United Nations, New York) and are reproduced with the permission of the United Nations.

```
30.3  8.1 107.7 Pakistan          33.2  7.7     45 Philippines
17.8  5.2   7.5 Singapore         21.3  6.2   19.4 Sri_Lanka
22.3  7.7    28 Thailand          31.8  9.5     64 Vietnam
35.5  8.3    74 Algeria           47.2 20.2    137 Angola
48.5 11.6    67 Botswana          46.1 14.6     73 Congo
38.8  9.5  49.4 Egypt             48.6 20.7    137 Ethiopia
39.4 16.8   103 Gabon             47.4 21.4    143 Gambia
44.4 13.1    90 Ghana               47 11.3     72 Kenya
  44  9.4    82 Libya             48.3   25    130 Malawi
35.5  9.8    82 Morocco             45 18.5    141 Mozambique
  44 12.1   135 Namibia           48.5 15.6    105 Nigeria
48.2 23.4   154 Sierra_Leone      50.1 20.2    132 Somalia
32.1  9.9    72 South_Africa      44.6 15.8    108 Sudan
46.8 12.5   118 Swaziland         31.1  7.3     52 Tunisia
52.2 15.6   103 Uganda            50.5   14    106 Tanzania
45.6 14.2    83 Zaire             51.1 13.7     80 Zambia
41.7 10.3    66 Zimbabwe
;
```

The data set Poverty contains the character variable Country and the numeric variables Birth, Death, and InfantDeath, which represent the birth rate per thousand, death rate per thousand, and infant death rate per thousand. The `$20.` in the INPUT statement specifies that the variable Country is a character variable with a length of 20. The double trailing at sign (@@) in the INPUT statement holds the input line for further iterations of the DATA step, specifying that observations are input from each line until all values are read.

Because the variables in the data set do not have equal variance, you must perform some form of scaling or transformation. One method is to standardize the variables to mean zero and variance one. However, when you suspect that the data contain elliptical clusters, you can use the ACECLUS procedure to transform the data such that the resulting within-cluster covariance matrix is spherical. The procedure obtains approximate estimates of the pooled within-cluster covariance matrix and then computes canonical variables to be used in subsequent analyses.

The following statements perform the ACECLUS transformation using the SAS data set Poverty. The OUT= option creates an output SAS data set called Ace to contain the canonical variable scores.

```
proc aceclus data=Poverty out=Ace p=.03 noprint;
   var Birth Death InfantDeath;
run;
```

The P= option specifies that approximately three percent of the pairs are included in the estimation of the within-cluster covariance matrix. The NOPRINT option suppresses the display of the output. The VAR statement specifies that the variables Birth, Death, and InfantDeath are used in computing the canonical variables.

The following statements invoke the CLUSTER procedure, using the SAS data set ACE created in the previous PROC ACECLUS run.

```
proc cluster data=Ace outtree=Tree method=ward
             ccc pseudo print=15;
   var can1 can2 can3 ;
   id Country;
run;
```

The OUTTREE= option creates an output SAS data set called Tree that can be used by the TREE procedure to draw a tree diagram. Ward's minimum-variance clustering method is specified by the METHOD= option. The CCC option displays the cubic clustering criterion, and the PSEUDO option displays pseudo F and t^2 statistics. Only the last 15 generations of the cluster history are displayed, as defined by the PRINT= option.

The VAR statement specifies that the canonical variables computed in the ACECLUS procedure are used in the cluster analysis. The ID statement specifies that the variable Country should be added to the Tree output data set.

The results of this analysis are displayed in the following figures.

PROC CLUSTER first displays the table of eigenvalues of the covariance matrix for the three canonical variables (Figure 23.1). The first two columns list each eigenvalue and the difference between the eigenvalue and its successor. The last two columns display the individual and cumulative proportion of variation associated with each eigenvalue.

```
                         The CLUSTER Procedure
                 Ward's Minimum Variance Cluster Analysis

                    Eigenvalues of the Covariance Matrix

            Eigenvalue    Difference    Proportion    Cumulative

        1   64.5500051    54.7313223        0.8091        0.8091
        2    9.8186828     4.4038309        0.1231        0.9321
        3    5.4148519                      0.0679        1.0000


    Root-Mean-Square Total-Sample Standard Deviation = 5.156987
    Root-Mean-Square Distance Between Observations   = 12.63199
```

Figure 23.1. Table of Eigenvalues of the Covariance Matrix

As displayed in the last column, the first two canonical variables account for about 93% of the total variation. Figure 23.1 also displays the root mean square of the total sample standard deviation and the root mean square distance between observations.

Figure 23.2 displays the last 15 generations of the cluster history. First listed are the number of clusters and the names of the clusters joined. The observations are identified either by the ID value or by CLn, where n is the number of the cluster. Next, PROC CLUSTER displays the number of observations in the new cluster and the semipartial R^2. The latter value represents the decrease in the proportion of variance accounted for by joining the two clusters.

The CLUSTER Procedure
Ward's Minimum Variance Cluster Analysis

Root-Mean-Square Total-Sample Standard Deviation = 5.156987
Root-Mean-Square Distance Between Observations = 12.63199

Cluster History

NCL	Clusters Joined		FREQ	SPRSQ	RSQ	ERSQ	CCC	PSF	PST2	Tie
15	Oman	CL37	5	0.0039	.957	.933	6.03	132	12.1	
14	CL31	CL22	13	0.0040	.953	.928	5.81	131	9.7	
13	CL41	CL17	32	0.0041	.949	.922	5.70	131	13.1	
12	CL19	CL21	10	0.0045	.945	.916	5.65	132	6.4	
11	CL39	CL15	9	0.0052	.940	.909	5.60	134	6.3	
10	CL76	CL27	6	0.0075	.932	.900	5.25	133	18.1	
9	CL23	CL11	15	0.0130	.919	.890	4.20	125	12.4	
8	CL10	Afghanistan	7	0.0134	.906	.879	3.55	122	7.3	
7	CL9	CL25	17	0.0217	.884	.864	2.26	114	11.6	
6	CL8	CL20	14	0.0239	.860	.846	1.42	112	10.5	
5	CL14	CL13	45	0.0307	.829	.822	0.65	112	59.2	
4	CL16	CL7	28	0.0323	.797	.788	0.57	122	14.8	
3	CL12	CL6	24	0.0323	.765	.732	1.84	153	11.6	
2	CL3	CL4	52	0.1782	.587	.613	-.82	135	48.9	
1	CL5	CL2	97	0.5866	.000	.000	0.00	.	135	

Figure 23.2. Cluster Generation History and R-Square Values

Next listed is the squared multiple correlation, R^2, which is the proportion of variance accounted for by the clusters. Figure 23.2 shows that, when the data are grouped into three clusters, the proportion of variance accounted for by the clusters (R^2) is about 77%. The approximate expected value of R^2 is given in the column labeled "ERSQ."

The next three columns display the values of the cubic clustering criterion (CCC), pseudo F (PSF), and t^2 (PST2) statistics. These statistics are useful in determining the number of clusters in the data.

Values of the cubic clustering criterion greater than 2 or 3 indicate good clusters; values between 0 and 2 indicate potential clusters, but they should be considered with caution; large negative values can indicate outliers. In Figure 23.2, there is a local peak of the CCC when the number of clusters is 3. The CCC drops at 4 clusters and then steadily increases, levelling off at 11 clusters.

Another method of judging the number of clusters in a data set is to look at the pseudo F statistic (PSF). Relatively large values indicate a stopping point. Reading down the PSF column, you can see that this method indicates a possible stopping point at 11 clusters and another at 3 clusters.

A general rule for interpreting the values of the pseudo t^2 statistic is to move down the column until you find the first value markedly larger than the previous value and move back up the column by one cluster. Moving down the PST2 column, you can see possible clustering levels at 11 clusters, 6 clusters, 3 clusters, and 2 clusters.

The final column in Figure 23.2 lists ties for minimum distance; a blank value indicates the absence of a tie.

These statistics indicate that the data can be clustered into 11 clusters or 3 clusters. The following statements examine the results of clustering the data into 3 clusters.

A graphical view of the clustering process can often be helpful in interpreting the clusters. The following statements use the TREE procedure to produce a tree diagram of the clusters:

```
goptions vsize=8in htext=1pct htitle=2.5pct;
axis1 order=(0 to 1 by 0.2);
proc tree data=Tree out=New nclusters=3
          graphics haxis=axis1 horizontal;
   height _rsq_;
   copy can1 can2 ;
   id country;
run;
```

The AXIS1 statement defines axis parameters that are used in the TREE procedure. The ORDER= option specifies the data values in the order in which they should appear on the axis.

The preceding statements use the SAS data set Tree as input. The OUT= option creates an output SAS data set named New to contain information on cluster membership. The NCLUSTERS= option specifies the number of clusters desired in the data set New.

The GRAPHICS option directs the procedure to use high resolution graphics. The HAXIS= option specifies AXIS1 to customize the appearance of the horizontal axis. Use this option only when the GRAPHICS option is in effect. The HORIZONTAL option orients the tree diagram horizontally. The HEIGHT statement specifies the variable _RSQ_ (R^2) as the height variable.

The COPY statement copies the canonical variables can1 and can2 (computed in the ACECLUS procedure) into the output SAS data set New. Thus, the SAS output data set New contains information for three clusters and the first two of the original canonical variables.

Figure 23.3 displays the tree diagram. The figure provides a graphical view of the information in Figure 23.2. As the number of branches grows to the left from the root, the R^2 approaches 1; the first three clusters (branches of the tree) account for over half of the variation (about 77%, from Figure 23.2). In other words, only three clusters are necessary to explain over three-fourths of the variation.

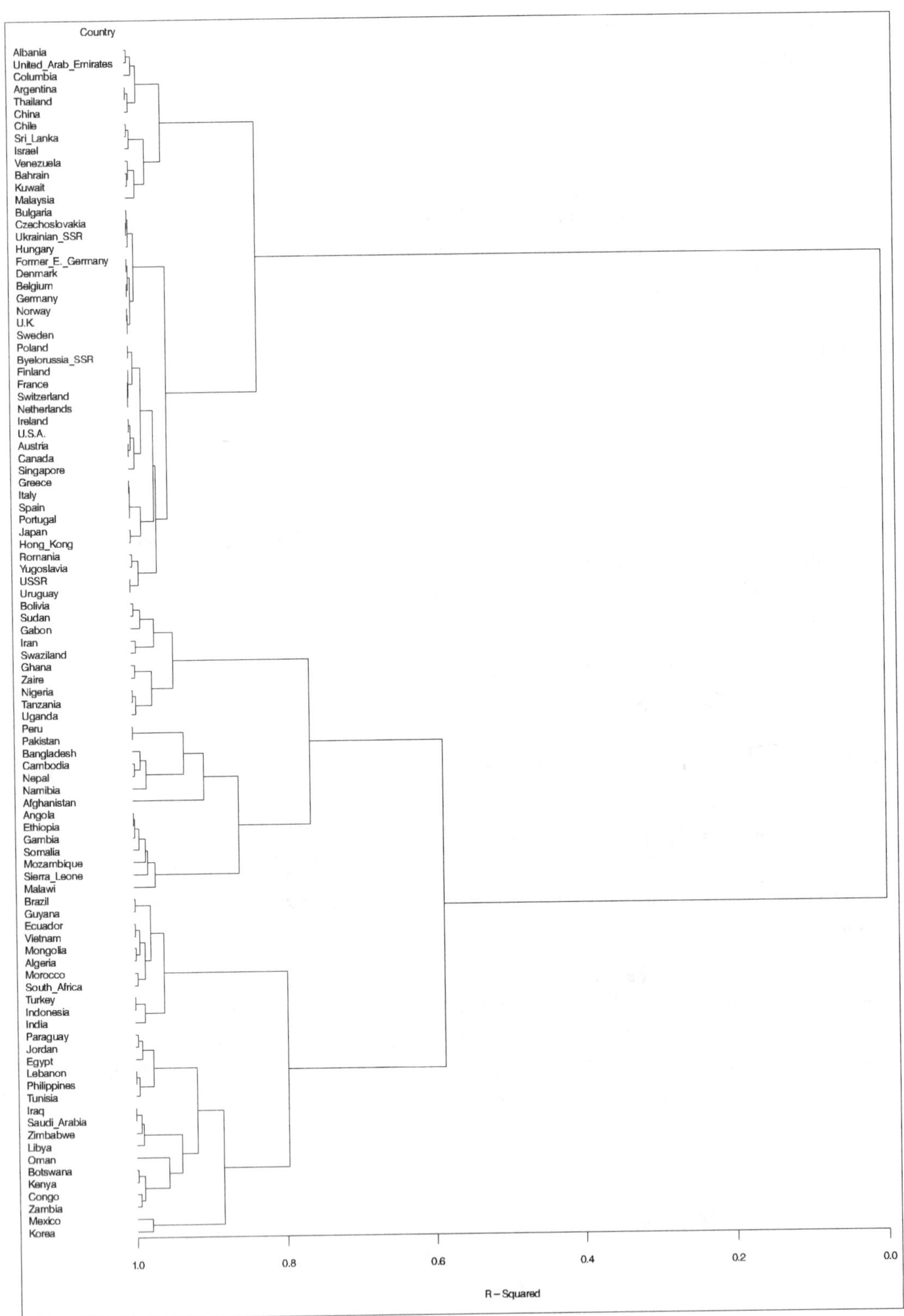

Figure 23.3. Tree Diagram of Clusters versus R-Square Values

The following statements invoke the GPLOT procedure on the SAS data set New.

```
legend1 frame cframe=ligr cborder=black
        position=center value=(justify=center);

axis1 label=(angle=90 rotate=0) minor=none order=(-10 to 20 by 5);
axis2 minor=none order=(-10 to 20 by 5);

proc gplot data=New ;
   plot can2*can1=cluster/frame cframe=ligr
                  legend=legend1 vaxis=axis1 haxis=axis2;
run;
```

The PLOT statement requests a plot of the two canonical variables, using the value of the variable cluster as the identification variable.

Figure 23.4 displays the separation of the clusters when three clusters are calculated. The plotting symbol is the cluster number.

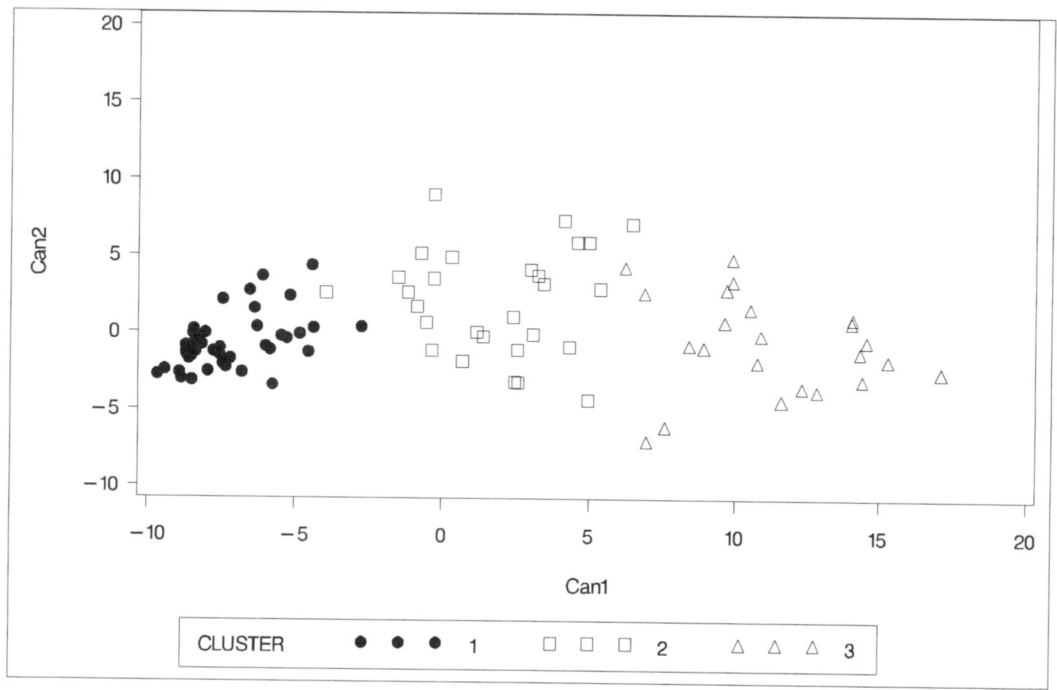

Figure 23.4. Plot of Canonical Variables and Cluster for Three Clusters

The statistics in Figure 23.2, the tree diagram in Figure 23.3, and the plot of the canonical variables assist in the determination of clusters in the data. There seems to be reasonable separation in the clusters. However, you must use this information, along with experience and knowledge of the field, to help in deciding the correct number of clusters.

Syntax

The following statements are available in the CLUSTER procedure.

PROC CLUSTER *METHOD = name < options >* **;**
BY *variables* **;**
COPY *variables* **;**
FREQ *variable* **;**
ID *variable* **;**
RMSSTD *variable* **;**
VAR *variables* **;**

Only the PROC CLUSTER statement is required, except that the FREQ statement is required when the RMSSTD statement is used; otherwise the FREQ statement is optional. Usually only the VAR statement and possibly the ID and COPY statements are needed in addition to the PROC CLUSTER statement. The rest of this section provides detailed syntax information for each of the preceding statements, beginning with the PROC CLUSTER statement. The remaining statements are covered in alphabetical order.

PROC CLUSTER Statement

PROC CLUSTER *METHOD=name < options >* **;**

The PROC CLUSTER statement starts the CLUSTER procedure, identifies a clustering method, and optionally identifies details for clustering methods, data sets, data processing, and displayed output. The METHOD= specification determines the clustering method used by the procedure. Any one of the following 11 methods can be specified for *name*:

AVERAGE | AVE
requests average linkage (group average, unweighted pair-group method using arithmetic averages, UPGMA). Distance data are squared unless you specify the NOSQUARE option.

CENTROID | CEN
requests the centroid method (unweighted pair-group method using centroids, UPGMC, centroid sorting, weighted-group method). Distance data are squared unless you specify the NOSQUARE option.

COMPLETE | COM
requests complete linkage (furthest neighbor, maximum method, diameter method, rank order typal analysis). To reduce distortion of clusters by outliers, the TRIM= option is recommended.

DENSITY | DEN
requests density linkage, which is a class of clustering methods using nonparametric probability density estima-

	tion. You must also specify one of the K=, R=, or HYBRID options to indicate the type of density estimation to be used. See also the MODE= and DIM= options in this section.
EML	requests maximum-likelihood hierarchical clustering for mixtures of spherical multivariate normal distributions with equal variances but possibly unequal mixing proportions. Use METHOD=EML only with coordinate data. See the PENALTY= option on page 849. The NONORM option does not affect the reported likelihood values but does affect other unrelated criteria. The EML method is much slower than the other methods in the CLUSTER procedure.
FLEXIBLE | FLE	requests the Lance-Williams flexible-beta method. See the BETA= option in this section.
MCQUITTY | MCQ	requests McQuitty's similarity analysis, which is weighted average linkage, weighted pair-group method using arithmetic averages (WPGMA).
MEDIAN | MED	requests Gower's median method, which is weighted pair-group method using centroids (WPGMC). Distance data are squared unless you specify the NOSQUARE option.
SINGLE | SIN	requests single linkage (nearest neighbor, minimum method, connectedness method, elementary linkage analysis, or dendritic method). To reduce chaining, you can use the TRIM= option with METHOD=SINGLE.
TWOSTAGE | TWO	requests two-stage density linkage. You must also specify the K=, R=, or HYBRID option to indicate the type of density estimation to be used. See also the MODE= and DIM= options in this section.
WARD | WAR	requests Ward's minimum-variance method (error sum of squares, trace W). Distance data are squared unless you specify the NOSQUARE option. To reduce distortion by outliers, the TRIM= option is recommended. See the NONORM option.

The following table summarizes the options in the PROC CLUSTER statement.

Tasks	Options
Specify input and output data sets	
specify input data set	DATA=
create output data set	OUTTREE=
Specify clustering methods	
specify clustering method	METHOD=
beta for flexible beta method	BETA=
minimum number of members for modal clusters	MODE=
penalty coefficient for maximum-likelihood	PENALTY=
Wong's hybrid clustering method	HYBRID
Control data processing prior to clustering	
suppress computation of eigenvalues	NOEIGEN
suppress normalizing of distances	NONORM
suppress squaring of distances	NOSQUARE
standardize variables	STANDARD
omit points with low probability densities	TRIM=
Control density estimation	
dimensionality for estimates	DIM=
number of neighbors for kth-nearest-neighbor	K=
radius of sphere of support for uniform-kernel	R=
Suppress checking for ties	NOTIE
Control display of the cluster history	
display cubic clustering criterion	CCC
suppress display of ID values	NOID
specify number of generations to display	PRINT=
display pseudo F and t^2 statistics	PSEUDO
display root-mean-square standard deviation	RMSSTD
display R^2 and semipartial R^2	RSQUARE
Control other aspects of output	
suppress display of all output	NOPRINT
display simple summary statistics	SIMPLE

The following list provides details on these options.

BETA=*n*

specifies the beta parameter for METHOD=FLEXIBLE. The value of n should be less than 1, usually between 0 and -1. By default, BETA=-0.25. Milligan (1987) suggests a somewhat smaller value, perhaps -0.5, for data with many outliers.

CCC

displays the cubic clustering criterion and approximate expected R^2 under the uniform null hypothesis (Sarle 1983). The statistics associated with the RSQUARE option, R^2 and semipartial R^2, are also displayed. The CCC option applies only to coordinate data. The CCC option is not appropriate with METHOD=SINGLE because of the method's tendency to chop off tails of distributions.

DATA=*SAS-data-set*

names the input data set containing observations to be clustered. By default, the procedure uses the most recently created SAS data set. If the data set is TYPE=DISTANCE, the data are interpreted as a distance matrix; the number of variables must equal the number of observations in the data set or in each BY group. The distances are assumed to be Euclidean, but the procedure accepts other types of distances or dissimilarities. If the data set is not TYPE=DISTANCE, the data are interpreted as coordinates in a Euclidean space, and Euclidean distances are computed. For more on TYPE=DISTANCE data sets, see Appendix A, "Special SAS Data Sets."

You cannot use a TYPE=CORR data set as input to PROC CLUSTER, since the procedure uses dissimilarity measures. Instead, you can use a DATA step or the IML procedure to extract the correlation matrix from a TYPE=CORR data set and transform the values to dissimilarities such as $1-r$ or $1-r^2$, where r is the correlation.

All methods produce the same results when used with coordinate data as when used with Euclidean distances computed from the coordinates. However, the DIM= option must be used with distance data if you specify METHOD=TWOSTAGE or METHOD=DENSITY or if you specify the TRIM= option.

Certain methods that are most naturally defined in terms of coordinates require *squared* Euclidean distances to be used in the combinatorial distance formulas (Lance and Williams 1967). For this reason, distance data are automatically squared when used with METHOD=AVERAGE, METHOD=CENTROID, METHOD=MEDIAN, or METHOD=WARD. If you want the combinatorial formulas to be applied to the (unsquared) distances with these methods, use the NOSQUARE option.

DIM=*n*

specifies the dimensionality used when computing density estimates with the TRIM= option, METHOD=DENSITY, or METHOD=TWOSTAGE. The values of n must be greater than or equal to 1. The default is the number of variables if the data are coordinates; the default is 1 if the data are distances.

HYBRID

requests Wong's (1982) hybrid clustering method in which density estimates are computed from a preliminary cluster analysis using the k-means method. The DATA= data set must contain means, frequencies, and root-mean-square standard deviations of the preliminary clusters (see the FREQ and RMSSTD statements). To use HYBRID, you must use either a FREQ statement or a DATA= data set that contains a _FREQ_ variable, and you must also use either an RMSSTD statement or a DATA= data set that contains a _RMSSTD_ variable.

The MEAN= data set produced by the FASTCLUS procedure is suitable for input to the CLUSTER procedure for hybrid clustering. Since this data set contains _FREQ_ and _RMSSTD_ variables, you can use it as input and then omit the FREQ and RMSSTD statements.

You must specify either METHOD=DENSITY or METHOD=TWOSTAGE with the HYBRID option. You cannot use this option in combination with the TRIM=, K=, or R= option.

K=*n*

specifies the number of neighbors to use for kth-nearest-neighbor density estimation (Silverman 1986, pp. 19–21 and 96–99). The number of neighbors (n) must be at least two but less than the number of observations. See the MODE= option, which follows.

If you request an analysis that requires density estimation (the TRIM= option, METHOD=DENSITY, or METHOD=TWOSTAGE), you must specify one of the K=, HYBRID, or R= options.

MODE=*n*

specifies that, when two clusters are joined, each must have at least n members for either cluster to be designated a modal cluster. If you specify MODE=1, each cluster must also have a maximum density greater than the fusion density for either cluster to be designated a modal cluster.

Use the MODE= option only with METHOD=DENSITY or METHOD=TWOSTAGE. With METHOD=TWOSTAGE, the MODE= option affects the number of modal clusters formed. With METHOD=DENSITY, the MODE= option does not affect the clustering process but does determine the number of modal clusters reported on the output and identified by the _MODE_ variable in the output data set.

If you specify the K= option, the default value of MODE= is the same as the value of K= because the use of kth-nearest-neighbor density estimation limits the resolution that can be obtained for clusters with fewer than k members. If you do not specify the K= option, the default is MODE=2.

If you specify MODE=0, the default value is used instead of 0.

If you specify a FREQ statement or if a _FREQ_ variable appears in the input data set, the MODE= value is compared with the number of actual observations in the clusters being joined, not with the sum of the frequencies in the clusters.

NOEIGEN

suppresses computation of eigenvalues for the cubic clustering criterion. Specifying the NOEIGEN option saves time if the number of variables is large, but it should be used only if the variables are nearly uncorrelated or if you are not interested in the cubic clustering criterion. If you specify the NOEIGEN option and the variables are highly correlated, the cubic clustering criterion may be very liberal. The NOEIGEN option applies only to coordinate data.

NOID

suppresses the display of ID values for the clusters joined at each generation of the cluster history.

NONORM

prevents the distances from being normalized to unit mean or unit root mean square with most methods. With METHOD=WARD, the NONORM option prevents the between-cluster sum of squares from being normalized by the total sum of squares to yield a squared semipartial correlation. The NONORM option does not affect the reported likelihood values with METHOD=EML, but it does affect other unrelated criteria, such as the _DIST_ variable.

NOPRINT

suppresses the display of all output. Note that this option temporarily disables the Output Delivery System (ODS). For more information, see Chapter 15, "Using the Output Delivery System."

NOSQUARE

prevents input distances from being squared with METHOD=AVERAGE, METHOD=CENTROID, METHOD=MEDIAN, or METHOD=WARD.

If you specify the NOSQUARE option with distance data, the data are assumed to be squared Euclidean distances for computing R-squared and related statistics defined in a Euclidean coordinate system.

If you specify the NOSQUARE option with coordinate data with METHOD=CENTROID, METHOD=MEDIAN, or METHOD=WARD, then the combinatorial formula is applied to unsquared Euclidean distances. The resulting cluster distances do not have their usual Euclidean interpretation and are, therefore, labeled "False" in the output.

NOTIE

prevents PROC CLUSTER from checking for ties for minimum distance between clusters at each generation of the cluster history. If your data are measured with such sufficient precision that ties are unlikely, then you can specify the NOTIE option to reduce slightly the time and space required by the procedure. See the section "Ties" on page 865.

OUTTREE=*SAS-data-set*

creates an output data set that can be used by the TREE procedure to draw a tree diagram. You must give the data set a two-level name to save it. Refer to *SAS Language Reference: Concepts* for a discussion of permanent data sets. If you omit the OUTTREE= option, the data set is named using the DATAn convention and is not permanently saved. If you do not want to create an output data set, use OUTTREE=_NULL_.

PENALTY=*p*

specifies the penalty coefficient used with METHOD=EML. See the section "Clustering Methods" on page 854. Values for p must be greater than zero. By default, PENALTY=2.

PRINT=*n* | P=*n*

specifies the number of generations of the cluster history to display. The P= option displays the latest n generations; for example, P=5 displays the cluster history from 1 cluster through 5 clusters. The value of P= must be a nonnegative integer. The default is to display all generations. Specify PRINT=0 to suppress the cluster history.

PSEUDO

displays pseudo F and t^2 statistics. This option is effective only when the data are coordinates or when METHOD=AVERAGE, METHOD=CENTROID, or METHOD=WARD. See the section "Miscellaneous Formulas" on page 861. The PSEUDO option is not appropriate with METHOD=SINGLE because of the method's tendency to chop off tails of distributions.

R=*n*

specifies the radius of the sphere of support for uniform-kernel density estimation (Silverman 1986, pp. 11–13 and 75–94). The value of R= must be greater than zero.

If you request an analysis that requires density estimation (the TRIM= option, METHOD=DENSITY, or METHOD=TWOSTAGE), you must specify one of the K=, HYBRID, or R= options.

RMSSTD

displays the root-mean-square standard deviation of each cluster. This option is effective only when the data are coordinates or when METHOD=AVERAGE, METHOD=CENTROID, or METHOD=WARD. See the section "Miscellaneous Formulas" on page 861.

RSQUARE | RSQ

displays the R^2 and semipartial R^2. This option is effective only when the data are coordinates or when METHOD=AVERAGE or METHOD=CENTROID. The R^2 and semipartial R^2 statistics are always displayed with METHOD=WARD. See the section "Miscellaneous Formulas" on page 861.

SIMPLE | S

displays means, standard deviations, skewness, kurtosis, and a coefficient of bimodality. The SIMPLE option applies only to coordinate data. See the section "Miscellaneous Formulas" on page 861.

STANDARD | STD

standardizes the variables to mean 0 and standard deviation 1. The STANDARD option applies only to coordinate data.

TRIM=*p*

omits points with low estimated probability densities from the analysis. Valid values for the TRIM= option are $0 \leq p < 100$. If $p < 1$, then p is the proportion of observations omitted. If $p \geq 1$, then p is interpreted as a percentage. A specification of TRIM=10, which trims 10 percent of the points, is a reasonable value for many data sets. Densities are estimated by the kth-nearest-neighbor or uniform-kernel methods. Trimmed points are indicated by a negative value of the _FREQ_ variable in the OUTTREE= data set.

You must use either the K= or R= option when you use TRIM=. You cannot use the HYBRID option in combination with TRIM=, so you may want to use the DIM= option instead. If you specify the STANDARD option in combination with TRIM=, the variables are standardized both before and after trimming.

The TRIM= option is useful for removing outliers and reducing chaining. Trimming is highly recommended with METHOD=WARD or METHOD=COMPLETE because clusters from these methods can be severely distorted by outliers. Trimming is also valuable with METHOD=SINGLE since single linkage is the method most susceptible to chaining. Most other methods also benefit from trimming. However, trimming is unnecessary with METHOD=TWOSTAGE or METHOD=DENSITY when kth-nearest-neighbor density estimation is used.

Use of the TRIM= option may spuriously inflate the cubic clustering criterion and the pseudo F and t^2 statistics. Trimming only outliers improves the accuracy of the statistics, but trimming saddle regions between clusters yields excessively large values.

BY Statement

BY *variables* ;

You can specify a BY statement with PROC CLUSTER to obtain separate analyses on observations in groups defined by the BY variables. When a BY statement appears, the procedure expects the input data set to be sorted in order of the BY variables.

If your input data set is not sorted in ascending order, use one of the following alternatives:

- Sort the data using the SORT procedure with a similar BY statement.
- Specify the BY statement option NOTSORTED or DESCENDING in the BY statement for the CLUSTER procedure. The NOTSORTED option does not mean that the data are unsorted but rather that the data are arranged in groups (according to values of the BY variables) and that these groups are not necessarily in alphabetical or increasing numeric order.
- Create an index on the BY variables using the DATASETS procedure.

For more information on the BY statement, refer to the discussion in *SAS Language Reference: Concepts*. For more information on the DATASETS procedure, refer to the discussion in the *SAS Procedures Guide*.

COPY Statement

COPY *variables* ;

The variables in the COPY statement are copied from the input data set to the OUTTREE= data set. Observations in the OUTTREE= data set that represent clusters of more than one observation from the input data set have missing values for the COPY variables.

FREQ Statement

FREQ *variable* ;

If one variable in the input data set represents the frequency of occurrence for other values in the observation, specify the variable's name in a FREQ statement. PROC CLUSTER then treats the data set as if each observation appeared n times, where n is the value of the FREQ variable for the observation. Noninteger values of the FREQ variable are truncated to the largest integer less than the FREQ value.

If you omit the FREQ statement but the DATA= data set contains a variable called _FREQ_, then frequencies are obtained from the _FREQ_ variable. If neither a FREQ statement nor a _FREQ_ variable is present, each observation is assumed to have a frequency of one.

If each observation in the DATA= data set represents a cluster (for example, clusters formed by PROC FASTCLUS), the variable specified in the FREQ statement should give the number of original observations in each cluster.

If you specify the RMSSTD statement, a FREQ statement is required. A FREQ statement or _FREQ_ variable is required when you specify the HYBRID option.

With most clustering methods, the same clusters are obtained from a data set with a FREQ variable as from a similar data set without a FREQ variable, if each observation is repeated as many times as the value of the FREQ variable in the first data set. The FLEXIBLE method can yield different results due to the nature of the combinatorial formula. The DENSITY and TWOSTAGE methods are also exceptions because two identical observations can be absorbed one at a time by a cluster with a higher density. If you are using a FREQ statement with either the DENSITY or TWOSTAGE method, see the MODE=option on page 848.

ID Statement

ID *variable* ;

The values of the ID variable identify observations in the displayed cluster history and in the OUTTREE= data set. If the ID statement is omitted, each observation is denoted by OBn, where n is the observation number.

RMSSTD Statement

RMSSTD *variable* ;

If the coordinates in the DATA= data set represent cluster means (for example, formed by the FASTCLUS procedure), you can obtain accurate statistics in the cluster histories for METHOD=AVERAGE, METHOD=CENTROID, or METHOD=WARD if the data set contains

- a variable giving the number of original observations in each cluster (see the discussion of the FREQ statement earlier in this chapter)
- a variable giving the root-mean-square standard deviation of each cluster

Specify the name of the variable containing root-mean-square standard deviations in the RMSSTD statement. If you specify the RMSSTD statement, you must also specify a FREQ statement.

If you omit the RMSSTD statement but the DATA= data set contains a variable called _RMSSTD_, then root-mean-square standard deviations are obtained from the _RMSSTD_ variable.

An RMSSTD statement or _RMSSTD_ variable is required when you specify the HYBRID option.

A data set created by FASTCLUS using the MEAN= option contains _FREQ_ and _RMSSTD_ variables, so you do not have to use FREQ and RMSSTD statements when using such a data set as input to the CLUSTER procedure.

VAR Statement

VAR *variables* ;

The VAR statement lists numeric variables to be used in the cluster analysis. If you omit the VAR statement, all numeric variables not listed in other statements are used.

Details

Clustering Methods

The following notation is used, with lowercase symbols generally pertaining to observations and uppercase symbols pertaining to clusters:

n	number of observations
v	number of variables if data are coordinates
G	number of clusters at any given level of the hierarchy
x_i or $\mathbf{x}_i$	ith observation (row vector if coordinate data)
C_K	Kth cluster, subset of $\{1, 2, \ldots, n\}$
N_K	number of observations in C_K
$\bar{\mathbf{x}}$	sample mean vector
$\bar{\mathbf{x}}_K$	mean vector for cluster C_K
$\lVert\mathbf{x}\rVert$	Euclidean length of the vector $\mathbf{x}$, that is, the square root of the sum of the squares of the elements of $\mathbf{x}$
T	$\sum_{i=1}^{n} \lVert\mathbf{x}_i - \bar{\mathbf{x}}\rVert^2$
W_K	$\sum_{i \in C_k} \lVert\mathbf{x}_i - \bar{\mathbf{x}}_K\rVert^2$
P_G	$\sum W_J$, where summation is over the G clusters at the Gth level of the hierarchy
B_{KL}	$W_M - W_K - W_L$ if $C_M = C_K \cup C_L$
$d(\mathbf{x}, \mathbf{y})$	any distance or dissimilarity measure between observations or vectors $\mathbf{x}$ and $\mathbf{y}$
D_{KL}	any distance or dissimilarity measure between clusters C_K and C_L

The distance between two clusters can be defined either directly or combinatorially (Lance and Williams 1967), that is, by an equation for updating a distance matrix when two clusters are joined. In all of the following combinatorial formulas, it is assumed that clusters C_K and C_L are merged to form C_M, and the formula gives the distance between the new cluster C_M and any other cluster C_J.

For an introduction to most of the methods used in the CLUSTER procedure, refer to Massart and Kaufman (1983).

Average Linkage

The following method is obtained by specifying METHOD=AVERAGE. The distance between two clusters is defined by

$$D_{KL} = \frac{1}{N_K N_L} \sum_{i \in C_K} \sum_{j \in C_L} d(x_i, x_j)$$

If $d(\mathbf{x},\mathbf{y}) = \|\mathbf{x}-\mathbf{y}\|^2$, then

$$D_{KL} = \|\bar{\mathbf{x}}_K - \bar{\mathbf{x}}_L\|^2 + \frac{W_K}{N_K} + \frac{W_L}{N_L}$$

The combinatorial formula is

$$D_{JM} = \frac{N_K D_{JK} + N_L D_{JL}}{N_M}$$

In average linkage the distance between two clusters is the average distance between pairs of observations, one in each cluster. Average linkage tends to join clusters with small variances, and it is slightly biased toward producing clusters with the same variance.

Average linkage was originated by Sokal and Michener (1958).

Centroid Method

The following method is obtained by specifying METHOD=CENTROID. The distance between two clusters is defined by

$$D_{KL} = \|\bar{\mathbf{x}}_K - \bar{\mathbf{x}}_L\|^2$$

If $d(\mathbf{x},\mathbf{y}) = \|\mathbf{x}-\mathbf{y}\|^2$, then the combinatorial formula is

$$D_{JM} = \frac{N_K D_{JK} + N_L D_{JL}}{N_M} - \frac{N_K N_L D_{KL}}{N_M^2}$$

In the centroid method, the distance between two clusters is defined as the (squared) Euclidean distance between their centroids or means. The centroid method is more robust to outliers than most other hierarchical methods but in other respects may not perform as well as Ward's method or average linkage (Milligan 1980).

The centroid method was originated by Sokal and Michener (1958).

Complete Linkage

The following method is obtained by specifying METHOD=COMPLETE. The distance between two clusters is defined by

$$D_{KL} = \max_{i \in C_K} \max_{j \in C_L} d(x_i, x_j)$$

The combinatorial formula is

$$D_{JM} = \max(D_{JK}, D_{JL})$$

In complete linkage, the distance between two clusters is the maximum distance between an observation in one cluster and an observation in the other cluster. Complete linkage is strongly biased toward producing clusters with roughly equal diameters, and it can be severely distorted by moderate outliers (Milligan 1980).

Complete linkage was originated by Sorensen (1948).

Density Linkage

The phrase *density linkage* is used here to refer to a class of clustering methods using nonparametric probability density estimates (for example, Hartigan 1975, pp. 205–212; Wong 1982; Wong and Lane 1983). Density linkage consists of two steps:

1. A new dissimilarity measure, d^*, based on density estimates and adjacencies is computed. If x_i and x_j are adjacent (the definition of *adjacency* depends on the method of density estimation), then $d^*(x_i, x_j)$ is the reciprocal of an estimate of the density midway between x_i and x_j; otherwise, $d^*(x_i, x_j)$ is infinite.

2. A single linkage cluster analysis is performed using d^*.

The CLUSTER procedure supports three types of density linkage: the kth-nearest-neighbor method, the uniform kernel method, and Wong's hybrid method. These are obtained by using METHOD=DENSITY and the K=, R=, and HYBRID options, respectively.

kth-Nearest Neighbor Method

The kth-nearest-neighbor method (Wong and Lane 1983) uses kth-nearest neighbor density estimates. Let $r_k(x)$ be the distance from point x to the kth-nearest observation, where k is the value specified for the K= option. Consider a closed sphere centered at x with radius $r_k(x)$. The estimated density at x, $f(x)$, is the proportion of observations within the sphere divided by the volume of the sphere. The new dissimilarity measure is computed as

$$d^*(x_i, x_j) = \begin{cases} \frac{1}{2}\left(\frac{1}{f(x_i)} + \frac{1}{f(x_j)}\right) & \text{if } d(x_i, x_j) \le \max(r_k(x_i), r_k(x_j)) \\ \infty & \text{otherwise} \end{cases}$$

Wong and Lane (1983) show that kth-nearest-neighbor density linkage is strongly set consistent for high-density (density-contour) clusters if k is chosen such that $k/n \to 0$ and $k/\ln(n) \to \infty$ as $n \to \infty$. Wong and Schaack (1982) discuss methods for estimating the number of population clusters using kth-nearest-neighbor clustering.

Uniform-Kernel Method

The uniform-kernel method uses uniform-kernel density estimates. Let r be the value specified for the R= option. Consider a closed sphere centered at point x with radius r. The estimated density at x, $f(x)$, is the proportion of observations within the sphere divided by the volume of the sphere. The new dissimilarity measure is computed as

$$d^*(x_i, x_j) = \begin{cases} \frac{1}{2}\left(\frac{1}{f(x_i)} + \frac{1}{f(x_j)}\right) & \text{if } d(x_i, x_j) \le r \\ \infty & \text{otherwise} \end{cases}$$

Wong's Hybrid Method

Wong's (1982) hybrid clustering method uses density estimates based on a preliminary cluster analysis by the k-means method. The preliminary clustering can be done by the FASTCLUS procedure, using the MEAN= option to create a data set containing cluster means, frequencies, and root-mean-square standard deviations. This data set is used as input to the CLUSTER procedure, and the HYBRID option is specified with METHOD=DENSITY to request the hybrid analysis. The hybrid method is appropriate for very large data sets but should not be used with small data sets, say fewer than 100 observations in the original data. The term *preliminary cluster* refers to an observation in the DATA= data set.

For preliminary cluster C_K, N_K and W_K are obtained from the input data set, as are the cluster means or the distances between the cluster means. Preliminary clusters C_K and C_L are considered adjacent if the midpoint between $\bar{x}_K$ and $\bar{\mathbf{x}}_L$ is closer to either $\bar{\mathbf{x}}_K$ or $\bar{\mathbf{x}}_L$ than to any other preliminary cluster mean or, equivalently, if $d^2(\bar{\mathbf{x}}_K, \bar{\mathbf{x}}_L) < d^2(\bar{\mathbf{x}}_K, \bar{\mathbf{x}}_M) + d^2(\bar{\mathbf{x}}_L, \bar{\mathbf{x}}_M)$ for all other preliminary clusters C_M, $M \neq K$ or L. The new dissimilarity measure is computed as

$$d^*(\bar{\mathbf{x}}_K, \bar{\mathbf{x}}_L) = \begin{cases} \frac{\left(W_K + W_L + \frac{1}{4}(N_K+N_L)d^2(\bar{\mathbf{x}}_K, \bar{\mathbf{x}}_L)\right)^{\frac{v}{2}}}{(N_K+N_L)^{1+\frac{v}{2}}} & \text{if } C_K \text{ and } C_L \text{ are adjacent} \\ \infty & \text{otherwise} \end{cases}$$

Using the K= and R= Options

The values of the K= and R= options are called *smoothing parameters*. Small values of K= or R= produce jagged density estimates and, as a consequence, many modes. Large values of K= or R= produce smoother density estimates and fewer modes. In the hybrid method, the smoothing parameter is the number of clusters in the preliminary cluster analysis. The number of modes in the final analysis tends to increase as the number of clusters in the preliminary analysis increases. Wong (1982) suggests using $n^{0.3}$ preliminary clusters, where n is the number of observations in the original data set. There is no general rule-of-thumb for selecting K= values. For all types of density linkage, you should repeat the analysis with several different values of the smoothing parameter (Wong and Schaack 1982).

There is no simple answer to the question of which smoothing parameter to use (Silverman 1986, pp. 43–61, 84–88, and 98–99). It is usually necessary to try several different smoothing parameters. A reasonable first guess for the R= option in many coordinate data sets is given by

$$\left[\frac{2^{v+2}(v+2)\Gamma(\frac{v}{2}+1)}{nv^2}\right]^{\frac{1}{v+4}} \sqrt{\sum_{l=1}^{v} s_l^2}$$

where s_l^2 is the standard deviation of the lth variable. The estimate for R= can be computed in a DATA step using the GAMMA function for Γ. This formula is derived under the assumption that the data are sampled from a multivariate normal distribution and tends, therefore, to be too large (oversmooth) if the true distribution is multimodal. Robust estimates of the standard deviations may be preferable if there are outliers. If the data are distances, the factor $\sum s_l^2$ can be replaced by an average (mean, trimmed mean, median, root-mean-square, and so on) distance divided by $\sqrt{2}$. To prevent outliers from appearing as separate clusters, you can also specify K=2, or more generally K=m, $m \geq 2$, which in most cases forces clusters to have at least m members.

If the variables all have unit variance (for example, if the STANDARD option is used), Table 23.1 can be used to obtain an initial guess for the R= option:

Table 23.1. Reasonable First Guess for the R= Option for Standardized Data

Number of	Number of Variables									
Observations	1	2	3	4	5	6	7	8	9	10
20	1.01	1.36	1.77	2.23	2.73	3.25	3.81	4.38	4.98	5.60
35	0.91	1.24	1.64	2.08	2.56	3.08	3.62	4.18	4.77	5.38
50	0.84	1.17	1.56	1.99	2.46	2.97	3.50	4.06	4.64	5.24
75	0.78	1.09	1.47	1.89	2.35	2.85	3.38	3.93	4.50	5.09
100	0.73	1.04	1.41	1.82	2.28	2.77	3.29	3.83	4.40	4.99
150	0.68	0.97	1.33	1.73	2.18	2.66	3.17	3.71	4.27	4.85
200	0.64	0.93	1.28	1.67	2.11	2.58	3.09	3.62	4.17	4.75
350	0.57	0.85	1.18	1.56	1.98	2.44	2.93	3.45	4.00	4.56
500	0.53	0.80	1.12	1.49	1.91	2.36	2.84	3.35	3.89	4.45
750	0.49	0.74	1.06	1.42	1.82	2.26	2.74	3.24	3.77	4.32
1000	0.46	0.71	1.01	1.37	1.77	2.20	2.67	3.16	3.69	4.23
1500	0.43	0.66	0.96	1.30	1.69	2.11	2.57	3.06	3.57	4.11
2000	0.40	0.63	0.92	1.25	1.63	2.05	2.50	2.99	3.49	4.03

Since infinite d^* values occur in density linkage, the final number of clusters can exceed one when there are wide gaps between the clusters or when the smoothing parameter results in little smoothing.

Density linkage applies no constraints to the shapes of the clusters and, unlike most other hierarchical clustering methods, is capable of recovering clusters with elongated or irregular shapes. Since density linkage employs less prior knowledge about the shape of the clusters than do methods restricted to compact clusters, density linkage is less effective at recovering compact clusters from small samples than are methods that always recover compact clusters, regardless of the data.

EML

The following method is obtained by specifying METHOD=EML. The distance between two clusters is given by

$$D_{KL} = nv \ln \left(1 + \frac{B_{KL}}{P_G} \right) - 2\left(N_M \ln(N_M) - N_K \ln(N_K) - N_L \ln(N_L)\right)$$

The EML method joins clusters to maximize the likelihood at each level of the hierarchy under the following assumptions.

- multivariate normal mixture
- equal spherical covariance matrices
- unequal sampling probabilities

The EML method is similar to Ward's minimum-variance method but removes the bias toward equal-sized clusters. Practical experience has indicated that EML is somewhat biased toward unequal-sized clusters. You can specify the PENALTY= option to adjust the degree of bias. If you specify PENALTY=p, the formula is modified to

$$D_{KL} = nv \ln \left(1 + \frac{B_{KL}}{P_G}\right) - p\left(N_M \ln(N_M) - N_K \ln(N_K) - N_L \ln(N_L)\right)$$

The EML method was derived by W.S. Sarle of SAS Institute Inc. from the maximum-likelihood formula obtained by Symons (1981, p. 37, equation 8) for disjoint clustering. There are currently no other published references on the EML method.

Flexible-Beta Method

The following method is obtained by specifying METHOD=FLEXIBLE. The combinatorial formula is

$$D_{JM} = (D_{JK} + D_{JL})\frac{1-b}{2} + D_{KL}b$$

where b is the value of the BETA= option, or -0.25 by default.

The flexible-beta method was developed by Lance and Williams (1967). See also Milligan (1987).

McQuitty's Similarity Analysis

The following method is obtained by specifying METHOD=MCQUITTY. The combinatorial formula is

$$D_{JM} = \frac{D_{JK} + D_{JL}}{2}$$

The method was independently developed by Sokal and Michener (1958) and McQuitty (1966).

Median Method

The following method is obtained by specifying METHOD=MEDIAN. If $d(\mathbf{x}, \mathbf{y}) = \|\mathbf{x} - \mathbf{y}\|^2$, then the combinatorial formula is

$$D_{JM} = \frac{D_{JK} + D_{JL}}{2} - \frac{D_{KL}}{4}$$

The median method was developed by Gower (1967).

Single Linkage

The following method is obtained by specifying METHOD=SINGLE. The distance between two clusters is defined by

$$D_{KL} = \min_{i \in C_K} \min_{j \in C_L} d(x_i, x_j)$$

The combinatorial formula is

$$D_{JM} = \min(D_{JK}, D_{JL})$$

In single linkage, the distance between two clusters is the minimum distance between an observation in one cluster and an observation in the other cluster. Single linkage has many desirable theoretical properties (Jardine and Sibson 1971; Fisher and Van Ness 1971; Hartigan 1981) but has fared poorly in Monte Carlo studies (for example, Milligan 1980). By imposing no constraints on the shape of clusters, single linkage sacrifices performance in the recovery of compact clusters in return for the ability to detect elongated and irregular clusters. You must also recognize that single linkage tends to chop off the tails of distributions before separating the main clusters (Hartigan 1981). The notorious chaining tendency of single linkage can be alleviated by specifying the TRIM= option (Wishart 1969, pp. 296–298).

Density linkage and two-stage density linkage retain most of the virtues of single linkage while performing better with compact clusters and possessing better asymptotic properties (Wong and Lane 1983).

Single linkage was originated by Florek et al. (1951a, 1951b) and later reinvented by McQuitty (1957) and Sneath (1957).

Two-Stage Density Linkage

If you specify METHOD=DENSITY, the modal clusters often merge before all the points in the tails have clustered. The option METHOD=TWOSTAGE is a modification of density linkage that ensures that all points are assigned to modal clusters before the modal clusters are allowed to join. The CLUSTER procedure supports the same three varieties of two-stage density linkage as of ordinary density linkage: kth-nearest neighbor, uniform kernel, and hybrid.

In the first stage, disjoint modal clusters are formed. The algorithm is the same as the single linkage algorithm ordinarily used with density linkage, with one exception: two clusters are joined only if at least one of the two clusters has fewer members than the number specified by the MODE= option. At the end of the first stage, each point belongs to one modal cluster.

In the second stage, the modal clusters are hierarchically joined by single linkage. The final number of clusters can exceed one when there are wide gaps between the clusters or when the smoothing parameter is small.

Each stage forms a tree that can be plotted by the TREE procedure. By default, the TREE procedure plots the tree from the first stage. To obtain the tree for the second stage, use the option HEIGHT=MODE in the PROC TREE statement. You can also produce a single tree diagram containing both stages, with the number of clusters as the height axis, by using the option HEIGHT=N in the PROC TREE statement. To produce an output data set from PROC TREE containing the modal clusters, use _HEIGHT_ for the HEIGHT variable (the default) and specify LEVEL=0.

Two-stage density linkage was developed by W.S. Sarle of SAS Institute Inc. There are currently no other published references on two-stage density linkage.

Ward's Minimum-Variance Method

The following method is obtained by specifying METHOD=WARD. The distance between two clusters is defined by

$$D_{KL} = B_{KL} = \frac{\|\bar{\mathbf{x}}_K - \bar{\mathbf{x}}_L\|^2}{\frac{1}{N_K} + \frac{1}{N_L}}$$

If $d(\mathbf{x}, \mathbf{y}) = \frac{1}{2}\|\mathbf{x} - \mathbf{y}\|^2$, then the combinatorial formula is

$$D_{JM} = \frac{(N_J + N_K)D_{JK} + (N_J + N_L)D_{JL} - N_J D_{KL}}{N_J + N_M}$$

In Ward's minimum-variance method, the distance between two clusters is the *ANOVA* sum of squares between the two clusters added up over all the variables. At each generation, the within-cluster sum of squares is minimized over all partitions obtainable by merging two clusters from the previous generation. The sums of squares are easier to interpret when they are divided by the total sum of squares to give proportions of variance (squared semipartial correlations).

Ward's method joins clusters to maximize the likelihood at each level of the hierarchy under the following assumptions:

- multivariate normal mixture
- equal spherical covariance matrices
- equal sampling probabilities

Ward's method tends to join clusters with a small number of observations, and it is strongly biased toward producing clusters with roughly the same number of observations. It is also very sensitive to outliers (Milligan 1980).

Ward (1963) describes a class of hierarchical clustering methods including the minimum variance method.

Miscellaneous Formulas

The root-mean-square standard deviation of a cluster C_K is

$$\text{RMSSTD} = \sqrt{\frac{W_K}{v(N_K - 1)}}$$

The R^2 statistic for a given level of the hierarchy is

$$R^2 = 1 - \frac{P_G}{T}$$

The squared semipartial correlation for joining clusters C_K and C_L is

$$\text{semipartial } R^2 = \frac{B_{KL}}{T}$$

The bimodality coefficient is

$$b = \frac{m_3^2 + 1}{m_4 + \frac{3(n-1)^2}{(n-2)(n-3)}}$$

where m_3 is skewness and m_4 is kurtosis. Values of b greater than 0.555 (the value for a uniform population) may indicate bimodal or multimodal marginal distributions. The maximum of 1.0 (obtained for the Bernoulli distribution) is obtained for a population with only two distinct values. Very heavy-tailed distributions have small values of b regardless of the number of modes.

Formulas for the cubic-clustering criterion and approximate expected R^2 are given in Sarle (1983).

The pseudo F statistic for a given level is

$$\text{pseudo } F = \frac{\frac{T-P_G}{G-1}}{\frac{P_G}{n-G}}$$

The pseudo t^2 statistic for joining C_K and C_L is

$$\text{pseudo } t^2 = \frac{B_{KL}}{\frac{W_K+W_L}{N_K+N_L-2}}$$

The pseudo F and t^2 statistics may be useful indicators of the number of clusters, but they are *not* distributed as F and t^2 random variables. If the data are independently sampled from a multivariate normal distribution with a scalar covariance matrix and if the clustering method allocates observations to clusters randomly (which no clustering method actually does), then the pseudo F statistic is distributed as an F random variable with $v(G-1)$ and $v(n-G)$ degrees of freedom. Under the same assumptions, the pseudo t^2 statistic is distributed as an F random variable with v and $v(N_K + N_L - 2)$ degrees of freedom. The pseudo t^2 statistic differs computationally from Hotelling's T^2 in that the latter uses a general symmetric covariance matrix instead of a scalar covariance matrix. The pseudo F statistic was suggested by Calinski and Harabasz (1974). The pseudo t^2 statistic is related to the $J_e(2)/J_e(1)$ statistic of Duda and Hart (1973) by

$$\frac{J_e(2)}{J_e(1)} = \frac{W_K + W_L}{W_M} = \frac{1}{1 + \frac{t^2}{N_K+N_L-2}}$$

See Milligan and Cooper (1985) and Cooper and Milligan (1988) regarding the performance of these statistics in estimating the number of population clusters. Conservative tests for the number of clusters using the pseudo F and t^2 statistics can be obtained by the Bonferroni approach (Hawkins, Muller, and ten Krooden 1982, pp. 337–340).

Ultrametrics

A dissimilarity measure $d(x, y)$ is called an *ultrametric* if it satisfies the following conditions:

- $d(x, x) = 0$ for all x
- $d(x, y) \geq 0$ for all x, y
- $d(x, y) = d(y, x)$ for all x, y
- $d(x, y) \leq \max(d(x, z), d(y, z))$ for all x, y, and z

Any hierarchical clustering method induces a dissimilarity measure on the observations, say $h(x_i, x_j)$. Let C_M be the cluster with the fewest members that contains both x_i and x_j. Assume C_M was formed by joining C_K and C_L. Then define $h(x_i, x_j) = D_{KL}$.

If the fusion of C_K and C_L reduces the number of clusters from g to $g-1$, then define $D_{(g)} = D_{KL}$. Johnson (1967) shows that if

$$0 \leq D_{(n)} \leq D_{(n-1)} \leq \cdots \leq D_{(2)}$$

then $h(\cdot, \cdot)$ is an ultrametric. A method that always satisfies this condition is said to be a *monotonic* or *ultrametric clustering method*. All methods implemented in PROC CLUSTER except CENTROID, EML, and MEDIAN are ultrametric (Milligan 1979; Batagelj 1981).

Algorithms

Anderberg (1973) describes three algorithms for implementing agglomerative hierarchical clustering: stored data, stored distance, and sorted distance. The algorithms used by PROC CLUSTER for each method are indicated in Table 23.2. For METHOD=AVERAGE, METHOD=CENTROID, or METHOD=WARD, either the stored data or the stored distance algorithm can be used. For these methods, if the data are distances or if you specify the NOSQUARE option, the stored distance algorithm is used; otherwise, the stored data algorithm is used.

Table 23.2. Three Algorithms for Implementing Agglomerative Hierarchical Clustering

Stored Method	Algorithm Stored Data	Stored Distance	Sorted Distance
AVERAGE	x	x	
CENTROID	x	x	
COMPLETE		x	
DENSITY			x
EML	x		
FLEXIBLE		x	
MCQUITTY		x	
MEDIAN		x	
SINGLE		x	
TWOSTAGE			x
WARD	x	x	

Computational Resources

The CLUSTER procedure stores the data (including the COPY and ID variables) in memory or, if necessary, on disk. If eigenvalues are computed, the covariance matrix is stored in memory. If the stored distance or sorted distance algorithm is used, the distances are stored in memory or, if necessary, on disk.

With coordinate data, the increase in CPU time is roughly proportional to the number of variables. The VAR statement should list the variables in order of decreasing variance for greatest efficiency.

For both coordinate and distance data, the dominant factor determining CPU time is the number of observations. For density methods with coordinate data, the asymptotic time requirements are somewhere between $n \ln(n)$ and n^2, depending on how the smoothing parameter increases. For other methods except EML, time is roughly proportional to n^2. For the EML method, time is roughly proportional to n^3.

PROC CLUSTER runs much faster if the data can be stored in memory and, if the stored distance algorithm is used, the distance matrix can be stored in memory as well. To estimate the bytes of memory needed for the data, use the following equation and round up to the nearest multiple of d.

$n(vd$	$+ \quad 8d + i$	
	$+ \quad i$	if density estimation or the sorted distance algorithm used
	$+ \quad 3d$	if stored data algorithm used
	$+ \quad 3d$	if density estimation used
	+ max(8, length of ID variable)	if ID variable used
	+ length of ID variable	if ID variable used
	+ sum of lengths of COPY variables)	if COPY variables used

where

n is the number of observations

v is the number of variables

d is the size of a C variable of type *double*. For most computers, $d = 8$.

i is the size of a C variable of type *int*. For most computers, $i = 4$.

The number of bytes needed for the distance matrix is $dn(n + 1)/2$.

Missing Values

If the data are coordinates, observations with missing values are excluded from the analysis. If the data are distances, missing values are not allowed in the lower triangle of the distance matrix. The upper triangle is ignored. For more on TYPE=DISTANCE data sets, see Appendix A, "Special SAS Data Sets."

Ties

At each level of the clustering algorithm, PROC CLUSTER must identify the pair of clusters with the minimum distance. Sometimes, usually when the data are discrete, there may be two or more pairs with the same minimum distance. In such cases the tie must be broken in some arbitrary way. If there are ties, then the results of the cluster analysis depend on the order of the observations in the data set. The presence of ties is reported in the SAS log and in the column of the cluster history labeled "Tie" unless the NOTIE option is specified.

PROC CLUSTER breaks ties as follows. Each cluster is identified by the smallest observation number among its members. For each pair of clusters, there is a smaller identification number and a larger identification number. If two or more pairs of clusters are tied for minimum distance between clusters, the pair that has the minimum larger identification number is merged. If there is a tie for minimum larger identification number, the pair that has the minimum smaller identification number is merged. This method for breaking ties is different from that used in Version 5. The change in the algorithm may produce changes in the resulting clusters.

A tie means that the level in the cluster history at which the tie occurred and possibly some of the subsequent levels are not uniquely determined. Ties that occur early in the cluster history usually have little effect on the later stages. Ties that occur in the middle part of the cluster history are cause for further investigation. Ties late in the cluster history indicate important indeterminacies.

The importance of ties can be assessed by repeating the cluster analysis for several different random permutations of the observations. The discrepancies at a given level can be examined by crosstabulating the clusters obtained at that level for all of the permutations. See Example 23.4 for details.

Size, Shape, and Correlation

In some biological applications, the organisms that are being clustered may be at different stages of growth. Unless it is the growth process itself that is being studied, differences in size among such organisms are not of interest. Therefore, distances among organisms should be computed in such a way as to control for differences in size while retaining information about differences in shape.

If coordinate data are measured on an interval scale, you can control for size by subtracting a measure of the overall size of each observation from each datum. For example, if no other direct measure of size is available, you could subtract the mean of each row of the data matrix, producing a row-centered coordinate matrix. An easy way to subtract the mean of each row is to use PROC STANDARD on the transposed coordinate matrix:

```
proc transpose data= coordinate-datatype ;
proc standard m=0;
proc transpose out=row-centered-coordinate-data;
```

Another way to remove size effects from interval-scale coordinate data is to do a principal component analysis and discard the first component (Blackith and Reyment 1971).

If the data are measured on a ratio scale, you can control for size by dividing each datum by a measure of overall size; in this case, the geometric mean is a more natural measure of size than the arithmetic mean. However, it is often more meaningful to analyze the logarithms of ratio-scaled data, in which case you can subtract the arithmetic mean after taking logarithms. You must also consider the dimensions of measurement. For example, if you have measures of both length and weight, you may need to cube the measures of length or take the cube root of the weights. Various other complications may also arise in real applications, such as different growth rates for different parts of the body (Sneath and Sokal 1973).

Issues of size and shape are pertinent to many areas besides biology (for example, Hamer and Cunningham 1981). Suppose you have data consisting of subjective ratings made by several different raters. Some raters may tend to give higher overall ratings than other raters. Some raters may also tend to spread out their ratings over more of the scale than do other raters. If it is impossible for you to adjust directly for rater differences, then distances should be computed in such a way as to control for both differences in size and variability. For example, if the data are considered to be measured on an interval scale, you can subtract the mean of each observation and divide by the standard deviation, producing a row-standardized coordinate matrix. With some clustering methods, analyzing squared Euclidean distances from a row-standardized coordinate matrix is equivalent to analyzing the matrix of correlations among rows, since squared Euclidean distance is an affine transformation of the correlation (Hartigan 1975, p. 64).

If you do an analysis of row-centered or row-standardized data, you need to consider whether the columns (variables) should be standardized before centering or standardizing the rows, after centering or standardizing the rows, or both before and after. If you standardize the columns after standardizing the rows, then strictly speaking you are not analyzing shape because the profiles are distorted by standardizing the columns; however, this type of double standardization may be necessary in practice to get reasonable results. It is not clear whether iterating the standardization of rows and columns may be of any benefit.

The choice of distance or correlation measure should depend on the meaning of the data and the purpose of the analysis. Simulation studies that compare distance and correlation measures are useless unless the data are generated to mimic data from your field of application; conclusions drawn from artificial data cannot be generalized because it is possible to generate data such that distances that include size effects work better or such that correlations work better.

You can standardize the rows of a data set by using a DATA step or by using the TRANSPOSE and STANDARD procedures. You can also use PROC TRANSPOSE and then have PROC CORR create a TYPE=CORR data set containing a correlation matrix. If you want to analyze a TYPE=CORR data set with PROC CLUSTER, you must use a DATA step to perform the following steps:

1. Set the data set TYPE= to DISTANCE.
2. Convert the correlations to dissimilarities by computing $1 - r$, $\sqrt{1 - r}$, $1 - r^2$, or some other decreasing function.
3. Delete observations for which the variable _TYPE_ does not have the value 'CORR'.

See Example 23.6 for an analysis of a data set in which size information is detrimental to the classification.

Output Data Set

The OUTTREE= data set contains one observation for each observation in the input data set, plus one observation for each cluster of two or more observations (that is, one observation for each node of the cluster tree). The total number of output observations is usually $2n - 1$, where n is the number of input observations. The density methods may produce fewer output observations when the number of clusters cannot be reduced to one.

The label of the OUTTREE= data set identifies the type of cluster analysis performed and is automatically displayed when the TREE procedure is invoked.

The variables in the OUTTREE= data set are as follows:

- the BY variables, if you use a BY statement
- the ID variable, if you use an ID statement
- the COPY variables, if you use a COPY statement
- _NAME_, a character variable giving the name of the node. If the node is a cluster, the name is CLn, where n is the number of the cluster. If the node is an observation, the name is OBn, where n is the observation number. If the node is an observation and the ID statement is used, the name is the formatted value of the ID variable.
- _PARENT_, a character variable giving the value of _NAME_ of the parent of the node
- _NCL_, the number of clusters
- _FREQ_, the number of observations in the current cluster
- _HEIGHT_, the distance or similarity between the last clusters joined, as defined in the section "Clustering Methods" on page 854. The variable _HEIGHT_ is used by the TREE procedure as the default height axis. The label of the _HEIGHT_ variable identifies the between-cluster distance measure. For METHOD=TWOSTAGE, the _HEIGHT_ variable contains the densities at which clusters joined in the first stage; for clusters formed in the second stage, _HEIGHT_ is a very small negative number.

If the input data set contains coordinates, the following variables appear in the output data set:

- the variables containing the coordinates used in the cluster analysis. For output observations that correspond to input observations, the values of the coordinates are the same in both data sets except for some slight numeric error possibly introduced by standardizing and unstandardizing if the STANDARD option is used. For output observations that correspond to clusters of more than one input observation, the values of the coordinates are the cluster means.
- _ERSQ_, the approximate expected value of R^2 under the uniform null hypothesis
- _RATIO_, equal to $\frac{1-\text{\_ERSQ\_}}{1-\text{\_RSQ\_}}$
- _LOGR_, natural logarithm of _RATIO_
- _CCC_, the cubic clustering criterion

The variables _ERSQ_, _RATIO_, _LOGR_, and _CCC_ have missing values when the number of clusters is greater than one-fifth the number of observations.

If the input data set contains coordinates and METHOD=AVERAGE, METHOD=CENTROID, or METHOD=WARD, then the following variables appear in the output data set.

- _DIST_, the Euclidean distance between the means of the last clusters joined
- _AVLINK_, the average distance between the last clusters joined

If the input data set contains coordinates or METHOD=AVERAGE, METHOD=CENTROID, or METHOD=WARD, then the following variables appear in the output data set:

- _RMSSTD_, the root-mean-square standard deviation of the current cluster
- _SPRSQ_, the semipartial squared multiple correlation or the decrease in the proportion of variance accounted for due to joining two clusters to form the current cluster
- _RSQ_, the squared multiple correlation
- _PSF_, the pseudo F statistic
- _PST2_, the pseudo t^2 statistic

If METHOD=EML, then the following variable appears in the output data set:

- _LNLR_, the log-likelihood ratio

If METHOD=TWOSTAGE or METHOD=DENSITY, the following variable appears in the output data set:

- _MODE_, pertaining to the modal clusters. With METHOD=DENSITY, the _MODE_ variable indicates the number of modal clusters contained by the current cluster. With METHOD=TWOSTAGE, the _MODE_ variable gives the maximum density in each modal cluster and the fusion density, d^*, for clusters containing two or more modal clusters; for clusters containing no modal clusters, _MODE_ is missing.

If nonparametric density estimates are requested (when METHOD=DENSITY or METHOD=TWOSTAGE and the HYBRID option is not used; or when the TRIM= option is used), the output data set contains

- _DENS_, the maximum density in the current cluster

Displayed Output

If you specify the SIMPLE option and the data are coordinates, PROC CLUSTER produces simple descriptive statistics for each variable:

- the Mean
- the standard deviation, Std Dev
- the Skewness
- the Kurtosis
- a coefficient of Bimodality

If the data are coordinates and you do not specify the NOEIGEN option, PROC CLUSTER displays

- the Eigenvalues of the Correlation or Covariance Matrix
- the Difference between successive eigenvalues
- the Proportion of variance explained by each eigenvalue
- the Cumulative proportion of variance explained

If the data are coordinates, PROC CLUSTER displays the Root-Mean-Square Total-Sample Standard Deviation of the variables

If the distances are normalized, PROC CLUSTER displays one of the following, depending on whether squared or unsquared distances are used:

- the Root-Mean-Square Distance Between Observations
- the Mean Distance Between Observations

For the generations in the clustering process specified by the PRINT= option, PROC CLUSTER displays

- the Number of Clusters or NCL
- the names of the Clusters Joined. The observations are identified by the formatted value of the ID variable, if any; otherwise, the observations are identified by OBn, where n is the observation number. The CLUSTER procedure displays the entire value of the ID variable in the cluster history instead of truncating at 16 characters. Long ID values may be flowed onto several lines. Clusters of two or more observations are identified as CLn, where n is the number of clusters existing after the cluster in question is formed.
- the number of observations in the new cluster, Frequency of New Cluster or FREQ

If you specify the RMSSTD option and if the data are coordinates or if you specify METHOD=AVERAGE, METHOD=CENTROID, or METHOD=WARD, then PROC CLUSTER displays the root-mean-square standard deviation of the new cluster, RMS Std of New Cluster or RMS Std.

PROC CLUSTER displays the following items if you specify METHOD=WARD. It also displays them if you specify the RSQUARE option and either the data are coordinates or you specify METHOD=AVERAGE or METHOD=CENTROID:

- the decrease in the proportion of variance accounted for resulting from joining the two clusters, Semipartial R-Squared or SPRSQ. This equals the between-cluster sum of squares divided by the corrected total sum of squares.
- the squared multiple correlation, R-Squared or RSQ. R^2 is the proportion of variance accounted for by the clusters.

If you specify the CCC option and the data are coordinates, PROC CLUSTER displays

- Approximate Expected R-Squared or ERSQ, the approximate expected value of R^2 under the uniform null hypothesis
- the Cubic Clustering Criterion or CCC. The cubic clustering criterion and approximate expected R^2 are given missing values when the number of clusters is greater than one-fifth the number of observations.

If you specify the PSEUDO option and if the data are coordinates or METHOD=AVERAGE, METHOD=CENTROID, or METHOD=WARD, then PROC CLUSTER displays

- Pseudo F or PSF, the pseudo F statistic measuring the separation among all the clusters at the current level
- Pseudo t^2 or PST2, the pseudo t^2 statistic measuring the separation between the two clusters most recently joined

If you specify the NOSQUARE option and METHOD=AVERAGE, PROC CLUSTER displays the (Normalized) Average Distance or (Norm) Aver Dist, the average distance between pairs of objects in the two clusters joined with one object from each cluster.

If you do not specify the NOSQUARE option and METHOD=AVERAGE, PROC CLUSTER displays the (Normalized) RMS Distance or (Norm) RMS Dist, the root-mean-square distance between pairs of objects in the two clusters joined with one object from each cluster.

If METHOD=CENTROID, PROC CLUSTER displays the (Normalized) Centroid Distance or (Norm) Cent Dist, the distance between the two cluster centroids.

If METHOD=COMPLETE, PROC CLUSTER displays the (Normalized) Maximum Distance or (Norm) Max Dist, the maximum distance between the two clusters.

If METHOD=DENSITY or METHOD=TWOSTAGE, PROC CLUSTER displays

- Normalized Fusion Density or Normalized Fusion Dens, the value of d^* as defined in the section "Clustering Methods" on page 854
- the Normalized Maximum Density in Each Cluster joined, including the Lesser or Min, and the Greater or Max, of the two maximum density values

If METHOD=EML, PROC CLUSTER displays

- Log Likelihood Ratio or LNLR
- Log Likelihood or LNLIKE

If METHOD=FLEXIBLE, PROC CLUSTER displays the (Normalized) Flexible Distance or (Norm) Flex Dist, the distance between the two clusters based on the Lance-Williams flexible formula.

If METHOD=MEDIAN, PROC CLUSTER displays the (Normalized) Median Distance or (Norm) Med Dist, the distance between the two clusters based on the median method.

If METHOD=MCQUITTY, PROC CLUSTER displays the (Normalized) McQuitty's Similarity or (Norm) MCQ, the distance between the two clusters based on McQuitty's similarity method.

If METHOD=SINGLE, PROC CLUSTER displays the (Normalized) Minimum Distance or (Norm) Min Dist, the minimum distance between the two clusters.

If you specify the NONORM option and METHOD=WARD, PROC CLUSTER displays the Between-Cluster Sum of Squares or BSS, the *ANOVA* sum of squares between the two clusters joined.

If you specify neither the NOTIE option nor METHOD=TWOSTAGE or METHOD=DENSITY, PROC CLUSTER displays Tie, where a T in the column indicates a tie for minimum distance and a blank indicates the absence of a tie.

After the cluster history, if METHOD=TWOSTAGE or METHOD=DENSITY, PROC CLUSTER displays the number of modal clusters.

ODS Table Names

PROC CLUSTER assigns a name to each table it creates. You can use these names to reference the table when using the Output Delivery System (ODS) to select tables and create output data sets. These names are listed in the following table. For more information on ODS, see Chapter 15, "Using the Output Delivery System."

Table 23.3. ODS Tables Produced in PROC CLUSTER

ODS Table Name	Description	Statement	Option
ClusterHistory	Obs or clusters joined, frequencies and other cluster statistics	PROC	default
SimpleStatistics	Simple statistics, before or after trimming	PROC	SIMPLE
EigenvalueTable	Eigenvalues of the CORR or COV matrix	PROC	default

Examples

Example 23.1. Cluster Analysis of Flying Mileages between Ten American Cities

This first example clusters ten American cities based on the flying mileages between them. Six clustering methods are shown with corresponding tree diagrams produced by the TREE procedure. The EML method cannot be used because it requires coordinate data. The other omitted methods produce the same clusters, although not the same distances between clusters, as one of the illustrated methods: complete linkage and the flexible-beta method yield the same clusters as Ward's method, McQuitty's similarity analysis produces the same clusters as average linkage, and the median method corresponds to the centroid method.

All of the methods suggest a division of the cities into two clusters along the east-west dimension. There is disagreement, however, about which cluster Denver should belong to. Some of the methods indicate a possible third cluster containing Denver and Houston. The following statements produce Output 23.1.1:

```
title 'Cluster Analysis of Flying Mileages Between 10 American Cities';
data mileages(type=distance);
   input (atlanta chicago denver houston losangeles
         miami newyork sanfran seattle washdc) (5.)
         @55 city $15.;
   datalines;
    0                                                ATLANTA
  587    0                                           CHICAGO
 1212  920    0                                      DENVER
  701  940  879    0                                 HOUSTON
 1936 1745  831 1374    0                            LOS ANGELES
  604 1188 1726  968 2339    0                       MIAMI
  748  713 1631 1420 2451 1092    0                  NEW YORK
 2139 1858  949 1645  347 2594 2571    0             SAN FRANCISCO
 2182 1737 1021 1891  959 2734 2408  678    0        SEATTLE
  543  597 1494 1220 2300  923  205 2442 2329    0   WASHINGTON D.C.
;
```

```
/*---------------------- Average linkage --------------------*/
proc cluster data=mileages method=average pseudo;
   id city;
run;

proc tree horizontal spaces=2;
   id city;
run;

/*---------------------- Centroid method --------------------*/
proc cluster data=mileages method=centroid pseudo;
   id city;
run;

proc tree horizontal spaces=2;
   id city;
run;

/*-------- Density linkage with 3rd-nearest-neighbor --------*/
proc cluster data=mileages method=density k=3;
   id city;
run;

proc tree horizontal spaces=2;
   id city;
run;

/*--------------------- Single linkage ----------------------*/
proc cluster data=mileages method=single;
   id city;
run;

proc tree horizontal spaces=2;
   id city;
run;

/*--- Two-stage density linkage with 3rd-nearest-neighbor ---*/
proc cluster data=mileages method=twostage k=3;
   id city;
run;

proc tree horizontal spaces=2;
   id city;
run;

/* Ward's minimum variance with pseudo $F$ and $t^2$ statistics */
proc cluster data=mileages method=ward pseudo;
   id city;
run;

proc tree horizontal spaces=2;
   id city;
run;
```

Output 23.1.1. Statistics and Tree Diagrams for Six Different Clustering Methods

```
                 Cluster Analysis of Flying Mileages Between 10 American Cities

                                    The CLUSTER Procedure
                                 Average Linkage Cluster Analysis

                  Root-Mean-Square Distance Between Observations   = 1580.242


                                        Cluster History
                                                                                Norm    T
                                                                                 RMS    i
     NCL    ---------Clusters Joined----------      FREQ     PSF    PST2        Dist    e

       9    NEW YORK            WASHINGTON D.C.        2    66.7       .      0.1297
       8    LOS ANGELES         SAN FRANCISCO          2    39.2       .      0.2196
       7    ATLANTA             CHICAGO                2    21.7       .      0.3715
       6    CL7                 CL9                    4    14.5     3.4      0.4149
       5    CL8                 SEATTLE                3    12.4     7.3      0.5255
       4    DENVER              HOUSTON                2    13.9       .      0.5562
       3    CL6                 MIAMI                  5    15.5     3.8      0.6185
       2    CL3                 CL4                    7    16.0     5.3      0.8005
       1    CL2                 CL5                   10       .    16.0      1.2967
```

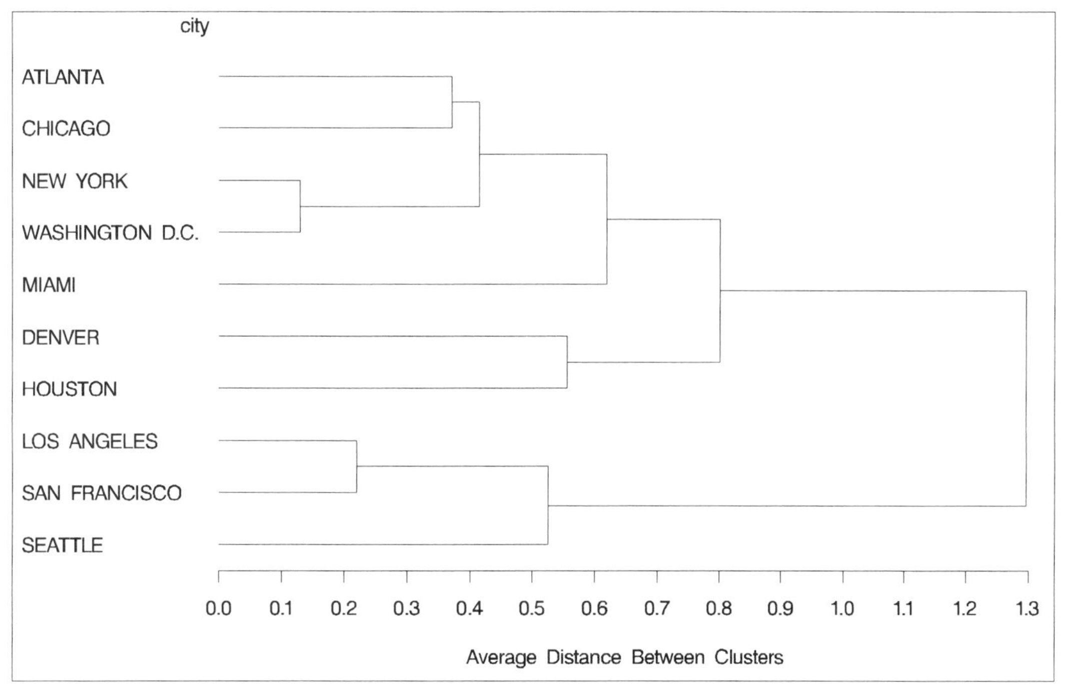

```
          Cluster Analysis of Flying Mileages Between 10 American Cities

                              The CLUSTER Procedure
                       Centroid Hierarchical Cluster Analysis

           Root-Mean-Square Distance Between Observations    = 1580.242


                                  Cluster History
                                                                     Norm    T
                                                                     Cent    i
NCL    ---------Clusters Joined----------    FREQ     PSF    PST2    Dist    e

  9    NEW YORK           WASHINGTON D.C.       2    66.7       .  0.1297
  8    LOS ANGELES        SAN FRANCISCO         2    39.2       .  0.2196
  7    ATLANTA            CHICAGO               2    21.7       .  0.3715
  6    CL7                CL9                   4    14.5     3.4  0.3652
  5    CL8                SEATTLE               3    12.4     7.3  0.5139
  4    DENVER             CL5                   4    12.4     2.1  0.5337
  3    CL6                MIAMI                 5    14.2     3.8  0.5743
  2    CL3                HOUSTON               6    22.1     2.6  0.6091
  1    CL2                CL4                  10       .    22.1   1.173
```

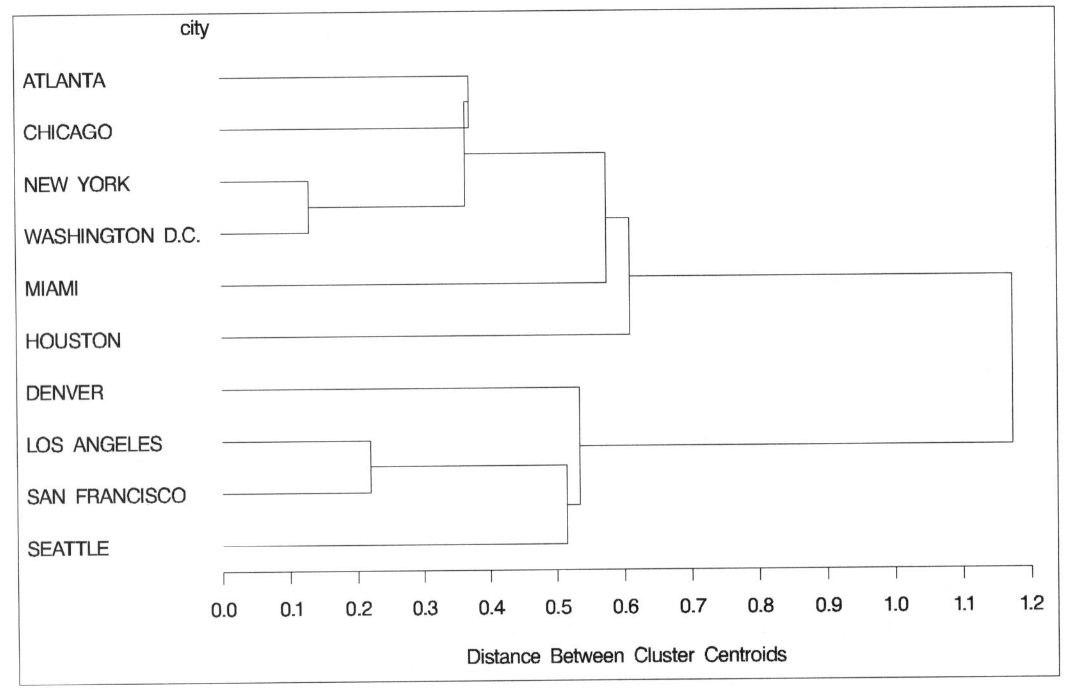

```
                   Cluster Analysis of Flying Mileages Between 10 American Cities

                                    The CLUSTER Procedure
                                Density Linkage Cluster Analysis

                                            K = 3


                                       Cluster History
                                                      Normalized             Maximum Density      T
                                                          Fusion             in Each Cluster      i
  NCL    ---------Clusters Joined----------      FREQ    Density             Lesser    Greater    e

    9    ATLANTA            WASHINGTON D.C.         2     96.106            92.5043      100.0
    8    CL9                CHICAGO                 3     95.263            90.9548      100.0
    7    CL8                NEW YORK                4     86.465            76.1571      100.0
    6    CL7                MIAMI                   5     74.079            58.8299      100.0    T
    5    CL6                HOUSTON                 6     74.079            61.7747      100.0
    4    LOS ANGELES        SAN FRANCISCO           2     71.968            65.3430    80.0885
    3    CL4                SEATTLE                 3     66.341            56.6215    80.0885
    2    CL3                DENVER                  4     63.509            61.7747    80.0885
    1    CL5                CL2                    10     61.775      *     80.0885      100.0

                       * indicates fusion of two modal or multimodal clusters
                                 2 modal clusters have been formed.
```

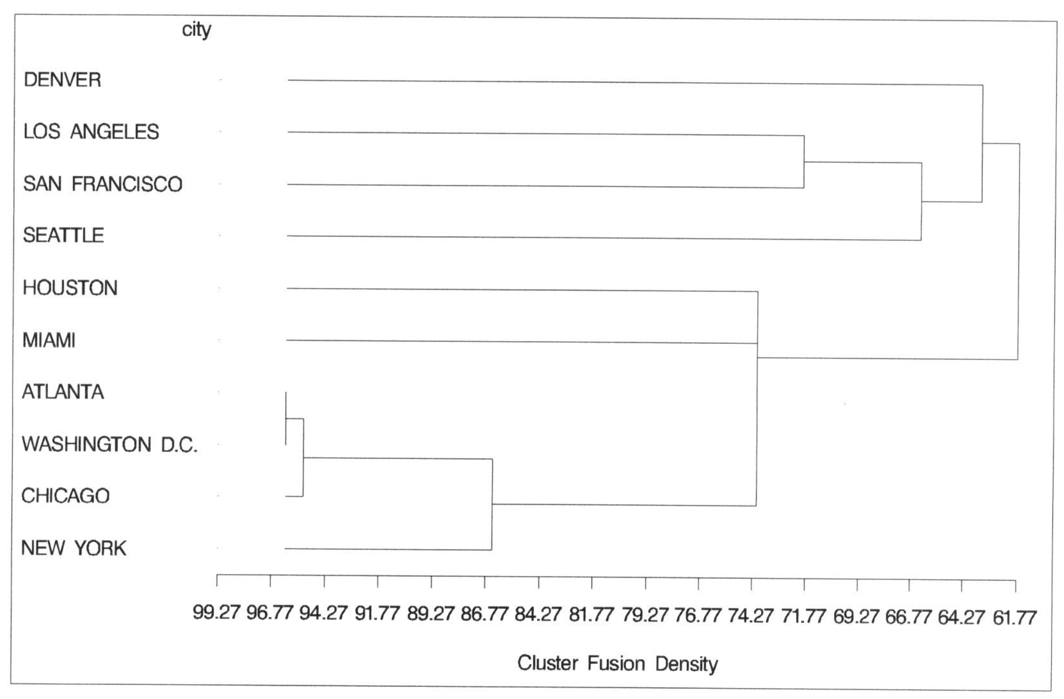

```
              Cluster Analysis of Flying Mileages Between 10 American Cities

                                 The CLUSTER Procedure
                             Single Linkage Cluster Analysis

               Mean Distance Between Observations              = 1417.133


                                    Cluster History
                                                                      Norm    T
                                                                       Min    i
             NCL    ---------Clusters Joined----------       FREQ     Dist    e

               9    NEW YORK            WASHINGTON D.C.         2   0.1447
               8    LOS ANGELES         SAN FRANCISCO           2   0.2449
               7    ATLANTA             CL9                     3   0.3832
               6    CL7                 CHICAGO                 4   0.4142
               5    CL6                 MIAMI                   5   0.4262
               4    CL8                 SEATTLE                 3   0.4784
               3    CL5                 HOUSTON                 6   0.4947
               2    DENVER              CL4                     4   0.5864
               1    CL3                 CL2                    10   0.6203
```

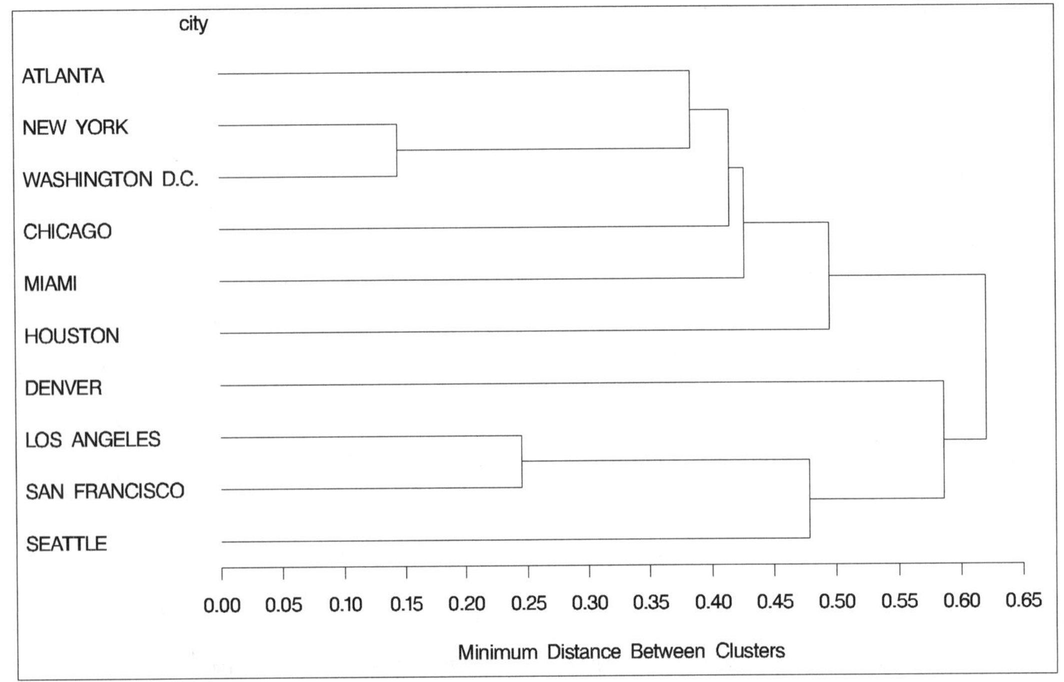

```
                Cluster Analysis of Flying Mileages Between 10 American Cities

                                    The CLUSTER Procedure
                              Two-Stage Density Linkage Clustering

                                            K = 3


                                       Cluster History
                                                            Normalized        Maximum Density       T
                                                              Fusion          in Each Cluster       i
   NCL     ---------Clusters Joined----------      FREQ       Density       Lesser      Greater     e

     9     ATLANTA             WASHINGTON D.C.        2        96.106      92.5043        100.0
     8     CL9                 CHICAGO                3        95.263      90.9548        100.0
     7     CL8                 NEW YORK               4        86.465      76.1571        100.0
     6     CL7                 MIAMI                  5        74.079      58.8299        100.0     T
     5     CL6                 HOUSTON                6        74.079      61.7747        100.0
     4     LOS ANGELES         SAN FRANCISCO          2        71.968      65.3430      80.0885
     3     CL4                 SEATTLE                3        66.341      56.6215      80.0885
     2     CL3                 DENVER                 4        63.509      61.7747      80.0885
     1     CL5                 CL2                   10        61.775      80.0885        100.0
                              2 modal clusters have been formed.
```

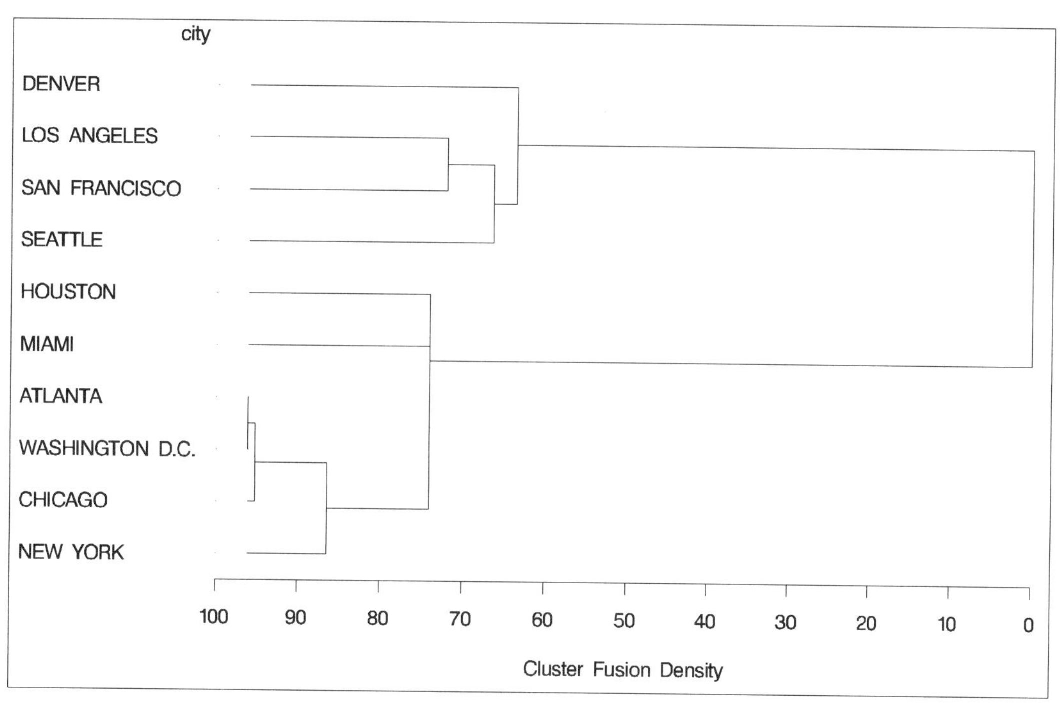

```
                    Cluster Analysis of Flying Mileages Between 10 American Cities

                                        The CLUSTER Procedure
                               Ward's Minimum Variance Cluster Analysis

                     Root-Mean-Square Distance Between Observations    = 1580.242


                                           Cluster History
                                                                                              T
                                                                                              i
NCL    ---------Clusters Joined---------         FREQ     SPRSQ      RSQ      PSF     PST2    e

  9    NEW YORK           WASHINGTON D.C.           2    0.0019     .998     66.7       .
  8    LOS ANGELES        SAN FRANCISCO             2    0.0054     .993     39.2       .
  7    ATLANTA            CHICAGO                   2    0.0153     .977     21.7       .
  6    CL7                CL9                       4    0.0296     .948     14.5      3.4
  5    DENVER             HOUSTON                   2    0.0344     .913     13.2       .
  4    CL8                SEATTLE                   3    0.0391     .874     13.9      7.3
  3    CL6                MIAMI                     5    0.0586     .816     15.5      3.8
  2    CL3                CL5                       7    0.1488     .667     16.0      5.3
  1    CL2                CL4                      10    0.6669     .000        .     16.0
```

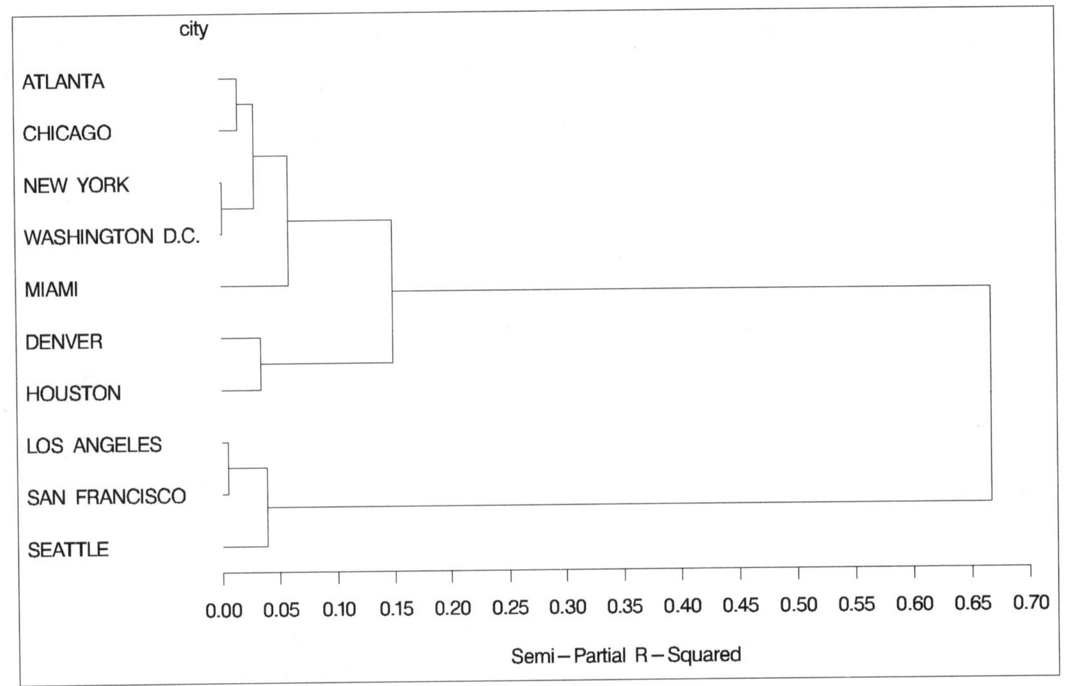

Example 23.2. Crude Birth and Death Rates

The following example uses the SAS data set Poverty created in the "Getting Started" section beginning on page 837. The data, from Rouncefield (1995), are birth rates, death rates, and infant death rates for 97 countries. Six cluster analyses are performed with eight methods. Scatter plots showing cluster membership at selected levels are produced instead of tree diagrams.

Each cluster analysis is performed by a macro called ANALYZE. The macro takes two arguments. The first, &METHOD, specifies the value of the METHOD= option to be used in the PROC CLUSTER statement. The second, &NCL, must be specified as a list of integers, separated by blanks, indicating the number of clusters desired in each scatter plot. For example, the first invocation of ANALYZE specifies the AVERAGE method and requests plots of 3 and 8 clusters. When two-stage density linkage is used, the K= and R= options are specified as part of the first argument.

The ANALYZE macro first invokes the CLUSTER procedure with METHOD=&METHOD, where &METHOD represents the value of the first argument to ANALYZE. This part of the macro produces the PROC CLUSTER output shown.

The %DO loop processes &NCL, the list of numbers of clusters to plot. The macro variable &K is a counter that indexes the numbers within &NCL. The %SCAN function picks out the &Kth number in &NCL, which is then assigned to the macro variable &N. When &K exceeds the number of numbers in &NCL, %SCAN returns a null string. Thus, the %DO loop executes while &N is not equal to a null string. In the %WHILE condition, a null string is indicated by the absence of any nonblank characters between the comparison operator (NE) and the right parenthesis that terminates the condition.

Within the %DO loop, the TREE procedure creates an output data set containing &N clusters. The GPLOT procedure then produces a scatter plot in which each observation is identified by the number of the cluster to which it belongs. The TITLE2 statement uses double quotes so that &N and &METHOD can be used within the title. At the end of the loop, &K is incremented by 1, and the next number is extracted from &NCL by %SCAN.

For this example, plots are obtained only for average linkage. To generate plots for other methods, follow the example shown in the first macro call. The following statements produce Output 23.2.1 through Output 23.2.7.

```
title 'Cluster Analysis of Birth and Death Rates';

%macro analyze(method,ncl);
proc cluster data=poverty outtree=tree method=&method p=15 ccc pseudo;
   var birth death;
   title2;
run;
%let k=1;
%let n=%scan(&ncl,&k);
%do %while(&n NE);
   proc tree data=tree noprint out=out ncl=&n;
      copy birth death;
   run;
   legend1 frame cframe=ligr cborder=black
           position=center value=(justify=center);
   axis1 label=(angle=90 rotate=0) minor=none;
   axis2 minor=none;
   proc gplot;
      plot death*birth=cluster /
      frame cframe=ligr legend=legend1 vaxis=axis1 haxis=axis2;
      title2 "Plot of &n Clusters from METHOD=&METHOD";
   run;
   %let k=%eval(&k+1);
   %let n=%scan(&ncl,&k);
%end;
%mend;
```

```
%analyze(average,3 8)
%analyze(complete,3)
%analyze(single,7 10)
%analyze(two k=10,3)
%analyze(two k=18,2)
```

For average linkage, the CCC has peaks at 3, 8, 10, and 12 clusters, but the 3-cluster peak is lower than the 8-cluster peak. The pseudo F statistic has peaks at 3, 8, and 12 clusters. The pseudo t^2 statistic drops sharply at 3 clusters, continues to fall at 4 clusters, and has a particularly low value at 12 clusters. However, there are not enough data to seriously consider as many as 12 clusters. Scatter plots are given for 3 and 8 clusters. The results are shown in Output 23.2.1 through Output 23.2.3. In Output 23.2.3, the eighth cluster consists of the two outlying observations, Mexico and Korea.

Output 23.2.1. Clusters for Birth and Death Rates: METHOD=AVERAGE

Cluster Analysis of Birth and Death Rates

The CLUSTER Procedure
Average Linkage Cluster Analysis

Eigenvalues of the Covariance Matrix

	Eigenvalue	Difference	Proportion	Cumulative
1	189.106588	173.101020	0.9220	0.9220
2	16.005568		0.0780	1.0000

Root-Mean-Square Total-Sample Standard Deviation = 10.127
Root-Mean-Square Distance Between Observations = 20.25399

Cluster History

NCL	--Clusters	Joined---	FREQ	SPRSQ	RSQ	ERSQ	CCC	PSF	PST2	Norm RMS Dist	Tie
15	CL27	CL20	18	0.0035	.980	.975	2.61	292	18.6	0.2325	
14	CL23	CL17	28	0.0034	.977	.972	1.97	271	17.7	0.2358	
13	CL18	CL54	8	0.0015	.975	.969	2.35	279	7.1	0.2432	
12	CL21	CL26	8	0.0015	.974	.966	2.85	290	6.1	0.2493	
11	CL19	CL24	12	0.0033	.971	.962	2.78	285	14.8	0.2767	
10	CL22	CL16	12	0.0036	.967	.957	2.84	284	17.4	0.2858	
9	CL15	CL28	22	0.0061	.961	.951	2.45	271	17.5	0.3353	
8	OB23	OB61	2	0.0014	.960	.943	3.59	302	.	0.3703	
7	CL25	CL11	17	0.0098	.950	.933	3.01	284	23.3	0.4033	
6	CL7	CL12	25	0.0122	.938	.920	2.63	273	14.8	0.4132	
5	CL10	CL14	40	0.0303	.907	.902	0.59	225	82.7	0.4584	
4	CL13	CL6	33	0.0244	.883	.875	0.77	234	22.2	0.5194	
3	CL9	CL8	24	0.0182	.865	.827	2.13	300	27.7	0.735	
2	CL5	CL3	64	0.1836	.681	.697	-.55	203	148	0.8402	
1	CL2	CL4	97	0.6810	.000	.000	0.00	.	203	1.3348	

Output 23.2.2. Plot of Three Clusters, METHOD=AVERAGE

Plot of 3 Clusters from METHOD=average

Output 23.2.3. Plot of Eight Clusters, METHOD=AVERAGE

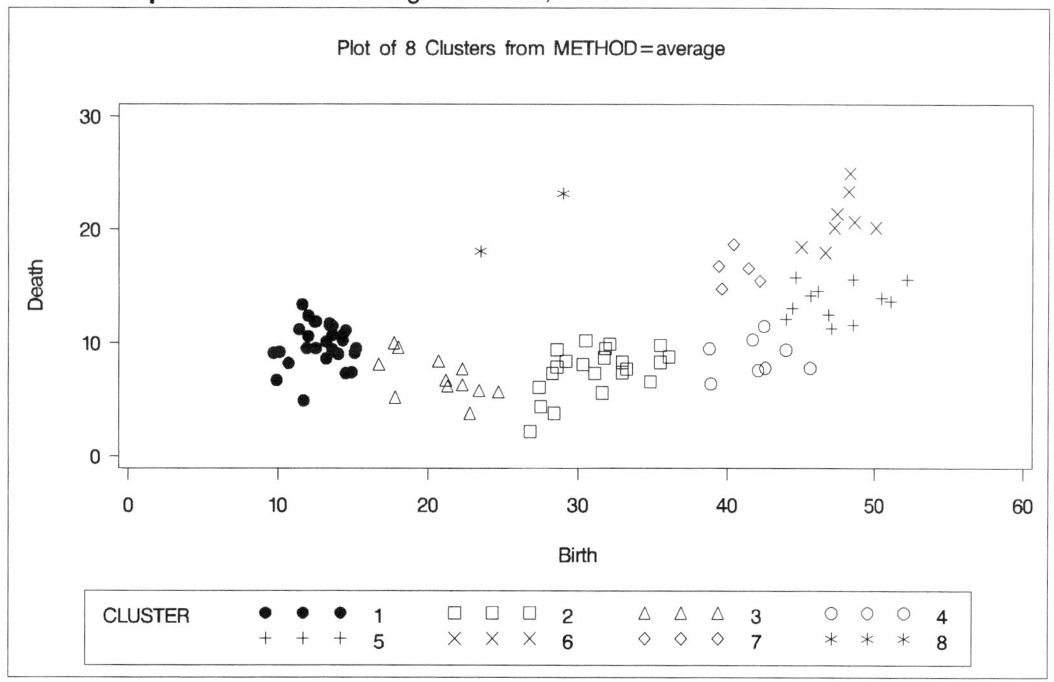

Complete linkage shows CCC peaks at 3, 8 and 12 clusters. The pseudo F statistic peaks at 3 and 12 clusters. The pseudo t^2 statistic indicates 3 clusters.

The scatter plot for 3 clusters is shown. The results are shown in Output 23.2.4.

Output 23.2.4. Clusters for Birth and Death Rates: METHOD=COMPLETE

```
                          Cluster Analysis of Birth and Death Rates

                                    The CLUSTER Procedure
                              Complete Linkage Cluster Analysis

                             Eigenvalues of the Covariance Matrix

                        Eigenvalue    Difference    Proportion    Cumulative

                   1    189.106588    173.101020        0.9220        0.9220
                   2     16.005568                      0.0780        1.0000

               Root-Mean-Square Total-Sample Standard Deviation =    10.127
               Mean Distance Between Observations               = 17.13099


                                       Cluster History
                                                                                  Norm    T
                                                                                   Max    i
NCL    --Clusters Joined---      FREQ     SPRSQ     RSQ    ERSQ     CCC     PSF   PST2    Dist    e

 15    CL22          CL33           8    0.0015    .983    .975    3.80     329    6.1  0.4092
 14    CL56          CL18           8    0.0014    .981    .972    3.97     331    6.6  0.4255
 13    CL30          CL44           8    0.0019    .979    .969    4.04     330   19.0  0.4332
 12    OB23          OB61           2    0.0014    .978    .966    4.45     340     .   0.4378
 11    CL19          CL24          24    0.0034    .974    .962    4.17     327   24.1  0.4962
 10    CL17          CL28          12    0.0033    .971    .957    4.18     325   14.8  0.5204
  9    CL20          CL13          16    0.0067    .964    .951    3.38     297   25.2  0.5236
  8    CL11          CL21          32    0.0054    .959    .943    3.44     297   19.7  0.6001
  7    CL26          CL15          13    0.0096    .949    .933    2.93     282   28.9  0.7233
  6    CL14          CL10          20    0.0128    .937    .920    2.46     269   27.7  0.8033
  5    CL9           CL16          30    0.0237    .913    .902    1.29     241   47.1  0.8993
  4    CL6           CL7           33    0.0240    .889    .875    1.38     248   21.7  1.2165
  3    CL5           CL12          32    0.0178    .871    .827    2.56     317   13.6  1.2326
  2    CL3           CL8           64    0.1900    .681    .697    -.55     203    167  1.5412
  1    CL2           CL4           97    0.6810    .000    .000    0.00       .    203  2.5233
```

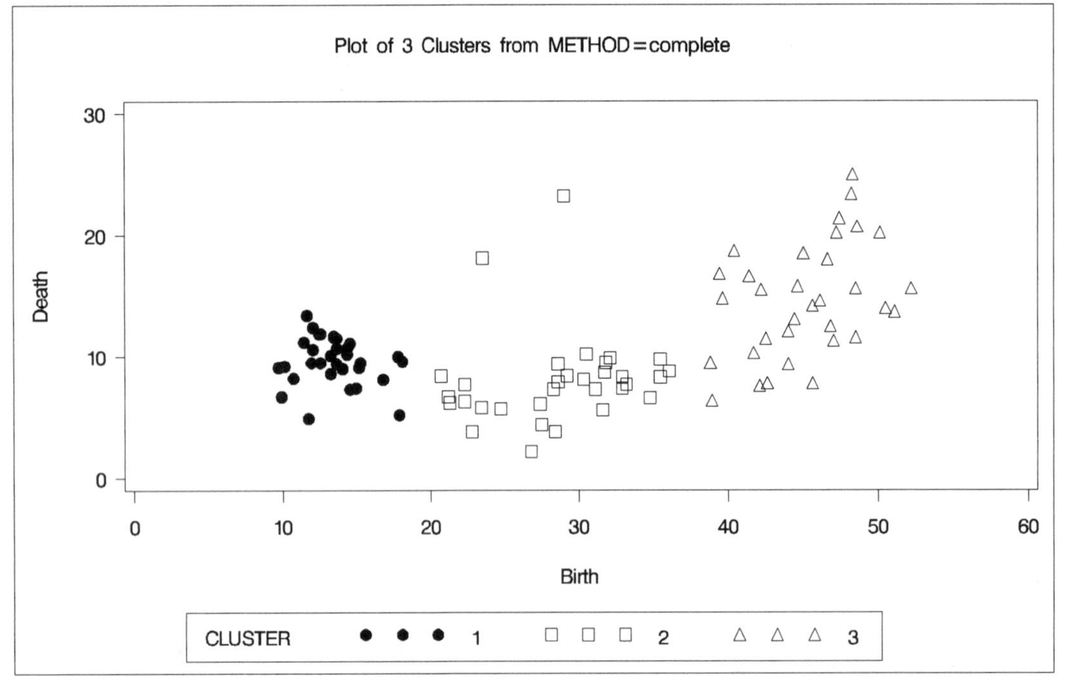

The CCC and pseudo F statistics are not appropriate for use with single linkage because of the method's tendency to chop off tails of distributions. The pseudo t^2 statistic can be used by looking for *large* values and taking the number of clusters to be one greater than the level at which the large pseudo t^2 value is displayed. For these data, there are large values at levels 6 and 9, suggesting 7 or 10 clusters.

The scatter plots for 7 and 10 clusters are shown. The results are shown in Output 23.2.5.

Output 23.2.5. Clusters for Birth and Death Rates: METHOD=SINGLE

Cluster Analysis of Birth and Death Rates

The CLUSTER Procedure
Single Linkage Cluster Analysis

Eigenvalues of the Covariance Matrix

	Eigenvalue	Difference	Proportion	Cumulative
1	189.106588	173.101020	0.9220	0.9220
2	16.005568		0.0780	1.0000

Root-Mean-Square Total-Sample Standard Deviation = 10.127
Mean Distance Between Observations = 17.13099

Cluster History

NCL	--Clusters	Joined---	FREQ	SPRSQ	RSQ	ERSQ	CCC	PSF	PST2	Norm Min Dist	Tie
15	CL37	CL19	8	0.0014	.968	.975	-2.3	178	6.6	0.1331	
14	CL20	CL23	15	0.0059	.962	.972	-3.1	162	18.7	0.1412	
13	CL14	CL16	19	0.0054	.957	.969	-3.4	155	8.8	0.1442	
12	CL26	OB58	31	0.0014	.955	.966	-2.7	165	4.0	0.1486	
11	OB86	CL18	4	0.0003	.955	.962	-1.6	183	3.8	0.1495	
10	CL13	CL11	23	0.0088	.946	.957	-2.3	170	11.3	0.1518	
9	CL22	CL17	30	0.0235	.923	.951	-4.7	131	45.7	0.1593	T
8	CL15	CL10	31	0.0210	.902	.943	-5.8	117	21.8	0.1593	
7	CL9	OB75	31	0.0052	.897	.933	-4.7	130	4.0	0.1628	
6	CL7	CL12	62	0.2023	.694	.920	-15	41.3	223	0.1725	
5	CL6	CL8	93	0.6681	.026	.902	-26	0.6	199	0.1756	
4	CL5	OB48	94	0.0056	.021	.875	-24	0.7	0.5	0.1811	T
3	CL4	OB67	95	0.0083	.012	.827	-15	0.6	0.8	0.1811	
2	OB23	OB61	2	0.0014	.011	.697	-13	1.0	.	0.4378	
1	CL3	CL2	97	0.0109	.000	.000	0.00	.	1.0	0.5815	

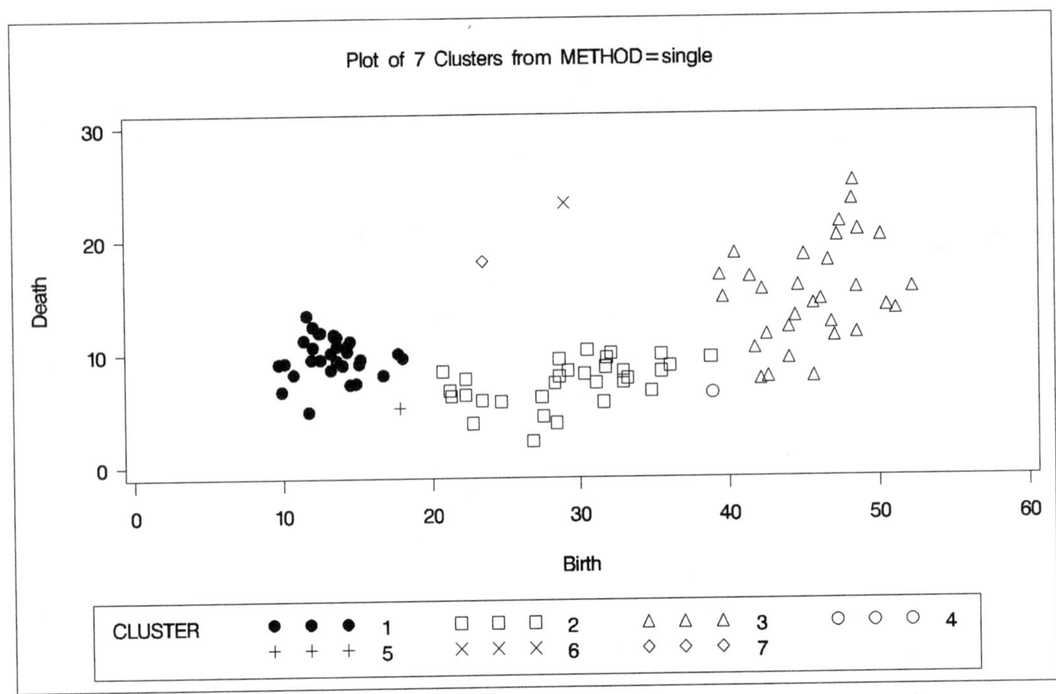
Plot of 7 Clusters from METHOD=single
Death
Birth
0
10
20
30
40
50
60
CLUSTER
1
2
3
4
5
6
7

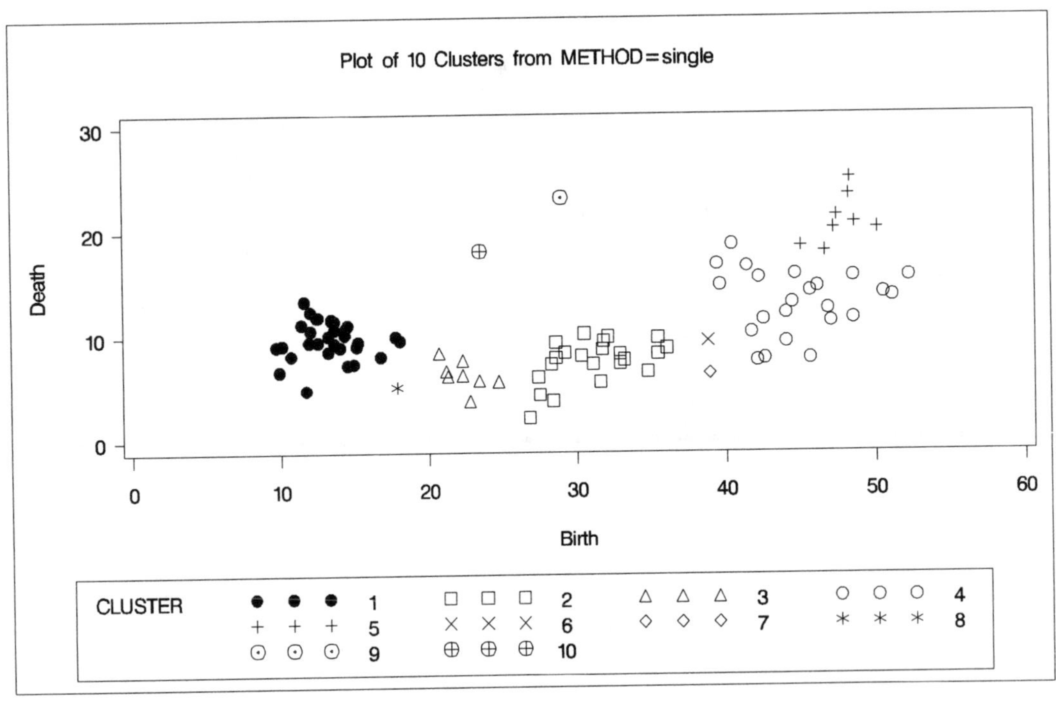
Plot of 10 Clusters from METHOD=single
Death
Birth
0
10
20
30
40
50
60
CLUSTER
1
2
3
4
5
6
7
8
9
10

For kth-nearest-neighbor density linkage, the number of modes as a function of k is as follows (not all of these analyses are shown):

k	**modes**
3	13
4	6
5-7	4
8-15	3
16-21	2
22+	1

Thus, there is strong evidence of 3 modes and an indication of the possibility of 2 modes. Uniform-kernel density linkage gives similar results. For K=10 (10th-nearest-neighbor density linkage), the scatter plot for 3 clusters is shown; and for K=18, the scatter plot for 2 clusters is shown. The results are shown in Output 23.2.6.

Output 23.2.6. Clusters for Birth and Death Rates: METHOD=TWOSTAGE, K=10

Cluster Analysis of Birth and Death Rates

The CLUSTER Procedure
Two-Stage Density Linkage Clustering

Eigenvalues of the Covariance Matrix

	Eigenvalue	Difference	Proportion	Cumulative
1	189.106588	173.101020	0.9220	0.9220
2	16.005568		0.0780	1.0000

K = 10
Root-Mean-Square Total-Sample Standard Deviation = 10.127

Cluster History

NCL	--Clusters	Joined--	FREQ	SPRSQ	RSQ	ERSQ	CCC	PSF	PST2	Normalized Fusion Density	Maximum Density in Each Cluster Lesser	Greater	Tie
15	CL16	OB94	22	0.0015	.921	.975	-11	68.4	1.4	9.2234	6.7927	15.3069	
14	CL19	OB49	28	0.0021	.919	.972	-11	72.4	1.8	8.7369	5.9334	33.4385	
13	CL15	OB52	23	0.0024	.917	.969	-10	76.9	2.3	8.5847	5.9651	15.3069	
12	CL13	OB96	24	0.0018	.915	.966	-9.3	83.0	1.6	7.9252	5.4724	15.3069	
11	CL12	OB93	25	0.0025	.912	.962	-8.5	89.5	2.2	7.8913	5.4401	15.3069	
10	CL11	OB78	26	0.0031	.909	.957	-7.7	96.9	2.5	7.787	5.4082	15.3069	
9	CL10	OB76	27	0.0026	.907	.951	-6.7	107	2.1	7.7133	5.4401	15.3069	
8	CL9	OB77	28	0.0023	.904	.943	-5.5	120	1.7	7.4256	4.9017	15.3069	
7	CL8	OB43	29	0.0022	.902	.933	-4.1	138	1.6	6.927	4.4764	15.3069	
6	CL7	OB87	30	0.0043	.898	.920	-2.7	160	3.1	4.932	2.9977	15.3069	
5	CL6	OB82	31	0.0055	.892	.902	-1.1	191	3.7	3.7331	2.1560	15.3069	
4	CL22	OB61	37	0.0079	.884	.875	0.93	237	10.6	3.1713	1.6308	100.0	
3	CL14	OB23	29	0.0126	.872	.827	2.60	320	10.4	2.0654	1.0744	33.4385	
2	CL4	CL3	66	0.2129	.659	.697	-1.3	183	172	12.409	33.4385	100.0	
1	CL2	CL5	97	0.6588	.000	.000	0.00	.	183	10.071	15.3069	100.0	

3 modal clusters have been formed.

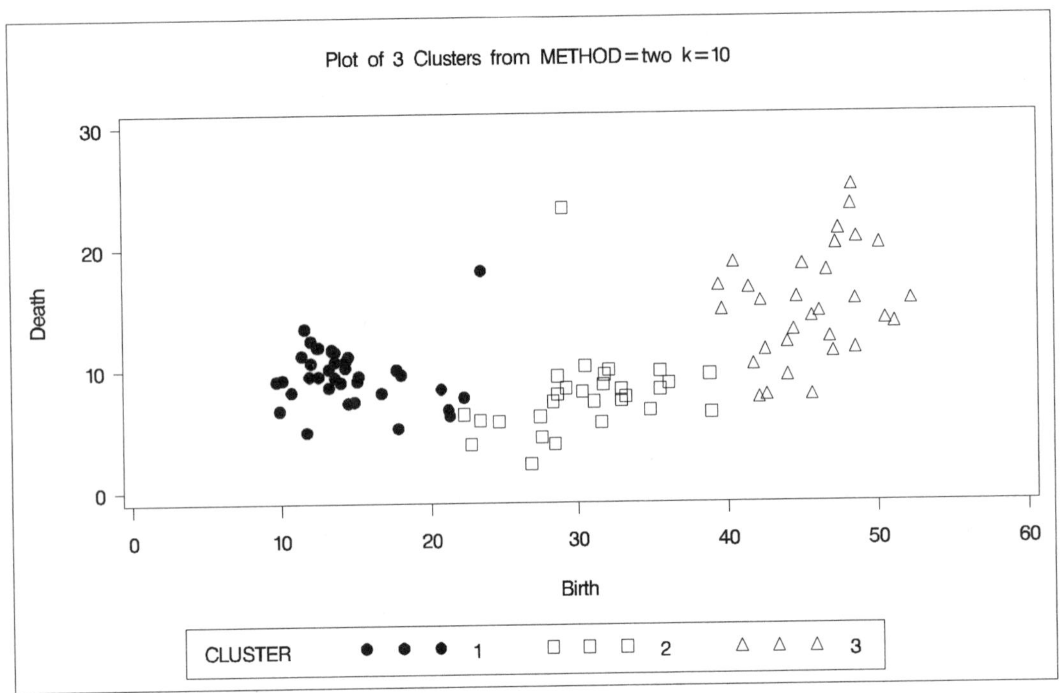

Output 23.2.7. Clusters for Birth and Death Rates: METHOD=TWOSTAGE, K=18

Cluster Analysis of Birth and Death Rates

The CLUSTER Procedure
Two-Stage Density Linkage Clustering

Eigenvalues of the Covariance Matrix

	Eigenvalue	Difference	Proportion	Cumulative
1	189.106588	173.101020	0.9220	0.9220
2	16.005568		0.0780	1.0000

K = 18

Root-Mean-Square Total-Sample Standard Deviation = 10.127

Cluster History

NCL	--Clusters Joined--		FREQ	SPRSQ	RSQ	ERSQ	CCC	PSF	PST2	Normalized Fusion Density	Maximum Density in Each Cluster Lesser	Greater	Tie
15	CL16	OB72	46	0.0107	.799	.975	-21	23.3	3.0	10.118	7.7445	23.4457	
14	CL15	OB94	47	0.0098	.789	.972	-21	23.9	2.7	9.676	7.1257	23.4457	
13	CL14	OB51	48	0.0037	.786	.969	-20	25.6	1.0	9.409	6.8398	23.4457	T
12	CL13	OB96	49	0.0099	.776	.966	-19	26.7	2.6	9.409	6.8398	23.4457	
11	CL12	OB76	50	0.0114	.764	.962	-19	27.9	2.9	8.8136	6.3138	23.4457	
10	CL11	OB77	51	0.0021	.762	.957	-18	31.0	0.5	8.6593	6.0751	23.4457	
9	CL10	OB78	52	0.0103	.752	.951	-17	33.3	2.5	8.6007	6.0976	23.4457	
8	CL9	OB43	53	0.0034	.748	.943	-16	37.8	0.8	8.4964	5.9160	23.4457	
7	CL8	OB93	54	0.0109	.737	.933	-15	42.1	2.6	8.367	5.7913	23.4457	
6	CL7	OB88	55	0.0110	.726	.920	-13	48.3	2.6	7.916	5.3679	23.4457	
5	CL6	OB87	56	0.0120	.714	.902	-12	57.5	2.7	6.6917	4.3415	23.4457	
4	CL20	OB61	39	0.0077	.707	.875	-9.8	74.7	8.3	6.2578	3.2882	100.0	
3	CL5	OB82	57	0.0138	.693	.827	-5.0	106	3.0	5.3605	3.2834	23.4457	
2	CL3	OB23	58	0.0117	.681	.697	-.54	203	2.5	3.2687	1.7568	23.4457	
1	CL2	CL4	97	0.6812	.000	.000	0.00	.	203	13.764	23.4457	100.0	

2 modal clusters have been formed.

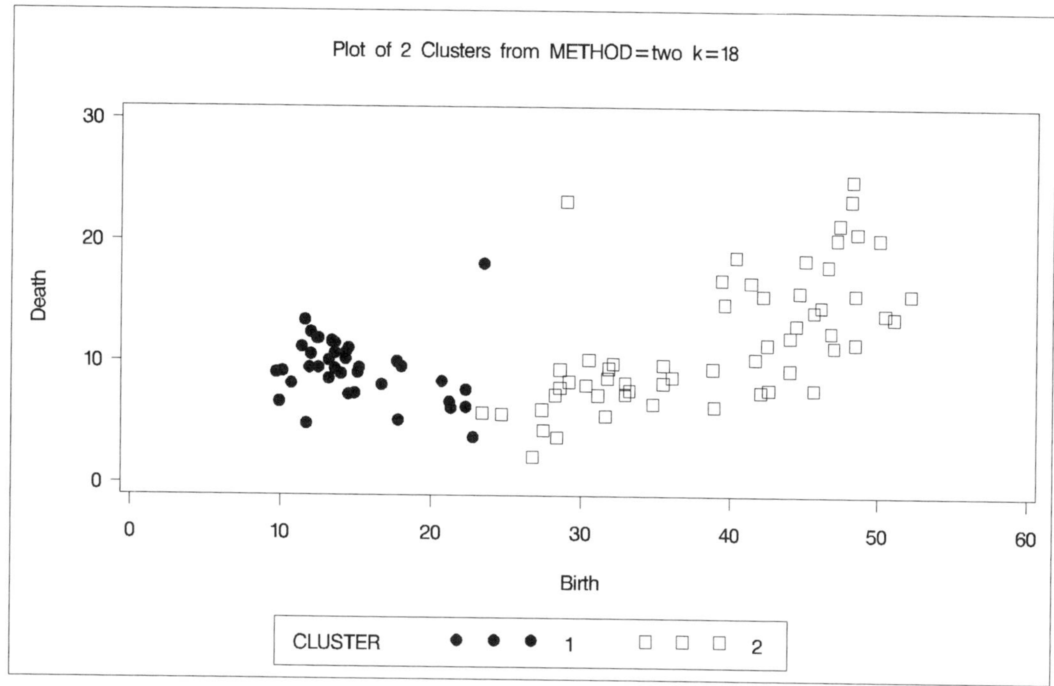

In summary, most of the clustering methods indicate 3 or 8 clusters. Most methods agree at the 3-cluster level, but at the other levels, there is considerable disagreement about the composition of the clusters. The presence of numerous ties also complicates the analysis; see Example 23.4.

Example 23.3. Cluster Analysis of Fisher Iris Data

The iris data published by Fisher (1936) have been widely used for examples in discriminant analysis and cluster analysis. The sepal length, sepal width, petal length, and petal width are measured in millimeters on fifty iris specimens from each of three species, *Iris setosa, I. versicolor,* and *I. virginica*. Mezzich and Solomon (1980) discuss a variety of cluster analyses of the iris data.

This example analyzes the iris data by Ward's method and two-stage density linkage and then illustrates how the FASTCLUS procedure can be used in combination with PROC CLUSTER to analyze large data sets.

```
title 'Cluster Analysis of Fisher (1936) Iris Data';
proc format;
   value specname
      1='Setosa    '
      2='Versicolor'
      3='Virginica ';
run;

data iris;
   input SepalLength SepalWidth PetalLength PetalWidth Species @@;
   format Species specname.;
   label SepalLength='Sepal Length in mm.'
```

```
          SepalWidth ='Sepal Width in mm.'
          PetalLength='Petal Length in mm.'
          PetalWidth ='Petal Width in mm.';
   symbol = put(species, specname10.);
   datalines;
50 33 14 02 1 64 28 56 22 3 65 28 46 15 2 67 31 56 24 3
63 28 51 15 3 46 34 14 03 1 69 31 51 23 3 62 22 45 15 2
59 32 48 18 2 46 36 10 02 1 61 30 46 14 2 60 27 51 16 2
65 30 52 20 3 56 25 39 11 2 65 30 55 18 3 58 27 51 19 3
68 32 59 23 3 51 33 17 05 1 57 28 45 13 2 62 34 54 23 3
77 38 67 22 3 63 33 47 16 2 67 33 57 25 3 76 30 66 21 3
49 25 45 17 3 55 35 13 02 1 67 30 52 23 3 70 32 47 14 2
64 32 45 15 2 61 28 40 13 2 48 31 16 02 1 59 30 51 18 3
55 24 38 11 2 63 25 50 19 3 64 32 53 23 3 52 34 14 02 1
49 36 14 01 1 54 30 45 15 2 79 38 64 20 3 44 32 13 02 1
67 33 57 21 3 50 35 16 06 1 58 26 40 12 2 44 30 13 02 1
77 28 67 20 3 63 27 49 18 3 47 32 16 02 1 55 26 44 12 2
50 23 33 10 2 72 32 60 18 3 48 30 14 03 1 51 38 16 02 1
61 30 49 18 3 48 34 19 02 1 50 30 16 02 1 50 32 12 02 1
61 26 56 14 3 64 28 56 21 3 43 30 11 01 1 58 40 12 02 1
51 38 19 04 1 67 31 44 14 2 62 28 48 18 3 49 30 14 02 1
51 35 14 02 1 56 30 45 15 2 58 27 41 10 2 50 34 16 04 1
46 32 14 02 1 60 29 45 15 2 57 26 35 10 2 57 44 15 04 1
50 36 14 02 1 77 30 61 23 3 63 34 56 24 3 58 27 51 19 3
57 29 42 13 2 72 30 58 16 3 54 34 15 04 1 52 41 15 01 1
71 30 59 21 3 64 31 55 18 3 60 30 48 18 3 63 29 56 18 3
49 24 33 10 2 56 27 42 13 2 57 30 42 12 2 55 42 14 02 1
49 31 15 02 1 77 26 69 23 3 60 22 50 15 3 54 39 17 04 1
66 29 46 13 2 52 27 39 14 2 60 34 45 16 2 50 34 15 02 1
44 29 14 02 1 50 20 35 10 2 55 24 37 10 2 58 27 39 12 2
47 32 13 02 1 46 31 15 02 1 69 32 57 23 3 62 29 43 13 2
74 28 61 19 3 59 30 42 15 2 51 34 15 02 1 50 35 13 03 1
56 28 49 20 3 60 22 40 10 2 73 29 63 18 3 67 25 58 18 3
49 31 15 01 1 67 31 47 15 2 63 23 44 13 2 54 37 15 02 1
56 30 41 13 2 63 25 49 15 2 61 28 47 12 2 64 29 43 13 2
51 25 30 11 2 57 28 41 13 2 65 30 58 22 3 69 31 54 21 3
54 39 13 04 1 51 35 14 03 1 72 36 61 25 3 65 32 51 20 3
61 29 47 14 2 56 29 36 13 2 69 31 49 15 2 64 27 53 19 3
68 30 55 21 3 55 25 40 13 2 48 34 16 02 1 48 30 14 01 1
45 23 13 03 1 57 25 50 20 3 57 38 17 03 1 51 38 15 03 1
55 23 40 13 2 66 30 44 14 2 68 28 48 14 2 54 34 17 02 1
51 37 15 04 1 52 35 15 02 1 58 28 51 24 3 67 30 50 17 2
63 33 60 25 3 53 37 15 02 1
;
```

The following macro, SHOW, is used in the subsequent analyses to display cluster results. It invokes the FREQ procedure to crosstabulate clusters and species. The CANDISC procedure computes canonical variables for discriminating among the clusters, and the first two canonical variables are plotted to show cluster membership. See Chapter 21, "The CANDISC Procedure," for a canonical discriminant analysis of the iris species.

```
%macro show;
proc freq;
   tables cluster*species;
run;
proc candisc noprint out=can;
   class cluster;
   var petal: sepal:;
run;
legend1 frame cframe=ligr cborder=black
        position=center value=(justify=center);
axis1 label=(angle=90 rotate=0) minor=none;
axis2 minor=none;
proc gplot;
   plot can2*can1=cluster /
      frame cframe=ligr legend=legend1 vaxis=axis1 haxis=axis2;
run;
%mend;
```

The first analysis clusters the iris data by Ward's method and plots the CCC and pseudo F and t^2 statistics. The CCC has a local peak at 3 clusters but a higher peak at 5 clusters. The pseudo F statistic indicates 3 clusters, while the pseudo t^2 statistic suggests 3 or 6 clusters. For large numbers of clusters, Version 6 of the SAS System produces somewhat different results than previous versions of PROC CLUSTER. This is due to changes in the treatment of ties. Results are identical for 5 or fewer clusters.

The TREE procedure creates an output data set containing the 3-cluster partition for use by the SHOW macro. The FREQ procedure reveals 16 misclassifications. The results are shown in Output 23.3.1.

```
title2 'By Ward''s Method';
proc cluster data=iris method=ward print=15 ccc pseudo;
   var petal: sepal:;
   copy species;
run;
legend1 frame cframe=ligr cborder=black
        position=center value=(justify=center);
axis1 label=(angle=90 rotate=0) minor=none order=(0 to 600 by 100);
axis2 minor=none order=(1 to 30 by 1);
axis3 label=(angle=90 rotate=0) minor=none order=(0 to 7 by 1);
proc gplot;
   plot _ccc_*_ncl_  /
      frame cframe=ligr legend=legend1 vaxis=axis3 haxis=axis2;
   plot _psf_*_ncl_  _pst2_*_ncl_  /overlay
      frame cframe=ligr legend=legend1 vaxis=axis1 haxis=axis2;
run;

proc tree noprint ncl=3 out=out;
   copy petal: sepal: species;
run;

%show;
```

Output 23.3.1. Cluster Analysis of Fisher Iris Data: CLUSTER with METHOD=WARD

Cluster Analysis of Fisher (1936) Iris Data
By Ward's Method

The CLUSTER Procedure
Ward's Minimum Variance Cluster Analysis

Eigenvalues of the Covariance Matrix

	Eigenvalue	Difference	Proportion	Cumulative
1	422.824171	398.557096	0.9246	0.9246
2	24.267075	16.446125	0.0531	0.9777
3	7.820950	5.437441	0.0171	0.9948
4	2.383509		0.0052	1.0000

Root-Mean-Square Total-Sample Standard Deviation = 10.69224
Root-Mean-Square Distance Between Observations = 30.24221

Cluster History

NCL	--Clusters Joined---		FREQ	SPRSQ	RSQ	ERSQ	CCC	PSF	PST2	Tie
15	CL24	CL28	15	0.0016	.971	.958	5.93	324	9.8	
14	CL21	CL53	7	0.0019	.969	.955	5.85	329	5.1	
13	CL18	CL48	15	0.0023	.967	.953	5.69	334	8.9	
12	CL16	CL23	24	0.0023	.965	.950	4.63	342	9.6	
11	CL14	CL43	12	0.0025	.962	.946	4.67	353	5.8	
10	CL26	CL20	22	0.0027	.959	.942	4.81	368	12.9	
9	CL27	CL17	31	0.0031	.956	.936	5.02	387	17.8	
8	CL35	CL15	23	0.0031	.953	.930	5.44	414	13.8	
7	CL10	CL47	26	0.0058	.947	.921	5.43	430	19.1	
6	CL8	CL13	38	0.0060	.941	.911	5.81	463	16.3	
5	CL9	CL19	50	0.0105	.931	.895	5.82	488	43.2	
4	CL12	CL11	36	0.0172	.914	.872	3.99	515	41.0	
3	CL6	CL7	64	0.0301	.884	.827	4.33	558	57.2	
2	CL4	CL3	100	0.1110	.773	.697	3.83	503	116	
1	CL5	CL2	150	0.7726	.000	.000	0.00	.	503	

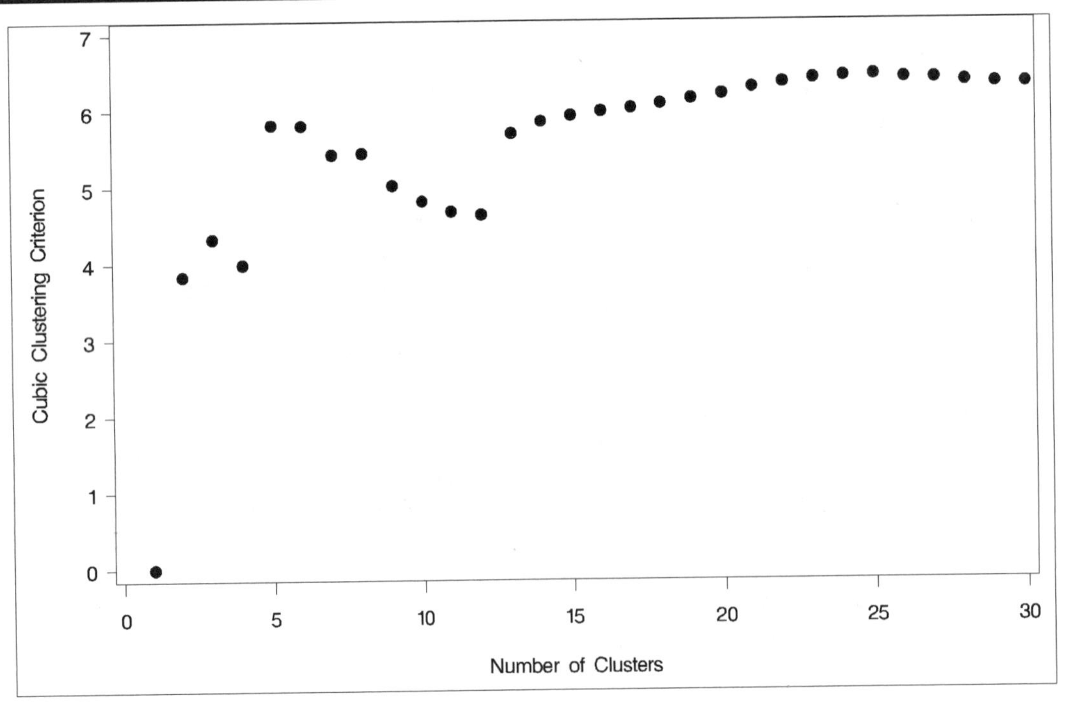

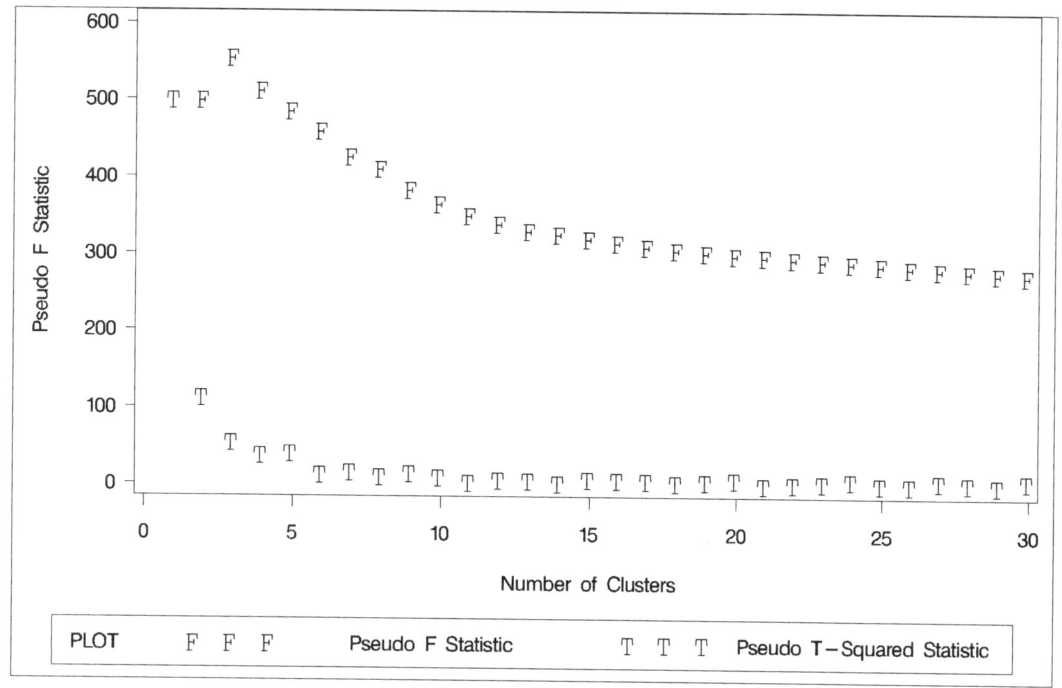

Cluster Analysis of Fisher (1936) Iris Data

The FREQ Procedure

Table of CLUSTER by Species

CLUSTER / Species Frequency Percent Row Pct Col Pct	Setosa	Versicolor	Virginica	Total
1	0 0.00 0.00 0.00	49 32.67 76.56 98.00	15 10.00 23.44 30.00	64 42.67
2	0 0.00 0.00 0.00	1 0.67 2.78 2.00	35 23.33 97.22 70.00	36 24.00
3	50 33.33 100.00 100.00	0 0.00 0.00 0.00	0 0.00 0.00 0.00	50 33.33
Total	50 33.33	50 33.33	50 33.33	150 100.00

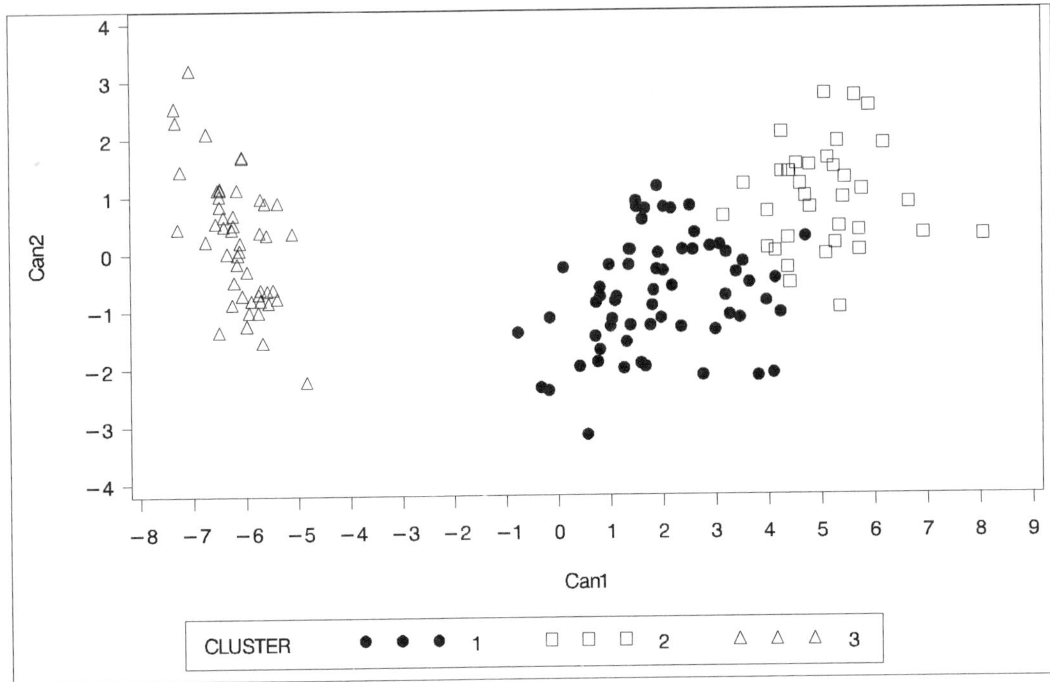

The second analysis uses two-stage density linkage. The raw data suggest 2 or 6 modes instead of 3:

k	**modes**
3	12
4-6	6
7	4
8	3
9-50	2
51+	1

However, the ACECLUS procedure can be used to reveal 3 modes. This analysis uses K=8 to produce 3 clusters for comparison with other analyses. There are only 6 misclassifications. The results are shown in Output 23.3.2.

```
title2 'By Two-Stage Density Linkage';
proc cluster data=iris method=twostage k=8 print=15 ccc pseudo;
   var petal: sepal:;
   copy species;
run;

proc tree noprint ncl=3 out=out;
   copy petal: sepal: species;
run;

%show;
```

Output 23.3.2. Cluster Analysis of Fisher Iris Data: CLUSTER with METHOD=TWOSTAGE

Cluster Analysis of Fisher (1936) Iris Data
By Two-Stage Density Linkage

The CLUSTER Procedure
Two-Stage Density Linkage Clustering

Eigenvalues of the Covariance Matrix

	Eigenvalue	Difference	Proportion	Cumulative
1	422.824171	398.557096	0.9246	0.9246
2	24.267075	16.446125	0.0531	0.9777
3	7.820950	5.437441	0.0171	0.9948
4	2.383509		0.0052	1.0000

K = 8
Root-Mean-Square Total-Sample Standard Deviation = 10.69224

Cluster History

NCL	--Clusters	Joined--	FREQ	SPRSQ	RSQ	ERSQ	CCC	PSF	PST2	Normalized Fusion Density	Maximum Density in Each Cluster Lesser	Greater	Tie
15	CL17	OB127	44	0.0025	.916	.958	-11	105	3.4	0.3903	0.2066	3.5156	
14	CL16	OB137	50	0.0023	.913	.955	-11	110	5.6	0.3637	0.1837	100.0	
13	CL15	OB74	45	0.0029	.910	.953	-10	116	3.7	0.3553	0.2130	3.5156	
12	CL28	OB49	46	0.0036	.907	.950	-8.0	122	5.2	0.3223	0.1736	8.3678	T
11	CL12	OB85	47	0.0036	.903	.946	-7.6	130	4.8	0.3223	0.1736	8.3678	
10	CL11	OB98	48	0.0033	.900	.942	-7.1	140	4.1	0.2879	0.1479	8.3678	
9	CL13	OB24	46	0.0037	.896	.936	-6.5	152	4.4	0.2802	0.2005	3.5156	
8	CL10	OB25	49	0.0019	.894	.930	-5.5	171	2.2	0.2699	0.1372	8.3678	
7	CL8	OB121	50	0.0035	.891	.921	-4.5	194	4.0	0.2586	0.1372	8.3678	
6	CL9	OB45	47	0.0042	.886	.911	-3.3	225	4.6	0.1412	0.0832	3.5156	
5	CL6	OB39	48	0.0049	.882	.895	-1.7	270	5.0	0.107	0.0605	3.5156	
4	CL5	OB21	49	0.0049	.877	.872	0.35	346	4.7	0.0969	0.0541	3.5156	
3	CL4	OB90	50	0.0047	.872	.827	3.28	500	4.1	0.0715	0.0370	3.5156	
2	CL3	CL7	100	0.0993	.773	.697	3.83	503	91.9	2.6277	3.5156	8.3678	

3 modal clusters have been formed.

Cluster Analysis of Fisher (1936) Iris Data

The FREQ Procedure

Table of CLUSTER by Species

```
CLUSTER     Species

Frequency|
Percent  |
Row Pct  |
Col Pct  |Setosa  |Versicol|Virginic|  Total
         |        |or      |a       |
---------+--------+--------+--------+
       1 |     50 |      0 |      0 |     50
         |  33.33 |   0.00 |   0.00 |  33.33
         | 100.00 |   0.00 |   0.00 |
         | 100.00 |   0.00 |   0.00 |
---------+--------+--------+--------+
       2 |      0 |     47 |      3 |     50
         |   0.00 |  31.33 |   2.00 |  33.33
         |   0.00 |  94.00 |   6.00 |
         |   0.00 |  94.00 |   6.00 |
---------+--------+--------+--------+
       3 |      0 |      3 |     47 |     50
         |   0.00 |   2.00 |  31.33 |  33.33
         |   0.00 |   6.00 |  94.00 |
         |   0.00 |   6.00 |  94.00 |
---------+--------+--------+--------+
Total          50       50       50      150
            33.33    33.33    33.33   100.00
```

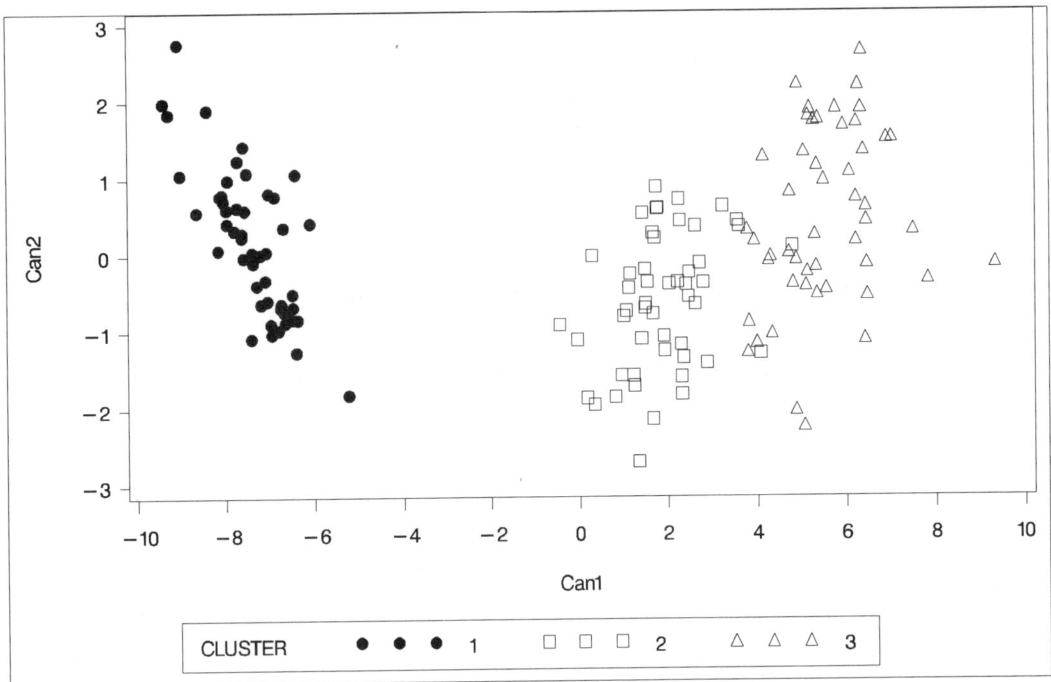

The CLUSTER procedure is not practical for very large data sets because, with most methods, the CPU time varies as the square or cube of the number of observations. The FASTCLUS procedure requires time proportional to the number of observations and can, therefore, be used with much larger data sets than PROC CLUSTER. If you want to hierarchically cluster a very large data set, you can use PROC FASTCLUS for a preliminary cluster analysis producing a large number of clusters and then use PROC CLUSTER to hierarchically cluster the preliminary clusters.

FASTCLUS automatically creates variables _FREQ_ and _RMSSTD_ in the MEAN= output data set. These variables are then automatically used by PROC CLUSTER in the computation of various statistics.

The iris data are used to illustrate the process of clustering clusters. In the preliminary analysis, PROC FASTCLUS produces ten clusters, which are then crosstabulated with species. The data set containing the preliminary clusters is sorted in preparation for later merges. The results are shown in Output 23.3.3.

```
title2 'Preliminary Analysis by FASTCLUS';
proc fastclus data=iris summary maxc=10 maxiter=99 converge=0
              mean=mean out=prelim cluster=preclus;
   var petal: sepal:;
run;

proc freq;
   tables preclus*species;
run;

proc sort data=prelim;
   by preclus;
run;
```

Output 23.3.3. Preliminary Analysis of Fisher Iris Data

Cluster Analysis of Fisher (1936) Iris Data
Preliminary Analysis by FASTCLUS

The FASTCLUS Procedure
Replace=FULL Radius=0 Maxclusters=10 Maxiter=99 Converge=0

Cluster Summary

Cluster	Frequency	RMS Std Deviation	Maximum Distance from Seed to Observation	Radius Exceeded	Nearest Cluster	Distance Between Cluster Centroids
1	9	2.7067	8.2027		5	8.7362
2	19	2.2001	7.7340		4	6.2243
3	18	2.1496	6.2173		8	7.5049
4	4	2.5249	5.3268		2	6.2243
5	3	2.7234	5.8214		1	8.7362
6	7	2.2939	5.1508		2	9.3318
7	17	2.0274	6.9576		10	7.9503
8	18	2.2628	7.1135		3	7.5049
9	22	2.2666	7.5029		8	9.0090
10	33	2.0594	10.0033		7	7.9503

Pseudo F Statistic = 370.58

Observed Over-All R-Squared = 0.95971

Approximate Expected Over-All R-Squared = 0.82928

Cubic Clustering Criterion = 27.077

WARNING: The two values above are invalid for correlated variables.

```
              Cluster Analysis of Fisher (1936) Iris Data
                   Preliminary Analysis by FASTCLUS

                         The FREQ Procedure

                   Table of PRECLUS by Species

          PRECLUS(Cluster)     Species

          Frequency|
          Percent  |
          Row Pct  |
          Col Pct  |Setosa  |Versicol|Virginic|  Total
                   |        |or      |a       |
          ---------+--------+--------+--------+
                 1 |      0 |      0 |      9 |      9
                   |   0.00 |   0.00 |   6.00 |   6.00
                   |   0.00 |   0.00 | 100.00 |
                   |   0.00 |   0.00 |  18.00 |
          ---------+--------+--------+--------+
                 2 |      0 |     19 |      0 |     19
                   |   0.00 |  12.67 |   0.00 |  12.67
                   |   0.00 | 100.00 |   0.00 |
                   |   0.00 |  38.00 |   0.00 |
          ---------+--------+--------+--------+
                 3 |      0 |     18 |      0 |     18
                   |   0.00 |  12.00 |   0.00 |  12.00
                   |   0.00 | 100.00 |   0.00 |
                   |   0.00 |  36.00 |   0.00 |
          ---------+--------+--------+--------+
                 4 |      0 |      3 |      1 |      4
                   |   0.00 |   2.00 |   0.67 |   2.67
                   |   0.00 |  75.00 |  25.00 |
                   |   0.00 |   6.00 |   2.00 |
          ---------+--------+--------+--------+
                 5 |      0 |      0 |      3 |      3
                   |   0.00 |   0.00 |   2.00 |   2.00
                   |   0.00 |   0.00 | 100.00 |
                   |   0.00 |   0.00 |   6.00 |
          ---------+--------+--------+--------+
                 6 |      0 |      7 |      0 |      7
                   |   0.00 |   4.67 |   0.00 |   4.67
                   |   0.00 | 100.00 |   0.00 |
                   |   0.00 |  14.00 |   0.00 |
          ---------+--------+--------+--------+
                 7 |     17 |      0 |      0 |     17
                   |  11.33 |   0.00 |   0.00 |  11.33
                   | 100.00 |   0.00 |   0.00 |
                   |  34.00 |   0.00 |   0.00 |
          ---------+--------+--------+--------+
                 8 |      0 |      3 |     15 |     18
                   |   0.00 |   2.00 |  10.00 |  12.00
                   |   0.00 |  16.67 |  83.33 |
                   |   0.00 |   6.00 |  30.00 |
          ---------+--------+--------+--------+
                 9 |      0 |      0 |     22 |     22
                   |   0.00 |   0.00 |  14.67 |  14.67
                   |   0.00 |   0.00 | 100.00 |
                   |   0.00 |   0.00 |  44.00 |
          ---------+--------+--------+--------+
                10 |     33 |      0 |      0 |     33
                   |  22.00 |   0.00 |   0.00 |  22.00
                   | 100.00 |   0.00 |   0.00 |
                   |  66.00 |   0.00 |   0.00 |
          ---------+--------+--------+--------+
          Total          50       50       50      150
                      33.33    33.33    33.33   100.00
```

The following macro, CLUS, clusters the preliminary clusters. There is one argument to choose the METHOD= specification to be used by PROC CLUSTER. The TREE procedure creates an output data set containing the 3-cluster partition, which is sorted and merged with the OUT= data set from PROC FASTCLUS to determine to which cluster each of the original 150 observations belongs. The SHOW macro is then used to display the results. In this example, the CLUS macro is invoked using

Ward's method, which produces 16 misclassifications, and Wong's hybrid method, which produces 22 misclassifications. The results are shown in Output 23.3.4 and Output 23.3.5.

```
%macro clus(method);
proc cluster data=mean method=&method ccc pseudo;
   var petal: sepal:;
   copy preclus;
run;
proc tree noprint ncl=3 out=out;
   copy petal: sepal: preclus;
run;
proc sort data=out;
   by preclus;
run;
data clus;
   merge prelim out;
   by preclus;
run;
%show;
%mend;

title2 'Clustering Clusters by Ward''s Method';
%clus(ward);

title2 'Clustering Clusters by Wong''s Hybrid Method';
%clus(twostage hybrid);
```

Output 23.3.4. Clustering Clusters: with Ward's Method

```
                       Cluster Analysis of Fisher (1936) Iris Data
                          Clustering Clusters by Ward's Method

                                 The CLUSTER Procedure
                         Ward's Minimum Variance Cluster Analysis

                           Eigenvalues of the Covariance Matrix

                       Eigenvalue    Difference    Proportion    Cumulative

                  1    416.976349    398.666421        0.9501        0.9501
                  2     18.309928     14.952922        0.0417        0.9918
                  3      3.357006      3.126943        0.0076        0.9995
                  4      0.230063                      0.0005        1.0000


              Root-Mean-Square Total-Sample Standard Deviation = 10.69224
              Root-Mean-Square Distance Between Observations   = 30.24221


                                     Cluster History
                                                                                          T
                                                                                          i
NCL    --Clusters Joined---       FREQ    SPRSQ     RSQ    ERSQ     CCC     PSF    PST2   e

  9    OB2          OB4             23    0.0019   .958    .932    6.26     400     6.3
  8    OB1          OB5             12    0.0025   .955    .926    6.75     434     5.8
  7    CL9          OB6             30    0.0069   .948    .918    6.28     438    19.5
  6    OB3          OB8             36    0.0074   .941    .907    6.21     459    26.0
  5    OB7          OB10            50    0.0104   .931    .892    6.15     485    42.2
  4    CL8          OB9             34    0.0162   .914    .870    4.28     519    39.3
  3    CL7          CL6             66    0.0318   .883    .824    4.39     552    59.7
  2    CL4          CL3            100    0.1099   .773    .695    3.94     503     113
  1    CL2          CL5            150    0.7726   .000    .000    0.00       .     503
```

```
Cluster Analysis of Fisher (1936) Iris Data

                  The FREQ Procedure

             Table of CLUSTER by Species

CLUSTER      Species

Frequency|
Percent  |
Row Pct  |
Col Pct  |Setosa  |Versicol|Virginic|  Total
         |        |or      |a       |
---------+--------+--------+--------+
       1 |      0 |     50 |     16 |     66
         |   0.00 |  33.33 |  10.67 |  44.00
         |   0.00 |  75.76 |  24.24 |
         |   0.00 | 100.00 |  32.00 |
---------+--------+--------+--------+
       2 |      0 |      0 |     34 |     34
         |   0.00 |   0.00 |  22.67 |  22.67
         |   0.00 |   0.00 | 100.00 |
         |   0.00 |   0.00 |  68.00 |
---------+--------+--------+--------+
       3 |     50 |      0 |      0 |     50
         |  33.33 |   0.00 |   0.00 |  33.33
         | 100.00 |   0.00 |   0.00 |
         | 100.00 |   0.00 |   0.00 |
---------+--------+--------+--------+
Total          50       50       50      150
            33.33    33.33    33.33   100.00
```

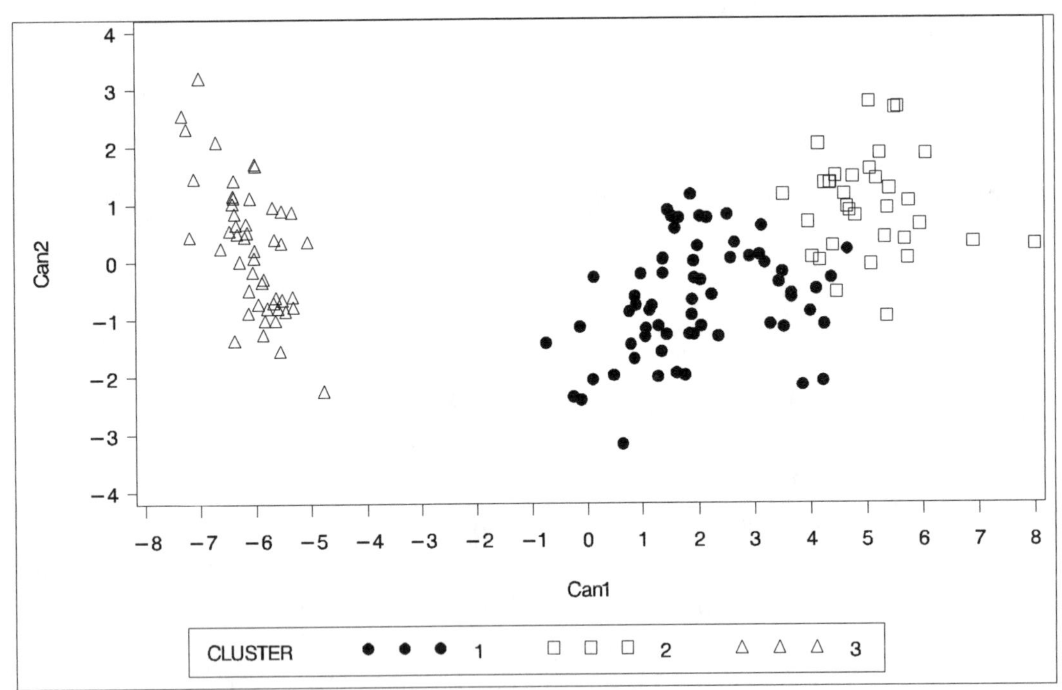

Output 23.3.5. Clustering Clusters: PROC CLUSTER with Wong's Hybrid Method

Cluster Analysis of Fisher (1936) Iris Data
Clustering Clusters by Wong's Hybrid Method

The CLUSTER Procedure
Two-Stage Density Linkage Clustering

Eigenvalues of the Covariance Matrix

	Eigenvalue	Difference	Proportion	Cumulative
1	416.976349	398.666421	0.9501	0.9501
2	18.309928	14.952922	0.0417	0.9918
3	3.357006	3.126943	0.0076	0.9995
4	0.230063		0.0005	1.0000

Root-Mean-Square Total-Sample Standard Deviation = 10.69224

Cluster History

NCL	--Clusters Joined--		FREQ	SPRSQ	RSQ	ERSQ	CCC	PSF	PST2	Normalized Fusion Density	Maximum Density in Each Cluster Lesser	Greater	Tie
9	OB10	OB7	50	0.0104	.949	.932	3.81	330	42.2	40.24	58.2179	100.0	
8	OB3	OB8	36	0.0074	.942	.926	3.22	329	26.0	27.981	39.4511	48.4350	
7	OB2	OB4	23	0.0019	.940	.918	4.24	373	6.3	23.775	8.9675	46.3026	
6	CL8	OB9	58	0.0194	.921	.907	2.13	334	46.3	20.724	46.8846	48.4350	
5	CL7	OB6	30	0.0069	.914	.892	3.09	383	19.5	13.303	17.6360	46.3026	
4	CL6	OB1	67	0.0292	.884	.870	1.21	372	41.0	8.4137	10.8758	48.4350	
3	CL4	OB5	70	0.0138	.871	.824	3.33	494	12.3	5.1855	6.2890	48.4350	
2	CL3	CL5	100	0.0979	.773	.695	3.94	503	89.5	19.513	46.3026	48.4350	
1	CL2	CL9	150	0.7726	.000	.000	0.00	.	503	1.3337	48.4350	100.0	

3 modal clusters have been formed.

Cluster Analysis of Fisher (1936) Iris Data

The FREQ Procedure

Table of CLUSTER by Species

CLUSTER (Frequency / Percent / Row Pct / Col Pct)	Species: Setosa	Versicolor	Virginica	Total
1	50	0	0	50
	33.33	0.00	0.00	33.33
	100.00	0.00	0.00	
	100.00	0.00	0.00	
2	0	21	49	70
	0.00	14.00	32.67	46.67
	0.00	30.00	70.00	
	0.00	42.00	98.00	
3	0	29	1	30
	0.00	19.33	0.67	20.00
	0.00	96.67	3.33	
	0.00	58.00	2.00	
Total	50	50	50	150
	33.33	33.33	33.33	100.00

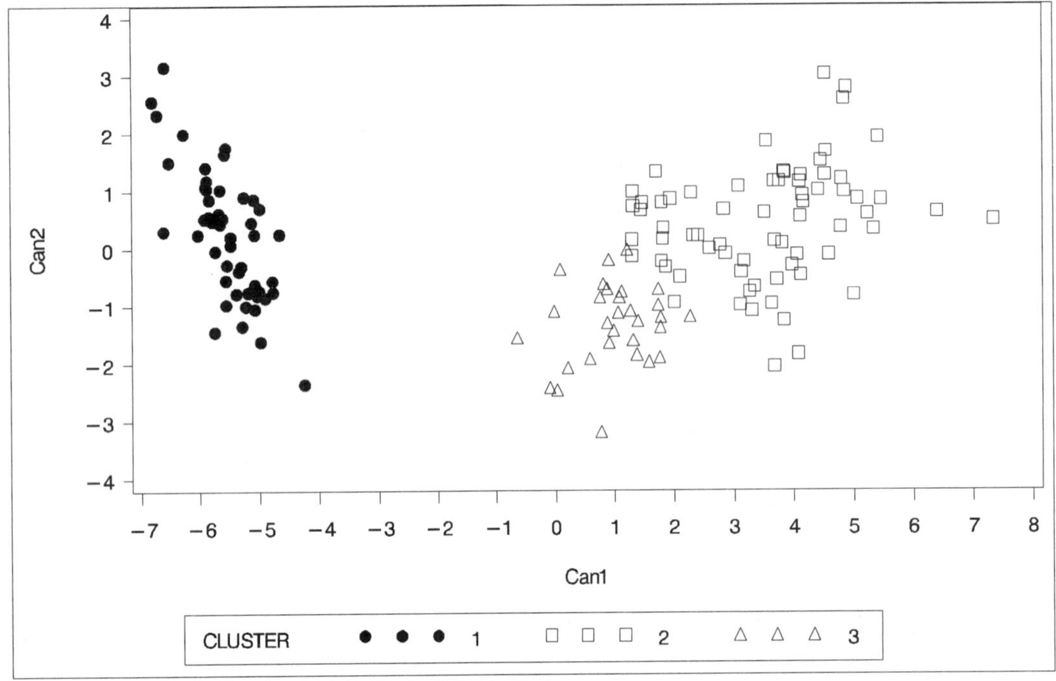

Example 23.4. Evaluating the Effects of Ties

If, at some level of the cluster history, there is a tie for minimum distance between clusters, then one or more levels of the sample cluster tree are not uniquely determined. This example shows how the degree of indeterminacy can be assessed.

Mammals have four kinds of teeth: incisors, canines, premolars, and molars. The following data set gives the number of teeth of each kind on one side of the top and bottom jaws for 32 mammals.

Since all eight variables are measured in the same units, it is not strictly necessary to rescale the data. However, the canines have much less variance than the other kinds of teeth and, therefore, have little effect on the analysis if the variables are not standardized. An average linkage cluster analysis is run with and without standardization to allow comparison of the results. The results are shown in Output 23.4.1 and Output 23.4.2.

```
title 'Hierarchical Cluster Analysis of Mammals'' Teeth Data';
title2 'Evaluating the Effects of Ties';
data teeth;
   input mammal $ 1-16
         @21 (v1-v8) (1.);
   label v1='Top incisors'
         v2='Bottom incisors'
         v3='Top canines'
         v4='Bottom canines'
         v5='Top premolars'
         v6='Bottom premolars'
         v7='Top molars'
         v8='Bottom molars';
```

```
   datalines;
BROWN BAT          23113333
MOLE               32103333
SILVER HAIR BAT    23112333
PIGMY BAT          23112233
HOUSE BAT          23111233
RED BAT            13112233
PIKA               21002233
RABBIT             21003233
BEAVER             11002133
GROUNDHOG          11002133
GRAY SQUIRREL      11001133
HOUSE MOUSE        11000033
PORCUPINE          11001133
WOLF               33114423
BEAR               33114423
RACCOON            33114432
MARTEN             33114412
WEASEL             33113312
WOLVERINE          33114412
BADGER             33113312
RIVER OTTER        33114312
SEA OTTER          32113312
JAGUAR             33113211
COUGAR             33113211
FUR SEAL           32114411
SEA LION           32114411
GREY SEAL          32113322
ELEPHANT SEAL      21114411
REINDEER           04103333
ELK                04103333
DEER               04003333
MOOSE              04003333
;

proc cluster data=teeth method=average nonorm
             outtree=_null_;
   var v1-v8;
   id mammal;
   title3 'Raw Data';
run;

proc cluster data=teeth std method=average nonorm
             outtree=_null_;
   var v1-v8;
   id mammal;
   title3 'Standardized Data';
run;
```

Output 23.4.1. Average Linkage Analysis of Mammals' Teeth Data: Raw Data

```
              Hierarchical Cluster Analysis of Mammals' Teeth Data
                          Evaluating the Effects of Ties
                                     Raw Data

                              The CLUSTER Procedure
                         Average Linkage Cluster Analysis

                        Eigenvalues of the Covariance Matrix

            Eigenvalue    Difference    Proportion    Cumulative

     1      3.76799365    2.33557185        0.5840        0.5840
     2      1.43242180    0.91781899        0.2220        0.8061
     3      0.51460281    0.08414950        0.0798        0.8858
     4      0.43045331    0.30021485        0.0667        0.9525
     5      0.13023846    0.03814626        0.0202        0.9727
     6      0.09209220    0.04216914        0.0143        0.9870
     7      0.04992305    0.01603541        0.0077        0.9947
     8      0.03388764                      0.0053        1.0000


     Root-Mean-Square Total-Sample Standard Deviation = 0.898027


                                 Cluster History
                                                                       T
                                                                RMS    i
NCL     ----------Clusters Joined-----------      FREQ         Dist    e

 31     BEAVER              GROUNDHOG                2            0    T
 30     GRAY SQUIRREL       PORCUPINE                2            0    T
 29     WOLF                BEAR                     2            0    T
 28     MARTEN              WOLVERINE                2            0    T
 27     WEASEL              BADGER                   2            0    T
 26     JAGUAR              COUGAR                   2            0    T
 25     FUR SEAL            SEA LION                 2            0    T
 24     REINDEER            ELK                      2            0    T
 23     DEER                MOOSE                    2            0
 22     BROWN BAT           SILVER HAIR BAT          2            1    T
 21     PIGMY BAT           HOUSE BAT                2            1    T
 20     PIKA                RABBIT                   2            1    T
 19     CL31                CL30                     4            1    T
 18     CL28                RIVER OTTER              3            1    T
 17     CL27                SEA OTTER                3            1    T
 16     CL24                CL23                     4            1
 15     CL21                RED BAT                  3       1.2247
 14     CL17                GREY SEAL                4        1.291
 13     CL29                RACCOON                  3       1.4142    T
 12     CL25                ELEPHANT SEAL            3       1.4142
 11     CL18                CL14                     7       1.5546
 10     CL22                CL15                     5       1.5811
  9     CL20                CL19                     6       1.8708    T
  8     CL11                CL26                     9       1.9272
  7     CL8                 CL12                    12       2.2278
  6     MOLE                CL13                     4       2.2361
  5     CL9                 HOUSE MOUSE              7       2.4833
  4     CL6                 CL7                     16       2.5658
  3     CL10                CL16                     9       2.8107
  2     CL3                 CL5                     16       3.7054
  1     CL2                 CL4                     32       4.2939
```

Output 23.4.2. Average Linkage Analysis of Mammals' Teeth Data: Standardized Data

```
                     Hierarchical Cluster Analysis of Mammals' Teeth Data
                                Evaluating the Effects of Ties
                                       Standardized Data

                                    The CLUSTER Procedure
                               Average Linkage Cluster Analysis

                              Eigenvalues of the Correlation Matrix

                       Eigenvalue     Difference     Proportion     Cumulative

                  1    4.74153902     3.27458808         0.5927         0.5927
                  2    1.46695094     0.70824118         0.1834         0.7761
                  3    0.75870977     0.25146252         0.0948         0.8709
                  4    0.50724724     0.30264737         0.0634         0.9343
                  5    0.20459987     0.05925818         0.0256         0.9599
                  6    0.14534169     0.03450100         0.0182         0.9780
                  7    0.11084070     0.04606994         0.0139         0.9919
                  8    0.06477076                        0.0081         1.0000


              The data have been standardized to mean 0 and variance 1
              Root-Mean-Square Total-Sample Standard Deviation =        1


                                      Cluster History
                                                                                T
                                                                     RMS        i
          NCL     ----------Clusters Joined-----------      FREQ      Dist      e

           31     BEAVER              GROUNDHOG                 2         0     T
           30     GRAY SQUIRREL       PORCUPINE                 2         0     T
           29     WOLF                BEAR                      2         0     T
           28     MARTEN              WOLVERINE                 2         0     T
           27     WEASEL              BADGER                    2         0     T
           26     JAGUAR              COUGAR                    2         0     T
           25     FUR SEAL            SEA LION                  2         0     T
           24     REINDEER            ELK                       2         0     T
           23     DEER                MOOSE                     2         0
           22     PIGMY BAT           RED BAT                   2    0.9157
           21     CL28                RIVER OTTER               3    0.9169
           20     CL31                CL30                      4    0.9428     T
           19     BROWN BAT           SILVER HAIR BAT           2    0.9428     T
           18     PIKA                RABBIT                    2    0.9428
           17     CL27                SEA OTTER                 3    0.9847
           16     CL22                HOUSE BAT                 3    1.1437
           15     CL21                CL17                      6    1.3314
           14     CL25                ELEPHANT SEAL             3    1.3447
           13     CL19                CL16                      5    1.4688
           12     CL15                GREY SEAL                 7    1.6314
           11     CL29                RACCOON                   3     1.692
           10     CL18                CL20                      6    1.7357
            9     CL12                CL26                      9    2.0285
            8     CL24                CL23                      4    2.1891
            7     CL9                 CL14                     12    2.2674
            6     CL10                HOUSE MOUSE               7     2.317
            5     CL11                CL7                      15    2.6484
            4     CL13                MOLE                      6    2.8624
            3     CL4                 CL8                      10    3.5194
            2     CL3                 CL6                      17    4.1265
            1     CL2                 CL5                      32    4.7753
```

There are ties at 16 levels for the raw data but at only 10 levels for the standardized data. There are more ties for the raw data because the increments between successive values are the same for all of the raw variables but different for the standardized variables.

One way to assess the importance of the ties in the analysis is to repeat the analysis on several random permutations of the observations and then to see to what extent the results are consistent at the interesting levels of the cluster history. Three macros are presented to facilitate this process.

```
/* -------------------------------------------------------- */
/*                                                          */
/* The macro CLUSPERM randomly permutes observations and    */
/* does a cluster analysis for each permutation.            */
/* The arguments are as follows:                            */
/*                                                          */
/*    data    data set name                                 */
/*    var     list of variables to cluster                  */
/*    id      id variable for proc cluster                  */
/*    method  clustering method (and possibly other options) */
/*    nperm   number of random permutations.                */
/*                                                          */
/* -------------------------------------------------------- */
%macro CLUSPERM(data,var,id,method,nperm);
/* ------CREATE TEMPORARY DATA SET WITH RANDOM NUMBERS------ */
data _temp_;
   set &data;
   array _random_ _ran_1-_ran_&nperm;
   do over _random_;
     _random_=ranuni(835297461);
   end;
run;
/* ------PERMUTE AND CLUSTER THE DATA----------------------- */
%do n=1 %to &nperm;
    proc sort data=_temp_(keep=_ran_&n &var &id) out=_perm_;
       by _ran_&n;
    run;
    proc cluster method=&method noprint outtree=_tree_&n;
       var &var;
       id &id;
    run;
%end;
%mend;

/* -------------------------------------------------------- */
/*                                                          */
/* The macro PLOTPERM plots various cluster statistics      */
/* against the number of clusters for each permutation.     */
/* The arguments are as follows:                            */
/*                                                          */
/*    stats   names of variables from tree data set         */
/*    nclus   maximum number of clusters to be plotted      */
/*    nperm   number of random permutations.                */
/*                                                          */
/* -------------------------------------------------------- */
%macro PLOTPERM(stat,nclus,nperm);
/* ---CONCATENATE TREE DATA SETS FOR 20 OR FEWER CLUSTERS--- */
data _plot_;
   set %do n=1 %to &nperm; _tree_&n(in=_in_&n) %end; ;
   if _ncl_<=&nclus;
   %do n=1 %to &nperm;
      if _in_&n then _perm_=&n;
   %end;
   label _perm_='permutation number';
```

```
   keep _ncl_ &stat _perm_;
run;
/* ---PLOT THE REQUESTED STATISTICS BY NUMBER OF CLUSTERS--- */

proc plot;
   plot (&stat)*_ncl_=_perm_ /vpos=26;
title2 'Symbol is value of _PERM_';
run;
%mend;

/* -------------------------------------------------------- */
/*                                                          */
/* The macro TREEPERM generates cluster-membership variables */
/* for a specified number of clusters for each permutation.  */
/* PROC PRINT lists the objects in each cluster-combination, */
/* and PROC TABULATE gives the frequencies and means.  The   */
/* arguments are as follows:                                 */
/*                                                          */
/*    var     list of variables to cluster                  */
/*            (no "-" or ":" allowed)                        */
/*    id      id variable for proc cluster                  */
/*    meanfmt format for printing means in PROC TABULATE    */
/*    nclus   number of clusters desired                    */
/*    nperm   number of random permutations.                */
/*                                                          */
/* -------------------------------------------------------- */
%macro TREEPERM(var,id,meanfmt,nclus,nperm);
/* ------CREATE DATA SETS GIVING CLUSTER MEMBERSHIP--------- */
%do n=1 %to &nperm;
   proc tree data=_tree_&n noprint n=&nclus
             out=_out_&n(drop=clusname
                          rename=(cluster=_clus_&n));
      copy &var;
      id &id;
   run;
   proc sort;
      by &id &var;
   run;
%end;
/* ------MERGE THE CLUSTER VARIABLES------------------------ */
data _merge_;
   merge
      %do n=1 %to &nperm;
         _out_&n
      %end; ;
   by &id &var;
   length all_clus $ %eval(3*&nperm);
   %do n=1 %to &nperm;
      substr( all_clus, %eval(1+(&n-1)*3), 3) =
         put( _clus_&n, 3.);
   %end;
run;
```

```
/* ------PRINT AND TABULATE CLUSTER COMBINATIONS----------- */
proc sort;
   by _clus_:;
run;
proc print;
   var &var;
   id &id;
   by all_clus notsorted;
run;
proc tabulate order=data formchar='           ';
   class all_clus;
   var &var;
   table all_clus, n='FREQ'*f=5. mean*f=&meanfmt*(&var) /
      rts=%eval(&nperm*3+1);
run;
%mend;
```

To use these, it is first convenient to define a macro, VLIST, listing the teeth variables, since the forms V1-V8 or V: cannot be used with the TABULATE procedure in the TREEPERM macro:

```
/* -TABULATE does not accept hyphens or colons in VAR lists- */
%let vlist=v1 v2 v3 v4 v5 v6 v7 v8;
```

The CLUSPERM macro is then called to analyze ten random permutations. The PLOTPERM macro plots the pseudo F and t^2 statistics and the cubic clustering criterion. Since the data are discrete, the pseudo F statistic and the cubic clustering criterion can be expected to increase as the number of clusters increases, so local maxima or large jumps in these statistics are more relevant than the global maximum in determining the number of clusters. For the raw data, only the pseudo t^2 statistic indicates the possible presence of clusters, with the 4-cluster level being suggested. Hence, the TREEPERM macro is used to analyze the results at the 4-cluster level:

```
title3 'Raw Data';

/* ------CLUSTER RAW DATA WITH AVERAGE LINKAGE-------------- */
%clusperm( teeth, &vlist, mammal, average, 10);

/* -----PLOT STATISTICS FOR THE LAST 20 LEVELS-------------- */
%plotperm( _psf_ _pst2_ _ccc_, 20, 10);

/* ------ANALYZE THE 4-CLUSTER LEVEL----------------------- */
%treeperm( &vlist, mammal, 9.1, 4, 10);
```

The results are shown in Output 23.4.3.

Output 23.4.3. Analysis of Ten Random Permutations of Raw Mammals' Teeth Data: Indeterminacy at the 4-Cluster Level

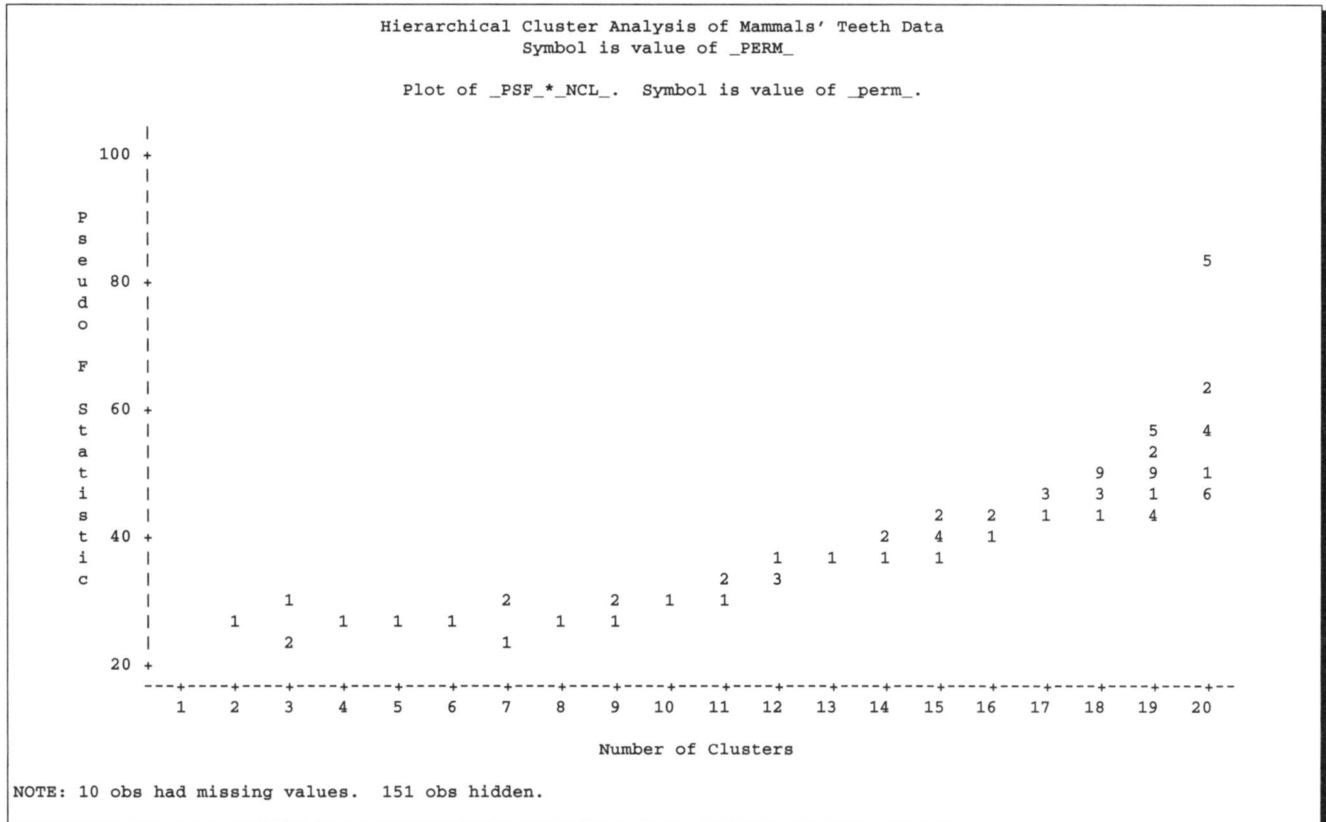

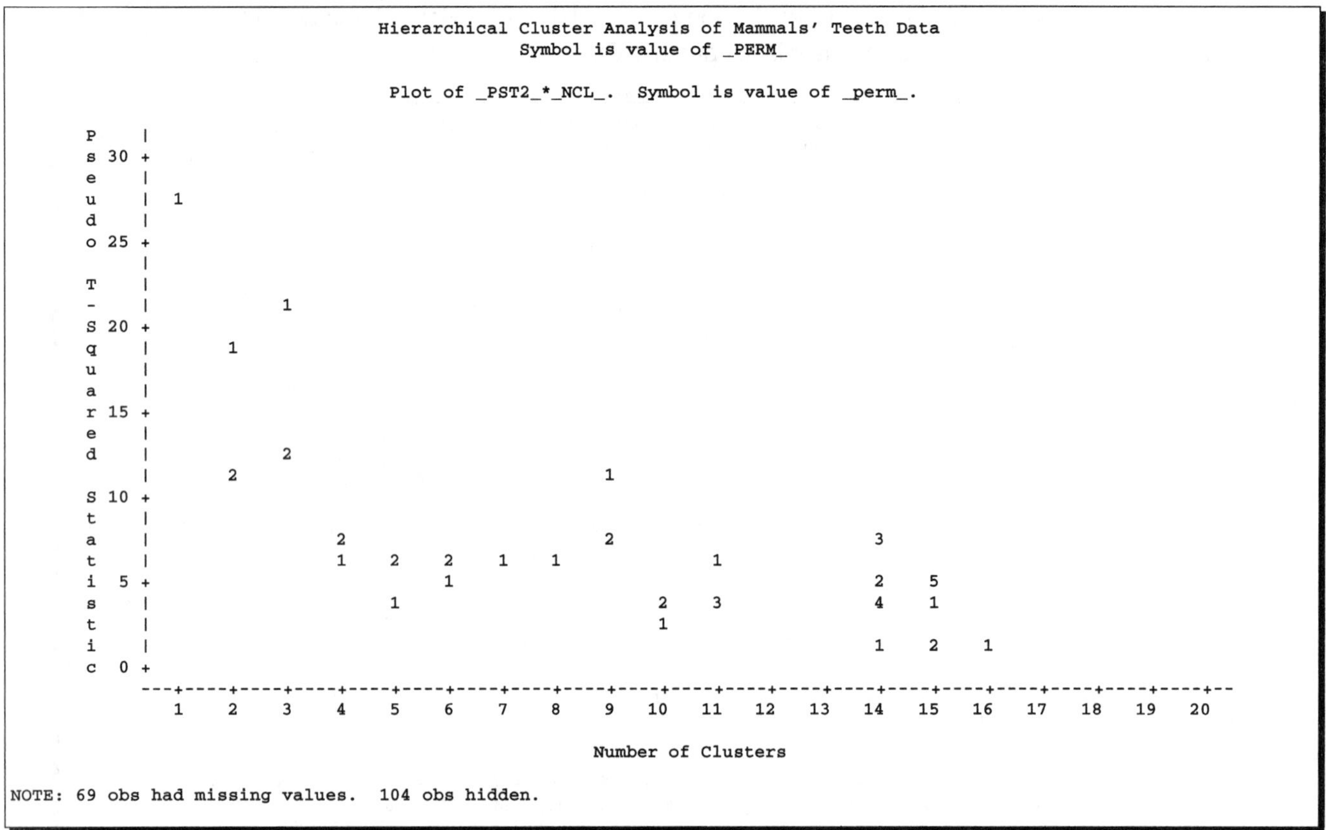
Hierarchical Cluster Analysis of Mammals' Teeth Data
Symbol is value of _PERM_
Plot of _PST2_*_NCL_. Symbol is value of _perm_.
Pseudo T-Squared Statistic
Number of Clusters
NOTE: 69 obs had missing values. 104 obs hidden.

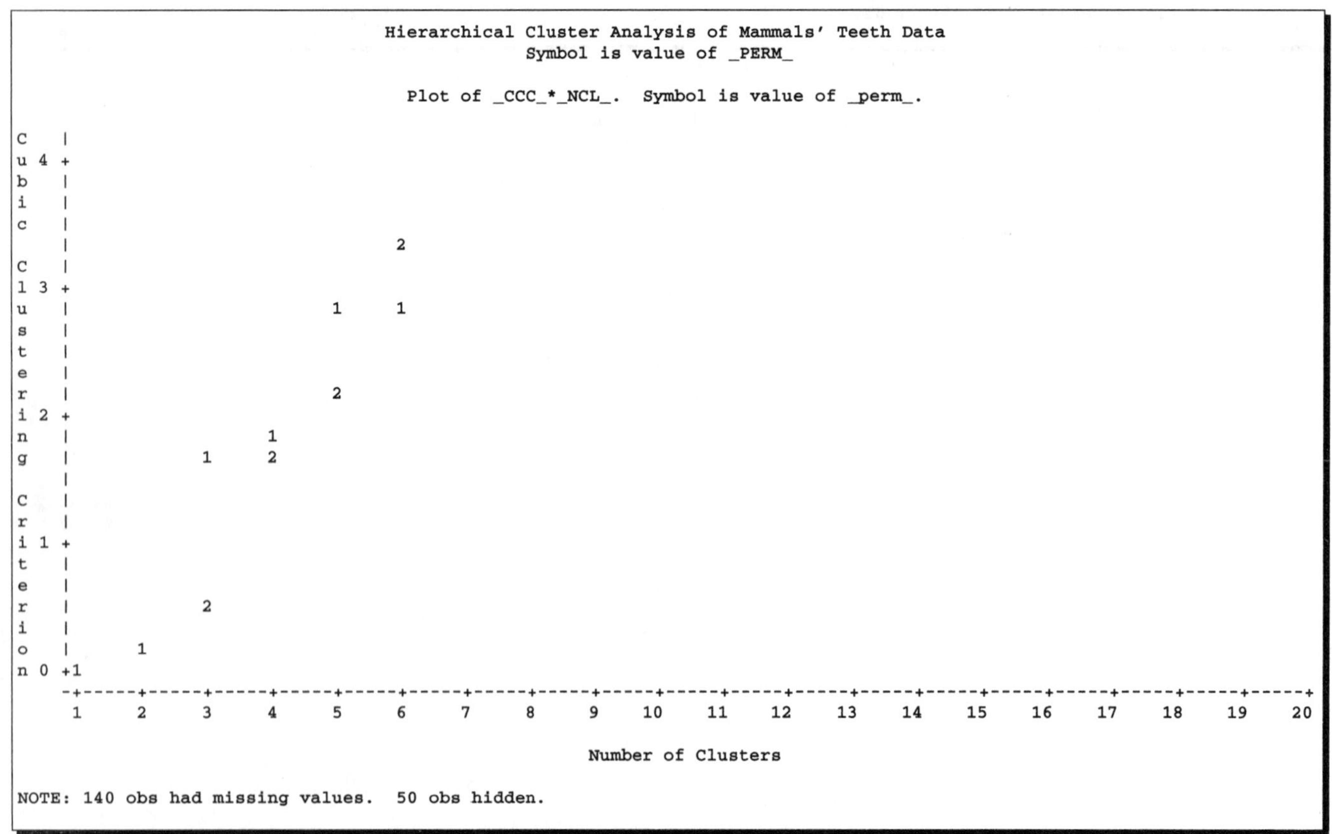
Hierarchical Cluster Analysis of Mammals' Teeth Data
Symbol is value of _PERM_
Plot of _CCC_*_NCL_. Symbol is value of _perm_.
Cubic Clustering Criterion
Number of Clusters
NOTE: 140 obs had missing values. 50 obs hidden.

------------------------------------- all_clus=' 1 3 1 1 1 3 3 3 2 3' -------------------------------------

mammal	v1	v2	v3	v4	v5	v6	v7	v8
DEER	0	4	0	0	3	3	3	3
ELK	0	4	1	0	3	3	3	3
MOOSE	0	4	0	0	3	3	3	3
REINDEER	0	4	1	0	3	3	3	3

------------------------------------- all_clus=' 2 2 2 2 2 2 1 2 1 1' -------------------------------------

mammal	v1	v2	v3	v4	v5	v6	v7	v8
BADGER	3	3	1	1	3	3	1	2
BEAR	3	3	1	1	4	4	2	3
COUGAR	3	3	1	1	3	2	1	1
ELEPHANT SEAL	2	1	1	1	4	4	1	1
FUR SEAL	3	2	1	1	4	4	1	1
GREY SEAL	3	2	1	1	3	3	2	2
JAGUAR	3	3	1	1	3	2	1	1
MARTEN	3	3	1	1	4	4	1	2
RACCOON	3	3	1	1	4	4	3	2
RIVER OTTER	3	3	1	1	4	3	1	2
SEA LION	3	2	1	1	4	4	1	1
SEA OTTER	3	2	1	1	3	3	1	2
WEASEL	3	3	1	1	3	3	1	2
WOLF	3	3	1	1	4	4	2	3
WOLVERINE	3	3	1	1	4	4	1	2

------------------------------------- all_clus=' 2 4 2 2 4 2 1 2 1 1' -------------------------------------

mammal	v1	v2	v3	v4	v5	v6	v7	v8
MOLE	3	2	1	0	3	3	3	3

------------------------------------- all_clus=' 3 1 3 3 3 1 2 1 3 2' -------------------------------------

mammal	v1	v2	v3	v4	v5	v6	v7	v8
BEAVER	1	1	0	0	2	1	3	3
GRAY SQUIRREL	1	1	0	0	1	1	3	3
GROUNDHOG	1	1	0	0	2	1	3	3
HOUSE MOUSE	1	1	0	0	0	0	3	3
PORCUPINE	1	1	0	0	1	1	3	3

------------------------------------- all_clus=' 3 4 3 3 4 1 2 1 3 2' -------------------------------------

mammal	v1	v2	v3	v4	v5	v6	v7	v8
PIKA	2	1	0	0	2	2	3	3
RABBIT	2	1	0	0	3	2	3	3

------------------------------------- all_clus=' 4 4 4 4 4 4 4 4 4 4' -------------------------------------

mammal	v1	v2	v3	v4	v5	v6	v7	v8
BROWN BAT	2	3	1	1	3	3	3	3
HOUSE BAT	2	3	1	1	1	2	3	3
PIGMY BAT	2	3	1	1	2	2	3	3
RED BAT	1	3	1	1	2	2	3	3
SILVER HAIR BAT	2	3	1	1	2	3	3	3

all_clus	FREQ	Mean Top incisors	Bottom incisors	Top canines	Bottom canines	Top premolars	Bottom premolars	Top molars	Bottom molars
1 3 1 1 1 3 3 3 2 3	4	0.0	4.0	0.5	0.0	3.0	3.0	3.0	3.0
2 2 2 2 2 2 1 2 1 1	15	2.9	2.6	1.0	1.0	3.6	3.4	1.3	1.8
2 4 2 2 4 2 1 2 1 1	1	3.0	2.0	1.0	0.0	3.0	3.0	3.0	3.0
3 1 3 3 3 1 2 1 3 2	5	1.0	1.0	0.0	0.0	1.2	0.8	3.0	3.0
3 4 3 3 4 1 2 1 3 2	2	2.0	1.0	0.0	0.0	2.5	2.0	3.0	3.0
4 4 4 4 4 4 4 4 4 4	5	1.8	3.0	1.0	1.0	2.0	2.4	3.0	3.0

From the TABULATE and PRINT output, you can see that two types of clustering are obtained. In one case, the mole is grouped with the carnivores, while the pika and rabbit are grouped with the rodents. In the other case, both the mole and the lagomorphs are grouped with the bats.

Next, the analysis is repeated with the standardized data. The pseudo F and t^2 statistics indicate 3 or 4 clusters, while the cubic clustering criterion shows a sharp rise up to 4 clusters and then levels off up to 6 clusters. So the TREEPERM macro is used again at the 4-cluster level. In this case, there is no indeterminacy, as the same four clusters are obtained with every permutation, although in different orders. It must be emphasized, however, that lack of indeterminacy in no way indicates validity. The results are shown in Output 23.4.4.

```
title3 'Standardized Data';

/*------CLUSTER STANDARDIZED DATA WITH AVERAGE LINKAGE------*/
%clusperm( teeth, &vlist, mammal, average std, 10);

/*------PLOT STATISTICS FOR THE LAST 20 LEVELS--------------*/
%plotperm( _psf_ _pst2_ _ccc_, 20, 10);

/*------ANALYZE THE 4-CLUSTER LEVEL-------------------------*/
%treeperm( &vlist, mammal, 9.1, 4, 10);
```

Output 23.4.4. Analysis of Ten Random Permutations of Standardized Mammals' Teeth Data: No Indeterminacy at the 4-Cluster Level

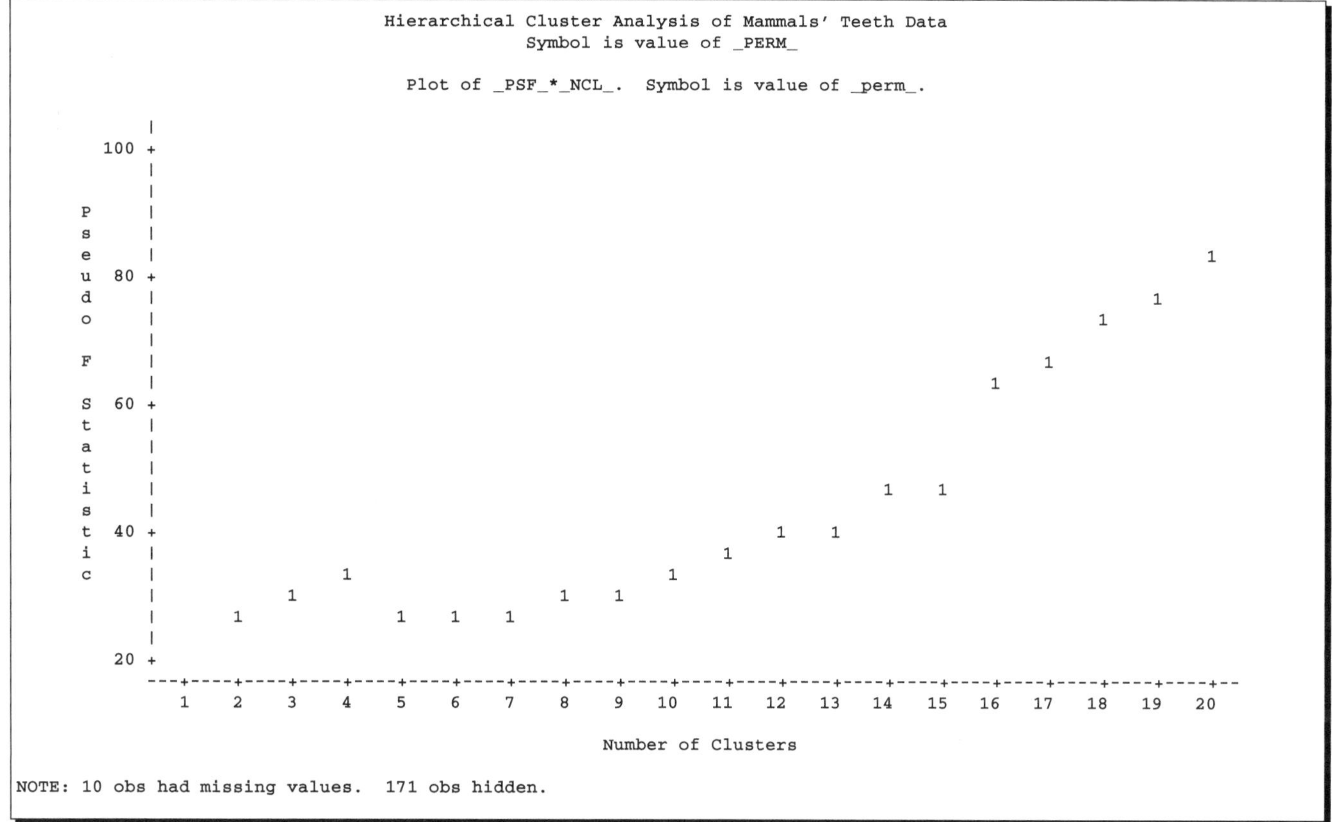

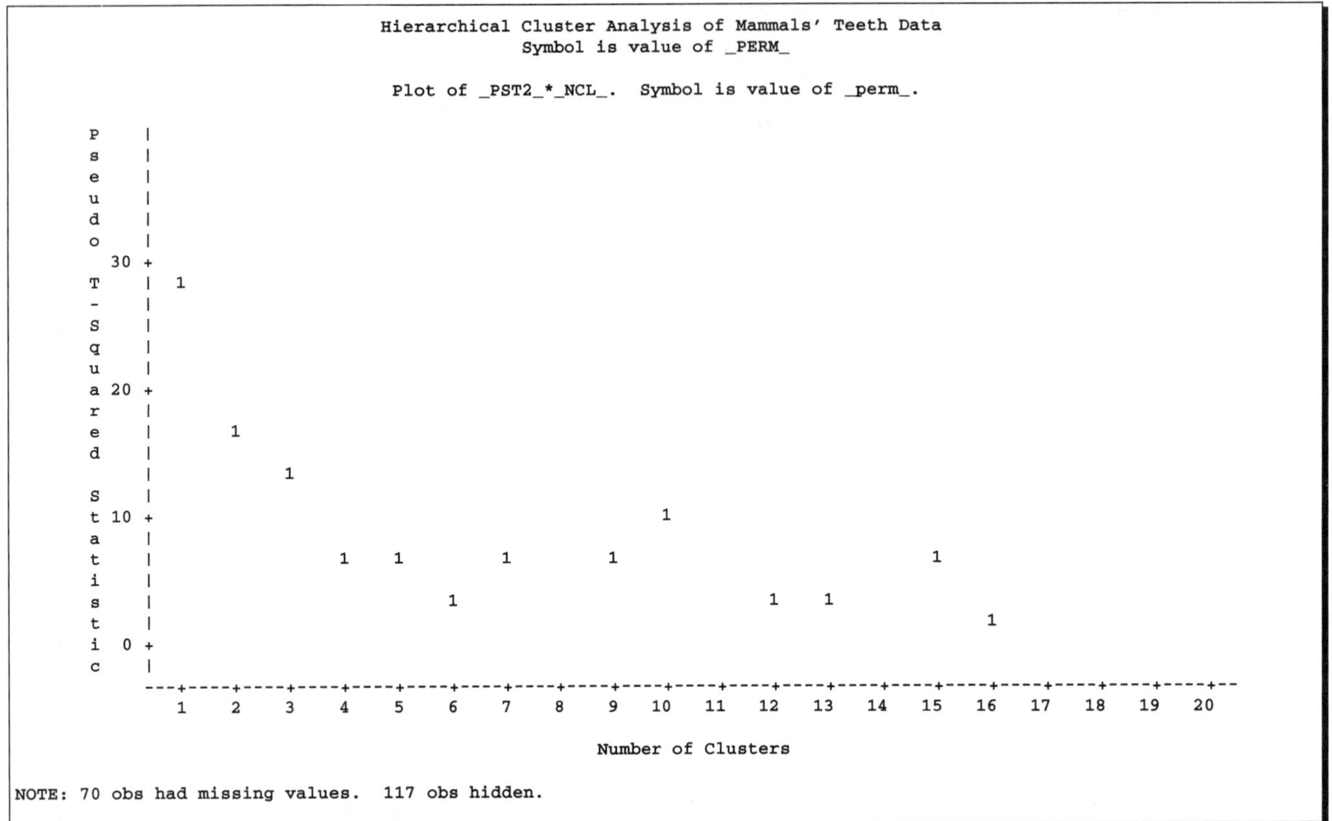
Hierarchical Cluster Analysis of Mammals' Teeth Data
Symbol is value of _PERM_
Plot of _PST2_*_NCL_. Symbol is value of _perm_.
Pseudo T-Squared Statistic
30
20
10
0
1 2 3 4 5 6 7 8 9 10 11 12 13 14 15 16 17 18 19 20
Number of Clusters
NOTE: 70 obs had missing values. 117 obs hidden.

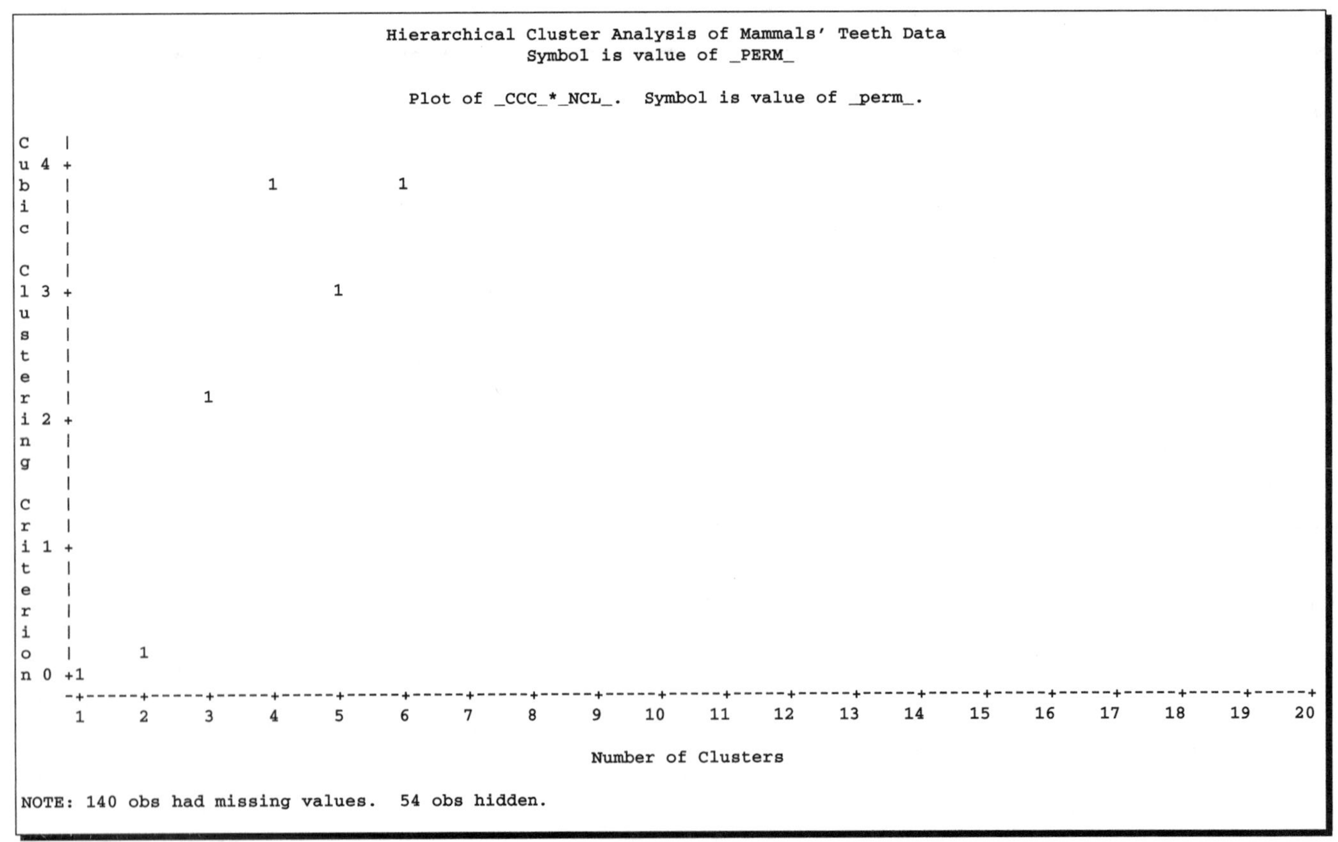
Hierarchical Cluster Analysis of Mammals' Teeth Data
Symbol is value of _PERM_
Plot of _CCC_*_NCL_. Symbol is value of _perm_.
Cubic Clustering Criterion
4
3
2
1
0
1 2 3 4 5 6 7 8 9 10 11 12 13 14 15 16 17 18 19 20
Number of Clusters
NOTE: 140 obs had missing values. 54 obs hidden.

------------------------------------- all_clus=' 1 3 1 1 1 3 3 3 2 3' -------------------------------------

mammal	v1	v2	v3	v4	v5	v6	v7	v8
DEER	0	4	0	0	3	3	3	3
ELK	0	4	1	0	3	3	3	3
MOOSE	0	4	0	0	3	3	3	3
REINDEER	0	4	1	0	3	3	3	3

------------------------------------- all_clus=' 2 2 2 2 2 2 1 2 1 1' -------------------------------------

mammal	v1	v2	v3	v4	v5	v6	v7	v8
BADGER	3	3	1	1	3	3	1	2
BEAR	3	3	1	1	4	4	2	3
COUGAR	3	3	1	1	3	2	1	1
ELEPHANT SEAL	2	1	1	1	4	4	1	1
FUR SEAL	3	2	1	1	4	4	1	1
GREY SEAL	3	2	1	1	3	3	2	2
JAGUAR	3	3	1	1	3	2	1	1
MARTEN	3	3	1	1	4	4	1	2
RACCOON	3	3	1	1	4	4	3	2
RIVER OTTER	3	3	1	1	4	3	1	2
SEA LION	3	2	1	1	4	4	1	1
SEA OTTER	3	2	1	1	3	3	1	2
WEASEL	3	3	1	1	3	3	1	2
WOLF	3	3	1	1	4	4	2	3
WOLVERINE	3	3	1	1	4	4	1	2

------------------------------------- all_clus=' 3 1 3 3 3 1 2 1 3 2' -------------------------------------

mammal	v1	v2	v3	v4	v5	v6	v7	v8
BEAVER	1	1	0	0	2	1	3	3
GRAY SQUIRREL	1	1	0	0	1	1	3	3
GROUNDHOG	1	1	0	0	2	1	3	3
HOUSE MOUSE	1	1	0	0	0	0	3	3
PIKA	2	1	0	0	2	2	3	3
PORCUPINE	1	1	0	0	1	1	3	3
RABBIT	2	1	0	0	3	2	3	3

------------------------------------- all_clus=' 4 4 4 4 4 4 4 4 4 4' -------------------------------------

mammal	v1	v2	v3	v4	v5	v6	v7	v8
BROWN BAT	2	3	1	1	3	3	3	3
HOUSE BAT	2	3	1	1	1	2	3	3
MOLE	3	2	1	0	3	3	3	3
PIGMY BAT	2	3	1	1	2	2	3	3
RED BAT	1	3	1	1	2	2	3	3
SILVER HAIR BAT	2	3	1	1	2	3	3	3

		Mean							
all_clus	FREQ	Top incisors	Bottom incisors	Top canines	Bottom canines	Top premolars	Bottom premolars	Top molars	Bottom molars
1 3 1 1 1 3 3 3 2 3	4	0.0	4.0	0.5	0.0	3.0	3.0	3.0	3.0
2 2 2 2 2 2 1 2 1 1	15	2.9	2.6	1.0	1.0	3.6	3.4	1.3	1.8
3 1 3 3 3 1 2 1 3 2	7	1.3	1.0	0.0	0.0	1.6	1.1	3.0	3.0
4 4 4 4 4 4 4 4 4 4	6	2.0	2.8	1.0	0.8	2.2	2.5	3.0	3.0

Example 23.5. Computing a Distance Matrix

A wide variety of distance and similarity measures are used in cluster analysis (Anderberg 1973, Sneath and Sokal 1973). If your data are in coordinate form and you want to use a non-Euclidean distance for clustering, you can compute a distance matrix using a DATA step or the IML procedure.

Similarity measures must be converted to dissimilarities before being used in PROC CLUSTER. Such conversion can be done in a variety of ways, such as taking reciprocals or subtracting from a large value. The choice of conversion method depends on the application and the similarity measure.

In the following example, the observations are states. Binary-valued variables correspond to various grounds for divorce and indicate whether the grounds for divorce apply in each of the states.

The %DISTANCE* macro is used to compute the Jaccard coefficient (Anderberg 1973, pp. 89, 115, and 117) between each pair of states. The Jaccard coefficient is defined as the number of variables that are coded as 1 for both states divided by the number of variables that are coded as 1 for either or both states. The Jaccard coefficient is converted to a distance measure by subtracting it from 1.

```
%include  '<location of  SAS/STAT sample library>/xmacro.sas';
%include  '<location of  SAS/STAT sample library>/distnew.sas';

options ls=120 ps=60;
data divorce;
   title 'Grounds for Divorce';
   input state $15.
         (incompat cruelty desertn non_supp alcohol
          felony impotenc insanity separate) (1.) @@;
   if mod(_n_,2) then input +4 @@; else input;
   datalines;
ALABAMA         111111111    ALASKA          111011110
ARIZONA         100000000    ARKANSAS        011111111
CALIFORNIA      100000010    COLORADO        100000000
CONNECTICUT     111111011    DELAWARE        100000001
FLORIDA         100000010    GEORGIA         111011110
HAWAII          100000001    IDAHO           111111011
ILLINOIS        011011100    INDIANA         100001110
IOWA            100000000    KANSAS          111011110
KENTUCKY        100000000    LOUISIANA       000001001
MAINE           111110110    MARYLAND        011001111
MASSACHUSETTS   111111101    MICHIGAN        100000000
MINNESOTA       100000000    MISSISSIPPI     111011110
MISSOURI        100000000    MONTANA         100000000
```

*The %DISTANCE macro computes various measures of distance, dissimilarity, or similarity between the observations (rows) of a SAS data set. These proximity measures are stored as a lower triangular matrix or a square matrix in an output data set that can then be used as input to the CLUSTER, MDS or MODECLUS procedures. The input data sets may contain numeric or character variables or both, depending on which proximity measure is used. The macro is documented in the macro comments and can be found in the SAS/STAT sample library.

```
NEBRASKA        100000000    NEVADA          100000011
NEW HAMPSHIRE   111111100    NEW JERSEY      011011011
NEW MEXICO      111000000    NEW YORK        011001001
NORTH CAROLINA  000000111    NORTH DAKOTA    111111110
OHIO            111011101    OKLAHOMA        111111110
OREGON          100000000    PENNSYLVANIA    011001110
RHODE ISLAND    111111101    SOUTH CAROLINA  011010001
SOUTH DAKOTA    011111000    TENNESSEE       111111100
TEXAS           111001011    UTAH            011111110
VERMONT         011101011    VIRGINIA        010001001
WASHINGTON      100000001    WEST VIRGINIA   111011011
WISCONSIN       100000001    WYOMING         100000011
;

%distance(data=divorce, id=state, options=nomiss, out=distjacc,
          shape=square, method=djaccard, var=incompat--separate);

proc print data=distjacc(obs=10);
   id state; var alabama--georgia;
   title2 'First 10 states';
run;
title2;

proc cluster data=distjacc method=centroid
             pseudo outtree=tree;
   id state;
   var alabama--wyoming;
run;

proc tree data=tree noprint n=9 out=out;
   id state;
run;

proc sort;
   by state;
run;

data clus;
   merge divorce out;
   by state;
run;

proc sort;
   by cluster;
run;

proc print;
   id state;
   var incompat--separate;
   by cluster;
run;
```

Output 23.5.1. Computing a Distance Matrix

Grounds for Divorce
First 10 states

state	ALABAMA	ALASKA	ARIZONA	ARKANSAS	CALIFORNIA	COLORADO	CONNECTICUT	DELAWARE	FLORIDA	GEORGIA
ALABAMA	0.00000	0.22222	0.88889	0.11111	0.77778	0.88889	0.11111	0.77778	0.77778	0.22222
ALASKA	0.22222	0.00000	0.85714	0.33333	0.71429	0.85714	0.33333	0.87500	0.71429	0.00000
ARIZONA	0.88889	0.85714	0.00000	1.00000	0.50000	0.00000	0.87500	0.50000	0.50000	0.85714
ARKANSAS	0.11111	0.33333	1.00000	0.00000	0.88889	1.00000	0.22222	0.88889	0.88889	0.33333
CALIFORNIA	0.77778	0.71429	0.50000	0.88889	0.00000	0.50000	0.75000	0.66667	0.00000	0.71429
COLORADO	0.88889	0.85714	0.00000	1.00000	0.50000	0.00000	0.87500	0.50000	0.50000	0.85714
CONNECTICUT	0.11111	0.33333	0.87500	0.22222	0.75000	0.87500	0.00000	0.75000	0.75000	0.33333
DELAWARE	0.77778	0.87500	0.50000	0.88889	0.66667	0.50000	0.75000	0.00000	0.66667	0.87500
FLORIDA	0.77778	0.71429	0.50000	0.88889	0.00000	0.50000	0.75000	0.66667	0.00000	0.71429
GEORGIA	0.22222	0.00000	0.85714	0.33333	0.71429	0.85714	0.33333	0.87500	0.71429	0.00000

Grounds for Divorce

The CLUSTER Procedure
Centroid Hierarchical Cluster Analysis

Root-Mean-Square Distance Between Observations = 0.694873

Cluster History

NCL	---------Clusters Joined---------		FREQ	PSF	PST2	Norm Cent Dist	T i e
49	ARIZONA	COLORADO	2	.	.	0	T
48	CALIFORNIA	FLORIDA	2	.	.	0	T
47	ALASKA	GEORGIA	2	.	.	0	T
46	DELAWARE	HAWAII	2	.	.	0	T
45	CONNECTICUT	IDAHO	2	.	.	0	T
44	CL49	IOWA	3	.	.	0	T
43	CL47	KANSAS	3	.	.	0	T
42	CL44	KENTUCKY	4	.	.	0	T
41	CL42	MICHIGAN	5	.	.	0	T
40	CL41	MINNESOTA	6	.	.	0	T
39	CL43	MISSISSIPPI	4	.	.	0	T
38	CL40	MISSOURI	7	.	.	0	T
37	CL38	MONTANA	8	.	.	0	T
36	CL37	NEBRASKA	9	.	.	0	T
35	NORTH DAKOTA	OKLAHOMA	2	.	.	0	T
34	CL36	OREGON	10	.	.	0	T
33	MASSACHUSETTS	RHODE ISLAND	2	.	.	0	T
32	NEW HAMPSHIRE	TENNESSEE	2	.	.	0	T
31	CL46	WASHINGTON	3	.	.	0	T
30	CL31	WISCONSIN	4	.	.	0	T
29	NEVADA	WYOMING	2	.	.	0	
28	ALABAMA	ARKANSAS	2	1561	.	0.1599	T
27	CL33	CL32	4	479	.	0.1799	T
26	CL39	CL35	6	265	.	0.1799	T
25	CL45	WEST VIRGINIA	3	231	.	0.1799	
24	MARYLAND	PENNSYLVANIA	2	199	.	0.2399	
23	CL28	UTAH	3	167	3.2	0.2468	
22	CL27	OHIO	5	136	5.4	0.2698	
21	CL26	MAINE	7	111	8.9	0.2998	
20	CL23	CL21	10	75.2	8.7	0.3004	
19	CL25	NEW JERSEY	4	71.8	6.5	0.3053	T
18	CL19	TEXAS	5	69.1	2.5	0.3077	
17	CL20	CL22	15	48.7	9.9	0.3219	
16	NEW YORK	VIRGINIA	2	50.1	.	0.3598	
15	CL18	VERMONT	6	49.4	2.9	0.3797	
14	CL17	ILLINOIS	16	47.0	3.2	0.4425	
13	CL14	CL15	22	29.2	15.3	0.4722	
12	CL48	CL29	4	29.5	.	0.4797	T
11	CL13	CL24	24	27.6	4.5	0.5042	
10	CL11	SOUTH DAKOTA	25	28.4	2.4	0.5449	
9	LOUISIANA	CL16	3	30.3	3.5	0.5844	
8	CL34	CL30	14	23.3	3.3	0.7196	
7	CL8	CL12	18	19.3	15.0	0.7175	
6	CL10	SOUTH CAROLINA	26	21.4	4.2	0.7384	
5	CL6	NEW MEXICO	27	24.0	4.7	0.8303	
4	CL5	INDIANA	28	28.9	4.1	0.8343	
3	CL4	CL9	31	31.7	10.9	0.8472	
2	CL3	NORTH CAROLINA	32	55.1	4.1	1.0017	
1	CL2	CL7	50	.	55.1	1.0663	

Grounds for Divorce

CLUSTER=1

state	incompat	cruelty	desertn	non_supp	alcohol	felony	impotenc	insanity	separate
ARIZONA	1	0	0	0	0	0	0	0	0
COLORADO	1	0	0	0	0	0	0	0	0
IOWA	1	0	0	0	0	0	0	0	0
KENTUCKY	1	0	0	0	0	0	0	0	0
MICHIGAN	1	0	0	0	0	0	0	0	0
MINNESOTA	1	0	0	0	0	0	0	0	0
MISSOURI	1	0	0	0	0	0	0	0	0
MONTANA	1	0	0	0	0	0	0	0	0
NEBRASKA	1	0	0	0	0	0	0	0	0
OREGON	1	0	0	0	0	0	0	0	0

CLUSTER=2

state	incompat	cruelty	desertn	non_supp	alcohol	felony	impotenc	insanity	separate
CALIFORNIA	1	0	0	0	0	0	0	1	0
FLORIDA	1	0	0	0	0	0	0	1	0
NEVADA	1	0	0	0	0	0	0	1	1
WYOMING	1	0	0	0	0	0	0	1	1

CLUSTER=3

state	incompat	cruelty	desertn	non_supp	alcohol	felony	impotenc	insanity	separate
ALABAMA	1	1	1	1	1	1	1	1	1
ALASKA	1	1	1	0	1	1	1	1	0
ARKANSAS	0	1	1	1	1	1	1	1	1
CONNECTICUT	1	1	1	1	1	1	0	1	1
GEORGIA	1	1	1	0	1	1	1	1	0
IDAHO	1	1	1	1	1	1	0	1	1
ILLINOIS	0	1	1	0	1	1	1	0	0
KANSAS	1	1	1	0	1	1	1	1	0
MAINE	1	1	1	1	1	0	1	1	0
MARYLAND	0	1	1	0	0	1	1	1	1
MASSACHUSETTS	1	1	1	1	1	1	1	0	1
MISSISSIPPI	1	1	1	0	1	1	1	1	0
NEW HAMPSHIRE	1	1	1	1	1	1	1	0	0
NEW JERSEY	0	1	1	0	1	1	0	1	1
NORTH DAKOTA	1	1	1	1	1	1	1	1	0
OHIO	1	1	1	0	1	1	1	0	1
OKLAHOMA	1	1	1	1	1	1	1	1	0
PENNSYLVANIA	0	1	1	0	0	1	1	1	0
RHODE ISLAND	1	1	1	1	1	1	1	0	1
SOUTH DAKOTA	0	1	1	1	1	1	0	0	0
TENNESSEE	1	1	1	1	1	1	1	0	0
TEXAS	1	1	1	0	0	1	0	1	1
UTAH	0	1	1	1	1	1	1	1	0
VERMONT	0	1	1	1	0	1	0	1	1
WEST VIRGINIA	1	1	1	0	1	1	0	1	1

CLUSTER=4

state	incompat	cruelty	desertn	non_supp	alcohol	felony	impotenc	insanity	separate
DELAWARE	1	0	0	0	0	0	0	0	1
HAWAII	1	0	0	0	0	0	0	0	1
WASHINGTON	1	0	0	0	0	0	0	0	1
WISCONSIN	1	0	0	0	0	0	0	0	1

CLUSTER=5

state	incompat	cruelty	desertn	non_supp	alcohol	felony	impotenc	insanity	separate
LOUISIANA	0	0	0	0	0	1	0	0	1
NEW YORK	0	1	1	0	0	1	0	0	1
VIRGINIA	0	1	0	0	0	1	0	0	1

CLUSTER=6

state	incompat	cruelty	desertn	non_supp	alcohol	felony	impotenc	insanity	separate
SOUTH CAROLINA	0	1	1	0	1	0	0	0	1

CLUSTER=7

state	incompat	cruelty	desertn	non_supp	alcohol	felony	impotenc	insanity	separate
NEW MEXICO	1	1	1	0	0	0	0	0	0

CLUSTER=8

state	incompat	cruelty	desertn	non_supp	alcohol	felony	impotenc	insanity	separate
INDIANA	1	0	0	0	0	1	1	1	0

CLUSTER=9

state	incompat	cruelty	desertn	non_supp	alcohol	felony	impotenc	insanity	separate
NORTH CAROLINA	0	0	0	0	0	0	1	1	1

Example 23.6. Size, Shape, and Correlation

The following example shows the analysis of a data set in which size information is detrimental to the classification. Imagine that an archaeologist of the future is excavating a 20th century grocery store. The archaeologist has discovered a large number of boxes of various sizes, shapes, and colors and wants to do a preliminary classification based on simple external measurements: height, width, depth, weight, and the predominant color of the box. It is known that a given product may have been sold in packages of different size, so the archaeologist wants to remove the effect of size from the classification. It is not known whether color is relevant to the use of the products, so the analysis should be done both with and without color information.

Unknown to the archaeologist, the boxes actually fall into six general categories according to the use of the product: breakfast cereals, crackers, laundry detergents, Little Debbie snacks, tea, and toothpaste. These categories are shown in the analysis so that you can evaluate the effectiveness of the classification.

Since there is no reason for the archaeologist to assume that the true categories have equal sample sizes or variances, the centroid method is used to avoid undue bias. Each analysis is done with Euclidean distances after suitable transformations of the data. Color is coded as five dummy variables with values of 0 or 1. The DATA step is as follows:

```
options ls=120;
title 'Cluster Analysis of Grocery Boxes';
data grocery2;
```

```
   length name $35   /* name of product */
          class $16  /* category of product */
          unit $1    /* unit of measurement for weights:
                           g=gram
                           o=ounce
                           l=lb
                        all weights are converted to grams */
          color $8   /* predominant color of box */
          height 8   /* height of box in cm. */
          width 8    /* width of box in cm. */
          depth 8    /* depth of box (front to back) in cm. */
          weight 8   /* weight of box in grams */
          c_white c_yellow c_red c_green c_blue 4;
                     /* dummy variables */
   retain class;
   drop unit;

   /*--- read name with possible embedded blanks ---*/
   input name & @;

   /*--- if name starts with "---",                ---*/
   /*--- it's really a category value              ---*/
   if substr(name,1,3) = '---' then do;
      class = substr(name,4,index(substr(name,4),'-')-1);
      delete;
      return;
   end;

   /*--- read the rest of the variables ---*/
   input height width depth weight unit color;

   /*--- convert weights to grams ---*/
   select (unit);
      when ('l') weight = weight * 454;
      when ('o') weight = weight * 28.3;
      when ('g') ;
      otherwise put 'Invalid unit ' unit;
   end;

   /*--- use 0/1 coding for dummy variables for colors ---*/
   c_white  = (color = 'w');
   c_yellow = (color = 'y');
   c_red    = (color = 'r');
   c_green  = (color = 'g');
   c_blue   = (color = 'b');

datalines;

---Breakfast cereals---

Cheerios                               32.5 22.4  8.4  567 g y
Cheerios                               30.3 20.4  7.2  425 g y
Cheerios                               27.5 19    6.2  283 g y
Cheerios                               24.1 17.2  5.3  198 g y
```

```
Special K                              30.1 20.5  8.5    18 o w
Special K                              29.6 19.2  6.7    12 o w
Special K                              23.4 16.6  5.7     7 o w
Corn Flakes                            33.7 25.4  8      24 o w
Corn Flakes                            30.2 20.6  8.4    18 o w
Corn Flakes                            30   19.1  6.6    12 o w
Grape Nuts                             21.7 16.3  4.9   680 g w
Shredded Wheat                         19.7 19.9  7.5   283 g y
Shredded Wheat, Spoon Size             26.6 19.6  5.6   510 g r
All-Bran                               21.1 14.3  5.2  13.8 o y
Froot Loops                            30.2 20.8  8.5  19.7 o r
Froot Loops                            25   17.7  6.4    11 o r

---Crackers---

Wheatsworth                            11.1 25.2  5.5   326 g w
Ritz                                   23.1 16    5.3   340 g r
Ritz                                   23.1 20.7  5.2   454 g r
Premium Saltines                       11   25   10.7   454 g w
Waverly Wafers                         14.4 22.5  6.2   454 g g

---Detergent---

Arm & Hammer Detergent                 38.8 30   16.9    25 l y
Arm & Hammer Detergent                 39.5 25.8 11    14.2 l y
Arm & Hammer Detergent                 33.7 22.8  7       7 l y
Arm & Hammer Detergent                 27.8 19.4  6.3     4 l y
Tide                                   39.4 24.8 11.3   9.2 l r
Tide                                   32.5 23.2  7.3   4.5 l r
Tide                                   26.5 19.9  6.3    42 o r
Tide                                   19.3 14.6  4.7    17 o r

---Little Debbie---

Figaroos                               13.5 18.6  3.7    12 o y
Swiss Cake Rolls                       10.1 21.8  5.8    13 o w
Fudge Brownies                         11   30.8  2.5    12 o w
Marshmallow Supremes                    9.4 32    7      10 o w
Apple Delights                         11.2 30.1  4.9    15 o w
Snack Cakes                            13.4 32    3.4    13 o b
Nutty Bar                              13.2 18.5  4.2    12 o y
Lemon Stix                             13.2 18.5  4.2     9 o w
Fudge Rounds                            8.1 28.3  5.4   9.5 o w

---Tea---

Celestial Saesonings Mint Magic         7.8 13.8  6.3    49 g b
Celestial Saesonings Cranberry Cove     7.8 13.8  6.3    46 g r
Celestial Saesonings Sleepy Time        7.8 13.8  6.3    37 g g
Celestial Saesonings Lemon Zinger       7.8 13.8  6.3    56 g y
Bigelow Lemon Lift                      7.7 13.4  6.9    40 g y
Bigelow Plantation Mint                 7.7 13.4  6.9    35 g g
Bigelow Earl Grey                       7.7 13.4  6.9    35 g b
Luzianne                                8.9 22.8  6.4     6 o r
```

```
Luzianne                            18.4 20.2  6.9    8 o r
Luzianne Decaffeinated               8.9 22.8  6.4 5.25 o g
Lipton Tea Bags                     17.1 20    6.7    8 o r
Lipton Tea Bags                     11.5 14.4  6.6 3.75 o r
Lipton Tea Bags                      6.7 10    5.7 1.25 o r
Lipton Family Size Tea Bags         13.7 24    9     12 o r
Lipton Family Size Tea Bags          8.7 20.8  8.2    6 o r
Lipton Family Size Tea Bags          8.9 11.1  8.2    3 o r
Lipton Loose Tea                    12.7 10.9  5.4    8 o r

---Paste, Tooth---

Colgate                              4.4 22    3.5    7 o r
Colgate                              3.6 15.6  3.3    3 o r
Colgate                              4.2 18.3  3.5    5 o r
Crest                                4.3 21.7  3.7  6.4 o w
Crest                                4.3 17.4  3.6  4.6 o w
Crest                                3.5 15.2  3.2  2.7 o w
Crest                                3.0 10.9  2.8  .85 o w
Arm & Hammer                         4.4 17    3.7    5 o w
;


data grocery;
   length name $16;
   set grocery2;
```

The FORMAT procedure is used to define to formats to make the output easier to read. The STARS. format is used for graphical crosstabulations in the TABULATE procedure. The $COLOR format displays the names of the colors instead of just the first letter.

```
     /*------ formats and macros for displaying ------*/
     /*------ cluster results                    ------*/
proc format; value stars
       0='              '
       1='             #'
       2='            ##'
       3='           ###'
       4='          ####'
       5='         #####'
       6='        ######'
       7='       #######'
       8='      ########'
       9='     #########'
      10='    ##########'
      11='   ###########'
      12='  ############'
      13=' #############'
      14='##############'
 15-high='>##############';
 run;
```

```
proc format; value $color
   'w'='White'
   'y'='Yellow'
   'r'='Red'
   'g'='Green'
   'b'='Blue';
run;
```

Since a full display of the results of each cluster analysis would be very long, a macro is used with five macro variables to select parts of the output. The macro variables are set to select only the PROC CLUSTER output and the crosstabulation of clusters and true categories for the first two analyses. The example could be run with different settings of the macro variables to show the full output or other selected parts.

```
%let cluster=1;    /* 1=show CLUSTER output, 0=don't */
%let tree=0;       /* 1=print TREE diagram, 0=don't */
%let list=0;       /* 1=list clusters, 0=don't */
%let crosstab=1;   /* 1=crosstabulate clusters and classes,
                      0=don't                              */
%let crosscol=0;   /* 1=crosstabulate clusters and colors,
                      0=don't                              */

   /*--- define macro with options for TREE ---*/
%macro treeopt;
   %if &tree %then h page=1;
   %else noprint;
%mend;

   /*--- define macro with options for CLUSTER ---*/
%macro clusopt;
   %if &cluster %then pseudo ccc p=20;
   %else noprint;
%mend;

   /*------ macro for showing cluster results ------*/
%macro show(n); /* n=number of clusters
                   to show results for */

proc tree data=tree %treeopt n=&n out=out;
   id name;
   copy class height width depth weight color;
run;

%if &list %then %do;
   proc sort;
      by cluster;
   run;

   proc print;
      var class name height width depth weight color;
      by cluster clusname;
   run;
%end;
```

```
%if &crosstab %then %do;
   proc tabulate noseps /* formchar='           ' */;
         class class cluster;
         table cluster, class*n='
               '*f=stars./rts=10 misstext=' ';
run;
%end;

%if &crosscol %then %do;
   proc tabulate noseps /* formchar='           ' */;
       class color cluster;
       table cluster, color*n='
             '*f=stars./rts=10 misstext=' ';
       format color $color.;
run;
%end;
%mend;
```

The first analysis uses the variables height, width, depth, and weight in standardized form to show the effect of including size information. The CCC, pseudo F, and pseudo t^2 statistics indicate 10 clusters. Most of the clusters do not correspond closely to the true categories, and four of the clusters have only one or two observations.

```
/*********************************************************/
/*                                                       */
/*        Analysis 1: standardized box measurements      */
/*                                                       */
/*********************************************************/
title2 'Analysis 1: Standardized data';
proc cluster data=grocery m=cen std %clusopt outtree=tree;
   var height width depth weight;
   id name;
   copy class color;
run;

%show(10);
```

Output 23.6.1. Analysis of Standardized Data

```
                    Cluster Analysis of Grocery Boxes
                     Analysis 1: Standardized data

                        The CLUSTER Procedure
                  Centroid Hierarchical Cluster Analysis

                   Eigenvalues of the Correlation Matrix

            Eigenvalue    Difference    Proportion    Cumulative

       1    2.44512438    1.64456210        0.6113        0.6113
       2    0.80056228    0.33149770        0.2001        0.8114
       3    0.46906458    0.18381582        0.1173        0.9287
       4    0.28524876                      0.0713        1.0000

    The data have been standardized to mean 0 and variance 1
    Root-Mean-Square Total-Sample Standard Deviation =        1
    Root-Mean-Square Distance Between Observations   = 2.828427
```

```
                    Cluster Analysis of Grocery Boxes
                     Analysis 1: Standardized data

                        The CLUSTER Procedure
                  Centroid Hierarchical Cluster Analysis

    The data have been standardized to mean 0 and variance 1
    Root-Mean-Square Total-Sample Standard Deviation =        1
    Root-Mean-Square Distance Between Observations   = 2.828427


                              Cluster History
                                                                                 Norm  T
                                                                                 Cent  i
NCL  ----------Clusters Joined----------   FREQ   SPRSQ   RSQ  ERSQ   CCC   PSF  PST2   Dist  e

 20  CL22               Lipton Family Si     11  0.0028  .974     .     .  85.4   4.5 0.3073
 19  CL36               Corn Flakes           5  0.0026  .972     .     .  83.7  15.3 0.3146
 18  CL24               CL41                 12  0.0080  .964     .     .  70.2  10.0 0.3316
 17  CL18               CL30                 18  0.0144  .949     .     .  53.8  12.7 0.3343
 16  Marshmallow Supr   CL29                  3  0.0024  .947     .     .  55.8   4.7 0.3363
 15  CL50               CL33                  7  0.0055  .941     .     .  55.0  24.4  0.346
 14  CL46               CL15                 10  0.0069  .934     .     .  53.7   8.1 0.3192
 13  CL27               Lipton Family Si      6  0.0035  .931     .     .  56.1   6.3  0.362
 12  CL31               CL16                  5  0.0075  .923  .861  8.03  55.8   6.6 0.4416
 11  CL19               CL23                  7  0.0102  .913  .848  7.59  54.6  12.7 0.4713
 10  Arm & Hammer Det   Tide                  2  0.0037  .909  .835  8.36  59.1     . 0.4781
  9  CL11               CL17                 25  0.0393  .870  .819  4.72  45.2  19.3 0.4918
  8  CL13               CL14                 16  0.0329  .837  .801  2.95  40.4  23.7 0.5215
  7  CL8                CL20                 27  0.0629  .774  .779  -.31  32.0  25.9 0.5467
  6  CL7                Crest                28  0.0112  .763  .752  0.61  36.7   2.4 0.6003
  5  CL9                CL6                  53  0.1879  .575  .718  -5.9  19.6  43.4 0.6641
  4  CL5                CL21                 55  0.0345  .541  .672  -5.2  23.2   4.5  0.745
  3  CL4                CL12                 60  0.1137  .427  .602  -5.3  22.4  14.5 0.8769
  2  CL3                CL10                 62  0.1511  .276  .471  -4.3  23.2  15.8 1.5559
  1  CL2                Arm & Hammer Det     63  0.2759  .000  .000  0.00     .  23.2  2.948
```

	class					
	Breakfast cereal	Crackers	Detergent	Little Debbie	Paste, Tooth	Tea
CLUSTER						
1						###########
2		##		#		###
3	#####		##			
4				###	#######	
5	###########	##	###			##
6				#####		
7		#				#
8			##			
9					#	
10			#			

The second analysis uses logarithms of height, width, depth, and the cube root of weight; the cube root is used for consistency with the linear measures. The rows are then centered to remove size information. Finally, the columns are standardized to have a standard deviation of 1. There is no compelling a priori reason to standardize the columns, but if they are not standardized, height dominates the analysis because of its large variance. The STANDARD procedure is used instead of the STD option in PROC CLUSTER so that a subsequent analysis can separately standardize the dummy variables for color.

```
/*****************************************************************/
/*                                                               */
/*      Analysis 2: standardized row-centered logarithms         */
/*                                                               */
/*****************************************************************/

title2 'Row-centered logarithms';
data shape;
   set grocery;
   array x height width depth weight;
   array l l_height l_width l_depth l_weight;
                           /* logarithms */
   weight=weight**(1/3);   /* take cube root to conform with
                              the other linear measurements */
   do over l;              /* take logarithms */
      l=log(x);
   end;
   mean=mean( of l(*));    /* find row mean of logarithms */
   do over l;
      l=l-mean;            /* center row */
   end;
run;

title2 'Analysis 2: Standardized row-centered logarithms';
proc standard data=shape out=shapstan m=0 s=1;
   var l_height l_width l_depth l_weight;
run;
```

```
proc cluster data=shapstan m=cen %clusopt outtree=tree;
   var l_height l_width l_depth l_weight;
   id name;
   copy class height width depth weight color;
run;

%show(8);
```

The results of the second analysis are shown for eight clusters. Clusters 1 through 4 correspond fairly well to tea, toothpaste, breakfast cereals, and detergents. Crackers and Little Debbie products are scattered among several clusters.

Output 23.6.2. Analysis of Standardized Row-Centered Logarithms

Cluster Analysis of Grocery Boxes
Analysis 2: Standardized row-centered logarithms

The CLUSTER Procedure
Centroid Hierarchical Cluster Analysis

Eigenvalues of the Covariance Matrix

	Eigenvalue	Difference	Proportion	Cumulative
1	1.94931049	0.34845395	0.4873	0.4873
2	1.60085654	1.15102358	0.4002	0.8875
3	0.44983296	0.44983296	0.1125	1.0000
4	0.00000000		0.0000	1.0000

Root-Mean-Square Total-Sample Standard Deviation = 1
Root-Mean-Square Distance Between Observations = 2.828427

Cluster History

NCL	----------Clusters	Joined----------	FREQ	SPRSQ	RSQ	ERSQ	CCC	PSF	PST2	Norm Cent Dist	Tie
20	CL29	All-Bran	4	0.0017	.977	.	.	94.7	2.9	0.2658	
19	CL26	CL27	8	0.0045	.972	.	.	85.4	8.4	0.3047	
18	Fudge Rounds	Crest	2	0.0016	.971	.	.	87.2	.	0.3193	
17	Fudge Brownies	Snack Cakes	2	0.0018	.969	.	.	89.1	.	0.3331	
16	Arm & Hammer Det	Lipton Loose Tea	2	0.0019	.967	.	.	91.3	.	0.3434	
15	CL23	CL18	5	0.0050	.962	.	.	86.5	4.8	0.3587	
14	CL37	CL21	5	0.0051	.957	.	.	83.5	10.4	0.3613	
13	CL30	CL24	9	0.0068	.950	.	.	79.2	12.9	0.3682	
12	CL32	CL20	16	0.0142	.936	.892	5.75	67.6	29.3	0.3826	
11	CL22	Apple Delights	4	0.0037	.932	.881	6.31	71.4	3.2	0.3901	
10	CL11	CL31	7	0.0090	.923	.869	6.17	70.8	6.3	0.4032	
9	CL33	CL13	11	0.0092	.914	.853	6.25	71.7	7.6	0.4181	
8	CL19	CL16	10	0.0131	.901	.835	6.12	71.4	10.9	0.503	
7	CL14	CL9	16	0.0297	.871	.813	4.63	63.1	15.6	0.5173	
6	CL10	CL15	12	0.0329	.838	.785	3.69	59.1	13.6	0.5916	
5	CL6	CL28	19	0.0557	.783	.748	2.01	52.2	15.8	0.6252	
4	CL12	CL8	26	0.0885	.694	.697	-.16	44.6	48.8	0.6679	
3	CL5	CL17	21	0.0459	.648	.617	1.21	55.3	7.4	0.8863	
2	CL4	CL7	42	0.2841	.364	.384	-.56	34.9	60.3	0.9429	
1	CL2	CL3	63	0.3640	.000	.000	0.00	.	34.9	0.8978	

```
---------------------------------------------------------------------------------------------------------------------
|        |                                        class                                                              |
|        |-----------------------------------------------------------------------------------------------------------|
|        |  Breakfast     |                |                |                |                |                      |
|        |   cereal       |   Crackers     |   Detergent    | Little Debbie  | Paste, Tooth   |         Tea          |
|--------+----------------+----------------+----------------+----------------+----------------+----------------------|
|CLUSTER |                |                |                |                |                |                      |
|        |                |                |                |                |                |          ##########  |
|1       |                |               #|                |                |                |                      |
|        |                |                |                |                |         #######|                      |
|2       |                |                |                |                |                |                      |
|3       | ############## |              ##|                |                |                |                      |
|        |                |                |        ########|                |                |                     #|
|4       |               #|                |                |                |                |                      |
|        |                |                |                |              ##|               #|                    ##|
|5       |                |                |                |                |                |                      |
|        |                |                |                |                |                |                  ####|
|6       |               #|                |                |                |                |                      |
|        |                |                |                |           #####|                |                      |
|7       |                |              ##|                |                |                |                      |
|        |                |                |                |              ##|                |                      |
|8       |                |                |                |                |                |                      |
---------------------------------------------------------------------------------------------------------------------
```

The third analysis is similar to the second analysis except that the rows are standardized rather than just centered. There is a clear indication of seven clusters from the CCC, pseudo F, and pseudo t^2 statistics. The clusters are listed as well as crosstabulated with the true categories and colors.

```
/******************************************************************/
/*                                                                */
/*   Analysis 3: standardized row-standardized logarithms         */
/*                                                                */
/******************************************************************/

%let list=1;
%let crosscol=1;

title2 'Row-standardized logarithms';
data std;
   set grocery;
   array x height width depth weight;
   array l l_height l_width l_depth l_weight;
                           /* logarithms */
   weight=weight**(1/3);  /* take cube root to conform with
                              the other linear measurements */
   do over l;
      l=log(x);            /* take logarithms */
   end;
   mean=mean( of l(*));    /* find row mean of logarithms */
   std=std( of l(*));      /* find row standard deviation */
   do over l;
      l=(l-mean)/std;      /* standardize row */
   end;
run;

title2 'Analysis 3: Standardized row-standardized logarithms';
proc standard data=std out=stdstan m=0 s=1;
   var l_height l_width l_depth l_weight;
run;

proc cluster data=stdstan m=cen %clusopt outtree=tree;
   var l_height l_width l_depth l_weight;
   id name;
```

```
   copy class height width depth weight color;
run;

%show(7);
```

The output from the third analysis shows that cluster 1 contains 9 of the 17 teas. Cluster 2 contains all of the detergents plus Grape Nuts, a very heavy cereal. Cluster 3 includes all of the toothpastes and one Little Debbie product that is of very similar shape, although roughly twice as large. Cluster 4 has most of the cereals, Ritz crackers (which come in a box very similar to most of the cereal boxes), and Lipton Loose Tea (all the other teas in the sample come in tea bags). Clusters 5 and 6 each contain several Luzianne and Lipton teas and one or two miscellaneous items. Cluster 7 includes most of the Little Debbie products and two types of crackers. Thus, the crackers are not identified and the teas are broken up into three clusters, but the other categories correspond to single clusters. This analysis classifies toothpaste and Little Debbie products slightly better than the second analysis,

Output 23.6.3. Analysis of Standardized Row-Standardized Logarithms

Cluster Analysis of Grocery Boxes
Analysis 3: Standardized row-standardized logarithms

The CLUSTER Procedure
Centroid Hierarchical Cluster Analysis

Eigenvalues of the Covariance Matrix

	Eigenvalue	Difference	Proportion	Cumulative
1	2.42684848	0.94583675	0.6067	0.6067
2	1.48101173	1.38887193	0.3703	0.9770
3	0.09213980	0.09213980	0.0230	1.0000
4	-.00000000		-0.0000	1.0000

Root-Mean-Square Total-Sample Standard Deviation = 1
Root-Mean-Square Distance Between Observations = 2.828427

Cluster History

NCL	Clusters Joined		FREQ	SPRSQ	RSQ	ERSQ	CCC	PSF	PST2	Norm Cent Dist	Tie
20	CL35	CL33	8	0.0024	.990	.	.	229	32.0	0.1923	
19	CL22	Ritz	5	0.0010	.989	.	.	224	2.9	0.2014	
18	CL44	CL27	6	0.0018	.987	.	.	206	20.5	0.2073	
17	CL18	CL26	9	0.0025	.985	.	.	187	6.4	0.1956	
16	Fudge Rounds	Crest	2	0.0009	.984	.	.	192	.	0.24	
15	CL24	CL23	5	0.0029	.981	.	.	177	7.8	0.2753	
14	CL25	Waverly Wafers	4	0.0021	.979	.	.	175	7.7	0.2917	
13	CL30	CL19	17	0.0101	.969	.	.	130	41.0	0.2974	
12	CL16	CL31	9	0.0049	.964	.932	5.49	124	20.5	0.3121	
11	CL21	Lipton Family Si	4	0.0029	.961	.924	5.81	129	8.2	0.3445	
10	CL41	CL11	6	0.0045	.957	.915	5.94	130	5.0	0.323	
9	CL29	Lipton Tea Bags	4	0.0031	.953	.904	6.52	138	20.3	0.3603	
8	CL14	CL15	9	0.0101	.943	.890	6.08	131	10.7	0.3761	
7	CL20	Lipton Family Si	9	0.0047	.939	.872	6.89	143	11.7	0.4063	
6	CL13	CL9	21	0.0272	.911	.848	5.23	117	30.0	0.5101	
5	CL6	CL17	30	0.0746	.837	.814	1.30	74.3	42.2	0.606	
4	CL10	CL7	15	0.0440	.793	.764	1.40	75.3	36.4	0.6152	
3	CL8	CL12	18	0.0642	.729	.681	2.02	80.6	44.0	0.6648	
2	CL3	CL4	33	0.2580	.471	.470	0.01	54.2	54.4	0.9887	
1	CL5	CL2	63	0.4707	.000	.000	0.00	.	54.2	0.9636	

-- CLUSTER=1 CLUSNAME=CL7 --

Obs	class	name	height	width	depth	weight	color
1	Tea	Bigelow Plantati	7.7	13.4	6.9	3.27107	g
2	Tea	Bigelow Earl Gre	7.7	13.4	6.9	3.27107	b
3	Tea	Celestial Saeson	7.8	13.8	6.3	3.65931	b
4	Tea	Celestial Saeson	7.8	13.8	6.3	3.58305	r
5	Tea	Bigelow Lemon Li	7.7	13.4	6.9	3.41995	y
6	Tea	Celestial Saeson	7.8	13.8	6.3	3.82586	y
7	Tea	Celestial Saeson	7.8	13.8	6.3	3.33222	g
8	Tea	Lipton Tea Bags	6.7	10.0	5.7	3.28271	r
9	Tea	Lipton Family Si	8.9	11.1	8.2	4.39510	r

-- CLUSTER=2 CLUSNAME=CL17 --

Obs	class	name	height	width	depth	weight	color
10	Detergent	Tide	26.5	19.9	6.3	10.5928	r
11	Detergent	Tide	19.3	14.6	4.7	7.8357	r
12	Detergent	Tide	32.5	23.2	7.3	12.6889	r
13	Breakfast cereal	Grape Nuts	21.7	16.3	4.9	8.7937	w
14	Detergent	Arm & Hammer Det	33.7	22.8	7.0	14.7023	y
15	Detergent	Arm & Hammer Det	27.8	19.4	6.3	12.2003	y
16	Detergent	Arm & Hammer Det	38.8	30.0	16.9	22.4732	y
17	Detergent	Tide	39.4	24.8	11.3	16.1045	r
18	Detergent	Arm & Hammer Det	39.5	25.8	11.0	18.6115	y

-- CLUSTER=3 CLUSNAME=CL12 --

Obs	class	name	height	width	depth	weight	color
19	Paste, Tooth	Colgate	3.6	15.6	3.3	4.39510	r
20	Paste, Tooth	Crest	3.5	15.2	3.2	4.24343	w
21	Paste, Tooth	Crest	4.3	17.4	3.6	5.06813	w
22	Paste, Tooth	Arm & Hammer	4.4	17.0	3.7	5.21097	w
23	Paste, Tooth	Colgate	4.2	18.3	3.5	5.21097	r
24	Paste, Tooth	Crest	4.3	21.7	3.7	5.65790	w
25	Paste, Tooth	Colgate	4.4	22.0	3.5	5.82946	r
26	Little Debbie	Fudge Rounds	8.1	28.3	5.4	6.45411	w
27	Paste, Tooth	Crest	3.0	10.9	2.8	2.88670	w

```
---------------------------------------------- CLUSTER=4 CLUSNAME=CL13 ----------------------------------------------

        Obs    class              name                 height    width    depth    weight     color

         28    Breakfast cereal   Cheerios              27.5      19.0      6.2    6.56541      y
         29    Breakfast cereal   Froot Loops           25.0      17.7      6.4    6.77735      r
         30    Breakfast cereal   Special K             30.1      20.5      8.5    7.98644      w
         31    Breakfast cereal   Corn Flakes           30.2      20.6      8.4    7.98644      w
         32    Breakfast cereal   Special K             29.6      19.2      6.7    6.97679      w
         33    Breakfast cereal   Corn Flakes           30.0      19.1      6.6    6.97679      w
         34    Breakfast cereal   Froot Loops           30.2      20.8      8.5    8.23034      r
         35    Breakfast cereal   Cheerios              30.3      20.4      7.2    7.51847      y
         36    Breakfast cereal   Cheerios              24.1      17.2      5.3    5.82848      y
         37    Breakfast cereal   Corn Flakes           33.7      25.4      8.0    8.79021      w
         38    Breakfast cereal   Special K             23.4      16.6      5.7    5.82946      w
         39    Breakfast cereal   Cheerios              32.5      22.4      8.4    8.27677      y
         40    Breakfast cereal   Shredded Wheat,       26.6      19.6      5.6    7.98957      r
         41    Crackers           Ritz                  23.1      16.0      5.3    6.97953      r
         42    Breakfast cereal   All-Bran              21.1      14.3      5.2    7.30951      y
         43    Tea                Lipton Loose Tea      12.7      10.9      5.4    6.09479      r
         44    Crackers           Ritz                  23.1      20.7      5.2    7.68573      r

---------------------------------------------- CLUSTER=5 CLUSNAME=CL10 ----------------------------------------------

        Obs    class              name                 height    width    depth    weight     color

         45    Tea                Luzianne               8.9      22.8      6.4    5.53748      r
         46    Tea                Luzianne Decaffe       8.9      22.8      6.4    5.29641      g
         47    Crackers           Premium Saltines      11.0      25.0     10.7    7.68573      w
         48    Tea                Lipton Family Si       8.7      20.8      8.2    5.53748      r
         49    Little Debbie      Marshmallow Supr       9.4      32.0      7.0    6.56541      w
         50    Tea                Lipton Family Si      13.7      24.0      9.0    6.97679      r
```

```
---------------------------------------------- CLUSTER=6 CLUSNAME=CL9 ----------------------------------------------

        Obs    class              name                 height    width    depth    weight     color

         51    Tea                Luzianne              18.4      20.2      6.9    6.09479      r
         52    Tea                Lipton Tea Bags       17.1      20.0      6.7    6.09479      r
         53    Breakfast cereal   Shredded Wheat        19.7      19.9      7.5    6.56541      y
         54    Tea                Lipton Tea Bags       11.5      14.4      6.6    4.73448      r

---------------------------------------------- CLUSTER=7 CLUSNAME=CL8 ----------------------------------------------

        Obs    class              name                 height    width    depth    weight     color

         55    Crackers           Wheatsworth           11.1      25.2      5.5    6.88239      w
         56    Little Debbie      Swiss Cake Rolls      10.1      21.8      5.8    7.16545      w
         57    Little Debbie      Figaroos              13.5      18.6      3.7    6.97679      y
         58    Little Debbie      Nutty Bar             13.2      18.5      4.2    6.97679      y
         59    Little Debbie      Apple Delights        11.2      30.1      4.9    7.51552      w
         60    Little Debbie      Lemon Stix            13.2      18.5      4.2    6.33884      w
         61    Little Debbie      Fudge Brownies        11.0      30.8      2.5    6.97679      w
         62    Little Debbie      Snack Cakes           13.4      32.0      3.4    7.16545      b
         63    Crackers           Waverly Wafers        14.4      22.5      6.2    7.68573      g
```

```
------------------------------------------------------------------------------------------------------------
|        |                                            class                                                 |
|        |--------------------------------------------------------------------------------------------------|
|        |   Breakfast    |                |                |                |                |             |
|        |    cereal      |    Crackers    |   Detergent    | Little Debbie  | Paste, Tooth   |     Tea     |
|--------+----------------+----------------+----------------+----------------+----------------+-------------|
|CLUSTER |                |                |                |                |                |             |
|1       |                |                |                |                |                |  #########  |
|2       |               #|                |        ########|                |                |             |
|3       |                |                |                |               #|        ########|             |
|4       | ###############|              ##|                |                |                |            #|
|5       |                |               #|                |               #|                |         ####|
|6       |               #|                |                |                |                |          ###|
|7       |                |              ##|                |         #######|                |             |
------------------------------------------------------------------------------------------------------------
```

```
---------------------------------------------------------------------------
|        |                             color                              |
|        |----------------------------------------------------------------|
|        |    Blue     |    Green    |     Red     |   White     | Yellow  |
|--------+-------------+-------------+-------------+-------------+---------|
|CLUSTER |             |             |             |             |         |
|1       |          ## |          ## |         ### |             |      ## |
|2       |             |             |        #### |           # |    #### |
|3       |             |             |         ### |      ###### |         |
|4       |             |             |      ###### |      ###### |   ##### |
|5       |             |           # |         ### |          ## |         |
|6       |             |             |         ### |             |       # |
|7       |           # |           # |             |       ##### |      ## |
---------------------------------------------------------------------------
```

The last several analyses include color. Obviously, the dummy variables must not be included in calculations to standardize the rows. If the five dummy variables are simply standardized to variance 1.0 and included with the other variables, color dominates the analysis. The dummy variables should be scaled to a smaller variance, which must be determined by trial and error. Four analyses are done using PROC STANDARD to scale the dummy variables to a standard deviation of 0.2, 0.3, 0.4, or 0.8. The cluster listings are suppressed.

Since dummy variables drastically violate the normality assumption on which the CCC depends, the CCC tends to indicate an excessively large number of clusters.

```
/*****************************************************************/
/*                                                               */
/* Analyses 4-7: standardized row-standardized logs & color      */
/*                                                               */
/*****************************************************************/
%let list=0;
%let crosscol=1;

title2
   'Analysis 4: Standardized row-standardized
                logarithms and color (s=.2)';
proc standard data=stdstan out=stdstan m=0 s=.2;
   var c_:;
run;

proc cluster data=stdstan m=cen %clusopt outtree=tree;
   var l_height l_width l_depth l_weight c_:;
   id name;
   copy class height width depth weight color;
run;

%show(7);

title2
   'Analysis 5: Standardized row-standardized
                logarithms and color (s=.3)';
proc standard data=stdstan out=stdstan m=0 s=.3;
   var c_:;
run;
```

```
proc cluster data=stdstan m=cen %clusopt outtree=tree;
   var l_height l_width l_depth l_weight c_:;
   id name;
   copy class height width depth weight color;
run;

%show(6);

title2
  'Analysis 6: Standardized row-standardized
               logarithms and color (s=.4)';
proc standard data=stdstan out=stdstan m=0 s=.4;
   var c_:;
run;

proc cluster data=stdstan m=cen %clusopt outtree=tree;
   var l_height l_width l_depth l_weight c_:;
   id name;
   copy class height width depth weight color;
run;

%show(3);

title2
  'Analysis 7: Standardized row-standardized
               logarithms and color (s=.8)';
proc standard data=stdstan out=stdstan m=0 s=.8;
   var c_:;
run;

proc cluster data=stdstan m=cen %clusopt outtree=tree;
   var l_height l_width l_depth l_weight c_:;
   id name;
   copy class height width depth weight color;
run;

%show(10);
```

Using PROC STANDARD on the dummy variables with S=0.2 causes four of the Little Debbie products to join the toothpastes. Using S=0.3 causes one of the tea clusters to merge with the breakfast cereals while three cereals defect to the detergents. Using S=0.4 produces three clusters consisting of (1) cereals and detergents, (2) Little Debbie products and toothpaste, and (3) teas, with crackers divided among all three clusters and a few other misclassifications. With S=0.8, ten clusters are indicated, each entirely monochrome. So, S=0.2 or S=0.3 degrades the classification, S=0.4 yields a good but perhaps excessively coarse classification, and higher values of the S= option produce clusters that are determined mainly by color.

Output 23.6.4. Analysis of Standardized Row-Standardized Logarithms and Color

Cluster Analysis of Grocery Boxes
Analysis 4: Standardized row-standardized logarithms and color (s=.2)

The CLUSTER Procedure
Centroid Hierarchical Cluster Analysis

Eigenvalues of the Covariance Matrix

	Eigenvalue	Difference	Proportion	Cumulative
1	2.43584975	0.94791932	0.5800	0.5800
2	1.48793042	1.39363531	0.3543	0.9342
3	0.09429511	0.03686218	0.0225	0.9567
4	0.05743293	0.01036136	0.0137	0.9704
5	0.04707157	0.00489503	0.0112	0.9816
6	0.04217654	0.00693298	0.0100	0.9916
7	0.03524355	0.03524355	0.0084	1.0000
8	-.00000000	0.00000000	-0.0000	1.0000
9	-.00000000		-0.0000	1.0000

Root-Mean-Square Total-Sample Standard Deviation = 0.68313
Root-Mean-Square Distance Between Observations = 2.898275

Cluster History

NCL	----------Clusters	Joined----------	FREQ	SPRSQ	RSQ	ERSQ	CCC	PSF	PST2	Norm Cent Dist	Tie
20	CL46	Lemon Stix	3	0.0016	.968	.	.	67.5	11.9	0.2706	
19	Luzianne	Lipton Family Si	2	0.0014	.966	.	.	69.7	.	0.2995	
18	CL25	CL37	6	0.0041	.962	.	.	67.1	5.0	0.3081	
17	CL33	CL35	16	0.0099	.952	.	.	57.2	16.7	0.3196	
16	CL19	Luzianne Decaffe	3	0.0024	.950	.	.	59.2	1.7	0.3357	
15	CL30	CL16	5	0.0042	.946	.	.	59.5	2.7	0.3299	
14	CL27	CL18	8	0.0057	.940	.	.	58.9	4.2	0.3429	
13	CL20	Fudge Brownies	4	0.0031	.937	.	.	61.7	3.6	0.3564	
12	CL24	Lipton Tea Bags	4	0.0031	.934	.905	3.23	65.2	4.7	0.359	
11	CL39	CL28	6	0.0068	.927	.896	3.17	65.9	12.1	0.3743	
10	CL13	Snack Cakes	5	0.0036	.923	.886	3.62	70.8	2.3	0.3755	
9	CL11	CL32	13	0.0176	.906	.874	2.70	64.8	16.0	0.4107	
8	CL14	Lipton Family Si	9	0.0052	.900	.859	3.29	71.0	2.6	0.4265	
7	Waverly Wafers	CL10	6	0.0052	.895	.841	4.09	79.8	2.4	0.4378	
6	CL17	CL12	20	0.0248	.870	.817	3.52	76.6	19.7	0.4898	
5	CL15	CL8	14	0.0326	.838	.783	3.08	75.0	14.0	0.5607	
4	CL6	CL21	30	0.0743	.764	.734	1.35	63.5	35.6	0.5877	
3	CL9	CL7	19	0.0579	.706	.653	2.17	72.0	22.8	0.6611	
2	CL4	CL3	49	0.3632	.343	.450	-2.6	31.8	73.0	0.9838	
1	CL2	CL5	63	0.3426	.000	.000	0.00	.	31.8	0.9876	

	class					
	Breakfast cereal	Crackers	Detergent	Little Debbie	Paste, Tooth	Tea
CLUSTER						
1	##		########			
2		#		####	########	
3	#############	##				#
4	#					###
5		#		#####		
6						#########
7		#				####

```
------------------------------------------------------------------------------------
|        |                                 color                                    |
|        |--------------------------------------------------------------------------|
|        |    Blue      |     Green     |      Red      |     White     |   Yellow    |
|--------+--------------+---------------+---------------+---------------+-------------|
|CLUSTER |              |               |               |               |             |
|1       |              |               |           ####|              #|        #####|
|2       |              |               |            ###|     ##########|             |
|3       |              |               |         ######|         ######|         ####|
|4       |              |               |            ###|               |            #|
|5       |             #|              #|               |             ##|           ##|
|6       |            ##|             ##|            ###|               |           ##|
|7       |              |              #|            ###|              #|             |
------------------------------------------------------------------------------------
```

Cluster Analysis of Grocery Boxes
Analysis 5: Standardized row-standardized logarithms and color (s=.3)

The CLUSTER Procedure
Centroid Hierarchical Cluster Analysis

Eigenvalues of the Covariance Matrix

	Eigenvalue	Difference	Proportion	Cumulative
1	2.44752302	0.95026671	0.5500	0.5500
2	1.49725632	1.36701945	0.3365	0.8865
3	0.13023687	0.02135049	0.0293	0.9157
4	0.10888637	0.00867367	0.0245	0.9402
5	0.10021271	0.00628821	0.0225	0.9627
6	0.09392449	0.02196469	0.0211	0.9838
7	0.07195981	0.07195981	0.0162	1.0000
8	0.00000000	0.00000000	0.0000	1.0000
9	-.00000000		-0.0000	1.0000

Root-Mean-Square Total-Sample Standard Deviation = 0.703167
Root-Mean-Square Distance Between Observations = 2.983287

Cluster History

NCL	Clusters Joined		FREQ	SPRSQ	RSQ	ERSQ	CCC	PSF	PST2	Norm Cent Dist	Tie
20	CL24	CL28	4	0.0038	.953	.	.	45.7	2.7	0.3448	
19	Grape Nuts	CL23	6	0.0033	.950	.	.	46.0	3.5	0.3477	
18	CL46	Lemon Stix	3	0.0027	.947	.	.	47.1	21.9	0.3558	
17	CL21	Lipton Tea Bags	4	0.0031	.944	.	.	48.2	2.5	0.3577	
16	CL39	CL33	6	0.0064	.937	.	.	46.9	12.1	0.3637	
15	CL19	CL29	14	0.0152	.922	.	.	40.6	12.4	0.3707	
14	CL18	Fudge Brownies	4	0.0035	.919	.	.	42.5	2.5	0.3813	
13	CL16	CL25	13	0.0175	.901	.	.	38.0	13.7	0.4103	
12	CL22	Lipton Family Si	5	0.0049	.896	.875	1.76	40.0	3.2	0.4353	
11	CL12	CL37	7	0.0089	.887	.865	1.71	40.9	4.6	0.4397	
10	CL20	Luzianne Decaffe	5	0.0056	.882	.854	2.02	43.9	2.5	0.4669	
9	CL26	CL17	16	0.0222	.859	.841	1.20	41.3	16.6	0.479	
8	CL32	CL11	9	0.0125	.847	.826	1.31	43.5	4.5	0.4988	
7	CL14	Snack Cakes	5	0.0070	.840	.806	1.95	49.0	3.3	0.519	
6	Waverly Wafers	CL7	6	0.0077	.832	.782	2.79	56.6	2.3	0.5366	
5	CL9	CL15	30	0.0716	.761	.749	0.54	46.1	28.3	0.5452	
4	CL10	CL8	14	0.0318	.729	.700	1.21	52.9	8.6	0.5542	
3	CL5	CL6	36	0.0685	.660	.622	1.50	58.3	14.2	0.6516	
2	CL13	CL4	27	0.2008	.460	.427	0.90	51.9	46.6	0.9611	
1	CL3	CL2	63	0.4595	.000	.000	0.00	.	51.9	0.9609	

```
-------------------------------------------------------------------------------------------------------------------
|         |                                              class                                                    |
|         |-------------------------------------------------------------------------------------------------------|
|         |  Breakfast   |              |              |              |              |                            |
|         |    cereal    |   Crackers   |  Detergent   | Little Debbie| Paste, Tooth |            Tea             |
|---------+--------------+--------------+--------------+--------------+--------------+----------------------------|
|CLUSTER  |              |              |              |              |              |                            |
|1        |           ###|            ##|      ########|              |              |                           #|
|2        |              |             #|              |          ####|      ########|                            |
|3        |##############|              |              |              |              |                         ###|
|4        |              |             #|              |         #####|              |                            |
|5        |              |              |              |              |              |                   #########|
|6        |              |             #|              |              |              |                        ####|
-------------------------------------------------------------------------------------------------------------------
```

```
------------------------------------------------------------------------------------------
|         |                                   color                                      |
|         |------------------------------------------------------------------------------|
|         |      Blue      |     Green      |      Red       |     White      |  Yellow    |
|---------+----------------+----------------+----------------+----------------+------------|
|CLUSTER  |                |                |                |                |            |
|1        |                |                |        ########|               #|       #####|
|2        |                |                |             ###|     ###########|            |
|3        |                |                |           #####|          ######|       #####|
|4        |               #|               #|                |              ##|          ##|
|5        |              ##|              ##|             ###|                |          ##|
|6        |                |               #|             ###|               #|            |
------------------------------------------------------------------------------------------
```

```
                         Cluster Analysis of Grocery Boxes
        Analysis 6: Standardized row-standardized logarithms and color (s=.4)

                              The CLUSTER Procedure
                       Centroid Hierarchical Cluster Analysis

                         Eigenvalues of the Covariance Matrix

                  Eigenvalue    Difference    Proportion    Cumulative

             1    2.46469435    0.95296119        0.5135        0.5135
             2    1.51173316    1.28149311        0.3149        0.8284
             3    0.23024005    0.04306536        0.0480        0.8764
             4    0.18717469    0.01766446        0.0390        0.9154
             5    0.16951023    0.01827481        0.0353        0.9507
             6    0.15123542    0.06582379        0.0315        0.9822
             7    0.08541162    0.08541162        0.0178        1.0000
             8    -.00000000    0.00000000       -0.0000        1.0000
             9    -.00000000                    -0.0000        1.0000


          Root-Mean-Square Total-Sample Standard Deviation = 0.730297
          Root-Mean-Square Distance Between Observations   = 3.098387
```

Cluster History

NCL	----------Clusters Joined----------		FREQ	SPRSQ	RSQ	ERSQ	CCC	PSF	PST2	Norm Cent Dist	Tie
20	CL29	CL44	10	0.0074	.955	.	.	47.7	8.2	0.3789	
19	CL38	Lipton Family Si	3	0.0031	.952	.	.	48.1	9.3	0.3792	
18	CL25	CL41	11	0.0155	.936	.	.	38.8	36.7	0.4192	
17	CL23	CL43	10	0.0120	.924	.	.	35.0	11.6	0.4208	
16	Grape Nuts	CL26	6	0.0050	.919	.	.	35.6	5.8	0.4321	
15	CL19	CL31	5	0.0074	.912	.	.	35.4	5.3	0.4362	
14	Premium Saltines	CL27	4	0.0046	.907	.	.	36.8	2.9	0.4374	
13	CL18	CL20	21	0.0352	.872	.	.	28.4	19.7	0.4562	
12	CL13	CL16	27	0.0372	.835	.839	-.37	23.4	12.0	0.4968	
11	CL21	CL17	15	0.0289	.806	.828	-1.5	21.6	13.6	0.5183	
10	CL14	CL15	9	0.0200	.786	.815	-1.8	21.6	7.2	0.5281	
9	Waverly Wafers	Luzianne Decaffe	2	0.0047	.781	.801	-1.2	24.1	.	0.5425	
8	CL10	CL24	12	0.0243	.757	.785	-1.3	24.5	5.8	0.5783	
7	CL12	CL46	29	0.0224	.735	.765	-1.3	25.8	5.3	0.6105	
6	CL8	CL37	14	0.0220	.712	.740	-1.1	28.3	4.0	0.6313	
5	CL6	CL32	16	0.0251	.687	.707	-.78	31.9	3.9	0.6664	
4	CL11	CL9	17	0.0287	.659	.660	-.04	38.0	7.0	0.7098	
3	CL4	Snack Cakes	18	0.0180	.641	.584	2.21	53.5	3.2	0.7678	
2	CL3	CL5	34	0.2175	.423	.400	0.67	44.8	31.4	0.8923	
1	CL7	CL2	63	0.4232	.000	.000	0.00	.	44.8	0.9156	

```
-------------------------------------------------------------------------------------------------------
|        |                                              class                                          |
|        |---------------------------------------------------------------------------------------------|
|        |  Breakfast   |              |              |               |               |               |
|        |   cereal     |   Crackers   |  Detergent   | Little Debbie | Paste, Tooth  |      Tea      |
|--------+--------------+--------------+--------------+---------------+---------------+---------------|
|CLUSTER |              |              |              |               |               |               |
|1       |>##############|           ##|      ########|             ##|               |              #|
|2       |              |            ##|              |        #######|       ########|              #|
|3       |              |             #|              |               |               |>##############|
-------------------------------------------------------------------------------------------------------
```

```
-------------------------------------------------------------------------------------
|        |                                     color                                |
|        |--------------------------------------------------------------------------|
|        |     Blue     |    Green     |     Red      |    White     |    Yellow    |
|--------+--------------+--------------+--------------+--------------+--------------|
|CLUSTER |              |              |              |              |              |
|1       |              |              |    ##########|       #######|  ############|
|2       |             #|            ##|           ###| ############|              |
|3       |            ##|            ##|     #########|             #|            ##|
-------------------------------------------------------------------------------------
```

Cluster Analysis of Grocery Boxes
Analysis 7: Standardized row-standardized logarithms and color (s=.8)

The CLUSTER Procedure
Centroid Hierarchical Cluster Analysis

Eigenvalues of the Covariance Matrix

	Eigenvalue	Difference	Proportion	Cumulative
1	2.61400794	0.93268930	0.3631	0.3631
2	1.68131864	0.77645948	0.2335	0.5966
3	0.90485916	0.22547234	0.1257	0.7222
4	0.67938683	0.00292216	0.0944	0.8166
5	0.67646466	0.12119211	0.0940	0.9106
6	0.55527255	0.46658428	0.0771	0.9877
7	0.08868827	0.08868827	0.0123	1.0000
8	-.00000000	0.00000000	-0.0000	1.0000
9	-.00000000		-0.0000	1.0000

Root-Mean-Square Total-Sample Standard Deviation = 0.894427
Root-Mean-Square Distance Between Observations = 3.794733

Cluster History

NCL	--Clusters	Joined--	FREQ	SPRSQ	RSQ	ERSQ	CCC	PSF	PST2	Norm Cent Dist	Tie
20	CL29	CL44	10	0.0049	.970	.	.	72.7	8.2	0.3094	
19	CL38	Lipton Family Si	3	0.0021	.968	.	.	73.3	9.3	0.3096	
18	CL21	CL23	12	0.0153	.952	.	.	53.0	15.0	0.4029	
17	Waverly Wafers	Luzianne Decaffe	2	0.0032	.949	.	.	53.8	.	0.443	
16	CL27	CL24	6	0.0095	.940	.	.	48.9	10.4	0.444	
15	CL19	CL16	9	0.0136	.926	.	.	43.0	6.1	0.4587	
14	CL41	Grape Nuts	7	0.0058	.920	.	.	43.6	51.2	0.4591	
13	CL26	CL46	7	0.0105	.910	.	.	42.1	22.0	0.4769	
12	CL25	CL13	12	0.0205	.889	.743	16.5	37.3	13.8	0.467	
11	CL18	Premium Saltines	13	0.0093	.880	.726	16.7	38.2	4.0	0.5586	
10	CL17	CL37	4	0.0134	.867	.706	16.5	38.3	7.9	0.6454	
9	CL14	CL20	17	0.0567	.810	.684	11.0	28.8	52.6	0.6534	
8	CL12	CL9	29	0.0828	.727	.659	5.03	20.9	20.7	0.604	
7	CL11	CL43	16	0.0359	.691	.631	4.25	20.9	14.4	0.6758	
6	CL15	CL31	11	0.0263	.665	.598	4.24	22.6	8.0	0.7065	
5	CL7	CL6	27	0.1430	.522	.557	-1.7	15.8	28.2	0.8247	
4	CL8	CL5	56	0.2692	.253	.507	-9.1	6.6	31.5	0.7726	
3	Snack Cakes	CL32	3	0.0216	.231	.435	-6.6	9.0	46.0	1.0027	
2	CL4	CL10	60	0.1228	.108	.289	-5.6	7.4	9.5	1.0096	
1	CL2	CL3	63	0.1083	.000	.000	0.00	.	7.4	1.0839	

```
---------------------------------------------------------------------------------------------------------
|        |                                          class                                               |
|        |----------------------------------------------------------------------------------------------|
|        | Breakfast     |               |               |               |               |              |
|        |   cereal      |   Crackers    |   Detergent   | Little Debbie | Paste, Tooth  |     Tea      |
|--------+---------------+---------------+---------------+---------------+---------------+--------------|
|CLUSTER |               |               |               |               |               |              |
|1       |            ###|             ##|           ####|               |               |             #|
|2       |               |             ##|               |         ######|          #####|              |
|3       |        #######|               |               |               |               |              |
|4       |         ######|               |           ####|             ##|               |              |
|5       |               |               |               |               |            ###|              |
|6       |               |               |               |               |               |     #########|
|7       |               |              #|               |               |               |           ###|
|8       |               |               |               |               |               |            ##|
|9       |               |               |               |               |               |            ##|
|10      |               |               |               |              #|               |              |
---------------------------------------------------------------------------------------------------------
```

```
--------------------------------------------------------------------------------
|        |                             color                                  |
|        |--------------------------------------------------------------------|
|        |     Blue      |     Green     |      Red      |     White     |    Yellow     |
|--------+---------------+---------------+---------------+---------------+---------------|
|CLUSTER |               |               |               |               |               |
|1       |               |               |     ##########|               |               |
|2       |               |               |               |  #############|               |
|3       |               |               |               |        #######|               |
|4       |               |               |               |               |   ############|
|5       |               |               |            ###|               |               |
|6       |               |               |      #########|               |               |
|7       |               |           ####|               |               |               |
|8       |             ##|               |               |               |               |
|9       |               |               |               |               |             ##|
|10      |              #|               |               |               |               |
--------------------------------------------------------------------------------
```

References

Anderberg, M.R. (1973), *Cluster Analysis for Applications*, New York: Academic Press, Inc.

Batagelj, V. (1981), "Note on Ultrametric Hierarchical Clustering Algorithms," *Psychometrika*, 46, 351–352.

Blackith, R.E. and Reyment, R.A. (1971), *Multivariate Morphometrics*, London: Academic Press.

Blashfield, R.K. and Aldenderfer, M.S. (1978), "The Literature on Cluster Analysis," *Multivariate Behavioral Research*, 13, 271–295.

Calinski, T. and Harabasz, J. (1974), "A Dendrite Method for Cluster Analysis," *Communications in Statistics*, 3, 1–27.

Cooper, M.C. and Milligan, G.W. (1988), "The Effect of Error on Determining the Number of Clusters," *Proceedings of the International Workship on Data Analysis, Decision Support, and Expert Knowledge Representation in Marketing and Related Areas of Research*, 319–328.

Duda, R.O. and Hart, P.E. (1973), *Pattern Classification and Scene Analysis*, New York: John Wiley & Sons, Inc.

Everitt, B.S. (1980), *Cluster Analysis*, Second Edition, London: Heineman Educational Books Ltd.

Fisher, L. and Van Ness, J.W. (1971), "Admissible Clustering Procedures," *Biometrika*, 58, 91–104.

Fisher, R.A. (1936), "The Use of Multiple Measurements in Taxonomic Problems," *Annals of Eugenics*, 7, 179–188.

Florek, K., Lukaszewicz, J., Perkal, J., and Zubrzycki, S. (1951a), "Sur la Liaison et la Division des Points d'un Ensemble Fini," *Colloquium Mathematicae*, 2, 282–285.

Florek, K., Lukaszewicz, J., Perkal, J., and Zubrzycki, S. (1951b), "Taksonomia Wroclawska," *Przeglad Antropol.*, 17, 193–211.

Gower, J.C. (1967), "A Comparison of Some Methods of Cluster Analysis," *Biometrics*, 23, 623–637.

Hamer, R.M. and Cunningham, J.W. (1981), "Cluster analyzing profile data with interrater differences: A comparison of profile association measures," *Applied Psychological Measurement*, 5, 63–72.

Hartigan, J.A. (1975), *Clustering Algorithms*, New York: John Wiley & Sons, Inc.

Hartigan, J.A. (1977), "Distribution Problems in Clustering," in *Classification and Clustering*, ed. J. Van Ryzin, New York: Academic Press, Inc.

Hartigan, J.A. (1981), "Consistency of Single Linkage for High-density Clusters," *Journal of the American Statistical Association*, 76, 388–394.

Hawkins, D.M., Muller, M.W., and ten Krooden, J.A. (1982), "Cluster Analysis," in *Topics in Applied Multivariate Analysis*, ed. D.M. Hawkins, Cambridge: Cambridge University Press.

Jardine, N. and Sibson, R. (1971), *Mathematical Taxonomy*, New York: John Wiley & Sons, Inc.

Johnson, S.C. (1967), "Hierarchical Clustering Schemes," *Psychometrika*, 32, 241–254.

Lance, G.N. and Williams, W.T. (1967), "A General Theory of Classificatory Sorting Strategies. I. Hierarchical Systems," *Computer Journal*, 9, 373–380.

Massart, D.L. and Kaufman, L. (1983), *The Interpretation of Analytical Chemical Data by the Use of Cluster Analysis*, New York: John Wiley & Sons, Inc.

McQuitty, L.L. (1957), "Elementary Linkage Analysis for Isolating Orthogonal and Oblique Types and Typal Relevancies," *Educational and Psychological Measurement*, 17, 207–229.

McQuitty, L.L. (1966), "Similarity Analysis by Reciprocal Pairs for Discrete and Continuous Data," *Educational and Psychological Measurement*, 26, 825–831.

Mezzich, J.E and Solomon, H. (1980), *Taxonomy and Behavioral Science*, New York: Academic Press, Inc.

Milligan, G.W. (1979), "Ultrametric Hierarchical Clustering Algorithms," *Psychometrika*, 44, 343–346.

Milligan, G.W. (1980), "An Examination of the Effect of Six Types of Error Perturbation on Fifteen Clustering Algorithms," *Psychometrika*, 45, 325–342.

Milligan, G.W. (1987), "A Study of the Beta-Flexible Clustering Method," *College of Administrative Science Working Paper Series*, 87–61 Columbus, OH: The Ohio State University.

Milligan, G.W. and Cooper, M.C. (1985), "An Examination of Procedures for Determining the Number of Clusters in a Data Set," *Psychometrika*, 50,159–179.

Milligan, G.W. and Cooper, M.C. (1987), "A Study of Variable Standardization," *College of Administrative Science Working Paper Series*, 87–63, Columbus, OH: The Ohio State University.

Rouncefield, M. (1995), "The Statistics of Poverty and Inequality," *Journal of Statistics Education*, 3(2). [Online]: [http://www.stat.ncsu.edu/info/jse], accessed Dec. 19, 1997.

Sarle, W.S. (1983), *Cubic Clustering Criterion*, SAS Technical Report A-108, Cary, NC: SAS Institute Inc.

Silverman, B.W. (1986), *Density Estimation*, New York: Chapman and Hall.

Sneath, P.H.A. (1957), "The Application of Computers to Taxonomy," *Journal of General Microbiology*, 17, 201–226.

Sneath, P.H.A. and Sokal, R.R. (1973), *Numerical Taxonomy*, San Francisco: Freeman.

Sokal, R.R. and Michener, C.D. (1958), "A Statistical Method for Evaluating Systematic Relationships," *University of Kansas Science Bulletin*, 38, 1409–1438.

Sorensen, T. (1948), "A Method of Establishing Groups of Equal Amplitude in Plant Sociology Based on Similarity of Species Content and Its Application to Analyses of the Vegetation on Danish Commons," *Biologiske Skrifter*, 5, 1–34.

Spath, H. (1980), *Cluster Analysis Algorithms*, Chichester, England: Ellis Horwood.

Symons, M.J. (1981), "Clustering Criteria and Multivariate Normal Mixtures," *Biometrics*, 37, 35–43.

Ward, J.H. (1963), "Hierarchical Grouping to Optimize an Objective Function," *Journal of the American Statistical Association*, 58, 236–244.

Wishart, D. (1969), "Mode Analysis: A Generalisation of Nearest Neighbour Which Reduces Chaining Effects," in *Numerical Taxonomy*, ed. A.J. Cole, London: Academic Press.

Wong, M.A. (1982), "A Hybrid Clustering Method for Identifying High-Density Clusters," *Journal of the American Statistical Association*, 77, 841–847.

Wong, M.A. and Lane, T. (1983), "A kth Nearest Neighbor Clustering Procedure," *Journal of the Royal Statistical Society*, Series B, 45, 362–368.

Wong, M.A. and Schaack, C. (1982), "Using the kth Nearest Neighbor Clustering Procedure to Determine the Number of Subpopulations," *American Statistical Association 1982 Proceedings of the Statistical Computing Section*, 40–48.

Chapter 24
The CORRESP Procedure

Chapter Table of Contents

Chapter 24
The CORRESP Procedure

Overview

The CORRESP procedure performs simple and multiple correspondence analysis. You can use correspondence analysis to find a low-dimensional graphical representation of the rows and columns of a crosstabulation or contingency table. Each row and column is represented by a point in a plot determined from the cell frequencies. PROC CORRESP can also compute coordinates for supplementary rows and columns.

PROC CORRESP can read two kinds of input: raw categorical responses on two or more classification variables, and a two-way contingency table. The correspondence analysis results can be output and displayed with the %PLOTIT macro.

Background

Correspondence analysis is a popular data analysis method in France and Japan. In France, correspondence analysis was developed under the strong influence of Jean-Paul Benzécri; in Japan, it was developed under Chikio Hayashi. The name *correspondence analysis* is a translation of the French *analyse des correspondances*. The technique apparently has many independent beginnings (for example, Richardson and Kuder 1933; Hirshfeld 1935; Horst 1935; Fisher 1940; Guttman 1941; Burt 1950; Hayashi 1950). It has had many other names, including optimal scaling, reciprocal averaging, optimal scoring, and appropriate scoring in the United States; quantification method in Japan; homogeneity analysis in the Netherlands; dual scaling in Canada; and scalogram analysis in Israel.

Correspondence analysis is described in more detail in French in Benzécri (1973) and Lebart, Morineau, and Tabard (1977). In Japanese, the subject is described in Komazawa (1982), Nishisato (1982), and Kobayashi (1981). In English, correspondence analysis is described in Lebart, Morineau, and Warwick (1984), Greenacre (1984), Nishisato (1980), Tenenhaus and Young (1985); Gifi (1990); Greenacre and Hastie (1987); and many other sources. Hoffman and Franke (1986) offer a short, introductory treatment using examples from the field of market research.

Getting Started

Data are available containing the numbers of Ph.Ds awarded in the United States during the years 1973 through 1978 (U.S. Bureau of the Census 1979). The table has six rows, one for each of six academic disciplines, and six columns for the six years. The following DATA step reads the complete table into a SAS data set, and PROC CORRESP displays correspondence analysis results including the inertia decomposition and coordinates. The concept of *inertia* in correspondence analysis is analogous to the concept of variance in principal component analysis, and it is proportional to the chi-square information. The %PLOTIT macro creates a graphical scatterplot of the results. See Appendix B, "Using the %PLOTIT Macro," for more information on the %PLOTIT macro.

```
title "Number of Ph.D's Awarded from 1973 to 1978";
data PhD;
   input Science $ 1-19 y1973-y1978;
   label y1973 = '1973'
         y1974 = '1974'
         y1975 = '1975'
         y1976 = '1976'
         y1977 = '1977'
         y1978 = '1978';
   datalines;
Life Sciences       4489 4303 4402 4350 4266 4361
Physical Sciences   4101 3800 3749 3572 3410 3234
Social Sciences     3354 3286 3344 3278 3137 3008
Behavioral Sciences 2444 2587 2749 2878 2960 3049
Engineering         3338 3144 2959 2791 2641 2432
Mathematics         1222 1196 1149 1003  959  959
;

proc corresp data=PhD out=Results short;
   var y1973-y1978;
   id Science;
run;

%plotit(data=Results, datatype=corresp, plotvars=Dim1 Dim2)
```

```
                  Number of Ph.D's Awarded from 1973 to 1978

                            The CORRESP Procedure

                      Inertia and Chi-Square Decomposition

Singular  Principal     Chi-            Cumulative
   Value    Inertia   Square  Percent      Percent    19   38   57   76   95
                                                  ----+----+----+----+----+---
 0.05845    0.00342  368.653    96.04        96.04  ************************
 0.00861    0.00007    7.995     2.08        98.12  *
 0.00694    0.00005    5.197     1.35        99.48
 0.00414    0.00002    1.852     0.48        99.96
 0.00122    0.00000    0.160     0.04       100.00

   Total    0.00356  383.856   100.00

Degrees of Freedom = 25
```

Figure 24.1. Inertia and Chi-Square Decomposition

The total chi-square statistic, which is a measure of the association between the rows and columns in the full five dimensions of the (centered) table, is 383.856. The maximum number of dimensions (or axes) is the minimum of the number of rows and columns, minus one. Over 96% of the total chi-square and inertia is explained by the first dimension, indicating that the association between the row and column categories is essentially one dimensional. The plot shows how the number of doctorates in the different areas changes over time. The plot shows that the number of doctorates in the behavioral sciences is associated with later years, and the number of doctorates in mathematics and engineering is associated with earlier years. This is consistent with the data which shows that number of doctorates in the behavioral sciences is increasing, the number of doctorates in every other discipline is decreasing, and the rate of decrease is greatest for mathematics and engineering.

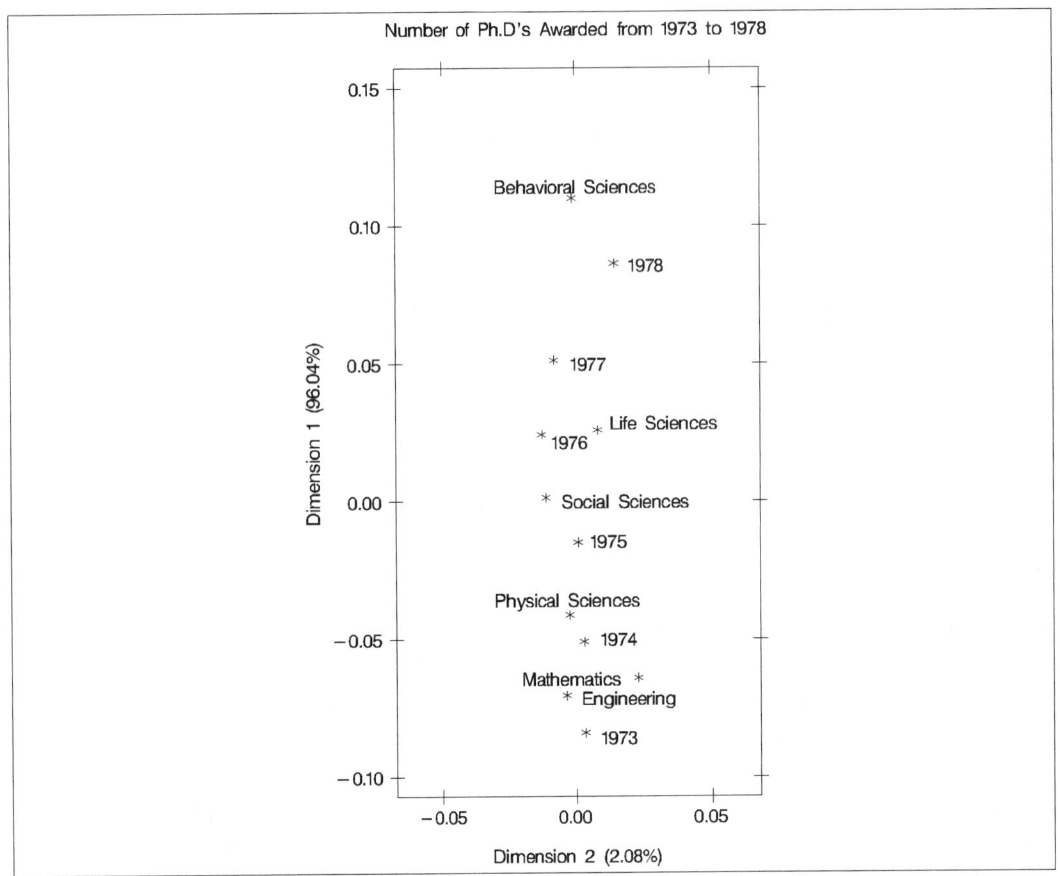

Figure 24.2. Plot of Dimension 1 versus Dimension 2 for Ph.D. Data

Syntax

The following statements are available in the CORRESP procedure.

> **PROC CORRESP** < *options* > **;**
>   **TABLES** < *row-variables,* > *column-variables* **;**
>   **VAR** *variables* **;**
>   **BY** *variables* **;**
>   **ID** *variable* **;**
>   **SUPPLEMENTARY** *variables* **;**
>   **WEIGHT** *variable* **;**

There are two separate forms of input to PROC CORRESP. One form is specified in the TABLES statement, the other in the VAR statement. You must specify either the TABLES or the VAR statement, but not both, each time you run PROC CORRESP.

Specify the TABLES statement if you are using raw, categorical data, the levels of which define the rows and columns of a table.

Specify the VAR statement if your data are already in tabular form. PROC CORRESP is generally more efficient with VAR statement input than with TABLES statement input.

The other statements are optional. Each of the statements is explained in alphabetical order following the PROC CORRESP statement. All of the options in PROC CORRESP can be abbreviated to their first three letters, except for the OUTF= option. This is a special feature of PROC CORRESP and is not generally true of SAS/STAT procedures.

PROC CORRESP Statement

PROC CORRESP < *options* > **;**

The PROC CORRESP statement invokes the procedure. You can specify the following options in the PROC CORRESP statement. These options are described following Table 24.1.

Table 24.1. Summary of PROC CORRESP Statement Options

Task	Options
Specify data sets	
specify input SAS data set	DATA=
specify output coordinate SAS data set	OUTC=
specify output frequency SAS data set	OUTF=
Compute row and column coordinates	
specify the number of dimensions or axes	DIMENS=
perform multiple correspondence analysis	MCA
standardize the row and column coordinates	PROFILE=
Construct tables	
specify binary table	BINARY
specify cross levels of TABLES variables	CROSS=
specify input data in PROC FREQ output	FREQOUT
include observations with missing values	MISSING
Display output	
display all output	ALL
display inertias adjusted by Benzécri's method	BENZECRI
display cell contributions to chi-square	CELLCHI2
display column profile matrix	CP
display observed minus expected values	DEVIATION
display chi-square expected values	EXPECTED
display inertias adjusted by Greenacre's method	GREENACRE
suppress the display of column coordinates	NOCOLUMN=
suppress the display of all output	NOPRINT
suppress the display of row coordinates	NOROW=
display contingency table of observed frequencies	OBSERVED
display percentages or frequencies	PRINT=

Task	Options
display row profile matrix	RP
suppress all point and coordinate statistics	SHORT
display unadjusted inertias	UNADJUSTED
Other tasks	
specify rarely used column coordinate standardizations	COLUMN=
specify minimum inertia	MININERTIA=
specify number of classification variables	NVARS=
specify rarely used row coordinate standardizations	ROW=
specify effective zero	SINGULAR=
include level source in the OUTC= data set	SOURCE

The display options control the amount of displayed output. The CELLCHI2, EXPECTED, and DEVIATION options display additional chi-square information. See the "Details" section on page 961 for more information. The unit of the matrices displayed by the CELLCHI2, CP, DEVIATION, EXPECTED, OBSERVED, and RP options depends on the value of the PRINT= option. The table construction options control the construction of the contingency table; these options are valid only when you also specify a TABLES statement.

You can specify the following options in the PROC CORRESP statement. They are described in alphabetical order.

ALL

is equivalent to specifying the OBSERVED, RP, CP, CELLCHI2, EXPECTED, and DEVIATION options. Specifying the ALL option does not affect the PRINT= option. Therefore, only frequencies (not percentages) for these options are displayed unless you specify otherwise with the PRINT= option.

BENZECRI | BEN

displays adjusted inertias when performing multiple correspondence analysis. By default, unadjusted inertias, the usual inertias from multiple correspondence analysis, are displayed. However, adjusted inertias using a method proposed by Benzécri (1979) and described by Greenacre (1984, p. 145) can be displayed by specifying the BENZECRI option. Specify the UNADJUSTED option to output the usual table of unadjusted inertias as well. See the section "MCA Adjusted Inertias" on page 981 for more information.

BINARY

enables you to create binary tables easily. When you specify the BINARY option, specify only column variables in the TABLES statement. Each input data set observation forms a single row in the constructed table.

CELLCHI2 | CEL

displays the contribution to the total chi-square test statistic for each cell. See also the descriptions of the DEVIATION, EXPECTED, and OBSERVED options.

COLUMN=B | BD | DB | DBD | DBD1/2 | DBID1/2
COL=B | BD | DB | DBD | DBD1/2 | DBID1/2

provides other standardizations of the column coordinates. The COLUMN= option is rarely needed. Typically, you should use the PROFILE= option instead (see the section "The PROFILE=, ROW=, and COLUMN= Options" on page 978). By default, COLUMN=DBD.

CP

displays the column profile matrix. Column profiles contain the observed conditional probabilities of row membership given column membership. See also the RP option.

CROSS=BOTH | COLUMN | NONE | ROW
CRO=BOT | COL | NON | ROW

specifies the method of crossing (factorially combining) the levels of the TABLES variables. The default is CROSS=NONE.

- CROSS=NONE causes each level of every row variable to become a row label and each level of every column variable to become a column label.
- CROSS=ROW causes each combination of levels for all row variables to become a row label, whereas each level of every column variable becomes a column label.
- CROSS=COLUMN causes each combination of levels for all column variables to become a column label, whereas each level of every row variable becomes a row label.
- CROSS=BOTH causes each combination of levels for all row variables to become a row label and each combination of levels for all column variables to become a column label.

The "TABLES Statement" section on page 959 provides a more detailed description of this option.

DATA=*SAS-data-set*

specifies the SAS data set to be used by PROC CORRESP. If you do not specify the DATA= option, PROC CORRESP uses the most recently created SAS data set.

DEVIATION | DEV

displays the matrix of deviations between the observed frequency matrix and the product of its row marginals and column marginals divided by its grand frequency. For ordinary two-way contingency tables, these are the observed minus expected frequencies under the hypothesis of row and column independence and are components of the chi-square test statistic. See also the CELLCHI2, EXPECTED, and OBSERVED options.

DIMENS=*n*
DIM=*n*

specifies the number of dimensions or axes to use. The default is DIMENS=2. The maximum value of the DIMENS= option in an $(n_r \times n_c)$ table is $n_r - 1$ or $n_c - 1$, whichever is smaller. For example, in a table with 4 rows and 5 columns, the maximum specification is DIMENS=3. If your table has 2 rows or 2 columns, specify DIMENS=1.

EXPECTED | EXP

displays the product of the row marginals and the column marginals divided by the grand frequency of the observed frequency table. For ordinary two-way contingency tables, these are the expected frequencies under the hypothesis of row and column independence and are components of the chi-square test statistic. In other situations, this interpretation is not strictly valid. See also the CELLCHI2, DEVIATION, and OBSERVED options.

FREQOUT | FRE

indicates that the PROC CORRESP input data set has the same form as an output data set from the FREQ procedure, even if it was not directly produced by PROC FREQ. The FREQOUT option enables PROC CORRESP to take shortcuts in constructing the contingency table.

When you specify the FREQOUT option, you must also specify a WEIGHT statement. The cell frequencies in a PROC FREQ output data set are contained in a variable called COUNT, so specify COUNT in a WEIGHT statement with PROC CORRESP. The FREQOUT option may produce unexpected results if the DATA= data set is structured incorrectly. Each of the two variable lists specified in the TABLES statement must consist of a single variable, and observations must be grouped by the levels of the row variable and then by the levels of the column variable. It is not required that the observations be sorted by the row variable and column variable, but they must be grouped consistently. There must be as many observations in the input data set (or BY group) as there are cells in the completed contingency table. Zero cells must be specified with zero weights. When you use PROC FREQ to create the PROC CORRESP input data set, you must specify the SPARSE option in the FREQ procedure's TABLES statement so that the zero cells are written to the output data set.

GREENACRE | GRE

displays adjusted inertias when performing multiple correspondence analysis. By default, unadjusted inertias, the usual inertias from multiple correspondence analysis, are displayed. However, adjusted inertias using a method proposed by Greenacre (1994, p. 156) can be displayed by specifying the GREENACRE option. Specify the UNADJUSTED option to output the usual table of unadjusted inertias as well. See the section "MCA Adjusted Inertias" on page 981 for more information.

MCA

requests a multiple correspondence analysis. This option requires that the input table be a Burt table, which is a symmetric matrix of crosstabulations among several categorical variables. If you specify the MCA option and a VAR statement, you must also specify the NVARS= option, which gives the number of categorical variables that were used to create the table. With raw categorical data, if you want results for the individuals as well as the categories, use the BINARY option instead.

MININERTIA=*n*
MIN=*n*

specifies the minimum inertia ($0 \leq n \leq 1$) used to create the "best" tables—the indicator of which points best explain the inertia of each dimension. By default, MININERTIA=0.8. See the "Algorithm and Notation" section on page 976 for more information.

MISSING | MIS

specifies that observations with missing values for the TABLES statement variables are included in the analysis. Missing values are treated as a distinct level of each categorical variable. By default, observations with missing values are excluded from the analysis.

NOCOLUMN < = BOTH | DATA | PRINT >
NOC < = BOT | DAT | PRI >

suppresses the display of the column coordinates and statistics and omits them from the output coordinate data set.

BOTH	suppresses all column information from both the SAS listing and the output data set. The NOCOLUMN option is equivalent to the option NOCOLUMN=BOTH.
DATA	suppresses all column information from the output data set.
PRINT	suppresses all column information from the SAS listing.

NOPRINT | NOP

suppresses the display of all output. This option is useful when you need only an output data set. Note that this option temporarily disables the Output Delivery System (ODS). For more information, see Chapter 15, "Using the Output Delivery System."

NOROW < = BOTH | DATA | PRINT >
NOR < = BOT | DAT | PRI >

suppresses the display of the row coordinates and statistics and omits them from the output coordinate data set.

BOTH	suppresses all row information from both the SAS listing and the output data set. The NOROW option is equivalent to the option NOROW=BOTH.
DATA	suppresses all row information from the output data set.
PRINT	suppresses all row information from the SAS listing.

The NOROW option can be useful when the rows of the contingency table are replications.

NVARS=*n*
NVA=*n*

specifies the number of classification variables that were used to create the Burt table. For example, if the Burt table was originally created with the statement

```
tables a b c;
```

you must specify NVARS=3 to read the table with a VAR statement.

The NVARS= option is required when you specify both the MCA option and a VAR statement. (See the section "VAR Statement" on page 960 for an example.)

OBSERVED | OBS

displays the contingency table of observed frequencies and its row, column, and grand totals. If you do not specify the OBSERVED or ALL option, the contingency table is not displayed.

OUTC=*SAS-data-set*
OUT=*SAS-data-set*

creates an output coordinate SAS data set to contain the row, column, supplementary observation, and supplementary variable coordinates. This data set also contains the masses, squared cosines, quality of each point's representation in the DIMENS=n dimensional display, relative inertias, partial contributions to inertia, and best indicators.

OUTF=*SAS-data-set*

creates an output frequency SAS data set to contain the contingency table, row, and column profiles, the expected values, and the observed minus expected values and contributions to the chi-square statistic.

PRINT=BOTH | FREQ | PERCENT
PRI=BOT | FRE | PER

affects the OBSERVED, RP, CP, CELLCHI2, EXPECTED, and DEVIATION options. The default is PRINT=FREQ.

- The PRINT=FREQ option displays output in the appropriate raw or natural units. (That is, PROC CORRESP displays raw frequencies for the OBSERVED option, relative frequencies with row marginals of 1.0 for the RP option, and so on.)
- The PRINT=PERCENT option scales results to percentages for the display of the output. (All elements in the OBSERVED matrix sum to 100.0, the row marginals are 100.0 for the RP option, and so on.)
- The PRINT=BOTH option displays both percentages and frequencies.

PROFILE=BOTH | COLUMN | NONE | ROW
PRO=BOT | COL | NON | ROW

specifies the standardization for the row and column coordinates. The default is PROFILE=BOTH.

PROFILE=BOTH specifies a standard correspondence analysis, which jointly displays the principal row and column coordinates. Row coordinates are computed from the row profile matrix, and column coordinates are computed from the column profile matrix.

PROFILE=ROW specifies a correspondence analysis of the row profile matrix. The row coordinates are weighted centroids of the column coordinates.

PROFILE=COLUMN specifies a correspondence analysis of the column profile matrix. The column coordinates are weighted centroids of the row coordinates.

PROFILE=NONE is rarely needed. Row and column coordinates are the generalized singular vectors, without the customary standardizations.

ROW=A | AD | DA | DAD | DAD1/2 | DAID1/2

provides other standardizations of the row coordinates. The ROW= option is rarely needed. Typically, you should use the PROFILE= option instead (see the section "The PROFILE=, ROW=, and COLUMN= Options" on page 978). By default, ROW=DAD.

RP

displays the row profile matrix. Row profiles contain the observed conditional probabilities of column membership given row membership. See also the CP option.

SHORT | SHO

suppresses the display of all point and coordinate statistics except the coordinates. The following information is suppressed: each point's mass, relative contribution to the total inertia, and quality of representation in the DIMENS=n dimensional display; the squared cosines of the angles between each axis and a vector from the origin to the point; the partial contributions of each point to the inertia of each dimension; and the best indicators.

SINGULAR=*n*
SIN=*n*

specifies the largest value that is considered to be within rounding error of zero. The default value is 1E−8. This parameter is used when checking for zero rows and columns, when checking Burt table diagonal sums for equality, when checking denominators before dividing, and so on. Typically, you should not assign a value outside the range 1E−6 to 1E−12.

SOURCE | SOU

adds the variable _VAR_, which contains the name or label of the variable corresponding to the current level, to the OUTC= and OUTF= data sets.

UNADJUSTED | UNA

displays unadjusted inertias when performing multiple correspondence analysis. By default, unadjusted inertias, the usual inertias from multiple correspondence analysis, are displayed. However, if adjusted inertias are requested by either the GREENACRE option or the BENZECRI option, then the unadjusted inertia table is not displayed unless the UNADJUSTED option is specified. See the section "MCA Adjusted Inertias" on page 981 for more information.

BY Statement

BY *variables* ;

You can specify a BY statement with PROC CORRESP to obtain separate analyses on observations in groups defined by the BY variables. When a BY statement appears, the procedure expects the input data set to be sorted in order of the BY variables.

If your input data set is not sorted in ascending order, use one of the following alternatives:

- Sort the data using the SORT procedure with a similar BY statement.
- Specify the BY statement option NOTSORTED or DESCENDING in the BY statement for the CORRESP procedure. The NOTSORTED option does not mean that the data are unsorted but rather that the data are arranged in groups (according to values of the BY variables) and that these groups are not necessarily in alphabetical or increasing numeric order.
- Create an index on the BY variables using the DATASETS procedure.

For more information on the BY statement, refer to the discussion in *SAS Language Reference: Concepts*. For more information on the DATASETS procedure, refer to the discussion in the *SAS Procedures Guide*.

ID Statement

ID *variable* ;

You specify the ID statement only in conjunction with the VAR statement. You cannot specify the ID statement when you use the TABLES statement or the MCA option. When you specify an ID variable, PROC CORRESP labels the rows of the tables with the ID values and places the ID variable in the output data set.

SUPPLEMENTARY Statement

SUPPLEMENTARY *variables* ;
SUP *variables* ;

The SUPPLEMENTARY statement specifies variables that are to be represented as points in the joint row and column space but that are not used when determining the locations of the other, active row and column points of the contingency table. Supplementary observations on supplementary variables are ignored in simple correspondence analysis but are needed to compute the squared cosines for multiple correspondence analysis. Variables that are specified in the SUPPLEMENTARY statement must also be specified in the TABLES or VAR statement.

When you specify a VAR statement, each SUPPLEMENTARY variable indicates one supplementary column of the table. Supplementary variables must be numeric with VAR statement input.

When you specify a TABLES statement, each SUPPLEMENTARY variable indicates a set of rows or columns of the table that is supplementary. Supplementary variables can be either character or numeric with TABLES statement input.

TABLES Statement

TABLES < *row-variables,* > *column-variables* **;**

The TABLES statement instructs PROC CORRESP to create a contingency table, Burt table, or binary table from the values of two or more categorical variables. The TABLES statement specifies classification variables that are used to construct the rows and columns of the contingency table. The variables can be either numeric or character. The variable lists in the TABLES statement and the CROSS= option together determine the row and column labels of the contingency table.

You can specify both row variables and column variables separated by a comma, or you can specify only column variables and no comma. If you do not specify row variables (that is, if you list variables but do not use the comma as a delimiter), then you should specify either the MCA or the BINARY option. With the MCA option, PROC CORRESP creates a Burt table, which is a crosstabulation of each variable with itself and every other variable. The Burt table is symmetric. With the BINARY option, PROC CORRESP creates a binary table, which consists of one row for each input data set observation and one column for each category of each TABLES statement variable. If the binary matrix is $\mathbf{Z}$, then the Burt table is $\mathbf{Z}'\mathbf{Z}$. Specifying the BINARY option with the NOROWS option produces the same results as specifying the MCA option (except for the chi-square statistics).

See Figure 24.3 for an example or see the section "The MCA Option" on page 980 for a detailed description of Burt tables.

You can use the WEIGHT statement with the TABLES statement to read category frequencies. Specify the SUPPLEMENTARY statement to name variables with categories that are supplementary rows or columns. You cannot specify the ID or VAR statement with the TABLES statement.

See the section "Using the TABLES Statement" on page 967 for an example.

VAR Statement

VAR *variables* ;

You should specify the VAR statement when your data are in tabular form. The VAR variables must be numeric. The VAR statement instructs PROC CORRESP to read an existing contingency table, binary indicator matrix, fuzzy-coded indicator matrix, or Burt table, rather than raw data. See the "Algorithm and Notation" section on page 976 for a description of a binary indicator matrix and a fuzzy-coded indicator matrix.

You can specify the WEIGHT statement with the VAR statement to read category frequencies and designate supplementary rows. Specify the SUPPLEMENTARY statement to name supplementary variables. You cannot specify the TABLES statement with the VAR statement.

WEIGHT Statement

WEIGHT *variable* ;

The WEIGHT statement specifies weights for each observation and indicates supplementary observations for simple correspondence analyses with VAR statement input. You can include only one WEIGHT statement, and the weight variable must be numeric.

If you omit the WEIGHT statement, each observation contributes a value of 1 to the frequency count for its category. That is, each observation represents one subject. When you specify a WEIGHT statement, each observation contributes the value of the weighting variable for that observation. For example, a weight of 3 means that the observation represents 3 subjects. Weight values are not required to be integers.

You can specify the WEIGHT statement with a TABLES statement to indicate category frequencies, as in the following example:

```
proc freq;
   tables a*b / out=outfreq sparse;
run;

proc corresp freqout;
   tables a, b;
   weight count;
run;
```

If you specify a VAR statement, you can specify the WEIGHT statement to indicate supplementary observations and to weight some rows of the table more heavily than others. When the value of the WEIGHT variable is negative, the observation is treated as supplementary, and the absolute value of the weight is used as the weighting value.

You cannot specify a WEIGHT statement with a VAR statement and the MCA option, because the table must be symmetric. Supplementary variables are indicated with the SUPPLEMENTARY statement, so differential weighting of rows is inappropriate.

Details

Input Data Set

PROC CORRESP can read two kinds of input:

- raw category responses on two or more classification variables with the TABLES statement
- a two-way contingency table with the VAR statement

You can use output from PROC FREQ as input for PROC CORRESP.

The classification variables referred to by the TABLES statement can be either numeric or character variables. Normally, all observations for a given variable that have the same formatted value are placed in the same level, and observations with different values are placed in different levels.

The variables in the VAR statement must be numeric. The values of the observations specify the cell frequencies. These values are not required to be integers, but only those observations with all nonnegative, nonmissing values are used in the correspondence analysis. Observations with one or more negative values are removed from the analysis.

The WEIGHT variable must be numeric. Observations with negative weights are treated as supplementary observations. The absolute values of the weights are used to weight the observations.

Types of Tables Used as Input

The following example explains correspondence analysis and illustrates some capabilities of PROC CORRESP.

```
data Neighbor;
   input Name $ 1-10 Age $ 12-18 Sex $ 19-25
         Height $ 26-30 Hair $ 32-37;
   datalines;
Jones      Old    Male   Short White
Smith      Young  Female Tall  Brown
Kasavitz   Old    Male   Short Brown
Ernst      Old    Female Tall  White
Zannoria   Old    Female Short Brown
Spangel    Young  Male   Tall  Blond
Myers      Young  Male   Tall  Brown
Kasinski   Old    Male   Short Blond
Colman     Young  Female Short Blond
Delafave   Old    Male   Tall  Brown
```

```
Singer     Young  Male   Tall  Brown
Igor       Old           Short
;
```

There are several types of tables, **N**, that can be used as input to correspondence analysis —all tables can be defined using a binary matrix, **Z**.

With the BINARY option, $\mathbf{N} = \mathbf{Z}$ is directly analyzed. The binary matrix has one column for each category and one row for each individual or case. A binary table constructed from m categorical variables has m partitions. The following table has four partitions, one for each of the four categorical variables. Each partition has a 1 in each row, and each row contains exactly four 1s since there are four categorical variables. More generally, the binary design matrix has exactly m 1s in each row. The 1s indicate the categories to which the observation applies.

Table 24.2. $\mathbf{Z}$, The Binary Coding of Neighbor Data Set

$\mathbf{Z}_{\text{Hair}}$			$\mathbf{Z}_{\text{Height}}$		$\mathbf{Z}_{\text{Sex}}$		$\mathbf{Z}_{\text{Age}}$	
Blond	Brown	White	Short	Tall	Female	Male	Old	Young
0	0	1	1	0	0	1	1	0
0	1	0	0	1	1	0	0	1
0	1	0	1	0	0	1	1	0
0	0	1	0	1	1	0	1	0
0	1	0	1	0	1	0	1	0
1	0	0	0	1	0	1	0	1
0	1	0	0	1	0	1	0	1
1	0	0	1	0	0	1	1	0
1	0	0	1	0	1	0	0	1
0	1	0	0	1	0	1	1	0
0	1	0	0	1	0	1	0	1

With the MCA option, the Burt table ($\mathbf{Z}'\mathbf{Z}$) is analyzed. A Burt table is a partitioned symmetric matrix containing all pairs of crosstabulations among a set of categorical variables. Each diagonal partition is a diagonal matrix containing marginal frequencies (a crosstabulation of a variable with itself). Each off-diagonal partition is an ordinary contingency table. Each contingency table above the diagonal has a transposed counterpart below the diagonal.

Table 24.3. $\mathbf{Z'Z}$, The Burt Table

	Blond	Brown	White	Short	Tall	Female	Male	Old	Young
Blond	3	0	0	2	1	1	2	1	2
Brown	0	6	0	2	4	2	4	3	3
White	0	0	2	1	1	1	1	2	0
Short	2	2	1	5	0	2	3	4	1
Tall	1	4	1	0	6	2	4	2	4
Female	1	2	1	2	2	4	0	2	2
Male	2	4	1	3	4	0	7	4	3
Old	1	3	2	4	2	2	4	6	0
Young	2	3	0	1	4	2	3	0	5

This Burt table is composed of all pairs of crosstabulations among the variables Hair, Height, Sex, and Age. It is composed of sixteen individual subtables —the number of variables squared. Both the rows and the columns have the same nine categories (in this case Blond, Brown, White, Short, Tall, Female, Male, Old, and Young). The off-diagonal partitions are crosstabulations of each variable with every other variable. Below the diagonal are the following crosstabulations (from left to right, top to bottom): Height * Hair, Sex * Hair, Sex * Height, Age * Hair, Age * Height, and Age * Sex. Each crosstabulation below the diagonal has a transposed counterpart above the diagonal. Each diagonal partition contains a crosstabulation of a variable with itself (Hair * Hair, Height * Height, Sex * Sex, and Age * Age). The diagonal elements of the diagonal partitions contain marginal frequencies of the off-diagonal partitions.

For example, the table Hair * Height has three rows for Hair and two columns for Height. The values of the Hair * Height table, summed across rows, sum to the diagonal values of the Height * Height table, as displayed in the following table.

Table 24.4. $\mathbf{Z}_{\mathbf{Hair,Height}}{}'\mathbf{Z}_{\mathbf{Height}}$, The (Hair Height) × Height Crosstabulation

	Short	Tall
Blond	2	1
Brown	2	4
White	1	1
Short	5	0
Tall	0	6

A simple crosstabulation of Hair × Height is $\mathbf{N} = \mathbf{Z}_{\mathbf{Hair}}{}'\mathbf{Z}_{\mathbf{Height}}$. Crosstabulations such as this, involving only two variables, are the input to simple correspondence analysis.

Table 24.5. $\mathbf{Z}_{\mathbf{Hair}}{}'\mathbf{Z}_{\mathbf{Height}}$, The Hair × Height Crosstabulation

	Short	Tall
Blond	2	1
Brown	2	4
White	1	1

Tables such as the following ($\mathbf{N} = \mathbf{Z_{Hair}}'\mathbf{Z_{Height,Sex}}$), made up of several crosstabulations, can also be analyzed in simple correspondence analysis.

Table 24.6. $\mathbf{Z_{Hair}}'\mathbf{Z_{Height,Sex}}$, The Hair × (Height Sex) Crosstabulation

	Short	Tall	Female	Male
Blond	2	1	1	2
Brown	2	4	2	4
White	1	1	1	1

Coding, Fuzzy Coding, and Doubling

You can use an indicator matrix as input to PROC CORRESP using the VAR statement. An indicator matrix is composed of several submatrices, each of which is a design matrix with one column for each category of a categorical variable. In order to create an indicator matrix, you must code an indicator variable for each level of each categorical variable. For example, the categorical variable Sex, with two levels (Female and Male), would be coded using two indicator variables.

A binary indicator variable is coded 1 to indicate the presence of an attribute and 0 to indicate its absence. For the variable Sex, a male would be coded Female=0 and Male=1, and a female would be coded Female=1 and Male=0. The indicator variables representing a categorical variable must sum to 1.0. You can specify the BINARY option to create a binary table.

Sometimes binary data such as Yes/No data are available. For example, 1 means "Yes, I have bought this brand in the last month" and 0 means "No, I have not bought this brand in the last month".

```
title 'Doubling Yes/No Data';

proc format;
   value yn 0 = 'No '  1 = 'Yes';
   run;

data BrandChoice;
   input a b c;
   label a = 'Brand A' b = 'Brand B' c = 'Brand B';
   format a b c yn.;
   datalines;
0 0 1
1 1 0
0 1 1
0 1 0
1 0 0
;
```

Data such as these cannot be analyzed directly because the raw data do not consist of partitions, each with one column per level and exactly one 1 in each row. The data must be *doubled* so that both Yes and No are both represented by a column in the data matrix. The TRANSREG procedure provides one way of doubling. In the following statements, the DESIGN option specifies that PROC TRANSREG is being used only for coding, not analysis. The option SEPARATORS=': ' specifies that labels for the coded columns are constructed from input variable labels, followed by a colon and space, followed by the formatted value. The variables are designated in the MODEL statement as CLASS variables, and the ZERO=NONE option creates binary variables for all levels. The OUTPUT statement specifies the output data set and drops the _NAME_, _TYPE_, and Intercept variables. PROC TRANSREG stores a list of coded variable names in a macro variable &_TRGIND, which in this case has the value "aNo aYes bNo bYes cNo cYes". This macro can be used directly in the VAR statement in PROC CORRESP.

```
proc transreg data=BrandChoice design separators=': ';
   model class(a b c / zero=none);
   output out=Doubled(drop=_: Intercept);
run;

proc print label;
run;

proc corresp data=Doubled norow short;
   var &_trgind;
run;
```

A fuzzy-coded indicator also sums to 1.0 across levels of the categorical variable, but it is coded with fractions rather than with 1 and 0. The fractions represent the distribution of the attribute across several levels of the categorical variable.

Ordinal variables, such as survey responses of 1 to 3 can be represented as two design variables.

Table 24.7. Coding an Ordinal Variable

Ordinal Values	Coding	
1	0.25	0.75
2	0.50	0.50
3	0.75	0.25

Values of the coding sum to one across the two coded variables.

This next example illustrates the use of binary and fuzzy-coded indicator variables. Fuzzy-coded indicators are used to represent missing data. Note that the missing values in the observation Igor are coded with equal proportions.

```
proc transreg data=Neighbor design cprefix=0;
   model class(Age Sex Height Hair / zero=none);
   output out=Neighbor2(drop=_: Intercept);
   id Name;
   run;

data Neighbor3;
   set Neighbor2;
```

```
      if Sex = ' ' then do;
         Female = 0.5;
         Male   = 0.5;
         end;
      if Hair = ' ' then do;
         White = 1/3;
         Brown = 1/3;
         Blond = 1/3;
         end;
run;

proc print label;
run;
```

Obs	Age Old	Age Young	Sex Female	Sex Male	Height Short	Height Tall	Hair Blond	Hair Brown	Hair White	Age	Sex	Height	Hair	Name
1	1	0	0.0	1.0	1	0	0.00000	0.00000	1.00000	Old	Male	Short	White	Jones
2	0	1	1.0	0.0	0	1	0.00000	1.00000	0.00000	Young	Female	Tall	Brown	Smith
3	1	0	0.0	1.0	1	0	0.00000	1.00000	0.00000	Old	Male	Short	Brown	Kasavitz
4	1	0	1.0	0.0	0	1	0.00000	0.00000	1.00000	Old	Female	Tall	White	Ernst
5	1	0	1.0	0.0	1	0	0.00000	1.00000	0.00000	Old	Female	Short	Brown	Zannoria
6	0	1	0.0	1.0	0	1	1.00000	0.00000	0.00000	Young	Male	Tall	Blond	Spangel
7	0	1	0.0	1.0	0	1	0.00000	1.00000	0.00000	Young	Male	Tall	Brown	Myers
8	1	0	0.0	1.0	1	0	1.00000	0.00000	0.00000	Old	Male	Short	Blond	Kasinski
9	0	1	1.0	0.0	1	0	1.00000	0.00000	0.00000	Young	Female	Short	Blond	Colman
10	1	0	0.0	1.0	0	1	0.00000	1.00000	0.00000	Old	Male	Tall	Brown	Delafave
11	0	1	0.0	1.0	0	1	0.00000	1.00000	0.00000	Young	Male	Tall	Brown	Singer
12	1	0	0.5	0.5	1	0	0.33333	0.33333	0.33333	Old		Short		Igor

Figure 24.3. Fuzzy Coding of Missing Values

There is one set of coded variables for each input categorical variable. If observation 12 is excluded, each set is a binary design matrix. Each design matrix has one column for each category and exactly one 1 in each row.

Fuzzy-coding is shown in the final observation, Igor. The observation Igor has missing values for the variables Sex and Hair. The design matrix variables are coded with fractions that sum to one within each categorical variable.

An alternative way to represent missing data is to treat missing values as an additional level of the categorical variable. This alternative is available with the MISSING option in the PROC statement. This approach yields coordinates for missing responses, allowing the comparison of "missing" along with the other levels of the categorical variables.

Greenacre and Hastie (1987) discuss additional coding schemes, including one for continuous variables. Continuous variables can be coded with PROC TRANSREG by specifying BSPLINE(*variables* / degree=1) in the MODEL statement.

Using the TABLES Statement

In the following TABLES statement, each variable list consists of a single variable:

```
proc corresp data=Neighbor dimens=1 observed short;
   ods select observed;
   tables Sex, Age;
run;
```

These statements create a contingency table with two rows (Female and Male) and two columns (Old and Young) and show the neighbors broken down by age and sex. The DIMENS=1 option overrides the default, which is DIMENS=2. The OBSERVED option displays the contingency table. The SHORT option limits the displayed output. Because it contains missing values, the observation where Name='Igor' is omitted from the analysis. Figure 24.4 displays the contingency table.

```
                         The CORRESP Procedure

                           Contingency Table

                            Old          Young           Sum

          Female              2              2             4
          Male                4              3             7
          Sum                 6              5            11
```

Figure 24.4. Contingency Table for Sex, Age

The following statements create a table with six rows (**Blond*Short**, **Blond*Tall**, **Brown*Short**, **Brown*Tall**, **White*Short**, and **White*Tall**), and four columns (**Female**, **Male**, **Old**, and **Young**). The levels of the row variables are crossed, forming mutually exclusive categories, whereas the categories of the column variables overlap.

```
proc corresp data=Neighbor cross=row observed short;
   ods select observed;
   tables Hair Height, Sex Age;
run;
```

```
                        The CORRESP Procedure

                          Contingency Table

                     Female        Male         Old       Young         Sum

Blond * Short             1           1           1           1           4
Blond * Tall              0           1           0           1           2
Brown * Short             1           1           2           0           4
Brown * Tall              1           3           1           3           8
White * Short             0           1           1           0           2
White * Tall              1           0           1           0           2
Sum                       4           7           6           5          22
```

Figure 24.5. Contingency Table for Hair Height, Sex Age

You can enter supplementary variables with TABLES input by including a SUPPLEMENTARY statement. Variables named in the SUPPLEMENTARY statement indicate TABLES variables with categories that are supplementary. In other words, the categories of the variable Age are represented in the row and column space, but they are not used in determining the scores of the categories of the variables Hair, Height, and Sex. The variable used in the SUPPLEMENTARY statement must be listed in the TABLES statement as well. For example, the following statements create a Burt table with seven active rows and columns (`Blond`, `Brown`, `White`, `Short`, `Tall`, `Female`, `Male`) and two supplementary rows and columns (`Old` and `Young`).

```
proc corresp data=Neighbor observed short mca;
   ods select burt supcols;
   tables Hair Height Sex Age;
   supplementary Age;
run;
```

The CORRESP Procedure

Burt Table

	Blond	Brown	White	Short	Tall	Female	Male
Blond	3	0	0	2	1	1	2
Brown	0	6	0	2	4	2	4
White	0	0	2	1	1	1	1
Short	2	2	1	5	0	2	3
Tall	1	4	1	0	6	2	4
Female	1	2	1	2	2	4	0
Male	2	4	1	3	4	0	7

Supplementary Columns

	Old	Young
Blond	1	2
Brown	3	3
White	2	0
Short	4	1
Tall	2	4
Female	2	2
Male	4	3

Figure 24.6. Burt Table from PROC CORRESP

The following statements create a binary table with 7 active columns (`Blond`, `Brown`, `White`, `Short`, `Tall`, `Female`, `Male`), 2 supplementary columns (`Old` and `Young`), and 11 rows for the 11 observations with nonmissing values.

```
proc corresp data=Neighbor observed short binary;
   ods select binary supcols;
   tables Hair Height Sex Age;
   supplementary Age;
run;
```

The CORRESP Procedure

Binary Table

	Blond	Brown	White	Short	Tall	Female	Male
1	0	0	1	1	0	0	1
2	0	1	0	0	1	1	0
3	0	1	0	1	0	0	1
4	0	0	1	0	1	1	0
5	0	1	0	1	0	1	0
6	1	0	0	0	1	0	1
7	0	1	0	0	1	0	1
8	1	0	0	1	0	0	1
9	1	0	0	1	0	1	0
10	0	1	0	0	1	0	1
11	0	1	0	0	1	0	1

Supplementary Columns

	Old	Young
1	1	0
2	0	1
3	1	0
4	1	0
5	1	0
6	0	1
7	0	1
8	1	0
9	0	1
10	1	0
11	0	1

Figure 24.7. Binary Table from PROC CORRESP

Using the VAR Statement

With VAR statement input, the rows of the contingency table correspond to the observations of the input data set, and the columns correspond to the VAR statement variables. The values of the variables typically contain the table frequencies. The example displayed in Figure 24.4 could be run with VAR statement input using the following code:

```
data Ages;
   input Sex $ Old Young;
   datalines;
Female  2 2
Male    4 3
;

proc corresp data=Ages dimens=1 observed short;
   var Old Young;
   id Sex;
run;
```

Only nonnegative values are accepted. Negative values are treated as missing, causing the observation to be excluded from the analysis. The values are not required to be integers. Row labels for the table are specified with an ID variable. Column labels are constructed from the variable name or variable label if one is specified. When you specify multiple correspondence analysis (MCA), the row and column labels are the same and are constructed from the variable names or labels, so you cannot include an ID statement. With MCA, the VAR statement must list the variables in the order in which the rows occur. For example, the table displayed in Figure 24.6, which was created with the following TABLES statement,

```
tables Hair Height Sex Age;
```

is input as follows with the VAR statement:

```
proc corresp data=table nvars=4 mca;
   var Blond Brown White Short Tall Female Male Old Young;
run;
```

You must specify the NVARS= option to specify the number of original categorical variables with the MCA option. The option NVARS=n is needed to find boundaries between the subtables of the Burt table. If f is the sum of all elements in the Burt table $\mathbf{Z}'\mathbf{Z}$, then fn^{-2} is the number of rows in the binary matrix $\mathbf{Z}$. The sum of all elements in each diagonal subtable of the Burt table must be fn^{-2}.

To enter supplementary observations, include a WEIGHT statement with negative weights for those observations. Specify the SUPPLEMENTARY statement to include supplementary variables. You must list supplementary variables in both the VAR and SUPPLEMENTARY statements.

Missing and Invalid Data

With VAR statement input, observations with missing or negative frequencies are excluded from the analysis. Supplementary variables and supplementary observations with missing or negative frequencies are also excluded. Negative weights are valid with VAR statement input.

With TABLES statement input, observations with negative weights are excluded from the analysis. With this form of input, missing cell frequencies cannot occur. Observations with missing values on the categorical variables are excluded unless you specify the MISSING option. If you specify the MISSING option, ordinary missing values and special missing values are treated as additional levels of a categorical variable. In all cases, if any row or column of the constructed table contains only zeros, that row or column is excluded from the analysis.

Observations with missing weights are excluded from the analysis.

Creating a Data Set Containing the Crosstabulation

The CORRESP procedure can read or create a contingency or Burt table. PROC CORRESP is generally more efficient with VAR statement input than with TABLES statement input. TABLES statement input requires that the table be created from raw categorical variables, whereas the VAR statement is used to read an existing table. If PROC CORRESP runs out of memory, it may be possible to use some other method to create the table and then use VAR statement input with PROC CORRESP.

The following example uses the CORRESP, FREQ, and TRANSPOSE procedures to create rectangular tables from a SAS data set WORK.A that contains the categorical variables V1–V5. The Burt table examples assume that no categorical variable has a value found in any of the other categorical variables (that is, that each row and column label is unique).

You can use PROC CORRESP and ODS to create a rectangular two-way contingency table from two categorical variables.

```
proc corresp data=a observed short;
   ods listing close;
   ods output Observed=Obs(drop=Sum where=(Label ne 'Sum'));
   tables v1, v2;
run;

ods listing;
```

You can use PROC FREQ and PROC TRANSPOSE to create a rectangular two-way contingency table from two categorical variables.

```
proc freq data=a;
   tables v1 * v2 / sparse noprint out=freqs;
run;

proc transpose data=freqs out=rfreqs;
   id  v2;
   var count;
   by  v1;
run;
```

You can use PROC CORRESP and ODS to create a Burt table from five categorical variables.

```
proc corresp data=a observed short mca;
   ods listing close;
   ods output Burt=Obs;
   tables v1-v5;
run;

ods listing;
```

You can use a DATA step, PROC FREQ, and PROC TRANSPOSE to create a Burt table from five categorical variables.

```
data b;
   set a;
   array v[5] $ v1-v5;
   do i = 1 to 5;
      row = v[i];
      do j = 1 to 5;
         column = v[j];
         output;
         end;
      end;
   keep row column;
run;

proc freq data=b;
   tables row * column / sparse  noprint out=freqs;
run;

proc transpose data=freqs out=rfreqs;
   id  column;
   var count;
   by  row;
run;
```

Output Data Sets

The OUTC= Data Set

The OUTC= data set contains two or three character variables and $4n + 4$ numeric variables, where n is the number of axes from DIMENS=n (two by default). The OUTC= data set contains one observation for each row, column, supplementary row, and supplementary column point, and one observation for inertias.

The first variable is named _TYPE_ and identifies the type of observation. The values of _TYPE_ are as follows:

- The 'INERTIA' observation contains the total inertia in the INERTIA variable, and each dimension's inertia in the Contr1–Contr$n$ variables.
- The 'OBS' observations contain the coordinates and statistics for the rows of the table.
- The 'SUPOBS' observations contain the coordinates and statistics for the supplementary rows of the table.
- The 'VAR' observations contain the coordinates and statistics for the columns of the table.
- The 'SUPVAR' observations contain the coordinates and statistics for the supplementary columns of the table.

If you specify the SOURCE option, then the data set also contains a variable _VAR_ containing the name or label of the input variable from which that row originates. The name of the next variable is either _NAME_ or (if you specify an ID statement) the name of the ID variable.

For observations with a value of 'OBS' or 'SUPOBS' for the _TYPE_ variable, the values of the second variable are constructed as follows:

- When you use a VAR statement without an ID statement, the values are 'Row1', 'Row2', and so on.
- When you specify a VAR statement with an ID statement, the values are set equal to the values of the ID variable.
- When you specify a TABLES statement, the _NAME_ variable has values formed from the appropriate row variable values.

For observations with a value of 'VAR' or 'SUPVAR' for the _TYPE_ variable, the values of the second variable are equal to the names or labels of the VAR (or SUPPLEMENTARY) variables. When you specify a TABLES statement, the values are formed from the appropriate column variable values.

The third and subsequent variables contain the numerical results of the correspondence analysis.

- Quality contains the quality of each point's representation in the DIMENS=n dimensional display, which is the sum of squared cosines over the first n dimensions.
- Mass contains the masses or marginal sums of the relative frequency matrix.
- Inertia contains each point's relative contribution to the total inertia.
- Dim1–Dim$n$ contain the point coordinates.
- Contr1–Contr$n$ contain the partial contributions to inertia.
- SqCos1–SqCos$n$ contain the squared cosines.
- Best1–Best$n$ and Best contain the summaries of the partial contributions to inertia.

The OUTF= Data Set

The OUTF= data set contains frequencies and percentages. It is similar to a PROC FREQ output data set. The OUTF= data set begins with a variable called _TYPE_, which contains the observation type. If the SOURCE option is specified, the data set contains two variables _ROWVAR_ and _COLVAR_ that contain the names or labels of the row and column input variables from which each cell originates. The next two variables are classification variables that contain the row and column levels. If you use TABLES statement input and each variable list consists of a single variable, the names of the first two variables match the names of the input variables; otherwise, these variables are named Row and Column. The next two variables are Count and Percent, which contain frequencies and percentages.

The _TYPE_ variable can have the following values:

- 'OBSERVED' observations contain the contingency table.
- 'SUPOBS' observations contain the supplementary rows.
- 'SUPVAR' observations contain the supplementary columns.
- 'EXPECTED' observations contain the product of the row marginals and the column marginals divided by the grand frequency of the observed frequency table. For ordinary two-way contingency tables, these are the expected frequency matrix under the hypothesis of row and column independence.
- 'DEVIATION' observations contain the matrix of deviations between the observed frequency matrix and the product of its row marginals and column marginals divided by its grand frequency. For ordinary two-way contingency tables, these are the observed minus expected frequencies under the hypothesis of row and column independence.
- 'CELLCHI2' observations contain contributions to the total chi-square test statistic.
- 'RP' observations contain the row profiles.
- 'SUPRP' observations contain supplementary row profiles.
- 'CP' observations contain the column profiles.
- 'SUPCP' observations contain supplementary column profiles.

Computational Resources

Let

$$\begin{aligned}
n_r &= \text{number of rows in the table} \\
n_c &= \text{number of columns in the table} \\
n &= \text{number of observations} \\
v &= \text{number of VAR statement variables} \\
t &= \text{number of TABLES statement variables} \\
c &= \max(n_r, n_c) \\
d &= \min(n_r, n_c)
\end{aligned}$$

For TABLES statement input, more than

$$32(t+1) + 8(\max(2tn, (n_r+3)(n_c+3)))$$

bytes of array space are required.

For VAR statement input, more than

$$16(v+2) + 8(n_r+3)(n_c+3)$$

bytes of array space are required.

Memory

The computational resources formulas are underestimates of the amounts of memory needed to handle most problems. If you use a utility data set, and if memory could be used with perfect efficiency, then roughly the stated amount of memory would be needed. In reality, most problems require at least two or three times the minimum.

PROC CORRESP tries to store the raw data (TABLES input) and the contingency table in memory. If there is not enough memory, a utility data set is used, potentially resulting in a large increase in execution time.

Time

The time required to perform the generalized singular value decomposition is roughly proportional to $2cd^2 + 5d^3$. Overall computation time increases with table size at a rate roughly proportional to $(n_r n_c)^{\frac{3}{2}}$.

Algorithm and Notation

This section is primarily based on the theory of correspondence analysis found in Greenacre (1984). If you are interested in other references, see the "Background" section on page 947.

Let $\mathbf{N}$ be the contingency table formed from those observations and variables that are not supplementary and from those observations that have no missing values and have a positive weight. This table is an $(n_r \times n_c)$ rank q matrix of nonnegative numbers with nonzero row and column sums. If $\mathbf{Z}_a$ is the binary coding for variable A, and $\mathbf{Z}_b$ is the binary coding for variable B, then $\mathbf{N} = \mathbf{Z}_a'\mathbf{Z}_b$ is a contingency table. Similarly, if $\mathbf{Z}_{b,c}$ contains the binary coding for both variables B and C, then $\mathbf{N} = \mathbf{Z}_a'\mathbf{Z}_{b,c}$ can also be input to a correspondence analysis. With the BINARY option, $\mathbf{N} = \mathbf{Z}$, and the analysis is based on a binary table. In multiple correspondence analysis, the analysis is based on a Burt table, $\mathbf{Z}'\mathbf{Z}$.

Let $\mathbf{1}$ be a vector of 1s of the appropriate order, let $\mathbf{I}$ be an identity matrix, and let $\text{diag}(\cdot)$ be a matrix-valued function that creates a diagonal matrix from a vector. Let

$$\begin{aligned} f &= \mathbf{1}'\mathbf{N}\mathbf{1} \\ \mathbf{P} &= \frac{1}{f}\mathbf{N} \\ \mathbf{r} &= \mathbf{P}\mathbf{1} \end{aligned}$$

$$\begin{aligned} \mathbf{c} &= \mathbf{P}'\mathbf{1} \\ \mathbf{D_r} &= \text{diag}(\mathbf{r}) \\ \mathbf{D_c} &= \text{diag}(\mathbf{c}) \\ \mathbf{R} &= \mathbf{D_r^{-1}P} \\ \mathbf{C}' &= \mathbf{D_c^{-1}P}' \end{aligned}$$

The scalar f is the sum of all elements in $\mathbf{N}$. The matrix $\mathbf{P}$ is a matrix of relative frequencies. The vector $\mathbf{r}$ contains row marginal proportions or row "masses." The vector $\mathbf{c}$ contains column marginal proportions or column masses. The matrices $\mathbf{D_r}$ and $\mathbf{D_c}$ are diagonal matrices of marginals.

The rows of $\mathbf{R}$ contain the "row profiles." The elements of each row of $\mathbf{R}$ sum to one. Each (i, j) element of $\mathbf{R}$ contains the observed probability of being in column j given membership in row i. Similarly, the columns of $\mathbf{C}$ contain the column profiles. The coordinates in correspondence analysis are based on the generalized singular value decomposition of $\mathbf{P}$,

$$\mathbf{P} = \mathbf{AD_uB}'$$

where

$$\mathbf{A}'\mathbf{D_r^{-1}A} = \mathbf{B}'\mathbf{D_c^{-1}B} = \mathbf{I}$$

In multiple correspondence analysis,

$$\mathbf{P} = \mathbf{BD_u^2B}'$$

The matrix $\mathbf{A}$, which is the rectangular matrix of left generalized singular vectors, has n_r rows and q columns; the matrix $\mathbf{D_u}$, which is a diagonal matrix of singular values, has q rows and columns; and the matrix $\mathbf{B}$, which is the rectangular matrix of right generalized singular vectors, has n_c rows and q columns. The columns of $\mathbf{A}$ and $\mathbf{B}$ define the principal axes of the column and row point clouds, respectively.

The generalized singular value decomposition of $\mathbf{P} - \mathbf{rc}'$, discarding the last singular value (which is zero) and the last left and right singular vectors, is exactly the same as a generalized singular value decomposition of $\mathbf{P}$, discarding the first singular value (which is one), the first left singular vector, $\mathbf{r}$, and the first right singular vector, $\mathbf{c}$. The first (trivial) column of $\mathbf{A}$ and $\mathbf{B}$ and the first singular value in $\mathbf{D_u}$ are discarded before any results are displayed. You can obtain the generalized singular value decomposition of $\mathbf{P} - \mathbf{rc}'$ from the ordinary singular value decomposition of $\mathbf{D_r^{-1/2}(P - rc')D_c^{-1/2}}$.

$$\mathbf{D_r^{-1/2}(P - rc')D_c^{-1/2}} = \mathbf{UD_uV}' = (\mathbf{D_r^{-1/2}A})\mathbf{D_u}(\mathbf{D_c^{-1/2}B})'$$

$$\mathbf{P} - \mathbf{rc}' = \mathbf{D_r^{1/2}UD_uV'D_c^{1/2}} = (\mathbf{D_r^{1/2}U})\mathbf{D_u}(\mathbf{D_c^{1/2}V})' = \mathbf{AD_uB}'$$

Hence, $\mathbf{A} = \mathbf{D_r^{1/2} U}$ and $\mathbf{B} = \mathbf{D_c^{1/2} V}$.

The default row coordinates are $\mathbf{D_r^{-1} A D_u}$, and the default column coordinates are $\mathbf{D_c^{-1} B D_u}$. Typically the first two columns of $\mathbf{D_r^{-1} A D_u}$ and $\mathbf{D_c^{-1} B D_u}$ are plotted to display graphically associations between the row and column categories. The plot consists of two overlaid plots, one for rows and one for columns. The row points are row profiles, rescaled so that distances between profiles can be displayed as ordinary Euclidean distances, then orthogonally rotated to a principal axes orientation. The column points are column profiles, rescaled so that distances between profiles can be displayed as ordinary Euclidean distances, then orthogonally rotated to a principal axes orientation. Distances between row points and other row points have meaning. Distances between column points and other column points have meaning. However, distances between column points and row points are not interpretable.

The PROFILE=, ROW=, and COLUMN= Options

The PROFILE=, ROW=, and COLUMN= options standardize the coordinates before they are displayed and placed in the output data set. The options PROFILE=BOTH, PROFILE=ROW, and PROFILE=COLUMN provide the standardizations that are typically used in correspondence analysis. There are six choices each for row and column coordinates. However, most of the combinations of the ROW= and COLUMN= options are not useful. The ROW= and COLUMN= options are provided for completeness, but they are not intended for general use.

ROW=	Matrix Formula
A	$\mathbf{A}$
AD	$\mathbf{A D_u}$
DA	$\mathbf{D_r^{-1} A}$
DAD	$\mathbf{D_r^{-1} A D_u}$
DAD1/2	$\mathbf{D_r^{-1} A D_u^{1/2}}$
DAID1/2	$\mathbf{D_r^{-1} A (I + D_u)^{1/2}}$

COLUMN=	Matrix Formula
B	$\mathbf{B}$
BD	$\mathbf{B D_u}$
DB	$\mathbf{D_c^{-1} B}$
DBD	$\mathbf{D_c^{-1} B D_u}$
DBD1/2	$\mathbf{D_c^{-1} B D_u^{1/2}}$
DBID1/2	$\mathbf{D_c^{-1} B (I + D_u)^{1/2}}$

When PROFILE=ROW (ROW=DAD and COLUMN=DB), the row coordinates $\mathbf{D_r^{-1} A D_u}$ and column coordinates $\mathbf{D_c^{-1} B}$ provide a correspondence analysis based on the row profile matrix. The row profile (conditional probability) matrix is defined as $\mathbf{R} = \mathbf{D_r^{-1} P} = \mathbf{D_r^{-1} A D_u B'}$. The elements of each row of $\mathbf{R}$ sum to one. Each (i, j) element of $\mathbf{R}$ contains the observed probability of being in column

j given membership in row i. The "principal" row coordinates $\mathbf{D_r^{-1}AD_u}$ and "standard" column coordinates $\mathbf{D_c^{-1}B}$ provide a decomposition of $\mathbf{D_r^{-1}AD_uB'D_c^{-1}} = \mathbf{D_r^{-1}PD_c^{-1}} = \mathbf{RD_c^{-1}}$. Since $\mathbf{D_r^{-1}AD_u} = \mathbf{RD_c^{-1}B}$, the row coordinates are weighted centroids of the column coordinates. Each column point, with coordinates scaled to standard coordinates, defines a vertex in $(n_c - 1)$-dimensional space. All of the principal row coordinates are located in the space defined by the standard column coordinates. Distances among row points have meaning, but distances among column points and distances between row and column points are not interpretable.

The option PROFILE=COLUMN can be described as applying the PROFILE=ROW formulas to the transpose of the contingency table. When PROFILE=COLUMN (ROW=DA and COLUMN=DBD), the principal column coordinates $\mathbf{D_c^{-1}BD_u}$ are weighted centroids of the standard row coordinates $\mathbf{D_r^{-1}A}$. Each row point, with coordinates scaled to standard coordinates, defines a vertex in $(n_r - 1)$-dimensional space. All of the principal column coordinates are located in the space defined by the standard row coordinates. Distances among column points have meaning, but distances among row points and distances between row and column points are not interpretable.

The usual sets of coordinates are given by the default PROFILE=BOTH (ROW=DAD and COLUMN=DBD). All of the summary statistics, such as the squared cosines and contributions to inertia, apply to these two sets of points. One advantage to using these coordinates is that both sets ($\mathbf{D_r^{-1}AD_u}$ and $\mathbf{D_c^{-1}BD_u}$) are postmultiplied by the diagonal matrix $\mathbf{D_u}$, which has diagonal values that are all less than or equal to one. When $\mathbf{D_u}$ is a part of the definition of only one set of coordinates, that set forms a tight cluster near the centroid whereas the other set of points is more widely dispersed. Including $\mathbf{D_u}$ in both sets makes a better graphical display. However, care must be taken in interpreting such a plot. No correct interpretation of distances between row points and column points can be made.

Another property of this choice of coordinates concerns the geometry of distances between points within each set. The default row coordinates can be decomposed into $\mathbf{D_r^{-1}AD_u} = \mathbf{D_r^{-1}AD_uB'D_c^{-1}B} = (\mathbf{D_r^{-1}P})(\mathbf{D_c^{-1/2}})(\mathbf{D_c^{-1/2}B})$. The row coordinates are row profiles $(\mathbf{D_r^{-1}P})$, rescaled by $\mathbf{D_c^{-1/2}}$ (rescaled so that distances between profiles are transformed from a chi-square metric to a Euclidean metric), then orthogonally rotated (with $\mathbf{D_c^{-1/2}B}$) to a principal axes orientation. Similarly, the column coordinates are column profiles rescaled to a Euclidean metric and orthogonally rotated to a principal axes orientation.

The rationale for computing distances between row profiles using the non-Euclidean chi-square metric is as follows. Each row of the contingency table can be viewed as a realization of a multinomial distribution conditional on its row marginal frequency. The null hypothesis of row and column independence is equivalent to the hypothesis of homogeneity of the row profiles. A significant chi-square statistic is geometrically interpreted as a significant deviation of the row profiles from their centroid, $\mathbf{c}'$. The chi-square metric is the Mahalanobis metric between row profiles based on their estimated covariance matrix under the homogeneity assumption (Greenacre and Hastie 1987). A parallel argument can be made for the column profiles.

When ROW=DAD1/2 and COLUMN=DBD1/2 (Gifi 1990; van der Heijden and de Leeuw 1985), the row coordinates $\mathbf{D_r^{-1}AD_u^{1/2}}$ and column coordinates $\mathbf{D_c^{-1}BD_u^{1/2}}$ are a decomposition of $\mathbf{D_r^{-1}PD_c^{-1}}$.

In all of the preceding pairs, distances between row and column points are not meaningful. This prompted Carroll, Green, and Schaffer (1986) to propose that row coordinates $\mathbf{D_r^{-1}A(I + D_u)^{1/2}}$ and column coordinates $\mathbf{D_c^{-1}B(I + D_u)^{1/2}}$ be used. These coordinates are (except for a constant scaling) the coordinates from a multiple correspondence analysis of a Burt table created from two categorical variables. This standardization is available with ROW=DAID1/2 and COLUMN=DBID1/2. However, this approach has been criticized on both theoretical and empirical grounds by Greenacre (1989). The Carroll, Green, and Schaffer standardization relies on the assumption that the chi-square metric is an appropriate metric for measuring the distance between the columns of a bivariate indicator matrix. See the section "Types of Tables Used as Input" on page 961 for a description of indicator matrices. Greenacre (1989) showed that this assumption cannot be justified.

The MCA Option

MCA= option) The MCA option performs a multiple correspondence analysis (MCA). This option requires a Burt table. You can specify the MCA option with a table created from a design matrix with fuzzy coding schemes as long as every row of every partition of the design matrix has the same marginal sum. For example, each row of each partition could contain the probabilities that the observation is a member of each level. Then the Burt table constructed from this matrix no longer contains all integers, and the diagonal partitions are no longer diagonal matrices, but MCA is still valid.

A TABLES statement with a single variable list creates a Burt table. Thus, you can always specify the MCA option with this type of input. If you use the MCA option when reading an existing table with a VAR statement, you must ensure that the table is a Burt table.

If you perform MCA on a table that is not a Burt table, the results of the analysis are invalid. If the table is not symmetric, or if the sums of all elements in each diagonal partition are not equal, PROC CORRESP displays an error message and quits.

A subset of the columns of a Burt table is not necessarily a Burt table, so in MCA it is not appropriate to designate arbitrary columns as supplementary. You can, however, designate all columns from one or more categorical variables as supplementary.

The results of a multiple correspondence analysis of a Burt table $\mathbf{Z'Z}$ are the same as the column results from a simple correspondence analysis of the binary (or fuzzy) matrix $\mathbf{Z}$. Multiple correspondence analysis is not a simple correspondence analysis of the Burt table. It is not appropriate to perform a simple correspondence analysis of a Burt table. The MCA option is based on $\mathbf{P} = \mathbf{BD_u^2B'}$, whereas a simple correspondence analysis of the Burt table would be based on $\mathbf{P} = \mathbf{BD_uB'}$.

Since the rows and columns of the Burt table are the same, no row information is displayed or written to the output data sets. The resulting inertias and the default (COLUMN=DBD) column coordinates are the appropriate inertias and coordinates for an MCA. The supplementary column coordinates, cosines, and quality of representation formulas for MCA differ from the simple correspondence analysis formulas because the design matrix column profiles and left singular vectors are not available.

The following statements create a Burt table and perform a multiple correspondence analysis:

```
proc corresp data=Neighbor observed short mca;
   tables Hair Height Sex Age;
run;
```

Both the rows and the columns have the same nine categories (Blond, Brown, White, Short, Tall, Female, Male, Old, and Young).

MCA Adjusted Inertias

The usual principal inertias of a Burt Table constructed from m categorical variables in MCA are the eigenvalues u_k from $\mathbf{D}_\mathbf{u}^2$. The problem with these inertias is that they provide a pessimistic indication of fit. Benzécri (1979) proposed the following inertia adjustment, which is also described by Greenacre (1984, p. 145):

$$\left(\frac{m}{m-1}\right)^2 \times \left(u_k - \frac{1}{m}\right)^2 \qquad \text{for } u_k > \frac{1}{m}$$

The Benzécri adjustment is available with the BENZECRI option.

Greenacre (1994, p. 156) argues that the Benzécri adjustment overestimates the quality of fit. Greenacre proposes instead the following inertia adjustment:

$$\left(\frac{m}{m-1}\right)^2 \times \left(\sqrt{u_k} - \frac{1}{m}\right)^2 \qquad \text{for } \sqrt{u_k} > \frac{1}{m}$$

The Greenacre adjustment is available with the GREENACRE option.

Ordinary unadjusted inertias are printed by default with MCA when neither the BENZECRI nor the GREENACRE option is specified. However, the unadjusted inertias are not printed by default when either the BENZECRI or the GREENACRE option is specified. To display both adjusted and unadjusted inertias, specify the UNADJUSTED option in addition to the relevant adjusted inertia option (BENZECRI, GREENACRE, or both).

Supplementary Rows and Columns

Supplementary rows and columns are represented as points in the joint row and column space, but they are not used when determining the locations of the other active rows and columns of the table. The formulas that are used to compute coordinates for the supplementary rows and columns depend on the PROFILE= option or on the ROW= and COLUMN= options. Let $\mathbf{S_o}$ be the matrix with rows that contain the supplementary observations and $\mathbf{S_v}$ be a matrix with rows that contain the supplementary variables. Note that $\mathbf{S_v}$ is defined to be the transpose of the supplementary variable partition of the table. Let $\mathbf{R_s} = \text{diag}(\mathbf{S_o 1})^{-1}\mathbf{S_o}$ be the supplementary observation profile matrix and $\mathbf{C_s} = \text{diag}(\mathbf{S_v 1})^{-1}\mathbf{S_v}$ be the supplementary variable profile matrix. Note that the notation $\text{diag}(\cdot)^{-1}$ means to convert the vector to a diagonal matrix, then invert the diagonal matrix. The coordinates for the supplementary observations and variables are as follows.

ROW=	Matrix Formula
A	$\frac{1}{f}\mathbf{S_o D_c^{-1} B D_u^{-1}}$
AD	$\frac{1}{f}\mathbf{S_o D_c^{-1} B}$
DA	$\mathbf{R_s D_c^{-1} B D_u^{-1}}$
DAD	$\mathbf{R_s D_c^{-1} B}$
DAD1/2	$\mathbf{R_s D_c^{-1} B D_u^{-1/2}}$
DAID1/2	$\mathbf{R_s D_c^{-1} B D_u^{-1} (I + D_u)^{1/2}}$

COLUMN=	Matrix Formula
B	$\frac{1}{f}\mathbf{S_v D_r^{-1} A D_u^{-1}}$
BD	$\frac{1}{f}\mathbf{S_v D_r^{-1} A}$
DB	$\mathbf{C_s D_r^{-1} A D_u^{-1}}$
DBD	$\mathbf{C_s D_r^{-1} A}$
DBD1/2	$\mathbf{C_s D_r^{-1} A D_u^{-1/2}}$
DBID1/2	$\mathbf{C_s D_r^{-1} A D_u^{-1} (I + D_u)^{1/2}}$

MCA COLUMN=	Matrix Formula
B	not allowed
BD	not allowed
DB	$\mathbf{C_s D_r^{-1} B D_u^{-2}}$
DBD	$\mathbf{C_s D_r^{-1} B D_u^{-1}}$
DBD1/2	$\mathbf{C_s D_r^{-1} B D_u^{-3/2}}$
DBID1/2	$\mathbf{C_s D_r^{-1} B D_u^{-2} (I + D_u)^{1/2}}$

Statistics that Aid Interpretation

The partial contributions to inertia, squared cosines, quality of representation, inertia, and mass provide additional information about the coordinates. These statistics are displayed by default. Include the SHORT or NOPRINT option in the PROC CORRESP statement to avoid having these statistics displayed.

These statistics pertain to the default PROFILE=BOTH coordinates, no matter what values you specify for the ROW=, COLUMN=, or PROFILE= option. Let $\mathrm{sq}(\cdot)$ be a matrix-valued function denoting elementwise squaring of the argument matrix. Let t be the total inertia (the sum of the elements in $\mathbf{D_u^2}$).

In MCA, let $\mathbf{D_s}$ be the Burt table partition containing the intersection of the supplementary columns and the supplementary rows. The matrix $\mathbf{D_s}$ is a diagonal matrix of marginal frequencies of the supplemental columns of the binary matrix $\mathbf{Z}$. Let p be the number of rows in this design matrix.

Statistic	Matrix Formula
Row partial contributions to inertia	$\mathbf{D_r^{-1}}\text{sq}(\mathbf{A})$
Column partial contributions to inertia	$\mathbf{D_c^{-1}}\text{sq}(\mathbf{B})$
Row squared cosines	$\text{diag}(\text{sq}(\mathbf{AD_u})\mathbf{1})^{-1}\text{sq}(\mathbf{AD_u})$
Column squared cosines	$\text{diag}(\text{sq}(\mathbf{BD_u})\mathbf{1})^{-1}\text{sq}(\mathbf{BD_u})$
Row mass	$\mathbf{r}$
Column mass	$\mathbf{c}$
Row inertia	$\frac{1}{t}\mathbf{D_r^{-1}}\ \text{sq}(\mathbf{AD_u})\mathbf{1}$
Column inertia	$\frac{1}{t}\mathbf{D_c^{-1}}\ \text{sq}(\mathbf{BD_u})\mathbf{1}$
Supplementary row squared cosines	$\text{diag}(\text{sq}(\mathbf{R_s} - \mathbf{1c}')\mathbf{D_c^{-1}}\mathbf{1})^{-1}\text{sq}(\mathbf{R_s D_c^{-1} B})$
Supplementary column squared cosines	$\text{diag}(\text{sq}(\mathbf{C_s} - \mathbf{1r}')\mathbf{D_r^{-1}}\mathbf{1})^{-1}\text{sq}(\mathbf{C_s D_r^{-1} A})$
MCA supplementary column squared cosines	$\mathbf{D_s}(p\mathbf{I} - \mathbf{D_s})^{-1}\ \text{sq}(\mathbf{C_s D_r^{-1} B D_u^{-1}})$

The quality of representation in the DIMENS=n dimensional display of any point is the sum of its squared cosines over only the n dimensions. Inertia and mass are not defined for supplementary points.

A table that summarizes the partial contributions to inertia table is also computed. The points that best explain the inertia of each dimension and the dimension to which each point contributes the most inertia are indicated. The output data set variable names for this table are Best1–Best$n$ (where DIMENS=n) and Best. The Best column contains the dimension number of the largest partial contribution to inertia for each point (the index of the maximum value in each row of $\mathbf{D_r^{-1}}\text{sq}(\mathbf{A})$ or $\mathbf{D_c^{-1}}\text{sq}(\mathbf{B})$).

For each row, the Best1–Best$n$ columns contain either the corresponding value of Best if the point is one of the biggest contributors to the dimension's inertia or 0 if it is not. Specifically, Best1 contains the value of Best for the point with the largest contribution to dimension one's inertia. A cumulative proportion sum is initialized to this point's partial contribution to the inertia of dimension one. If this sum is less than the value for the MININERTIA= option, then Best1 contains the value of Best for the point with the second largest contribution to dimension one's inertia. Otherwise, this point's Best1 is 0. This point's partial contribution to inertia is added to the sum. This process continues for the point with the third largest partial contribution, and so on, until adding a point's contribution to the sum increases the sum beyond the value of the MININERTIA= option. This same algorithm is then used for Best2, and so on.

For example, the following table contains contributions to inertia and the corresponding Best variables. The contribution to inertia variables are proportions that sum to 1 within each column. The first point makes its greatest contribution to the inertia of dimension two, so Best for point one is set to 2 and Best1–Best3 for point one must all be 0 or 2. The second point also makes its greatest contribution to the inertia of dimension two, so Best for point two is set to 2 and Best1–Best3 for point two must all be 0 or 2, and so on.

Assume MININERTIA=0.8, the default. In dimension one, the largest contribution is 0.41302 for the fourth point, so Best1 is set to 1, the value of Best for the fourth point. Because this value is less than 0.8, the second largest value (0.36456 for point five) is found and its Best1 is set to its Best's value of 1. Because $0.41302 + 0.36456 = 0.77758$ is less than 0.8, the third point (0.0882 at point eight) is found and Best1 is set to 3 since the contribution to dimension 3 for that point is greater than the contribution to dimension 1. This increases the sum of the partial contributions to greater than 0.8, so the remaining Best1 values are all 0.

Contr1	Contr2	Contr3	Best1	Best2	Best3	Best
0.01593	0.32178	0.07565	0	2	2	2
0.03014	0.24826	0.07715	0	2	2	2
0.00592	0.02892	0.02698	0	0	0	2
0.41302	0.05191	0.05773	1	0	0	1
0.36456	0.00344	0.15565	1	0	1	1
0.03902	0.30966	0.11717	0	2	2	2
0.00019	0.01840	0.00734	0	0	0	2
0.08820	0.00527	0.16555	3	0	3	3
0.01447	0.00024	0.03851	0	0	0	3
0.02855	0.01213	0.27827	0	0	3	3

Displayed Output

The display options control the amount of displayed output. By default, the following information is displayed:

- an inertia and chi-square decomposition table including the total inertia, the principal inertias of each dimension (eigenvalues), the singular values (square roots of the eigenvalues), each dimension's percentage of inertia, a horizontal bar chart of the percentages, and the total chi-square with its degrees of freedom and decomposition. The chi-square statistics and degrees of freedom are valid only when the constructed table is an ordinary two-way contingency table.
- the coordinates of the rows and columns on the dimensions
- the mass, relative contribution to the total inertia, and quality of representation in the DIMENS=n dimensional display of each row and column
- the squared cosines of the angles between each axis and a vector from the origin to the point
- the partial contributions of each point to each dimension's inertia
- the Best table, indicators of which points best explain the inertia of each dimension

Specific display options and combinations of options display output as follows.

If you specify the OBSERVED or ALL option and you do not specify PRINT=PERCENT, PROC CORRESP displays

- the contingency table including the row and column marginal frequencies; or with BINARY, the binary table; or the Burt table in MCA
- the supplementary rows
- the supplementary columns

If you specify the OBSERVED or ALL option, with the PRINT=PERCENT or PRINT=BOTH option, PROC CORRESP displays

- the contingency table or Burt table in MCA, scaled to percentages, including the row and column marginal percentages
- the supplementary rows, scaled to percentages
- the supplementary columns, scaled to percentages

If you specify the EXPECTED or ALL option and you do not specify PRINT=PERCENT, PROC CORRESP displays the product of the row marginals and the column marginals divided by the grand frequency of the observed frequency table. For ordinary two-way contingency tables, these are the expected frequencies under the hypothesis of row and column independence.

If you specify the EXPECTED or ALL option with the PRINT=PERCENT or PRINT=BOTH option, PROC CORRESP displays the product of the row marginals and the column marginals divided by the grand frequency of the observed percentages table. For ordinary two-way contingency tables, these are the expected percentages under the hypothesis of row and column independence.

If you specify the DEVIATION or ALL option and you do not specify PRINT=PERCENT, PROC CORRESP displays the observed minus expected frequencies. For ordinary two-way contingency tables, these are the expected frequencies under the hypothesis of row and column independence.

If you specify the DEVIATION or ALL option with the PRINT=PERCENT or PRINT=BOTH option, PROC CORRESP displays the observed minus expected percentages. For ordinary two-way contingency tables, these are the expected percentages under the hypothesis of row and column independence.

If you specify the CELLCHI2 or ALL option and you do not specify PRINT=PERCENT, PROC CORRESP displays contributions to the total chi-square test statistic, including the row and column marginals. The intersection of the marginals contains the total chi-square statistic.

If you specify the CELLCHI2 or ALL option with the PRINT=PERCENT or the PRINT=BOTH option, PROC CORRESP displays contributions to the total chi-square, scaled to percentages, including the row and column marginals.

If you specify the RP or ALL option and you do not specify PRINT=PERCENT, PROC CORRESP displays the row profiles and the supplementary row profiles.

If you specify the RP or ALL option with the PRINT=PERCENT or the PRINT=BOTH option, PROC CORRESP displays the row profiles (scaled to percentages) and the supplementary row profiles (scaled to percentages).

If you specify the CP or ALL option and you do not specify PRINT=PERCENT, PROC CORRESP displays the column profiles and the supplementary column profiles.

If you specify the CP or ALL option with the PRINT=PERCENT or PRINT=BOTH option, PROC CORRESP displays the column profiles (scaled to percentages) and the supplementary column profiles (scaled to percentages).

If you do not specify the NOPRINT option, PROC CORRESP displays the inertia and chi-square decomposition table. This includes the nonzero singular values of the contingency table (or, in MCA, the binary matrix **Z** used to create the Burt table), the nonzero principal inertias (or eigenvalues) for each dimension, the total inertia, the total chi-square, the decomposition of chi-square, the chi-square degrees of freedom (appropriate only when the table is an ordinary two-way contingency table), the percent of the total chi-square and inertia for each dimension, and a bar chart of the percents.

If you specify the MCA option and you do not specify the NOPRINT option, PROC CORRESP displays the adjusted inertias. This includes the nonzero adjusted inertias, percents, cumulative percents, and a bar chart of the percents.

If you do not specify the NOROW, NOPRINT, or MCA option, PROC CORRESP displays the row coordinates and the supplementary row coordinates (displayed when there are supplementary row points).

If you do not specify the NOROW, NOPRINT, MCA, or SHORT option, PROC CORRESP displays

- the summary statistics for the row points including the quality of representation of the row points in the n-dimensional display, the mass, and the relative contributions to inertia
- the quality of representation of the supplementary row points in the n-dimensional display (displayed when there are supplementary row points)
- the partial contributions to inertia for the row points
- the row Best table, indicators of which row points best explain the inertia of each dimension
- the squared cosines for the row points
- the squared cosines for the supplementary row points (displayed when there are supplementary row points)

If you do not specify the NOCOLUMN or NOPRINT option, PROC CORRESP displays the column coordinates and the supplementary column coordinates (displayed when there are supplementary column points).

If you do not specify the NOCOLUMN, NOPRINT, or SHORT option, PROC CORRESP displays

- the summary statistics for the column points including the quality of representation of the column points in the n-dimensional display, the mass, and the relative contributions to inertia for the supplementary column points
- the quality of representation of the supplementary column points in the n-dimensional display (displayed when there are supplementary column points)
- the partial contributions to inertia for the column points
- the column Best table, indicators of which column points best explain the inertia of each dimension
- the squared cosines for the column points
- the squared cosines for the supplementary column points

ODS Table Names

PROC CORRESP assigns a name to each table it creates. You can use these names to reference the table when using the Output Delivery System (ODS) to select tables and create output data sets. These names are listed in the following table. For more information on ODS, see Chapter 15, "Using the Output Delivery System."

Table 24.8. ODS Tables Produced in PROC CORRESP

ODS Table Name	Description	Option
AdjInGreenacre	Greenacre Inertia Adjustment	GREENACRE
AdjInBenzecri	Benzécri Inertia Adjustment	BENZECRI
Binary	Binary table	OBSERVED, BINARY
BinaryPct	Binary table percents	OBSERVED, BINARY *
Burt	Burt table	OBSERVED, MCA
BurtPct	Burt table percents	OBSERVED, MCA *
CellChiSq	Contributions to Chi Square	CELLCHI2
CellChiSqPct	Contributions, pcts	CELLCHI2 *
ColBest	Col best indicators	default
ColContr	Col contributions to inertia	default
ColCoors	Col coordinates	default
ColProfiles	Col profiles	CP
ColProfilesPct	Col profiles, pcts	CP *
ColQualMassIn	Col quality, mass, inertia	default
ColSqCos	Col squared cosines	default
DF	DF, Chi Square (not displayed)	default
Deviations	Observed - expected freqs	DEVIATIONS
DeviationsPct	Observed - expected pcts	DEVIATIONS *
Expected	Expected frequencies	EXPECTED
ExpectedPct	Expected percents	EXPECTED *
Inertias	Inertia decomposition table	default

Table 24.8. (continued)

ODS Table Name	Description	Option
Observed	Observed frequencies	OBSERVED
ObservedPct	Observed percents	OBSERVED *
RowBest	Row best indicators	default
RowContr	Row contributions to inertia	default
RowCoors	Row coordinates	default
RowProfiles	Row profiles	RP
RowProfilesPct	Row profiles, pcts	RP *
RowQualMassIn	Row quality, mass, inertia	default
RowSqCos	Row squared cosines	default
SupColCoors	Supp col coordinates	default
SupColProfiles	Supp col profiles	CP
SupColProfilesPct	Supp col profiles, pcts	CP *
SupColQuality	Supp col quality	default
SupCols	Supplementary col freq	OBSERVED
SupColsPct	Supplementary col pcts	OBSERVED *
SupColSqCos	Supp col squared cosines	default
SupRows	Supplementary row freqs	OBSERVED
SupRowCoors	Supp row coordinates	default
SupRowProfiles	Supp row profiles	RP
SupRowProfilesPct	Supp row profiles, pcts	RP *
SupRowQuality	Supp row quality	default
SupRowsPct	Supplementary row pcts	OBSERVED *
SupRowSqCos	Supp row squared cosines	default

*Percents are displayed when you specify the PRINT=PERCENT or PRINT=BOTH option.

Examples

Example 24.1. Simple Correspondence Analysis of Cars and Their Owners

In this example, PROC CORRESP creates a contingency table from categorical data and performs a simple correspondence analysis. The data are from a sample of individuals who were asked to provide information about themselves and their cars. The questions included origin of the car (American, Japanese, European) and family status (single, married, single and living with children, and married living with children). These data are used again in Example 24.2.

The first steps read the input data and assign formats. PROC CORRESP is used to perform the simple correspondence analysis. The ALL option displays all tables including the contingency table, chi-square information, profiles, and all results of the correspondence analysis. The OUTC= option creates an output coordinate data set. The TABLES statement specifies the row and column categorical variables. The %PLOTIT macro is used to plot the results.

Normally, you only need to tell the %PLOTIT macro the name of the input data set, DATA=Coor, and the type of analysis performed on the data, DATATYPE=CORRESP.

The following statements produce Output 24.1.1:

```
title 'Car Owners and Car Origin';

proc format;
   value Origin  1 = 'American' 2 = 'Japanese' 3 = 'European';
   value Size    1 = 'Small'    2 = 'Medium'   3 = 'Large';
   value Type    1 = 'Family'   2 = 'Sporty'   3 = 'Work';
   value Home    1 = 'Own'      2 = 'Rent';
   value Sex     1 = 'Male'     2 = 'Female';
   value Income  1 = '1 Income' 2 = '2 Incomes';
   value Marital 1 = 'Single with Kids' 2 = 'Married with Kids'
                 3 = 'Single'           4 = 'Married';
   run;

data Cars;
   missing a;
   input (Origin Size Type Home Income Marital Kids Sex) (1.) @@;
   * Check for End of Line;
   if n(of Origin -- Sex) eq 0 then do; input; return; end;
   marital = 2 * (kids le 0) + marital;
   format Origin Origin. Size Size. Type Type. Home Home.
          Sex Sex. Income Income. Marital Marital.;
   output;
   datalines;
131112212121110121112201131211011211221122112121131122123211222212212201
121122023121221232211101122122022121110122112102131112211121110112311101
211112113211223121122202221122111311123131211102321122223221220221221101
122122022121220211212201221122021122110132112202213112111331226122221101
1212110231AA2202321122121131121121212202122122021121110222221102121212 21
211211012211222212211101313112113121220121112212121112212211222221112211
221111011112220122212201131211013121220113112222131112012131110221112211
121112212211121121112201321122311311221113112212213211013121220221221101
133211011212220233311102213111023211122121312222212212111111222121112211
133112011212112212112212212222022131222222121101111122022211220113112212
211112012232220121221102213211011131220121212201211122112331220233312202
222122012111220212112201221122112212220222212211311122012111110112212212
112222011131112221212202322211021222110121221101333211012232110132212101
223222013111220112211101211211022112110212211102221122021111220112111211
111122022121110113311122322111122221210222211101212122021211221232112202
133111011311221121322201213122121111221222112202133122021212111212 1.2212
121122.221212102331122122221210113111221212111022111221121211101212 12101
311212022231221112112211211211312221221213112212221122022222110131212202
213122211311221212112222113122221221220213111221121211221211221221221102
131122211211220221222101223112012111221212111102223122111311222121111102
212111012111220213312222231112212131221211 2.210131212201211112211211 2202
111212023121110111112221212111012211220221321101221211122121220112111112
212221102211111012222110112111211212211012212223222112221221122121211 2202
213122112211110212121201113211012221110232111102212211012112220121212202
221112011211220121221101211211022211221112121101111112212121221111221201
211122122122111212112221111122312132110113121101121122222111220222121102
221211012122110221221102312111012122220121121101121122221111222212221102
212122021222120113112202121122212121110113111101123112212111220113111101
221112211321210131212211121211011222110122112222123122023121223112212202
```

```
311211012131110131221102112211021131220213122201222111022121221221312202
131.225232211101222122211311124122112202211211121312220221222201221222 01
212111011311220221312202221122123221210121222202223122121211221221111112
211111121211221221212201113122122131220222112222211122011311110112312211
211222013221220121211211312122122222122012211220111122201121111012231 1112
312111021231220122121101211112112.221102221122121211221222111101211121 01
121211013211222121112222321112112112110121321101113111012221220121312201
213211012212220221211101321122121111220221121101122211021122110213112212
21212201121112213122110112121102221222021212110 1
;

*---Perform Simple Correspondence Analysis---;
proc corresp all data=Cars outc=Coor;
   tables Marital, Origin;
   run;

*---Plot the Simple Correspondence Analysis Results---;
%plotit(data=Coor, datatype=corresp)
```

Correspondence analysis locates all the categories in a Euclidean space. The first two dimensions of this space are plotted to examine the associations among the categories. Since the smallest dimension of this table is three, there is no loss of information when only two dimensions are plotted. The plot should be thought of as two different overlaid plots, one for each categorical variable. Distances between points within a variable have meaning, but distances between points from different variables do not.

Output 24.1.1. Simple Correspondence Analysis of a Contingency Table

Car Owners and Car Origin

The CORRESP Procedure

Contingency Table

	American	European	Japanese	Sum
Married	37	14	51	102
Married with Kids	52	15	44	111
Single	33	15	63	111
Single with Kids	6	1	8	15
Sum	128	45	166	339

Chi-Square Statistic Expected Values

	American	European	Japanese
Married	38.5133	13.5398	49.9469
Married with Kids	41.9115	14.7345	54.3540
Single	41.9115	14.7345	54.3540
Single with Kids	5.6637	1.9912	7.3451

Observed Minus Expected Values

	American	European	Japanese
Married	-1.5133	0.4602	1.0531
Married with Kids	10.0885	0.2655	-10.3540
Single	-8.9115	0.2655	8.6460
Single with Kids	0.3363	-0.9912	0.6549

Contributions to the Total Chi-Square Statistic

	American	European	Japanese	Sum
Married	0.05946	0.01564	0.02220	0.09730
Married with Kids	2.42840	0.00478	1.97235	4.40553
Single	1.89482	0.00478	1.37531	3.27492
Single with Kids	0.01997	0.49337	0.05839	0.57173
Sum	4.40265	0.51858	3.42825	8.34947

```
                    Car Owners and Car Origin

                     The CORRESP Procedure

                         Row Profiles

                              American      European      Japanese

Married                       0.362745      0.137255      0.500000
Married with Kids             0.468468      0.135135      0.396396
Single                        0.297297      0.135135      0.567568
Single with Kids              0.400000      0.066667      0.533333


                       Column Profiles

                              American      European      Japanese

Married                       0.289063      0.311111      0.307229
Married with Kids             0.406250      0.333333      0.265060
Single                        0.257813      0.333333      0.379518
Single with Kids              0.046875      0.022222      0.048193
```

```
                    Car Owners and Car Origin

                     The CORRESP Procedure

               Inertia and Chi-Square Decomposition

Singular  Principal    Chi-              Cumulative
   Value    Inertia   Square  Percent       Percent    19   38   57   76   95
                                                    ----+----+----+----+----+---
 0.15122    0.02287  7.75160    92.84         92.84  ************************
 0.04200    0.00176  0.59787     7.16        100.00  **

   Total    0.02463  8.34947   100.00

Degrees of Freedom = 6


                        Row Coordinates

                                        Dim1        Dim2

           Married                   -0.0278      0.0134
           Married with Kids          0.1991      0.0064
           Single                    -0.1716      0.0076
           Single with Kids          -0.0144     -0.1947


             Summary Statistics for the Row Points

                                 Quality        Mass     Inertia

      Married                     1.0000      0.3009      0.0117
      Married with Kids           1.0000      0.3274      0.5276
      Single                      1.0000      0.3274      0.3922
      Single with Kids            1.0000      0.0442      0.0685
```

Car Owners and Car Origin

The CORRESP Procedure

Partial Contributions to Inertia for the Row Points

	Dim1	Dim2
Married	0.0102	0.0306
Married with Kids	0.5678	0.0076
Single	0.4217	0.0108
Single with Kids	0.0004	0.9511

Indices of the Coordinates that Contribute Most to Inertia for the Row Points

	Dim1	Dim2	Best
Married	0	0	2
Married with Kids	1	0	1
Single	1	0	1
Single with Kids	0	2	2

Squared Cosines for the Row Points

	Dim1	Dim2
Married	0.8121	0.1879
Married with Kids	0.9990	0.0010
Single	0.9980	0.0020
Single with Kids	0.0054	0.9946

Car Owners and Car Origin

The CORRESP Procedure

Column Coordinates

	Dim1	Dim2
American	0.1847	-0.0166
European	0.0013	0.1073
Japanese	-0.1428	-0.0163

Summary Statistics for the Column Points

	Quality	Mass	Inertia
American	1.0000	0.3776	0.5273
European	1.0000	0.1327	0.0621
Japanese	1.0000	0.4897	0.4106

Car Owners and Car Origin

The CORRESP Procedure

Partial Contributions to Inertia for the Column Points

	Dim1	Dim2
American	0.5634	0.0590
European	0.0000	0.8672
Japanese	0.4366	0.0737

Indices of the Coordinates that Contribute Most to Inertia for the Column Points

	Dim1	Dim2	Best
American	1	0	1
European	0	2	2
Japanese	1	0	1

Squared Cosines for the Column Points

	Dim1	Dim2
American	0.9920	0.0080
European	0.0001	0.9999
Japanese	0.9871	0.0129

Output 24.1.2. Plot of Simple Correspondence Analysis of a Contingency Table

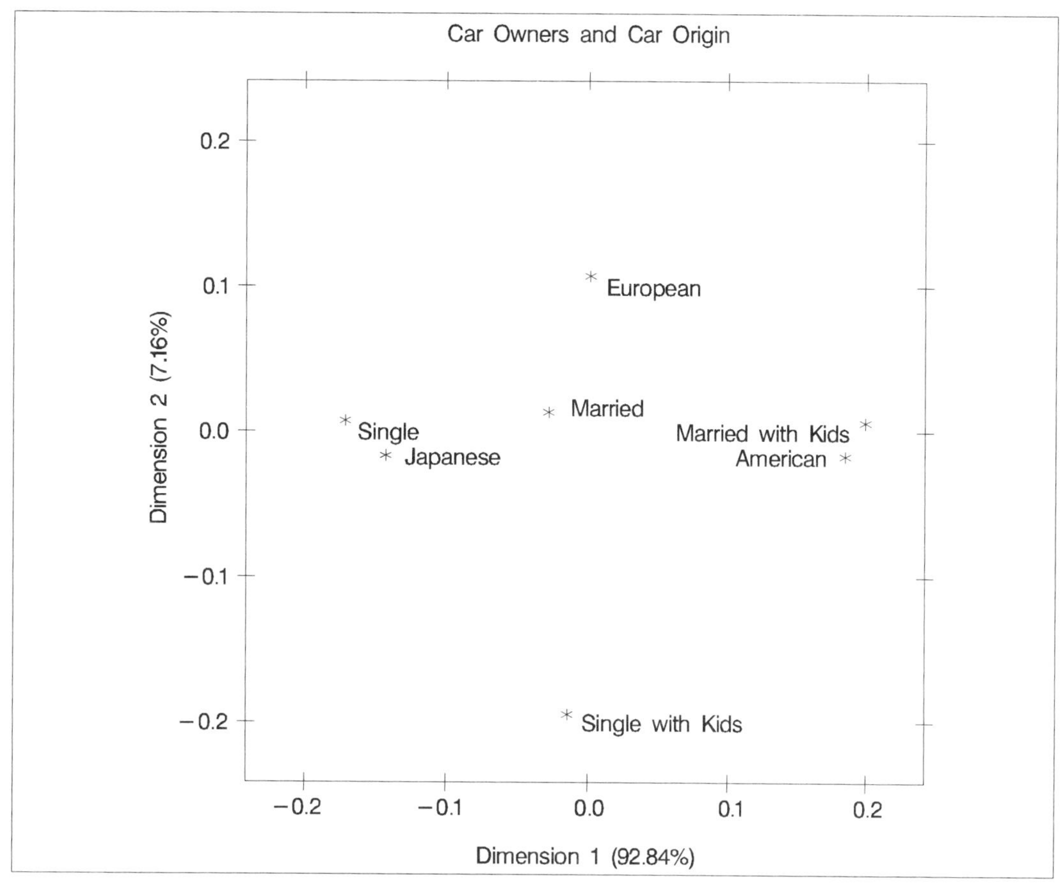

To interpret the plot, start by interpreting the row points separately from the column points. The European point is near and to the left of the centroid, so it makes a relatively small contribution to the chi-square statistic (because it is near the centroid), it contributes almost nothing to the inertia of dimension one (since its coordinate on dimension one has a small absolute value relative to the other column points), and it makes a relatively large contribution to the inertia of dimension two (since its coordinate on dimension two has a large absolute value relative to the other column points). Its squared cosines for dimension one and two, approximately 0 and 1, respectively, indicate that its position is almost completely determined by its location on dimension two. Its quality of display is 1.0, indicating perfect quality, since the table is two-dimensional after the centering. The American and Japanese points are far from the centroid, and they lie along dimension one. They make relatively large contributions to the chi-square statistic and the inertia of dimension one. The horizontal dimension seems to be largely determined by Japanese versus American car ownership.

In the row points, the Married point is near the centroid, and the Single with Kids point has a small coordinate on dimension one that is near zero. The horizontal dimension seems to be largely determined by the Single versus the Married with Kids points. The two interpretations of dimension one show the association with being Married with Kids and owning an American car, and being single and owning a Japanese car. The fact that the Married with Kids point is close to the American point and the fact that the Japanese point is near the Single point should be ignored. Distances between row and column points are not defined. The plot shows that more people who are married with kids than you would expect if the rows and columns were independent drive an American car, and more people who are single than you would expect if the rows and columns were independent drive a Japanese car.

Example 24.2. Multiple Correspondence Analysis of Cars and Their Owners

In this example, PROC CORRESP creates a Burt table from categorical data and performs a multiple correspondence analysis. The data are from a sample of individuals who were asked to provide information about themselves and their cars. The questions included origin of the car (American, Japanese, European), size of car (Small, Medium, Large), type of car (Family, Sporty, Work Vehicle), home ownership (Owns, Rents), marital/family status (single, married, single and living with children, and married living with children), and sex (Male, Female).

The data are read and formats assigned in a previous step, displayed in Example 24.1. The variables used in this example are Origin, Size, Type, Income, Home, Marital, and Sex. MCA specifies multiple correspondence analysis, OBSERVED displays the Burt table, and the OUTC= option creates an output coordinate data set. The TABLES statement with only a single variable list and no comma creates the Burt table. The %PLOTIT macro is used to plot the results with vertical and horizontal reference lines.

The data used to produce Output 24.2.1 and Output 24.2.2 can be found in Example 24.1.

```
title 'MCA of Car Owners and Car Attributes';

*---Perform Multiple Correspondence Analysis---;
proc corresp mca observed data=Cars outc=Coor;
   tables Origin Size Type Income Home Marital Sex;
run;

*---Plot the Multiple Correspondence Analysis Results---;
%plotit(data=Coor, datatype=corresp, href=0, vref=0)
```

Output 24.2.1. Multiple Correspondence Analysis of a Burt Table

MCA of Car Owners and Car Attributes

The CORRESP Procedure

Burt Table

	American	European	Japanese	Large	Medium	Small	Family	Sporty	Work	1 Income
American	125	0	0	36	60	29	81	24	20	58
European	0	44	0	4	20	20	17	23	4	18
Japanese	0	0	165	2	61	102	76	59	30	74
Large	36	4	2	42	0	0	30	1	11	20
Medium	60	20	61	0	141	0	89	39	13	57
Small	29	20	102	0	0	151	55	66	30	73
Family	81	17	76	30	89	55	174	0	0	69
Sporty	24	23	59	1	39	66	0	106	0	55
Work	20	4	30	11	13	30	0	0	54	26
1 Income	58	18	74	20	57	73	69	55	26	150
2 Incomes	67	26	91	22	84	78	105	51	28	0
Own	93	38	111	35	106	101	130	71	41	80
Rent	32	6	54	7	35	50	44	35	13	70
Married	37	13	51	9	42	50	50	35	16	10
Married with Kids	50	15	44	21	51	37	79	12	18	27
Single	32	15	62	11	40	58	35	57	17	99
Single with Kids	6	1	8	1	8	6	10	2	3	14
Female	58	21	70	17	70	62	83	44	22	47
Male	67	23	95	25	71	89	91	62	32	103

Burt Table

	2 Incomes	Own	Rent	Married	Married with Kids	Single	Single with Kids	Female	Male
American	67	93	32	37	50	32	6	58	67
European	26	38	6	13	15	15	1	21	23
Japanese	91	111	54	51	44	62	8	70	95
Large	22	35	7	9	21	11	1	17	25
Medium	84	106	35	42	51	40	8	70	71
Small	78	101	50	50	37	58	6	62	89
Family	105	130	44	50	79	35	10	83	91
Sporty	51	71	35	35	12	57	2	44	62
Work	28	41	13	16	18	17	3	22	32
1 Income	0	80	70	10	27	99	14	47	103
2 Incomes	184	162	22	91	82	10	1	102	82
Own	162	242	0	76	106	52	8	114	128
Rent	22	0	92	25	3	57	7	35	57
Married	91	76	25	101	0	0	0	53	48
Married with Kids	82	106	3	0	109	0	0	48	61
Single	10	52	57	0	0	109	0	35	74
Single with Kids	1	8	7	0	0	0	15	13	2
Female	102	114	35	53	48	35	13	149	0
Male	82	128	57	48	61	74	2	0	185

```
                      MCA of Car Owners and Car Attributes

                             The CORRESP Procedure

                      Inertia and Chi-Square Decomposition

Singular  Principal    Chi-              Cumulative
   Value    Inertia  Square  Percent        Percent    4    8   12   16   20
                                                    ----+----+----+----+----+---
 0.56934    0.32415  970.77    18.91          18.91 ************************
 0.48352    0.23380  700.17    13.64          32.55 *****************
 0.42716    0.18247  546.45    10.64          43.19 *************
 0.41215    0.16987  508.73     9.91          53.10 ************
 0.38773    0.15033  450.22     8.77          61.87 ***********
 0.38520    0.14838  444.35     8.66          70.52 ***********
 0.34066    0.11605  347.55     6.77          77.29 ********
 0.32983    0.10879  325.79     6.35          83.64 ********
 0.31517    0.09933  297.47     5.79          89.43 *******
 0.28069    0.07879  235.95     4.60          94.03 ******
 0.26115    0.06820  204.24     3.98          98.01 *****
 0.18477    0.03414  102.24     1.99         100.00 **

   Total    1.71429 5133.92   100.00

Degrees of Freedom = 324
```

MCA of Car Owners and Car Attributes

The CORRESP Procedure

Column Coordinates

	Dim1	Dim2
American	-0.4035	0.8129
European	-0.0568	-0.5552
Japanese	0.3208	-0.4678
Large	-0.6949	1.5666
Medium	-0.2562	0.0965
Small	0.4326	-0.5258
Family	-0.4201	0.3602
Sporty	0.6604	-0.6696
Work	0.0575	0.1539
1 Income	0.8251	0.5472
2 Incomes	-0.6727	-0.4461
Own	-0.3887	-0.0943
Rent	1.0225	0.2480
Married	-0.4169	-0.7954
Married with Kids	-0.8200	0.3237
Single	1.1461	0.2930
Single with Kids	0.4373	0.8736
Female	-0.3365	-0.2057
Male	0.2710	0.1656

Summary Statistics for the Column Points

	Quality	Mass	Inertia
American	0.4925	0.0535	0.0521
European	0.0473	0.0188	0.0724
Japanese	0.3141	0.0706	0.0422
Large	0.4224	0.0180	0.0729
Medium	0.0548	0.0603	0.0482
Small	0.3825	0.0646	0.0457
Family	0.3330	0.0744	0.0399
Sporty	0.4112	0.0453	0.0569
Work	0.0052	0.0231	0.0699
1 Income	0.7991	0.0642	0.0459
2 Incomes	0.7991	0.0787	0.0374
Own	0.4208	0.1035	0.0230
Rent	0.4208	0.0393	0.0604
Married	0.3496	0.0432	0.0581
Married with Kids	0.3765	0.0466	0.0561
Single	0.6780	0.0466	0.0561
Single with Kids	0.0449	0.0064	0.0796
Female	0.1253	0.0637	0.0462
Male	0.1253	0.0791	0.0372

MCA of Car Owners and Car Attributes

The CORRESP Procedure

Partial Contributions to Inertia for the Column Points

	Dim1	Dim2
American	0.0268	0.1511
European	0.0002	0.0248
Japanese	0.0224	0.0660
Large	0.0268	0.1886
Medium	0.0122	0.0024
Small	0.0373	0.0764
Family	0.0405	0.0413
Sporty	0.0610	0.0870
Work	0.0002	0.0023
1 Income	0.1348	0.0822
2 Incomes	0.1099	0.0670
Own	0.0482	0.0039
Rent	0.1269	0.0103
Married	0.0232	0.1169
Married with Kids	0.0967	0.0209
Single	0.1889	0.0171
Single with Kids	0.0038	0.0209
Female	0.0223	0.0115
Male	0.0179	0.0093

MCA of Car Owners and Car Attributes

The CORRESP Procedure

Indices of the Coordinates that Contribute Most to Inertia for the Column Points

	Dim1	Dim2	Best
American	0	2	2
European	0	0	2
Japanese	0	2	2
Large	0	2	2
Medium	0	0	1
Small	0	2	2
Family	2	0	2
Sporty	2	2	2
Work	0	0	2
1 Income	1	1	1
2 Incomes	1	1	1
Own	1	0	1
Rent	1	0	1
Married	0	2	2
Married with Kids	1	0	1
Single	1	0	1
Single with Kids	0	0	2
Female	0	0	1
Male	0	0	1

Squared Cosines for the Column Points

	Dim1	Dim2
American	0.0974	0.3952
European	0.0005	0.0468
Japanese	0.1005	0.2136
Large	0.0695	0.3530
Medium	0.0480	0.0068
Small	0.1544	0.2281
Family	0.1919	0.1411
Sporty	0.2027	0.2085
Work	0.0006	0.0046
1 Income	0.5550	0.2441
2 Incomes	0.5550	0.2441
Own	0.3975	0.0234
Rent	0.3975	0.0234
Married	0.0753	0.2742
Married with Kids	0.3258	0.0508
Single	0.6364	0.0416
Single with Kids	0.0090	0.0359
Female	0.0912	0.0341
Male	0.0912	0.0341

Multiple correspondence analysis locates all the categories in a Euclidean space. The first two dimensions of this space are plotted to examine the associations among the categories. The top-right quadrant of the plot shows that the categories single, single with kids, 1 income, and renting a home are associated. Proceeding clockwise, the categories sporty, small, and Japanese are associated. The bottom-left quadrant shows the association between being married, owning your own home, and having two incomes. Having children is associated with owning a large American family car. Such information could be used in market research to identify target audiences for advertisements.

This interpretation is based on points found in approximately the same direction from the origin and in approximately the same region of the space. Distances between points do not have a straightforward interpretation in multiple correspondence analysis. The geometry of multiple correspondence analysis is not a simple generalization of the geometry of simple correspondence analysis (Greenacre and Hastie 1987; Greenacre 1988).

Output 24.2.2. Plot of Multiple Correspondence Analysis of a Burt Table

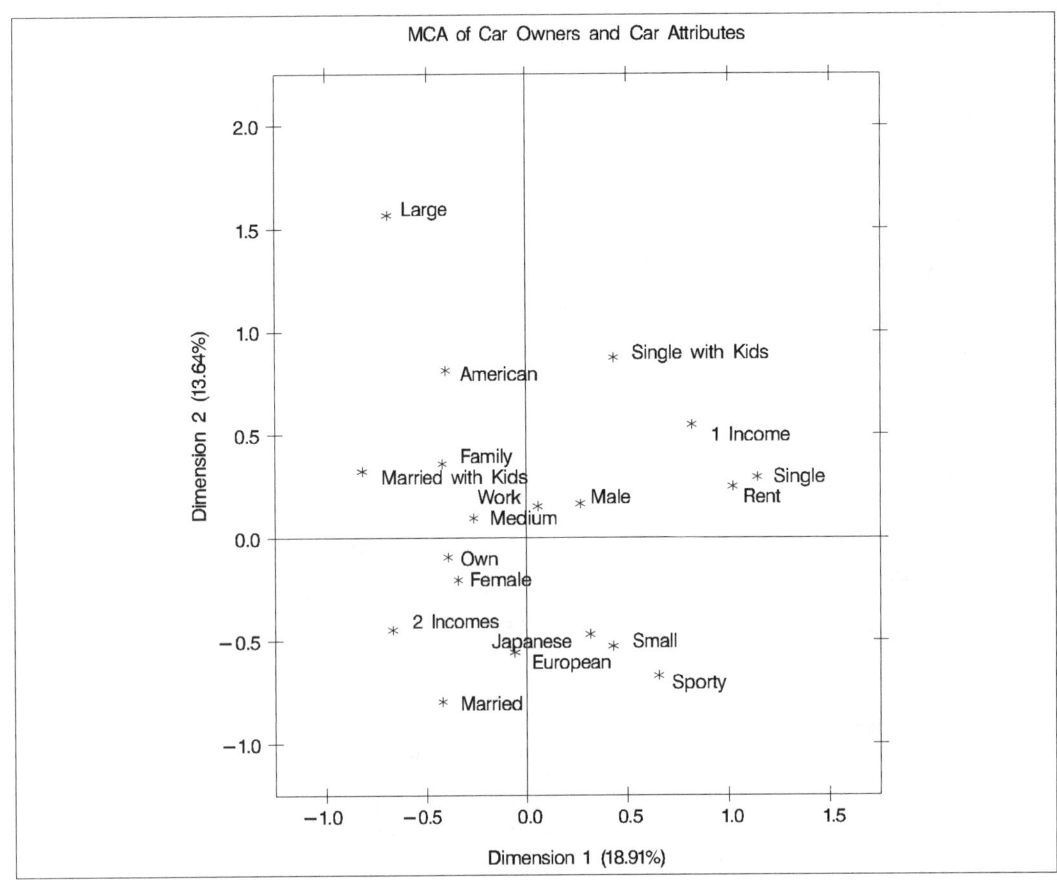

If you want to perform a multiple correspondence analysis and get scores for the individuals, you can specify the BINARY option to analyze the binary table. In the interest of space, only the first ten rows of coordinates are printed.

```
title 'Car Owners and Car Attributes';
title2 'Binary Table';

*---Perform Multiple Correspondence Analysis---;
proc corresp data=Cars binary;
   ods select RowCoors;
   tables Origin Size Type Income Home Marital Sex;
run;
```

Output 24.2.3. Correspondence Analysis of a Binary Table

```
                    Car Owners and Car Attributes
                            Binary Table

                        The CORRESP Procedure

                           Row Coordinates

                                   Dim1         Dim2

                    1           -0.4093       1.0878
                    2            0.8198      -0.2221
                    3           -0.2193      -0.5328
                    4            0.4382       1.1799
                    5           -0.6750       0.3600
                    6           -0.1778       0.1441
                    7           -0.9375       0.6846
                    8           -0.7405      -0.1539
                    9           -0.3027      -0.2749
                   10           -0.7263      -0.0803
```

Example 24.3. Simple Correspondence Analysis of U.S. Population

In this example, PROC CORRESP reads an existing contingency table with supplementary observations and performs a simple correspondence analysis. The data are populations of the fifty states, grouped into regions, for each of the census years from 1920 to 1970 (U.S. Bureau of the Census 1979). Alaska and Hawaii are treated as supplementary regions. They were not states during this entire period and they are not physically connected to the other 48 states. Consequently, it is reasonable to expect that population changes in these two states operate differently from population changes in the other states. The correspondence analysis is performed giving the supplementary points negative weight, then the coordinates for the supplementary points are computed in the solution defined by the other points.

The initial DATA step reads the table, provides labels for the years, flags the supplementary rows with negative weights, and specifies absolute weights of 1000 for all observations since the data were originally reported in units of 1000 people.

In the PROC CORRESP statement, PRINT=PERCENT and the display options display the table of cell percentages (OBSERVED), cell contributions to the total chi-square scaled to sum to 100 (CELLCHI2), row profile rows that sum to 100 (RP), and column profile columns that sum to 100 (CP). The SHORT option specifies that the correspondence analysis summary statistics, contributions to inertia, and squared cosines should not be displayed. The option OUTC=COOR creates the output coordinate data set. Since the data are already in table form, a VAR statement is used to read the table. Row labels are specified with the ID statement, and column labels come from the variable labels. The WEIGHT statement flags the supplementary observations and restores the table values to populations.

The %PLOTIT macro is used to plot the results. Normally, you only need to tell the %PLOTIT macro the name of the input data set, DATA=Coor, and the type of analysis performed on the data, DATATYPE=CORRESP. In this case, PLOTVARS=Dim1

Dim2 is also specified to indicate that Dim1 is the vertical axis variable, as opposed to the default PLOTVARS=Dim2 Dim1.

For an essentially one-dimensional plot such as this, specifying PLOTVARS=Dim1 Dim2 improves the graphical display.

The following statements produce Output 24.3.1 and Output 24.3.2:

```
title 'United States Population';

data USPop;

   * Regions:
   * New England      - ME, NH, VT, MA, RI, CT.
   * Great Lake       - OH, IN, IL, MI, WI.
   * South Atlantic   - DE, MD, DC, VA, WV, NC, SC, GA, FL.
   * Mountain         - MT, ID, WY, CO, NM, AZ, UT, NV.
   * Pacific          - WA, OR, CA.
   *
   * Note: Multiply data values by 1000 to get populations.;

   input Region $14. y1920 y1930 y1940 y1950 y1960 y1970;

   label y1920 = '1920'    y1930 = '1930'    y1940 = '1940'
         y1950 = '1950'    y1960 = '1960'    y1970 = '1970';

   if region = 'Hawaii' or region = 'Alaska'
      then w = -1000;       /* Flag Supplementary Observations */
      else w =  1000;

   datalines;
New England        7401  8166  8437  9314 10509 11842
NY, NJ, PA        22261 26261 27539 30146 34168 37199
Great Lake        21476 25297 26626 30399 36225 40252
Midwest           12544 13297 13517 14061 15394 16319
South Atlantic    13990 15794 17823 21182 25972 30671
KY, TN, AL, MS     8893  9887 10778 11447 12050 12803
AR, LA, OK, TX    10242 12177 13065 14538 16951 19321
Mountain           3336  3702  4150  5075  6855  8282
Pacific            5567  8195  9733 14486 20339 25454
Alaska               55    59    73   129   226   300
Hawaii              256   368   423   500   633   769
;

*---Perform Simple Correspondence Analysis---;
proc corresp print=percent observed cellchi2 rp cp
     short outc=Coor;
   var y1920 -- y1970;
   id Region;
   weight w;
   run;

*---Plot the Simple Correspondence Analysis Results---;
%plotit(data=Coor, datatype=corresp, plotvars=Dim1 Dim2)
```

The contingency table shows that the population of all regions increased over this time period. The row profiles show that population is increasing at a different rate for the different regions. There is a small increase in population in the Midwest, for example, but the population has more than quadrupled in the Pacific region over the same period. The column profiles show that in 1920, the US population was concentrated in the NY, NJ, PA, Great Lakes, Midwest, and South Atlantic regions. With time, the population is shifting more to the South Atlantic, Mountain, and Pacific regions. This is also clear from the correspondence analysis. The inertia and chi-square decomposition table shows that there are five nontrivial dimensions in the table, but the association between the rows and columns is almost entirely one-dimensional.

Output 24.3.1. Simple Correspondence Analysis of a Contingency Table with Supplementary Observations

United States Population

The CORRESP Procedure

Contingency Table

Percents	1920	1930	1940	1950	1960	1970	Sum
New England	0.830	0.916	0.946	1.045	1.179	1.328	6.245
NY, NJ, PA	2.497	2.946	3.089	3.382	3.833	4.173	19.921
Great Lake	2.409	2.838	2.987	3.410	4.064	4.516	20.224
Midwest	1.407	1.492	1.516	1.577	1.727	1.831	9.550
South Atlantic	1.569	1.772	1.999	2.376	2.914	3.441	14.071
KY, TN, AL, MS	0.998	1.109	1.209	1.284	1.352	1.436	7.388
AR, LA, OK, TX	1.149	1.366	1.466	1.631	1.902	2.167	9.681
Mountain	0.374	0.415	0.466	0.569	0.769	0.929	3.523
Pacific	0.625	0.919	1.092	1.625	2.282	2.855	9.398
Sum	11.859	13.773	14.771	16.900	20.020	22.677	100.000

Supplementary Rows

Percents	1920	1930	1940	1950	1960	1970
Alaska	0.006170	0.006619	0.008189	0.014471	0.025353	0.033655
Hawaii	0.028719	0.041283	0.047453	0.056091	0.071011	0.086268

Contributions to the Total Chi-Square Statistic

Percents	1920	1930	1940	1950	1960	1970	Sum
New England	0.937	0.314	0.054	0.009	0.352	0.469	2.135
NY, NJ, PA	0.665	1.287	0.633	0.006	0.521	2.265	5.378
Great Lake	0.004	0.085	0.000	0.001	0.005	0.094	0.189
Midwest	5.749	2.039	0.684	0.072	1.546	4.472	14.563
South Atlantic	0.509	1.231	0.259	0.000	0.285	1.688	3.973
KY, TN, AL, MS	1.454	0.711	1.098	0.087	0.946	2.945	7.242
AR, LA, OK, TX	0.000	0.069	0.077	0.001	0.059	0.030	0.238
Mountain	0.391	0.868	0.497	0.098	0.498	1.834	4.187
Pacific	18.591	9.380	5.458	0.074	7.346	21.248	62.096
Sum	28.302	15.986	8.761	0.349	11.558	35.046	100.000

United States Population

The CORRESP Procedure

Row Profiles

Percents	1920	1930	1940	1950	1960	1970
New England	13.2947	14.6688	15.1557	16.7310	18.8777	21.2722
NY, NJ, PA	12.5362	14.7888	15.5085	16.9766	19.2416	20.9484
Great Lake	11.9129	14.0325	14.7697	16.8626	20.0943	22.3281
Midwest	14.7348	15.6193	15.8777	16.5167	18.0825	19.1691
South Atlantic	11.1535	12.5917	14.2093	16.8872	20.7060	24.4523
KY, TN, AL, MS	13.5033	15.0126	16.3655	17.3813	18.2969	19.4403
AR, LA, OK, TX	11.8687	14.1111	15.1401	16.8471	19.6433	22.3897
Mountain	10.6242	11.7898	13.2166	16.1624	21.8312	26.3758
Pacific	6.6453	9.7823	11.6182	17.2918	24.2784	30.3841

Supplementary Row Profiles

Percents	1920	1930	1940	1950	1960	1970
Alaska	6.5321	7.0071	8.6698	15.3207	26.8409	35.6295
Hawaii	8.6809	12.4788	14.3438	16.9549	21.4649	26.0766

Column Profiles

Percents	1920	1930	1940	1950	1960	1970
New England	7.0012	6.6511	6.4078	6.1826	5.8886	5.8582
NY, NJ, PA	21.0586	21.3894	20.9155	20.0109	19.1457	18.4023
Great Lake	20.3160	20.6042	20.2221	20.1788	20.2983	19.9126
Midwest	11.8664	10.8303	10.2660	9.3337	8.6259	8.0730
South Atlantic	13.2343	12.8641	13.5363	14.0606	14.5532	15.1729
KY, TN, AL, MS	8.4126	8.0529	8.1857	7.5985	6.7521	6.3336
AR, LA, OK, TX	9.6888	9.9181	9.9227	9.6503	9.4983	9.5581
Mountain	3.1558	3.0152	3.1519	3.3688	3.8411	4.0971
Pacific	5.2663	6.6748	7.3921	9.6158	11.3968	12.5921

```
                           United States Population

                            The CORRESP Procedure

                     Inertia and Chi-Square Decomposition

Singular  Principal     Chi-               Cumulative
   Value    Inertia   Square  Percent         Percent    20   40   60   80  100
                                                        ----+----+----+----+----+---
 0.10664    0.01137  1.014E7    98.16           98.16   *************************
 0.01238    0.00015   136586     1.32           99.48
 0.00658    0.00004    38540     0.37           99.85
 0.00333    0.00001   9896.6     0.10           99.95
 0.00244    0.00001   5309.9     0.05          100.00

   Total    0.01159  1.033E7   100.00

Degrees of Freedom = 40


                               Row Coordinates

                                        Dim1        Dim2

                     New England      0.0611      0.0132
                     NY, NJ, PA       0.0546     -0.0117
                     Great Lake       0.0074     -0.0028
                     Midwest          0.1315      0.0186
                     South Atlantic  -0.0553      0.0105
                     KY, TN, AL, MS   0.1044     -0.0144
                     AR, LA, OK, TX   0.0131     -0.0067
                     Mountain        -0.1121      0.0338
                     Pacific         -0.2766     -0.0070


                         Supplementary Row Coordinates

                                    Dim1        Dim2

                         Alaska   -0.4152      0.0912
                         Hawaii   -0.1198     -0.0321


                              Column Coordinates

                                    Dim1        Dim2

                         1920      0.1642      0.0263
                         1930      0.1149     -0.0089
                         1940      0.0816     -0.0108
                         1950     -0.0046     -0.0125
                         1960     -0.0815     -0.0007
                         1970     -0.1335      0.0086
```

The plot shows that the first dimension correctly orders the years. There is nothing in the correspondence analysis that forces this to happen; PROC CORRESP knows nothing about the inherent ordering of the column categories. The ordering of the regions and the ordering of the years reflect the shift over time of the US population from the Northeast quadrant of the country to the South and to the West. The results show that the West and Southeast are growing faster than the rest of the contiguous 48 states.

The plot also shows that the growth pattern for Hawaii is similar to the growth pattern for the mountain states and that Alaska's growth is even more extreme than the Pacific states' growth. The row profiles confirm this interpretation.

The Pacific region is farther from the origin than all other active points. The Midwest is the extreme region in the other direction. The table of contributions to the total chi-square shows that 62% of the total chi-square statistic is contributed by the Pacific region, which is followed by the Midwest at over 14%. Similarly the two extreme years, 1920 and 1970, together contribute over 63% to the total chi-square, whereas the years nearer the origin of the plot contribute less.

Output 24.3.2. Plot of Simple Correspondence Analysis of a Contingency Table with Supplementary Observations

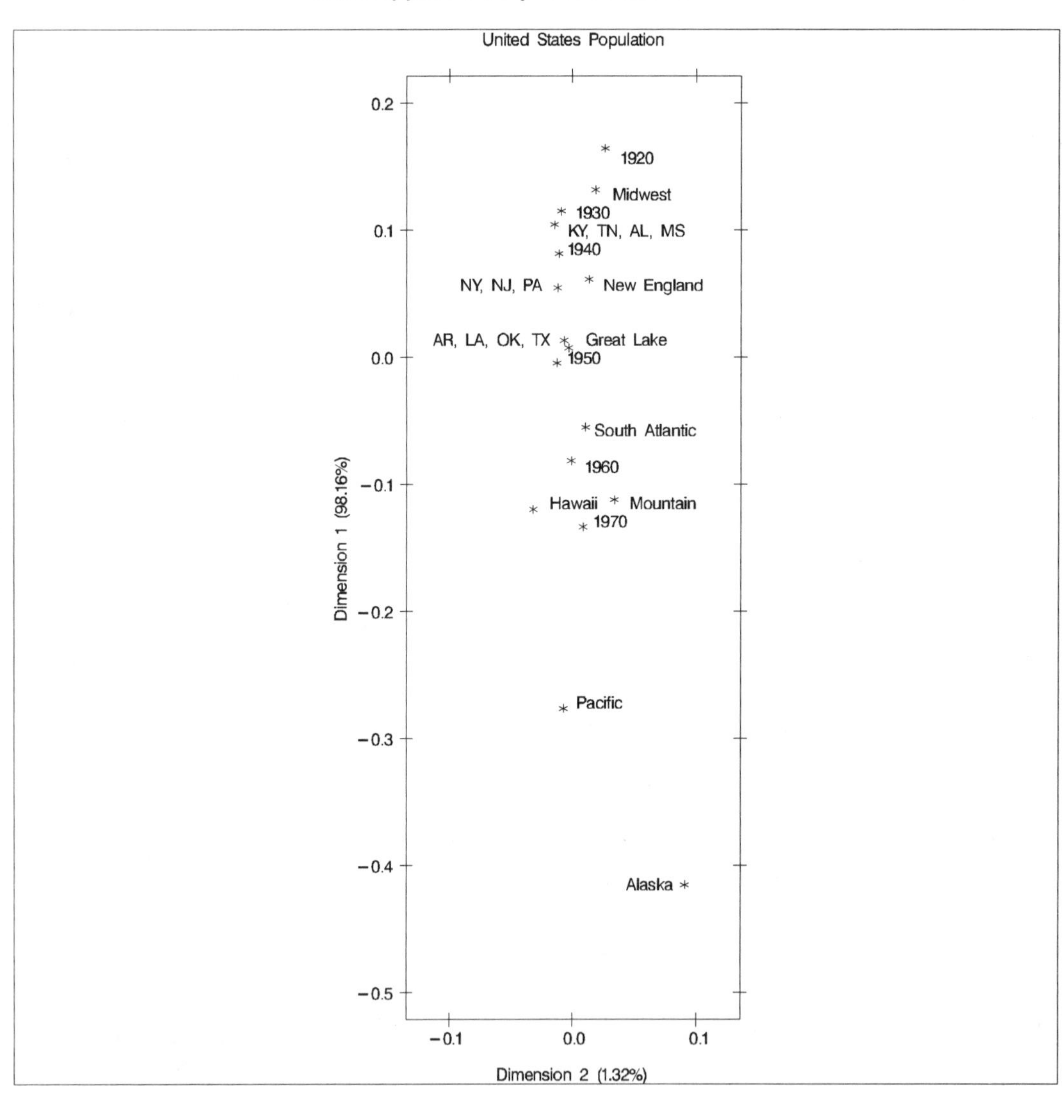

References

Benzécri, J.P. (1973), *L'Analyse des Données: T. 2, l'Analyse des Correspondances*, Paris: Dunod.

Benzécri, J.P. (1979), *Sur le Calcul des taux d'inertie dans l'analyse d'un questionaire,* Addendum et erratum á [BIN.MULT.]. Cahiers de l'Analyse des Données 4, 377–378.

Burt, C. (1950), "The Factorial Analysis of Qualitative Data," *British Journal of Psychology*, 3, 166–185.

Carroll, J.D, Green, P.E., and Schaffer, C.M. (1986), "Interpoint Distance Comparisons in Correspondence Analysis," *Journal of Marketing Research*, 23, 271–280.

Fisher, R.A. (1940), "The Precision of Discriminant Functions," *Annals of Eugenics*, 10, 422–429.

Gifi, A. (1990), *Nonlinear Multivariate Analysis*, New York: John Wiley & Sons, Inc.

Greenacre, M.J. (1984), *Theory and Applications of Correspondence Analysis*, London: Academic Press.

Greenacre, M.J. (1988), "Correspondence Analysis of Multivariate Categorical Data by Weighted Least-Squares," *Biometrika,* 75, 457–467.

Greenacre, M.J. (1989), "The Carroll-Green-Schaffer Scaling in Correspondence Analysis: A Theoretical and Empirical Appraisal," *Journal of Market Research*,26, 358–365.

Greenacre, M.J. (1994), "Multiple and Joint Correspondence Analysis," in Greenacre, M.J. and Blasius, J. (ed) *Correspondence Analysis in the Social Sciences*, London: Academic Press.

Greenacre, M.J. and Hastie, T. (1987), "The Geometric Interpretation of Correspondence Analysis," *Journal of the American Statistical Association*, 82, 437–447.

Guttman, L. (1941), "The Quantification of a Class of Attributes: A Theory and Method of Scale Construction," in P. Horst, et al. (ed)., *The Prediction of Personal Adjustment*, New York: Social Science Research Council.

Hayashi, C. (1950), "On the Quantification of Qualitative Data from the Mathematico-Statistical Point of View," *Annals of the Institute of Statistical Mathematics*, 2 (1), 35–47.

van der Heijden, P.G.M, and de Leeuw, J. (1985), "Correspondence Analysis Used Complementary to Loglinear Analysis," *Psychometrika*, 50, 429–447.

Hirshfield, H.O. (1935), "A Connection Between Correlation and Contingency," *Cambridge Philosophical Society Proceedings*, 31, 520–524.

Hoffman, D.L. and Franke, G.R. (1986), "Correspondence Analysis: Graphical Representation of Categorical Data in Marketing Research," *Journal of Marketing Research*, 23, 213–227.

Horst, P. (1935), "Measuring Complex Attitudes," *Journal of Social Psychology*, 6, 369–374.

Kobayashi, R. (1981), *An Introduction to Quantification Theory*, Tokyo: Japan Union of Scientists and Engineers.

Komazawa, T. (1982), *Quantification Theory and Data Processing*, Tokyo: Asakura-shoten.

Lebart, L., Morineau, A., and Tabard, N. (1977), *Techniques de la Description Statistique*, Paris: Dunod.

Lebart, L., Morineau, A., and Warwick, K.M. (1984), *Multivariate Descriptive Statistical Analysis: Correspondence Analysis and Related Techniques for Large Matrices*, New York: John Wiley & Sons, Inc.

Nishisato, S. (1980), *Analysis of Categorical Data: Dual Scaling and Its Applications*, Toronto: University of Toronto Press.

Nishisato, S. (1982), *Quantification of Qualitative Data - Dual Scaling and Its Applications*, Tokyo: Asakura-shoten.

Richardson, M., and Kuder, G.F. (1933), "Making a Rating Scale that Measures," *Personnel Journal*, 12, 36–40.

Tenenhaus, M. and Young, F.W. (1985), "An Analysis and Synthesis of Multiple Correspondence Analysis, Optimal Scaling, Dual Scaling, Homogeneity Analysis, and Other Methods of Quantifying Categorical Multivariate Data," *Psychometrika*, 50, 91–119.

U.S. Bureau of the Census (1979), *Statistical Abstract of the United States*, (100th Edition), Washington DC.

Chapter 25

The DISCRIM Procedure

Chapter Table of Contents

Chapter 25
The DISCRIM Procedure

Overview

For a set of observations containing one or more quantitative variables and a classification variable defining groups of observations, the DISCRIM procedure develops a discriminant criterion to classify each observation into one of the groups. The derived discriminant criterion from this data set can be applied to a second data set during the same execution of PROC DISCRIM. The data set that PROC DISCRIM uses to derive the discriminant criterion is called the *training* or *calibration* data set.

When the distribution within each group is assumed to be multivariate normal, a parametric method can be used to develop a discriminant function. The discriminant function, also known as a classification criterion, is determined by a measure of generalized squared distance (Rao 1973). The classification criterion can be based on either the individual within-group covariance matrices (yielding a quadratic function) or the pooled covariance matrix (yielding a linear function); it also takes into account the prior probabilities of the groups. The calibration information can be stored in a special SAS data set and applied to other data sets.

When no assumptions can be made about the distribution within each group, or when the distribution is assumed not to be multivariate normal, nonparametric methods can be used to estimate the group-specific densities. These methods include the kernel and k-nearest-neighbor methods (Rosenblatt 1956; Parzen 1962). The DISCRIM procedure uses uniform, normal, Epanechnikov, biweight, or triweight kernels for density estimation.

Either Mahalanobis or Euclidean distance can be used to determine proximity. Mahalanobis distance can be based on either the full covariance matrix or the diagonal matrix of variances. With a k-nearest-neighbor method, the pooled covariance matrix is used to calculate the Mahalanobis distances. With a kernel method, either the individual within-group covariance matrices or the pooled covariance matrix can be used to calculate the Mahalanobis distances. With the estimated group-specific densities and their associated prior probabilities, the posterior probability estimates of group membership for each class can be evaluated.

Canonical discriminant analysis is a dimension-reduction technique related to principal component analysis and canonical correlation. Given a classification variable and several quantitative variables, PROC DISCRIM derives canonical variables (linear combinations of the quantitative variables) that summarize between-class variation in much the same way that principal components summarize total variation. (See Chapter 21, "The CANDISC Procedure," for more information on canonical discriminant analysis.) A discriminant criterion is always derived in PROC DISCRIM. If you want canonical discriminant analysis without the use of a discriminant criterion, you should use the CANDISC procedure.

The DISCRIM procedure can produce an output data set containing various statistics such as means, standard deviations, and correlations. If a parametric method is used, the discriminant function is also stored in the data set to classify future observations. When canonical discriminant analysis is performed, the output data set includes canonical coefficients that can be rotated by the FACTOR procedure. PROC DISCRIM can also create a second type of output data set containing the classification results for each observation. When canonical discriminant analysis is performed, this output data set also includes canonical variable scores. A third type of output data set containing the group-specific density estimates at each observation can also be produced.

PROC DISCRIM evaluates the performance of a discriminant criterion by estimating error rates (probabilities of misclassification) in the classification of future observations. These error-rate estimates include error-count estimates and posterior probability error-rate estimates. When the input data set is an ordinary SAS data set, the error rate can also be estimated by cross validation.

Do not confuse discriminant analysis with cluster analysis. All varieties of discriminant analysis require prior knowledge of the classes, usually in the form of a sample from each class. In cluster analysis, the data do not include information on class membership; the purpose is to construct a classification.

See Chapter 7, "Introduction to Discriminant Procedures," for a discussion of discriminant analysis and the SAS/STAT procedures available.

Getting Started

The data in this example are measurements taken on 159 fish caught off the coast of Finland. The species, weight, three different length measurements, height, and width of each fish are tallied. The full data set is displayed in Chapter 60, "The STEPDISC Procedure." The STEPDISC procedure identifies all the variables as significant indicators of the differences among the seven fish species. The goal now is to find a discriminant function based on these six variables that best classifies the fish into species.

First, assume that the data are normally distributed within each group with equal covariances across groups. The following program uses PROC DISCRIM to analyze the Fish data and create Figure 25.1 through Figure 25.5.

```
proc format;
   value specfmt
      1='Bream'
      2='Roach'
      3='Whitefish'
      4='Parkki'
      5='Perch'
      6='Pike'
      7='Smelt';
data fish (drop=HtPct WidthPct);
   title 'Fish Measurement Data';
   input Species Weight Length1 Length2 Length3 HtPct
         WidthPct @@;
   Height=HtPct*Length3/100;
   Width=WidthPct*Length3/100;
   format Species specfmt.;
   symbol = put(Species, specfmt.);
   datalines;
1  242.0 23.2 25.4 30.0 38.4 13.4
1  290.0 24.0 26.3 31.2 40.0 13.8
1  340.0 23.9 26.5 31.1 39.8 15.1
1  363.0 26.3 29.0 33.5 38.0 13.3
 ...[155 more records]
;
proc discrim data=fish;
   class Species;
run;
```

The DISCRIM procedure begins by displaying summary information about the variables in the analysis. This information includes the number of observations, the number of quantitative variables in the analysis (specified with the VAR statement), and the number of classes in the classification variable (specified with the CLASS statement). The frequency of each class, its weight, proportion of the total sample, and prior probability are also displayed. Equal priors are assigned by default.

```
                              Fish Measurement Data

                              The DISCRIM Procedure

             Observations     158          DF Total                 157
             Variables          6          DF Within Classes        151
             Classes            7          DF Between Classes         6


                             Class Level Information

              Variable                                                  Prior
 Species      Name           Frequency       Weight    Proportion    Probability

 Bream        Bream                 34      34.0000      0.215190       0.142857
 Parkki       Parkki                11      11.0000      0.069620       0.142857
 Perch        Perch                 56      56.0000      0.354430       0.142857
 Pike         Pike                  17      17.0000      0.107595       0.142857
 Roach        Roach                 20      20.0000      0.126582       0.142857
 Smelt        Smelt                 14      14.0000      0.088608       0.142857
 Whitefish    Whitefish              6       6.0000      0.037975       0.142857
```

Figure 25.1. Summary Information

The natural log of the determinant of the pooled covariance matrix is displayed next (Figure 25.2). The squared distances between the classes are shown in Figure 25.3.

```
                          Fish Measurement Data

                          The DISCRIM Procedure

                   Pooled Covariance Matrix Information

                                 Natural Log of the
                   Covariance    Determinant of the
                   Matrix Rank    Covariance Matrix

                             6              4.17613
```

Figure 25.2. Pooled Covariance Matrix Information

```
                                    Fish Measurement Data

                                    The DISCRIM Procedure

                     Pairwise Generalized Squared Distances Between Groups

                              2         _   _       -1  _   _
                             D (i|j) = (X - X )' COV   (X - X )
                                         i   j           i   j


                            Generalized Squared Distance to Species

From
Species           Bream      Parkki       Perch        Pike       Roach       Smelt   Whitefish

Bream                 0    83.32523   243.66688   310.52333   133.06721   252.75503   132.05820
Parkki         83.32523           0    57.09760   174.20918    27.00096    60.52076    26.54855
Perch         243.66688    57.09760           0   101.06791    29.21632    29.26806    20.43791
Pike          310.52333   174.20918   101.06791           0    92.40876   127.82177    99.90673
Roach         133.06721    27.00096    29.21632    92.40876           0    33.84280     6.31997
Smelt         252.75503    60.52076    29.26806   127.82177    33.84280           0    46.37326
Whitefish     132.05820    26.54855    20.43791    99.90673     6.31997    46.37326           0
```

Figure 25.3. Squared Distances

The coefficients of the linear discriminant function are displayed (in Figure 25.4) with the default options METHOD=NORMAL and POOL=YES.

```
                         Linear Discriminant Function

                     _      -1 _                           -1 _
     Constant = -.5 X' COV    X        Coefficient Vector = COV    X
                     j          j                                   j


                 Linear Discriminant Function for Species

Variable        Bream       Parkki       Perch        Pike       Roach       Smelt   Whitefish

Constant   -185.91682    -64.92517   -48.68009  -148.06402   -62.65963   -19.70401   -67.44603
Weight       -0.10912     -0.09031    -0.09418    -0.13805    -0.09901    -0.05778    -0.09948
Length1     -23.02273    -13.64180   -19.45368   -20.92442   -14.63635    -4.09257   -22.57117
Length2     -26.70692     -5.38195    17.33061     6.19887    -7.47195    -3.63996     3.83450
Length3      50.55780     20.89531     5.25993    22.94989    25.00702    10.60171    21.12638
Height       13.91638      8.44567    -1.42833    -8.99687    -0.26083    -1.84569     0.64957
Width       -23.71895    -13.38592     1.32749    -9.13410    -3.74542    -3.43630    -2.52442
```

Figure 25.4. Linear Discriminant Function

A summary of how the discriminant function classifies the data used to develop the function is displayed last. In Figure 25.5, you see that only three of the observations are misclassified. The error-count estimates give the proportion of misclassified observations in each group. Since you are classifying the same data that are used to derive the discriminant function, these error-count estimates are biased. One way to reduce the bias of the error-count estimates is to split the Fish data into two sets, use one set to derive the discriminant function, and use the other to run validation tests; Example 25.4 on page 1106 shows how to analyze a test data set. Another method of reducing bias is to classify each observation using a discriminant function computed from all of the other observations; this method is invoked with the CROSSVALIDATE option.

```
                         The DISCRIM Procedure
            Classification Summary for Calibration Data: WORK.FISH
           Resubstitution Summary using Linear Discriminant Function

                   Generalized Squared Distance Function

                        2         _       -1   _
                       D (X) = (X-X )' COV   (X-X )
                        j          j             j

            Posterior Probability of Membership in Each Species

                               2                     2
               Pr(j|X) = exp(-.5 D (X)) / SUM exp(-.5 D (X))
                                  j        k          k
```

Number of Observations and Percent Classified into Species

From Species	Bream	Parkki	Perch	Pike	Roach	Smelt	Whitefish	Total
Bream	34 100.00	0 0.00	0 0.00	0 0.00	0 0.00	0 0.00	0 0.00	34 100.00
Parkki	0 0.00	11 100.00	0 0.00	0 0.00	0 0.00	0 0.00	0 0.00	11 100.00
Perch	0 0.00	0 0.00	53 94.64	0 0.00	0 0.00	3 5.36	0 0.00	56 100.00
Pike	0 0.00	0 0.00	0 0.00	17 100.00	0 0.00	0 0.00	0 0.00	17 100.00
Roach	0 0.00	0 0.00	0 0.00	0 0.00	20 100.00	0 0.00	0 0.00	20 100.00
Smelt	0 0.00	0 0.00	0 0.00	0 0.00	0 0.00	14 100.00	0 0.00	14 100.00
Whitefish	0 0.00	0 0.00	0 0.00	0 0.00	0 0.00	0 0.00	6 100.00	6 100.00
Total	34 21.52	11 6.96	53 33.54	17 10.76	20 12.66	17 10.76	6 3.80	158 100.00
Priors	0.14286	0.14286	0.14286	0.14286	0.14286	0.14286	0.14286	

Error Count Estimates for Species

	Bream	Parkki	Perch	Pike	Roach	Smelt	Whitefish	Total
Rate	0.0000	0.0000	0.0536	0.0000	0.0000	0.0000	0.0000	0.0077
Priors	0.1429	0.1429	0.1429	0.1429	0.1429	0.1429	0.1429	

Figure 25.5. Resubstitution Misclassification Summary

Syntax

The following statements are available in PROC DISCRIM.

PROC DISCRIM < *options* > **;**
CLASS *variable* **;**
BY *variables* **;**
FREQ *variable* **;**
ID *variable* **;**
PRIORS *probabilities* **;**
TESTCLASS *variable* **;**
TESTFREQ *variable* **;**
TESTID *variable* **;**
VAR *variables* **;**
WEIGHT *variable* **;**

Only the PROC DISCRIM and CLASS statements are required. The following sections describe the PROC DISCRIM statement and then describe the other statements in alphabetical order.

PROC DISCRIM Statement

PROC DISCRIM < *options* > **;**

This statement invokes the DISCRIM procedure. You can specify the following options in the PROC DISCRIM statement.

Tasks	Options
Specify Input Data Set	DATA=
	TESTDATA=
Specify Output Data Set	OUTSTAT=
	OUT=
	OUTCROSS=
	OUTD=
	TESTOUT=
	TESTOUTD=
Discriminant Analysis	METHOD=
	POOL=
	SLPOOL=
Nonparametric Methods	K=
	R=
	KERNEL=
	METRIC=

Tasks	Options
Classification Rule	THRESHOLD=
Determine Singularity	SINGULAR=
Canonical Discriminant Analysis	CANONICAL CANPREFIX= NCAN=
Resubstitution Classification	LIST LISTERR NOCLASSIFY
Cross Validation Classification	CROSSLIST CROSSLISTERR CROSSVALIDATE
Test Data Classification	TESTLIST TESTLISTERR
Estimate Error Rate	POSTERR
Control Displayed Output	
Correlations	BCORR PCORR TCORR WCORR
Covariances	BCOV PCOV TCOV WCOV
SSCP Matrix	BSSCP PSSCP TSSCP WSSCP
Miscellaneous	ALL ANOVA DISTANCE MANOVA SIMPLE STDMEAN
Suppress output	NOPRINT SHORT

ALL

activates all options that control displayed output. When the derived classification criterion is used to classify observations, the ALL option also activates the POSTERR option.

ANOVA

displays univariate statistics for testing the hypothesis that the class means are equal in the population for each variable.

BCORR

displays between-class correlations.

BCOV

displays between-class covariances. The between-class covariance matrix equals the between-class SSCP matrix divided by $n(c-1)/c$, where n is the number of observations and c is the number of classes. You should interpret the between-class covariances in comparison with the total-sample and within-class covariances, not as formal estimates of population parameters.

BSSCP

displays the between-class SSCP matrix.

CANONICAL
CAN

performs canonical discriminant analysis.

CANPREFIX=*name*

specifies a prefix for naming the canonical variables. By default, the names are Can1, Can2, ... , Can$n$. If you specify CANPREFIX=ABC, the components are named ABC1, ABC2, ABC3, and so on. The number of characters in the prefix, plus the number of digits required to designate the canonical variables, should not exceed 32. The prefix is truncated if the combined length exceeds 32.

The CANONICAL option is activated when you specify either the NCAN= or the CANPREFIX= option. A discriminant criterion is always derived in PROC DISCRIM. If you want canonical discriminant analysis without the use of discriminant criteria, you should use PROC CANDISC.

CROSSLIST

displays the cross validation classification results for each observation.

CROSSLISTERR

displays the cross validation classification results for misclassified observations only.

CROSSVALIDATE

specifies the cross validation classification of the input DATA= data set. When a parametric method is used, PROC DISCRIM classifies each observation in the DATA= data set using a discriminant function computed from the other observations in the DATA= data set, excluding the observation being classified. When a nonparametric method is used, the covariance matrices used to compute the distances are based on all observations in the data set and do not exclude the observation being classified. However, the observation being classified is excluded from the nonparametric density estimation (if you specify the R= option) or the k nearest neighbors (if you specify the K= option) of that observation. The CROSSVALIDATE option is set when you specify the CROSSLIST, CROSSLISTERR, or OUTCROSS= option.

DATA=*SAS-data-set*

specifies the data set to be analyzed. The data set can be an ordinary SAS data set or one of several specially structured data sets created by SAS/STAT procedures. These specially structured data sets include TYPE=CORR, TYPE=COV, TYPE=CSSCP, TYPE=SSCP, TYPE=LINEAR, TYPE=QUAD, and TYPE=MIXED. The input data set must be an ordinary SAS data set if you specify METHOD=NPAR. If you omit the DATA= option, the procedure uses the most recently created SAS data set.

DISTANCE

MAHALANOBIS displays the squared Mahalanobis distances between the group means, F statistics, and the corresponding probabilities of greater Mahalanobis squared distances between the group means. The squared distances are based on the specification of the POOL= and METRIC= options.

K=*k*

specifies a k value for the k-nearest-neighbor rule. An observation $\mathbf{x}$ is classified into a group based on the information from the k nearest neighbors of $\mathbf{x}$. Do not specify both the K= and R= options.

KERNEL=BIWEIGHT | BIW
KERNEL=EPANECHNIKOV | EPA
KERNEL=NORMAL | NOR
KERNEL=TRIWEIGHT | TRI
KERNEL=UNIFORM | UNI

specifies a kernel density to estimate the group-specific densities. You can specify the KERNEL= option only when the R= option is specified. The default is KERNEL=UNIFORM.

LIST

displays the resubstitution classification results for each observation. You can specify this option only when the input data set is an ordinary SAS data set.

LISTERR

displays the resubstitution classification results for misclassified observations only. You can specify this option only when the input data set is an ordinary SAS data set.

MANOVA

displays multivariate statistics for testing the hypothesis that the class means are equal in the population.

METHOD=NORMAL | NPAR

determines the method to use in deriving the classification criterion. When you specify METHOD=NORMAL, a parametric method based on a multivariate normal distribution within each class is used to derive a linear or quadratic discriminant function. The default is METHOD=NORMAL. When you specify METHOD=NPAR, a nonparametric method is used and you must also specify either the K= or R= option.

METRIC=DIAGONAL | FULL | IDENTITY

specifies the metric in which the computations of squared distances are performed. If you specify METRIC=FULL, PROC DISCRIM uses either the pooled covariance matrix (POOL=YES) or individual within-group covariance matrices (POOL=NO) to compute the squared distances. If you specify METRIC=DIAGONAL, PROC DISCRIM uses either the diagonal matrix of the pooled covariance matrix (POOL=YES) or diagonal matrices of individual within-group covariance matrices (POOL=NO) to compute the squared distances. If you specify METRIC=IDENTITY, PROC DISCRIM uses Euclidean distance. The default is METRIC=FULL. When you specify METHOD=NORMAL, the option METRIC=FULL is used.

NCAN=*number*

specifies the number of canonical variables to compute. The value of *number* must be less than or equal to the number of variables. If you specify the option NCAN=0, the procedure displays the canonical correlations but not the canonical coefficients, structures, or means. Let v be the number of variables in the VAR statement and c be the number of classes. If you omit the NCAN= option, only $\min(v, c-1)$ canonical variables are generated. If you request an output data set (OUT=, OUTCROSS=, TESTOUT=), v canonical variables are generated. In this case, the last $v-(c-1)$ canonical variables have missing values.

The CANONICAL option is activated when you specify either the NCAN= or the CANPREFIX= option. A discriminant criterion is always derived in PROC DISCRIM. If you want canonical discriminant analysis without the use of discriminant criterion, you should use PROC CANDISC.

NOCLASSIFY

suppresses the resubstitution classification of the input DATA= data set. You can specify this option only when the input data set is an ordinary SAS data set.

NOPRINT

suppresses the normal display of results. Note that this option temporarily disables the Output Delivery System (ODS); see Chapter 15, "Using the Output Delivery System," for more information.

OUT=*SAS-data-set*

creates an output SAS data set containing all the data from the DATA= data set, plus the posterior probabilities and the class into which each observation is classified by resubstitution. When you specify the CANONICAL option, the data set also contains new variables with canonical variable scores. See the "OUT= Data Set" section on page 1044.

OUTCROSS=*SAS-data-set*

creates an output SAS data set containing all the data from the DATA= data set, plus the posterior probabilities and the class into which each observation is classified by cross validation. When you specify the CANONICAL option, the data set also contains new variables with canonical variable scores. See the "OUT= Data Set" section on page 1044.

OUTD=*SAS-data-set*
creates an output SAS data set containing all the data from the DATA= data set, plus the group-specific density estimates for each observation. See the "OUT= Data Set" section on page 1044.

OUTSTAT=*SAS-data-set*
creates an output SAS data set containing various statistics such as means, standard deviations, and correlations. When the input data set is an ordinary SAS data set or when TYPE=CORR, TYPE=COV, TYPE=CSSCP, or TYPE=SSCP, this option can be used to generate discriminant statistics. When you specify the CANONICAL option, canonical correlations, canonical structures, canonical coefficients, and means of canonical variables for each class are included in the data set. If you specify METHOD=NORMAL, the output data set also includes coefficients of the discriminant functions, and the output data set is TYPE=LINEAR (POOL=YES), TYPE=QUAD (POOL=NO), or TYPE=MIXED (POOL=TEST). If you specify METHOD=NPAR, this output data set is TYPE=CORR. This data set also holds calibration information that can be used to classify new observations. See the "Saving and Using Calibration Information" section on page 1041 and the "OUT= Data Set" section on page 1044.

PCORR
displays pooled within-class correlations.

PCOV
displays pooled within-class covariances.

POOL=NO | TEST | YES
determines whether the pooled or within-group covariance matrix is the basis of the measure of the squared distance. If you specify POOL=YES, PROC DISCRIM uses the pooled covariance matrix in calculating the (generalized) squared distances. Linear discriminant functions are computed. If you specify POOL=NO, the procedure uses the individual within-group covariance matrices in calculating the distances. Quadratic discriminant functions are computed. The default is POOL=YES.

When you specify METHOD=NORMAL, the option POOL=TEST requests Bartlett's modification of the likelihood ratio test (Morrison 1976; Anderson 1984) of the homogeneity of the within-group covariance matrices. The test is unbiased (Perlman 1980). However, it is not robust to nonnormality. If the test statistic is significant at the level specified by the SLPOOL= option, the within-group covariance matrices are used. Otherwise, the pooled covariance matrix is used. The discriminant function coefficients are displayed only when the pooled covariance matrix is used.

POSTERR
displays the posterior probability error-rate estimates of the classification criterion based on the classification results.

PSSCP
displays the pooled within-class corrected SSCP matrix.

R=*r*

specifies a radius r value for kernel density estimation. With uniform, Epanechnikov, biweight, or triweight kernels, an observation $\mathbf{x}$ is classified into a group based on the information from observations $\mathbf{y}$ in the training set within the radius r of $\mathbf{x}$, that is, the group t observations $\mathbf{y}$ with squared distance $d_t^2(\mathbf{x}, \mathbf{y}) \leq r^2$. When a normal kernel is used, the classification of an observation $\mathbf{x}$ is based on the information of the estimated group-specific densities from all observations in the training set. The matrix $r^2\mathbf{V}_t$ is used as the group t covariance matrix in the normal-kernel density, where $\mathbf{V}_t$ is the matrix used in calculating the squared distances. Do not specify both the K= and R= options. For more information on selecting r, see the "Nonparametric Methods" section on page 1033.

SHORT

suppresses the display of certain items in the default output. If you specify METHOD= NORMAL, PROC DISCRIM suppresses the display of determinants, generalized squared distances between-class means, and discriminant function coefficients. When you specify the CANONICAL option, PROC DISCRIM suppresses the display of canonical structures, canonical coefficients, and class means on canonical variables; only tables of canonical correlations are displayed.

SIMPLE

displays simple descriptive statistics for the total sample and within each class.

SINGULAR=*p*

specifies the criterion for determining the singularity of a matrix, where $0 < p < 1$. The default is SINGULAR=1E−8.

Let $\mathbf{S}$ be the total-sample correlation matrix. If the R^2 for predicting a quantitative variable in the VAR statement from the variables preceding it exceeds $1 - p$, then $\mathbf{S}$ is considered singular. If $\mathbf{S}$ is singular, the probability levels for the multivariate test statistics and canonical correlations are adjusted for the number of variables with R^2 exceeding $1 - p$.

Let $\mathbf{S}_t$ be the group t covariance matrix and $\mathbf{S}_p$ be the pooled covariance matrix. In group t, if the R^2 for predicting a quantitative variable in the VAR statement from the variables preceding it exceeds $1 - p$, then $\mathbf{S}_t$ is considered singular. Similarly, if the partial R^2 for predicting a quantitative variable in the VAR statement from the variables preceding it, after controlling for the effect of the CLASS variable, exceeds $1 - p$, then $\mathbf{S}_p$ is considered singular.

If PROC DISCRIM needs to compute either the inverse or the determinant of a matrix that is considered singular, then it uses a quasi-inverse or a quasi-determinant. For details, see the "Quasi-Inverse" section on page 1038.

SLPOOL=*p*

specifies the significance level for the test of homogeneity. You can specify the SLPOOL= option only when POOL=TEST is also specified. If you specify POOL= TEST but omit the SLPOOL= option, PROC DISCRIM uses 0.10 as the significance level for the test.

STDMEAN
displays total-sample and pooled within-class standardized class means.

TCORR
displays total-sample correlations.

TCOV
displays total-sample covariances.

TESTDATA=*SAS-data-set*
names an ordinary SAS data set with observations that are to be classified. The quantitative variable names in this data set must match those in the DATA= data set. When you specify the TESTDATA= option, you can also specify the TESTCLASS, TESTFREQ, and TESTID statements. When you specify the TESTDATA= option, you can use the TESTOUT= and TESTOUTD= options to generate classification results and group-specific density estimates for observations in the test data set.

TESTLIST
lists classification results for all observations in the TESTDATA= data set.

TESTLISTERR
lists only misclassified observations in the TESTDATA= data set but only if a TEST-CLASS statement is also used.

TESTOUT=*SAS-data-set*
creates an output SAS data set containing all the data from the TESTDATA= data set, plus the posterior probabilities and the class into which each observation is classified. When you specify the CANONICAL option, the data set also contains new variables with canonical variable scores. See the "OUT= Data Set" section on page 1044.

TESTOUTD=*SAS-data-set*
creates an output SAS data set containing all the data from the TESTDATA= data set, plus the group-specific density estimates for each observation. See the "OUT= Data Set" section on page 1044.

THRESHOLD=*p*
specifies the minimum acceptable posterior probability for classification, where $0 \leq p \leq 1$. If the largest posterior probability of group membership is less than the THRESHOLD value, the observation is classified into group OTHER. The default is THRESHOLD=0.

TSSCP
displays the total-sample corrected SSCP matrix.

WCORR
displays within-class correlations for each class level.

WCOV
displays within-class covariances for each class level.

WSSCP
displays the within-class corrected SSCP matrix for each class level.

BY Statement

BY *variables* **;**

You can specify a BY statement with PROC DISCRIM to obtain separate analyses on observations in groups defined by the BY variables. When a BY statement appears, the procedure expects the input data set to be sorted in order of the BY variables.

If your input data set is not sorted in ascending order, use one of the following alternatives:

- Sort the data using the SORT procedure with a similar BY statement.
- Specify the BY statement option NOTSORTED or DESCENDING in the BY statement for the DISCRIM procedure. The NOTSORTED option does not mean that the data are unsorted but rather that the data are arranged in groups (according to values of the BY variables) and that these groups are not necessarily in alphabetical or increasing numeric order.
- Create an index on the BY variables using the DATASETS procedure (in base SAS software).

For more information on the BY statement, refer to *SAS Language Reference: Concepts*. For more information on the DATASETS procedure, see the discussion in the *SAS Procedures Guide*.

If you specify the TESTDATA= option and the TESTDATA= data set does not contain any of the BY variables, then the entire TESTDATA= data set is classified according to the discriminant functions computed in each BY group in the DATA= data set.

If the TESTDATA= data set contains some but not all of the BY variables, or if some BY variables do not have the same type or length in the TESTDATA= data set as in the DATA= data set, then PROC DISCRIM displays an error message and stops.

If all BY variables appear in the TESTDATA= data set with the same type and length as in the DATA= data set, then each BY group in the TESTDATA= data set is classified by the discriminant function from the corresponding BY group in the DATA= data set. The BY groups in the TESTDATA= data set must be in the same order as in the DATA= data set. If you specify the NOTSORTED option in the BY statement, there must be exactly the same BY groups in the same order in both data sets. If you omit the NOTSORTED option, some BY groups may appear in one data set but not in the other. If some BY groups appear in the TESTDATA= data set but not in the DATA= data set, and you request an output test data set using the TESTOUT= or TESTOUTD= option, these BY groups are not included in the output data set.

CLASS Statement

CLASS *variable* **;**

The values of the classification variable define the groups for analysis. Class levels are determined by the formatted values of the CLASS variable. The specified variable can be numeric or character. A CLASS statement is required.

FREQ Statement

FREQ *variable* **;**

If a variable in the data set represents the frequency of occurrence for the other values in the observation, include the variable's name in a FREQ statement. The procedure then treats the data set as if each observation appears n times, where n is the value of the FREQ variable for the observation. The total number of observations is considered to be equal to the sum of the FREQ variable when the procedure determines degrees of freedom for significance probabilities.

If the value of the FREQ variable is missing or is less than one, the observation is not used in the analysis. If the value is not an integer, it is truncated to an integer.

ID Statement

ID *variable* **;**

The ID statement is effective only when you specify the LIST or LISTERR option in the PROC DISCRIM statement. When the DISCRIM procedure displays the classification results, the ID variable (rather than the observation number) is displayed for each observation.

PRIORS Statement

PRIORS EQUAL;

PRIORS PROPORTIONAL | PROP;

PRIORS *probabilities* **;**

The PRIORS statement specifies the prior probabilities of group membership. To set the prior probabilities equal, use

```
priors equal;
```

To set the prior probabilities proportional to the sample sizes, use

```
priors proportional;
```

For other than equal or proportional priors, specify the prior probability for each level of the classification variable. Each class level can be written as either a SAS name or a quoted string, and it must be followed by an equal sign and a numeric constant between zero and one. A SAS name begins with a letter or an underscore and can contain digits as well. Lowercase character values and data values with leading blanks must be enclosed in quotes. For example, to define prior probabilities for each level of Grade, where Grade's values are A, B, C, and D, the PRIORS statement can be

```
priors A=0.1 B=0.3 C=0.5 D=0.1;
```

If Grade's values are 'a', 'b', 'c', and 'd', each class level must be written as a quoted string:

```
priors 'a'=0.1  'b'=0.3  'c'=0.5  'd'=0.1;
```

If Grade is numeric, with formatted values of '1', '2', and '3', the PRIORS statement can be

```
priors '1'=0.3  '2'=0.6  '3'=0.1;
```

The specified class levels must exactly match the formatted values of the CLASS variable. For example, if a CLASS variable C has the format 4.2 and a value 5, the PRIORS statement must specify '5.00', not '5.0' or '5'. If the prior probabilities do not sum to one, these probabilities are scaled proportionally to have the sum equal to one. The default is PRIORS EQUAL.

TESTCLASS Statement

TESTCLASS *variable* ;

The TESTCLASS statement names the variable in the TESTDATA= data set that is used to determine whether an observation in the TESTDATA= data set is misclassified. The TESTCLASS variable should have the same type (character or numeric) and length as the variable given in the CLASS statement. PROC DISCRIM considers an observation misclassified when the formatted value of the TESTCLASS variable does not match the group into which the TESTDATA= observation is classified. When the TESTCLASS statement is missing and the TESTDATA= data set contains the variable given in the CLASS statement, the CLASS variable is used as the TESTCLASS variable.

TESTFREQ Statement

TESTFREQ *variable* **;**

If a variable in the TESTDATA= data set represents the frequency of occurrence for the other values in the observation, include the variable's name in a TESTFREQ statement. The procedure then treats the data set as if each observation appears n times, where n is the value of the TESTFREQ variable for the observation.

If the value of the TESTFREQ variable is missing or is less than one, the observation is not used in the analysis. If the value is not an integer, it is truncated to an integer.

TESTID Statement

TESTID *variable* **;**

The TESTID statement is effective only when you specify the TESTLIST or TESTLISTERR option in the PROC DISCRIM statement. When the DISCRIM procedure displays the classification results for the TESTDATA= data set, the TESTID variable (rather than the observation number) is displayed for each observation. The variable given in the TESTID statement must be in the TESTDATA= data set.

VAR Statement

VAR *variables* **;**

The VAR statement specifies the quantitative variables to be included in the analysis. The default is all numeric variables not listed in other statements.

WEIGHT Statement

WEIGHT *variable* **;**

To use relative weights for each observation in the input data set, place the weights in a variable in the data set and specify the name in a WEIGHT statement. This is often done when the variance associated with each observation is different and the values of the weight variable are proportional to the reciprocals of the variances. If the value of the WEIGHT variable is missing or is less than zero, then a value of zero for the weight is used.

The WEIGHT and FREQ statements have a similar effect except that the WEIGHT statement does not alter the degrees of freedom.

Details

Missing Values

Observations with missing values for variables in the analysis are excluded from the development of the classification criterion. When the values of the classification variable are missing, the observation is excluded from the development of the classification criterion, but if no other variables in the analysis have missing values for that observation, the observation is classified and displayed with the classification results.

Background

The following notation is used to describe the classification methods:

$\mathbf{x}$	a p-dimensional vector containing the quantitative variables of an observation
$\mathbf{S}_p$	the pooled covariance matrix
t	a subscript to distinguish the groups
n_t	the number of training set observations in group t
$\mathbf{m}_t$	the p-dimensional vector containing variable means in group t
$\mathbf{S}_t$	the covariance matrix within group t
$\lvert\mathbf{S}_t\rvert$	the determinant of $\mathbf{S}_t$
q_t	the prior probability of membership in group t
$p(t\lvert\mathbf{x})$	the posterior probability of an observation $\mathbf{x}$ belonging to group t
f_t	the probability density function for group t
$f_t(\mathbf{x})$	the group-specific density estimate at $\mathbf{x}$ from group t
$f(\mathbf{x})$	$\sum_t q_t f_t(\mathbf{x})$, the estimated unconditional density at $\mathbf{x}$
e_t	the classification error rate for group t

Bayes' Theorem

Assuming that the prior probabilities of group membership are known and that the group-specific densities at $\mathbf{x}$ can be estimated, PROC DISCRIM computes $p(t|\mathbf{x})$, the probability of $\mathbf{x}$ belonging to group t, by applying Bayes' theorem:

$$p(t|\mathbf{x}) = \frac{q_t f_t(\mathbf{x})}{f(\mathbf{x})}$$

PROC DISCRIM partitions a p-dimensional vector space into regions R_t, where the region R_t is the subspace containing all p-dimensional vectors $\mathbf{y}$ such that $p(t|\mathbf{y})$ is the largest among all groups. An observation is classified as coming from group t if it lies in region R_t.

Parametric Methods

Assuming that each group has a multivariate normal distribution, PROC DISCRIM develops a discriminant function or classification criterion using a measure of generalized squared distance. The classification criterion is based on either the individual within-group covariance matrices or the pooled covariance matrix; it also takes into account the prior probabilities of the classes. Each observation is placed in the class from which it has the smallest generalized squared distance. PROC DISCRIM also computes the posterior probability of an observation belonging to each class.

The squared Mahalanobis distance from $\mathbf{x}$ to group t is

$$d_t^2(\mathbf{x}) = (\mathbf{x} - \mathbf{m}_t)'\mathbf{V}_t^{-1}(\mathbf{x} - \mathbf{m}_t)$$

where $\mathbf{V}_t = \mathbf{S}_t$ if the within-group covariance matrices are used, or $\mathbf{V}_t = \mathbf{S}_p$ if the pooled covariance matrix is used.

The group-specific density estimate at $\mathbf{x}$ from group t is then given by

$$f_t(\mathbf{x}) = (2\pi)^{-\frac{p}{2}}|\mathbf{V}_t|^{-\frac{1}{2}} \exp\left(-0.5d_t^2(\mathbf{x})\right)$$

Using Bayes' theorem, the posterior probability of $\mathbf{x}$ belonging to group t is

$$p(t|\mathbf{x}) = \frac{q_t f_t(\mathbf{x})}{\sum_u q_u f_u(\mathbf{x})}$$

where the summation is over all groups.

The generalized squared distance from $\mathbf{x}$ to group t is defined as

$$D_t^2(\mathbf{x}) = d_t^2(\mathbf{x}) + g_1(t) + g_2(t)$$

where

$$g_1(t) = \begin{cases} \ln|\mathbf{S}_t| & \text{if the within-group covariance matrices are used} \\ 0 & \text{if the pooled covariance matrix is used} \end{cases}$$

and

$$g_2(t) = \begin{cases} -2\ln(q_t) & \text{if the prior probabilities are not all equal} \\ 0 & \text{if the prior probabilities are all equal} \end{cases}$$

The posterior probability of $\mathbf{x}$ belonging to group t is then equal to

$$p(t|\mathbf{x}) = \frac{\exp\left(-0.5D_t^2(\mathbf{x})\right)}{\sum_u \exp\left(-0.5D_u^2(\mathbf{x})\right)}$$

The discriminant scores are $-0.5D_u^2(\mathbf{x})$. An observation is classified into group u if setting $t = u$ produces the largest value of $p(t|\mathbf{x})$ or the smallest value of $D_t^2(\mathbf{x})$. If this largest posterior probability is less than the threshold specified, $\mathbf{x}$ is classified into group OTHER.

Nonparametric Methods

Nonparametric discriminant methods are based on nonparametric estimates of group-specific probability densities. Either a kernel method or the k-nearest-neighbor method can be used to generate a nonparametric density estimate in each group and to produce a classification criterion. The kernel method uses uniform, normal, Epanechnikov, biweight, or triweight kernels in the density estimation.

Either Mahalanobis distance or Euclidean distance can be used to determine proximity. When the k-nearest-neighbor method is used, the Mahalanobis distances are based on the pooled covariance matrix. When a kernel method is used, the Mahalanobis distances are based on either the individual within-group covariance matrices or the pooled covariance matrix. Either the full covariance matrix or the diagonal matrix of variances can be used to calculate the Mahalanobis distances.

The squared distance between two observation vectors, $\mathbf{x}$ and $\mathbf{y}$, in group t is given by

$$d_t^2(\mathbf{x},\mathbf{y}) = (\mathbf{x}-\mathbf{y})'V_t^{-1}(\mathbf{x}-\mathbf{y})$$

where $\mathbf{V}_t$ has one of the following forms:

$$V_t = \begin{cases} \mathbf{S}_p & \text{the pooled covariance matrix} \\ \text{diag}(\mathbf{S}_p) & \text{the diagonal matrix of the pooled covariance matrix} \\ \mathbf{S}_t & \text{the covariance matrix within group } t \\ \text{diag}(\mathbf{S}_t) & \text{the diagonal matrix of the covariance matrix within group } t \\ \mathbf{I} & \text{the identity matrix} \end{cases}$$

The classification of an observation vector $\mathbf{x}$ is based on the estimated group-specific densities from the training set. From these estimated densities, the posterior probabilities of group membership at $\mathbf{x}$ are evaluated. An observation $\mathbf{x}$ is classified into group u if setting $t = u$ produces the largest value of $p(t|\mathbf{x})$. If there is a tie for the largest probability or if this largest probability is less than the threshold specified, $\mathbf{x}$ is classified into group OTHER.

The kernel method uses a fixed radius, r, and a specified kernel, K_t, to estimate the group t density at each observation vector $\mathbf{x}$. Let $\mathbf{z}$ be a p-dimensional vector. Then the volume of a p-dimensional unit sphere bounded by $\mathbf{z}'\mathbf{z} = 1$ is

$$v_0 = \frac{\pi^{\frac{p}{2}}}{\Gamma\left(\frac{p}{2}+1\right)}$$

where Γ represents the gamma function (refer to *SAS Language Reference: Dictionary*).

Thus, in group t, the volume of a p-dimensional ellipsoid bounded by $\{\mathbf{z} \mid \mathbf{z}'\mathbf{V}_t^{-1}\mathbf{z} = r^2\}$ is

$$v_r(t) = r^p |V_t|^{\frac{1}{2}} v_0$$

The kernel method uses one of the following densities as the kernel density in group t.

Uniform Kernel

$$K_t(\mathbf{z}) = \begin{cases} \dfrac{1}{v_r(t)} & \text{if } \mathbf{z}'\mathbf{V}_t^{-1}\mathbf{z} \le r^2 \\ 0 & \text{elsewhere} \end{cases}$$

Normal Kernel (with mean zero, variance $r^2\mathbf{V}_t$)

$$K_t(\mathbf{z}) = \frac{1}{c_0(t)} \exp\left(-\frac{1}{2r^2}\mathbf{z}'\mathbf{V}_t^{-1}\mathbf{z}\right)$$

where $c_0(t) = (2\pi)^{\frac{p}{2}} r^p |\mathbf{V}_t|^{\frac{1}{2}}$.

Epanechnikov Kernel

$$K_t(\mathbf{z}) = \begin{cases} c_1(t)\left(1 - \dfrac{1}{r^2}\mathbf{z}'\mathbf{V}_t^{-1}\mathbf{z}\right) & \text{if } \mathbf{z}'\mathbf{V}_t^{-1}\mathbf{z} \le r^2 \\ 0 & \text{elsewhere} \end{cases}$$

where $c_1(t) = \dfrac{1}{v_r(t)}\left(1 + \dfrac{p}{2}\right)$.

Biweight Kernel

$$K_t(\mathbf{z}) = \begin{cases} c_2(t)\left(1 - \dfrac{1}{r^2}\mathbf{z}'\mathbf{V}_t^{-1}\mathbf{z}\right)^2 & \text{if } \mathbf{z}'\mathbf{V}_t^{-1}\mathbf{z} \le r^2 \\ 0 & \text{elsewhere} \end{cases}$$

where $c_2(t) = \left(1 + \dfrac{p}{4}\right) c_1(t)$.

Triweight Kernel

$$K_t(\mathbf{z}) = \begin{cases} c_3(t)\left(1 - \dfrac{1}{r^2}\mathbf{z}'\mathbf{V}_t^{-1}\mathbf{z}\right)^3 & \text{if } \mathbf{z}'\mathbf{V}_t^{-1}\mathbf{z} \le r^2 \\ 0 & \text{elsewhere} \end{cases}$$

where $c_3(t) = \left(1 + \dfrac{p}{6}\right) c_2(t)$.

The group t density at $\mathbf{x}$ is estimated by

$$f_t(\mathbf{x}) = \frac{1}{n_t} \sum_{\mathbf{y}} K_t(\mathbf{x} - \mathbf{y})$$

where the summation is over all observations $\mathbf{y}$ in group t, and K_t is the specified kernel function. The posterior probability of membership in group t is then given by

$$p(t|\mathbf{x}) = \frac{q_t f_t(\mathbf{x})}{f(\mathbf{x})}$$

where $f(\mathbf{x}) = \sum_u q_u f_u(\mathbf{x})$ is the estimated unconditional density. If $f(\mathbf{x})$ is zero, the observation $\mathbf{x}$ is classified into group OTHER.

The uniform-kernel method treats $K_t(\mathbf{z})$ as a multivariate uniform function with density uniformly distributed over $\mathbf{z}'\mathbf{V}_t^{-1}\mathbf{z} \leq r^2$. Let k_t be the number of training set observations $\mathbf{y}$ from group t within the closed ellipsoid centered at $\mathbf{x}$ specified by $d_t^2(\mathbf{x}, \mathbf{y}) \leq r^2$. Then the group t density at $\mathbf{x}$ is estimated by

$$f_t(\mathbf{x}) = \frac{k_t}{n_t v_r(t)}$$

When the identity matrix or the pooled within-group covariance matrix is used in calculating the squared distance, $v_r(t)$ is a constant, independent of group membership. The posterior probability of $\mathbf{x}$ belonging to group t is then given by

$$p(t|\mathbf{x}) = \frac{\frac{q_t k_t}{n_t}}{\sum_u \frac{q_u k_u}{n_u}}$$

If the closed ellipsoid centered at $\mathbf{x}$ does not include any training set observations, $f(\mathbf{x})$ is zero and $\mathbf{x}$ is classified into group OTHER. When the prior probabilities are equal, $p(t|\mathbf{x})$ is proportional to k_t/n_t and $\mathbf{x}$ is classified into the group that has the highest proportion of observations in the closed ellipsoid. When the prior probabilities are proportional to the group sizes, $p(t|\mathbf{x}) = k_t / \sum_u k_u$, $\mathbf{x}$ is classified into the group that has the largest number of observations in the closed ellipsoid.

The nearest-neighbor method fixes the number, k, of training set points for each observation $\mathbf{x}$. The method finds the radius $r_k(\mathbf{x})$ that is the distance from $\mathbf{x}$ to the kth nearest training set point in the metric $\mathbf{V}_t^{-1}$. Consider a closed ellipsoid centered at $\mathbf{x}$ bounded by $\{\mathbf{z} \mid (\mathbf{z} - \mathbf{x})'\mathbf{V}_t^{-1}(\mathbf{z} - \mathbf{x}) = r_k^2(\mathbf{x})\}$; the nearest-neighbor method is equivalent to the uniform-kernel method with a location-dependent radius $r_k(\mathbf{x})$. Note that, with ties, more than k training set points may be in the ellipsoid.

Using the k-nearest-neighbor rule, the k_n (or more with ties) smallest distances are saved. Of these k distances, let k_t represent the number of distances that are associated with group t. Then, as in the uniform-kernel method, the estimated group t density at $\mathbf{x}$ is

$$f_t(\mathbf{x}) = \frac{k_t}{n_t v_k(\mathbf{x})}$$

where $v_k(\mathbf{x})$ is the volume of the ellipsoid bounded by $\{\mathbf{z} \mid (\mathbf{z}-\mathbf{x})'\mathbf{V}_t^{-1}(\mathbf{z}-\mathbf{x}) = r_k^2(\mathbf{x})\}$. Since the pooled within-group covariance matrix is used to calculate the distances used in the nearest-neighbor method, the volume $v_k(\mathbf{x})$ is a constant independent of group membership. When $k = 1$ is used in the nearest-neighbor rule, $\mathbf{x}$ is classified into the group associated with the $\mathbf{y}$ point that yields the smallest squared distance $d_t^2(\mathbf{x}, \mathbf{y})$. Prior probabilities affect nearest-neighbor results in the same way that they affect uniform-kernel results.

With a specified squared distance formula (METRIC=, POOL=), the values of r and k determine the degree of irregularity in the estimate of the density function, and they are called smoothing parameters. Small values of r or k produce jagged density estimates, and large values of r or k produce smoother density estimates. Various methods for choosing the smoothing parameters have been suggested, and there is as yet no simple solution to this problem.

For a fixed kernel shape, one way to choose the smoothing parameter r is to plot estimated densities with different values of r and to choose the estimate that is most in accordance with the prior information about the density. For many applications, this approach is satisfactory.

Another way of selecting the smoothing parameter r is to choose a value that optimizes a given criterion. Different groups may have different sets of optimal values. Assume that the unknown density has bounded and continuous second derivatives and that the kernel is a symmetric probability density function. One criterion is to minimize an approximate mean integrated square error of the estimated density (Rosenblatt 1956). The resulting optimal value of r depends on the density function and the kernel. A reasonable choice for the smoothing parameter r is to optimize the criterion with the assumption that group t has a normal distribution with covariance matrix $\mathbf{V}_t$. Then, in group t, the resulting optimal value for r is given by

$$\left(\frac{A(K_t)}{n_t}\right)^{\frac{1}{p+4}}$$

where the optimal constant $A(K_t)$ depends on the kernel K_t (Epanechnikov 1969). For some useful kernels, the constants $A(K_t)$ are given by

$$A(K_t) = \frac{1}{p}2^{p+1}(p+2)\Gamma\left(\frac{p}{2}\right) \quad \text{with a uniform kernel}$$

$$A(K_t) = \frac{4}{2p+1} \quad \text{with a normal kernel}$$

$$A(K_t) = \frac{2^{p+2}p^2(p+2)(p+4)}{2p+1}\Gamma\left(\frac{p}{2}\right) \quad \text{with an Epanechnikov kernel}$$

These selections of $A(K_t)$ are derived under the assumption that the data in each group are from a multivariate normal distribution with covariance matrix $\mathbf{V}_t$. However, when the Euclidean distances are used in calculating the squared distance

($\mathbf{V}_t = I$), the smoothing constant should be multiplied by s, where s is an estimate of standard deviations for all variables. A reasonable choice for s is

$$s = \left(\frac{1}{p}\sum s_{jj}\right)^{\frac{1}{2}}$$

where s_{jj} are group t marginal variances.

The DISCRIM procedure uses only a single smoothing parameter for all groups. However, with the selection of the matrix to be used in the distance formula (using the METRIC= or POOL= option), individual groups and variables can have different scalings. When $\mathbf{V}_t$, the matrix used in calculating the squared distances, is an identity matrix, the kernel estimate on each data point is scaled equally for all variables in all groups. When $\mathbf{V}_t$ is the diagonal matrix of a covariance matrix, each variable in group t is scaled separately by its variance in the kernel estimation, where the variance can be the pooled variance ($\mathbf{V}_t = \mathbf{S}_p$) or an individual within-group variance ($\mathbf{V}_t = \mathbf{S}_t$). When $\mathbf{V}_t$ is a full covariance matrix, the variables in group t are scaled simultaneously by $\mathbf{V}_t$ in the kernel estimation.

In nearest-neighbor methods, the choice of k is usually relatively uncritical (Hand 1982). A practical approach is to try several different values of the smoothing parameters within the context of the particular application and to choose the one that gives the best cross validated estimate of the error rate.

Classification Error-Rate Estimates

A classification criterion can be evaluated by its performance in the classification of future observations. PROC DISCRIM uses two types of error-rate estimates to evaluate the derived classification criterion based on parameters estimated by the training sample:

- error-count estimates
- posterior probability error-rate estimates.

The error-count estimate is calculated by applying the classification criterion derived from the training sample to a test set and then counting the number of misclassified observations. The group-specific error-count estimate is the proportion of misclassified observations in the group. When the test set is independent of the training sample, the estimate is unbiased. However, it can have a large variance, especially if the test set is small.

When the input data set is an ordinary SAS data set and no independent test sets are available, the same data set can be used both to define and to evaluate the classification criterion. The resulting error-count estimate has an optimistic bias and is called an *apparent error rate*. To reduce the bias, you can split the data into two sets, one set for deriving the discriminant function and the other set for estimating the error rate. Such a split-sample method has the unfortunate effect of reducing the effective sample size.

Another way to reduce bias is cross validation (Lachenbruch and Mickey 1968). Cross validation treats $n - 1$ out of n training observations as a training set. It determines the discriminant functions based on these $n - 1$ observations and then applies them to classify the one observation left out. This is done for each of the n training observations. The misclassification rate for each group is the proportion of sample observations in that group that are misclassified. This method achieves a nearly unbiased estimate but with a relatively large variance.

To reduce the variance in an error-count estimate, smoothed error-rate estimates are suggested (Glick 1978). Instead of summing terms that are either zero or one as in the error-count estimator, the smoothed estimator uses a continuum of values between zero and one in the terms that are summed. The resulting estimator has a smaller variance than the error-count estimate. The posterior probability error-rate estimates provided by the POSTERR option in the PROC DISCRIM statement (see the following section, "Posterior Probability Error-Rate Estimates") are smoothed error-rate estimates. The posterior probability estimates for each group are based on the posterior probabilities of the observations classified into that same group. The posterior probability estimates provide good estimates of the error rate when the posterior probabilities are accurate. When a parametric classification criterion (linear or quadratic discriminant function) is derived from a nonnormal population, the resulting posterior probability error-rate estimators may not be appropriate.

The overall error rate is estimated through a weighted average of the individual group-specific error-rate estimates, where the prior probabilities are used as the weights.

To reduce both the bias and the variance of the estimator, Hora and Wilcox (1982) compute the posterior probability estimates based on cross validation. The resulting estimates are intended to have both low variance from using the posterior probability estimate and low bias from cross validation. They use Monte Carlo studies on two-group multivariate normal distributions to compare the cross validation posterior probability estimates with three other estimators: the apparent error rate, cross validation estimator, and posterior probability estimator. They conclude that the cross validation posterior probability estimator has a lower mean squared error in their simulations.

Quasi-Inverse

Consider the plot shown in Figure 25.6 with two variables, X1 and X2, and two classes, A and B. The within-class covariance matrix is diagonal, with a positive value for X1 but zero for X2. Using a Moore-Penrose pseudo-inverse would effectively ignore X2 completely in doing the classification, and the two classes would have a zero generalized distance and could not be discriminated at all. The quasi-inverse used by PROC DISCRIM replaces the zero variance for X2 by a small positive number to remove the singularity. This allows X2 to be used in the discrimination and results correctly in a large generalized distance between the two classes and a zero error rate. It also allows new observations, such as the one indicated by N, to be classified in a reasonable way. PROC CANDISC also uses a quasi-inverse when the total-sample covariance matrix is considered to be singular and Mahalanobis distances are requested. This problem with singular within-class covariance matrices is discussed in Ripley (1996, p. 38). The use of the quasi-inverse is an innovation introduced by SAS Institute Inc.

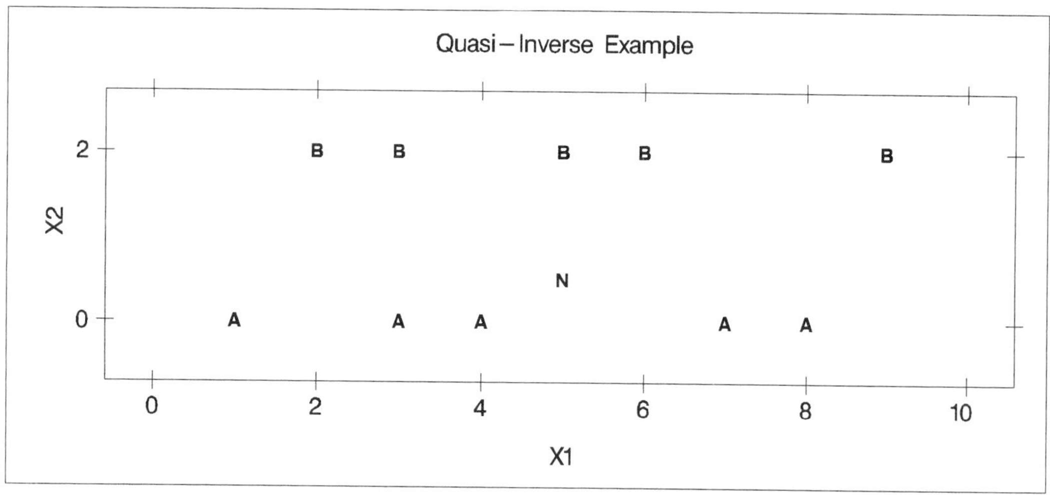

Figure 25.6. Plot of Data with Singular Within-Class Covariance Matrix

Let $\mathbf{S}$ be a singular covariance matrix. The matrix $\mathbf{S}$ can be either a within-group covariance matrix, a pooled covariance matrix, or a total-sample covariance matrix. Let v be the number of variables in the VAR statement and the nullity n be the number of variables among them with (partial) R^2 exceeding $1 - p$. If the determinant of $\mathbf{S}$ (Testing of Homogeneity of Within Covariance Matrices) or the inverse of $\mathbf{S}$ (Squared Distances and Generalized Squared Distances) is required, a quasi-determinant or quasi-inverse is used instead. PROC DISCRIM scales each variable to unit total-sample variance before calculating this quasi-inverse. The calculation is based on the spectral decomposition $\mathbf{S} = \mathbf{\Gamma\Lambda\Gamma}'$, where $\mathbf{\Lambda}$ is a diagonal matrix of eigenvalues λ_j, $j = 1, \ldots, v$, where $\lambda_i \geq \lambda_j$ when $i < j$, and $\mathbf{\Gamma}$ is a matrix with the corresponding orthonormal eigenvectors of $\mathbf{S}$ as columns. When the nullity n is less than v, set $\lambda_j^0 = \lambda_j$ for $j = 1, \ldots, v - n$, and $\lambda_j^0 = p\bar{\lambda}$ for $j = v - n + 1, \ldots, v$, where

$$\bar{\lambda} = \frac{1}{v - n} \sum_{k=1}^{v-n} \lambda_k$$

When the nullity n is equal to v, set $\lambda_j^0 = p$, for $j = 1, \ldots, v$. A quasi-determinant is then defined as the product of λ_j^0, $j = 1, \ldots, v$. Similarly, a quasi-inverse is then defined as $\mathbf{S}^* = \mathbf{\Gamma\Lambda}^*\mathbf{\Gamma}'$, where $\mathbf{\Lambda}^*$ is a diagonal matrix of values $1/\lambda_j^0$, $j = 1, \ldots, v$.

Posterior Probability Error-Rate Estimates

The posterior probability error-rate estimates (Fukunaga and Kessell 1973; Glick 1978; Hora and Wilcox 1982) for each group are based on the posterior probabilities of the observations classified into that same group.

A sample of observations with classification results can be used to estimate the posterior error rates. The following notation is used to describe the sample.

$\mathcal{S}$ the set of observations in the (training) sample

n the number of observations in $\mathcal{S}$

n_t the number of observations in $\mathcal{S}$ in group t

$\mathcal{R}_t$ the set of observations such that the posterior probability belonging to group t is the largest

$\mathcal{R}_{ut}$ the set of observations from group u such that the posterior probability belonging to group t is the largest.

The classification error rate for group t is defined as

$$e_t = 1 - \int_{\mathcal{R}_t} f_t(\mathbf{x})d\mathbf{x}$$

The posterior probability of $\mathbf{x}$ for group t can be written as

$$p(t|\mathbf{x}) = \frac{q_t f_t(\mathbf{x})}{f(\mathbf{x})}$$

where $f(\mathbf{x}) = \sum_u q_u f_u(\mathbf{x})$ is the unconditional density of $\mathbf{x}$.

Thus, if you replace $f_t(\mathbf{x})$ with $p(t|\mathbf{x})f(\mathbf{x})/q_t$, the error rate is

$$e_t = 1 - \frac{1}{q_t}\int_{\mathcal{R}_t} p(t|\mathbf{x})f(\mathbf{x})d\mathbf{x}$$

An estimator of e_t, unstratified over the groups from which the observations come, is then given by

$$\hat{e}_t \text{ (unstratified)} = 1 - \frac{1}{nq_t}\sum_{\mathcal{R}_t} p(t|\mathbf{x})$$

where $p(t|\mathbf{x})$ is estimated from the classification criterion, and the summation is over all sample observations of $\mathcal{S}$ classified into group t. The true group membership of each observation is not required in the estimation. The term nq_t is the number of observations that are expected to be classified into group t, given the priors. If more observations than expected are classified into group t, then $\hat{e}_t$ can be negative.

Further, if you replace $f(\mathbf{x})$ with $\sum_u q_u f_u(\mathbf{x})$, the error rate can be written as

$$e_t = 1 - \frac{1}{q_t}\sum_u q_u \int_{\mathcal{R}_{ut}} p(t|\mathbf{x})f_u(\mathbf{x})d\mathbf{x}$$

and an estimator stratified over the group from which the observations come is given by

$$\hat{e}_t \text{ (stratified)} = 1 - \frac{1}{q_t}\sum_u q_u \frac{1}{n_u}\left(\sum_{\mathcal{R}_{ut}} p(t|\mathbf{x})\right)$$

The inner summation is over all sample observations of $\mathcal{S}$ coming from group u and classified into group t, and n_u is the number of observations originally from group u. The stratified estimate uses only the observations with known group membership. When the prior probabilities of the group membership are proportional to the group sizes, the stratified estimate is the same as the unstratified estimator.

The estimated group-specific error rates can be less than zero, usually due to a large discrepancy between prior probabilities of group membership and group sizes. To have a reliable estimate for group-specific error rate estimates, you should use group sizes that are at least approximately proportional to the prior probabilities of group membership.

A total error rate is defined as a weighted average of the individual group error rates

$$e = \sum_t q_t e_t$$

and can be estimated from

$$\hat{e}\ (\text{unstratified}) = \sum_t q_t \hat{e}_t\ (\text{unstratified})$$

or

$$\hat{e}\ (\text{stratified}) = \sum_t q_t \hat{e}_t\ (\text{stratified})$$

The total unstratified error-rate estimate can also be written as

$$\hat{e}\ (\text{unstratified}) = 1 - \frac{1}{n} \sum_t \sum_{\mathcal{R}_t} p(t|\mathbf{x})$$

which is one minus the average value of the maximum posterior probabilities for each observation in the sample. The prior probabilities of group membership do not appear explicitly in this overall estimate.

Saving and Using Calibration Information

When you specify METHOD=NORMAL to derive a linear or quadratic discriminant function, you can save the calibration information developed by the DISCRIM procedure in a SAS data set by using the OUTSTAT= option in the procedure. PROC DISCRIM then creates a specially structured SAS data set of TYPE=LINEAR, TYPE=QUAD, or TYPE=MIXED that contains the calibration information. For more information on these data sets, see Appendix A, "Special SAS Data Sets." Calibration information cannot be saved when METHOD=NPAR, but you can classify a TESTDATA= data set in the same step. For an example of this, see Example 25.1 on page 1055.

To use this calibration information to classify observations in another data set, specify both of the following:

- the name of the calibration data set after the DATA= option in the PROC DISCRIM statement
- the name of the data set to be classified after the TESTDATA= option in the PROC DISCRIM statement.

Here is an example:

```
data original;
   input position x1 x2;
   datalines;
  ...[data lines]
;

proc discrim outstat=info;
   class position;
run;

data check;
   input position x1 x2;
   datalines;
  ...[second set of data lines]
;

proc discrim data=info testdata=check testlist;
   class position;
run;
```

The first DATA step creates the SAS data set Original, which the DISCRIM procedure uses to develop a classification criterion. Specifying OUTSTAT=INFO in the PROC DISCRIM statement causes the DISCRIM procedure to store the calibration information in a new data set called Info. The next DATA step creates the data set Check. The second PROC DISCRIM statement specifies DATA=INFO and TESTDATA=CHECK so that the classification criterion developed earlier is applied to the Check data set.

Input Data Sets

DATA= Data Set

When you specify METHOD=NPAR, an ordinary SAS data set is required as the input DATA= data set. When you specify METHOD=NORMAL, the DATA= data set can be an ordinary SAS data set or one of several specially structured data sets created by SAS/STAT procedures. These specially structured data sets include

- TYPE=CORR data sets created by PROC CORR using a BY statement
- TYPE=COV data sets created by PROC PRINCOMP using both the COV option and a BY statement

- TYPE=CSSCP data sets created by PROC CORR using the CSSCP option and a BY statement, where the OUT= data set is assigned TYPE=CSSCP with the TYPE= data set option
- TYPE=SSCP data sets created by PROC REG using both the OUTSSCP= option and a BY statement
- TYPE=LINEAR, TYPE=QUAD, and TYPE=MIXED data sets produced by previous runs of PROC DISCRIM that used both METHOD=NORMAL and OUTSTAT= options

When the input data set is TYPE=CORR, TYPE=COV, TYPE=CSSCP, or TYPE=SSCP, the BY variable in these data sets becomes the CLASS variable in the DISCRIM procedure.

When the input data set is TYPE=CORR, TYPE=COV, or TYPE=CSSCP, PROC DISCRIM reads the number of observations for each class from the observations with _TYPE_='N' and reads the variable means in each class from the observations with _TYPE_='MEAN'. PROC DISCRIM then reads the within-class correlations from the observations with _TYPE_='CORR' and reads the standard deviations from the observations with _TYPE_='STD' (data set TYPE=CORR), the within-class covariances from the observations with _TYPE_='COV' (data set TYPE=COV), or the within-class corrected sums of squares and cross products from the observations with _TYPE_='CSSCP' (data set TYPE=CSSCP).

When you specify POOL=YES and the data set does not include any observations with _TYPE_='CSSCP' (data set TYPE=CSSCP), _TYPE_='COV' (data set TYPE=COV), or _TYPE_='CORR' (data set TYPE=CORR) for each class, PROC DISCRIM reads the pooled within-class information from the data set. In this case, PROC DISCRIM reads the pooled within-class covariances from the observations with _TYPE_='PCOV' (data set TYPE=COV) or reads the pooled within-class correlations from the observations with _TYPE_='PCORR' and the pooled within-class standard deviations from the observations with _TYPE_='PSTD' (data set TYPE=CORR) or the pooled within-class corrected SSCP matrix from the observations with _TYPE_='PSSCP' (data set TYPE=CSSCP).

When the input data set is TYPE=SSCP, the DISCRIM procedure reads the number of observations for each class from the observations with _TYPE_='N', the sum of weights of observations for each class from the variable INTERCEP in observations with _TYPE_='SSCP' and _NAME_='INTERCEPT', the variable sums from the variable=*variablenames* in observations with _TYPE_='SSCP' and _NAME_='INTERCEPT', and the uncorrected sums of squares and cross products from the variable=*variablenames* in observations with _TYPE_='SSCP' and _NAME_='variablenames'.

When the input data set is TYPE=LINEAR, TYPE=QUAD, or TYPE=MIXED, PROC DISCRIM reads the prior probabilities for each class from the observations with variable _TYPE_='PRIOR'.

When the input data set is TYPE=LINEAR, PROC DISCRIM reads the coefficients of the linear discriminant functions from the observations with variable _TYPE_='LINEAR' (see page 1048).

When the input data set is TYPE=QUAD, PROC DISCRIM reads the coefficients of the quadratic discriminant functions from the observations with variable _TYPE_='QUAD' (see page 1048).

When the input data set is TYPE=MIXED, PROC DISCRIM reads the coefficients of the linear discriminant functions from the observations with variable _TYPE_='LINEAR'. If there are no observations with _TYPE_='LINEAR', PROC DISCRIM then reads the coefficients of the quadratic discriminant functions from the observations with variable _TYPE_='QUAD' (see page 1048).

TESTDATA= Data Set

The TESTDATA= data set is an ordinary SAS data set with observations that are to be classified. The quantitative variable names in this data set must match those in the DATA= data set. The TESTCLASS statement can be used to specify the variable containing group membership information of the TESTDATA= data set observations. When the TESTCLASS statement is missing and the TESTDATA= data set contains the variable given in the CLASS statement, this variable is used as the TESTCLASS variable. The TESTCLASS variable should have the same type (character or numeric) and length as the variable given in the CLASS statement. PROC DISCRIM considers an observation misclassified when the value of the TESTCLASS variable does not match the group into which the TESTDATA= observation is classified.

Output Data Sets

When an output data set includes variables containing the posterior probabilities of group membership (OUT=, OUTCROSS=, or TESTOUT= data sets) or group-specific density estimates (OUTD= or TESTOUTD= data sets), the names of these variables are constructed from the formatted values of the class levels converted to valid SAS variable names.

OUT= Data Set

The OUT= data set contains all the variables in the DATA= data set, plus new variables containing the posterior probabilities and the resubstitution classification results. The names of the new variables containing the posterior probabilities are constructed from the formatted values of the class levels converted to SAS names. A new variable, _INTO_, with the same attributes as the CLASS variable, specifies the class to which each observation is assigned. If an observation is classified into group OTHER, the variable _INTO_ has a missing value. When you specify the CANONICAL option, the data set also contains new variables with canonical variable scores. The NCAN= option determines the number of canonical variables. The names of the canonical variables are constructed as described in the CANPREFIX= option. The canonical variables have means equal to zero and pooled within-class variances equal to one.

An OUT= data set cannot be created if the DATA= data set is not an ordinary SAS data set.

OUTD= Data Set

The OUTD= data set contains all the variables in the DATA= data set, plus new variables containing the group-specific density estimates. The names of the new variables containing the density estimates are constructed from the formatted values of the class levels.

An OUTD= data set cannot be created if the DATA= data set is not an ordinary SAS data set.

OUTCROSS= Data Set

The OUTCROSS= data set contains all the variables in the DATA= data set, plus new variables containing the posterior probabilities and the classification results of cross validation. The names of the new variables containing the posterior probabilities are constructed from the formatted values of the class levels. A new variable, _INTO_, with the same attributes as the CLASS variable, specifies the class to which each observation is assigned. When an observation is classified into group OTHER, the variable _INTO_ has a missing value. When you specify the CANONICAL option, the data set also contains new variables with canonical variable scores. The NCAN= option determines the number of new variables. The names of the new variables are constructed as described in the CANPREFIX= option. The new variables have mean zero and pooled within-class variance equal to one.

An OUTCROSS= data set cannot be created if the DATA= data set is not an ordinary SAS data set.

TESTOUT= Data Set

The TESTOUT= data set contains all the variables in the TESTDATA= data set, plus new variables containing the posterior probabilities and the classification results. The names of the new variables containing the posterior probabilities are formed from the formatted values of the class levels. A new variable, _INTO_, with the same attributes as the CLASS variable, gives the class to which each observation is assigned. If an observation is classified into group OTHER, the variable _INTO_ has a missing value. When you specify the CANONICAL option, the data set also contains new variables with canonical variable scores. The NCAN= option determines the number of new variables. The names of the new variables are formed as described in the CANPREFIX= option.

TESTOUTD= Data Set

The TESTOUTD= data set contains all the variables in the TESTDATA= data set, plus new variables containing the group-specific density estimates. The names of the new variables containing the density estimates are formed from the formatted values of the class levels.

OUTSTAT= Data Set

The OUTSTAT= data set is similar to the TYPE=CORR data set produced by the CORR procedure. The data set contains various statistics such as means, standard deviations, and correlations. For an example of an OUTSTAT= data set, see Example 25.3 on page 1097. When you specify the CANONICAL option, canonical correlations, canonical structures, canonical coefficients, and means of canonical variables for each class are included in the data set.

If you specify METHOD=NORMAL, the output data set also includes coefficients of the discriminant functions, and the data set is TYPE=LINEAR (POOL=YES), TYPE=QUAD (POOL=NO), or TYPE=MIXED (POOL=TEST). If you specify METHOD=NPAR, this output data set is TYPE=CORR.

The OUTSTAT= data set contains the following variables:

- the BY variables, if any
- the CLASS variable
- _TYPE_, a character variable of length 8 that identifies the type of statistic
- _NAME_, a character variable of length 32 that identifies the row of the matrix, the name of the canonical variable, or the type of the discriminant function coefficients
- the quantitative variables, that is, those in the VAR statement, or, if there is no VAR statement, all numeric variables not listed in any other statement

The observations, as identified by the variable _TYPE_, have the following _TYPE_ values:

TYPE	**Contents**
N	number of observations both for the total sample (CLASS variable missing) and within each class (CLASS variable present)
SUMWGT	sum of weights both for the total sample (CLASS variable missing) and within each class (CLASS variable present), if a WEIGHT statement is specified
MEAN	means both for the total sample (CLASS variable missing) and within each class (CLASS variable present)
PRIOR	prior probability for each class
STDMEAN	total-standardized class means
PSTDMEAN	pooled within-class standardized class means
STD	standard deviations both for the total sample (CLASS variable missing) and within each class (CLASS variable present)
PSTD	pooled within-class standard deviations
BSTD	between-class standard deviations
RSQUARED	univariate R^2s
LNDETERM	the natural log of the determinant or the natural log of the quasi-determinant of the within-class covariance matrix either pooled (CLASS variable missing) or not pooled (CLASS variable present)

The following kinds of observations are identified by the combination of the variables _TYPE_ and _NAME_. When the _TYPE_ variable has one of the following values, the _NAME_ variable identifies the row of the matrix.

TYPE	Contents
CSSCP	corrected SSCP matrix both for the total sample (CLASS variable missing) and within each class (CLASS variable present)
PSSCP	pooled within-class corrected SSCP matrix
BSSCP	between-class SSCP matrix
COV	covariance matrix both for the total sample (CLASS variable missing) and within each class (CLASS variable present)
PCOV	pooled within-class covariance matrix
BCOV	between-class covariance matrix
CORR	correlation matrix both for the total sample (CLASS variable missing) and within each class (CLASS variable present)
PCORR	pooled within-class correlation matrix
BCORR	between-class correlation matrix

When you request canonical discriminant analysis, the _TYPE_ variable can have one of the following values. The _NAME_ variable identifies a canonical variable.

TYPE	Contents
CANCORR	canonical correlations
STRUCTUR	canonical structure
BSTRUCT	between canonical structure
PSTRUCT	pooled within-class canonical structure
SCORE	standardized canonical coefficients
RAWSCORE	raw canonical coefficients
CANMEAN	means of the canonical variables for each class

When you specify METHOD=NORMAL, the _TYPE_ variable can have one of the following values. The _NAME_ variable identifies different types of coefficients in the discriminant function.

TYPE	Contents
LINEAR	coefficients of the linear discriminant functions
QUAD	coefficients of the quadratic discriminant functions

The values of the _NAME_ variable are as follows:

NAME	Contents
variable names	quadratic coefficients of the quadratic discriminant functions (a symmetric matrix for each class)
LINEAR	linear coefficients of the discriminant functions
CONST	constant coefficients of the discriminant functions

Computational Resources

In the following discussion, let

$n =$ number of observations in the training data set

$v =$ number of variables

$c =$ number of class levels

$k =$ number of canonical variables

$l =$ length of the CLASS variable

Memory Requirements

The amount of temporary storage required depends on the discriminant method used and the options specified. The least amount of temporary storage in bytes needed to process the data is approximately

$$c(32v + 3l + 128) + 8v^2 + 104v + 4l$$

A parametric method (METHOD=NORMAL) requires an additional temporary memory of $12v^2 + 100v$ bytes. When you specify the CROSSVALIDATE option, this temporary storage must be increased by $4v^2 + 44v$ bytes. When a nonparametric method (METHOD=NPAR) is used, an additional temporary storage of $10v^2 + 94v$ bytes is needed if you specify METRIC=FULL to evaluate the distances.

With the MANOVA option, the temporary storage must be increased by $8v^2 + 96v$ bytes. The CANONICAL option requires a temporary storage of $2v^2+94v+8k(v+c)$ bytes. The POSTERR option requires a temporary storage of $8c^2 + 64c + 96$ bytes. Additional temporary storage is also required for classification summary and for each output data set.

For example, in the following statements,

```
proc discrim manova;
   class gp;
   var x1 x2 x3;
run;
```

if the CLASS variable gp has a length of eight and the input data set contains two class levels, the procedure requires a temporary storage of 1992 bytes. This includes 1104 bytes for data processing, 480 bytes for using a parametric method, and 408 bytes for specifying the MANOVA option.

Time Requirements

The following factors determine the time requirements of discriminant analysis.

- The time needed for reading the data and computing covariance matrices is proportional to nv^2. PROC DISCRIM must also look up each class level in the list. This is faster if the data are sorted by the CLASS variable. The time for looking up class levels is proportional to a value ranging from n to $n \ln(c)$.
- The time for inverting a covariance matrix is proportional to v^3.
- With a parametric method, the time required to classify each observation is proportional to cv for a linear discriminant function and is proportional to cv^2 for a quadratic discriminant function. When you specify the CROSSVALIDATE option, the discriminant function is updated for each observation in the classification. A substantial amount of time is required.
- With a nonparametric method, the data are stored in a tree structure (Friedman, Bentley, and Finkel 1977). The time required to organize the observations into the tree structure is proportional to $nv \ln(n)$. The time for performing each tree search is proportional to $\ln(n)$. When you specify the normal KERNEL= option, all observations in the training sample contribute to the density estimation and more computer time is needed.
- The time required for the canonical discriminant analysis is proportional to v^3.

Each of the preceding factors has a different machine-dependent constant of proportionality.

Displayed Output

The displayed output from PROC DISCRIM includes the following:

- Class Level Information, including the values of the classification variable, Variable Name constructed from each class value, the Frequency and Weight of each value, its Proportion in the total sample, and the Prior Probability for each class level.

Optional output includes the following:

- Within-Class SSCP Matrices for each group
- Pooled Within-Class SSCP Matrix
- Between-Class SSCP Matrix
- Total-Sample SSCP Matrix
- Within-Class Covariance Matrices, $\mathbf{S}_t$, for each group
- Pooled Within-Class Covariance Matrix, $\mathbf{S}_p$
- Between-Class Covariance Matrix, equal to the between-class SSCP matrix divided by $n(c-1)/c$, where n is the number of observations and c is the number of classes

- Total-Sample Covariance Matrix
- Within-Class Correlation Coefficients and Pr $> |r|$ to test the hypothesis that the within-class population correlation coefficients are zero
- Pooled Within-Class Correlation Coefficients and Pr $> |r|$ to test the hypothesis that the partial population correlation coefficients are zero
- Between-Class Correlation Coefficients and Pr $> |r|$ to test the hypothesis that the between-class population correlation coefficients are zero
- Total-Sample Correlation Coefficients and Pr $> |r|$ to test the hypothesis that the total population correlation coefficients are zero
- Simple descriptive Statistics including N (the number of observations), Sum, Mean, Variance, and Standard Deviation both for the total sample and within each class
- Total-Sample Standardized Class Means, obtained by subtracting the grand mean from each class mean and dividing by the total sample standard deviation
- Pooled Within-Class Standardized Class Means, obtained by subtracting the grand mean from each class mean and dividing by the pooled within-class standard deviation
- Pairwise Squared Distances Between Groups
- Univariate Test Statistics, including Total-Sample Standard Deviations, Pooled Within-Class Standard Deviations, Between-Class Standard Deviations, R^2, $R^2/(1-R^2)$, F, and Pr $> F$ (univariate F values and probability levels for one-way analyses of variance)
- Multivariate Statistics and F Approximations, including Wilks' Lambda, Pillai's Trace, Hotelling-Lawley Trace, and Roy's Greatest Root with F approximations, degrees of freedom (Num DF and Den DF), and probability values (Pr $> F$). Each of these four multivariate statistics tests the hypothesis that the class means are equal in the population. See Chapter 3, "Introduction to Regression Procedures," for more information.

If you specify METHOD=NORMAL, the following three statistics are displayed:

- Covariance Matrix Information, including Covariance Matrix Rank and Natural Log of Determinant of the Covariance Matrix for each group (POOL=TEST, POOL=NO) and for the pooled within-group (POOL=TEST, POOL=YES)
- Optionally, Test of Homogeneity of Within Covariance Matrices (the results of a chi-square test of homogeneity of the within-group covariance matrices) (Morrison 1976; Kendall, Stuart, and Ord 1983; Anderson 1984)
- Pairwise Generalized Squared Distances Between Groups

If the CANONICAL option is specified, the displayed output contains these statistics:

- Canonical Correlations
- Adjusted Canonical Correlations (Lawley 1959). These are asymptotically less biased than the raw correlations and can be negative. The adjusted canonical correlations may not be computable and are displayed as missing values if two canonical correlations are nearly equal or if some are close to zero. A missing value is also displayed if an adjusted canonical correlation is larger than a previous adjusted canonical correlation.
- Approximate Standard Error of the canonical correlations
- Squared Canonical Correlations
- Eigenvalues of $\mathbf{E}^{-1}\mathbf{H}$. Each eigenvalue is equal to $\rho^2/(1-\rho^2)$, where ρ^2 is the corresponding squared canonical correlation and can be interpreted as the ratio of between-class variation to within-class variation for the corresponding canonical variable. The table includes Eigenvalues, Differences between successive eigenvalues, the Proportion of the sum of the eigenvalues, and the Cumulative proportion.
- Likelihood Ratio for the hypothesis that the current canonical correlation and all smaller ones are zero in the population. The likelihood ratio for all canonical correlations equals Wilks' lambda.
- Approximate F statistic based on Rao's approximation to the distribution of the likelihood ratio (Rao 1973, p. 556; Kshirsagar 1972, p. 326)
- Num DF (numerator degrees of freedom), Den DF (denominator degrees of freedom), and $\Pr > F$, the probability level associated with the F statistic

The following statistic concerns the classification criterion:

- the Linear Discriminant Function, but only if you specify METHOD=NORMAL and the pooled covariance matrix is used to calculate the (generalized) squared distances

When the input DATA= data set is an ordinary SAS data set, the displayed output includes the following:

- Optionally, the Resubstitution Results including Obs, the observation number (if an ID statement is included, the values of the ID variable are displayed instead of the observation number), the actual group for the observation, the group into which the developed criterion would classify it, and the Posterior Probability of its Membership in each group
- Resubstitution Summary, a summary of the performance of the classification criterion based on resubstitution classification results
- Error Count Estimate of the resubstitution classification results

- Optionally, Posterior Probability Error Rate Estimates of the resubstitution classification results

If you specify the CROSSVALIDATE option, the displayed output contains these statistics:

- Optionally, the Cross-validation Results including Obs, the observation number (if an ID statement is included, the values of the ID variable are displayed instead of the observation number), the actual group for the observation, the group into which the developed criterion would classify it, and the Posterior Probability of its Membership in each group
- Cross-validation Summary, a summary of the performance of the classification criterion based on cross validation classification results
- Error Count Estimate of the cross validation classification results
- Optionally, Posterior Probability Error Rate Estimates of the cross validation classification results

If you specify the TESTDATA= option, the displayed output contains these statistics:

- Optionally, the Classification Results including Obs, the observation number (if a TESTID statement is included, the values of the ID variable are displayed instead of the observation number), the actual group for the observation (if a TESTCLASS statement is included), the group into which the developed criterion would classify it, and the Posterior Probability of its Membership in each group
- Classification Summary, a summary of the performance of the classification criterion
- Error Count Estimate of the test data classification results
- Optionally, Posterior Probability Error Rate Estimates of the test data classification results

ODS Table Names

PROC DISCRIM assigns a name to each table it creates. You can use these names to reference the table when using the Output Delivery System (ODS) to select tables and create output data sets. These names are listed in the following table. For more information on ODS, see Chapter 15, "Using the Output Delivery System."

Table 25.1. ODS Tables Produced by PROC DISCRIM

ODS Table Name	Description	PROC DISCRIM Option
ANOVA	Univariate statistics	ANOVA
AvePostCrossVal	Average posterior probabilities, cross validation	POSTERR & CROSSVALIDATE
AvePostResub	Average posterior probabilities, resubstitution	POSTERR
AvePostTestClass	Average posterior probabilities, test classification	POSTERR & TEST=
AveRSquare	Average R-Square	ANOVA
BCorr	Between-class correlations	BCORR
BCov	Between-class covariances	BCOV
BSSCP	Between-class SSCP matrix	BSSCP
BStruc	Between canonical structure	CANONICAL
CanCorr	Canonical correlations	CANONICAL
CanonicalMeans	Class means on canonical variables	CANONICAL
ChiSq	Chi-square information	POOL=TEST
ClassifiedCrossVal	Number of observations and percent classified, cross validation	CROSSVALIDATE
ClassifiedResub	Number of observations and percent classified, resubstitution	default
ClassifiedTestClass	Number of observations and percent classified, test classification	TEST=
Counts	Number of observations, variables, classes, df	default
CovDF	DF for covariance matrices, not displayed	any *COV option
Dist	Squared distances	MAHALANOBIS
DistFValues	F values based on squared distances	MAHALANOBIS
DistGeneralized	Generalized squared distances	default
DistProb	Probabilities for F values from squared distances	MAHALANOBIS
ErrorCrossVal	Error count estimates, cross validation	CROSSVALIDATE
ErrorResub	Error count estimates, resubstitution	default
ErrorTestClass	Error count estimates, test classification	TEST=
Levels	Class level information	default
LinearDiscFunc	Linear discriminant function	POOL=YES
LogDet	Log determinant of the covariance matrix	default
MultStat	MANOVA	MANOVA
PCoef	Pooled standard canonical coefficients	CANONICAL

Table 25.1. (continued)

ODS Table Name	Description	PROC DISCRIM Option
PCorr	Pooled within-class correlations	PCORR
PCov	Pooled within-class covariances	PCOV
PSSCP	Pooled within-class SSCP matrix	PSSCP
PStdMeans	Pooled standardized class means	STDMEAN
PStruc	Pooled within canonical structure	CANONICAL
PostCrossVal	Posterior probabilities, cross validation	CROSSLIST or CROSSLISTERR
PostErrCrossVal	Posterior error estimates, cross validation	POSTERR & CROSSVALIDATE
PostErrResub	Posterior error estimates, resubstitution	POSTERR
PostErrTestClass	Posterior error estimates, test classification	POSTERR & TEST=
PostResub	Posterior probabilities, resubstitution	LIST or LISTERR
PostTestClass	Posterior probabilities, test classification	TESTLIST or TESTLISTERR
RCoef	Raw canonical coefficients	CANONICAL
SimpleStatistics	Simple statistics	SIMPLE
TCoef	Total-sample standard canonical coefficients	CANONICAL
TCorr	Total-sample correlations	TCORR
TCov	Total-sample covariances	TCOV
TSSCP	Total-sample SSCP matrix	TSSCP
TStdMeans	Total standardized class means	STDMEAN
TStruc	Total canonical structure	CANONICAL
WCorr	Within-class correlations	WCORR
WCov	Within-class covariances	WCOV
WSSCP	Within-class SSCP matrices	WSSCP

Examples

The iris data published by Fisher (1936) are widely used for examples in discriminant analysis and cluster analysis. The sepal length, sepal width, petal length, and petal width are measured in millimeters on fifty iris specimens from each of three species, *Iris setosa, I. versicolor, and I. virginica.* The iris data are used in Example 25.1 through Example 25.3.

Example 25.4 and Example 25.5 use remote-sensing data on crops. In this data set, the observations are grouped into five crops: clover, corn, cotton, soybeans, and sugar beets. Four measures called X1 through X4 make up the descriptive variables.

Example 25.1. Univariate Density Estimates and Posterior Probabilities

In this example, several discriminant analyses are run with a single quantitative variable, petal width, so that density estimates and posterior probabilities can be plotted easily. The example produces Output 25.1.1 through Output 25.1.5. The GCHART procedure is used to display the sample distribution of petal width in the three species. Note the overlap between species *I. versicolor* and *I. virginica* that the bar chart shows. These statements produce Output 25.1.1:

```
proc format;
   value specname
      1='Setosa    '
      2='Versicolor'
      3='Virginica ';
run;

data iris;
   title 'Discriminant Analysis of Fisher (1936) Iris Data';
   input SepalLength SepalWidth PetalLength PetalWidth
         Species @@;
   format Species specname.;
   label SepalLength='Sepal Length in mm.'
         SepalWidth ='Sepal Width in mm.'
         PetalLength='Petal Length in mm.'
         PetalWidth ='Petal Width in mm.';
   symbol = put(Species, specname10.);
   datalines;
50 33 14 02 1 64 28 56 22 3 65 28 46 15 2 67 31 56 24 3
63 28 51 15 3 46 34 14 03 1 69 31 51 23 3 62 22 45 15 2
59 32 48 18 2 46 36 10 02 1 61 30 46 14 2 60 27 51 16 2
65 30 52 20 3 56 25 39 11 2 65 30 55 18 3 58 27 51 19 3
68 32 59 23 3 51 33 17 05 1 57 28 45 13 2 62 34 54 23 3
77 38 67 22 3 63 33 47 16 2 67 33 57 25 3 76 30 66 21 3
49 25 45 17 3 55 35 13 02 1 67 30 52 23 3 70 32 47 14 2
64 32 45 15 2 61 28 40 13 2 48 31 16 02 1 59 30 51 18 3
55 24 38 11 2 63 25 50 19 3 64 32 53 23 3 52 34 14 02 1
49 36 14 01 1 54 30 45 15 2 79 38 64 20 3 44 32 13 02 1
67 33 57 21 3 50 35 16 06 1 58 26 40 12 2 44 30 13 02 1
77 28 67 20 3 63 27 49 18 3 47 32 16 02 1 55 26 44 12 2
```

```
50 23 33 10 2 72 32 60 18 3 48 30 14 03 1 51 38 16 02 1
61 30 49 18 3 48 34 19 02 1 50 30 16 02 1 50 32 12 02 1
61 26 56 14 3 64 28 56 21 3 43 30 11 01 1 58 40 12 02 1
51 38 19 04 1 67 31 44 14 2 62 28 48 18 3 49 30 14 02 1
51 35 14 02 1 56 30 45 15 2 58 27 41 10 2 50 34 16 04 1
46 32 14 02 1 60 29 45 15 2 57 26 35 10 2 57 44 15 04 1
50 36 14 02 1 77 30 61 23 3 63 34 56 24 3 58 27 51 19 3
57 29 42 13 2 72 30 58 16 3 54 34 15 04 1 52 41 15 01 1
71 30 59 21 3 64 31 55 18 3 60 30 48 18 3 63 29 56 18 3
49 24 33 10 2 56 27 42 13 2 57 30 42 12 2 55 42 14 02 1
49 31 15 02 1 77 26 69 23 3 60 22 50 15 3 54 39 17 04 1
66 29 46 13 2 52 27 39 14 2 60 34 45 16 2 50 34 15 02 1
44 29 14 02 1 50 20 35 10 2 55 24 37 10 2 58 27 39 12 2
47 32 13 02 1 46 31 15 02 1 69 32 57 23 3 62 29 43 13 2
74 28 61 19 3 59 30 42 15 2 51 34 15 02 1 50 35 13 03 1
56 28 49 20 3 60 22 40 10 2 73 29 63 18 3 67 25 58 18 3
49 31 15 01 1 67 31 47 15 2 63 23 44 13 2 54 37 15 02 1
56 30 41 13 2 63 25 49 15 2 61 28 47 12 2 64 29 43 13 2
51 25 30 11 2 57 28 41 13 2 65 30 58 22 3 69 31 54 21 3
54 39 13 04 1 51 35 14 03 1 72 36 61 25 3 65 32 51 20 3
61 29 47 14 2 56 29 36 13 2 69 31 49 15 2 64 27 53 19 3
68 30 55 21 3 55 25 40 13 2 48 34 16 02 1 48 30 14 01 1
45 23 13 03 1 57 25 50 20 3 57 38 17 03 1 51 38 15 03 1
55 23 40 13 2 66 30 44 14 2 68 28 48 14 2 54 34 17 02 1
51 37 15 04 1 52 35 15 02 1 58 28 51 24 3 67 30 50 17 2
63 33 60 25 3 53 37 15 02 1
;

pattern1 c=red    /*v=l1   */;
pattern2 c=yellow /*v=empty*/;
pattern3 c=blue   /*v=r1   */;
axis1 label=(angle=90);
axis2 value=(height=.6);
legend1 frame label=none;

proc gchart data=iris;
   vbar PetalWidth / subgroup=Species midpoints=0 to 25
        raxis=axis1 maxis=axis2 legend=legend1 cframe=ligr;
run;
```

Output 25.1.1. Sample Distribution of Petal Width in Three Species

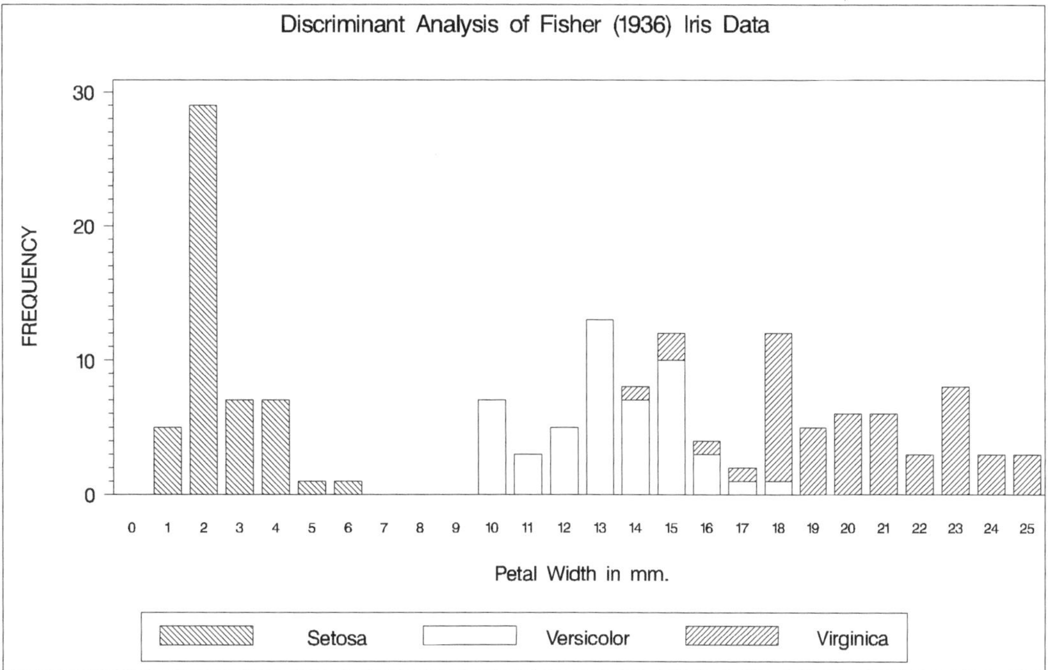

In order to plot the density estimates and posterior probabilities, a data set called plotdata is created containing equally spaced values from -5 to 30, covering the range of petal width with a little to spare on each end. The plotdata data set is used with the TESTDATA= option in PROC DISCRIM.

```
data plotdata;
   do PetalWidth=-5 to 30 by .5;
      output;
   end;
run;
```

The same plots are produced after each discriminant analysis, so a macro can be used to reduce the amount of typing required. The macro PLOT uses two data sets. The data set plotd, containing density estimates, is created by the TESTOUTD= option in PROC DISCRIM. The data set plotp, containing posterior probabilities, is created by the TESTOUT= option. For each data set, the macro PLOT removes uninteresting values (near zero) and does an overlay plot showing all three species on a single plot. The following statements create the macro PLOT

```
%macro plot;
   data plotd;
      set plotd;
      if setosa<.002 then setosa=.;
      if versicolor<.002 then versicolor=.;
      if virginica <.002 then virginica=.;
      label PetalWidth='Petal Width in mm.';
   run;
```

```
   symbol1 i=join v=none c=red    l=1 /*l=21*/;
   symbol2 i=join v=none c=yellow l=1 /*l= 1*/;
   symbol3 i=join v=none c=blue   l=1 /*l= 2*/;
   legend1 label=none frame;
   axis1 label=(angle=90 'Density') order=(0 to .6 by .1);

   proc gplot data=plotd;
      plot setosa*PetalWidth
           versicolor*PetalWidth
           virginica*PetalWidth
           / overlay vaxis=axis1 legend=legend1 frame
             cframe=ligr;
      title3 'Plot of Estimated Densities';
   run;

   data plotp;
      set plotp;
      if setosa<.01 then setosa=.;
      if versicolor<.01 then versicolor=.;
      if virginica<.01 then virginica=.;
      label PetalWidth='Petal Width in mm.';
   run;

   axis1 label=(angle=90 'Posterior Probability')
         order=(0 to 1 by .2);

   proc gplot data=plotp;
      plot setosa*PetalWidth
           versicolor*PetalWidth
           virginica*PetalWidth
           / overlay vaxis=axis1 legend=legend1 frame
             cframe=ligr;
      title3 'Plot of Posterior Probabilities';
   run;
%mend;
```

The first analysis uses normal-theory methods (METHOD=NORMAL) assuming equal variances (POOL=YES) in the three classes. The NOCLASSIFY option suppresses the resubstitution classification results of the input data set observations. The CROSSLISTERR option lists the observations that are misclassified under cross validation and displays cross validation error-rate estimates. The following statements produce Output 25.1.2:

```
proc discrim data=iris method=normal pool=yes
             testdata=plotdata testout=plotp testoutd=plotd
             short noclassify crosslisterr;
   class Species;
   var PetalWidth;
   title2 'Using Normal Density Estimates with Equal Variance';
run;
%plot
```

Output 25.1.2. Normal Density Estimates with Equal Variance

```
              Discriminant Analysis of Fisher (1936) Iris Data
             Using Normal Density Estimates with Equal Variance

                          The DISCRIM Procedure

            Observations    150          DF Total               149
            Variables         1          DF Within Classes      147
            Classes           3          DF Between Classes       2


                         Class Level Information

              Variable                                                Prior
Species       Name          Frequency       Weight    Proportion    Probability

Setosa        Setosa               50      50.0000      0.333333       0.333333
Versicolor    Versicolor           50      50.0000      0.333333       0.333333
Virginica     Virginica            50      50.0000      0.333333       0.333333
```

```
              Discriminant Analysis of Fisher (1936) Iris Data
             Using Normal Density Estimates with Equal Variance

                          The DISCRIM Procedure
          Classification Results for Calibration Data: WORK.IRIS
       Cross-validation Results using Linear Discriminant Function

                 Generalized Squared Distance Function

                   2         _            -1       _
                  D (X) = (X-X    )' COV    (X-X    )
                   j          (X)j      (X)     (X)j

          Posterior Probability of Membership in Each Species

                                2                     2
             Pr(j|X) = exp(-.5 D (X)) / SUM exp(-.5 D (X))
                                j        k            k


              Posterior Probability of Membership in Species

        From          Classified
 Obs    Species       into Species          Setosa    Versicolor     Virginica

   5    Virginica     Versicolor *          0.0000        0.9610        0.0390
   9    Versicolor    Virginica  *          0.0000        0.0952        0.9048
  57    Virginica     Versicolor *          0.0000        0.9940        0.0060
  78    Virginica     Versicolor *          0.0000        0.8009        0.1991
  91    Virginica     Versicolor *          0.0000        0.9610        0.0390
 148    Versicolor    Virginica  *          0.0000        0.3828        0.6172

                      * Misclassified observation
```

```
             Discriminant Analysis of Fisher (1936) Iris Data
             Using Normal Density Estimates with Equal Variance

                           The DISCRIM Procedure
           Classification Summary for Calibration Data: WORK.IRIS
        Cross-validation Summary using Linear Discriminant Function

                 Generalized Squared Distance Function

                  2         _              -1   _
                 D (X) = (X-X    )' COV    (X-X    )
                  j          (X)j       (X)     (X)j

           Posterior Probability of Membership in Each Species

                              2                     2
         Pr(j|X) = exp(-.5 D (X)) / SUM exp(-.5 D (X))
                              j       k             k


        Number of Observations and Percent Classified into Species

  From
  Species          Setosa     Versicolor     Virginica        Total

  Setosa               50              0             0           50
                   100.00           0.00          0.00       100.00

  Versicolor            0             48             2           50
                     0.00          96.00          4.00       100.00

  Virginica             0              4            46           50
                     0.00           8.00         92.00       100.00

  Total                50             52            48          150
                    33.33          34.67         32.00       100.00

  Priors          0.33333        0.33333       0.33333


                  Error Count Estimates for Species

                     Setosa    Versicolor    Virginica        Total

    Rate             0.0000        0.0400       0.0800       0.0400
    Priors           0.3333        0.3333       0.3333
```

```
            Discriminant Analysis of Fisher (1936) Iris Data
          Using Normal Density Estimates with Equal Variance

                        The DISCRIM Procedure
          Classification Summary for Test Data: WORK.PLOTDATA
      Classification Summary using Linear Discriminant Function

               Generalized Squared Distance Function

                        2         _         -1  _
                       D (X) = (X-X )' COV   (X-X )
                        j          j             j

          Posterior Probability of Membership in Each Species

                                2                     2
             Pr(j|X) = exp(-.5 D (X)) / SUM exp(-.5 D (X))
                                j          k          k


    Number of Observations and Percent Classified into Species

                       Setosa     Versicolor     Virginica        Total

    Total                  26             18            27           71
                        36.62          25.35         38.03       100.00

    Priors            0.33333        0.33333       0.33333
```

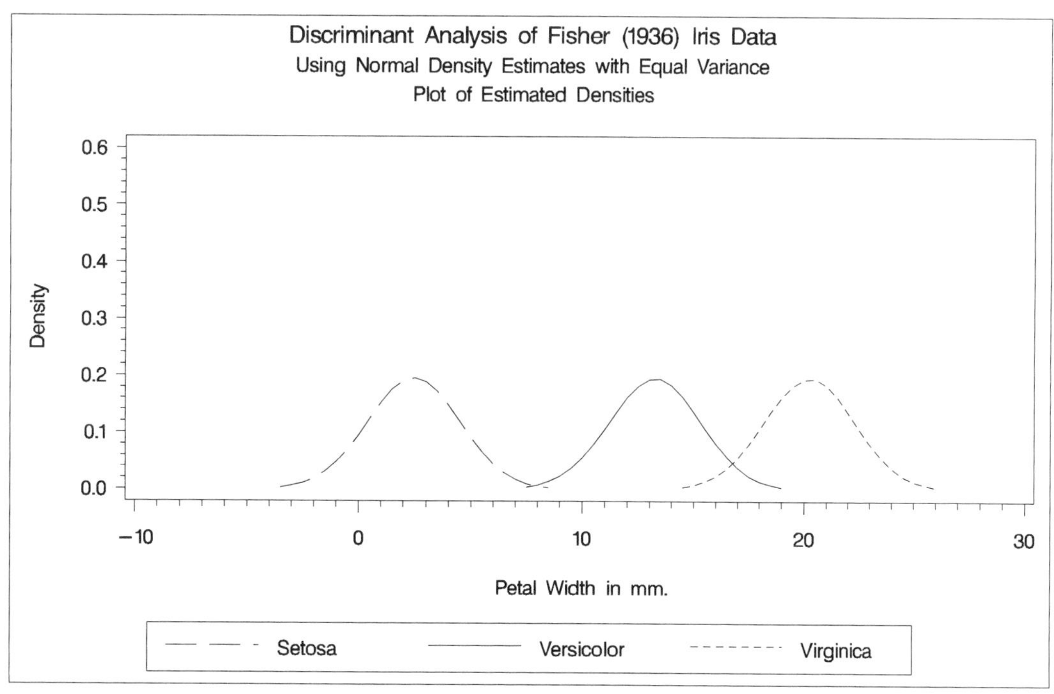

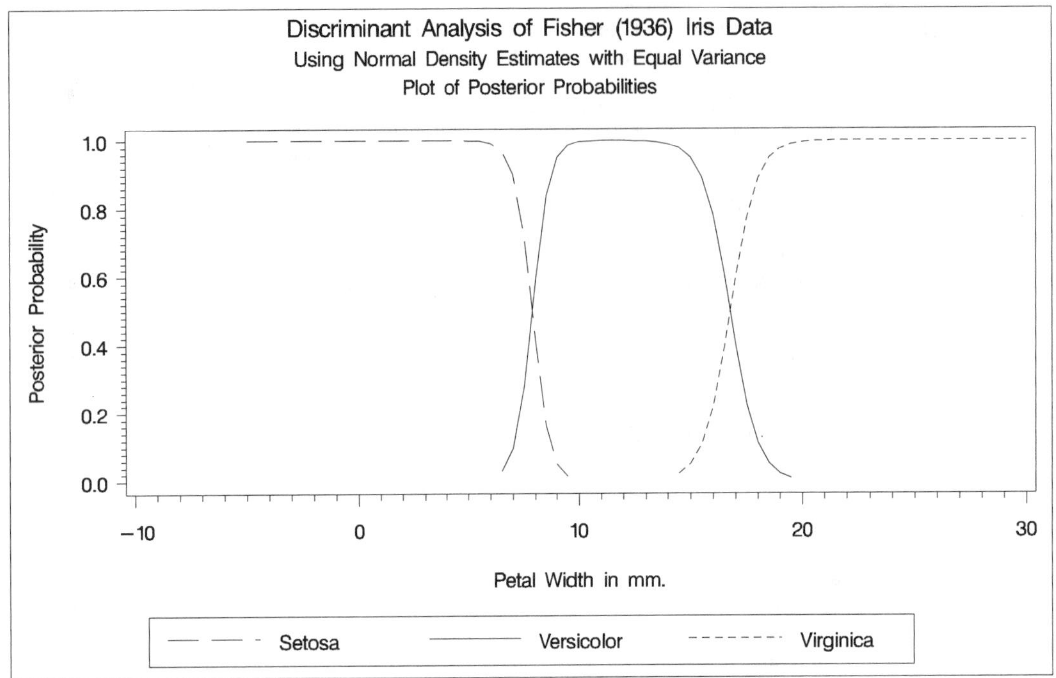

The next analysis uses normal-theory methods assuming unequal variances (POOL=NO) in the three classes. The following statements produce Output 25.1.3:

```
proc discrim data=iris method=normal pool=no
             testdata=plotdata testout=plotp testoutd=plotd
             short noclassify crosslisterr;
   class Species;
   var PetalWidth;
   title2 'Using Normal Density Estimates with Unequal Variance';
run;
%plot
```

Output 25.1.3. Normal Density Estimates with Unequal Variance

```
             Discriminant Analysis of Fisher (1936) Iris Data
           Using Normal Density Estimates with Unequal Variance

                          The DISCRIM Procedure

          Observations     150          DF Total               149
          Variables          1          DF Within Classes      147
          Classes            3          DF Between Classes       2


                         Class Level Information

            Variable                                                  Prior
Species     Name           Frequency       Weight    Proportion    Probability

Setosa      Setosa                50      50.0000      0.333333       0.333333
Versicolor  Versicolor            50      50.0000      0.333333       0.333333
Virginica   Virginica             50      50.0000      0.333333       0.333333
```

```
              Discriminant Analysis of Fisher (1936) Iris Data
            Using Normal Density Estimates with Unequal Variance

                           The DISCRIM Procedure
           Classification Results for Calibration Data: WORK.IRIS
        Cross-validation Results using Quadratic Discriminant Function

                  Generalized Squared Distance Function

             2             _          -1      _
            D (X) = (X-X      )' COV    (X-X     ) + ln |COV     |
             j           (X)j       (X)j    (X)j            (X)j

            Posterior Probability of Membership in Each Species

                                   2                      2
              Pr(j|X) = exp(-.5 D (X)) / SUM exp(-.5 D (X))
                                   j        k             k


              Posterior Probability of Membership in Species

         From          Classified
  Obs    Species       into Species        Setosa    Versicolor     Virginica

    5    Virginica     Versicolor *        0.0000        0.8740        0.1260
    9    Versicolor    Virginica  *        0.0000        0.0686        0.9314
   42    Setosa        Versicolor *        0.4923        0.5073        0.0004
   57    Virginica     Versicolor *        0.0000        0.9602        0.0398
   78    Virginica     Versicolor *        0.0000        0.6558        0.3442
   91    Virginica     Versicolor *        0.0000        0.8740        0.1260
  148    Versicolor    Virginica  *        0.0000        0.2871        0.7129

                       * Misclassified observation
```

```
               Discriminant Analysis of Fisher (1936) Iris Data
             Using Normal Density Estimates with Unequal Variance

                           The DISCRIM Procedure
            Classification Summary for Calibration Data: WORK.IRIS
        Cross-validation Summary using Quadratic Discriminant Function

                   Generalized Squared Distance Function

             2           _            -1    _
             D (X) = (X-X     )' COV     (X-X     ) + ln |COV     |
             j           (X)j       (X)j    (X)j              (X)j

             Posterior Probability of Membership in Each Species

                                  2                     2
               Pr(j|X) = exp(-.5 D (X)) / SUM exp(-.5 D (X))
                                  j         k            k


          Number of Observations and Percent Classified into Species

     From
     Species          Setosa    Versicolor     Virginica        Total

     Setosa               49             1             0           50
                       98.00          2.00          0.00       100.00

     Versicolor            0            48             2           50
                        0.00         96.00          4.00       100.00

     Virginica             0             4            46           50
                        0.00          8.00         92.00       100.00

     Total                49            53            48          150
                       32.67         35.33         32.00       100.00

     Priors          0.33333       0.33333       0.33333


                     Error Count Estimates for Species

                        Setosa    Versicolor    Virginica        Total

       Rate             0.0200        0.0400       0.0800       0.0467
       Priors           0.3333        0.3333       0.3333
```

```
             Discriminant Analysis of Fisher (1936) Iris Data
            Using Normal Density Estimates with Unequal Variance

                          The DISCRIM Procedure
            Classification Summary for Test Data: WORK.PLOTDATA
        Classification Summary using Quadratic Discriminant Function

                  Generalized Squared Distance Function

                   2         _        -1   _
                  D (X) = (X-X )' COV  (X-X ) + ln |COV |
                  j          j      j    j            j

            Posterior Probability of Membership in Each Species

                                  2                    2
            Pr(j|X) = exp(-.5 D (X)) / SUM exp(-.5 D (X))
                                  j        k           k


       Number of Observations and Percent Classified into Species

                     Setosa      Versicolor      Virginica         Total

   Total                 23              20             28            71
                      32.39           28.17          39.44        100.00

   Priors           0.33333         0.33333        0.33333
```

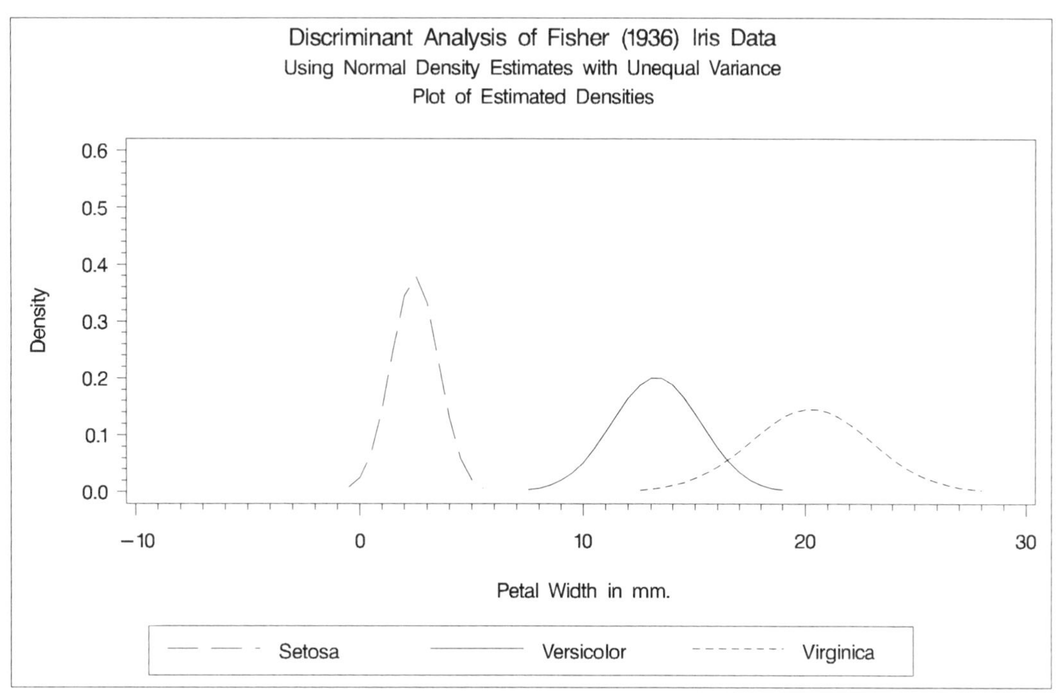

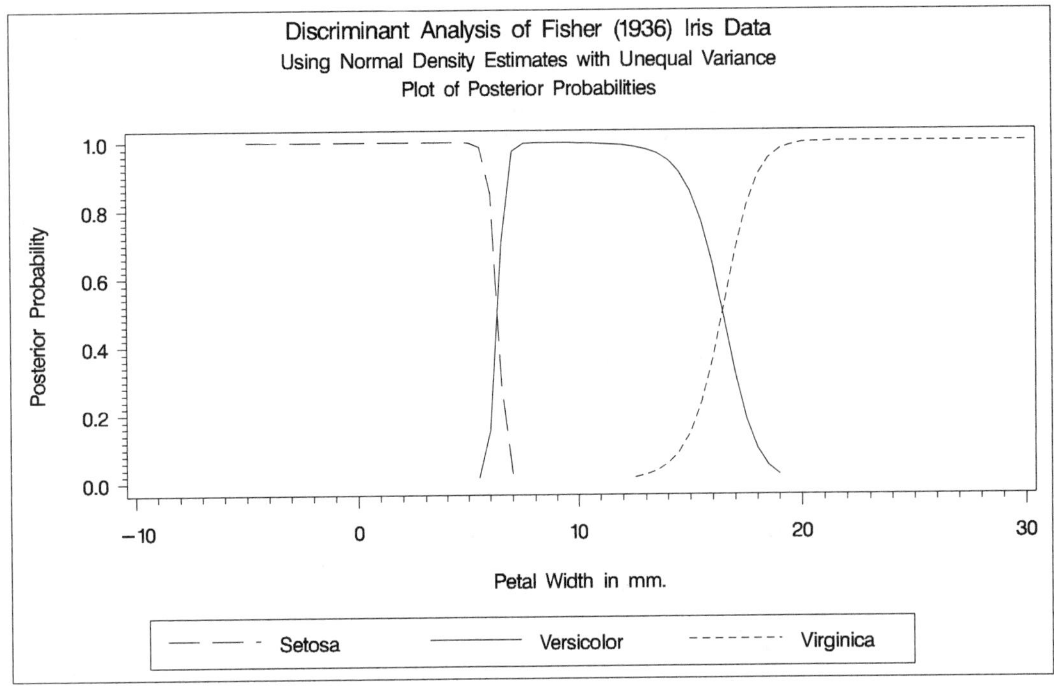

Two more analyses are run with nonparametric methods (METHOD=NPAR), specifically kernel density estimates with normal kernels (KERNEL=NORMAL). The first of these uses equal bandwidths (smoothing parameters) (POOL=YES) in each class. The use of equal bandwidths does not constrain the density estimates to be of equal variance. The value of the radius parameter that, assuming normality, minimizes an approximate mean integrated square error is 0.48 (see the "Nonparametric Methods" section on page 1033). Choosing $r = 0.4$ gives a more detailed look at the irregularities in the data. The following statements produce Output 25.1.4:

```
proc discrim data=iris method=npar kernel=normal
                r=.4 pool=yes
             testdata=plotdata testout=plotp
                testoutd=plotd
             short noclassify crosslisterr;
   class Species;
   var PetalWidth;
   title2 'Using Kernel Density Estimates with Equal
            Bandwidth';
run;
%plot
```

Output 25.1.4. Kernel Density Estimates with Equal Bandwidth

```
                Discriminant Analysis of Fisher (1936) Iris Data
              Using Kernel Density Estimates with Equal Bandwidth

                             The DISCRIM Procedure

            Observations     150          DF Total              149
            Variables          1          DF Within Classes     147
            Classes            3          DF Between Classes      2


                            Class Level Information

              Variable                                                  Prior
Species       Name              Frequency       Weight    Proportion    Probability

Setosa        Setosa                   50      50.0000      0.333333       0.333333
Versicolor    Versicolor               50      50.0000      0.333333       0.333333
Virginica     Virginica                50      50.0000      0.333333       0.333333
```

```
                Discriminant Analysis of Fisher (1936) Iris Data
              Using Kernel Density Estimates with Equal Bandwidth

                             The DISCRIM Procedure
             Classification Results for Calibration Data: WORK.IRIS
              Cross-validation Results using Normal Kernel Density

                           Squared Distance Function

                             2                    -1
                            D (X,Y) = (X-Y)' COV   (X-Y)

              Posterior Probability of Membership in Each Species

                             -1                  2          2
                   F(X|j) = n   SUM exp( -.5 D (X,Y  ) / R  )
                             j   i                  ji

                   Pr(j|X) = PRIOR  F(X|j) / SUM PRIOR  F(X|k)
                                  j              k      k


                Posterior Probability of Membership in Species

       From          Classified
Obs    Species       into Species          Setosa     Versicolor      Virginica

  5    Virginica     Versicolor *          0.0000         0.8827         0.1173
  9    Versicolor    Virginica  *          0.0000         0.0438         0.9562
 57    Virginica     Versicolor *          0.0000         0.9472         0.0528
 78    Virginica     Versicolor *          0.0000         0.8061         0.1939
 91    Virginica     Versicolor *          0.0000         0.8827         0.1173
148    Versicolor    Virginica  *          0.0000         0.2586         0.7414

                          * Misclassified observation
```

```
               Discriminant Analysis of Fisher (1936) Iris Data
             Using Kernel Density Estimates with Equal Bandwidth

                           The DISCRIM Procedure
            Classification Summary for Calibration Data: WORK.IRIS
             Cross-validation Summary using Normal Kernel Density

                          Squared Distance Function

                          2                   -1
                         D (X,Y) = (X-Y)' COV   (X-Y)

              Posterior Probability of Membership in Each Species

                          -1              2            2
                 F(X|j) = n    SUM exp( -.5 D (X,Y   ) / R  )
                           j    i                  ji

                   Pr(j|X) = PRIOR  F(X|j) / SUM PRIOR  F(X|k)
                                  j               k        k


         Number of Observations and Percent Classified into Species

     From
     Species          Setosa     Versicolor     Virginica       Total

     Setosa               50              0             0          50
                      100.00           0.00          0.00      100.00

     Versicolor            0             48             2          50
                        0.00          96.00          4.00      100.00

     Virginica             0              4            46          50
                        0.00           8.00         92.00      100.00

     Total                50             52            48         150
                       33.33          34.67         32.00      100.00

     Priors          0.33333        0.33333       0.33333


                      Error Count Estimates for Species

                        Setosa    Versicolor    Virginica       Total

       Rate             0.0000        0.0400       0.0800      0.0400
       Priors           0.3333        0.3333       0.3333
```

```
              Discriminant Analysis of Fisher (1936) Iris Data
            Using Kernel Density Estimates with Equal Bandwidth

                          The DISCRIM Procedure
            Classification Summary for Test Data: WORK.PLOTDATA
             Classification Summary using Normal Kernel Density

                        Squared Distance Function

                          2                    -1
                         D (X,Y) = (X-Y)' COV   (X-Y)

            Posterior Probability of Membership in Each Species

                         -1                2           2
              F(X|j) = n    SUM exp( -.5 D (X,Y   ) / R  )
                         j   i                 ji

              Pr(j|X) = PRIOR  F(X|j) / SUM PRIOR  F(X|k)
                             j           k       k


        Number of Observations and Percent Classified into Species

                      Setosa     Versicolor     Virginica        Total

    Total                 26             18            27           71
                       36.62          25.35         38.03       100.00

    Priors           0.33333        0.33333       0.33333
```

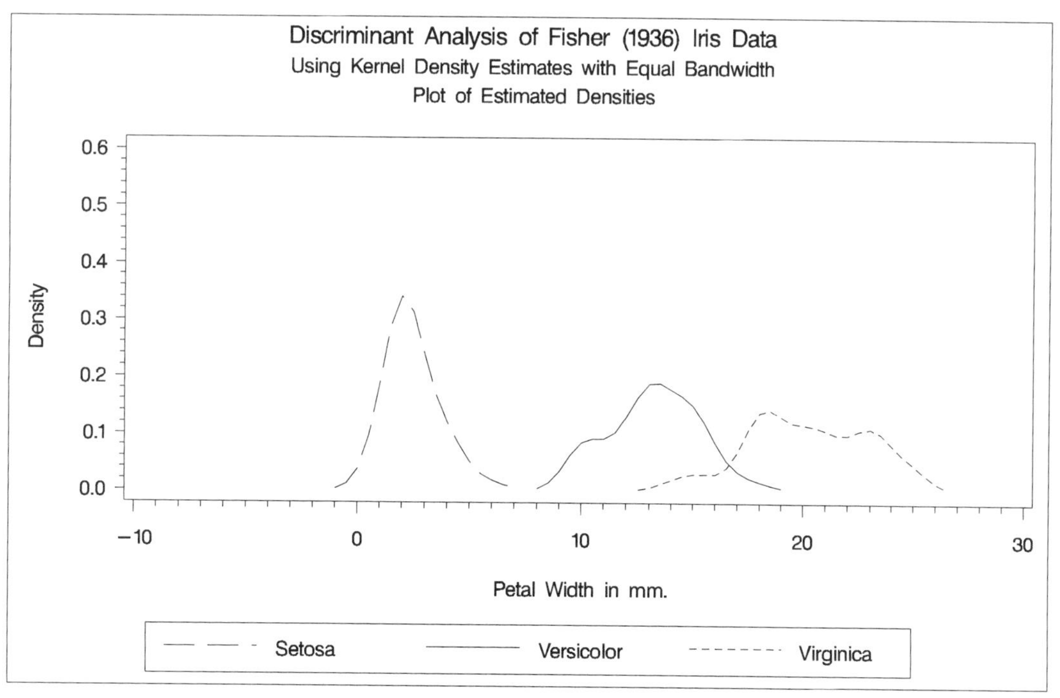

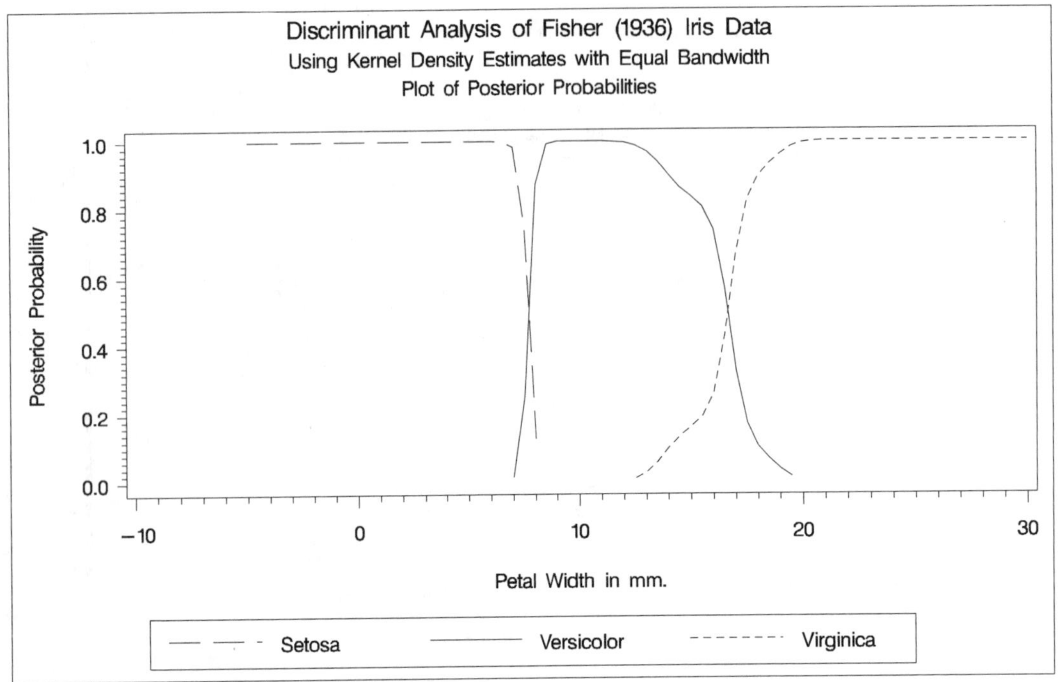

Another nonparametric analysis is run with unequal bandwidths (POOL=NO). These statements produce Output 25.1.5:

```
proc discrim data=iris method=npar kernel=normal
                r=.4 pool=no
             testdata=plotdata testout=plotp
                testoutd=plotd
             short noclassify crosslisterr;
   class Species;
   var PetalWidth;
   title2 'Using Kernel Density Estimates with Unequal
           Bandwidth';
run;
%plot
```

Output 25.1.5. Kernel Density Estimates with Unequal Bandwidth

```
                Discriminant Analysis of Fisher (1936) Iris Data
             Using Kernel Density Estimates with Unequal Bandwidth

                             The DISCRIM Procedure

            Observations    150           DF Total                149
            Variables         1           DF Within Classes       147
            Classes           3           DF Between Classes        2


                            Class Level Information

              Variable                                                    Prior
Species       Name              Frequency        Weight    Proportion    Probability

Setosa        Setosa                   50       50.0000      0.333333       0.333333
Versicolor    Versicolor               50       50.0000      0.333333       0.333333
Virginica     Virginica                50       50.0000      0.333333       0.333333
```

```
                Discriminant Analysis of Fisher (1936) Iris Data
             Using Kernel Density Estimates with Unequal Bandwidth

                             The DISCRIM Procedure
             Classification Results for Calibration Data: WORK.IRIS
              Cross-validation Results using Normal Kernel Density

                            Squared Distance Function

                            2                   -1
                           D (X,Y) = (X-Y)' COV  (X-Y)
                                                j

              Posterior Probability of Membership in Each Species

                              -1              2          2
                     F(X|j) = n   SUM exp( -.5 D (X,Y  ) / R  )
                              j   i                  ji

                     Pr(j|X) = PRIOR  F(X|j) / SUM PRIOR  F(X|k)
                                    j             k       k


                Posterior Probability of Membership in Species

       From          Classified
 Obs   Species       into Species        Setosa    Versicolor      Virginica

   5   Virginica     Versicolor *        0.0000        0.8805         0.1195
   9   Versicolor    Virginica  *        0.0000        0.0466         0.9534
  57   Virginica     Versicolor *        0.0000        0.9394         0.0606
  78   Virginica     Versicolor *        0.0000        0.7193         0.2807
  91   Virginica     Versicolor *        0.0000        0.8805         0.1195
 148   Versicolor    Virginica  *        0.0000        0.2275         0.7725

                          * Misclassified observation
```

```
              Discriminant Analysis of Fisher (1936) Iris Data
           Using Kernel Density Estimates with Unequal Bandwidth

                          The DISCRIM Procedure
           Classification Summary for Calibration Data: WORK.IRIS
            Cross-validation Summary using Normal Kernel Density

                        Squared Distance Function

                        2                   -1
                       D (X,Y) = (X-Y)' COV  (X-Y)
                                            j

            Posterior Probability of Membership in Each Species

                    -1                   2           2
         F(X|j) = n   SUM exp( -.5 D (X,Y  ) / R  )
                    j   i                   ji

         Pr(j|X) = PRIOR  F(X|j) / SUM PRIOR  F(X|k)
                        j             k      k


        Number of Observations and Percent Classified into Species

    From
    Species           Setosa    Versicolor     Virginica        Total

    Setosa                50             0             0           50
                      100.00          0.00          0.00       100.00

    Versicolor             0            48             2           50
                        0.00         96.00          4.00       100.00

    Virginica              0             4            46           50
                        0.00          8.00         92.00       100.00

    Total                 50            52            48          150
                       33.33         34.67         32.00       100.00

    Priors           0.33333       0.33333       0.33333


                      Error Count Estimates for Species

                         Setosa    Versicolor    Virginica       Total

      Rate               0.0000        0.0400       0.0800      0.0400
      Priors             0.3333        0.3333       0.3333
```

```
              Discriminant Analysis of Fisher (1936) Iris Data
           Using Kernel Density Estimates with Unequal Bandwidth

                          The DISCRIM Procedure
            Classification Summary for Test Data: WORK.PLOTDATA
             Classification Summary using Normal Kernel Density

                        Squared Distance Function

                          2                   -1
                         D (X,Y) = (X-Y)' COV   (X-Y)
                                               j

           Posterior Probability of Membership in Each Species

                          -1                  2           2
                 F(X|j) = n   SUM exp( -.5 D (X,Y   ) / R   )
                           j   i                   ji

                 Pr(j|X) = PRIOR  F(X|j) / SUM PRIOR  F(X|k)
                                j             k       k


         Number of Observations and Percent Classified into Species

                       Setosa      Versicolor      Virginica        Total

     Total                 25              18             28           71
                        35.21           25.35          39.44       100.00

     Priors           0.33333         0.33333        0.33333
```

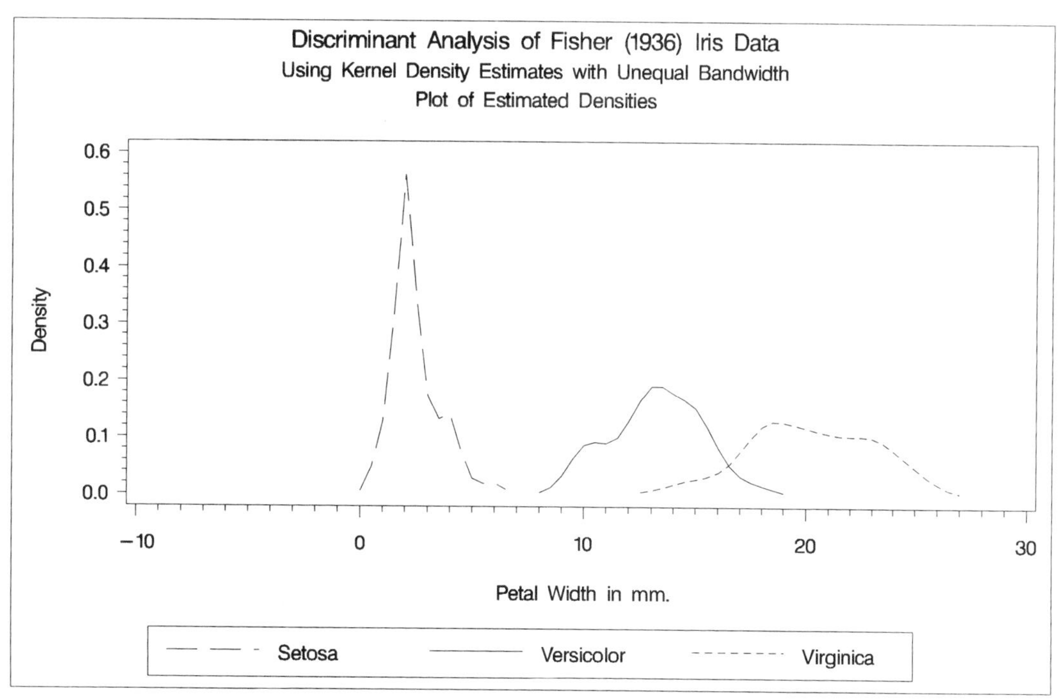

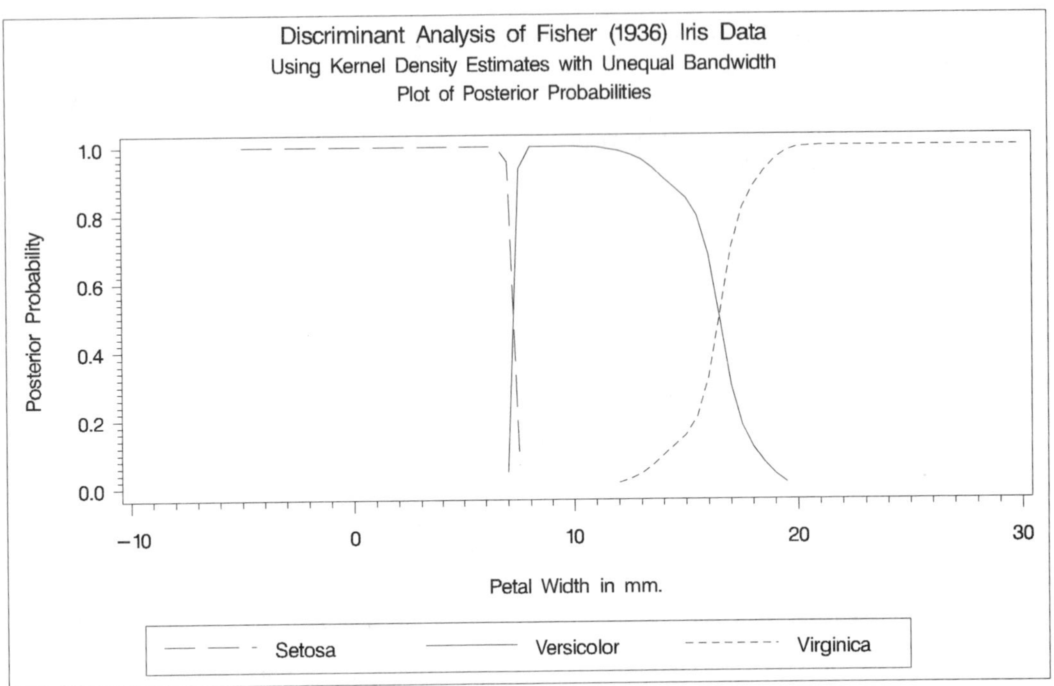

Example 25.2. Bivariate Density Estimates and Posterior Probabilities

In this example, four more discriminant analyses of iris data are run with two quantitative variables: petal width and petal length. The example produces Output 25.2.1 through Output 25.2.5. A scatter plot shows the joint sample distribution. See Appendix B, "Using the %PLOTIT Macro," for more information on the %PLOTIT macro.

```
%plotit(data=iris, plotvars=PetalWidth PetalLength,
        labelvar=_blank_, symvar=symbol, typevar=symbol,
        symsize=0.35, symlen=4, exttypes=symbol, ls=100);
```

Output 25.2.1. Joint Sample Distribution of Petal Width and Petal Length in Three Species

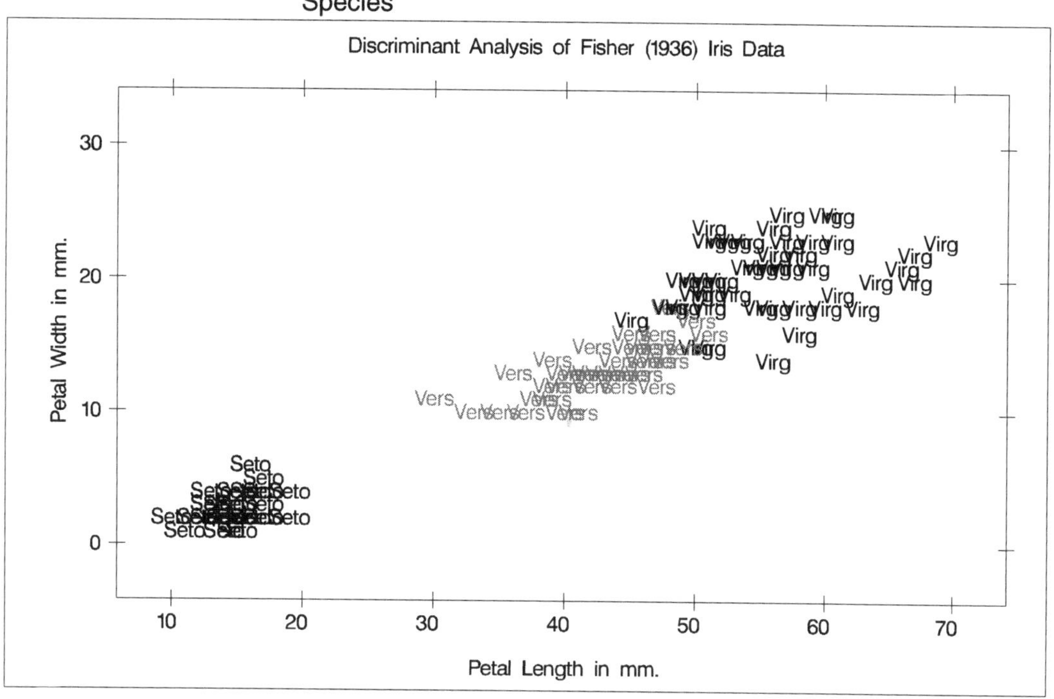

Another data set is created for plotting, containing a grid of points suitable for contour plots. The large number of points in the grid makes the following analyses very time-consuming. If you attempt to duplicate these examples, begin with a small number of points in the grid.

```
data plotdata;
   do PetalLength=-2 to 72 by 0.25;
      h + 1;     * Number of horizontal cells;
      do PetalWidth=-5 to 32 by 0.25;
         n + 1; * Total number of cells;
         output;
      end;
   end;
   * Make variables to contain H and V grid sizes;
   call symput('hnobs', compress(put(h    , best12.)));
   call symput('vnobs', compress(put(n / h, best12.)));
   drop n h;
run;
```

A macro CONTOUR is defined to make contour plots of density estimates and posterior probabilities. Classification results are also plotted on the same grid.

```
%macro contour;
   data contour(keep=PetalWidth PetalLength symbol density);
      set plotd(in=d) iris;
      if d then density = max(setosa,versicolor,virginica);
   run;

   title3 'Plot of Estimated Densities';
   %plotit(data=contour, plotvars=PetalWidth PetalLength,
           labelvar=_blank_, symvar=symbol, typevar=symbol,
           symlen=4, exttypes=symbol contour, ls=100,
           paint=density white black, rgbtypes=contour,
           hnobs=&hnobs, vnobs=&vnobs, excolors=white,
           rgbround=-16 1 1 1,  extend=close, options=noclip,
           types  =Setosa Versicolor Virginica  '',
           symtype=symbol symbol     symbol     contour,
           symsize=0.6    0.6        0.6        1,
           symfont=swiss  swiss      swiss      solid)

   data posterior(keep=PetalWidth PetalLength symbol
        prob _into_);
      set plotp(in=d) iris;
      if d then prob = max(setosa,versicolor,virginica);
   run;

   title3 'Plot of Posterior Probabilities '
          '(Black to White is Low to High Probability)';
   %plotit(data=posterior, plotvars=PetalWidth PetalLength,
           labelvar=_blank_, symvar=symbol, typevar=symbol,
           symlen=4, exttypes=symbol contour, ls=100,
           paint=prob black white 0.3 0.999, rgbtypes=contour,
           hnobs=&hnobs, vnobs=&vnobs,  excolors=white,
           rgbround=-16 1 1 1, extend=close, options=noclip,
           types  =Setosa Versicolor Virginica  '',
           symtype=symbol symbol     symbol     contour,
           symsize=0.6    0.6        0.6        1,
           symfont=swiss  swiss      swiss      solid)

   title3 'Plot of Classification Results';
   %plotit(data=posterior, plotvars=PetalWidth PetalLength,
           labelvar=_blank_, symvar=symbol, typevar=symbol,
           symlen=4, exttypes=symbol contour, ls=100,
           paint=_into_ CXCCCCCC CXDDDDDD white,
              rgbtypes=contour, hnobs=&hnobs, vnobs=&vnobs,
              excolors=white,
           extend=close, options=noclip,
           types  =Setosa Versicolor Virginica  '',
           symtype=symbol symbol     symbol     contour,
           symsize=0.6    0.6        0.6        1,
           symfont=swiss  swiss      swiss      solid)

%mend;
```

A normal-theory analysis (METHOD=NORMAL) assuming equal covariance matrices (POOL=YES) illustrates the linearity of the classification boundaries. These statements produce Output 25.2.2:

```
proc discrim data=iris method=normal pool=yes
             testdata=plotdata testout=plotp testoutd=plotd
             short noclassify crosslisterr;
   class Species;
   var Petal:;
   title2 'Using Normal Density Estimates with Equal
           Variance';
run;
%contour
```

Output 25.2.2. Normal Density Estimates with Equal Variance

```
                Discriminant Analysis of Fisher (1936) Iris Data
               Using Normal Density Estimates with Equal Variance

                             The DISCRIM Procedure

            Observations     150          DF Total               149
            Variables          2          DF Within Classes      147
            Classes            3          DF Between Classes       2


                            Class Level Information

              Variable                                                  Prior
Species       Name              Frequency       Weight    Proportion    Probability

Setosa        Setosa                   50      50.0000      0.333333       0.333333
Versicolor    Versicolor               50      50.0000      0.333333       0.333333
Virginica     Virginica                50      50.0000      0.333333       0.333333
```

```
                Discriminant Analysis of Fisher (1936) Iris Data
               Using Normal Density Estimates with Equal Variance

                             The DISCRIM Procedure
              Classification Results for Calibration Data: WORK.IRIS
            Cross-validation Results using Linear Discriminant Function

                      Generalized Squared Distance Function

                          2         _              -1     _
                         D (X) = (X-X    )' COV     (X-X    )
                          j           (X)j       (X)      (X)j

              Posterior Probability of Membership in Each Species

                                 2                         2
               Pr(j|X) = exp(-.5 D (X)) / SUM exp(-.5 D (X))
                                 j           k             k


                Posterior Probability of Membership in Species

          From          Classified
   Obs    Species       into Species          Setosa    Versicolor     Virginica

     5    Virginica     Versicolor *          0.0000        0.8453        0.1547
     9    Versicolor    Virginica  *          0.0000        0.2130        0.7870
    25    Virginica     Versicolor *          0.0000        0.8322        0.1678
    57    Virginica     Versicolor *          0.0000        0.8057        0.1943
    91    Virginica     Versicolor *          0.0000        0.8903        0.1097
   148    Versicolor    Virginica  *          0.0000        0.3118        0.6882

                         * Misclassified observation
```

```
              Discriminant Analysis of Fisher (1936) Iris Data
             Using Normal Density Estimates with Equal Variance

                         The DISCRIM Procedure
           Classification Summary for Calibration Data: WORK.IRIS
        Cross-validation Summary using Linear Discriminant Function

                  Generalized Squared Distance Function

                       2         _           -1     _
                      D (X) = (X-X    )' COV    (X-X    )
                       j          (X)j       (X)      (X)j

            Posterior Probability of Membership in Each Species

                                     2                     2
              Pr(j|X) = exp(-.5 D (X)) / SUM exp(-.5 D (X))
                                     j         k             k


      Number of Observations and Percent Classified into Species

  From
  Species          Setosa      Versicolor      Virginica        Total

  Setosa               50               0              0           50
                   100.00            0.00           0.00       100.00

  Versicolor            0              48              2           50
                     0.00           96.00           4.00       100.00

  Virginica             0               4             46           50
                     0.00            8.00          92.00       100.00

  Total                50              52             48          150
                    33.33           34.67          32.00       100.00

  Priors          0.33333         0.33333        0.33333


                    Error Count Estimates for Species

                     Setosa    Versicolor    Virginica        Total

   Rate              0.0000        0.0400       0.0800       0.0400
   Priors            0.3333        0.3333       0.3333
```

```
                  Discriminant Analysis of Fisher (1936) Iris Data
                  Using Normal Density Estimates with Equal Variance

                            The DISCRIM Procedure
               Classification Summary for Test Data: WORK.PLOTDATA
            Classification Summary using Linear Discriminant Function

                     Generalized Squared Distance Function

                          2         _       -1   _
                         D (X) = (X-X )' COV   (X-X )
                          j         j             j

                 Posterior Probability of Membership in Each Species

                                 2                     2
                 Pr(j|X) = exp(-.5 D (X)) / SUM exp(-.5 D (X))
                                    j        k            k


         Number of Observations and Percent Classified into Species

                        Setosa     Versicolor    Virginica        Total

      Total              14507          16888        12858        44253
                         32.78          38.16        29.06       100.00

      Priors           0.33333        0.33333      0.33333
```

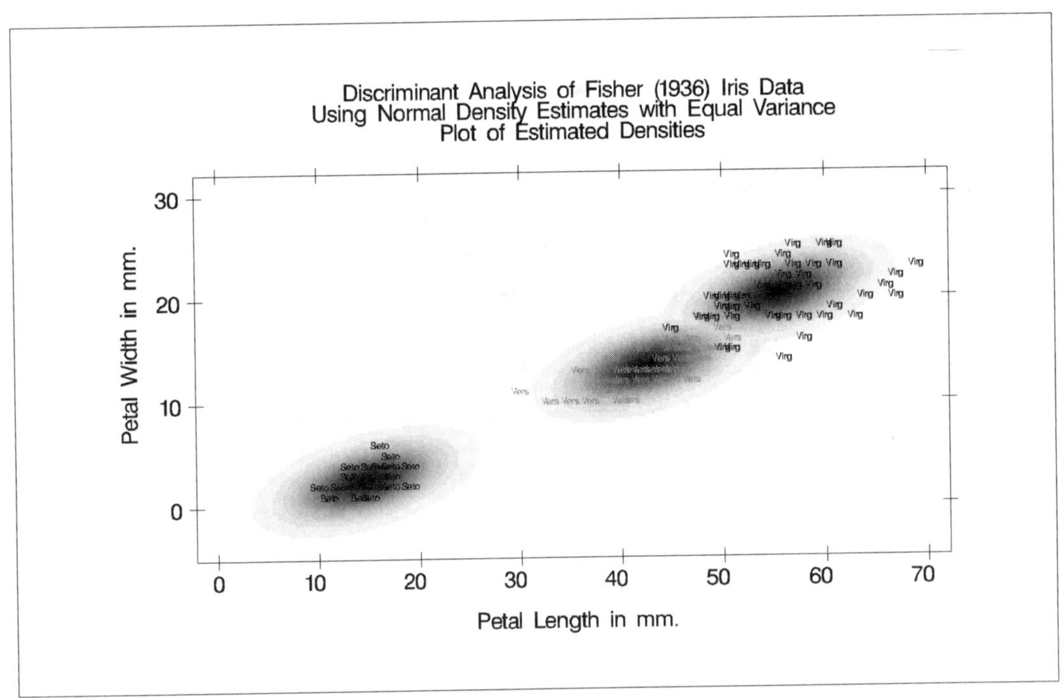

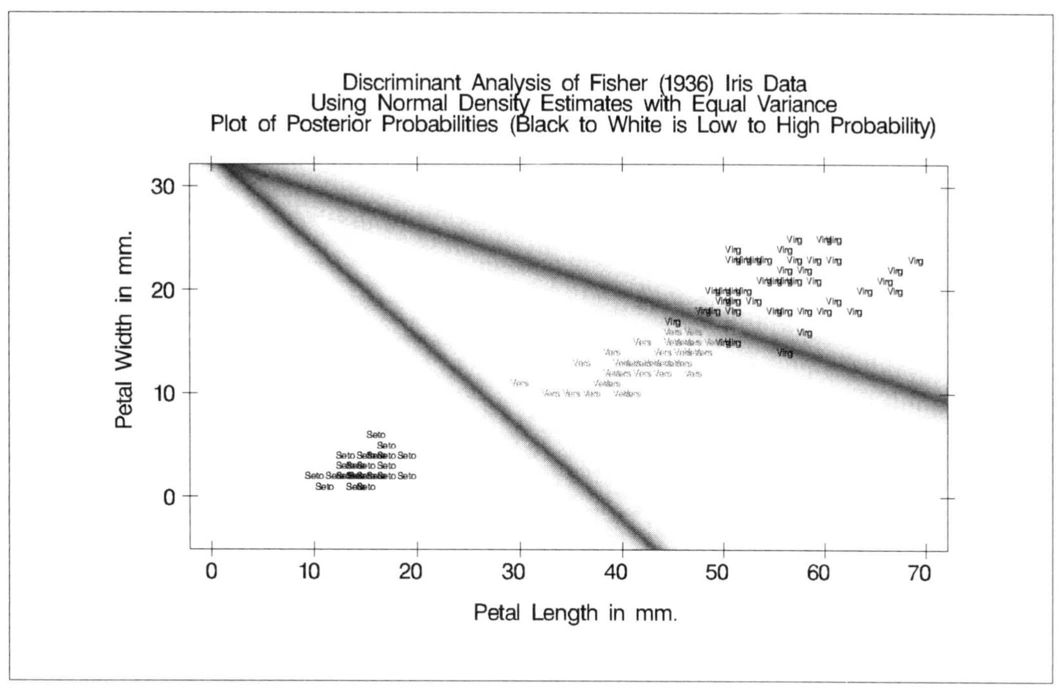
Discriminant Analysis of Fisher (1936) Iris Data
Using Normal Density Estimates with Equal Variance
Plot of Posterior Probabilities (Black to White is Low to High Probability)
Petal Width in mm.
Petal Length in mm.

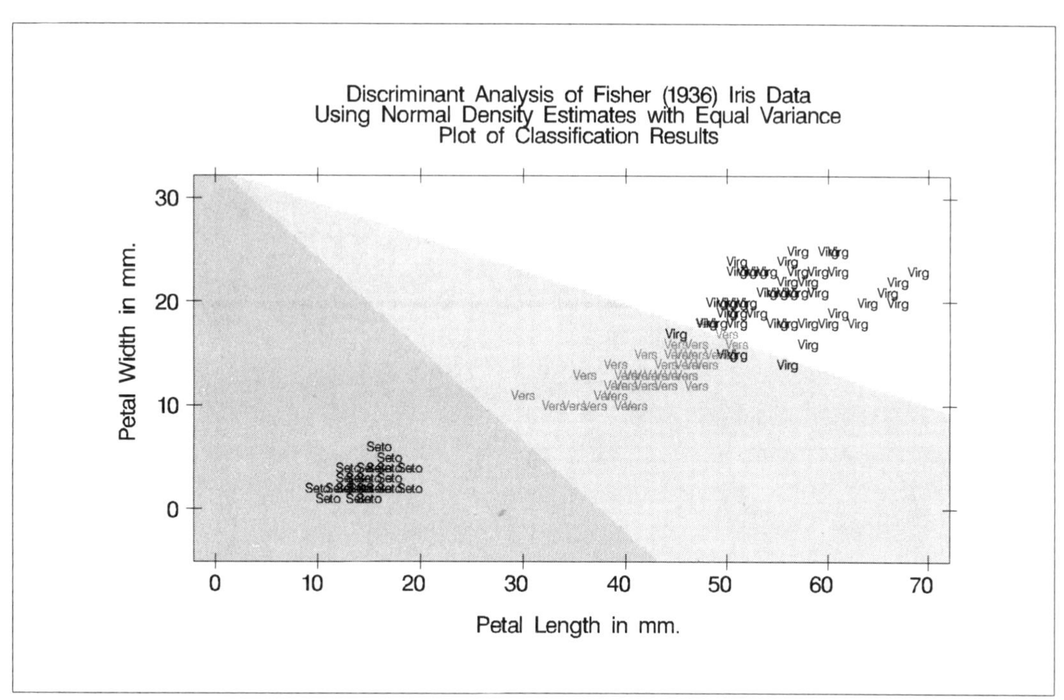
Discriminant Analysis of Fisher (1936) Iris Data
Using Normal Density Estimates with Equal Variance
Plot of Classification Results
Petal Width in mm.
Petal Length in mm.

A normal-theory analysis assuming unequal covariance matrices (POOL=NO) illustrates quadratic classification boundaries. These statements produce Output 25.2.3:

```
proc discrim data=iris method=normal pool=no
             testdata=plotdata testout=plotp testoutd=plotd
             short noclassify crosslisterr;
   class Species;
   var Petal:;
   title2 'Using Normal Density Estimates with Unequal
          Variance';
run;
%contour
```

Output 25.2.3. Normal Density Estimates with Unequal Variance

```
                  Discriminant Analysis of Fisher (1936) Iris Data
                Using Normal Density Estimates with Unequal Variance

                              The DISCRIM Procedure

             Observations     150          DF Total               149
             Variables          2          DF Within Classes      147
             Classes            3          DF Between Classes       2


                             Class Level Information

              Variable                                                          Prior
Species       Name              Frequency       Weight     Proportion     Probability

Setosa        Setosa                   50      50.0000       0.333333        0.333333
Versicolor    Versicolor               50      50.0000       0.333333        0.333333
Virginica     Virginica                50      50.0000       0.333333        0.333333
```

Discriminant Analysis of Fisher (1936) Iris Data
Using Normal Density Estimates with Unequal Variance

The DISCRIM Procedure
Classification Results for Calibration Data: WORK.IRIS
Cross-validation Results using Quadratic Discriminant Function

Generalized Squared Distance Function

$$D_j^2(X) = (X-\bar{X}_{(X)j})' \, COV_{(X)j}^{-1} \, (X-\bar{X}_{(X)j}) + \ln |COV_{(X)j}|$$

Posterior Probability of Membership in Each Species

$$Pr(j|X) = \exp(-.5 \, D_j^2(X)) \;/\; SUM_k \exp(-.5 \, D_k^2(X))$$

Posterior Probability of Membership in Species

Obs	From Species	Classified into Species	Setosa	Versicolor	Virginica
5	Virginica	Versicolor *	0.0000	0.7288	0.2712
9	Versicolor	Virginica *	0.0000	0.0903	0.9097
25	Virginica	Versicolor *	0.0000	0.5196	0.4804
91	Virginica	Versicolor *	0.0000	0.8335	0.1665
148	Versicolor	Virginica *	0.0000	0.4675	0.5325

* Misclassified observation

Discriminant Analysis of Fisher (1936) Iris Data
Using Normal Density Estimates with Unequal Variance

The DISCRIM Procedure
Classification Summary for Calibration Data: WORK.IRIS
Cross-validation Summary using Quadratic Discriminant Function

Generalized Squared Distance Function

$$D_j^2(X) = (X-\bar{X}_{(X)j})' \, COV_{(X)j}^{-1} (X-\bar{X}_{(X)j}) + \ln |COV_{(X)j}|$$

Posterior Probability of Membership in Each Species

$$Pr(j|X) = \exp(-.5 D_j^2(X)) / SUM_k \exp(-.5 D_k^2(X))$$

Number of Observations and Percent Classified into Species

From Species	Setosa	Versicolor	Virginica	Total
Setosa	50 100.00	0 0.00	0 0.00	50 100.00
Versicolor	0 0.00	48 96.00	2 4.00	50 100.00
Virginica	0 0.00	3 6.00	47 94.00	50 100.00
Total	50 33.33	51 34.00	49 32.67	150 100.00
Priors	0.33333	0.33333	0.33333	

Error Count Estimates for Species

	Setosa	Versicolor	Virginica	Total
Rate	0.0000	0.0400	0.0600	0.0333
Priors	0.3333	0.3333	0.3333	

```
           Discriminant Analysis of Fisher (1936) Iris Data
          Using Normal Density Estimates with Unequal Variance

                        The DISCRIM Procedure
          Classification Summary for Test Data: WORK.PLOTDATA
        Classification Summary using Quadratic Discriminant Function

                 Generalized Squared Distance Function

                  2          _         -1    _
                 D (X) = (X-X )' COV   (X-X ) + ln |COV |
                  j          j      j     j          j

          Posterior Probability of Membership in Each Species

                                 2                     2
            Pr(j|X) = exp(-.5 D (X)) / SUM exp(-.5 D (X))
                                 j         k           k


       Number of Observations and Percent Classified into Species

                      Setosa      Versicolor     Virginica        Total

  Total                 5461           5354          33438        44253
                       12.34          12.10          75.56       100.00

  Priors             0.33333        0.33333        0.33333
```

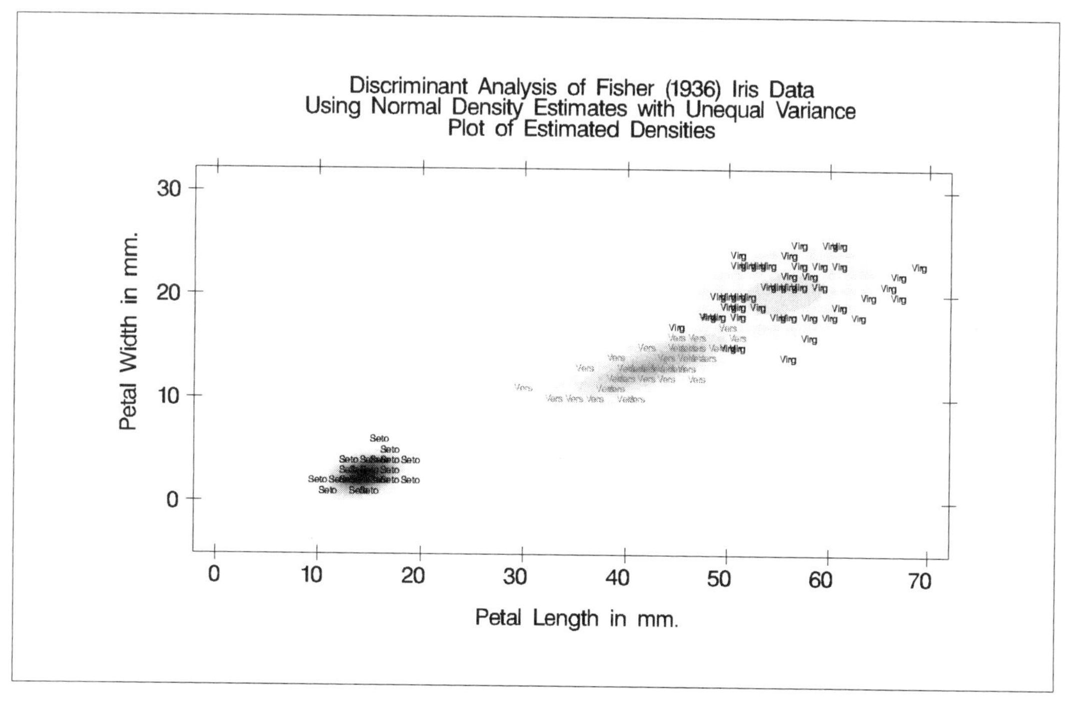

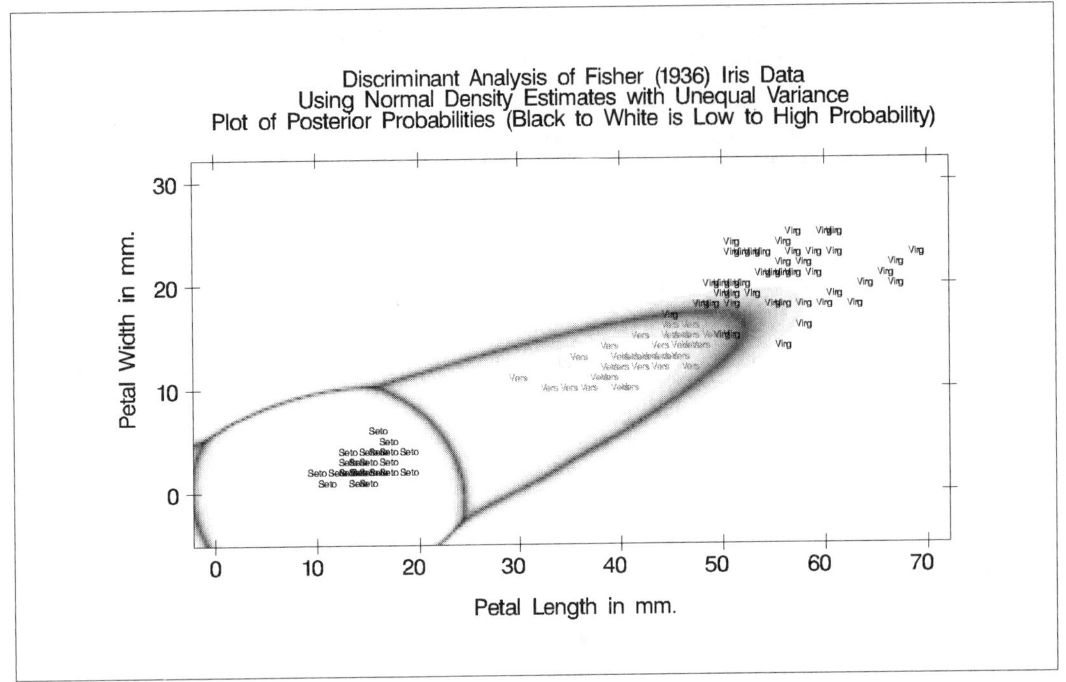
Discriminant Analysis of Fisher (1936) Iris Data
Using Normal Density Estimates with Unequal Variance
Plot of Posterior Probabilities (Black to White is Low to High Probability)
Petal Width in mm.
Petal Length in mm.
Seto
Vers
Virg

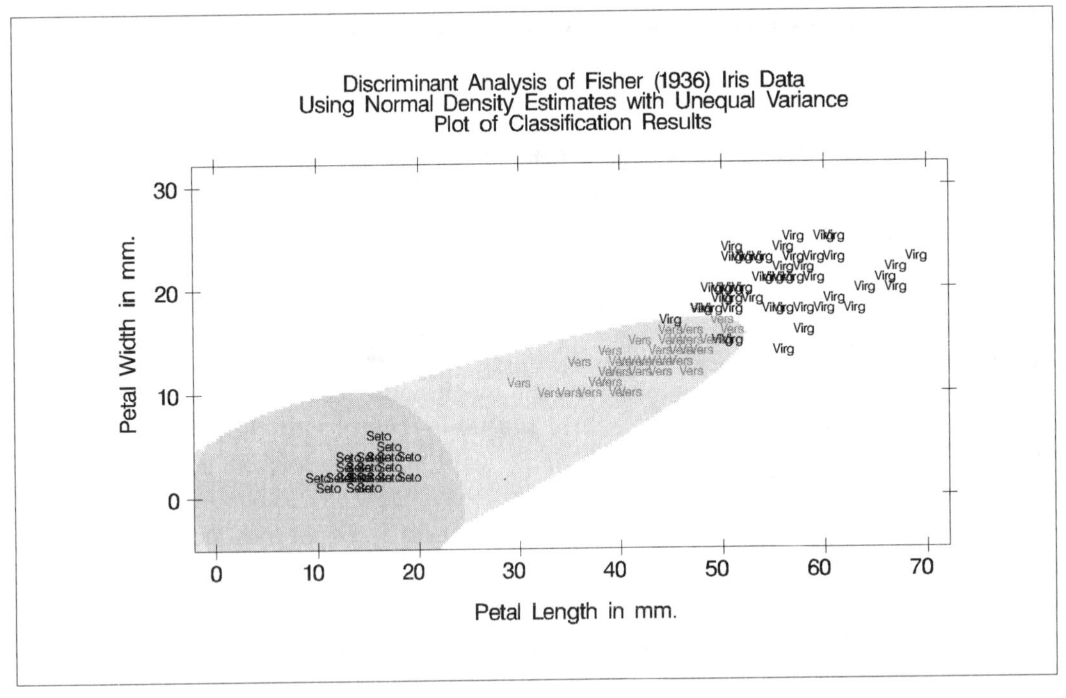
Discriminant Analysis of Fisher (1936) Iris Data
Using Normal Density Estimates with Unequal Variance
Plot of Classification Results
Petal Width in mm.
Petal Length in mm.
Seto
Vers
Virg

A nonparametric analysis (METHOD=NPAR) follows, using normal kernels (KERNEL=NORMAL) and equal bandwidths (POOL=YES) in each class. The value of the radius parameter r that, assuming normality, minimizes an approximate mean integrated square error is 0.50 (see the "Nonparametric Methods" section on page 1033). These statements produce Output 25.2.4:

```
proc discrim data=iris method=npar kernel=normal
                r=.5 pool=yes
             testdata=plotdata testout=plotp
                testoutd=plotd
             short noclassify crosslisterr;
   class Species;
   var Petal:;
   title2 'Using Kernel Density Estimates with Equal
           Bandwidth';
run;
%contour
```

Output 25.2.4. Kernel Density Estimates with Equal Bandwidth

```
            Discriminant Analysis of Fisher (1936) Iris Data
           Using Kernel Density Estimates with Equal Bandwidth

                        The DISCRIM Procedure

          Observations    150          DF Total               149
          Variables         2          DF Within Classes      147
          Classes           3          DF Between Classes       2


                       Class Level Information

              Variable                                                Prior
Species       Name             Frequency      Weight    Proportion    Probability

Setosa        Setosa                  50     50.0000      0.333333       0.333333
Versicolor    Versicolor              50     50.0000      0.333333       0.333333
Virginica     Virginica               50     50.0000      0.333333       0.333333
```

```
                Discriminant Analysis of Fisher (1936) Iris Data
              Using Kernel Density Estimates with Equal Bandwidth

                             The DISCRIM Procedure
             Classification Results for Calibration Data: WORK.IRIS
              Cross-validation Results using Normal Kernel Density

                           Squared Distance Function

                            2                  -1
                           D (X,Y) = (X-Y)' COV  (X-Y)

              Posterior Probability of Membership in Each Species

                              -1               2           2
                    F(X|j) = n   SUM exp( -.5 D (X,Y  ) / R  )
                              j   i                ji

                   Pr(j|X) = PRIOR  F(X|j) / SUM PRIOR  F(X|k)
                                  j             k       k


                Posterior Probability of Membership in Species

        From          Classified
 Obs    Species       into Species         Setosa    Versicolor     Virginica

   5    Virginica     Versicolor *         0.0000        0.7474        0.2526
   9    Versicolor    Virginica  *         0.0000        0.0800        0.9200
  25    Virginica     Versicolor *         0.0000        0.5863        0.4137
  91    Virginica     Versicolor *         0.0000        0.8358        0.1642
 148    Versicolor    Virginica  *         0.0000        0.4123        0.5877

                           * Misclassified observation
```

```
          Discriminant Analysis of Fisher (1936) Iris Data
        Using Kernel Density Estimates with Equal Bandwidth

                       The DISCRIM Procedure
       Classification Summary for Calibration Data: WORK.IRIS
        Cross-validation Summary using Normal Kernel Density

                     Squared Distance Function

                        2                   -1
                       D (X,Y) = (X-Y)' COV   (X-Y)

        Posterior Probability of Membership in Each Species

                        -1                2           2
            F(X|j) = n    SUM exp( -.5 D (X,Y   ) / R   )
                       j   i                   ji

            Pr(j|X) = PRIOR  F(X|j) / SUM PRIOR  F(X|k)
                           j               k       k


    Number of Observations and Percent Classified into Species

From
Species           Setosa     Versicolor      Virginica         Total

Setosa                50              0              0            50
                  100.00           0.00           0.00        100.00

Versicolor             0             48              2            50
                    0.00          96.00           4.00        100.00

Virginica              0              3             47            50
                    0.00           6.00          94.00        100.00

Total                 50             51             49           150
                   33.33          34.00          32.67        100.00

Priors           0.33333        0.33333        0.33333


                   Error Count Estimates for Species

                    Setosa    Versicolor    Virginica        Total

  Rate              0.0000        0.0400       0.0600       0.0333
  Priors            0.3333        0.3333       0.3333
```

```
              Discriminant Analysis of Fisher (1936) Iris Data
            Using Kernel Density Estimates with Equal Bandwidth

                           The DISCRIM Procedure
            Classification Summary for Test Data: WORK.PLOTDATA
             Classification Summary using Normal Kernel Density

                         Squared Distance Function

                          2                  -1
                         D (X,Y) = (X-Y)' COV   (X-Y)

            Posterior Probability of Membership in Each Species

                         -1               2           2
                 F(X|j) = n   SUM exp( -.5 D (X,Y  ) / R  )
                          j   i                  ji

                Pr(j|X) = PRIOR  F(X|j) / SUM PRIOR  F(X|k)
                               j            k      k


        Number of Observations and Percent Classified into Species

                       Setosa     Versicolor     Virginica        Total

    Total               12631           9941         21681        44253
                        28.54          22.46         48.99       100.00

    Priors            0.33333        0.33333       0.33333
```

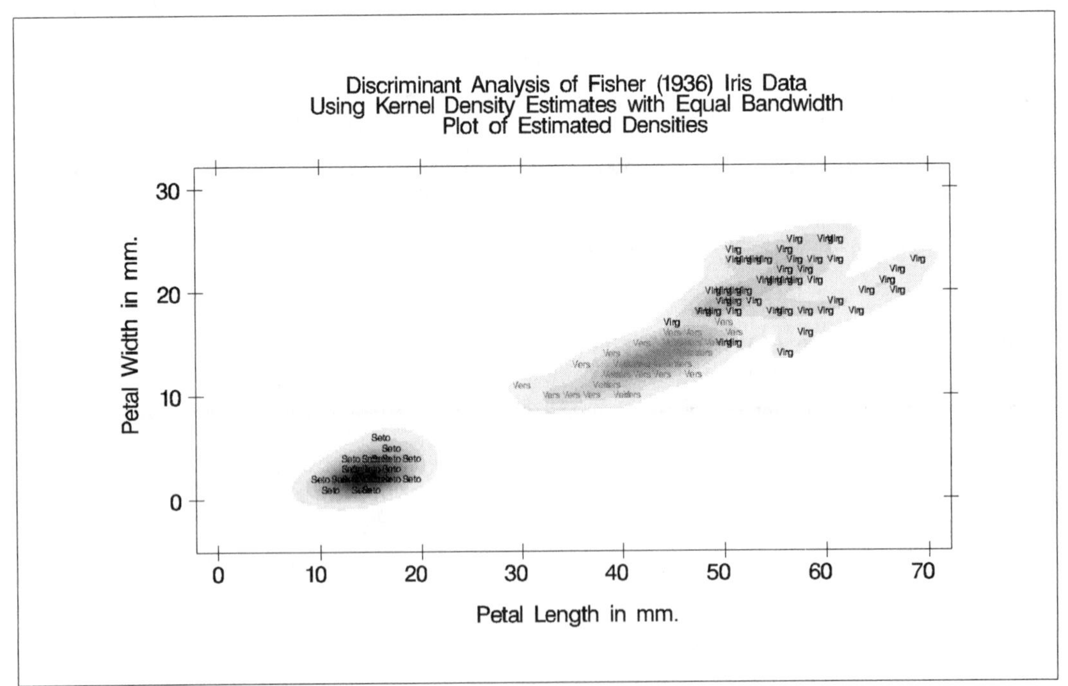

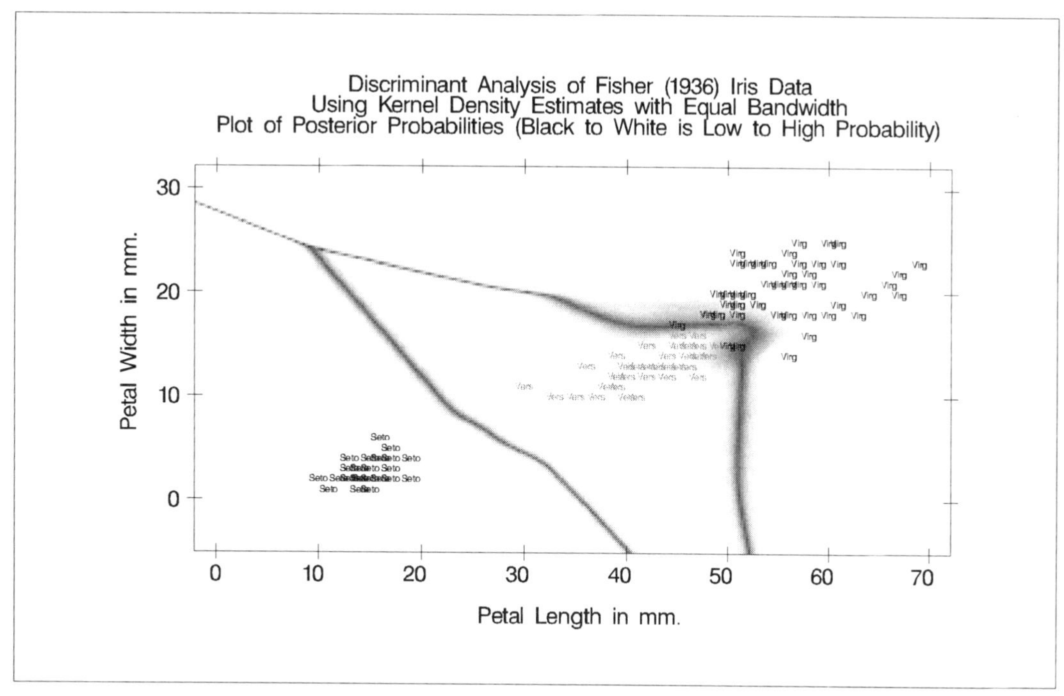
Discriminant Analysis of Fisher (1936) Iris Data
Using Kernel Density Estimates with Equal Bandwidth
Plot of Posterior Probabilities (Black to White is Low to High Probability)
Petal Width in mm.
Petal Length in mm.
0
10
20
30
40
50
60
70
Seto
Vers
Virg

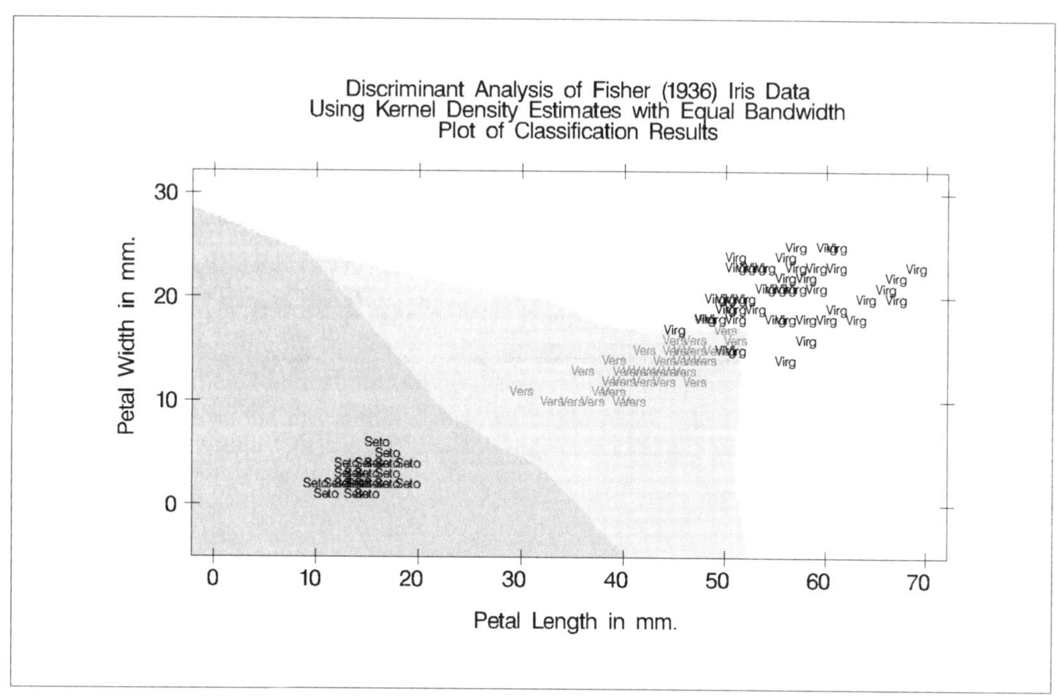
Discriminant Analysis of Fisher (1936) Iris Data
Using Kernel Density Estimates with Equal Bandwidth
Plot of Classification Results
Petal Width in mm.
Petal Length in mm.
0
10
20
30
40
50
60
70
Seto
Vers
Virg

Another nonparametric analysis is run with unequal bandwidths (POOL=NO). These statements produce Output 25.2.5:

```
proc discrim data=iris method=npar kernel=normal
                r=.5 pool=no
             testdata=plotdata testout=plotp
                testoutd=plotd
             short noclassify crosslisterr;
   class Species;
   var Petal:;
   title2 'Using Kernel Density Estimates with Unequal
           Bandwidth';
run;
%contour
```

Output 25.2.5. Kernel Density Estimates with Unequal Bandwidth

```
                Discriminant Analysis of Fisher (1936) Iris Data
             Using Kernel Density Estimates with Unequal Bandwidth

                            The DISCRIM Procedure

            Observations     150          DF Total               149
            Variables          2          DF Within Classes      147
            Classes            3          DF Between Classes       2


                           Class Level Information

               Variable                                                  Prior
Species        Name             Frequency        Weight    Proportion    Probability

Setosa         Setosa                  50       50.0000      0.333333       0.333333
Versicolor     Versicolor              50       50.0000      0.333333       0.333333
Virginica      Virginica               50       50.0000      0.333333       0.333333
```

```
              Discriminant Analysis of Fisher (1936) Iris Data
           Using Kernel Density Estimates with Unequal Bandwidth

                          The DISCRIM Procedure
           Classification Results for Calibration Data: WORK.IRIS
            Cross-validation Results using Normal Kernel Density

                        Squared Distance Function

                          2                    -1
                         D (X,Y) = (X-Y)' COV   (X-Y)
                                               j

            Posterior Probability of Membership in Each Species

                        -1                 2             2
                F(X|j) = n    SUM exp( -.5 D (X,Y   ) / R   )
                          j    i                  ji

                Pr(j|X) = PRIOR  F(X|j) / SUM PRIOR  F(X|k)
                               j             k       k


              Posterior Probability of Membership in Species

       From          Classified
Obs    Species       into Species        Setosa    Versicolor    Virginica

  5    Virginica     Versicolor *        0.0000        0.7826       0.2174
  9    Versicolor    Virginica  *        0.0000        0.0506       0.9494
 91    Virginica     Versicolor *        0.0000        0.8802       0.1198
148    Versicolor    Virginica  *        0.0000        0.3726       0.6274

                     * Misclassified observation
```

```
            Discriminant Analysis of Fisher (1936) Iris Data
         Using Kernel Density Estimates with Unequal Bandwidth

                        The DISCRIM Procedure
         Classification Summary for Calibration Data: WORK.IRIS
          Cross-validation Summary using Normal Kernel Density

                      Squared Distance Function

                       2                   -1
                      D (X,Y) = (X-Y)' COV   (X-Y)
                                           j

          Posterior Probability of Membership in Each Species

                    -1              2           2
            F(X|j) = n   SUM exp( -.5 D (X,Y  ) / R  )
                      j   i                  ji

            Pr(j|X) = PRIOR  F(X|j) / SUM PRIOR  F(X|k)
                           j              k       k


      Number of Observations and Percent Classified into Species

 From
 Species           Setosa     Versicolor     Virginica        Total

 Setosa                50              0             0           50
                   100.00           0.00          0.00       100.00

 Versicolor             0             48             2           50
                     0.00          96.00          4.00       100.00

 Virginica              0              2            48           50
                     0.00           4.00         96.00       100.00

 Total                 50             50            50          150
                    33.33          33.33         33.33       100.00

 Priors           0.33333        0.33333       0.33333


                   Error Count Estimates for Species

                      Setosa    Versicolor    Virginica       Total

   Rate               0.0000        0.0400       0.0400      0.0267
   Priors             0.3333        0.3333       0.3333
```

```
                  Discriminant Analysis of Fisher (1936) Iris Data
               Using Kernel Density Estimates with Unequal Bandwidth

                             The DISCRIM Procedure
                Classification Summary for Test Data: WORK.PLOTDATA
                 Classification Summary using Normal Kernel Density

                           Squared Distance Function

                          2                   -1
                         D (X,Y) = (X-Y)' COV   (X-Y)
                                              j

                Posterior Probability of Membership in Each Species

                    -1                2           2
        F(X|j) = n    SUM exp( -.5 D (X,Y   ) / R   )
                  j    i                 ji

        Pr(j|X) = PRIOR  F(X|j) / SUM PRIOR  F(X|k)
                       j             k       k


          Number of Observations and Percent Classified into Species

                      Setosa     Versicolor     Virginica        Total

      Total             5447           5984         32822        44253
                       12.31          13.52         74.17       100.00

      Priors         0.33333        0.33333       0.33333
```

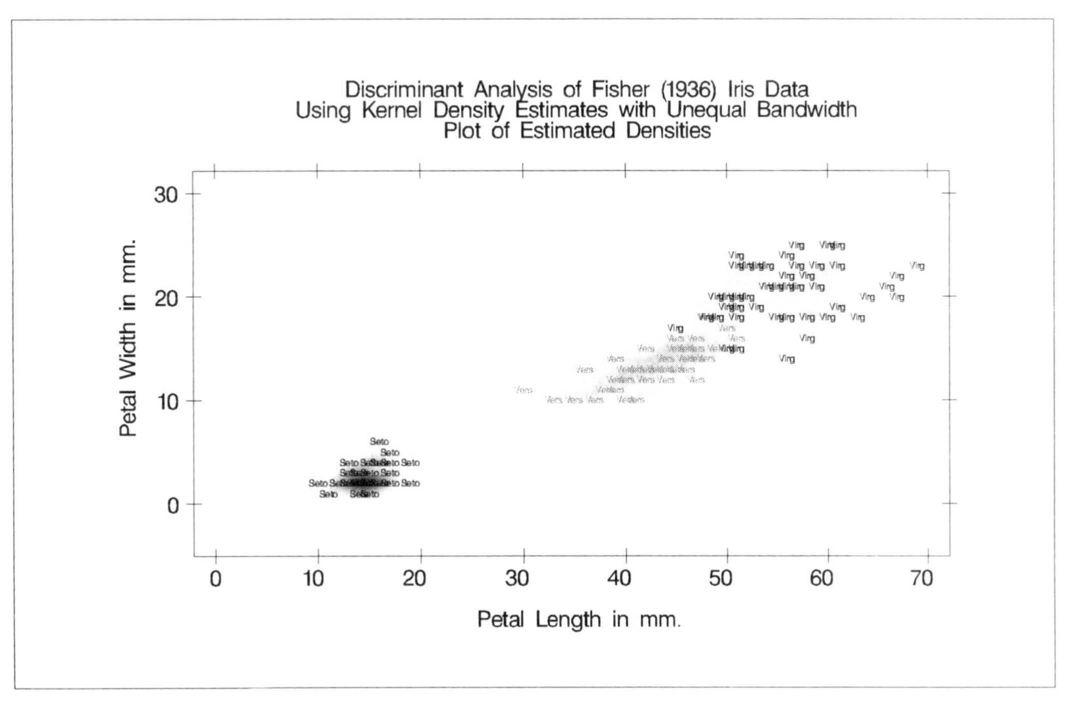

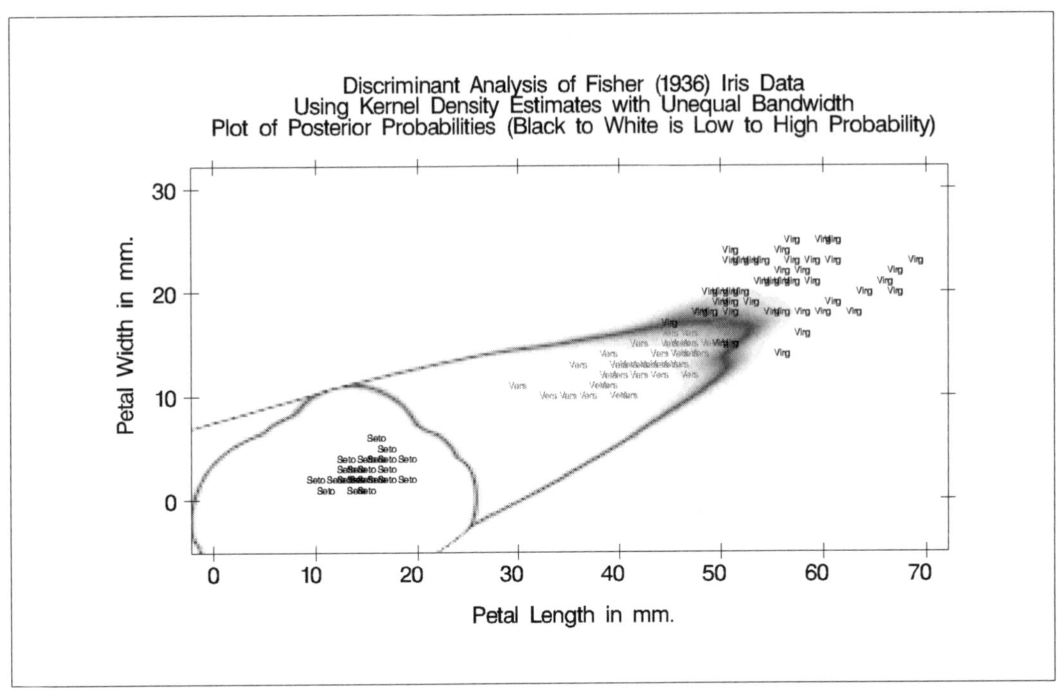
Discriminant Analysis of Fisher (1936) Iris Data
Using Kernel Density Estimates with Unequal Bandwidth
Plot of Posterior Probabilities (Black to White is Low to High Probability)
Petal Width in mm.
Petal Length in mm.

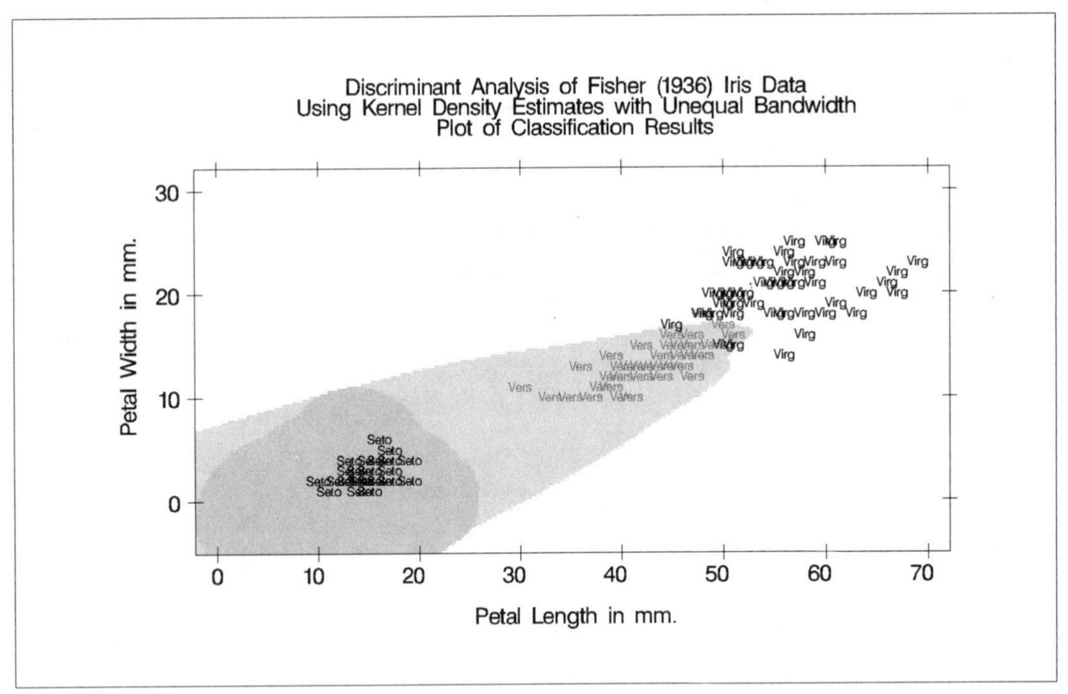
Discriminant Analysis of Fisher (1936) Iris Data
Using Kernel Density Estimates with Unequal Bandwidth
Plot of Classification Results
Petal Width in mm.
Petal Length in mm.

Example 25.3. Normal-Theory Discriminant Analysis of Iris Data

In this example, PROC DISCRIM uses normal-theory methods to classify the iris data used in Example 25.1. The POOL=TEST option tests the homogeneity of the within-group covariance matrices (Output 25.3.3). Since the resulting test statistic is significant at the 0.10 level, the within-group covariance matrices are used to derive the quadratic discriminant criterion. The WCOV and PCOV options display the within-group covariance matrices and the pooled covariance matrix (Output 25.3.2). The DISTANCE option displays squared distances between classes (Output 25.3.4). The ANOVA and MANOVA options test the hypothesis that the class means are equal, using univariate statistics and multivariate statistics; all statistics are significant at the 0.0001 level (Output 25.3.5). The LISTERR option lists the misclassified observations under resubstitution (Output 25.3.6). The CROSSLISTERR option lists the observations that are misclassified under cross validation and displays cross validation error-rate estimates (Output 25.3.7). The resubstitution error count estimate, 0.02, is not larger than the cross validation error count estimate, 0.0267, as would be expected because the resubstitution estimate is optimistically biased. The OUTSTAT= option generates a TYPE=MIXED (because POOL=TEST) output data set containing various statistics such as means, covariances, and coefficients of the discriminant function (Output 25.3.8).

The following statements produce Output 25.3.1 through Output 25.3.8:

```
proc discrim data=iris outstat=irisstat
             wcov pcov method=normal pool=test
             distance anova manova listerr crosslisterr;
   class Species;
   var SepalLength SepalWidth PetalLength PetalWidth;
   title2 'Using Quadratic Discriminant Function';
run;

proc print data=irisstat;
   title2 'Output Discriminant Statistics';
run;
```

Output 25.3.1. Quadratic Discriminant Analysis of Iris Data

```
                 Discriminant Analysis of Fisher (1936) Iris Data
                      Using Quadratic Discriminant Function

                             The DISCRIM Procedure

            Observations     150          DF Total               149
            Variables          4          DF Within Classes      147
            Classes            3          DF Between Classes       2


                            Class Level Information

               Variable                                                 Prior
Species        Name            Frequency       Weight    Proportion    Probability

Setosa         Setosa                 50      50.0000      0.333333       0.333333
Versicolor     Versicolor             50      50.0000      0.333333       0.333333
Virginica      Virginica              50      50.0000      0.333333       0.333333
```

Output 25.3.2. Covariance Matrices

Discriminant Analysis of Fisher (1936) Iris Data
Using Quadratic Discriminant Function

The DISCRIM Procedure
Within-Class Covariance Matrices

Species = Setosa, DF = 49

Variable	Label	SepalLength	SepalWidth	PetalLength	PetalWidth
SepalLength	Sepal Length in mm.	12.42489796	9.92163265	1.63551020	1.03306122
SepalWidth	Sepal Width in mm.	9.92163265	14.36897959	1.16979592	0.92979592
PetalLength	Petal Length in mm.	1.63551020	1.16979592	3.01591837	0.60693878
PetalWidth	Petal Width in mm.	1.03306122	0.92979592	0.60693878	1.11061224

Species = Versicolor, DF = 49

Variable	Label	SepalLength	SepalWidth	PetalLength	PetalWidth
SepalLength	Sepal Length in mm.	26.64326531	8.51836735	18.28979592	5.57795918
SepalWidth	Sepal Width in mm.	8.51836735	9.84693878	8.26530612	4.12040816
PetalLength	Petal Length in mm.	18.28979592	8.26530612	22.08163265	7.31020408
PetalWidth	Petal Width in mm.	5.57795918	4.12040816	7.31020408	3.91061224

Species = Virginica, DF = 49

Variable	Label	SepalLength	SepalWidth	PetalLength	PetalWidth
SepalLength	Sepal Length in mm.	40.43428571	9.37632653	30.32897959	4.90938776
SepalWidth	Sepal Width in mm.	9.37632653	10.40040816	7.13795918	4.76285714
PetalLength	Petal Length in mm.	30.32897959	7.13795918	30.45877551	4.88244898
PetalWidth	Petal Width in mm.	4.90938776	4.76285714	4.88244898	7.54326531

Discriminant Analysis of Fisher (1936) Iris Data
Using Quadratic Discriminant Function

The DISCRIM Procedure

Pooled Within-Class Covariance Matrix, DF = 147

Variable	Label	SepalLength	SepalWidth	PetalLength	PetalWidth
SepalLength	Sepal Length in mm.	26.50081633	9.27210884	16.75142857	3.84013605
SepalWidth	Sepal Width in mm.	9.27210884	11.53877551	5.52435374	3.27102041
PetalLength	Petal Length in mm.	16.75142857	5.52435374	18.51877551	4.26653061
PetalWidth	Petal Width in mm.	3.84013605	3.27102041	4.26653061	4.18816327

Within Covariance Matrix Information

Species	Covariance Matrix Rank	Natural Log of the Determinant of the Covariance Matrix
Setosa	4	5.35332
Versicolor	4	7.54636
Virginica	4	9.49362
Pooled	4	8.46214

Output 25.3.3. Homogeneity Test

```
              Discriminant Analysis of Fisher (1936) Iris Data
                    Using Quadratic Discriminant Function

                           The DISCRIM Procedure
              Test of Homogeneity of Within Covariance Matrices

Notation: K     = Number of Groups

          P     = Number of Variables

          N     = Total Number of Observations - Number of Groups

          N(i)  = Number of Observations in the i'th Group - 1

                     __                  N(i)/2
                     ||   |Within SS Matrix(i)|
          V     = -----------------------------------
                                       N/2
                        |Pooled SS Matrix|

                        _                 _      2
                       |       1        1  |  2P + 3P - 1
          RHO   = 1.0 - | SUM -----  -  --- | -------------
                       |_      N(i)     N _|  6(P+1)(K-1)

          DF    = .5(K-1)P(P+1)
                                              _                  _
                                             |    PN/2            |
                                             |   N        V       |
Under the null hypothesis:      -2 RHO ln   | ------------------ |
                                             |   __       PN(i)/2  |
                                             |_  ||  N(i)         _|

is distributed approximately as Chi-Square(DF).


                Chi-Square        DF    Pr > ChiSq

                140.943050        20        <.0001

Since the Chi-Square value is significant at the 0.1 level, the within
covariance matrices will be used in the discriminant function.
Reference: Morrison, D.F. (1976) Multivariate Statistical Methods
p252.
```

Output 25.3.4. Squared Distances

```
             Discriminant Analysis of Fisher (1936) Iris Data
                   Using Quadratic Discriminant Function

                           The DISCRIM Procedure

                 Pairwise Squared Distances Between Groups

                    2         _   _          -1  _   _
                   D (i|j) = (X - X )' COV     (X - X )
                               i   j      j     i   j

                        Squared Distance to Species

         From
         Species            Setosa    Versicolor     Virginica

         Setosa                  0     103.19382     168.76759
         Versicolor      323.06203             0      13.83875
         Virginica       706.08494      17.86670             0

         Pairwise Generalized Squared Distances Between Groups

              2         _   _          -1  _   _
             D (i|j) = (X - X )' COV     (X - X ) + ln |COV |
                         i   j      j     i   j             j

                  Generalized Squared Distance to Species

         From
         Species            Setosa    Versicolor     Virginica

         Setosa            5.35332     110.74017     178.26121
         Versicolor      328.41535       7.54636      23.33238
         Virginica       711.43826      25.41306       9.49362
```

Output 25.3.5. Tests of Equal Class Means

```
                   Discriminant Analysis of Fisher (1936) Iris Data
                         Using Quadratic Discriminant Function

                                The DISCRIM Procedure

                             Univariate Test Statistics

                      F Statistics,    Num DF=2,    Den DF=147

                                Total    Pooled   Between
                             Standard  Standard  Standard             R-Square
Variable    Label           Deviation Deviation Deviation R-Square / (1-RSq) F Value Pr > F

SepalLength Sepal Length in mm.   8.2807    5.1479    7.9506   0.6187    1.6226  119.26 <.0001
SepalWidth  Sepal Width in mm.    4.3587    3.3969    3.3682   0.4008    0.6688   49.16 <.0001
PetalLength Petal Length in mm.  17.6530    4.3033   20.9070   0.9414   16.0566 1180.16 <.0001
PetalWidth  Petal Width in mm.    7.6224    2.0465    8.9673   0.9289   13.0613  960.01 <.0001


                                  Average R-Square

                          Unweighted               0.7224358
                          Weighted by Variance     0.8689444


                     Multivariate Statistics and F Approximations

                               S=2     M=0.5     N=71

        Statistic                      Value     F Value    Num DF    Den DF    Pr > F

        Wilks' Lambda             0.02343863      199.15         8       288    <.0001
        Pillai's Trace            1.19189883       53.47         8       290    <.0001
        Hotelling-Lawley Trace   32.47732024      582.20         8     203.4    <.0001
        Roy's Greatest Root      32.19192920     1166.96         4       145    <.0001

                NOTE: F Statistic for Roy's Greatest Root is an upper bound.
                        NOTE: F Statistic for Wilks' Lambda is exact.
```

Output 25.3.6. Misclassified Observations: Resubstitution

```
                   Discriminant Analysis of Fisher (1936) Iris Data
                         Using Quadratic Discriminant Function

                                The DISCRIM Procedure
                Classification Results for Calibration Data: WORK.IRIS
             Resubstitution Results using Quadratic Discriminant Function

                         Generalized Squared Distance Function

                             2         _          -1    _
                            D (X) = (X-X )' COV   (X-X ) + ln |COV |
                             j          j      j      j          j

                 Posterior Probability of Membership in Each Species

                                            2                    2
                     Pr(j|X) = exp(-.5 D (X)) / SUM exp(-.5 D (X))
                                            j         k          k


                   Posterior Probability of Membership in Species

              From          Classified
      Obs     Species       into Species         Setosa    Versicolor     Virginica

        5     Virginica     Versicolor *         0.0000        0.6050        0.3950
        9     Versicolor    Virginica  *         0.0000        0.3359        0.6641
       12     Versicolor    Virginica  *         0.0000        0.1543        0.8457

                              * Misclassified observation
```

```
          Discriminant Analysis of Fisher (1936) Iris Data
                Using Quadratic Discriminant Function

                        The DISCRIM Procedure
       Classification Summary for Calibration Data: WORK.IRIS
    Resubstitution Summary using Quadratic Discriminant Function

                Generalized Squared Distance Function

                 2         _          -1   _
                D (X) = (X-X )' COV   (X-X ) + ln |COV |
                j           j      j     j            j

        Posterior Probability of Membership in Each Species

                           2                        2
        Pr(j|X) = exp(-.5 D (X)) / SUM exp(-.5 D (X))
                           j         k              k


   Number of Observations and Percent Classified into Species

From
Species          Setosa    Versicolor    Virginica       Total

Setosa               50             0            0          50
                 100.00          0.00         0.00      100.00

Versicolor            0            48            2          50
                   0.00         96.00         4.00      100.00

Virginica             0             1           49          50
                   0.00          2.00        98.00      100.00

Total                50            49           51         150
                  33.33         32.67        34.00      100.00

Priors          0.33333       0.33333      0.33333


                 Error Count Estimates for Species

                    Setosa    Versicolor    Virginica       Total

  Rate              0.0000        0.0400       0.0200      0.0200
  Priors            0.3333        0.3333       0.3333
```

Output 25.3.7. Misclassified Observations: Cross validation

```
                   Discriminant Analysis of Fisher (1936) Iris Data
                         Using Quadratic Discriminant Function

                                 The DISCRIM Procedure
                   Classification Results for Calibration Data: WORK.IRIS
               Cross-validation Results using Quadratic Discriminant Function

                         Generalized Squared Distance Function

                      2          _         -1      _
                      D (X) = (X-X    )' COV    (X-X    ) + ln |COV    |
                      j           (X)j      (X)j    (X)j             (X)j

                      Posterior Probability of Membership in Each Species

                                             2                    2
                         Pr(j|X) = exp(-.5 D (X)) / SUM exp(-.5 D (X))
                                             j        k           k


                        Posterior Probability of Membership in Species

                 From          Classified
          Obs    Species       into Species         Setosa     Versicolor     Virginica

            5    Virginica     Versicolor *         0.0000         0.6632        0.3368
            8    Versicolor    Virginica  *         0.0000         0.3134        0.6866
            9    Versicolor    Virginica  *         0.0000         0.1616        0.8384
           12    Versicolor    Virginica  *         0.0000         0.0713        0.9287

                               * Misclassified observation
```

```
              Discriminant Analysis of Fisher (1936) Iris Data
                    Using Quadratic Discriminant Function

                           The DISCRIM Procedure
           Classification Summary for Calibration Data: WORK.IRIS
      Cross-validation Summary using Quadratic Discriminant Function

                  Generalized Squared Distance Function

             2           _            -1      _
            D (X) = (X-X     )' COV      (X-X     ) + ln |COV     |
             j           (X)j       (X)j     (X)j            (X)j

            Posterior Probability of Membership in Each Species

                                 2                   2
               Pr(j|X) = exp(-.5 D (X)) / SUM exp(-.5 D (X))
                                   j         k         k


        Number of Observations and Percent Classified into Species

    From
    Species          Setosa     Versicolor      Virginica        Total

    Setosa               50              0              0           50
                     100.00           0.00           0.00       100.00

    Versicolor            0             47              3           50
                       0.00          94.00           6.00       100.00

    Virginica             0              1             49           50
                       0.00           2.00          98.00       100.00

    Total                50             48             52          150
                      33.33          32.00          34.67       100.00

    Priors          0.33333        0.33333        0.33333


                      Error Count Estimates for Species

                         Setosa    Versicolor    Virginica        Total

      Rate               0.0000        0.0600       0.0200       0.0267
      Priors             0.3333        0.3333       0.3333
```

Output 25.3.8. Output Statistics from Iris Data

Discriminant Analysis of Fisher (1936) Iris Data
Output Discriminant Statistics

Obs	Species	_TYPE_	_NAME_	Sepal Length	Sepal Width	Petal Length	Petal Width
1	.	N		150.00	150.00	150.00	150.00
2	Setosa	N		50.00	50.00	50.00	50.00
3	Versicolor	N		50.00	50.00	50.00	50.00
4	Virginica	N		50.00	50.00	50.00	50.00
5	.	MEAN		58.43	30.57	37.58	11.99
6	Setosa	MEAN		50.06	34.28	14.62	2.46
7	Versicolor	MEAN		59.36	27.70	42.60	13.26
8	Virginica	MEAN		65.88	29.74	55.52	20.26
9	Setosa	PRIOR		0.33	0.33	0.33	0.33
10	Versicolor	PRIOR		0.33	0.33	0.33	0.33
11	Virginica	PRIOR		0.33	0.33	0.33	0.33
12	Setosa	CSSCP	SepalLength	608.82	486.16	80.14	50.62
13	Setosa	CSSCP	SepalWidth	486.16	704.08	57.32	45.56
14	Setosa	CSSCP	PetalLength	80.14	57.32	147.78	29.74
15	Setosa	CSSCP	PetalWidth	50.62	45.56	29.74	54.42
16	Versicolor	CSSCP	SepalLength	1305.52	417.40	896.20	273.32
17	Versicolor	CSSCP	SepalWidth	417.40	482.50	405.00	201.90
18	Versicolor	CSSCP	PetalLength	896.20	405.00	1082.00	358.20
19	Versicolor	CSSCP	PetalWidth	273.32	201.90	358.20	191.62
20	Virginica	CSSCP	SepalLength	1981.28	459.44	1486.12	240.56
21	Virginica	CSSCP	SepalWidth	459.44	509.62	349.76	233.38
22	Virginica	CSSCP	PetalLength	1486.12	349.76	1492.48	239.24
23	Virginica	CSSCP	PetalWidth	240.56	233.38	239.24	369.62
24	.	PSSCP	SepalLength	3895.62	1363.00	2462.46	564.50
25	.	PSSCP	SepalWidth	1363.00	1696.20	812.08	480.84
26	.	PSSCP	PetalLength	2462.46	812.08	2722.26	627.18
27	.	PSSCP	PetalWidth	564.50	480.84	627.18	615.66
28	.	BSSCP	SepalLength	6321.21	-1995.27	16524.84	7127.93
29	.	BSSCP	SepalWidth	-1995.27	1134.49	-5723.96	-2293.27
30	.	BSSCP	PetalLength	16524.84	-5723.96	43710.28	18677.40
31	.	BSSCP	PetalWidth	7127.93	-2293.27	18677.40	8041.33
32	.	CSSCP	SepalLength	10216.83	-632.27	18987.30	7692.43
33	.	CSSCP	SepalWidth	-632.27	2830.69	-4911.88	-1812.43
34	.	CSSCP	PetalLength	18987.30	-4911.88	46432.54	19304.58
35	.	CSSCP	PetalWidth	7692.43	-1812.43	19304.58	8656.99
36	.	RSQUARED		0.62	0.40	0.94	0.93
37	Setosa	COV	SepalLength	12.42	9.92	1.64	1.03
38	Setosa	COV	SepalWidth	9.92	14.37	1.17	0.93
39	Setosa	COV	PetalLength	1.64	1.17	3.02	0.61
40	Setosa	COV	PetalWidth	1.03	0.93	0.61	1.11
41	Versicolor	COV	SepalLength	26.64	8.52	18.29	5.58
42	Versicolor	COV	SepalWidth	8.52	9.85	8.27	4.12
43	Versicolor	COV	PetalLength	18.29	8.27	22.08	7.31
44	Versicolor	COV	PetalWidth	5.58	4.12	7.31	3.91
45	Virginica	COV	SepalLength	40.43	9.38	30.33	4.91
46	Virginica	COV	SepalWidth	9.38	10.40	7.14	4.76
47	Virginica	COV	PetalLength	30.33	7.14	30.46	4.88
48	Virginica	COV	PetalWidth	4.91	4.76	4.88	7.54
49	.	PCOV	SepalLength	26.50	9.27	16.75	3.84
50	.	PCOV	SepalWidth	9.27	11.54	5.52	3.27
51	.	PCOV	PetalLength	16.75	5.52	18.52	4.27
52	.	PCOV	PetalWidth	3.84	3.27	4.27	4.19
53	.	BCOV	SepalLength	63.21	-19.95	165.25	71.28
54	.	BCOV	SepalWidth	-19.95	11.34	-57.24	-22.93
55	.	BCOV	PetalLength	165.25	-57.24	437.10	186.77
56	.	BCOV	PetalWidth	71.28	-22.93	186.77	80.41
57	.	COV	SepalLength	68.57	-4.24	127.43	51.63
58	.	COV	SepalWidth	-4.24	19.00	-32.97	-12.16
59	.	COV	PetalLength	127.43	-32.97	311.63	129.56
60	.	COV	PetalWidth	51.63	-12.16	129.56	58.10
61	Setosa	STD		3.52	3.79	1.74	1.05
62	Versicolor	STD		5.16	3.14	4.70	1.98
63	Virginica	STD		6.36	3.22	5.52	2.75
64	.	PSTD		5.15	3.40	4.30	2.05
65	.	BSTD		7.95	3.37	20.91	8.97
66	.	STD		8.28	4.36	17.65	7.62
67	Setosa	CORR	SepalLength	1.00	0.74	0.27	0.28
68	Setosa	CORR	SepalWidth	0.74	1.00	0.18	0.23
69	Setosa	CORR	PetalLength	0.27	0.18	1.00	0.33
70	Setosa	CORR	PetalWidth	0.28	0.23	0.33	1.00

71	Versicolor	CORR	SepalLength	1.00	0.53	0.75	0.55
72	Versicolor	CORR	SepalWidth	0.53	1.00	0.56	0.66
73	Versicolor	CORR	PetalLength	0.75	0.56	1.00	0.79
74	Versicolor	CORR	PetalWidth	0.55	0.66	0.79	1.00
75	Virginica	CORR	SepalLength	1.00	0.46	0.86	0.28
76	Virginica	CORR	SepalWidth	0.46	1.00	0.40	0.54
77	Virginica	CORR	PetalLength	0.86	0.40	1.00	0.32
78	Virginica	CORR	PetalWidth	0.28	0.54	0.32	1.00
79	.	PCORR	SepalLength	1.00	0.53	0.76	0.36
80	.	PCORR	SepalWidth	0.53	1.00	0.38	0.47
81	.	PCORR	PetalLength	0.76	0.38	1.00	0.48
82	.	PCORR	PetalWidth	0.36	0.47	0.48	1.00
83	.	BCORR	SepalLength	1.00	-0.75	0.99	1.00
84	.	BCORR	SepalWidth	-0.75	1.00	-0.81	-0.76
85	.	BCORR	PetalLength	0.99	-0.81	1.00	1.00
86	.	BCORR	PetalWidth	1.00	-0.76	1.00	1.00
87	.	CORR	SepalLength	1.00	-0.12	0.87	0.82
88	.	CORR	SepalWidth	-0.12	1.00	-0.43	-0.37
89	.	CORR	PetalLength	0.87	-0.43	1.00	0.96
90	.	CORR	PetalWidth	0.82	-0.37	0.96	1.00
91	Setosa	STDMEAN		-1.01	0.85	-1.30	-1.25
92	Versicolor	STDMEAN		0.11	-0.66	0.28	0.17
93	Virginica	STDMEAN		0.90	-0.19	1.02	1.08
94	Setosa	PSTDMEAN		-1.63	1.09	-5.34	-4.66
95	Versicolor	PSTDMEAN		0.18	-0.85	1.17	0.62
96	Virginica	PSTDMEAN		1.45	-0.25	4.17	4.04
97	.	LNDETERM		8.46	8.46	8.46	8.46
98	Setosa	LNDETERM		5.35	5.35	5.35	5.35
99	Versicolor	LNDETERM		7.55	7.55	7.55	7.55
100	Virginica	LNDETERM		9.49	9.49	9.49	9.49
101	Setosa	QUAD	SepalLength	-0.09	0.06	0.02	0.02
102	Setosa	QUAD	SepalWidth	0.06	-0.08	-0.01	0.01
103	Setosa	QUAD	PetalLength	0.02	-0.01	-0.19	0.09
104	Setosa	QUAD	PetalWidth	0.02	0.01	0.09	-0.53
105	Setosa	QUAD	_LINEAR_	4.46	-0.76	3.36	-3.13
106	Setosa	QUAD	_CONST_	-121.83	-121.83	-121.83	-121.83
107	Versicolor	QUAD	SepalLength	-0.05	0.02	0.04	-0.03
108	Versicolor	QUAD	SepalWidth	0.02	-0.10	-0.01	0.10
109	Versicolor	QUAD	PetalLength	0.04	-0.01	-0.10	0.13
110	Versicolor	QUAD	PetalWidth	-0.03	0.10	0.13	-0.44
111	Versicolor	QUAD	_LINEAR_	1.80	1.60	0.33	-1.47
112	Versicolor	QUAD	_CONST_	-76.55	-76.55	-76.55	-76.55
113	Virginica	QUAD	SepalLength	-0.05	0.02	0.05	-0.01
114	Virginica	QUAD	SepalWidth	0.02	-0.08	-0.01	0.04
115	Virginica	QUAD	PetalLength	0.05	-0.01	-0.07	0.01
116	Virginica	QUAD	PetalWidth	-0.01	0.04	0.01	-0.10
117	Virginica	QUAD	_LINEAR_	0.74	1.32	0.62	0.97
118	Virginica	QUAD	_CONST_	-75.82	-75.82	-75.82	-75.82

Example 25.4. Linear Discriminant Analysis of Remote-Sensing Data on Crops

In this example, the remote-sensing data described at the beginning of the section are used. In the first PROC DISCRIM statement, the DISCRIM procedure uses normal-theory methods (METHOD=NORMAL) assuming equal variances (POOL=YES) in five crops. The PRIORS statement, PRIORS PROP, sets the prior probabilities proportional to the sample sizes. The LIST option lists the resubstitution classification results for each observation (Output 25.4.2). The CROSSVALIDATE option displays cross validation error-rate estimates (Output 25.4.3). The OUTSTAT= option stores the calibration information in a new data set to classify future observations. A second PROC DISCRIM statement uses this calibration information to classify a test data set. Note that the values of the identification variable, xvalues, are obtained by rereading the x1 through x4 fields in the data lines as a single character variable. The following statements produce Output 25.4.1 through Output 25.4.3.

```
data crops;
   title 'Discriminant Analysis of Remote Sensing Data
          on Five Crops';
   input Crop $ 4-13 x1-x4 xvalues $ 14-24;
   datalines;
Corn      16 27 31 33
Corn      15 23 30 30
Corn      16 27 27 26
Corn      18 20 25 23
Corn      15 15 31 32
Corn      15 32 32 15
Corn      12 15 16 73
Soybeans  20 23 23 25
Soybeans  24 24 25 32
Soybeans  21 25 23 24
Soybeans  27 45 24 12
Soybeans  12 13 15 42
Soybeans  22 32 31 43
Cotton    31 32 33 34
Cotton    29 24 26 28
Cotton    34 32 28 45
Cotton    26 25 23 24
Cotton    53 48 75 26
Cotton    34 35 25 78
Sugarbeets22 23 25 42
Sugarbeets25 25 24 26
Sugarbeets34 25 16 52
Sugarbeets54 23 21 54
Sugarbeets25 43 32 15
Sugarbeets26 54  2 54
Clover    12 45 32 54
Clover    24 58 25 34
Clover    87 54 61 21
Clover    51 31 31 16
Clover    96 48 54 62
Clover    31 31 11 11
Clover    56 13 13 71
Clover    32 13 27 32
Clover    36 26 54 32
Clover    53 08 06 54
Clover    32 32 62 16
;
proc discrim data=crops outstat=cropstat
             method=normal pool=yes
             list crossvalidate;
   class Crop;
   priors prop;
   id xvalues;
   var x1-x4;
   title2 'Using Linear Discriminant Function';
run;
```

Output 25.4.1. Linear Discriminant Function on Crop Data

```
          Discriminant Analysis of Remote Sensing Data on Five Crops
                      Using Linear Discriminant Function

                            The DISCRIM Procedure

           Observations     36          DF Total                 35
           Variables         4          DF Within Classes        31
           Classes           5          DF Between Classes        4


                           Class Level Information

              Variable                                                 Prior
 Crop         Name           Frequency         Weight    Proportion    Probability

 Clover       Clover                11        11.0000      0.305556       0.305556
 Corn         Corn                   7         7.0000      0.194444       0.194444
 Cotton       Cotton                 6         6.0000      0.166667       0.166667
 Soybeans     Soybeans               6         6.0000      0.166667       0.166667
 Sugarbeets   Sugarbeets             6         6.0000      0.166667       0.166667
```

```
          Discriminant Analysis of Remote Sensing Data on Five Crops
                      Using Linear Discriminant Function

                            The DISCRIM Procedure

                     Pooled Covariance Matrix Information

                                    Natural Log of the
                       Covariance   Determinant of the
                      Matrix Rank    Covariance Matrix

                                4             21.30189
```

```
          Discriminant Analysis of Remote Sensing Data on Five Crops
                      Using Linear Discriminant Function

                            The DISCRIM Procedure

              Pairwise Generalized Squared Distances Between Groups

                2         _   _          -1  _   _
              D (i|j) = (X - X )' COV   (X - X ) - 2 ln PRIOR
                             i   j           i   j              j


                      Generalized Squared Distance to Crop

From Crop          Clover          Corn        Cotton      Soybeans    Sugarbeets

Clover            2.37125       7.52830       4.44969       6.16665       5.07262
Corn              6.62433       3.27522       5.46798       4.31383       6.47395
Cotton            3.23741       5.15968       3.58352       5.01819       4.87908
Soybeans          4.95438       4.00552       5.01819       3.58352       4.65998
Sugarbeets        3.86034       6.16564       4.87908       4.65998       3.58352
```

Linear Discriminant Function

$$\text{Constant} = -.5\,\bar{X}_j'\,\text{COV}^{-1}\,\bar{X}_j + \ln \text{PRIOR}_j \qquad \text{Coefficient Vector} = \text{COV}^{-1}\,\bar{X}_j$$

Linear Discriminant Function for Crop

Variable	Clover	Corn	Cotton	Soybeans	Sugarbeets
Constant	-10.98457	-7.72070	-11.46537	-7.28260	-9.80179
x1	0.08907	-0.04180	0.02462	0.0000369	0.04245
x2	0.17379	0.11970	0.17596	0.15896	0.20988
x3	0.11899	0.16511	0.15880	0.10622	0.06540
x4	0.15637	0.16768	0.18362	0.14133	0.16408

Output 25.4.2. Misclassified Observations: Resubstitution

```
Discriminant Analysis of Remote Sensing Data on Five Crops
            Using Linear Discriminant Function

                  The DISCRIM Procedure
      Classification Results for Calibration Data: WORK.CROPS
     Resubstitution Results using Linear Discriminant Function

             Generalized Squared Distance Function

              2           _        -1   _
             D (X) = (X-X )' COV   (X-X ) - 2 ln PRIOR
              j           j             j             j

         Posterior Probability of Membership in Each Crop

                              2                    2
           Pr(j|X) = exp(-.5 D (X)) / SUM exp(-.5 D (X))
                              j          k         k


           Posterior Probability of Membership in Crop
```

xvalues	From Crop	Classified into Crop		Clover	Corn	Cotton	Soybeans	Sugarbeets
16 27 31 33	Corn	Corn		0.0894	0.4054	0.1763	0.2392	0.0897
15 23 30 30	Corn	Corn		0.0769	0.4558	0.1421	0.2530	0.0722
16 27 27 26	Corn	Corn		0.0982	0.3422	0.1365	0.3073	0.1157
18 20 25 23	Corn	Corn		0.1052	0.3634	0.1078	0.3281	0.0955
15 15 31 32	Corn	Corn		0.0588	0.5754	0.1173	0.2087	0.0398
15 32 32 15	Corn	Soybeans	*	0.0972	0.3278	0.1318	0.3420	0.1011
12 15 16 73	Corn	Corn		0.0454	0.5238	0.1849	0.1376	0.1083
20 23 23 25	Soybeans	Soybeans		0.1330	0.2804	0.1176	0.3305	0.1385
24 24 25 32	Soybeans	Soybeans		0.1768	0.2483	0.1586	0.2660	0.1502
21 25 23 24	Soybeans	Soybeans		0.1481	0.2431	0.1200	0.3318	0.1570
27 45 24 12	Soybeans	Sugarbeets	*	0.2357	0.0547	0.1016	0.2721	0.3359
12 13 15 42	Soybeans	Corn	*	0.0549	0.4749	0.0920	0.2768	0.1013
22 32 31 43	Soybeans	Cotton	*	0.1474	0.2606	0.2624	0.1848	0.1448
31 32 33 34	Cotton	Clover	*	0.2815	0.1518	0.2377	0.1767	0.1523
29 24 26 28	Cotton	Soybeans	*	0.2521	0.1842	0.1529	0.2549	0.1559
34 32 28 45	Cotton	Clover	*	0.3125	0.1023	0.2404	0.1357	0.2091
26 25 23 24	Cotton	Soybeans	*	0.2121	0.1809	0.1245	0.3045	0.1780
53 48 75 26	Cotton	Clover	*	0.4837	0.0391	0.4384	0.0223	0.0166
34 35 25 78	Cotton	Cotton		0.2256	0.0794	0.3810	0.0592	0.2548
22 23 25 42	Sugarbeets	Corn	*	0.1421	0.3066	0.1901	0.2231	0.1381
25 25 24 26	Sugarbeets	Soybeans	*	0.1969	0.2050	0.1354	0.2960	0.1667
34 25 16 52	Sugarbeets	Sugarbeets		0.2928	0.0871	0.1665	0.1479	0.3056
54 23 21 54	Sugarbeets	Clover	*	0.6215	0.0194	0.1250	0.0496	0.1845
25 43 32 15	Sugarbeets	Soybeans	*	0.2258	0.1135	0.1646	0.2770	0.2191
26 54 2 54	Sugarbeets	Sugarbeets		0.0850	0.0081	0.0521	0.0661	0.7887
12 45 32 54	Clover	Cotton	*	0.0693	0.2663	0.3394	0.1460	0.1789
24 58 25 34	Clover	Sugarbeets	*	0.1647	0.0376	0.1680	0.1452	0.4845
87 54 61 21	Clover	Clover		0.9328	0.0003	0.0478	0.0025	0.0165
51 31 31 16	Clover	Clover		0.6642	0.0205	0.0872	0.0959	0.1322
96 48 54 62	Clover	Clover		0.9215	0.0002	0.0604	0.0007	0.0173
31 31 11 11	Clover	Sugarbeets	*	0.2525	0.0402	0.0473	0.3012	0.3588
56 13 13 71	Clover	Clover		0.6132	0.0212	0.1226	0.0408	0.2023
32 13 27 32	Clover	Clover		0.2669	0.2616	0.1512	0.2260	0.0943
36 26 54 32	Clover	Cotton	*	0.2650	0.2645	0.3495	0.0918	0.0292
53 08 06 54	Clover	Clover		0.5914	0.0237	0.0676	0.0781	0.2392
32 32 62 16	Clover	Cotton	*	0.2163	0.3180	0.3327	0.1125	0.0206

* Misclassified observation

```
                Discriminant Analysis of Remote Sensing Data on Five Crops
                         Using Linear Discriminant Function

                              The DISCRIM Procedure
                 Classification Summary for Calibration Data: WORK.CROPS
                Resubstitution Summary using Linear Discriminant Function

                        Generalized Squared Distance Function

                          2         _       -1   _
                         D (X) = (X-X )' COV  (X-X ) - 2 ln PRIOR
                          j         j            j              j

                    Posterior Probability of Membership in Each Crop

                                         2                    2
                        Pr(j|X) = exp(-.5 D (X)) / SUM exp(-.5 D (X))
                                          j         k          k
```

Number of Observations and Percent Classified into Crop

From Crop	Clover	Corn	Cotton	Soybeans	Sugarbeets	Total
Clover	6 54.55	0 0.00	3 27.27	0 0.00	2 18.18	11 100.00
Corn	0 0.00	6 85.71	0 0.00	1 14.29	0 0.00	7 100.00
Cotton	3 50.00	0 0.00	1 16.67	2 33.33	0 0.00	6 100.00
Soybeans	0 0.00	1 16.67	1 16.67	3 50.00	1 16.67	6 100.00
Sugarbeets	1 16.67	1 16.67	0 0.00	2 33.33	2 33.33	6 100.00
Total	10 27.78	8 22.22	5 13.89	8 22.22	5 13.89	36 100.00
Priors	0.30556	0.19444	0.16667	0.16667	0.16667	

Error Count Estimates for Crop

	Clover	Corn	Cotton	Soybeans	Sugarbeets	Total
Rate	0.4545	0.1429	0.8333	0.5000	0.6667	0.5000
Priors	0.3056	0.1944	0.1667	0.1667	0.1667	

Output 25.4.3. Misclassified Observations: Cross Validation

```
                     Discriminant Analysis of Remote Sensing Data on Five Crops
                                Using Linear Discriminant Function

                                      The DISCRIM Procedure
                       Classification Summary for Calibration Data: WORK.CROPS
                     Cross-validation Summary using Linear Discriminant Function

                               Generalized Squared Distance Function

                           2           _              -1         _
                          D (X) = (X-X      )' COV       (X-X       ) - 2 ln PRIOR
                           j              (X)j      (X)       (X)j                  j

                           Posterior Probability of Membership in Each Crop

                                                   2                     2
                            Pr(j|X) = exp(-.5 D (X)) / SUM exp(-.5 D (X))
                                                   j         k           k


                     Number of Observations and Percent Classified into Crop

From Crop          Clover         Corn        Cotton      Soybeans     Sugarbeets        Total

Clover                  4            3             1             0              3           11
                    36.36        27.27          9.09          0.00          27.27       100.00

Corn                    0            4             1             2              0            7
                     0.00        57.14         14.29         28.57           0.00       100.00

Cotton                  3            0             0             2              1            6
                    50.00         0.00          0.00         33.33          16.67       100.00

Soybeans                0            1             1             3              1            6
                     0.00        16.67         16.67         50.00          16.67       100.00

Sugarbeets              2            1             0             2              1            6
                    33.33        16.67          0.00         33.33          16.67       100.00

Total                   9            9             3             9              6           36
                    25.00        25.00          8.33         25.00          16.67       100.00

Priors            0.30556      0.19444       0.16667       0.16667        0.16667


                                    Error Count Estimates for Crop

                        Clover         Corn       Cotton     Soybeans     Sugarbeets       Total

   Rate                 0.6364       0.4286       1.0000       0.5000         0.8333      0.6667
   Priors               0.3056       0.1944       0.1667       0.1667         0.1667
```

Now use the calibration information stored in the Cropstat data set to classify a test data set. The TESTLIST option lists the classification results for each observation in the test data set. The following statements produce Output 25.4.4 and Output 25.4.5:

```
data test;
   input Crop $ 1-10 x1-x4 xvalues $ 11-21;
   datalines;
Corn      16 27 31 33
Soybeans  21 25 23 24
Cotton    29 24 26 28
Sugarbeets54 23 21 54
Clover    32 32 62 16
;
```

```
proc discrim data=cropstat testdata=test testout=tout
             testlist;
   class Crop;
   testid xvalues;
   var x1-x4;
   title2 'Classification of Test Data';
run;
proc print data=tout;
   title2 'Output Classification Results of Test Data';
run;
```

Output 25.4.4. Classification of Test Data

```
               Discriminant Analysis of Remote Sensing Data on Five Crops
                              Classification of Test Data

                                The DISCRIM Procedure
                   Classification Results for Test Data: WORK.TEST
                Classification Results using Linear Discriminant Function

                        Generalized Squared Distance Function

                                  2         _       -1   _
                                 D (X) = (X-X )' COV  (X-X )
                                  j          j           j

                  Posterior Probability of Membership in Each Crop

                                         2                    2
                      Pr(j|X) = exp(-.5 D (X)) / SUM exp(-.5 D (X))
                                         j        k            k


                        Posterior Probability of Membership in Crop

                          Classified
xvalues      From Crop    into Crop          Clover        Corn      Cotton    Soybeans  Sugarbeets

16 27 31 33  Corn         Corn               0.0894      0.4054      0.1763      0.2392      0.0897
21 25 23 24  Soybeans     Soybeans           0.1481      0.2431      0.1200      0.3318      0.1570
29 24 26 28  Cotton       Soybeans     *     0.2521      0.1842      0.1529      0.2549      0.1559
54 23 21 54  Sugarbeets   Clover       *     0.6215      0.0194      0.1250      0.0496      0.1845
32 32 62 16  Clover       Cotton       *     0.2163      0.3180      0.3327      0.1125      0.0206

                              * Misclassified observation
```

```
                Discriminant Analysis of Remote Sensing Data on Five Crops
                              Classification of Test Data

                                The DISCRIM Procedure
                     Classification Summary for Test Data: WORK.TEST
                Classification Summary using Linear Discriminant Function

                          Generalized Squared Distance Function

                                   2         _       -1   _
                                  D (X) = (X-X )' COV   (X-X )
                                   j          j             j

                     Posterior Probability of Membership in Each Crop

                                            2                  2
                      Pr(j|X) = exp(-.5 D (X)) / SUM exp(-.5 D (X))
                                            j        k           k
```

Number of Observations and Percent Classified into Crop

From Crop	Clover	Corn	Cotton	Soybeans	Sugarbeets	Total
Clover	0 0.00	0 0.00	1 100.00	0 0.00	0 0.00	1 100.00
Corn	0 0.00	1 100.00	0 0.00	0 0.00	0 0.00	1 100.00
Cotton	0 0.00	0 0.00	0 0.00	1 100.00	0 0.00	1 100.00
Soybeans	0 0.00	0 0.00	0 0.00	1 100.00	0 0.00	1 100.00
Sugarbeets	1 100.00	0 0.00	0 0.00	0 0.00	0 0.00	1 100.00
Total	1 20.00	1 20.00	1 20.00	2 40.00	0 0.00	5 100.00
Priors	0.30556	0.19444	0.16667	0.16667	0.16667	

Error Count Estimates for Crop

	Clover	Corn	Cotton	Soybeans	Sugarbeets	Total
Rate	1.0000	0.0000	1.0000	0.0000	1.0000	0.6389
Priors	0.3056	0.1944	0.1667	0.1667	0.1667	

Output 25.4.5. Output Data Set of the Classification Results for Test Data

Discriminant Analysis of Remote Sensing Data on Five Crops
Output Classification Results of Test Data

Obs	Crop	x1	x2	x3	x4	xvalues				Clover	Corn	Cotton	Soybeans	Sugarbeets	_INTO_
1	Corn	16	27	31	33	16	27	31	33	0.08935	0.40543	0.17632	0.23918	0.08972	Corn
2	Soybeans	21	25	23	24	21	25	23	24	0.14811	0.24308	0.11999	0.33184	0.15698	Soybeans
3	Cotton	29	24	26	28	29	24	26	28	0.25213	0.18420	0.15294	0.25486	0.15588	Soybeans
4	Sugarbeets	54	23	21	54	54	23	21	54	0.62150	0.01937	0.12498	0.04962	0.18452	Clover
5	Clover	32	32	62	16	32	32	62	16	0.21633	0.31799	0.33266	0.11246	0.02056	Cotton

Example 25.5. Quadratic Discriminant Analysis of Remote-Sensing Data on Crops

In this example, PROC DISCRIM uses normal-theory methods (METHOD=NORMAL) assuming unequal variances (POOL=NO) for the remote-sensing data of Example 25.4. The PRIORS statement, PRIORS PROP, sets the prior probabilities proportional to the sample sizes. The CROSSVALIDATE option displays cross validation error-rate estimates. Note that the total error count estimate by cross validation (0.5556) is much larger than the total error count estimate by resubstitution (0.1111). The following statements produce Output 25.5.1:

```
proc discrim data=crops
             method=normal pool=no
             crossvalidate;
   class Crop;
   priors prop;
   id xvalues;
   var x1-x4;
   title2 'Using Quadratic Discriminant Function';
run;
```

Output 25.5.1. Quadratic Discriminant Function on Crop Data

```
        Discriminant Analysis of Remote Sensing Data on Five Crops
                  Using Quadratic Discriminant Function

                          The DISCRIM Procedure

          Observations     36          DF Total                35
          Variables         4          DF Within Classes       31
          Classes           5          DF Between Classes       4


                         Class Level Information

             Variable                                                 Prior
Crop         Name          Frequency       Weight    Proportion    Probability

Clover       Clover               11      11.0000      0.305556       0.305556
Corn         Corn                  7       7.0000      0.194444       0.194444
Cotton       Cotton                6       6.0000      0.166667       0.166667
Soybeans     Soybeans              6       6.0000      0.166667       0.166667
Sugarbeets   Sugarbeets            6       6.0000      0.166667       0.166667
```

```
        Discriminant Analysis of Remote Sensing Data on Five Crops
                  Using Quadratic Discriminant Function

                          The DISCRIM Procedure

                 Within Covariance Matrix Information

                                             Natural Log of the
                            Covariance       Determinant of the
             Crop           Matrix Rank       Covariance Matrix

             Clover                   4                23.64618
             Corn                     4                11.13472
             Cotton                   4                13.23569
             Soybeans                 4                12.45263
             Sugarbeets               4                17.76293
```

```
                Discriminant Analysis of Remote Sensing Data on Five Crops
                         Using Quadratic Discriminant Function

                                The DISCRIM Procedure

                   Pairwise Generalized Squared Distances Between Groups

             2                     -1   _   _
           D (i|j) = (X - X )' COV   (X - X ) + ln |COV | - 2 ln PRIOR
                       i   j       j    i   j          j              j


                          Generalized Squared Distance to Crop
```

From Crop	Clover	Corn	Cotton	Soybeans	Sugarbeets
Clover	26.01743	1320	104.18297	194.10546	31.40816
Corn	27.73809	14.40994	150.50763	38.36252	25.55421
Cotton	26.38544	588.86232	16.81921	52.03266	37.15560
Soybeans	27.07134	46.42131	41.01631	16.03615	23.15920
Sugarbeets	26.80188	332.11563	43.98280	107.95676	21.34645

```
                Discriminant Analysis of Remote Sensing Data on Five Crops
                         Using Quadratic Discriminant Function

                                The DISCRIM Procedure
                 Classification Summary for Calibration Data: WORK.CROPS
              Resubstitution Summary using Quadratic Discriminant Function

                          Generalized Squared Distance Function

               2                  -1   _
              D (X) = (X-X )' COV   (X-X ) + ln |COV | - 2 ln PRIOR
               j            j     j     j           j              j

                    Posterior Probability of Membership in Each Crop

                                        2                  2
                    Pr(j|X) = exp(-.5 D (X)) / SUM exp(-.5 D (X))
                                        j           k       k


                 Number of Observations and Percent Classified into Crop
```

From Crop	Clover	Corn	Cotton	Soybeans	Sugarbeets	Total
Clover	9 81.82	0 0.00	0 0.00	0 0.00	2 18.18	11 100.00
Corn	0 0.00	7 100.00	0 0.00	0 0.00	0 0.00	7 100.00
Cotton	0 0.00	0 0.00	6 100.00	0 0.00	0 0.00	6 100.00
Soybeans	0 0.00	0 0.00	0 0.00	6 100.00	0 0.00	6 100.00
Sugarbeets	0 0.00	0 0.00	1 16.67	1 16.67	4 66.67	6 100.00
Total	9 25.00	7 19.44	7 19.44	7 19.44	6 16.67	36 100.00
Priors	0.30556	0.19444	0.16667	0.16667	0.16667	

Error Count Estimates for Crop

	Clover	Corn	Cotton	Soybeans	Sugarbeets	Total
Rate	0.1818	0.0000	0.0000	0.0000	0.3333	0.1111
Priors	0.3056	0.1944	0.1667	0.1667	0.1667	

```
              Discriminant Analysis of Remote Sensing Data on Five Crops
                   Using Quadratic Discriminant Function

                           The DISCRIM Procedure
             Classification Summary for Calibration Data: WORK.CROPS
          Cross-validation Summary using Quadratic Discriminant Function

                    Generalized Squared Distance Function

          2          _              -1      _
          D (X) = (X-X     )' COV      (X-X     ) + ln |COV     | - 2 ln PRIOR
          j           (X)j       (X)j      (X)j            (X)j              j

               Posterior Probability of Membership in Each Crop

                                   2                   2
               Pr(j|X) = exp(-.5 D (X)) / SUM exp(-.5 D (X))
                                   j           k         k
```

Number of Observations and Percent Classified into Crop

From Crop	Clover	Corn	Cotton	Soybeans	Sugarbeets	Total
Clover	9 81.82	0 0.00	0 0.00	0 0.00	2 18.18	11 100.00
Corn	3 42.86	2 28.57	0 0.00	0 0.00	2 28.57	7 100.00
Cotton	3 50.00	0 0.00	2 33.33	0 0.00	1 16.67	6 100.00
Soybeans	3 50.00	0 0.00	0 0.00	2 33.33	1 16.67	6 100.00
Sugarbeets	3 50.00	0 0.00	1 16.67	1 16.67	1 16.67	6 100.00
Total	21 58.33	2 5.56	3 8.33	3 8.33	7 19.44	36 100.00
Priors	0.30556	0.19444	0.16667	0.16667	0.16667	

Error Count Estimates for Crop

	Clover	Corn	Cotton	Soybeans	Sugarbeets	Total
Rate	0.1818	0.7143	0.6667	0.6667	0.8333	0.5556
Priors	0.3056	0.1944	0.1667	0.1667	0.1667	

References

Anderson, T.W. (1984), *An Introduction to Multivariate Statistical Analysis, Second Edition*, New York: John Wiley & Sons, Inc.

Cover, T.M. and Hart, P.E. (1967), "Nearest Neighbor Pattern Classification," *IEEE Transactions on Information Theory*, IT-13, 21–27.

Epanechnikov, V.A. (1969), "Nonparametric Estimation of a Multivariate Probability Density," *Theory of Probability and Its Applications*, 14, 153–158.

Fisher, R.A. (1936), "The Use of Multiple Measurements in Taxonomic Problems," *Annals of Eugenics*, 7, 179–188.

Fix, E. and Hodges, J.L., Jr. (1959), "Discriminatory Analysis: Nonparametric Discrimination: Consistency Properties," *Report No. 4, Project No. 21-49-004*, School of Aviation Medicine, Randolph Air Force Base, TX.

Friedman, J.H., Bentley, J.L., and Finkel, R.A. (1977), "An Algorithm for Finding Best Matches in Logarithmic Expected Time," *ACM Transactions on Mathematical Software*, 3, 209–226.

Fukunaga, K. and Kessel, D.L. (1973), "Nonparametric Bayes Error Estimation Using Unclassified Samples," *IEEE Transactions on Information Theory*, 19, 434–440.

Glick, N. (1978), "Additive Estimators for Probabilities of Correct Classification," *Pattern Recognition*, 10, 211–222.

Hand, D.J. (1981), *Discrimination and Classification*, New York: John Wiley & Sons, Inc.

Hand, D.J. (1982), *Kernel Discriminant Analysis*, New York: Research Studies Press.

Hand, D.J. (1986), "Recent Advances in Error Rate Estimation," *Pattern Recognition Letters*, 4, 335–346.

Hora, S.C. and Wilcox, J.B. (1982), "Estimation of Error Rates in Several-Population Discriminant Analysis," *Journal of Marketing Research*, XIX, 57–61.

Kendall, M.G., Stuart, A., and Ord, J.K. (1983), *The Advanced Theory of Statistics, Vol. 3, Fourth Edition*, New York: Macmillan Publishing Co., Inc.

Kshirsagar, A.M. (1972), *Multivariate Analysis*, New York: Marcel Dekker.

Lachenbruch, P.A. and Mickey, M.A. (1968), "Estimation of Error Rates in Discriminant Analysis," *Technometrics*, 10, 1–10.

Lawley, D.N. (1959), "Tests of Significance in Canonical Analysis," *Biometrika*, 46, 59–66.

Morrison, D.F. (1976), *Multivariate Statistical Methods*, New York: McGraw-Hill.

Parzen, E. (1962), "On Estimation of a Probability Density Function and Mode," *Annals of Mathematical Statistics*, 33, 1065–1076.

Perlman, M.D. (1980), "Unbiasedness of the Likelihood Ratio Tests for Equality of Several Covariance Matrices and Equality of Several Multivariate Normal Populations," *Annals of Statistics*, 8, 247–263.

Rao, C. R. (1973), *Linear Statistical Inference and Its Applications, Second Edition*, New York: John Wiley & Sons, Inc.

Ripley, B.D. (1996), *Pattern Recognition and Neural Networks*, Cambridge: Cambridge University Press.

Rosenblatt, M. (1956), "Remarks on Some Nonparametric Estimates of a Density Function," *Annals of Mathematical Statistics*, 27, 832–837.

Silverman, B. W. (1986), *Density Estimation for Statistics and Data Analysis*, New York: Chapman and Hall.

Snapinn, S.M. and Knoke, J.D. (1985), "An Evaluation of Smoothed Classification Error-Rate Estimators," *Technometrics*, 27, 199–206.

Chapter 26
The FACTOR Procedure

Chapter Table of Contents

Chapter 26
The FACTOR Procedure

Overview

The FACTOR procedure performs a variety of common factor and component analyses and rotations. Input can be multivariate data, a correlation matrix, a covariance matrix, a factor pattern, or a matrix of scoring coefficients. The procedure can factor either the correlation or covariance matrix, and you can save most results in an output data set.

PROC FACTOR can process output from other procedures. For example, it can rotate the canonical coefficients from multivariate analyses in the GLM procedure.

The methods for factor extraction are principal component analysis, principal factor analysis, iterated principal factor analysis, unweighted least-squares factor analysis, maximum-likelihood (canonical) factor analysis, alpha factor analysis, image component analysis, and Harris component analysis. A variety of methods for prior communality estimation is also available.

The methods for rotation are varimax, quartimax, parsimax, equamax, orthomax with user-specified gamma, promax with user-specified exponent, Harris-Kaiser case II with user-specified exponent, and oblique Procrustean with a user-specified target pattern.

Output includes means, standard deviations, correlations, Kaiser's measure of sampling adequacy, eigenvalues, a scree plot, eigenvectors, prior and final communality estimates, the unrotated factor pattern, residual and partial correlations, the rotated primary factor pattern, the primary factor structure, interfactor correlations, the reference structure, reference axis correlations, the variance explained by each factor both ignoring and eliminating other factors, plots of both rotated and unrotated factors, squared multiple correlation of each factor with the variables, and scoring coefficients.

Any topics that are not given explicit references are discussed in Mulaik (1972) or Harman (1976).

Background

See Chapter 52, "The PRINCOMP Procedure," for a discussion of principal component analysis. See Chapter 19, "The CALIS Procedure," for a discussion of confirmatory factor analysis.

Common factor analysis was invented by Spearman (1904). Kim and Mueller (1978a,b) provide a very elementary discussion of the common factor model. Gorsuch (1974) contains a broad survey of factor analysis, and Gorsuch (1974) and

Cattell (1978) are useful as guides to practical research methodology. Harman (1976) gives a lucid discussion of many of the more technical aspects of factor analysis, especially oblique rotation. Morrison (1976) and Mardia, Kent, and Bibby (1979) provide excellent statistical treatments of common factor analysis. Mulaik (1972) is the most thorough and authoritative general reference on factor analysis and is highly recommended to anyone familiar with matrix algebra. Stewart (1981) gives a nontechnical presentation of some issues to consider when deciding whether or not a factor analysis may be appropriate.

A frequent source of confusion in the field of factor analysis is the term *factor*. It sometimes refers to a hypothetical, unobservable variable, as in the phrase *common factor*. In this sense, *factor analysis* must be distinguished from component analysis since a component is an observable linear combination. *Factor* is also used in the sense of *matrix factor,* in that one matrix is a factor of a second matrix if the first matrix multiplied by its transpose equals the second matrix. In this sense, *factor analysis* refers to all methods of data analysis using matrix factors, including component analysis and common factor analysis.

A *common factor* is an unobservable, hypothetical variable that contributes to the variance of at least two of the observed variables. The unqualified term "factor" often refers to a common factor. A *unique factor* is an unobservable, hypothetical variable that contributes to the variance of only one of the observed variables. The model for common factor analysis posits one unique factor for each observed variable.

The equation for the common factor model is

$$y_{ij} = x_{i1}b_{1j} + x_{i2}b_{2j} + \cdots + x_{iq}b_{qj} + e_{ij}$$

where

y_{ij}	is the value of the ith observation on the jth variable
x_{ik}	is the value of the ith observation on the kth common factor
b_{kj}	is the regression coefficient of the kth common factor for predicting the jth variable
e_{ij}	is the value of the ith observation on the jth unique factor
q	is the number of common factors

It is assumed, for convenience, that all variables have a mean of 0. In matrix terms, these equations reduce to

$$\mathbf{Y} = \mathbf{XB} + \mathbf{E}$$

In the preceding equation, $\mathbf{X}$ is the matrix of factor scores, and $\mathbf{B}'$ is the factor pattern.

There are two critical assumptions:

- The unique factors are uncorrelated with each other.
- The unique factors are uncorrelated with the common factors.

In principal component analysis, the residuals are generally correlated with each other. In common factor analysis, the unique factors play the role of residuals and are defined to be uncorrelated both with each other and with the common factors. Each common factor is assumed to contribute to at least two variables; otherwise, it would be a unique factor.

When the factors are initially extracted, it is also assumed, for convenience, that the common factors are uncorrelated with each other and have unit variance. In this case, the common factor model implies that the covariance s_{jk} between the jth and kth variables, $j \neq k$, is given by

$$s_{jk} = b_{1j}b_{1k} + b_{2j}b_{2k} + \cdots + b_{qj}b_{qk}$$

or

$$\mathbf{S} = \mathbf{B}'\mathbf{B} + \mathbf{U}^2$$

where $\mathbf{S}$ is the covariance matrix of the observed variables, and $\mathbf{U}^2$ is the diagonal covariance matrix of the unique factors.

If the original variables are standardized to unit variance, the preceding formula yields correlations instead of covariances. It is in this sense that common factors explain the correlations among the observed variables. The difference between the correlation predicted by the common factor model and the actual correlation is the *residual correlation*. A good way to assess the goodness-of-fit of the common factor model is to examine the residual correlations.

The common factor model implies that the partial correlations among the variables, removing the effects of the common factors, must all be 0. When the common factors are removed, only unique factors, which are by definition uncorrelated, remain.

The assumptions of common factor analysis imply that the common factors are, in general, not linear combinations of the observed variables. In fact, even if the data contain measurements on the entire population of observations, you cannot compute the scores of the observations on the common factors. Although the common factor scores cannot be computed directly, they can be estimated in a variety of ways.

The problem of factor score indeterminacy has led several factor analysts to propose methods yielding components that can be considered approximations to common factors. Since these components are defined as linear combinations, they are computable. The methods include Harris component analysis and image component analysis. The advantage of producing determinate component scores is offset by the fact that, even if the data fit the common factor model perfectly, component methods do not generally recover the correct factor solution. You should not use any type of component analysis if you really want a common factor analysis (Dziuban and Harris 1973; Lee and Comrey 1979).

After the factors are estimated, it is necessary to interpret them. Interpretation usually means assigning to each common factor a name that reflects the importance of the factor in predicting each of the observed variables, that is, the coefficients in the pattern matrix corresponding to the factor. Factor interpretation is a subjective process. It can sometimes be made less subjective by *rotating* the common factors, that is, by applying a nonsingular linear transformation. A rotated pattern matrix in which all the coefficients are close to 0 or ± 1 is easier to interpret than a pattern with many intermediate elements. Therefore, most rotation methods attempt to optimize a function of the pattern matrix that measures, in some sense, how close the elements are to 0 or ± 1.

After the initial factor extraction, the common factors are uncorrelated with each other. If the factors are rotated by an *orthogonal transformation,* the rotated factors are also uncorrelated. If the factors are rotated by an *oblique transformation,* the rotated factors become correlated. Oblique rotations often produce more useful patterns than do orthogonal rotations. However, a consequence of correlated factors is that there is no single unambiguous measure of the importance of a factor in explaining a variable. Thus, for oblique rotations, the pattern matrix does not provide all the necessary information for interpreting the factors; you must also examine the *factor structure* and the *reference structure*.

Rotating a set of factors does not change the statistical explanatory power of the factors. You cannot say that any rotation is better than any other rotation from a statistical point of view; all rotations are equally good statistically. Therefore, the choice among different rotations must be based on nonstatistical grounds. For most applications, the preferred rotation is that which is most easily interpretable.

If two rotations give rise to different interpretations, those two interpretations must not be regarded as conflicting. Rather, they are two different ways of looking at the same thing, two different points of view in the common-factor space. Any conclusion that depends on one and only one rotation being correct is invalid.

Outline of Use

Principal Component Analysis

One important type of analysis performed by the FACTOR procedure is principal component analysis. The statements

```
proc factor;
run;
```

result in a principal component analysis. The output includes all the eigenvalues and the pattern matrix for eigenvalues greater than one.

Most applications require additional output. For example, you may want to compute principal component scores for use in subsequent analyses or obtain a graphical aid to help decide how many components to keep. You can save the results of the analysis in a permanent SAS data library by using the OUTSTAT= option. (Refer to the *SAS Language Reference: Dictionary* for more information on permanent SAS data libraries and librefs.) Assuming that your SAS data library has the libref save and that the data are in a SAS data set called raw, you could do a principal component analysis as follows:

```
proc factor data=raw method=principal scree mineigen=0 score
     outstat=save.fact_all;
run;
```

The SCREE option produces a plot of the eigenvalues that is helpful in deciding how many components to use. The MINEIGEN=0 option causes all components with variance greater than zero to be retained. The SCORE option requests that scoring coefficients be computed. The OUTSTAT= option saves the results in a specially structured SAS data set. The name of the data set, in this case fact_all, is arbitrary. To compute principal component scores, use the SCORE procedure.

```
proc score data=raw score=save.fact_all out=save.scores;
run;
```

The SCORE procedure uses the data and the scoring coefficients that are saved in save.fact_all to compute principal component scores. The component scores are placed in variables named Factor1, Factor2, . . . , Factor$n$ and are saved in the data set save.scores. If you know ahead of time how many principal components you want to use, you can obtain the scores directly from PROC FACTOR by specifying the NFACTORS= and OUT= options. To get scores from three principal components, specify

```
proc factor data=raw method=principal
     nfactors=3 out=save.scores;
run;
```

To plot the scores for the first three components, use the PLOT procedure.

```
proc plot;
   plot factor2*factor1 factor3*factor1 factor3*factor2;
run;
```

Principal Factor Analysis

The simplest and computationally most efficient method of common factor analysis is principal factor analysis, which is obtained the same way as principal component analysis except for the use of the PRIORS= option. The usual form of the initial analysis is

```
proc factor data=raw method=principal scree
     mineigen=0 priors=smc outstat=save.fact_all;
run;
```

The squared multiple correlations (SMC) of each variable with all the other variables are used as the prior communality estimates. If your correlation matrix is singular, you should specify PRIORS=MAX instead of PRIORS=SMC. The SCREE and MINEIGEN= options serve the same purpose as in the preceding principal component analysis. Saving the results with the OUTSTAT= option enables you to examine the eigenvalues and scree plot before deciding how many factors to rotate and to try several different rotations without re-extracting the factors. The OUTSTAT= data set is automatically marked TYPE=FACTOR, so the FACTOR procedure realizes that it contains statistics from a previous analysis instead of raw data.

After looking at the eigenvalues to estimate the number of factors, you can try some rotations. Two and three factors can be rotated with the following statements:

```
proc factor data=save.fact_all method=principal n=2
     rotate=promax reorder score outstat=save.fact_2;
proc factor data=save.fact_all method=principal n=3
     rotate=promax reorder score outstat=save.fact_3;
run;
```

The output data set from the previous run is used as input for these analyses. The options N=2 and N=3 specify the number of factors to be rotated. The specification ROTATE=PROMAX requests a promax rotation, which has the advantage of providing both orthogonal and oblique rotations with only one invocation of PROC FACTOR. The REORDER option causes the variables to be reordered in the output so that variables associated with the same factor appear next to each other.

You can now compute and plot factor scores for the two-factor promax-rotated solution as follows:

```
proc score data=raw score=save.fact_2 out=save.scores;
proc plot;
   plot factor2*factor1;
run;
```

Maximum-Likelihood Factor Analysis

Although principal factor analysis is perhaps the most commonly used method of common factor analysis, most statisticians prefer maximum-likelihood (ML) factor analysis (Lawley and Maxwell 1971). The ML method of estimation has desirable asymptotic properties (Bickel and Doksum 1977) and produces better estimates than principal factor analysis in large samples. You can test hypotheses about the number of common factors using the ML method.

The ML solution is equivalent to Rao's (1955) canonical factor solution and Howe's solution maximizing the determinant of the partial correlation matrix (Morrison 1976). Thus, as a descriptive method, ML factor analysis does not require a multivariate normal distribution. The validity of Bartlett's χ^2 test for the number of factors does require approximate normality plus additional regularity conditions that are usually satisfied in practice (Geweke and Singleton 1980).

The ML method is more computationally demanding than principal factor analysis for two reasons. First, the communalities are estimated iteratively, and each iteration takes about as much computer time as principal factor analysis. The number of iterations typically ranges from about five to twenty. Second, if you want to extract different numbers of factors, as is often the case, you must run the FACTOR procedure once for each number of factors. Therefore, an ML analysis can take 100 times as long as a principal factor analysis.

You can use principal factor analysis to get a rough idea of the number of factors before doing an ML analysis. If you think that there are between one and three factors, you can use the following statements for the ML analysis:

```
proc factor data=raw method=ml n=1
     outstat=save.fact1;
run;
proc factor data=raw method=ml n=2 rotate=promax
     outstat=save.fact2;
run;
proc factor data=raw method=ml n=3 rotate=promax
     outstat=save.fact3;
run;
```

The output data sets can be used for trying different rotations, computing scoring coefficients, or restarting the procedure in case it does not converge within the allotted number of iterations.

The ML method cannot be used with a singular correlation matrix, and it is especially prone to Heywood cases. (See the section "Heywood Cases and Other Anomalies" on page 1153 for a discussion of Heywood cases.) If you have problems with ML, the best alternative is to use the METHOD=ULS option for unweighted least-squares factor analysis.

Getting Started

The following example demonstrates how you can use the FACTOR procedure to perform common factor analysis and use a transformation to rotate the extracted factors.

Suppose that you want to use factor analysis to explore the relationship among assessment scores of a group of students. For each student in the group, you record six homework scores, two midterm examination scores, and the final exam score.

The following DATA step creates the SAS data set Grades:

```
data Grades;
   input HomeWork1 - HomeWork6 MidTerm1 MidTerm2 FinalExam;
   datalines;
15  18  36  29  44  30  78  87  70
15  16  24  30  41  30  71  73  89
15  14  23  34  28  24  84  72  76
15  20  39  35  50  30  74  79  96
15  20  39  35  46  30  76  77  94
15  20  28  30  49  28  40  44  66
15  15  29  25  36  30  88  69  93
15  20  37  35  50  30  97  95  98
14  16  24  30  44  28  57  78  85
15  17  29  26  38  28  56  78  76
15  17  31  34  40  27  72  67  84
11  16  29  34  31  27  83  68  75
15  18  31  18  40  30  75  43  67
14  14  29  25  49  30  71  93  93
15  18  36  29  44  30  85  64  75
;
```

The data set Grades contains the variables representing homework scores (HomeWork1—HomeWork6), the two midterm exam scores (MidTerm1 and MidTerm2), and the final exam score (FinalExam).

The following statements invoke the FACTOR procedure:

```
proc factor data=Grades priors=smc rotate=varimax nfactors=2;
run;
```

The DATA= option in PROC FACTOR specifies the SAS data set Grades as the input data set. The PRIORS= option specifies that the squared multiple correlations (SMC) of each variable with all the other variables are used as the prior communality estimates and also that PROC FACTOR gives a principal factor solution to the common factor model. The ROTATE= option specifies the VARIMAX orthogonal factor rotation method. To see if two latent factors can explain the observed variation in the data, the NFACTOR= option specifies that two factors be retained. All variables in the data set are analyzed.

The output from this analysis is displayed in the following figures.

The SAS System

The FACTOR Procedure
Initial Factor Method: Principal Factors

Prior Communality Estimates: SMC

HomeWork1	HomeWork2	HomeWork3	HomeWork4	HomeWork5
0.27602335	0.86733312	0.82222517	0.79295256	0.80742053

HomeWork6	MidTerm1	MidTerm2	FinalExam
0.83330706	0.67135234	0.64889405	0.68860512

Eigenvalues of the Reduced Correlation Matrix:
Total = 6.40811331 Average = 0.71201259

	Eigenvalue	Difference	Proportion	Cumulative
1	3.00212450	1.21898414	0.4685	0.4685
2	1.78314036	0.71888817	0.2783	0.7468
3	1.06425218	0.34974843	0.1661	0.9128
4	0.71450375	0.55643869	0.1115	1.0243
5	0.15806506	0.10471212	0.0247	1.0490
6	0.05335294	0.15681933	0.0083	1.0573
7	-.10346639	0.01266761	-0.0161	1.0412
8	-.11613399	0.03159110	-0.0181	1.0231
9	-.14772509		-0.0231	1.0000

2 factors will be retained by the NFACTOR criterion.

Figure 26.1. Table of Eigenvalues from PROC FACTOR

As displayed in Figure 26.1, the prior communality estimates are set to the squared multiple correlations. Figure 26.1 also displays the table of eigenvalues, which are the variances of the principal factors, of the reduced correlation matrix. Each row of the table pertains to a single eigenvalue. Following the column of eigenvalues are three measures of each eigenvalue's relative size and importance. The first of these displays the difference between the eigenvalue and its successor. The last two columns display the individual and cumulative proportions that the corresponding factor contributes to the total variation. The last line displayed in Figure 26.1 states that two factors are retained, as specified by the NFACTORS= option in the PROC FACTOR statement.

The FACTOR Procedure
Initial Factor Method: Principal Factors

Factor Pattern

	Factor1	Factor2
HomeWork1	0.31105	-0.26516
HomeWork2	0.70521	-0.42151
HomeWork3	0.83281	-0.01966
HomeWork4	0.23315	0.54773
HomeWork5	0.79715	-0.29570
HomeWork6	0.73831	-0.24142
MidTerm1	0.21725	0.58751
MidTerm2	0.39266	0.64770
FinalExam	0.52745	0.56953

Figure 26.2. Factor Pattern Matrix from PROC FACTOR

Figure 26.2 displays the factor pattern matrix. The factor pattern matrix is the matrix of correlations between variables and the common factors. When the factors are orthogonal, the pattern matrix is also equal to the matrix of standardized regression coefficients for predicting the variables using the extracted factors.

The pattern matrix suggests that the first factor represents general ability, with positive loadings from all variables. The second factor is more difficult to interpret, but it may represent a contrast between exam and homework scores, with the exception of the score for HomeWork4.

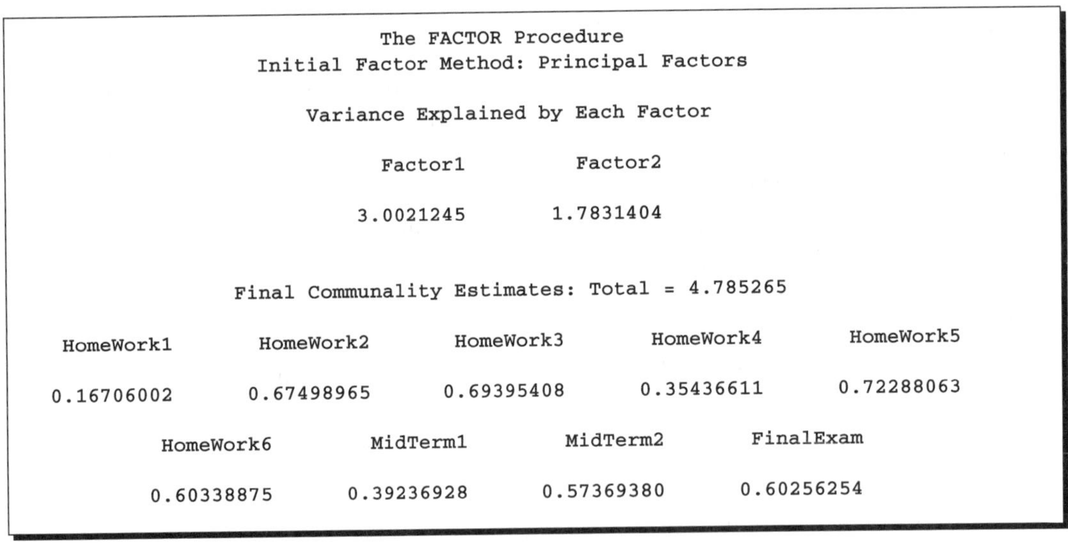

The FACTOR Procedure
Initial Factor Method: Principal Factors

Variance Explained by Each Factor

Factor1	Factor2
3.0021245	1.7831404

Final Communality Estimates: Total = 4.785265

HomeWork1	HomeWork2	HomeWork3	HomeWork4	HomeWork5
0.16706002	0.67498965	0.69395408	0.35436611	0.72288063

HomeWork6	MidTerm1	MidTerm2	FinalExam
0.60338875	0.39236928	0.57369380	0.60256254

Figure 26.3. Variance Explained and Final Communality Estimates

Figure 26.3 displays the variance explained by each factor and the final communality estimates, including the total communality. The final communality estimates are the proportion of variance of the variables accounted for by the common factors. When the factors are orthogonal, the final communalities are calculated by taking the sum of squares of each row of the factor pattern matrix. For example, the final communality estimate for the variable FinalExam is computed as follows:

$$0.60256254 = (0.52745)^2 + (0.56953)^2$$

Figure 26.4 displays the results of the VARIMAX rotation of the two extracted factors and the final communality estimates of the rotated factors.

The rotated factor pattern matrix is calculated by postmultiplying the original factor pattern matrix (Figure 26.2) by the orthogonal transformation matrix (Figure 26.4).

```
                    The FACTOR Procedure
                  Rotation Method: Varimax

              Orthogonal Transformation Matrix

                               1               2

                 1       0.89675         0.44254
                 2      -0.44254         0.89675


                   Rotated Factor Pattern

                         Factor1         Factor2

        HomeWork1        0.39628        -0.10013
        HomeWork2        0.81893        -0.06590
        HomeWork3        0.75552         0.35093
        HomeWork4       -0.03332         0.59435
        HomeWork5        0.84570         0.08761
        HomeWork6        0.76892         0.11024
        MidTerm1        -0.06518         0.62299
        MidTerm2         0.06549         0.75459
        FinalExam        0.22095         0.74414
```

Figure 26.4. Transformation Matrix and Rotated Factor Pattern

The rotated factor pattern matrix is somewhat simpler to interpret: the rotated Factor1 can now be interpreted as general ability in homework performance. The homework variables load higher on Factor1 (with the single exception of the variable HomeWork4), with small loadings for the exam score variables. The rotated Factor2 seems to measure exam performance or test-taking ability. The exam score variables load heavily on Factor2, as does HomeWork4.

```
                        The FACTOR Procedure
                      Rotation Method: Varimax

                  Variance Explained by Each Factor

                        Factor1         Factor2

                      2.7633918       2.0218731


             Final Communality Estimates: Total = 4.785265

    HomeWork1       HomeWork2       HomeWork3       HomeWork4       HomeWork5

   0.16706002      0.67498965      0.69395408      0.35436611      0.72288063

            HomeWork6       MidTerm1        MidTerm2       FinalExam

           0.60338875      0.39236928      0.57369380      0.60256254
```

Figure 26.5. Variance Explained and Final Communality Estimates after Rotation

Figure 26.5 displays the variance explained by each factor and the final communality estimates. Even though the variance explained by the rotated Factor1 is less than that explained by the unrotated factor (compare with Figure 26.3), the cumulative variance explained by both common factors remains the same after the orthogonal rotation. Also note that the VARIMAX rotation, as with any orthogonal rotation, has not changed the final communalities.

Syntax

You can specify the following statements with the FACTOR procedure.

> **PROC FACTOR** < *options* > ;
> **VAR** *variables* ;
> **PRIORS** *communalities* ;
> **PARTIAL** *variables* ;
> **FREQ** *variable* ;
> **WEIGHT** *variable* ;
> **BY** *variables* ;

Usually only the VAR statement is needed in addition to the PROC FACTOR statement. The descriptions of the BY, FREQ, PARTIAL, PRIORS, VAR, and WEIGHT statements follow the description of the PROC FACTOR statement in alphabetical order.

PROC FACTOR Statement

PROC FACTOR < *options* > **;**

The options available with the PROC FACTOR statement are listed in the following table and then are described in alphabetical order.

Table 26.1. Options Available in the PROC FACTOR Statement

Task	Option
Data sets	DATA=
	OUT=
	OUTSTAT=
	TARGET=
Extract factors and communalities	HEYWOOD
	METHOD=
	PRIORS=
	RANDOM=
	ULTRAHEYWOOD
Analyze data	COVARIANCE
	NOINT
	VARDEF=
	WEIGHT
Specify number of factors	MINEIGEN=
	NFACTORS=
	PROPORTION=
Specify numerical properties	CONVERGE=
	MAXITER=
	SINGULAR=
Specify rotation method	GAMMA=
	HKPOWER=
	NORM=
	POWER=
	PREROTATE=
	ROTATE=
Control displayed output	ALL
	CORR
	EIGENVECTORS
	MSA
	NOPRINT
	NPLOT=
	PLOT
	PREPLOT
	PRINT
	REORDER

Table 26.1. (continued)

Task	Option
	RESIDUALS
	SCORE
	SCREE
	SIMPLE
Exclude the correlation matrix from the OUTSTAT= data set	NOCORR
Miscellaneous	NOBS=

ALL

displays all optional output except plots. When the input data set is TYPE=CORR, TYPE=UCORR, TYPE=COV, TYPE=UCOV or TYPE=FACTOR, simple statistics, correlations, and MSA are not displayed.

CONVERGE=*p*
CONV=*p*

specifies the convergence criterion for the METHOD=PRINIT, METHOD=ULS, METHOD=ALPHA, or METHOD=ML option. Iteration stops when the maximum change in the communalities is less than the value of the CONVERGE= option. The default value is 0.001. Negative values are not allowed.

CORR
C

displays the correlation matrix or partial correlation matrix.

COVARIANCE
COV

requests factoring of the covariance matrix instead of the correlation matrix. The COV option can be used only with the METHOD=PRINCIPAL, METHOD=PRINIT, METHOD=ULS, or METHOD=IMAGE option.

DATA=*SAS-data-set*

specifies the input data set, which can be an ordinary SAS data set or a specially structured SAS data set as described in the section "Input Data Set" beginning on page 1146. If the DATA= option is omitted, the most recently created SAS data set is used.

EIGENVECTORS
EV

displays the eigenvectors. PROC FACTOR chooses the solution that makes the sum of the elements of each eigenvector nonnegative. If the sum of the elements is equal to zero, then the sign depends on how the number is rounded off.

GAMMA=*p*

specifies the orthomax weight used with the option ROTATE=ORTHOMAX or PREROTATE=ORTHOMAX. There is no restriction on valid values.

HEYWOOD
HEY

sets to 1 any communality greater than 1, allowing iterations to proceed.

HKPOWER=*p*
HKP=*p*

specifies the power of the square roots of the eigenvalues used to rescale the eigenvectors for Harris-Kaiser (ROTATE=HK) rotation. Values between 0.0 and 1.0 are reasonable. The default value is 0.0, yielding the independent cluster solution (each variable tends to have a large loading on only one factor). A value of 1.0 is equivalent to a varimax rotation. You can also specify the HKPOWER= option with the ROTATE=QUARTIMAX, ROTATE=VARIMAX, ROTATE=EQUAMAX, or ROTATE=ORTHOMAX option, in which case the Harris-Kaiser rotation uses the specified orthogonal rotation method.

MAXITER=*n*

specifies the maximum number of iterations. You can use the MAXITER= option with the PRINIT, ULS, ALPHA, or ML methods. The default is 30.

METHOD=*name*
M=*name*

specifies the method for extracting factors. The default is METHOD=PRINCIPAL unless the DATA= data set is TYPE=FACTOR, in which case the default is METHOD=PATTERN. Valid values for *name* are as follows:

ALPHA | A	produces alpha factor analysis.
HARRIS | H	yields Harris component analysis of $\mathbf{S}^{-1}\mathbf{R}\mathbf{S}^{-1}$ (Harris 1962), a noniterative approximation to canonical component analysis.
IMAGE | I	yields principal component analysis of the image covariance matrix, not Kaiser's (1963, 1970) or Kaiser and Rice's (1974) image analysis. A nonsingular correlation matrix is required.
ML | M	performs maximum-likelihood factor analysis with an algorithm due, except for minor details, to Fuller (1987). The option METHOD=ML requires a nonsingular correlation matrix.
PATTERN	reads a factor pattern from a TYPE=FACTOR, TYPE=CORR, TYPE=UCORR, TYPE=COV or TYPE=UCOV data set. If you create a TYPE=FACTOR data set in a DATA step, only observations containing the factor pattern (_TYPE_='PATTERN') and, if the factors are correlated, the interfactor correlations (_TYPE_='FCORR') are required.
PRINCIPAL | PRIN | P	yields principal component analysis if no PRIORS option or statement is used or if you specify PRIORS=ONE; if you specify a PRIORS statement or a PRIORS= value other than PRIORS=ONE, a principal factor analysis is performed.
PRINIT	yields iterated principal factor analysis.
SCORE	reads scoring coefficients (_TYPE_='SCORE') from a TYPE=FACTOR, TYPE=CORR, TYPE=UCORR, TYPE=COV,

or TYPE=UCOV data set. The data set must also contain either a correlation or a covariance matrix. Scoring coefficients are also displayed if you specify the OUT= option.

ULS | U produces unweighted least squares factor analysis.

MINEIGEN=*p*
MIN=*p*

specifies the smallest eigenvalue for which a factor is retained. If you specify two or more of the MINEIGEN=, NFACTORS=, and PROPORTION= options, the number of factors retained is the minimum number satisfying any of the criteria. The MINEIGEN= option cannot be used with either the METHOD=PATTERN or the METHOD=SCORE option. Negative values are not allowed. The default is 0 unless you omit both the NFACTORS= and the PROPORTION= options and one of the following conditions holds:

- If you specify the METHOD=ALPHA or METHOD=HARRIS option, then MINEIGEN=1.
- If you specify the METHOD=IMAGE option, then

$$\text{MINEIGEN} = \frac{\text{total image variance}}{\text{number of variables}}$$

- For any other METHOD= specification, if prior communality estimates of 1.0 are used, then

$$\text{MINEIGEN} = \frac{\text{total weighted variance}}{\text{number of variables}}$$

When an unweighted correlation matrix is factored, this value is 1.

MSA

produces the partial correlations between each pair of variables controlling for all other variables (the negative anti-image correlations) and Kaiser's measure of sampling adequacy (Kaiser 1970; Kaiser and Rice 1974; Cerny and Kaiser 1977).

NFACTORS=*n*
NFACT=*n*
N=*n*

specifies the maximum number of factors to be extracted and determines the amount of memory to be allocated for factor matrices. The default is the number of variables. Specifying a number that is small relative to the number of variables can substantially decrease the amount of memory required to run PROC FACTOR, especially with oblique rotations. If you specify two or more of the NFACTORS=, MINEIGEN=, and PROPORTION= options, the number of factors retained is the minimum number satisfying any of the criteria. If you specify the option NFACTORS=0, eigenvalues are computed, but no factors are extracted. If you specify the option NFACTORS=-1, neither eigenvalues nor factors are computed. You can use the NFACTORS= option with the METHOD=PATTERN or METHOD=SCORE option to specify a smaller number of factors than are present in the data set.

NOBS=*n*

specifies the number of observations. If the DATA= input data set is a raw data set, *nobs* is defined by default to be the number of observations in the raw data set. The NOBS= option overrides this default definition. If the DATA= input data set contains a covariance, correlation, or scalar product matrix, the number of observations can be specified either by using the NOBS= option in the PROC FACTOR statement or by including a _TYPE_='N' observation in the DATA= input data set.

NOCORR

prevents the correlation matrix from being transferred to the OUTSTAT= data set when you specify the METHOD=PATTERN option. The NOCORR option greatly reduces memory requirements when there are many variables but few factors. The NOCORR option is not effective if the correlation matrix is required for other requested output; for example, if the scores or the residual correlations are displayed (using SCORE, RESIDUALS, ALL options).

NOINT

omits the intercept from the analysis; covariances or correlations are not corrected for the mean.

NOPRINT

suppresses the display of all output. Note that this option temporarily disables the Output Delivery System (ODS). For more information, see Chapter 15, "Using the Output Delivery System."

NORM=COV | KAISER | NONE | RAW | WEIGHT

specifies the method for normalizing the rows of the factor pattern for rotation. If you specify the option NORM=KAISER, Kaiser's normalization is used ($\sum_j p_{ij}^2 = 1$). If you specify the option NORM=WEIGHT, the rows are weighted by the Cureton-Mulaik technique (Cureton and Mulaik 1975). If you specify the option NORM=COV, the rows of the pattern matrix are rescaled to represent covariances instead of correlations. If you specify the option NORM=NONE or NORM=RAW, normalization is not performed. The default is NORM=KAISER.

NPLOT=*n*

specifies the number of factors to be plotted. The default is to plot all factors. The smallest allowable value is 2. If you specify the option NPLOT=n, all pairs of the first n factors are plotted, producing a total of $n(n-1)/2$ plots.

OUT=*SAS-data-set*

creates a data set containing all the data from the DATA= data set plus variables called Factor1, Factor2, and so on, containing estimated factor scores. The DATA= data set must contain multivariate data, not correlations or covariances. You must also specify the NFACTORS= option to determine the number of factor score variables. If you want to create a permanent SAS data set, you must specify a two-level name. Refer to "SAS Files" in *SAS Language Reference: Concepts* for more information on permanent data sets.

OUTSTAT=*SAS-data-set*

specifies an output data set containing most of the results of the analysis. The output data set is described in detail in the section "Output Data Sets" on page 1149. If you want to create a permanent SAS data set, you must specify a two-level name. Refer to "SAS Files" in *SAS Language Reference: Concepts* for more information on permanent data sets.

PLOT

plots the factor pattern after rotation.

POWER=*n*

specifies the power to be used in computing the target pattern for the option ROTATE=PROMAX. Valid values must be integers ≥ 1. The default value is 3.

PREPLOT

plots the factor pattern before rotation.

PREROTATE=*name*
PRE=*name*

specifies the prerotation method for the option ROTATE=PROMAX. Any rotation method other than PROMAX or PROCRUSTES can be used. The default is PREROTATE=VARIMAX. If a previously rotated pattern is read using the option METHOD=PATTERN, you should specify the PREROTATE=NONE option.

PRINT

displays the input factor pattern or scoring coefficients and related statistics. In oblique cases, the reference and factor structures are computed and displayed. The PRINT option is effective only with the option METHOD=PATTERN or METHOD=SCORE.

PRIORS=*name*

specifies a method for computing prior communality estimates. You can specify numeric values for the prior communality estimates by using the PRIORS statement. Valid values for *name* are as follows:

ASMC | A	sets the prior communality estimates proportional to the squared multiple correlations but adjusted so that their sum is equal to that of the maximum absolute correlations (Cureton 1968).
INPUT | I	reads the prior communality estimates from the first observation with either _TYPE_='PRIORS' or _TYPE_='COMMUNAL' in the DATA= data set (which must be TYPE=FACTOR).
MAX | M	sets the prior communality estimate for each variable to its maximum absolute correlation with any other variable.
ONE | O	sets all prior communalities to 1.0.
RANDOM | R	sets the prior communality estimates to pseudo-random numbers uniformly distributed between 0 and 1.
SMC | S	sets the prior communality estimate for each variable to its squared multiple correlation with all other variables.

The default prior communality estimates are as follows.

METHOD=	**PRIORS=**
PRINCIPAL	ONE
PRINIT	ONE
ALPHA	SMC
ULS	SMC
ML	SMC
HARRIS	(not applicable)
IMAGE	(not applicable)
PATTERN	(not applicable)
SCORE	(not applicable)

By default, the options METHOD=PRINIT, METHOD=ULS, METHOD=ALPHA, and METHOD=ML stop iterating and set the number of factors to 0 if an estimated communality exceeds 1. The options HEYWOOD and ULTRAHEYWOOD allow processing to continue.

PROPORTION=*p*
PERCENT=*p*
P=*p*

specifies the proportion of common variance to be accounted for by the retained factors using the prior communality estimates. If the value is greater than one, it is interpreted as a percentage and divided by 100. The options PROPORTION=0.75 and PERCENT=75 are equivalent. The default value is 1.0 or 100%. You cannot specify the PROPORTION= option with the METHOD=PATTERN or METHOD=SCORE option. If you specify two or more of the PROPORTION=, NFACTORS=, and MINEIGEN= options, the number of factors retained is the minimum number satisfying any of the criteria.

RANDOM=*n*

specifies a positive integer as a starting value for the pseudo-random number generator for use with the option PRIORS=RANDOM. If you do not specify the RANDOM= option, the time of day is used to initialize the pseudo-random number sequence. Valid values must be integers ≥ 1.

REORDER
RE

causes the rows (variables) of various factor matrices to be reordered on the output. Variables with their highest absolute loading (reference structure loading for oblique rotations) on the first factor are displayed first, from largest to smallest loading, followed by variables with their highest absolute loading on the second factor, and so on. The order of the variables in the output data set is not affected. The factors are not reordered.

RESIDUALS
RES

displays the residual correlation matrix and the associated partial correlation matrix. The diagonal elements of the residual correlation matrix are the unique variances.

ROTATE=*name*
R=*name*

specifies the rotation method. The default is ROTATE=NONE. The following orthogonal rotation methods are available in the FACTOR procedure: EQUAMAX, ORTHOMAX, QUARTIMAX, PARSIMAX, and VARIMAX.

After the initial factor extraction, the common factors are uncorrelated with each other. If the factors are rotated by an *orthogonal transformation,* the rotated factors are also uncorrelated. If the factors are rotated by an *oblique transformation,* the rotated factors become correlated. Oblique rotations often produce more useful patterns than do orthogonal rotations. However, a consequence of correlated factors is that there is no single unambiguous measure of the importance of a factor in explaining a variable. Thus, for oblique rotations, the pattern matrix does not provide all the necessary information for interpreting the factors; you must also examine the *factor structure* and the *reference structure*. Refer to Harman (1976) and Mulaik (1972) for further information.

Valid values for *name* are as follows:

EQUAMAX | E — specifies orthogonal equamax rotation. This corresponds to the specification ROTATE=ORTHOMAX with GAMMA=*number of factors*/2.

HK — specifies Harris-Kaiser case II orthoblique rotation. You can use the HKPOWER= option to set the power of the square roots of the eigenvalues by which the eigenvectors are scaled.

NONE | N — specifies that no rotation be performed.

ORTHOMAX — specifies general orthomax rotation with the weight specified by the GAMMA= option.

PARSIMAX — specifies orthogonal Parsimax rotation. This corresponds to the specification ROTATE=ORTHOMAX with

$$\text{GAMMA} = \frac{nvar \times (nfact - 1)}{nvar + nfact - 2}$$

where *nvar* is the number of variables, and *nfact* is the number of factors.

PROCRUSTES — specifies oblique Procrustes rotation with target pattern provided by the TARGET= data set. The unrestricted least squares method is used with factors scaled to unit variance after rotation.

PROMAX | P — specifies oblique promax rotation. The PREROTATE= and POWER= options can be used with the option ROTATE=PROMAX.

QUARTIMAX | Q specifies orthogonal quartimax rotation. This corresponds to the specification ROTATE=ORTHOMAX with GAMMA=0.

VARIMAX | V specifies orthogonal varimax rotation. This corresponds to the specification ROTATE=ORTHOMAX with GAMMA=1.

SCORE

displays the factor scoring coefficients. The squared multiple correlation of each factor with the variables is also displayed except in the case of unrotated principal components.

SCREE

displays a scree plot of the eigenvalues (Cattell 1966, 1978; Cattell and Vogelman 1977; Horn and Engstrom 1979).

SIMPLE
S

displays means, standard deviations, and the number of observations.

SINGULAR=*p*
SING=*p*

specifies the singularity criterion, where $0 < p < 1$. The default value is 1E−8.

TARGET=*SAS-data-set*

specifies an input data set containing the target pattern for Procrustes rotation (see the description of the ROTATE= option). The TARGET= data set must contain variables with the same names as those being factored. Each observation in the TARGET= data set becomes one column of the target factor pattern. Missing values are treated as zeros. The _NAME_ and _TYPE_ variables are not required and are ignored if present.

ULTRAHEYWOOD
ULTRA

allows communalities to exceed 1. The ULTRAHEYWOOD option can cause convergence problems because communalities can become extremely large, and ill-conditioned Hessians may occur.

VARDEF=DF | N | WDF | WEIGHT | WGT

specifies the divisor used in the calculation of variances and covariances. The default value is VARDEF=DF. The values and associated divisors are displayed in the following table where i= 0 if the NOINT option is used and i= 1 otherwise, and where k is the number of partial variables specified in the PARTIAL statement.

Value	Description	Divisor
DF	degrees of freedom	$n - k - i$
N	number of observations	$n - k$
WDF	sum of weights DF	$\sum_i w_i - k - i$
WEIGHT | WGT	sum of weights	$\sum_i w_i - k$

WEIGHT
: factors a weighted correlation or covariance matrix. The WEIGHT option can be used only with the METHOD=PRINCIPAL, METHOD=PRINIT, METHOD=ULS, or METHOD=IMAGE option. The input data set must be of type CORR, UCORR, COV, UCOV or FACTOR, and the variable weights are obtained from an observation with _TYPE_='WEIGHT'.

BY Statement

BY *variables* **;**

You can specify a BY statement with PROC FACTOR to obtain separate analyses on observations in groups defined by the BY variables. When a BY statement appears, the procedure expects the input data set to be sorted in order of the BY variables.

If your input data set is not sorted in ascending order, use one of the following alternatives:

- Sort the data using the SORT procedure with a similar BY statement.
- Specify the BY statement option NOTSORTED or DESCENDING in the BY statement for the FACTOR procedure. The NOTSORTED option does not mean that the data are unsorted but rather that the data are arranged in groups (according to values of the BY variables) and that these groups are not necessarily in alphabetical or increasing numeric order.
- Create an index on the BY variables using the DATASETS procedure (in Base SAS software). For more information on creating indexes and using the BY statement with indexed datasets, refer to "SAS Files" in *SAS Language Reference: Concepts*.

If you specify the TARGET= option and the TARGET= data set does not contain any of the BY variables, then the entire TARGET= data set is used as a Procrustean target for each BY group in the DATA= data set.

If the TARGET= data set contains some but not all of the BY variables, or if some BY variables do not have the same type or length in the TARGET= data set as in the DATA= data set, then PROC FACTOR displays an error message and stops.

If all the BY variables appear in the TARGET= data set with the same type and length as in the DATA= data set, then each BY group in the TARGET= data set is used as a Procrustean target for the corresponding BY group in the DATA= data set. The BY groups in the TARGET= data set must be in the same order as in the DATA= data set. If you specify the NOTSORTED option in the BY statement, there must be identical BY groups in the same order in both data sets. If you do not specify the NOTSORTED option, some BY groups can appear in one data set but not in the other.

For more information on the BY statement, refer to the discussion in *SAS Language Reference: Concepts*. For more information on the DATASETS procedure, refer to the discussion in the *SAS Procedures Guide*.

FREQ Statement

FREQ *variable* ;

If a variable in the data set represents the frequency of occurrence for the other values in the observation, include the variable's name in a FREQ statement. The procedure then treats the data set as if each observation appears n times, where n is the value of the FREQ variable for the observation. The total number of observations is considered to be equal to the sum of the FREQ variable when the procedure determines degrees of freedom for significance probabilities.

If the value of the FREQ variable is missing or is less than one, the observation is not used in the analysis. If the value is not an integer, the value is truncated to an integer.

The WEIGHT and FREQ statements have a similar effect, except in determining the number of observations for significance tests.

PARTIAL Statement

PARTIAL *variables* ;

If you want the analysis to be based on a partial correlation or covariance matrix, use the PARTIAL statement to list the variables that are used to partial out the variables in the analysis.

PRIORS Statement

PRIORS *communalities* ;

The PRIORS statement specifies numeric values between 0.0 and 1.0 for the prior communality estimates for each variable. The first numeric value corresponds to the first variable in the VAR statement, the second value to the second variable, and so on. The number of numeric values must equal the number of variables. For example,

```
proc factor;
   var     x  y  z;
   priors .7 .8 .9;
run;
```

You can specify various methods for computing prior communality estimates with the PRIORS= option of the PROC FACTOR statement. Refer to the description of that option for more information on the default prior communality estimates.

VAR Statement

VAR *variables* ;

The VAR statement specifies the numeric variables to be analyzed. If the VAR statement is omitted, all numeric variables not specified in other statements are analyzed.

WEIGHT Statement

WEIGHT *variable* ;

If you want to use relative weights for each observation in the input data set, specify a variable containing weights in a WEIGHT statement. This is often done when the variance associated with each observation is different and the values of the weight variable are proportional to the reciprocals of the variances. If a variable value is negative or is missing, it is excluded from the analysis.

Details

Incompatibilities with Earlier Versions of PROC FACTOR

PROC FACTOR no longer supports the FUZZ, FLAG, and ROUND options. However, a more flexible form of formatting is available. For an example of creating customized output, see Example 26.2.

Input Data Set

The FACTOR procedure can read an ordinary SAS data set containing raw data or a special data set specified as a TYPE=CORR, TYPE=UCORR, TYPE=SSCP, TYPE=COV, TYPE=UCOV, or TYPE=FACTOR data set containing previously computed statistics. A TYPE=CORR data set can be created by the CORR procedure or various other procedures such as the PRINCOMP procedure. It contains means, standard deviations, the sample size, the correlation matrix, and possibly other statistics if it is created by some procedure other than PROC CORR. A TYPE=COV data set is similar to a TYPE=CORR data set but contains a covariance matrix. A TYPE=UCORR or TYPE=UCOV data set contains a correlation or covariance matrix that is not corrected for the mean. The default VAR variable list does not include Intercept if the DATA= data set is TYPE=SSCP. If the Intercept variable is explicitly specified in the VAR statement with a TYPE=SSCP data set, the NOINT option is activated. A TYPE=FACTOR data set can be created by the FACTOR procedure and is described in the section "Output Data Sets" on page 1149.

If your data set has many observations and you plan to run FACTOR several times, you can save computer time by first creating a TYPE=CORR data set and using it as input to PROC FACTOR.

```
proc corr data=raw out=correl;      /* create TYPE=CORR data set */
proc factor data=correl method=ml; /* maximum likelihood        */
proc factor data=correl;           /* principal components      */
```

The data set created by the CORR procedure is automatically given the TYPE=CORR data set option, so you do not have to specify TYPE=CORR. However, if you use a DATA step with a SET statement to modify the correlation data set, you must use the TYPE=CORR attribute in the new data set. You can use a VAR statement with PROC FACTOR when reading a TYPE=CORR data set to select a subset of the variables or change the order of the variables.

Problems can arise from using the CORR procedure when there are missing data. By default, PROC CORR computes each correlation from all observations that have values present for the pair of variables involved (pairwise deletion). The resulting correlation matrix may have negative eigenvalues. If you specify the NOMISS option with the CORR procedure, observations with any missing values are completely omitted from the calculations (listwise deletion), and there is no danger of negative eigenvalues.

PROC FACTOR can also create a TYPE=FACTOR data set, which includes all the information in a TYPE=CORR data set, and use it for repeated analyses. For a TYPE=FACTOR data set, the default value of the METHOD= option is PATTERN. The following statements produce the same PROC FACTOR results as the previous example:

```
proc factor data=raw method=ml outstat=fact; /* max. likelihood */
proc factor data=fact method=prin;      /* principal components */
```

You can use a TYPE=FACTOR data set to try several different rotation methods on the same data without repeatedly extracting the factors. In the following example, the second and third PROC FACTOR statements use the data set fact created by the first PROC FACTOR statement:

```
proc factor data=raw outstat=fact; /* principal components */
proc factor rotate=varimax;        /* varimax rotation     */
proc factor rotate=quartimax;      /* quartimax rotation   */
```

You can create a TYPE=CORR, TYPE=UCORR, or TYPE=FACTOR data set in a DATA step. Be sure to specify the TYPE= option in parentheses after the data set name in the DATA statement and include the _TYPE_ and _NAME_ variables. In a TYPE=CORR data set, only the correlation matrix (_TYPE_='CORR') is necessary. It can contain missing values as long as every pair of variables has at least one nonmissing value.

```
data correl(type=corr);
   _TYPE_='CORR';
   input _NAME_ $ x y z;
   datalines;
x  1.0  .   .
y   .7 1.0  .
z   .5  .4 1.0
;
proc factor;
run;
```

You can create a TYPE=FACTOR data set containing only a factor pattern (_TYPE_='PATTERN') and use the FACTOR procedure to rotate it.

```
data pat(type=factor);
   _TYPE_='PATTERN';
   input _NAME_ $ x y z;
   datalines;
factor1  .5  .7  .3
factor2  .8  .2  .8
;
proc factor rotate=promax prerotate=none;
run;
```

If the input factors are oblique, you must also include the interfactor correlation matrix with _TYPE_='FCORR'.

```
data pat(type=factor);
   input _TYPE_ $ _NAME_ $ x y z;
   datalines;
pattern factor1  .5  .7  .3
pattern factor2  .8  .2  .8
fcorr   factor1 1.0  .2  .
fcorr   factor2  .2 1.0  .
;
proc factor rotate=promax prerotate=none;
run;
```

Some procedures, such as the PRINCOMP and CANDISC procedures, produce TYPE=CORR or TYPE=UCORR data sets containing scoring coefficients (_TYPE_='SCORE' or _TYPE_= 'USCORE'). These coefficients can be input to PROC FACTOR and rotated by using the METHOD=SCORE option. The input data set must contain the correlation matrix as well as the scoring coefficients.

```
proc princomp data=raw n=2 outstat=prin;
run;
proc factor data=prin method=score rotate=varimax;
run;
```

Output Data Sets

The OUT= Data Set

The OUT= data set contains all the data in the DATA= data set plus new variables called Factor1, Factor2, and so on, containing estimated factor scores. If more than 99 factors are requested, the new variable names are Fact1, Fact2, and so on. Each estimated factor score is computed as a linear combination of the standardized values of the variables that are factored. The coefficients are always displayed if the OUT= option is specified and are labeled "Standardized Scoring Coefficients."

The OUTSTAT= Data Set

The OUTSTAT= data set is similar to the TYPE=CORR or TYPE=UCORR data set produced by the CORR procedure, but it is a TYPE=FACTOR data set and it contains many results in addition to those produced by PROC CORR. The OUTSTAT= data set contains observations with _TYPE_='UCORR' and _TYPE_='USTD' if you specify the NOINT option.

The output data set contains the following variables:

- the BY variables, if any
- two new character variables, _TYPE_ and _NAME_
- the variables analyzed, that is, those in the VAR statement, or, if there is no VAR statement, all numeric variables not listed in any other statement.

Each observation in the output data set contains some type of statistic as indicated by the _TYPE_ variable. The _NAME_ variable is blank except where otherwise indicated. The values of the _TYPE_ variable are as follows:

TYPE	Contents
MEAN	means
STD	standard deviations
USTD	uncorrected standard deviations
N	sample size
CORR	correlations. The _NAME_ variable contains the name of the variable corresponding to each row of the correlation matrix.
UCORR	uncorrected correlations. The _NAME_ variable contains the name of the variable corresponding to each row of the uncorrected correlation matrix.
IMAGE	image coefficients. The _NAME_ variable contains the name of the variable corresponding to each row of the image coefficient matrix.
IMAGECOV	image covariance matrix. The _NAME_ variable contains the name of the variable corresponding to each row of the image covariance matrix.

COMMUNAL	final communality estimates
PRIORS	prior communality estimates, or estimates from the last iteration for iterative methods
WEIGHT	variable weights
SUMWGT	sum of the variable weights
EIGENVAL	eigenvalues
UNROTATE	unrotated factor pattern. The _NAME_ variable contains the name of the factor.
RESIDUAL	residual correlations. The _NAME_ variable contains the name of the variable corresponding to each row of the residual correlation matrix.
PRETRANS	transformation matrix from prerotation. The _NAME_ variable contains the name of the factor.
PREROTAT	factor pattern from prerotation. The _NAME_ variable contains the name of the factor.
TRANSFOR	transformation matrix from rotation. The _NAME_ variable contains the name of the factor.
FCORR	interfactor correlations. The _NAME_ variable contains the name of the factor.
PATTERN	factor pattern. The _NAME_ variable contains the name of the factor.
RCORR	reference axis correlations. The _NAME_ variable contains the name of the factor.
REFERENC	reference structure. The _NAME_ variable contains the name of the factor.
STRUCTUR	factor structure. The _NAME_ variable contains the name of the factor.
SCORE	scoring coefficients. The _NAME_ variable contains the name of the factor.
USCORE	scoring coefficients to be applied without subtracting the mean from the raw variables. The _NAME_ variable contains the name of the factor.

Missing Values

If the DATA= data set contains data (rather than a matrix or factor pattern), then observations with missing values for any variables in the analysis are omitted from the computations. If a correlation or covariance matrix is read, it can contain missing values as long as every pair of variables has at least one nonmissing entry. Missing values in a pattern or scoring coefficient matrix are treated as zeros.

Cautions

- The amount of time that FACTOR takes is roughly proportional to the cube of the number of variables. Factoring 100 variables, therefore, takes about 1000 times as long as factoring 10 variables. Iterative methods (PRINIT, ALPHA, ULS, ML) can also take 100 times as long as noniterative methods (PRINCIPAL, IMAGE, HARRIS).
- No computer program is capable of reliably determining the optimal number of factors since the decision is ultimately subjective. You should not blindly accept the number of factors obtained by default; instead, use your own judgment to make a decision.
- Singular correlation matrices cause problems with the options PRIORS=SMC and METHOD=ML. Singularities can result from using a variable that is the sum of other variables, coding too many dummy variables from a classification variable, or having more variables than observations.
- If you use the CORR procedure to compute the correlation matrix and there are missing data and the NOMISS option is not specified, then the correlation matrix may have negative eigenvalues.
- If a TYPE=CORR, TYPE=UCORR or TYPE=FACTOR data set is copied or modified using a DATA step, the new data set does not automatically have the same TYPE as the old data set. You must specify the TYPE= data set option in the DATA statement. If you try to analyze a data set that has lost its TYPE=CORR attribute, PROC FACTOR displays a warning message saying that the data set contains _NAME_ and _TYPE_ variables but analyzes the data set as an ordinary SAS data set.
- For a TYPE=FACTOR data set, the default is METHOD=PATTERN, not METHOD=PRIN.

Factor Scores

The FACTOR procedure can compute estimated factor scores directly if you specify the NFACTORS= and OUT= options, or indirectly using the SCORE procedure. The latter method is preferable if you use the FACTOR procedure interactively to determine the number of factors, the rotation method, or various other aspects of the analysis. To compute factor scores for each observation using the SCORE procedure,

- use the SCORE option in the PROC FACTOR statement
- create a TYPE=FACTOR output data set with the OUTSTAT= option
- use the SCORE procedure with both the raw data and the TYPE=FACTOR data set
- do not use the TYPE= option in the PROC SCORE statement

For example, the following statements could be used:

```
proc factor data=raw score outstat=fact;
run;
proc score  data=raw score=fact out=scores;
run;
```

or

```
proc corr   data=raw out=correl;
run;
proc factor data=correl score outstat=fact;
run;
proc score  data=raw score=fact out=scores;
run;
```

A component analysis (principal, image, or Harris) produces scores with mean zero and variance one. If you have done a common factor analysis, the true factor scores have mean zero and variance one, but the computed factor scores are only estimates of the true factor scores. These estimates have mean zero but variance equal to the squared multiple correlation of the factor with the variables. The estimated factor scores may have small nonzero correlations even if the true factors are uncorrelated.

Variable Weights and Variance Explained

A principal component analysis of a correlation matrix treats all variables as equally important. A principal component analysis of a covariance matrix gives more weight to variables with larger variances. A principal component analysis of a covariance matrix is equivalent to an analysis of a weighted correlation matrix, where the weight of each variable is equal to its variance. Variables with large weights tend to have larger loadings on the first component and smaller residual correlations than variables with small weights.

You may want to give weights to variables using values other than their variances. Mulaik (1972) explains how to obtain a maximally reliable component by means of a weighted principal component analysis. With the FACTOR procedure, you can indirectly give arbitrary weights to the variables by using the COV option and rescaling the variables to have variance equal to the desired weight, or you can give arbitrary weights directly by using the WEIGHT option and including the weights in a TYPE=CORR data set.

Arbitrary variable weights can be used with the METHOD=PRINCIPAL, METHOD=PRINIT, METHOD=ULS, or METHOD=IMAGE option. Alpha and ML factor analyses compute variable weights based on the communalities (Harman 1976, pp. 217-218). For alpha factor analysis, the weight of a variable is the reciprocal of its communality. In ML factor analysis, the weight is the reciprocal of the uniqueness. Harris component analysis uses weights equal to the reciprocal of one minus the squared multiple correlation of each variable with the other variables.

For uncorrelated factors, the variance explained by a factor can be computed with or without taking the weights into account. The usual method for computing variance accounted for by a factor is to take the sum of squares of the corresponding column of the factor pattern, yielding an unweighted result. If the square of each loading is multiplied by the weight of the variable before the sum is taken, the result is the weighted variance explained, which is equal to the corresponding eigenvalue except in image analysis. Whether the weighted or unweighted result is more important depends on the purpose of the analysis.

In the case of correlated factors, the variance explained by a factor can be computed with or without taking the other factors into account. If you want to ignore the other factors, the variance explained is given by the weighted or unweighted sum of squares of the appropriate column of the factor structure since the factor structure contains simple correlations. If you want to subtract the variance explained by the other factors from the amount explained by the factor in question (the Type II variance explained), you can take the weighted or unweighted sum of squares of the appropriate column of the reference structure because the reference structure contains semipartial correlations. There are other ways of measuring the variance explained. For example, given a prior ordering of the factors, you can eliminate from each factor the variance explained by previous factors and compute a Type I variance explained. Harman (1976, pp. 268-270) provides another method, which is based on direct and joint contributions.

Heywood Cases and Other Anomalies

Since communalities are squared correlations, you would expect them always to lie between 0 and 1. It is a mathematical peculiarity of the common factor model, however, that final communality estimates may exceed 1. If a communality equals 1, the situation is referred to as a Heywood case, and if a communality exceeds 1, it is an ultra-Heywood case. An ultra-Heywood case implies that some unique factor has negative variance, a clear indication that something is wrong. Possible causes include

- bad prior communality estimates
- too many common factors
- too few common factors
- not enough data to provide stable estimates
- the common factor model is not an appropriate model for the data

An ultra-Heywood case renders a factor solution invalid. Factor analysts disagree about whether or not a factor solution with a Heywood case can be considered legitimate.

Theoretically, the communality of a variable should not exceed its reliability. Violation of this condition is called a quasi-Heywood case and should be regarded with the same suspicion as an ultra-Heywood case.

Elements of the factor structure and reference structure matrices can exceed 1 only in the presence of an ultra-Heywood case. On the other hand, an element of the factor pattern may exceed 1 in an oblique rotation.

The maximum-likelihood method is especially susceptible to quasi- or ultra-Heywood cases. During the iteration process, a variable with high communality is given a high weight; this tends to increase its communality, which increases its weight, and so on.

It is often stated that the squared multiple correlation of a variable with the other variables is a lower bound to its communality. This is true if the common factor model fits the data perfectly, but it is not generally the case with real data. A final communality estimate that is less than the squared multiple correlation can, therefore, indicate poor fit, possibly due to not enough factors. It is by no means as serious a problem as an ultra-Heywood case. Factor methods using the Newton-Raphson method can actually produce communalities less than 0, a result even more disastrous than an ultra-Heywood case.

The squared multiple correlation of a factor with the variables may exceed 1, even in the absence of ultra-Heywood cases. This situation is also cause for alarm. Alpha factor analysis seems to be especially prone to this problem, but it does not occur with maximum likelihood. If a squared multiple correlation is negative, there are too many factors retained.

With data that do not fit the common factor model perfectly, you can expect some of the eigenvalues to be negative. If an iterative factor method converges properly, the sum of the eigenvalues corresponding to rejected factors should be 0; hence, some eigenvalues are positive and some negative. If a principal factor analysis fails to yield any negative eigenvalues, the prior communality estimates are probably too large. Negative eigenvalues cause the cumulative proportion of variance explained to exceed 1 for a sufficiently large number of factors. The cumulative proportion of variance explained by the retained factors should be approximately 1 for principal factor analysis and should converge to 1 for iterative methods. Occasionally, a single factor can explain more than 100 percent of the common variance in a principal factor analysis, indicating that the prior communality estimates are too low.

If a squared canonical correlation or a coefficient alpha is negative, there are too many factors retained.

Principal component analysis, unlike common factor analysis, has none of these problems if the covariance or correlation matrix is computed correctly from a data set with no missing values. Various methods for missing value correlation or severe rounding of the correlations can produce negative eigenvalues in principal components.

Time Requirements

$$
\begin{aligned}
n &= \text{number of observations} \\
v &= \text{number of variables} \\
f &= \text{number of factors} \\
i &= \text{number of iterations during factor extraction} \\
r &= \text{length of iterations during factor rotation}
\end{aligned}
$$

The time required to compute...	**is roughly proportional to**
an overall factor analysis	iv^3
the correlation matrix	nv^2
PRIORS=SMC or ASMC	v^3
PRIORS=MAX	v^2
eigenvalues	v^3
final eigenvectors	fv^2
ROTATE=VARIMAX, QUARTIMAX, EQUAMAX, ORTHOMAX, PARSIMAX, PROMAX, or HK	rvf^2
ROTATE=PROCRUSTES	vf^2

Each iteration in the PRINIT or ALPHA method requires computation of eigenvalues and f eigenvectors.

Each iteration in the ML or ULS method requires computation of eigenvalues and $v - f$ eigenvectors.

The amount of time that PROC FACTOR takes is roughly proportional to the cube of the number of variables. Factoring 100 variables, therefore, takes about 1000 times as long as factoring 10 variables. Iterative methods (PRINIT, ALPHA, ULS, ML) can also take 100 times as long as noniterative methods (PRINCIPAL, IMAGE, HARRIS).

Displayed Output

PROC FACTOR output includes

- Mean and Std Dev (standard deviation) of each variable and the number of observations, if you specify the SIMPLE option
- Correlations, if you specify the CORR option
- Inverse Correlation Matrix, if you specify the ALL option
- Partial Correlations Controlling all other Variables (negative anti-image correlations), if you specify the MSA option. If the data are appropriate for the common factor model, the partial correlations should be small.

- Kaiser's Measure of Sampling Adequacy (Kaiser 1970; Kaiser and Rice 1974; Cerny and Kaiser 1977) both overall and for each variable, if you specify the MSA option. The MSA is a summary of how small the partial correlations are relative to the ordinary correlations. Values greater than 0.8 can be considered good. Values less than 0.5 require remedial action, either by deleting the offending variables or by including other variables related to the offenders.
- Prior Communality Estimates, unless 1.0s are used or unless you specify the METHOD=IMAGE, METHOD=HARRIS, METHOD=PATTERN, or METHOD=SCORE option
- Squared Multiple Correlations of each variable with all the other variables, if you specify the METHOD=IMAGE or METHOD=HARRIS option
- Image Coefficients, if you specify the METHOD=IMAGE option
- Image Covariance Matrix, if you specify the METHOD=IMAGE option
- Preliminary Eigenvalues based on the prior communalities, if you specify the METHOD=PRINIT, METHOD=ALPHA, METHOD=ML, or METHOD=ULS option. The table produced includes the Total and the Average of the eigenvalues, the Difference between successive eigenvalues, the Proportion of variation represented, and the Cumulative proportion of variation.
- the number of factors that are retained, unless you specify the METHOD=PATTERN or METHOD=SCORE option
- the Scree Plot of Eigenvalues, if you specify the SCREE option. The preliminary eigenvalues are used if you specify the METHOD=PRINIT, METHOD=ALPHA, METHOD=ML, or METHOD=ULS option.
- the iteration history, if you specify the METHOD=PRINIT, METHOD=ALPHA, METHOD=ML, or METHOD=ULS option. The table produced contains the iteration number (Iter); the Criterion being optimized (Joreskog 1977); the Ridge value for the iteration if you specify the METHOD=ML or METHOD=ULS option; the maximum Change in any communality estimate; and the Communalities
- Significance tests, if you specify the option METHOD=ML, including Bartlett's Chi-square, df, and Prob $> \chi^2$ for H_0: No common factors and H_0: factors retained are sufficient to explain the correlations. The variables should have an approximate multivariate normal distribution for the probability levels to be valid. Lawley and Maxwell (1971) suggest that the number of observations should exceed the number of variables by fifty or more, although Geweke and Singleton (1980) claim that as few as ten observations are adequate with five variables and one common factor. Certain regularity conditions must also be satisfied for Bartlett's χ^2 test to be valid (Geweke and Singleton 1980), but in practice these conditions usually are satisfied. The notation Prob>chi**2 means "the probability under the null hypothesis of obtaining a greater χ^2 statistic than that observed." The Chi-square value is displayed with and without Bartlett's correction.
- Akaike's Information Criterion, if you specify the METHOD=ML option. Akaike's information criterion (AIC) (Akaike 1973, 1974, 1987) is a general

criterion for estimating the best number of parameters to include in a model when maximum-likelihood estimation is used. The number of factors that yields the smallest value of AIC is considered best. Like the chi-square test, AIC tends to include factors that are statistically significant but inconsequential for practical purposes.

- Schwarz's Bayesian Criterion, if you specify the METHOD=ML option. Schwarz's Bayesian Criterion (SBC) (Schwarz 1978) is another criterion, similar to AIC, for determining the best number of parameters. The number of factors that yields the smallest value of SBC is considered best; SBC seems to be less inclined to include trivial factors than either AIC or the chi-square test.
- Tucker and Lewis's Reliability Coefficient, if you specify the METHOD=ML option (Tucker and Lewis 1973)
- Squared Canonical Correlations, if you specify the METHOD=ML option. These are the same as the squared multiple correlations for predicting each factor from the variables.
- Coefficient Alpha for Each Factor, if you specify the METHOD=ALPHA option
- Eigenvectors, if you specify the EIGENVECTORS or ALL option, unless you also specify the METHOD=PATTERN or METHOD=SCORE option
- Eigenvalues of the (Weighted) (Reduced) (Image) Correlation or Covariance Matrix, unless you specify the METHOD=PATTERN or METHOD=SCORE option. Included are the Total and the Average of the eigenvalues, the Difference between successive eigenvalues, the Proportion of variation represented, and the Cumulative proportion of variation.
- the Factor Pattern, which is equal to both the matrix of standardized regression coefficients for predicting variables from common factors and the matrix of correlations between variables and common factors since the extracted factors are uncorrelated
- Variance explained by each factor, both Weighted and Unweighted, if variable weights are used
- Final Communality Estimates, including the Total communality; or Final Communality Estimates and Variable Weights, including the Total communality, both Weighted and Unweighted, if variable weights are used. Final communality estimates are the squared multiple correlations for predicting the variables from the estimated factors, and they can be obtained by taking the sum of squares of each row of the factor pattern, or a weighted sum of squares if variable weights are used.
- Residual Correlations with Uniqueness on the Diagonal, if you specify the RESIDUAL or ALL option
- Root Mean Square Off-diagonal Residuals, both Over-all and for each variable, if you specify the RESIDUAL or ALL option
- Partial Correlations Controlling Factors, if you specify the RESIDUAL or ALL option

- Root Mean Square Off-diagonal Partials, both Over-all and for each variable, if you specify the RESIDUAL or ALL option
- Plots of Factor Pattern for unrotated factors, if you specify the PREPLOT option. The number of plots is determined by the NPLOT= option.
- Variable Weights for Rotation, if you specify the NORM=WEIGHT option
- Factor Weights for Rotation, if you specify the HKPOWER= option
- Orthogonal Transformation Matrix, if you request an orthogonal rotation
- Rotated Factor Pattern, if you request an orthogonal rotation
- Variance explained by each factor after rotation. If you request an orthogonal rotation and if variable weights are used, both weighted and unweighted values are produced.
- Target Matrix for Procrustean Transformation, if you specify the ROTATE=PROCRUSTES or ROTATE=PROMAX option
- the Procrustean Transformation Matrix, if you specify the ROTATE=PROCRUSTES or ROTATE=PROMAX option
- the Normalized Oblique Transformation Matrix, if you request an oblique rotation, which, for the option ROTATE=PROMAX, is the product of the prerotation and the Procrustean rotation
- Inter-factor Correlations, if you specify an oblique rotation
- Rotated Factor Pattern (Std Reg Coefs), if you specify an oblique rotation, giving standardized regression coefficients for predicting the variables from the factors
- Reference Axis Correlations if you specify an oblique rotation. These are the partial correlations between the primary factors when all factors other than the two being correlated are partialled out.
- Reference Structure (Semipartial Correlations), if you request an oblique rotation. The reference structure is the matrix of semipartial correlations (Kerlinger and Pedhazur 1973) between variables and common factors, removing from each common factor the effects of other common factors. If the common factors are uncorrelated, the reference structure is equal to the factor pattern.
- Variance explained by each factor eliminating the effects of all other factors, if you specify an oblique rotation. Both Weighted and Unweighted values are produced if variable weights are used. These variances are equal to the (weighted) sum of the squared elements of the reference structure corresponding to each factor.
- Factor Structure (Correlations), if you request an oblique rotation. The (primary) factor structure is the matrix of correlations between variables and common factors. If the common factors are uncorrelated, the factor structure is equal to the factor pattern.
- Variance explained by each factor ignoring the effects of all other factors, if you request an oblique rotation. Both Weighted and Unweighted values are produced if variable weights are used. These variances are equal to the (weighted)

sum of the squared elements of the factor structure corresponding to each factor.

- Final Communality Estimates for the rotated factors if you specify the ROTATE= option. The estimates should equal the unrotated communalities.
- Squared Multiple Correlations of the Variables with Each Factor, if you specify the SCORE or ALL option, except for unrotated principal components
- Standardized Scoring Coefficients, if you specify the SCORE or ALL option
- Plots of the Factor Pattern for rotated factors, if you specify the PLOT option and you request an orthogonal rotation. The number of plots is determined by the NPLOT= option.
- Plots of the Reference Structure for rotated factors, if you specify the PLOT option and you request an oblique rotation. The number of plots is determined by the NPLOT= option. Included are the Reference Axis Correlation and the Angle between the Reference Axes for each pair of factors plotted.

If you specify the ROTATE=PROMAX option, the output includes results for both the prerotation and the Procrustean rotation.

ODS Table Names

PROC FACTOR assigns a name to each table it creates. You can use these names to reference the table when using the Output Delivery System (ODS) to select tables and create output data sets. These names are listed in the following table. For more information on ODS, see Chapter 15, "Using the Output Delivery System."

Table 26.2. ODS Tables Produced in PROC FACTOR

ODS Table Name	Description	Option
AlphaCoef	Coefficient alpha for each factor	METHOD=ALPHA
CanCorr	Squared canonical correlations	METHOD=ML
CondStdDev	Conditional standard deviations	SIMPLE w/PARTIAL
ConvergenceStatus	Convergence status	METHOD=PRINIT, =ALPHA, =ML, or =ULS
Corr	Correlations	CORR
Eigenvalues	Eigenvalues	default, SCREE
Eigenvectors	Eigenvectors	EIGENVECTORS
FactorWeightRotate	Factor weights for rotation	HKPOWER=
FactorPattern	Factor pattern	default
FactorStructure	Factor structure	ROTATE= any oblique rotation
FinalCommun	Final communalities	default
FinalCommunWgt	Final communalities with weights	METHOD=ML, METHOD=ALPHA
FitMeasures	Measures of fit	METHOD=ML
ImageCoef	Image coefficients	METHOD=IMAGE

Table 26.2. (continued)

ODS Table Name	Description	Option
ImageCov	Image covariance matrix	METHOD=IMAGE
ImageFactors	Image factor matrix	METHOD=IMAGE
InputFactorPattern	Input factor pattern	PRINT
InputScoreCoef	Standardized input scoring coefficients	METHOD=SCORE
InterFactorCorr	Inter-factor correlations	ROTATE= any oblique rotation
InvCorr	Inverse correlation matrix	ALL
IterHistory	Iteration history	METHOD=PRINIT, =ALPHA, =ML, or =ULS
MultipleCorr	Squared multiple correlations	METHOD=IMAGE or METHOD=HARRIS
NormObliqueTrans	Normalized oblique transformation matrix	ROTATE= any oblique rotation
ObliqueRotFactPat	Rotated factor pattern	ROTATE= any oblique rotation
ObliqueTrans	Oblique transformation matrix	HKPOWER=
OrthRotFactPat	Rotated factor pattern	ROTATE= any orthogonal rotation
OrthTrans	Orthogonal transformation matrix	ROTATE= any orthogonal rotation
ParCorrControlFactor	Partial correlations controlling factors	RESIDUAL
ParCorrControlVar	Partial correlations controlling other variables	MSA
PartialCorr	Partial correlations	MSA, CORR w/PARTIAL
PriorCommunalEst	Prior communality estimates	PRIORS=, METHOD=ML, METHOD=ALPHA
ProcrustesTarget	Target matrix for Procrustean transformation	ROTATE=PROCRUSTES, ROTATE=PROMAX
ProcrustesTrans	Procrustean transformation matrix	ROTATE=PROCRUSTES, ROTATE=PROMAX
RMSOffDiagPartials	Root mean square off-diagonal partials	RESIDUAL
RMSOffDiagResids	Root mean square off-diagonal residuals	RESIDUAL
ReferenceAxisCorr	Reference axis correlations	ROTATE= any oblique rotation
ReferenceStructure	Reference structure	ROTATE= any oblique rotation
ResCorrUniqueDiag	Residual correlations with uniqueness on the diagonal	RESIDUAL
SamplingAdequacy	Kaiser's measure of sampling adequacy	MSA
SignifTests	Significance tests	METHOD=ML
SimpleStatistics	Simple statistics	SIMPLE
StdScoreCoef	Standardized scoring coefficients	SCORE
VarExplain	Variance explained	default

Table 26.2. (continued)

ODS Table Name	Description	Option
VarExplainWgt	Variance explained with weights	METHOD=ML, METHOD=ALPHA
VarFactorCorr	Squared multiple correlations of the variables with each factor	SCORE
VarWeightRotate	Variable weights for rotation	NORM=WEIGHT, ROTATE=

Examples

Example 26.1. Principal Component Analysis

The following example analyzes socioeconomic data provided by Harman (1976). The five variables represent total population, median school years, total employment, miscellaneous professional services, and median house value. Each observation represents one of twelve census tracts in the Los Angeles Standard Metropolitan Statistical Area.

The first analysis is a principal component analysis. Simple descriptive statistics and correlations are also displayed. This example produces Output 26.1.1:

```
data SocioEconomics;
   title 'Five Socioeconomic Variables';
   title2 'See Page 14 of Harman: Modern Factor Analysis, 3rd Ed';
   input Population School Employment Services HouseValue;
   datalines;
5700     12.8     2500     270     25000
1000     10.9     600      10      10000
3400     8.8      1000     10      9000
3800     13.6     1700     140     25000
4000     12.8     1600     140     25000
8200     8.3      2600     60      12000
1200     11.4     400      10      16000
9100     11.5     3300     60      14000
9900     12.5     3400     180     18000
9600     13.7     3600     390     25000
9600     9.6      3300     80      12000
9400     11.4     4000     100     13000
;
proc factor data=SocioEconomics simple corr;
   title3 'Principal Component Analysis';
run;
```

There are two large eigenvalues, 2.8733 and 1.7967, which together account for 93.4% of the standardized variance. Thus, the first two principal components provide an adequate summary of the data for most purposes. Three components, explaining 97.7% of the variation, should be sufficient for almost any application.

PROC FACTOR retains two components on the basis of the eigenvalues-greater-than-one rule since the third eigenvalue is only 0.2148.

The first component has large positive loadings for all five variables. The correlation with Services (0.93239) is especially high. The second component is a contrast of Population (0.80642) and Employment (0.72605) against School (−0.54476) and HouseValue (−0.55818), with a very small loading on Services (−0.10431).

The final communality estimates show that all the variables are well accounted for by two components, with final communality estimates ranging from 0.880236 for Services to 0.987826 for Population.

Output 26.1.1. Principal Component Analysis

```
                    Five Socioeconomic Variables
        See Page 14 of Harman: Modern Factor Analysis, 3rd Ed
                    Principal Component Analysis

                        The FACTOR Procedure

          Means and Standard Deviations from 12 Observations

                Variable              Mean         Std Dev

                Population        6241.667       3439.9943
                School              11.442          1.7865
                Employment        2333.333       1241.2115
                Services           120.833        114.9275
                HouseValue       17000.000       6367.5313


                            Correlations

             Population        School    Employment      Services    HouseValue

Population      1.00000       0.00975       0.97245       0.43887       0.02241
School          0.00975       1.00000       0.15428       0.69141       0.86307
Employment      0.97245       0.15428       1.00000       0.51472       0.12193
Services        0.43887       0.69141       0.51472       1.00000       0.77765
HouseValue      0.02241       0.86307       0.12193       0.77765       1.00000
```

Principal Component Analysis

The FACTOR Procedure
Initial Factor Method: Principal Components

Eigenvalues of the Correlation Matrix: Total = 5 Average = 1

	Eigenvalue	Difference	Proportion	Cumulative
1	2.87331359	1.07665350	0.5747	0.5747
2	1.79666009	1.58182321	0.3593	0.9340
3	0.21483689	0.11490283	0.0430	0.9770
4	0.09993405	0.08467868	0.0200	0.9969
5	0.01525537		0.0031	1.0000

Factor Pattern

	Factor1	Factor2
Population	0.58096	0.80642
School	0.76704	-0.54476
Employment	0.67243	0.72605
Services	0.93239	-0.10431
HouseValue	0.79116	-0.55818

Variance Explained by Each Factor

Factor1	Factor2
2.8733136	1.7966601

Final Communality Estimates: Total = 4.669974

Population	School	Employment	Services	HouseValue
0.98782629	0.88510555	0.97930583	0.88023562	0.93750041

Example 26.2. Principal Factor Analysis

The following example uses the data presented in Example 26.1, and performs a principal factor analysis with squared multiple correlations for the prior communality estimates (PRIORS=SMC).

To help determine if the common factor model is appropriate, Kaiser's measure of sampling adequacy (MSA) is requested, and the residual correlations and partial correlations are computed (RESIDUAL). To help determine the number of factors, a scree plot (SCREE) of the eigenvalues is displayed, and the PREPLOT option plots the unrotated factor pattern.

The ROTATE= and REORDER options are specified to enhance factor interpretability. The ROTATE=PROMAX option produces an orthogonal varimax prerotation followed by an oblique rotation, and the REORDER option reorders the variables according to their largest factor loadings. The PLOT procedure is used to produce a plot of the reference structure. An OUTSTAT= data set is created by PROC FACTOR and displayed in Output 26.2.15.

This example also demonstrates how to define a picture format with the FORMAT procedure and use the PRINT procedure to produce customized factor pattern output. Small elements of the Rotated Factor Pattern matrix are displayed as '.'. Large values are multiplied by 100, truncated at the decimal, and flagged with an asterisk '*'. Intermediate values are scaled by 100 and truncated. For more information on picture formats, refer to "Formats" in *SAS Language Reference: Dictionary*.

```
ods output ObliqueRotFactPat = rotfacpat;
proc factor data=SocioEconomics
     priors=smc msa scree residual preplot
     rotate=promax reorder plot
     outstat=fact_all;
   title3 'Principal Factor Analysis with Promax Rotation';

proc print;
   title3 'Factor Output Data Set';
run;

proc format;
   picture FuzzFlag
   low  - 0.1  = '   .  '
   0.10 - 0.90 = '009   ' (mult = 100)
   0.90 - high = '009 *' (mult = 100);
run;

proc print data = rotfacpat;
   format factor1-factor2 FuzzFlag.;
run;
```

Output 26.2.1. Principal Factor Analysis

```
                 Principal Factor Analysis with Promax Rotation

                              The FACTOR Procedure
                   Initial Factor Method: Principal Factors

              Partial Correlations Controlling all other Variables

              Population         School    Employment       Services     HouseValue

Population       1.00000       -0.54465       0.97083        0.09612        0.15871
School          -0.54465        1.00000       0.54373        0.04996        0.64717
Employment       0.97083        0.54373       1.00000        0.06689       -0.25572
Services         0.09612        0.04996       0.06689        1.00000        0.59415
HouseValue       0.15871        0.64717      -0.25572        0.59415        1.00000


         Kaiser's Measure of Sampling Adequacy: Overall MSA = 0.57536759

   Population          School        Employment          Services        HouseValue

   0.47207897      0.55158839        0.48851137        0.80664365        0.61281377

             2 factors will be retained by the PROPORTION criterion.
```

```
                 Principal Factor Analysis with Promax Rotation

                              The FACTOR Procedure
                   Initial Factor Method: Principal Factors

                      Prior Communality Estimates: SMC

   Population          School        Employment          Services        HouseValue

   0.96859160      0.82228514        0.96918082        0.78572440        0.84701921


                 Eigenvalues of the Reduced Correlation Matrix:
                    Total = 4.39280116  Average = 0.87856023

                  Eigenvalue    Difference    Proportion    Cumulative

             1    2.73430084    1.01823217        0.6225        0.6225
             2    1.71606867    1.67650586        0.3907        1.0131
             3    0.03956281    0.06408626        0.0090        1.0221
             4    -.02452345    0.04808427       -0.0056        1.0165
             5    -.07260772                     -0.0165        1.0000

             2 factors will be retained by the PROPORTION criterion.
```

Output 26.2.1 displays the results of the principal factor extraction.

If the data are appropriate for the common factor model, the partial correlations controlling the other variables should be small compared to the original correlations. The partial correlation between the variables School and HouseValue, for example, is 0.65, slightly less than the original correlation of 0.86. The partial correlation between Population and School is -0.54, which is much larger in absolute value than the original correlation; this is an indication of trouble. Kaiser's MSA is a summary, for each variable and for all variables together, of how much smaller the partial correlations are than the original correlations. Values of 0.8 or 0.9 are considered good, while MSAs below 0.5 are unacceptable. The variables Population, School, and Employment have very poor MSAs. Only the Services variable has a good MSA. The overall MSA of 0.58 is sufficiently poor that additional variables should be included in the analysis to better define the common factors. A commonly used rule is that there should be at least three variables per factor. In the following analysis, there seems to be two common factors in these data, so more variables are needed for a reliable analysis.

The SMCs are all fairly large; hence, the factor loadings do not differ greatly from the principal component analysis.

The eigenvalues show clearly that two common factors are present. There are two large positive eigenvalues that together account for 101.31% of the common variance, which is as close to 100% as you are ever likely to get without iterating. The scree plot displays a sharp bend at the third eigenvalue, reinforcing the preceding conclusion.

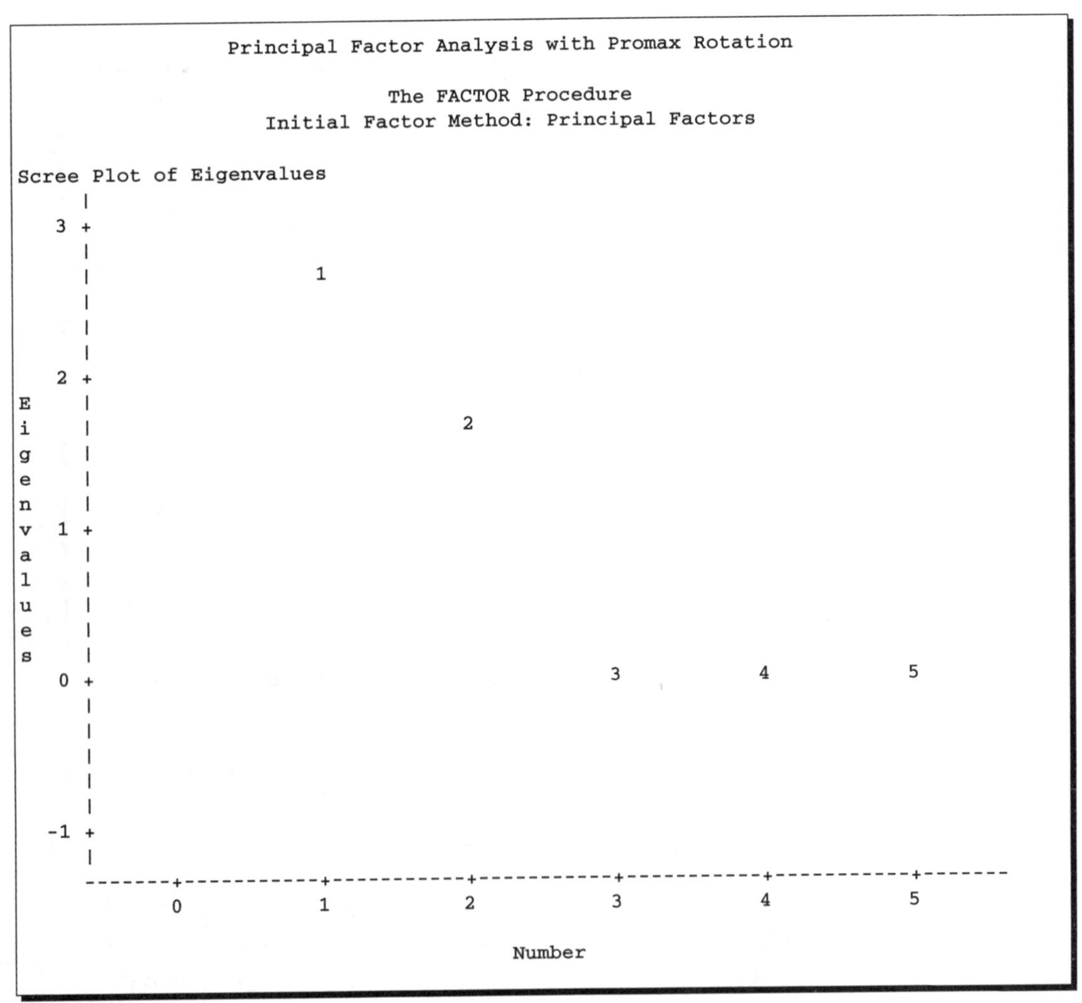

Output 26.2.2. Factor Pattern Matrix and Communalities

```
                Principal Factor Analysis with Promax Rotation

                            The FACTOR Procedure
                   Initial Factor Method: Principal Factors

                               Factor Pattern

                                 Factor1         Factor2

                 Services        0.87899        -0.15847
                 HouseValue      0.74215        -0.57806
                 Employment      0.71447         0.67936
                 School          0.71370        -0.55515
                 Population      0.62533         0.76621


                    Variance Explained by Each Factor

                          Factor1         Factor2

                        2.7343008       1.7160687


             Final Communality Estimates: Total = 4.450370

Population         School       Employment        Services        HouseValue

0.97811334     0.81756387      0.97199928      0.79774304      0.88494998
```

As displayed in Output 26.2.2, the principal factor pattern is similar to the principal component pattern seen in Example 26.1. For example, the variable Services has the largest loading on the first factor, and the Population variable has the smallest. The variables Population and Employment have large positive loadings on the second factor, and the HouseValue and School variables have large negative loadings.

The final communality estimates are all fairly close to the priors. Only the communality for the variable HouseValue increased appreciably, from 0.847019 to 0.884950. Nearly 100% of the common variance is accounted for. The residual correlations (off-diagonal elements) are low, the largest being 0.03 (Output 26.2.3). The partial correlations are not quite as impressive, since the uniqueness values are also rather small. These results indicate that the SMCs are good but not quite optimal communality estimates.

Output 26.2.3. Residual and Partial Correlations

Principal Factor Analysis with Promax Rotation

The FACTOR Procedure
Initial Factor Method: Principal Factors

Residual Correlations With Uniqueness on the Diagonal

	Population	School	Employment	Services	HouseValue
Population	0.02189	-0.01118	0.00514	0.01063	0.00124
School	-0.01118	0.18244	0.02151	-0.02390	0.01248
Employment	0.00514	0.02151	0.02800	-0.00565	-0.01561
Services	0.01063	-0.02390	-0.00565	0.20226	0.03370
HouseValue	0.00124	0.01248	-0.01561	0.03370	0.11505

Root Mean Square Off-Diagonal Residuals: Overall = 0.01693282

Population	School	Employment	Services	HouseValue
0.00815307	0.01813027	0.01382764	0.02151737	0.01960158

Partial Correlations Controlling Factors

	Population	School	Employment	Services	HouseValue
Population	1.00000	-0.17693	0.20752	0.15975	0.02471
School	-0.17693	1.00000	0.30097	-0.12443	0.08614
Employment	0.20752	0.30097	1.00000	-0.07504	-0.27509
Services	0.15975	-0.12443	-0.07504	1.00000	0.22093
HouseValue	0.02471	0.08614	-0.27509	0.22093	1.00000

Output 26.2.4. Root Mean Square Off-Diagonal Partials

Principal Factor Analysis with Promax Rotation

The FACTOR Procedure
Initial Factor Method: Principal Factors

Root Mean Square Off-Diagonal Partials: Overall = 0.18550132

Population	School	Employment	Services	HouseValue
0.15850824	0.19025867	0.23181838	0.15447043	0.18201538

Output 26.2.5. Unrotated Factor Pattern Plot

```
                 Principal Factor Analysis with Promax Rotation

                             The FACTOR Procedure
                      Initial Factor Method: Principal Factors

Plot of Factor Pattern for Factor1 and Factor2

                                  Factor1
                                     1

                                D   .9

                                    .8
                 E
                  B                 .7                  C
                                                          A
                                    .6

                                    .5

                                    .4

                                    .3

                                    .2
                                                                  F
                                    .1                            a
                                                                  c
      -1 -.9-.8-.7-.6-.5-.4-.3-.2-.1  0 .1 .2 .3 .4 .5 .6 .7 .8 .9 1.0t
                                                                  o
                                   -.1                            r
                                                                  2
                                   -.2

                                   -.3

                                   -.4

                                   -.5

                                   -.6

                                   -.7

                                   -.8

                                   -.9

                                    -1

      Population=A  School=B     Employment=C  Services=D    HouseValue=E
```

As displayed in Output 26.2.5, the unrotated factor pattern reveals two tight clusters of variables, with the variables HouseValue and School at the negative end of Factor2 axis and the variables Employment and Population at the positive end. The Services variable is in between but closer to the HouseValue and School variables. A good rotation would put the reference axes through the two clusters.

Output 26.2.6. Varimax Rotation: Transform Matrix and Rotated Pattern

```
                Principal Factor Analysis with Promax Rotation

                            The FACTOR Procedure
                        Prerotation Method: Varimax

                      Orthogonal Transformation Matrix

                                   1               2

                     1         0.78895         0.61446
                     2        -0.61446         0.78895


                          Rotated Factor Pattern

                                Factor1         Factor2

            HouseValue          0.94072        -0.00004
            School              0.90419         0.00055
            Services            0.79085         0.41509
            Population          0.02255         0.98874
            Employment          0.14625         0.97499
```

Output 26.2.7. Varimax Rotation: Variance Explained and Communalities

```
                Principal Factor Analysis with Promax Rotation

                            The FACTOR Procedure
                        Prerotation Method: Varimax

                      Variance Explained by Each Factor

                          Factor1         Factor2

                        2.3498567       2.1005128


            Final Communality Estimates: Total = 4.450370

Population         School      Employment        Services      HouseValue

0.97811334     0.81756387      0.97199928      0.79774304      0.88494998
```

Output 26.2.8. Varimax Rotated Factor Pattern Plot

```
                 Principal Factor Analysis with Promax Rotation

                               The FACTOR Procedure
                            Prerotation Method: Varimax

Plot of Factor Pattern for Factor1 and Factor2

                                     Factor1
                                       1
                                      E
                                      .B

                                      .8          D

                                      .7

                                      .6

                                      .5

                                      .4

                                      .3

                                      .2
                                                                C  F
                                      .1                           a
                                                                   c
     -1 -.9-.8-.7-.6-.5-.4-.3-.2-.1  0 .1 .2 .3 .4 .5 .6 .7 .8 .9 A.0t
                                                                   o
                                     -.1                           r
                                                                   2
                                     -.2

                                     -.3

                                     -.4

                                     -.5

                                     -.6

                                     -.7

                                     -.8

                                     -.9

                                      -1

     Population=A  School=B     Employment=C  Services=D    HouseValue=E
```

Output 26.2.6, Output 26.2.7 and Output 26.2.8 display the results of the varimax rotation. This rotation puts one axis through the variables HouseValue and School but misses the Population and Employment variables slightly.

Output 26.2.9. Promax Rotation: Procrustean Target and Transform Matrix

```
               Principal Factor Analysis with Promax Rotation

                          The FACTOR Procedure
                        Rotation Method: Promax

               Target Matrix for Procrustean Transformation

                                   Factor1         Factor2

               HouseValue          1.00000        -0.00000
               School              1.00000         0.00000
               Services            0.69421         0.10045
               Population          0.00001         1.00000
               Employment          0.00326         0.96793


                    Procrustean Transformation Matrix

                                     1               2

                      1      1.04116598      -0.0986534
                      2      -0.1057226      0.96303019
```

Output 26.2.10. Promax Rotation: Oblique Transform Matrix and Correlation

```
               Principal Factor Analysis with Promax Rotation

                          The FACTOR Procedure
                        Rotation Method: Promax

                 Normalized Oblique Transformation Matrix

                                     1               2

                      1         0.73803         0.54202
                      2        -0.70555         0.86528


                      Inter-Factor Correlations

                                Factor1         Factor2

                 Factor1        1.00000         0.20188
                 Factor2        0.20188         1.00000
```

Output 26.2.11. Promax Rotation: Rotated Factor Pattern and Correlations

```
              Principal Factor Analysis with Promax Rotation

                          The FACTOR Procedure
                       Rotation Method: Promax

       Rotated Factor Pattern (Standardized Regression Coefficients)

                                Factor1          Factor2

            HouseValue        0.95558485       -0.0979201
            School            0.91842142       -0.0935214
            Services          0.76053238        0.33931804
            Population       -0.0790832         1.00192402
            Employment          0.04799         0.97509085


                     Reference Axis Correlations

                              Factor1          Factor2

             Factor1          1.00000         -0.20188
             Factor2         -0.20188          1.00000
```

Output 26.2.12. Promax Rotation: Variance Explained and Factor Structure

```
              Principal Factor Analysis with Promax Rotation

                          The FACTOR Procedure
                       Rotation Method: Promax

              Reference Structure (Semipartial Correlations)

                                Factor1          Factor2

            HouseValue          0.93591         -0.09590
            School              0.89951         -0.09160
            Services            0.74487          0.33233
            Population         -0.07745          0.98129
            Employment          0.04700          0.95501


       Variance Explained by Each Factor Eliminating Other Factors

                          Factor1          Factor2

                        2.2480892        2.0030200


                     Factor Structure (Correlations)

                                Factor1          Factor2

            HouseValue          0.93582          0.09500
            School              0.89954          0.09189
            Services            0.82903          0.49286
            Population          0.12319          0.98596
            Employment          0.24484          0.98478
```

Output 26.2.13. Promax Rotation: Variance Explained and Final Communalities

```
                 Principal Factor Analysis with Promax Rotation

                            The FACTOR Procedure
                          Rotation Method: Promax

            Variance Explained by Each Factor Ignoring Other Factors

                            Factor1         Factor2

                          2.4473495       2.2022803


                 Final Community Estimates: Total = 4.450370

Population          School      Employment         Services       HouseValue

0.97811334      0.81756387      0.97199928       0.79774304       0.88494998
```

Output 26.2.14. Promax Rotated Factor Pattern Plot

```
                 Principal Factor Analysis with Promax Rotation

                              The FACTOR Procedure
                            Rotation Method: Promax

Plot of Reference Structure for Factor1 and Factor2
Reference Axis Correlation = -0.2019  Angle = 101.6471

                                   Factor1
                                      1
                                   E
                                   B .9

                                     .8
                                              D
                                     .7

                                     .6

                                     .5

                                     .4

                                     .3

                                     .2
                                                                       F
                                     .1                                a
                                                                    C  c
      -1 -.9-.8-.7-.6-.5-.4-.3-.2-.1  0 .1 .2 .3 .4 .5 .6 .7 .8 .9 1.0t
                                                                       o
                                    -.1                              A r
                                                                       2
                                    -.2

                                    -.3

                                    -.4

                                    -.5

                                    -.6

                                    -.7

                                    -.8

                                    -.9

                                     -1

    Population=A  School=B     Employment=C  Services=D    HouseValue=E
```

The oblique promax rotation (Output 26.2.9 through Output 26.2.14) places an axis through the variables Population and Employment but misses the HouseValue and School variables. Since an independent-cluster solution would be possible if it were not for the variable Services, a Harris-Kaiser rotation weighted by the Cureton-Mulaik technique should be used.

Output 26.2.15. Output Data Set

Factor Output Data Set

Obs	_TYPE_	_NAME_	Population	School	Employment	Services	House Value
1	MEAN		6241.67	11.4417	2333.33	120.833	17000.00
2	STD		3439.99	1.7865	1241.21	114.928	6367.53
3	N		12.00	12.0000	12.00	12.000	12.00
4	CORR	Population	1.00	0.0098	0.97	0.439	0.02
5	CORR	School	0.01	1.0000	0.15	0.691	0.86
6	CORR	Employment	0.97	0.1543	1.00	0.515	0.12
7	CORR	Services	0.44	0.6914	0.51	1.000	0.78
8	CORR	HouseValue	0.02	0.8631	0.12	0.778	1.00
9	COMMUNAL		0.98	0.8176	0.97	0.798	0.88
10	PRIORS		0.97	0.8223	0.97	0.786	0.85
11	EIGENVAL		2.73	1.7161	0.04	-0.025	-0.07
12	UNROTATE	Factor1	0.63	0.7137	0.71	0.879	0.74
13	UNROTATE	Factor2	0.77	-0.5552	0.68	-0.158	-0.58
14	RESIDUAL	Population	0.02	-0.0112	0.01	0.011	0.00
15	RESIDUAL	School	-0.01	0.1824	0.02	-0.024	0.01
16	RESIDUAL	Employment	0.01	0.0215	0.03	-0.006	-0.02
17	RESIDUAL	Services	0.01	-0.0239	-0.01	0.202	0.03
18	RESIDUAL	HouseValue	0.00	0.0125	-0.02	0.034	0.12
19	PRETRANS	Factor1	0.79	-0.6145	.	.	.
20	PRETRANS	Factor2	0.61	0.7889	.	.	.
21	PREROTAT	Factor1	0.02	0.9042	0.15	0.791	0.94
22	PREROTAT	Factor2	0.99	0.0006	0.97	0.415	-0.00
23	TRANSFOR	Factor1	0.74	-0.7055	.	.	.
24	TRANSFOR	Factor2	0.54	0.8653	.	.	.
25	FCORR	Factor1	1.00	0.2019	.	.	.
26	FCORR	Factor2	0.20	1.0000	.	.	.
27	PATTERN	Factor1	-0.08	0.9184	0.05	0.761	0.96
28	PATTERN	Factor2	1.00	-0.0935	0.98	0.339	-0.10
29	RCORR	Factor1	1.00	-0.2019	.	.	.
30	RCORR	Factor2	-0.20	1.0000	.	.	.
31	REFERENC	Factor1	-0.08	0.8995	0.05	0.745	0.94
32	REFERENC	Factor2	0.98	-0.0916	0.96	0.332	-0.10
33	STRUCTUR	Factor1	0.12	0.8995	0.24	0.829	0.94
34	STRUCTUR	Factor2	0.99	0.0919	0.98	0.493	0.09

The output data set displayed in Output 26.2.15 can be used for Harris-Kaiser rotation by deleting observations with _TYPE_='PATTERN' and _TYPE_='FCORR', which are for the promax-rotated factors, and changing _TYPE_='UNROTATE' to _TYPE_='PATTERN'.

Output 26.2.16 displays the rotated factor pattern output formatted with the picture format 'FuzzFlag'.

Output 26.2.16. Picture Format Output

Obs	RowName	Factor1	Factor2
1	HouseValue	95 *	.
2	School	91 *	.
3	Services	76	33
4	Population	.	100 *
5	Employment	.	97 *

The following statements produce Output 26.2.17:

```
data fact2(type=factor);
   set fact_all;
   if _TYPE_ in('PATTERN' 'FCORR') then delete;
   if _TYPE_='UNROTATE' then _TYPE_='PATTERN';

proc factor rotate=hk norm=weight reorder plot;
   title3 'Harris-Kaiser Rotation with Cureton-Mulaik Weights';
run;
```

The results of the Harris-Kaiser rotation are displayed in Output 26.2.17:

Output 26.2.17. Harris-Kaiser Rotation

```
            Harris-Kaiser Rotation with Cureton-Mulaik Weights

                          The FACTOR Procedure
                     Rotation Method: Harris-Kaiser

                      Variable Weights for Rotation

Population          School      Employment        Services      HouseValue

0.95982747      0.93945424      0.99746396      0.12194766      0.94007263


                     Oblique Transformation Matrix

                                    1               2

                     1        0.73537         0.61899
                     2       -0.68283         0.78987


                       Inter-Factor Correlations

                              Factor1         Factor2

                Factor1       1.00000         0.08358
                Factor2       0.08358         1.00000
```

```
         Harris-Kaiser Rotation with Cureton-Mulaik Weights

                       The FACTOR Procedure
                  Rotation Method: Harris-Kaiser

   Rotated Factor Pattern (Standardized Regression Coefficients)

                               Factor1         Factor2

        HouseValue             0.94048         0.00279
        School                 0.90391         0.00327
        Services               0.75459         0.41892
        Population            -0.06335         0.99227
        Employment             0.06152         0.97885


               Reference Axis Correlations

                             Factor1         Factor2

         Factor1             1.00000        -0.08358
         Factor2            -0.08358         1.00000


        Reference Structure (Semipartial Correlations)

                               Factor1         Factor2

        HouseValue             0.93719         0.00278
        School                 0.90075         0.00326
        Services               0.75195         0.41745
        Population            -0.06312         0.98880
        Employment             0.06130         0.97543


    Variance Explained by Each Factor Eliminating Other Factors

                       Factor1         Factor2

                     2.2628537       2.1034731
```

```
              Harris-Kaiser Rotation with Cureton-Mulaik Weights

                          The FACTOR Procedure
                     Rotation Method: Harris-Kaiser

                    Factor Structure (Correlations)

                                  Factor1         Factor2

                HouseValue        0.94071         0.08139
                School            0.90419         0.07882
                Services          0.78960         0.48198
                Population        0.01958         0.98698
                Employment        0.14332         0.98399


          Variance Explained by Each Factor Ignoring Other Factors

                          Factor1         Factor2

                        2.3468965       2.1875158


               Final Community Estimates: Total = 4.450370

Population          School     Employment        Services      HouseValue

0.97811334      0.81756387     0.97199928      0.79774304      0.88494998
```

```
                 Harris-Kaiser Rotation with Cureton-Mulaik Weights

                              The FACTOR Procedure
                        Rotation Method: Harris-Kaiser

Plot of Reference Structure for Factor1 and Factor2
Reference Axis Correlation = -0.0836  Angle = 94.7941

                                    Factor1
                                       1
                                       E
                                      .B

                                      .8
                                                D
                                      .7

                                      .6

                                      .5

                                      .4

                                      .3

                                      .2
                                                                   F
                                      .1                           a
                                                                 C c
     -1 -.9-.8-.7-.6-.5-.4-.3-.2-.1   0 .1 .2 .3 .4 .5 .6 .7 .8 .9 1.0t
                                                                 A o
                                     -.1                           r
                                                                   2
                                     -.2

                                     -.3

                                     -.4

                                     -.5

                                     -.6

                                     -.7

                                     -.8

                                     -.9

                                      -1

       Population=A   School=B       Employment=C   Services=D      HouseValue=E
```

In the results of the Harris-Kaiser rotation, the variable Services receives a small weight, and the axes are placed as desired.

Example 26.3. Maximum-Likelihood Factor Analysis

This example uses maximum-likelihood factor analyses for one, two, and three factors. It is already apparent from the principal factor analysis that the best number of common factors is almost certainly two. The one- and three-factor ML solutions reinforce this conclusion and illustrate some of the numerical problems that can occur. The following statements produce Output 26.3.1:

```
proc factor data=SocioEconomics method=ml heywood n=1;
   title3 'Maximum-Likelihood Factor Analysis with One Factor';
run;
proc factor data=SocioEconomics method=ml heywood n=2;
   title3 'Maximum-Likelihood Factor Analysis with Two Factors';
run;
proc factor data=SocioEconomics method=ml heywood n=3;
   title3 'Maximum-Likelihood Factor Analysis with Three Factors';
run;
```

Output 26.3.1. Maximum-Likelihood Factor Analysis

```
             Maximum-Likelihood Factor Analysis with One Factor

                           The FACTOR Procedure
                  Initial Factor Method: Maximum Likelihood

                    Prior Communality Estimates: SMC

 Population         School      Employment        Services      HouseValue

 0.96859160     0.82228514      0.96918082      0.78572440      0.84701921


      Preliminary Eigenvalues: Total = 76.1165859  Average = 15.2233172

                Eigenvalue    Difference    Proportion    Cumulative

           1    63.7010086    50.6462895        0.8369        0.8369
           2    13.0547191    12.7270798        0.1715        1.0084
           3     0.3276393     0.6749199        0.0043        1.0127
           4    -0.3472805     0.2722202       -0.0046        1.0081
           5    -0.6195007                     -0.0081        1.0000

           1 factor will be retained by the NFACTOR criterion.


Iteration    Criterion     Ridge    Change              Communalities

    1        6.5429218    0.0000    0.1033    0.93828   0.72227   1.00000   0.71940
                                              0.74371
    2        3.1232699    0.0000    0.7288    0.94566   0.02380   1.00000   0.26493
                                              0.01487


        Convergence criterion satisfied.
```

```
             Maximum-Likelihood Factor Analysis with One Factor

                            The FACTOR Procedure
                   Initial Factor Method: Maximum Likelihood

                  Significance Tests Based on 12 Observations

                                                                  Pr >
               Test                        DF     Chi-Square     ChiSq

      H0: No common factors                10        54.2517    <.0001
      HA: At least one common factor
      H0: 1 Factor is sufficient            5        24.4656    0.0002
      HA: More factors are needed


          Chi-Square without Bartlett's Correction       34.355969
          Akaike's Information Criterion                 24.355969
          Schwarz's Bayesian Criterion                   21.931436
          Tucker and Lewis's Reliability Coefficient      0.120231


                       Squared Canonical Correlations

                                  Factor1

                                 1.0000000


Eigenvalues of the Weighted Reduced Correlation Matrix: Total = 0  Average = 0

                             Eigenvalue     Difference

                       1          Infty          Infty
                       2     1.92716032     2.15547340
                       3     -.22831308     0.56464322
                       4     -.79295630     0.11293464
                       5     -.90589094
```

```
           Maximum-Likelihood Factor Analysis with One Factor

                         The FACTOR Procedure
               Initial Factor Method: Maximum Likelihood

                            Factor Pattern

                                         Factor1

                   Population            0.97245
                   School                0.15428
                   Employment            1.00000
                   Services              0.51472
                   HouseValue            0.12193


                 Variance Explained by Each Factor

                Factor          Weighted      Unweighted

                Factor1       17.8010629      2.24926004


           Final Communality Estimates and Variable Weights
  Total Communality: Weighted = 17.801063   Unweighted = 2.249260

              Variable       Communality          Weight

              Population      0.94565561      18.4011648
              School          0.02380349       1.0243839
              Employment      1.00000000           Infty
              Services        0.26493499       1.3604239
              HouseValue      0.01486595       1.0150903
```

Output 26.3.1 displays the results of the analysis with one factor. The solution on the second iteration is so close to the optimum that PROC FACTOR cannot find a better solution, hence you receive this message:

```
Convergence criterion satisfied.
```

When this message appears, you should try rerunning PROC FACTOR with different prior communality estimates to make sure that the solution is correct. In this case, other prior estimates lead to the same solution or possibly to worse local optima, as indicated by the information criteria or the Chi-square values.

The variable Employment has a communality of 1.0 and, therefore, an infinite weight that is displayed next to the final communality estimate as a missing/infinite value. The first eigenvalue is also infinite. Infinite values are ignored in computing the total of the eigenvalues and the total final communality.

Output 26.3.2. Maximum-Likelihood Factor Analysis: Two Factors

```
              Maximum-Likelihood Factor Analysis with Two Factors

                              The FACTOR Procedure
                     Initial Factor Method: Maximum Likelihood

                        Prior Communality Estimates: SMC

  Population          School        Employment          Services        HouseValue

  0.96859160      0.82228514        0.96918082        0.78572440        0.84701921


       Preliminary Eigenvalues: Total = 76.1165859  Average = 15.2233172

                  Eigenvalue    Difference    Proportion    Cumulative

             1    63.7010086    50.6462895        0.8369        0.8369
             2    13.0547191    12.7270798        0.1715        1.0084
             3     0.3276393     0.6749199        0.0043        1.0127
             4    -0.3472805     0.2722202       -0.0046        1.0081
             5    -0.6195007                     -0.0081        1.0000

              2 factors will be retained by the NFACTOR criterion.


Iteration     Criterion     Ridge    Change                 Communalities

    1         0.3431221    0.0000    0.0471    1.00000    0.80672    0.95058    0.79348
                                               0.89412
    2         0.3072178    0.0000    0.0307    1.00000    0.80821    0.96023    0.81048
                                               0.92480
    3         0.3067860    0.0000    0.0063    1.00000    0.81149    0.95948    0.81677
                                               0.92023
    4         0.3067373    0.0000    0.0022    1.00000    0.80985    0.95963    0.81498
                                               0.92241
    5         0.3067321    0.0000    0.0007    1.00000    0.81019    0.95955    0.81569
                                               0.92187


        Convergence criterion satisfied.
```

```
            Maximum-Likelihood Factor Analysis with Two Factors

                          The FACTOR Procedure
                 Initial Factor Method: Maximum Likelihood

               Significance Tests Based on 12 Observations

                                                                  Pr >
             Test                            DF    Chi-Square     ChiSq

      H0: No common factors                  10       54.2517     <.0001
      HA: At least one common factor
      H0: 2 Factors are sufficient            1        2.1982     0.1382
      HA: More factors are needed


          Chi-Square without Bartlett's Correction      3.3740530
          Akaike's Information Criterion                1.3740530
          Schwarz's Bayesian Criterion                  0.8891463
          Tucker and Lewis's Reliability Coefficient    0.7292200


                     Squared Canonical Correlations

                         Factor1          Factor2

                       1.0000000        0.9518891


              Eigenvalues of the Weighted Reduced Correlation
             Matrix: Total = 19.7853157  Average = 4.94632893

               Eigenvalue    Difference    Proportion    Cumulative

          1         Infty         Infty
          2    19.7853143    19.2421292        1.0000        1.0000
          3     0.5431851     0.5829564        0.0275        1.0275
          4    -0.0397713     0.4636411       -0.0020        1.0254
          5    -0.5034124                     -0.0254        1.0000
```

```
          Maximum-Likelihood Factor Analysis with Two Factors

                        The FACTOR Procedure
               Initial Factor Method: Maximum Likelihood

                           Factor Pattern

                                Factor1          Factor2

               Population       1.00000          0.00000
               School           0.00975          0.90003
               Employment       0.97245          0.11797
               Services         0.43887          0.78930
               HouseValue       0.02241          0.95989


                  Variance Explained by Each Factor

                  Factor        Weighted     Unweighted

                  Factor1     24.4329707     2.13886057
                  Factor2     19.7853143     2.36835294


             Final Communality Estimates and Variable Weights
      Total Communality: Weighted = 44.218285   Unweighted = 4.507214

                Variable      Communality         Weight

                Population     1.00000000          Infty
                School         0.81014489      5.2682940
                Employment     0.95957142     24.7246669
                Services       0.81560348      5.4256462
                HouseValue     0.92189372     12.7996793
```

Output 26.3.2 displays the results of the analysis using two factors. The analysis converges without incident. This time, however, the Population variable is a Heywood case.

Output 26.3.3. Maximum-Likelihood Factor Analysis: Three Factors

```
          Maximum-Likelihood Factor Analysis with Three Factors

                          The FACTOR Procedure
                 Initial Factor Method: Maximum Likelihood

                    Prior Communality Estimates: SMC

   Population          School       Employment         Services        HouseValue

   0.96859160      0.82228514       0.96918082       0.78572440        0.84701921


        Preliminary Eigenvalues: Total = 76.1165859  Average = 15.2233172

                  Eigenvalue    Difference    Proportion    Cumulative

              1   63.7010086    50.6462895        0.8369        0.8369
              2   13.0547191    12.7270798        0.1715        1.0084
              3    0.3276393     0.6749199        0.0043        1.0127
              4   -0.3472805     0.2722202       -0.0046        1.0081
              5   -0.6195007                     -0.0081        1.0000

             3 factors will be retained by the NFACTOR criterion.


               WARNING: Too many factors for a unique solution.


Iteration    Criterion    Ridge    Change              Communalities

    1        0.1798029   0.0313    0.0501    0.96081   0.84184   1.00000   0.80175
                                             0.89716
    2        0.0016405   0.0313    0.0678    0.98081   0.88713   1.00000   0.79559
                                             0.96500
    3        0.0000041   0.0313    0.0094    0.98195   0.88603   1.00000   0.80498
                                             0.96751
    4        0.0000000   0.0313    0.0006    0.98202   0.88585   1.00000   0.80561
                                             0.96735


        ERROR: Converged, but not to a proper optimum.
                      Try a different 'PRIORS' statement.
```

```
        Maximum-Likelihood Factor Analysis with Three Factors

                         The FACTOR Procedure
               Initial Factor Method: Maximum Likelihood

              Significance Tests Based on 12 Observations

                                                                 Pr >
             Test                            DF     Chi-Square    ChiSq

HO: No common factors                        10        54.2517    <.0001
HA: At least one common factor
HO: 3 Factors are sufficient                 -2         0.0000         .
HA: More factors are needed


    Chi-Square without Bartlett's Correction          0.0000003
    Akaike's Information Criterion                    4.0000003
    Schwarz's Bayesian Criterion                      4.9698136
    Tucker and Lewis's Reliability Coefficient        0.0000000


                   Squared Canonical Correlations

              Factor1          Factor2          Factor3

            1.0000000        0.9751895        0.6894465


          Eigenvalues of the Weighted Reduced Correlation
         Matrix: Total = 41.5254193   Average = 10.3813548

             Eigenvalue    Difference    Proportion    Cumulative

     1            Infty         Infty
     2       39.3054826    37.0854258        0.9465        0.9465
     3        2.2200568     2.2199693        0.0535        1.0000
     4        0.0000875     0.0002949        0.0000        1.0000
     5       -0.0002075                     -0.0000        1.0000
```

```
          Maximum-Likelihood Factor Analysis with Three Factors

                         The FACTOR Procedure
               Initial Factor Method: Maximum Likelihood

                            Factor Pattern

                         Factor1         Factor2         Factor3

     Population          0.97245        -0.11233        -0.15409
     School              0.15428         0.89108         0.26083
     Employment          1.00000         0.00000         0.00000
     Services            0.51472         0.72416        -0.12766
     HouseValue          0.12193         0.97227        -0.08473


               Variance Explained by Each Factor

               Factor        Weighted      Unweighted

               Factor1     54.6115241      2.24926004
               Factor2     39.3054826      2.27634375
               Factor3      2.2200568      0.11525433


         Final Communality Estimates and Variable Weights
  Total Communality: Weighted = 96.137063   Unweighted = 4.640858

             Variable       Communality         Weight

             Population      0.98201660      55.6066901
             School          0.88585165       8.7607194
             Employment      1.00000000           Infty
             Services        0.80564301       5.1444261
             HouseValue      0.96734687      30.6251078
```

The three-factor analysis displayed in Output 26.3.3 generates this message:

```
WARNING:  Too many factors for a unique solution.
```

The number of parameters in the model exceeds the number of elements in the correlation matrix from which they can be estimated, so an infinite number of different perfect solutions can be obtained. The Criterion approaches zero at an improper optimum, as indicated by this message:

```
Converged, but not to a proper optimum.
```

The degrees of freedom for the chi-square test are -2, so a probability level cannot be computed for three factors. Note also that the variable Employment is a Heywood case again.

The probability levels for the chi-square test are 0.0001 for the hypothesis of no common factors, 0.0002 for one common factor, and 0.1382 for two common factors. Therefore, the two-factor model seems to be an adequate representation. Akaike's information criterion and Schwarz's Bayesian criterion attain their minimum values at two common factors, so there is little doubt that two factors are appropriate for these data.

References

Akaike, H. (1973), "Information Theory and the Extension of the Maximum Likelihood Principle," in *Second International Symposium on Information Theory,* eds. V.N. Petrov and F. Csaki, Budapest: Akailseoniai-Kiudo, 267–281.

Akaike, H. (1974), "A New Look at the Statistical Identification Model," *IEEE Transactions on Automatic Control,* 19, 716–723.

Akaike, H. (1987), "Factor Analysis and AIC," *Psychometrika* 52, 317–332.

Bickel, P.J. and Doksum, K.A. (1977), *Mathematical Statistics,* San Francisco: Holden-Day.

Cattell, R.B. (1966), "The Scree Test for the Number of Factors," *Multivariate Behavioral Research,* 1, 245–276.

Cattell, R.B. (1978), *The Scientific Use of Factor Analysis,* New York: Plenum.

Cattell, R.B. and Vogelman, S. (1977), "A Comprehensive Trial of the Scree and KG Criteria for Determining the Number of Factors," *Multivariate Behavioral Research,* 12, 289–325.

Cerny, B.A. and Kaiser, H.F. (1977), "A Study of a Measure of Sampling Adequacy for Factor-Analytic Correlation Matrices," *Multivariate Behavioral Research,* 12, 43–47.

Cureton, E.E. (1968), *A Factor Analysis of Project TALENT Tests and Four Other Test Batteries,* (Interim Report 4 to the U.S. Office of Education, Cooperative Research Project No. 3051.) Palo Alto: Project TALENT Office, American Institutes for Research and University of Pittsburgh.

Cureton, E.E. and Mulaik, S.A. (1975), "The Weighted Varimax Rotation and the Promax Rotation," *Psychometrika,* 40, 183–195.

Dziuban, C.D. and Harris, C.W. (1973), "On the Extraction of Components and the Applicability of the Factor Model," *American Educational Research Journal,* 10, 93–99.

Fuller (1987), *Measurement Error Models*, New York: John Wiley & Sons, Inc.

Geweke, J.F. and Singleton, K.J. (1980), "Interpreting the Likelihood Ratio Statistic in Factor Models When Sample Size Is Small," *Journal of the American Statistical Association,* 75, 133–137.

Gorsuch, R.L. (1974), *Factor Analysis,* Philadelphia: W.B. Saunders Co.

Harman, H.H. (1976), *Modern Factor Analysis,* Third Edition, Chicago: University of Chicago Press.

Harris, C.W. (1962), "Some Rao-Guttman Relationships," *Psychometrika,* 27, 247–263.

Horn, J.L. and Engstrom, R. (1979), "Cattell's Scree Test in Relation to Bartlett's Chi-Square Test and Other Observations on the Number of Factors Problem," *Multivariate Behavioral Research,* 14, 283–300.

Joreskog, K.G. (1962), "On the Statistical Treatment of Residuals in Factor Analysis," *Psychometrika,* 27, 335–354.

Joreskog, K.G. (1977), "Factor Analysis by Least-Squares and Maximum Likelihood Methods," in *Statistical Methods for Digital Computers,* eds. K. Enslein, A. Ralston, and H.S. Wilf, New York: John Wiley & Sons, Inc.

Kaiser, H.F. (1963), "Image Analysis," in *Problems in Measuring Change,* ed. C.W. Harris, Madison, WI: University of Wisconsin Press.

Kaiser, H.F. (1970), "A Second Generation Little Jiffy," *Psychometrika,* 35, 401–415.

Kaiser, H.F. and Cerny, B.A. (1979), "Factor Analysis of the Image Correlation Matrix," *Educational and Psychological Measurement,* 39, 711–714.

Kaiser, H.F. and Rice, J. (1974), "Little Jiffy, Mark IV," *Educational and Psychological Measurement,* 34, 111–117.

Kerlinger, F.N. and Pedhazur, E.J. (1973), *Multiple Regression in Behavioral Research,* New York: Holt, Rinehart & Winston, Inc.

Kim, J.O. and Mueller, C.W. (1978a), *Introduction to Factor Analysis: What It Is and How To Do It,* Sage University Paper Series on Quantitative Applications in the Social Sciences, series no. 07-013, Beverly Hills: Sage Publications.

Kim, J.O. and Mueller, C.W. (1978b), *Factor Analysis: Statistical Methods and Practical Issues,* Sage University Paper Series on Quantitative Applications in the Social Sciences, series no. 07-014, Beverly Hills: Sage Publications.

Lawley, D.N. and Maxwell, A.E. (1971), *Factor Analysis as a Statistical Method,* New York: Macmillan Publishing Co., Inc.

Lee, H.B. and Comrey, A.L. (1979), "Distortions in a Commonly Used Factor Analytic Procedure," *Multivariate Behavioral Research,* 14, 301–321.

Mardia, K.V., Kent, J.T., and Bibby, J.M. (1979), *Multivariate Analysis,* London: Academic Press.

McDonald, R.P. (1975), "A Note on Rippe's Test of Significance in Common Factor Analysis," *Psychometrika,* 40, 117–119.

McDonald, R.P. (1985), *Factor Analysis and Related Methods,* New Jersey: Lawrence Erlbaum Associates, Publishers.

Morrison, D.F. (1976), *Multivariate Statistical Methods,* Second Edition, New York: McGraw-Hill Book Co.

Mulaik, S.A. (1972), *The Foundations of Factor Analysis,* New York: McGraw-Hill Book Co.

Rao, C.R. (1955), "Estimation and Tests of Significance in Factor Analysis," *Psychometrika,* 20, 93–111.

Schwarz, G. (1978), "Estimating the Dimension of a Model," *Annals of Statistics,* 6, 461–464.

Spearman, C. (1904), "General Intelligence Objectively Determined and Measured," *American Journal of Psychology,* 15, 201–293.

Stewart, D.W. (1981), "The Application and Misapplication of Factor Analysis in Marketing Research," *Journal of Marketing Research,* 18, 51–62.

Tucker, L.R. and Lewis, C. (1973), "A Reliability Coefficient for Maximum Likelihood Factor Analysis," *Psychometrika,* 38, 1–10.

Chapter 27
The FASTCLUS Procedure

Chapter Table of Contents

Chapter 27
The FASTCLUS Procedure

Overview

The FASTCLUS procedure performs a disjoint cluster analysis on the basis of distances computed from one or more quantitative variables. The observations are divided into clusters such that every observation belongs to one and only one cluster; the clusters do not form a tree structure as they do in the CLUSTER procedure. If you want separate analyses for different numbers of clusters, you can run PROC FASTCLUS once for each analysis. Alternatively, to do hierarchical clustering on a large data set, use PROC FASTCLUS to find initial clusters, then use those initial clusters as input to PROC CLUSTER.

By default, the FASTCLUS procedure uses Euclidean distances, so the cluster centers are based on least-squares estimation. This kind of clustering method is often called a *k-means model*, since the cluster centers are the means of the observations assigned to each cluster when the algorithm is run to complete convergence. Each iteration reduces the least-squares criterion until convergence is achieved.

Often there is no need to run the FASTCLUS procedure to convergence. PROC FASTCLUS is designed to find good clusters (but not necessarily the best possible clusters) with only two or three passes over the data set. The initialization method of PROC FASTCLUS guarantees that, if there exist clusters such that all distances between observations in the same cluster are less than all distances between observations in different clusters, and if you tell PROC FASTCLUS the correct number of clusters to find, it can always find such a clustering without iterating. Even with clusters that are not as well separated, PROC FASTCLUS usually finds initial seeds that are sufficiently good so that few iterations are required. Hence, by default, PROC FASTCLUS performs only one iteration.

The initialization method used by the FASTCLUS procedure makes it sensitive to outliers. PROC FASTCLUS can be an effective procedure for detecting outliers because outliers often appear as clusters with only one member.

The FASTCLUS procedure can use an L_p (least pth powers) clustering criterion (Spath 1985, pp. 62–63) instead of the least-squares (L_2) criterion used in k-means clustering methods. The LEAST=p option specifies the power p to be used. Using the LEAST= option increases execution time since more iterations are usually required, and the default iteration limit is increased when you specify LEAST=p. Values of p less than 2 reduce the effect of outliers on the cluster centers compared with least-squares methods; values of p greater than 2 increase the effect of outliers.

The FASTCLUS procedure is intended for use with large data sets, with 100 or more observations. With small data sets, the results may be highly sensitive to the order of the observations in the data set.

PROC FASTCLUS produces brief summaries of the clusters it finds. For more extensive examination of the clusters, you can request an output data set containing a cluster membership variable.

Background

The FASTCLUS procedure combines an effective method for finding initial clusters with a standard iterative algorithm for minimizing the sum of squared distances from the cluster means. The result is an efficient procedure for disjoint clustering of large data sets. PROC FASTCLUS was directly inspired by Hartigan's (1975) *leader algorithm* and MacQueen's (1967) *k-means algorithm*. PROC FASTCLUS uses a method that Anderberg (1973) calls *nearest centroid sorting*. A set of points called *cluster seeds* is selected as a first guess of the means of the clusters. Each observation is assigned to the nearest seed to form temporary clusters. The seeds are then replaced by the means of the temporary clusters, and the process is repeated until no further changes occur in the clusters. Similar techniques are described in most references on clustering (Anderberg 1973; Hartigan 1975; Everitt 1980; Spath 1980).

The FASTCLUS procedure differs from other nearest centroid sorting methods in the way the initial cluster seeds are selected. The importance of initial seed selection is demonstrated by Milligan (1980).

The clustering is done on the basis of Euclidean distances computed from one or more numeric variables. If there are missing values, PROC FASTCLUS computes an adjusted distance using the nonmissing values. Observations that are very close to each other are usually assigned to the same cluster, while observations that are far apart are in different clusters.

The FASTCLUS procedure operates in four steps:

1. Observations called *cluster seeds* are selected.
2. If you specify the DRIFT option, temporary clusters are formed by assigning each observation to the cluster with the nearest seed. Each time an observation is assigned, the cluster seed is updated as the current mean of the cluster. This method is sometimes called *incremental*, *on-line*, or *adaptive* training.
3. If the maximum number of iterations is greater than zero, clusters are formed by assigning each observation to the nearest seed. After all observations are assigned, the cluster seeds are replaced by either the cluster means or other location estimates (cluster centers) appropriate to the LEAST=p option. This step can be repeated until the changes in the cluster seeds become small or zero (MAXITER=$n \geq 1$).
4. Final clusters are formed by assigning each observation to the nearest seed.

If PROC FASTCLUS runs to complete convergence, the final cluster seeds will equal the cluster means or cluster centers. If PROC FASTCLUS terminates before complete convergence, which often happens with the default settings, the final cluster seeds may not equal the cluster means or cluster centers. If you want complete converegnce, specify CONVERGE=0 and a large value for the MAXITER= option.

The initial cluster seeds must be observations with no missing values. You can specify the maximum number of seeds (and, hence, clusters) using the MAXCLUSTERS= option. You can also specify a minimum distance by which the seeds must be separated using the RADIUS= option.

PROC FASTCLUS always selects the first complete (no missing values) observation as the first seed. The next complete observation that is separated from the first seed by at least the distance specified in the RADIUS= option becomes the second seed. Later observations are selected as new seeds if they are separated from all previous seeds by at least the radius, as long as the maximum number of seeds is not exceeded.

If an observation is complete but fails to qualify as a new seed, PROC FASTCLUS considers using it to replace one of the old seeds. Two tests are made to see if the observation can qualify as a new seed.

First, an old seed is replaced if the distance between the observation and the closest seed is greater than the minimum distance between seeds. The seed that is replaced is selected from the two seeds that are closest to each other. The seed that is replaced is the one of these two with the shortest distance to the closest of the remaining seeds when the other seed is replaced by the current observation.

If the observation fails the first test for seed replacement, a second test is made. The observation replaces the nearest seed if the smallest distance from the observation to all seeds other than the nearest one is greater than the shortest distance from the nearest seed to all other seeds. If the observation fails this test, PROC FASTCLUS goes on to the next observation.

You can specify the REPLACE= option to limit seed replacement. You can omit the second test for seed replacement (REPLACE=PART), causing PROC FASTCLUS to run faster, but the seeds selected may not be as widely separated as those obtained by the default method. You can also suppress seed replacement entirely by specifying REPLACE=NONE. In this case, PROC FASTCLUS runs much faster, but you must choose a good value for the RADIUS= option in order to get good clusters. This method is similar to Hartigan's (1975, pp. 74–78) leader algorithm and the *simple cluster seeking algorithm* described by Tou and Gonzalez (1974, pp. 90–92).

Getting Started

The following example demonstrates how to use the FASTCLUS procedure to compute disjoint clusters of observations in a SAS data set.

The data in this example are measurements taken on 159 fish caught off the coast of Finland; this data set is available from the Data Archive of the *Journal of Statistics Education*. The complete data set is displayed in Chapter 60, "The STEPDISC Procedure."

The species (bream, parkki, pike, perch, roach, smelt, and whitefish), weight, three different length measurements (measured from the nose of the fish to the beginning of its tail, the notch of its tail, and the end of its tail), height, and width of each fish are tallied. The height and width are recorded as percentages of the third length variable.

Suppose that you want to group empirically the fish measurements into clusters and that you want to associate the clusters with the species. You can use the FASTCLUS procedure to perform a cluster analysis.

The following DATA step creates the SAS data set Fish.

```
proc format;
   value specfmt
      1='Bream'
      2='Roach'
      3='Whitefish'
      4='Parkki'
      5='Perch'
      6='Pike'
      7='Smelt';
data Fish (drop=HtPct WidthPct);
   title 'Fish Measurement Data';
   input Species Weight Length1 Length2 Length3 HtPct
         WidthPct @@;
   if Weight <=0 or Weight = . then delete;
   Weight3=Weight**(1/3);
   Height=HtPct*Length3/(Weight3*100);
   Width=WidthPct*Length3/(Weight3*100);
   Length1=Length1/Weight3;
   Length3=Length3/Weight3;
   logLengthRatio=log(Length3/Length1);

   format Species specfmt.;
   symbol = put(Species, specfmt2.);
   datalines;
1  242.0 23.2 25.4 30.0 38.4 13.4
1  290.0 24.0 26.3 31.2 40.0 13.8
1  340.0 23.9 26.5 31.1 39.8 15.1
1  363.0 26.3 29.0 33.5 38.0 13.3
 ... [155 more records]
;
run;
```

The double trailing at sign (@@) in the INPUT statement specifies that observations are input from each line until all values are read. The variables are rescaled in order to adjust for dimensionality. Because the new variables Weight3–logLengthRatio depend on the variable Weight, observations with missing values for Weight are not added to the data set. Consequently, there are 157 observations in the SAS data set Fish.

Variables with larger variances exert a larger influence in calculating the clusters. In the Fish data set, the variables are not measured in the same units and cannot be assumed to have equal variance. Therefore, it is necessary to standardize the variables before performing the cluster analysis.

The following statements standardize the variables and perform a cluster analysis on the standardized data.

```
proc standard data=Fish out=Stand mean=0 std=1;
   var Length1 logLengthRatio Height Width Weight3;
proc fastclus data=Stand out=Clust
              maxclusters=7 maxiter=100 ;
   var Length1 logLengthRatio Height Width Weight3;
run;
```

The STANDARD procedure is first used to standardize all the analytical variables to a mean of 0 and standard deviation of 1. The procedure creates the output data set Stand to contain the transformed variables.

The FASTCLUS procedure then uses the data set Stand as input and creates the data set Clust. This output data set contains the original variables and two new variables, Cluster and Distance. The variable Cluster contains the cluster number to which each observation has been assigned. The variable Distance gives the distance from the observation to its cluster seed.

It is usually desirable to try several values of the MAXCLUSTERS= option. A reasonable beginning for this example is to use MAXCLUSTERS=7, since there are seven species of fish represented in the data set Fish.

The VAR statement specifies the variables used in the cluster analysis.

The results from this analysis are displayed in the following figures.

```
                              Fish Measurement Data

                             The FASTCLUS Procedure
            Replace=FULL  Radius=0  Maxclusters=7 Maxiter=100  Converge=0.02

                                  Initial Seeds

                                  logLength
Cluster          Length1              Ratio           Height           Width          Weight3
-------------------------------------------------------------------------------------------------
   1          1.388338414      -0.979577858     -1.594561848    -2.254050655      2.103447062
   2         -1.117178039      -0.877218192     -0.336166276     2.528114070      1.170706464
   3          2.393997461      -0.662642015     -0.930738701    -2.073879107     -1.839325419
   4         -0.495085516      -0.964041012     -0.265106856    -0.028245072      1.536846394
   5         -0.728772773       0.540096664      1.130501398    -1.207930053     -1.107018207
   6         -0.506924177       0.748211648      1.762482687     0.211507596      1.368987826
   7          1.573996573      -0.796593995     -0.824217424     1.561715851     -1.607942726

                      Criterion Based on Final Seeds =    0.3979
```

Figure 27.1. Initial Seeds Used in the FASTCLUS Procedure

Figure 27.1 displays the table of initial seeds used for each variable and cluster. The first line in the figure displays the option settings for REPLACE, RADIUS, MAXCLUSTERS, and MAXITER. These options, with the exception of MAXCLUSTERS and MAXITER, are set at their respective default values (REPLACE=FULL, RADIUS=0). Both the MAXCLUSTERS= and MAXITER= options are set in the PROC FASTCLUS statement.

Next, PROC FASTCLUS produces a table of summary statistics for the clusters. Figure 27.2 displays the number of observations in the cluster (frequency) and the root mean square standard deviation. The next two columns display the largest Euclidean distance from the cluster seed to any observation within the cluster and the number of the nearest cluster.

The last column of the table displays the distance between the centroid of the nearest cluster and the centroid of the current cluster. A centroid is the point having coordinates that are the means of all the observations in the cluster.

```
                              Fish Measurement Data

                             The FASTCLUS Procedure
            Replace=FULL  Radius=0  Maxclusters=7 Maxiter=100  Converge=0.02

                                 Cluster Summary

                                   Maximum Distance
                       RMS Std            from Seed      Radius      Nearest      Distance Between
Cluster    Frequency  Deviation      to Observation    Exceeded      Cluster     Cluster Centroids
-------------------------------------------------------------------------------------------------
   1            17       0.5064              1.7781                        4                2.5106
   2            19       0.3696              1.5007                        4                1.5510
   3            13       0.3803              1.7135                        1                2.6704
   4            13       0.4161              1.3976                        7                1.4266
   5            11       0.2466              0.6966                        6                1.7301
   6            34       0.3563              1.5443                        5                1.7301
   7            50       0.4447              2.3915                        4                1.4266
```

Figure 27.2. Cluster Summary Table from the FASTCLUS Procedure

Figure 27.3 displays the table of statistics for the variables. The table lists for each variable the total standard deviation, the pooled within-cluster standard deviation and the R^2 value for predicting the variable from the cluster. The ratio of between-cluster variance to within-cluster variance (R^2 to $1 - R^2$) appears in the last column.

```
                          Fish Measurement Data

                          The FASTCLUS Procedure
      Replace=FULL  Radius=0  Maxclusters=7 Maxiter=100  Converge=0.02

                         Statistics for Variables

   Variable          Total STD    Within STD      R-Square     RSQ/(1-RSQ)
   -----------------------------------------------------------------------
   Length1             1.00000       0.31428      0.905030        9.529606
   logLengthRatio      1.00000       0.39276      0.851676        5.741989
   Height              1.00000       0.20917      0.957929       22.769295
   Width               1.00000       0.55558      0.703200        2.369270
   Weight3             1.00000       0.47251      0.785323        3.658162
   OVER-ALL            1.00000       0.40712      0.840631        5.274764


                     Pseudo F Statistic =    131.87


          Approximate Expected Over-All R-Squared =    0.57420


                  Cubic Clustering Criterion =    37.808

     WARNING: The two above values are invalid for correlated variables.
```

Figure 27.3. Statistics for Variables Used in the FASTCLUS Procedure

The pseudo F statistic, approximate expected overall R^2, and cubic clustering criterion (CCC) are listed at the bottom of the figure. You can compare values of these statistics by running PROC FASTCLUS with different values for the MAXCLUSTERS= option. The R^2 and CCC values are not valid for correlated variables.

Values of the cubic clustering criterion greater than 2 or 3 indicate good clusters. Values between 0 and 2 indicate potential clusters, but they should be taken with caution; large negative values may indicate outliers.

PROC FASTCLUS next produces the within-cluster means and standard deviations of the variables, displayed in Figure 27.4.

Fish Measurement Data

The FASTCLUS Procedure

Replace=FULL Radius=0 Maxclusters=7 Maxiter=100 Converge=0.02

Cluster Means

Cluster	Length1	logLength Ratio	Height	Width	Weight3
1	1.747808245	-0.868605685	-1.327226832	-1.128760946	0.806373599
2	-0.405231510	-0.979113021	-0.281064162	1.463094486	1.060450065
3	2.006796315	-0.652725165	-1.053213440	-1.224020795	-1.826752838
4	-0.136820952	-1.039312574	-0.446429482	0.162596336	0.278560318
5	-0.850130601	0.550190242	1.245156076	-0.836585750	-0.567022647
6	-0.843912827	1.522291347	1.511408739	-0.380323563	0.763114370
7	-0.165570970	-0.048881276	-0.353723615	0.546442064	-0.668780782

Cluster Standard Deviations

Cluster	Length1	logLength Ratio	Height	Width	Weight3
1	0.3418476428	0.3544065543	0.1666302451	0.6172880027	0.7944227150
2	0.3129902863	0.3592350778	0.1369052680	0.5467406493	0.3720119097
3	0.2962504486	0.1740941675	0.1736086707	0.7528475622	0.0905232968
4	0.3254364840	0.2836681149	0.1884592934	0.4543390702	0.6612055341
5	0.1781837609	0.0745984121	0.2056932592	0.2784540794	0.3832002850
6	0.2273744242	0.3385584051	0.2046010964	0.5143496067	0.4025849044
7	0.3734733622	0.5275768119	0.2551130680	0.5721303628	0.4223181710

Figure 27.4. Cluster Means and Standard Deviations from the FASTCLUS Procedure

It is useful to study further the clusters calculated by the FASTCLUS procedure. One method is to look at a frequency tabulation of the clusters with other classification variables. The following statements invoke the FREQ procedure to crosstabulate the empirical clusters with the variable Species:

```
proc freq data=Clust;
   tables Species*Cluster;
run;
```

These statements produce a frequency table of the variable Cluster versus the variable Species.

Figure 27.5 displays the marked division between clusters.

Fish Measurement Data

The FREQ Procedure

Table of Species by CLUSTER

Species / Frequency, Percent, Row Pct, Col Pct	CLUSTER(Cluster) 1	2	3	4	5	6	7	Total
Bream	0	0	0	0	0	34	0	34
	0.00	0.00	0.00	0.00	0.00	21.66	0.00	21.66
	0.00	0.00	0.00	0.00	0.00	100.00	0.00	
	0.00	0.00	0.00	0.00	0.00	100.00	0.00	
Roach	0	0	0	0	0	0	19	19
	0.00	0.00	0.00	0.00	0.00	0.00	12.10	12.10
	0.00	0.00	0.00	0.00	0.00	0.00	100.00	
	0.00	0.00	0.00	0.00	0.00	0.00	38.00	
Whitefish	0	2	0	1	0	0	3	6
	0.00	1.27	0.00	0.64	0.00	0.00	1.91	3.82
	0.00	33.33	0.00	16.67	0.00	0.00	50.00	
	0.00	10.53	0.00	7.69	0.00	0.00	6.00	
Parkki	0	0	0	0	11	0	0	11
	0.00	0.00	0.00	0.00	7.01	0.00	0.00	7.01
	0.00	0.00	0.00	0.00	100.00	0.00	0.00	
	0.00	0.00	0.00	0.00	100.00	0.00	0.00	
Perch	0	17	0	12	0	0	27	56
	0.00	10.83	0.00	7.64	0.00	0.00	17.20	35.67
	0.00	30.36	0.00	21.43	0.00	0.00	48.21	
	0.00	89.47	0.00	92.31	0.00	0.00	54.00	
Pike	17	0	0	0	0	0	0	17
	10.83	0.00	0.00	0.00	0.00	0.00	0.00	10.83
	100.00	0.00	0.00	0.00	0.00	0.00	0.00	
	100.00	0.00	0.00	0.00	0.00	0.00	0.00	
Smelt	0	0	13	0	0	0	1	14
	0.00	0.00	8.28	0.00	0.00	0.00	0.64	8.92
	0.00	0.00	92.86	0.00	0.00	0.00	7.14	
	0.00	0.00	100.00	0.00	0.00	0.00	2.00	
Total	17	19	13	13	11	34	50	157
	10.83	12.10	8.28	8.28	7.01	21.66	31.85	100.00

Figure 27.5. Frequency Table of Cluster versus Species

For cases in which you have three or more clusters, you can use the CANDISC and GPLOT procedures to obtain a graphical check on the distribution of the clusters. In the following statements, the CANDISC and GPLOT procedures are used to compute canonical variables and plot the clusters.

```
proc candisc data=Clust out=Can noprint;
   class Cluster;
   var Length1 logLengthRatio Height Width Weight3;

legend1 frame cframe=ligr label=none cborder=black
        position=center value=(justify=center);
axis1 label=(angle=90 rotate=0) minor=none;
axis2 minor=none;
```

```
proc gplot data=Can;
   plot Can2*Can1=Cluster/frame cframe=ligr
                    legend=legend1 vaxis=axis1 haxis=axis2;
run;
```

First, the CANDISC procedure is invoked to perform a canonical discriminant analysis using the data set Clust and creating the output SAS data set Can. The NOPRINT option suppresses display of the output. The CLASS statement specifies the variable Cluster to define groups for the analysis. The VAR statement specifies the variables used in the analysis.

Next, the GPLOT procedure plots the two canonical variables from PROC CANDISC, Can1 and Can2. The PLOT statement specifies the variable Cluster as the identification variable.

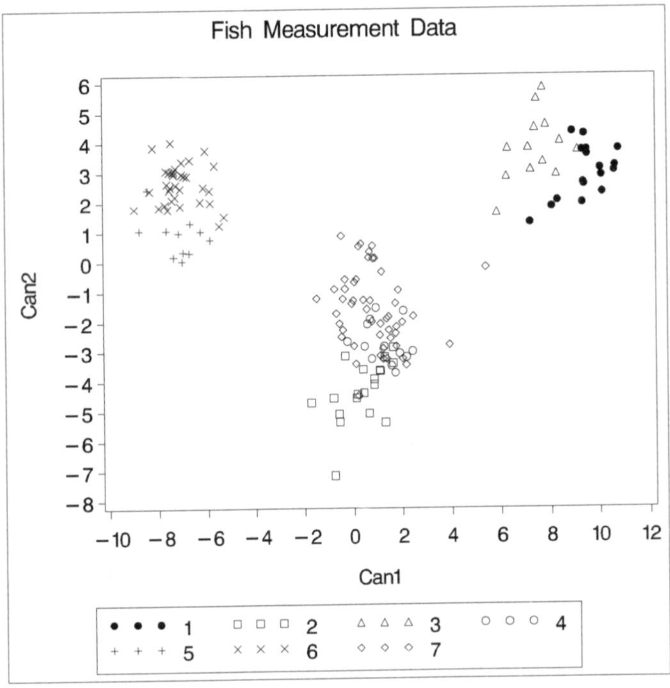

Figure 27.6. Plot of Canonical Variables and Cluster Value

The resulting plot (Figure 27.6) illustrates the spatial separation of the clusters calculated in the FASTCLUS procedure.

Syntax

The following statements are available in the FASTCLUS procedure:

> **PROC FASTCLUS MAXCLUSTERS=***n* | **RADIUS=***t* < *options* > **;**
>   **VAR** *variables* **;**
>   **ID** *variable* **;**
>   **FREQ** *variable* **;**
>   **WEIGHT** *variable* **;**
>   **BY** *variables* **;**

Usually you need only the VAR statement in addition to the PROC FASTCLUS statement. The BY, FREQ, ID, VAR, and WEIGHT statements are described in alphabetical order after the PROC FASTCLUS statement.

PROC FASTCLUS Statement

> **PROC FASTCLUS MAXCLUSTERS=***n* | **RADIUS=***t* < *options* > **;**

You must specify either the MAXCLUSTERS= or the RADIUS= argument in the PROC FASTCLUS statement.

MAXCLUSTERS=*n*
MAXC=*n*

specifies the maximum number of clusters allowed. If you omit the MAXCLUSTERS= option, a value of 100 is assumed.

RADIUS=*t*
R=*t*

establishes the minimum distance criterion for selecting new seeds. No observation is considered as a new seed unless its minimum distance to previous seeds exceeds the value given by the RADIUS= option. The default value is 0. If you specify the REPLACE=RANDOM option, the RADIUS= option is ignored.

You can specify the following options in the PROC FASTCLUS statement. Table 27.1 summarizes the options.

Table 27.1. Options Available in the PROC FASTCLUS Statement

Task	Options
Specify data set details	CLUSTER=
	DATA=
	MEAN=
	OUT=
	OUTITER
	OUTSEED=
	OUTSTAT=
	SEED=
Specify distance dimension	BINS=
	HC=
	HP=
	IRLS
	LEAST=
Select initial cluster seeds	RANDOM=
	REPLACE=
Compute final cluster seeds	CONVERGE=
	DELETE=
	DRIFT
	MAXCLUSTERS=
	MAXITER=
	RADIUS=
	STRICT
Work with missing values	IMPUTE
	NOMISS
Specify variance divisor	VARDEF
Control output	DISTANCE
	LIST
	NOPRINT
	SHORT
	SUMMARY

The following list provides details on these options. The list is in alphabetical order.

BINS=*n*

specifies the number of bins used in the bin-sort algorithm for computing medians for LEAST=1. By default, PROC FASTCLUS uses from 10 to 100 bins, depending on the amount of memory available. Larger values use more memory and make each iteration somewhat slower, but they may reduce the number of iterations. Smaller values have the opposite effect. The minimum value of n is 5.

CLUSTER=*name*

specifies a name for the variable in the OUTSEED= and OUT= data sets that indicates cluster membership. The default name for this variable is CLUSTER.

CONVERGE=*c*
CONV=*c*

specifies the convergence criterion. Any nonnegative value is allowed. The default value is 0.0001 for all values of p if LEAST=p is explicitly specified; otherwise, the default value is 0.02. Iterations stop when the maximum relative change in the cluster seeds is less than or equal to the convergence criterion and additional conditions on the homotopy parameter, if any, are satisfied (see the HP= option). The relative change in a cluster seed is the distance between the old seed and the new seed divided by a scaling factor. If you do not specify the LEAST= option, the scaling factor is the minimum distance between the initial seeds. If you specify the LEAST= option, the scaling factor is an L_1 scale estimate and is recomputed on each iteration. Specify the CONVERGE= option only if you specify a MAXITER= value greater than 1.

DATA=*SAS-data-set*

specifies the input data set containing observations to be clustered. If you omit the DATA= option, the most recently created SAS data set is used. The data must be coordinates, not distances, similarities, or correlations.

DELETE=*n*

deletes cluster seeds to which n or fewer observations are assigned. Deletion occurs after processing for the DRIFT option is completed and after each iteration specified by the MAXITER= option. Cluster seeds are not deleted after the final assignment of observations to clusters, so in rare cases a final cluster may not have more than n members. The DELETE= option is ineffective if you specify MAXITER=0 and do not specify the DRIFT option. By default, no cluster seeds are deleted.

DISTANCE | DIST

computes distances between the cluster means.

DRIFT

executes the second of the four steps described in the section "Background" on page 1196. After initial seed selection, each observation is assigned to the cluster with the nearest seed. After an observation is processed, the seed of the cluster to which it is assigned is recalculated as the mean of the observations currently assigned to the cluster. Thus, the cluster seeds drift about rather than remaining fixed for the duration of the pass.

HC=*c*
HP=p_1 <p_2>

pertains to the homotopy parameter for LEAST=p, where $1 < p < 2$. You should specify these options only if you encounter convergence problems using the default values.

For $1 < p < 2$, PROC FASTCLUS tries to optimize a perturbed variant of the L_p clustering criterion (Gonin and Money 1989, pp. 5–6). When the homotopy parameter is 0, the optimization criterion is equivalent to the clustering criterion. For a large homotopy parameter, the optimization criterion approaches the least-squares criterion and is, therefore, easy to optimize. Beginning with a large homotopy parameter, PROC FASTCLUS gradually decreases it by a factor in the range [0.01,0.5] over the course of the iterations. When both the homotopy parameter and the convergence measure are sufficiently small, the optimization process is declared to have converged.

If the initial homotopy parameter is too large or if it is decreased too slowly, the optimization may require many iterations. If the initial homotopy parameter is too small or if it is decreased too quickly, convergence to a local optimum is likely.

HC=c — specifies the criterion for updating the homotopy parameter. The homotopy parameter is updated when the maximum relative change in the cluster seeds is less than or equal to c. The default is the minimum of 0.01 and 100 times the value of the CONVERGE= option.

HP=p_1 — specifies p_1 as the initial value of the homotopy parameter. The default is 0.05 if the modified Ekblom-Newton method is used; otherwise, it is 0.25.

HP=p_1 p_2 — also specifies p_2 as the minimum value for the homotopy parameter, which must be reached for convergence. The default is the minimum of p_1 and 0.01 times the value of the CONVERGE= option.

IMPUTE

requests imputation of missing values after the final assignment of observations to clusters. If an observation has a missing value for a variable used in the cluster analysis, the missing value is replaced by the corresponding value in the cluster seed to which the observation is assigned. If the observation is not assigned to a cluster, missing values are not replaced. If you specify the IMPUTE option, the imputed values are not used in computing cluster statistics.

If you also request an OUT= data set, it contains the imputed values.

INSTAT=*SAS-data-set*

reads a SAS data set previously created by the FASTCLUS procedure using the OUTSTAT= option. If you specify the INSTAT= option, no clustering iterations are performed and no output is displayed. Only cluster assignment and imputation are performed as an OUT= data set is created.

IRLS

causes PROC FASTCLUS to use an iteratively reweighted least-squares method instead of the modified Ekblom-Newton method. If you specify the IRLS option, you must also specify LEAST=p, where $1 < p < 2$. Use the IRLS option only if you encounter convergence problems with the default method.

LEAST=*p* | MAX
L=*p* | MAX

causes PROC FASTCLUS to optimize an L_p criterion, where $1 \leq p \leq \infty$ (Spath 1985, pp. 62–63). Infinity is indicated by LEAST=MAX. The value of this clustering criterion is displayed in the iteration history.

If you do not specify the LEAST= option, PROC FASTCLUS uses the least-squares (L_2) criterion. However, the default number of iterations is only 1 if you omit the LEAST= option, so the optimization of the criterion is generally not completed. If you specify the LEAST= option, the maximum number of iterations is increased to allow the optimization process a chance to converge. See the MAXITER= option on page 1210.

Specifying the LEAST= option also changes the default convergence criterion from 0.02 to 0.0001. See the CONVERGE= option on page 1207.

When LEAST=2, PROC FASTCLUS tries to minimize the root mean square difference between the data and the corresponding cluster means.

When LEAST=1, PROC FASTCLUS tries to minimize the mean absolute difference between the data and the corresponding cluster medians.

When LEAST=MAX, PROC FASTCLUS tries to minimize the maximum absolute difference between the data and the corresponding cluster midranges.

For general values of p, PROC FASTCLUS tries to minimize the pth root of the mean of the pth powers of the absolute differences between the data and the corresponding cluster seeds.

The divisor in the clustering criterion is either the number of nonmissing data used in the analysis or, if there is a WEIGHT statement, the sum of the weights corresponding to all the nonmissing data used in the analysis (that is, an observation with n nonmissing data contributes n times the observation weight to the divisor). The divisor is not adjusted for degrees of freedom.

The method for updating cluster seeds during iteration depends on the LEAST= option, as follows (Gonin and Money 1989).

LEAST=*p*	**Algorithm for Computing Cluster Seeds**
$p = 1$	bin sort for median
$1 < p < 2$	modified Merle-Spath if you specify IRLS, otherwise modified Ekblom-Newton
$p = 2$	arithmetic mean
$2 < p < \infty$	Newton
$p = \infty$	midrange

During the final pass, a modified Merle-Spath step is taken to compute the cluster centers for $1 \leq p < 2$ or $2 < p < \infty$.

If you specify the LEAST=p option with a value other than 2, PROC FASTCLUS computes pooled scale estimates analogous to the root mean square standard deviation but based on pth power deviations instead of squared deviations.

LEAST=*p*	**Scale Estimate**
$p = 1$	mean absolute deviation
$1 < p < \infty$	root mean pth-power absolute deviation
$p = \infty$	maximum absolute deviation

The divisors for computing the mean absolute deviation or the root mean pth-power absolute deviation are adjusted for degrees of freedom just like the divisors for computing standard deviations. This adjustment can be suppressed by the VARDEF= option.

LIST

lists all observations, giving the value of the ID variable (if any), the number of the cluster to which the observation is assigned, and the distance between the observation and the final cluster seed.

MAXITER=*n*

specifies the maximum number of iterations for recomputing cluster seeds. When the value of the MAXITER= option is greater than 0, PROC FASTCLUS executes the third of the four steps described in the "Background" section on page 1196. In each iteration, each observation is assigned to the nearest seed, and the seeds are recomputed as the means of the clusters.

The default value of the MAXITER= option depends on the LEAST=p option.

LEAST=p	MAXITER=
not specified	1
$p = 1$	20
$1 < p < 1.5$	50
$1.5 \leq p < 2$	20
$p = 2$	10
$2 < p \leq \infty$	20

MEAN=*SAS-data-set*

creates an output data set to contain the cluster means and other statistics for each cluster. If you want to create a permanent SAS data set, you must specify a two-level name. Refer to "SAS Data Files" in *SAS Language Reference: Concepts* for more information on permanent data sets.

NOMISS

excludes observations with missing values from the analysis. However, if you also specify the IMPUTE option, observations with missing values are included in the final cluster assignments.

NOPRINT

suppresses the display of all output. Note that this option temporarily disables the Output Delivery System (ODS). For more information, see Chapter 15, "Using the Output Delivery System."

OUT=*SAS-data-set*

creates an output data set to contain all the original data, plus the new variables CLUSTER and DISTANCE. Refer to "SAS Data Files" in *SAS Language Reference: Concepts* for more information on permanent data sets.

OUTITER

outputs information from the iteration history to the OUTSEED= data set, including the cluster seeds at each iteration.

OUTSEED=*SAS-data-set*
OUTS=*SAS-data-set*

is another name for the MEAN= data set, provided because the data set may contain location estimates other than means. The MEAN= option is still accepted.

OUTSTAT=*SAS-data-set*

creates an output data set to contain various statistics, especially those not included in the OUTSEED= data set. Unlike the OUTSEED= data set, the OUTSTAT= data set is not suitable for use as a SEED= data set in a subsequent PROC FASTCLUS step.

RANDOM=*n*

specifies a positive integer as a starting value for the pseudo-random number generator for use with REPLACE=RANDOM. If you do not specify the RANDOM= option, the time of day is used to initialize the pseudo-random number sequence.

REPLACE=FULL | PART | NONE | RANDOM

specifies how seed replacement is performed.

FULL	requests default seed replacement as described in the section "Background" on page 1196.
PART	requests seed replacement only when the distance between the observation and the closest seed is greater than the minimum distance between seeds.
NONE	suppresses seed replacement.
RANDOM	selects a simple pseudo-random sample of complete observations as initial cluster seeds.

SEED=*SAS-data-set*

specifies an input data set from which initial cluster seeds are to be selected. If you do not specify the SEED= option, initial seeds are selected from the DATA= data set. The SEED= data set must contain the same variables that are used in the data analysis.

SHORT

suppresses the display of the initial cluster seeds, cluster means, and standard deviations.

STRICT
STRICT=*s*

prevents an observation from being assigned to a cluster if its distance to the nearest cluster seed exceeds the value of the STRICT= option. If you specify the STRICT option without a numeric value, you must also specify the RADIUS= option, and its value is used instead. In the OUT= data set, observations that are not assigned due to the STRICT= option are given a negative cluster number, the absolute value of which indicates the cluster with the nearest seed.

SUMMARY

suppresses the display of the initial cluster seeds, statistics for variables, cluster means, and standard deviations.

VARDEF=DF | N | WDF | WEIGHT | WGT

specifies the divisor to be used in the calculation of variances and covariances. The default value is VARDEF=DF. The possible values of the VARDEF= option and associated divisors are as follows.

Value	Description	Divisor
DF	error degrees of freedom	$n - c$
N	number of observations	n
WDF	sum of weights DF	$(\sum_i w_i) - c$
WEIGHT | WGT	sum of weights	$\sum_i w_i$

In the preceding definitions, c represents the number of clusters.

BY Statement

BY *variables* **;**

You can specify a BY statement with PROC FASTCLUS to obtain separate analyses on observations in groups defined by the BY variables. When a BY statement appears, the procedure expects the input data set to be sorted in order of the BY variables.

If your input data set is not sorted in ascending order, use one of the following alternatives:

- Sort the data using the SORT procedure with a similar BY statement.
- Specify the BY statement option NOTSORTED or DESCENDING in the BY statement for the FASTCLUS procedure. The NOTSORTED option does not mean that the data are unsorted but rather that the data are arranged in groups (according to values of the BY variables) and that these groups are not necessarily in alphabetical or increasing numeric order.
- Create an index on the BY variables using the DATASETS procedure.

If you specify the SEED= option and the SEED= data set does not contain any of the BY variables, then the entire SEED= data set is used to obtain initial cluster seeds for each BY group in the DATA= data set.

If the SEED= data set contains some but not all of the BY variables, or if some BY variables do not have the same type or length in the SEED= data set as in the DATA= data set, then PROC FASTCLUS displays an error message and stops.

If all the BY variables appear in the SEED= data set with the same type and length as in the DATA= data set, then each BY group in the SEED= data set is used to obtain initial cluster seeds for the corresponding BY group in the DATA= data set. All BY groups in the DATA= data set must also appear in the SEED= data set. The BY groups in the SEED= data set must be in the same order as in the DATA= data set. If you specify the NOTSORTED option in the BY statement, there must be exactly the same BY groups in the same order in both data sets. If you do not specify NOTSORTED, some BY groups can appear in the SEED= data set but not in the DATA= data set; such BY groups are not used in the analysis.

For more information on the BY statement, refer to the discussion in *SAS Language Reference: Concepts*. For more information on the DATASETS procedure, refer to the discussion in the *SAS Procedures Guide*.

FREQ Statement

FREQ *variable* ;

If a variable in the data set represents the frequency of occurrence for the other values in the observation, include the variable's name in a FREQ statement. The procedure then treats the data set as if each observation appears n times, where n is the value of the FREQ variable for the observation.

If the value of the FREQ variable is missing or ≤ 0, the observation is not used in the analysis. The exact values of the FREQ variable are used in computations: frequency values are not truncated to integers. The total number of observations is considered to be equal to the sum of the FREQ variable when the procedure determines degrees of freedom for significance probabilities.

The WEIGHT and FREQ statements have a similar effect, except in determining the number of observations for significance tests.

ID Statement

ID *variable* ;

The ID variable, which can be character or numeric, identifies observations on the output when you specify the LIST option.

VAR Statement

VAR *variables* ;

The VAR statement lists the numeric variables to be used in the cluster analysis. If you omit the VAR statement, all numeric variables not listed in other statements are used.

WEIGHT Statement

WEIGHT *variable* ;

The values of the WEIGHT variable are used to compute weighted cluster means. The WEIGHT and FREQ statements have a similar effect, except the WEIGHT statement does not alter the degrees of freedom or the number of observations. The WEIGHT variable can take nonintegral values. An observation is used in the analysis only if the value of the WEIGHT variable is greater than zero.

Details

Updates in the FASTCLUS Procedure

Some FASTCLUS procedure options and statements have changed from previous versions. The differences are as follows:

- Values of the FREQ variable are no longer truncated to integers. Noninteger variables specified in the FREQ statement produce results different than in previous releases.
- The IMPUTE option produces different cluster standard deviations and related statistics. When you specify the IMPUTE option, imputed values are no longer used in computing cluster statistics. This change causes the cluster standard deviations and other statistics computed from the standard deviations to be different than in previous releases.
- The INSTAT= option reads a SAS data set previously created by the FASTCLUS procedure using the OUTSTAT= option. If you specify the INSTAT= option, no clustering iterations are performed and no output is produced. Only cluster assignment and imputation are performed as an OUT= data set is created.
- The OUTSTAT= data set contains additional information used for imputation. _TYPE_=SEED corresponds to values that are cluster seeds. Observations previously designated _TYPE_='SCALE' are now _TYPE_='DISPERSION'.

Missing Values

Observations with all missing values are excluded from the analysis. If you specify the NOMISS option, observations with any missing values are excluded. Observations with missing values cannot be cluster seeds.

The distance between an observation with missing values and a cluster seed is obtained by computing the squared distance based on the nonmissing values, multiplying by the ratio of the number of variables, n, to the number of variables having nonmissing values, m, and taking the square root:

$$\sqrt{\left(\frac{n}{m}\right) \sum (x_i - s_i)^2}$$

where

n = number of variables

m = number of variables with nonmissing values

x_i = value of the ith variable for the observation

s_i = value of the ith variable for the seed

The summation is taken over variables with nonmissing values.

The IMPUTE option fills in missing values in the OUT= output data set.

Output Data Sets

OUT= Data Set

The OUT= data set contains

- the original variables
- a new variable taking values from 1 to the value specified in the MAXCLUSTERS= option, indicating the cluster to which each observation has been assigned. You can specify the variable name with the CLUSTER= option; the default name is CLUSTER.
- a new variable, DISTANCE, giving the distance from the observation to its cluster seed

If you specify the IMPUTE option, the OUT= data set also contains a new variable, _IMPUTE_, giving the number of imputed values in each observation.

OUTSEED= Data Set

The OUTSEED= data set contains one observation for each cluster. The variables are as follows:

- the BY variables, if any
- a new variable giving the cluster number. You can specify the variable name with the CLUSTER= option. The default name is CLUSTER.
- either the FREQ variable or a new variable called _FREQ_ giving the number of observations in the cluster
- the WEIGHT variable, if any

- a new variable, _RMSSTD_, giving the root mean square standard deviation for the cluster. See Chapter 23, "The CLUSTER Procedure," for details.
- a new variable, _RADIUS_, giving the maximum distance between any observation in the cluster and the cluster seed
- a new variable, _GAP_, containing the distance between the current cluster mean and the nearest other cluster mean. The value is the centroid distance given in the output.
- a new variable, _NEAR_, specifying the cluster number of the nearest cluster
- the VAR variables giving the cluster means

If you specify the LEAST=p option with a value other than 2, the _RMSSTD_ variable is replaced by the _SCALE_ variable, which contains the pooled scale estimate analogous to the root mean square standard deviation but based on pth power deviations instead of squared deviations:

LEAST=1	mean absolute deviation
LEAST=p	root mean pth-power absolute deviation
LEAST=MAX	maximum absolute deviation

If you specify the OUTITER option, there is one set of observations in the OUTSEED= data set for each pass through the data set (that is, one set for initial seeds, one for each iteration, and one for the final clusters). Also, several additional variables appear:

ITER	is the iteration number. For the initial seeds, the value is 0. For the final cluster means or centers, the _ITER_ variable is one greater than the last iteration reported in the iteration history.
CRIT	is the clustering criterion as described under the LEAST= option.
CHANGE	is the maximum over clusters of the relative change in the cluster seed from the previous iteration. The relative change in a cluster seed is the distance between the old seed and the new seed divided by a scaling factor. If you do not specify the LEAST= option, the scaling factor is the minimum distance between the initial seeds. If you specify the LEAST= option, the scaling factor is an L_1 scale estimate and is recomputed on each iteration.
HOMPAR	is the value of the homotopy parameter. This variable appears only for LEAST=p with $1 < p < 2$.
BINSIZ	is the maximum bin size used for estimating medians. This variable appears only for LEAST=1.

If you specify the OUTITER option, the variables _SCALE_ or _RMSSTD_, _RADIUS_, _NEAR_, and _GAP_ have missing values except for the last pass.

You can use the OUTSEED= data set as a SEED= input data set for a subsequent analysis.

OUTSTAT= Data Set

The variables in the OUTSTAT= data set are as follows:

- BY variables, if any
- a new character variable, _TYPE_, specifying the type of statistic given by other variables (see Table 27.2 and Table 27.3)
- a new numeric variable giving the cluster number. You can specify the variable name with the CLUSTER= option. The default name is CLUSTER.
- a new numeric variable, OVER_ALL, containing statistics that apply over all of the VAR variables
- the VAR variables giving statistics for particular variables

The values of _TYPE_ for all LEAST= options are given in the following table.

Table 27.2. _TYPE_ Values for all LEAST= Options

TYPE	**Contents of VAR variables**	**Contents of OVER_ALL**
INITIAL	Initial seeds	Missing
CRITERION	Missing	Optimization criterion; see the LEAST= option; this value is displayed just before the "Cluster Summary" table
CENTER	Cluster centers; see the LEAST= option	Missing
SEED	Cluster seeds: additional information used for imputation	
DISPERSION	Dispersion estimates for each cluster; see the LEAST= option; these values are displayed in a separate row with title depending on the LEAST= option	Dispersion estimates pooled over variables; see the LEAST= option; these values are displayed in the "Cluster Summary" table with label depending on the LEAST= option
FREQ	Frequency of each cluster omitting observations with missing values for the VAR variable; these values are not displayed	Frequency of each cluster based on all observations with any non-missing value; these values are displayed in the "Cluster Summary" table

Table 27.2. (continued)

TYPE	Contents of VAR variables	Contents of OVER_ALL
WEIGHT	Sum of weights for each cluster omitting observations with missing values for the VAR variable; these values are not displayed	Sum of weights for each cluster based on all observations with any nonmissing value; these values are displayed in the "Cluster Summary" table

Observations with _TYPE_='WEIGHT' are included only if you specify the WEIGHT statement.

The _TYPE_ values included only for least-squares clustering are given in the following table. Least-squares clustering is obtained by omitting the LEAST= option or by specifying LEAST=2.

Table 27.3. _TYPE_ Values for Least-Squares Clustering

TYPE	Contents of VAR variables	Contents of OVER_ALL
MEAN	Mean for the total sample; this is not displayed	Missing
STD	Standard deviation for the total sample; this is labeled "Total STD" in the output	Standard deviation pooled over all the VAR variables; this is labeled "Total STD" in the output
WITHIN_STD	Pooled within-cluster standard deviation	Within cluster standard deviation pooled over clusters and all the VAR variables
RSQ	R^2 for predicting the variable from the clusters; this is labeled "R-Squared" in the output	R^2 pooled over all the VAR variables; this is labeled "R-Squared" in the output
RSQ_RATIO	$\frac{R^2}{1-R^2}$; this is labeled "RSQ/(1-RSQ)" in the output	$\frac{R^2}{1-R^2}$; labeled "RSQ/(1-RSQ)" in the output
PSEUDO_F	Missing	Pseudo F statistic
ESRQ	Missing	Approximate expected value of R^2 under the null hypothesis of a single uniform cluster
CCC	Missing	The cubic clustering criterion

Computational Resources

Let

$$\begin{aligned} n &= \text{number of observations} \\ v &= \text{number of variables} \\ c &= \text{number of clusters} \\ p &= \text{number of passes over the data set} \end{aligned}$$

Memory

The memory required is approximately $4(19v + 12cv + 10c + 2\max(c+1, v))$ bytes.

If you request the DISTANCE option, an additional $4c(c+1)$ bytes of space is needed.

Time

The overall time required by PROC FASTCLUS is roughly proportional to $nvcp$ if c is small with respect to n.

Initial seed selection requires one pass over the data set. If the observations are in random order, the time required is roughly proportional to

$$nvc + vc^2$$

unless you specify REPLACE=NONE. In that case, a complete pass may not be necessary, and the time is roughly proportional to mvc, where $c \leq m \leq n$.

The DRIFT option, each iteration, and the final assignment of cluster seeds each require one pass, with time for each pass roughly proportional to nvc.

For greatest efficiency, you should list the variables in the VAR statement in order of decreasing variance.

Using PROC FASTCLUS

Before using PROC FASTCLUS, decide whether your variables should be standardized in some way, since variables with large variances tend to have more effect on the resulting clusters than those with small variances. If all variables are measured in the same units, standardization may not be necessary. Otherwise, some form of standardization is strongly recommended. The STANDARD procedure can standardize all variables to mean zero and variance one. The FACTOR or PRINCOMP procedures can compute standardized principal component scores. The ACECLUS procedure can transform the variables according to an estimated within-cluster covariance matrix.

Nonlinear transformations of the variables may change the number of population clusters and should, therefore, be approached with caution. For most applications, the variables should be transformed so that equal differences are of equal practical importance. An interval scale of measurement is required. Ordinal or ranked data are generally not appropriate.

PROC FASTCLUS produces relatively little output. In most cases you should create an output data set and use other procedures such as PRINT, PLOT, CHART, MEANS, DISCRIM, or CANDISC to study the clusters. It is usually desirable to try several values of the MAXCLUSTERS= option. Macros are useful for running PROC FASTCLUS repeatedly with other procedures.

A simple application of PROC FASTCLUS with two variables to examine the 2- and 3-cluster solutions may proceed as follows:

```
proc standard mean=0 std=1 out=stan;
   var v1 v2;
run;

proc fastclus data=stan out=clust maxclusters=2;
   var v1 v2;
run;

proc plot;
   plot v2*v1=cluster;
run;

proc fastclus data=stan out=clust maxclusters=3;
   var v1 v2;
run;

proc plot;
   plot v2*v1=cluster;
run;
```

If you have more than two variables, you can use the CANDISC procedure to compute canonical variables for plotting the clusters, for example,

```
proc standard mean=0 std=1 out=stan;
   var v1-v10;
run;

proc fastclus data=stan out=clust maxclusters=3;
   var v1-v10;
run;

proc candisc out=can;
   var v1-v10;
   class cluster;
run;

proc plot;
   plot can2*can1=cluster;
run;
```

If the data set is not too large, it may also be helpful to use

```
proc sort;
   by cluster distance;
run;
proc print;
   by cluster;
run;
```

to list the clusters. By examining the values of DISTANCE, you can determine if any observations are unusually far from their cluster seeds.

It is often advisable, especially if the data set is large or contains outliers, to make a preliminary PROC FASTCLUS run with a large number of clusters, perhaps 20 to 100. Use MAXITER=0 and OUTSEED=*SAS-data-set*. You can save time on subsequent runs by selecting cluster seeds from this output data set using the SEED= option.

You should check the preliminary clusters for outliers, which often appear as clusters with only one member. Use a DATA step to delete outliers from the data set created by the OUTSEED= option before using it as a SEED= data set in later runs. If there are severe outliers, the subsequent PROC FASTCLUS runs should specify the STRICT option to prevent the outliers from distorting the clusters.

You can use the OUTSEED= data set with the PLOT procedure to plot _GAP_ by _FREQ_. An overlay of _RADIUS_ by _FREQ_ provides a baseline against which to compare the values of _GAP_. Outliers appear in the upper left area of the plot, with large values of _GAP_ and small _FREQ_ values. Good clusters appear in the upper right area, with large values of both _GAP_ and _FREQ_. Good potential cluster seeds appear in the lower right, as well as in the upper right, since large _FREQ_ values indicate high density regions. Small _FREQ_ values in the left part of the plot indicate poor cluster seeds because the points are in low density regions. It often helps to remove all clusters with small frequencies even though the clusters may not be remote enough to be considered outliers. Removing points in low density regions improves cluster separation and provides visually sharper cluster outlines in scatter plots.

Displayed Output

Unless the SHORT or SUMMARY option is specified, PROC FASTCLUS displays

- Initial Seeds, cluster seeds selected after one pass through the data
- Change in Cluster Seeds for each iteration, if you specify MAXITER=$n > 1$

If you specify the LEAST=p option, with $(1 < p < 2)$, and you omit the IRLS option, an additional column is displayed in the Iteration History table. The column contains a character to identify the method used in each iteration. PROC FASTCLUS chooses the most efficient method to cluster the data at each iterative step, given the condition of the data. Thus, the method chosen is data dependent. The possible values are described as follows:

Value	Method
N	Newton's Method
I or L	iteratively weighted least squares (IRLS)
1	IRLS step, halved once
2	IRLS step, halved twice
3	IRLS step, halved three times

PROC FASTCLUS displays a Cluster Summary, giving the following for each cluster:

- Cluster number
- Frequency, the number of observations in the cluster
- Weight, the sum of the weights of the observations in the cluster, if you specify the WEIGHT statement
- RMS Std Deviation, the root mean square across variables of the cluster standard deviations, which is equal to the root mean square distance between observations in the cluster
- Maximum Distance from Seed to Observation, the maximum distance from the cluster seed to any observation in the cluster
- Nearest Cluster, the number of the cluster with mean closest to the mean of the current cluster
- Centroid Distance, the distance between the centroids (means) of the current cluster and the nearest other cluster

A table of statistics for each variable is displayed unless you specify the SUMMARY option. The table contains

- Total STD, the total standard deviation
- Within STD, the pooled within-cluster standard deviation

- R-Squared, the R^2 for predicting the variable from the cluster
- RSQ/(1 - RSQ), the ratio of between-cluster variance to within-cluster variance $(R^2/(1-R^2))$
- OVER-ALL, all of the previous quantities pooled across variables

PROC FASTCLUS also displays

- Pseudo F Statistic,

$$\frac{\frac{R^2}{c-1}}{\frac{1-R^2}{n-c}}$$

  where R^2 is the observed overall R^2, c is the number of clusters, and n is the number of observations. The pseudo F statistic was suggested by Calinski and Harabasz (1974). Refer to Milligan and Cooper (1985) and Cooper and Milligan (1988) regarding the use of the pseudo F statistic in estimating the number of clusters. See Example 23.2 in Chapter 23, "The CLUSTER Procedure," for a comparison of pseudo F statistics.
- Observed Overall R-Squared, if you specify the SUMMARY option
- Approximate Expected Overall R-Squared, the approximate expected value of the overall R^2 under the uniform null hypothesis assuming that the variables are uncorrelated. The value is missing if the number of clusters is greater than one-fifth the number of observations.
- Cubic Clustering Criterion, computed under the assumption that the variables are uncorrelated. The value is missing if the number of clusters is greater than one-fifth the number of observations.

  If you are interested in the approximate expected R^2 or the cubic clustering criterion but your variables are correlated, you should cluster principal component scores from the PRINCOMP procedure. Both of these statistics are described by Sarle (1983). The performance of the cubic clustering criterion in estimating the number of clusters is examined by Milligan and Cooper (1985) and Cooper and Milligan (1988).
- Distances Between Cluster Means, if you specify the DISTANCE option

Unless you specify the SHORT or SUMMARY option, PROC FASTCLUS displays

- Cluster Means for each variable
- Cluster Standard Deviations for each variable

ODS Table Names

PROC FASTCLUS assigns a name to each table it creates. You can use these names to reference the table when using the Output Delivery System (ODS) to select tables and create output data sets. These names are listed in the following table. For more information on ODS, see Chapter 15, "Using the Output Delivery System."

Table 27.4. ODS Tables Produced in PROC FASTCLUS

ODS Table Name	Description	Statement	Option
ApproxExpOverAllRSq	Approximate expected over-all R-squared, single number	PROC	default
CCC	CCC, Cubic Clustering Criterion, single number	PROC	default
ClusterList	Cluster listing, obs, id, and distances	PROC	LIST
ClusterSum	Cluster summary, cluster number, distances	PROC	PRINTALL
ClusterCenters	Cluster centers	PROC	default
ClusterDispersion	Cluster dispersion	PROC	default
ConvergenceStatus	Convergence status	PROC	PRINTALL
Criterion	Criterion based on final seeds, single number	PROC	default
DistBetweenClust	Distance between clusters	PROC	default
InitialSeeds	Initial seeds	PROC	default
IterHistory	Iteration history, various statistics for each iter	PROC	PRINTALL
MinDist	Minimum distance between initial seeds, single number	PROC	PRINTALL
NumberOfBins	Number of bins	PROC	default
ObsOverAllRSquare	Observed over-all R-squared, single number	PROC	SUMMARY
PrelScaleEst	Preliminary L(1) scale estimate, single number	PROC	PRINTALL
PseudoFStat	Pseudo F statistic, single number	PROC	default
SimpleStatistics	Simple statistics for input variables	PROC	default
VariableStat	Statistics for variables within clusters	PROC	default

Examples

Example 27.1. Fisher's Iris Data

The iris data published by Fisher (1936) have been widely used for examples in discriminant analysis and cluster analysis. The sepal length, sepal width, petal length, and petal width are measured in millimeters on fifty iris specimens from each of three species, *Iris setosa, I. versicolor,* and *I. virginica.* Mezzich and Solomon (1980) discuss a variety of cluster analyses of the iris data.

In this example, the FASTCLUS procedure is used to find two and, then, three clusters. An output data set is created, and PROC FREQ is invoked to compare the clusters with the species classification. See Output 27.1.1 and Output 27.1.2 for these results. For three clusters, you can use the CANDISC procedure to compute canonical variables for plotting the clusters. See Output 27.1.3 for the results.

```
proc format;
   value specname
      1='Setosa    '
      2='Versicolor'
      3='Virginica ';
run;

data iris;
   title 'Fisher (1936) Iris Data';
   input SepalLength SepalWidth PetalLength PetalWidth Species @@;
   format Species specname.;
   label SepalLength='Sepal Length in mm.'
         SepalWidth ='Sepal Width in mm.'
         PetalLength='Petal Length in mm.'
         PetalWidth ='Petal Width in mm.';
   symbol = put(species, specname10.);
   datalines;
50 33 14 02 1 64 28 56 22 3 65 28 46 15 2 67 31 56 24 3
63 28 51 15 3 46 34 14 03 1 69 31 51 23 3 62 22 45 15 2
59 32 48 18 2 46 36 10 02 1 61 30 46 14 2 60 27 51 16 2
65 30 52 20 3 56 25 39 11 2 65 30 55 18 3 58 27 51 19 3
68 32 59 23 3 51 33 17 05 1 57 28 45 13 2 62 34 54 23 3
77 38 67 22 3 63 33 47 16 2 67 33 57 25 3 76 30 66 21 3
49 25 45 17 3 55 35 13 02 1 67 30 52 23 3 70 32 47 14 2
64 32 45 15 2 61 28 40 13 2 48 31 16 02 1 59 30 51 18 3
55 24 38 11 2 63 25 50 19 3 64 32 53 23 3 52 34 14 02 1
49 36 14 01 1 54 30 45 15 2 79 38 64 20 3 44 32 13 02 1
67 33 57 21 3 50 35 16 06 1 58 26 40 12 2 44 30 13 02 1
77 28 67 20 3 63 27 49 18 3 47 32 16 02 1 55 26 44 12 2
50 23 33 10 2 72 32 60 18 3 48 30 14 03 1 51 38 16 02 1
61 30 49 18 3 48 34 19 02 1 50 30 16 02 1 50 32 12 02 1
61 26 56 14 3 64 28 56 21 3 43 30 11 01 1 58 40 12 02 1
51 38 19 04 1 67 31 44 14 2 62 28 48 18 3 49 30 14 02 1
51 35 14 02 1 56 30 45 15 2 58 27 41 10 2 50 34 16 04 1
46 32 14 02 1 60 29 45 15 2 57 26 35 10 2 57 44 15 04 1
50 36 14 02 1 77 30 61 23 3 63 34 56 24 3 58 27 51 19 3
```

```
57 29 42 13 2 72 30 58 16 3 54 34 15 04 1 52 41 15 01 1
71 30 59 21 3 64 31 55 18 3 60 30 48 18 3 63 29 56 18 3
49 24 33 10 2 56 27 42 13 2 57 30 42 12 2 55 42 14 02 1
49 31 15 02 1 77 26 69 23 3 60 22 50 15 3 54 39 17 04 1
66 29 46 13 2 52 27 39 14 2 60 34 45 16 2 50 34 15 02 1
44 29 14 02 1 50 20 35 10 2 55 24 37 10 2 58 27 39 12 2
47 32 13 02 1 46 31 15 02 1 69 32 57 23 3 62 29 43 13 2
74 28 61 19 3 59 30 42 15 2 51 34 15 02 1 50 35 13 03 1
56 28 49 20 3 60 22 40 10 2 73 29 63 18 3 67 25 58 18 3
49 31 15 01 1 67 31 47 15 2 63 23 44 13 2 54 37 15 02 1
56 30 41 13 2 63 25 49 15 2 61 28 47 12 2 64 29 43 13 2
51 25 30 11 2 57 28 41 13 2 65 30 58 22 3 69 31 54 21 3
54 39 13 04 1 51 35 14 03 1 72 36 61 25 3 65 32 51 20 3
61 29 47 14 2 56 29 36 13 2 69 31 49 15 2 64 27 53 19 3
68 30 55 21 3 55 25 40 13 2 48 34 16 02 1 48 30 14 01 1
45 23 13 03 1 57 25 50 20 3 57 38 17 03 1 51 38 15 03 1
55 23 40 13 2 66 30 44 14 2 68 28 48 14 2 54 34 17 02 1
51 37 15 04 1 52 35 15 02 1 58 28 51 24 3 67 30 50 17 2
63 33 60 25 3 53 37 15 02 1
;

proc fastclus data=iris maxc=2 maxiter=10 out=clus;
   var SepalLength SepalWidth PetalLength PetalWidth;
run;

proc freq;
   tables cluster*species;
run;

proc fastclus data=iris maxc=3 maxiter=10 out=clus;
   var SepalLength SepalWidth PetalLength PetalWidth;
run;

proc freq;
   tables cluster*Species;
run;

proc candisc anova out=can;
   class cluster;
   var SepalLength SepalWidth PetalLength PetalWidth;
   title2 'Canonical Discriminant Analysis of Iris Clusters';
run;
legend1 frame cframe=ligr label=none cborder=black
        position=center value=(justify=center);
axis1 label=(angle=90 rotate=0) minor=none;
axis2 minor=none;

proc gplot data=Can;
   plot Can2*Can1=Cluster/frame cframe=ligr
                  legend=legend1 vaxis=axis1 haxis=axis2;
   title2 'Plot of Canonical Variables Identified by Cluster';
run;
```

Output 27.1.1. Fisher's Iris Data: PROC FASTCLUS with MAXC=2 and PROC FREQ

Fisher (1936) Iris Data

The FASTCLUS Procedure
Replace=FULL Radius=0 Maxclusters=2 Maxiter=10 Converge=0.02

Initial Seeds

Cluster	SepalLength	SepalWidth	PetalLength	PetalWidth
1	43.00000000	30.00000000	11.00000000	1.00000000
2	77.00000000	26.00000000	69.00000000	23.00000000

Minimum Distance Between Initial Seeds = 70.85196

Fisher (1936) Iris Data

The FASTCLUS Procedure
Replace=FULL Radius=0 Maxclusters=2 Maxiter=10 Converge=0.02

Iteration History

Iteration	Criterion	Relative Change in Cluster Seeds 1	2
1	11.0638	0.1904	0.3163
2	5.3780	0.0596	0.0264
3	5.0718	0.0174	0.00766

Convergence criterion is satisfied.

Criterion Based on Final Seeds = 5.0417

Cluster Summary

Cluster	Frequency	RMS Std Deviation	Maximum Distance from Seed to Observation	Radius Exceeded	Nearest Cluster	Distance Between Cluster Centroids
1	53	3.7050	21.1621		2	39.2879
2	97	5.6779	24.6430		1	39.2879

Statistics for Variables

Variable	Total STD	Within STD	R-Square	RSQ/(1-RSQ)
SepalLength	8.28066	5.49313	0.562896	1.287784
SepalWidth	4.35866	3.70393	0.282710	0.394137
PetalLength	17.65298	6.80331	0.852470	5.778291
PetalWidth	7.62238	3.57200	0.781868	3.584390
OVER-ALL	10.69224	5.07291	0.776410	3.472463

Pseudo F Statistic = 513.92

Approximate Expected Over-All R-Squared = 0.51539

Cubic Clustering Criterion = 14.806

WARNING: The two above values are invalid for correlated variables.

```
                              Fisher (1936) Iris Data

                              The FASTCLUS Procedure
          Replace=FULL  Radius=0  Maxclusters=2 Maxiter=10  Converge=0.02

                                  Cluster Means

Cluster         SepalLength          SepalWidth         PetalLength          PetalWidth
-------------------------------------------------------------------------------------
   1            50.05660377         33.69811321         15.60377358          2.90566038
   2            63.01030928         28.86597938         49.58762887         16.95876289


                            Cluster Standard Deviations

Cluster         SepalLength          SepalWidth         PetalLength          PetalWidth
-------------------------------------------------------------------------------------
   1            3.427350930         4.396611045         4.404279486         2.105525249
   2            6.336887455         3.267991438         7.800577673         4.155612484
```

```
                              Fisher (1936) Iris Data

                                The FREQ Procedure

                            Table of CLUSTER by Species

                   CLUSTER(Cluster)     Species

                   Frequency|
                   Percent  |
                   Row Pct  |
                   Col Pct  |Setosa  |Versicol|Virginic|  Total
                            |        |or      |a       |
                   ---------+--------+--------+--------+
                          1 |     50 |      3 |      0 |     53
                            |  33.33 |   2.00 |   0.00 |  35.33
                            |  94.34 |   5.66 |   0.00 |
                            | 100.00 |   6.00 |   0.00 |
                   ---------+--------+--------+--------+
                          2 |      0 |     47 |     50 |     97
                            |   0.00 |  31.33 |  33.33 |  64.67
                            |   0.00 |  48.45 |  51.55 |
                            |   0.00 |  94.00 | 100.00 |
                   ---------+--------+--------+--------+
                   Total          50       50       50      150
                               33.33    33.33    33.33   100.00
```

Output 27.1.2. Fisher's Iris Data: PROC FASTCLUS with MAXC=3 and PROC FREQ

```
                              Fisher (1936) Iris Data

                              The FASTCLUS Procedure
          Replace=FULL  Radius=0  Maxclusters=3 Maxiter=10  Converge=0.02

                                  Initial Seeds

Cluster         SepalLength          SepalWidth         PetalLength          PetalWidth
-------------------------------------------------------------------------------------
   1            58.00000000         40.00000000         12.00000000          2.00000000
   2            77.00000000         38.00000000         67.00000000         22.00000000
   3            49.00000000         25.00000000         45.00000000         17.00000000


                 Minimum Distance Between Initial Seeds = 38.23611
```

```
                              Fisher (1936) Iris Data

                              The FASTCLUS Procedure
              Replace=FULL  Radius=0  Maxclusters=3 Maxiter=10  Converge=0.02

                                 Iteration History

                                       Relative Change in Cluster Seeds
                Iteration    Criterion            1            2            3
                -----------------------------------------------------------
                        1       6.7591       0.2652       0.3205       0.2985
                        2       3.7097            0       0.0459       0.0317
                        3       3.6427            0       0.0182       0.0124


              Convergence criterion is satisfied.


                        Criterion Based on Final Seeds =    3.6289


                                  Cluster Summary

                              Maximum Distance
                   RMS Std           from Seed      Radius      Nearest      Distance Between
Cluster     Frequency   Deviation      to Observation    Exceeded     Cluster     Cluster Centroids
-------------------------------------------------------------------------------------------------
      1            50      2.7803             12.4803                      3               33.5693
      2            38      4.0168             14.9736                      3               17.9718
      3            62      4.0398             16.9272                      2               17.9718


                              Statistics for Variables

             Variable         Total STD      Within STD       R-Square      RSQ/(1-RSQ)
             ----------------------------------------------------------------------
             SepalLength        8.28066         4.39488       0.722096         2.598359
             SepalWidth         4.35866         3.24816       0.452102         0.825156
             PetalLength       17.65298         4.21431       0.943773        16.784895
             PetalWidth         7.62238         2.45244       0.897872         8.791618
             OVER-ALL          10.69224         3.66198       0.884275         7.641194


                          Pseudo F Statistic =    561.63


                    Approximate Expected Over-All R-Squared =    0.62728


                           Cubic Clustering Criterion =    25.021

             WARNING: The two above values are invalid for correlated variables.
```

```
                              Fisher (1936) Iris Data

                              The FASTCLUS Procedure
              Replace=FULL  Radius=0  Maxclusters=3 Maxiter=10  Converge=0.02

                                   Cluster Means

       Cluster        SepalLength          SepalWidth         PetalLength          PetalWidth
       ------------------------------------------------------------------------------------
          1          50.06000000         34.28000000         14.62000000          2.46000000
          2          68.50000000         30.73684211         57.42105263         20.71052632
          3          59.01612903         27.48387097         43.93548387         14.33870968


                           Cluster Standard Deviations

       Cluster        SepalLength          SepalWidth         PetalLength          PetalWidth
       ------------------------------------------------------------------------------------
          1          3.524896872         3.790643691         1.736639965         1.053855894
          2          4.941550255         2.900924461         4.885895746         2.798724562
          3          4.664100551         2.962840548         5.088949673         2.974997167
```

```
                   Fisher (1936) Iris Data

                     The FREQ Procedure

                Table of CLUSTER by Species

        CLUSTER(Cluster)     Species

        Frequency|
        Percent  |
        Row Pct  |
        Col Pct  |Setosa  |Versicol|Virginic|  Total
                 |        |or      |a       |
        ---------+--------+--------+--------+
               1 |     50 |      0 |      0 |     50
                 |  33.33 |   0.00 |   0.00 |  33.33
                 | 100.00 |   0.00 |   0.00 |
                 | 100.00 |   0.00 |   0.00 |
        ---------+--------+--------+--------+
               2 |      0 |      2 |     36 |     38
                 |   0.00 |   1.33 |  24.00 |  25.33
                 |   0.00 |   5.26 |  94.74 |
                 |   0.00 |   4.00 |  72.00 |
        ---------+--------+--------+--------+
               3 |      0 |     48 |     14 |     62
                 |   0.00 |  32.00 |   9.33 |  41.33
                 |   0.00 |  77.42 |  22.58 |
                 |   0.00 |  96.00 |  28.00 |
        ---------+--------+--------+--------+
        Total          50       50       50      150
                    33.33    33.33    33.33   100.00
```

Output 27.1.3. Fisher's Iris Data: PROC CANDISC and PROC GPLOT

```
                   Fisher (1936) Iris Data
          Canonical Discriminant Analysis of Iris Clusters

                   The CANDISC Procedure

    Observations     150          DF Total               149
    Variables          4          DF Within Classes      147
    Classes            3          DF Between Classes       2


                   Class Level Information

              Variable
    CLUSTER   Name         Frequency       Weight     Proportion

          1   _1                  50      50.0000       0.333333
          2   _2                  38      38.0000       0.253333
          3   _3                  62      62.0000       0.413333
```

Fisher (1936) Iris Data
Canonical Discriminant Analysis of Iris Clusters

The CANDISC Procedure

Univariate Test Statistics

F Statistics, Num DF=2, Den DF=147

Variable	Label	Total Standard Deviation	Pooled Standard Deviation	Between Standard Deviation	R-Square	R-Square / (1-RSq)	F Value	Pr > F
SepalLength	Sepal Length in mm.	8.2807	4.3949	8.5893	0.7221	2.5984	190.98	<.0001
SepalWidth	Sepal Width in mm.	4.3587	3.2482	3.5774	0.4521	0.8252	60.65	<.0001
PetalLength	Petal Length in mm.	17.6530	4.2143	20.9336	0.9438	16.7849	1233.69	<.0001
PetalWidth	Petal Width in mm.	7.6224	2.4524	8.8164	0.8979	8.7916	646.18	<.0001

Average R-Square

Unweighted	0.7539604
Weighted by Variance	0.8842753

Multivariate Statistics and F Approximations

S=2 M=0.5 N=71

Statistic	Value	F Value	Num DF	Den DF	Pr > F
Wilks' Lambda	0.03222337	164.55	8	288	<.0001
Pillai's Trace	1.25669612	61.29	8	290	<.0001
Hotelling-Lawley Trace	21.06722883	377.66	8	203.4	<.0001
Roy's Greatest Root	20.63266809	747.93	4	145	<.0001

NOTE: F Statistic for Roy's Greatest Root is an upper bound.
NOTE: F Statistic for Wilks' Lambda is exact.

Fisher (1936) Iris Data
Canonical Discriminant Analysis of Iris Clusters

The CANDISC Procedure

	Canonical Correlation	Adjusted Canonical Correlation	Approximate Standard Error	Squared Canonical Correlation
1	0.976613	0.976123	0.003787	0.953774
2	0.550384	0.543354	0.057107	0.302923

Eigenvalues of Inv(E)*H
= CanRsq/(1-CanRsq)

Test of H0: The canonical correlations in the current row and all that follow are zero

	Eigenvalue	Difference	Proportion	Cumulative	Likelihood Ratio	Approximate F Value	Num DF	Den DF	Pr > F
1	20.6327	20.1981	0.9794	0.9794	0.03222337	164.55	8	288	<.0001
2	0.4346		0.0206	1.0000	0.69707749	21.00	3	145	<.0001

Fisher (1936) Iris Data
Canonical Discriminant Analysis of Iris Clusters

The CANDISC Procedure

Total Canonical Structure

Variable	Label	Can1	Can2
SepalLength	Sepal Length in mm.	0.831965	0.452137
SepalWidth	Sepal Width in mm.	-0.515082	0.810630
PetalLength	Petal Length in mm.	0.993520	0.087514
PetalWidth	Petal Width in mm.	0.966325	0.154745

Between Canonical Structure

Variable	Label	Can1	Can2
SepalLength	Sepal Length in mm.	0.956160	0.292846
SepalWidth	Sepal Width in mm.	-0.748136	0.663545
PetalLength	Petal Length in mm.	0.998770	0.049580
PetalWidth	Petal Width in mm.	0.995952	0.089883

Pooled Within Canonical Structure

Variable	Label	Can1	Can2
SepalLength	Sepal Length in mm.	0.339314	0.716082
SepalWidth	Sepal Width in mm.	-0.149614	0.914351
PetalLength	Petal Length in mm.	0.900839	0.308136
PetalWidth	Petal Width in mm.	0.650123	0.404282

Fisher (1936) Iris Data
Canonical Discriminant Analysis of Iris Clusters

The CANDISC Procedure

Total-Sample Standardized Canonical Coefficients

Variable	Label	Can1	Can2
SepalLength	Sepal Length in mm.	0.047747341	1.021487262
SepalWidth	Sepal Width in mm.	-0.577569244	0.864455153
PetalLength	Petal Length in mm.	3.341309573	-1.283043758
PetalWidth	Petal Width in mm.	0.996451144	0.900476563

Pooled Within-Class Standardized Canonical Coefficients

Variable	Label	Can1	Can2
SepalLength	Sepal Length in mm.	0.0253414487	0.5421446856
SepalWidth	Sepal Width in mm.	-.4304161258	0.6442092294
PetalLength	Petal Length in mm.	0.7976741592	-.3063023132
PetalWidth	Petal Width in mm.	0.3205998034	0.2897207865

Raw Canonical Coefficients

Variable	Label	Can1	Can2
SepalLength	Sepal Length in mm.	0.0057661265	0.1233581748
SepalWidth	Sepal Width in mm.	-.1325106494	0.1983303556
PetalLength	Petal Length in mm.	0.1892773419	-.0726814163
PetalWidth	Petal Width in mm.	0.1307270927	0.1181359305

Class Means on Canonical Variables

CLUSTER	Can1	Can2
1	-6.131527227	0.244761516
2	4.931414018	0.861972277
3	1.922300462	-0.725693908

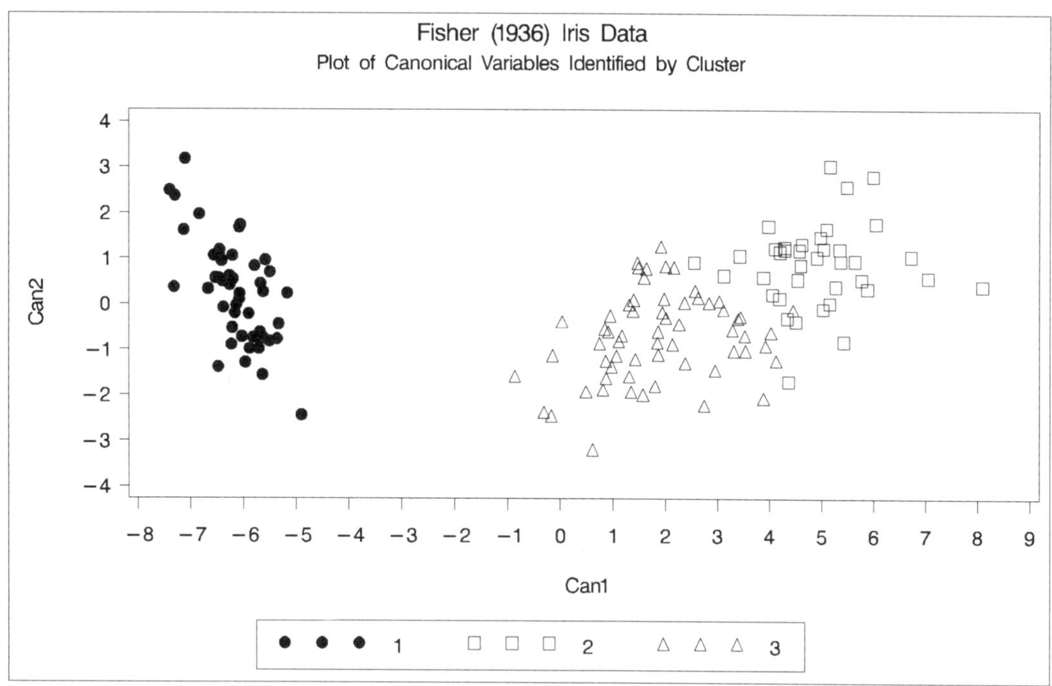

Example 27.2. Outliers

The second example involves data artificially generated to contain two clusters and several severe outliers. A preliminary analysis specifies twenty clusters and outputs an OUTSEED= data set to be used for a diagnostic plot. The exact number of initial clusters is not important; similar results could be obtained with ten or fifty initial clusters. Examination of the plot suggests that clusters with more than five (again, the exact number is not important) observations may yield good seeds for the main analysis. A DATA step deletes clusters with five or fewer observations, and the remaining cluster means provide seeds for the next PROC FASTCLUS analysis.

Two clusters are requested; the LEAST= option specifies the mean absolute deviation criterion (LEAST=1) . Values of the LEAST= option less than 2 reduce the effect of outliers on cluster centers.

The next analysis also requests two clusters; the STRICT= option is specified to prevent outliers from distorting the results. The STRICT= value is chosen to be close to the _GAP_ and _RADIUS_ values of the larger clusters in the diagnostic plot; the exact value is not critical.

A final PROC FASTCLUS run assigns the outliers to clusters. The results are displayed in Output 27.2.1 through Output 27.2.4.

```
/*   Create artificial data set with two clusters          */
/*   and some outliers.                                    */

data x;
title 'Using PROC FASTCLUS to Analyze Data with Outliers';
   drop n;
   do n=1 to 100;
      x=rannor(12345)+2;
      y=rannor(12345);
      output;
   end;
   do n=1 to 100;
      x=rannor(12345)-2;
      y=rannor(12345);
      output;
   end;
   do n=1 to 10;
      x=10*rannor(12345);
      y=10*rannor(12345);
      output;
   end;
run;

/* Run PROC FASTCLUS with many clusters and OUTSEED= output */
/* data set for diagnostic plot.                            */

title2 'Preliminary PROC FASTCLUS Analysis with 20 Clusters';
proc fastclus data=x outseed=mean1 maxc=20 maxiter=0 summary;
   var x y;
run;

legend1 frame cframe=ligr label=none cborder=black
        position=center value=(justify=center);

axis1 label=(angle=90 rotate=0) minor=none order=(0 to 10 by 2);
axis2 minor=none ;

proc gplot data=mean1;
     plot  _gap_*_freq_ _radius_*_freq_ /overlay frame
     cframe=ligr vaxis=axis1 haxis=axis2 legend=legend1;
run;
```

Output 27.2.1. Preliminary Analysis of Data with Outliers: PROC FASTCLUS and PROC GPLOT

```
                        Using PROC FASTCLUS to Analyze Data with Outliers
                       Preliminary PROC FASTCLUS Analysis with 20 Clusters

                                     The FASTCLUS Procedure
                         Replace=FULL  Radius=0  Maxclusters=20 Maxiter=0

                            Criterion Based on Final Seeds =    0.6873


                                        Cluster Summary

                                     Maximum Distance
                          RMS Std           from Seed     Radius     Nearest     Distance Between
Cluster     Frequency   Deviation      to Observation   Exceeded     Cluster    Cluster Centroids
-------------------------------------------------------------------------------------------------
      1             8      0.4753              1.1924                     19               1.7205
      2             1           .                   0                      6               6.2847
      3            44      0.6252              1.6774                      5               1.4386
      4             1           .                   0                     20               5.2130
      5            38      0.5603              1.4528                      3               1.4386
      6             2      0.0542              0.1085                      2               6.2847
      7             1           .                   0                     14               2.5094
      8             2      0.6480              1.2961                      1               1.8450
      9             1           .                   0                      7               9.4534
     10             1           .                   0                     18               4.2514
     11             1           .                   0                     16               4.7582
     12            20      0.5911              1.6291                     16               1.5601
     13             5      0.6682              1.4244                      3               1.9553
     14             1           .                   0                      7               2.5094
     15             5      0.4074              1.2678                      3               1.7609
     16            22      0.4168              1.5139                     19               1.4936
     17             8      0.4031              1.4794                      5               1.5564
     18             1           .                   0                     10               4.2514
     19            45      0.6475              1.6285                     16               1.4936
     20             3      0.5719              1.3642                     15               1.8999


                                 Pseudo F Statistic =   207.58


                        Approximate Expected Over-All R-Squared =   0.96103


                              Cubic Clustering Criterion =   -2.503

                WARNING: The two above values are invalid for correlated variables.
```

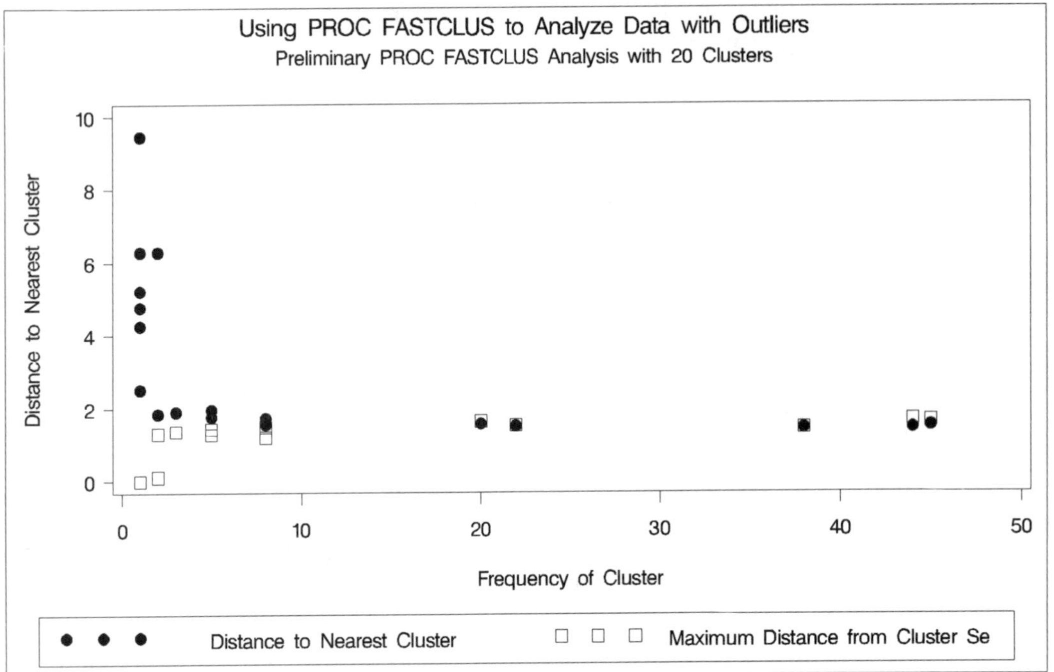


```
   /*    Remove low frequency clusters.  */
data seed;
   set mean1;
   if _freq_>5;
run;

   /*   Run PROC FASTCLUS again, selecting seeds from the          */
   /*   high frequency clusters in the previous analysis           */
   /*   using LEAST=1 Clustering Criterion                         */

title2 'PROC FASTCLUS Analysis Using LEAST= Clustering Criterion';
title3 'Values < 2 Reduce Effect of Outliers on Cluster Centers';
proc fastclus data=x seed=seed maxc=2 least=1 out=out;
   var x y;
run;

legend1 frame cframe=ligr label=none cborder=black
        position=center value=(justify=center);
axis1 label=(angle=90 rotate=0) minor=none;
axis2 minor=none;

proc gplot data=out;
   plot y*x=cluster/frame cframe=ligr
                legend=legend1 vaxis=axis1 haxis=axis2;
run;
```

Output 27.2.2. Analysis of Data with Outliers using the LEAST= Option

```
              Using PROC FASTCLUS to Analyze Data with Outliers
            PROC FASTCLUS Analysis Using LEAST= Clustering Criterion
            Values < 2 Reduce Effect of Outliers on Cluster Centers

                           The FASTCLUS Procedure
Replace=FULL  Radius=0  Maxclusters=2 Maxiter=20  Converge=0.0001  Least=1

                               Initial Seeds

                 Cluster                 x                 y
                 -------------------------------------------
                    1          2.794174248      -0.065970836
                    2         -2.027300384      -2.051208579


              Minimum Distance Between Initial Seeds = 6.806712


              Preliminary L(1) Scale Estimate =        2.796579
```

```
              Using PROC FASTCLUS to Analyze Data with Outliers
            PROC FASTCLUS Analysis Using LEAST= Clustering Criterion
            Values < 2 Reduce Effect of Outliers on Cluster Centers

                           The FASTCLUS Procedure
Replace=FULL  Radius=0  Maxclusters=2 Maxiter=20  Converge=0.0001  Least=1

                         Number of Bins =      100

                             Iteration History

                                                Relative Change
                                    Maximum     in Cluster Seeds
          Iteration    Criterion    Bin Size         1           2
          -------------------------------------------------------
                  1       1.3983      0.2263      0.4091      0.6696
                  2       1.0776      0.0226     0.00511      0.0452
                  3       1.0771     0.00226     0.00229     0.00234
                  4       1.0771    0.000396    0.000253    0.000144
                  5       1.0771    0.000396           0           0


       Convergence criterion is satisfied.
```

```
                  Using PROC FASTCLUS to Analyze Data with Outliers
                PROC FASTCLUS Analysis Using LEAST= Clustering Criterion
                Values < 2 Reduce Effect of Outliers on Cluster Centers

                              The FASTCLUS Procedure
      Replace=FULL  Radius=0  Maxclusters=2 Maxiter=20  Converge=0.0001  Least=1

                    Criterion Based on Final Seeds =    1.0771


                                  Cluster Summary

                           Mean   Maximum Distance
                       Absolute          from Seed      Radius    Nearest    Distance Between
Cluster    Frequency  Deviation     to Observation    Exceeded    Cluster     Cluster Medians
---------------------------------------------------------------------------------------------
  1              102     1.1278            24.1622                      2              4.2585
  2              108     1.0494            14.8292                      1              4.2585


                                  Cluster Medians

                      Cluster                x                 y
                      ------------------------------------------
                         1          1.923023887       0.222482918
                         2         -1.826721743      -0.286253041


                    Mean Absolute Deviations from Final Seeds

                      Cluster                x                 y
                      ------------------------------------------
                         1          1.113465261       1.142120480
                         2          0.890331835       1.208370913
```

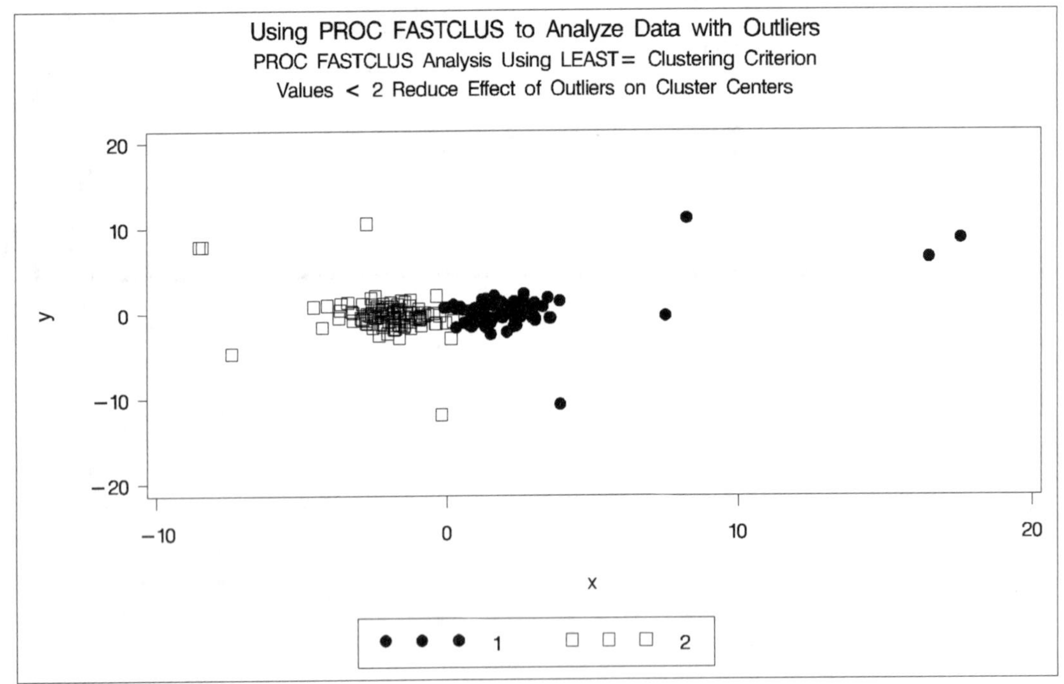

```
   /*   Run PROC FASTCLUS again, selecting seeds from the        */
   /*   high frequency clusters in the previous analysis         */
   /*   STRICT= prevents outliers from distorting the results.   */

title2 'PROC FASTCLUS Analysis Using STRICT= to Omit Outliers';
proc fastclus data=x seed=seed
     maxc=2 strict=3.0 out=out outseed=mean2;
   var x y;
run;

proc gplot data=out;
   plot y*x=cluster/frame cframe=ligr
                 legend=legend1 vaxis=axis1 haxis=axis2;
run;
```

Output 27.2.3. Cluster Analysis with Outliers Omitted: PROC FASTCLUS and PROC GPLOT

```
                      Using PROC FASTCLUS to Analyze Data with Outliers
                    PROC FASTCLUS Analysis Using STRICT= to Omit Outliers

                                   The FASTCLUS Procedure
                 Replace=FULL  Radius=0  Strict=3  Maxclusters=2 Maxiter=1

                                       Initial Seeds

                         Cluster                x                 y
                         -----------------------------------------
                            1          2.794174248      -0.065970836
                            2         -2.027300384      -2.051208579


                          Criterion Based on Final Seeds =    0.9515


                                      Cluster Summary

                                     Maximum Distance
                         RMS Std          from Seed      Radius      Nearest     Distance Between
Cluster     Frequency    Deviation     to Observation    Exceeded    Cluster     Cluster Centroids
-------------------------------------------------------------------------------------------------
   1              99       0.9501             2.9589                      2                 3.7666
   2              99       0.9290             2.8011                      1                 3.7666

 12 Observation(s) were not assigned to a cluster because the minimum distance to a cluster seed
                                exceeded the STRICT= value.

                                 Statistics for Variables

              Variable     Total STD    Within STD       R-Square      RSQ/(1-RSQ)
              -------------------------------------------------------------------
              x              2.06854       0.87098       0.823609         4.669219
              y              1.02113       1.00352       0.039093         0.040683
              OVER-ALL       1.63119       0.93959       0.669891         2.029303

                             Pseudo F Statistic =    397.74

                  Approximate Expected Over-All R-Squared =    0.60615

                           Cubic Clustering Criterion =     3.197

               WARNING: The two above values are invalid for correlated variables.
```

```
                 Using PROC FASTCLUS to Analyze Data with Outliers
               PROC FASTCLUS Analysis Using STRICT= to Omit Outliers

                             The FASTCLUS Procedure
          Replace=FULL  Radius=0  Strict=3  Maxclusters=2 Maxiter=1

                                 Cluster Means

                 Cluster                 x                   y
                 -------------------------------------------
                    1           1.825111432        0.141211701
                    2          -1.919910712       -0.261558725


                           Cluster Standard Deviations

                 Cluster                 x                   y
                 -------------------------------------------
                    1           0.889549271        1.006965219
                    2           0.852000588        1.000062579
```

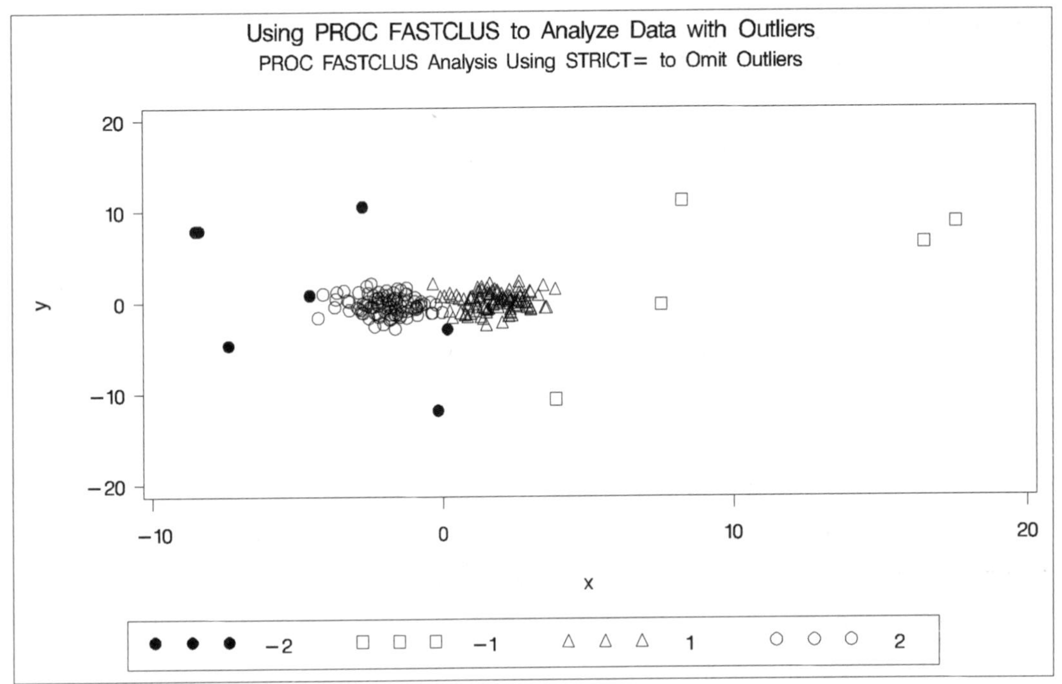


```
   /* Run PROC FASTCLUS one more time with zero iterations */
   /* to assign outliers and tails to clusters.            */
title2 'Final PROC FASTCLUS Analysis Assigning Outliers to '
       'Clusters';
proc fastclus data=x seed=mean2 maxc=2 maxiter=0 out=out;
   var x y;
run;


proc gplot data=out;
   plot y*x=cluster/frame cframe=ligr
                    legend=legend1 vaxis=axis1 haxis=axis2;
run;
```

Output 27.2.4. Final Analysis with Outliers Assigned to Clusters: PROC FASTCLUS and PROC GPLOT

```
                        Using PROC FASTCLUS to Analyze Data with Outliers
                   Final PROC FASTCLUS Analysis Assigning Outliers to Clusters

                                     The FASTCLUS Procedure
                         Replace=FULL  Radius=0  Maxclusters=2 Maxiter=0

                                         Initial Seeds

                            Cluster                  x                  y
                            -------------------------------------------
                               1           1.825111432        0.141211701
                               2          -1.919910712       -0.261558725


                             Criterion Based on Final Seeds =    2.0594


                                        Cluster Summary

                                     Maximum Distance
                           RMS Std            from Seed        Radius      Nearest      Distance Between
Cluster      Frequency    Deviation       to Observation      Exceeded     Cluster      Cluster Centroids
---------------------------------------------------------------------------------------------------------
   1               103       2.2569              17.9426                         2                 4.3753
   2               107       1.8371              11.7362                         1                 4.3753


                                    Statistics for Variables

                  Variable      Total STD     Within STD       R-Square      RSQ/(1-RSQ)
                  ------------------------------------------------------------------
                  x               2.92721        1.95529       0.555950         1.252000
                  y               2.15248        2.14754       0.009347         0.009435
                  OVER-ALL        2.56922        2.05367       0.364119         0.572621


                               Pseudo F Statistic =    119.11


                      Approximate Expected Over-All R-Squared =    0.49090


                              Cubic Clustering Criterion =    -5.338

                WARNING: The two above values are invalid for correlated variables.
```

```
                        Using PROC FASTCLUS to Analyze Data with Outliers
                   Final PROC FASTCLUS Analysis Assigning Outliers to Clusters

                                     The FASTCLUS Procedure
                         Replace=FULL  Radius=0  Maxclusters=2 Maxiter=0

                                         Cluster Means

                            Cluster                  x                  y
                            -------------------------------------------
                               1           2.280017469        0.263940765
                               2          -2.075547895       -0.151348765


                                  Cluster Standard Deviations

                            Cluster                  x                  y
                            -------------------------------------------
                               1           2.412264861        2.089922815
                               2           1.379355878        2.201567557
```

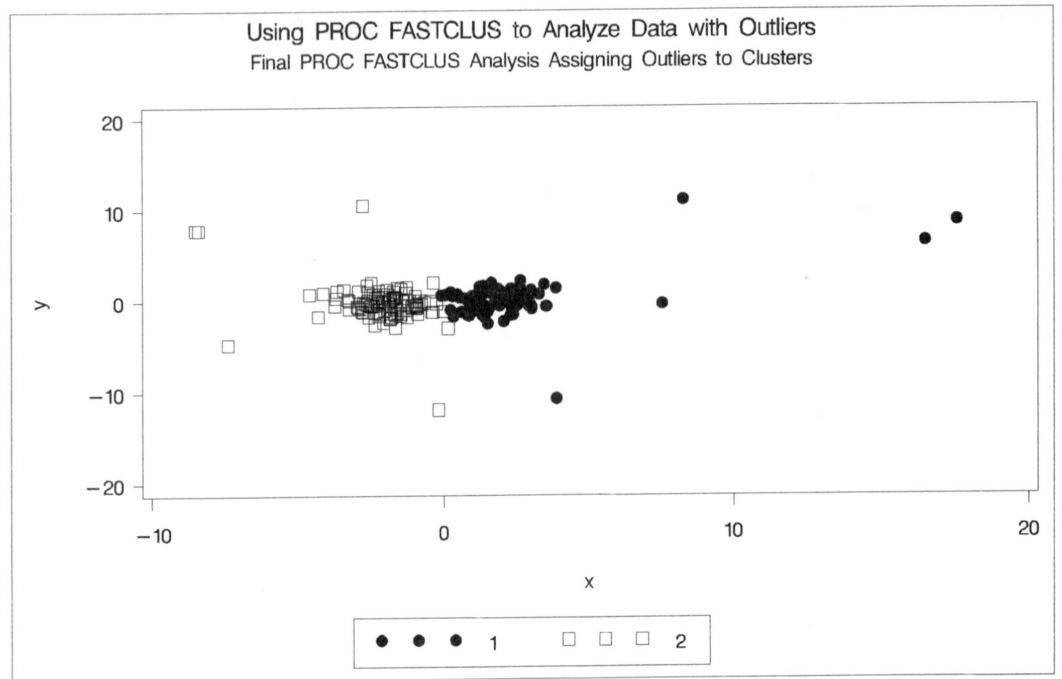

References

Anderberg, M.R. (1973), *Cluster Analysis for Applications*, New York: Academic Press, Inc.

Bock, H. H. (1985), "On Some Significance Tests in Cluster Analysis," *Journal of Classification*, 2, 77–108.

Calinski, T. and Harabasz, J. (1974), "A Dendrite Method for Cluster Analysis," *Communications in Statistics*, 3, 1–27.

Cooper, M.C. and Milligan, G.W. (1988), "The Effect of Error on Determining the Number of Clusters," Proceedings of the International Workshop on Data Analysis, Decision Support, and Expert Knowledge Representation in Marketing and Related Areas of Research.

Everitt, B.S. (1980), *Cluster Analysis*, Second Edition, London: Heineman Educational Books Ltd.

Fisher, R.A. (1936), "The Use of Multiple Measurements in Taxonomic Problems," *Annals of Eugenics*, 7, 179–188.

Gonin, R. and Money, A.H. (1989), *Nonlinear L_p-Norm Estimation*, New York: Marcel Dekker.

Hartigan, J.A. (1975), *Clustering Algorithms*, New York: John Wiley & Sons, Inc.

Hartigan, J.A. (1985), "Statistical Theory in Clustering," *Journal of Classification*, 2, 63–76.

Journal of Statistics Education, "Fish Catch Data Set," [http://www.stat.ncsu.edu/info/jse], accessed 4 December 1997.

MacQueen, J.B. (1967), "Some Methods for Classification and Analysis of Multivariate Observations," *Proceedings of the Fifth Berkeley Symposium on Mathematical Statistics and Probability*, 1, 281–297.

McLachlan, G. J. and Basford, K. E. (1988), *Mixture Models*, New York: Marcel Dekker, Inc.

Mezzich, J.E and Solomon, H. (1980), *Taxonomy and Behavioral Science*, New York: Academic Press, Inc.

Milligan, G.W. (1980), "An Examination of the Effect of Six Types of Error Perturbation on Fifteen Clustering Algorithms," *Psychometrika*, 45, 325–342.

Milligan, G.W. and Cooper, M.C. (1985), "An Examination of Procedures for Determining the Number of Clusters in a Data Set," *Psychometrika, 50,* 159–179.

Pollard, D. (1981), "Strong Consistency of *k* -Means Clustering," *Annals of Statistics*, 9, 135–140.

Sarle, W.S. (1983), "The Cubic Clustering Criterion," SAS Technical Report A-108, Cary, NC: SAS Institute Inc.

Spath, H. (1980), *Cluster Analysis Algorithms*, Chichester, England: Ellis Horwood.

Spath, H. (1985), *Cluster Dissection and Analysis*, Chichester, England: Ellis Horwood.

Titterington, D.M., Smith, A. F. M., and Makov, U. E. (1985), *Statistical Analysis of Finite Mixture Distributions*, New York: John Wiley & Sons.

Tou, J.T. and Gonzalez, R.C. (1974), *Pattern Recognition Principles*, Reading, MA: The Addison-Wesley Publishing Co.

All you need for
web-based
training!

SAS Institute

SAS Institute